STAR WARS

LEGENDS

THE OLD REPUBLIC

VOLUME 1

WRITER:
JOHN JACKSON MILLER

ARTISTS:
BRIAN CHING, TRAVEL FOREMAN, DUSTIN WEAVER & HARVEY TOLIBAO WITH
CRYSTAL FAITH CELESTIAL

COLORISTS:
**MICHAEL ATIYEH &
JAY DAVID RAMOS**

LETTERER:
MICHAEL HEISLER

ASSISTANT EDITOR:
DAVE MARSHALL

EDITOR:
JEREMY BARLOW

FRONT COVER ARTISTS:
**BRIAN CHING
& MICHAEL ATIYEH**

BACK COVER ARTIST:
TRAVIS CHAREST

COLLECTION EDITOR: MARK D. BEAZLEY
ASSISTANT MANAGING EDITOR: JOE HOCHSTEIN
ASSOCIATE MANAGING EDITOR: ALEX STARBUCK
EDITOR, SPECIAL PROJECTS: JENNIFER GRÜNWALD
SENIOR EDITOR, SPECIAL PROJECTS: JEFF YOUNGQUIST
RESEARCH: MIKE HANSEN
LAYOUT: JEPH YORK
PRODUCTION: RYAN DEVALL
BOOK DESIGNER: RODOLFO MURAGUCHI
SVP PRINT, SALES & MARKETING: DAVID GABRIEL

EDITOR IN CHIEF: AXEL ALONSO
CHIEF CREATIVE OFFICER: JOE QUESADA
PUBLISHER: DAN BUCKLEY
EXECUTIVE PRODUCER: ALAN FINE

SPECIAL THANKS TO FRANK PARISI & LUCASFILM, DEIDRE
HANSEN, GREGORY HECHT & STUART VANDAL

STAR WARS LEGENDS EPIC COLLECTION: THE OLD REPUBLIC VOL. 1. Contains material originally published in magazine form as STAR WARS: KNIGHTS OF THE OLD REPUBLIC #1-18 and STAR WARS: KNIGHTS OF THE OLD REPUBLIC/REBELLION #0. First printing 2015. ISBN# 978-0-7851-9717-1. Published by MARVEL WORLDWIDE, INC., a subsidiary of MARVEL ENTERTAINMENT, LLC. OFFICE OF PUBLICATION: 135 West 50th Street, New York, NY 10020. STAR WARS and related text and illustrations are trademarks and/or copyrights, in the United States and other countries, of Lucasfilm Ltd. and/or its affiliates. © & TM Lucasfilm Ltd. No similarity between any of the names, characters, persons, and/or institutions in this magazine with those of any living or dead person or institution is intended, and any such similarity which may exist is purely coincidental. Marvel and its logos are TM Marvel Characters, Inc. **Printed in the U.S.A.** ALAN FINE, President, Marvel Entertainment; DAN BUCKLEY, President, TV, Publishing and Brand Management; JOE QUESADA, Chief Creative Officer; TOM BREVOORT, SVP of Publishing; DAVID BOGART, SVP of Operations & Procurement, Publishing; C.B. CEBULSKI, VP of International Development & Brand Management; DAVID GABRIEL, SVP Print, Sales & Marketing; JIM O'KEEFE, VP of Operations & Logistics; DAN CARR, Executive Director of Publishing Technology; SUSAN CRESPI, Editorial Operations Manager; ALEX MORALES, Publishing Operations Manager; STAN LEE, Chairman Emeritus. For information regarding advertising in Marvel Comics or on Marvel.com, please contact Jonathan Rheingold, VP of Custom Solutions & Ad Sales, at jrheingold@marvel.com. For Marvel subscription inquiries, please call 800-217-9158. **Manufactured between 5/8/2015 and 6/15/2015 by R.R. DONNELLEY, INC., SALEM, VA, USA.**
10 9 8 7 6 5 4 3 2 1

THE OLD REPUBLIC — VOLUME 1

THE OLD REPUBLIC
VOLUME 1

It is a time of conflict. The Jedi Knights, guardians of peace and justice throughout the galaxy, have won a devastating war against the evil Sith and their leader, the Dark Lord Exar Kun. The Galactic Republic and the Jedi Order both suffered devastating losses during their hard-won victory.

As the Republic rebuilds itself, the warriors known as the Mandalorians have begun their own war against the Republic in retaliation for their defeat at the Jedi's hands during the Sith War. The Mandalorian Wars are now straining the Republic's resources to the breaking point.

With so many forces at the front, systems in the Outer Rim are on the brink of lawlessness — even the city-world of Taris, once a thriving commercial center. Here, as elsewhere, the Republic relies increasingly on Jedi Knights and their students to try to maintain order.

But some Jedi, frustrated with the ongoing wars, instead argue for a more active role in the conflict. These Jedi appeal to others for support, including the Jedi Masters — and their untested Padawan students — who are struggling to keep the peace and prevent an even darker future....

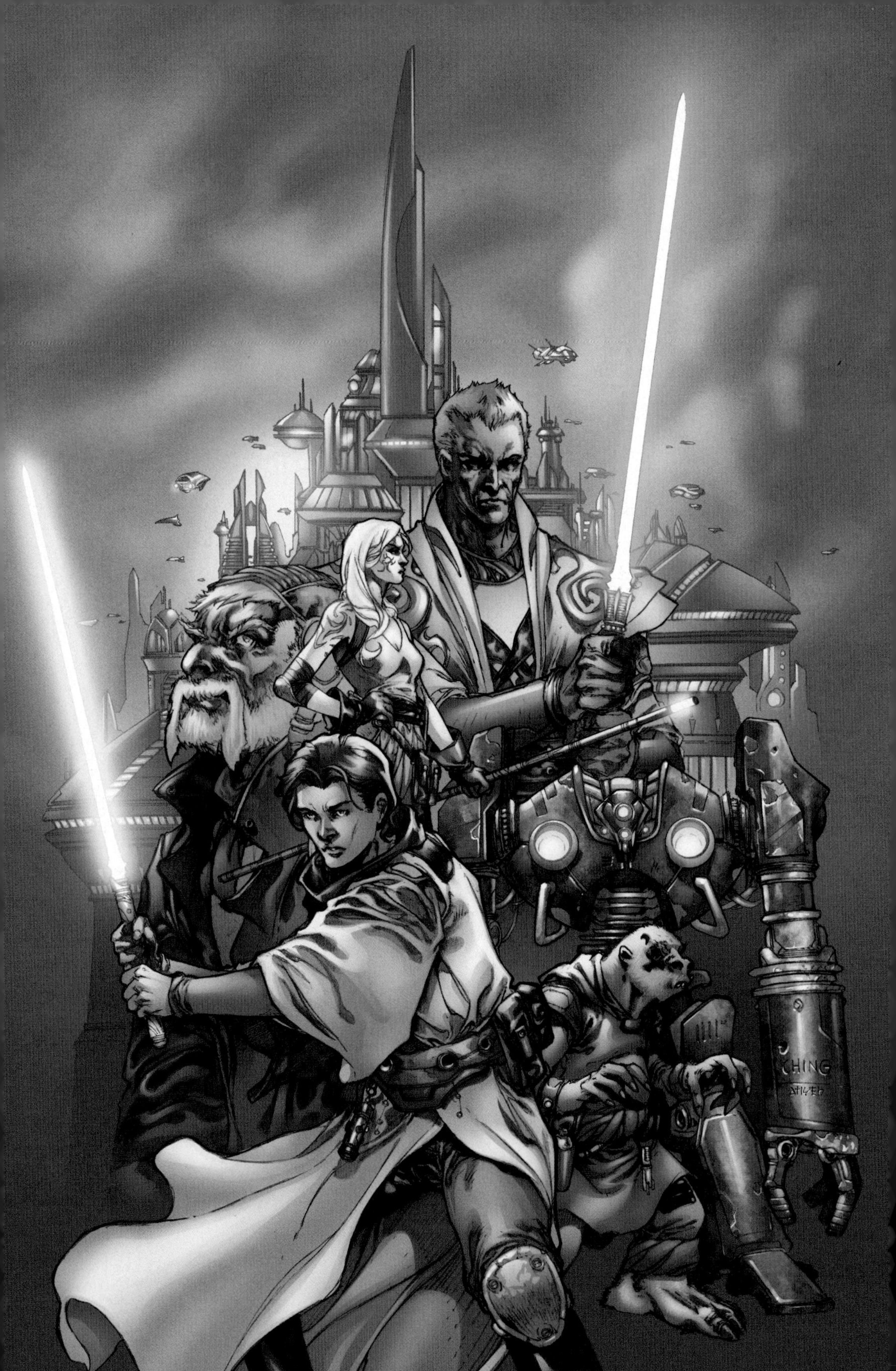

STAR WARS: KNIGHTS OF THE OLD REPUBLIC/REBELLION #0 — "CROSSROADS"

WRITER: JOHN JACKSON MILLER • ARTIST: BRIAN CHING • COLORIST: MICHAEL ATIYEH • LETTERER: MICHAEL HEISLER
ASSISTANT EDITOR: DAVE MARSHALL • EDITOR: JEREMY BARLOW • COVER ARTISTS: BRIAN CHING & MICHAEL ATIYEH

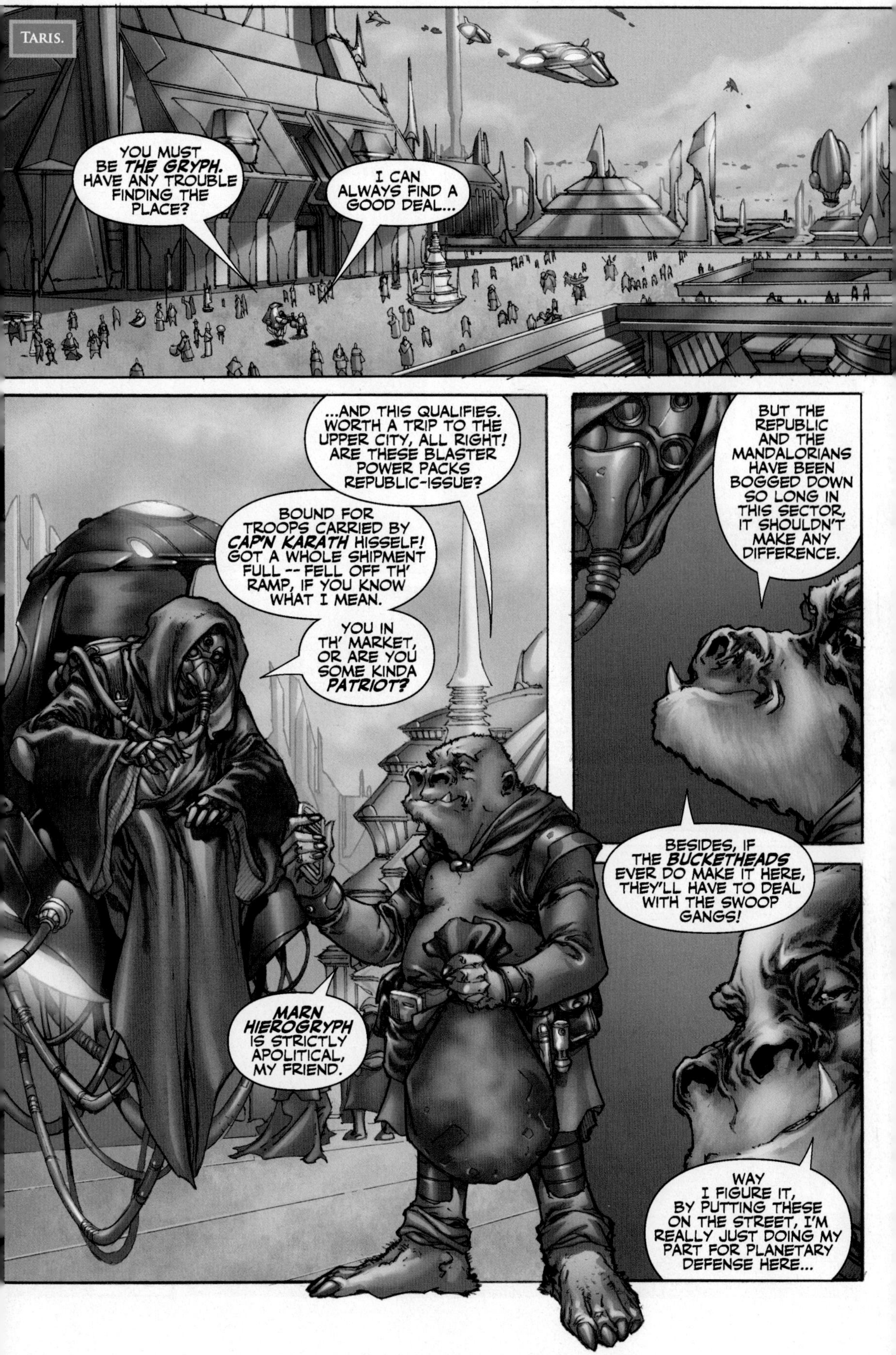
TARIS.
YOU MUST BE THE GRYPH. HAVE ANY TROUBLE FINDING THE PLACE?
I CAN ALWAYS FIND A GOOD DEAL...
...AND THIS QUALIFIES. WORTH A TRIP TO THE UPPER CITY, ALL RIGHT! ARE THESE BLASTER POWER PACKS REPUBLIC-ISSUE?
BOUND FOR TROOPS CARRIED BY CAP'N KARATH HISSELF! GOT A WHOLE SHIPMENT FULL -- FELL OFF TH' RAMP, IF YOU KNOW WHAT I MEAN.
YOU IN TH' MARKET, OR ARE YOU SOME KINDA PATRIOT?
MARN HIEROGRYPH IS STRICTLY APOLITICAL, MY FRIEND.
BUT THE REPUBLIC AND THE MANDALORIANS HAVE BEEN BOGGED DOWN SO LONG IN THIS SECTOR, IT SHOULDN'T MAKE ANY DIFFERENCE.
BESIDES, IF THE BUCKETHEADS EVER DO MAKE IT HERE, THEY'LL HAVE TO DEAL WITH THE SWOOP GANGS!
WAY I FIGURE IT, BY PUTTING THESE ON THE STREET, I'M REALLY JUST DOING MY PART FOR PLANETARY DEFENSE HERE...

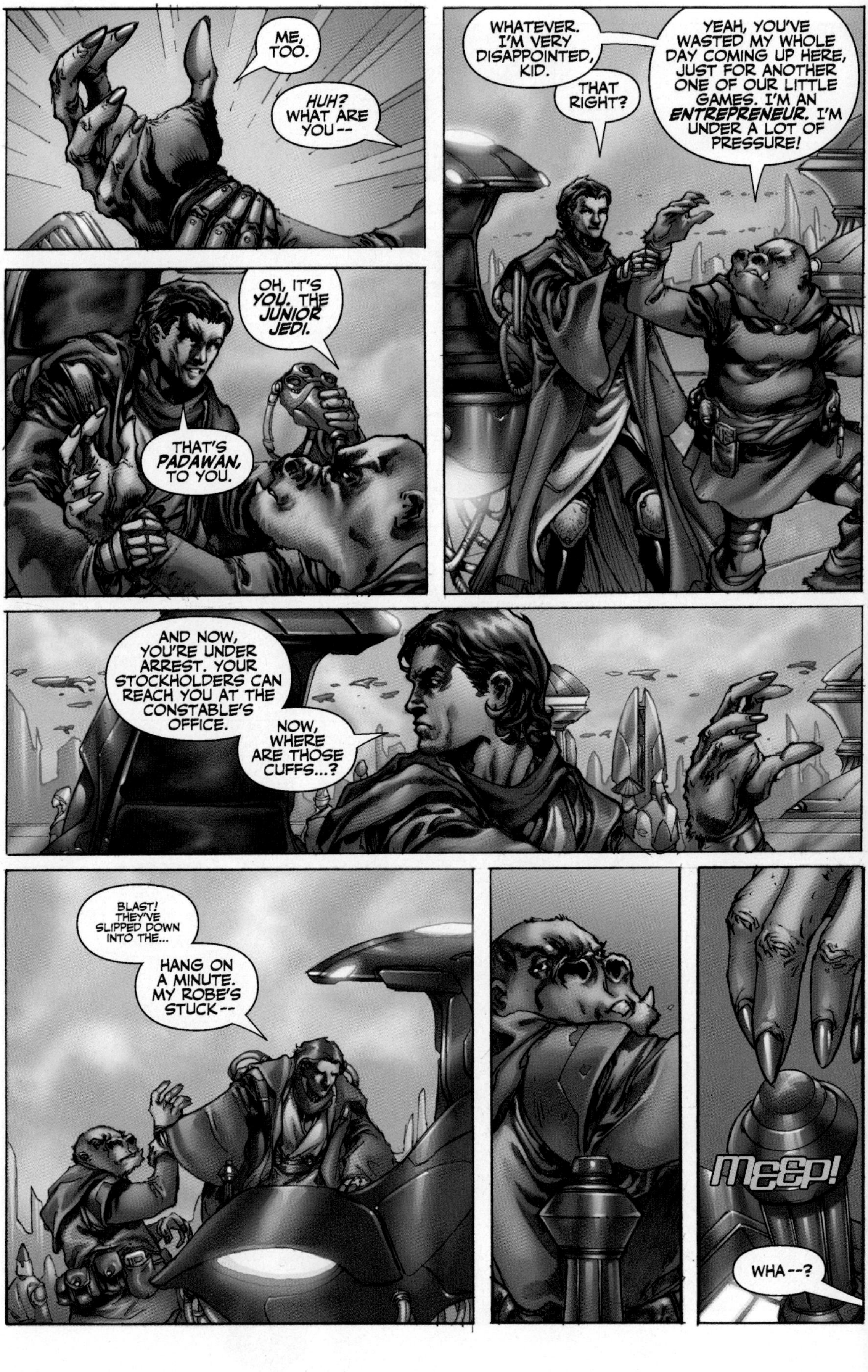
ME, TOO.
HUH? WHAT ARE YOU--
WHATEVER. I'M VERY DISAPPOINTED, KID.
THAT RIGHT?
YEAH, YOU'VE WASTED MY WHOLE DAY COMING UP HERE, JUST FOR ANOTHER ONE OF OUR LITTLE GAMES. I'M AN ENTREPRENEUR. I'M UNDER A LOT OF PRESSURE!
OH, IT'S YOU. THE JUNIOR JEDI.
THAT'S PADAWAN, TO YOU.
AND NOW, YOU'RE UNDER ARREST. YOUR STOCKHOLDERS CAN REACH YOU AT THE CONSTABLE'S OFFICE.
NOW, WHERE ARE THOSE CUFFS...?
BLAST! THEY'VE SLIPPED DOWN INTO THE...
HANG ON A MINUTE. MY ROBE'S STUCK--
MEEP!
WHA--?

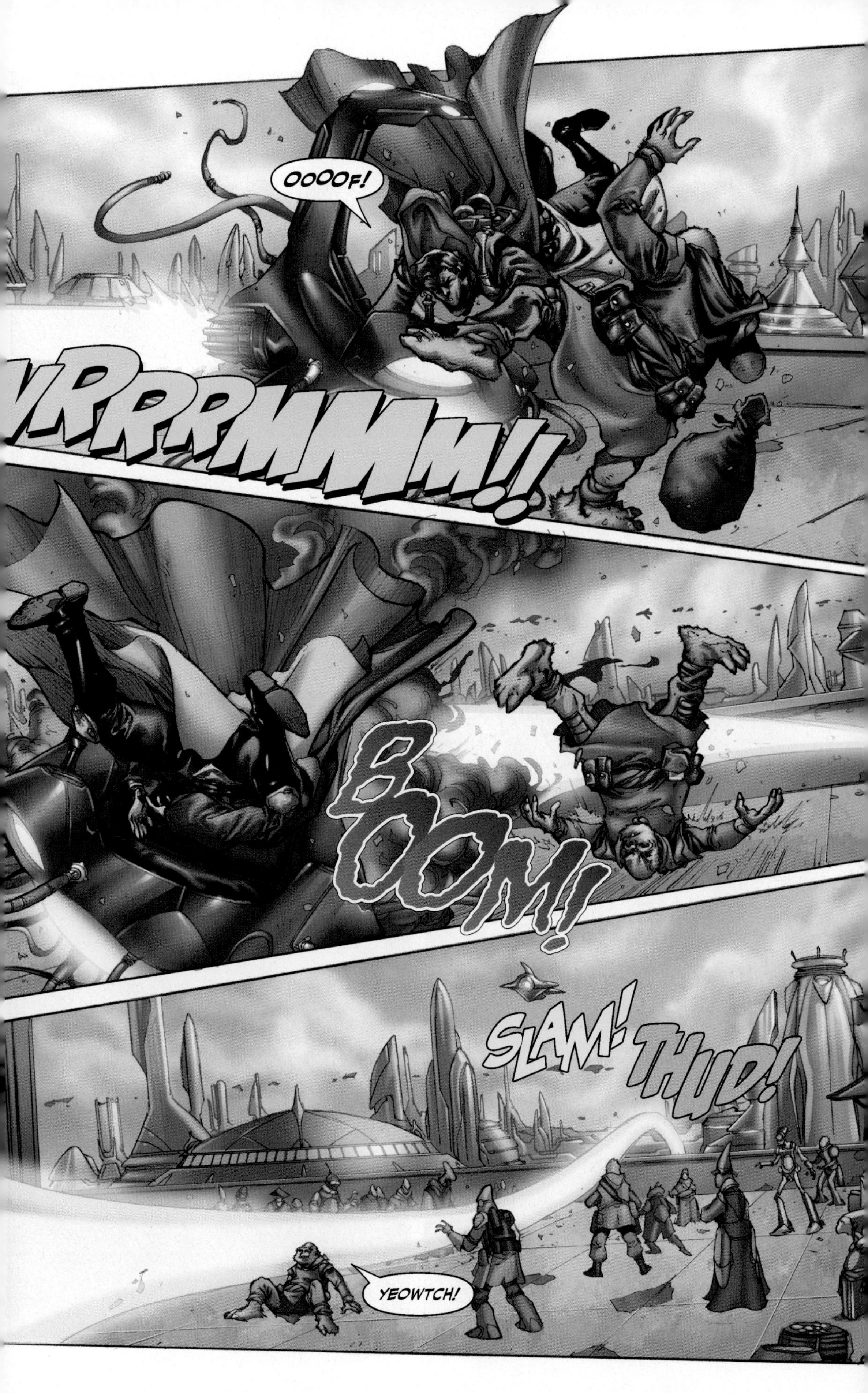
OOOOF!
VRRRMMMM!!
BOOM!
SLAM!
THUD!
YEOWTCH!

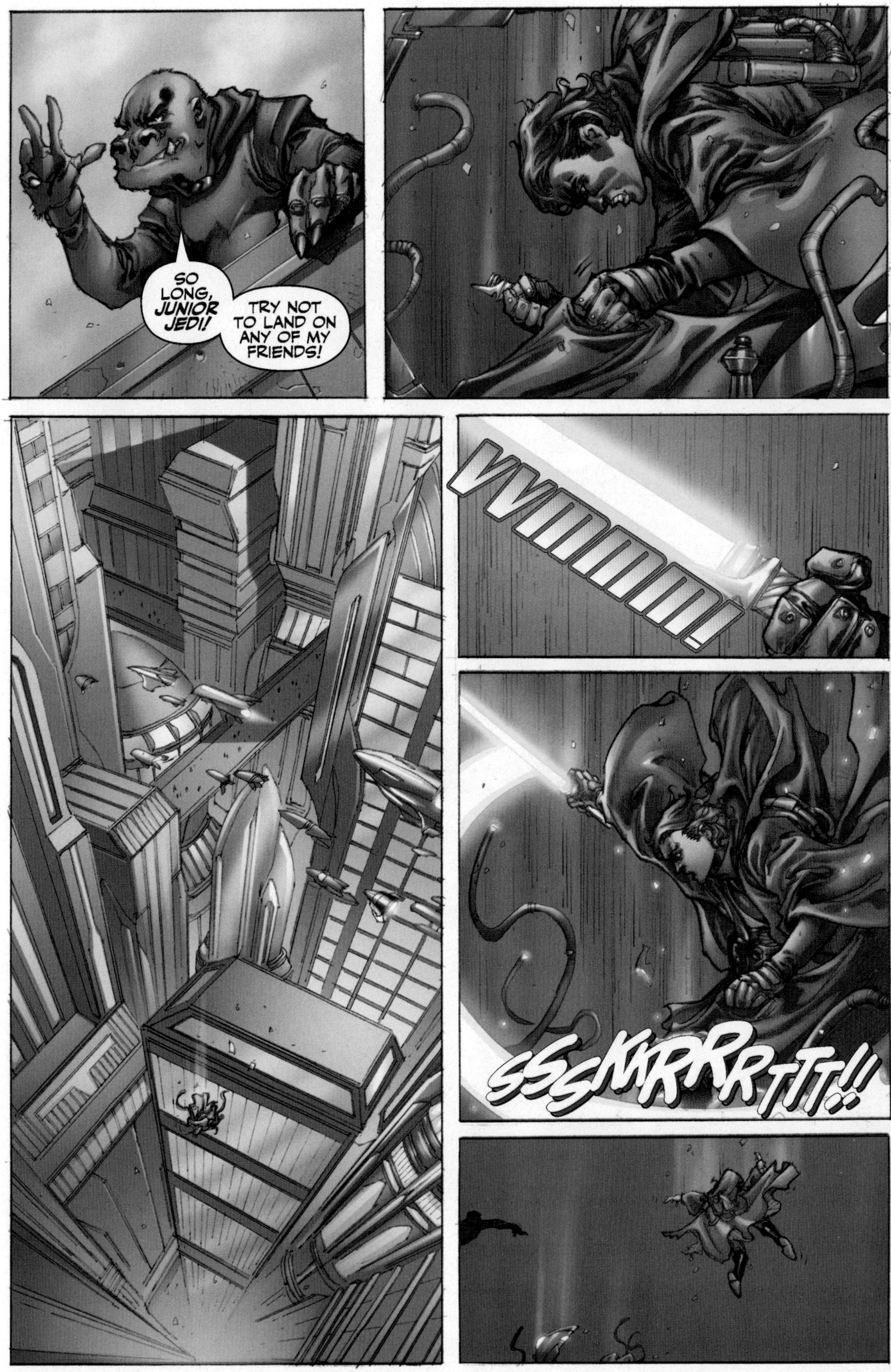
SO LONG, JUNIOR JEDI!
TRY NOT TO LAND ON ANY OF MY FRIENDS!
VVMMMMM!
SSSKKRRRRTTT!!

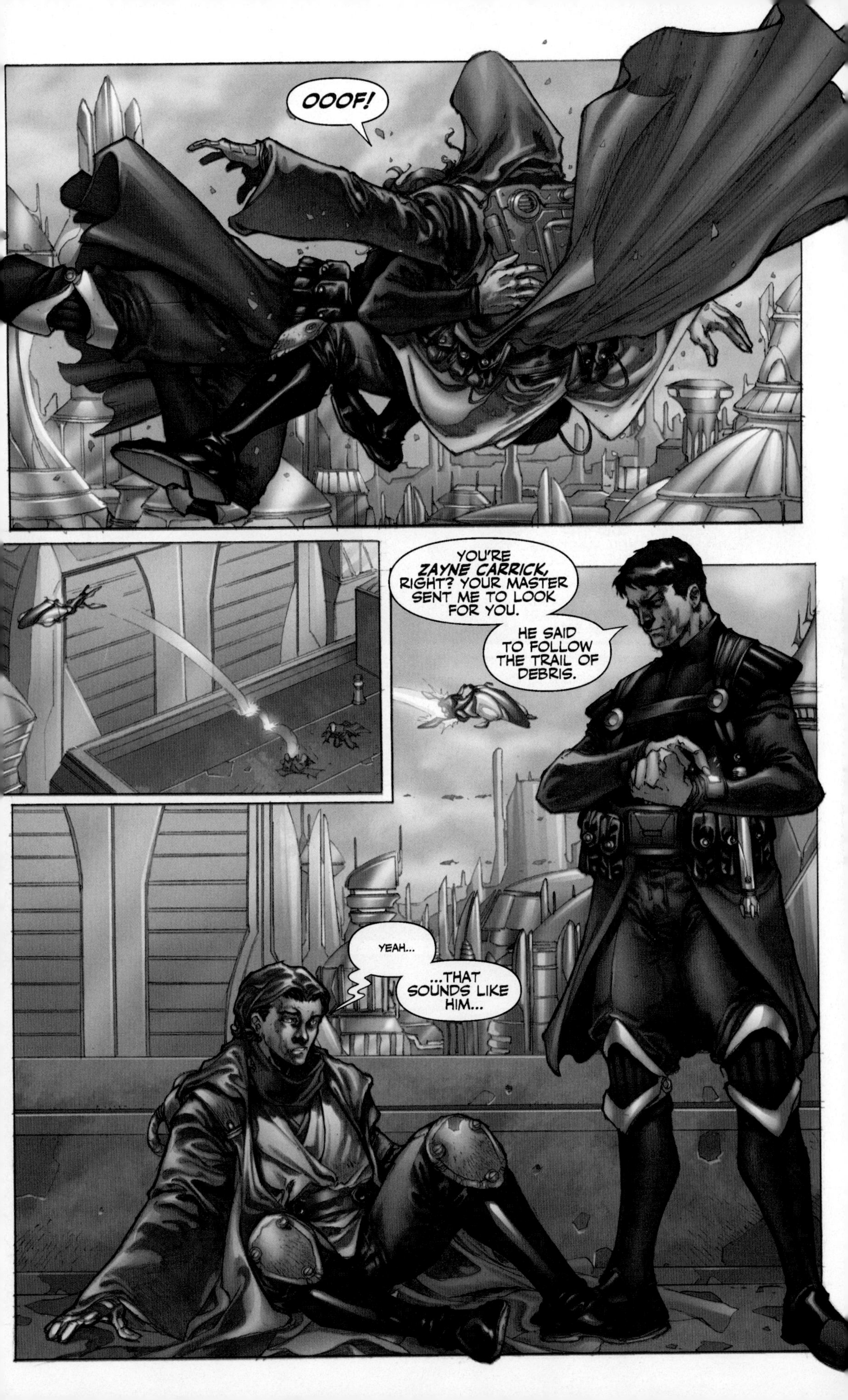
OOOF!
YOU'RE ZAYNE CARRICK, RIGHT? YOUR MASTER SENT ME TO LOOK FOR YOU.
HE SAID TO FOLLOW THE TRAIL OF DEBRIS.
YEAH...
...THAT SOUNDS LIKE HIM...

THANKS FOR THE SAVE. YOU'RE A JEDI? I DIDN'T KNOW THERE WERE OTHER JEDI ON TARIS -- BESIDES US AT THE ACADEMY.

A FEW OF US ARE PASSING THROUGH -- ON OUR WAY TO THE FRONT.

THE GUYS CALL ME SQUINT. OUR MASTER'S AN ACQUAINTANCE OF YOUR MASTER LUCIEN.

WE WERE HOPING TO RECRUIT SOME JEDI TO COME WITH US.

TO THE WAR? I'M AFRAID YOU'RE WASTING YOUR TIME.

MY MASTER DOESN'T THINK THE WAR WITH THE MANDALORIANS IS THE JEDI'S BUSINESS.

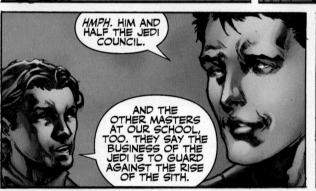

HMPH. HIM AND HALF THE JEDI COUNCIL.

AND THE OTHER MASTERS AT OUR SCHOOL, TOO. THEY SAY THE BUSINESS OF THE JEDI IS TO GUARD AGAINST THE RISE OF THE SITH.

THE SITH AGAIN! ZAYNE, YOU AND I COULD BE MANDALORIANS WITH OUR BOOTS AT YOUR MASTERS' THROATS --

-- BUT TO GET THEM TO NOTICE US, WE'D HAVE TO PAINT OUR HEADS AND BABBLE ABOUT THE DARK SIDE!

IT'S RIDICULOUS, DON'T YOU SEE? THE SITH THREAT ENDED, WHAT, 30 YEARS AGO? THE MANDALORIANS ARE THE THREAT. THE MANDALORIANS ARE HERE...

...ALMOST. WE NEED EVERY ABLE-BODIED JEDI WE CAN GET.

WELL, YOU'VE SEEN HOW ABLE-BODIED I AM -- AND I'M NOT A JEDI. NOT YET, ANYWAY. MY CLASS HAS A CHALLENGE TO FACE OFF-WORLD NEXT WEEK. IT MAY BE MY LAST CHANCE TO BECOME A KNIGHT.

YOU DON'T LIKE YOUR ODDS?

MY LUCK RANGES FROM BARELY TOLERABLE TO CATACLYSMIC. MASTER LUCIEN SAYS I'M LIVING PROOF THE FORCE HAS A SENSE OF HUMOR!

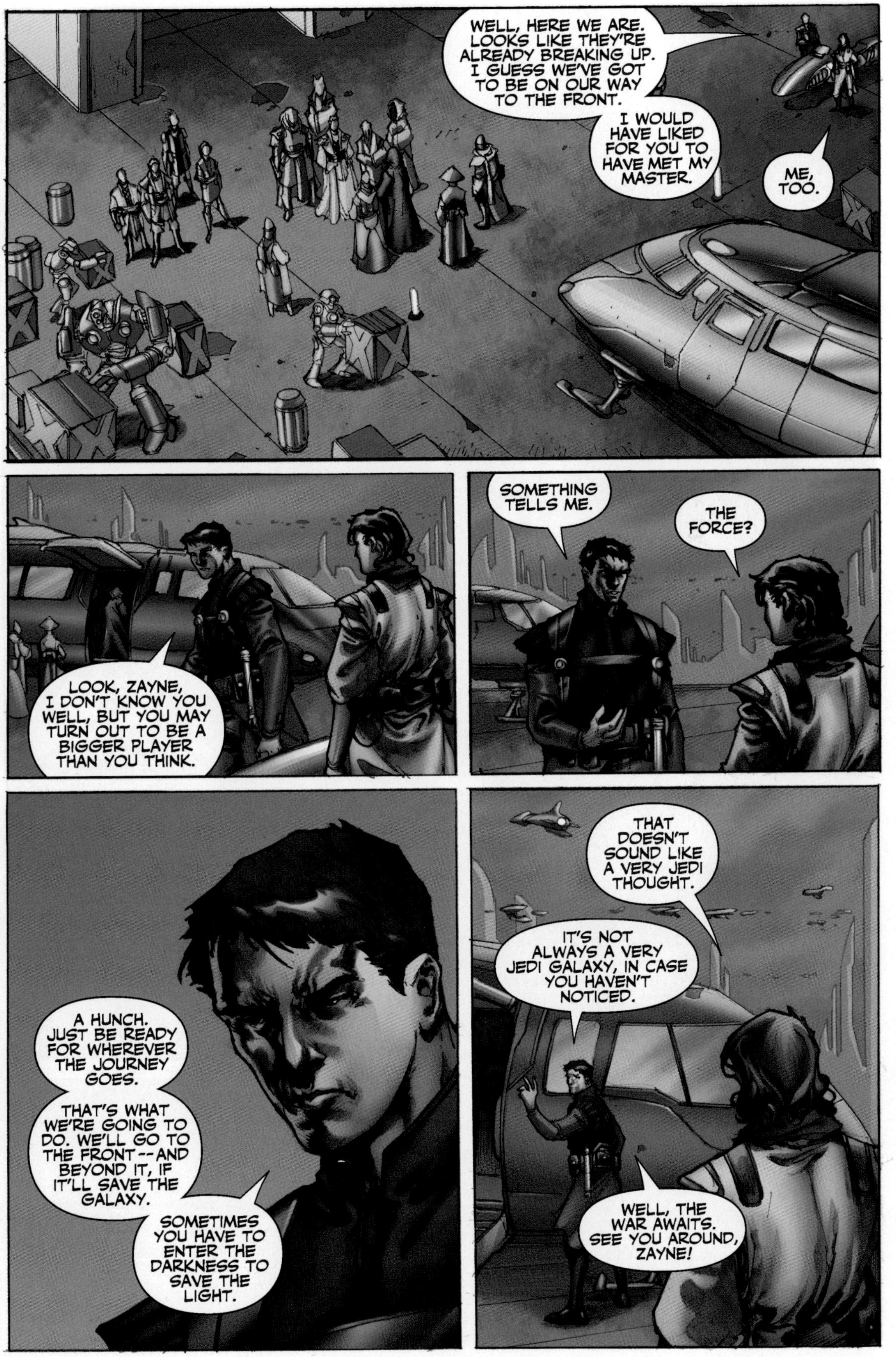

WELL, HERE WE ARE. LOOKS LIKE THEY'RE ALREADY BREAKING UP. I GUESS WE'VE GOT TO BE ON OUR WAY TO THE FRONT.
I WOULD HAVE LIKED FOR YOU TO HAVE MET MY MASTER.
ME, TOO.
LOOK, ZAYNE, I DON'T KNOW YOU WELL, BUT YOU MAY TURN OUT TO BE A BIGGER PLAYER THAN YOU THINK.
SOMETHING TELLS ME.
THE FORCE?
A HUNCH. JUST BE READY FOR WHEREVER THE JOURNEY GOES.
THAT'S WHAT WE'RE GOING TO DO. WE'LL GO TO THE FRONT--AND BEYOND IT, IF IT'LL SAVE THE GALAXY.
SOMETIMES YOU HAVE TO ENTER THE DARKNESS TO SAVE THE LIGHT.
THAT DOESN'T SOUND LIKE A VERY JEDI THOUGHT.
IT'S NOT ALWAYS A VERY JEDI GALAXY, IN CASE YOU HAVEN'T NOTICED.
WELL, THE WAR AWAITS. SEE YOU AROUND, ZAYNE!

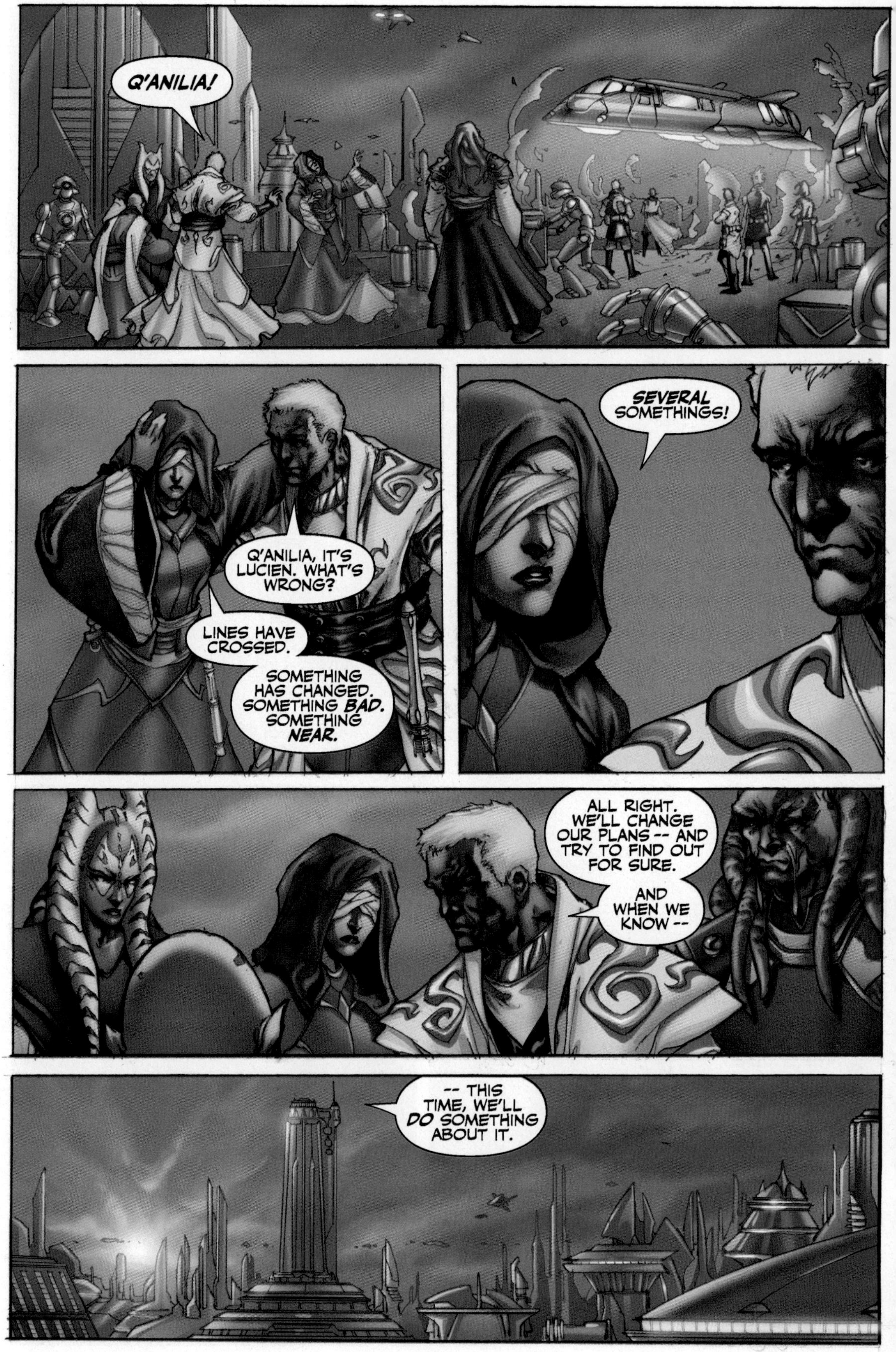
Q'ANILIA!
Q'ANILIA, IT'S LUCIEN. WHAT'S WRONG?
LINES HAVE CROSSED.
SOMETHING HAS CHANGED. SOMETHING *BAD.* SOMETHING *NEAR.*
SEVERAL SOMETHINGS!
ALL RIGHT. WE'LL CHANGE OUR PLANS -- AND TRY TO FIND OUT FOR SURE.
AND WHEN WE KNOW --
-- THIS TIME, WE'LL *DO* SOMETHING ABOUT IT.

39:56:1434
THE TARIS HOLOFEED
PRIME EDITION

STALEMATE ON SUURJA CONTINUES

FOURTH BATTLE IN SIX WEEKS INCONCLUSIVE

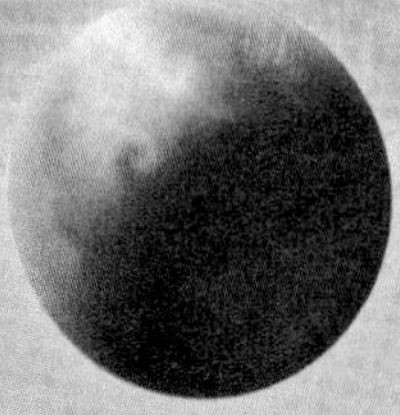

TARNITH STATION—Mandalorian and Republic forces have retired from the Outer Rim system of Suurja with neither gaining an advantage, according to embedded journalists with the Republic Fleet.

An agrarian world with a colonist population of 16 million, Suurja is the latest battlezone on the line of Jebble-Vanquo-Tarnith. It has been just over a year since the Mandalorians conquered their last populated system in the Outer Rim, not counting the Flashpoint stellar research station taken four months ago.

"This shows that the cordon that Captain [Saul] Karath has thrown up is holding," said Republic defense official Catronus Steffans. "It's only a matter of time before we begin pushing in the other direction."

Steffans chose not to respond to the recent controversy in the Jedi order over participation in the war. "Our relationship with the order is the most important the Republic has. We value their cooperation in any and all endeavors with us they choose to join."

Despite the official optimism, reports continue to surface of provisioning problems, despite the recent levy to keep the troops better supplied.

SELECT to learn more...

PATROL REDOUBLES HUNT FOR ZOVIUS MENDU

SELECT to learn more...

INVESTORS SOUGHT IN FISHING EXPEDITION

MARKET STREET, TARIS—Backers are being sought for a venture to return fleek eels from Hocekureem for the local restaurant trade. Baron Hieromarn, a Snivvian industrialist recently arrived on Taris, began soliciting investors yesterday in the Market Street Outdoor Exchange.

"There's nothing like a good fleek eel dripping in pepper oil—and, as inhabitants of your good world know, there's nothing like that here on Taris," the baron said. Once a tanker is hired and crewed, he said, backers can expect a three-for-one return on investment within a year.

"Within eight months, I guarantee eel will be the taste of the moment for the finer palates in the Upper City. Don't let this chance slip away!"

The baron said that, owing to a delay in transferring his accounts from Cadomai, only hard currency is being accepted at this time. He can be reached by leaving a message in care of the night desk clerk at the Middle City's Junavex Hotel—"a family friend," according to the baron.

SELECT to learn more...

TARIS PINS HOPES ON NEW JEDI CLASS

PATROL PLAZA, TARIS—With swoop-gang crime rampant in the Lower City, Taris officials increasingly looking towards another group of youths for possible relief: the five Padawans at the small satellite Jedi academy here.

The Padawans, should they become Knights, would traditionally be expected to be stationed to other systems. But while there is no agreement to the contrary, city officials—including the top law enforcement officer, Constable Sowrs—are hopeful the graduates will remain on duty here.

"They're already doing some policing as part of their training," Sowrs said. "If the number of Knights on Taris were to double overnight, it wouldn't trouble me in the least."

In a rare interview, the leader of the Jedi on Taris, Master Lucien Draay, spoke highly of the new class. Chief among the prospects are one of Taris' own, Shad Jelavan, a human orphaned two years ago after an accident claimed his parents' lives in the Middle City.

"Shad is the kind of apprentice every Master wishes he could have," Master Lucien said.

The other Padawans are Kamlin, the Falleen responsible for the capture of P'den Robalt; Gharn, one of the few Nagai Jedi candidates; Oojoh, the Ho'Din who brought down the Leverby smuggling ring; and Zayne Carrick, a human.

SELECT to learn more . . .

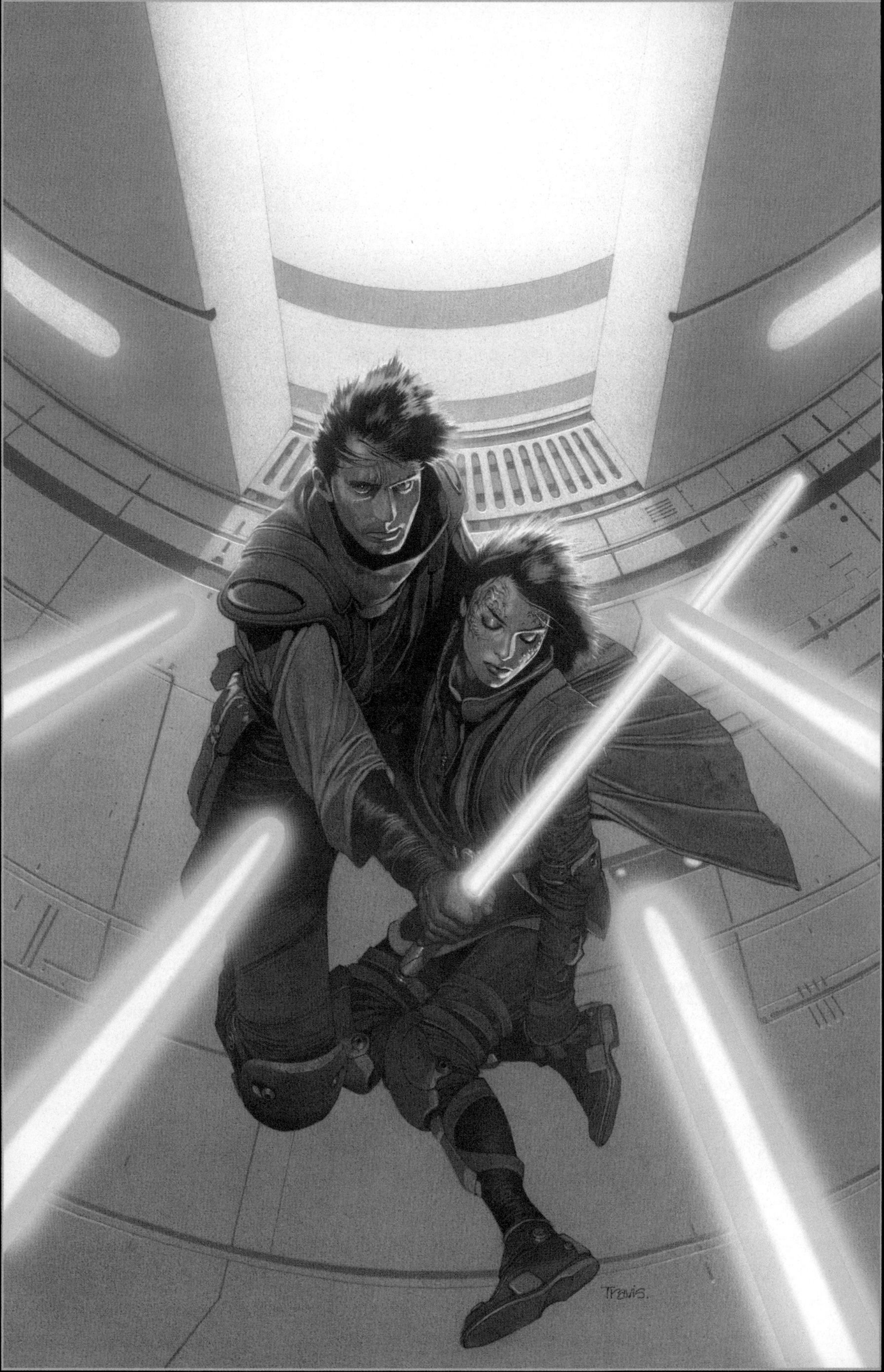
TRAVIS.

STAR WARS: KNIGHTS OF THE OLD REPUBLIC #1 **— "COMMENCEMENT, PART ONE"**

WRITER: JOHN JACKSON MILLER • ARTIST: BRIAN CHING • COLORIST: MICHAEL ATIYEH • LETTERER: MICHAEL HEISLER
ASSISTANT EDITOR: DAVE MARSHALL • EDITOR: JEREMY BARLOW • COVER ARTIST: TRAVIS CHAREST

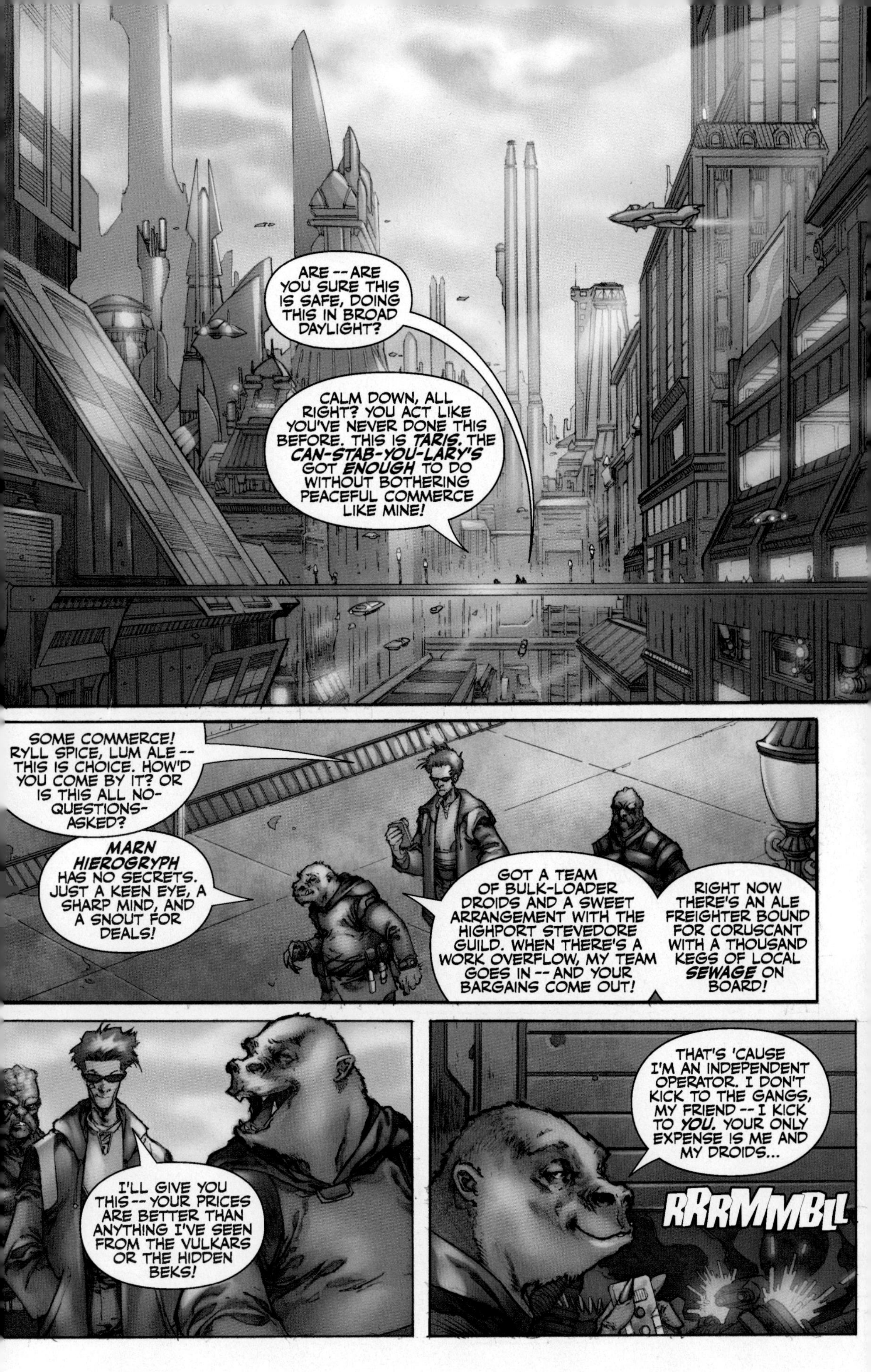
ARE -- ARE YOU SURE THIS IS SAFE, DOING THIS IN BROAD DAYLIGHT?
CALM DOWN, ALL RIGHT? YOU ACT LIKE YOU'VE NEVER DONE THIS BEFORE. THIS IS TARIS. THE CAN-STAB-YOU-LARY'S GOT ENOUGH TO DO WITHOUT BOTHERING PEACEFUL COMMERCE LIKE MINE!
SOME COMMERCE! RYLL SPICE, LUM ALE -- THIS IS CHOICE. HOW'D YOU COME BY IT? OR IS THIS ALL NO-QUESTIONS-ASKED?
MARN HIEROGRYPH HAS NO SECRETS. JUST A KEEN EYE, A SHARP MIND, AND A SNOUT FOR DEALS!
GOT A TEAM OF BULK-LOADER DROIDS AND A SWEET ARRANGEMENT WITH THE HIGHPORT STEVEDORE GUILD. WHEN THERE'S A WORK OVERFLOW, MY TEAM GOES IN -- AND YOUR BARGAINS COME OUT!
RIGHT NOW THERE'S AN ALE FREIGHTER BOUND FOR CORUSCANT WITH A THOUSAND KEGS OF LOCAL SEWAGE ON BOARD!
I'LL GIVE YOU THIS -- YOUR PRICES ARE BETTER THAN ANYTHING I'VE SEEN FROM THE VULKARS OR THE HIDDEN BEKS!
THAT'S 'CAUSE I'M AN INDEPENDENT OPERATOR. I DON'T KICK TO THE GANGS, MY FRIEND -- I KICK TO YOU. YOUR ONLY EXPENSE IS ME AND MY DROIDS...
RRRMMBLL

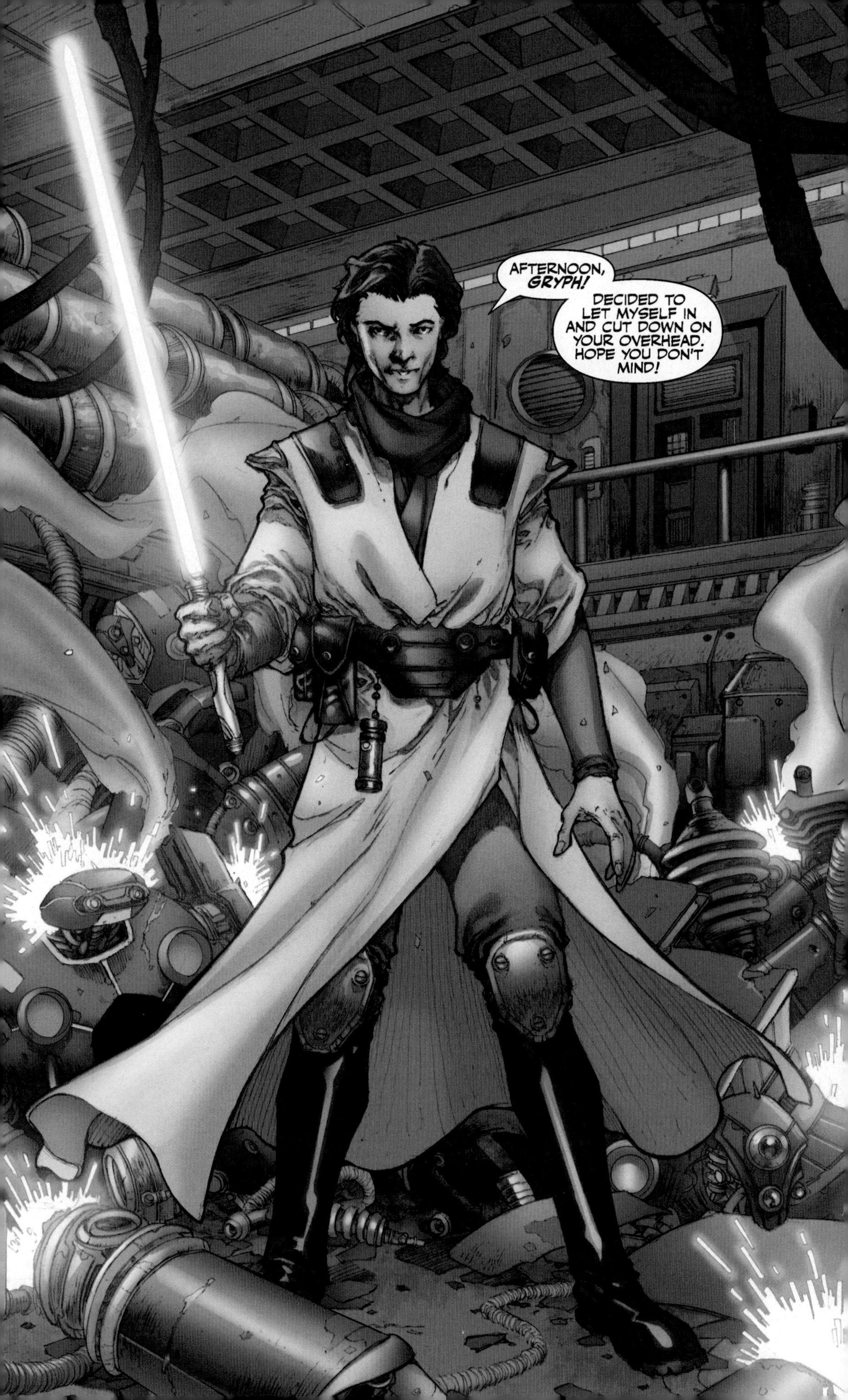
AFTERNOON, GRYPH!
DECIDED TO LET MYSELF IN AND CUT DOWN ON YOUR OVERHEAD. HOPE YOU DON'T MIND!

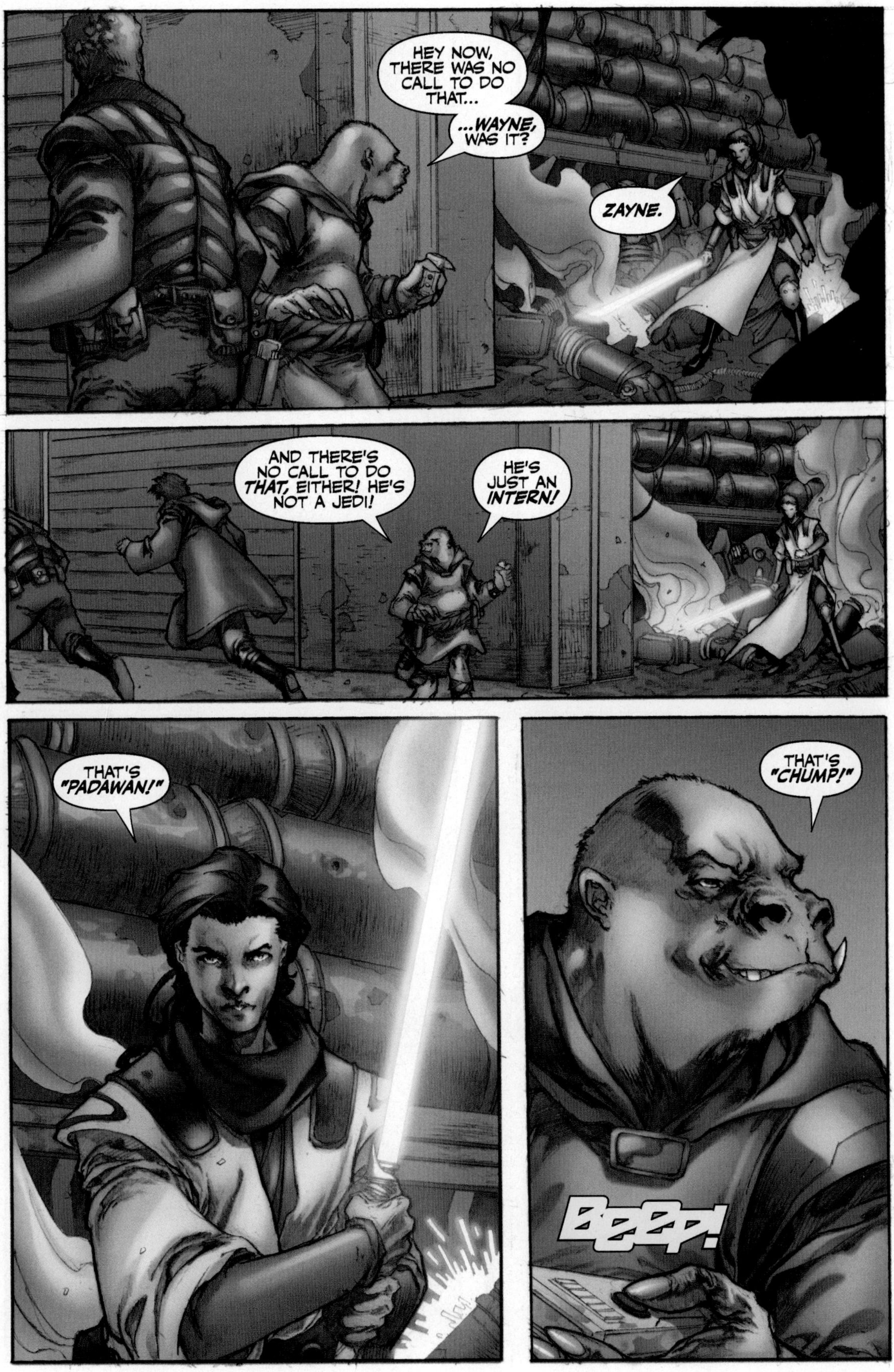

HEY NOW, THERE WAS NO CALL TO DO THAT...
...WAYNE, WAS IT?
ZAYNE.
AND THERE'S NO CALL TO DO THAT, EITHER! HE'S NOT A JEDI!
HE'S JUST AN INTERN!
THAT'S "PADAWAN!"
THAT'S "CHUMP!"
BEEP!

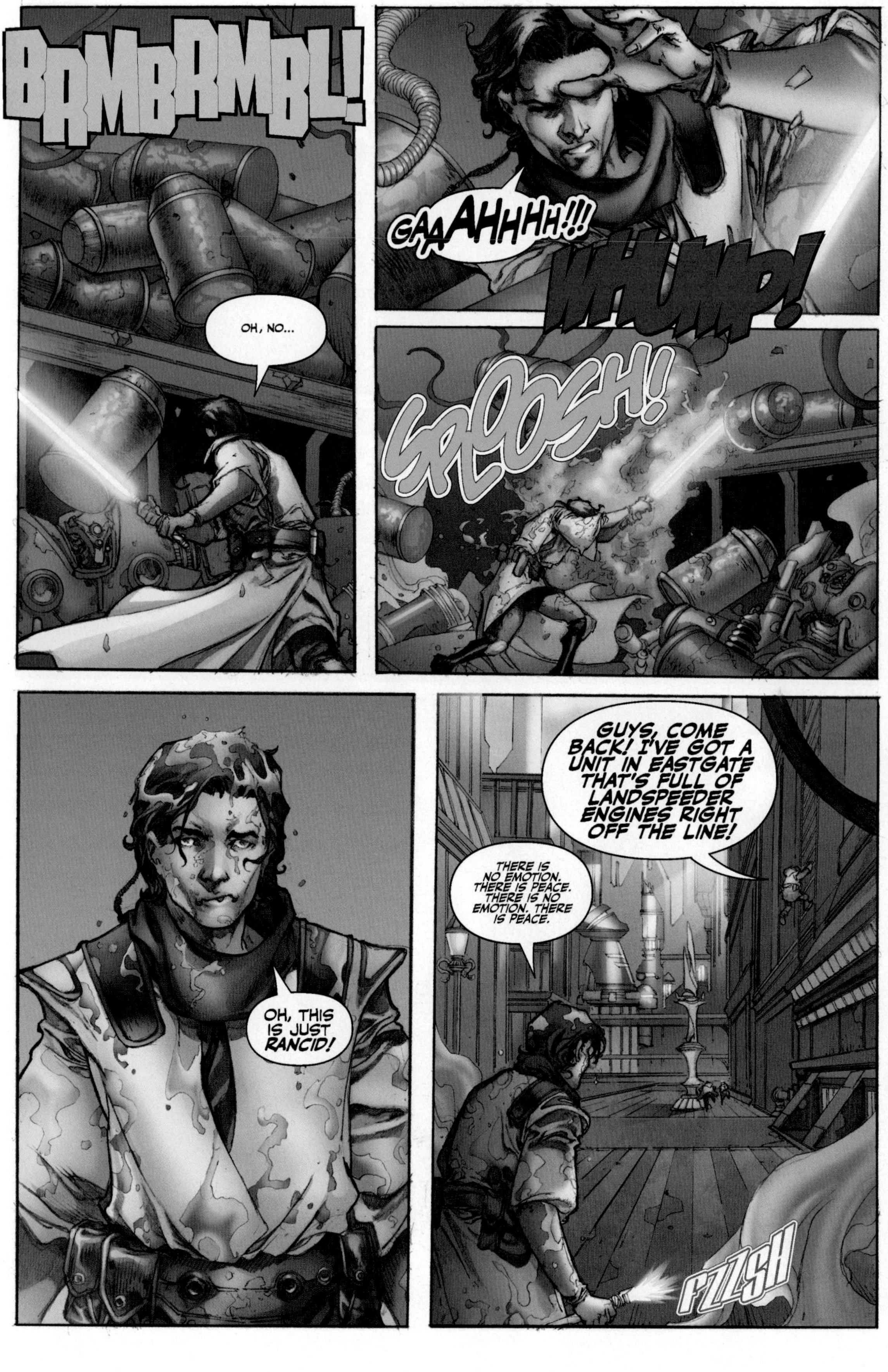
BRMBRMBL!
OH, NO...
GAAAHHHH!!!
WHUMP!
SPLOOSH!
OH, THIS IS JUST RANCID!
GUYS, COME BACK! I'VE GOT A UNIT IN EASTGATE THAT'S FULL OF LANDSPEEDER ENGINES RIGHT OFF THE LINE!
THERE IS NO EMOTION. THERE IS PEACE. THERE IS NO EMOTION. THERE IS PEACE.
FZZSH

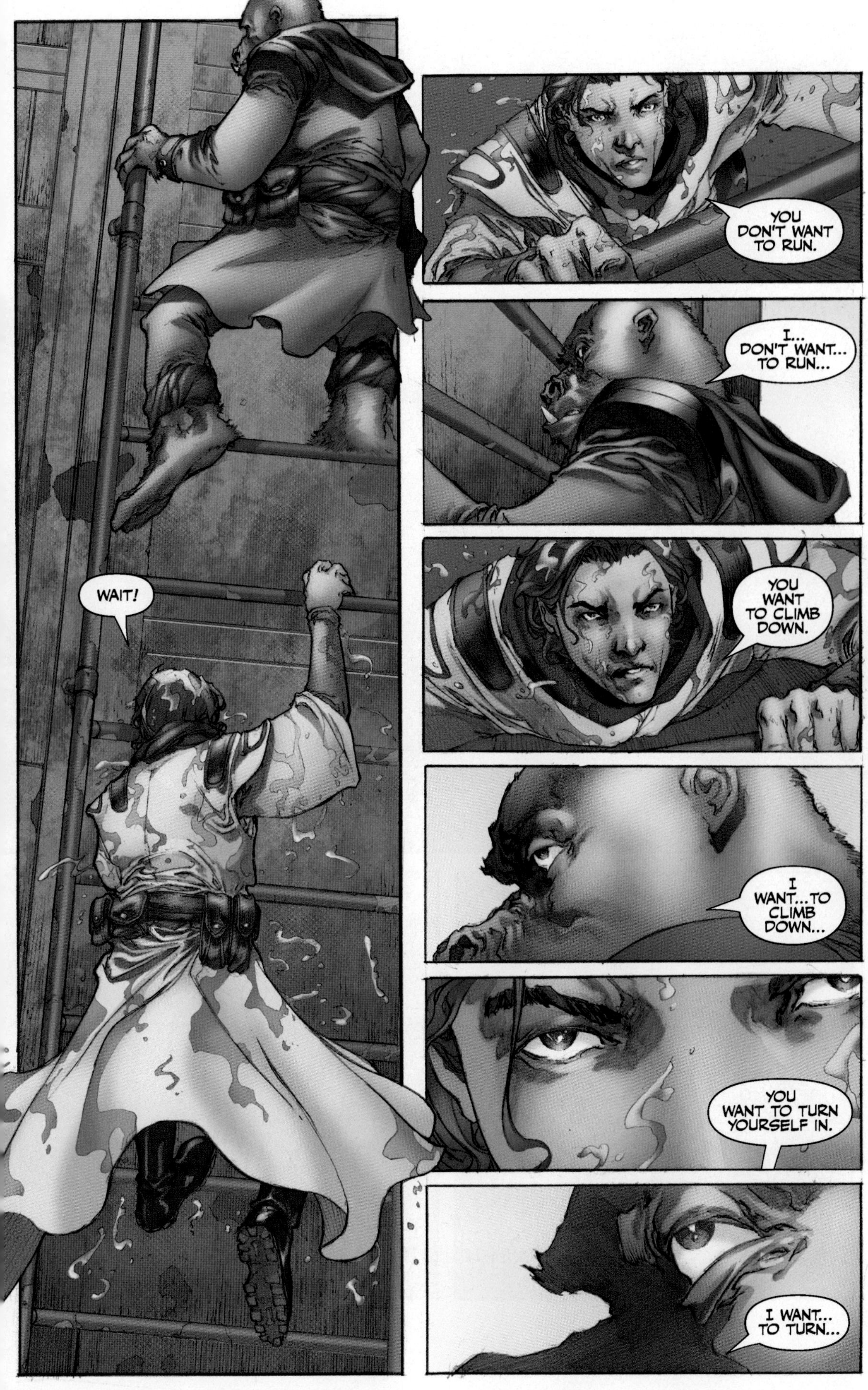
YOU DON'T WANT TO RUN.
I... DON'T WANT... TO RUN...
WAIT!
YOU WANT TO CLIMB DOWN.
I WANT...TO CLIMB DOWN...
YOU WANT TO TURN YOURSELF IN.
I WANT... TO TURN...

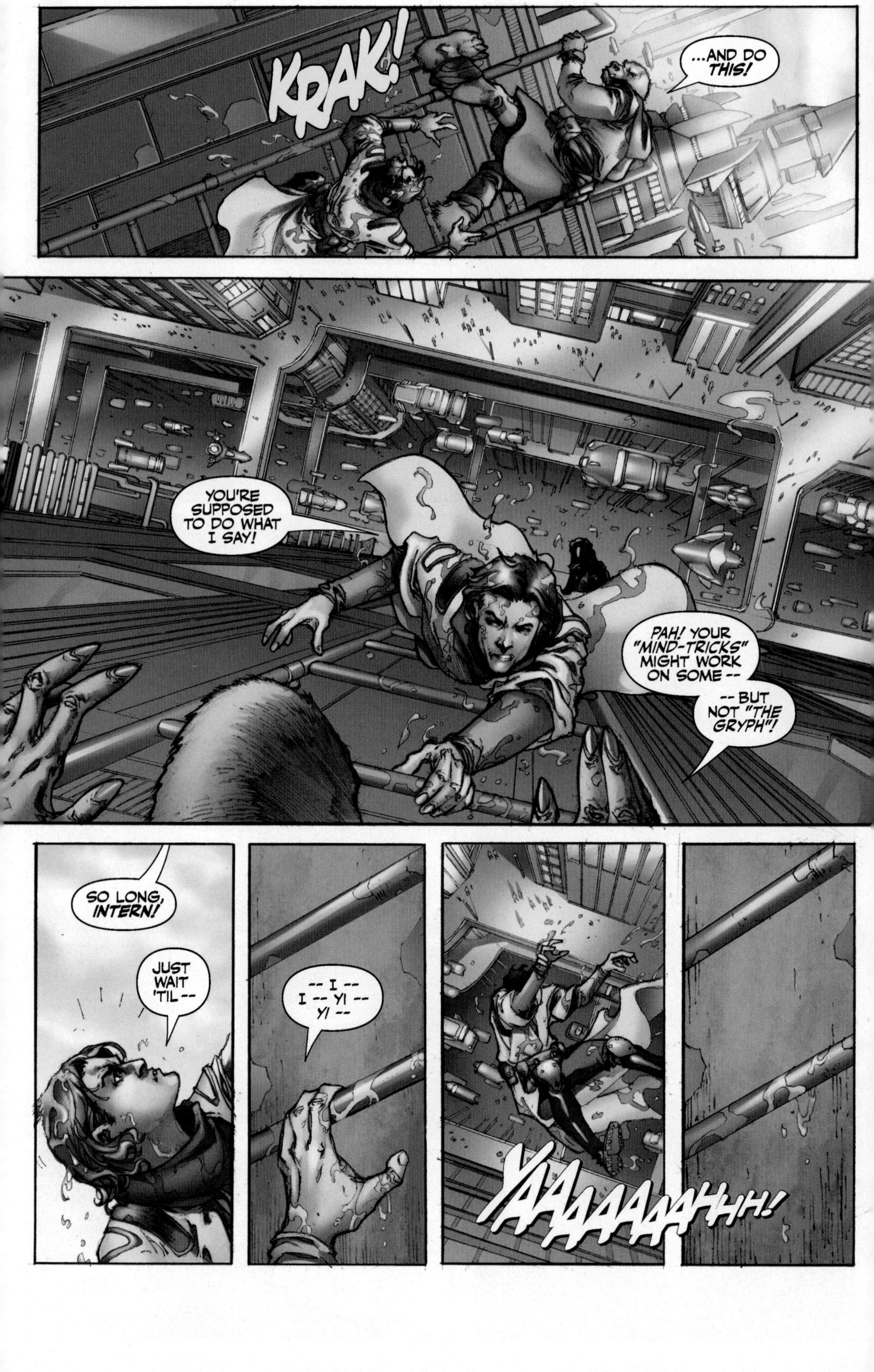
KRAK!
...AND DO THIS!
YOU'RE SUPPOSED TO DO WHAT I SAY!
PAH! YOUR "MIND-TRICKS" MIGHT WORK ON SOME --
-- BUT NOT "THE GRYPH"!
SO LONG, INTERN!
JUST WAIT 'TIL --
-- I -- I -- YI -- YI --
YAAAAAAAHHH!

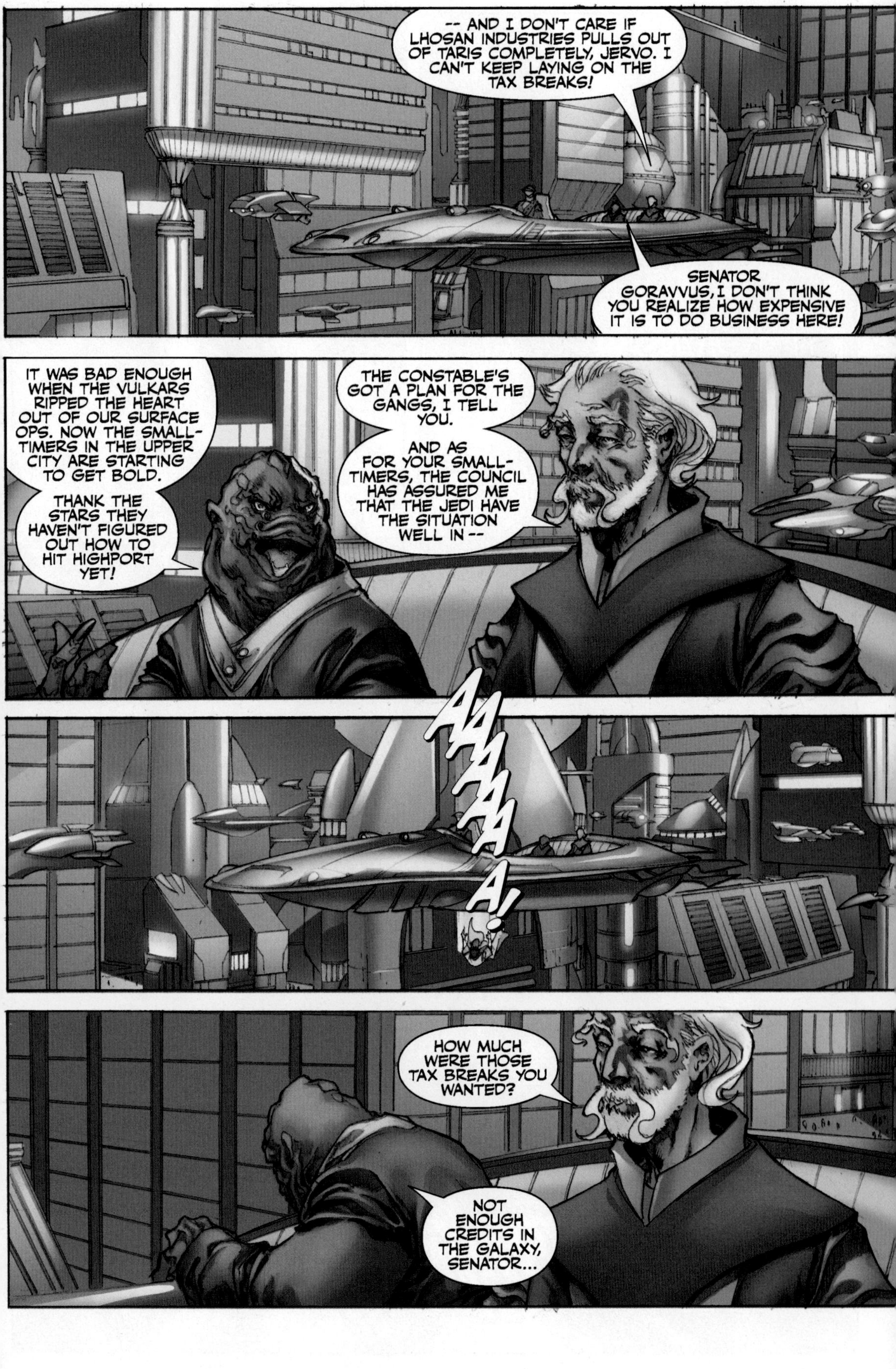
-- AND I DON'T CARE IF LHOSAN INDUSTRIES PULLS OUT OF TARIS COMPLETELY, JERVO. I CAN'T KEEP LAYING ON THE TAX BREAKS!
SENATOR GORAVVUS, I DON'T THINK YOU REALIZE HOW EXPENSIVE IT IS TO DO BUSINESS HERE!
IT WAS BAD ENOUGH WHEN THE VULKARS RIPPED THE HEART OUT OF OUR SURFACE OPS. NOW THE SMALL-TIMERS IN THE UPPER CITY ARE STARTING TO GET BOLD.
THANK THE STARS THEY HAVEN'T FIGURED OUT HOW TO HIT HIGHPORT YET!
THE CONSTABLE'S GOT A PLAN FOR THE GANGS, I TELL YOU.
AND AS FOR YOUR SMALL-TIMERS, THE COUNCIL HAS ASSURED ME THAT THE JEDI HAVE THE SITUATION WELL IN --
AAAAAAA!
HOW MUCH WERE THOSE TAX BREAKS YOU WANTED?
NOT ENOUGH CREDITS IN THE GALAXY, SENATOR...

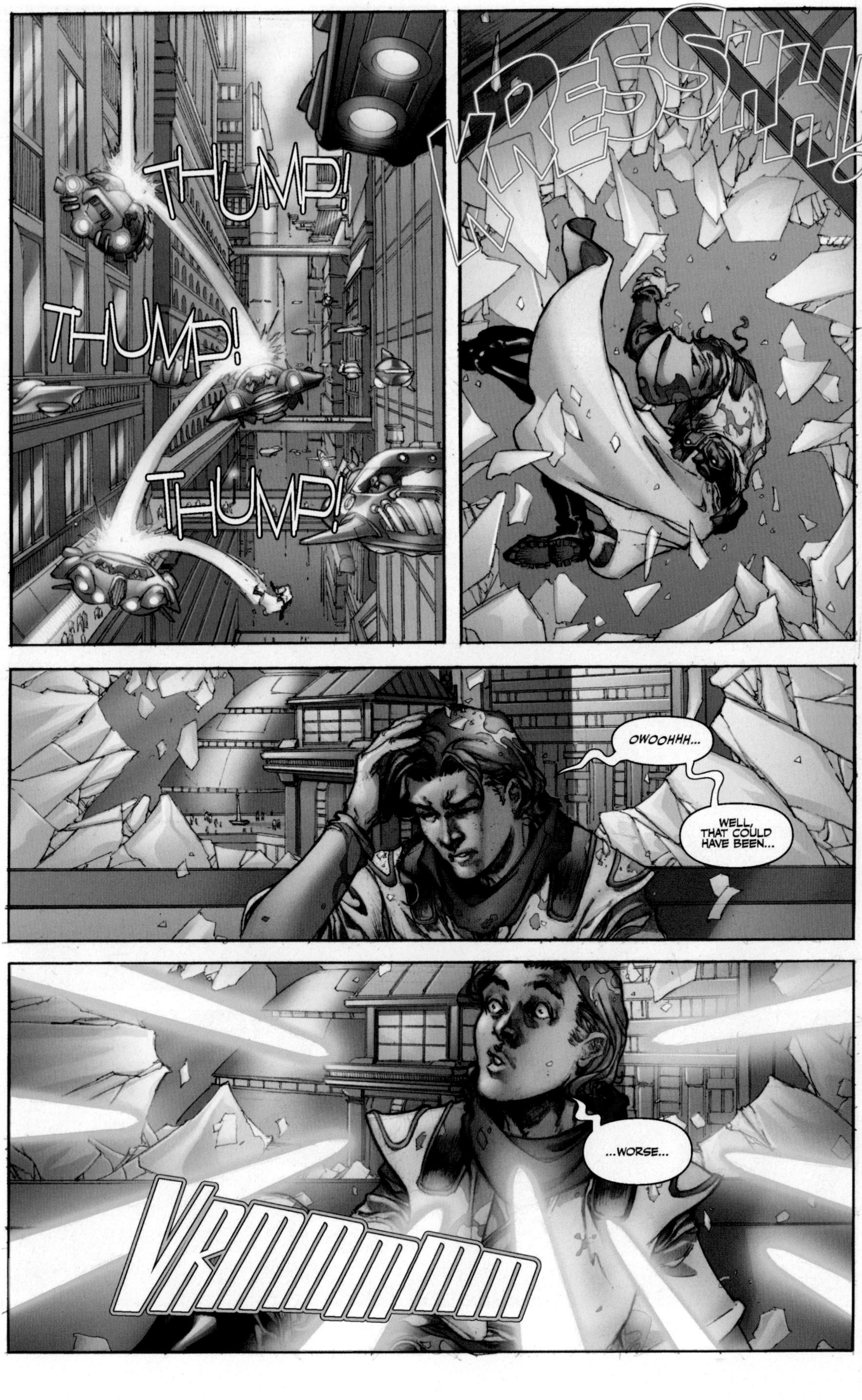
THUMP!
THUMP!
THUMP!
KRESSHH!
OWOOHHH...
WELL, THAT COULD HAVE BEEN...
...WORSE...
VRMMMMMM

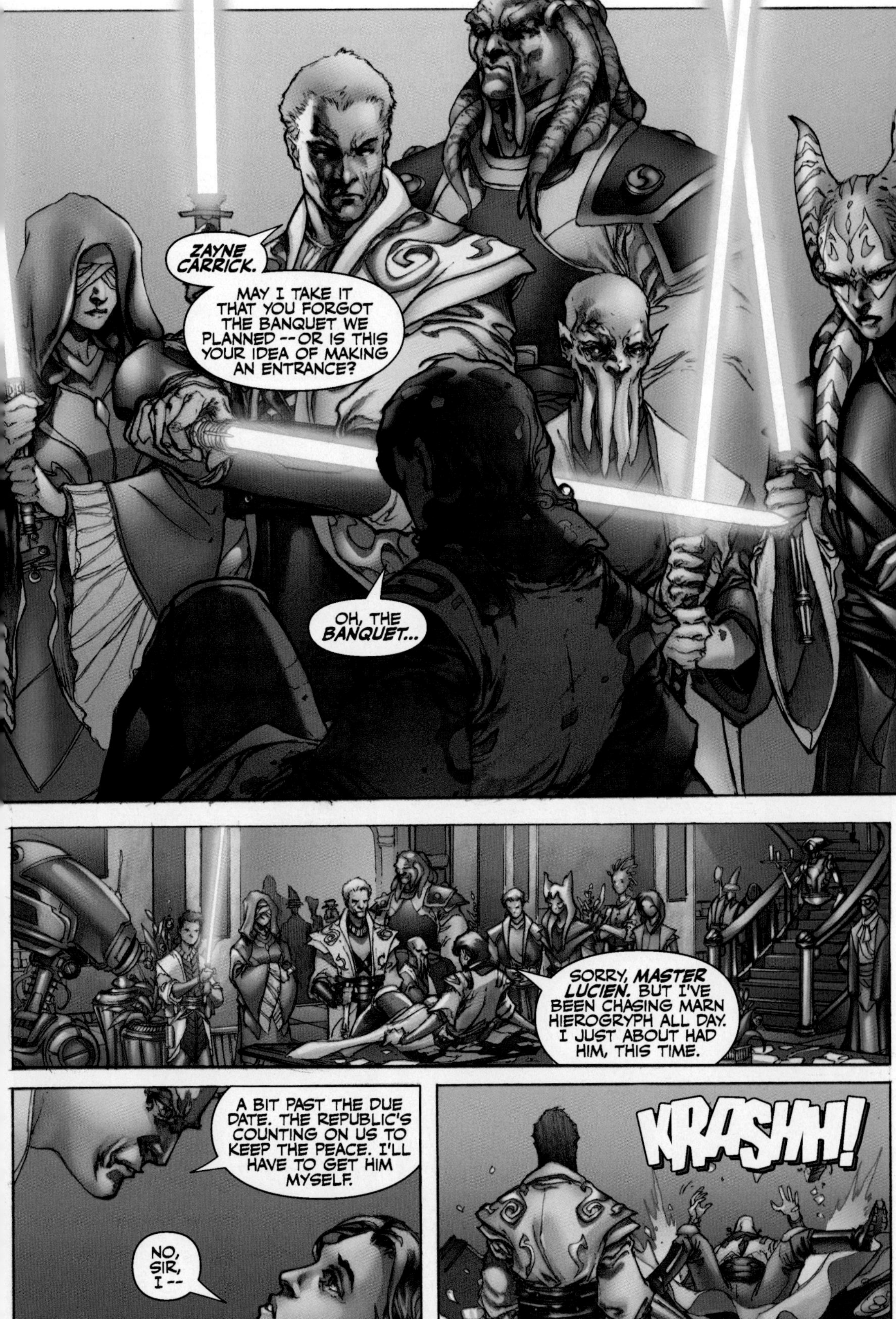
ZAYNE CARRICK.
MAY I TAKE IT THAT YOU FORGOT THE BANQUET WE PLANNED --OR IS THIS YOUR IDEA OF MAKING AN ENTRANCE?
OH, THE BANQUET...
SORRY, MASTER LUCIEN. BUT I'VE BEEN CHASING MARN HIEROGRYPH ALL DAY. I JUST ABOUT HAD HIM, THIS TIME.
A BIT PAST THE DUE DATE. THE REPUBLIC'S COUNTING ON US TO KEEP THE PEACE. I'LL HAVE TO GET HIM MYSELF.
NO, SIR, I --
KRASHH!

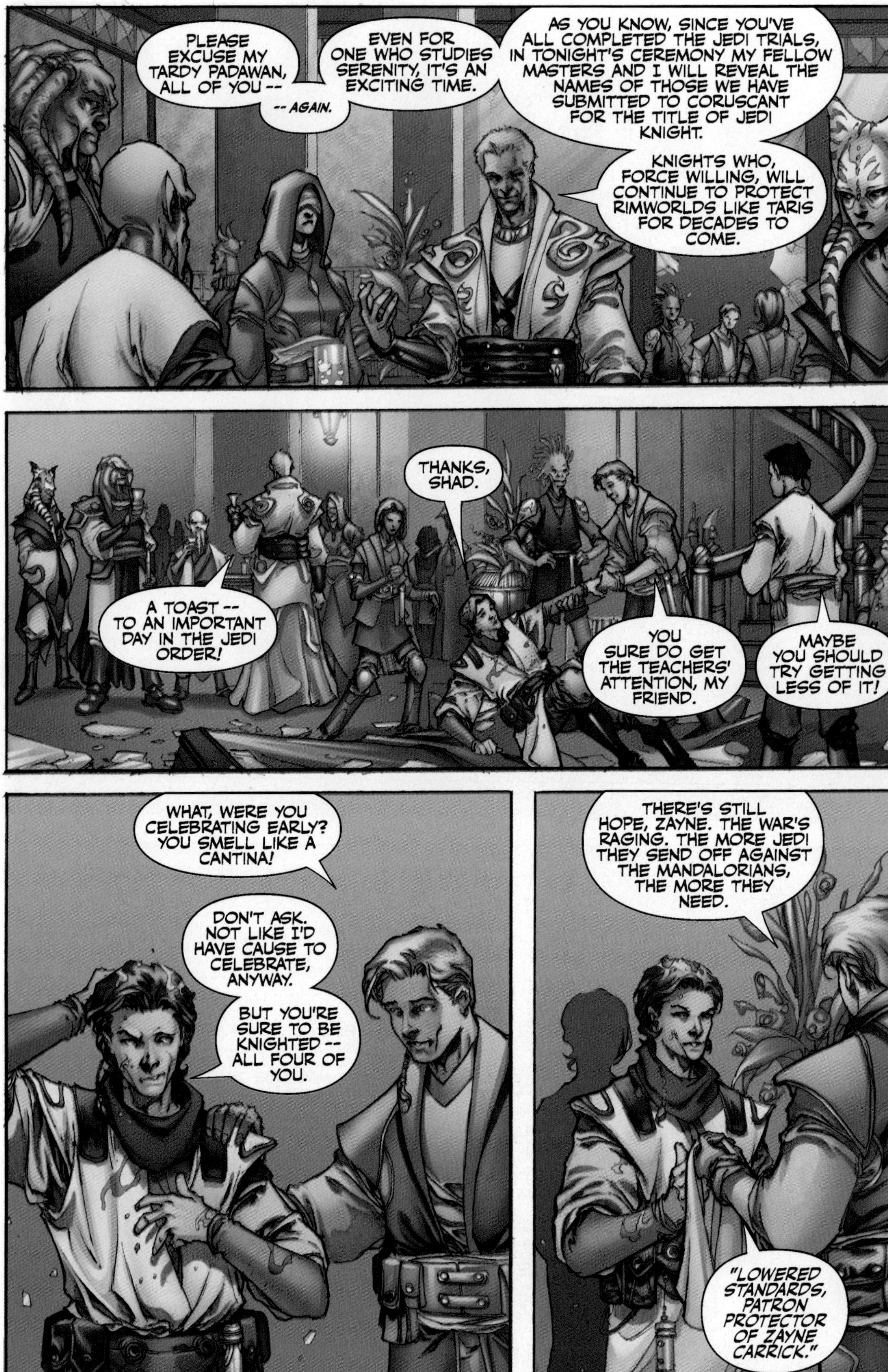
PLEASE EXCUSE MY TARDY PADAWAN, ALL OF YOU --
-- AGAIN.
EVEN FOR ONE WHO STUDIES SERENITY, IT'S AN EXCITING TIME.
AS YOU KNOW, SINCE YOU'VE ALL COMPLETED THE JEDI TRIALS, IN TONIGHT'S CEREMONY MY FELLOW MASTERS AND I WILL REVEAL THE NAMES OF THOSE WE HAVE SUBMITTED TO CORUSCANT FOR THE TITLE OF JEDI KNIGHT.
KNIGHTS WHO, FORCE WILLING, WILL CONTINUE TO PROTECT RIMWORLDS LIKE TARIS FOR DECADES TO COME.
THANKS, SHAD.
A TOAST -- TO AN IMPORTANT DAY IN THE JEDI ORDER!
YOU SURE DO GET THE TEACHERS' ATTENTION, MY FRIEND.
MAYBE YOU SHOULD TRY GETTING LESS OF IT!
WHAT, WERE YOU CELEBRATING EARLY? YOU SMELL LIKE A CANTINA!
DON'T ASK. NOT LIKE I'D HAVE CAUSE TO CELEBRATE, ANYWAY.
BUT YOU'RE SURE TO BE KNIGHTED -- ALL FOUR OF YOU.
THERE'S STILL HOPE, ZAYNE. THE WAR'S RAGING. THE MORE JEDI THEY SEND OFF AGAINST THE MANDALORIANS, THE MORE THEY NEED.
"LOWERED STANDARDS, PATRON PROTECTOR OF ZAYNE CARRICK."

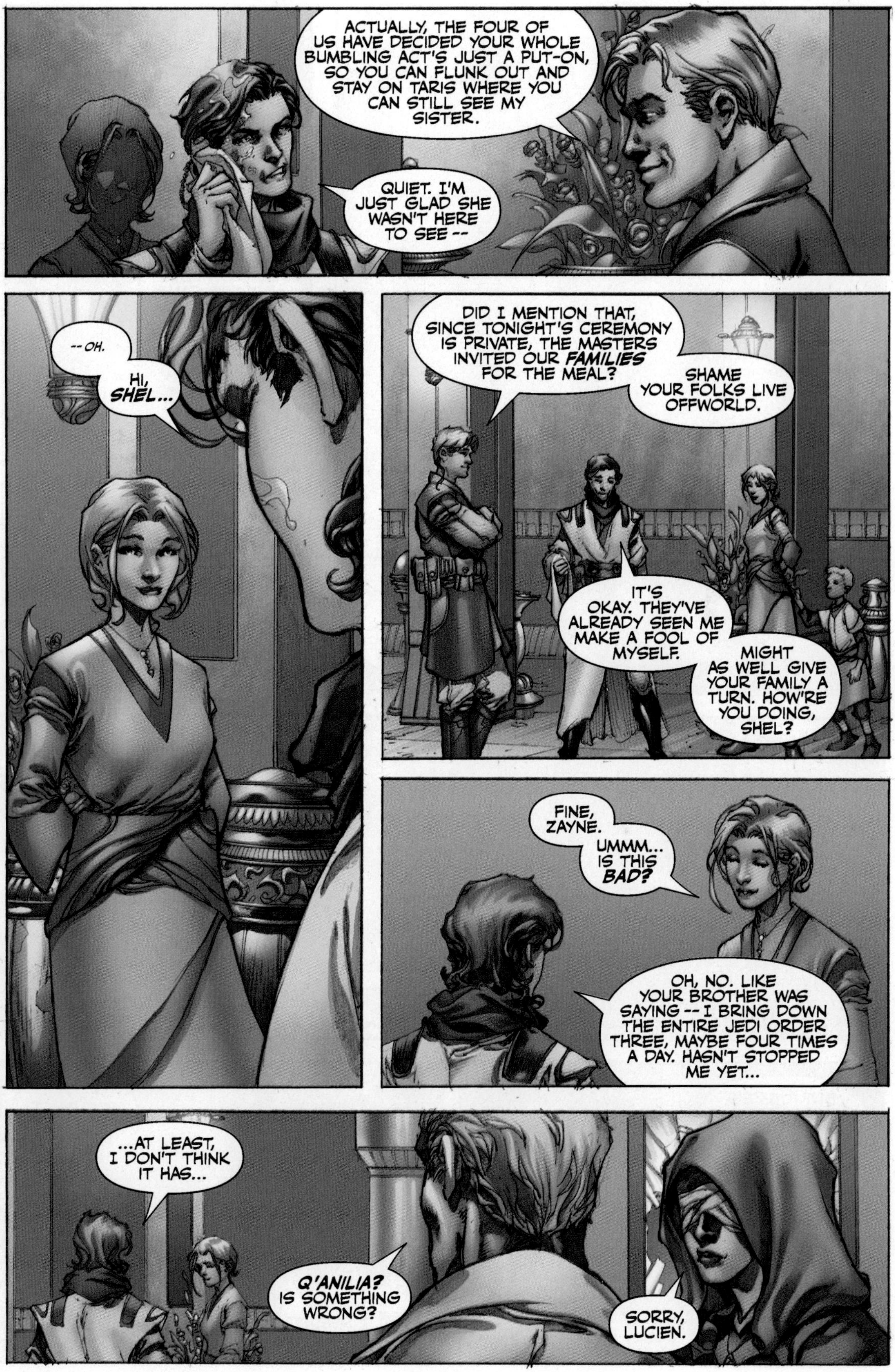
ACTUALLY, THE FOUR OF US HAVE DECIDED YOUR WHOLE BUMBLING ACT'S JUST A PUT-ON, SO YOU CAN FLUNK OUT AND STAY ON TARIS WHERE YOU CAN STILL SEE MY SISTER.
QUIET. I'M JUST GLAD SHE WASN'T HERE TO SEE --
--OH.
HI, SHEL...
DID I MENTION THAT, SINCE TONIGHT'S CEREMONY IS PRIVATE, THE MASTERS INVITED OUR FAMILIES FOR THE MEAL?
SHAME YOUR FOLKS LIVE OFFWORLD.
IT'S OKAY. THEY'VE ALREADY SEEN ME MAKE A FOOL OF MYSELF.
MIGHT AS WELL GIVE YOUR FAMILY A TURN. HOW'RE YOU DOING, SHEL?
FINE, ZAYNE.
UMMM... IS THIS BAD?
OH, NO. LIKE YOUR BROTHER WAS SAYING -- I BRING DOWN THE ENTIRE JEDI ORDER THREE, MAYBE FOUR TIMES A DAY. HASN'T STOPPED ME YET...
...AT LEAST, I DON'T THINK IT HAS...
Q'ANILIA? IS SOMETHING WRONG?
SORRY, LUCIEN.

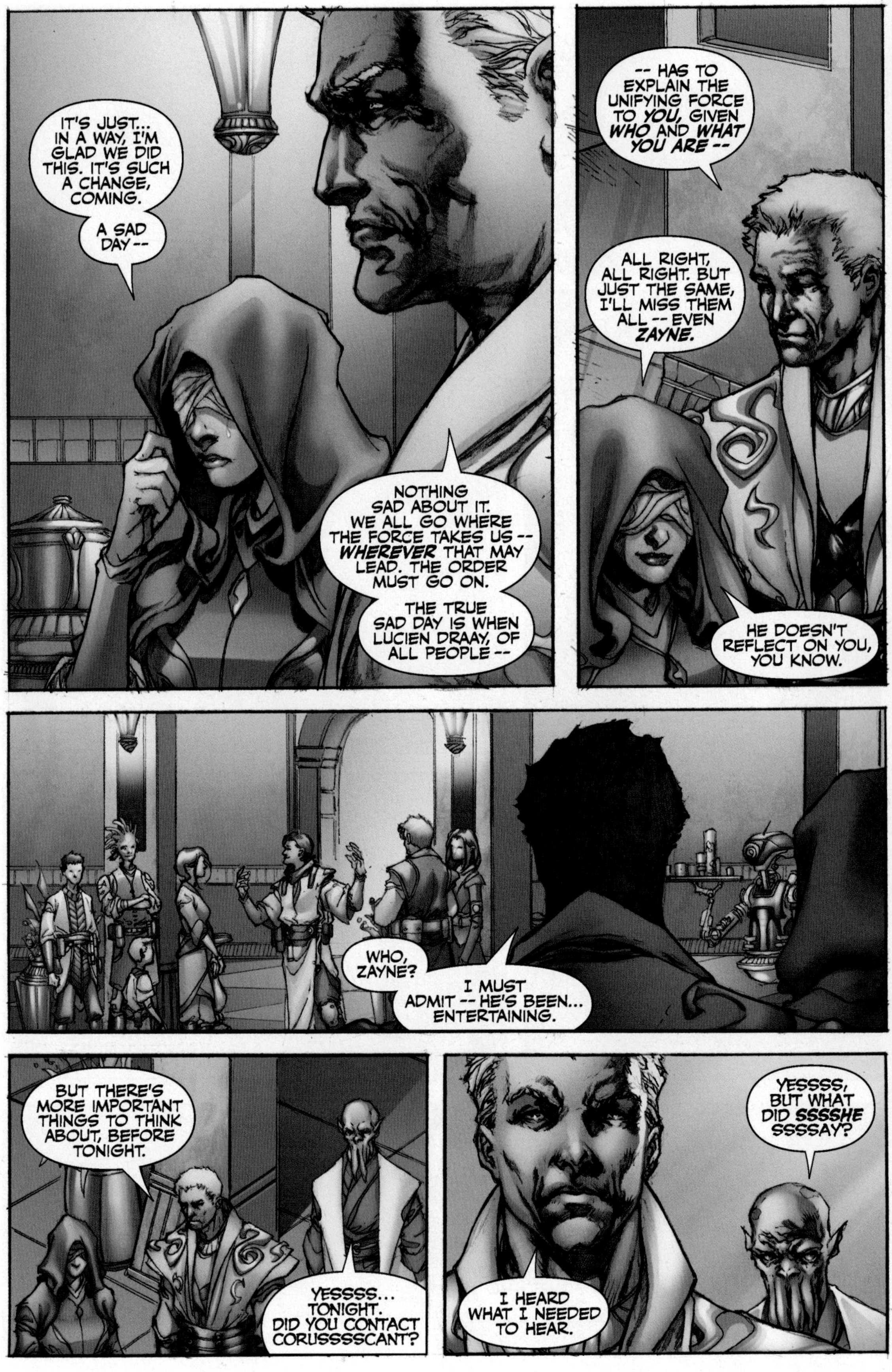
IT'S JUST... IN A WAY, I'M GLAD WE DID THIS. IT'S SUCH A CHANGE, COMING.
A SAD DAY --
NOTHING SAD ABOUT IT. WE ALL GO WHERE THE FORCE TAKES US -- *WHEREVER* THAT MAY LEAD. THE ORDER MUST GO ON.
THE TRUE SAD DAY IS WHEN LUCIEN DRAAY, OF ALL PEOPLE --
-- HAS TO EXPLAIN THE UNIFYING FORCE TO *YOU,* GIVEN *WHO* AND *WHAT YOU ARE* --
ALL RIGHT, ALL RIGHT. BUT JUST THE SAME, I'LL MISS THEM ALL -- EVEN *ZAYNE.*
HE DOESN'T REFLECT ON YOU, YOU KNOW.
WHO, ZAYNE?
I MUST ADMIT -- HE'S BEEN... ENTERTAINING.
BUT THERE'S MORE IMPORTANT THINGS TO THINK ABOUT, BEFORE TONIGHT.
YESSSS... TONIGHT. DID YOU CONTACT CORUSSSSCANT?
I HEARD WHAT I NEEDED TO HEAR.
YESSSS, BUT WHAT DID *SSSSHE* SSSSAY?

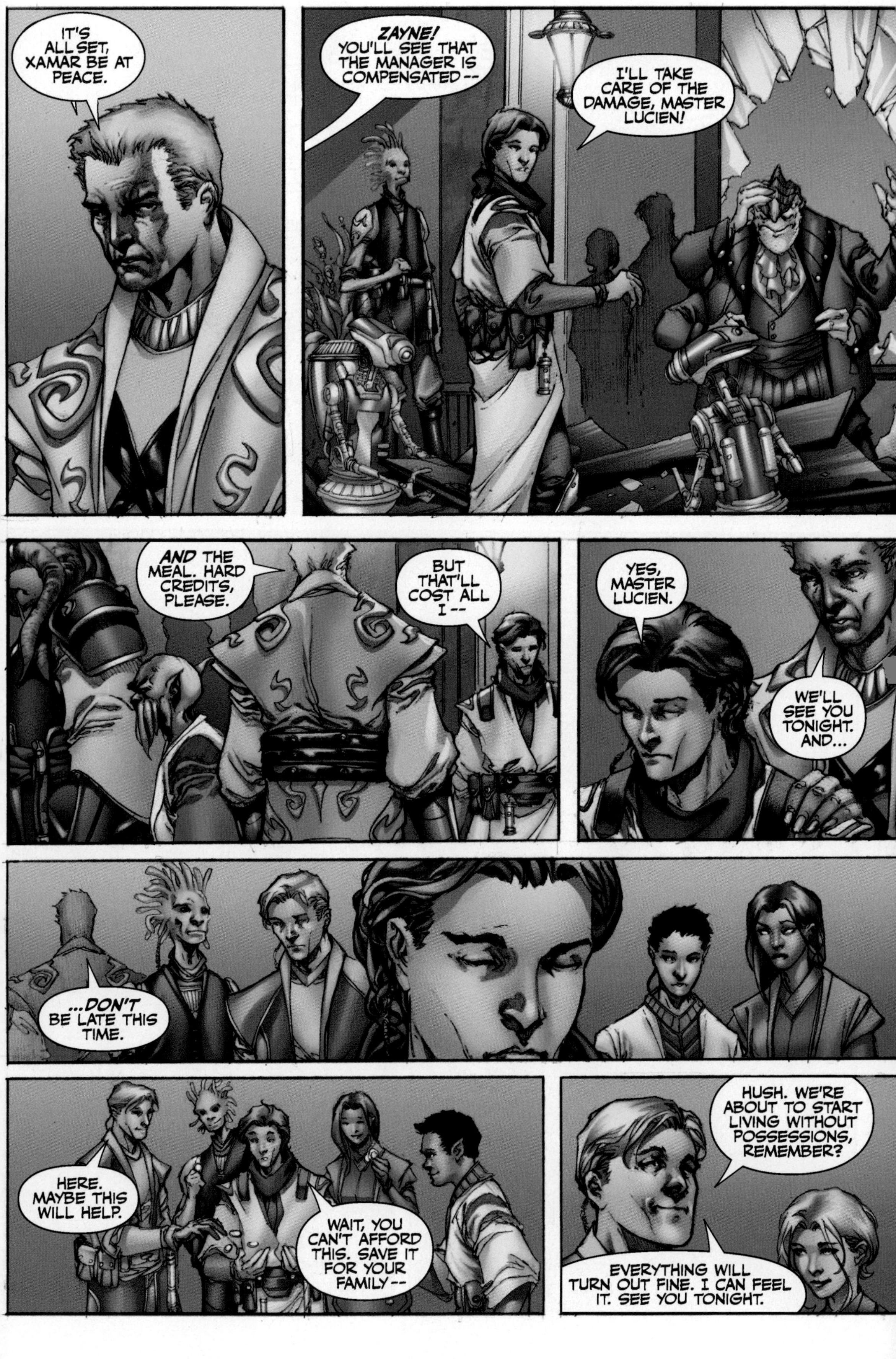
IT'S ALL SET, XAMAR BE AT PEACE.
ZAYNE! YOU'LL SEE THAT THE MANAGER IS COMPENSATED --
I'LL TAKE CARE OF THE DAMAGE, MASTER LUCIEN!
AND THE MEAL. HARD CREDITS, PLEASE.
BUT THAT'LL COST ALL I --
YES, MASTER LUCIEN.
WE'LL SEE YOU TONIGHT. AND...
...DON'T BE LATE THIS TIME.
HERE. MAYBE THIS WILL HELP.
WAIT, YOU CAN'T AFFORD THIS. SAVE IT FOR YOUR FAMILY --
HUSH. WE'RE ABOUT TO START LIVING WITHOUT POSSESSIONS, REMEMBER?
EVERYTHING WILL TURN OUT FINE. I CAN FEEL IT. SEE YOU TONIGHT.

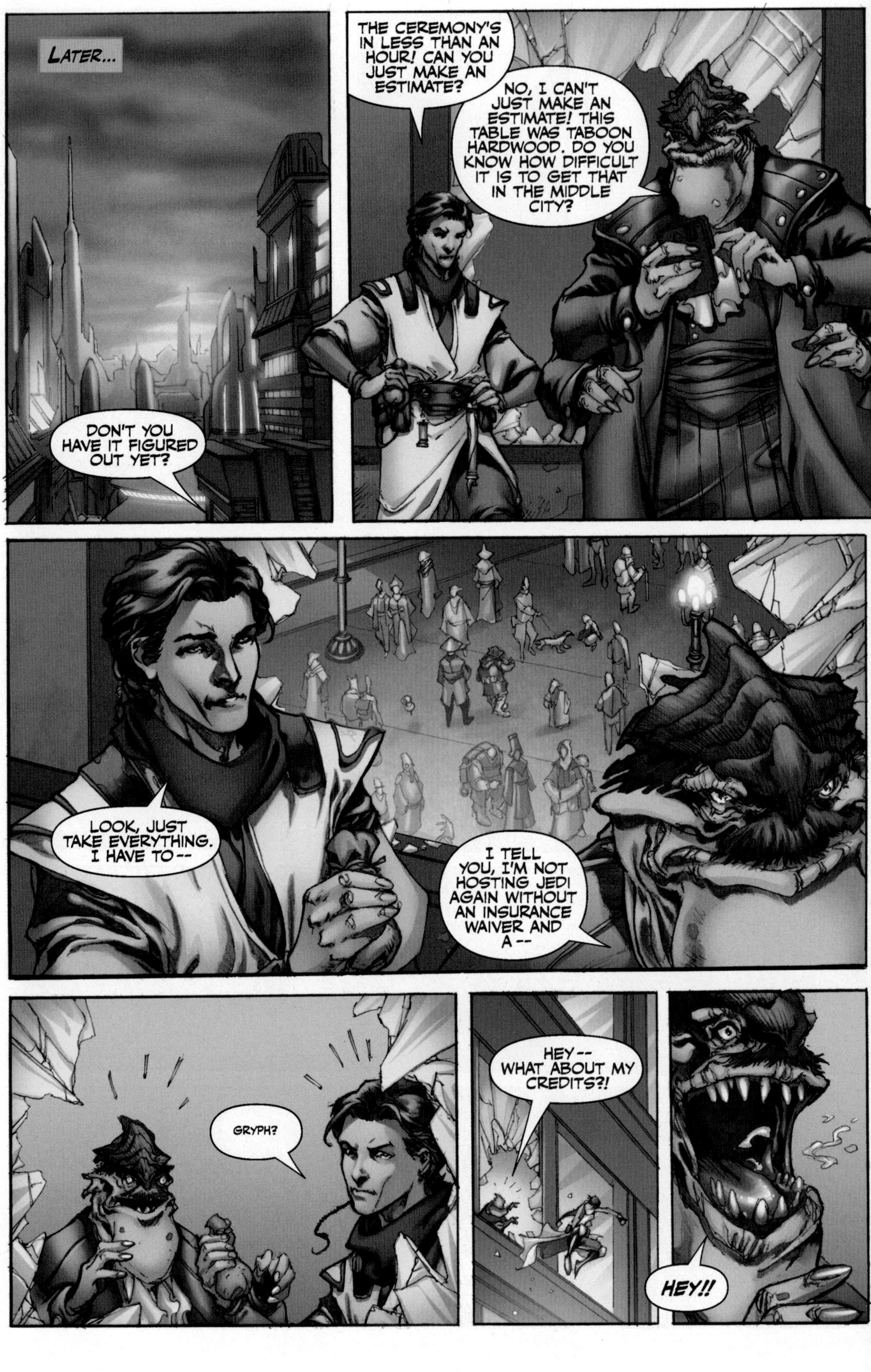
LATER...
DON'T YOU HAVE IT FIGURED OUT YET?
THE CEREMONY'S IN LESS THAN AN HOUR! CAN YOU JUST MAKE AN ESTIMATE?
NO, I CAN'T JUST MAKE AN ESTIMATE! THIS TABLE WAS TABOON HARDWOOD. DO YOU KNOW HOW DIFFICULT IT IS TO GET THAT IN THE MIDDLE CITY?
LOOK, JUST TAKE EVERYTHING. I HAVE TO--
I TELL YOU, I'M NOT HOSTING JEDI AGAIN WITHOUT AN INSURANCE WAIVER AND A--
GRYPH?
HEY-- WHAT ABOUT MY CREDITS?!
HEY!!

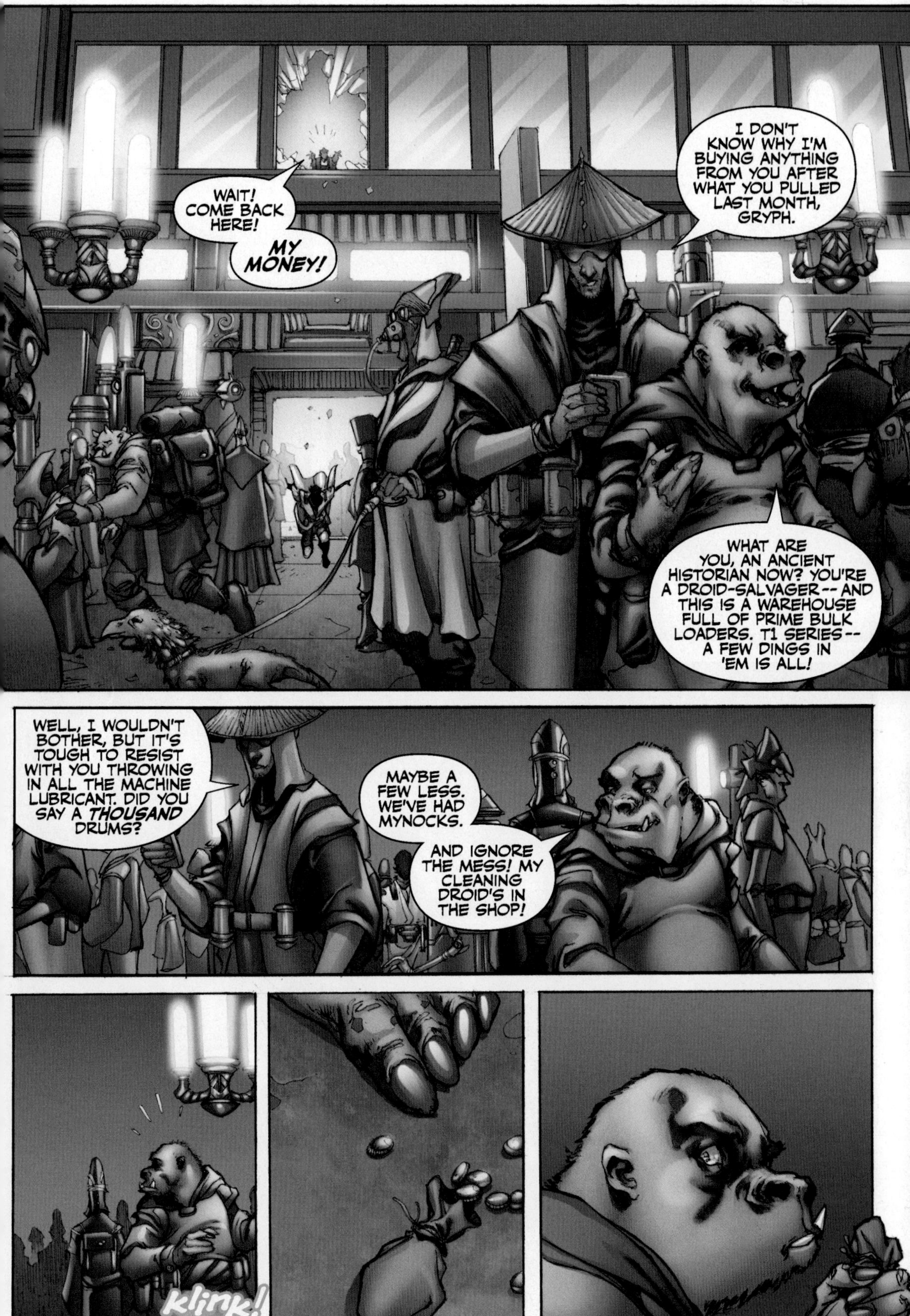
WAIT! COME BACK HERE!
MY MONEY!
I DON'T KNOW WHY I'M BUYING ANYTHING FROM YOU AFTER WHAT YOU PULLED LAST MONTH, GRYPH.
WHAT ARE YOU, AN ANCIENT HISTORIAN NOW? YOU'RE A DROID-SALVAGER -- AND THIS IS A WAREHOUSE FULL OF PRIME BULK LOADERS. T1 SERIES -- A FEW DINGS IN 'EM IS ALL!
WELL, I WOULDN'T BOTHER, BUT IT'S TOUGH TO RESIST WITH YOU THROWING IN ALL THE MACHINE LUBRICANT. DID YOU SAY A *THOUSAND* DRUMS?
MAYBE A FEW LESS. WE'VE HAD MYNOCKS.
AND IGNORE THE MESS! MY CLEANING DROID'S IN THE SHOP!
klink!

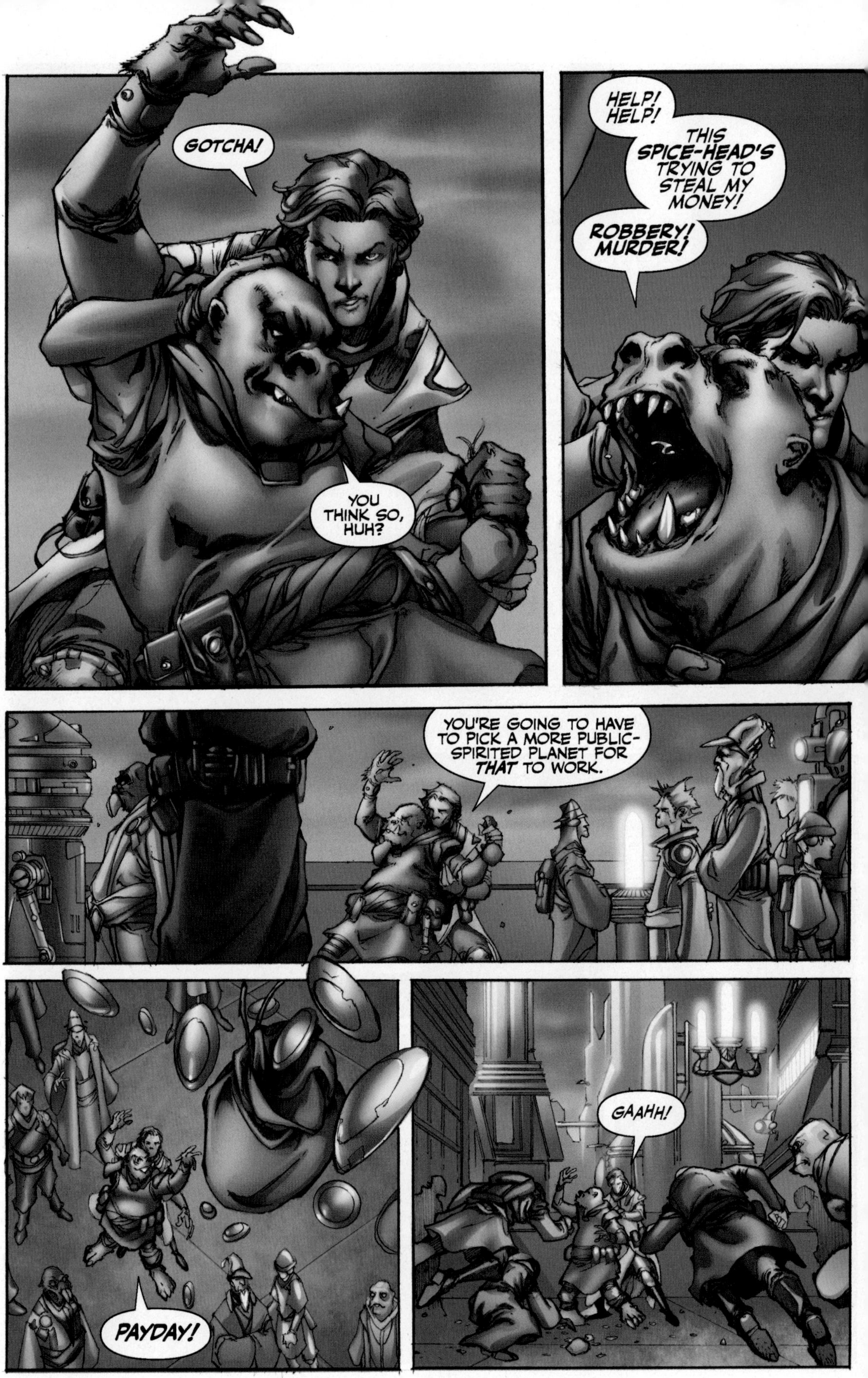
GOTCHA!
YOU THINK SO, HUH?
HELP! HELP!
THIS SPICE-HEAD'S TRYING TO STEAL MY MONEY!
ROBBERY! MURDER!
YOU'RE GOING TO HAVE TO PICK A MORE PUBLIC-SPIRITED PLANET FOR THAT TO WORK.
PAYDAY!
GAAHH!

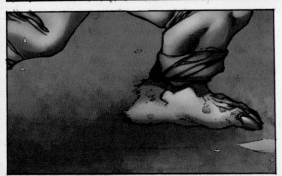

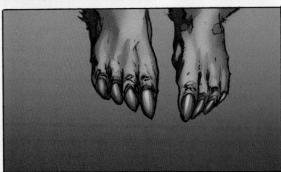

I -- UH -- SEEM TO HAVE LOST WEIGHT.

AND I SEEM TO HAVE LOST ALL MY MONEY.

GOT TO ADMIT, I WAS SURPRISED TO SEE YOU THROW IT AWAY.

AHHH, THAT'S SMALL CHANGE FOR A GUY LIKE ME.

THAT DIDN'T SEEM TO STOP YOU FROM GOING FOR IT IN THE FIRST PLACE.

NOW, WHERE DID I PARK...?

LISTEN, INTERN. YOU DON'T WANT TO DO THIS. WHATEVER THEY'RE PAYING YOU, I'LL BEAT IT!

THEY DON'T PAY JEDI.

AT LEAST, I DON'T THINK THEY DO. BY THE TIME *I* GET TO BE ONE, ALL THE RULES MAY HAVE CHANGED.

BET YOU'LL STILL GET TO LOSE THE BRAID, THOUGH, HUH? HOW MUCH YOU WANT FOR THAT? I KNOW COLLECTORS WHO GO FOR THAT KIND OF THING.

I'M HEADING TO A CEREMONY RIGHT NOW WHERE I'LL FIND OUT WHICH STUDENTS HAVE BEEN KNIGHTED. IF THEY CHOOSE ME, I'LL *GIVE* YOU MY BRAID.

IS THAT LIKELY?

ONLY IF THEY LOSE THEIR MINDS. IF YOU HAVEN'T NOTICED, I KIND OF STINK.

SNIVVIANS ARE ALL NOSTRIL, FRIEND. EVERYBODY STINKS TO ME.

SO WHAT'S NEXT? YOU TAKIN' ME TO SEE THE GRAND HIGH SABER-TWIRLER?

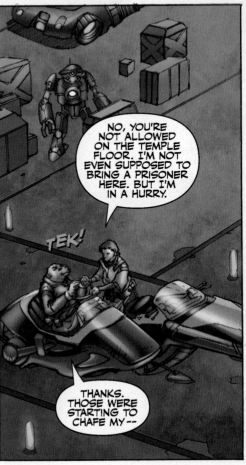

NO, YOU'RE NOT ALLOWED ON THE TEMPLE FLOOR. I'M NOT EVEN SUPPOSED TO BRING A PRISONER HERE. BUT I'M IN A HURRY.

TEK!

THANKS. THOSE WERE STARTING TO CHAFE MY--

IF I'M LUCKY, I CAN STILL CATCH THE END OF THE CEREMONY...

HEY! THIS HURTS!

COME BACK HERE!

WISH ME LUCK!

I DEMAND TO SEE THE SECTOR CONSTABLE! SHE MAY ARREST ME, BUT SHE'S SURE TO HAVE A LIGHTER TOUCH!

INTERN!

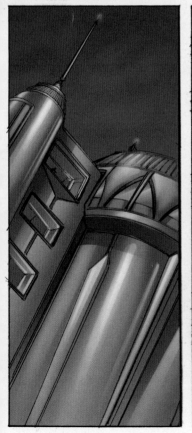

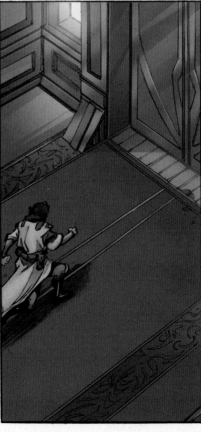

MASTERS, PLEASE --

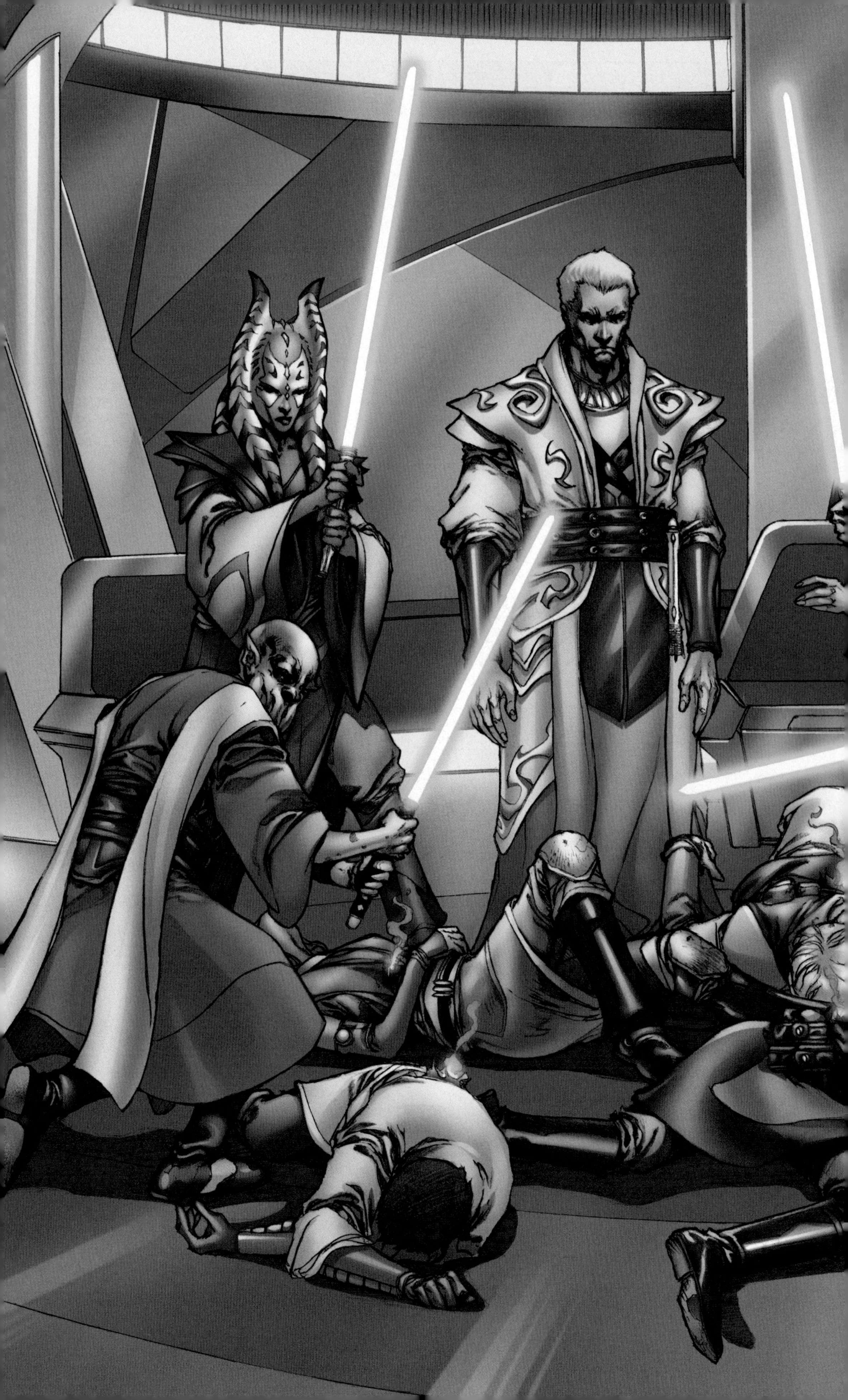

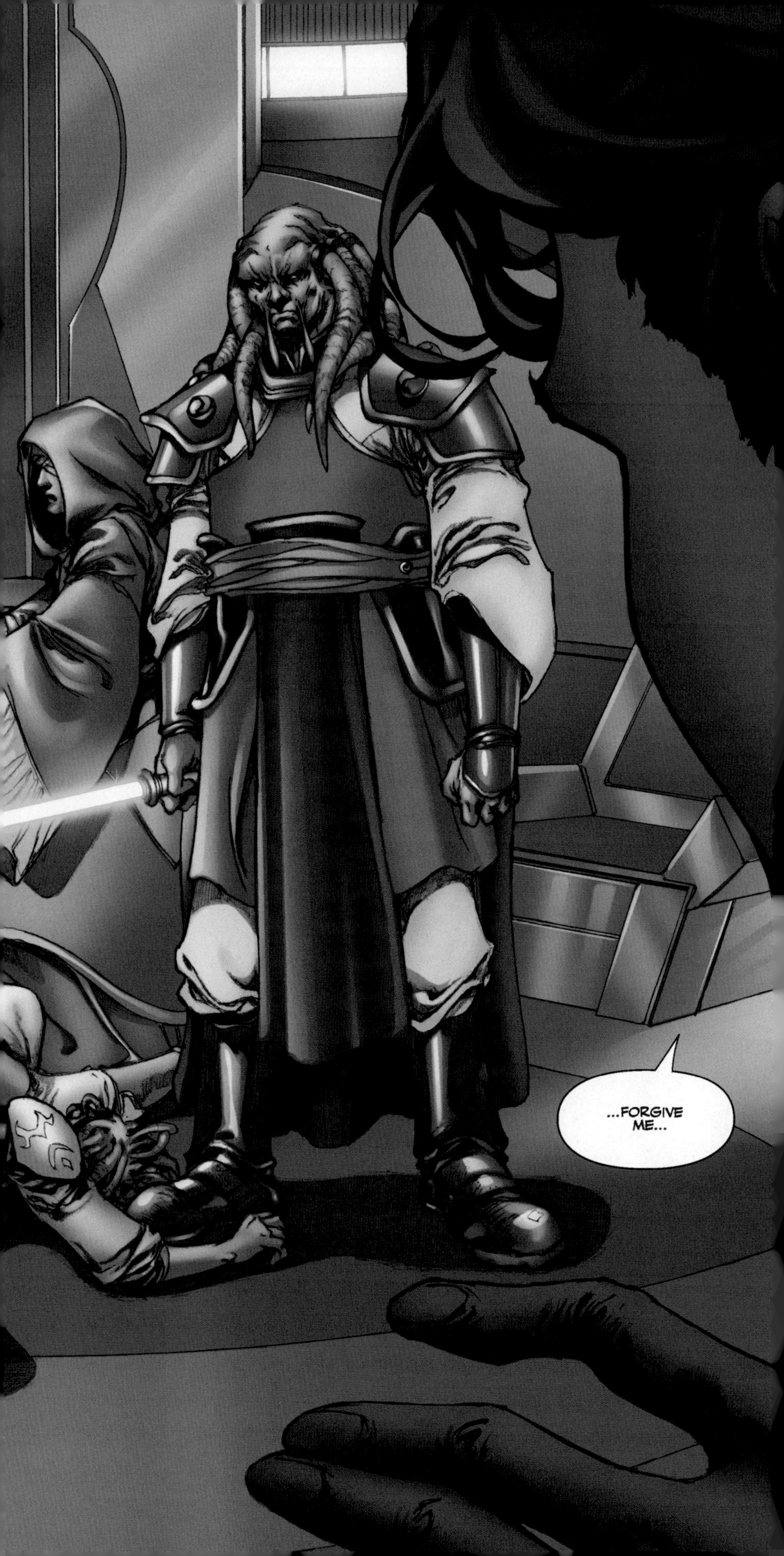
...FORGIVE ME...

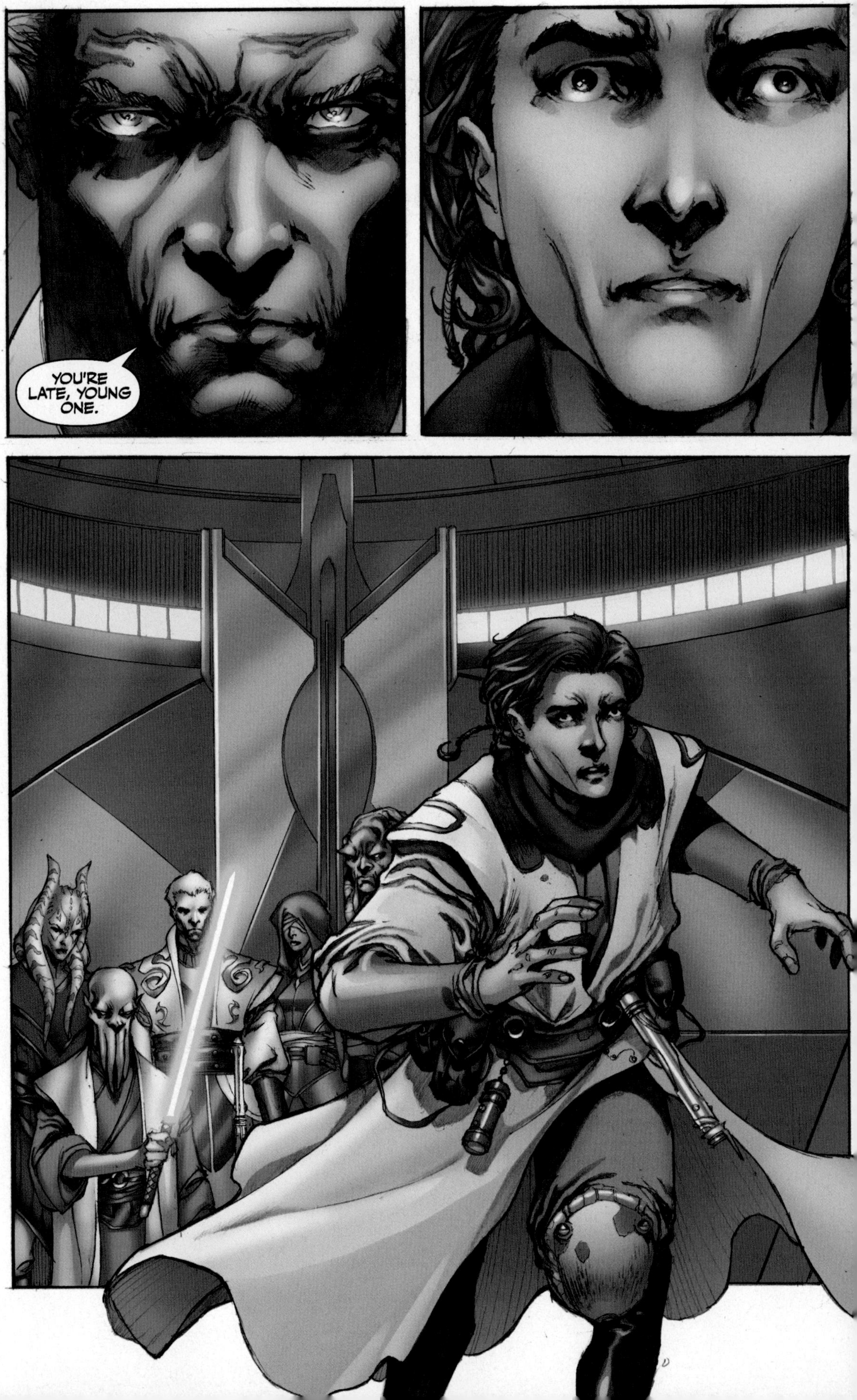
YOU'RE LATE, YOUNG ONE.

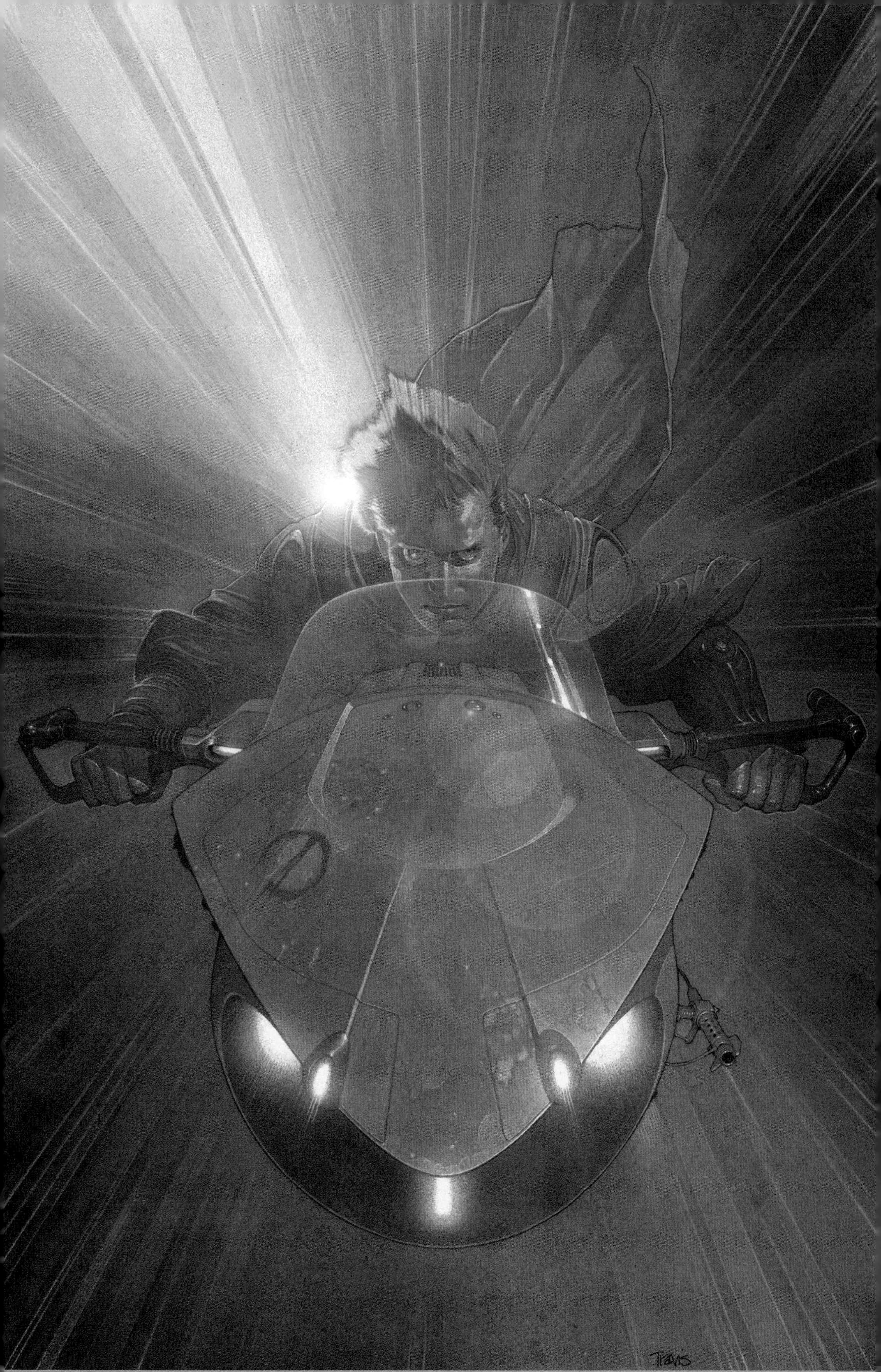
TRAVIS

STAR WARS: KNIGHTS OF THE OLD REPUBLIC #2 — "COMMENCEMENT, PART 2 (OF SIX)"

WRITER: JOHN JACKSON MILLER • ARTIST: BRIAN CHING • COLORIST: MICHAEL ATIYEH • LETTERER: MICHAEL HEISLER
ASSISTANT EDITOR: DAVE MARSHALL • EDITOR: JEREMY BARLOW • COVER ARTIST: TRAVIS CHAREST

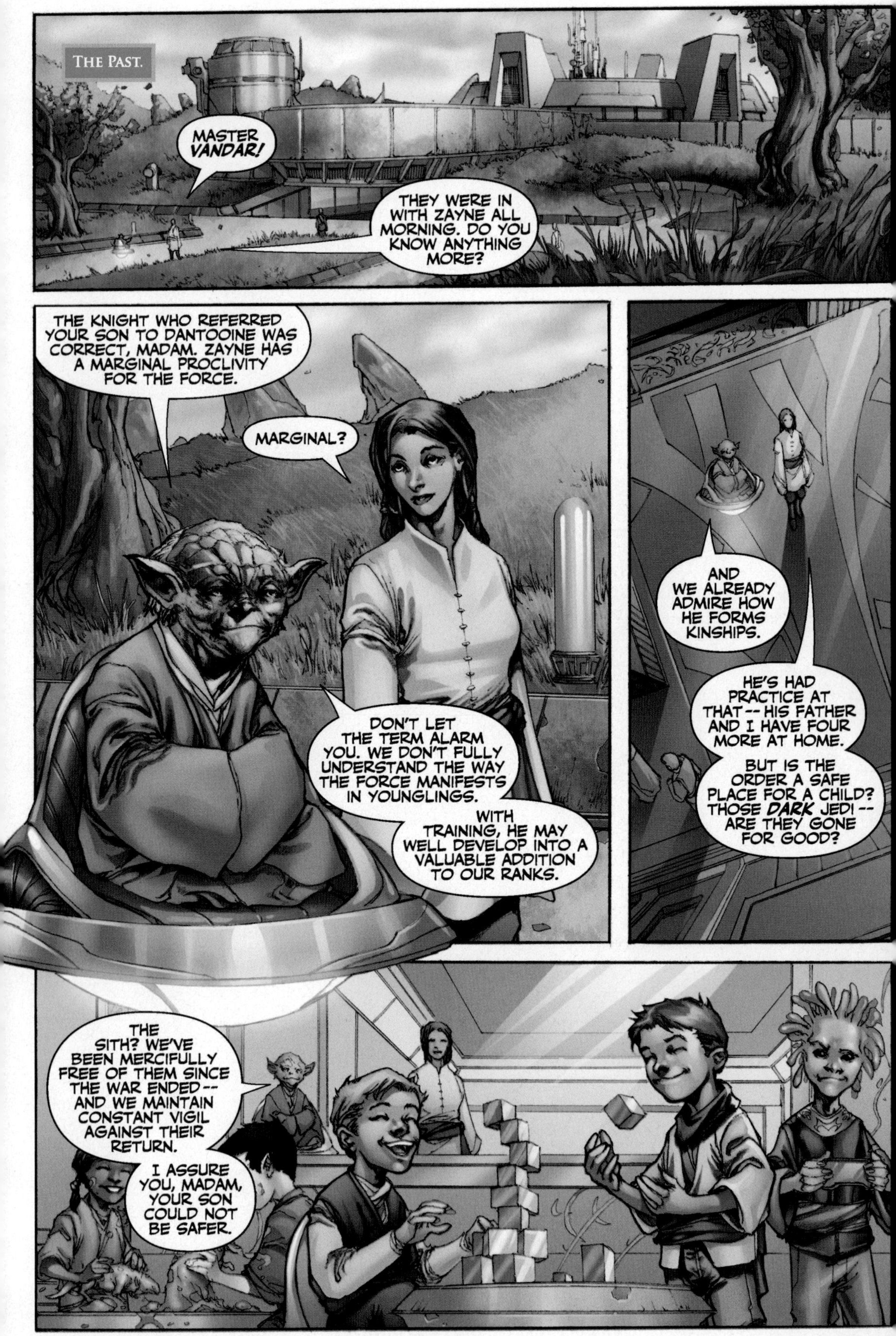

THE PAST.
MASTER *VANDAR!*
THEY WERE IN WITH ZAYNE ALL MORNING. DO YOU KNOW ANYTHING MORE?
THE KNIGHT WHO REFERRED YOUR SON TO DANTOOINE WAS CORRECT, MADAM. ZAYNE HAS A MARGINAL PROCLIVITY FOR THE FORCE.
MARGINAL?
DON'T LET THE TERM ALARM YOU. WE DON'T FULLY UNDERSTAND THE WAY THE FORCE MANIFESTS IN YOUNGLINGS.
WITH TRAINING, HE MAY WELL DEVELOP INTO A VALUABLE ADDITION TO OUR RANKS.
AND WE ALREADY ADMIRE HOW HE FORMS KINSHIPS.
HE'S HAD PRACTICE AT THAT -- HIS FATHER AND I HAVE FOUR MORE AT HOME.
BUT IS THE ORDER A SAFE PLACE FOR A CHILD? THOSE *DARK* JEDI -- ARE THEY GONE FOR GOOD?
THE SITH? WE'VE BEEN MERCIFULLY FREE OF THEM SINCE THE WAR ENDED -- AND WE MAINTAIN CONSTANT VIGIL AGAINST THEIR RETURN.
I ASSURE YOU, MADAM, YOUR SON COULD NOT BE SAFER.

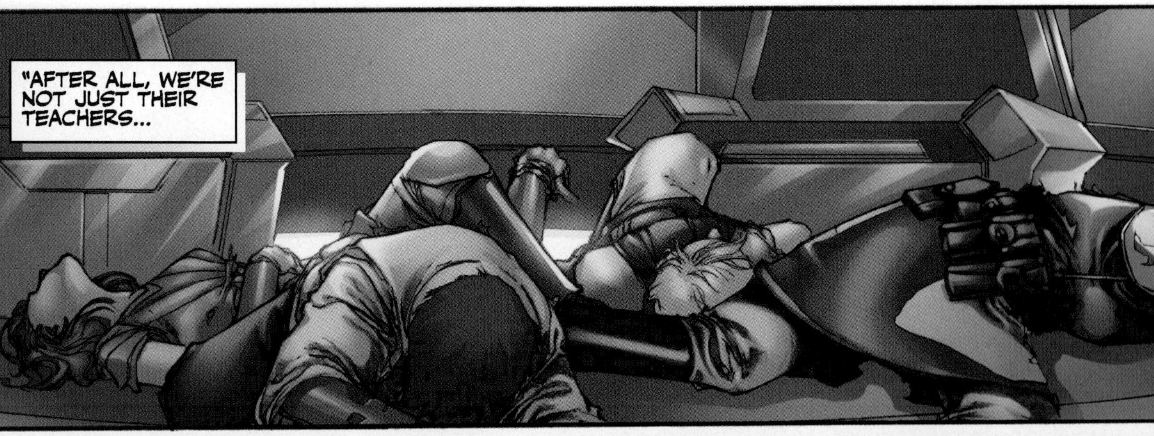
"AFTER ALL, WE'RE NOT JUST THEIR TEACHERS...

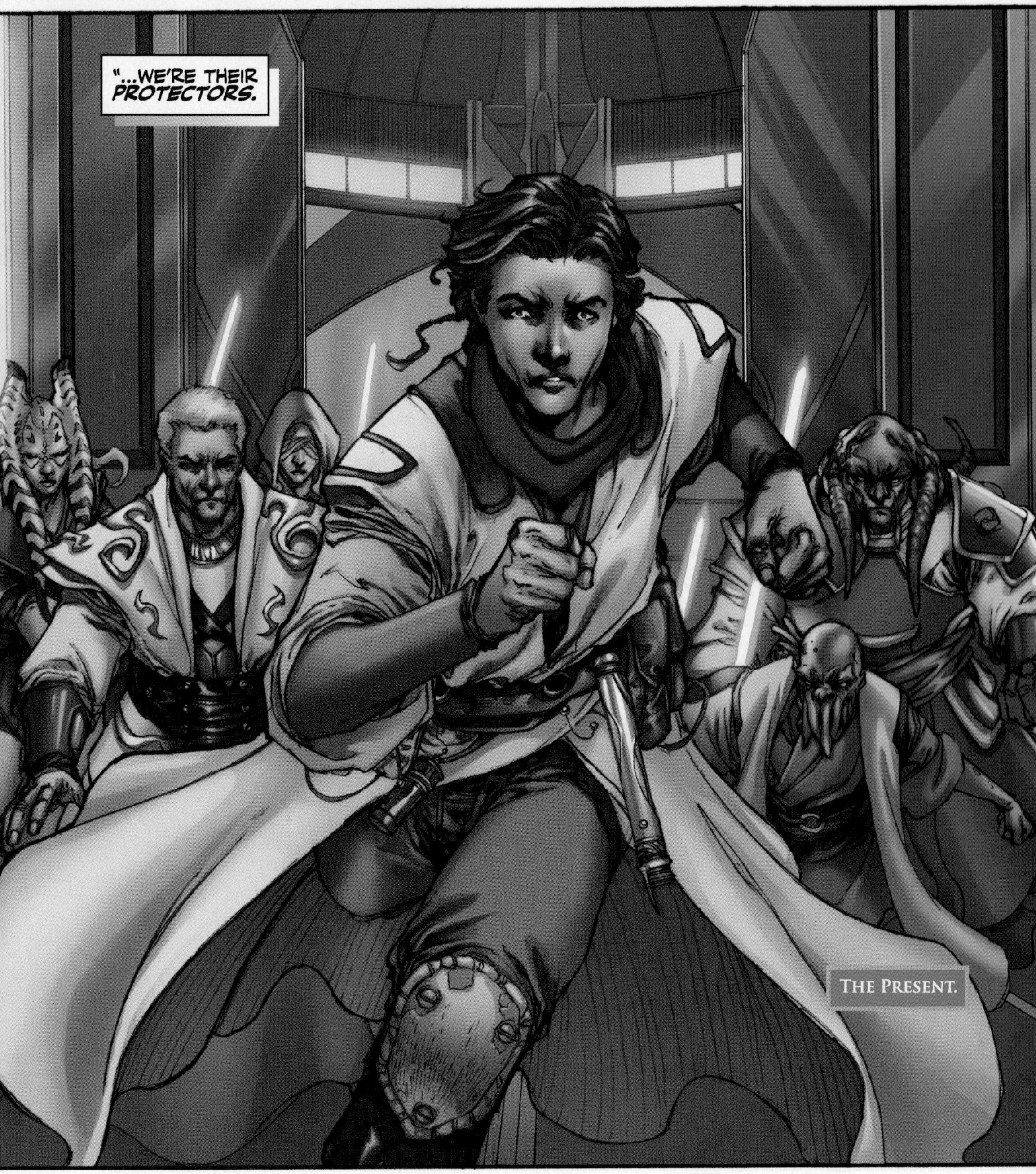
"...WE'RE THEIR PROTECTORS.
THE PRESENT.

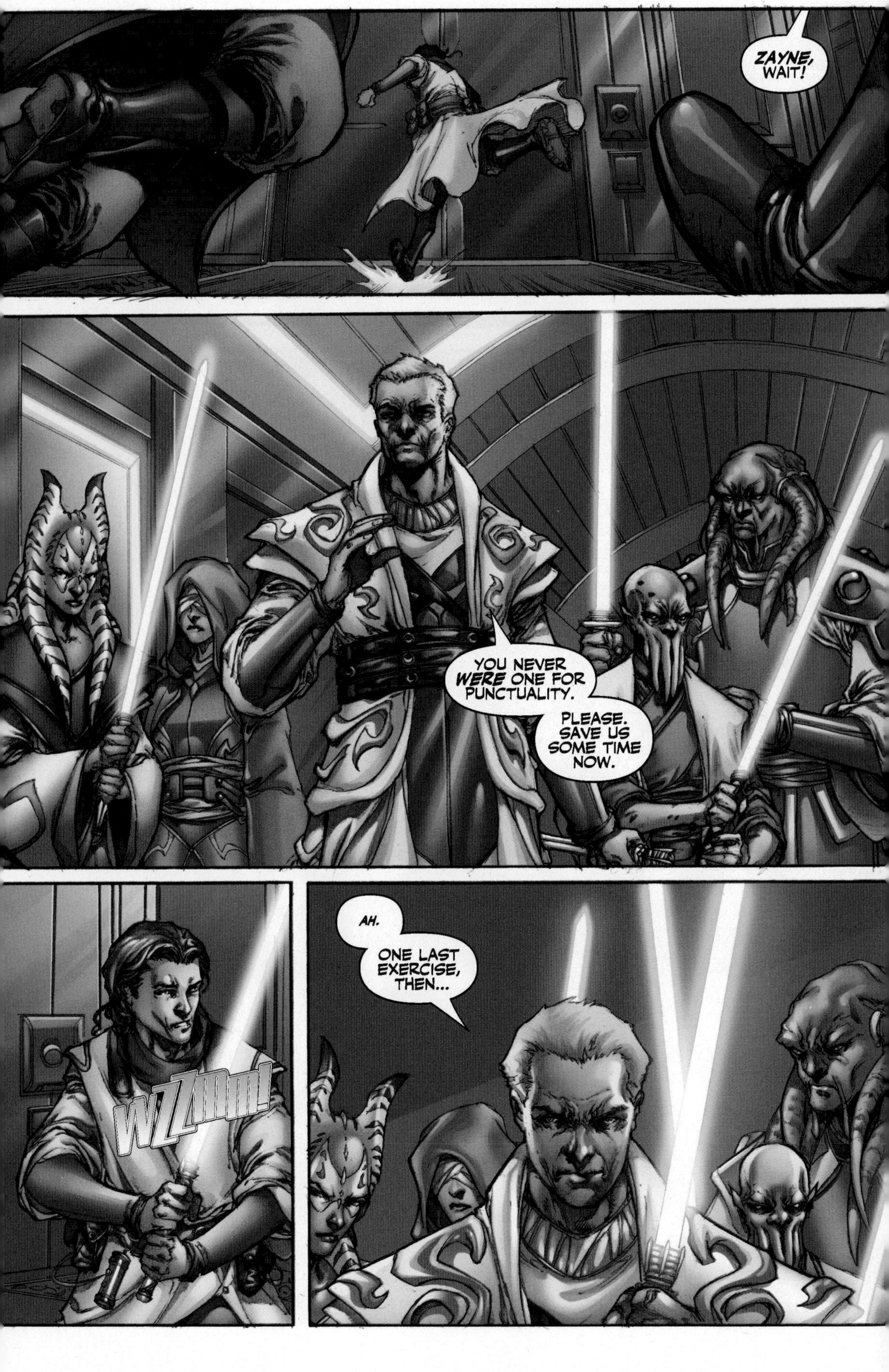
ZAYNE, WAIT!
YOU NEVER WERE ONE FOR PUNCTUALITY.
PLEASE. SAVE US SOME TIME NOW.
WZZMM!
AH.
ONE LAST EXERCISE, THEN...

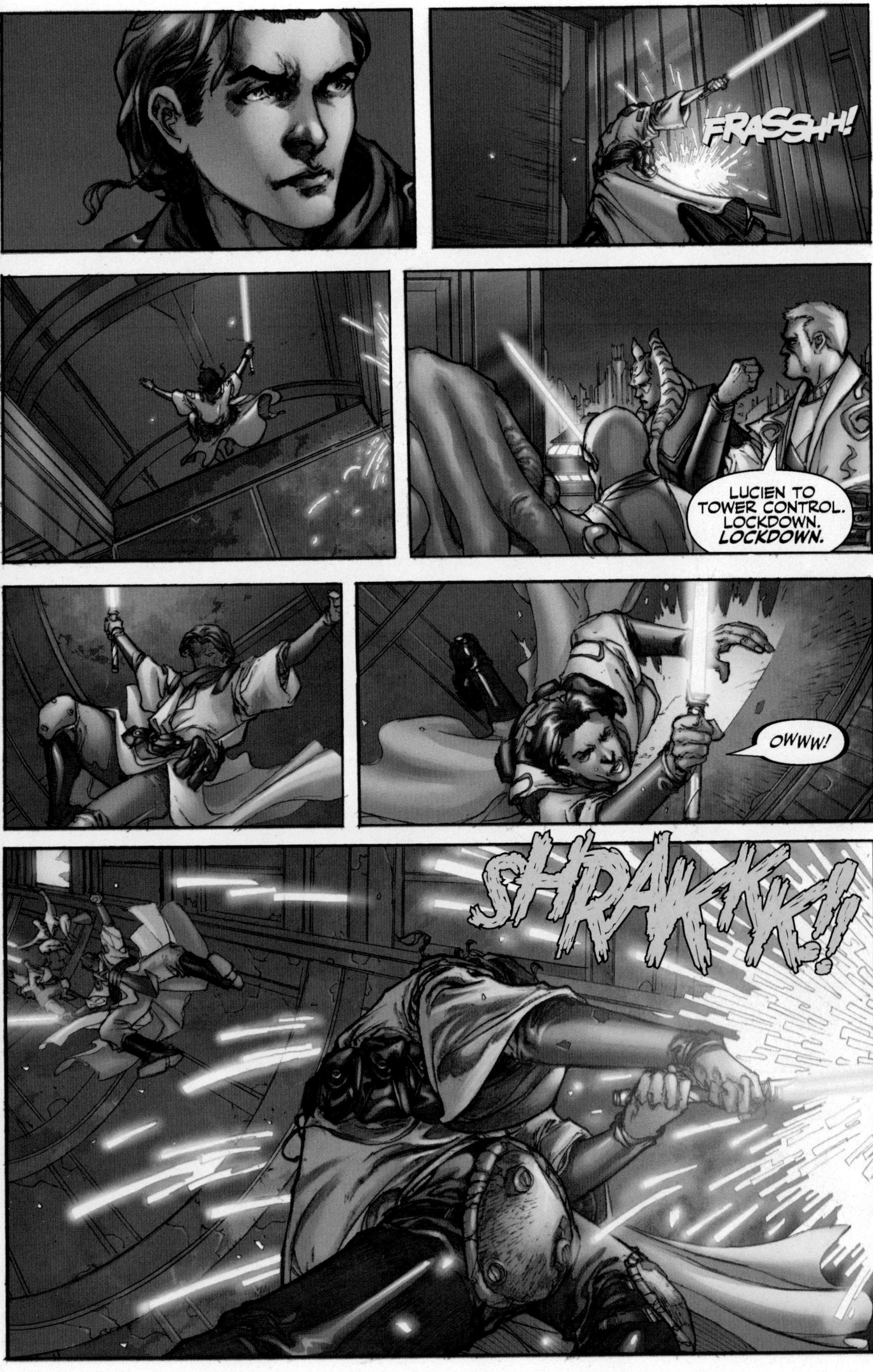
FRASSHH!
LUCIEN TO TOWER CONTROL. LOCKDOWN. LOCKDOWN.
OWWW!
SHRAKKK!!

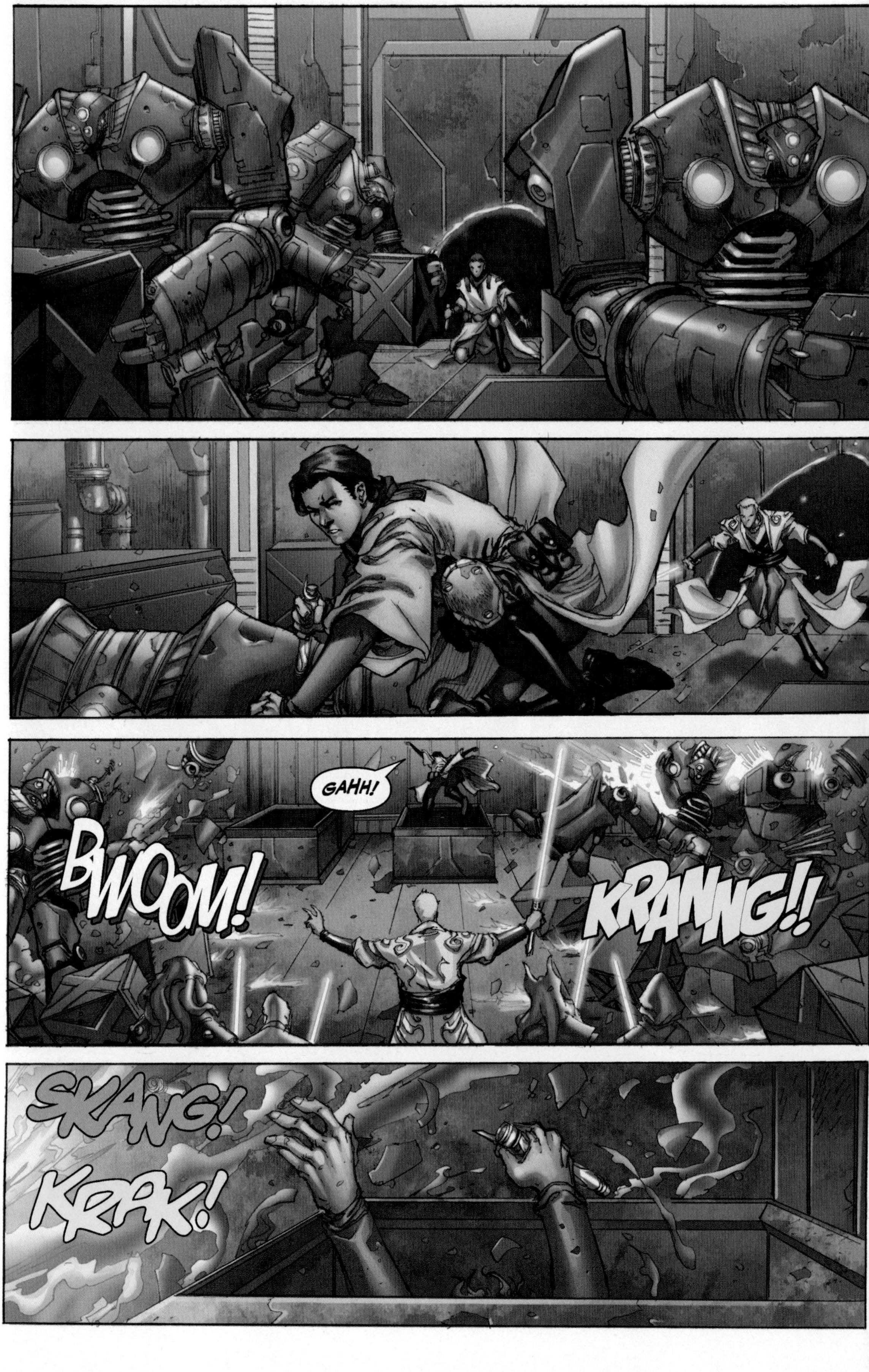
GAHH!
BWOOM!
KRANNG!!
SKANG!
KRAK!

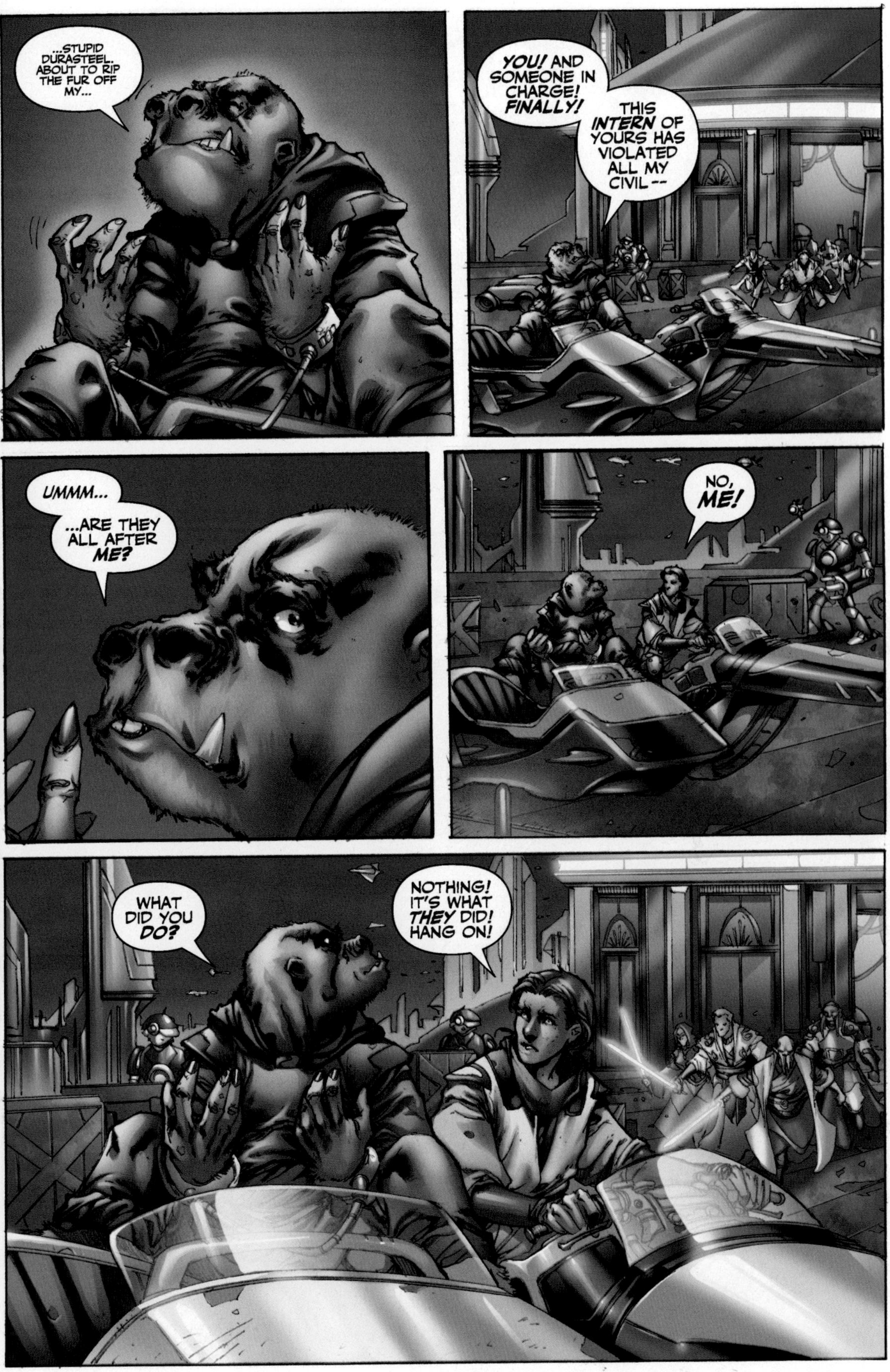
...STUPID DURASTEEL. ABOUT TO RIP THE FUR OFF MY...
YOU! AND SOMEONE IN CHARGE! FINALLY!
THIS INTERN OF YOURS HAS VIOLATED ALL MY CIVIL--
UMMM...
...ARE THEY ALL AFTER ME?
NO, ME!
WHAT DID YOU DO?
NOTHING! IT'S WHAT THEY DID! HANG ON!

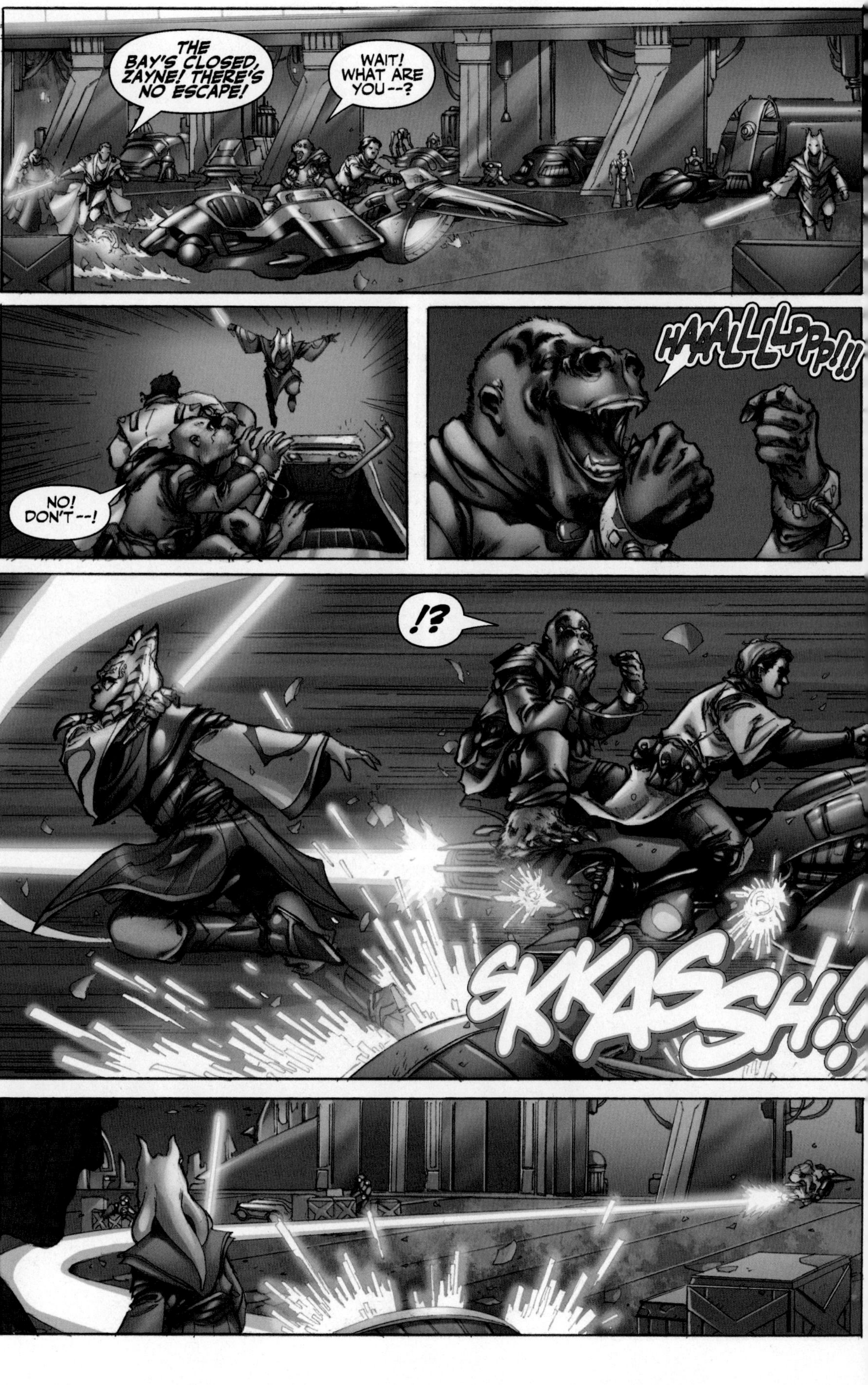
THE BAY'S CLOSED, ZAYNE! THERE'S NO ESCAPE!
WAIT! WHAT ARE YOU--?
NO! DON'T--!
HAAALLLPPP!!!
!?
SKKASSH!!

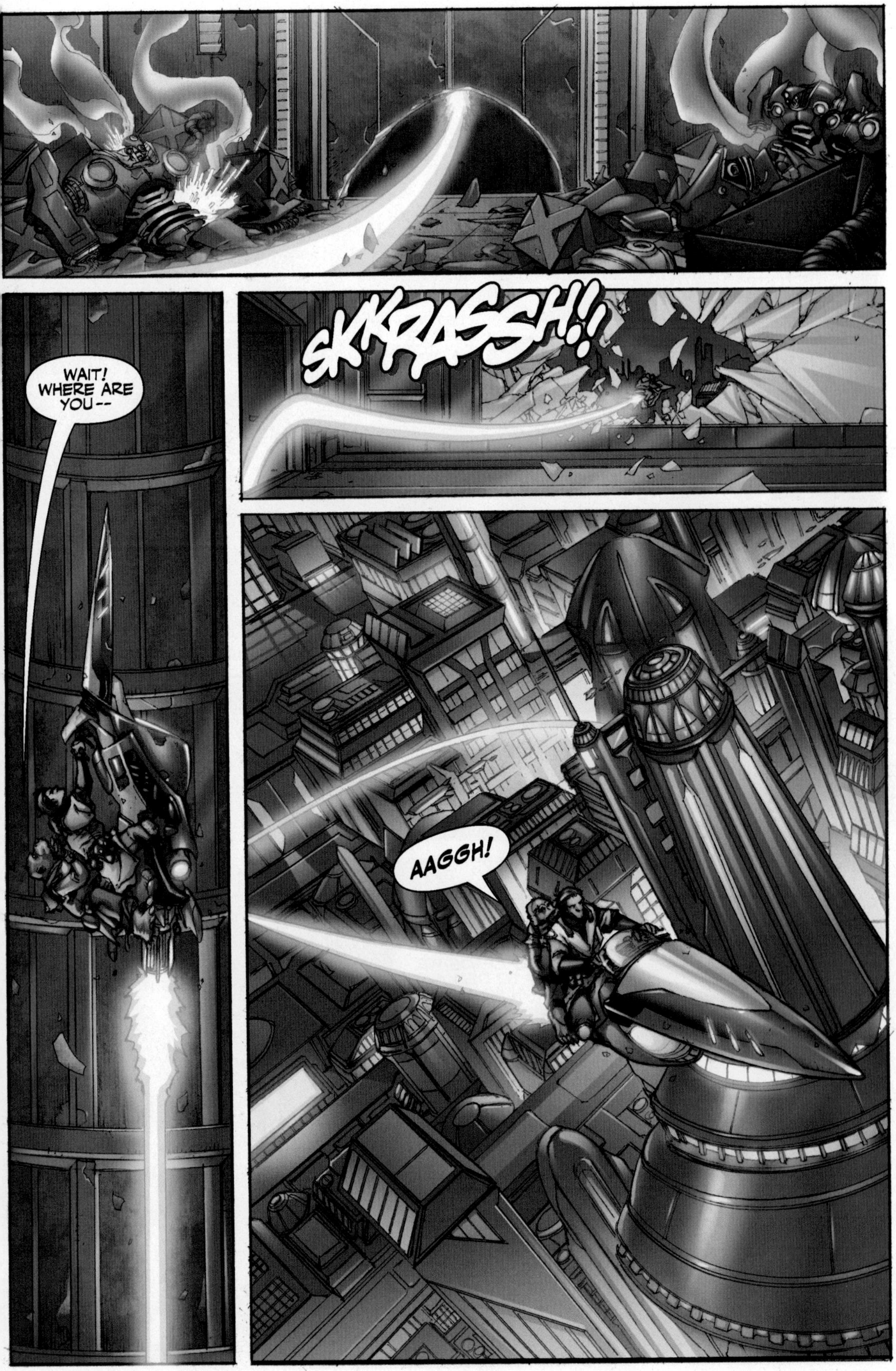
SKKRASSH!!
WAIT! WHERE ARE YOU--
AAGGH!

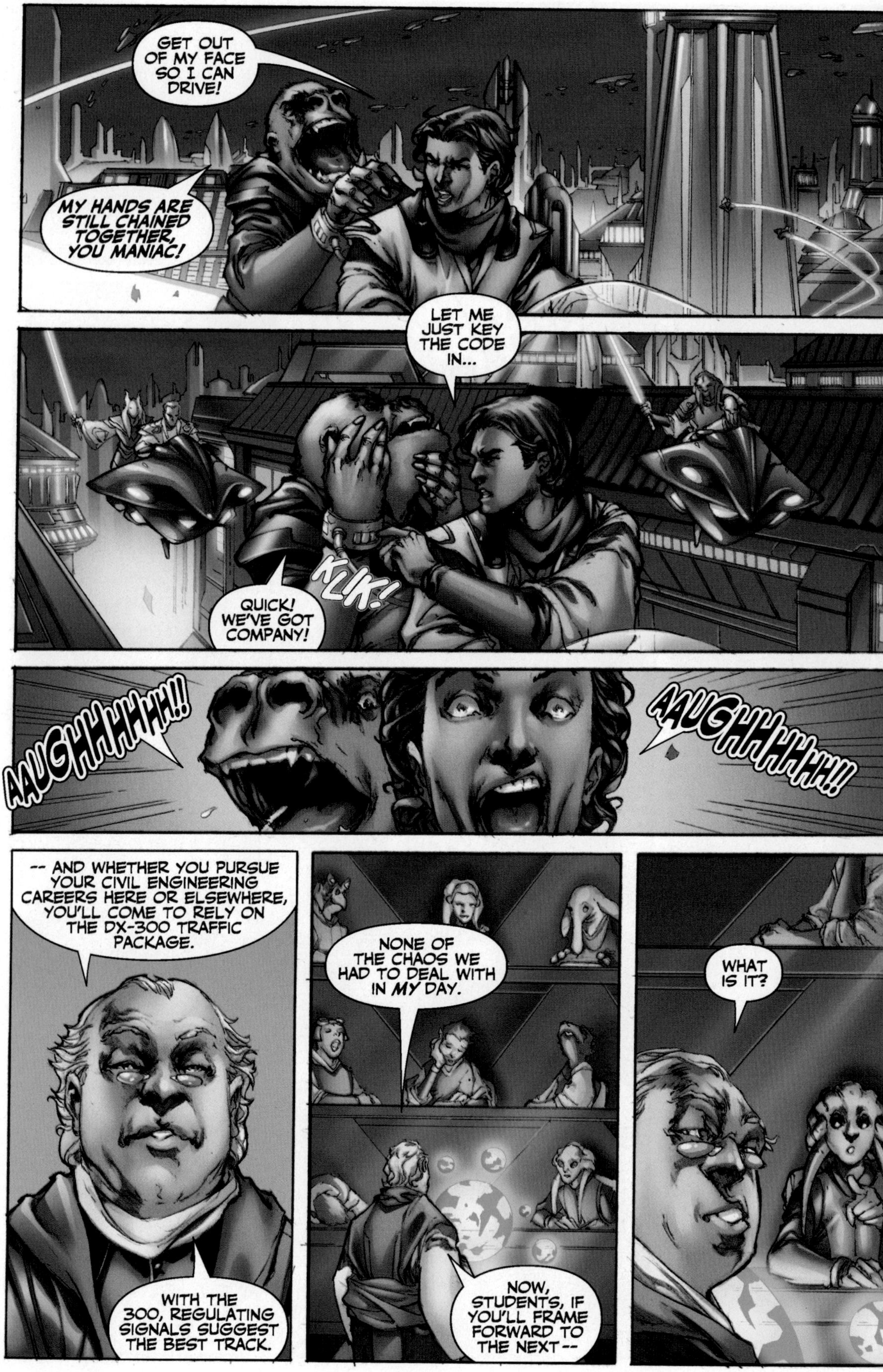
GET OUT OF MY FACE SO I CAN DRIVE!
MY HANDS ARE STILL CHAINED TOGETHER, YOU MANIAC!
LET ME JUST KEY THE CODE IN...
KLIK!
QUICK! WE'VE GOT COMPANY!
AAUGHHHHHH!!
AAUGHHHHHHH!!
-- AND WHETHER YOU PURSUE YOUR CIVIL ENGINEERING CAREERS HERE OR ELSEWHERE, YOU'LL COME TO RELY ON THE DX-300 TRAFFIC PACKAGE.
WITH THE 300, REGULATING SIGNALS SUGGEST THE BEST TRACK.
NONE OF THE CHAOS WE HAD TO DEAL WITH IN MY DAY.
NOW, STUDENTS, IF YOU'LL FRAME FORWARD TO THE NEXT--
WHAT IS IT?

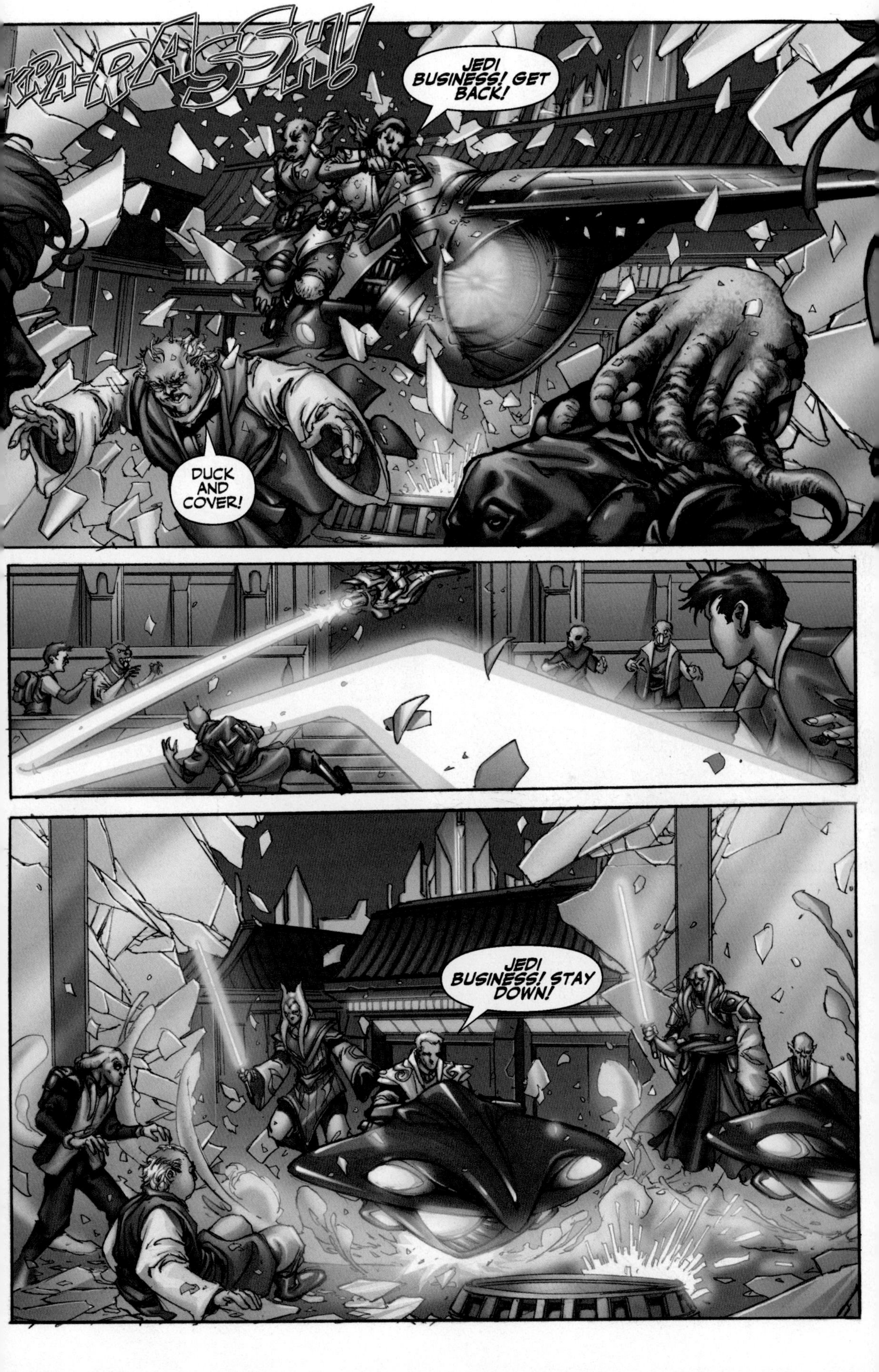
KRA-KRASSH!
JEDI BUSINESS! GET BACK!
DUCK AND COVER!
JEDI BUSINESS! STAY DOWN!

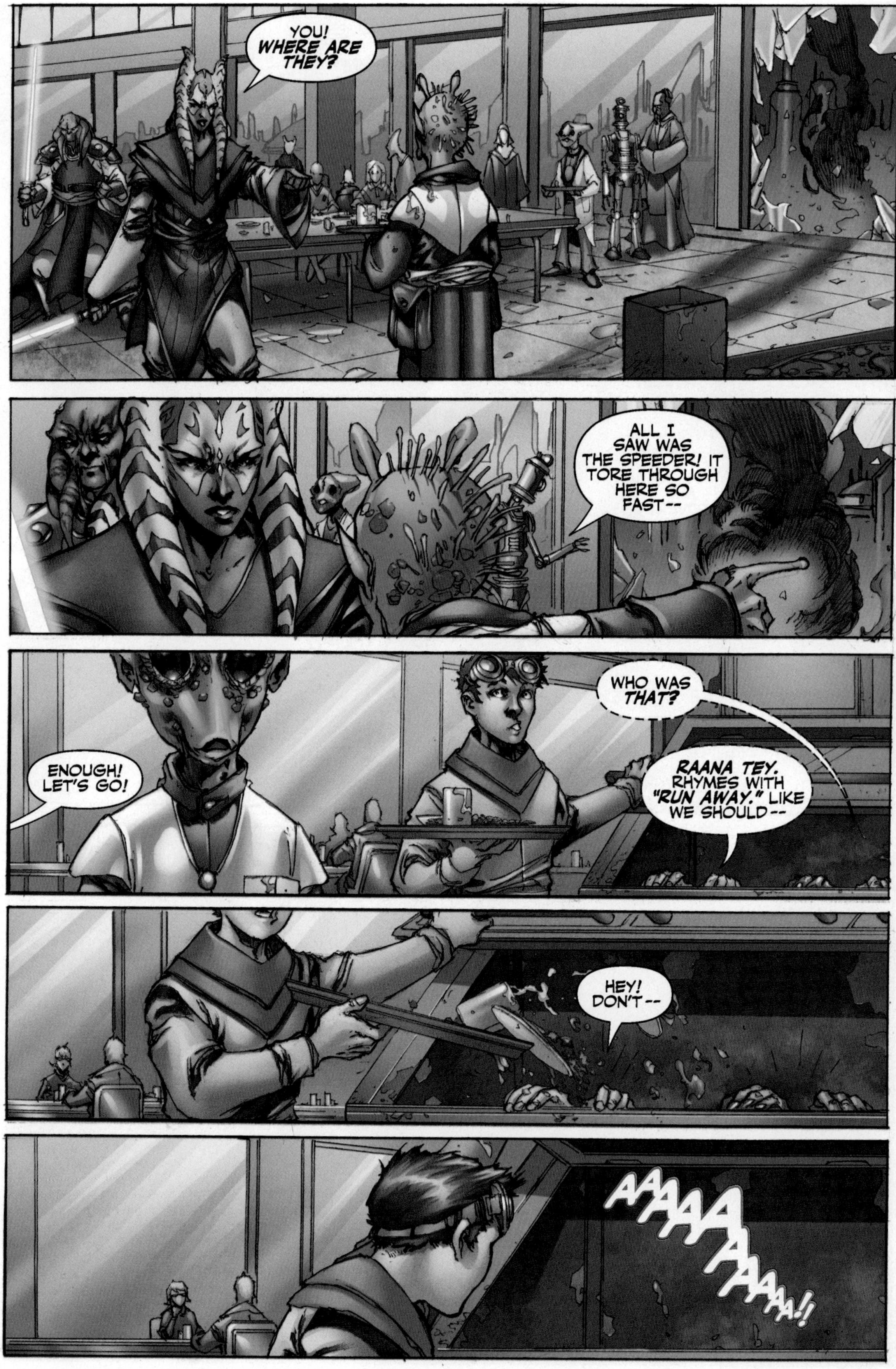
YOU! WHERE ARE THEY?
ALL I SAW WAS THE SPEEDER! IT TORE THROUGH HERE SO FAST--
WHO WAS THAT?
RAANA TEY. RHYMES WITH "RUN AWAY." LIKE WE SHOULD--
ENOUGH! LET'S GO!
HEY! DON'T--
AAAAAAAAAA!!

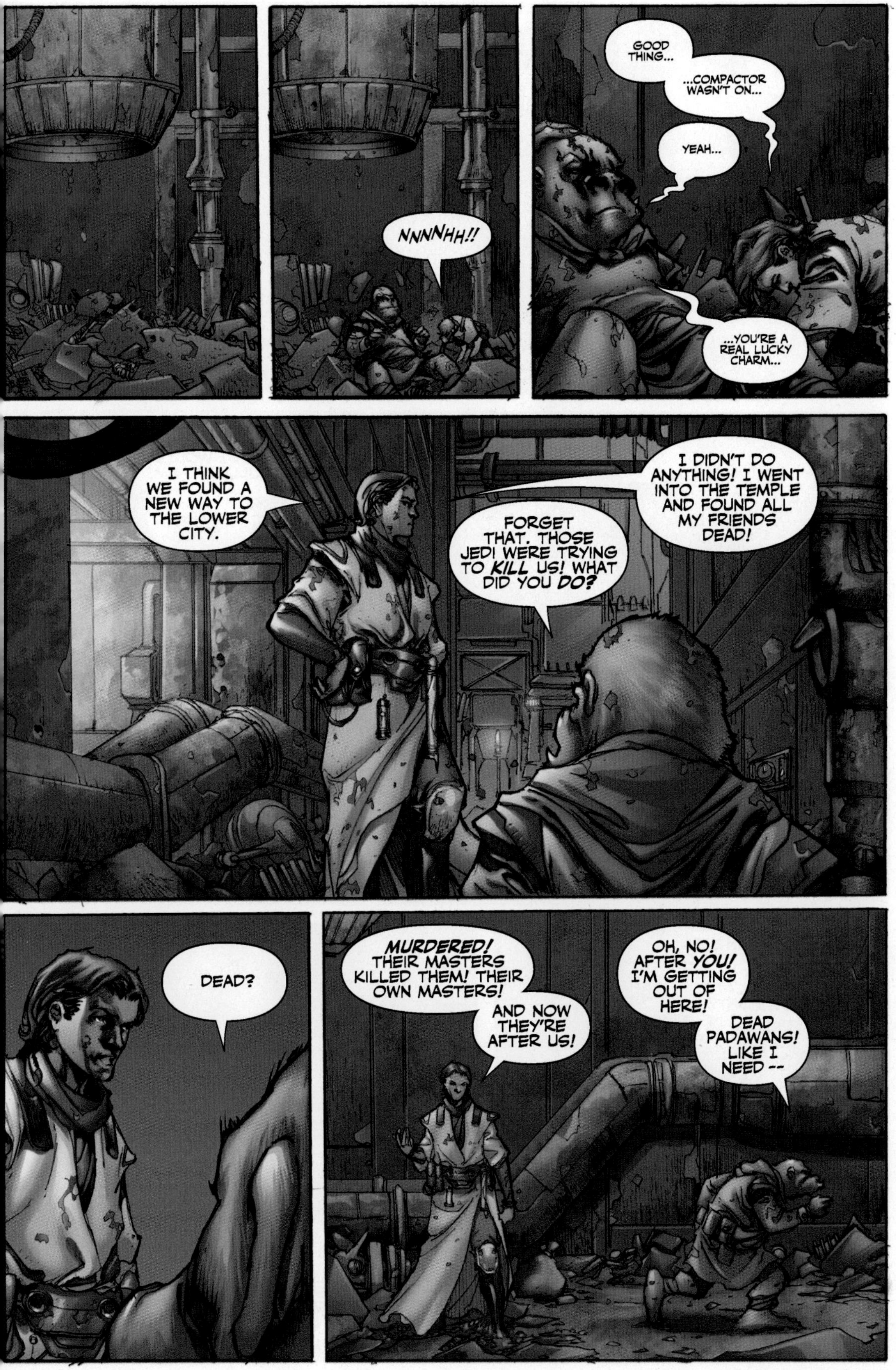
NNNNHH!!
GOOD THING...
...COMPACTOR WASN'T ON...
YEAH...
...YOU'RE A REAL LUCKY CHARM...
I THINK WE FOUND A NEW WAY TO THE LOWER CITY.
FORGET THAT. THOSE JEDI WERE TRYING TO KILL US! WHAT DID YOU DO?
I DIDN'T DO ANYTHING! I WENT INTO THE TEMPLE AND FOUND ALL MY FRIENDS DEAD!
DEAD?
MURDERED! THEIR MASTERS KILLED THEM! THEIR OWN MASTERS!
AND NOW THEY'RE AFTER US!
OH, NO! AFTER YOU! I'M GETTING OUT OF HERE!
DEAD PADAWANS! LIKE I NEED --

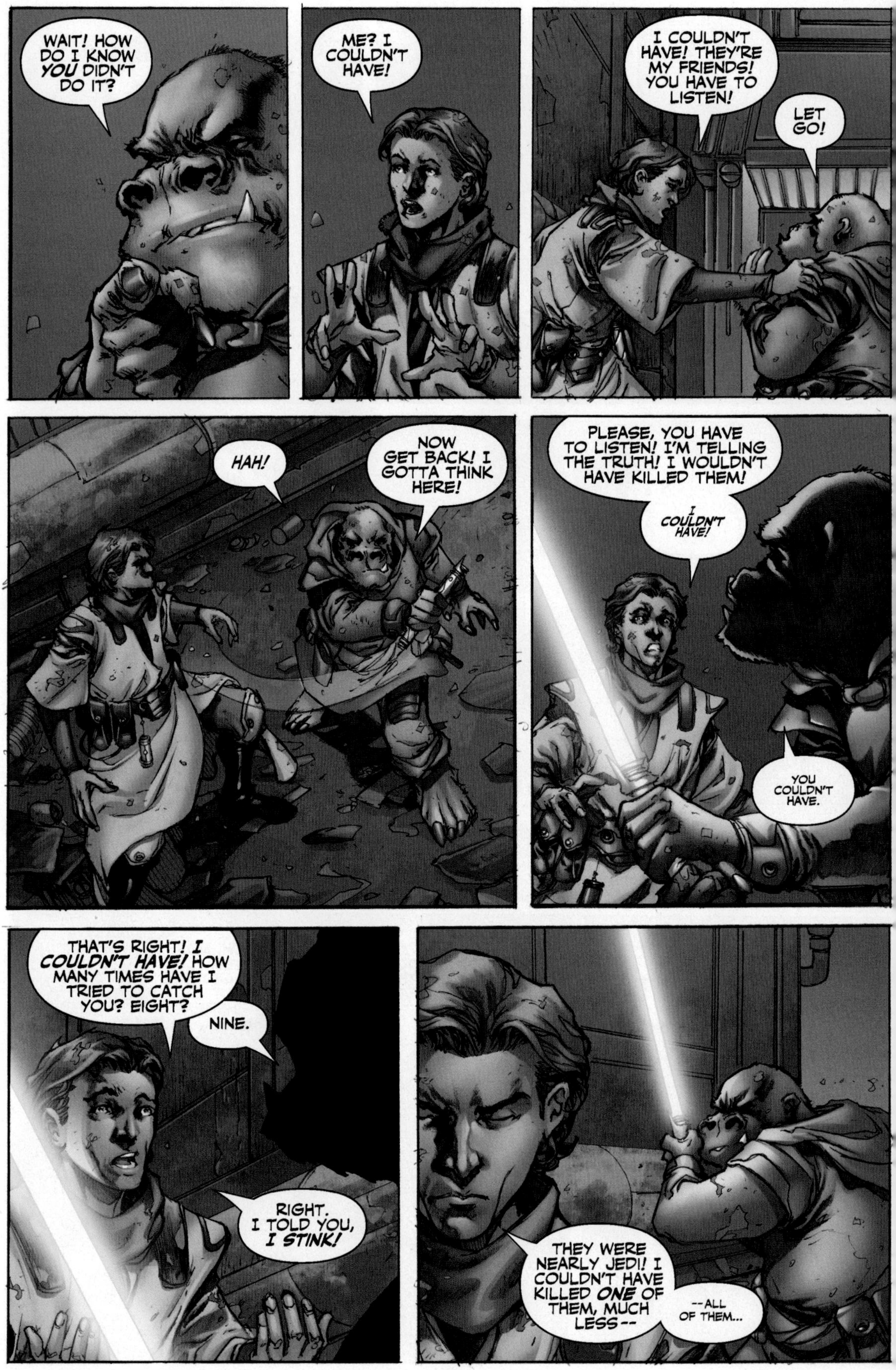
WAIT! HOW DO I KNOW *YOU* DIDN'T DO IT?
ME? I COULDN'T HAVE!
I COULDN'T HAVE! THEY'RE MY FRIENDS! YOU HAVE TO LISTEN!
LET GO!
HAH!
NOW GET BACK! I GOTTA THINK HERE!
PLEASE, YOU HAVE TO LISTEN! I'M TELLING THE TRUTH! I WOULDN'T HAVE KILLED THEM!
I COULDN'T HAVE!
YOU COULDN'T HAVE.
THAT'S RIGHT! *I COULDN'T HAVE!* HOW MANY TIMES HAVE I TRIED TO CATCH YOU? EIGHT?
NINE.
RIGHT. I TOLD YOU, *I STINK!*
THEY WERE NEARLY JEDI! I COULDN'T HAVE KILLED *ONE* OF THEM, MUCH LESS--
--ALL OF THEM...

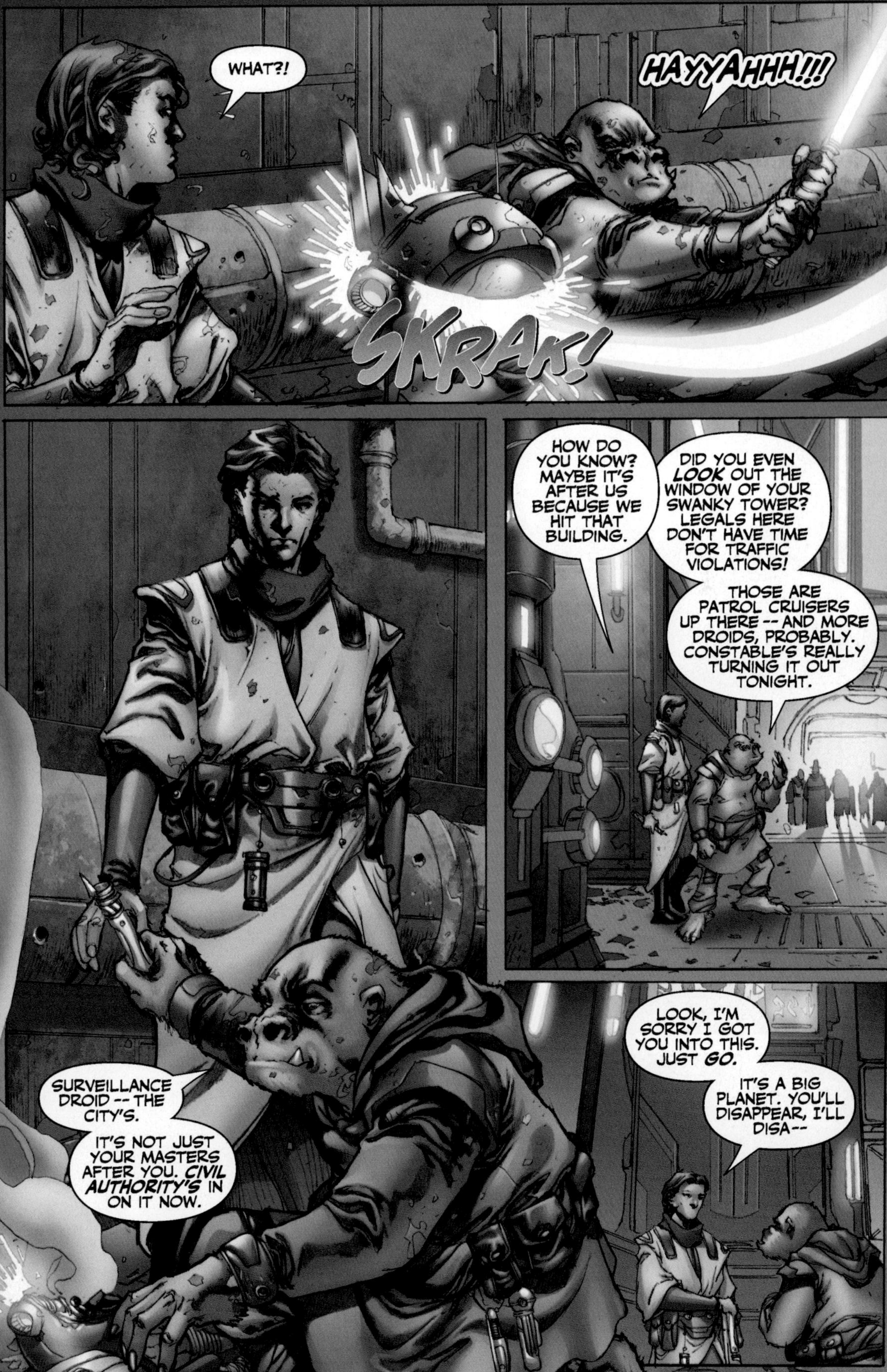
WHAT?!
HAYYAHHH!!!
SKRAK!
SURVEILLANCE DROID -- THE CITY'S.
IT'S NOT JUST YOUR MASTERS AFTER YOU. *CIVIL AUTHORITY'S* IN ON IT NOW.
HOW DO YOU KNOW? MAYBE IT'S AFTER US BECAUSE WE HIT THAT BUILDING.
DID YOU EVEN *LOOK* OUT THE WINDOW OF YOUR SWANKY TOWER? LEGALS HERE DON'T HAVE TIME FOR TRAFFIC VIOLATIONS!
THOSE ARE PATROL CRUISERS UP THERE -- AND MORE DROIDS, PROBABLY. CONSTABLE'S REALLY TURNING IT OUT TONIGHT.
LOOK, I'M SORRY I GOT YOU INTO THIS. JUST *GO*.
IT'S A BIG PLANET. YOU'LL DISAPPEAR, I'LL DISA--

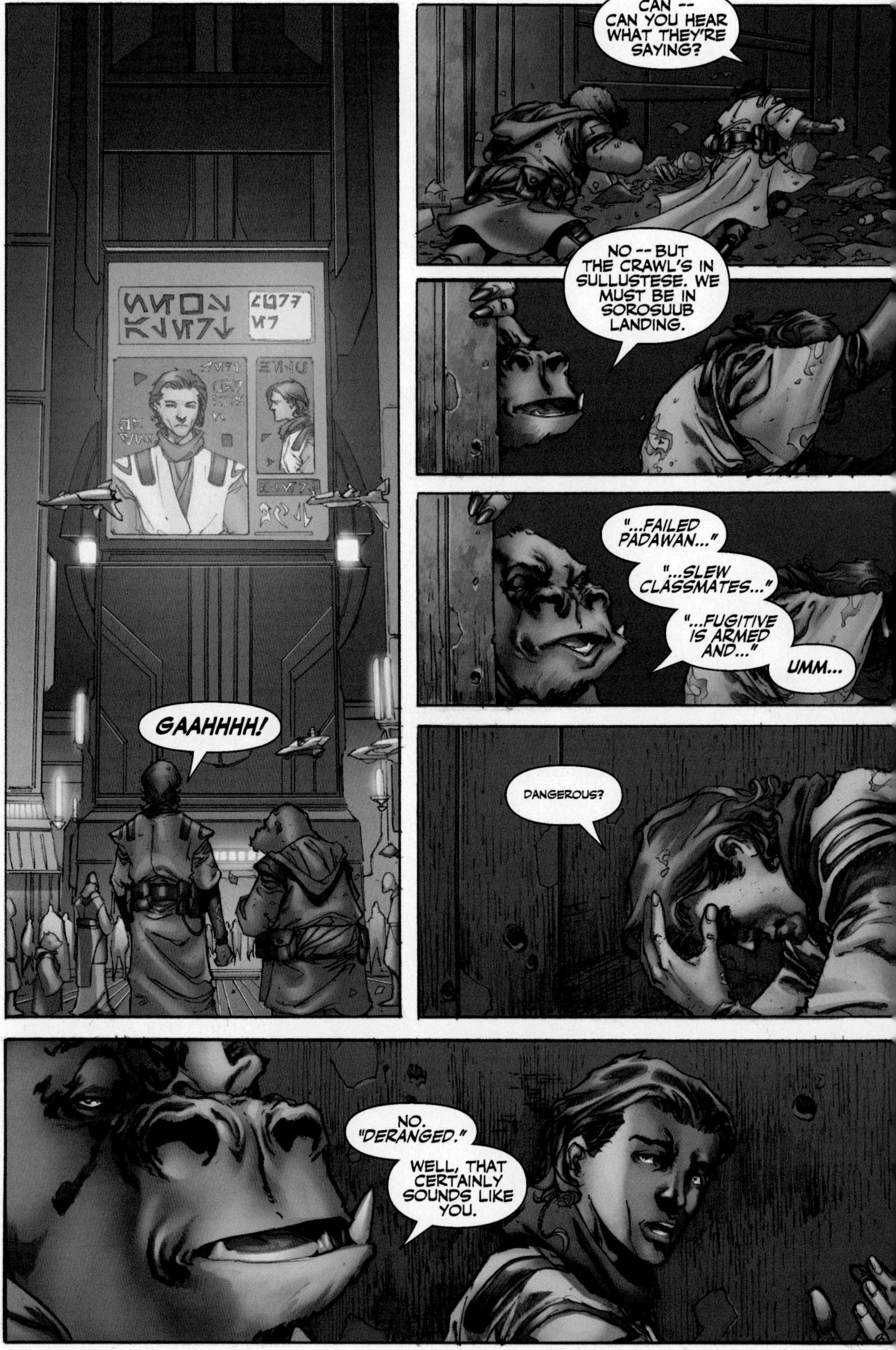
GAAHHHH!
CAN -- CAN YOU HEAR WHAT THEY'RE SAYING?
NO -- BUT THE CRAWL'S IN SULLUSTESE. WE MUST BE IN SOROSUUB LANDING.
"...FAILED PADAWAN..."
"...SLEW CLASSMATES..."
"...FUGITIVE IS ARMED AND..."
UMM...
DANGEROUS?
NO. "DERANGED."
WELL, THAT CERTAINLY SOUNDS LIKE YOU.

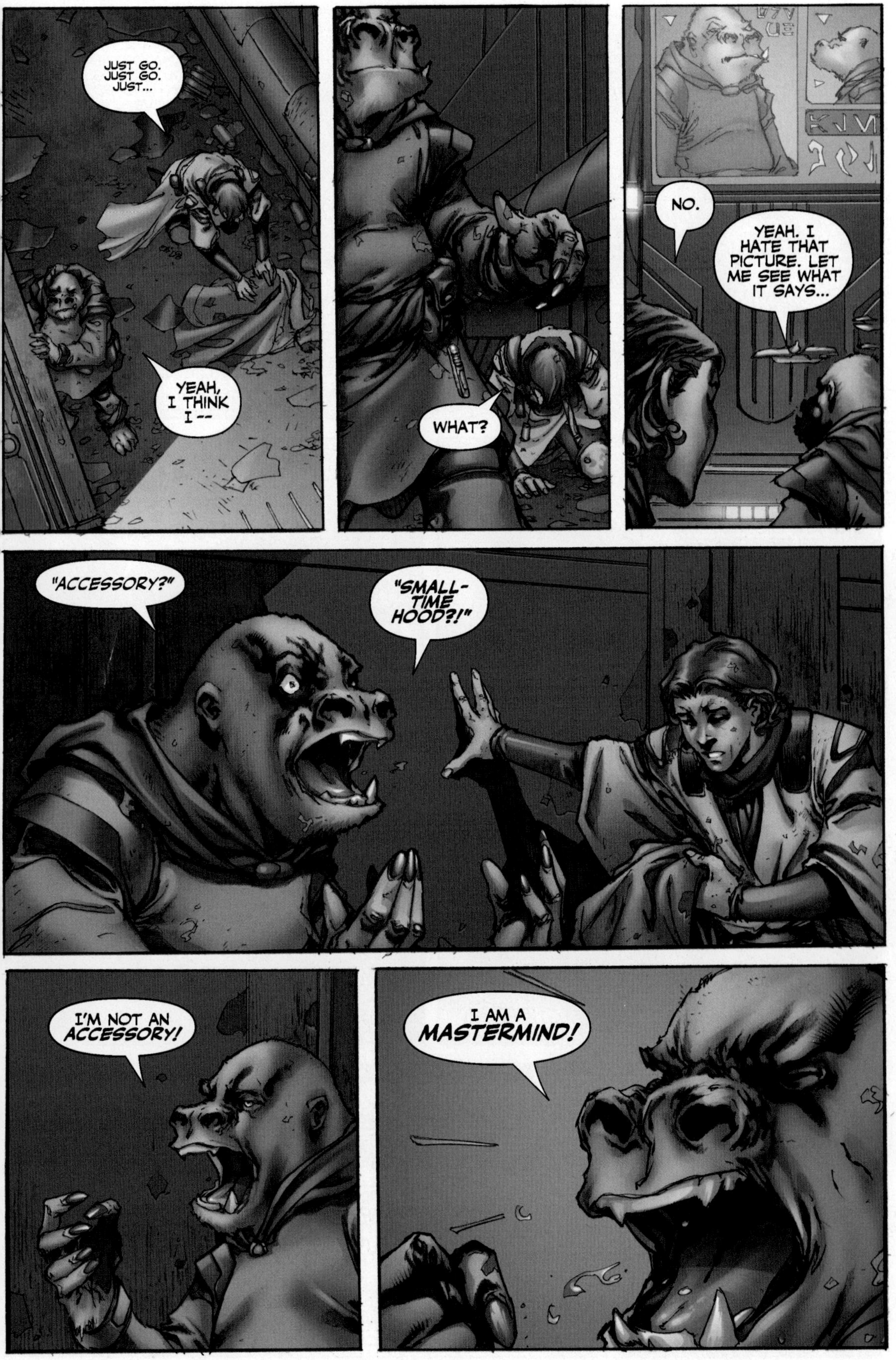
JUST GO. JUST GO. JUST...
YEAH, I THINK I --
WHAT?
NO.
YEAH. I HATE THAT PICTURE. LET ME SEE WHAT IT SAYS...
"ACCESSORY?"
"SMALL-TIME HOOD?!"
I'M NOT AN ACCESSORY!
I AM A MASTERMIND!

WAS THAT THE CONSTABLE CALLING BACK?

YES, *LUCIEN*. SHE SAYS THEY SHOULD HAVE ZAYNE RUN TO GROUND SOON.

THOUGH I'M NOT SURE I'M COMFORTABLE BRINGING OUTSIDERS IN ON SOMETHING SO SENSITIVE.

WELL, I'LL TELL YOU WHAT I JUST TOLD OUR...*ASSOCIATE* ON CORUSCANT. THE CIVIL AUTHORITIES WERE ALWAYS GOING TO BE INVOLVED -- IN ONE WAY OR ANOTHER. IT'S TO BE EXPECTED.

IT *WAS* EXPECTED.

THERE MUST BE A SHOW OF JUSTICE, *Q'ANILIA.* WE OWE THAT MUCH. TO THE FAMILIES.

OF COURSE, YOU'RE RIGHT. I JUST...WELL, I NEVER THOUGHT *ZAYNE* WOULD BE THE ONE.

HE STILL MAY *NOT* BE THE ONE. HE'S MY PADAWAN. I DON'T THINK HE'S THE ONE.

BUT WE HAVE TO MAKE SURE, DON'T WE?

OF COURSE.

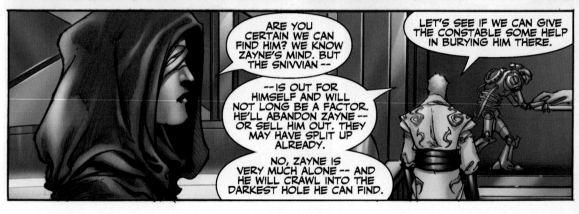

ARE YOU CERTAIN WE CAN FIND HIM? WE KNOW ZAYNE'S MIND. BUT THE SNIVVIAN --

LET'S SEE IF WE CAN GIVE THE CONSTABLE SOME HELP IN BURYING HIM THERE.

--IS OUT FOR HIMSELF AND WILL NOT LONG BE A FACTOR. HE'LL ABANDON ZAYNE -- OR SELL HIM OUT. THEY MAY HAVE SPLIT UP ALREADY.

NO, ZAYNE IS VERY MUCH ALONE -- AND HE WILL CRAWL INTO THE DARKEST HOLE HE CAN FIND.

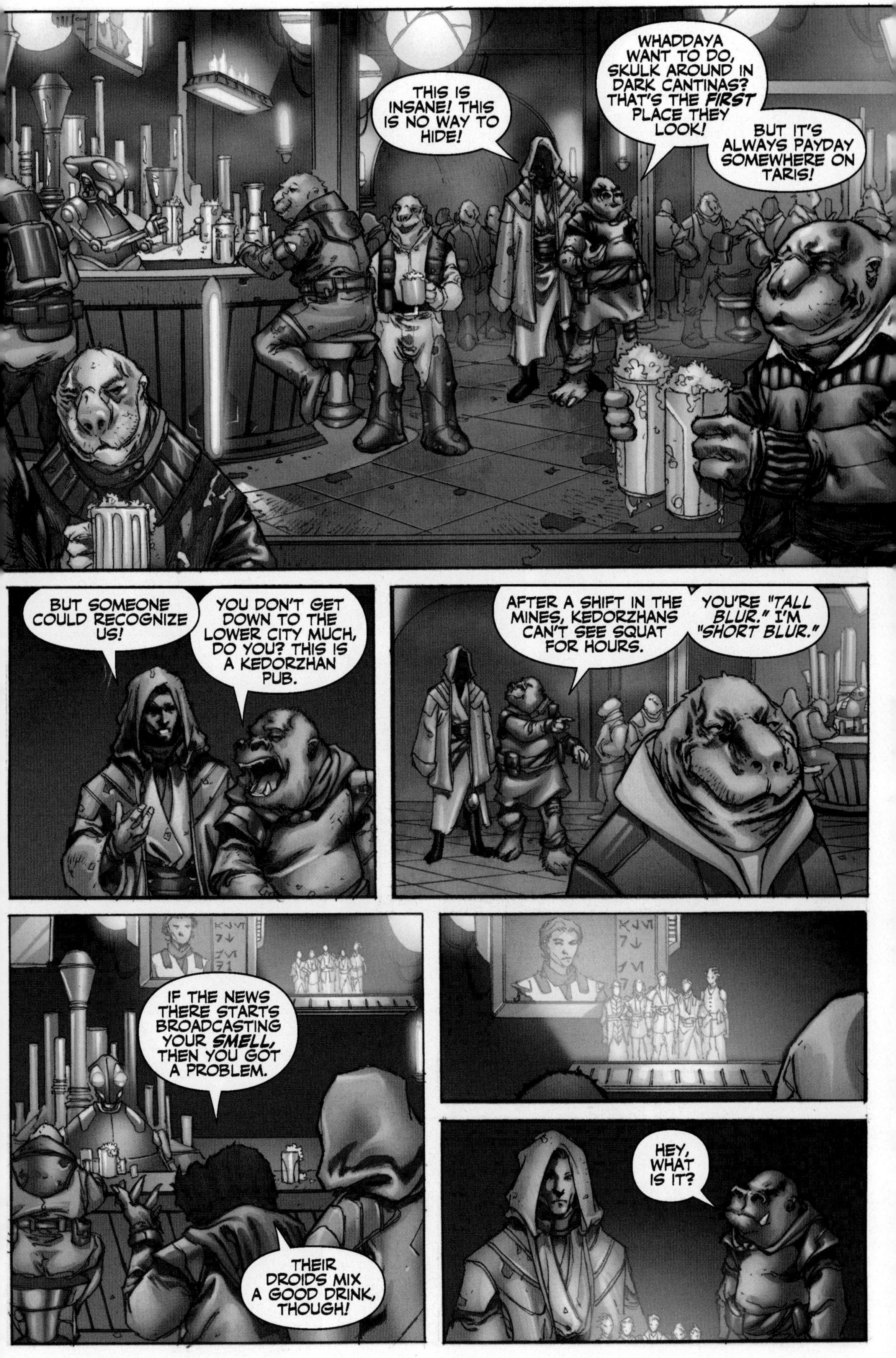
THIS IS INSANE! THIS IS NO WAY TO HIDE!
WHADDAYA WANT TO DO, SKULK AROUND IN DARK CANTINAS? THAT'S THE *FIRST* PLACE THEY LOOK!
BUT IT'S ALWAYS PAYDAY SOMEWHERE ON TARIS!
BUT SOMEONE COULD RECOGNIZE US!
YOU DON'T GET DOWN TO THE LOWER CITY MUCH, DO YOU? THIS IS A KEDORZHAN PUB.
AFTER A SHIFT IN THE MINES, KEDORZHANS CAN'T SEE SQUAT FOR HOURS.
YOU'RE "*TALL BLUR*." I'M "*SHORT BLUR*."
IF THE NEWS THERE STARTS BROADCASTING YOUR *SMELL*, THEN YOU GOT A PROBLEM.
THEIR DROIDS MIX A GOOD DRINK, THOUGH!
HEY, WHAT IS IT?

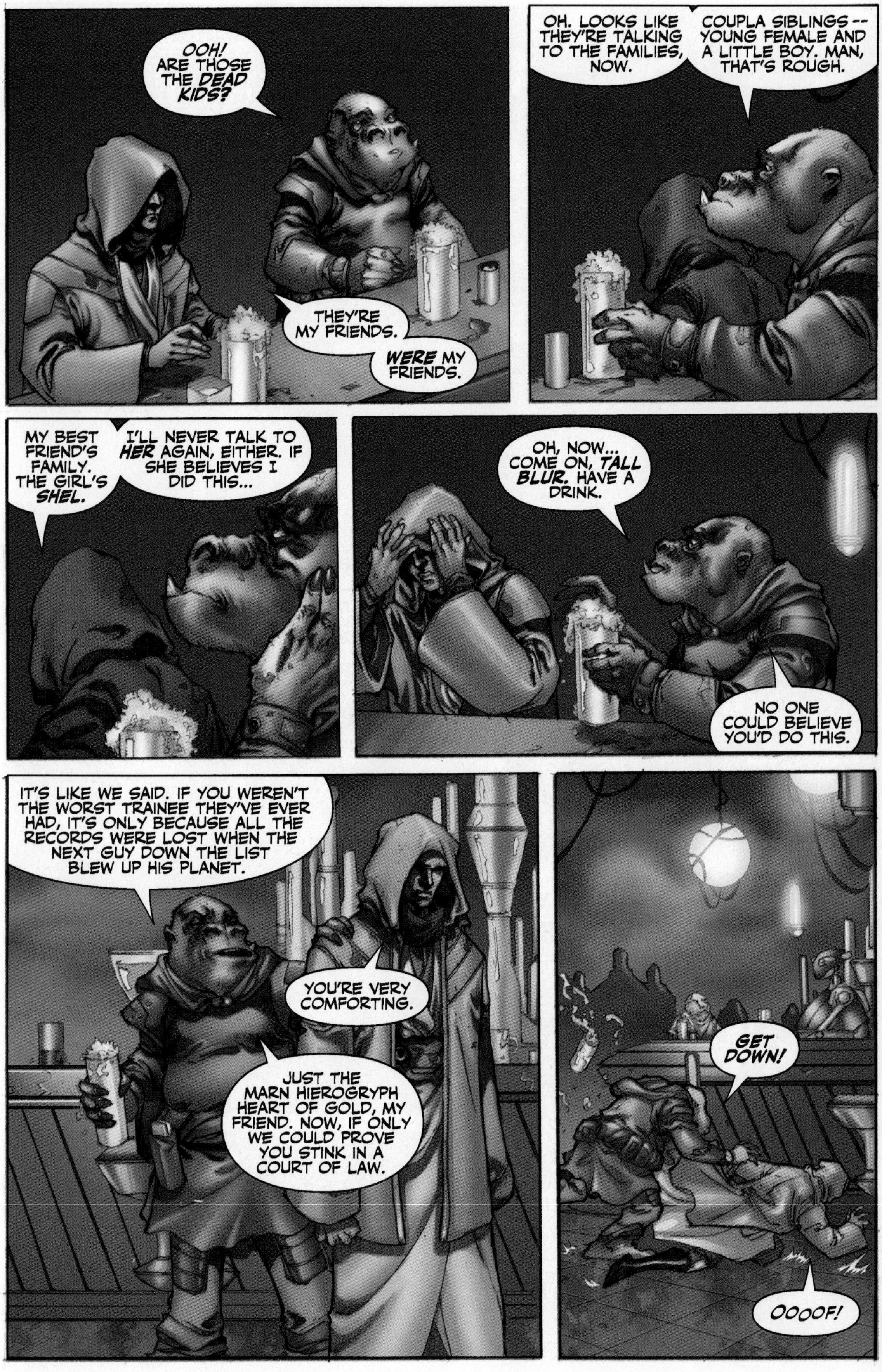

OOH! ARE THOSE THE DEAD KIDS?
THEY'RE MY FRIENDS.
WERE MY FRIENDS.
OH. LOOKS LIKE THEY'RE TALKING TO THE FAMILIES, NOW.
COUPLA SIBLINGS -- YOUNG FEMALE AND A LITTLE BOY. MAN, THAT'S ROUGH.
MY BEST FRIEND'S FAMILY. THE GIRL'S SHEL.
I'LL NEVER TALK TO HER AGAIN, EITHER. IF SHE BELIEVES I DID THIS...
OH, NOW... COME ON, TALL BLUR. HAVE A DRINK.
NO ONE COULD BELIEVE YOU'D DO THIS.
IT'S LIKE WE SAID. IF YOU WEREN'T THE WORST TRAINEE THEY'VE EVER HAD, IT'S ONLY BECAUSE ALL THE RECORDS WERE LOST WHEN THE NEXT GUY DOWN THE LIST BLEW UP HIS PLANET.
YOU'RE VERY COMFORTING.
JUST THE MARN HIEROGRYPH HEART OF GOLD, MY FRIEND. NOW, IF ONLY WE COULD PROVE YOU STINK IN A COURT OF LAW.
GET DOWN!
OOOOF!

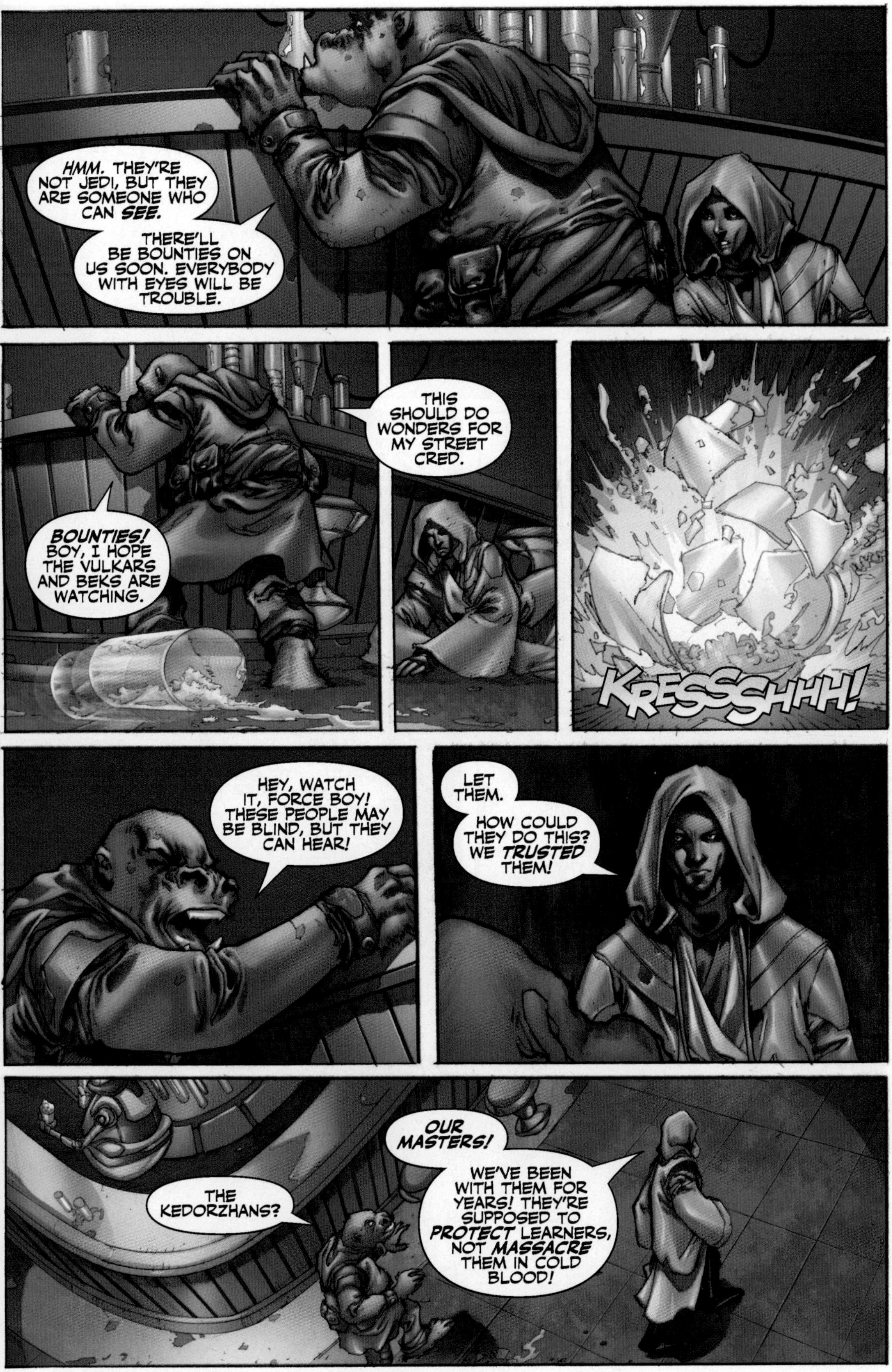
HMM. THEY'RE NOT JEDI, BUT THEY ARE SOMEONE WHO CAN *SEE*.
THERE'LL BE BOUNTIES ON US SOON. EVERYBODY WITH EYES WILL BE TROUBLE.
BOUNTIES! BOY, I HOPE THE VULKARS AND BEKS ARE WATCHING.
THIS SHOULD DO WONDERS FOR MY STREET CRED.
KRESSSHHH!
HEY, WATCH IT, FORCE BOY! THESE PEOPLE MAY BE BLIND, BUT THEY CAN HEAR!
LET THEM.
HOW COULD THEY DO THIS? WE *TRUSTED* THEM!
OUR MASTERS!
WE'VE BEEN WITH THEM FOR YEARS! THEY'RE SUPPOSED TO *PROTECT* LEARNERS, NOT *MASSACRE* THEM IN COLD BLOOD!
THE KEDORZHANS?

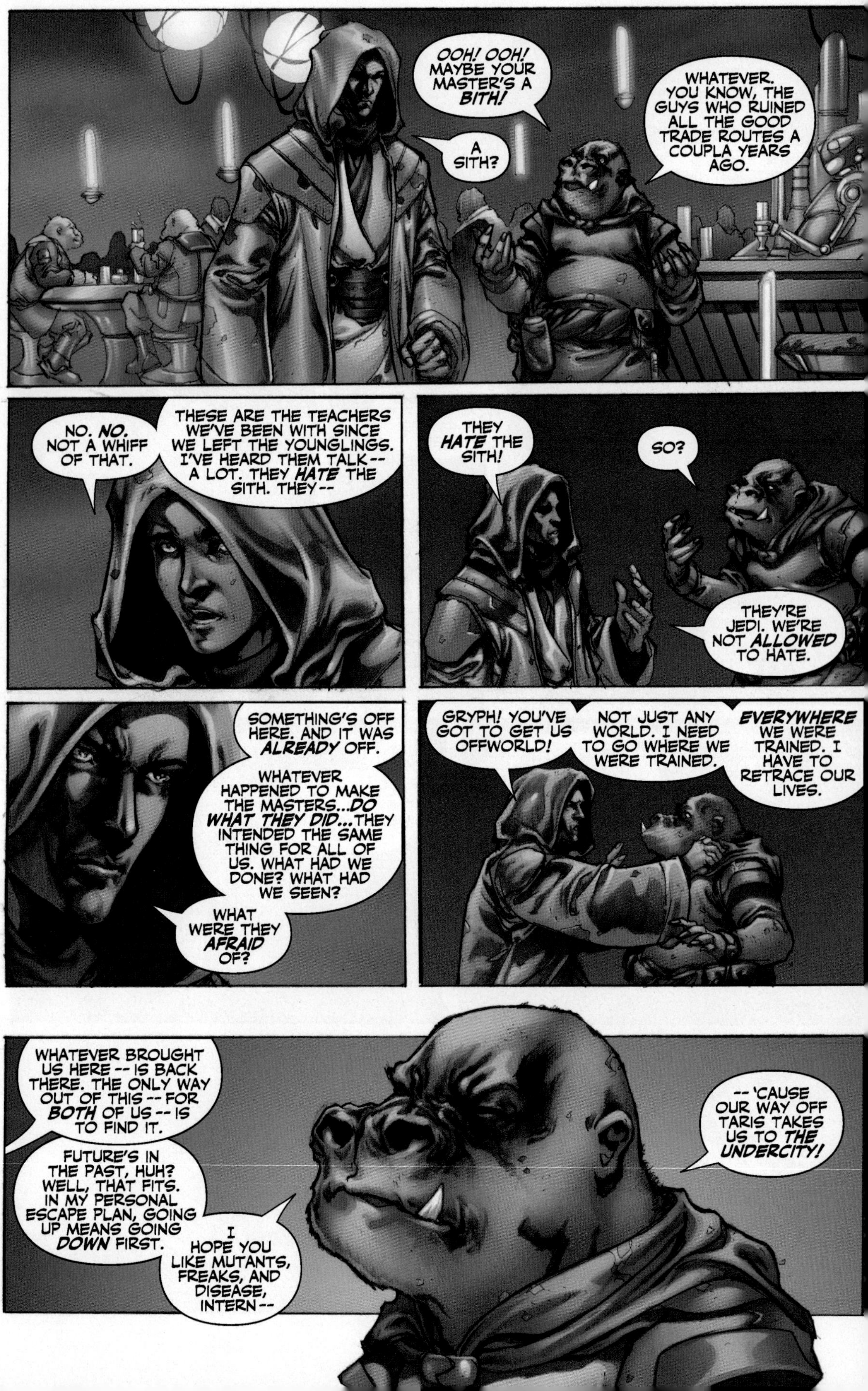
OOH! OOH! MAYBE YOUR MASTER'S A BITH!
A SITH?
WHATEVER. YOU KNOW, THE GUYS WHO RUINED ALL THE GOOD TRADE ROUTES A COUPLA YEARS AGO.
NO. NO. NOT A WHIFF OF THAT.
THESE ARE THE TEACHERS WE'VE BEEN WITH SINCE WE LEFT THE YOUNGLINGS. I'VE HEARD THEM TALK -- A LOT. THEY HATE THE SITH. THEY --
THEY HATE THE SITH!
SO?
THEY'RE JEDI. WE'RE NOT ALLOWED TO HATE.
SOMETHING'S OFF HERE. AND IT WAS ALREADY OFF.
WHATEVER HAPPENED TO MAKE THE MASTERS...DO WHAT THEY DID...THEY INTENDED THE SAME THING FOR ALL OF US. WHAT HAD WE DONE? WHAT HAD WE SEEN?
WHAT WERE THEY AFRAID OF?
GRYPH! YOU'VE GOT TO GET US OFFWORLD!
NOT JUST ANY WORLD. I NEED TO GO WHERE WE WERE TRAINED.
EVERYWHERE WE WERE TRAINED. I HAVE TO RETRACE OUR LIVES.
WHATEVER BROUGHT US HERE -- IS BACK THERE. THE ONLY WAY OUT OF THIS -- FOR BOTH OF US -- IS TO FIND IT.
FUTURE'S IN THE PAST, HUH? WELL, THAT FITS. IN MY PERSONAL ESCAPE PLAN, GOING UP MEANS GOING DOWN FIRST.
I HOPE YOU LIKE MUTANTS, FREAKS, AND DISEASE, INTERN --
-- 'CAUSE OUR WAY OFF TARIS TAKES US TO THE UNDERCITY!

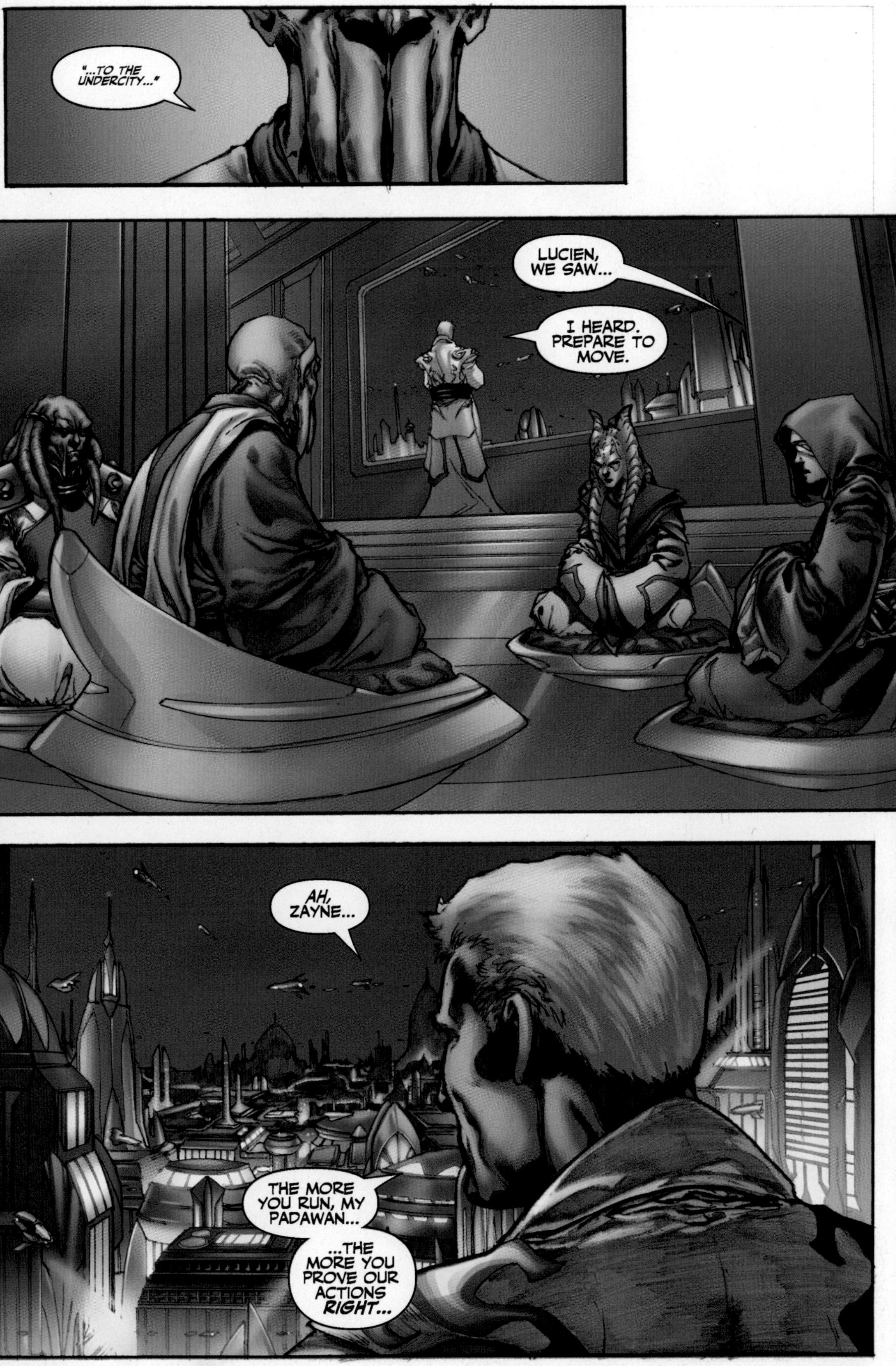
"...TO THE UNDERCITY..."
LUCIEN, WE SAW...
I HEARD. PREPARE TO MOVE.
AH, ZAYNE...
THE MORE YOU RUN, MY PADAWAN...
...THE MORE YOU PROVE OUR ACTIONS RIGHT...

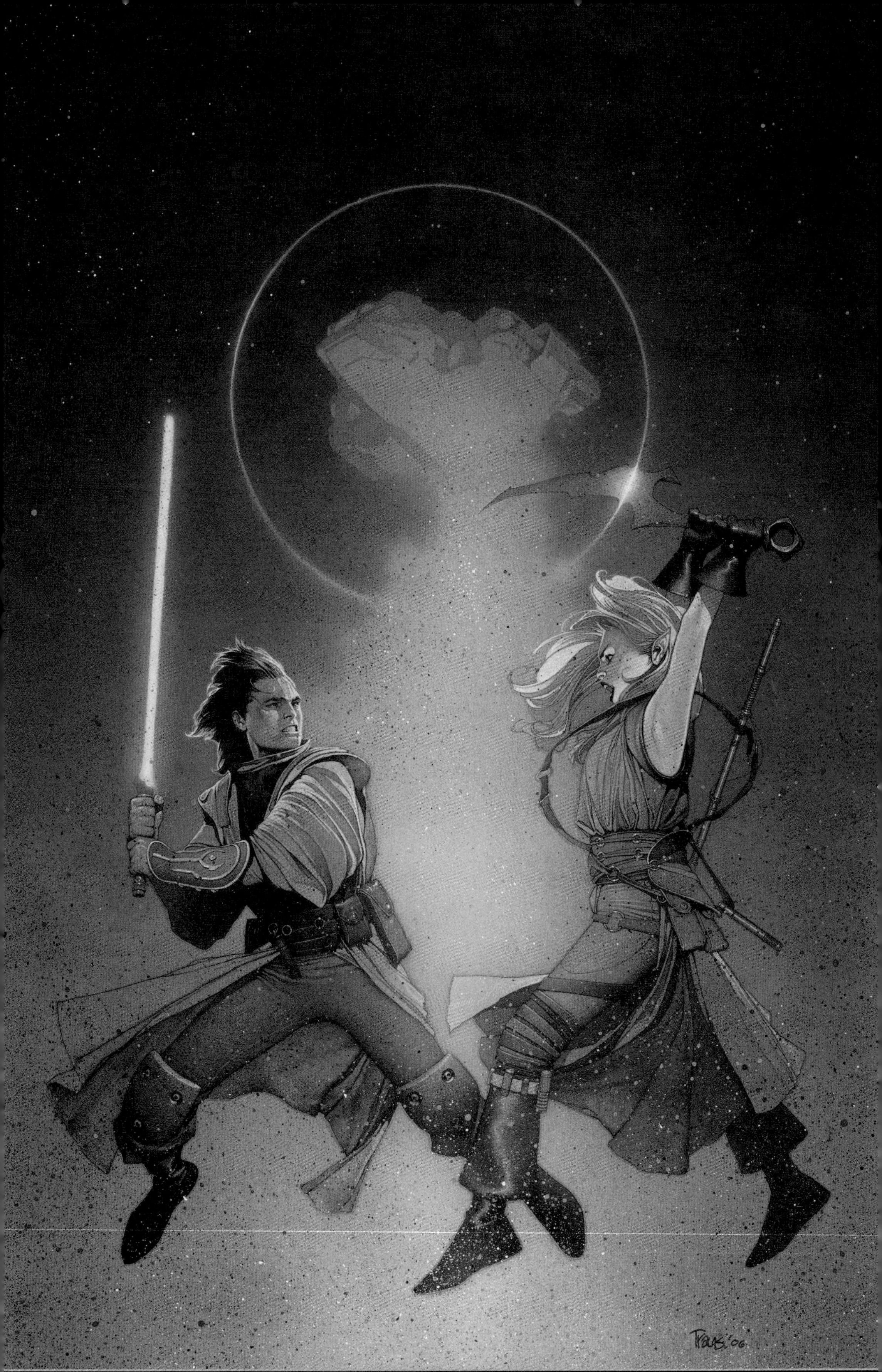

STAR WARS: KNIGHTS OF THE OLD REPUBLIC #3 — "COMMENCEMENT, PART 3 (OF SIX)"

WRITER: JOHN JACKSON MILLER • ARTIST: BRIAN CHING • COLORIST: MICHAEL ATIYEH • LETTERER: MICHAEL HEISLER
ASSISTANT EDITOR: DAVE MARSHALL • EDITOR: JEREMY BARLOW • COVER ARTIST: TRAVIS CHAREST

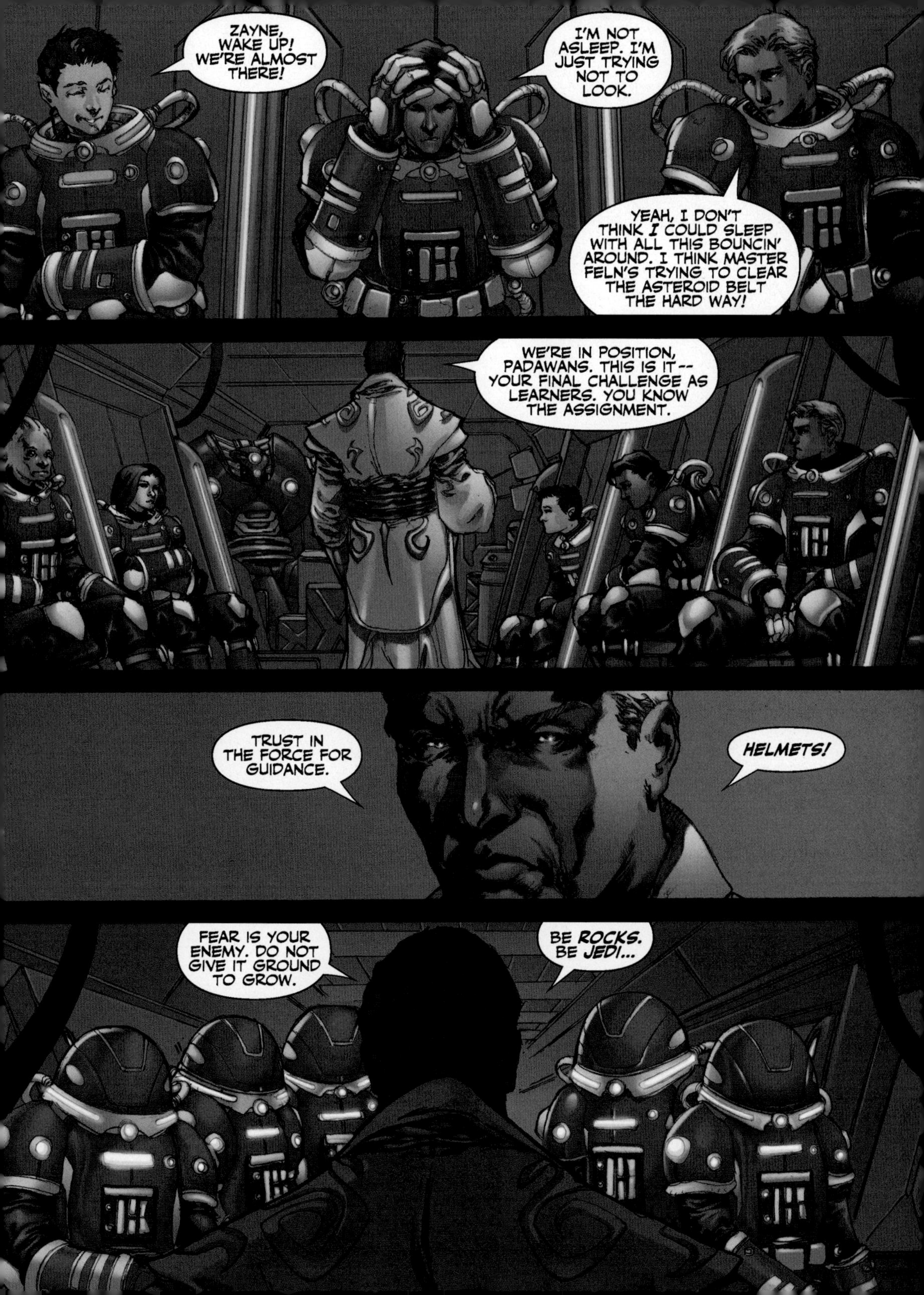
ZAYNE, WAKE UP! WE'RE ALMOST THERE!
I'M NOT ASLEEP. I'M JUST TRYING NOT TO LOOK.
YEAH, I DON'T THINK I COULD SLEEP WITH ALL THIS BOUNCIN' AROUND. I THINK MASTER FELN'S TRYING TO CLEAR THE ASTEROID BELT THE HARD WAY!
WE'RE IN POSITION, PADAWANS. THIS IS IT-- YOUR FINAL CHALLENGE AS LEARNERS. YOU KNOW THE ASSIGNMENT.
TRUST IN THE FORCE FOR GUIDANCE.
HELMETS!
FEAR IS YOUR ENEMY. DO NOT GIVE IT GROUND TO GROW.
BE ROCKS. BE JEDI...

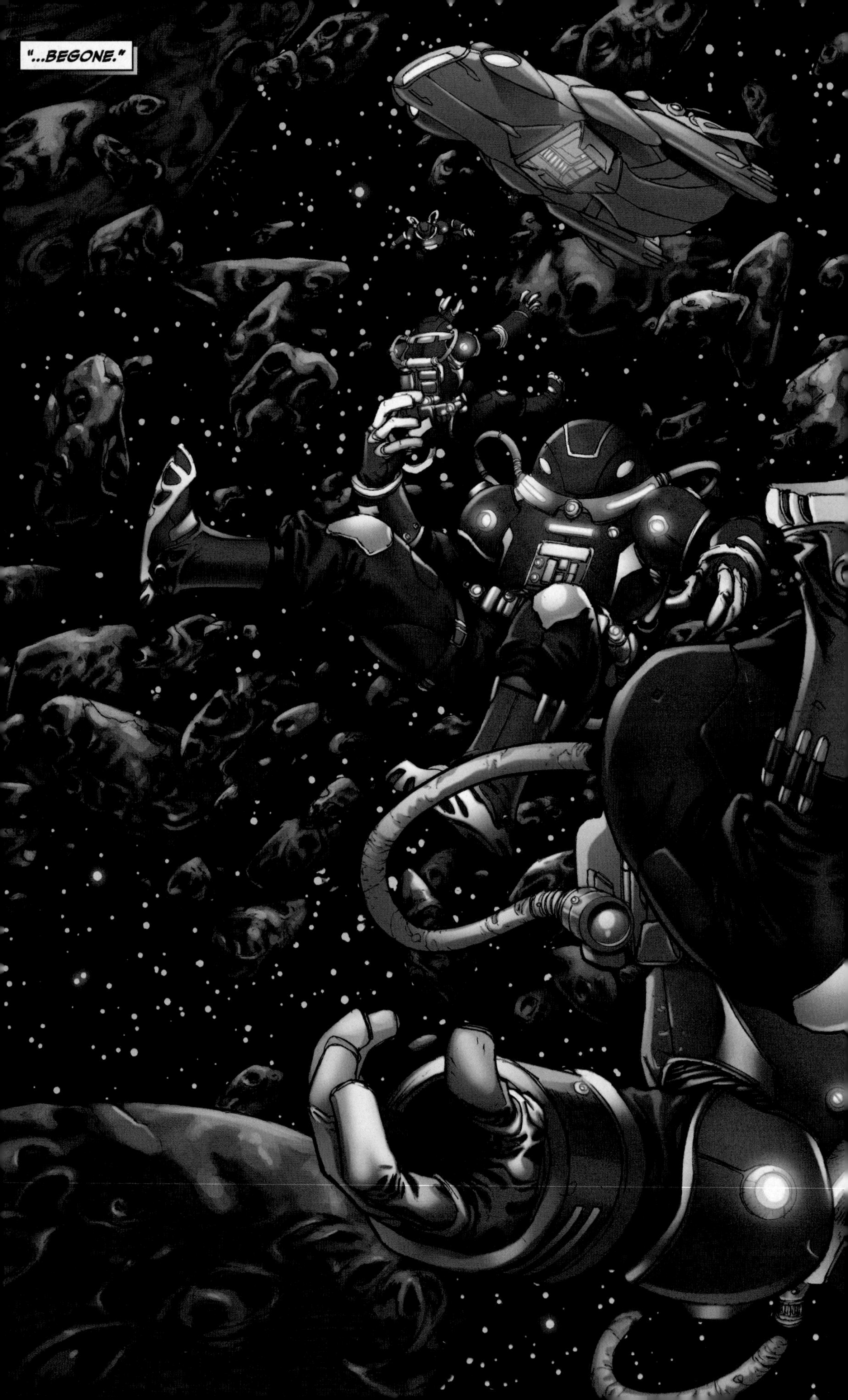
"...BEGONE."

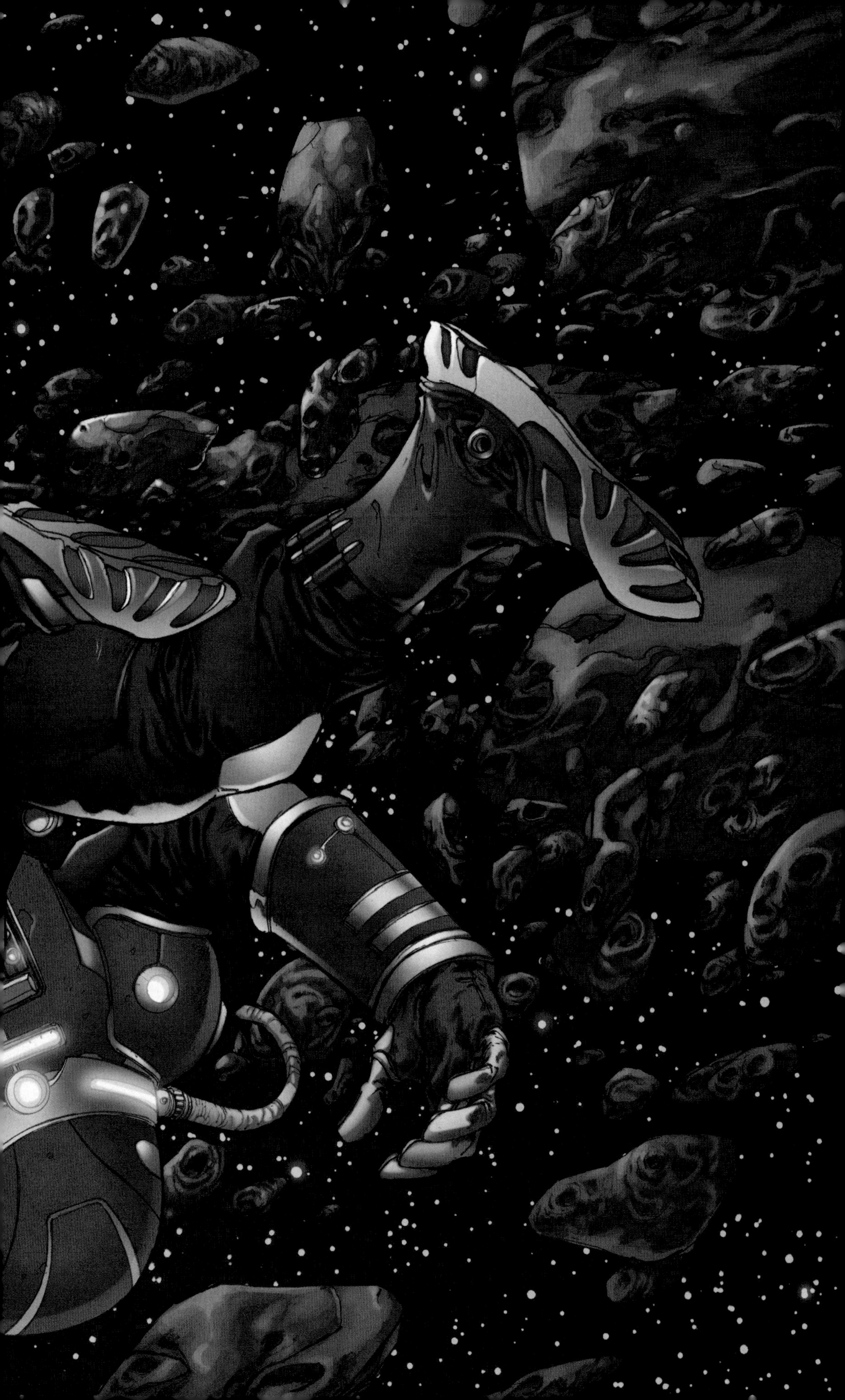

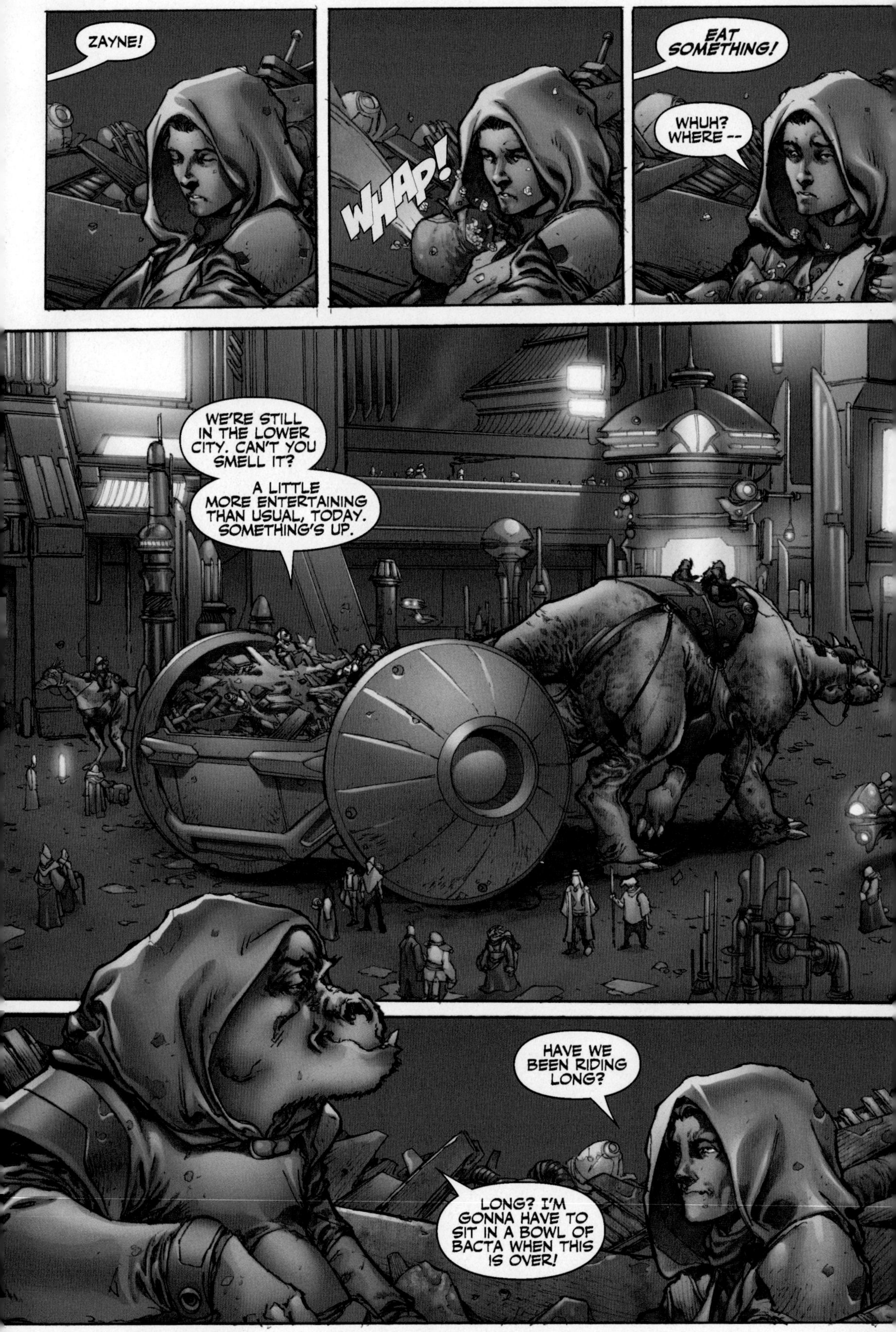
ZAYNE!
WHAP!
EAT SOMETHING!
WHUH? WHERE --
WE'RE STILL IN THE LOWER CITY. CAN'T YOU SMELL IT?
A LITTLE MORE ENTERTAINING THAN USUAL, TODAY. SOMETHING'S UP.
HAVE WE BEEN RIDING LONG?
LONG? I'M GONNA HAVE TO SIT IN A BOWL OF BACTA WHEN THIS IS OVER!

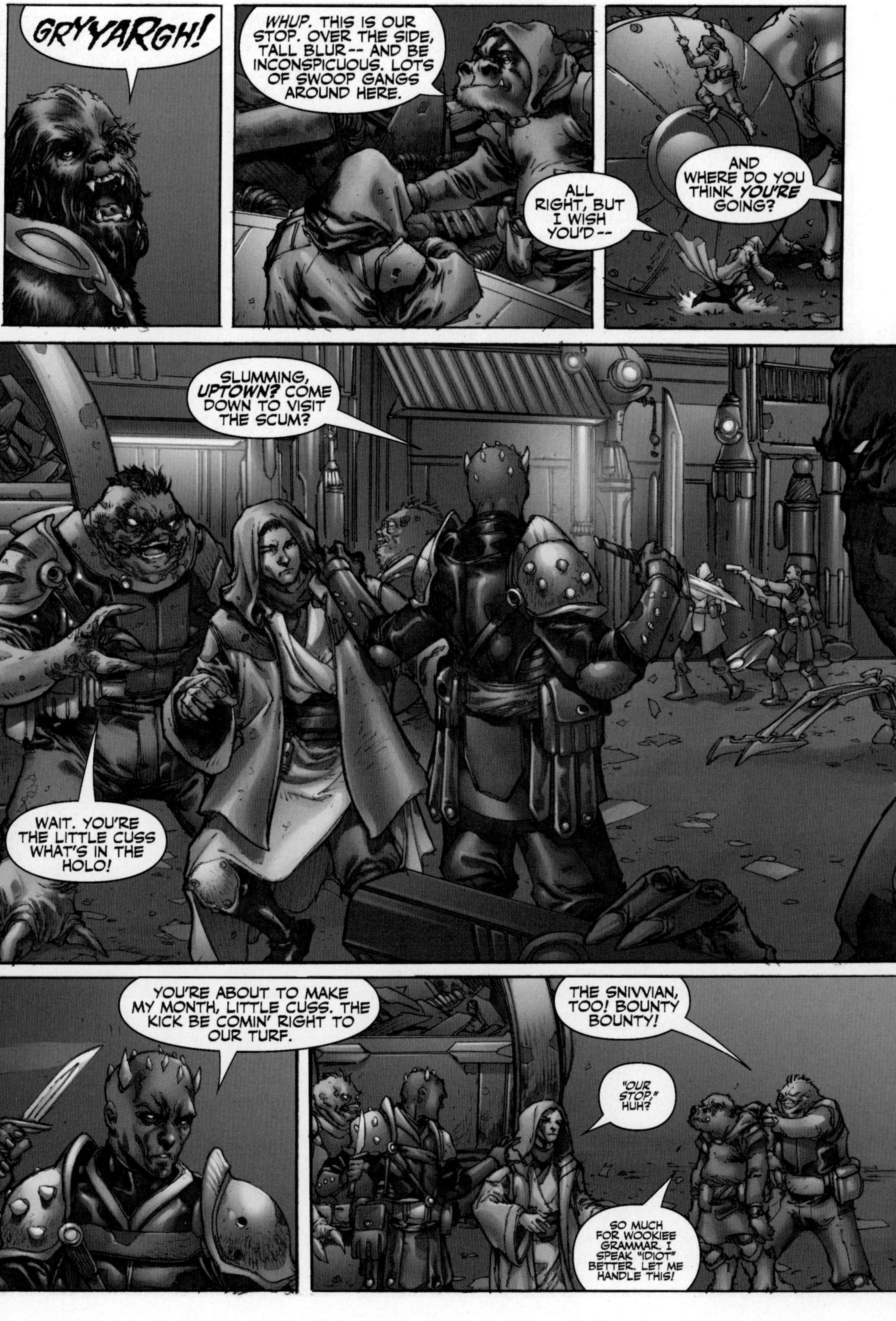
GRYYARGH!
WHUP. THIS IS OUR STOP. OVER THE SIDE, TALL BLUR-- AND BE INCONSPICUOUS. LOTS OF SWOOP GANGS AROUND HERE.
ALL RIGHT, BUT I WISH YOU'D--
AND WHERE DO YOU THINK YOU'RE GOING?
SLUMMING, UPTOWN? COME DOWN TO VISIT THE SCUM?
WAIT. YOU'RE THE LITTLE CUSS WHAT'S IN THE HOLO!
YOU'RE ABOUT TO MAKE MY MONTH, LITTLE CUSS. THE KICK BE COMIN' RIGHT TO OUR TURF.
THE SNIVVIAN, TOO! BOUNTY BOUNTY!
"OUR STOP," HUH?
SO MUCH FOR WOOKIEE GRAMMAR. I SPEAK "IDIOT" BETTER. LET ME HANDLE THIS!

JUST A MOMENT, MY FRIEND. I SEE THE COLORS -- YOU'RE WITH THE VULKARS. BENNO'S BOYS, MAYBE?
WHAT'S IT TO YOU, SIDE DISH?
BENNO HATES TO WAIT. CASHING A BOUNTY FROM THE CONSTABLE'S GONNA MEAN BUREAUCRACY, AUTHORIZATIONS, DELAY --
-- AND THEY MAY MAKE HIM COME UP-CITY TO TESTIFY. JUST PICTURE ***BENNO, UP-CITY!***
HRRMM. BENNO DON'T LIKE TO WEAR CITY CLOTHES.
AND THAT'D BE FOR WEEKS AT A TIME! AND ALL HE'S GONNA BE THINKING ABOUT IS THE GUYS WHO ***GOT*** HIM THERE.
BENNO DON'T ***LIKE*** THINKING!
WELL, YOU CAN KEEP THAT FROM HAPPENING. THERE'S AN EASIER WAY TO MAKE YOUR KICK FOR THE WHOLE YEAR -- IF YOU'LL LISTEN...

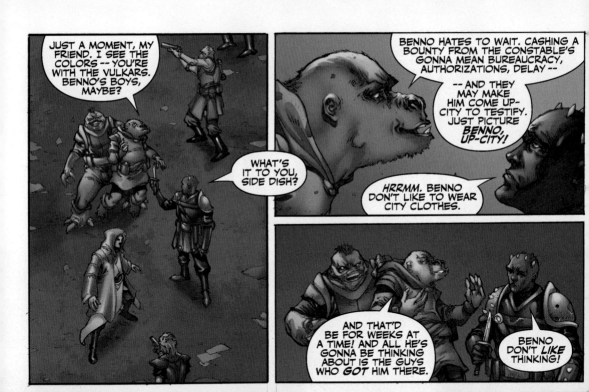

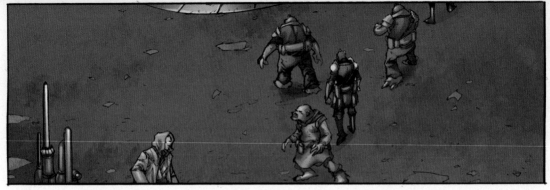

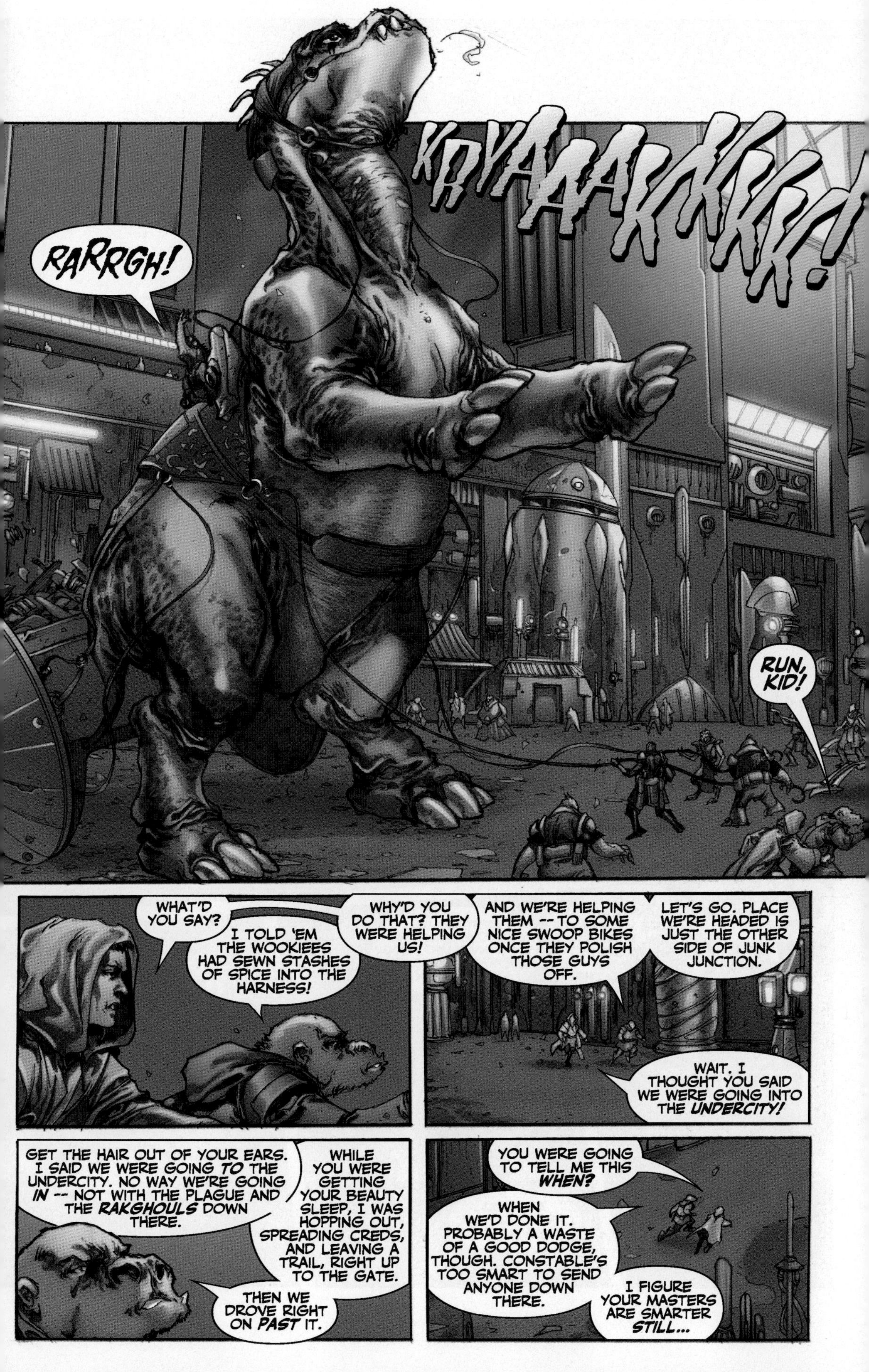
KRYAAAAKKKK!
RARRGH!
RUN, KID!
WHAT'D YOU SAY?
I TOLD 'EM THE WOOKIEES HAD SEWN STASHES OF SPICE INTO THE HARNESS!
WHY'D YOU DO THAT? THEY WERE HELPING US!
AND WE'RE HELPING THEM -- TO SOME NICE SWOOP BIKES ONCE THEY POLISH THOSE GUYS OFF.
LET'S GO. PLACE WE'RE HEADED IS JUST THE OTHER SIDE OF JUNK JUNCTION.
WAIT. I THOUGHT YOU SAID WE WERE GOING INTO THE UNDERCITY!
GET THE HAIR OUT OF YOUR EARS. I SAID WE WERE GOING TO THE UNDERCITY. NO WAY WE'RE GOING IN -- NOT WITH THE PLAGUE AND THE RAKGHOULS DOWN THERE.
WHILE YOU WERE GETTING YOUR BEAUTY SLEEP, I WAS HOPPING OUT, SPREADING CREDS, AND LEAVING A TRAIL, RIGHT UP TO THE GATE.
THEN WE DROVE RIGHT ON PAST IT.
YOU WERE GOING TO TELL ME THIS WHEN?
WHEN WE'D DONE IT. PROBABLY A WASTE OF A GOOD DODGE, THOUGH. CONSTABLE'S TOO SMART TO SEND ANYONE DOWN THERE.
I FIGURE YOUR MASTERS ARE SMARTER STILL...

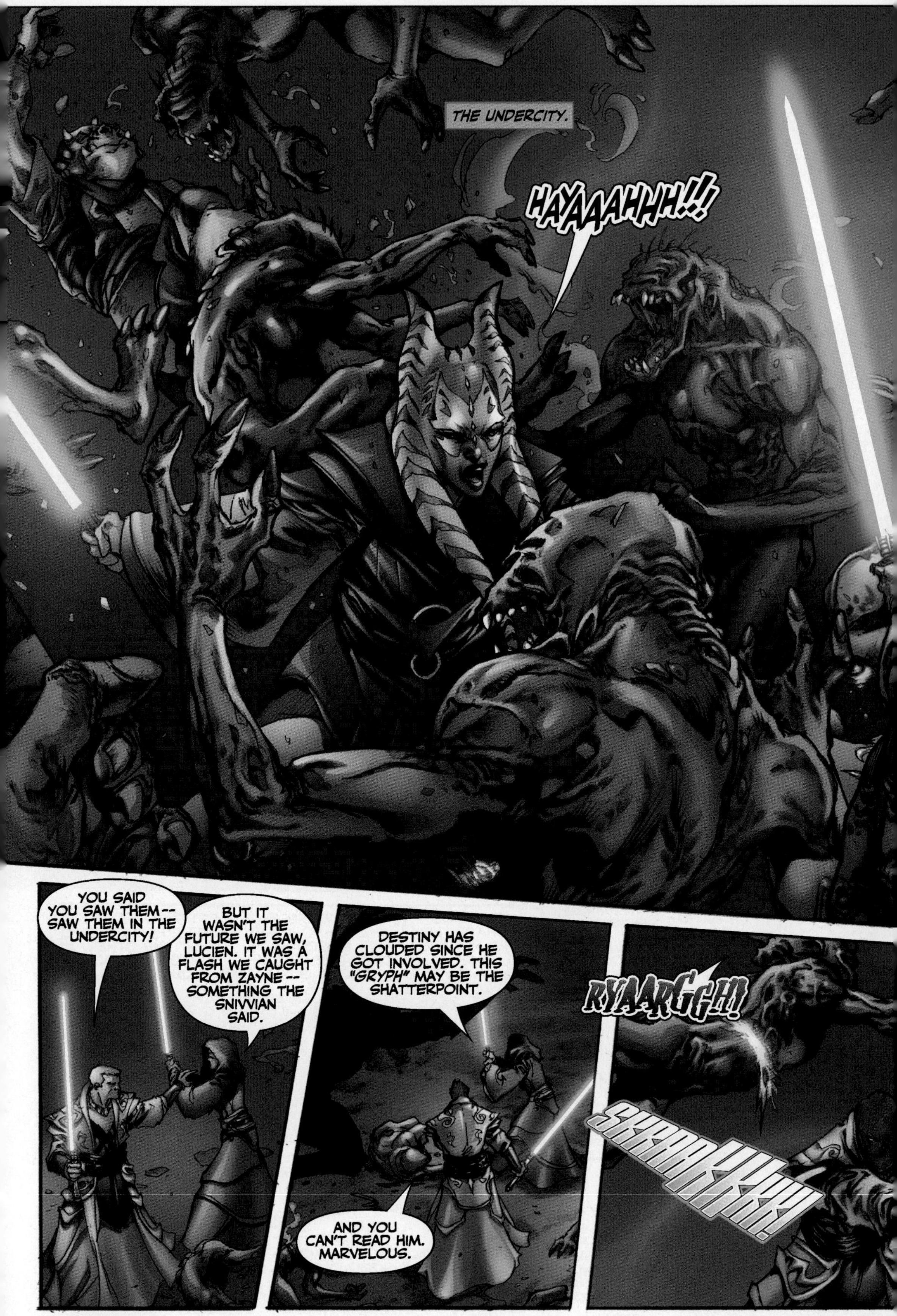
THE UNDERCITY.
HAYAAAHHH!!!
YOU SAID YOU SAW THEM-- SAW THEM IN THE UNDERCITY!
BUT IT WASN'T THE FUTURE WE SAW, LUCIEN. IT WAS A FLASH WE CAUGHT FROM ZAYNE -- SOMETHING THE SNIVVIAN SAID.
DESTINY HAS CLOUDED SINCE HE GOT INVOLVED. THIS "GRYPH" MAY BE THE SHATTERPOINT.
AND YOU CAN'T READ HIM. MARVELOUS.
RYAARGGH!!
SKRAKKKKH!

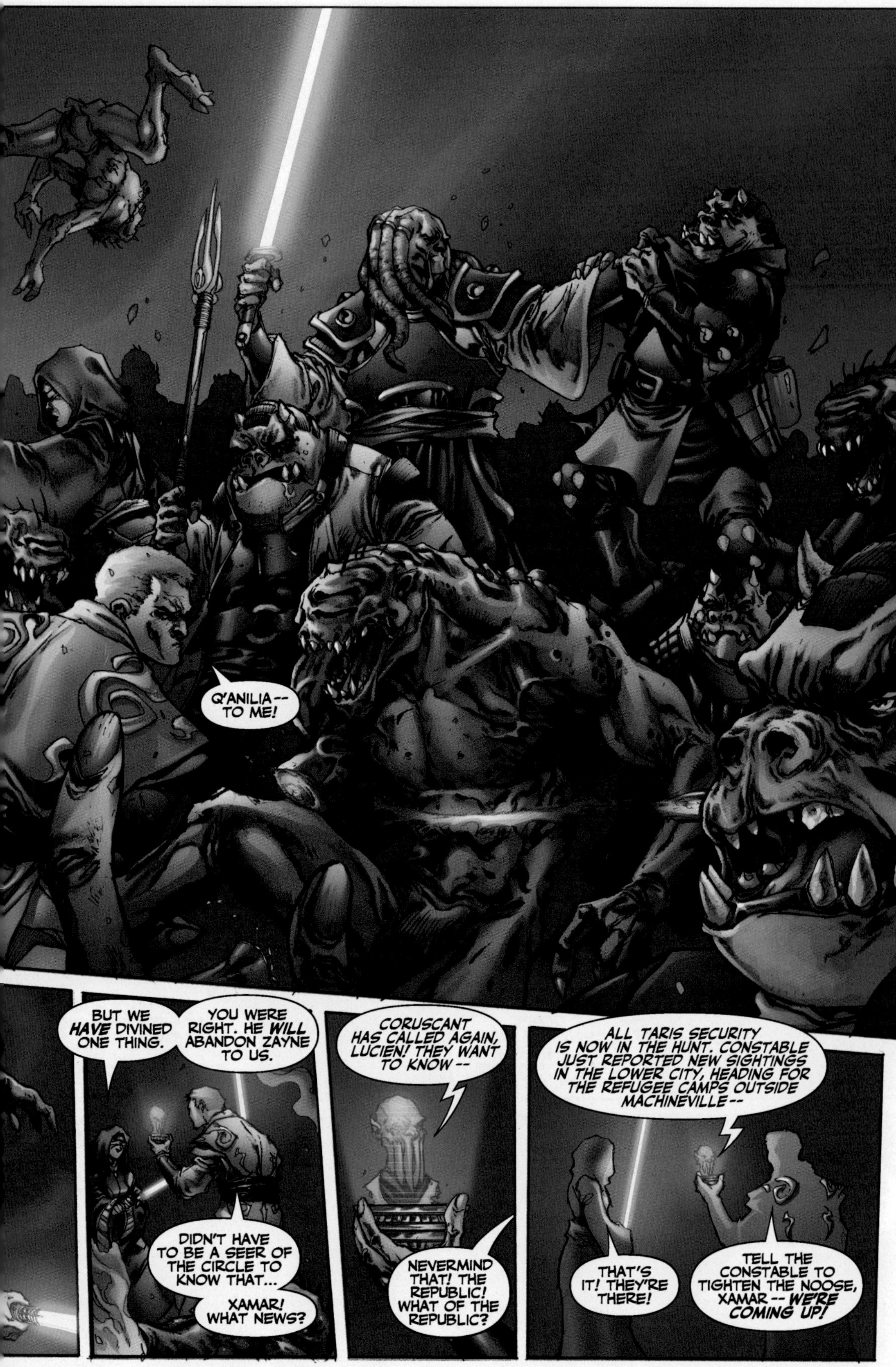
Q'ANILIA-- TO ME!
BUT WE HAVE DIVINED ONE THING.
YOU WERE RIGHT. HE WILL ABANDON ZAYNE TO US.
DIDN'T HAVE TO BE A SEER OF THE CIRCLE TO KNOW THAT...
XAMAR! WHAT NEWS?
CORUSCANT HAS CALLED AGAIN, LUCIEN! THEY WANT TO KNOW --
NEVERMIND THAT! THE REPUBLIC! WHAT OF THE REPUBLIC?
ALL TARIS SECURITY IS NOW IN THE HUNT. CONSTABLE JUST REPORTED NEW SIGHTINGS IN THE LOWER CITY, HEADING FOR THE REFUGEE CAMPS OUTSIDE MACHINEVILLE--
THAT'S IT! THEY'RE THERE!
TELL THE CONSTABLE TO TIGHTEN THE NOOSE, XAMAR -- WE'RE COMING UP!

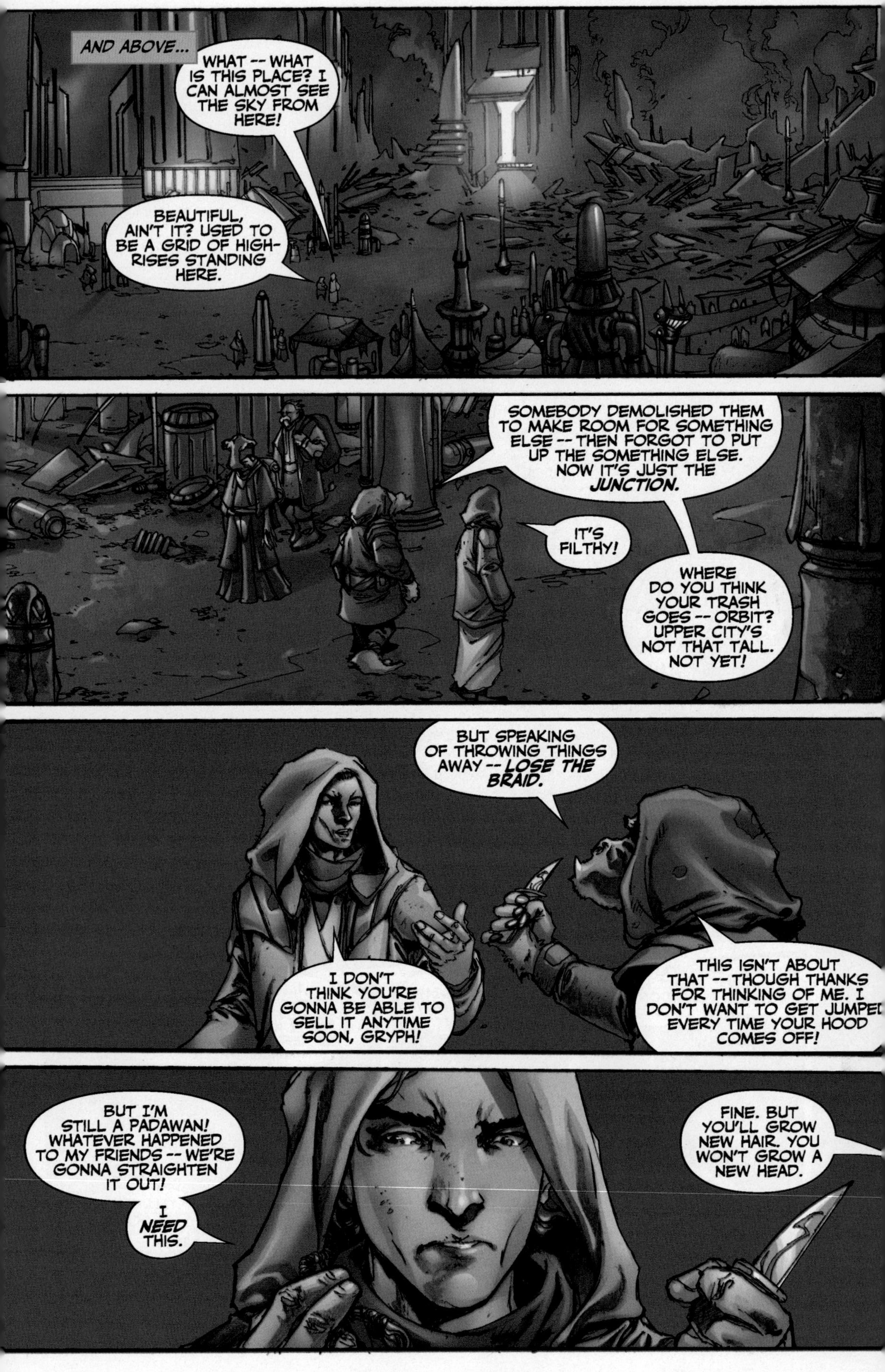
AND ABOVE...
WHAT -- WHAT IS THIS PLACE? I CAN ALMOST SEE THE SKY FROM HERE!
BEAUTIFUL, AIN'T IT? USED TO BE A GRID OF HIGH-RISES STANDING HERE.
SOMEBODY DEMOLISHED THEM TO MAKE ROOM FOR SOMETHING ELSE -- THEN FORGOT TO PUT UP THE SOMETHING ELSE. NOW IT'S JUST THE JUNCTION.
IT'S FILTHY!
WHERE DO YOU THINK YOUR TRASH GOES -- ORBIT? UPPER CITY'S NOT THAT TALL. NOT YET!
BUT SPEAKING OF THROWING THINGS AWAY -- LOSE THE BRAID.
I DON'T THINK YOU'RE GONNA BE ABLE TO SELL IT ANYTIME SOON, GRYPH!
THIS ISN'T ABOUT THAT -- THOUGH THANKS FOR THINKING OF ME. I DON'T WANT TO GET JUMPED EVERY TIME YOUR HOOD COMES OFF!
BUT I'M STILL A PADAWAN! WHATEVER HAPPENED TO MY FRIENDS -- WE'RE GONNA STRAIGHTEN IT OUT!
I NEED THIS.
FINE. BUT YOU'LL GROW NEW HAIR. YOU WON'T GROW A NEW HEAD.

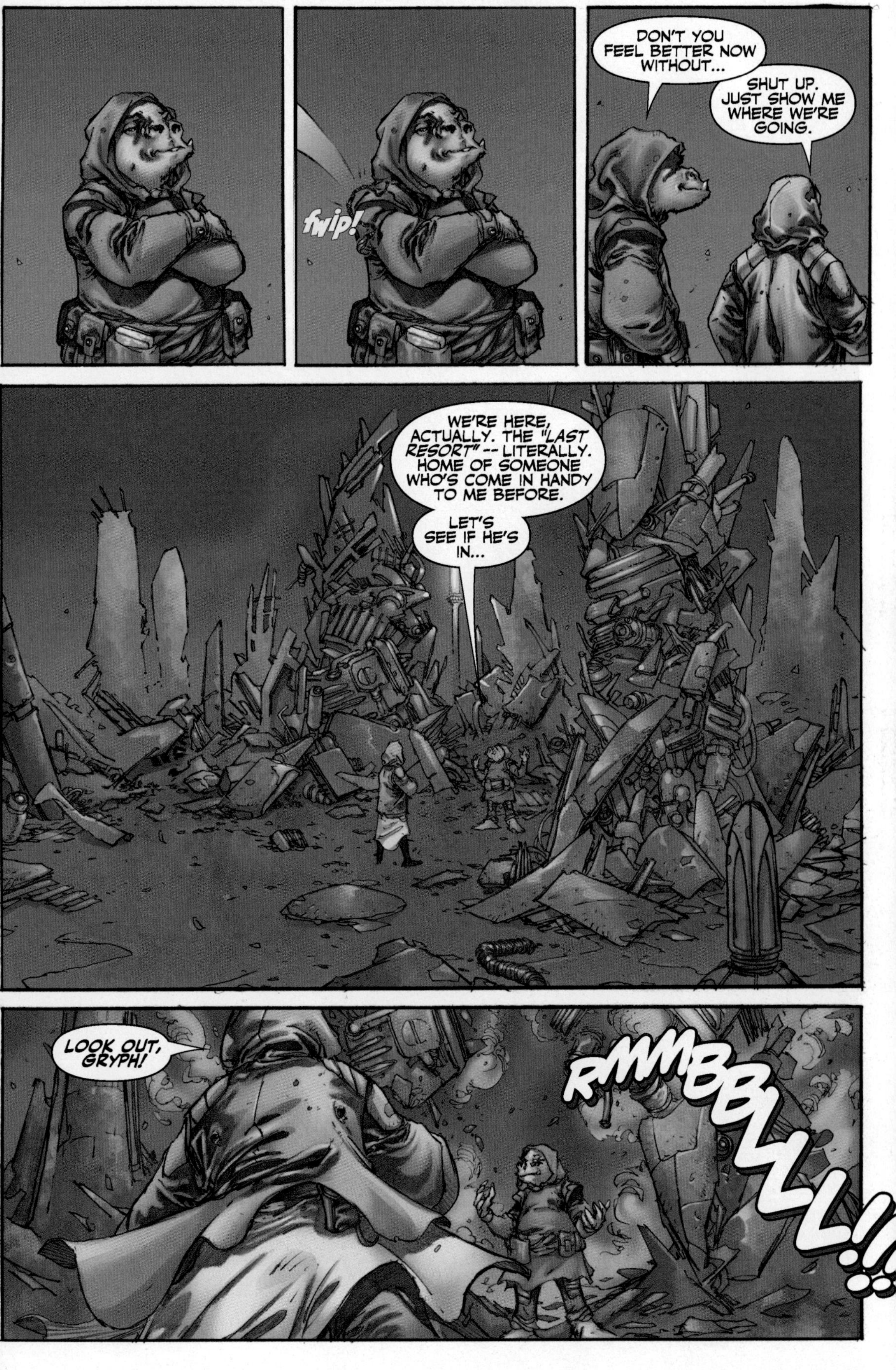
fwip!
DON'T YOU FEEL BETTER NOW WITHOUT...
SHUT UP. JUST SHOW ME WHERE WE'RE GOING.
WE'RE HERE, ACTUALLY. THE "LAST RESORT" -- LITERALLY. HOME OF SOMEONE WHO'S COME IN HANDY TO ME BEFORE.
LET'S SEE IF HE'S IN...
LOOK OUT, GRYPH!
RMMBBLLL!!!

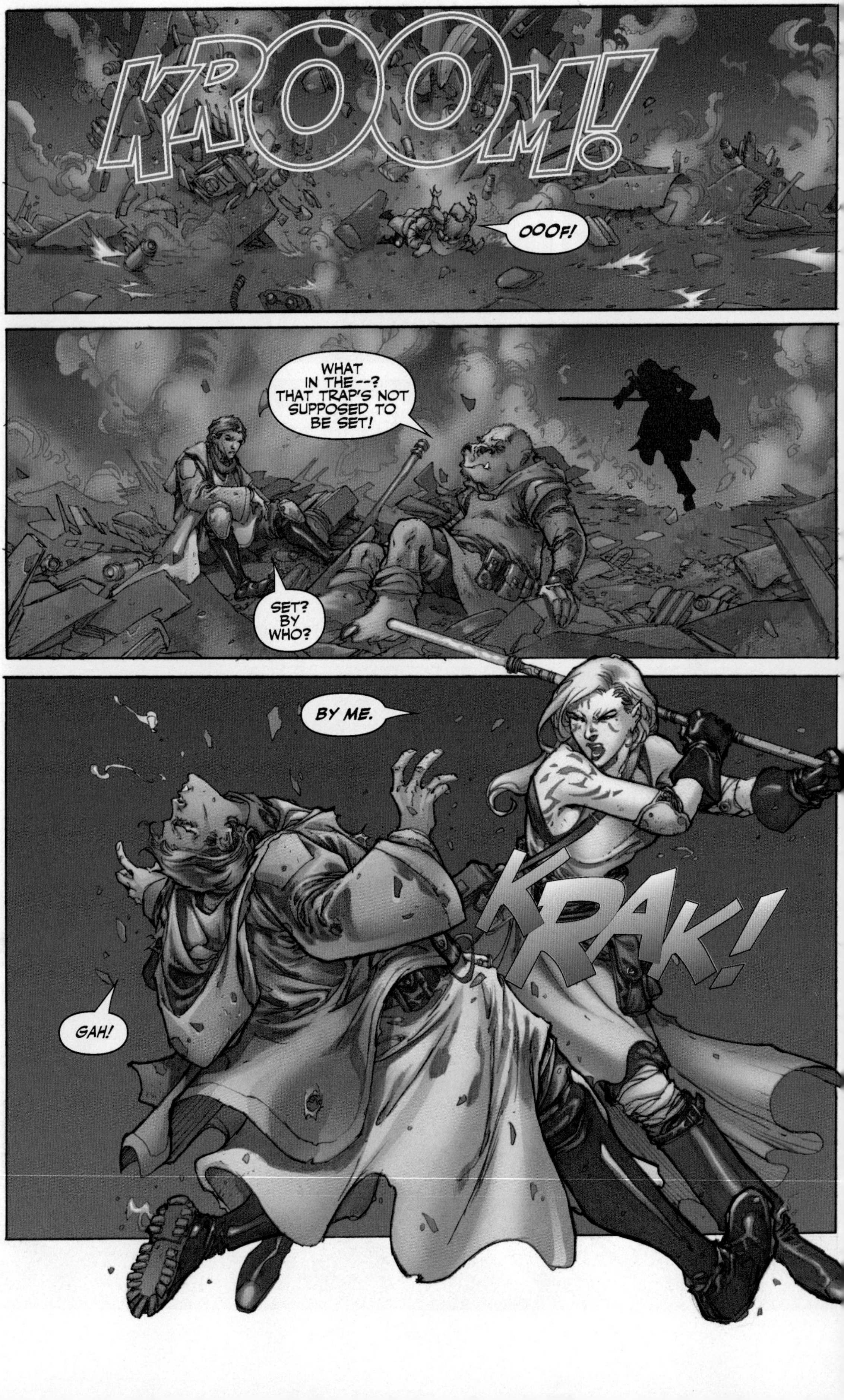
KROOOM!
OOOF!
WHAT IN THE--? THAT TRAP'S NOT SUPPOSED TO BE SET!
SET? BY WHO?
BY ME.
KRAK!
GAH!

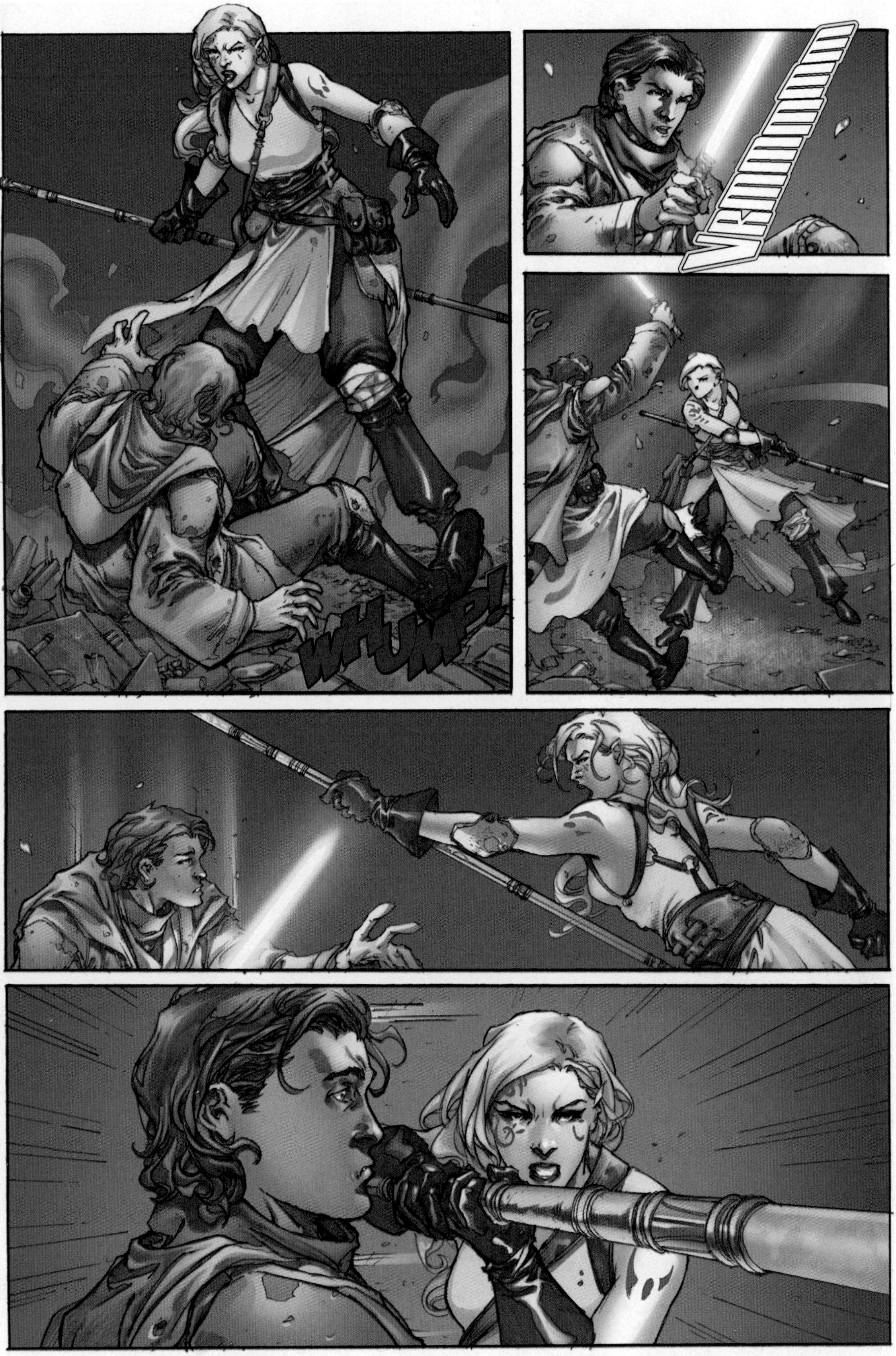
WHUMP!

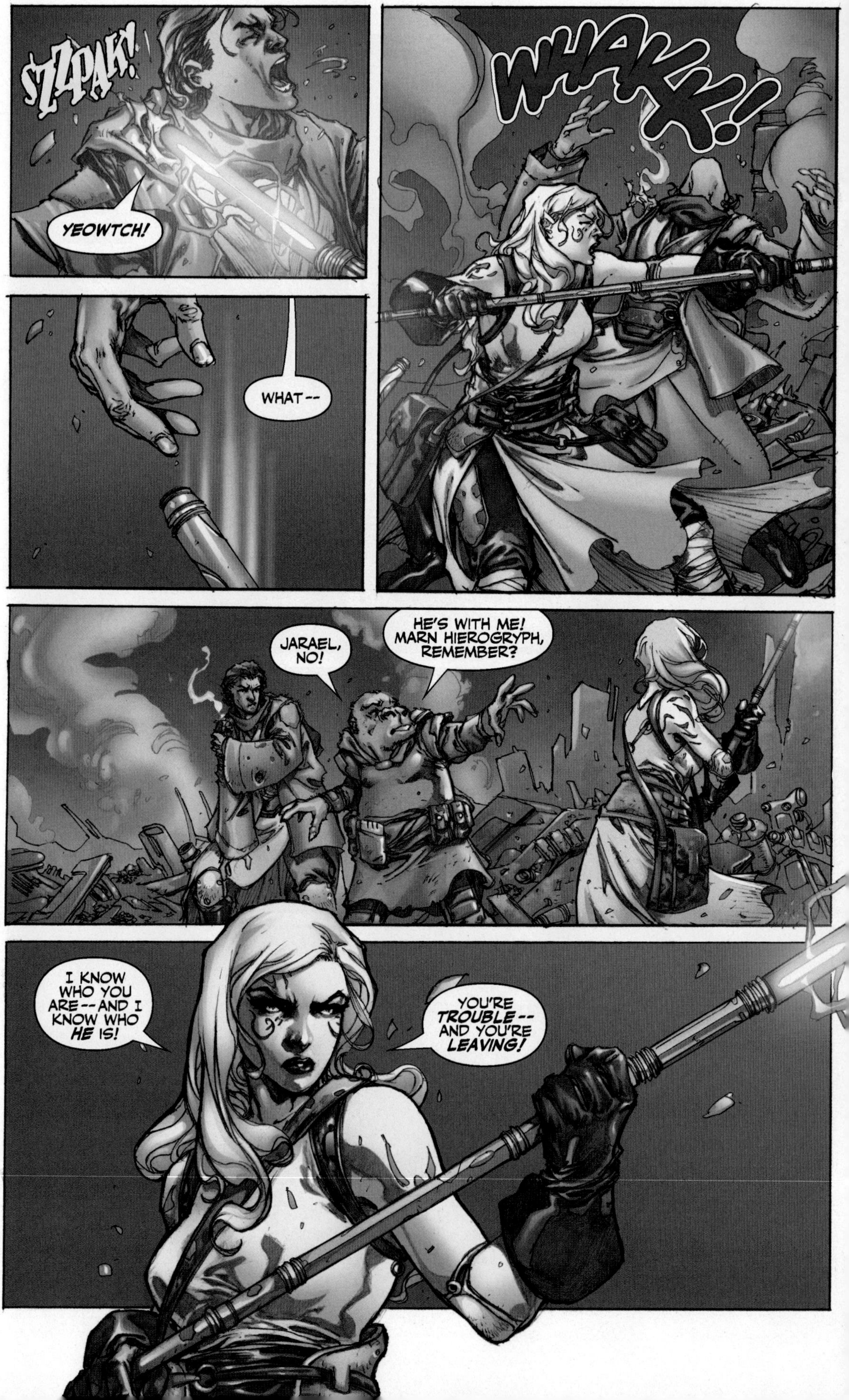
SZZPAK!
YEOWTCH!
WHAKK!!
WHAT--
JARAEL, NO!
HE'S WITH ME! MARN HIEROGRYPH, REMEMBER?
I KNOW WHO YOU ARE--AND I KNOW WHO HE IS!
YOU'RE TROUBLE--AND YOU'RE LEAVING!

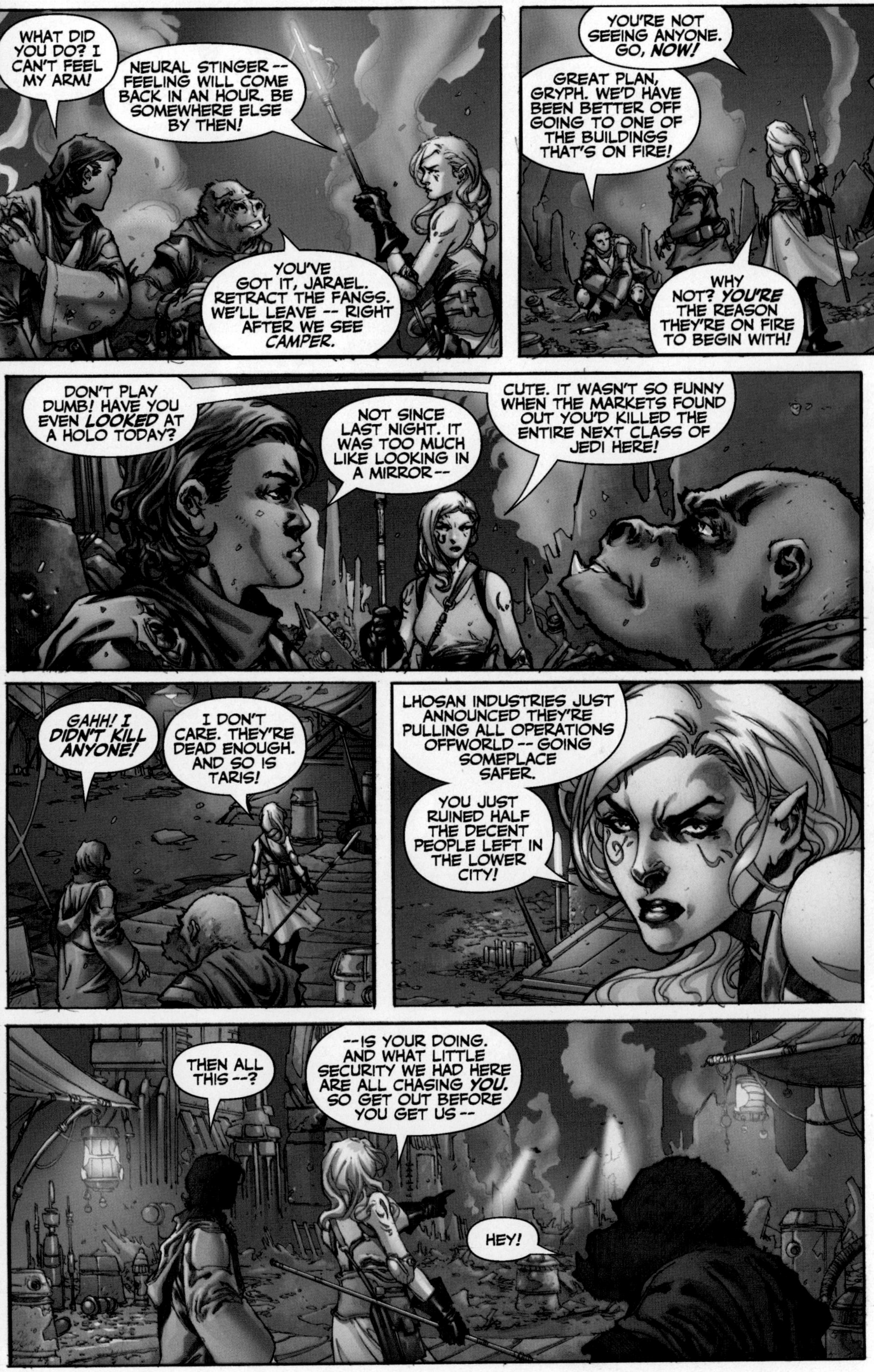
WHAT DID YOU DO? I CAN'T FEEL MY ARM!
NEURAL STINGER -- FEELING WILL COME BACK IN AN HOUR. BE SOMEWHERE ELSE BY THEN!
YOU'VE GOT IT, JARAEL. RETRACT THE FANGS. WE'LL LEAVE -- RIGHT AFTER WE SEE CAMPER.
YOU'RE NOT SEEING ANYONE. GO, NOW!
GREAT PLAN, GRYPH. WE'D HAVE BEEN BETTER OFF GOING TO ONE OF THE BUILDINGS THAT'S ON FIRE!
WHY NOT? YOU'RE THE REASON THEY'RE ON FIRE TO BEGIN WITH!
DON'T PLAY DUMB! HAVE YOU EVEN LOOKED AT A HOLO TODAY?
NOT SINCE LAST NIGHT. IT WAS TOO MUCH LIKE LOOKING IN A MIRROR--
CUTE. IT WASN'T SO FUNNY WHEN THE MARKETS FOUND OUT YOU'D KILLED THE ENTIRE NEXT CLASS OF JEDI HERE!
GAHH! I DIDN'T KILL ANYONE!
I DON'T CARE. THEY'RE DEAD ENOUGH. AND SO IS TARIS!
LHOSAN INDUSTRIES JUST ANNOUNCED THEY'RE PULLING ALL OPERATIONS OFFWORLD -- GOING SOMEPLACE SAFER.
YOU JUST RUINED HALF THE DECENT PEOPLE LEFT IN THE LOWER CITY!
THEN ALL THIS --?
--IS YOUR DOING. AND WHAT LITTLE SECURITY WE HAD HERE ARE ALL CHASING YOU. SO GET OUT BEFORE YOU GET US --
HEY!

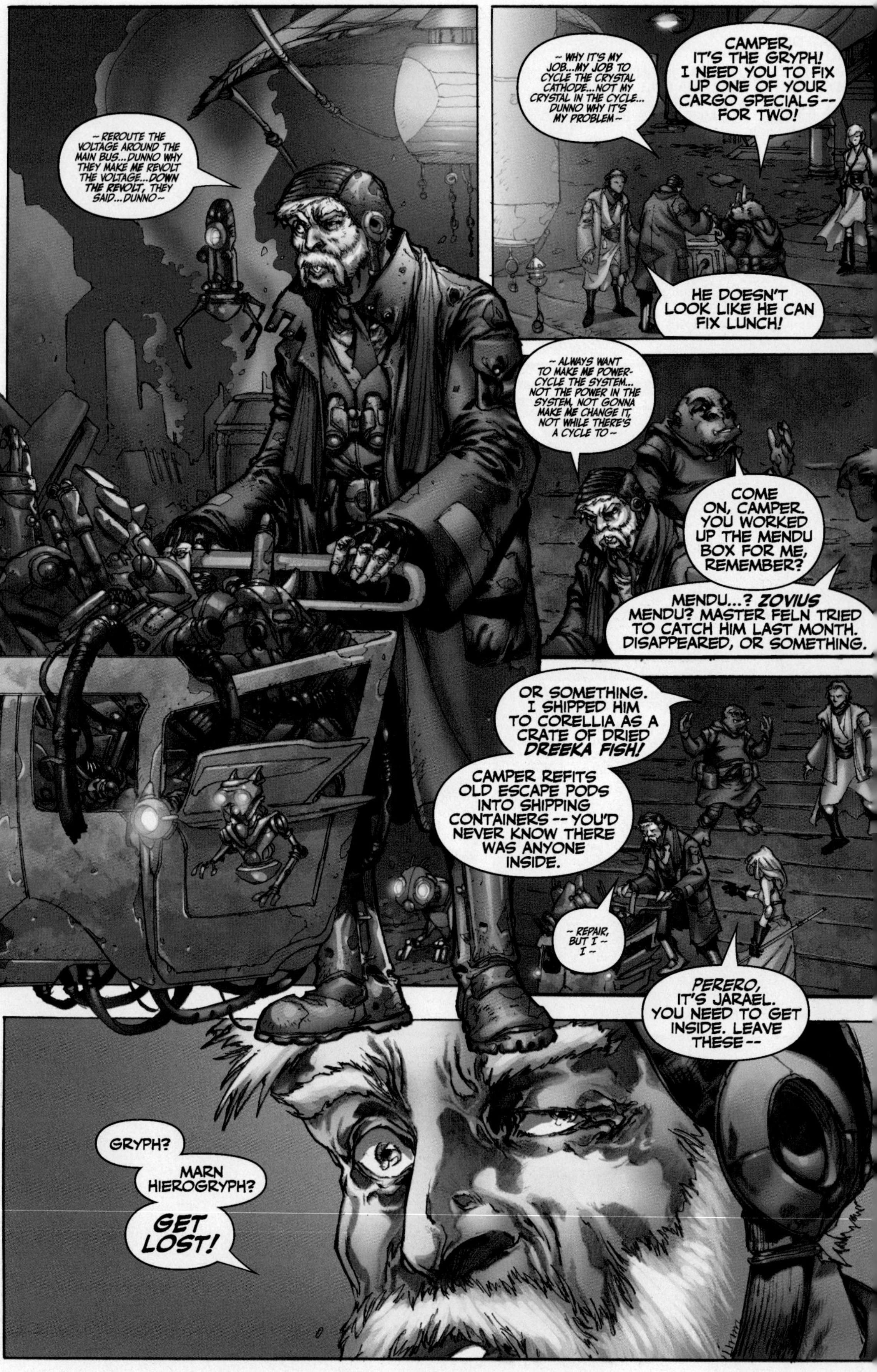
~ REROUTE THE VOLTAGE AROUND THE MAIN BUS...DUNNO WHY THEY MAKE ME REVOLT THE VOLTAGE...DOWN THE REVOLT, THEY SAID...DUNNO ~
~ WHY IT'S MY JOB...MY JOB TO CYCLE THE CRYSTAL CATHODE...NOT MY CRYSTAL IN THE CYCLE... DUNNO WHY IT'S MY PROBLEM ~
CAMPER, IT'S THE GRYPH! I NEED YOU TO FIX UP ONE OF YOUR CARGO SPECIALS -- FOR TWO!
HE DOESN'T LOOK LIKE HE CAN FIX LUNCH!
~ ALWAYS WANT TO MAKE ME POWER-CYCLE THE SYSTEM... NOT THE POWER IN THE SYSTEM, NOT GONNA MAKE ME CHANGE IT, NOT WHILE THERE'S A CYCLE TO ~
COME ON, CAMPER. YOU WORKED UP THE MENDU BOX FOR ME, REMEMBER?
MENDU...? ZOVIUS MENDU? MASTER FELN TRIED TO CATCH HIM LAST MONTH. DISAPPEARED, OR SOMETHING.
OR SOMETHING. I SHIPPED HIM TO CORELLIA AS A CRATE OF DRIED DREEKA FISH!
CAMPER REFITS OLD ESCAPE PODS INTO SHIPPING CONTAINERS -- YOU'D NEVER KNOW THERE WAS ANYONE INSIDE.
~ REPAIR, BUT I -- I ~
PERERO, IT'S JARAEL. YOU NEED TO GET INSIDE. LEAVE THESE --
GRYPH?
MARN HIEROGRYPH?
GET LOST!

OH, NOW, DID I NOT *PAY* YOU? I'VE BEEN MEANING TO GET YOU TO LOOK AT MY BOOKKEEPING DROID. YOU CAN DO THAT AFTER YOU--

NO TIME FOR YOU, SNOUT! I GOT JUST THE EQUIPMENT I NEED RIGHT HERE, *RIGHT HERE!*

YOU'RE A MAN WITH GRIEVANCES. I CAN COPE. WE JUST WANT--

YOU WANT--? I GIVE YOU WHAT *YOU* WANT. THEN I HAVE TO GIVE THEM WHAT *THEY* WANT. EVERYONE WANTS!

WELL, *I* WANT TO FINISH REROUTING THIS TEE-THREE'S RELAYS, WHILE I STILL REMEMBER HOW!

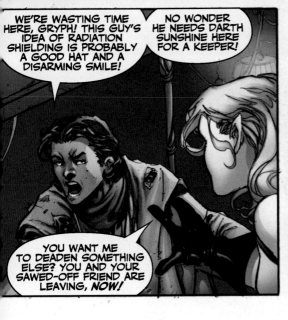

WE'RE WASTING TIME HERE, GRYPH! THIS GUY'S IDEA OF RADIATION SHIELDING IS PROBABLY A GOOD HAT AND A DISARMING SMILE!

NO WONDER HE NEEDS DARTH SUNSHINE HERE FOR A KEEPER!

YOU WANT ME TO DEADEN SOMETHING ELSE? YOU AND YOUR SAWED-OFF FRIEND ARE LEAVING, *NOW!*

WHAT'S YOUR PROBLEM? DON'T *YOU* WANT THE BOUNTY? EVERYONE ELSE WANTS A PIECE OF ME!

YOU THINK IT'S THAT SIMPLE FOR US, *HUH?* WELL, YOU'RE NOT THE ONLY--

NO!

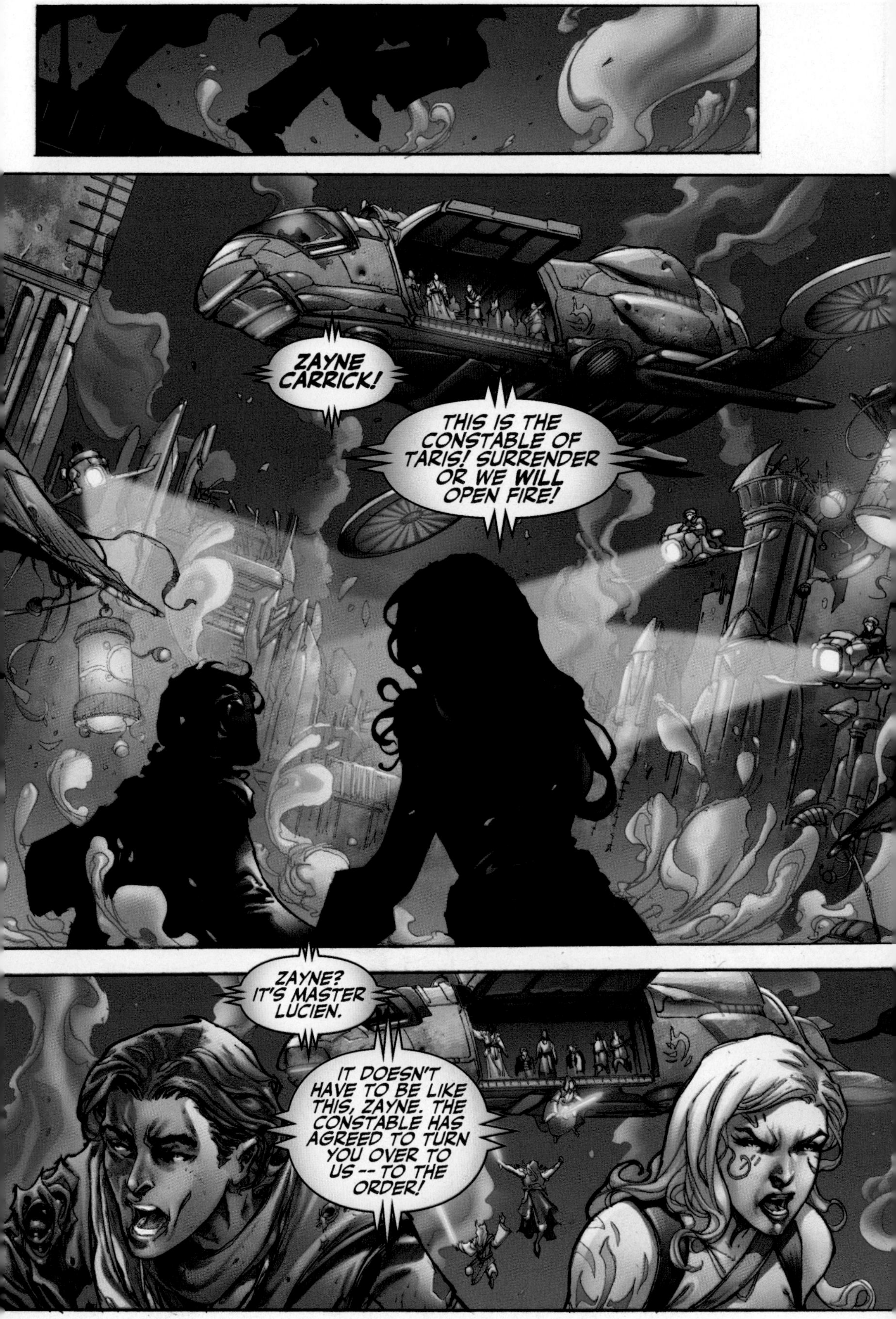
ZAYNE CARRICK!
THIS IS THE CONSTABLE OF TARIS! SURRENDER OR WE WILL OPEN FIRE!
ZAYNE? IT'S MASTER LUCIEN.
IT DOESN'T HAVE TO BE LIKE THIS, ZAYNE. THE CONSTABLE HAS AGREED TO TURN YOU OVER TO US -- TO THE ORDER!

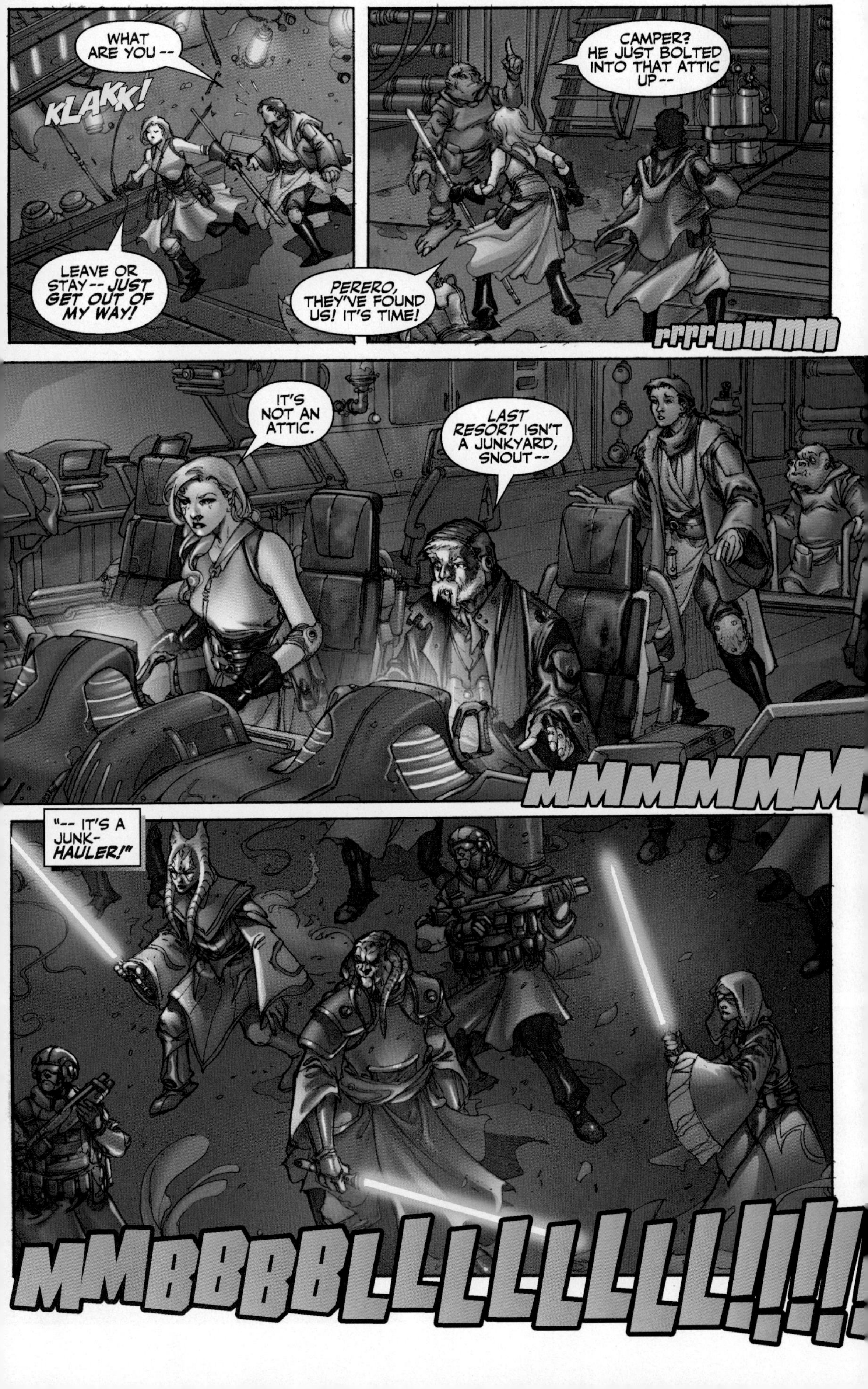
WHAT ARE YOU --
KLAKK!
LEAVE OR STAY -- JUST GET OUT OF MY WAY!
CAMPER? HE JUST BOLTED INTO THAT ATTIC UP --
PERERO, THEY'VE FOUND US! IT'S TIME!
rrrrMMMMM
IT'S NOT AN ATTIC.
LAST RESORT ISN'T A JUNKYARD, SNOUT --
MMMMMMM
"-- IT'S A JUNK-HAULER!"
MMBBBBLLLLLLLL!!!!!

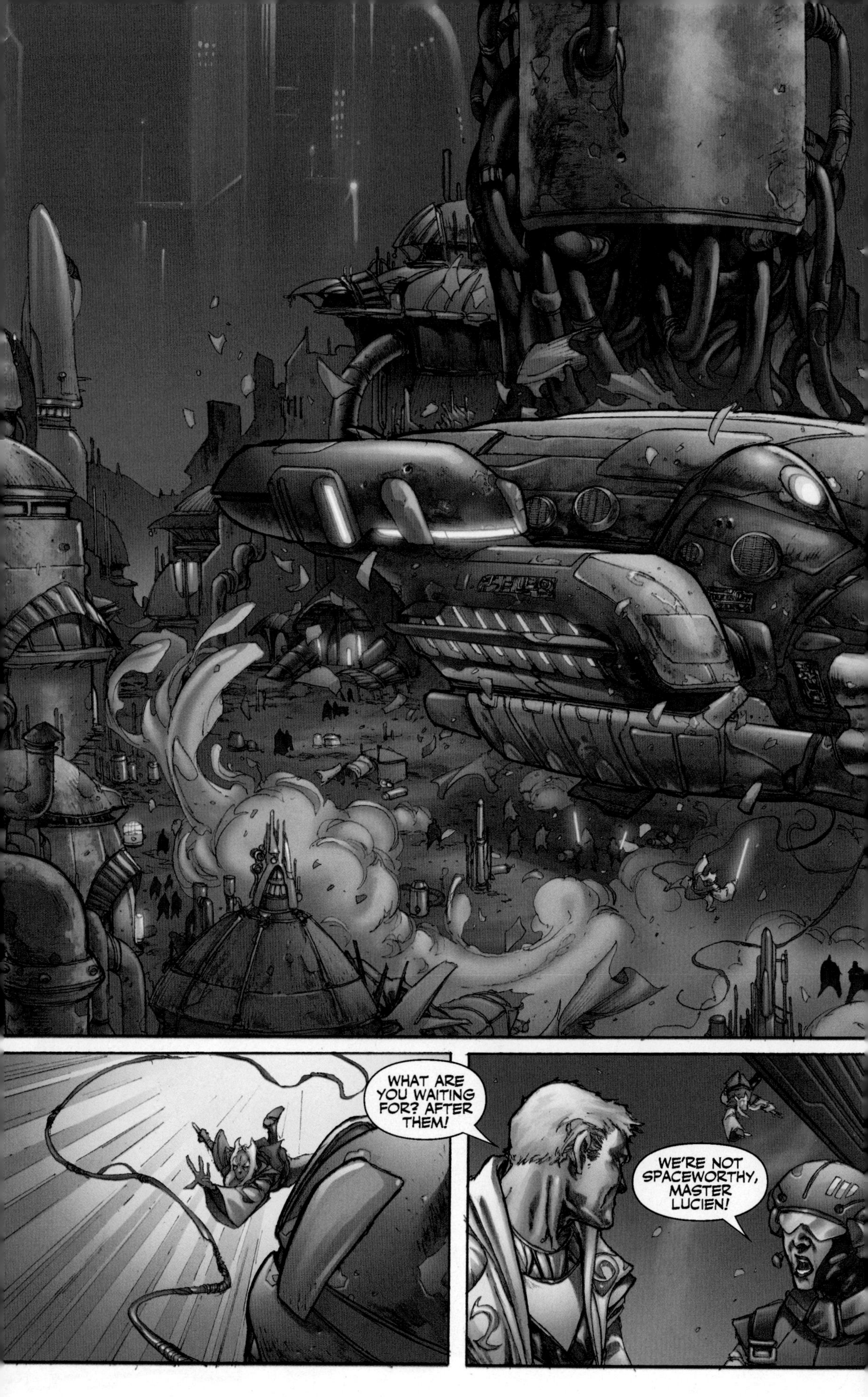
WHAT ARE YOU WAITING FOR? AFTER THEM!
WE'RE NOT SPACEWORTHY, MASTER LUCIEN!

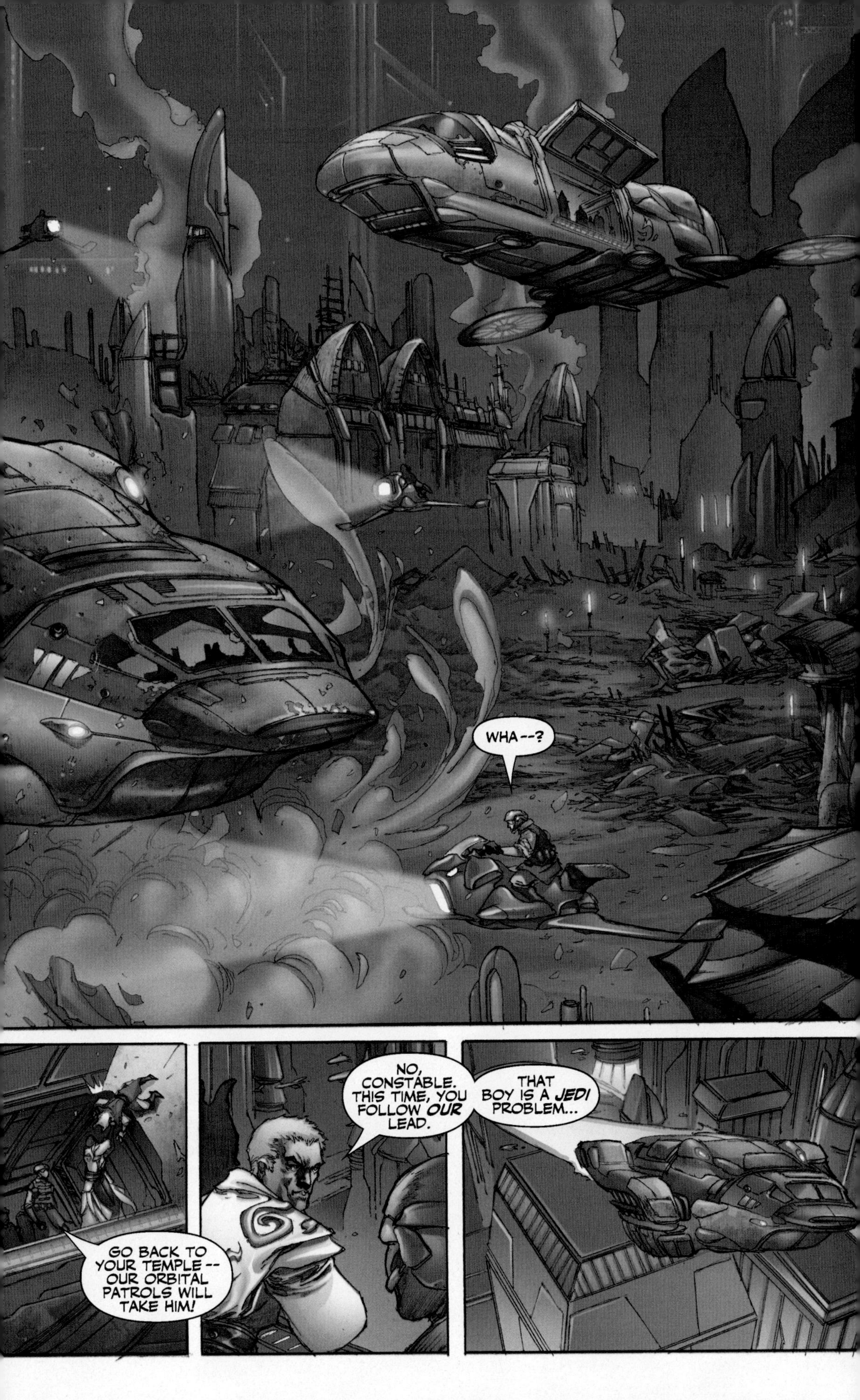
WHA--?
GO BACK TO YOUR TEMPLE -- OUR ORBITAL PATROLS WILL TAKE HIM!
NO, CONSTABLE. THIS TIME, YOU FOLLOW OUR LEAD.
THAT BOY IS A JEDI PROBLEM...

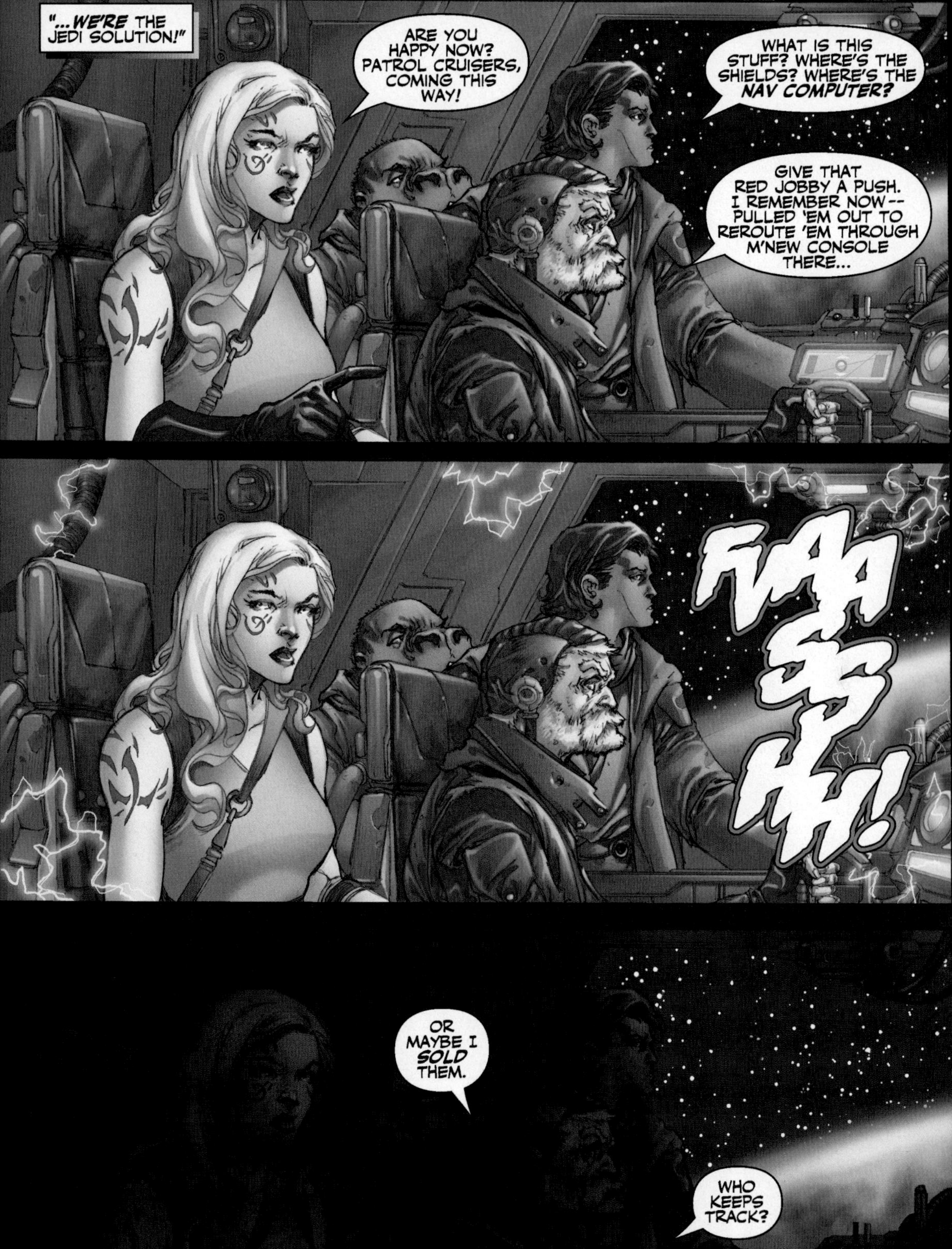
"...WE'RE THE JEDI SOLUTION!"
ARE YOU HAPPY NOW? PATROL CRUISERS, COMING THIS WAY!
WHAT IS THIS STUFF? WHERE'S THE SHIELDS? WHERE'S THE NAV COMPUTER?
GIVE THAT RED JOBBY A PUSH. I REMEMBER NOW-- PULLED 'EM OUT TO REROUTE 'EM THROUGH M'NEW CONSOLE THERE...
FWAASSHH!
OR MAYBE I SOLD THEM.
WHO KEEPS TRACK?

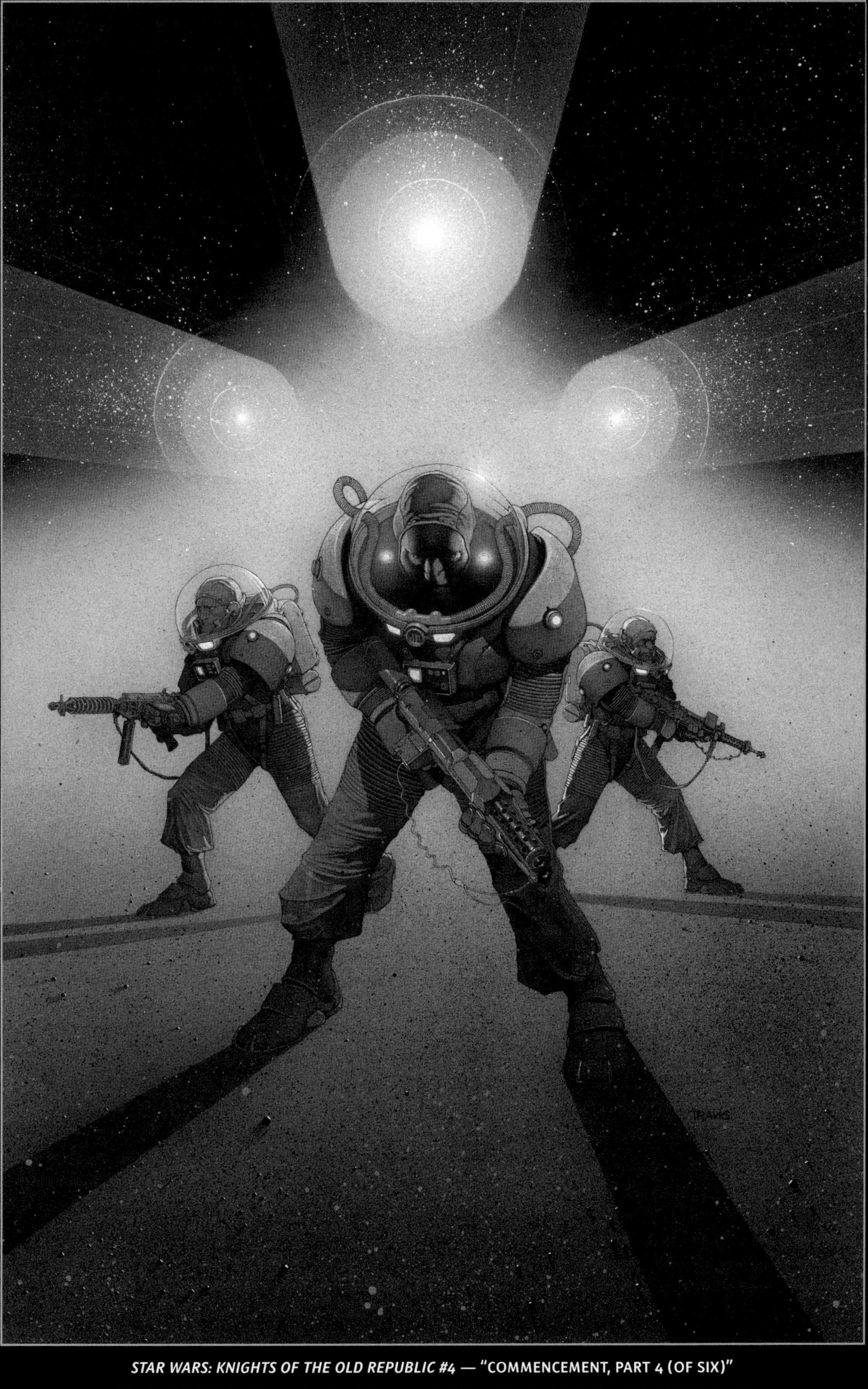
TRAVIS

STAR WARS: KNIGHTS OF THE OLD REPUBLIC #4 — "COMMENCEMENT, PART 4 (OF SIX)"

WRITER: JOHN JACKSON MILLER • ARTIST: BRIAN CHING • COLORIST: MICHAEL ATIYEH • LETTERER: MICHAEL HEISLER
ASSISTANT EDITOR: DAVE MARSHALL • EDITOR: JEREMY BARLOW • COVER ARTIST: TRAVIS CHAREST

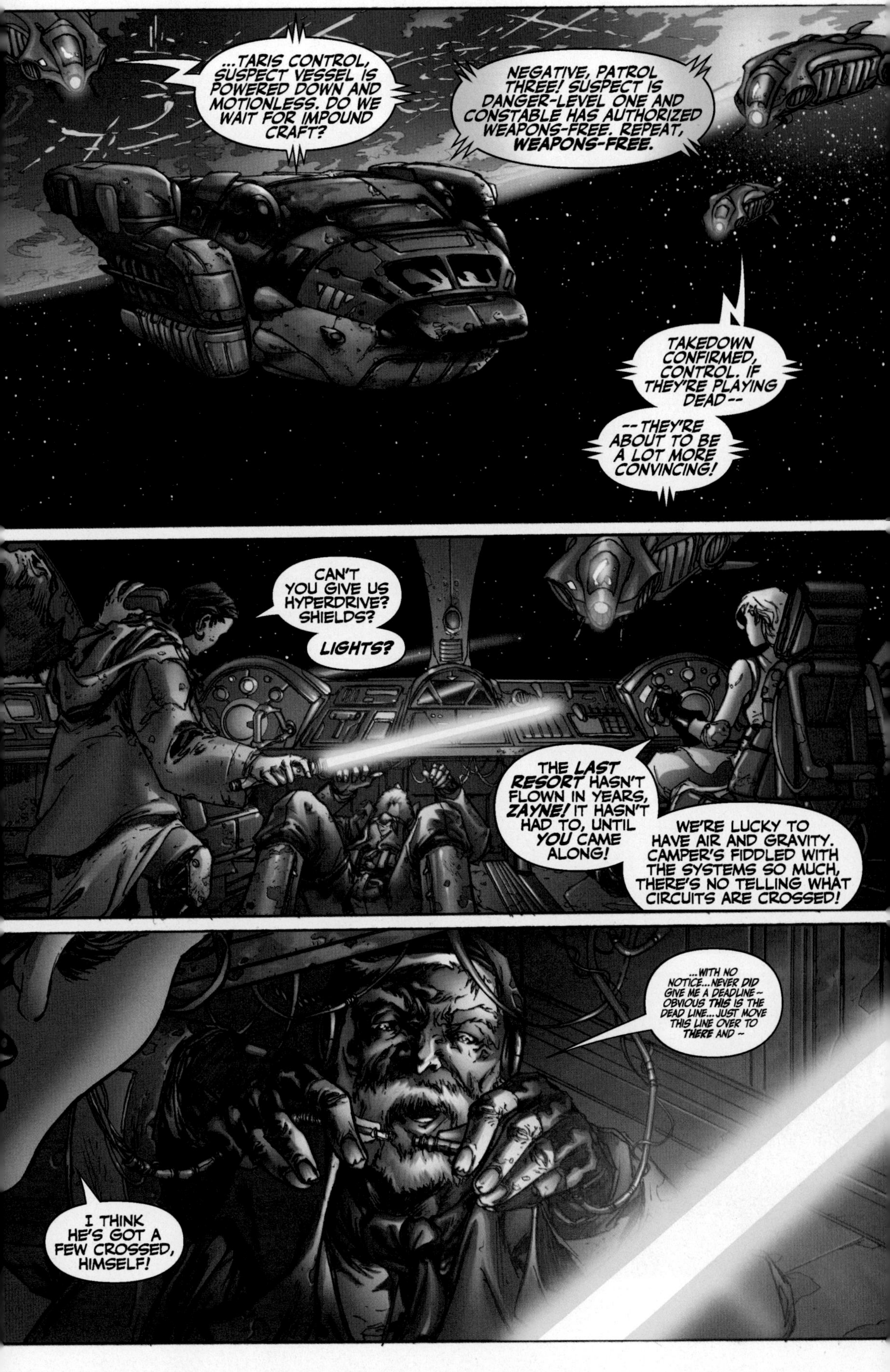
...TARIS CONTROL, SUSPECT VESSEL IS POWERED DOWN AND MOTIONLESS. DO WE WAIT FOR IMPOUND CRAFT?
NEGATIVE, PATROL THREE! SUSPECT IS DANGER-LEVEL ONE AND CONSTABLE HAS AUTHORIZED WEAPONS-FREE. REPEAT, **WEAPONS-FREE.**
TAKEDOWN CONFIRMED, CONTROL. IF THEY'RE PLAYING DEAD--
--THEY'RE ABOUT TO BE A LOT MORE CONVINCING!
CAN'T YOU GIVE US HYPERDRIVE? SHIELDS?
LIGHTS?
THE *LAST RESORT* HASN'T FLOWN IN YEARS, *ZAYNE!* IT HASN'T HAD TO, UNTIL *YOU* CAME ALONG!
WE'RE LUCKY TO HAVE AIR AND GRAVITY. CAMPER'S FIDDLED WITH THE SYSTEMS SO MUCH, THERE'S NO TELLING WHAT CIRCUITS ARE CROSSED!
...WITH NO NOTICE...NEVER DID GIVE ME A DEADLINE~ OBVIOUS THIS IS THE DEAD LINE...JUST MOVE THIS LINE OVER TO THERE AND ~
I THINK HE'S GOT A FEW CROSSED, HIMSELF!

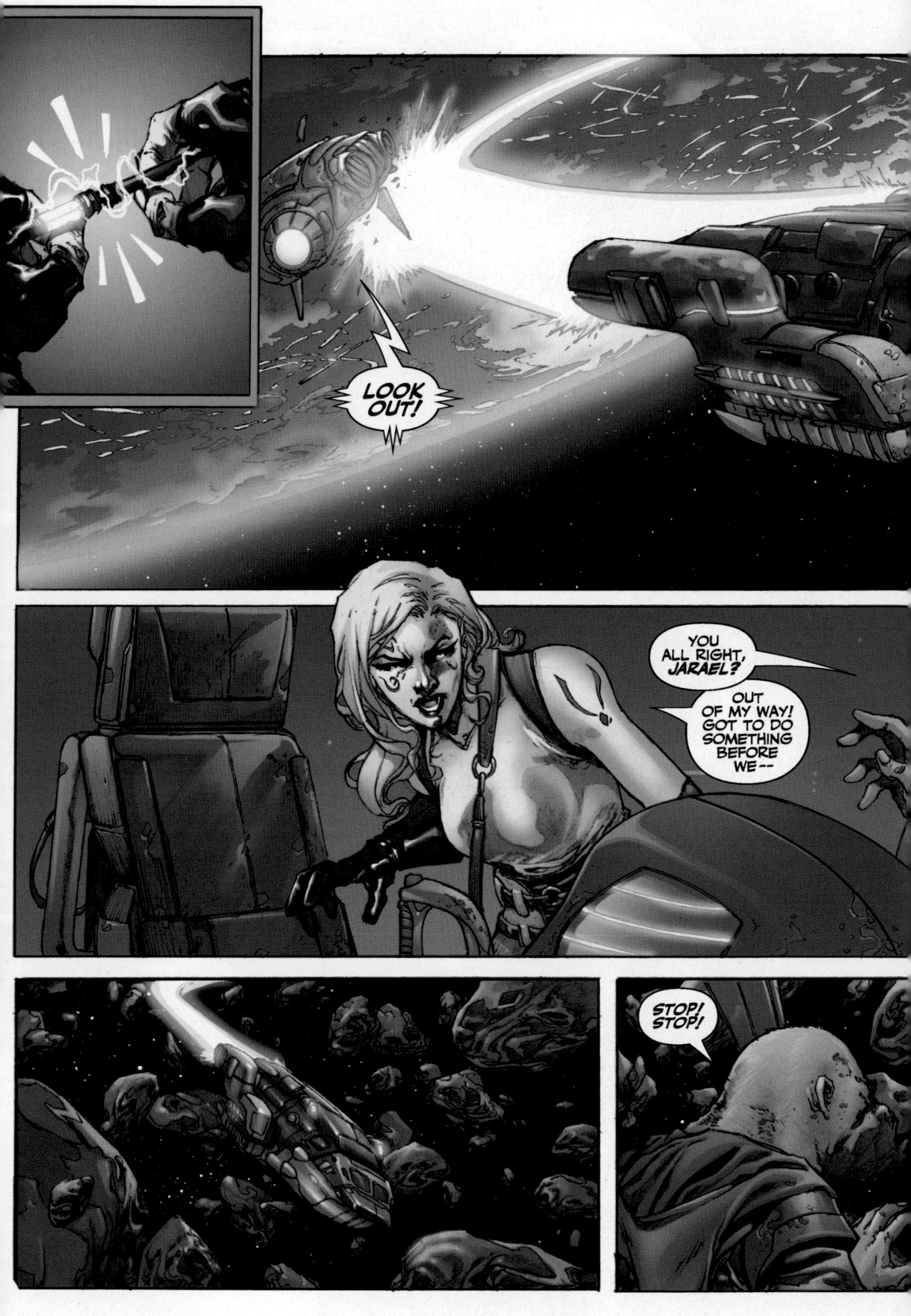
LOOK OUT!
YOU ALL RIGHT, JARAEL?
OUT OF MY WAY! GOT TO DO SOMETHING BEFORE WE--
STOP! STOP!

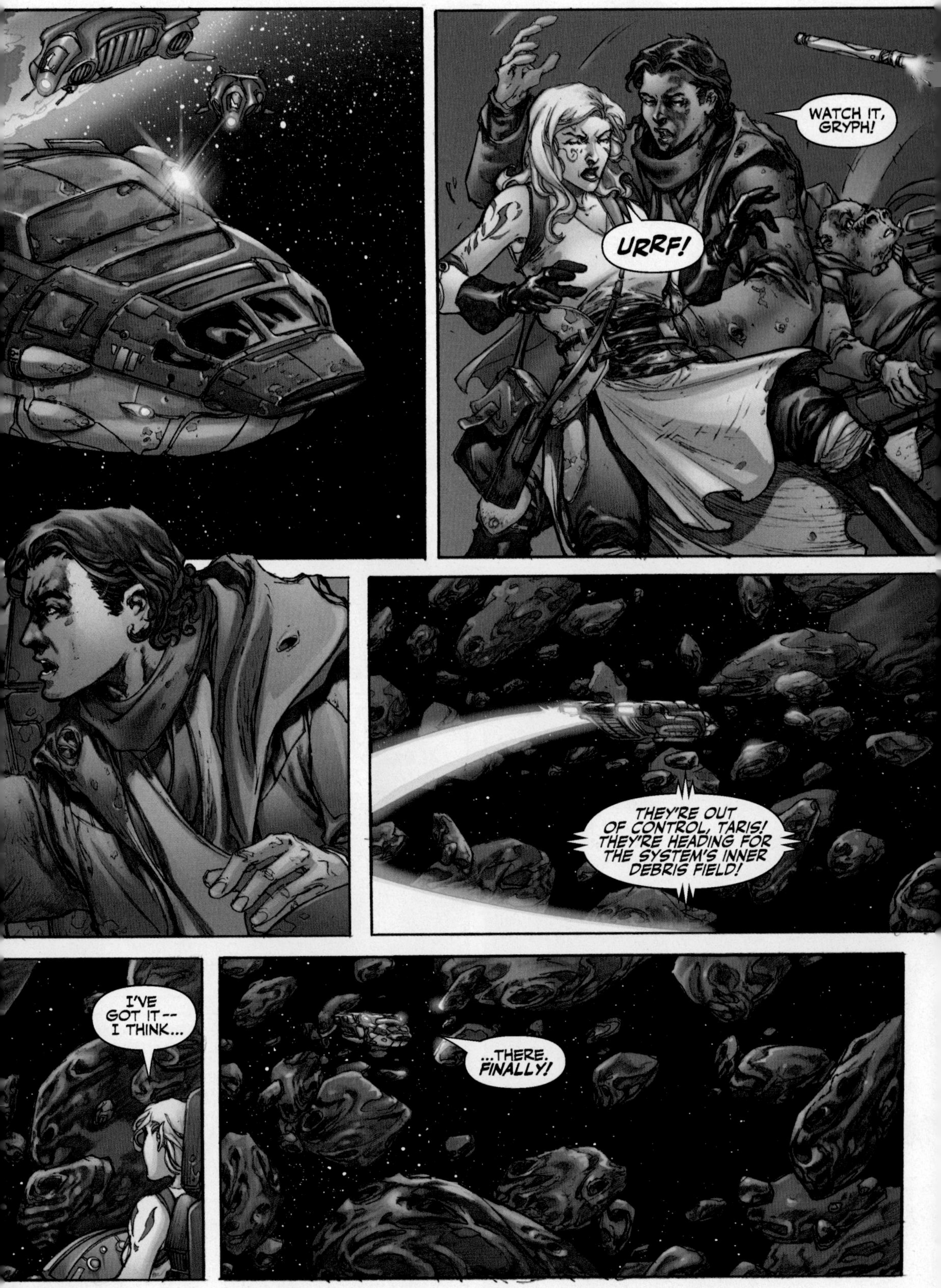
WATCH IT, GRYPH!
URRF!
THEY'RE OUT OF CONTROL, TARIS! THEY'RE HEADING FOR THE SYSTEM'S INNER DEBRIS FIELD!
I'VE GOT IT -- I THINK...
...THERE. FINALLY!

THEY'RE GOING PAST.

THEY'RE LAW ENFORCEMENT, NOT MILITARY. THEY'RE NOT GONNA RISK THEIR NECKS IN HERE. WE'RE SAFE.

SAFE? WE HAVEN'T BEEN SAFE SINCE WE MET YOU!

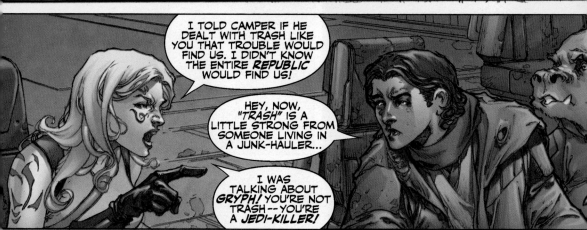

I TOLD CAMPER IF HE DEALT WITH TRASH LIKE YOU THAT TROUBLE WOULD FIND US. I DIDN'T KNOW THE ENTIRE REPUBLIC WOULD FIND US!

HEY, NOW, "TRASH" IS A LITTLE STRONG FROM SOMEONE LIVING IN A JUNK-HAULER...

I WAS TALKING ABOUT GRYPH! YOU'RE NOT TRASH -- YOU'RE A JEDI-KILLER!

WHAT IS THAT? IS HE DANGEROUS?

GAHHH!!!

ONLY TO HIMSELF.

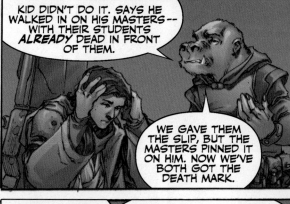

KID DIDN'T DO IT. SAYS HE WALKED IN ON HIS MASTERS -- WITH THEIR STUDENTS ALREADY DEAD IN FRONT OF THEM.

WE GAVE THEM THE SLIP, BUT THE MASTERS PINNED IT ON HIM. NOW WE'VE BOTH GOT THE DEATH MARK.

A DEATH MARK ON ME -- IMAGINE! AND I'M NOT EVEN A VIOLENT OFFENDER.

MY CAREER IS MADE! THIS'LL DEFINITELY LAND ME A NICE PERCH WITH THE BEKS OR THE VULKAR GANG WHEN I GET BACK TO--

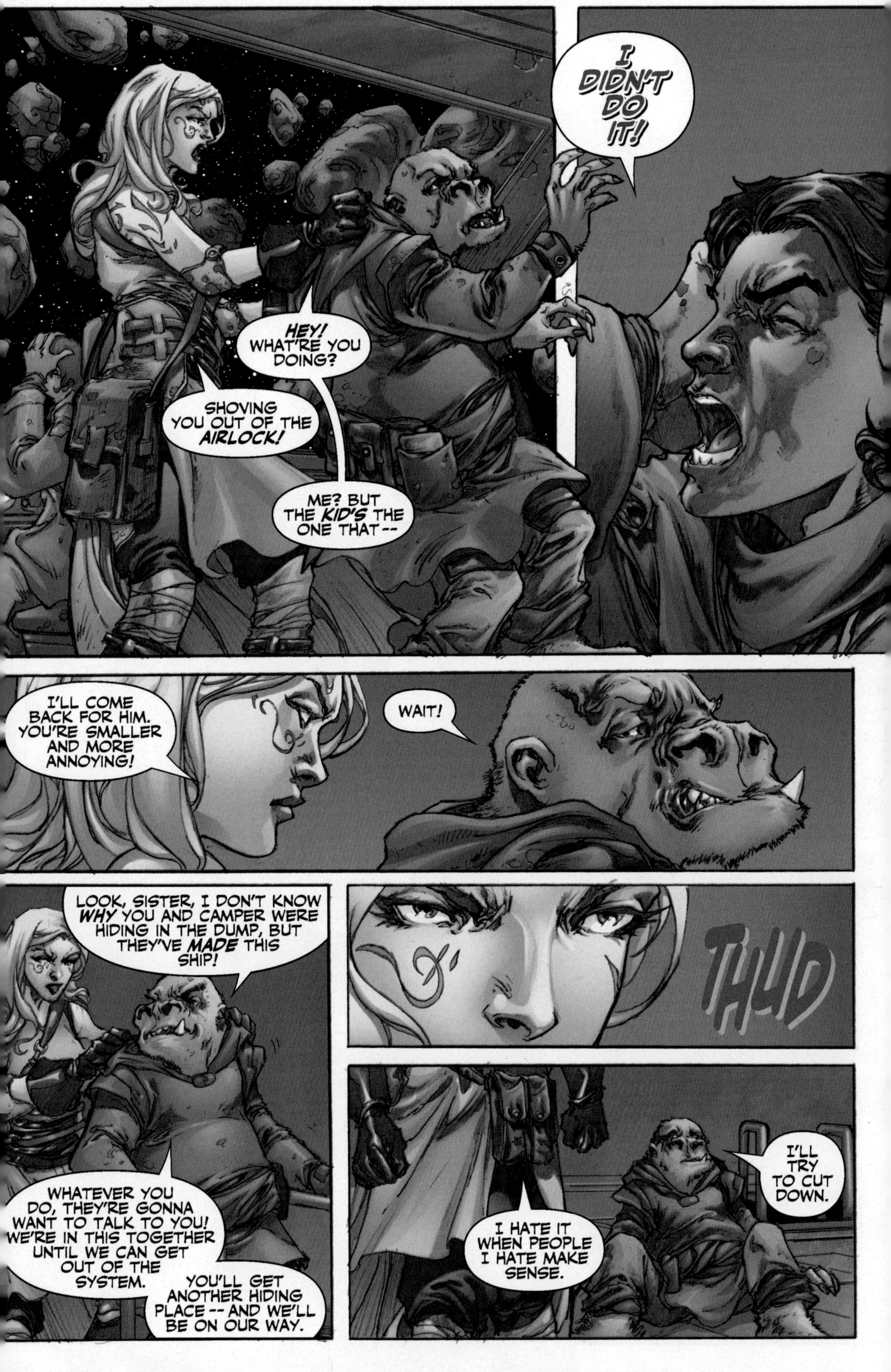
I DIDN'T DO IT!
HEY! WHAT'RE YOU DOING?
SHOVING YOU OUT OF THE AIRLOCK!
ME? BUT THE KID'S THE ONE THAT --
I'LL COME BACK FOR HIM. YOU'RE SMALLER AND MORE ANNOYING!
WAIT!
LOOK, SISTER, I DON'T KNOW WHY YOU AND CAMPER WERE HIDING IN THE DUMP, BUT THEY'VE MADE THIS SHIP!
WHATEVER YOU DO, THEY'RE GONNA WANT TO TALK TO YOU! WE'RE IN THIS TOGETHER UNTIL WE CAN GET OUT OF THE SYSTEM.
YOU'LL GET ANOTHER HIDING PLACE -- AND WE'LL BE ON OUR WAY.
THUD
I HATE IT WHEN PEOPLE I HATE MAKE SENSE.
I'LL TRY TO CUT DOWN.

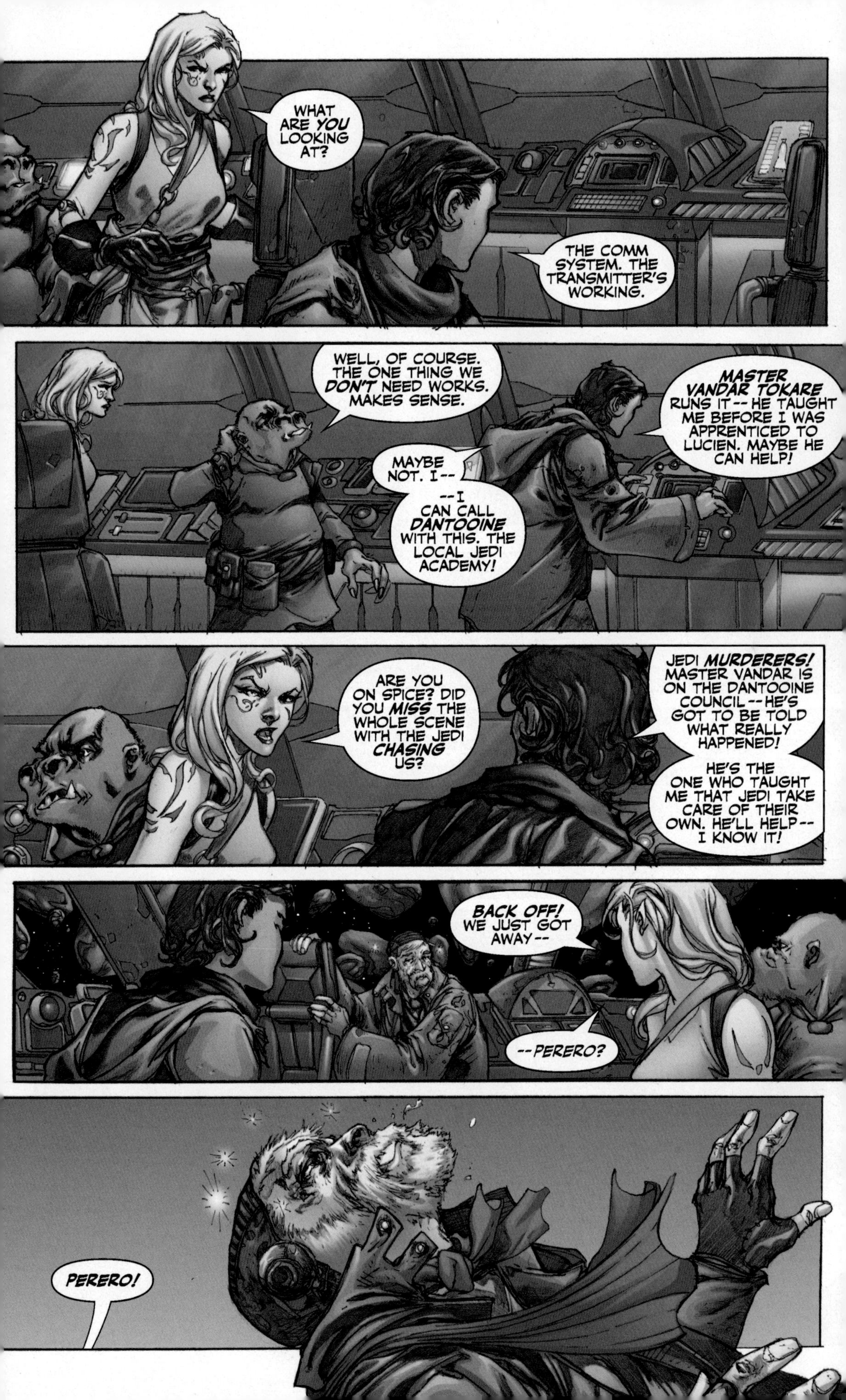
WHAT ARE YOU LOOKING AT?
THE COMM SYSTEM. THE TRANSMITTER'S WORKING.
WELL, OF COURSE. THE ONE THING WE DON'T NEED WORKS. MAKES SENSE.
MAYBE NOT. I--
--I CAN CALL DANTOOINE WITH THIS. THE LOCAL JEDI ACADEMY!
MASTER VANDAR TOKARE RUNS IT--HE TAUGHT ME BEFORE I WAS APPRENTICED TO LUCIEN. MAYBE HE CAN HELP!
ARE YOU ON SPICE? DID YOU MISS THE WHOLE SCENE WITH THE JEDI CHASING US?
JEDI MURDERERS! MASTER VANDAR IS ON THE DANTOOINE COUNCIL--HE'S GOT TO BE TOLD WHAT REALLY HAPPENED!
HE'S THE ONE WHO TAUGHT ME THAT JEDI TAKE CARE OF THEIR OWN. HE'LL HELP--I KNOW IT!
BACK OFF! WE JUST GOT AWAY--
--PERERO?
PERERO!

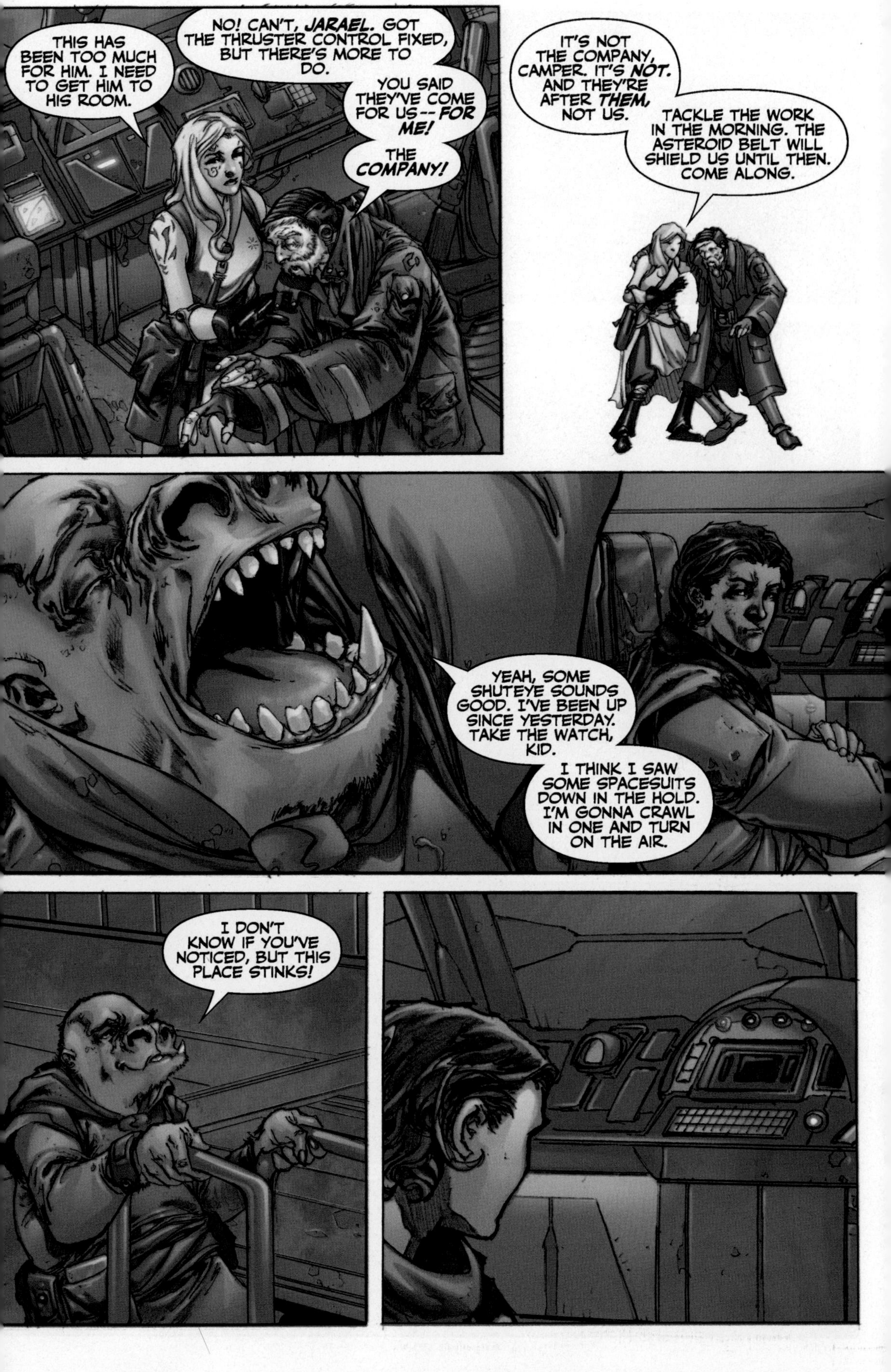
THIS HAS BEEN TOO MUCH FOR HIM. I NEED TO GET HIM TO HIS ROOM.
NO! CAN'T, JARAEL. GOT THE THRUSTER CONTROL FIXED, BUT THERE'S MORE TO DO.
YOU SAID THEY'VE COME FOR US-- FOR ME!
THE COMPANY!
IT'S NOT THE COMPANY, CAMPER. IT'S NOT. AND THEY'RE AFTER THEM, NOT US.
TACKLE THE WORK IN THE MORNING. THE ASTEROID BELT WILL SHIELD US UNTIL THEN. COME ALONG.
YEAH, SOME SHUTEYE SOUNDS GOOD. I'VE BEEN UP SINCE YESTERDAY. TAKE THE WATCH, KID.
I THINK I SAW SOME SPACESUITS DOWN IN THE HOLD. I'M GONNA CRAWL IN ONE AND TURN ON THE AIR.
I DON'T KNOW IF YOU'VE NOTICED, BUT THIS PLACE STINKS!

LATER...

DANTOOINE ACADEMY HERE. I CAN BARELY READ YOUR SIGNAL.

THERE'S SOME INTERFERENCE HERE-- I'M MOVING CLEAR OF IT. LET ME TALK TO MASTER *VANDAR TOKARE.*

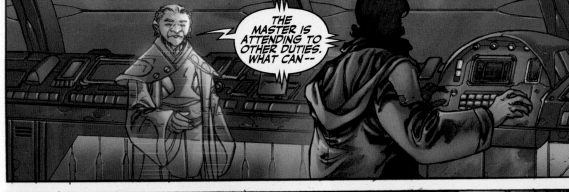

THE MASTER IS ATTENDING TO OTHER DUTIES. WHAT CAN--

TELL HIM IT'S *ZAYNE CARRICK.*

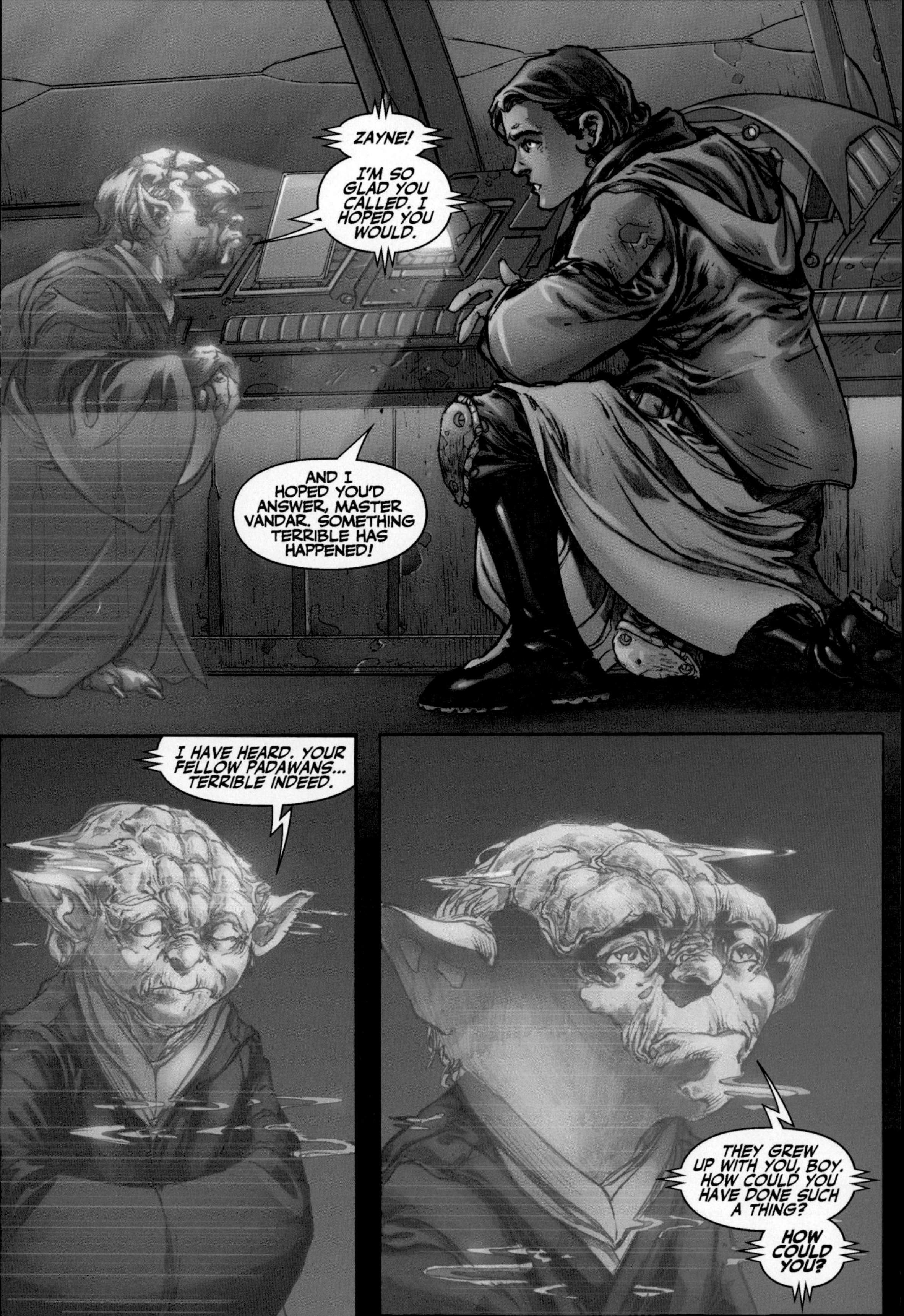
ZAYNE!
I'M SO GLAD YOU CALLED. I HOPED YOU WOULD.
AND I HOPED YOU'D ANSWER, MASTER VANDAR. SOMETHING TERRIBLE HAS HAPPENED!
I HAVE HEARD. YOUR FELLOW PADAWANS... TERRIBLE INDEED.
THEY GREW UP WITH YOU, BOY. HOW COULD YOU HAVE DONE SUCH A THING?
HOW COULD YOU?

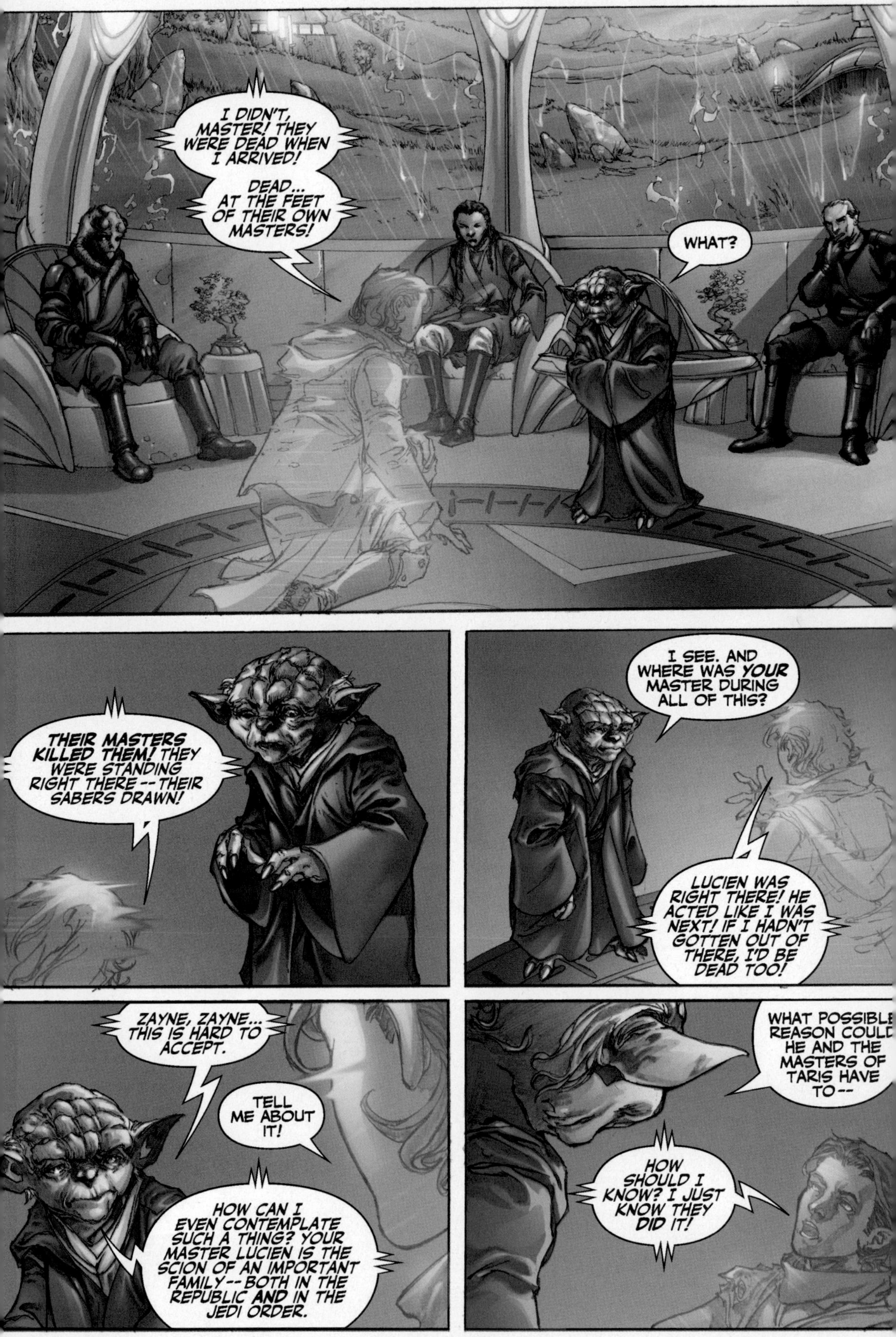
I DIDN'T, MASTER! THEY WERE DEAD WHEN I ARRIVED!
DEAD... AT THE FEET OF THEIR OWN MASTERS!
WHAT?
THEIR MASTERS KILLED THEM! THEY WERE STANDING RIGHT THERE -- THEIR SABERS DRAWN!
I SEE. AND WHERE WAS YOUR MASTER DURING ALL OF THIS?
LUCIEN WAS RIGHT THERE! HE ACTED LIKE I WAS NEXT! IF I HADN'T GOTTEN OUT OF THERE, I'D BE DEAD TOO!
ZAYNE, ZAYNE... THIS IS HARD TO ACCEPT.
TELL ME ABOUT IT!
HOW CAN I EVEN CONTEMPLATE SUCH A THING? YOUR MASTER LUCIEN IS THE SCION OF AN IMPORTANT FAMILY -- BOTH IN THE REPUBLIC AND IN THE JEDI ORDER.
WHAT POSSIBLE REASON COULD HE AND THE MASTERS OF TARIS HAVE TO --
HOW SHOULD I KNOW? I JUST KNOW THEY DID IT!

YES, I THINK YOU TRULY BELIEVE THAT.

BUT WE BOTH KNOW YOUR RELATIONSHIP WITH THE FORCE HAS ALWAYS BEEN...*COMPLICATED*. AND ITS DARK SIDE CAN BE SEDUCTIVE FOR THE LESS EXPERIENCED.

THE MIND CAN DECEIVE ITSELF. YOU...

...YOU *MAY* HAVE DONE SOMETHING YOU DON'T REMEMBER.

I COULDN'T HAVE!

ARE YOU SURE? I HAVE TO WONDER -- IF THIS IS TRUE, THEN WHAT ARE YOU DOING ALIVE?

YOU, ESCAPING FIVE MASTERS OF THE ORDER? YOU, ZAYNE? WITH *YOUR* SKILLS?

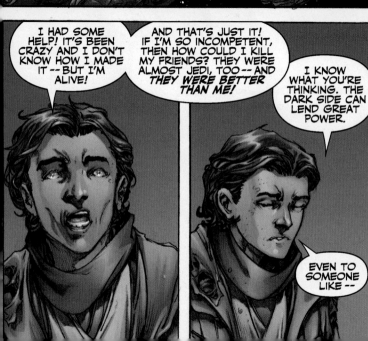

I HAD SOME HELP! IT'S BEEN CRAZY AND I DON'T KNOW HOW I MADE IT -- BUT I'M ALIVE!

AND THAT'S JUST IT! IF I'M SO INCOMPETENT, THEN HOW COULD I KILL MY FRIENDS? THEY WERE ALMOST JEDI, TOO -- AND *THEY WERE BETTER THAN ME!*

I KNOW WHAT YOU'RE THINKING. THE DARK SIDE CAN LEND GREAT POWER.

EVEN TO SOMEONE LIKE --

BUT I HAVEN'T FALLEN!

I DIDN'T KILL MY FRIENDS!

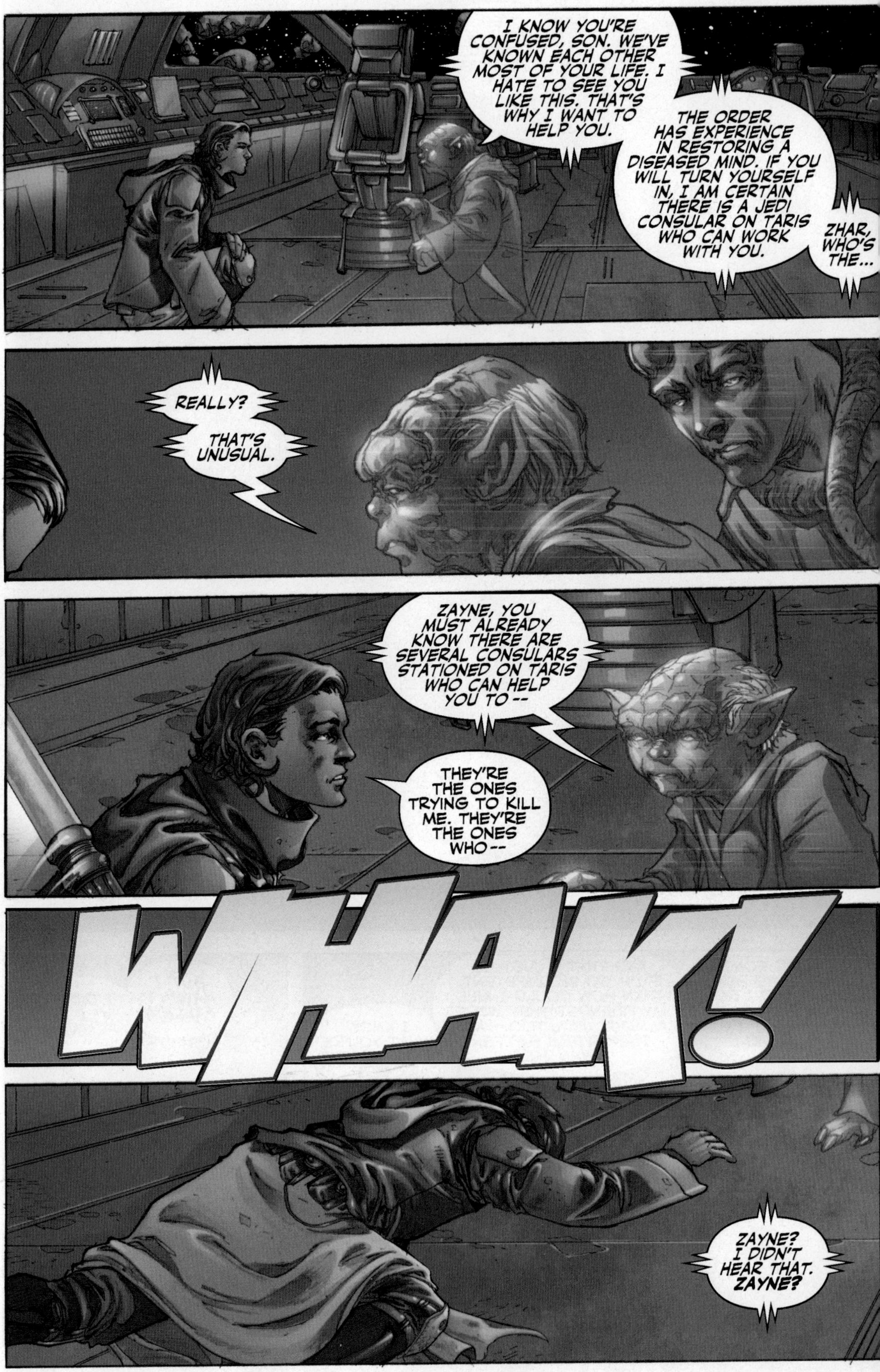
I KNOW YOU'RE CONFUSED, SON. WE'VE KNOWN EACH OTHER MOST OF YOUR LIFE. I HATE TO SEE YOU LIKE THIS. THAT'S WHY I WANT TO HELP YOU.
THE ORDER HAS EXPERIENCE IN RESTORING A DISEASED MIND. IF YOU WILL TURN YOURSELF IN, I AM CERTAIN THERE IS A JEDI CONSULAR ON TARIS WHO CAN WORK WITH YOU.
ZHAR, WHO'S THE...
REALLY?
THAT'S UNUSUAL.
ZAYNE, YOU MUST ALREADY KNOW THERE ARE SEVERAL CONSULARS STATIONED ON TARIS WHO CAN HELP YOU TO --
THEY'RE THE ONES TRYING TO KILL ME. THEY'RE THE ONES WHO --
WHAK!
ZAYNE? I DIDN'T HEAR THAT. ZAYNE?

OOOOHHHH-- WHAT HIT ME?

THAT'D BE MY SHOCKSTAFF TO THE BACK OF YOUR HEAD. ANY OTHER BRUISES ARE FROM ME FLYING US BACK INTO THE ASTEROID BELT.

I'M SORRY I DIDN'T HAVE TIME TO PICK A SAFER ROUTE. YOUR LITTLE STUNT ATTRACTED SOME ATTENTION.

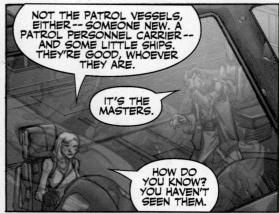

NOT THE PATROL VESSELS, EITHER -- SOMEONE NEW. A PATROL PERSONNEL CARRIER -- AND SOME LITTLE SHIPS. THEY'RE GOOD, WHOEVER THEY ARE.

IT'S THE MASTERS.

HOW DO YOU KNOW? YOU HAVEN'T SEEN THEM.

I CAN FEEL THEIR PRESENCE.

WELL, THEY FEEL YOURS. SEE? WE'RE BEING HAILED.

I'LL GET IT, BUT I'M PRETTY SURE IT'S FOR YOU.

HAAALLLPPP!!!

IT'S SO STRONG, IT'S LIKE THE SENDER'S RIGHT HERE WITH US.

I'M AFRAID HE IS. COME WITH ME...

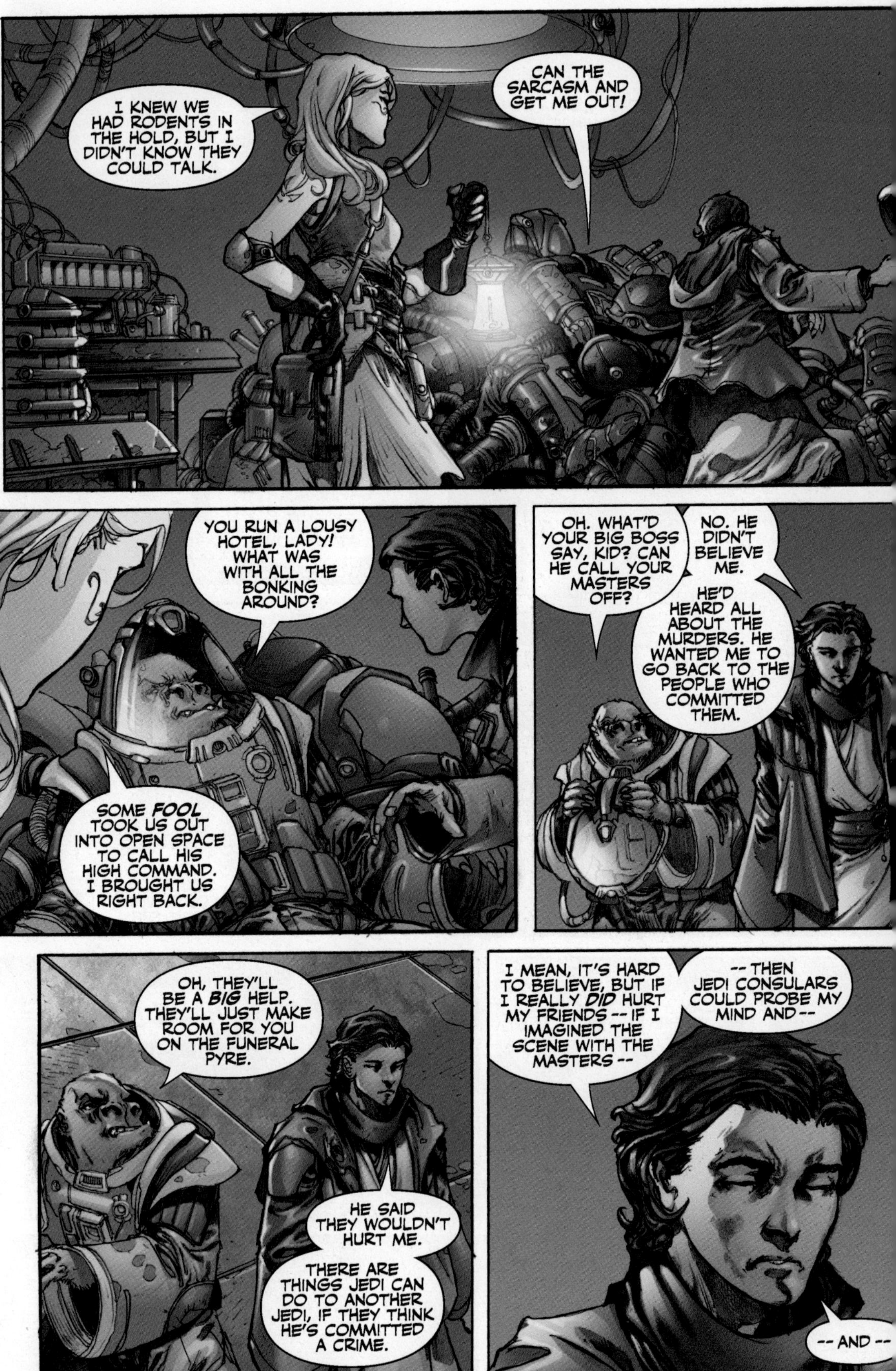
I KNEW WE HAD RODENTS IN THE HOLD, BUT I DIDN'T KNOW THEY COULD TALK.
CAN THE SARCASM AND GET ME OUT!
YOU RUN A LOUSY HOTEL, LADY! WHAT WAS WITH ALL THE BONKING AROUND?
SOME *FOOL* TOOK US OUT INTO OPEN SPACE TO CALL HIS HIGH COMMAND. I BROUGHT US RIGHT BACK.
OH. WHAT'D YOUR BIG BOSS SAY, KID? CAN HE CALL YOUR MASTERS OFF?
NO. HE DIDN'T BELIEVE ME.
HE'D HEARD ALL ABOUT THE MURDERS. HE WANTED ME TO GO BACK TO THE PEOPLE WHO COMMITTED THEM.
OH, THEY'LL BE A *BIG* HELP. THEY'LL JUST MAKE ROOM FOR YOU ON THE FUNERAL PYRE.
HE SAID THEY WOULDN'T HURT ME.
THERE ARE THINGS JEDI CAN DO TO ANOTHER JEDI, IF THEY THINK HE'S COMMITTED A CRIME.
I MEAN, IT'S HARD TO BELIEVE, BUT IF I REALLY *DID* HURT MY FRIENDS -- IF I IMAGINED THE SCENE WITH THE MASTERS --
-- THEN JEDI CONSULARS COULD PROBE MY MIND AND --
-- AND --

WHAT?

I JUST THOUGHT OF SOMETHING. THE MASTERS ON TARIS ARE *ALL* CONSULARS -- ALL BUT LUCIEN!

I DON'T FOLLOW.

A CONSULAR IS A SPECIALIZED KIND OF JEDI. THEY FOCUS MORE ON CEREBRAL FORCE SKILLS. THEY'RE OUR HEALERS, OUR RESEARCHERS, OUR SEERS.

THEY DON'T SOUND SO TOUGH.

THEY'RE STILL JEDI. YOU DON'T MESS WITH THEM.

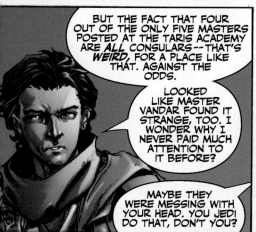

BUT THE FACT THAT FOUR OUT OF THE ONLY FIVE MASTERS POSTED AT THE TARIS ACADEMY ARE *ALL* CONSULARS -- THAT'S *WEIRD*, FOR A PLACE LIKE THAT. AGAINST THE ODDS.

LOOKED LIKE MASTER VANDAR FOUND IT STRANGE, TOO. I WONDER WHY I NEVER PAID MUCH ATTENTION TO IT BEFORE?

MAYBE THEY WERE MESSING WITH YOUR HEAD. YOU JEDI! DO THAT, DON'T YOU?

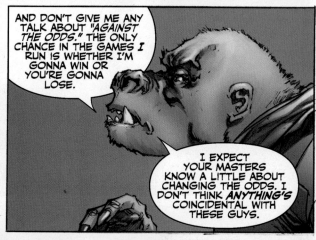

AND DON'T GIVE ME ANY TALK ABOUT *"AGAINST THE ODDS."* THE ONLY CHANCE IN THE GAMES *I* RUN IS WHETHER I'M GONNA WIN OR YOU'RE GONNA LOSE.

I EXPECT YOUR MASTERS KNOW A LITTLE ABOUT CHANGING THE ODDS. I DON'T THINK *ANYTHING'S* COINCIDENTAL WITH THESE GUYS.

WHAT NOW? WHERE ARE YOU GOING?

TO FIND SOME ANSWERS!

I CAN'T BELIEVE I DIDN'T THINK OF IT EARLIER. IT'S IN THE DEBRIS FIELD -- WE'RE ALMOST ON TOP OF IT!

THE LAST PLACE MY MASTERS AND FRIENDS WERE ALL TOGETHER BEFORE YESTERDAY.

THE ROGUE MOON...

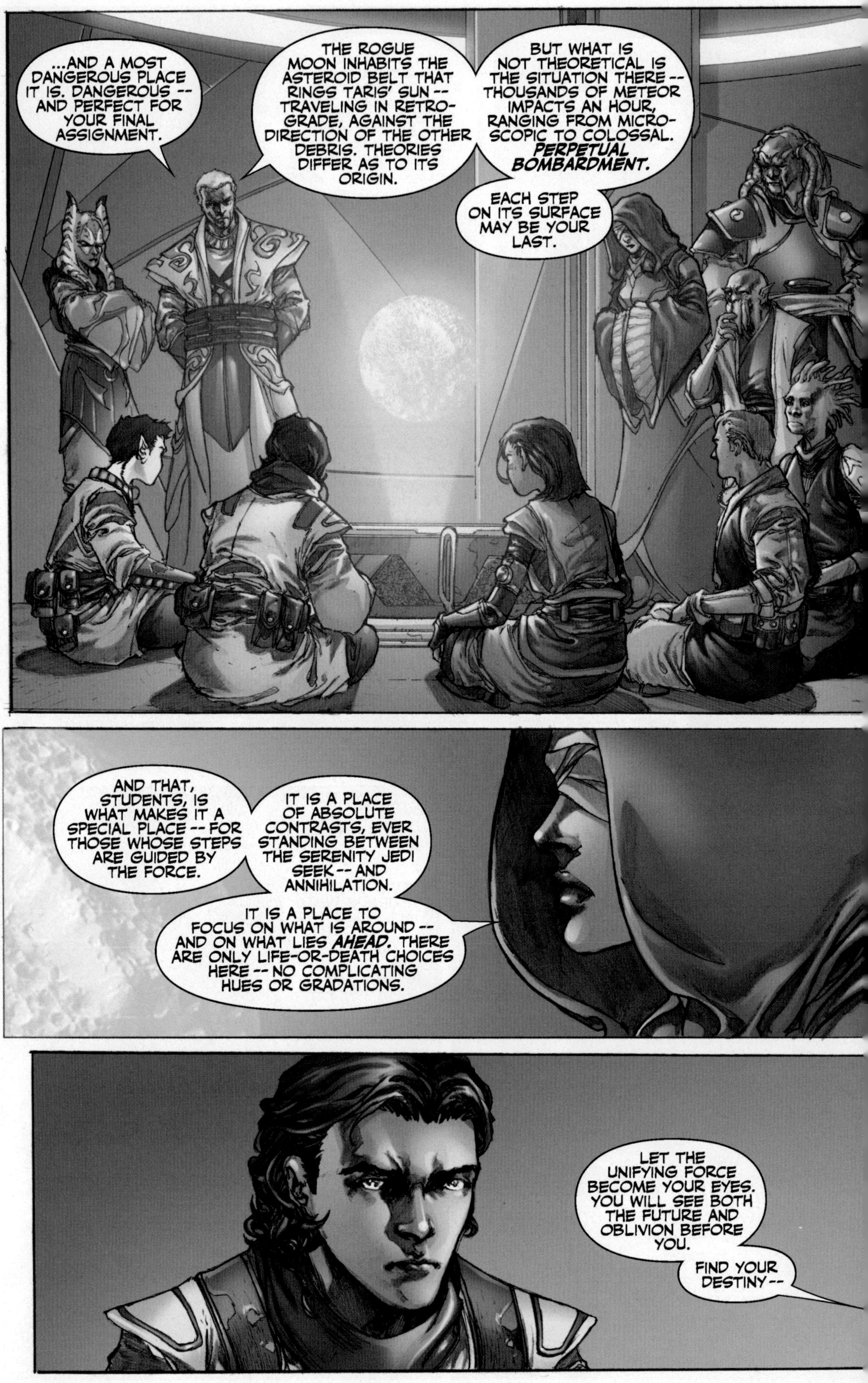

...AND A MOST DANGEROUS PLACE IT IS. DANGEROUS -- AND PERFECT FOR YOUR FINAL ASSIGNMENT.
THE ROGUE MOON INHABITS THE ASTEROID BELT THAT RINGS TARIS' SUN -- TRAVELING IN RETROGRADE, AGAINST THE DIRECTION OF THE OTHER DEBRIS. THEORIES DIFFER AS TO ITS ORIGIN.
BUT WHAT IS NOT THEORETICAL IS THE SITUATION THERE -- THOUSANDS OF METEOR IMPACTS AN HOUR, RANGING FROM MICROSCOPIC TO COLOSSAL. *PERPETUAL BOMBARDMENT.*
EACH STEP ON ITS SURFACE MAY BE YOUR LAST.
AND THAT, STUDENTS, IS WHAT MAKES IT A SPECIAL PLACE -- FOR THOSE WHOSE STEPS ARE GUIDED BY THE FORCE.
IT IS A PLACE OF ABSOLUTE CONTRASTS, EVER STANDING BETWEEN THE SERENITY JEDI SEEK -- AND ANNIHILATION.
IT IS A PLACE TO FOCUS ON WHAT IS AROUND -- AND ON WHAT LIES *AHEAD.* THERE ARE ONLY LIFE-OR-DEATH CHOICES HERE -- NO COMPLICATING HUES OR GRADATIONS.
LET THE UNIFYING FORCE BECOME YOUR EYES. YOU WILL SEE BOTH THE FUTURE AND OBLIVION BEFORE YOU.
FIND YOUR DESTINY --

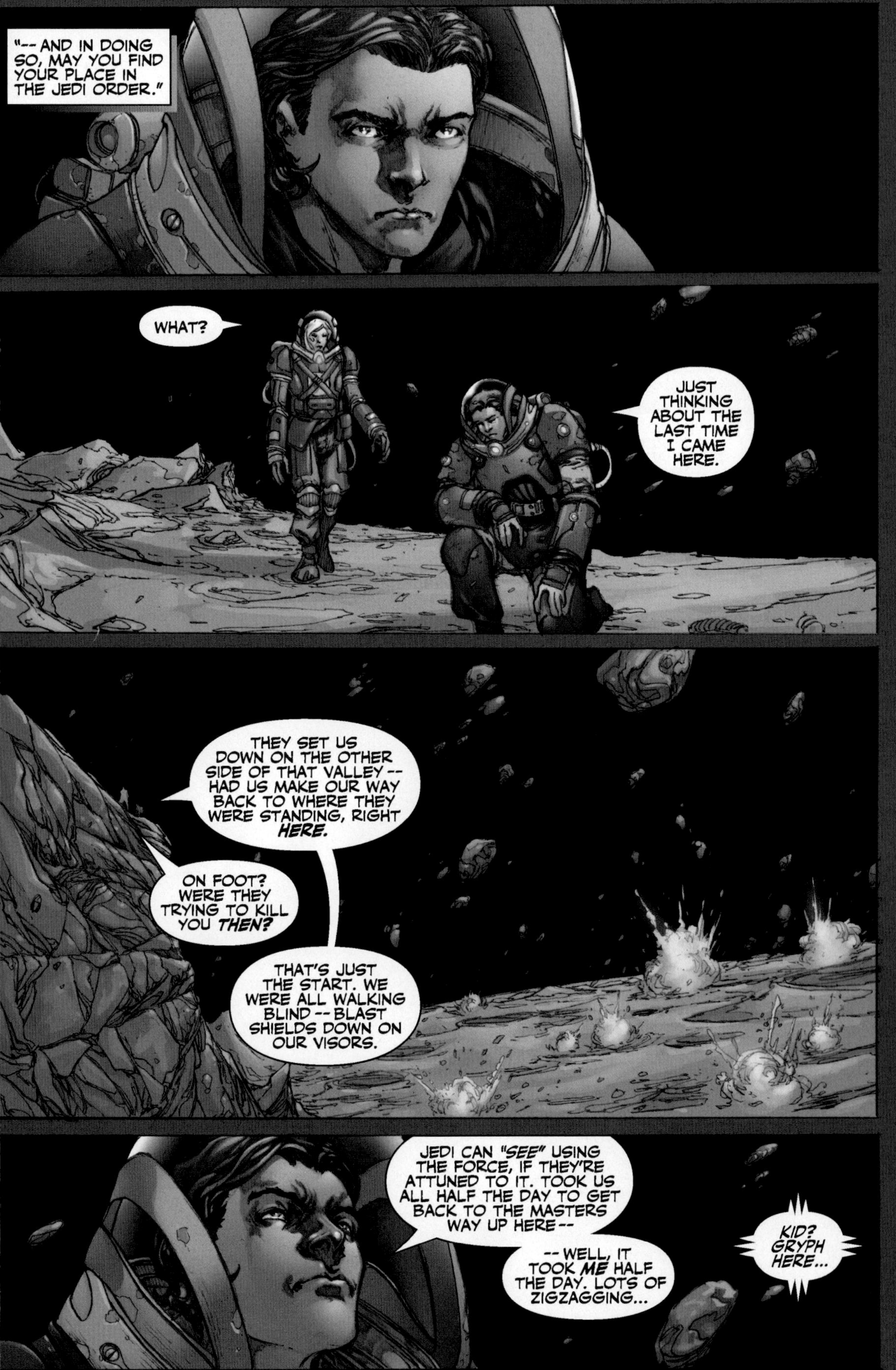
"-- AND IN DOING SO, MAY YOU FIND YOUR PLACE IN THE JEDI ORDER."
WHAT?
JUST THINKING ABOUT THE LAST TIME I CAME HERE.
THEY SET US DOWN ON THE OTHER SIDE OF THAT VALLEY -- HAD US MAKE OUR WAY BACK TO WHERE THEY WERE STANDING, RIGHT *HERE.*
ON FOOT? WERE THEY TRYING TO KILL YOU *THEN?*
THAT'S JUST THE START. WE WERE ALL WALKING BLIND -- BLAST SHIELDS DOWN ON OUR VISORS.
JEDI CAN *"SEE"* USING THE FORCE, IF THEY'RE ATTUNED TO IT. TOOK US ALL HALF THE DAY TO GET BACK TO THE MASTERS WAY UP HERE --
-- WELL, IT TOOK *ME* HALF THE DAY. LOTS OF ZIGZAGGING...
KID? GRYPH HERE...

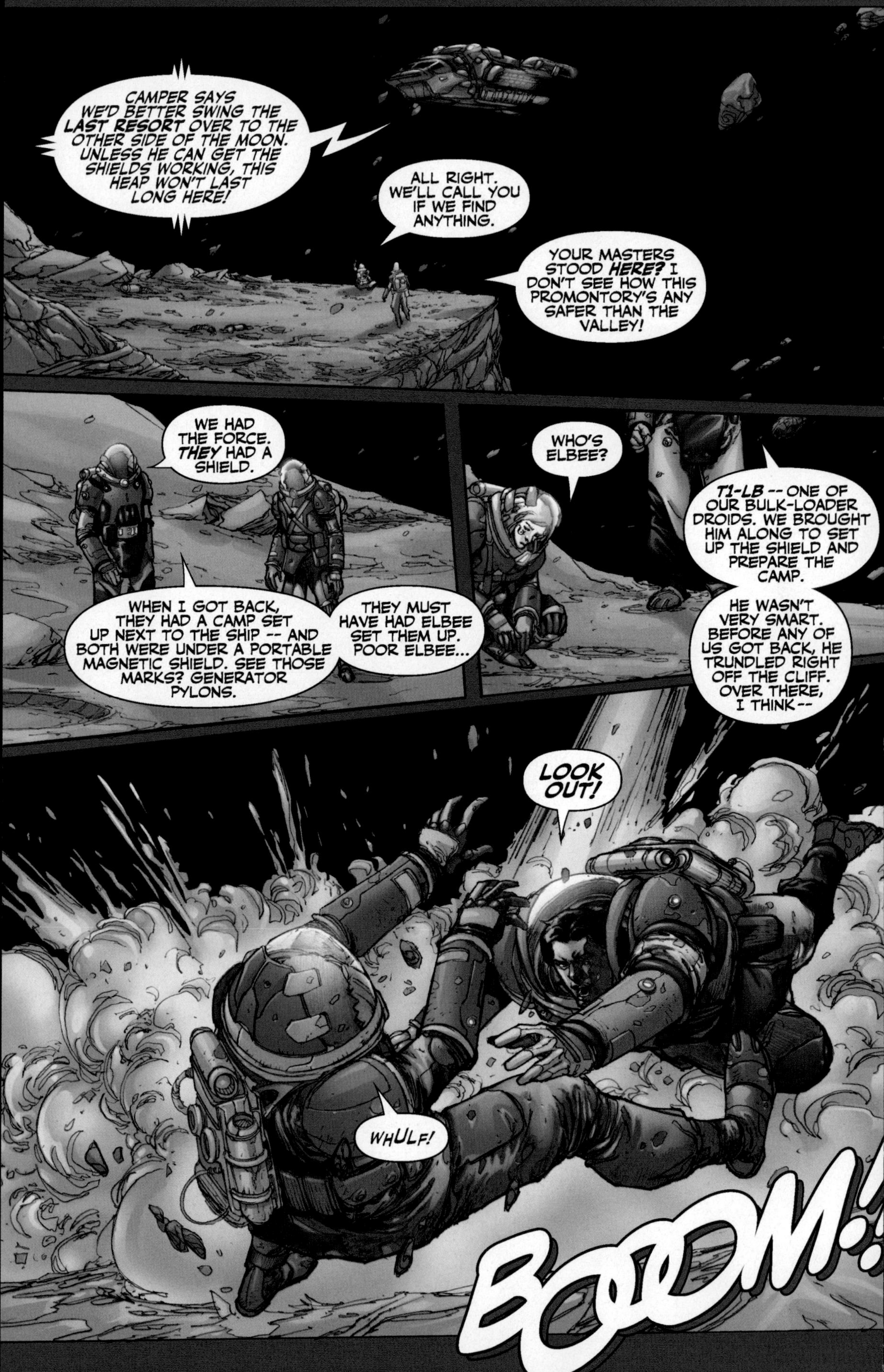
CAMPER SAYS WE'D BETTER SWING THE LAST RESORT OVER TO THE OTHER SIDE OF THE MOON. UNLESS HE CAN GET THE SHIELDS WORKING, THIS HEAP WON'T LAST LONG HERE!
ALL RIGHT. WE'LL CALL YOU IF WE FIND ANYTHING.
YOUR MASTERS STOOD HERE? I DON'T SEE HOW THIS PROMONTORY'S ANY SAFER THAN THE VALLEY!
WE HAD THE FORCE. THEY HAD A SHIELD.
WHEN I GOT BACK, THEY HAD A CAMP SET UP NEXT TO THE SHIP -- AND BOTH WERE UNDER A PORTABLE MAGNETIC SHIELD. SEE THOSE MARKS? GENERATOR PYLONS.
THEY MUST HAVE HAD ELBEE SET THEM UP. POOR ELBEE...
WHO'S ELBEE?
T1-LB -- ONE OF OUR BULK-LOADER DROIDS. WE BROUGHT HIM ALONG TO SET UP THE SHIELD AND PREPARE THE CAMP.
HE WASN'T VERY SMART. BEFORE ANY OF US GOT BACK, HE TRUNDLED RIGHT OFF THE CLIFF. OVER THERE, I THINK--
LOOK OUT!
WHULF!
BOOOM!!

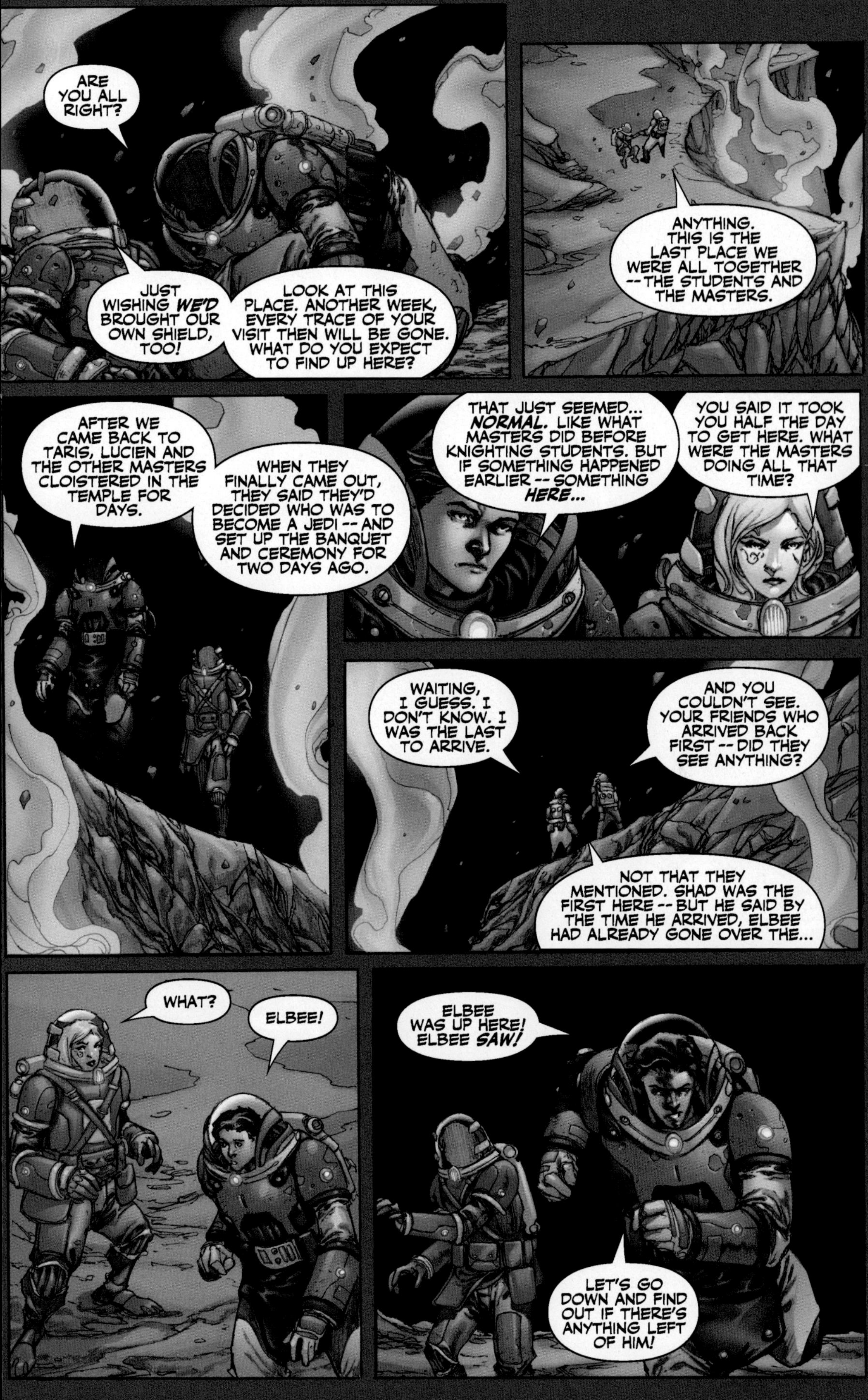
ARE YOU ALL RIGHT?
JUST WISHING *WE'D* BROUGHT OUR OWN SHIELD, TOO!
LOOK AT THIS PLACE. ANOTHER WEEK, EVERY TRACE OF YOUR VISIT THEN WILL BE GONE. WHAT DO YOU EXPECT TO FIND UP HERE?
ANYTHING. THIS IS THE LAST PLACE WE WERE ALL TOGETHER -- THE STUDENTS AND THE MASTERS.
AFTER WE CAME BACK TO TARIS, LUCIEN AND THE OTHER MASTERS CLOISTERED IN THE TEMPLE FOR DAYS.
WHEN THEY FINALLY CAME OUT, THEY SAID THEY'D DECIDED WHO WAS TO BECOME A JEDI -- AND SET UP THE BANQUET AND CEREMONY FOR TWO DAYS AGO.
YOU SAID IT TOOK YOU HALF THE DAY TO GET HERE. WHAT WERE THE MASTERS DOING ALL THAT TIME?
WAITING, I GUESS. I DON'T KNOW. I WAS THE LAST TO ARRIVE.
THAT JUST SEEMED... *NORMAL.* LIKE WHAT MASTERS DID BEFORE KNIGHTING STUDENTS. BUT IF SOMETHING HAPPENED EARLIER -- SOMETHING *HERE*...
AND YOU COULDN'T SEE. YOUR FRIENDS WHO ARRIVED BACK FIRST -- DID THEY SEE ANYTHING?
NOT THAT THEY MENTIONED. SHAD WAS THE FIRST HERE -- BUT HE SAID BY THE TIME HE ARRIVED, ELBEE HAD ALREADY GONE OVER THE...
WHAT?
ELBEE!
ELBEE WAS UP HERE! ELBEE *SAW!*
LET'S GO DOWN AND FIND OUT IF THERE'S ANYTHING LEFT OF HIM!

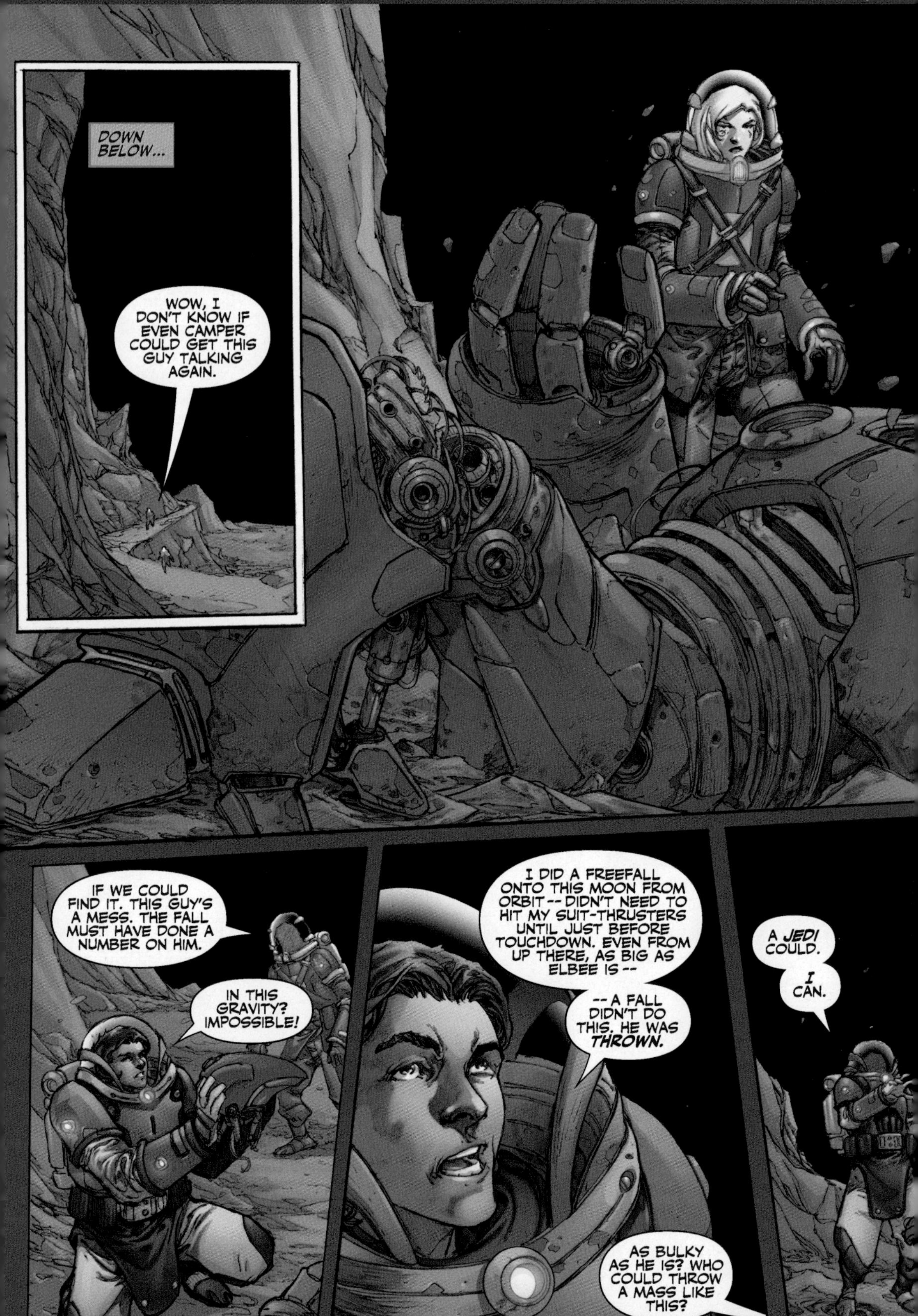
DOWN BELOW...
WOW, I DON'T KNOW IF EVEN CAMPER COULD GET THIS GUY TALKING AGAIN.
IF WE COULD FIND IT. THIS GUY'S A MESS. THE FALL MUST HAVE DONE A NUMBER ON HIM.
IN THIS GRAVITY? IMPOSSIBLE!
I DID A FREEFALL ONTO THIS MOON FROM ORBIT -- DIDN'T NEED TO HIT MY SUIT-THRUSTERS UNTIL JUST BEFORE TOUCHDOWN. EVEN FROM UP THERE, AS BIG AS ELBEE IS --
-- A FALL DIDN'T DO THIS. HE WAS THROWN.
AS BULKY AS HE IS? WHO COULD THROW A MASS LIKE THIS?
A JEDI COULD.
I CAN.

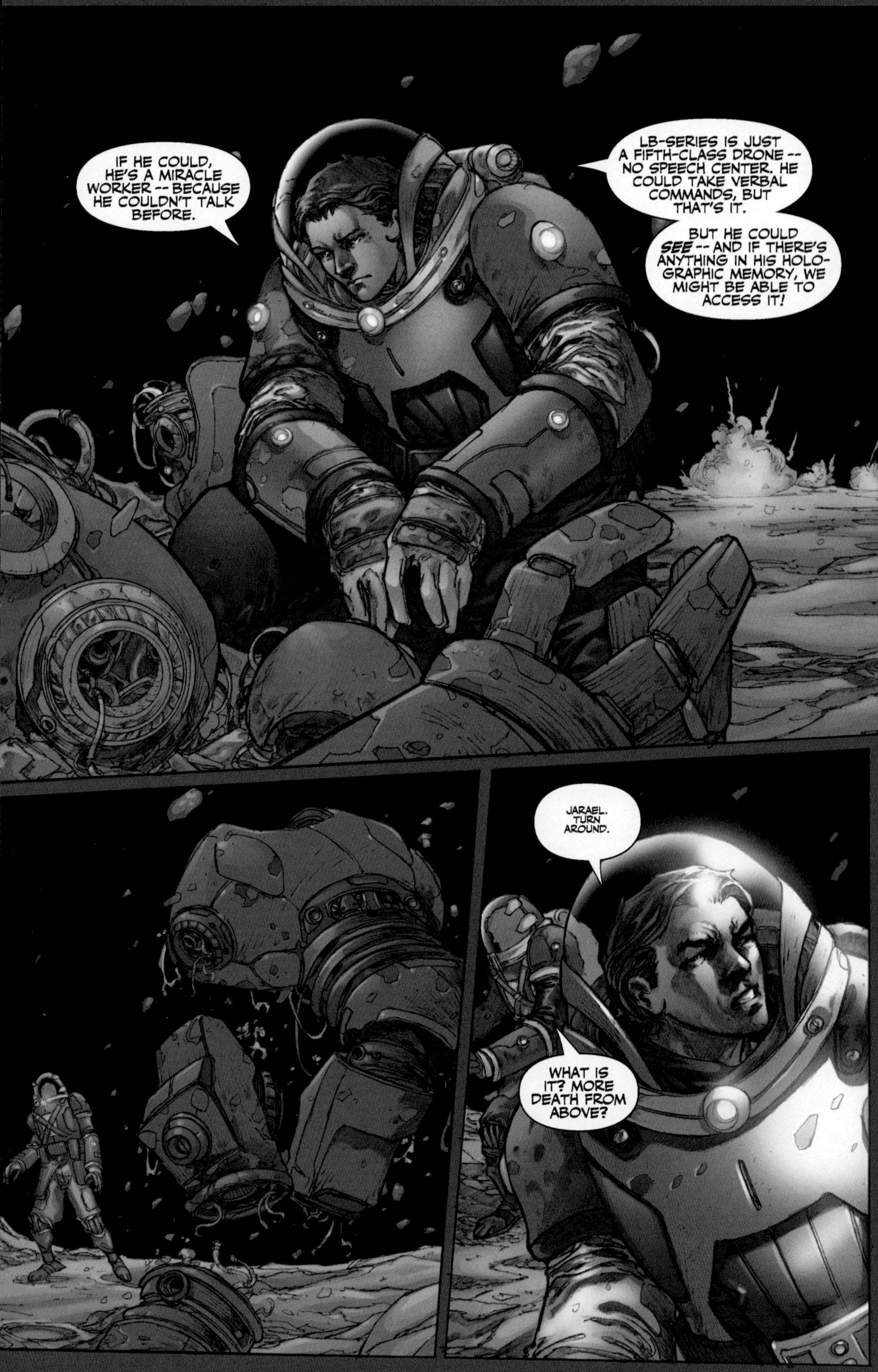
LB-SERIES IS JUST A FIFTH-CLASS DRONE -- NO SPEECH CENTER. HE COULD TAKE VERBAL COMMANDS, BUT THAT'S IT.
BUT HE COULD SEE -- AND IF THERE'S ANYTHING IN HIS HOLOGRAPHIC MEMORY, WE MIGHT BE ABLE TO ACCESS IT!
IF HE COULD, HE'S A MIRACLE WORKER -- BECAUSE HE COULDN'T TALK BEFORE.
JARAEL. TURN AROUND.
WHAT IS IT? MORE DEATH FROM ABOVE?

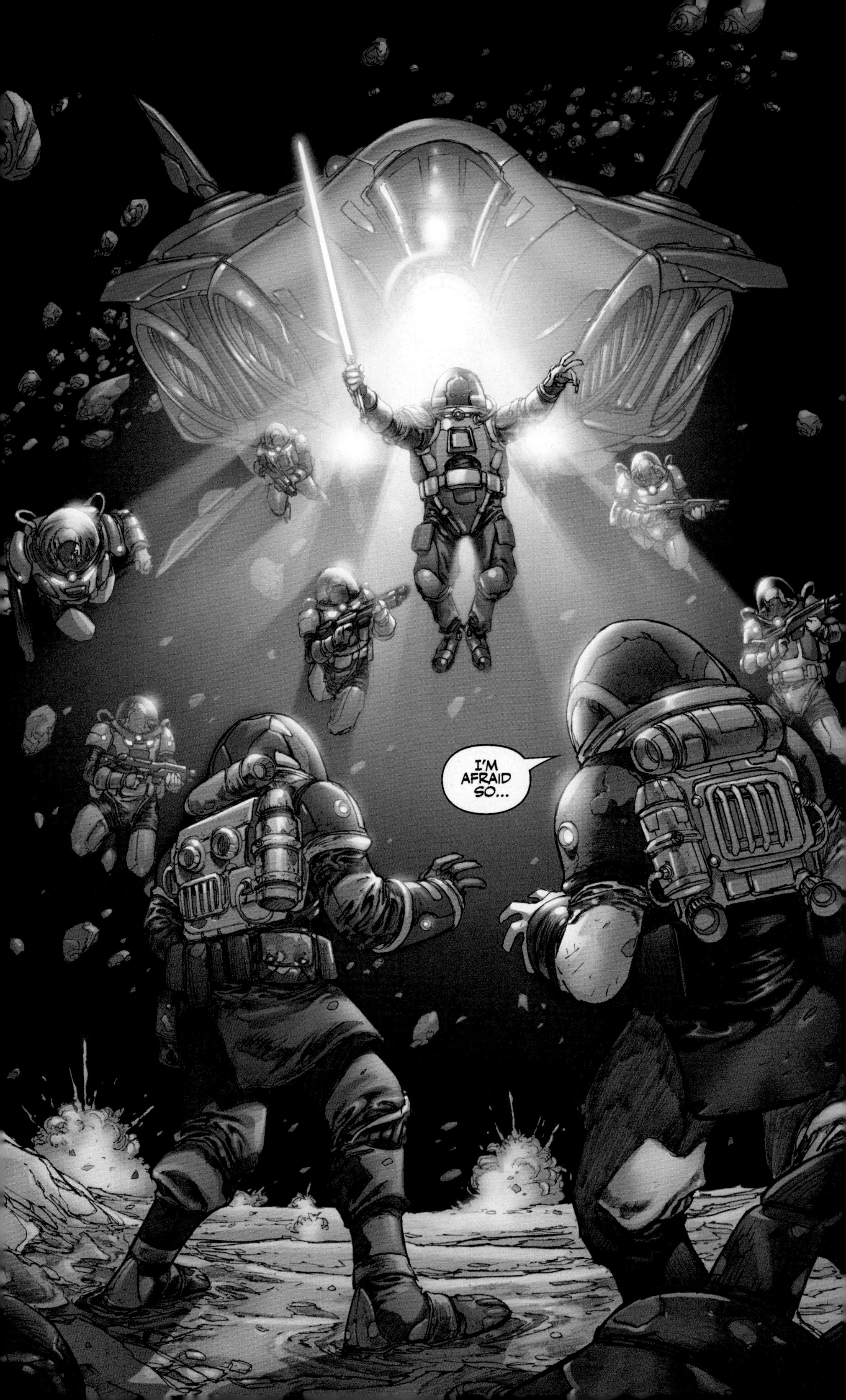
I'M AFRAID SO...

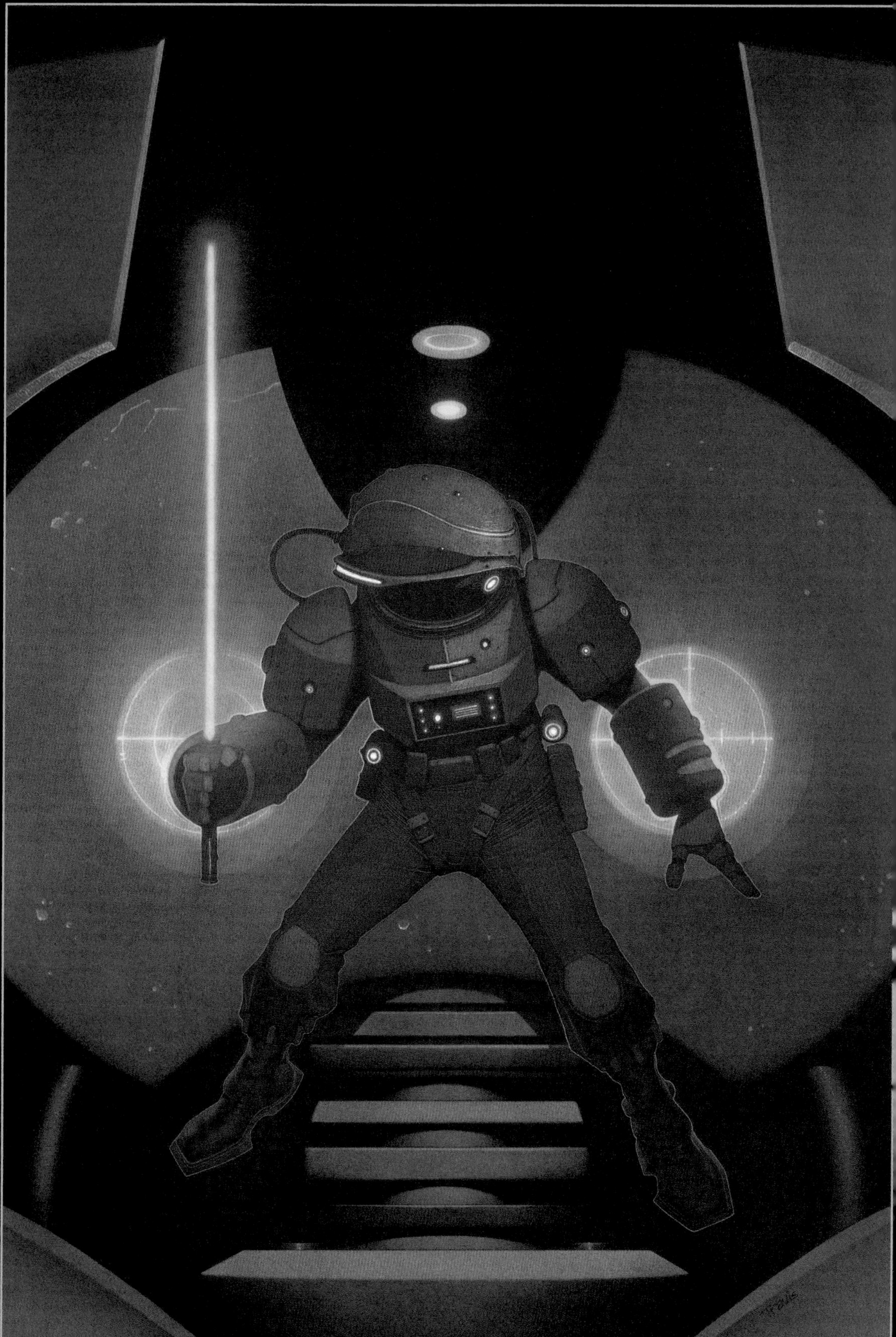

***STAR WARS: KNIGHTS OF THE OLD REPUBLIC #5* — "COMMENCEMENT, PART 5 (OF SIX)"**

WRITER: JOHN JACKSON MILLER • ARTIST: TRAVEL FOREMAN • COLORIST: MICHAEL ATIYEH • LETTERER: MICHAEL HEISLER
ASSISTANT EDITOR: DAVE MARSHALL • EDITOR: JEREMY BARLOW • COVER ARTIST: TRAVIS CHAREST

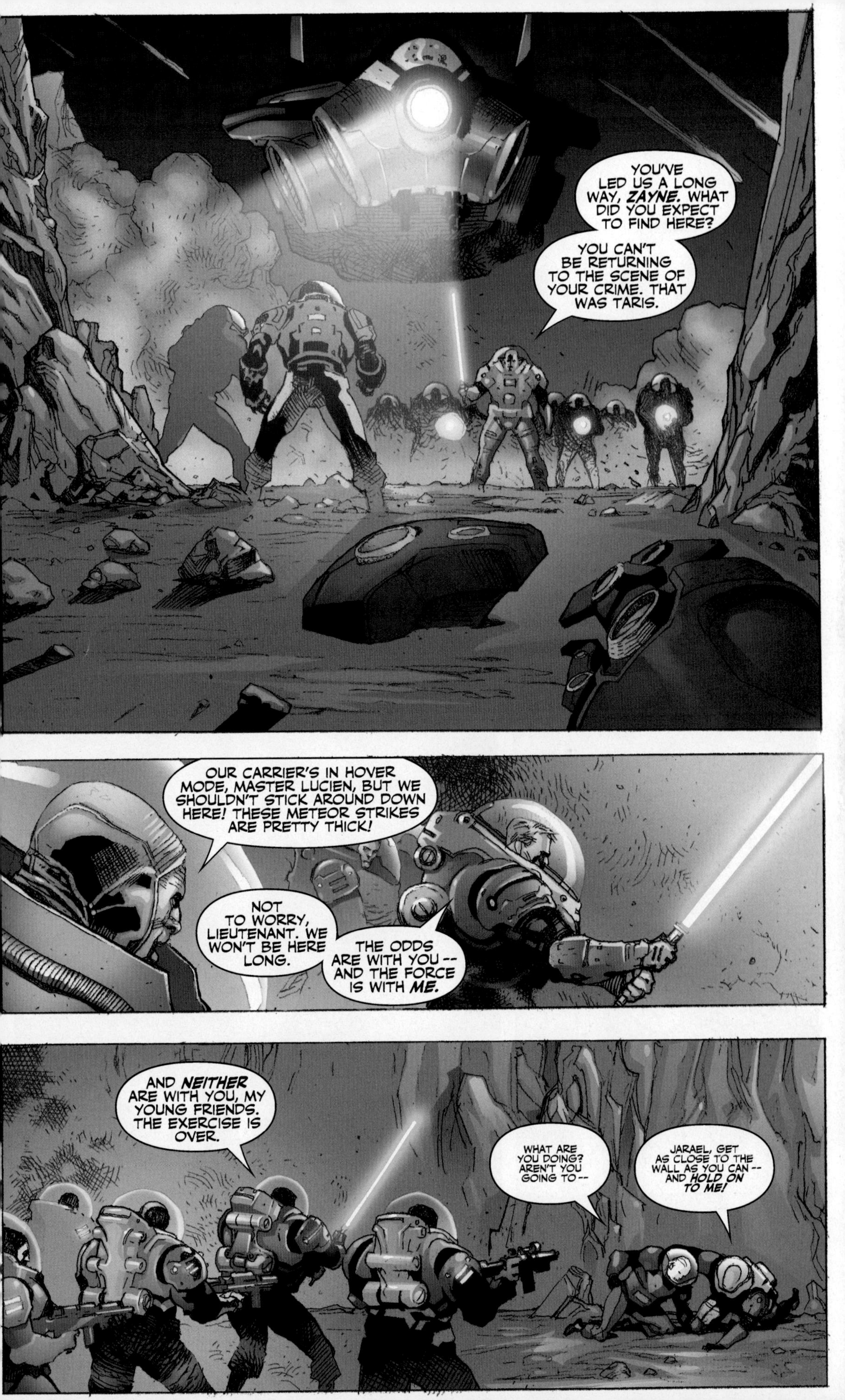
YOU'VE LED US A LONG WAY, ZAYNE. WHAT DID YOU EXPECT TO FIND HERE?
YOU CAN'T BE RETURNING TO THE SCENE OF YOUR CRIME. THAT WAS TARIS.
OUR CARRIER'S IN HOVER MODE, MASTER LUCIEN, BUT WE SHOULDN'T STICK AROUND DOWN HERE! THESE METEOR STRIKES ARE PRETTY THICK!
NOT TO WORRY, LIEUTENANT. WE WON'T BE HERE LONG.
THE ODDS ARE WITH YOU -- AND THE FORCE IS WITH ME.
AND NEITHER ARE WITH YOU, MY YOUNG FRIENDS. THE EXERCISE IS OVER.
WHAT ARE YOU DOING? AREN'T YOU GOING TO --
JARAEL, GET AS CLOSE TO THE WALL AS YOU CAN -- AND HOLD ON TO ME!

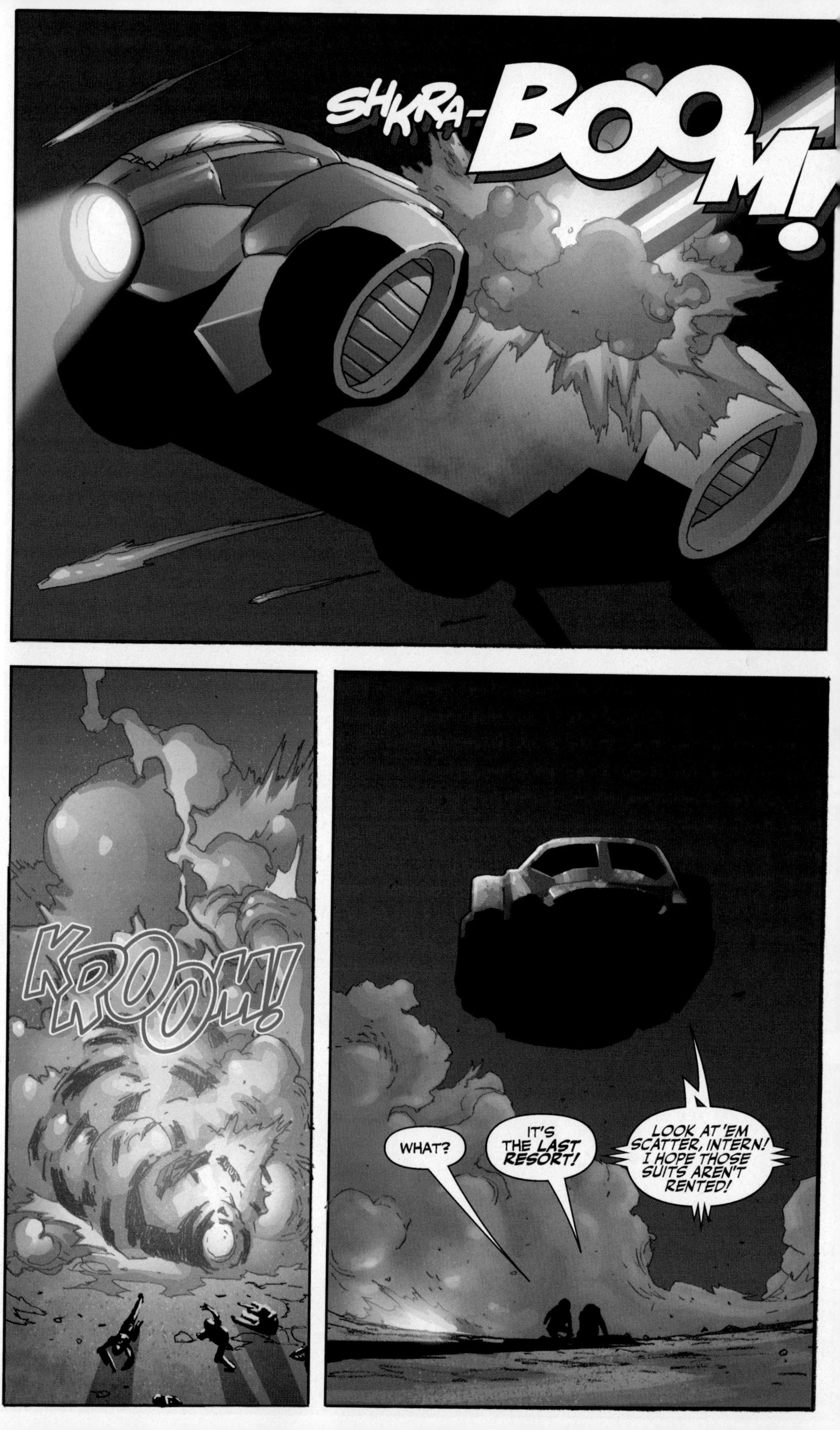
SHKRA-BOOM!
KROOOM!
WHAT?
IT'S THE LAST RESORT!
LOOK AT 'EM SCATTER, INTERN! I HOPE THOSE SUITS AREN'T RENTED!

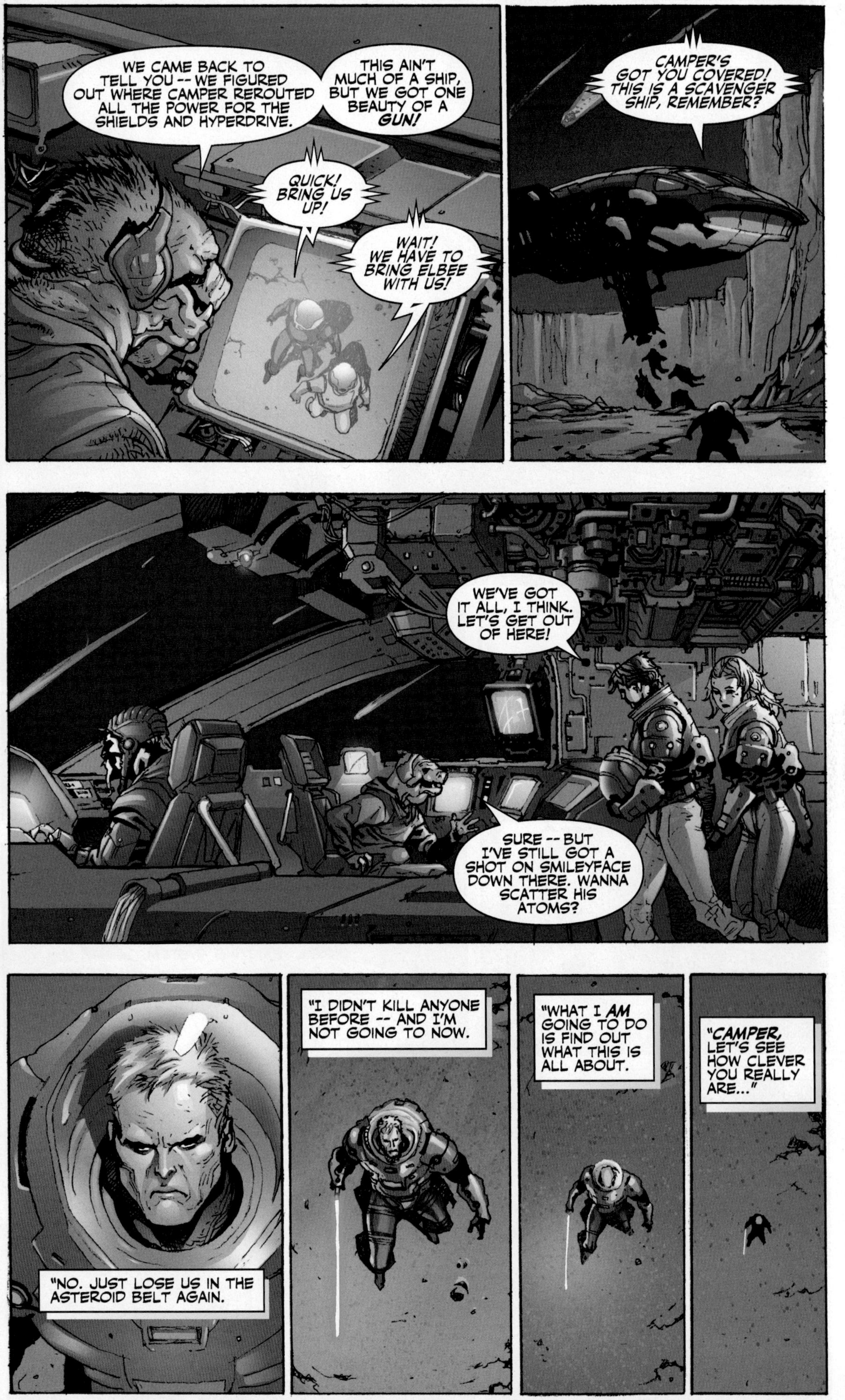
WE CAME BACK TO TELL YOU -- WE FIGURED OUT WHERE CAMPER REROUTED ALL THE POWER FOR THE SHIELDS AND HYPERDRIVE.
THIS AIN'T MUCH OF A SHIP, BUT WE GOT ONE BEAUTY OF A GUN!
QUICK! BRING US UP!
WAIT! WE HAVE TO BRING ELBEE WITH US!
CAMPER'S GOT YOU COVERED! THIS IS A SCAVENGER SHIP, REMEMBER?
WE'VE GOT IT ALL, I THINK. LET'S GET OUT OF HERE!
SURE -- BUT I'VE STILL GOT A SHOT ON SMILEYFACE DOWN THERE. WANNA SCATTER HIS ATOMS?
"NO. JUST LOSE US IN THE ASTEROID BELT AGAIN.
"I DIDN'T KILL ANYONE BEFORE -- AND I'M NOT GOING TO NOW.
"WHAT I AM GOING TO DO IS FIND OUT WHAT THIS IS ALL ABOUT.
"CAMPER, LET'S SEE HOW CLEVER YOU REALLY ARE..."

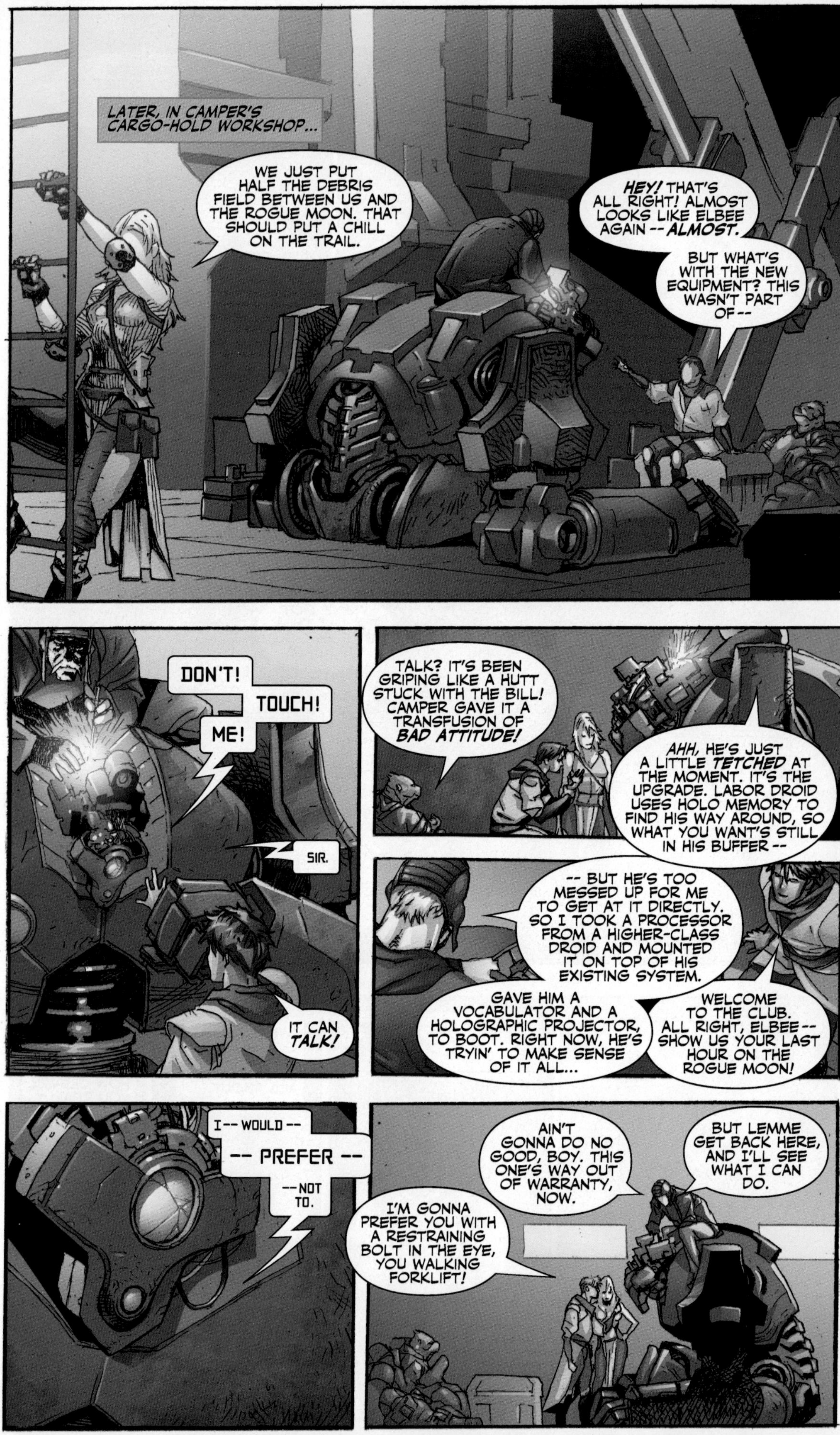

LATER, IN CAMPER'S CARGO-HOLD WORKSHOP...
WE JUST PUT HALF THE DEBRIS FIELD BETWEEN US AND THE ROGUE MOON. THAT SHOULD PUT A CHILL ON THE TRAIL.
HEY! THAT'S ALL RIGHT! ALMOST LOOKS LIKE ELBEE AGAIN -- ALMOST.
BUT WHAT'S WITH THE NEW EQUIPMENT? THIS WASN'T PART OF --
DON'T!
TOUCH!
ME!
SIR.
IT CAN TALK!
TALK? IT'S BEEN GRIPING LIKE A HUTT STUCK WITH THE BILL! CAMPER GAVE IT A TRANSFUSION OF BAD ATTITUDE!
AHH, HE'S JUST A LITTLE TETCHED AT THE MOMENT. IT'S THE UPGRADE. LABOR DROID USES HOLO MEMORY TO FIND HIS WAY AROUND, SO WHAT YOU WANT'S STILL IN HIS BUFFER --
-- BUT HE'S TOO MESSED UP FOR ME TO GET AT IT DIRECTLY. SO I TOOK A PROCESSOR FROM A HIGHER-CLASS DROID AND MOUNTED IT ON TOP OF HIS EXISTING SYSTEM.
GAVE HIM A VOCABULATOR AND A HOLOGRAPHIC PROJECTOR, TO BOOT. RIGHT NOW, HE'S TRYIN' TO MAKE SENSE OF IT ALL...
WELCOME TO THE CLUB. ALL RIGHT, ELBEE -- SHOW US YOUR LAST HOUR ON THE ROGUE MOON!
I -- WOULD --
-- PREFER --
-- NOT TO.
I'M GONNA PREFER YOU WITH A RESTRAINING BOLT IN THE EYE, YOU WALKING FORKLIFT!
AIN'T GONNA DO NO GOOD, BOY. THIS ONE'S WAY OUT OF WARRANTY, NOW.
BUT LEMME GET BACK HERE, AND I'LL SEE WHAT I CAN DO.

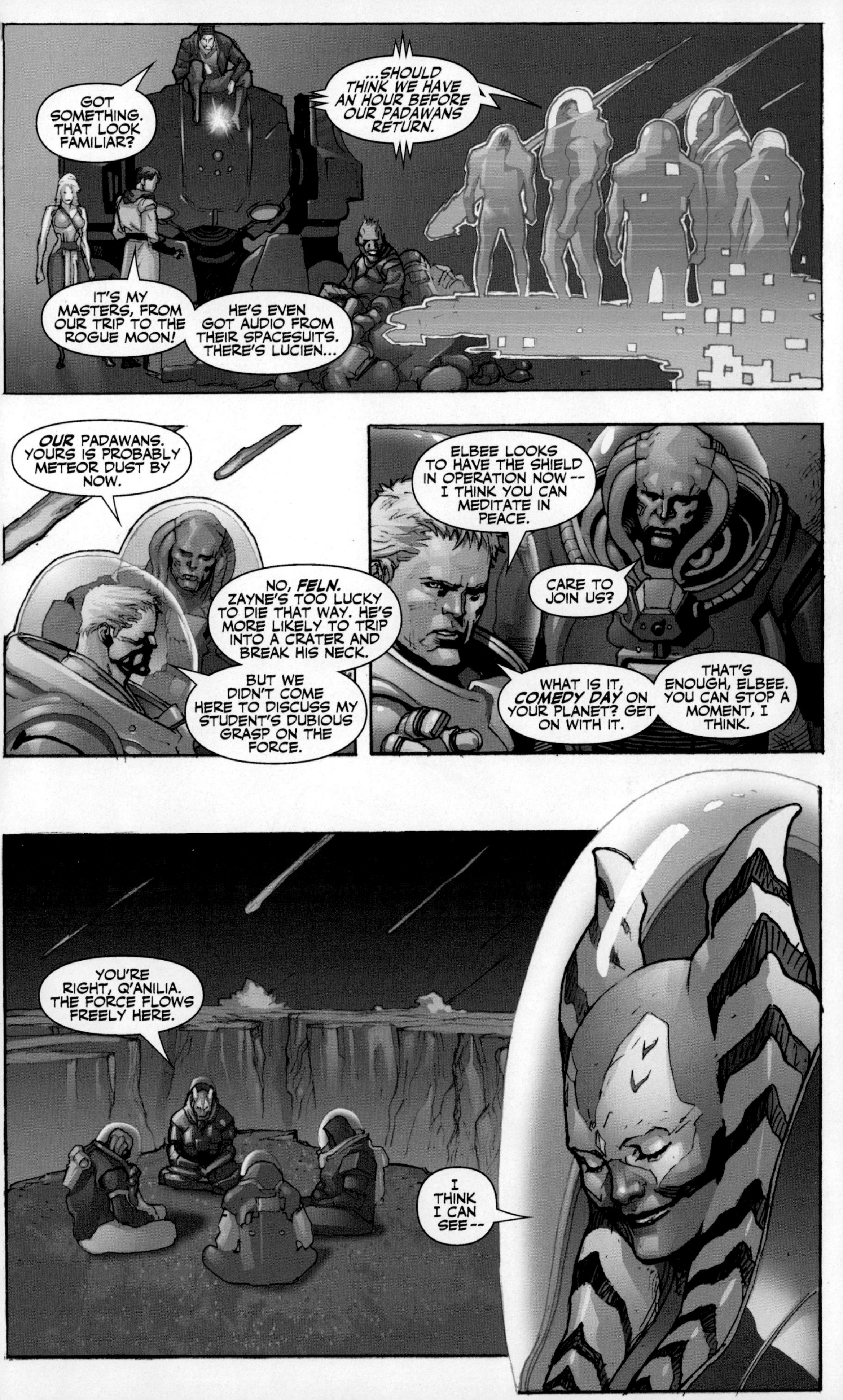
GOT SOMETHING. THAT LOOK FAMILIAR?
IT'S MY MASTERS, FROM OUR TRIP TO THE ROGUE MOON!
HE'S EVEN GOT AUDIO FROM THEIR SPACESUITS. THERE'S LUCIEN...
...SHOULD THINK WE HAVE AN HOUR BEFORE OUR PADAWANS RETURN.
OUR PADAWANS. YOURS IS PROBABLY METEOR DUST BY NOW.
NO, *FELN.* ZAYNE'S TOO LUCKY TO DIE THAT WAY. HE'S MORE LIKELY TO TRIP INTO A CRATER AND BREAK HIS NECK.
BUT WE DIDN'T COME HERE TO DISCUSS MY STUDENT'S DUBIOUS GRASP ON THE FORCE.
ELBEE LOOKS TO HAVE THE SHIELD IN OPERATION NOW -- I THINK YOU CAN MEDITATE IN PEACE.
CARE TO JOIN US?
WHAT IS IT, *COMEDY DAY* ON YOUR PLANET? GET ON WITH IT.
THAT'S ENOUGH, ELBEE. YOU CAN STOP A MOMENT, I THINK.
YOU'RE RIGHT, Q'ANILIA. THE FORCE FLOWS FREELY HERE.
I THINK I CAN SEE--

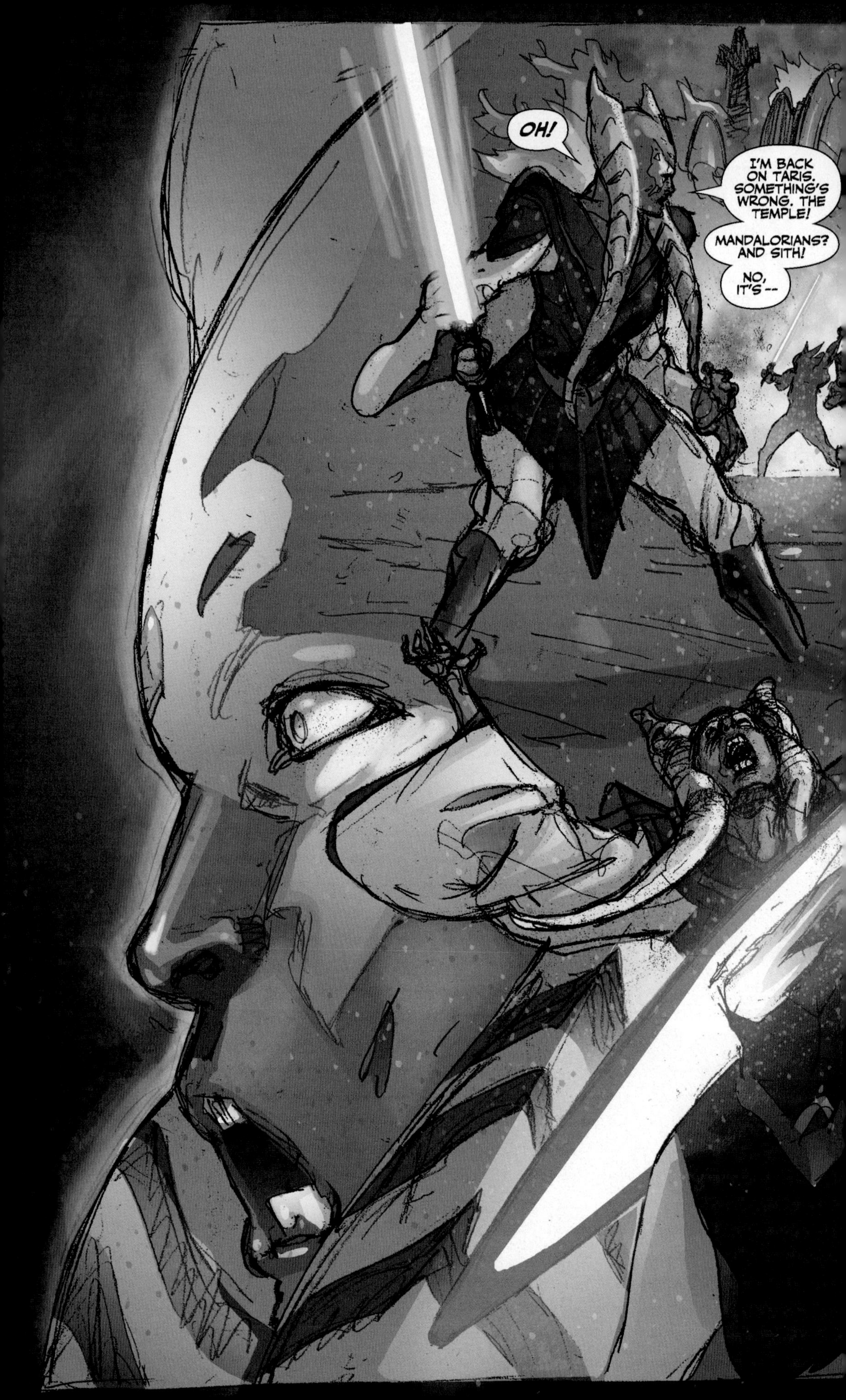
OH!
I'M BACK ON TARIS. SOMETHING'S WRONG. THE TEMPLE!
MANDALORIANS? AND SITH!
NO, IT'S--

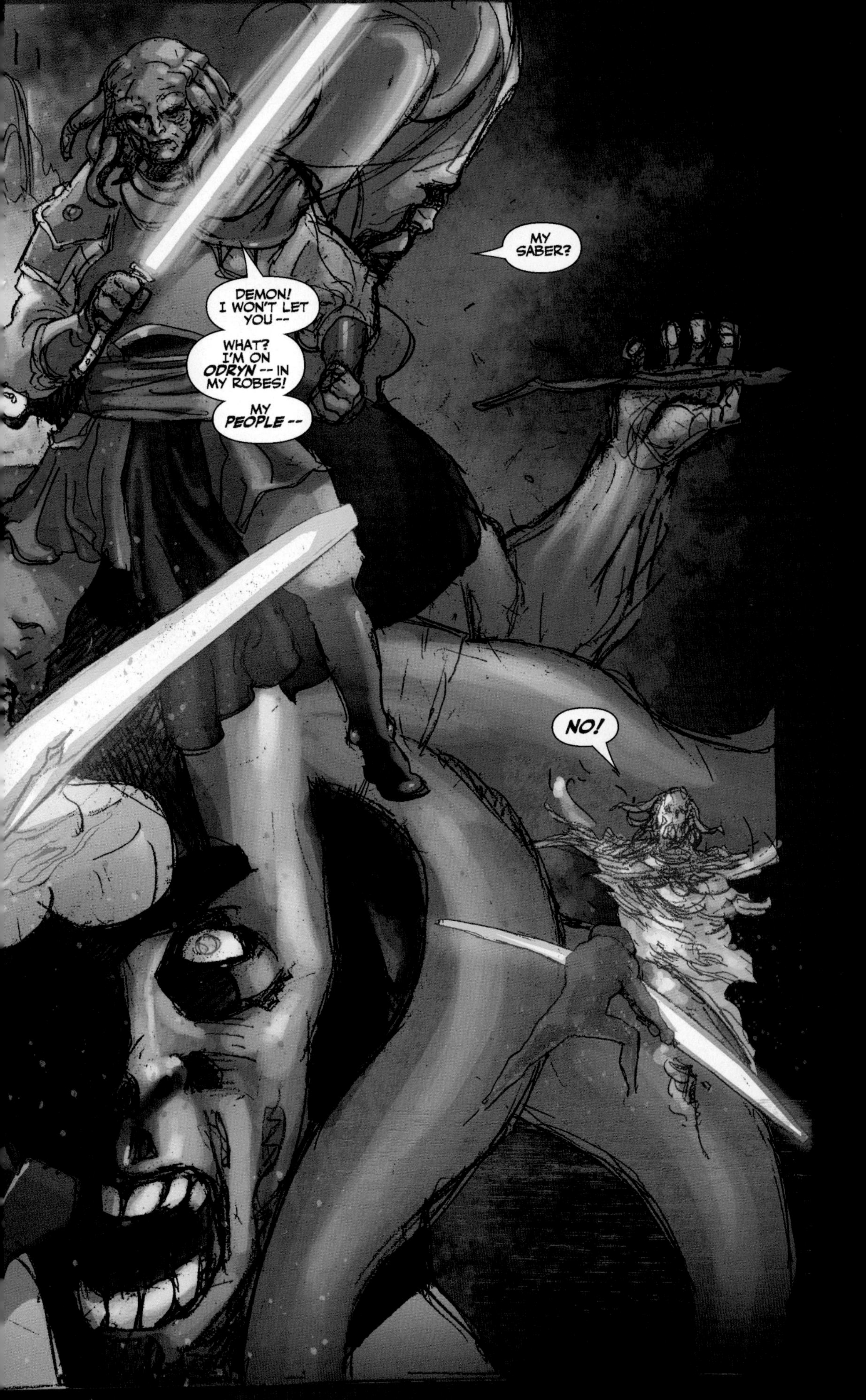
MY SABER?
DEMON! I WON'T LET YOU --
WHAT? I'M ON ODRYN -- IN MY ROBES!
MY PEOPLE --
NO!

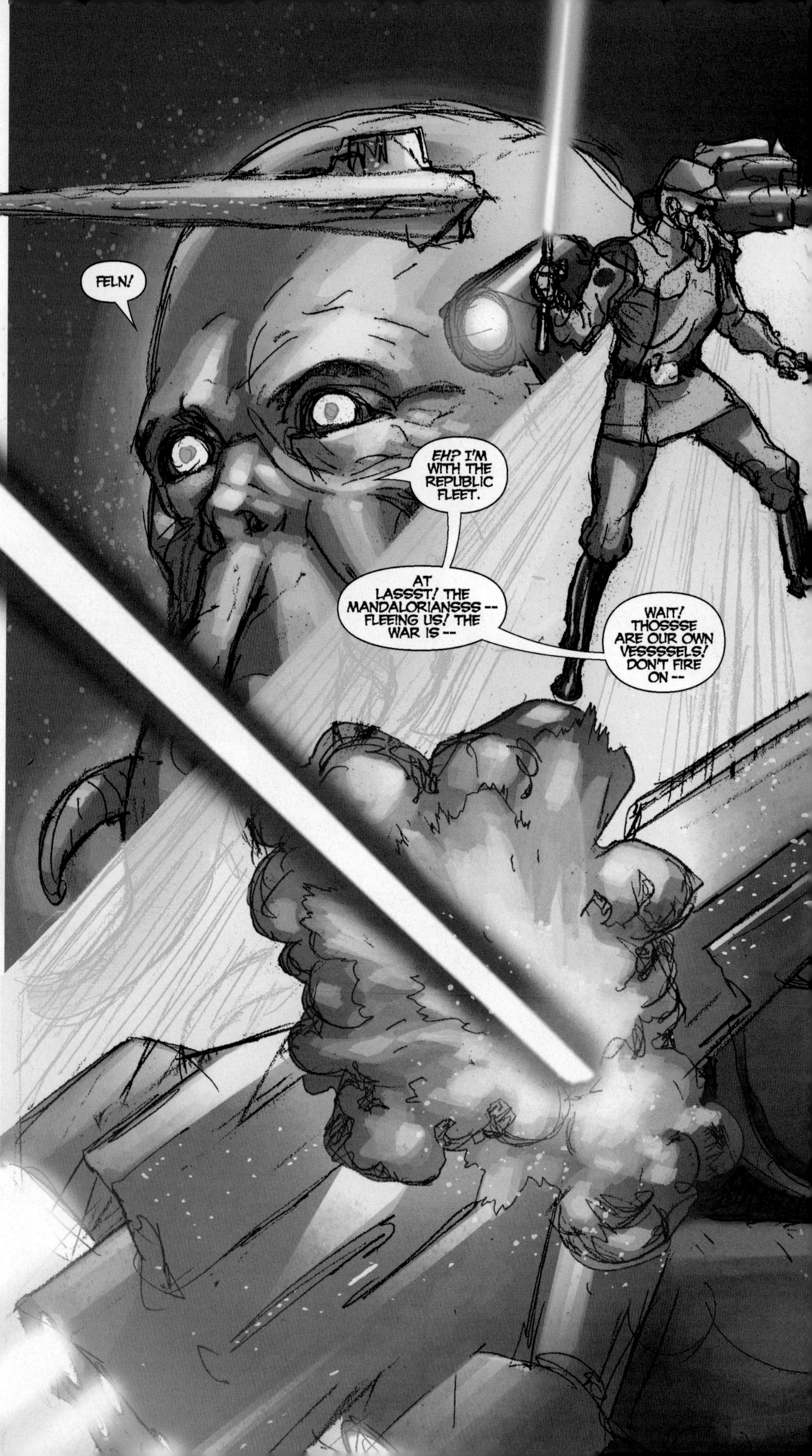
FELN!
EH? I'M WITH THE REPUBLIC FLEET.
AT LASSST! THE MANDALORIANSSS -- FLEEING US! THE WAR IS --
WAIT! THOSSSE ARE OUR OWN VESSSSELS! DON'T FIRE ON --

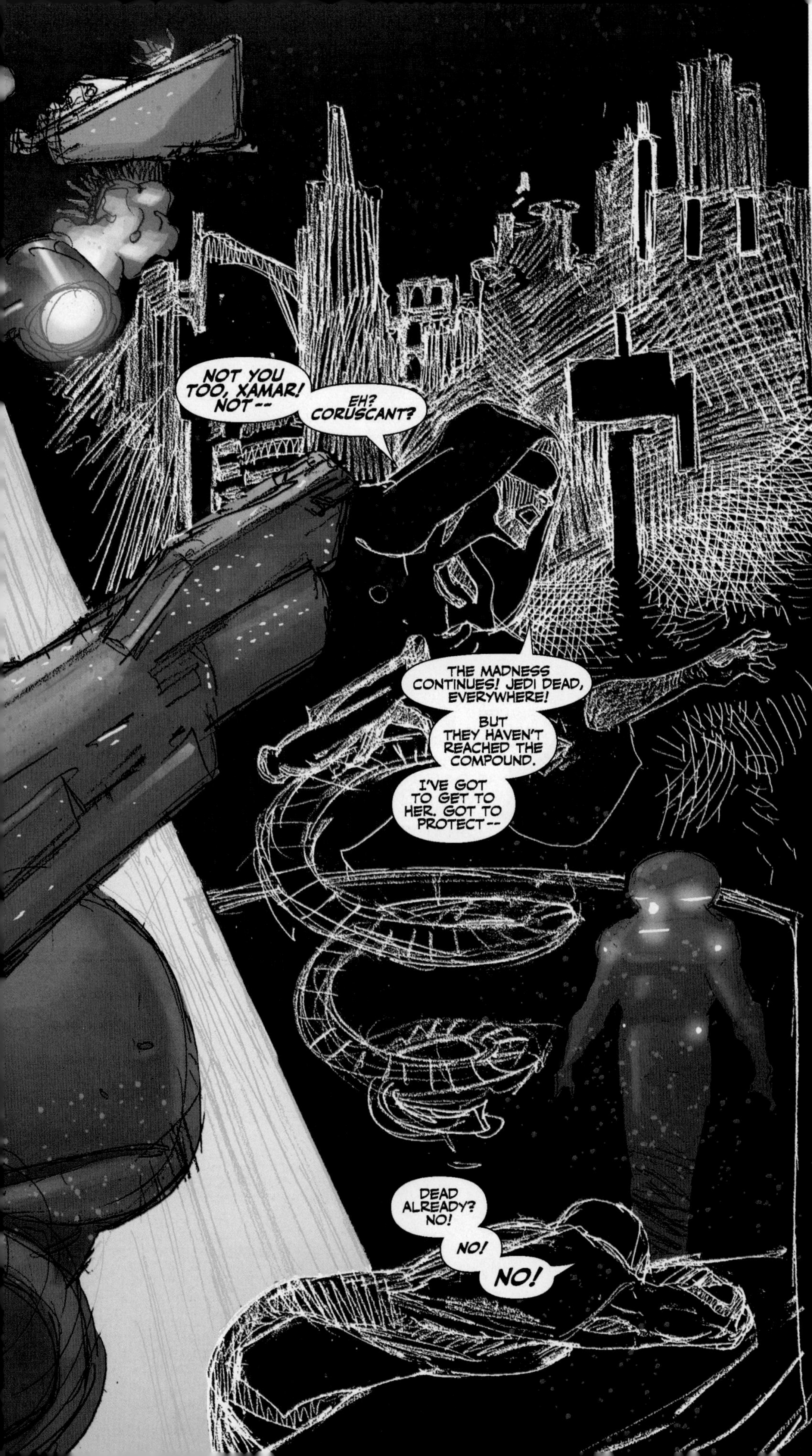
NOT YOU TOO, XAMAR! NOT--
EH? CORUSCANT?
THE MADNESS CONTINUES! JEDI DEAD, EVERYWHERE!
BUT THEY HAVEN'T REACHED THE COMPOUND.
I'VE GOT TO GET TO HER. GOT TO PROTECT--
DEAD ALREADY? NO!
NO!
NO!

NOOOO!!!!

WHAT? *WHAT?* YOU'VE BEEN FLAPPING AROUND LIKE MYNOCKS!

IT'S WHAT WE'VE BEEN WATCHING FOR!

THE SITH! THE SITH ARE RETURNING!

IN FLAMES, LUCIEN! THE ORDER! THE REPUBLIC! ALL IN FLAMES!

WHAT?

SITH! I SAW SITH ON TARIS! AND -- A *DARK LORD!*

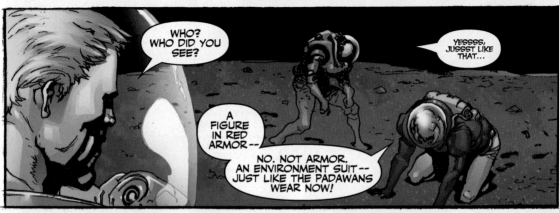

WHO? WHO DID YOU SEE?

YESSSS, JUSSST LIKE THAT...

A FIGURE IN RED ARMOR--

NO. NOT ARMOR. AN ENVIRONMENT SUIT-- JUST LIKE THE PADAWANS WEAR NOW!

LIKE THE PADAWANS WEAR NOW...

WE HAVE TO *KILL* THEM! NOW!

RAANA, NO! HOW CAN WE KNOW--

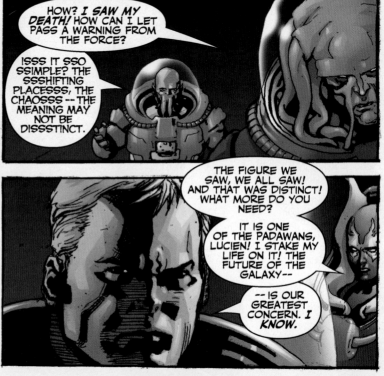

HOW? *I SAW MY DEATH!* HOW CAN I LET PASS A WARNING FROM THE FORCE?

ISSS IT SSO SSIMPLE? THE SSSHIFTING PLACESSS, THE CHAOSSS -- THE MEANING MAY NOT BE DISSSTINCT.

THE FIGURE WE SAW, WE ALL SAW! AND THAT WAS DISTINCT! WHAT MORE DO YOU NEED?

IT IS ONE OF THE PADAWANS, LUCIEN! I STAKE MY LIFE ON IT! THE FUTURE OF THE GALAXY--

-- IS OUR GREATEST CONCERN. *I KNOW.*

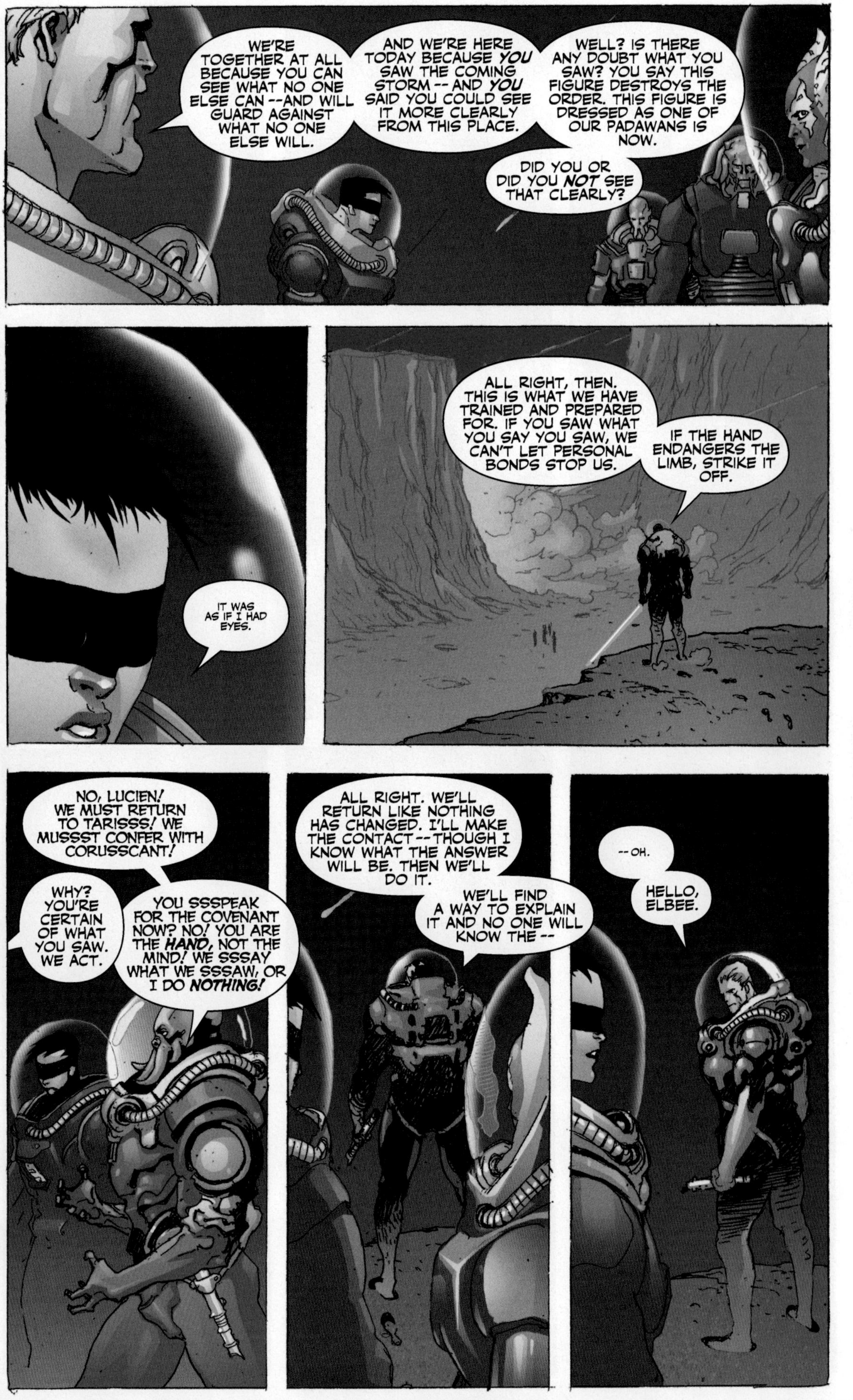
WE'RE TOGETHER AT ALL BECAUSE YOU CAN SEE WHAT NO ONE ELSE CAN--AND WILL GUARD AGAINST WHAT NO ONE ELSE WILL.
AND WE'RE HERE TODAY BECAUSE YOU SAW THE COMING STORM--AND YOU SAID YOU COULD SEE IT MORE CLEARLY FROM THIS PLACE.
WELL? IS THERE ANY DOUBT WHAT YOU SAW? YOU SAY THIS FIGURE DESTROYS THE ORDER. THIS FIGURE IS DRESSED AS ONE OF OUR PADAWANS IS NOW.
DID YOU OR DID YOU NOT SEE THAT CLEARLY?
IT WAS AS IF I HAD EYES.
ALL RIGHT, THEN. THIS IS WHAT WE HAVE TRAINED AND PREPARED FOR. IF YOU SAW WHAT YOU SAY YOU SAW, WE CAN'T LET PERSONAL BONDS STOP US.
IF THE HAND ENDANGERS THE LIMB, STRIKE IT OFF.
NO, LUCIEN! WE MUST RETURN TO TARISSS! WE MUSSST CONFER WITH CORUSSCANT!
WHY? YOU'RE CERTAIN OF WHAT YOU SAW. WE ACT.
YOU SSSPEAK FOR THE COVENANT NOW? NO! YOU ARE THE HAND, NOT THE MIND! WE SSSAY WHAT WE SSSAW, OR I DO NOTHING!
ALL RIGHT. WE'LL RETURN LIKE NOTHING HAS CHANGED. I'LL MAKE THE CONTACT--THOUGH I KNOW WHAT THE ANSWER WILL BE. THEN WE'LL DO IT.
WE'LL FIND A WAY TO EXPLAIN IT AND NO ONE WILL KNOW THE--
--OH.
HELLO, ELBEE.

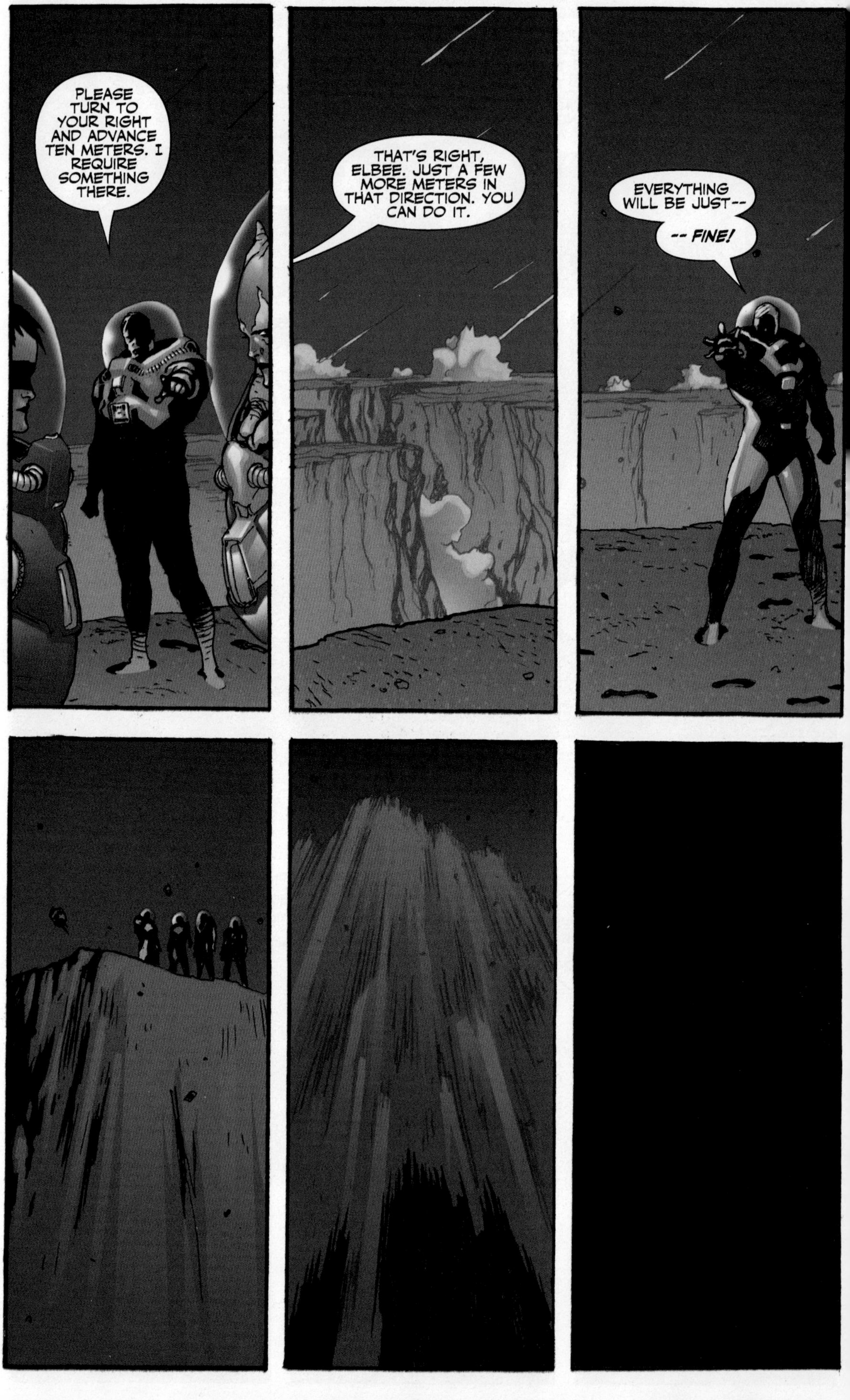
PLEASE TURN TO YOUR RIGHT AND ADVANCE TEN METERS. I REQUIRE SOMETHING THERE.
THAT'S RIGHT, ELBEE. JUST A FEW MORE METERS IN THAT DIRECTION. YOU CAN DO IT.
EVERYTHING WILL BE JUST--
-- FINE!

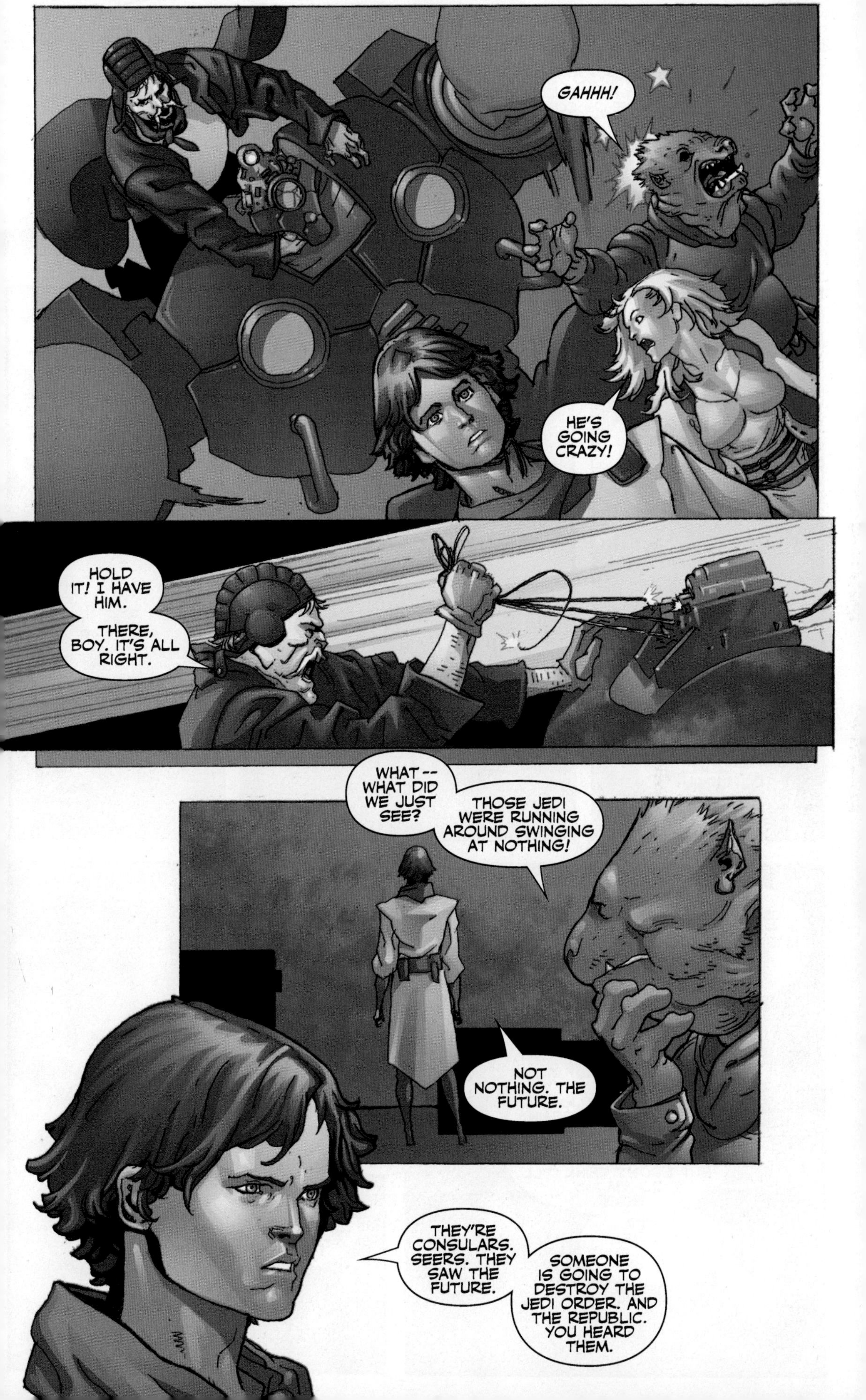
GAHHH!
HE'S GOING CRAZY!
HOLD IT! I HAVE HIM.
THERE, BOY. IT'S ALL RIGHT.
WHAT -- WHAT DID WE JUST SEE?
THOSE JEDI WERE RUNNING AROUND SWINGING AT NOTHING!
NOT NOTHING. THE FUTURE.
THEY'RE CONSULARS. SEERS. THEY SAW THE FUTURE.
SOMEONE IS GOING TO DESTROY THE JEDI ORDER. AND THE REPUBLIC. YOU HEARD THEM.

BUT I DON'T GET THE SPACESUIT THING. WHO DO YOU KNOW WHO WOULD NEED ONE ON CORUSCANT? OR THOSE OTHER PLACES?

JEDI VISIONS ARE COMPLICATED. YOU MIGHT SEE SOMETHING IN GREAT DETAIL, LIKE A SPACESUIT -- AND IT CAN BE JUST A SYMBOL.

AT THAT MOMENT, MY FRIENDS AND I WERE IN RED ENVIRONMENT SUITS -- JUST LIKE THAT ONE, OVER THERE.

I GUESS THEY TOOK THAT TO MEAN ONE OF *US* WAS THE --

WHOA!

BZZT!

WHAT HAPPENED?

OUR LITTLE FRIEND JUST DELETED THAT WHOLE STRETCH OF HOLOGRAPHIC MEMORY. *ON HIS OWN.*

WHAT? HOW --

THAT DEATH-MEMORY'S STUCK IN HIS CRAW -- IT'S WHAT'S TANGLED UP HIS MOTIVATION CENTER.

DROID ISN'T SUPPOSED TO DO ITSELF IN -- AND ITS MASTER ISN'T SUPPOSED TO *ORDER* IT TO DO SO, BY ITS LOGIC.

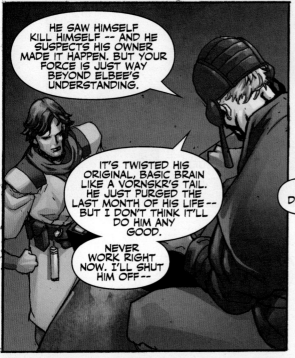

HE SAW HIMSELF KILL HIMSELF -- AND HE SUSPECTS HIS OWNER MADE IT HAPPEN. BUT YOUR FORCE IS JUST WAY BEYOND ELBEE'S UNDERSTANDING.

IT'S TWISTED HIS ORIGINAL, BASIC BRAIN LIKE A VORNSKR'S TAIL. HE JUST PURGED THE LAST MONTH OF HIS LIFE -- BUT I DON'T THINK IT'LL DO HIM ANY GOOD.

NEVER WORK RIGHT NOW. I'LL SHUT HIM OFF --

NO, DON'T. HE'S GIVEN ME WHAT I WANTED.

I ONLY WISH HE COULD TELL ME WHAT TO DO WITH IT.

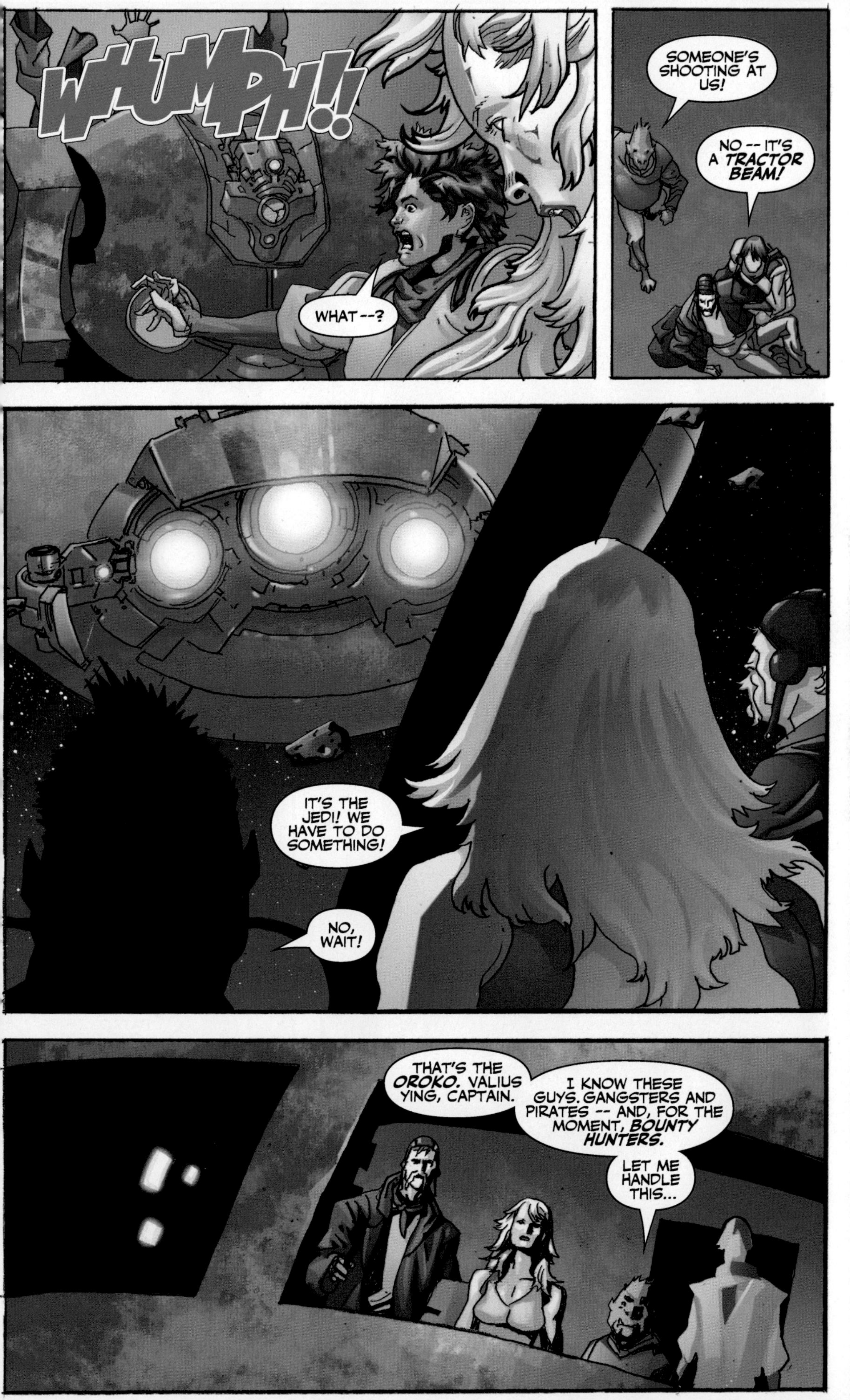
WHUMPH!!
WHAT --?
SOMEONE'S SHOOTING AT US!
NO -- IT'S A *TRACTOR BEAM!*
IT'S THE JEDI! WE HAVE TO DO SOMETHING!
NO, WAIT!
THAT'S THE *OROKO.* VALIUS YING, CAPTAIN.
I KNOW THESE GUYS. GANGSTERS AND PIRATES -- AND, FOR THE MOMENT, *BOUNTY HUNTERS.*
LET ME HANDLE THIS...

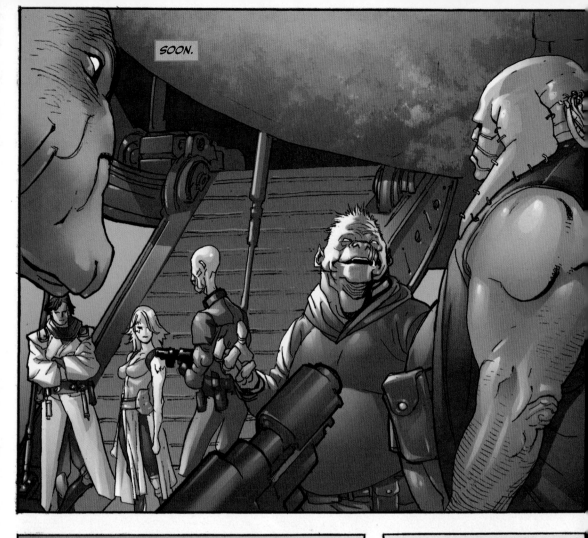

SOON.

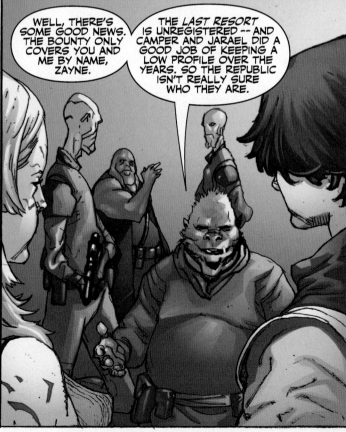

WELL, THERE'S SOME GOOD NEWS. THE BOUNTY ONLY COVERS YOU AND ME BY NAME, ZAYNE.

THE *LAST RESORT* IS UNREGISTERED -- AND CAMPER AND JARAEL DID A GOOD JOB OF KEEPING A LOW PROFILE OVER THE YEARS. SO THE REPUBLIC ISN'T REALLY SURE WHO THEY ARE.

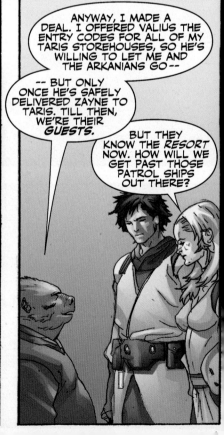

ANYWAY, I MADE A DEAL. I OFFERED VALIUS THE ENTRY CODES FOR ALL OF MY TARIS STOREHOUSES, SO HE'S WILLING TO LET ME AND THE ARKANIANS GO --

-- BUT ONLY ONCE HE'S SAFELY DELIVERED ZAYNE TO TARIS. TILL THEN, WE'RE THEIR *GUESTS.*

BUT THEY KNOW THE *RESORT* NOW. HOW WILL WE GET PAST THOSE PATROL SHIPS OUT THERE?

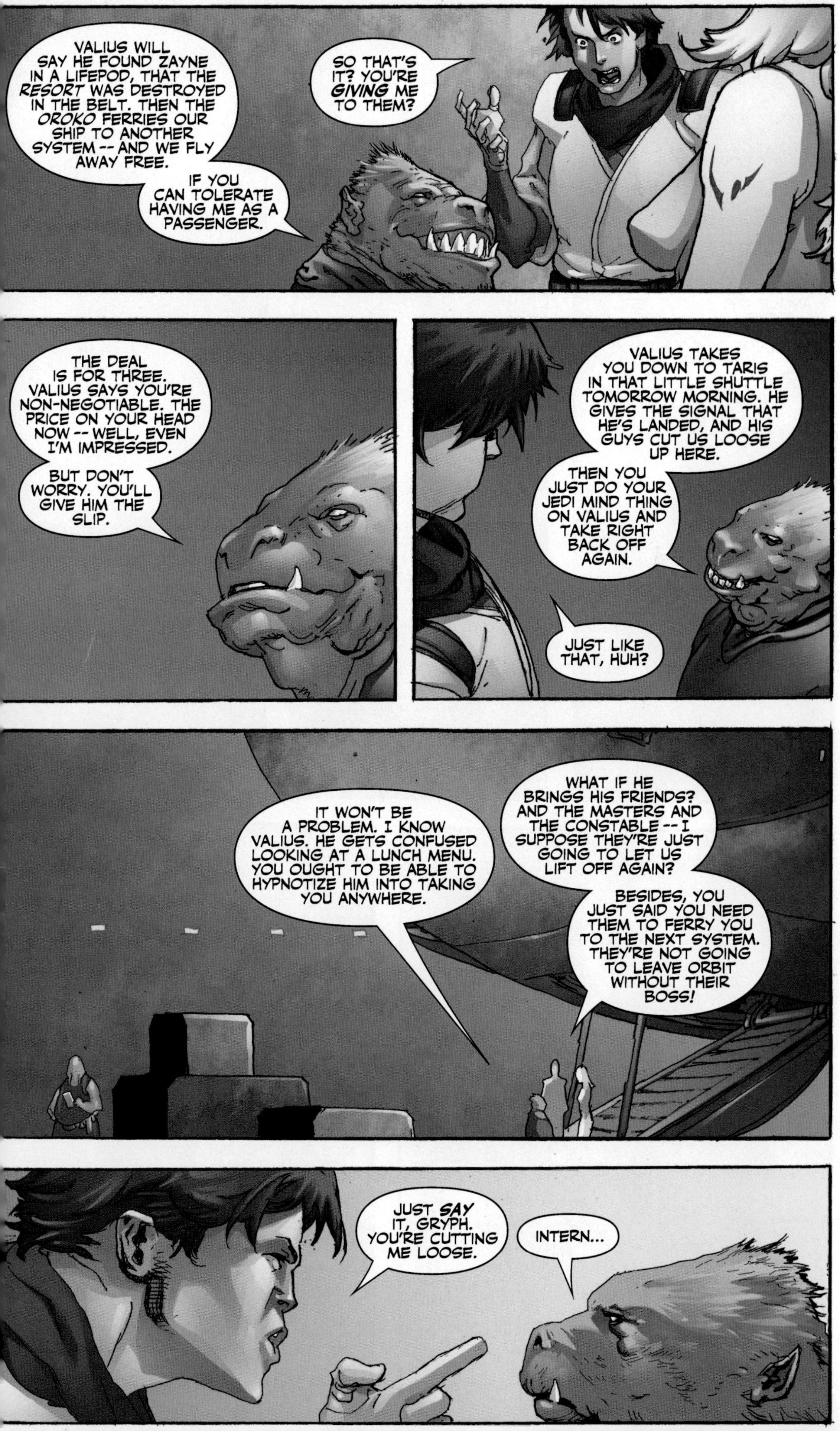
VALIUS WILL SAY HE FOUND ZAYNE IN A LIFEPOD, THAT THE RESORT WAS DESTROYED IN THE BELT. THEN THE OROKO FERRIES OUR SHIP TO ANOTHER SYSTEM -- AND WE FLY AWAY FREE.
SO THAT'S IT? YOU'RE GIVING ME TO THEM?
IF YOU CAN TOLERATE HAVING ME AS A PASSENGER.
THE DEAL IS FOR THREE. VALIUS SAYS YOU'RE NON-NEGOTIABLE. THE PRICE ON YOUR HEAD NOW -- WELL, EVEN I'M IMPRESSED.
BUT DON'T WORRY. YOU'LL GIVE HIM THE SLIP.
VALIUS TAKES YOU DOWN TO TARIS IN THAT LITTLE SHUTTLE TOMORROW MORNING. HE GIVES THE SIGNAL THAT HE'S LANDED, AND HIS GUYS CUT US LOOSE UP HERE.
THEN YOU JUST DO YOUR JEDI MIND THING ON VALIUS AND TAKE RIGHT BACK OFF AGAIN.
JUST LIKE THAT, HUH?
IT WON'T BE A PROBLEM. I KNOW VALIUS. HE GETS CONFUSED LOOKING AT A LUNCH MENU. YOU OUGHT TO BE ABLE TO HYPNOTIZE HIM INTO TAKING YOU ANYWHERE.
WHAT IF HE BRINGS HIS FRIENDS? AND THE MASTERS AND THE CONSTABLE -- I SUPPOSE THEY'RE JUST GOING TO LET US LIFT OFF AGAIN?
BESIDES, YOU JUST SAID YOU NEED THEM TO FERRY YOU TO THE NEXT SYSTEM. THEY'RE NOT GOING TO LEAVE ORBIT WITHOUT THEIR BOSS!
JUST SAY IT, GRYPH. YOU'RE CUTTING ME LOOSE.
INTERN...

...*ZAYNE.*
LISTEN.

SNIVVIANS -- MY PEOPLE -- WE *PLAY* AT THINGS. ADVENTURING, POLITICS, EVEN CRIME. AND I LOVE THE GAME. I'M *GOOD* AT IT. BUT *THIS* -- THIS IS TOO MUCH HEAT FOR ME.

YOU'RE A LOSING HAND. MARKS AND PUNKS I CAN HANDLE. I CAN'T ANGLE THE WHOLE JEDI ORDER -- MUCH LESS THE REPUBLIC AND A SWARM OF BOUNTY HUNTERS!

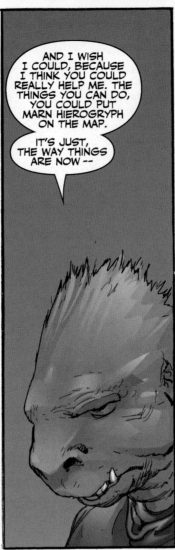

AND I WISH I COULD, BECAUSE I THINK YOU COULD REALLY HELP ME. THE THINGS YOU CAN DO, YOU COULD PUT MARN HIEROGRYPH ON THE MAP.

IT'S JUST, THE WAY THINGS ARE NOW --

IT'S ALL RIGHT.

YOU'VE GOTTEN MORE THAN YOU BARGAINED FOR. I UNDERSTAND.

WE HAD A NICE RUN, THOUGH. I COULDN'T HAVE GOTTEN THIS FAR WITHOUT YOU.

SEE YOU AROUND, GRYPH...

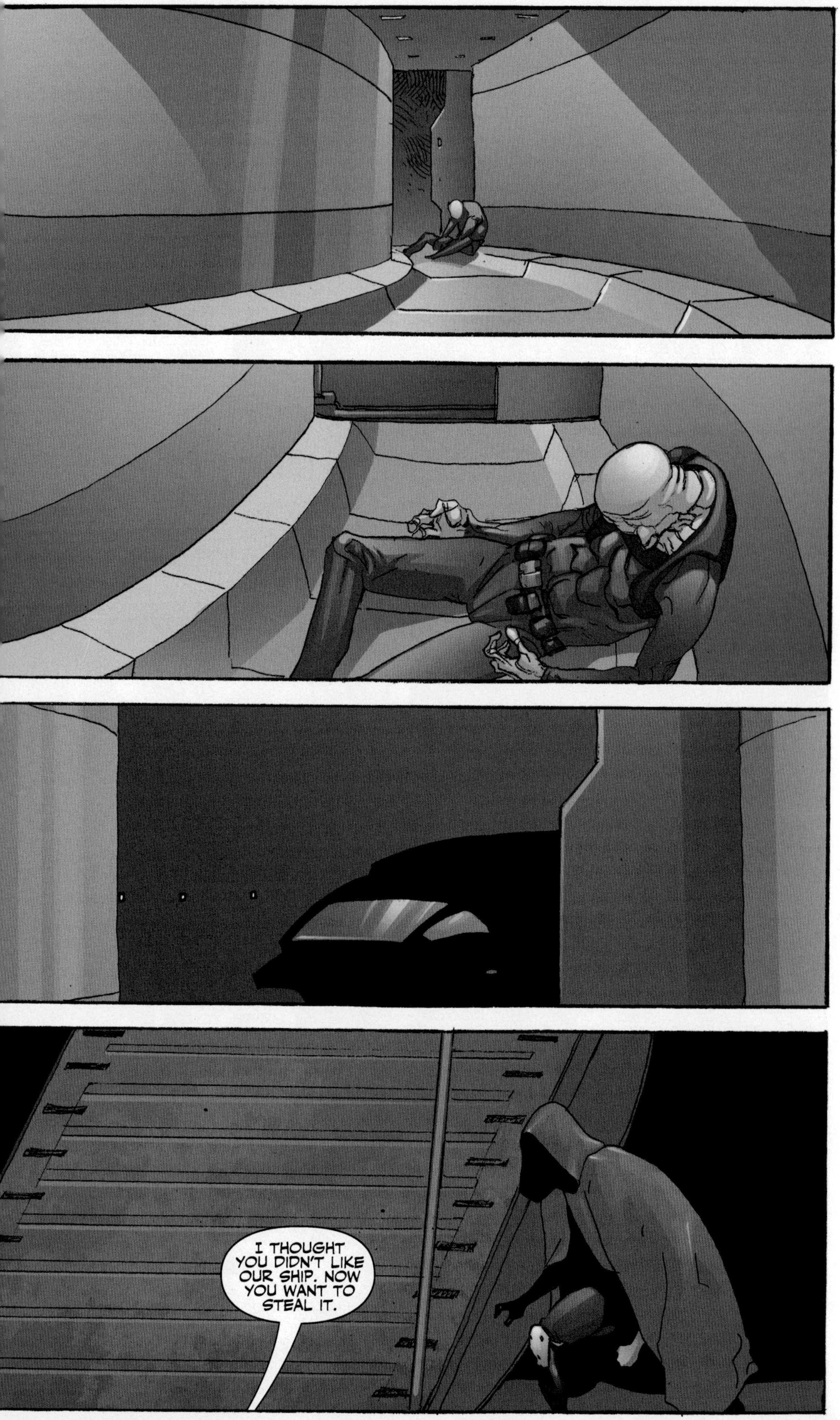
I THOUGHT YOU DIDN'T LIKE OUR SHIP. NOW YOU WANT TO STEAL IT.

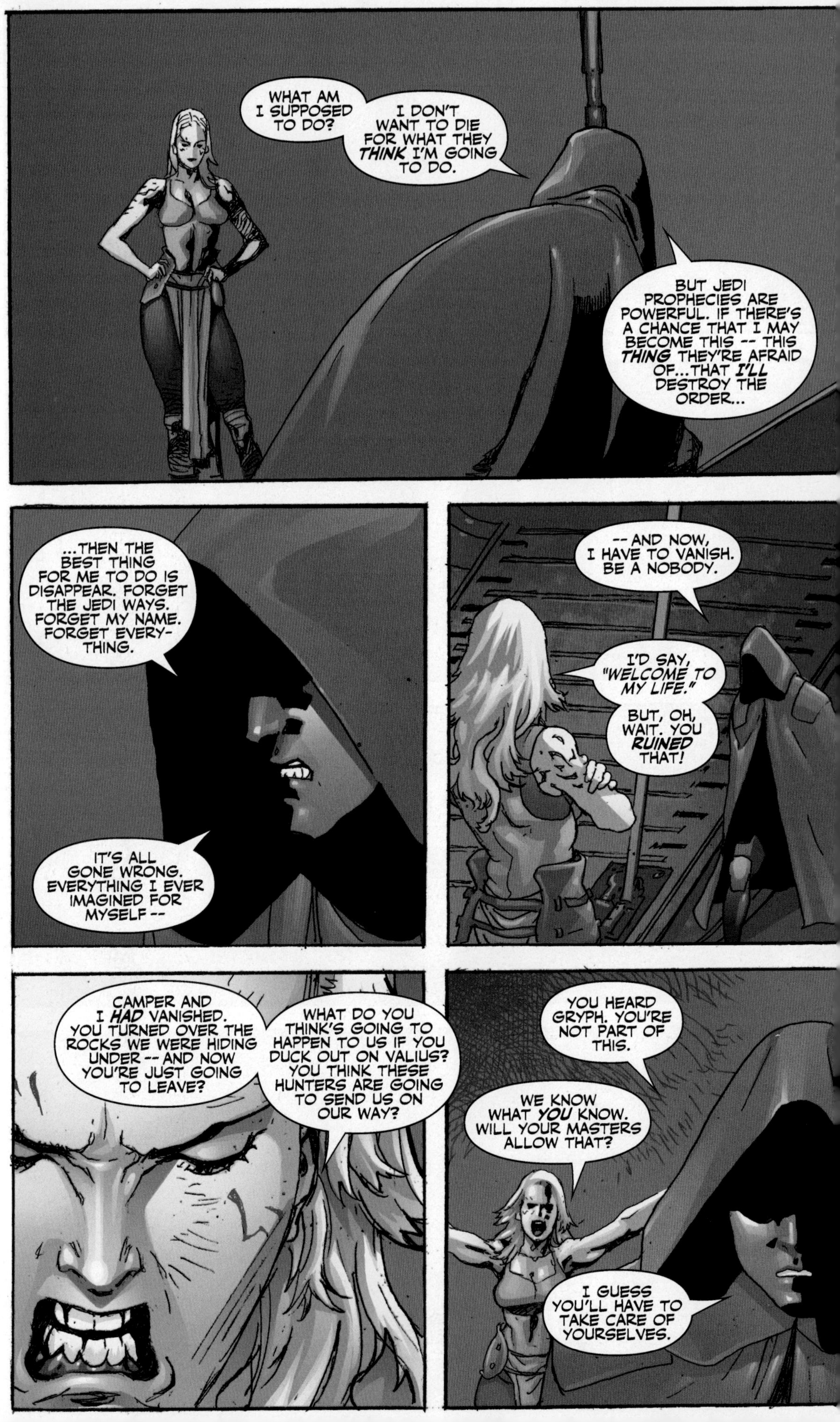
WHAT AM I SUPPOSED TO DO?
I DON'T WANT TO DIE FOR WHAT THEY THINK I'M GOING TO DO.
BUT JEDI PROPHECIES ARE POWERFUL. IF THERE'S A CHANCE THAT I MAY BECOME THIS -- THIS THING THEY'RE AFRAID OF...THAT I'LL DESTROY THE ORDER...
...THEN THE BEST THING FOR ME TO DO IS DISAPPEAR. FORGET THE JEDI WAYS. FORGET MY NAME. FORGET EVERY-THING.
IT'S ALL GONE WRONG. EVERYTHING I EVER IMAGINED FOR MYSELF --
-- AND NOW, I HAVE TO VANISH. BE A NOBODY.
I'D SAY, "WELCOME TO MY LIFE."
BUT, OH, WAIT. YOU RUINED THAT!
CAMPER AND I HAD VANISHED. YOU TURNED OVER THE ROCKS WE WERE HIDING UNDER -- AND NOW YOU'RE JUST GOING TO LEAVE?
WHAT DO YOU THINK'S GOING TO HAPPEN TO US IF YOU DUCK OUT ON VALIUS? YOU THINK THESE HUNTERS ARE GOING TO SEND US ON OUR WAY?
YOU HEARD GRYPH. YOU'RE NOT PART OF THIS.
WE KNOW WHAT YOU KNOW. WILL YOUR MASTERS ALLOW THAT?
I GUESS YOU'LL HAVE TO TAKE CARE OF YOURSELVES.

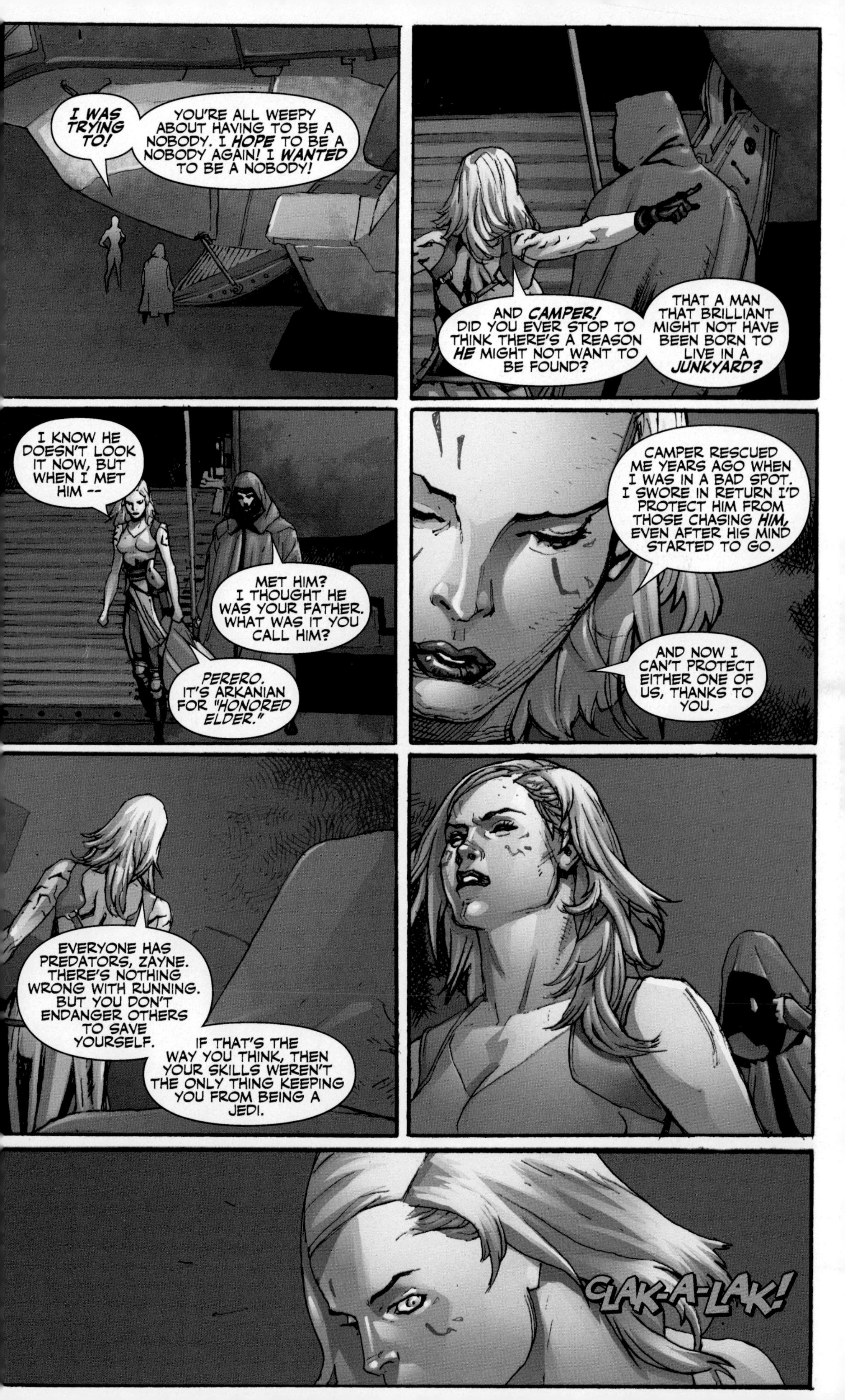

I WAS TRYING TO!
YOU'RE ALL WEEPY ABOUT HAVING TO BE A NOBODY. I HOPE TO BE A NOBODY AGAIN! I WANTED TO BE A NOBODY!
AND CAMPER! DID YOU EVER STOP TO THINK THERE'S A REASON HE MIGHT NOT WANT TO BE FOUND?
THAT A MAN THAT BRILLIANT MIGHT NOT HAVE BEEN BORN TO LIVE IN A JUNKYARD?
I KNOW HE DOESN'T LOOK IT NOW, BUT WHEN I MET HIM --
MET HIM? I THOUGHT HE WAS YOUR FATHER. WHAT WAS IT YOU CALL HIM?
PERERO. IT'S ARKANIAN FOR "HONORED ELDER."
CAMPER RESCUED ME YEARS AGO WHEN I WAS IN A BAD SPOT. I SWORE IN RETURN I'D PROTECT HIM FROM THOSE CHASING HIM, EVEN AFTER HIS MIND STARTED TO GO.
AND NOW I CAN'T PROTECT EITHER ONE OF US, THANKS TO YOU.
EVERYONE HAS PREDATORS, ZAYNE. THERE'S NOTHING WRONG WITH RUNNING. BUT YOU DON'T ENDANGER OTHERS TO SAVE YOURSELF.
IF THAT'S THE WAY YOU THINK, THEN YOUR SKILLS WEREN'T THE ONLY THING KEEPING YOU FROM BEING A JEDI.
CLAK-A-LAK!

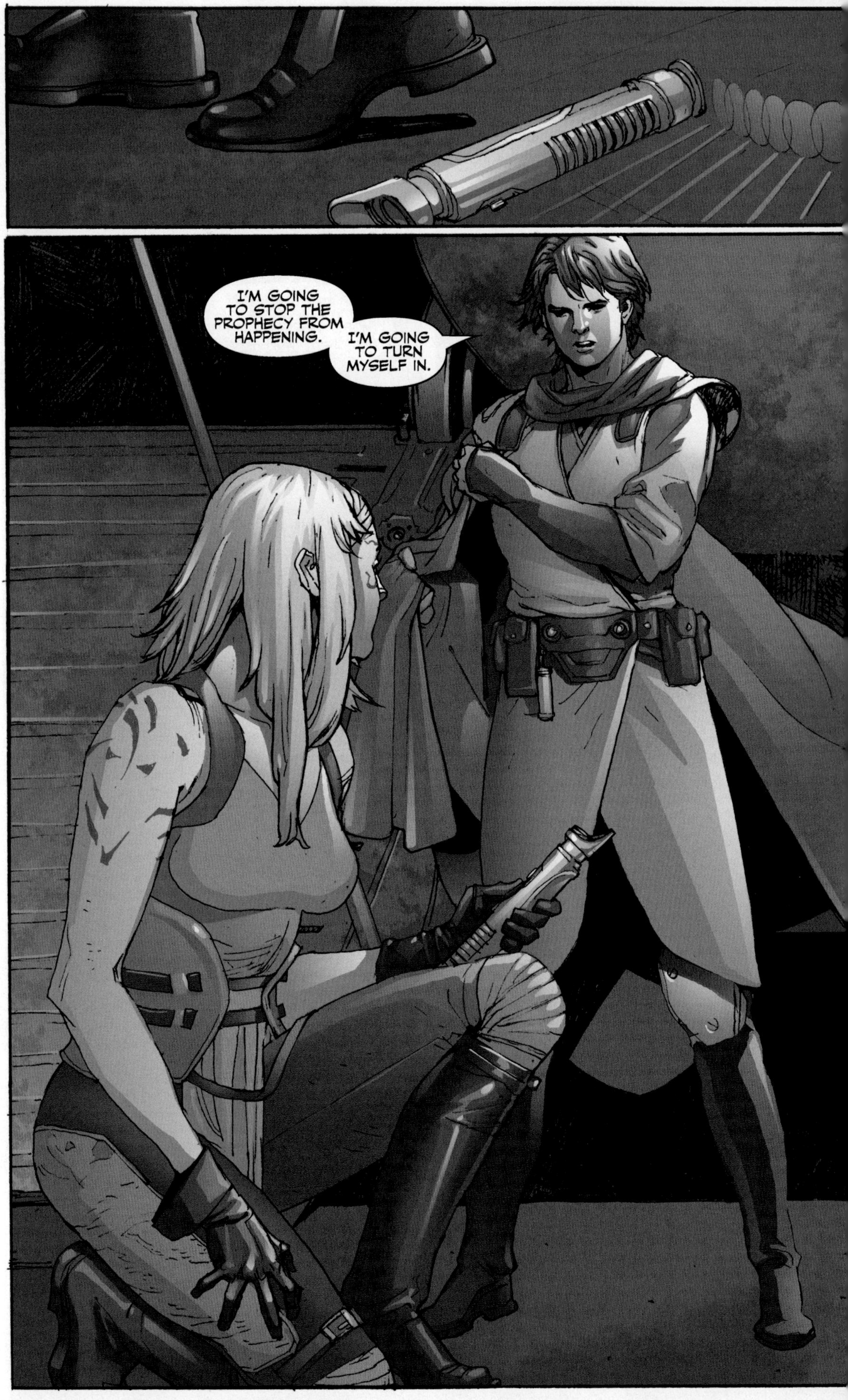
I'M GOING TO STOP THE PROPHECY FROM HAPPENING.
I'M GOING TO TURN MYSELF IN.

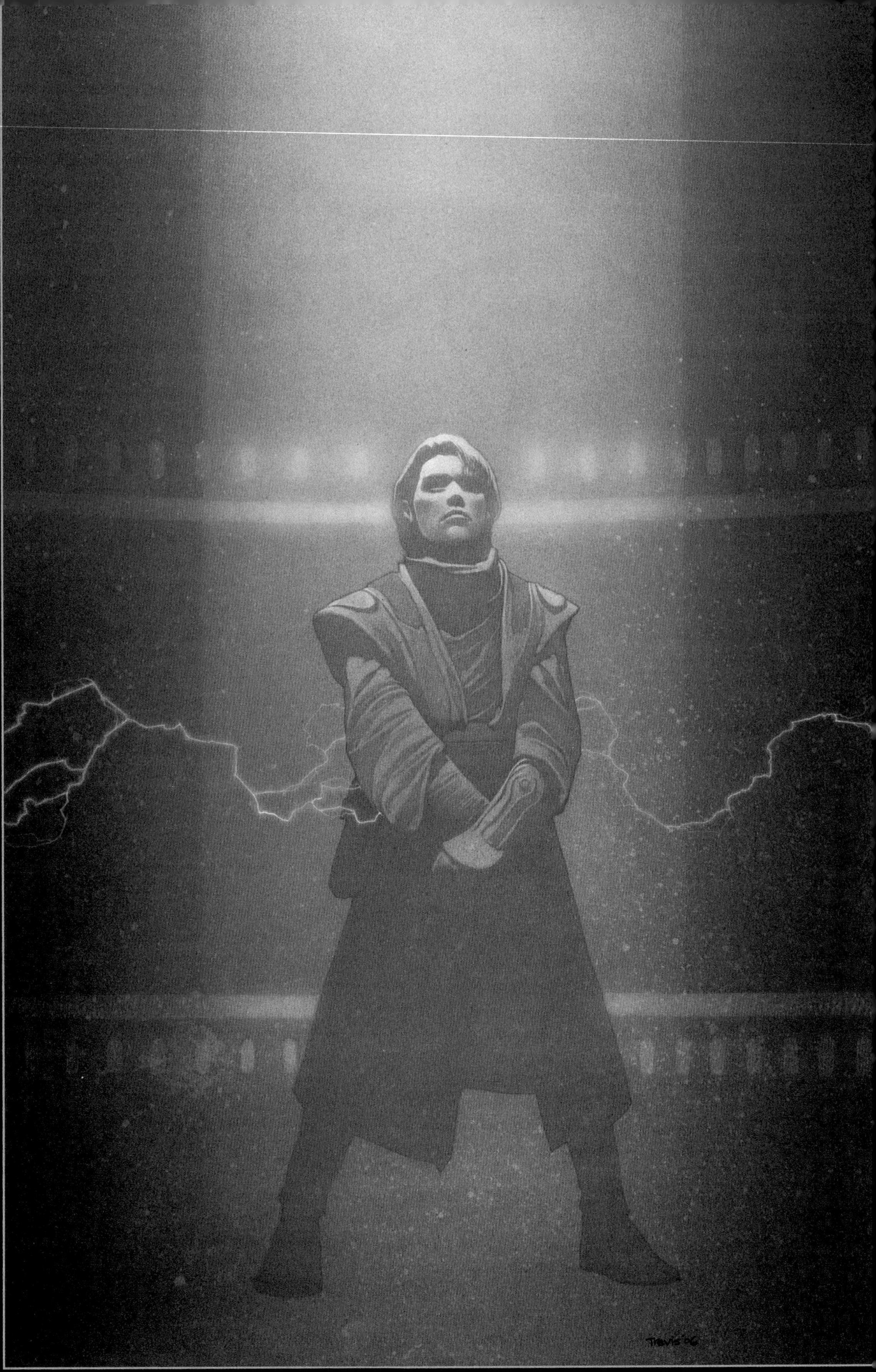

STAR WARS: KNIGHTS OF THE OLD REPUBLIC #6 **— "COMMENCEMENT, PART 6 (OF SIX)"**

WRITER: JOHN JACKSON MILLER • ARTIST: BRIAN CHING • COLORIST: MICHAEL ATIYEH • LETTERER: MICHAEL HEISLER
ASSISTANT EDITOR: DAVE MARSHALL • EDITOR: JEREMY BARLOW • COVER ARTIST: TRAVIS CHAREST

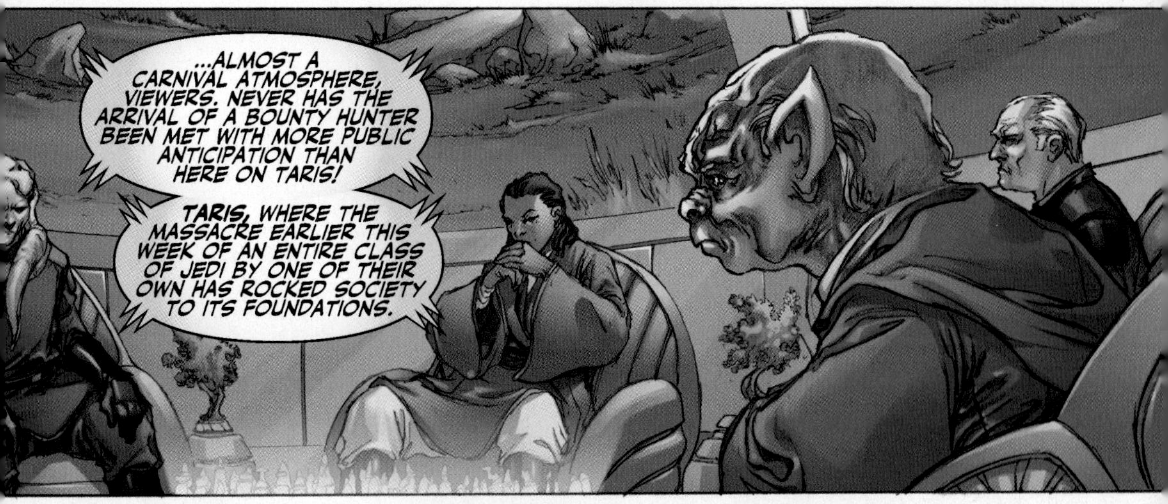
...ALMOST A CARNIVAL ATMOSPHERE, VIEWERS. NEVER HAS THE ARRIVAL OF A BOUNTY HUNTER BEEN MET WITH MORE PUBLIC ANTICIPATION THAN HERE ON TARIS!
TARIS, WHERE THE MASSACRE EARLIER THIS WEEK OF AN ENTIRE CLASS OF JEDI BY ONE OF THEIR OWN HAS ROCKED SOCIETY TO ITS FOUNDATIONS.

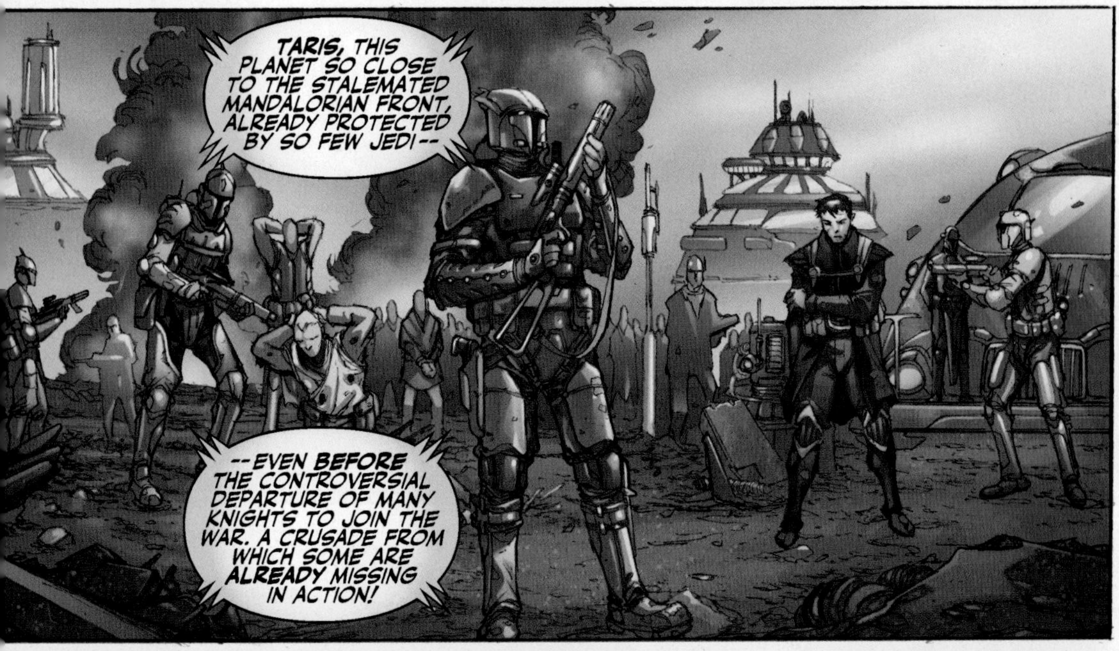
TARIS, THIS PLANET SO CLOSE TO THE STALEMATED MANDALORIAN FRONT, ALREADY PROTECTED BY SO FEW JEDI--
--EVEN BEFORE THE CONTROVERSIAL DEPARTURE OF MANY KNIGHTS TO JOIN THE WAR. A CRUSADE FROM WHICH SOME ARE ALREADY MISSING IN ACTION!

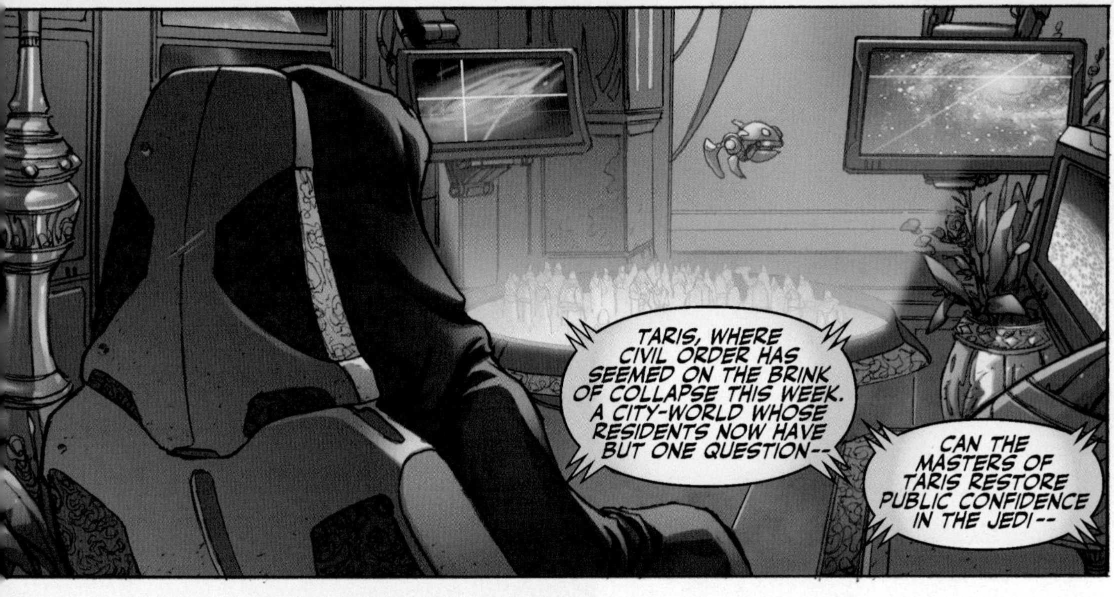
TARIS, WHERE CIVIL ORDER HAS SEEMED ON THE BRINK OF COLLAPSE THIS WEEK. A CITY-WORLD WHOSE RESIDENTS NOW HAVE BUT ONE QUESTION--
CAN THE MASTERS OF TARIS RESTORE PUBLIC CONFIDENCE IN THE JEDI--

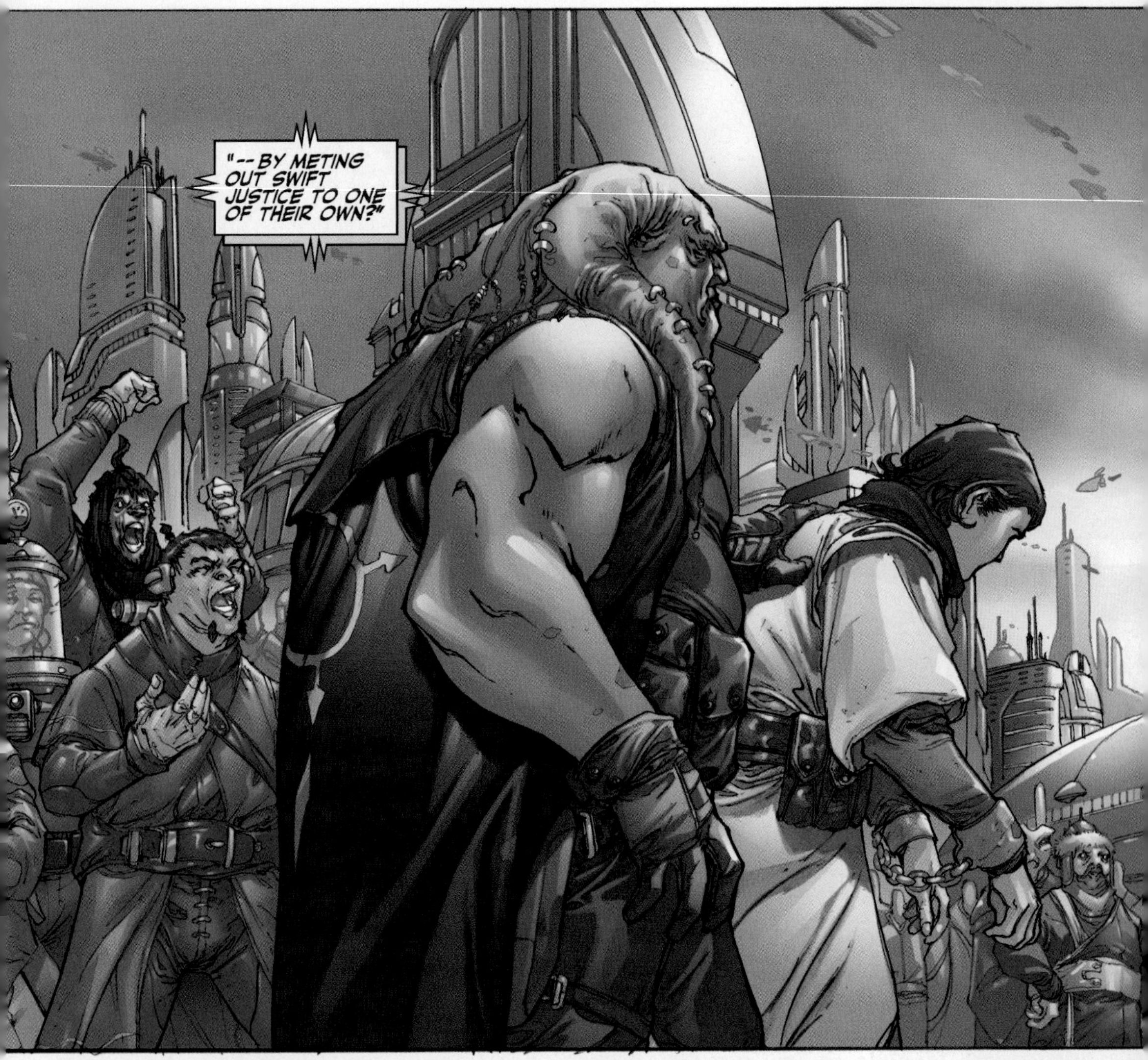
"-- BY METING OUT SWIFT JUSTICE TO ONE OF THEIR OWN?"

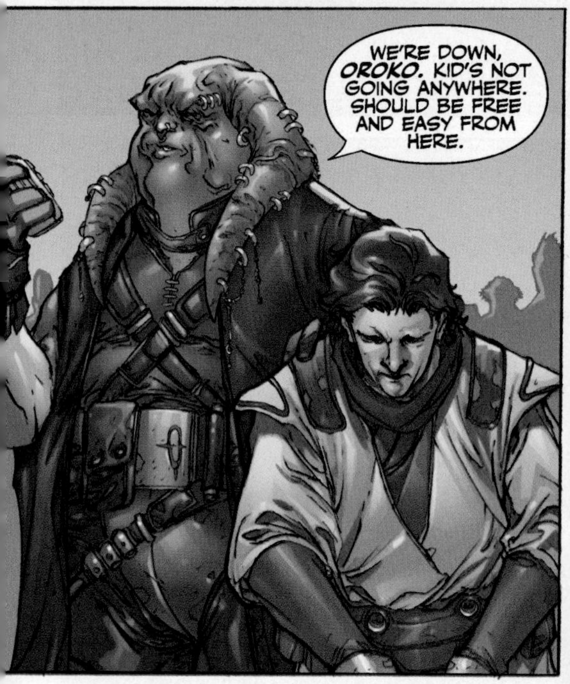
WE'RE DOWN, OROKO. KID'S NOT GOING ANYWHERE. SHOULD BE FREE AND EASY FROM HERE.

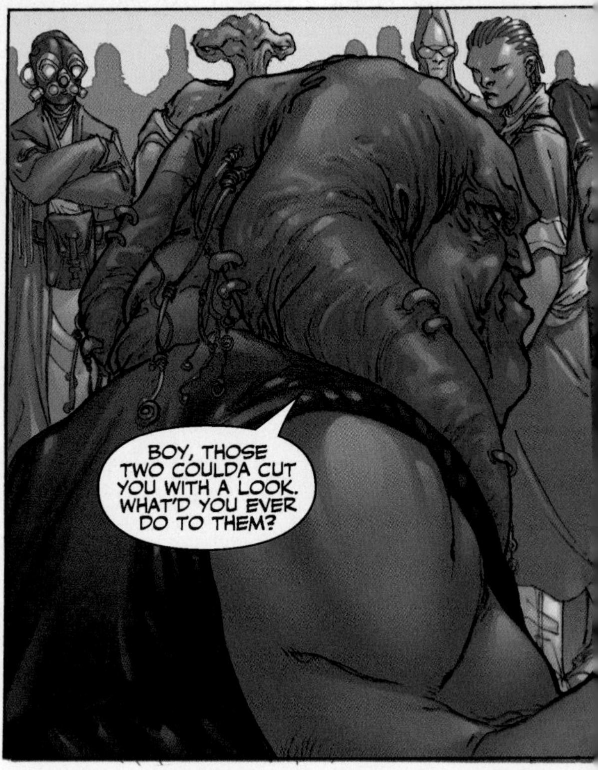
BOY, THOSE TWO COULDA CUT YOU WITH A LOOK. WHAT'D YOU EVER DO TO THEM?

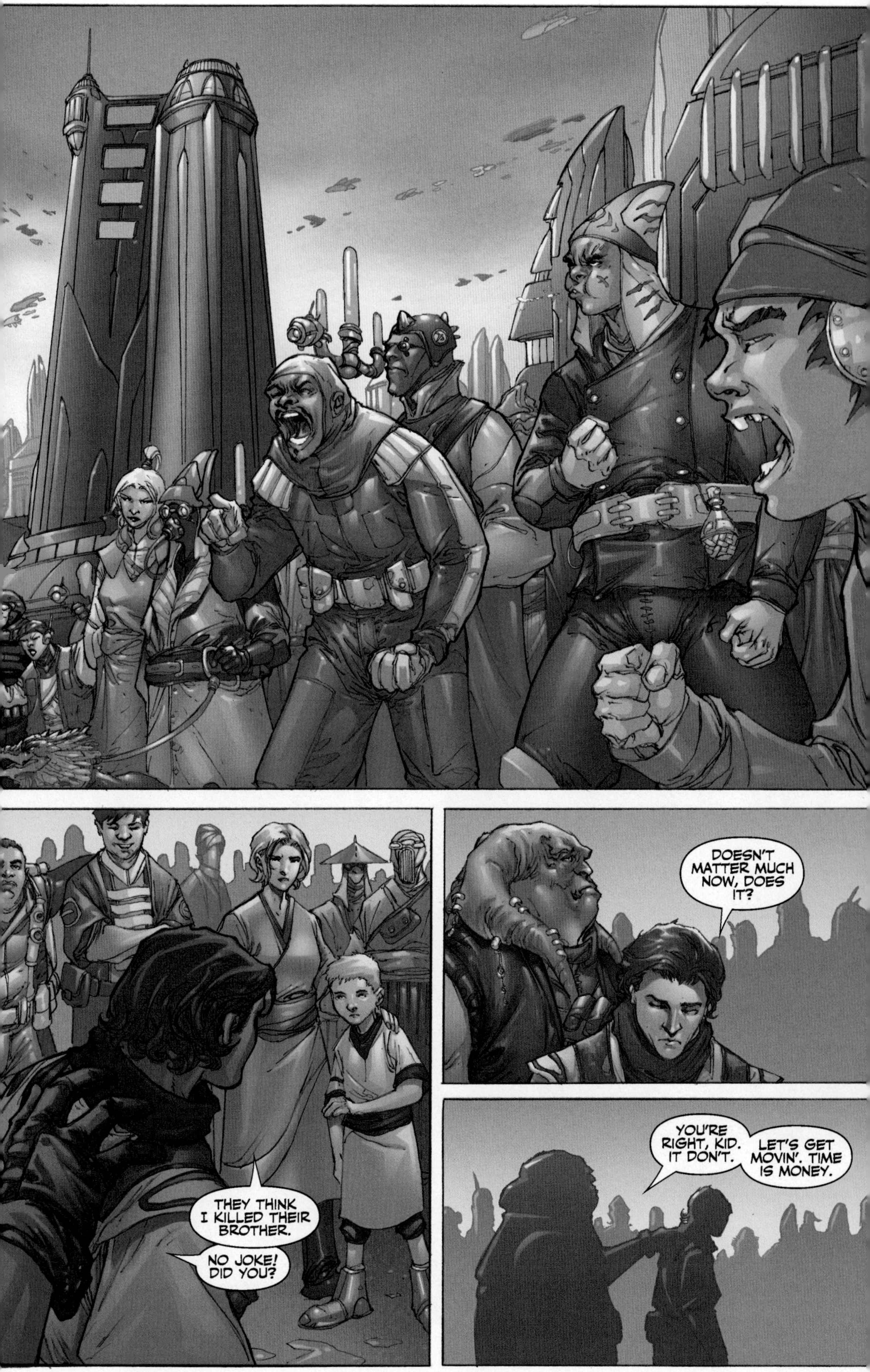
THEY THINK I KILLED THEIR BROTHER.
NO JOKE! DID YOU?
DOESN'T MATTER MUCH NOW, DOES IT?
YOU'RE RIGHT, KID. IT DON'T.
LET'S GET MOVIN'. TIME IS MONEY.

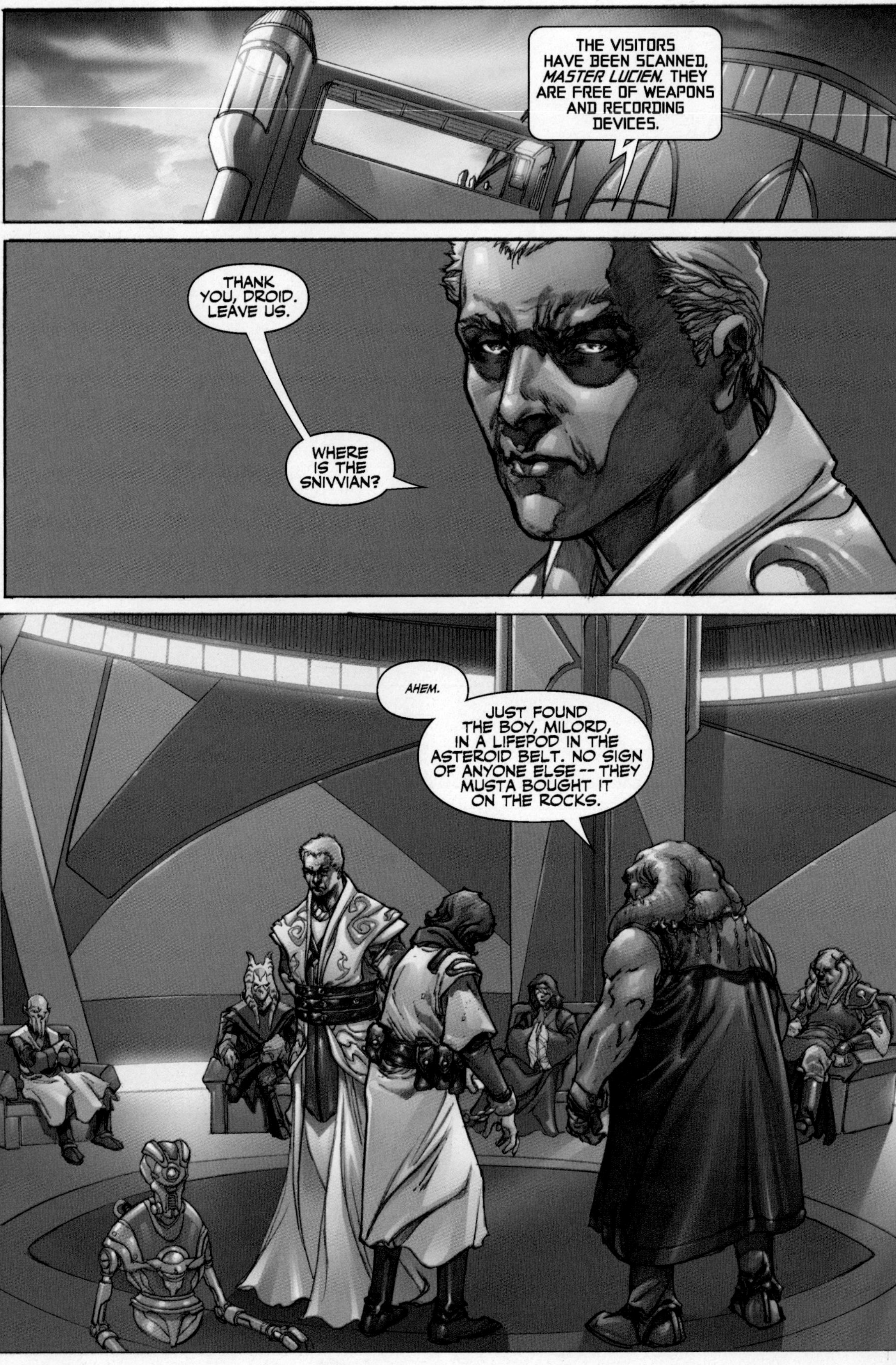

THE VISITORS HAVE BEEN SCANNED, MASTER LUCIEN. THEY ARE FREE OF WEAPONS AND RECORDING DEVICES.
THANK YOU, DROID. LEAVE US.
WHERE IS THE SNIVVIAN?
AHEM.
JUST FOUND THE BOY, MILORD, IN A LIFEPOD IN THE ASTEROID BELT. NO SIGN OF ANYONE ELSE -- THEY MUSTA BOUGHT IT ON THE ROCKS.

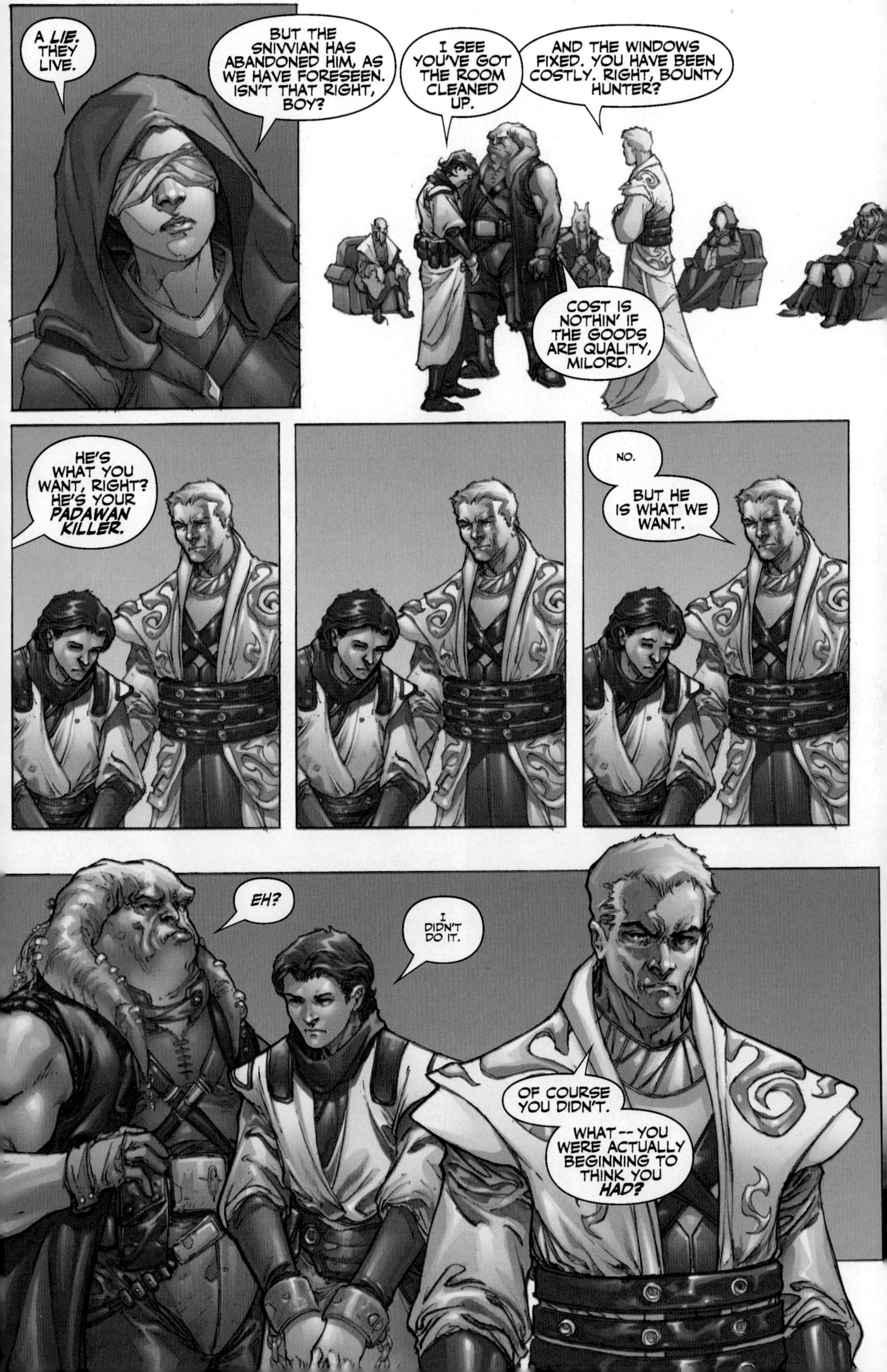
A LIE. THEY LIVE.
BUT THE SNIVVIAN HAS ABANDONED HIM, AS WE HAVE FORESEEN. ISN'T THAT RIGHT, BOY?
I SEE YOU'VE GOT THE ROOM CLEANED UP.
AND THE WINDOWS FIXED. YOU HAVE BEEN COSTLY. RIGHT, BOUNTY HUNTER?
COST IS NOTHIN' IF THE GOODS ARE QUALITY, MILORD.
HE'S WHAT YOU WANT, RIGHT? HE'S YOUR PADAWAN KILLER.
NO.
BUT HE IS WHAT WE WANT.
EH?
I DIDN'T DO IT.
OF COURSE YOU DIDN'T.
WHAT -- YOU WERE ACTUALLY BEGINNING TO THINK YOU HAD?

FOR A MOMENT. THEN I REMEMBERED *ELBEE.*

ELBEE SHOWED ME YOUR MEDITATION ON THE *ROGUE MOON.* I HEARD YOU TALK ABOUT THIS VISION OF YOURS, THE GREAT DESTROYER.

WEARING A SPACESUIT AND FACEMASK LIKE ONE OF *OURS.*

YES, *ELBEE.* REMARKABLE INSIGHT YOU SHOWED THERE, MY PADAWAN.

DON'T CALL ME THAT.

WHAT, WERE YOU KNIGHTED WITHOUT MY KNOWING?

STOP PLAYING GAMES.

I DON'T NEED DETAILS, GOOD PEOPLE, I JUST NEED MY *MONEY.* IF WE CAN--

OH, BUT KNOWLEDGE HAS VALUE, TOO, *CAPTAIN YING.*

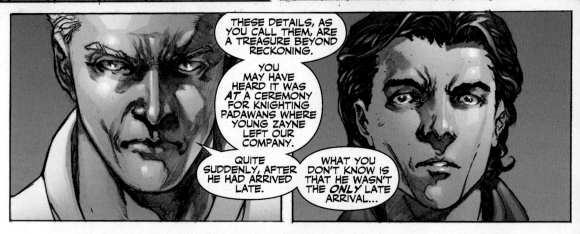

THESE DETAILS, AS YOU CALL THEM, ARE A TREASURE BEYOND RECKONING.

YOU MAY HAVE HEARD IT WAS *AT A CEREMONY* FOR KNIGHTING PADAWANS WHERE YOUNG ZAYNE LEFT OUR COMPANY.

QUITE SUDDENLY, AFTER HE HAD ARRIVED LATE.

WHAT YOU DON'T KNOW IS THAT HE WASN'T THE *ONLY* LATE ARRIVAL...

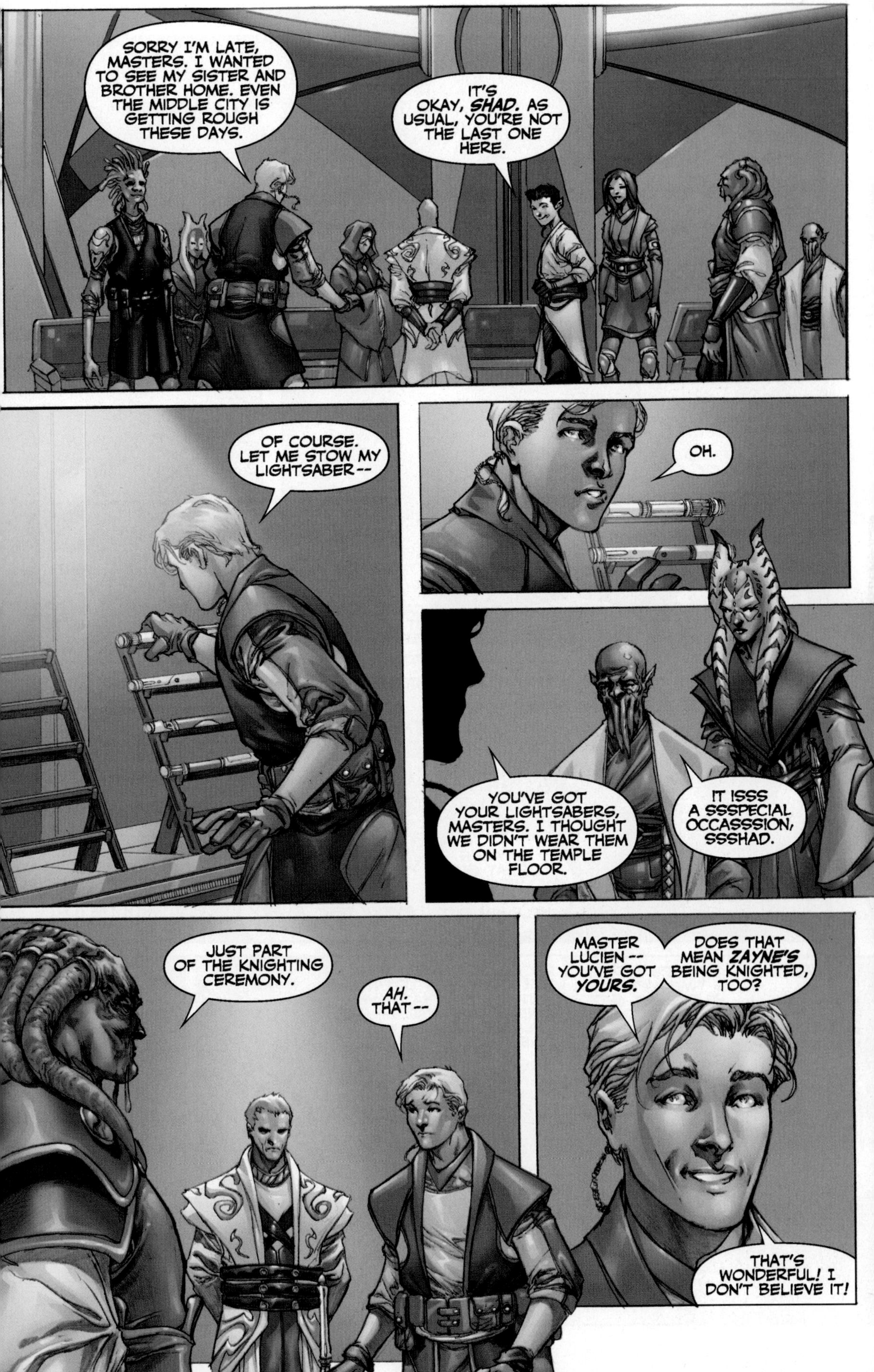
SORRY I'M LATE, MASTERS. I WANTED TO SEE MY SISTER AND BROTHER HOME. EVEN THE MIDDLE CITY IS GETTING ROUGH THESE DAYS.
IT'S OKAY, SHAD. AS USUAL, YOU'RE NOT THE LAST ONE HERE.
OF COURSE. LET ME STOW MY LIGHTSABER--
OH.
YOU'VE GOT YOUR LIGHTSABERS, MASTERS. I THOUGHT WE DIDN'T WEAR THEM ON THE TEMPLE FLOOR.
IT ISSS A SSSPECIAL OCCASSSION, SSSHAD.
JUST PART OF THE KNIGHTING CEREMONY.
AH. THAT--
MASTER LUCIEN -- YOU'VE GOT YOURS.
DOES THAT MEAN ZAYNE'S BEING KNIGHTED, TOO?
THAT'S WONDERFUL! I DON'T BELIEVE IT!

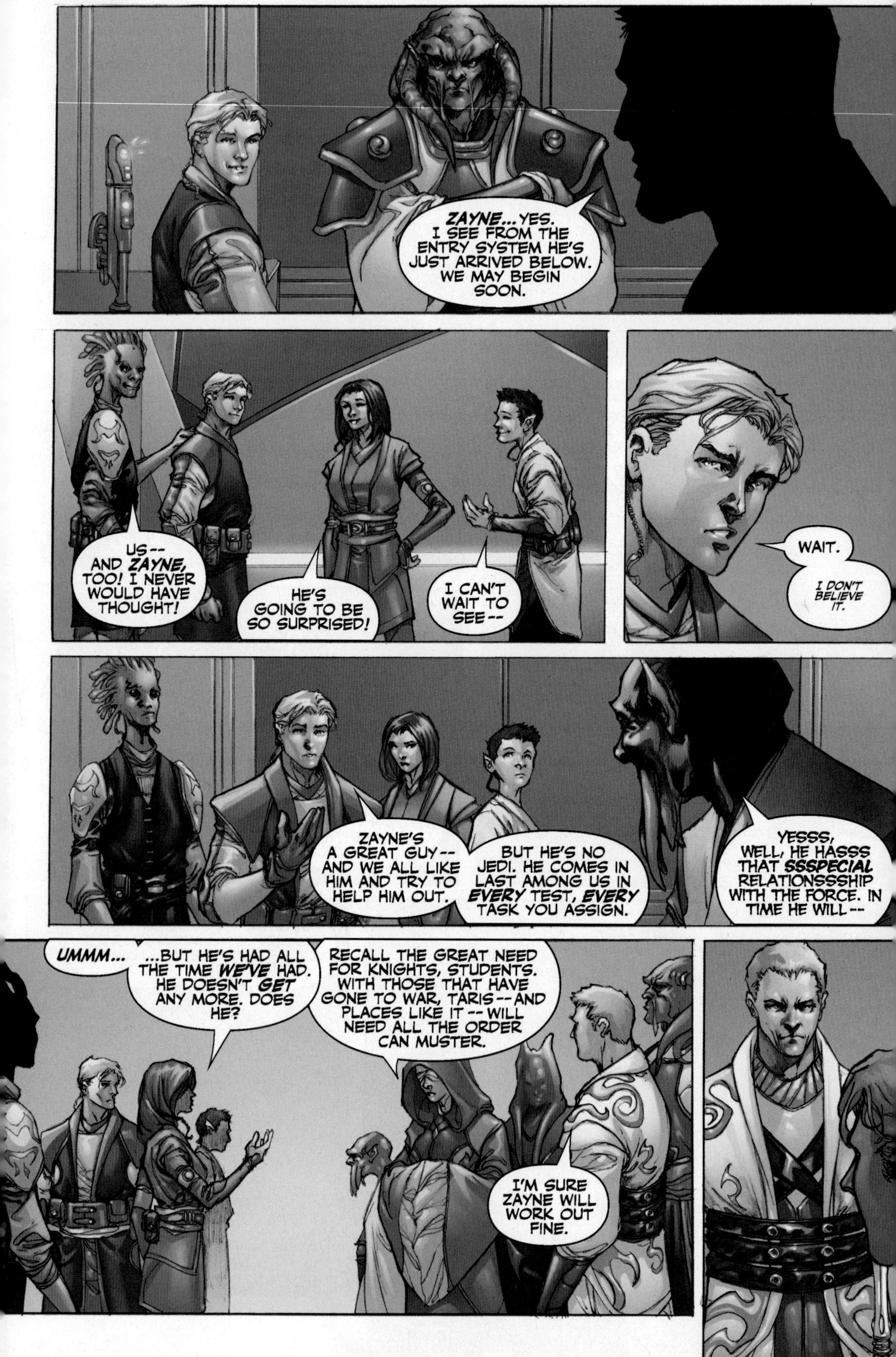
ZAYNE... YES. I SEE FROM THE ENTRY SYSTEM HE'S JUST ARRIVED BELOW. WE MAY BEGIN SOON.
US -- AND ZAYNE, TOO! I NEVER WOULD HAVE THOUGHT!
HE'S GOING TO BE SO SURPRISED!
I CAN'T WAIT TO SEE --
WAIT.
I DON'T BELIEVE IT.
ZAYNE'S A GREAT GUY -- AND WE ALL LIKE HIM AND TRY TO HELP HIM OUT.
BUT HE'S NO JEDI. HE COMES IN LAST AMONG US IN EVERY TEST, EVERY TASK YOU ASSIGN.
YESSS, WELL, HE HASSS THAT SSSPECIAL RELATIONSSSHIP WITH THE FORCE. IN TIME HE WILL --
UMMM...
...BUT HE'S HAD ALL THE TIME WE'VE HAD. HE DOESN'T GET ANY MORE. DOES HE?
RECALL THE GREAT NEED FOR KNIGHTS, STUDENTS. WITH THOSE THAT HAVE GONE TO WAR, TARIS -- AND PLACES LIKE IT -- WILL NEED ALL THE ORDER CAN MUSTER.
I'M SURE ZAYNE WILL WORK OUT FINE.

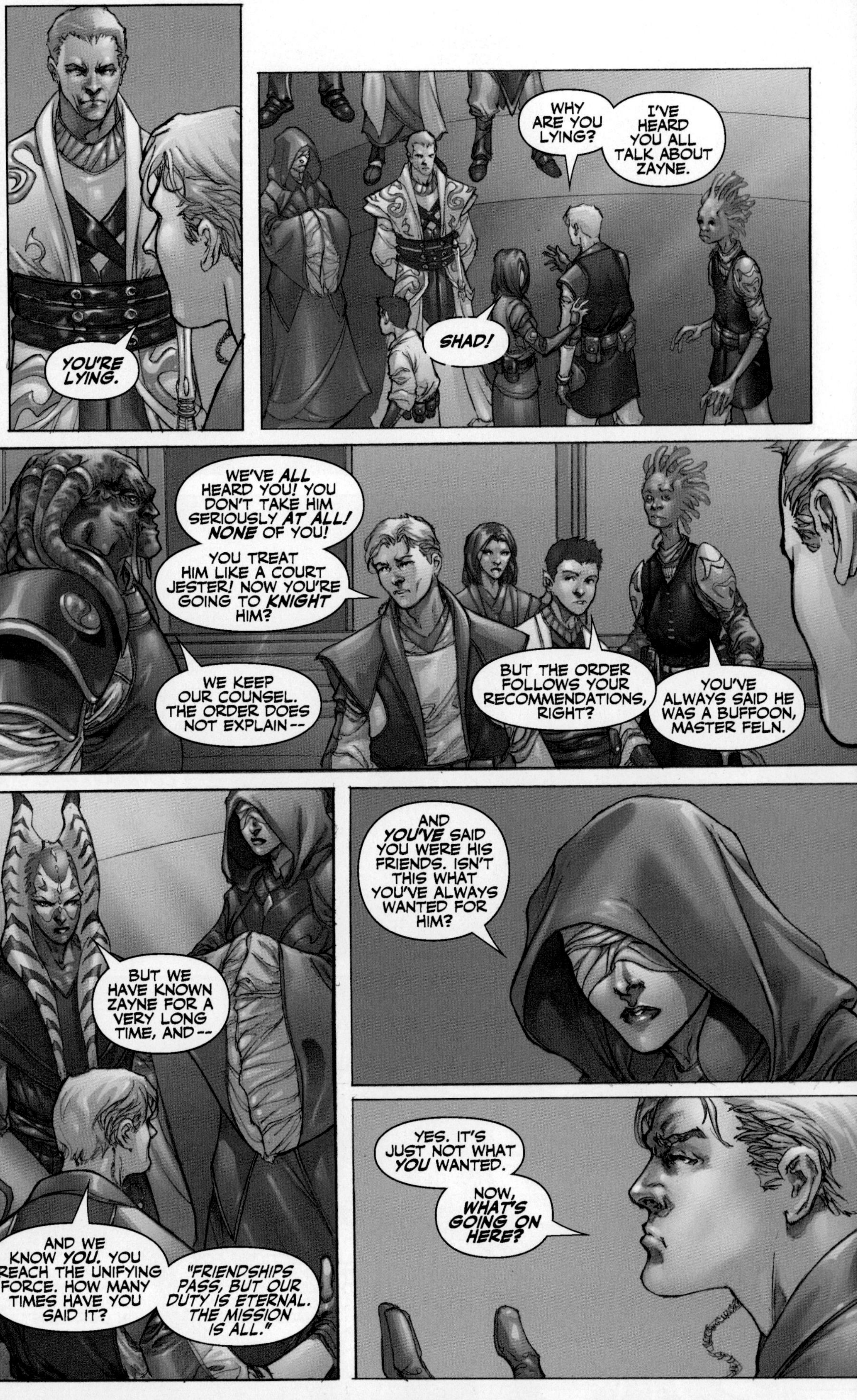

YOU'RE LYING.
WHY ARE YOU LYING?
I'VE HEARD YOU ALL TALK ABOUT ZAYNE.
SHAD!
WE'VE ALL HEARD YOU! YOU DON'T TAKE HIM SERIOUSLY AT ALL! NONE OF YOU!
YOU TREAT HIM LIKE A COURT JESTER! NOW YOU'RE GOING TO KNIGHT HIM?
WE KEEP OUR COUNSEL. THE ORDER DOES NOT EXPLAIN--
BUT THE ORDER FOLLOWS YOUR RECOMMENDATIONS, RIGHT?
YOU'VE ALWAYS SAID HE WAS A BUFFOON, MASTER FELN.
BUT WE HAVE KNOWN ZAYNE FOR A VERY LONG TIME, AND--
AND WE KNOW YOU. YOU PREACH THE UNIFYING FORCE. HOW MANY TIMES HAVE YOU SAID IT?
"FRIENDSHIPS PASS, BUT OUR DUTY IS ETERNAL. THE MISSION IS ALL."
AND YOU'VE SAID YOU WERE HIS FRIENDS. ISN'T THIS WHAT YOU'VE ALWAYS WANTED FOR HIM?
YES. IT'S JUST NOT WHAT YOU WANTED.
NOW, WHAT'S GOING ON HERE?

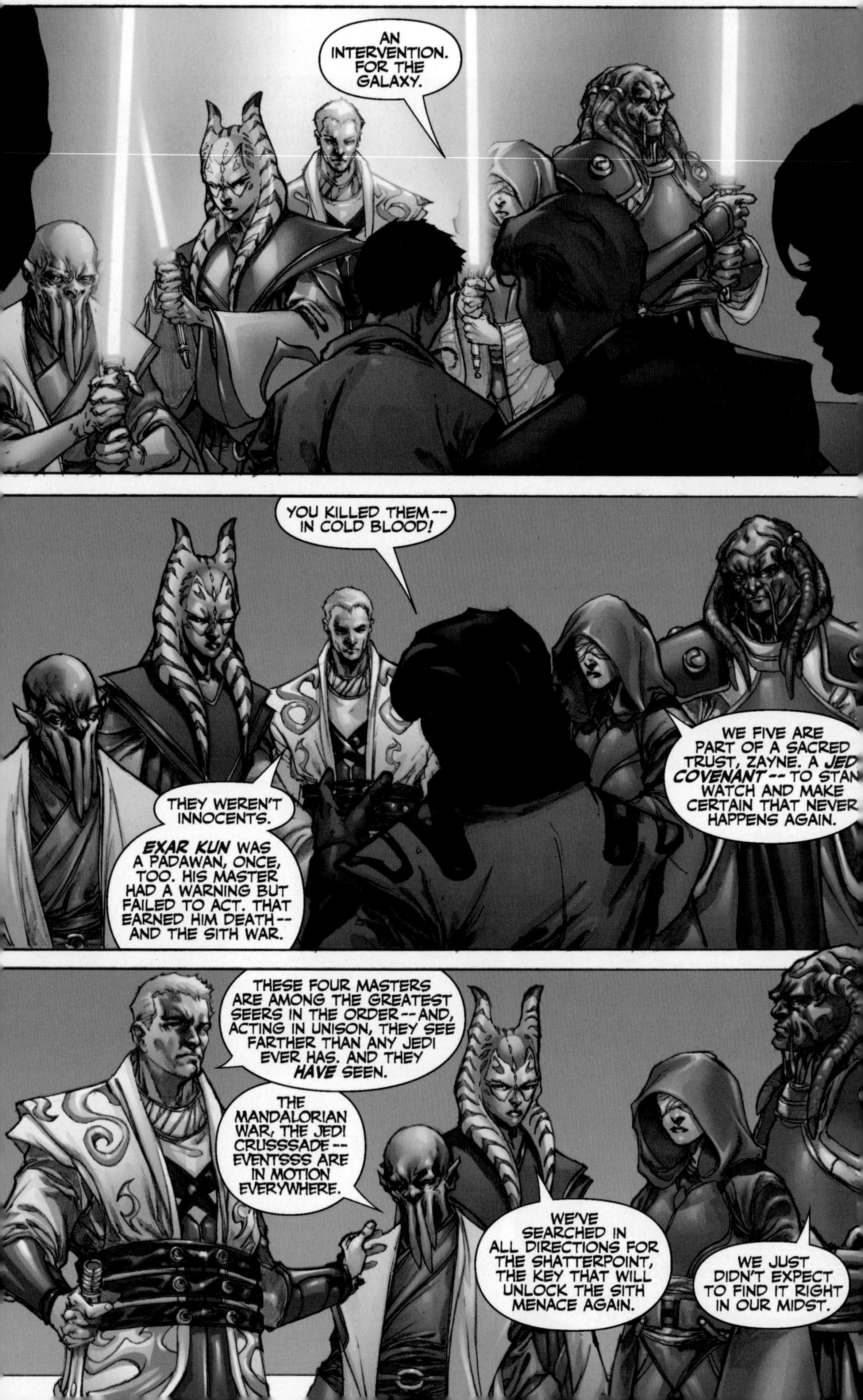
AN INTERVENTION. FOR THE GALAXY.
YOU KILLED THEM-- IN COLD BLOOD!
THEY WEREN'T INNOCENTS.
EXAR KUN WAS A PADAWAN, ONCE, TOO. HIS MASTER HAD A WARNING BUT FAILED TO ACT. THAT EARNED HIM DEATH-- AND THE SITH WAR.
WE FIVE ARE PART OF A SACRED TRUST, ZAYNE. A JED COVENANT-- TO STAN WATCH AND MAKE CERTAIN THAT NEVER HAPPENS AGAIN.
THESE FOUR MASTERS ARE AMONG THE GREATEST SEERS IN THE ORDER--AND, ACTING IN UNISON, THEY SEE FARTHER THAN ANY JEDI EVER HAS. AND THEY HAVE SEEN.
THE MANDALORIAN WAR, THE JEDI CRUSSSADE-- EVENTSSS ARE IN MOTION EVERYWHERE.
WE'VE SEARCHED IN ALL DIRECTIONS FOR THE SHATTERPOINT, THE KEY THAT WILL UNLOCK THE SITH MENACE AGAIN.
WE JUST DIDN'T EXPECT TO FIND IT RIGHT IN OUR MIDST.

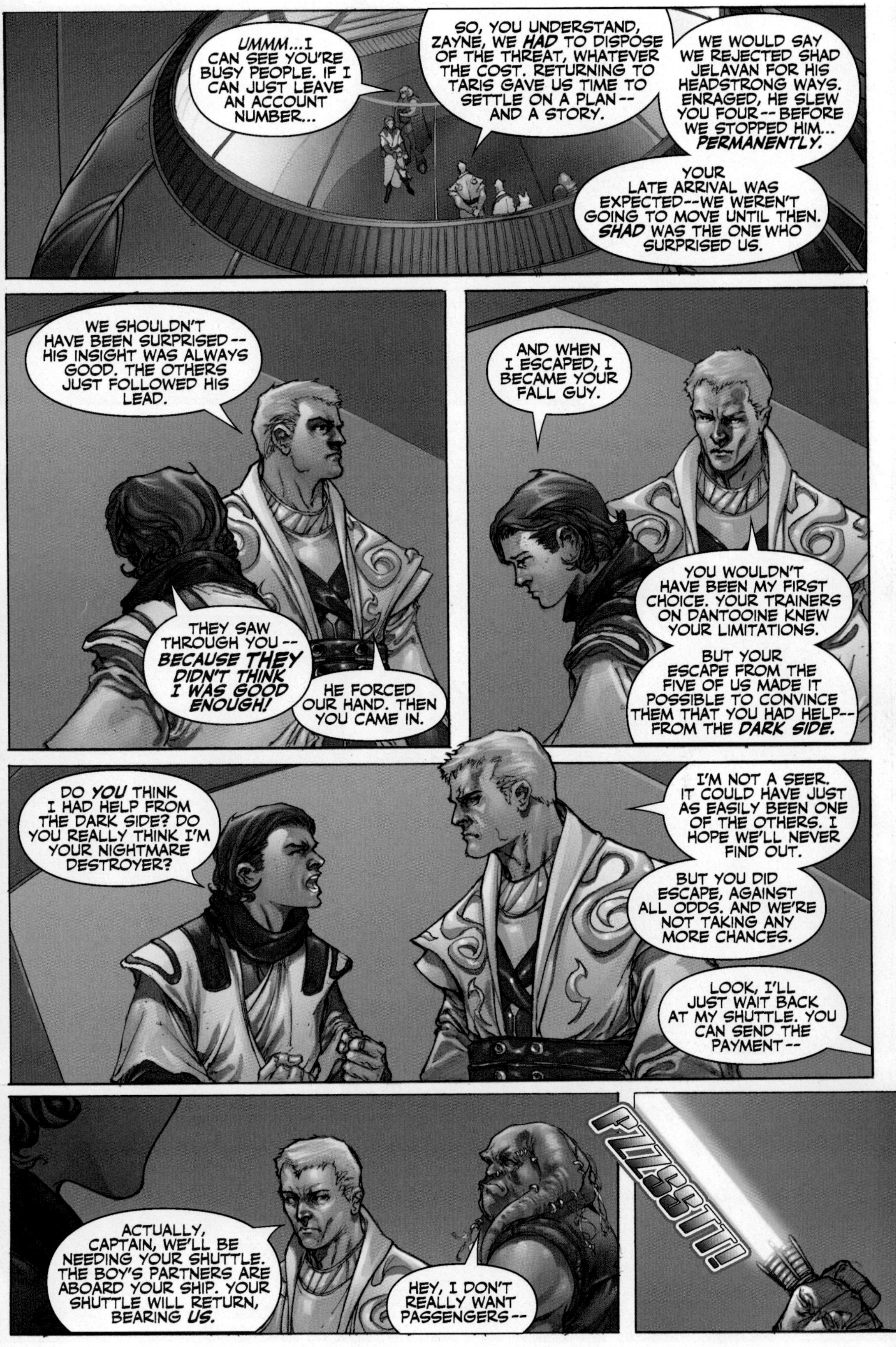
UMMM...I CAN SEE YOU'RE BUSY PEOPLE. IF I CAN JUST LEAVE AN ACCOUNT NUMBER...
SO, YOU UNDERSTAND, ZAYNE, WE HAD TO DISPOSE OF THE THREAT, WHATEVER THE COST. RETURNING TO TARIS GAVE US TIME TO SETTLE ON A PLAN-- AND A STORY.
WE WOULD SAY WE REJECTED SHAD JELAVAN FOR HIS HEADSTRONG WAYS. ENRAGED, HE SLEW YOU FOUR--BEFORE WE STOPPED HIM... PERMANENTLY.
YOUR LATE ARRIVAL WAS EXPECTED--WE WEREN'T GOING TO MOVE UNTIL THEN. SHAD WAS THE ONE WHO SURPRISED US.
WE SHOULDN'T HAVE BEEN SURPRISED-- HIS INSIGHT WAS ALWAYS GOOD. THE OTHERS JUST FOLLOWED HIS LEAD.
THEY SAW THROUGH YOU-- BECAUSE THEY DIDN'T THINK I WAS GOOD ENOUGH!
HE FORCED OUR HAND. THEN YOU CAME IN.
AND WHEN I ESCAPED, I BECAME YOUR FALL GUY.
YOU WOULDN'T HAVE BEEN MY FIRST CHOICE. YOUR TRAINERS ON DANTOOINE KNEW YOUR LIMITATIONS.
BUT YOUR ESCAPE FROM THE FIVE OF US MADE IT POSSIBLE TO CONVINCE THEM THAT YOU HAD HELP-- FROM THE DARK SIDE.
DO YOU THINK I HAD HELP FROM THE DARK SIDE? DO YOU REALLY THINK I'M YOUR NIGHTMARE DESTROYER?
I'M NOT A SEER. IT COULD HAVE JUST AS EASILY BEEN ONE OF THE OTHERS. I HOPE WE'LL NEVER FIND OUT.
BUT YOU DID ESCAPE, AGAINST ALL ODDS. AND WE'RE NOT TAKING ANY MORE CHANCES.
LOOK, I'LL JUST WAIT BACK AT MY SHUTTLE. YOU CAN SEND THE PAYMENT--
ACTUALLY, CAPTAIN, WE'LL BE NEEDING YOUR SHUTTLE. THE BOY'S PARTNERS ARE ABOARD YOUR SHIP. YOUR SHUTTLE WILL RETURN, BEARING US.
HEY, I DON'T REALLY WANT PASSENGERS--
PZZSSTT!

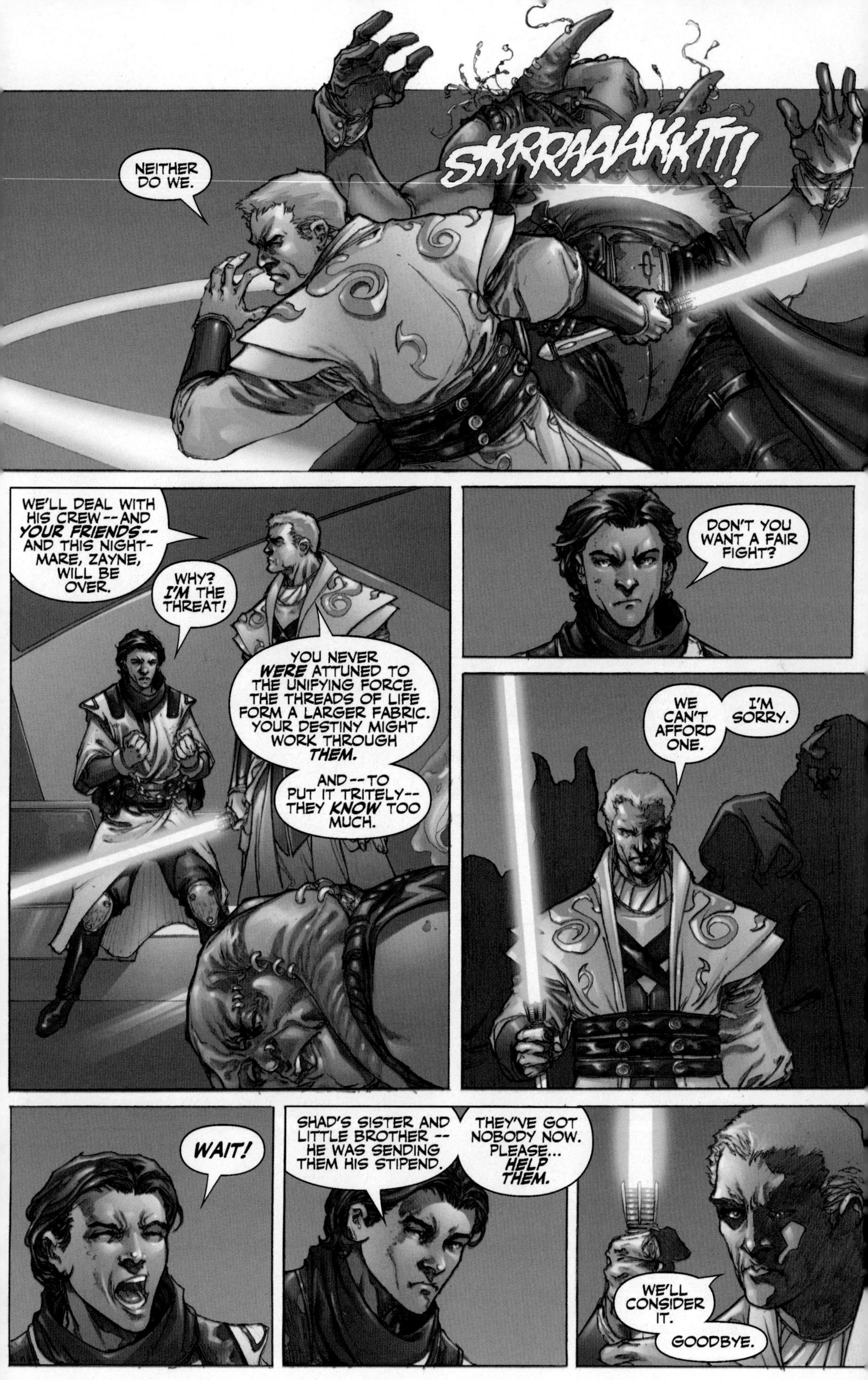

NEITHER DO WE.
SKRRAAAKKT!!
WE'LL DEAL WITH HIS CREW--AND YOUR FRIENDS--AND THIS NIGHT-MARE, ZAYNE, WILL BE OVER.
WHY? I'M THE THREAT!
YOU NEVER WERE ATTUNED TO THE UNIFYING FORCE. THE THREADS OF LIFE FORM A LARGER FABRIC. YOUR DESTINY MIGHT WORK THROUGH THEM.
AND--TO PUT IT TRITELY--THEY KNOW TOO MUCH.
DON'T YOU WANT A FAIR FIGHT?
WE CAN'T AFFORD ONE.
I'M SORRY.
WAIT!
SHAD'S SISTER AND LITTLE BROTHER -- HE WAS SENDING THEM HIS STIPEND.
THEY'VE GOT NOBODY NOW. PLEASE... HELP THEM.
WE'LL CONSIDER IT.
GOODBYE.

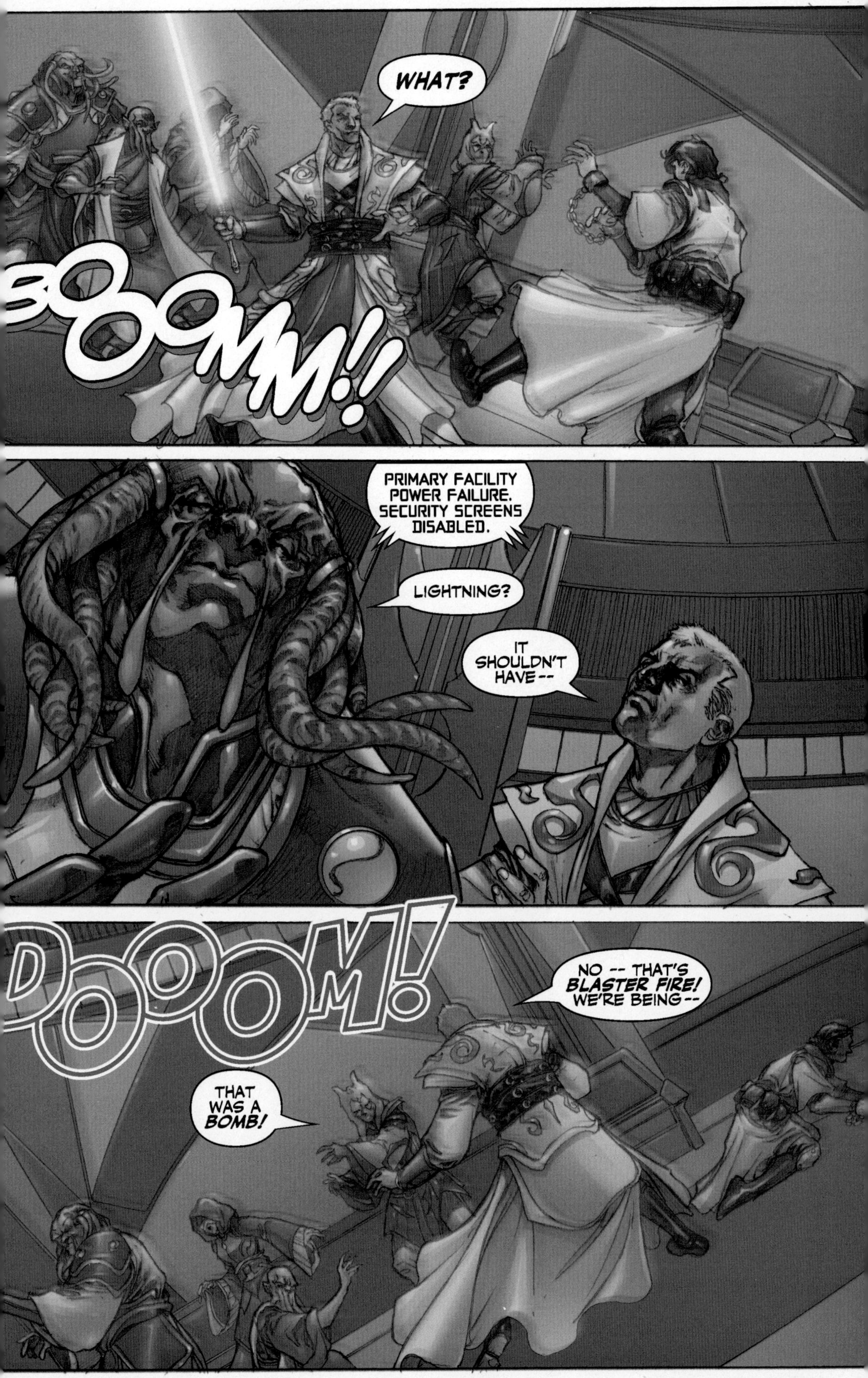
WHAT?
BOOOMM!!
PRIMARY FACILITY POWER FAILURE. SECURITY SCREENS DISABLED.
LIGHTNING?
IT SHOULDN'T HAVE--
DOOOOM!
NO -- THAT'S *BLASTER FIRE!* WE'RE BEING--
THAT WAS A *BOMB!*

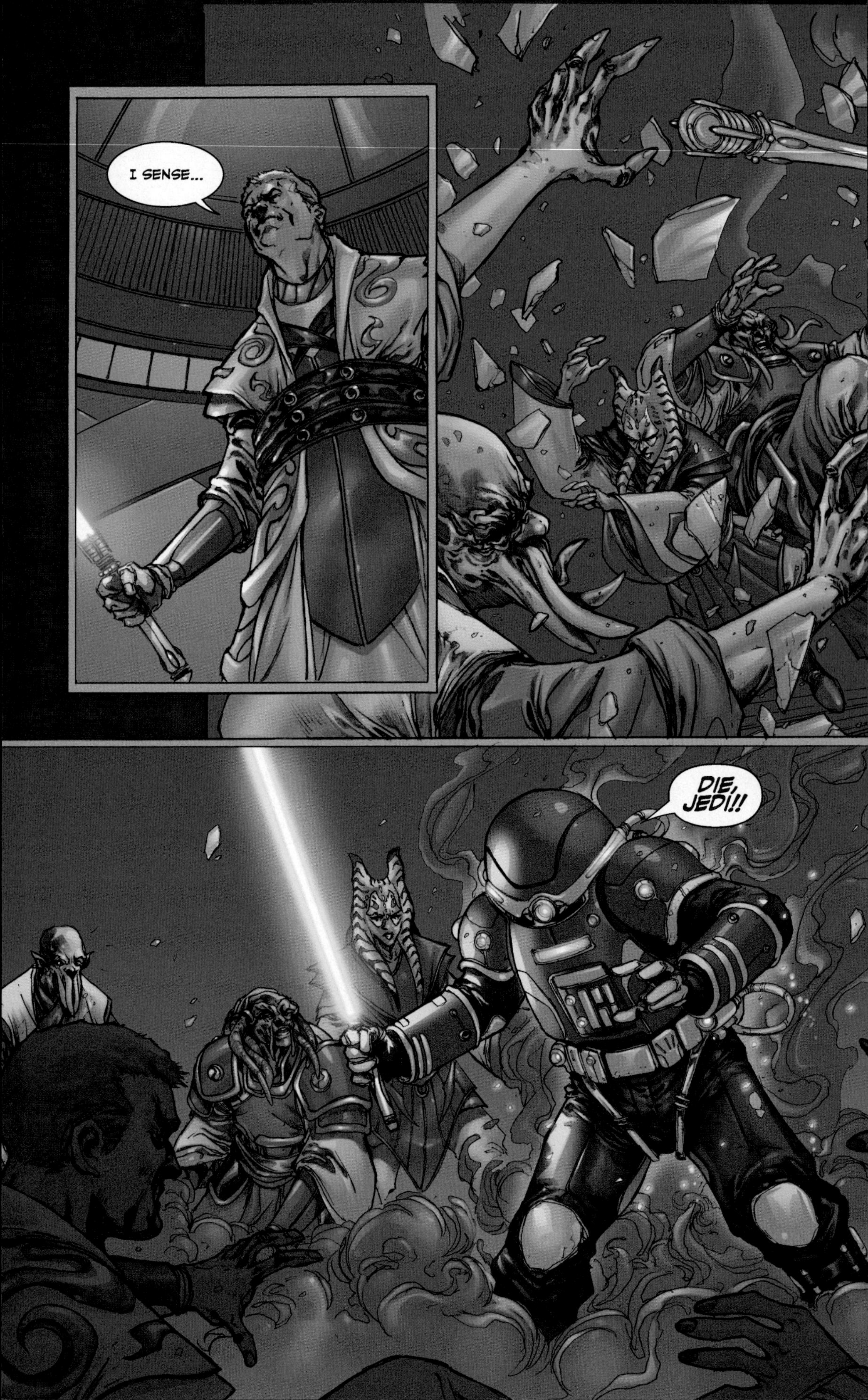
I SENSE...
DIE, JEDI!!

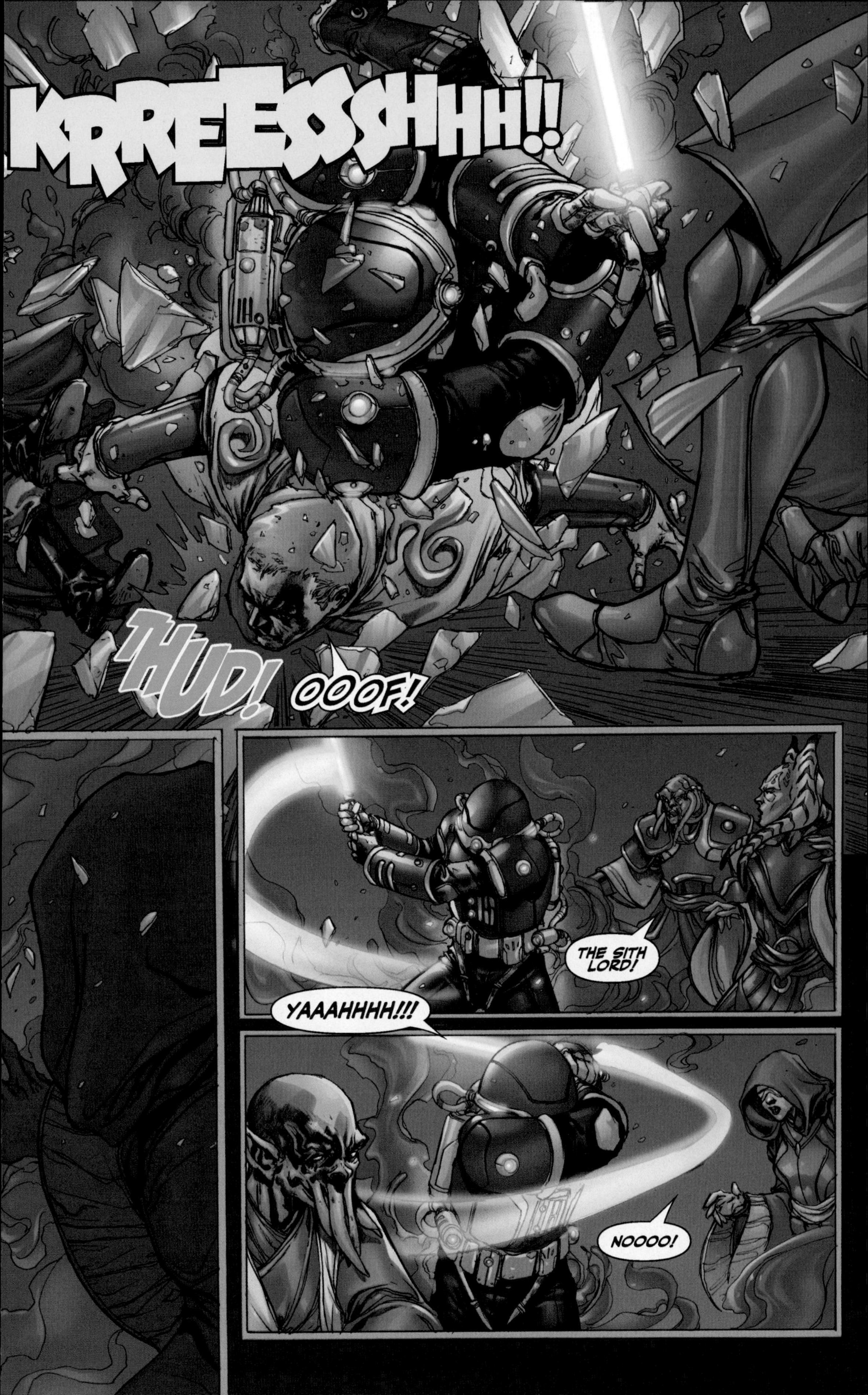
KRREESSHHH!!
THUD!
OOOF!
THE SITH LORD!
YAAAHHHH!!!
NOOOO!

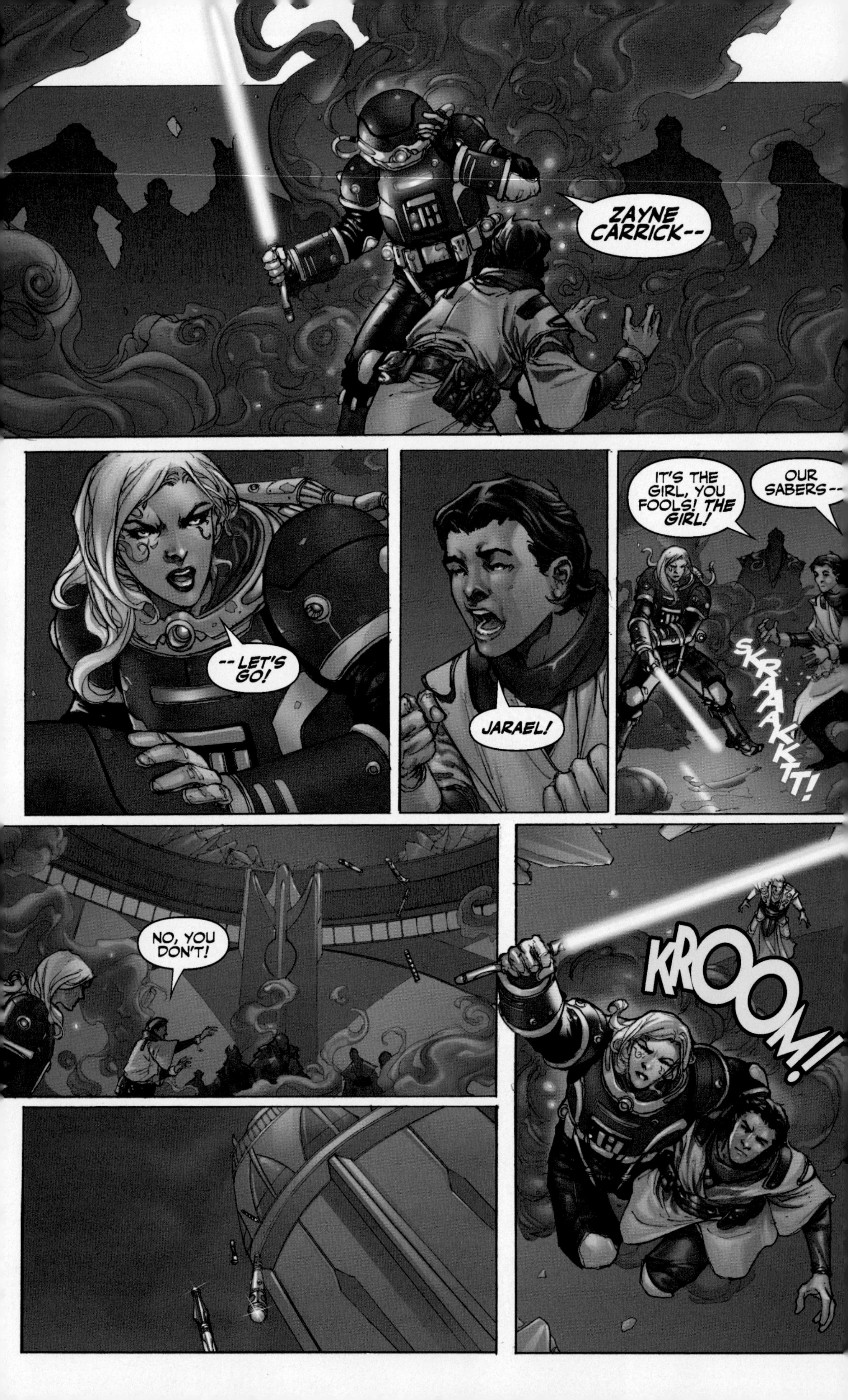
ZAYNE CARRICK--
--LET'S GO!
JARAEL!
IT'S THE GIRL, YOU FOOLS! THE GIRL!
OUR SABERS--
SKRAAAKKT!
NO, YOU DON'T!
KROOOM!

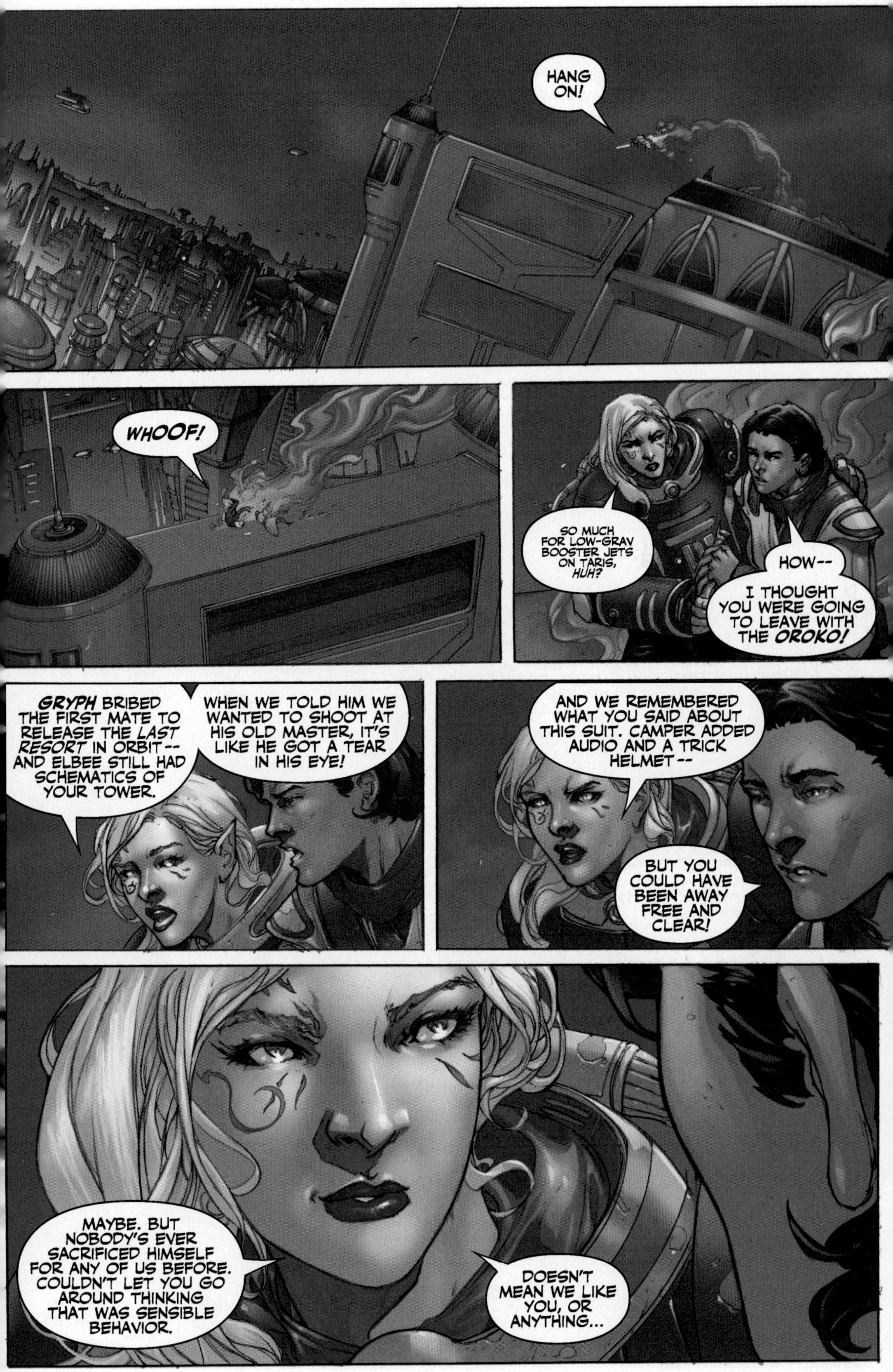
HANG ON!
WHOOF!
SO MUCH FOR LOW-GRAV BOOSTER JETS ON TARIS, HUH?
HOW--
I THOUGHT YOU WERE GOING TO LEAVE WITH THE OROKO!
GRYPH BRIBED THE FIRST MATE TO RELEASE THE LAST RESORT IN ORBIT-- AND ELBEE STILL HAD SCHEMATICS OF YOUR TOWER.
WHEN WE TOLD HIM WE WANTED TO SHOOT AT HIS OLD MASTER, IT'S LIKE HE GOT A TEAR IN HIS EYE!
AND WE REMEMBERED WHAT YOU SAID ABOUT THIS SUIT. CAMPER ADDED AUDIO AND A TRICK HELMET--
BUT YOU COULD HAVE BEEN AWAY FREE AND CLEAR!
MAYBE. BUT NOBODY'S EVER SACRIFICED HIMSELF FOR ANY OF US BEFORE. COULDN'T LET YOU GO AROUND THINKING THAT WAS SENSIBLE BEHAVIOR.
DOESN'T MEAN WE LIKE YOU, OR ANYTHING...

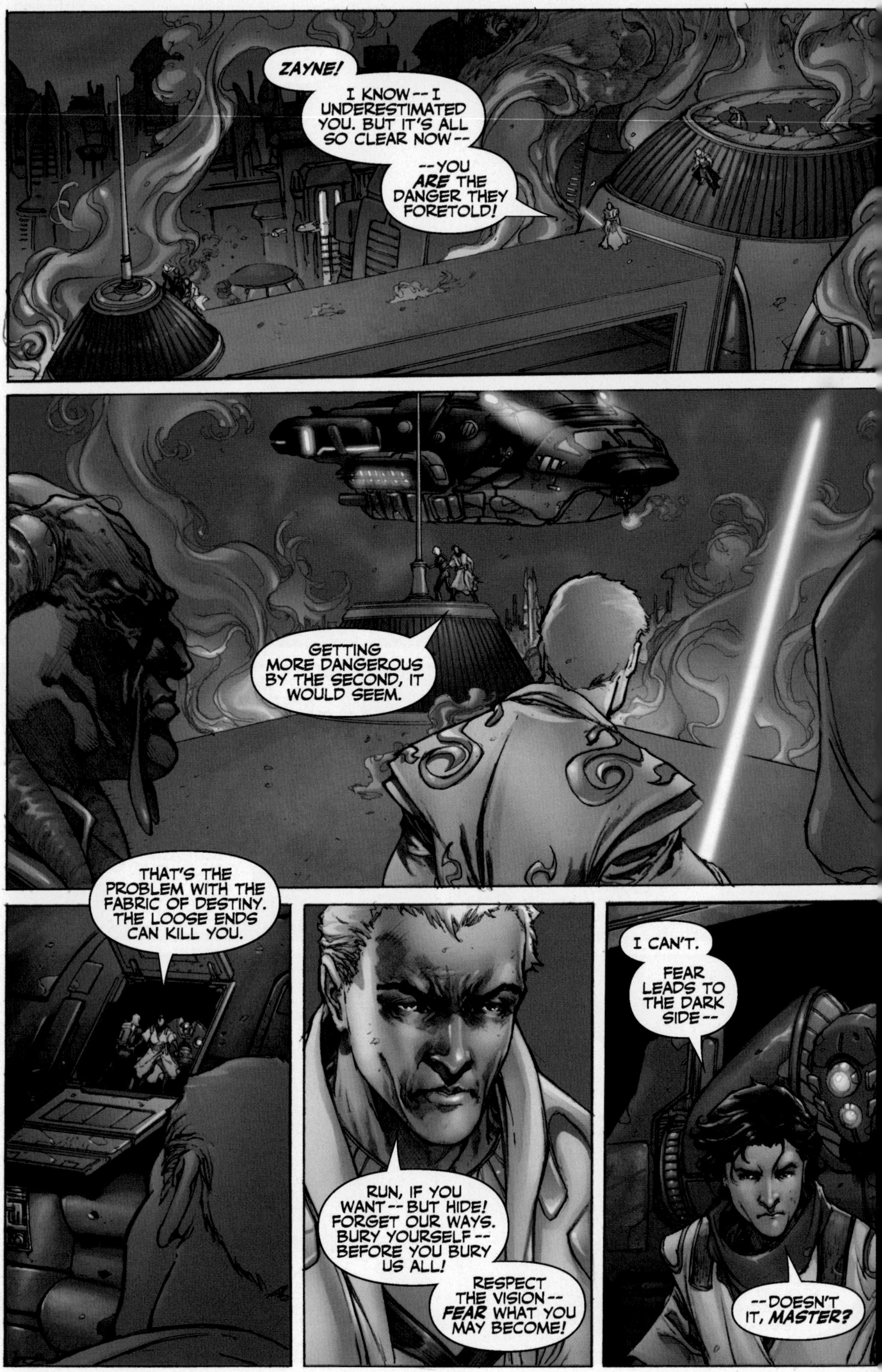
ZAYNE!
I KNOW -- I UNDERESTIMATED YOU. BUT IT'S ALL SO CLEAR NOW --
-- YOU ARE THE DANGER THEY FORETOLD!
GETTING MORE DANGEROUS BY THE SECOND, IT WOULD SEEM.
THAT'S THE PROBLEM WITH THE FABRIC OF DESTINY. THE LOOSE ENDS CAN KILL YOU.
RUN, IF YOU WANT -- BUT HIDE! FORGET OUR WAYS. BURY YOURSELF -- BEFORE YOU BURY US ALL!
RESPECT THE VISION -- FEAR WHAT YOU MAY BECOME!
I CAN'T.
FEAR LEADS TO THE DARK SIDE --
-- DOESN'T IT, MASTER?

GRYPH -- YOU CAME BACK! WHY DIDN'T YOU RUN?

UNFINISHED BUSINESS, *INTERN!* I'M HERE TO OFFER YOU A POSITION IN MY ORGANIZATION!

YOUR *ORGANIZATION?* IT'S JUST *YOU!*

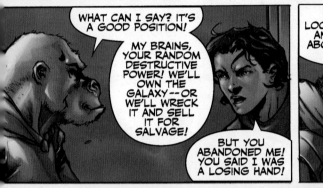

WHAT CAN I SAY? IT'S A GOOD POSITION!

MY BRAINS, YOUR RANDOM DESTRUCTIVE POWER! WE'LL OWN THE GALAXY -- OR WE'LL WRECK IT AND SELL IT FOR SALVAGE!

BUT YOU ABANDONED ME! YOU SAID I WAS A LOSING HAND!

AW, I NEVER LOOK AT MY CARDS, ANYWAY! I'M ALL ABOUT THE BLUFF, REMEMBER?

THERE'S NOTHING BETTER THAN MAKING SOMETHING OUT OF NOTHING. I'D FOR- GOTTEN -- UNTIL JARAEL REMINDED ME.

SO, ARE YOU IN?

THIS IS INSANE --

-- BUT THIS IS THE DAY FOR IT!

MY FAMILY, MY TEACHERS -- EVEN MY FRIENDS -- THEY ALL ASSUMED I'D FAIL. THEY NEVER TOOK A CHANCE ON ME THAT *MEANT* ANYTHING!

I'M TIRED OF BETTING AGAINST MYSELF. IF YOU GUYS CAN BET ON ME, MAYBE I CAN, TOO!

SO I'M *IN* -- ON ONE CONDITION. STOP CALLING ME *"INTERN"!*

YOU GOT IT... *HENCHMAN!*

HEY, TARIS! TELL THE VULKARS AND THE BEKS THERE'S A NEW POWER ON THE SCENE!

MARN HIEROGRYPH! JEDI JAILBREAKS, TWO FOR A CREDIT!

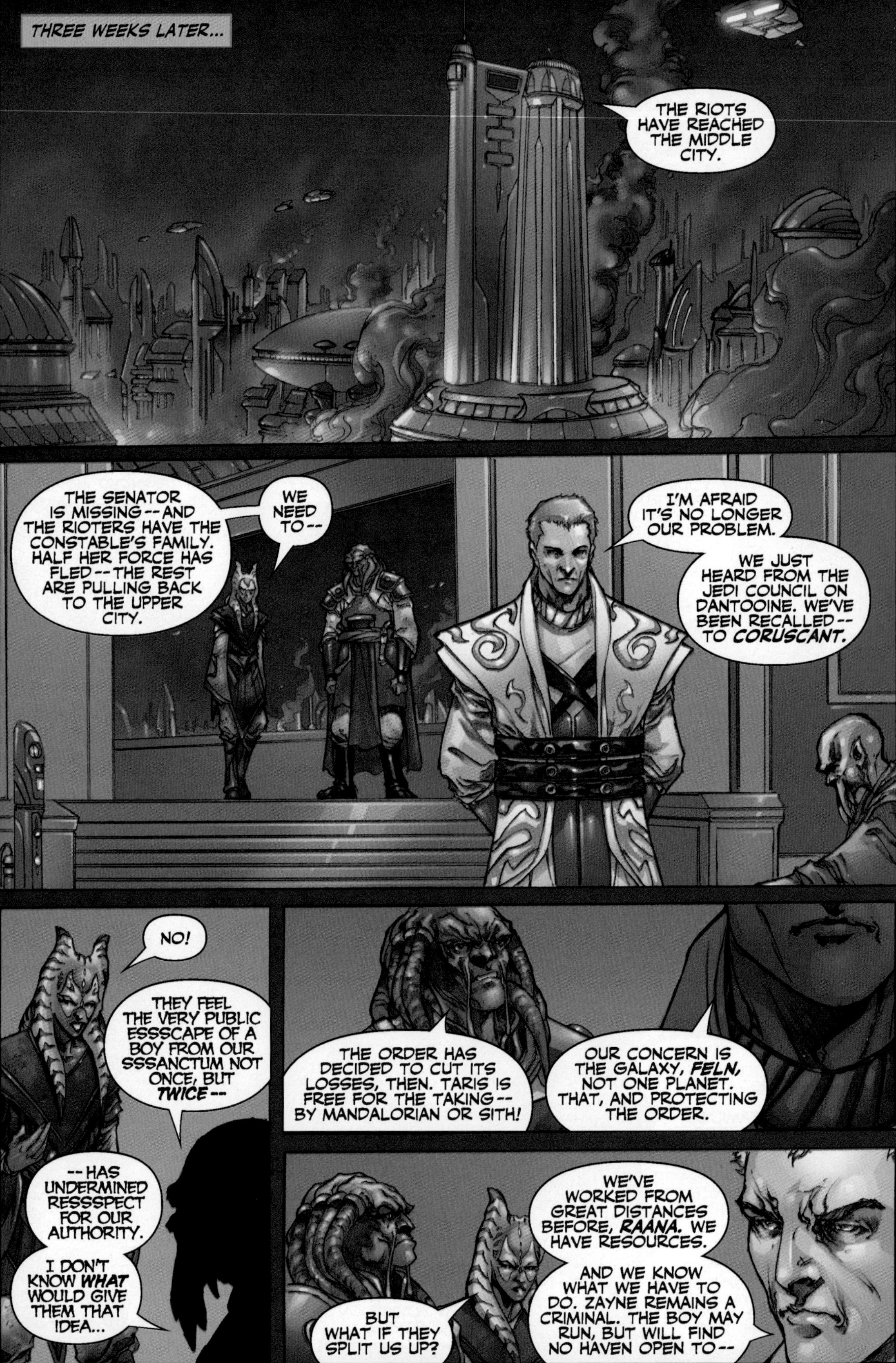
THREE WEEKS LATER...
THE RIOTS HAVE REACHED THE MIDDLE CITY.
THE SENATOR IS MISSING--AND THE RIOTERS HAVE THE CONSTABLE'S FAMILY. HALF HER FORCE HAS FLED--THE REST ARE PULLING BACK TO THE UPPER CITY.
WE NEED TO--
I'M AFRAID IT'S NO LONGER OUR PROBLEM.
WE JUST HEARD FROM THE JEDI COUNCIL ON DANTOOINE. WE'VE BEEN RECALLED--TO ***CORUSCANT.***
NO!
THEY FEEL THE VERY PUBLIC ESSSCAPE OF A BOY FROM OUR SSSANCTUM NOT ONCE, BUT ***TWICE***--
--HAS UNDERMINED RESSSPECT FOR OUR AUTHORITY.
I DON'T KNOW ***WHAT*** WOULD GIVE THEM THAT IDEA...
THE ORDER HAS DECIDED TO CUT ITS LOSSES, THEN. TARIS IS FREE FOR THE TAKING--BY MANDALORIAN OR SITH!
OUR CONCERN IS THE GALAXY, ***FELN,*** NOT ONE PLANET. THAT, AND PROTECTING THE ORDER.
WE'VE WORKED FROM GREAT DISTANCES BEFORE, ***RAANA.*** WE HAVE RESOURCES.
AND WE KNOW WHAT WE HAVE TO DO. ZAYNE REMAINS A CRIMINAL. THE BOY MAY RUN, BUT WILL FIND NO HAVEN OPEN TO--
BUT WHAT IF THEY SPLIT US UP?

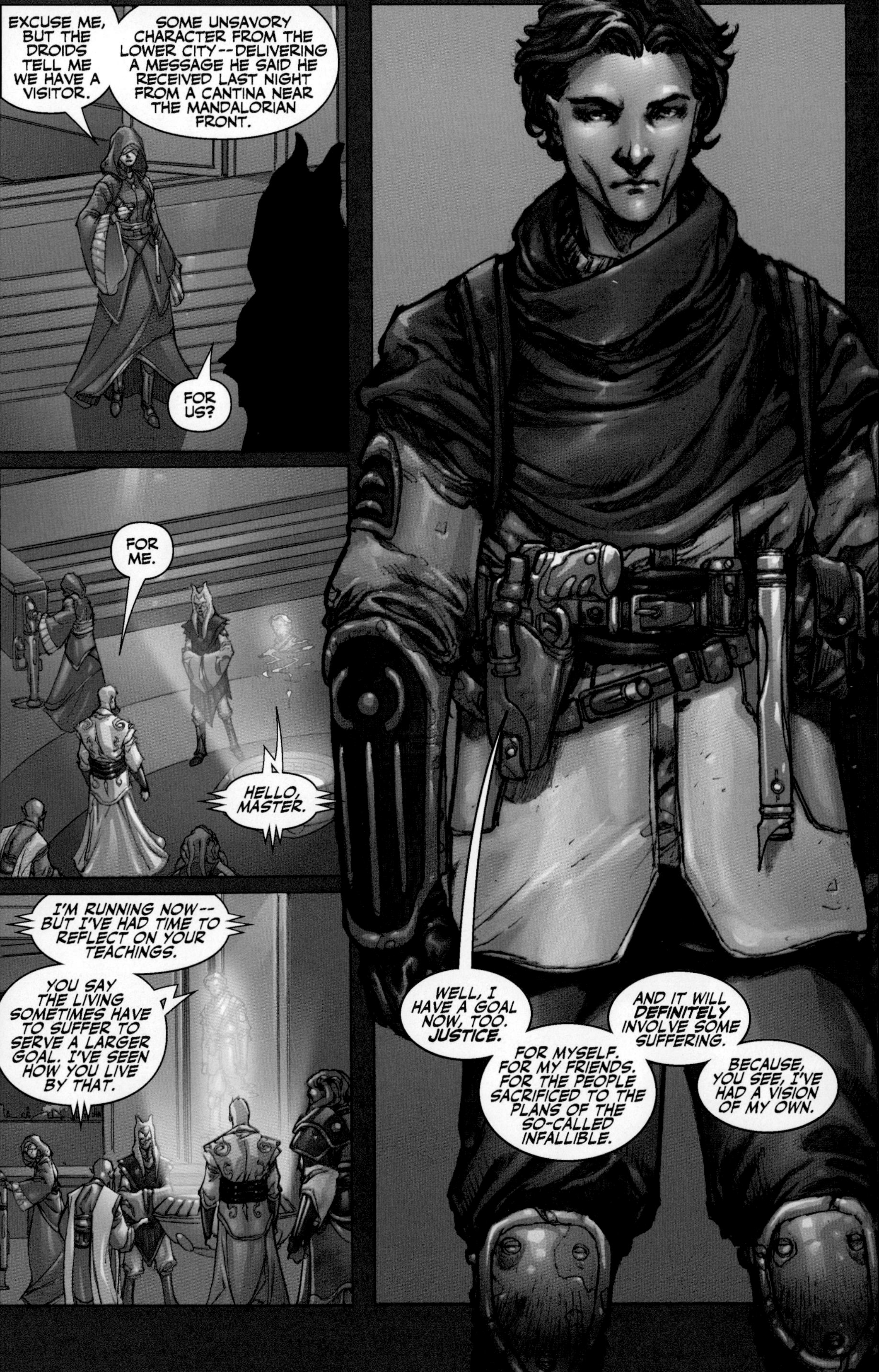
EXCUSE ME, BUT THE DROIDS TELL ME WE HAVE A VISITOR.
SOME UNSAVORY CHARACTER FROM THE LOWER CITY--DELIVERING A MESSAGE HE SAID HE RECEIVED LAST NIGHT FROM A CANTINA NEAR THE MANDALORIAN FRONT.
FOR US?
FOR ME.
HELLO, MASTER.
I'M RUNNING NOW--BUT I'VE HAD TIME TO REFLECT ON YOUR TEACHINGS.
YOU SAY THE LIVING SOMETIMES HAVE TO SUFFER TO SERVE A LARGER GOAL. I'VE SEEN HOW YOU LIVE BY THAT.
WELL, I HAVE A GOAL NOW, TOO. JUSTICE.
FOR MYSELF. FOR MY FRIENDS. FOR THE PEOPLE SACRIFICED TO THE PLANS OF THE SO-CALLED INFALLIBLE.
AND IT WILL DEFINITELY INVOLVE SOME SUFFERING.
BECAUSE, YOU SEE, I'VE HAD A VISION OF MY OWN.

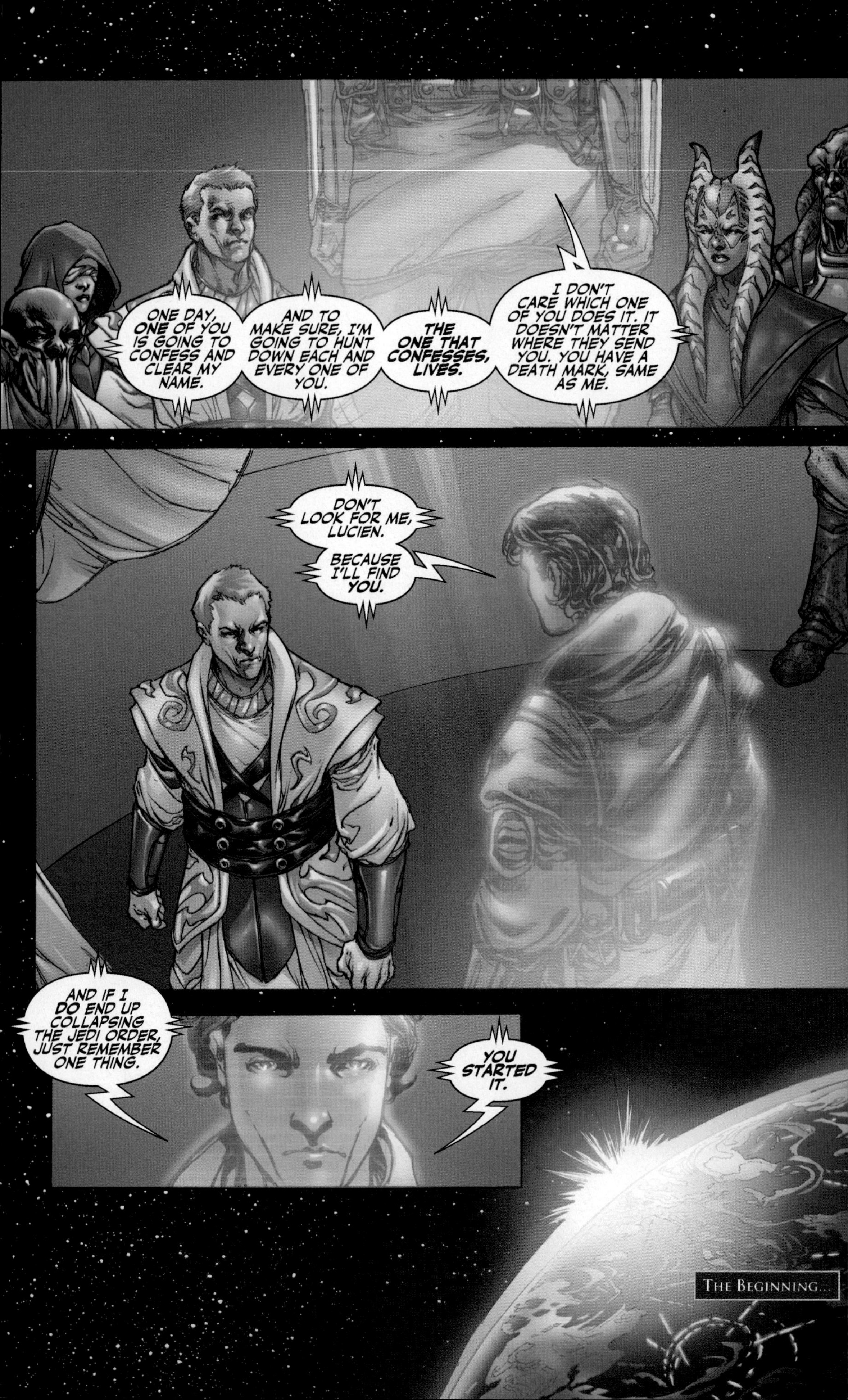

ONE DAY, ONE OF YOU IS GOING TO CONFESS AND CLEAR MY NAME.
AND TO MAKE SURE, I'M GOING TO HUNT DOWN EACH AND EVERY ONE OF YOU.
THE ONE THAT CONFESSES, LIVES.
I DON'T CARE WHICH ONE OF YOU DOES IT. IT DOESN'T MATTER WHERE THEY SEND YOU. YOU HAVE A DEATH MARK, SAME AS ME.
DON'T LOOK FOR ME, LUCIEN.
BECAUSE I'LL FIND YOU.
AND IF I DO END UP COLLAPSING THE JEDI ORDER, JUST REMEMBER ONE THING.
YOU STARTED IT.
THE BEGINNING...

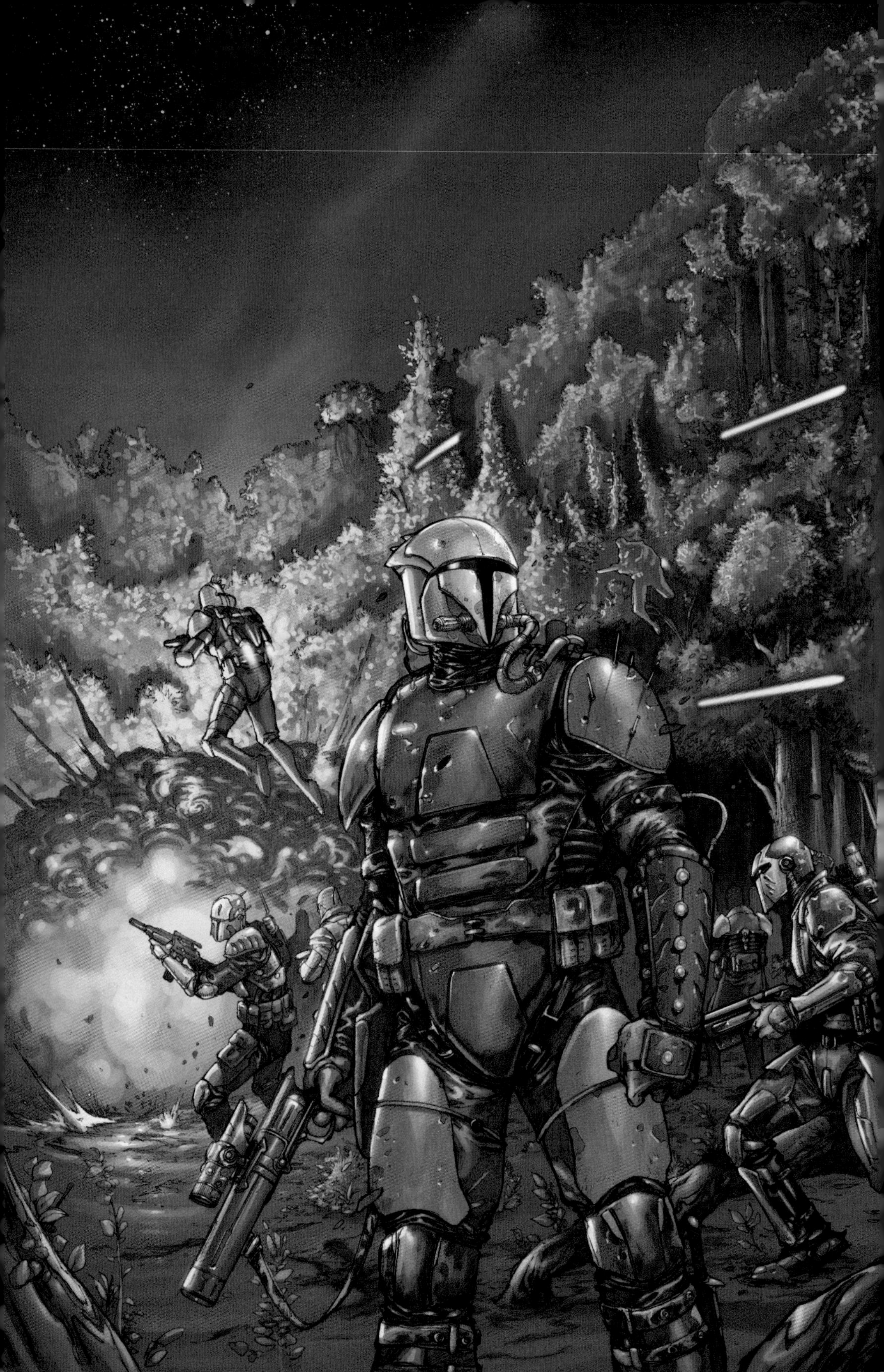

STAR WARS: KNIGHTS OF THE OLD REPUBLIC #7 — "FLASHPOINT, PART 1"

WRITER: JOHN JACKSON MILLER • ARTIST: DUSTIN WEAVER • COLORIST: MICHAEL ATIYEH • LETTERER: MICHAEL HEISLER
ASSISTANT EDITOR: DAVE MARSHALL • EDITOR: JEREMY BARLOW • COVER ARTISTS: BRIAN CHING & MICHAEL ATIYEH

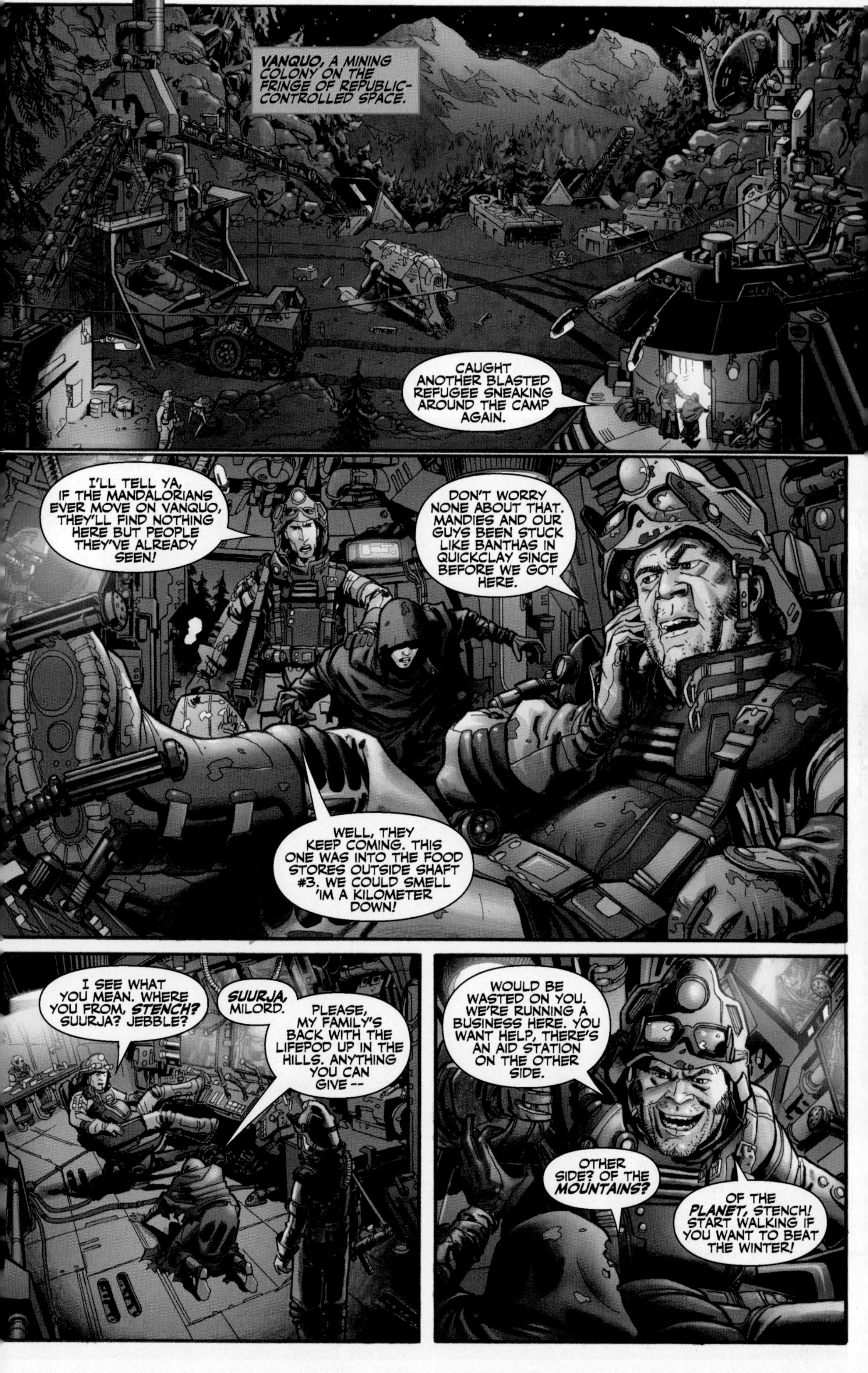
VANQUO, A MINING COLONY ON THE FRINGE OF REPUBLIC-CONTROLLED SPACE.
CAUGHT ANOTHER BLASTED REFUGEE SNEAKING AROUND THE CAMP AGAIN.
I'LL TELL YA, IF THE MANDALORIANS EVER MOVE ON VANQUO, THEY'LL FIND NOTHING HERE BUT PEOPLE THEY'VE ALREADY SEEN!
DON'T WORRY NONE ABOUT THAT. MANDIES AND OUR GUYS BEEN STUCK LIKE BANTHAS IN QUICKCLAY SINCE BEFORE WE GOT HERE.
WELL, THEY KEEP COMING. THIS ONE WAS INTO THE FOOD STORES OUTSIDE SHAFT #3. WE COULD SMELL 'IM A KILOMETER DOWN!
I SEE WHAT YOU MEAN. WHERE YOU FROM, STENCH? SUURJA? JEBBLE?
SUURJA, MILORD.
PLEASE, MY FAMILY'S BACK WITH THE LIFEPOD UP IN THE HILLS. ANYTHING YOU CAN GIVE --
WOULD BE WASTED ON YOU. WE'RE RUNNING A BUSINESS HERE. YOU WANT HELP, THERE'S AN AID STATION ON THE OTHER SIDE.
OTHER SIDE? OF THE MOUNTAINS?
OF THE PLANET, STENCH! START WALKING IF YOU WANT TO BEAT THE WINTER!

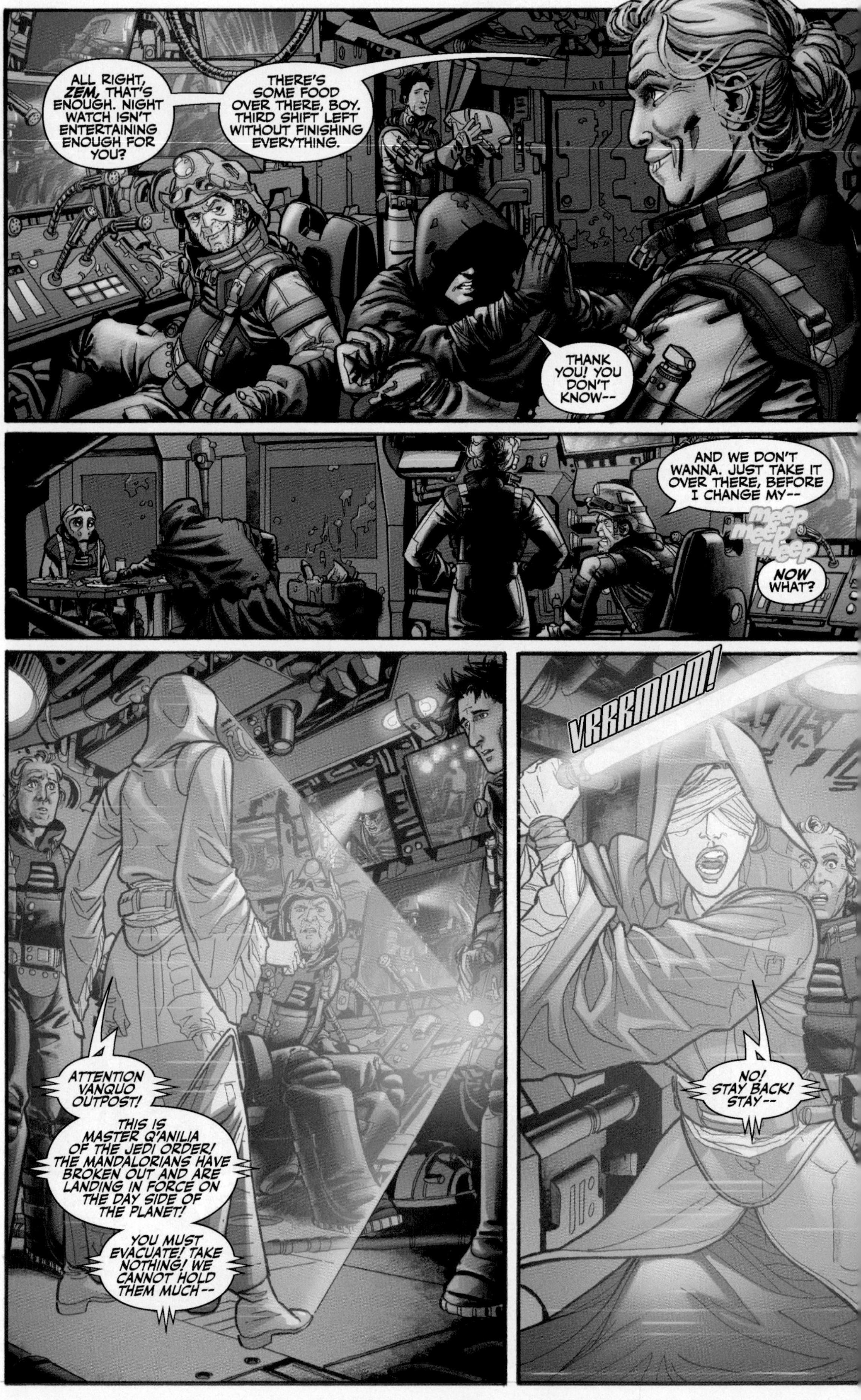
ALL RIGHT, ZEM, THAT'S ENOUGH. NIGHT WATCH ISN'T ENTERTAINING ENOUGH FOR YOU?
THERE'S SOME FOOD OVER THERE, BOY. THIRD SHIFT LEFT WITHOUT FINISHING EVERYTHING.
THANK YOU! YOU DON'T KNOW--
AND WE DON'T WANNA. JUST TAKE IT OVER THERE, BEFORE I CHANGE MY--
meep meep meep
NOW WHAT?
ATTENTION VANQUO OUTPOST!
THIS IS MASTER Q'ANILIA OF THE JEDI ORDER! THE MANDALORIANS HAVE BROKEN OUT AND ARE LANDING IN FORCE ON THE DAY SIDE OF THE PLANET!
YOU MUST EVACUATE! TAKE NOTHING! WE CANNOT HOLD THEM MUCH--
VRRRMMMM!
NO! STAY BACK! STAY--

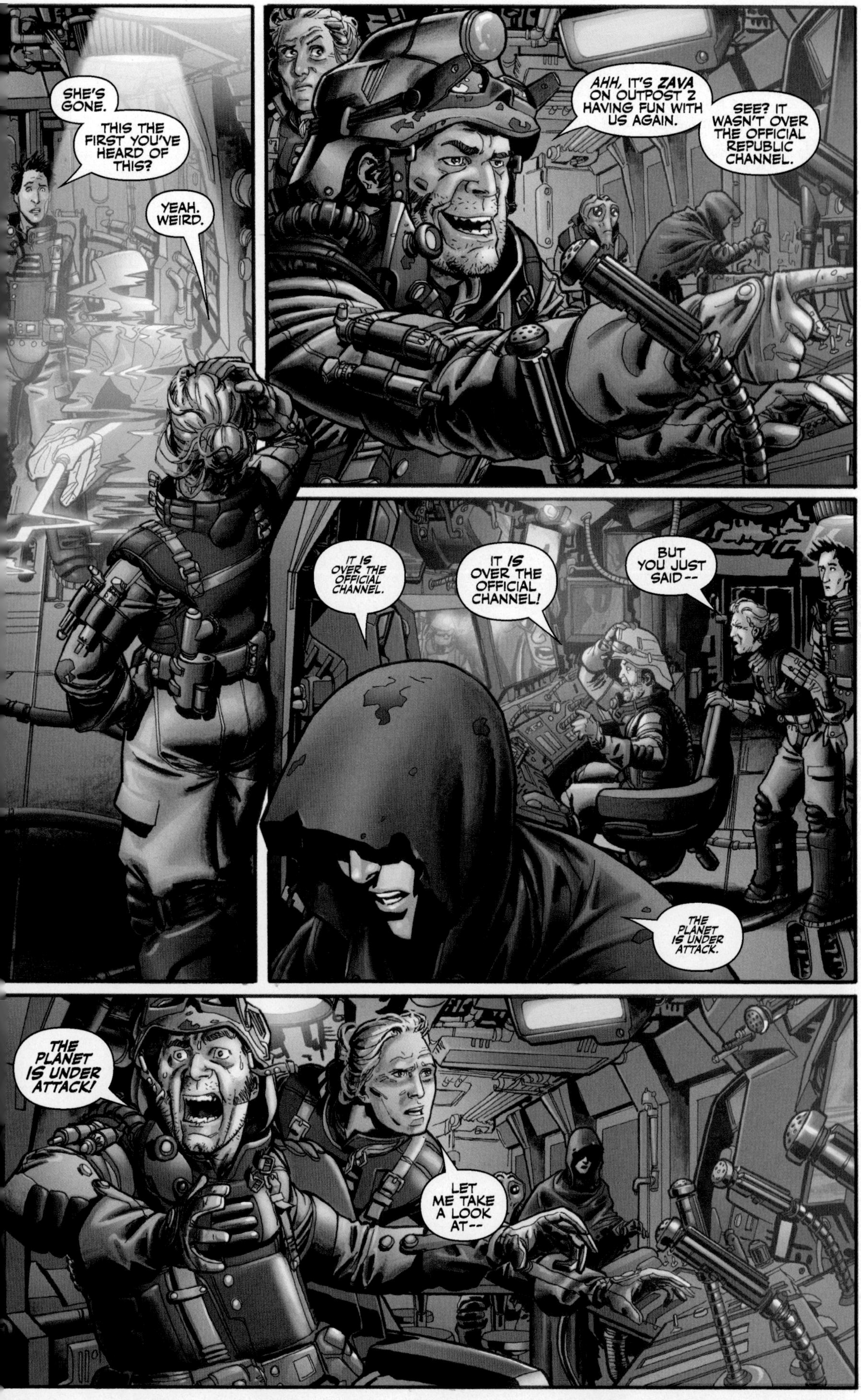
SHE'S GONE.
THIS THE FIRST YOU'VE HEARD OF THIS?
YEAH. WEIRD.
AHH, IT'S ZAVA ON OUTPOST 2 HAVING FUN WITH US AGAIN.
SEE? IT WASN'T OVER THE OFFICIAL REPUBLIC CHANNEL.
IT IS OVER THE OFFICIAL CHANNEL.
IT IS OVER THE OFFICIAL CHANNEL!
BUT YOU JUST SAID--
THE PLANET IS UNDER ATTACK.
THE PLANET IS UNDER ATTACK!
LET ME TAKE A LOOK AT--

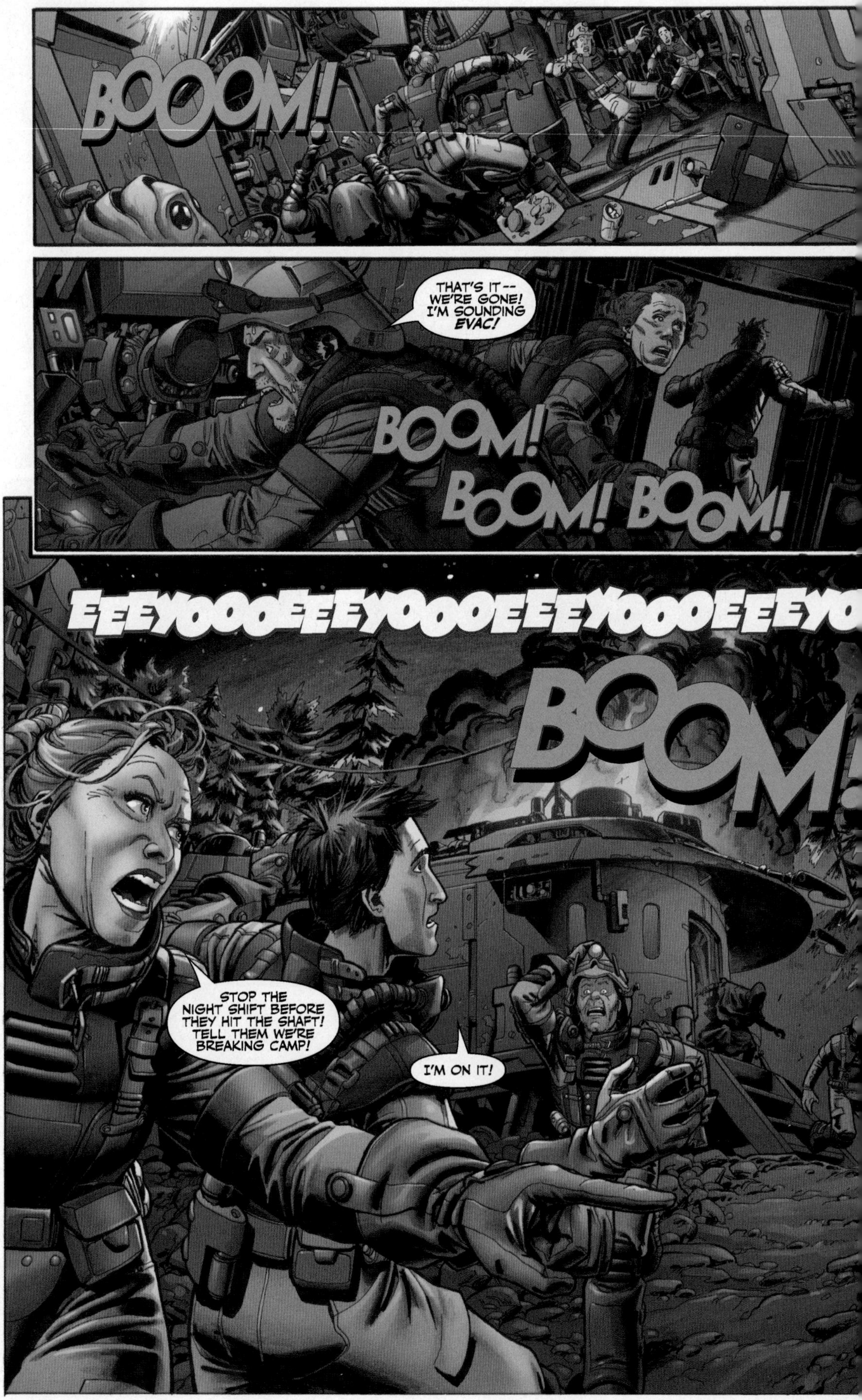
BOOOM!
THAT'S IT -- WE'RE GONE! I'M SOUNDING EVAC!
BOOM! BOOM! BOOM!
EEEYOOOEEEYOOOEEEYOOOEEEYO
BOOM!
STOP THE NIGHT SHIFT BEFORE THEY HIT THE SHAFT! TELL THEM WE'RE BREAKING CAMP!
I'M ON IT!

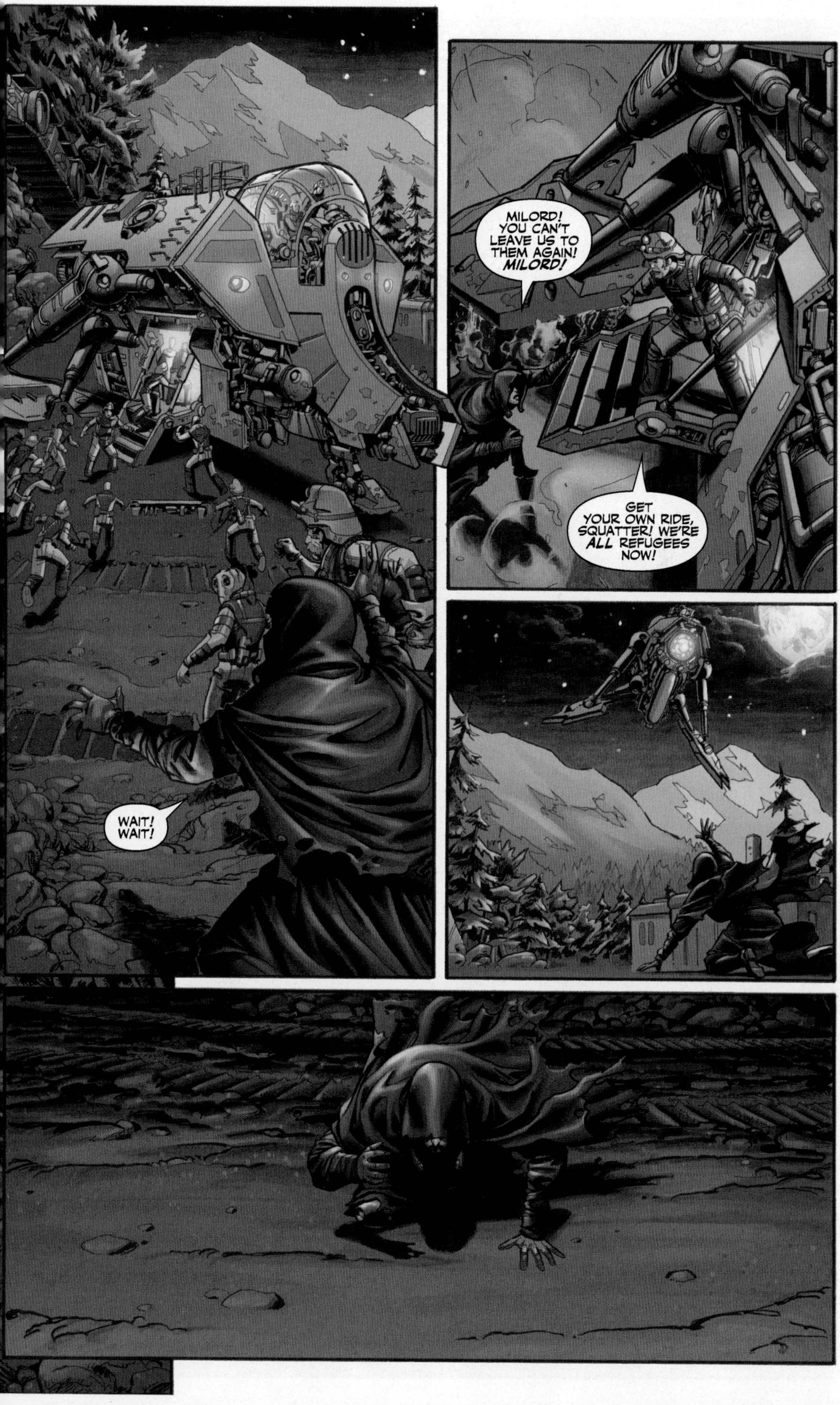
WAIT! WAIT!
MILORD! YOU CAN'T LEAVE US TO THEM AGAIN! MILORD!
GET YOUR OWN RIDE, SQUATTER! WE'RE ALL REFUGEES NOW!

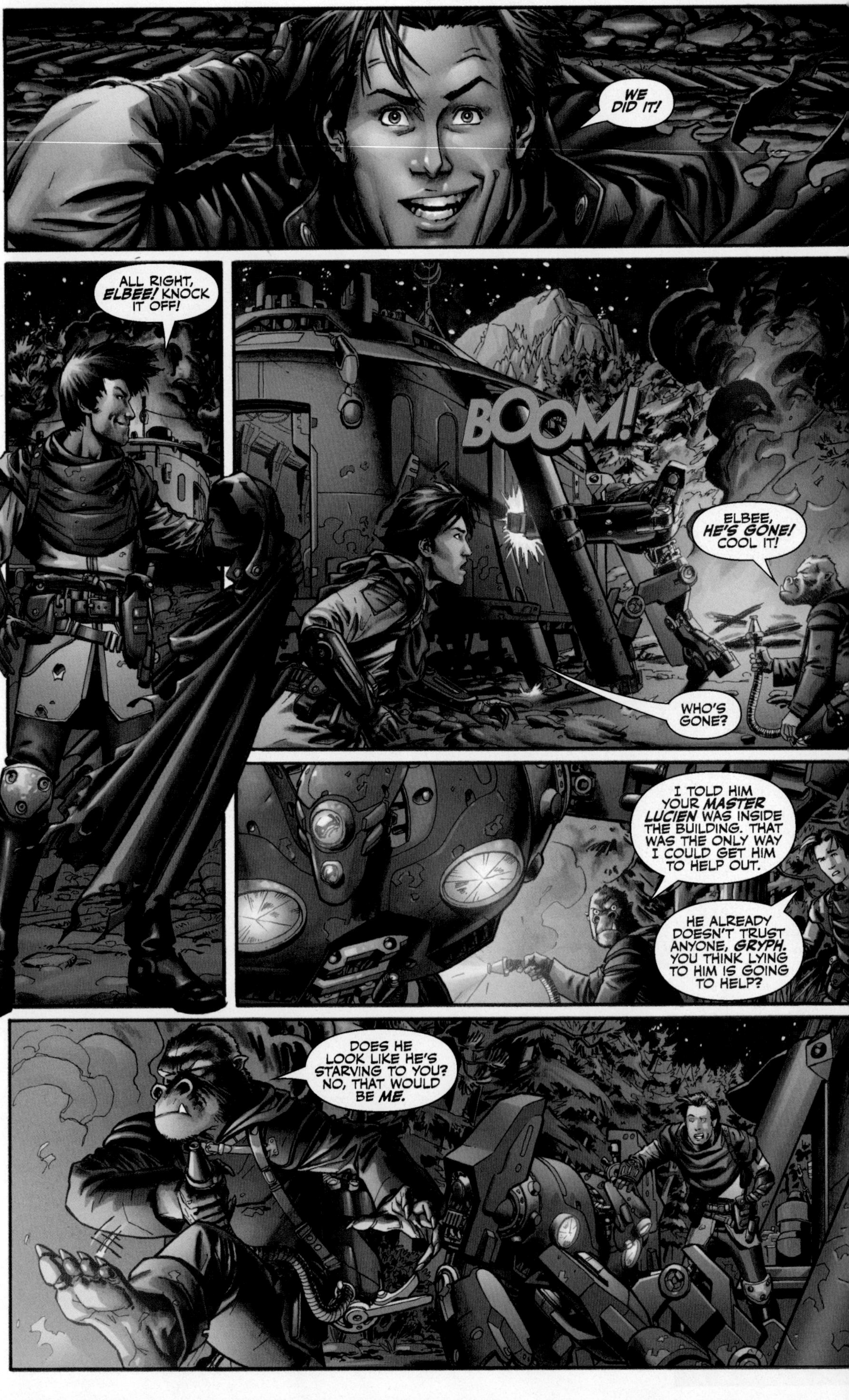

WE DID IT!
ALL RIGHT, ELBEE! KNOCK IT OFF!
BOOM!
ELBEE, HE'S GONE! COOL IT!
WHO'S GONE?
I TOLD HIM YOUR MASTER LUCIEN WAS INSIDE THE BUILDING. THAT WAS THE ONLY WAY I COULD GET HIM TO HELP OUT.
HE ALREADY DOESN'T TRUST ANYONE, GRYPH. YOU THINK LYING TO HIM IS GOING TO HELP?
DOES HE LOOK LIKE HE'S STARVING TO YOU? NO, THAT WOULD BE ME.

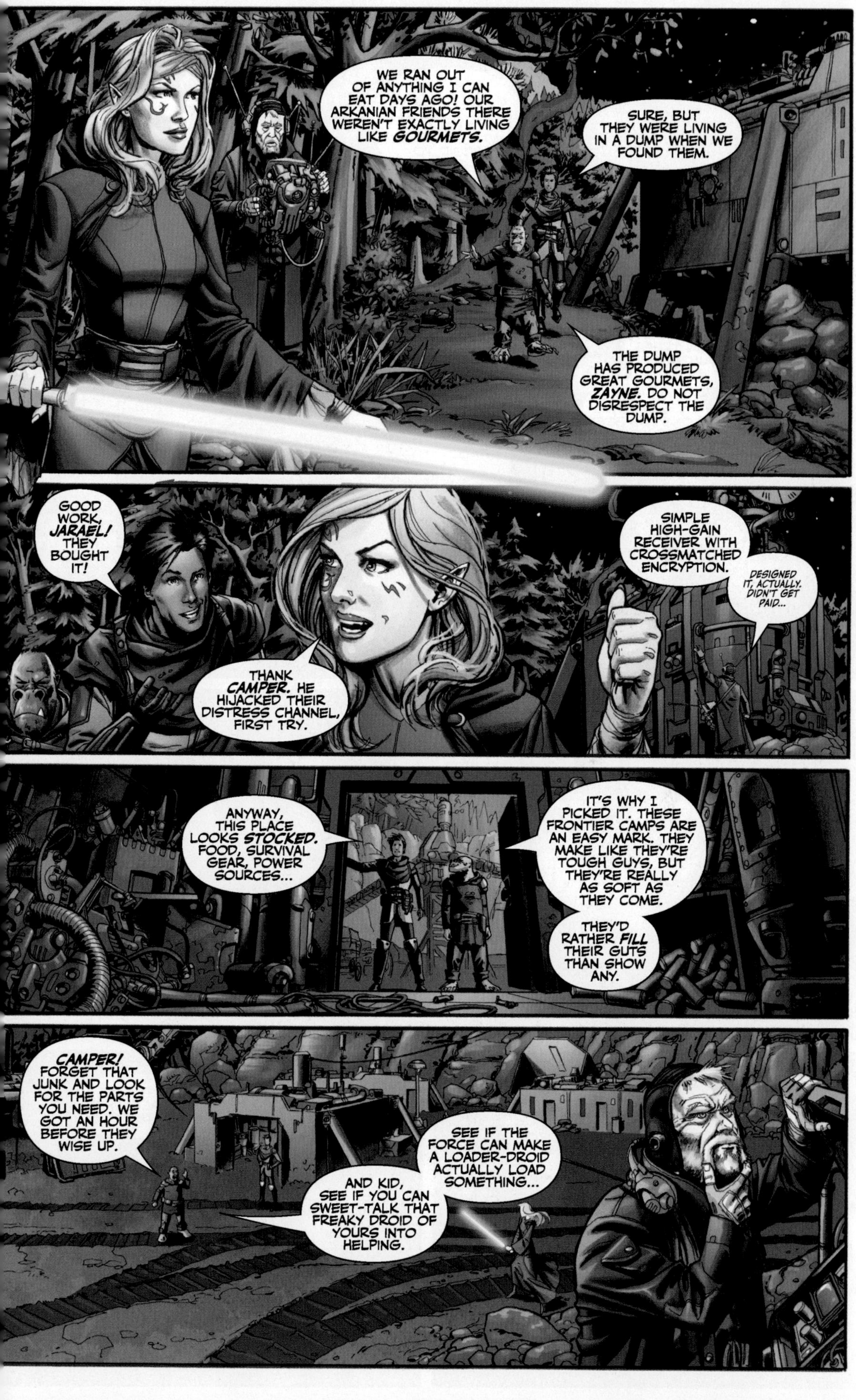

WE RAN OUT OF ANYTHING I CAN EAT DAYS AGO! OUR ARKANIAN FRIENDS THERE WEREN'T EXACTLY LIVING LIKE GOURMETS.
SURE, BUT THEY WERE LIVING IN A DUMP WHEN WE FOUND THEM.
THE DUMP HAS PRODUCED GREAT GOURMETS, ZAYNE. DO NOT DISRESPECT THE DUMP.
GOOD WORK, JARAEL! THEY BOUGHT IT!
THANK CAMPER. HE HIJACKED THEIR DISTRESS CHANNEL, FIRST TRY.
SIMPLE HIGH-GAIN RECEIVER WITH CROSSMATCHED ENCRYPTION.
DESIGNED IT, ACTUALLY. DIDN'T GET PAID...
ANYWAY, THIS PLACE LOOKS STOCKED. FOOD, SURVIVAL GEAR, POWER SOURCES...
IT'S WHY I PICKED IT. THESE FRONTIER CAMPS ARE AN EASY MARK. THEY MAKE LIKE THEY'RE TOUGH GUYS, BUT THEY'RE REALLY AS SOFT AS THEY COME.
THEY'D RATHER FILL THEIR GUTS THAN SHOW ANY.
CAMPER! FORGET THAT JUNK AND LOOK FOR THE PARTS YOU NEED. WE GOT AN HOUR BEFORE THEY WISE UP.
AND KID, SEE IF YOU CAN SWEET-TALK THAT FREAKY DROID OF YOURS INTO HELPING.
SEE IF THE FORCE CAN MAKE A LOADER-DROID ACTUALLY LOAD SOMETHING...

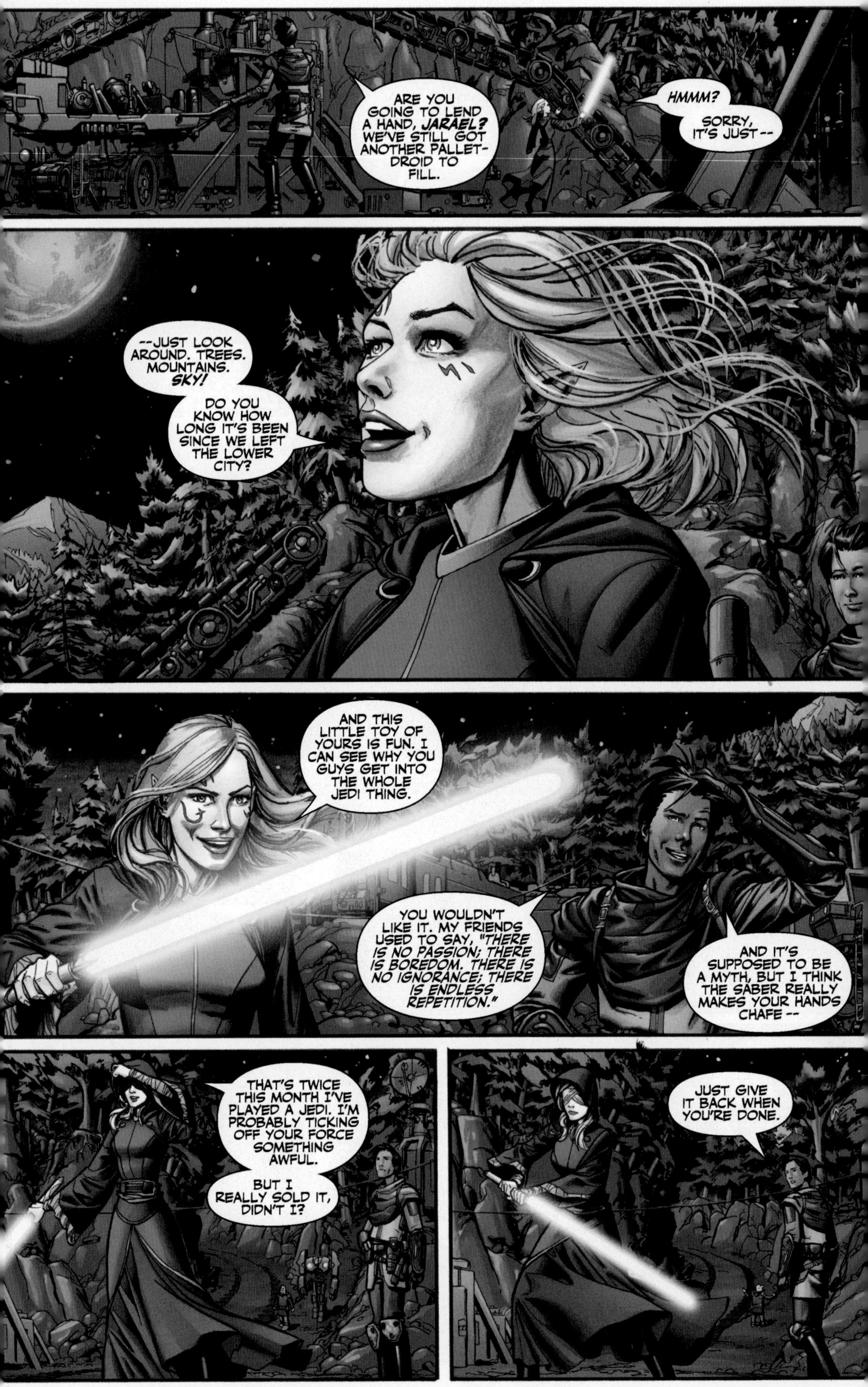
ARE YOU GOING TO LEND A HAND, JARAEL? WE'VE STILL GOT ANOTHER PALLET-DROID TO FILL.
HMMM?
SORRY, IT'S JUST --
--JUST LOOK AROUND. TREES. MOUNTAINS. SKY!
DO YOU KNOW HOW LONG IT'S BEEN SINCE WE LEFT THE LOWER CITY?
AND THIS LITTLE TOY OF YOURS IS FUN. I CAN SEE WHY YOU GUYS GET INTO THE WHOLE JEDI THING.
YOU WOULDN'T LIKE IT. MY FRIENDS USED TO SAY, "THERE IS NO PASSION; THERE IS BOREDOM. THERE IS NO IGNORANCE; THERE IS ENDLESS REPETITION."
AND IT'S SUPPOSED TO BE A MYTH, BUT I THINK THE SABER REALLY MAKES YOUR HANDS CHAFE --
THAT'S TWICE THIS MONTH I'VE PLAYED A JEDI. I'M PROBABLY TICKING OFF YOUR FORCE SOMETHING AWFUL.
BUT I REALLY SOLD IT, DIDN'T I?
JUST GIVE IT BACK WHEN YOU'RE DONE.

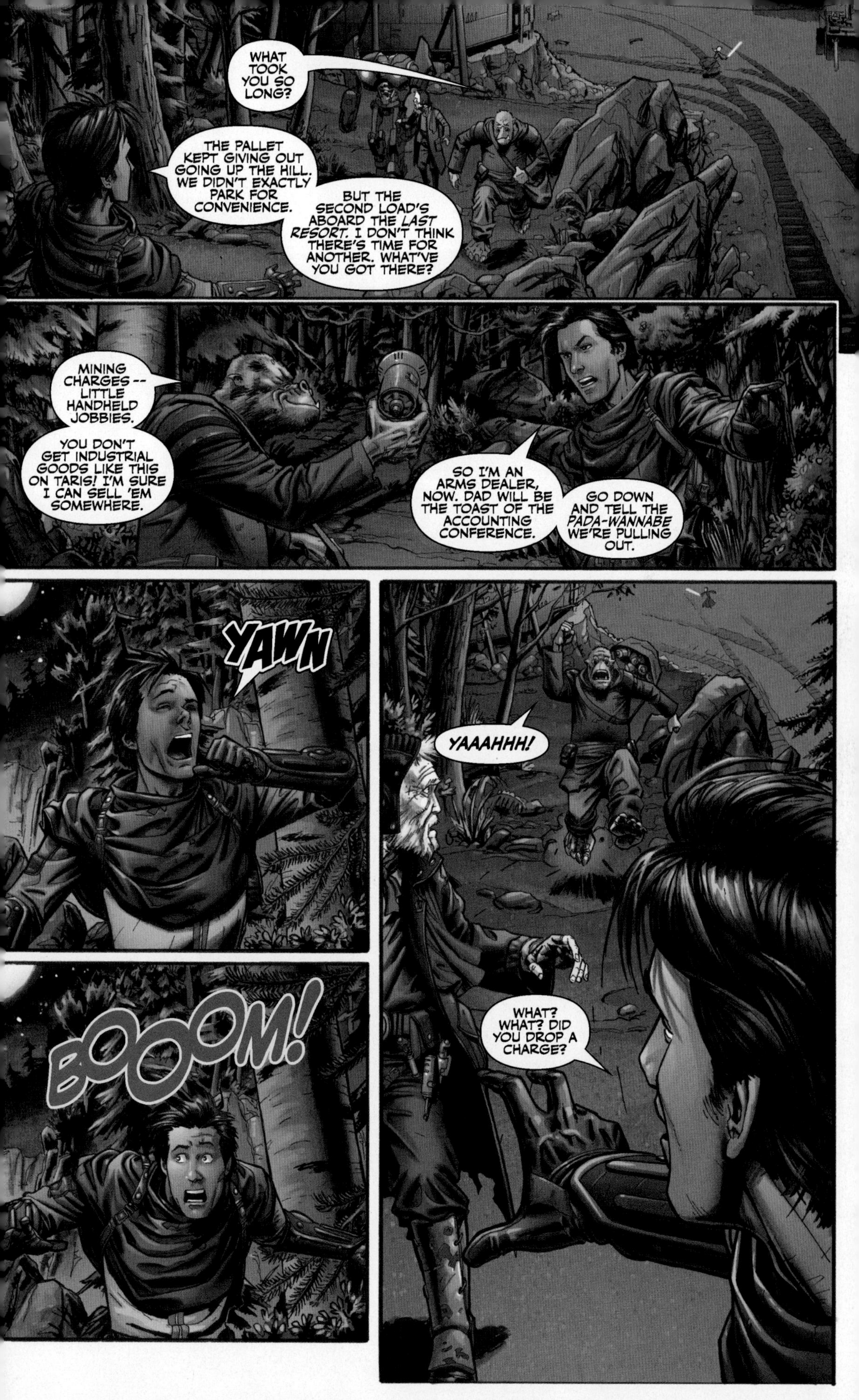
WHAT TOOK YOU SO LONG?
THE PALLET KEPT GIVING OUT GOING UP THE HILL. WE DIDN'T EXACTLY PARK FOR CONVENIENCE.
BUT THE SECOND LOAD'S ABOARD THE *LAST RESORT*. I DON'T THINK THERE'S TIME FOR ANOTHER. WHAT'VE YOU GOT THERE?
MINING CHARGES -- LITTLE HANDHELD JOBBIES.
YOU DON'T GET INDUSTRIAL GOODS LIKE THIS ON TARIS! I'M SURE I CAN SELL 'EM SOMEWHERE.
SO I'M AN ARMS DEALER, NOW. DAD WILL BE THE TOAST OF THE ACCOUNTING CONFERENCE.
GO DOWN AND TELL THE *PADA-WANNABE* WE'RE PULLING OUT.
YAWN
YAAAHHH!
BOOOM!
WHAT? WHAT? DID YOU DROP A CHARGE?

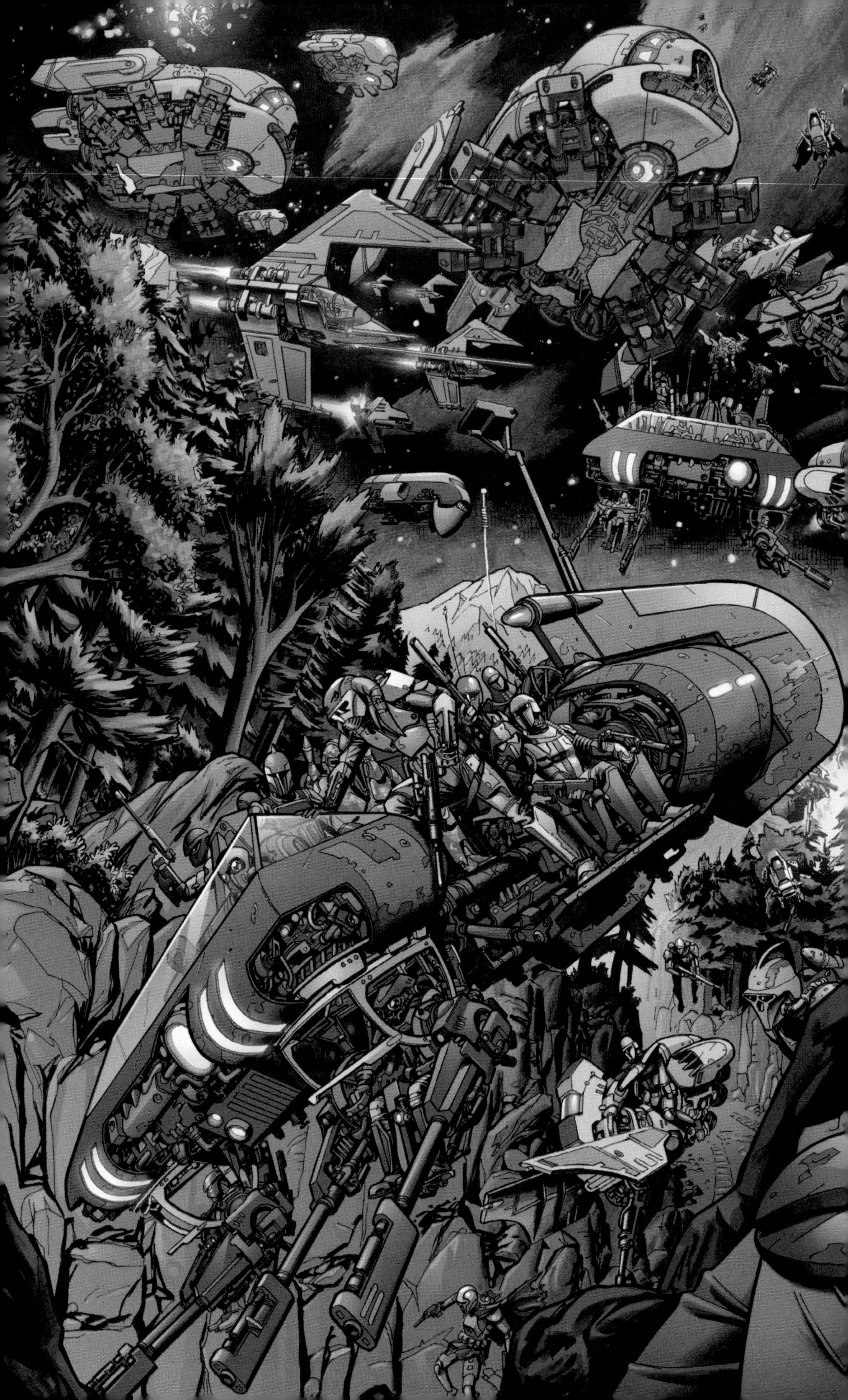

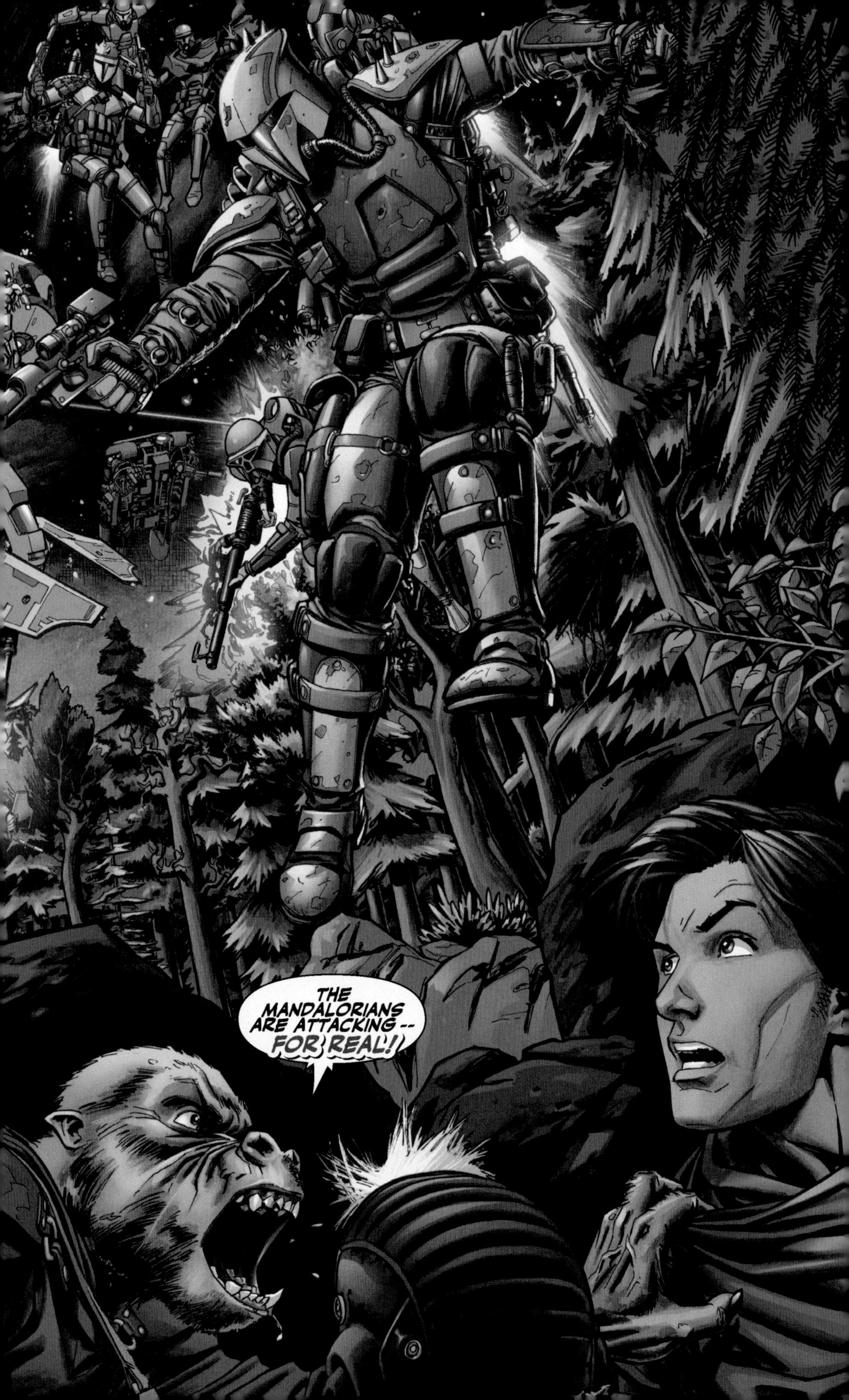
THE MANDALORIANS ARE ATTACKING -- FOR REAL!

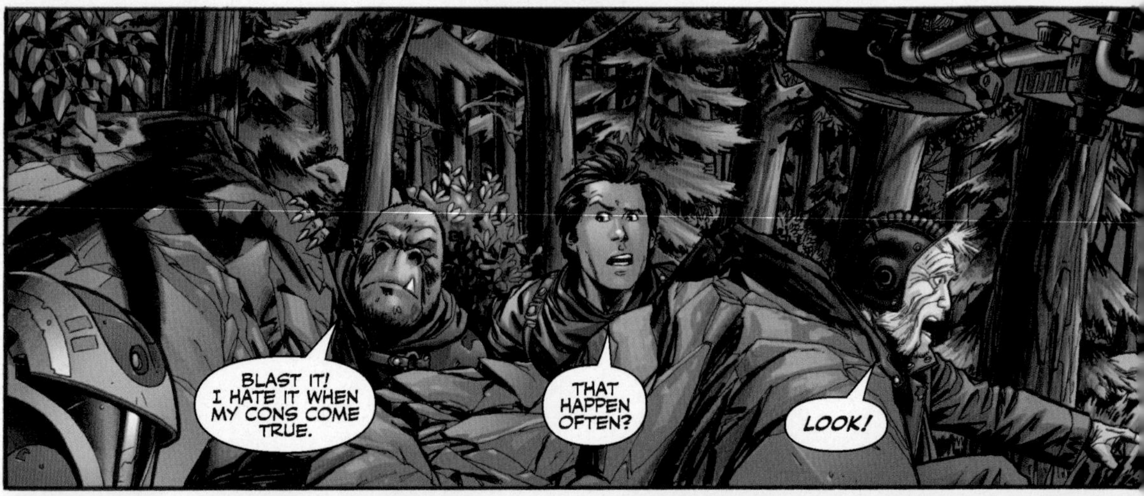
BLAST IT! I HATE IT WHEN MY CONS COME TRUE.
THAT HAPPEN OFTEN?
LOOK!

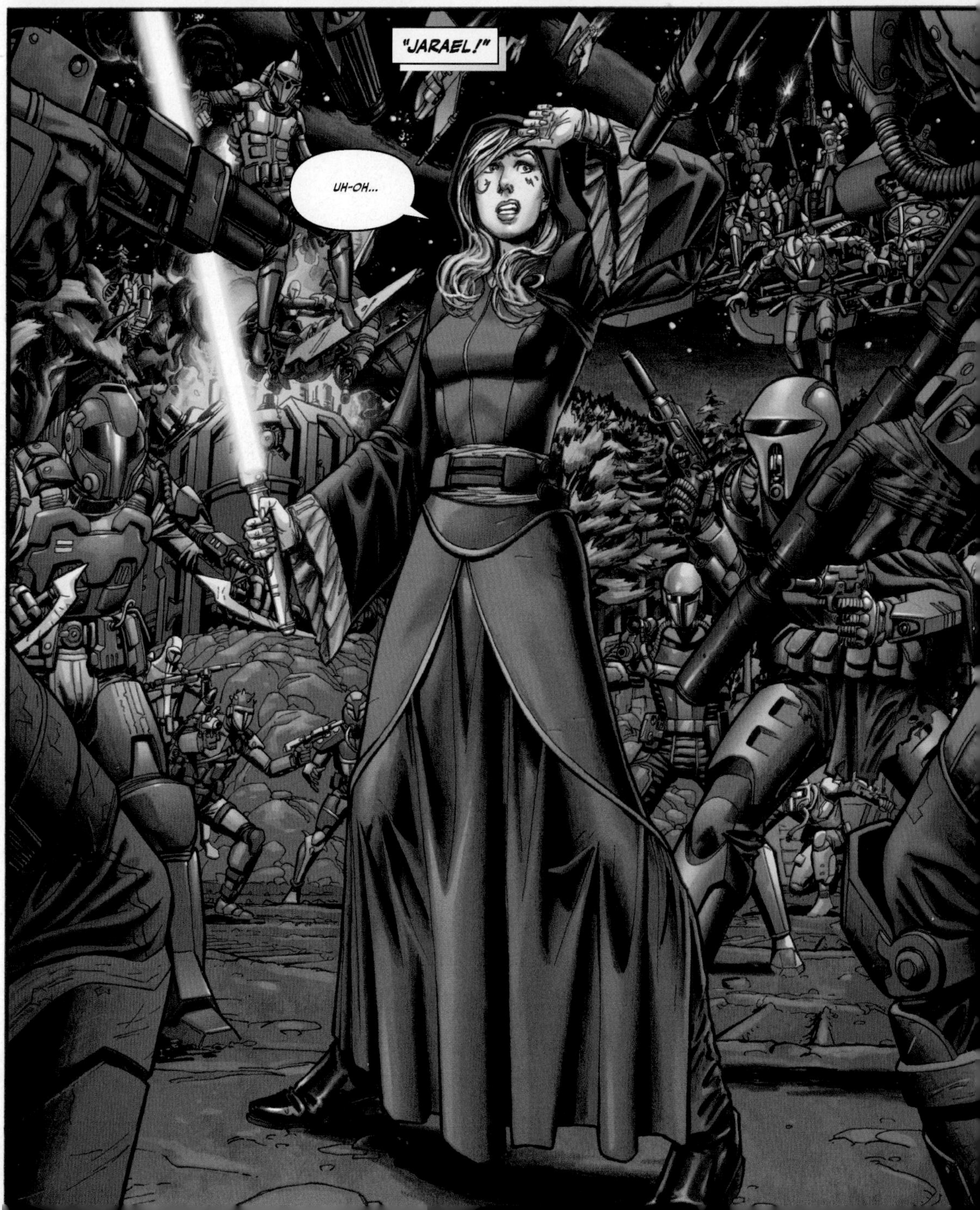
"JARAEL!"
UH-OH...

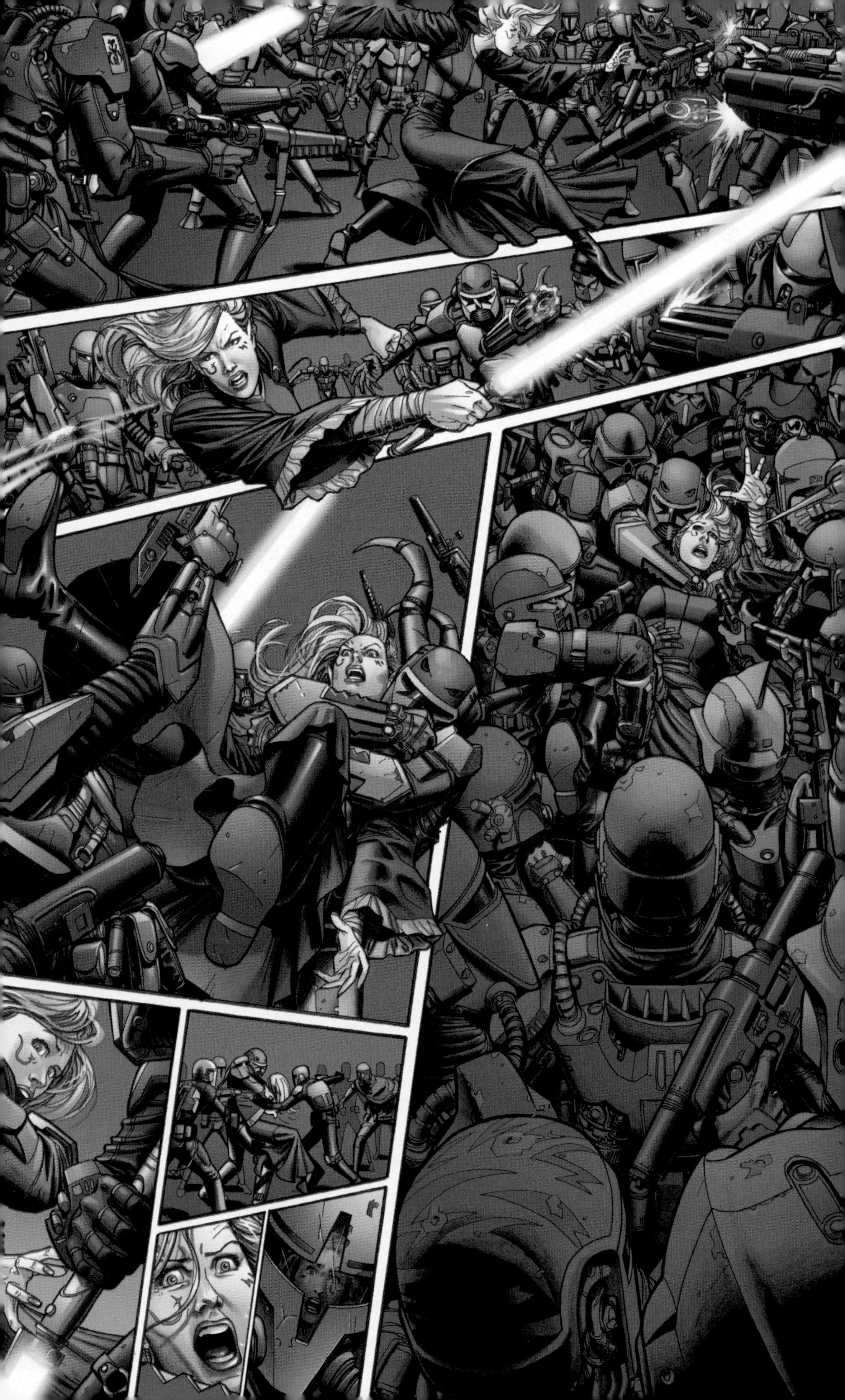

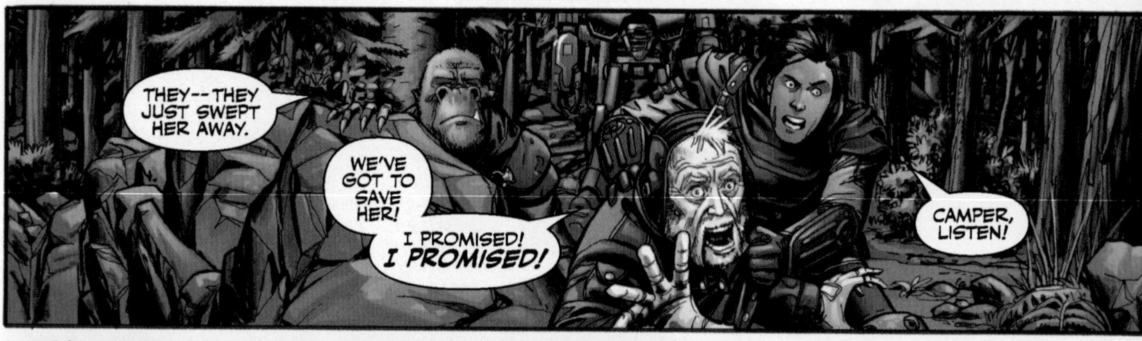
THEY--THEY JUST SWEPT HER AWAY.
WE'VE GOT TO SAVE HER!
I PROMISED! I PROMISED!
CAMPER, LISTEN!

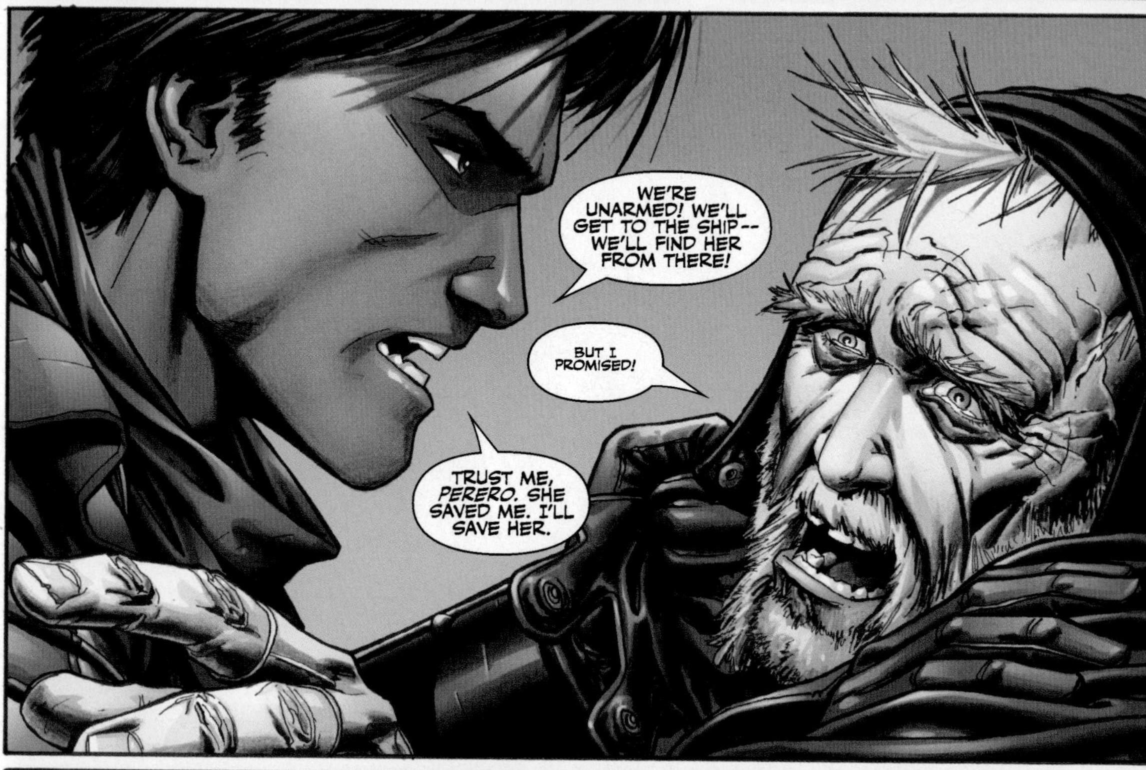
WE'RE UNARMED! WE'LL GET TO THE SHIP-- WE'LL FIND HER FROM THERE!
BUT I PROMISED!
TRUST ME, PERERO. SHE SAVED ME. I'LL SAVE HER.

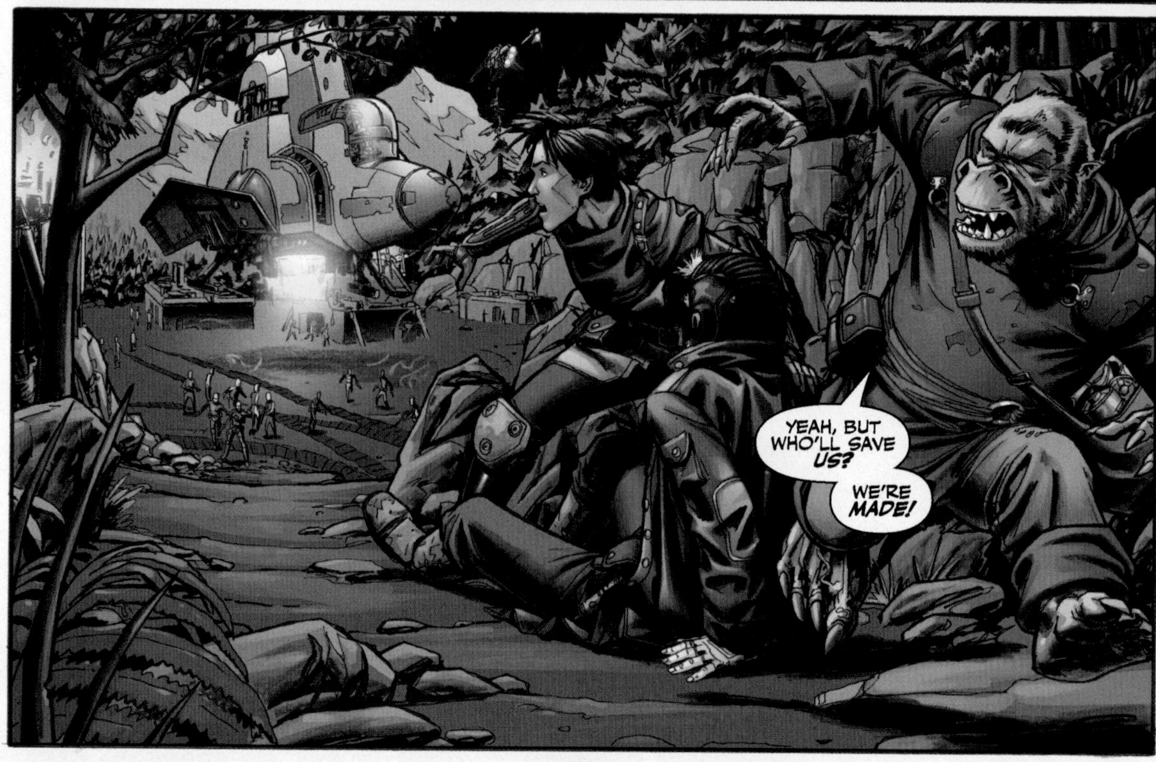
YEAH, BUT WHO'LL SAVE US?
WE'RE MADE!

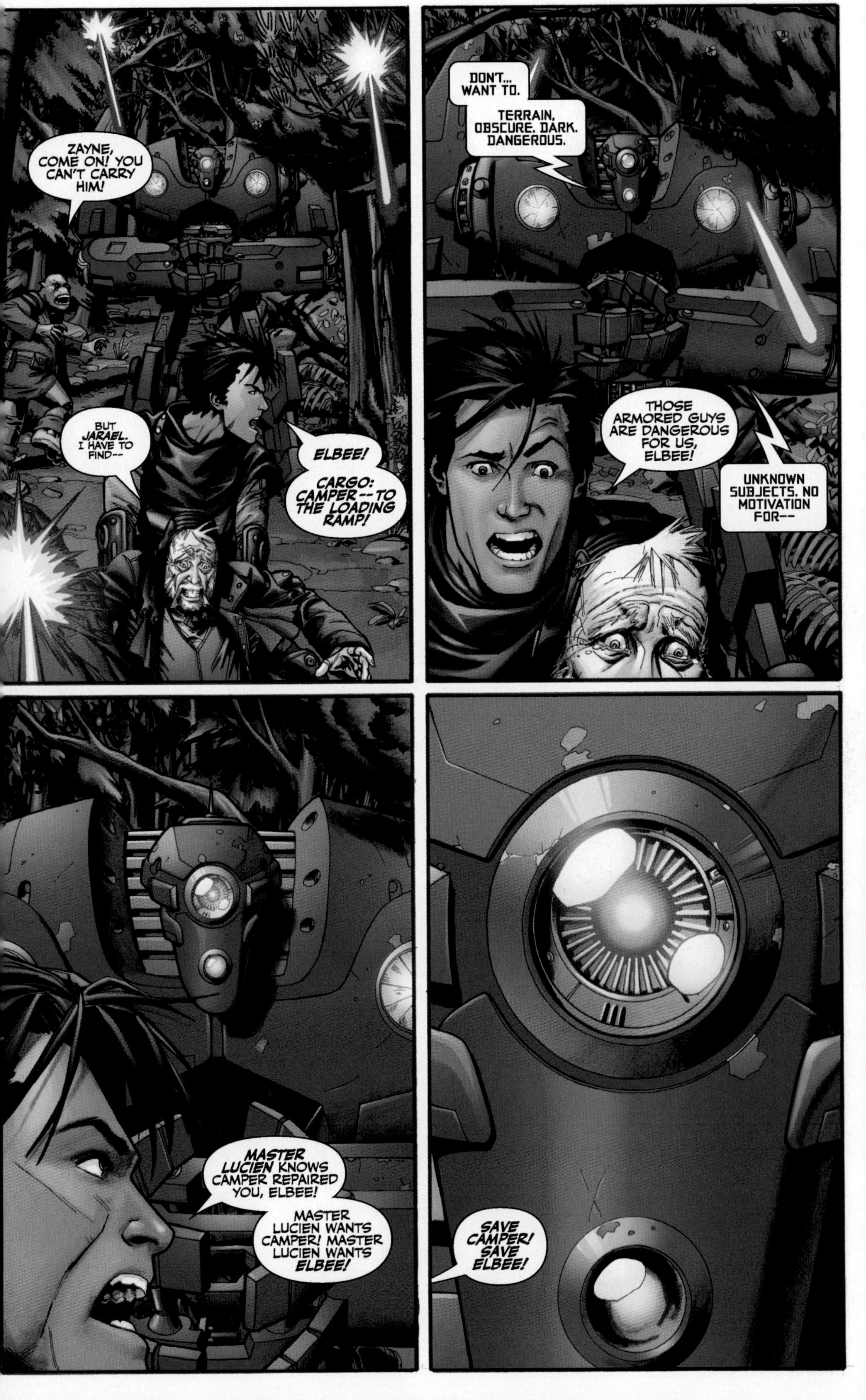
ZAYNE, COME ON! YOU CAN'T CARRY HIM!
BUT JARAEL. I HAVE TO FIND--
ELBEE!
CARGO: CAMPER--TO THE LOADING RAMP!
DON'T... WANT TO.
TERRAIN, OBSCURE. DARK. DANGEROUS.
THOSE ARMORED GUYS ARE DANGEROUS FOR US, ELBEE!
UNKNOWN SUBJECTS. NO MOTIVATION FOR--
MASTER LUCIEN KNOWS CAMPER REPAIRED YOU, ELBEE!
MASTER LUCIEN WANTS CAMPER! MASTER LUCIEN WANTS ELBEE!
SAVE CAMPER! SAVE ELBEE!

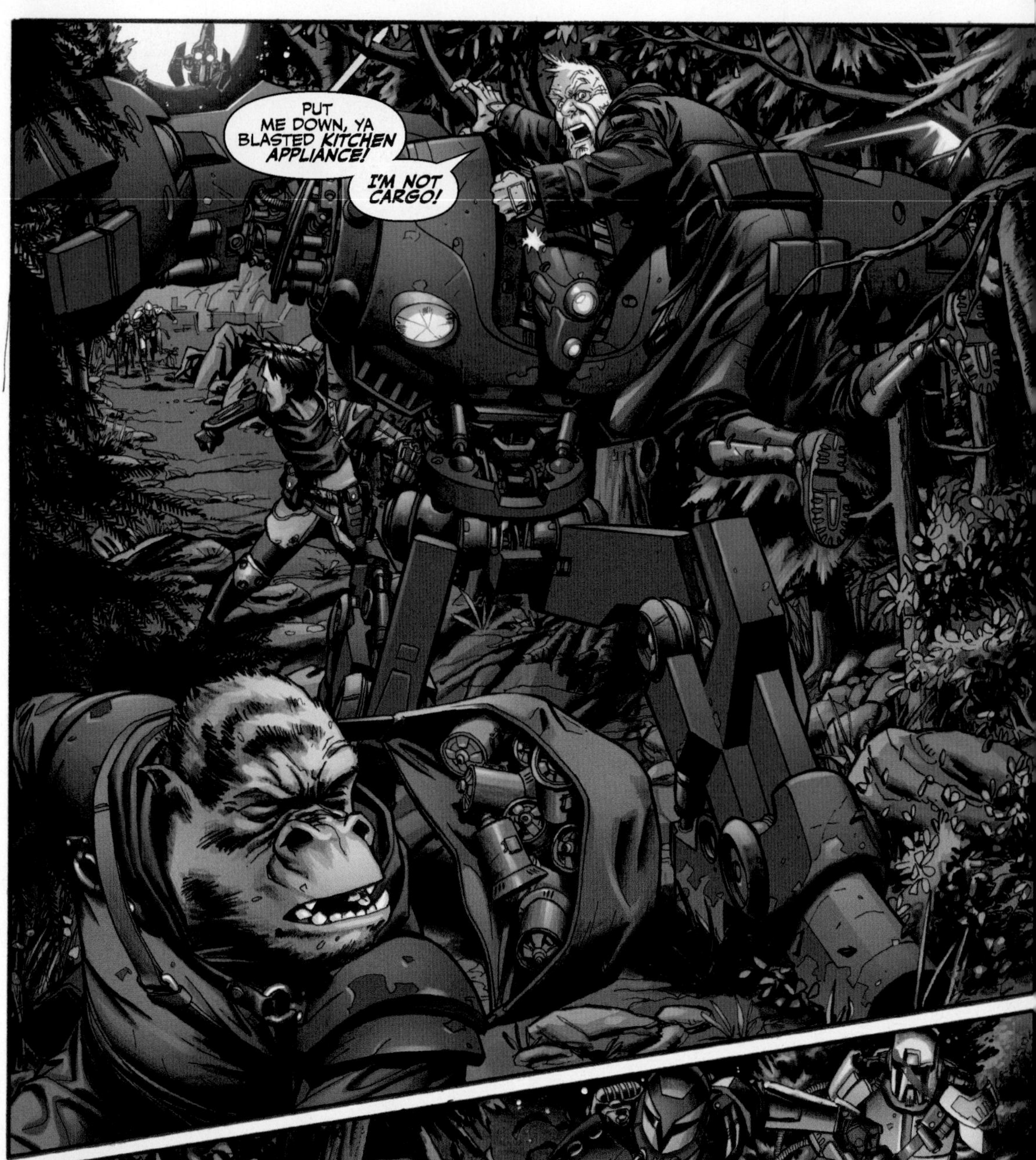
PUT ME DOWN, YA BLASTED *KITCHEN APPLIANCE!*
I'M NOT CARGO!

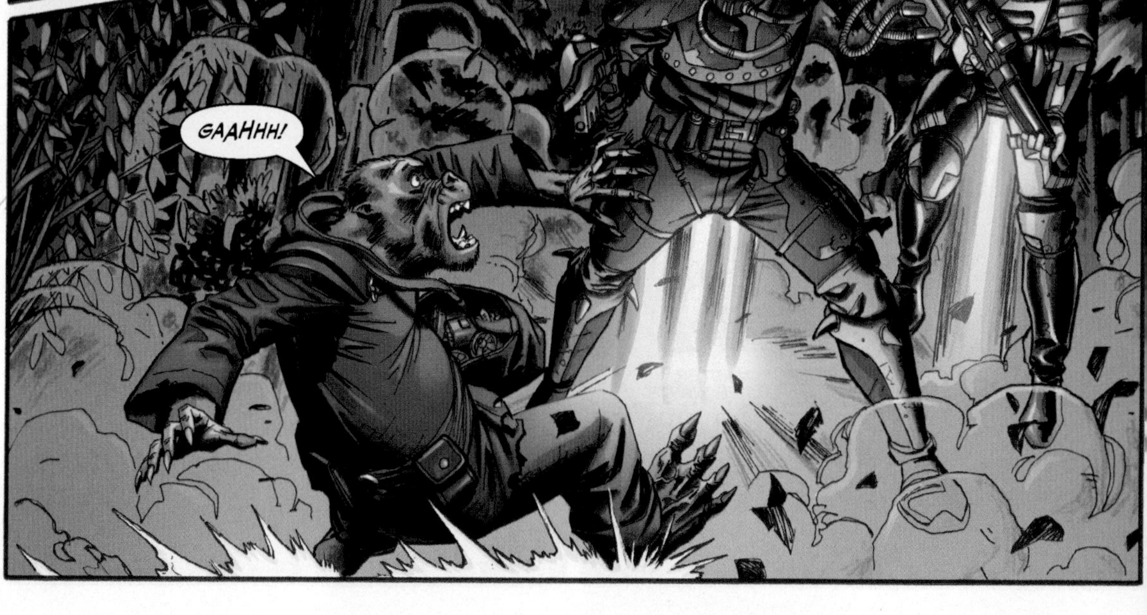
GAAHHH!

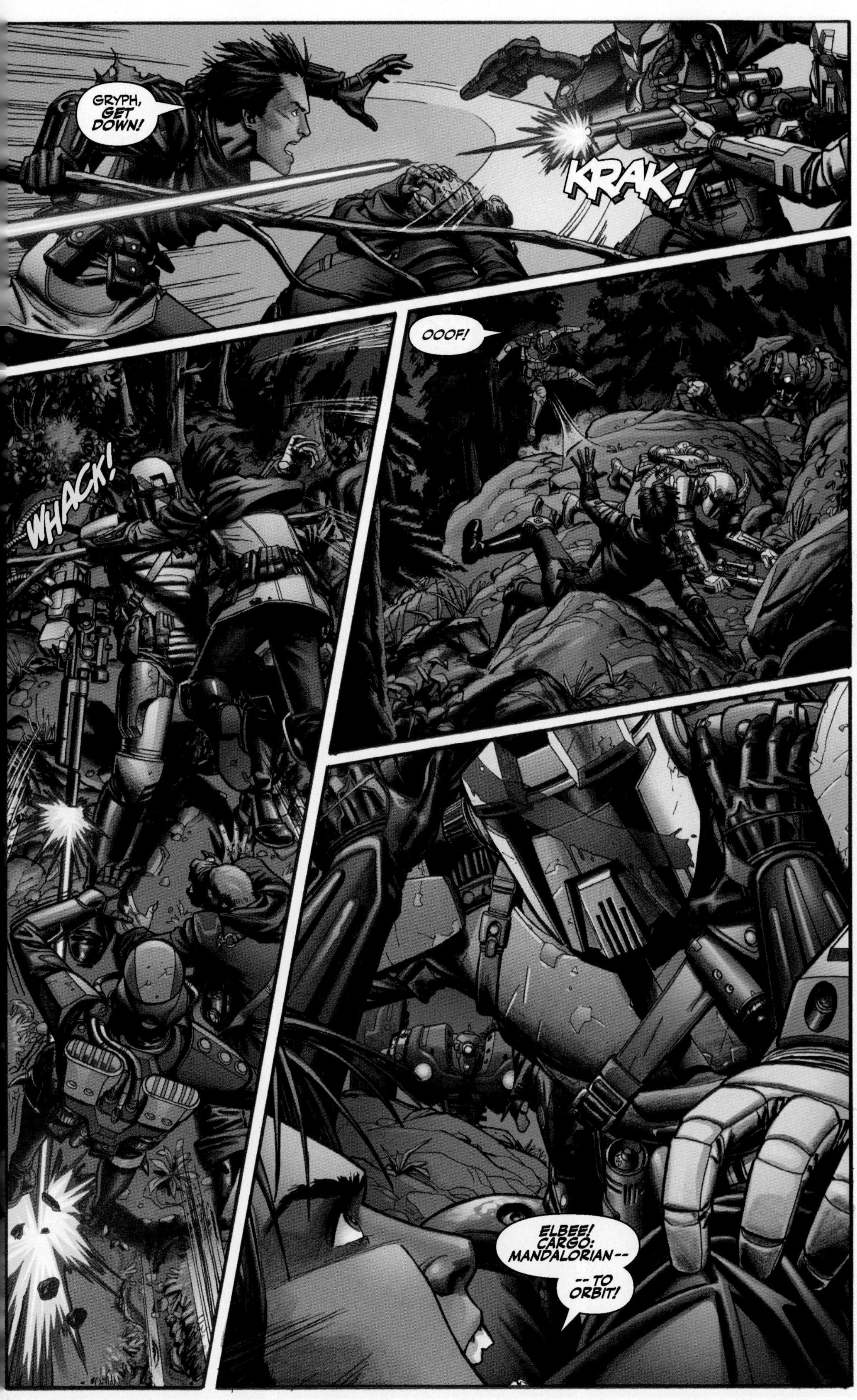
GRYPH, GET DOWN!
KRAK!
WHACK!
OOOF!
ELBEE! CARGO: MANDALORIAN--
--TO ORBIT!

-- SENT TWO TO THE CLEARING ABOVE, COMMANDER *ROHLAN.* WE'LL HAVE THEM SURROUNDED IN --

YAAAAAAHHHH!!!

WHUMPH!

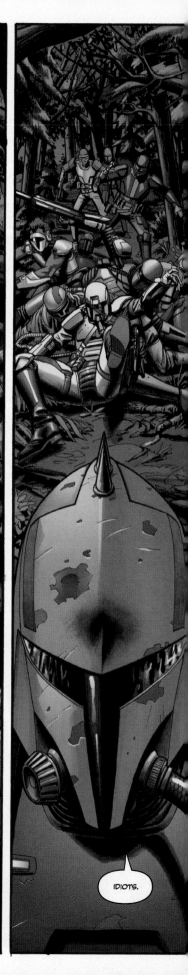

IDIOTS.

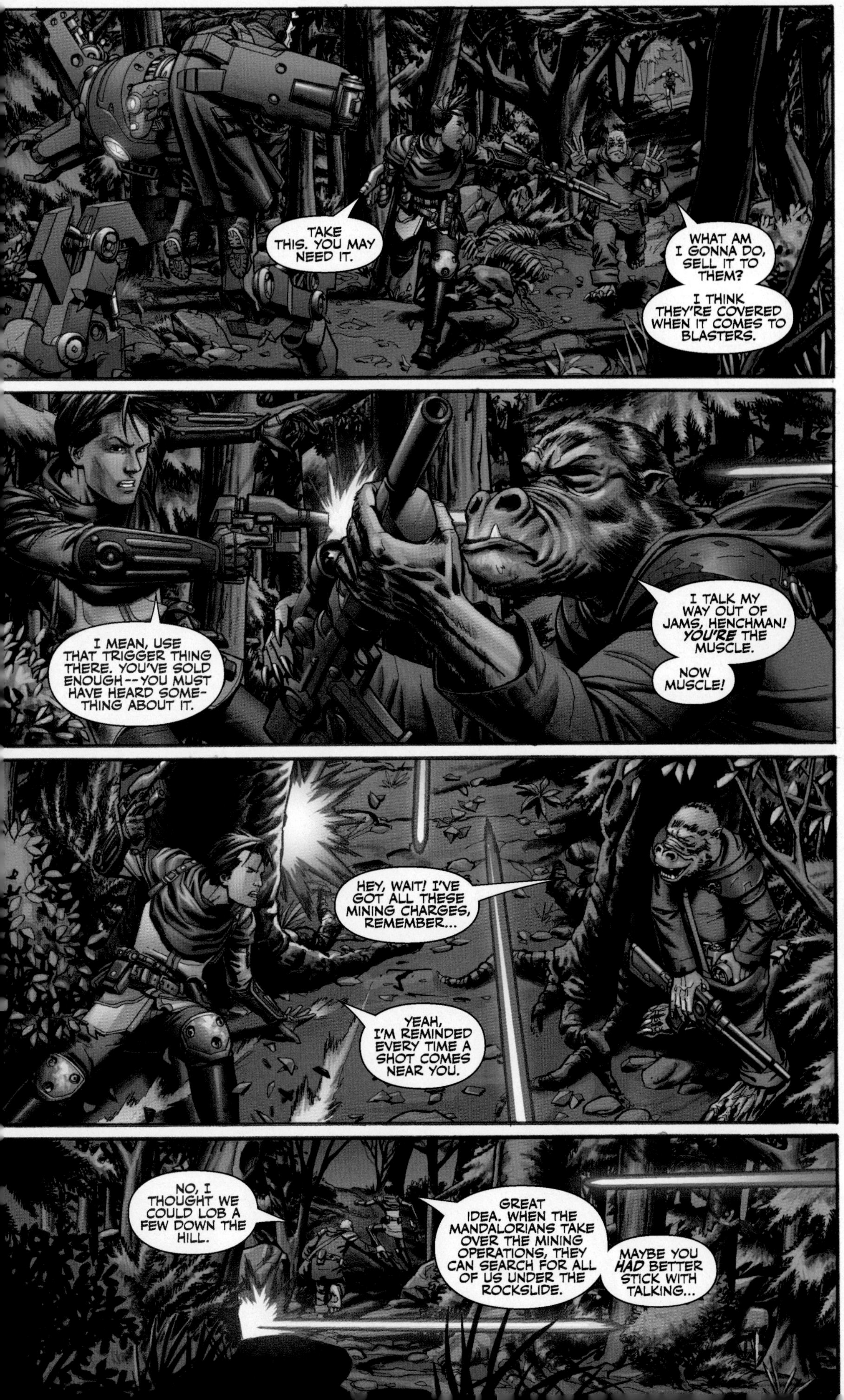
TAKE THIS. YOU MAY NEED IT.
WHAT AM I GONNA DO, SELL IT TO THEM?
I THINK THEY'RE COVERED WHEN IT COMES TO BLASTERS.
I MEAN, USE THAT TRIGGER THING THERE. YOU'VE SOLD ENOUGH--YOU MUST HAVE HEARD SOMETHING ABOUT IT.
I TALK MY WAY OUT OF JAMS, HENCHMAN! YOU'RE THE MUSCLE.
NOW MUSCLE!
HEY, WAIT! I'VE GOT ALL THESE MINING CHARGES, REMEMBER...
YEAH, I'M REMINDED EVERY TIME A SHOT COMES NEAR YOU.
NO, I THOUGHT WE COULD LOB A FEW DOWN THE HILL.
GREAT IDEA. WHEN THE MANDALORIANS TAKE OVER THE MINING OPERATIONS, THEY CAN SEARCH FOR ALL OF US UNDER THE ROCKSLIDE.
MAYBE YOU HAD BETTER STICK WITH TALKING...

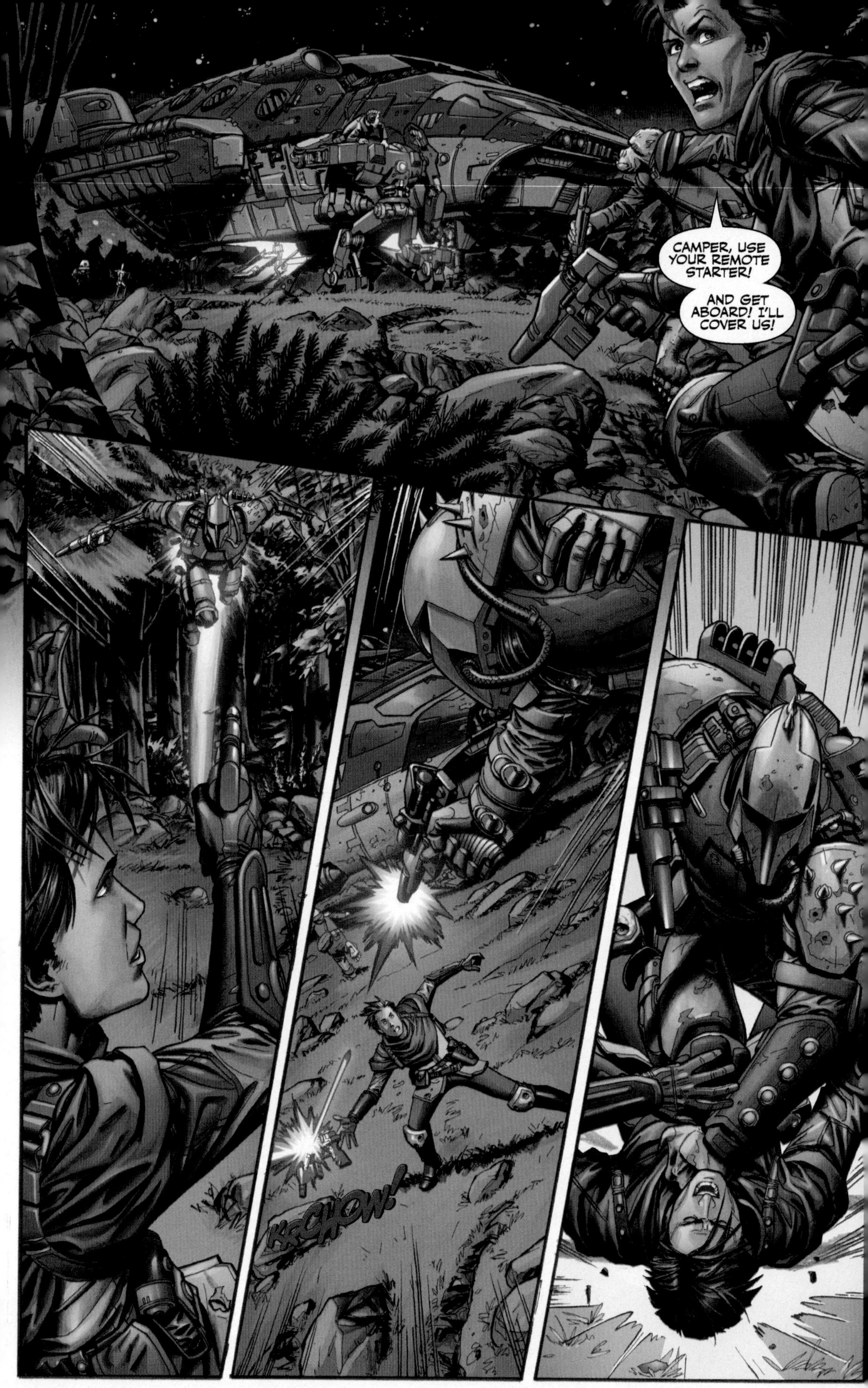
CAMPER, USE YOUR REMOTE STARTER!
AND GET ABOARD! I'LL COVER US!
KRCHOW!

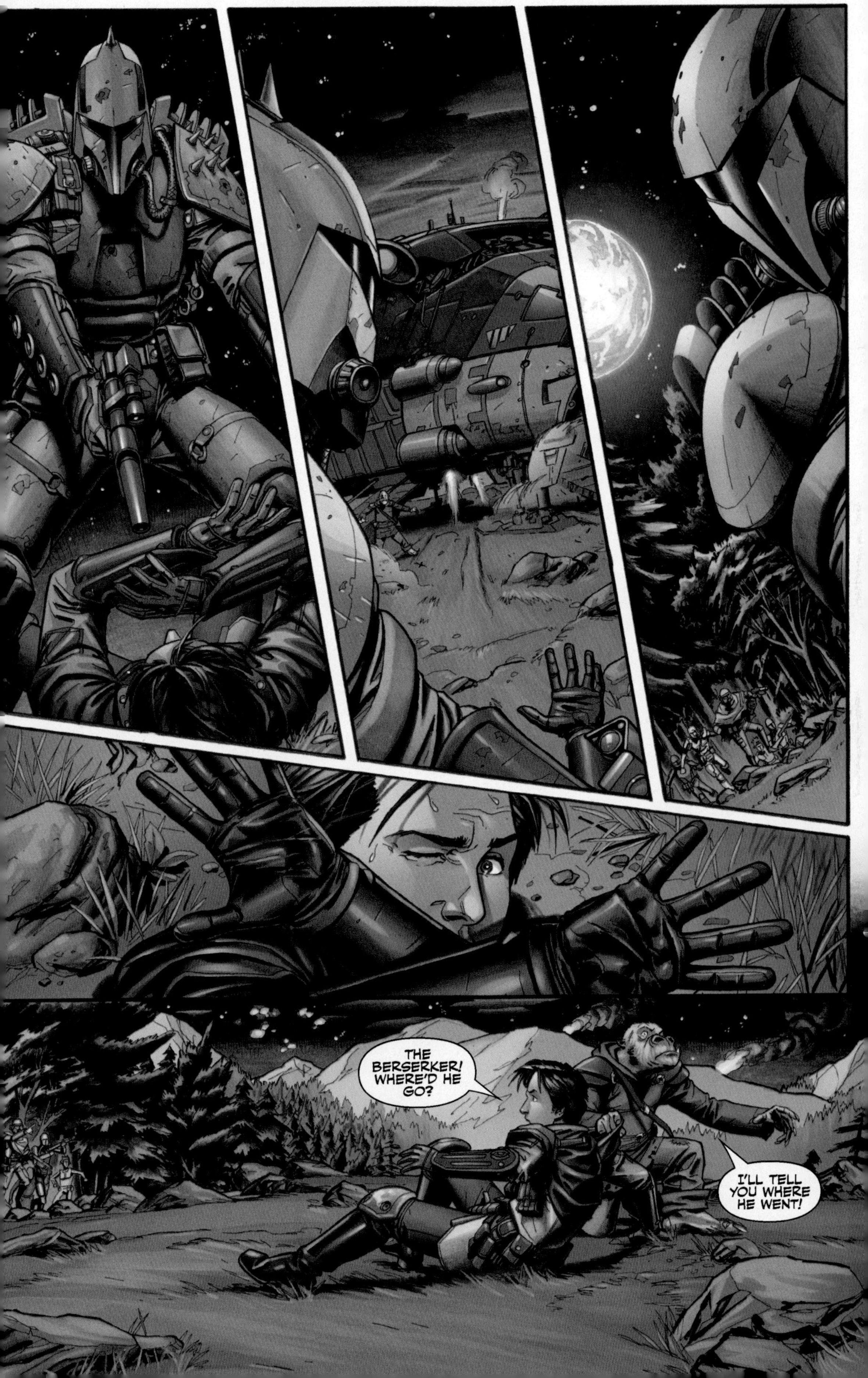
THE BERSERKER! WHERE'D HE GO?
I'LL TELL YOU WHERE HE WENT!

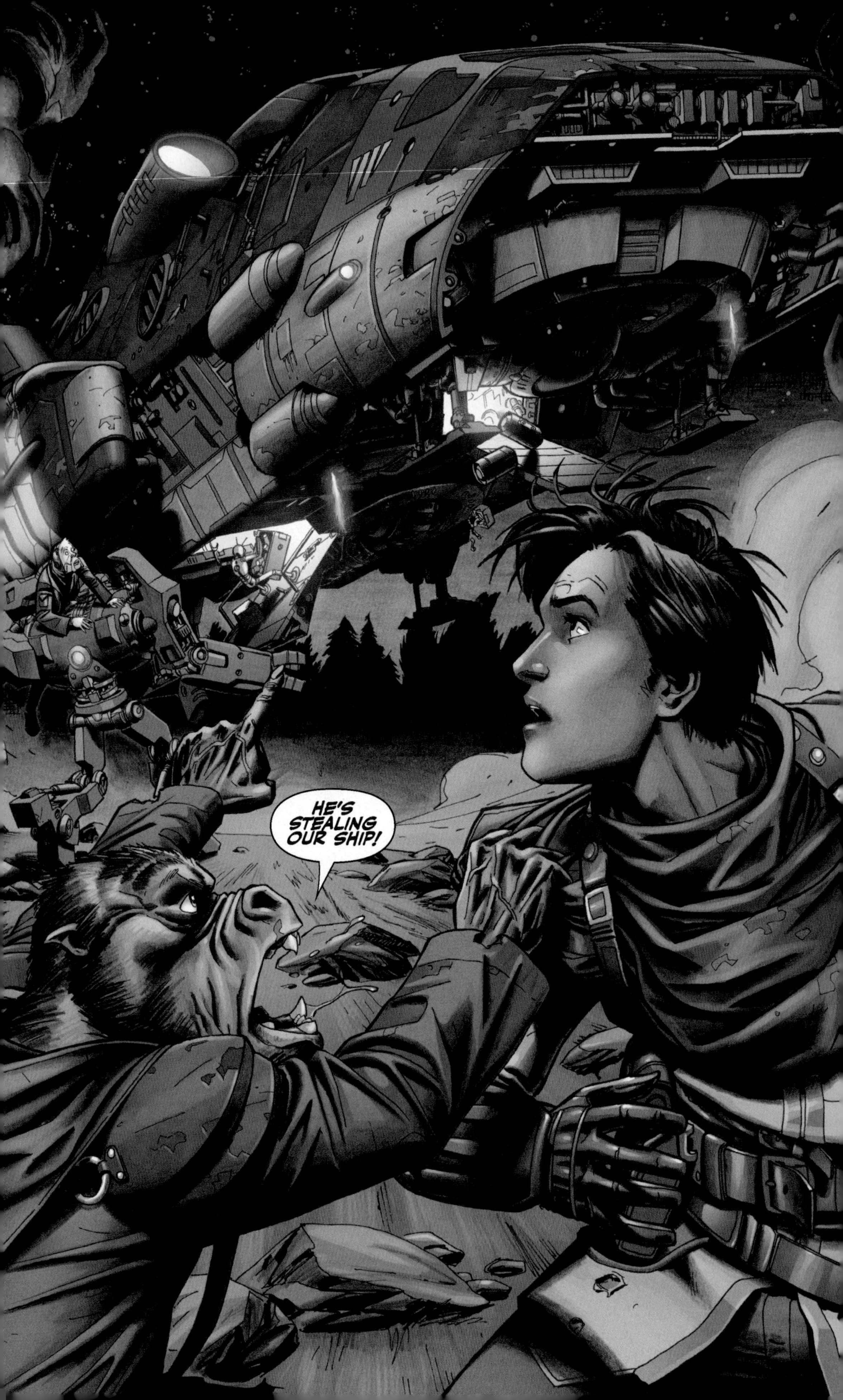
HE'S STEALING OUR SHIP!

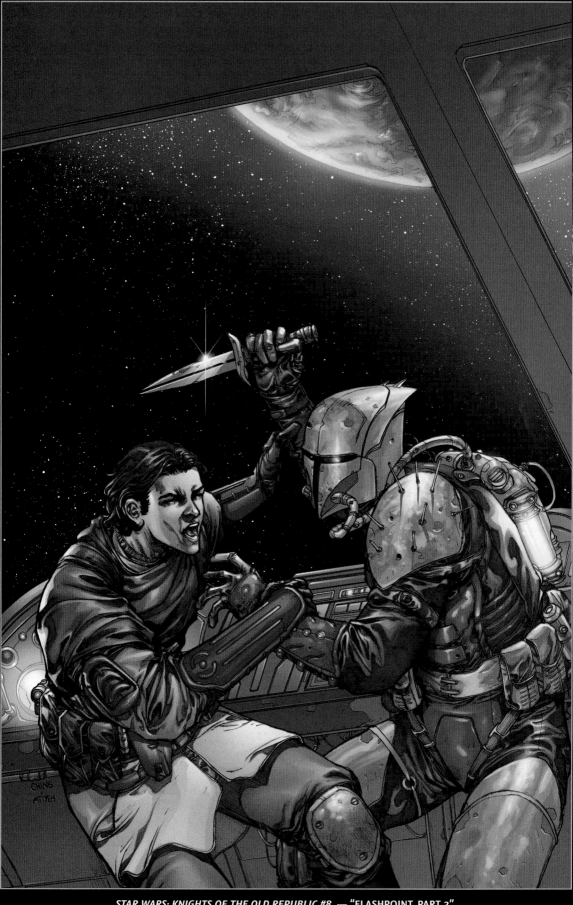

STAR WARS: KNIGHTS OF THE OLD REPUBLIC #8 — "FLASHPOINT, PART 2"

WRITER: JOHN JACKSON MILLER • ARTIST: DUSTIN WEAVER • COLORIST: MICHAEL ATIYEH • LETTERER: MICHAEL HEISLER
ASSISTANT EDITOR: DAVE MARSHALL • EDITOR: JEREMY BARLOW • COVER ARTISTS: BRIAN CHING & MICHAEL ATIYEH

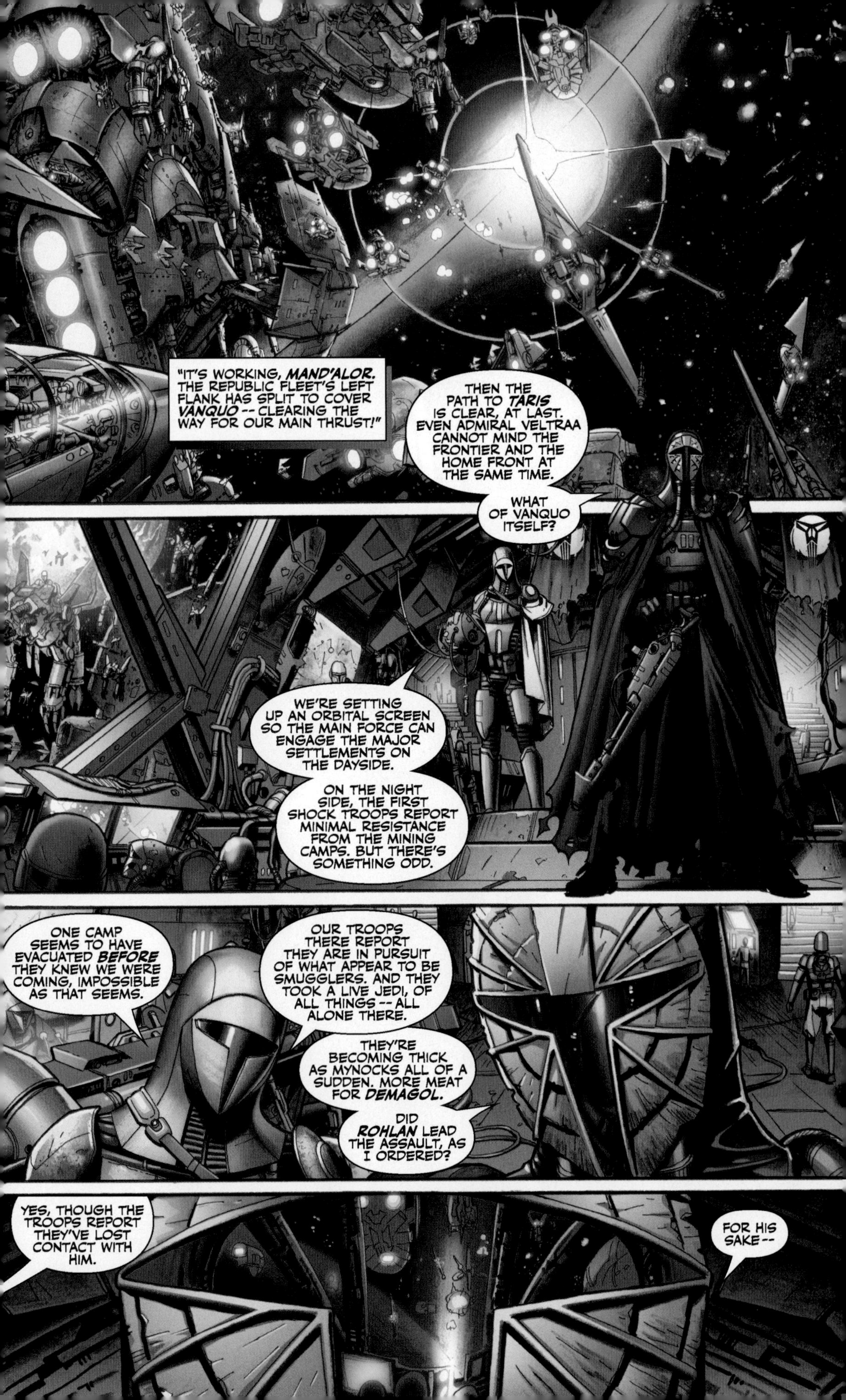
"IT'S WORKING, MAND'ALOR. THE REPUBLIC FLEET'S LEFT FLANK HAS SPLIT TO COVER VANQUO -- CLEARING THE WAY FOR OUR MAIN THRUST!"
THEN THE PATH TO TARIS IS CLEAR, AT LAST. EVEN ADMIRAL VELTRAA CANNOT MIND THE FRONTIER AND THE HOME FRONT AT THE SAME TIME.
WHAT OF VANQUO ITSELF?
WE'RE SETTING UP AN ORBITAL SCREEN SO THE MAIN FORCE CAN ENGAGE THE MAJOR SETTLEMENTS ON THE DAYSIDE.
ON THE NIGHT SIDE, THE FIRST SHOCK TROOPS REPORT MINIMAL RESISTANCE FROM THE MINING CAMPS. BUT THERE'S SOMETHING ODD.
ONE CAMP SEEMS TO HAVE EVACUATED BEFORE THEY KNEW WE WERE COMING, IMPOSSIBLE AS THAT SEEMS.
OUR TROOPS THERE REPORT THEY ARE IN PURSUIT OF WHAT APPEAR TO BE SMUGGLERS. AND THEY TOOK A LIVE JEDI, OF ALL THINGS -- ALL ALONE THERE.
THEY'RE BECOMING THICK AS MYNOCKS ALL OF A SUDDEN. MORE MEAT FOR DEMAGOL.
DID ROHLAN LEAD THE ASSAULT, AS I ORDERED?
YES, THOUGH THE TROOPS REPORT THEY'VE LOST CONTACT WITH HIM.
FOR HIS SAKE--

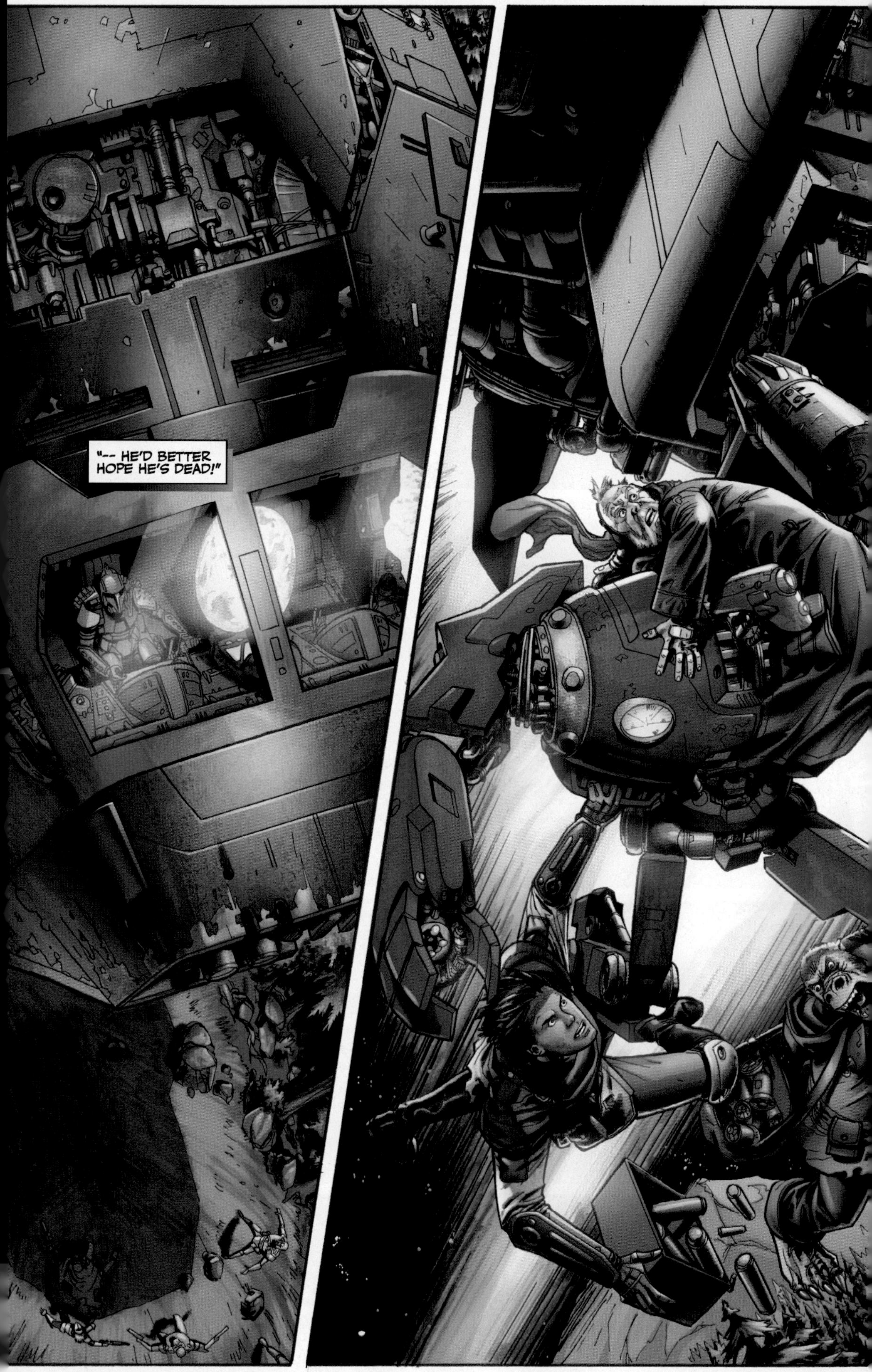
"-- HE'D BETTER HOPE HE'S DEAD!"

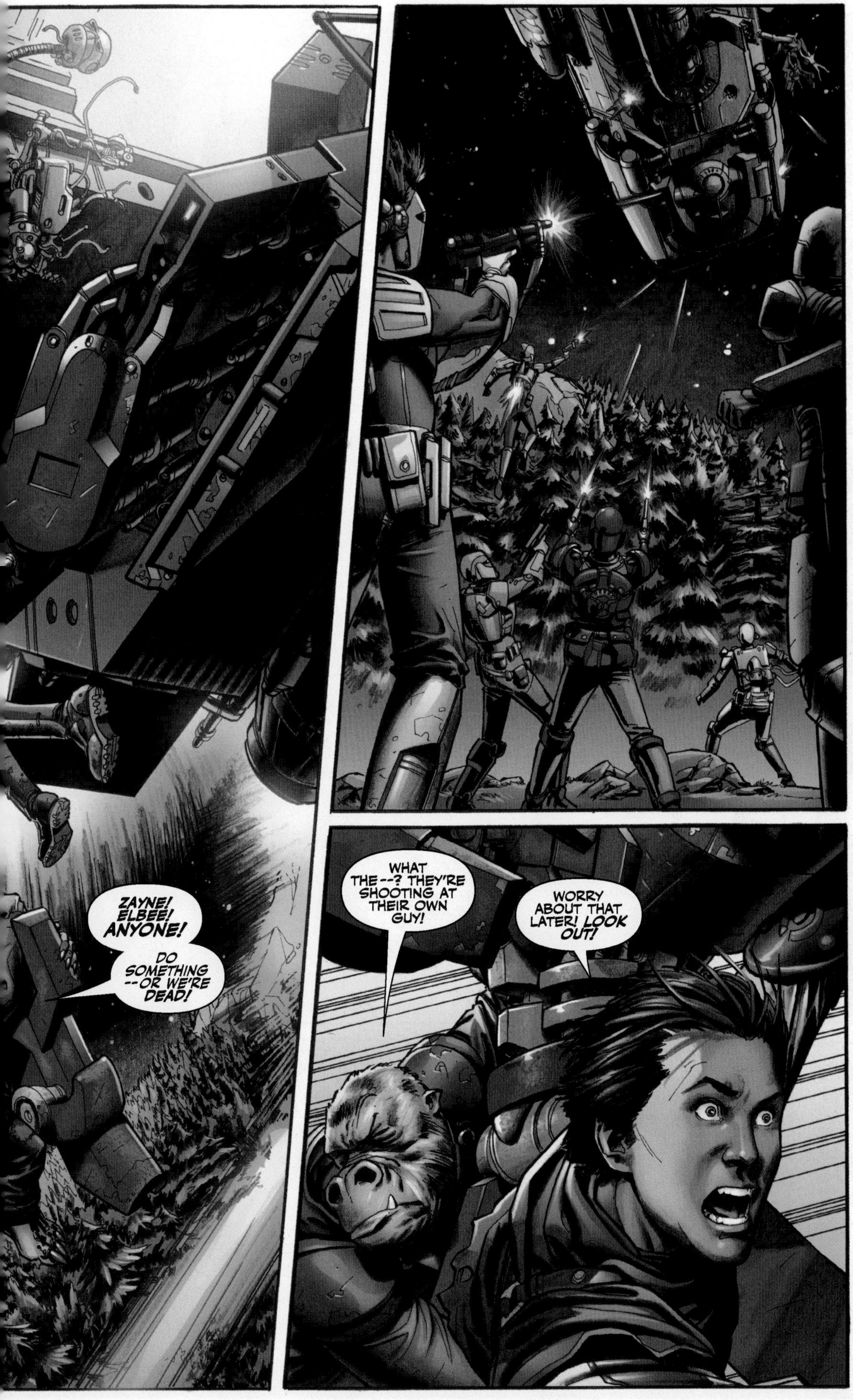
ZAYNE! ELBEE! ANYONE!
DO SOMETHING --OR WE'RE DEAD!
WHAT THE --? THEY'RE SHOOTING AT THEIR OWN GUY!
WORRY ABOUT THAT LATER! LOOK OUT!

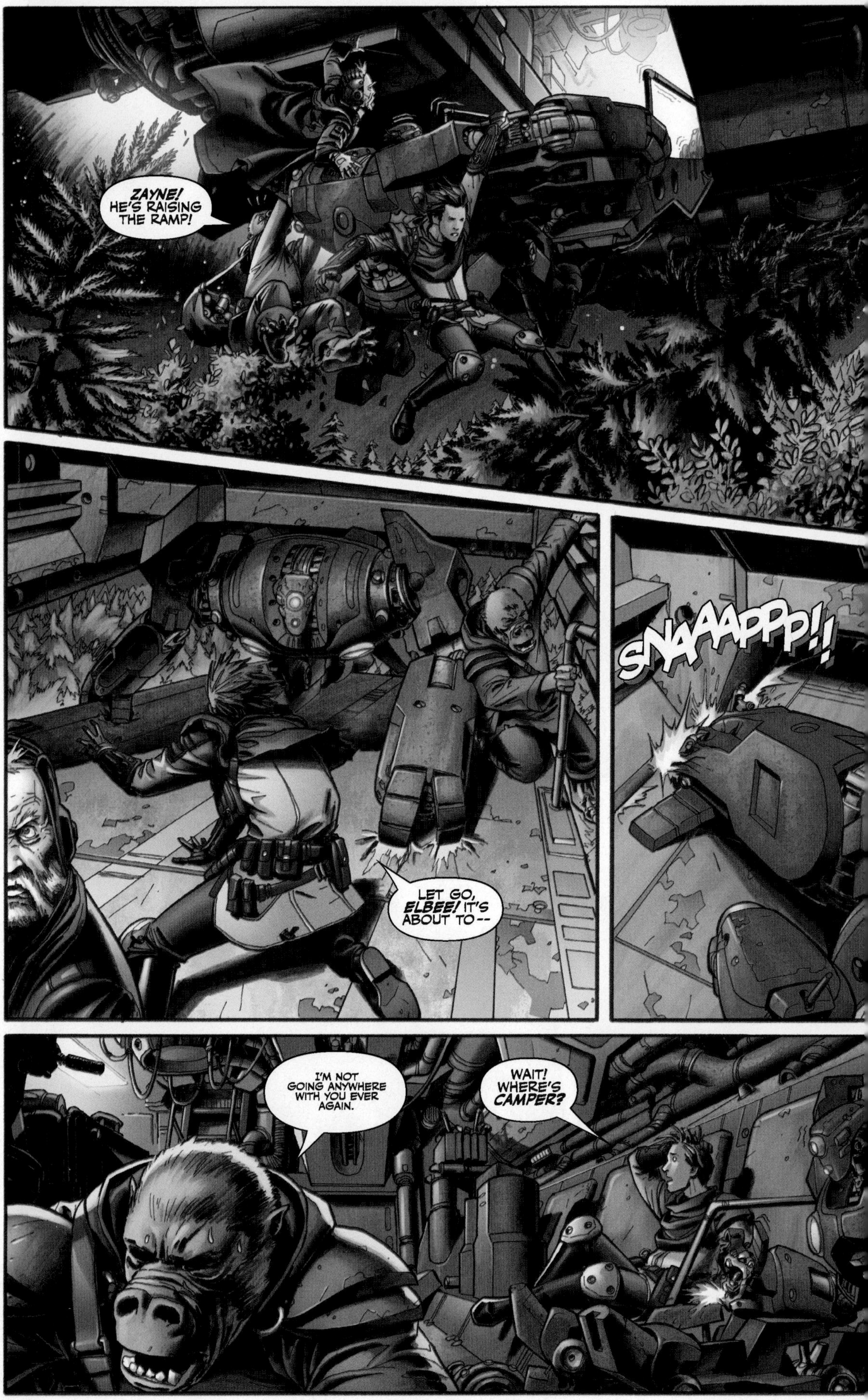
ZAYNE! HE'S RAISING THE RAMP!
LET GO, ELBEE! IT'S ABOUT TO--
SNAAAPPP!!
I'M NOT GOING ANYWHERE WITH YOU EVER AGAIN.
WAIT! WHERE'S CAMPER?

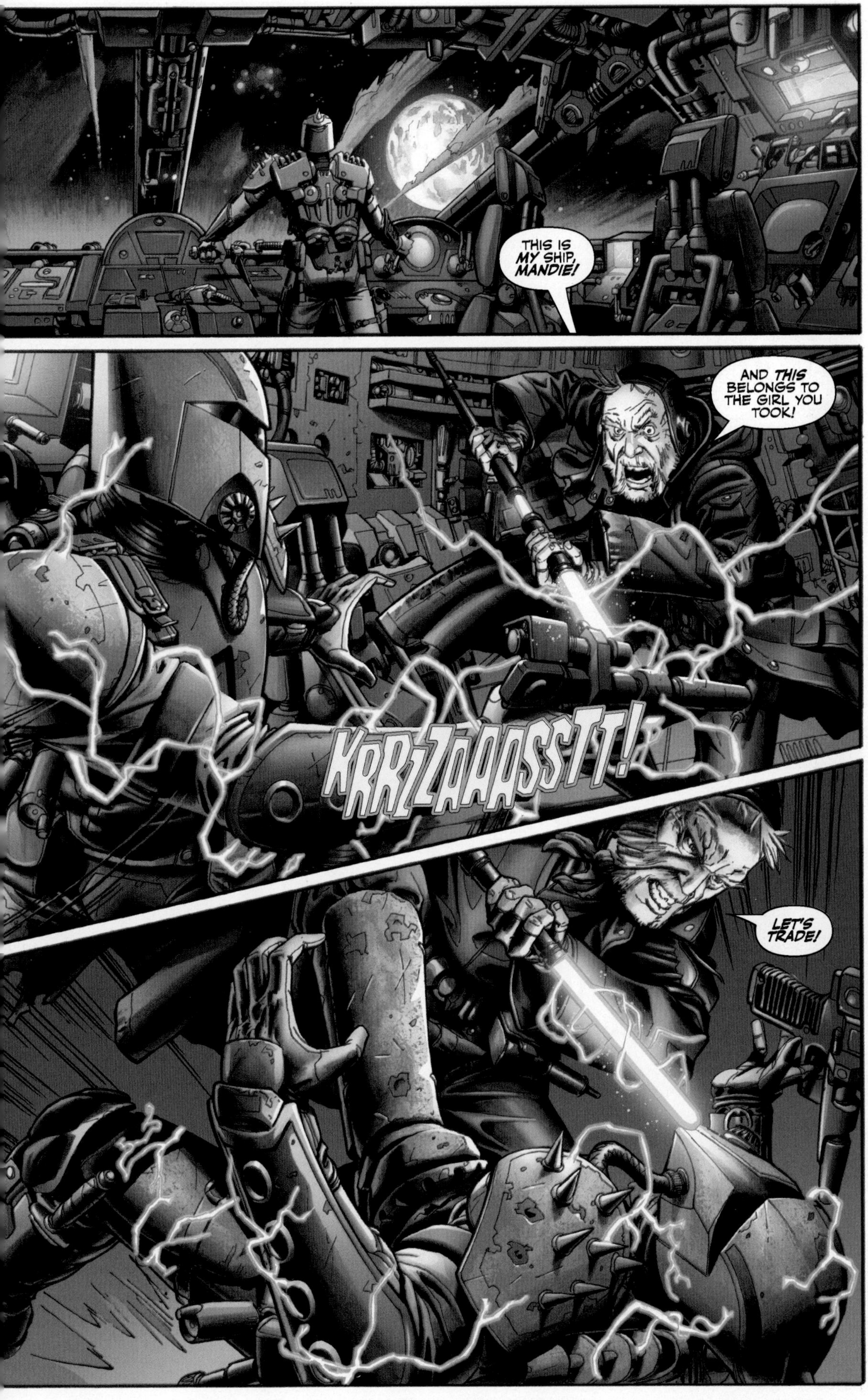
THIS IS MY SHIP, MANDIE!
AND THIS BELONGS TO THE GIRL YOU TOOK!
KRRZAAASSTT!
LET'S TRADE!

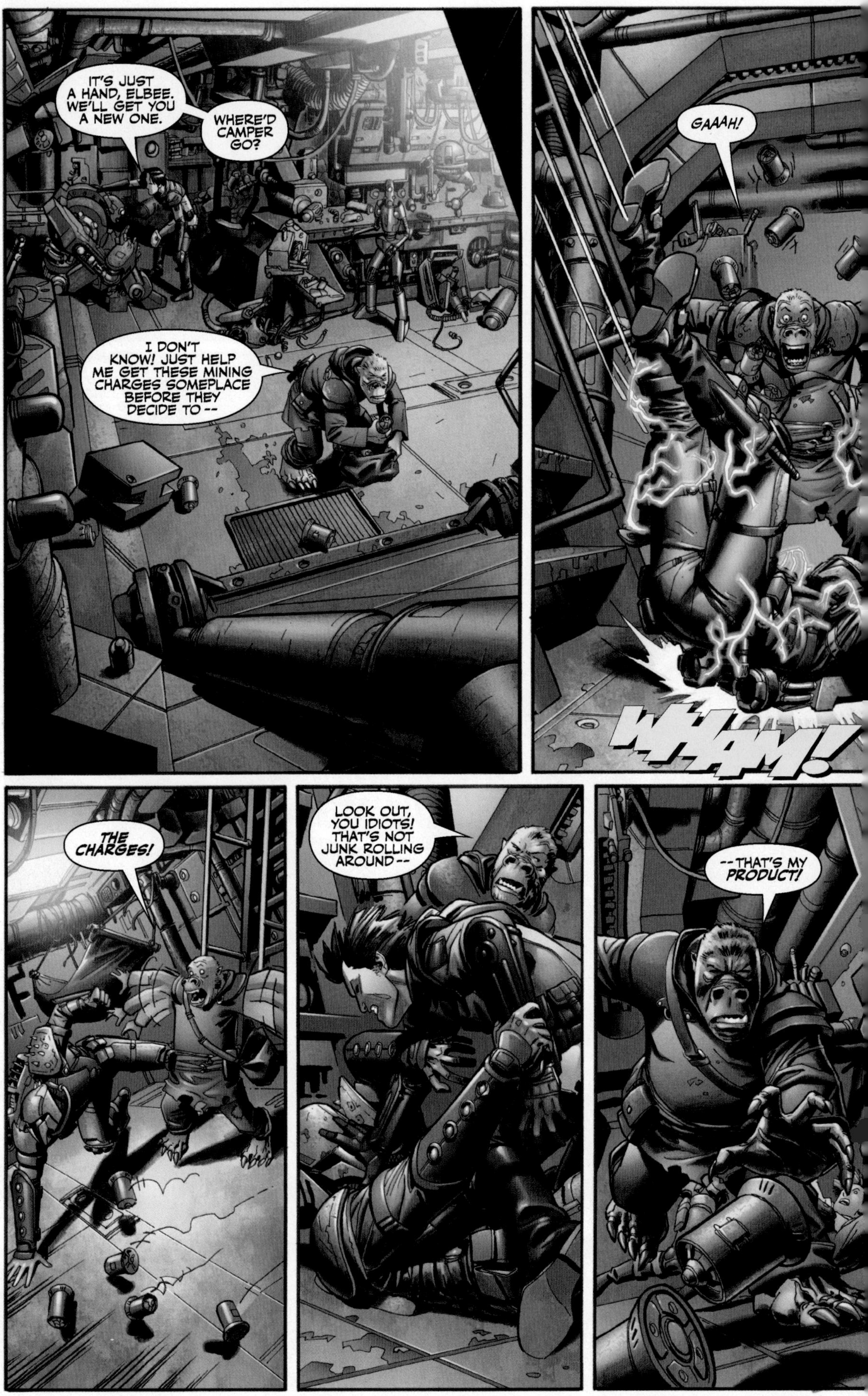
IT'S JUST A HAND, ELBEE. WE'LL GET YOU A NEW ONE.
WHERE'D CAMPER GO?
I DON'T KNOW! JUST HELP ME GET THESE MINING CHARGES SOMEPLACE BEFORE THEY DECIDE TO --
GAAAH!
WHAM!
THE CHARGES!
LOOK OUT, YOU IDIOTS! THAT'S NOT JUNK ROLLING AROUND --
--THAT'S MY PRODUCT!

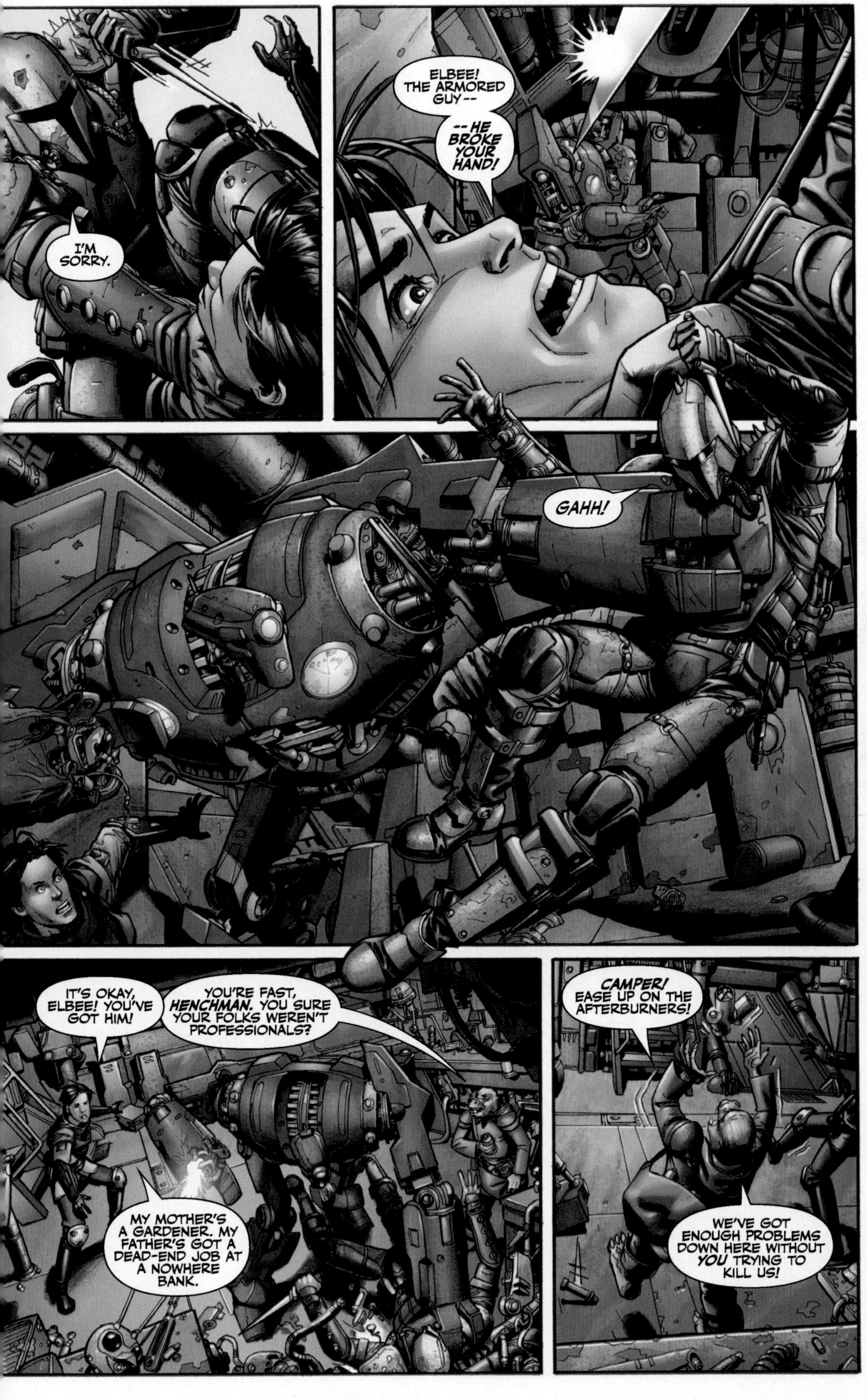
I'M SORRY.
ELBEE! THE ARMORED GUY--
--HE BROKE YOUR HAND!
GAHH!
IT'S OKAY, ELBEE! YOU'VE GOT HIM!
YOU'RE FAST, HENCHMAN. YOU SURE YOUR FOLKS WEREN'T PROFESSIONALS?
MY MOTHER'S A GARDENER. MY FATHER'S GOT A DEAD-END JOB AT A NOWHERE BANK.
CAMPER! EASE UP ON THE AFTERBURNERS!
WE'VE GOT ENOUGH PROBLEMS DOWN HERE WITHOUT YOU TRYING TO KILL US!

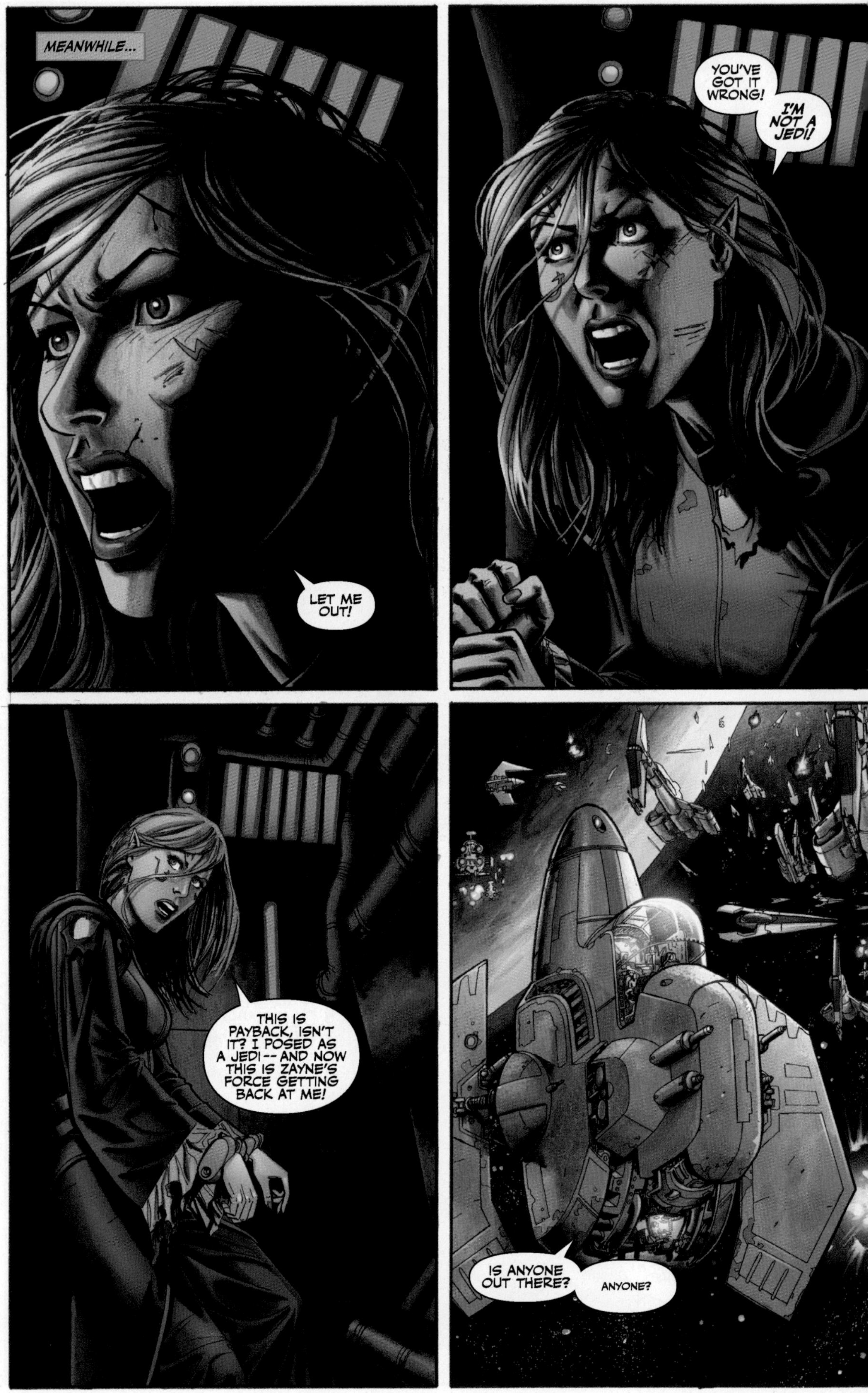
MEANWHILE...
LET ME OUT!
YOU'VE GOT IT WRONG!
I'M NOT A JEDI!
THIS IS PAYBACK, ISN'T IT? I POSED AS A JEDI-- AND NOW THIS IS ZAYNE'S FORCE GETTING BACK AT ME!
IS ANYONE OUT THERE?
ANYONE?

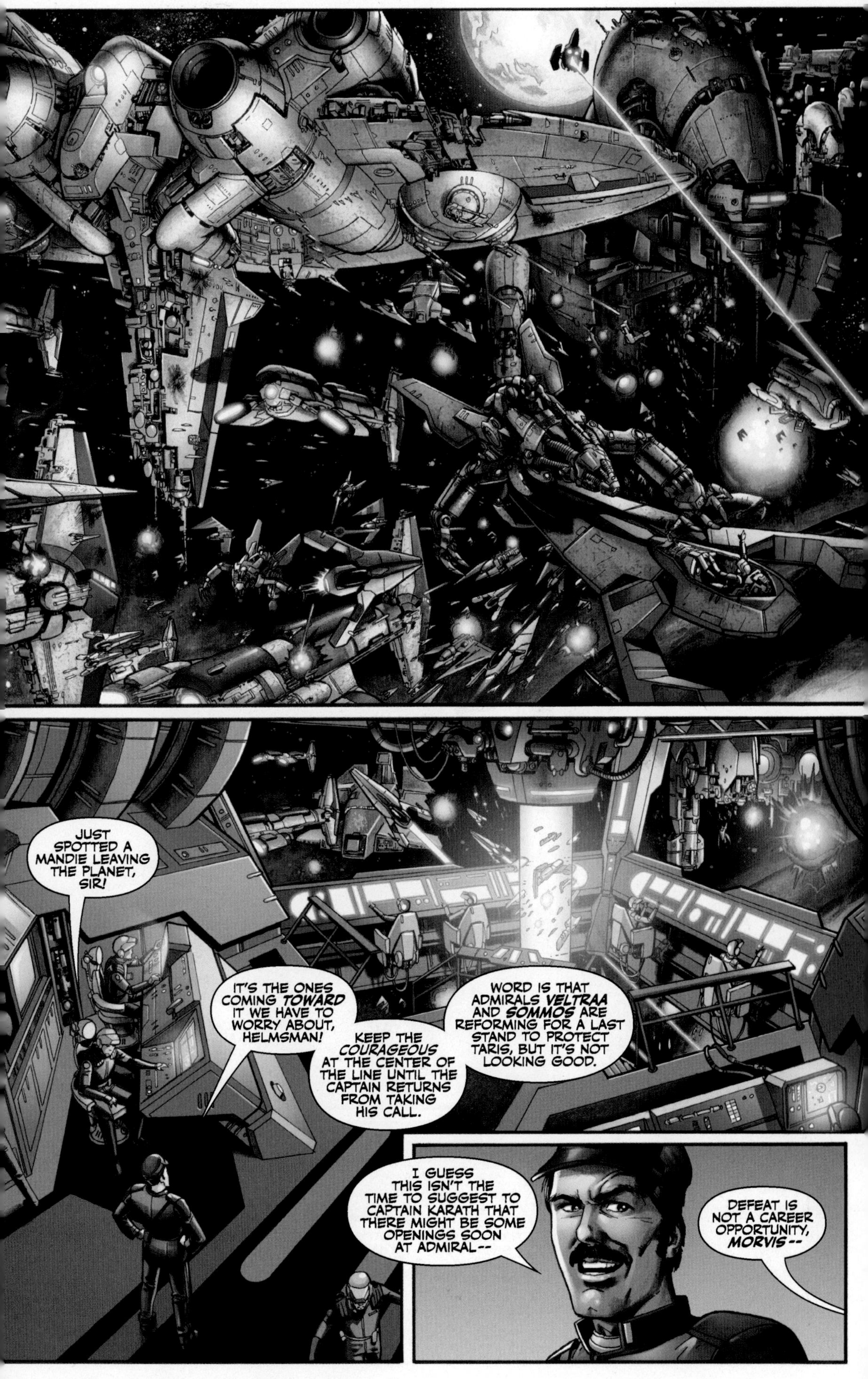
JUST SPOTTED A MANDIE LEAVING THE PLANET, SIR!
IT'S THE ONES COMING *TOWARD* IT WE HAVE TO WORRY ABOUT, HELMSMAN!
KEEP THE *COURAGEOUS* AT THE CENTER OF THE LINE UNTIL THE CAPTAIN RETURNS FROM TAKING HIS CALL.
WORD IS THAT ADMIRALS *VELTRAA* AND *SOMMOS* ARE REFORMING FOR A LAST STAND TO PROTECT TARIS, BUT IT'S NOT LOOKING GOOD.
I GUESS THIS ISN'T THE TIME TO SUGGEST TO CAPTAIN KARATH THAT THERE MIGHT BE SOME OPENINGS SOON AT ADMIRAL--
DEFEAT IS NOT A CAREER OPPORTUNITY, *MORVIS*--

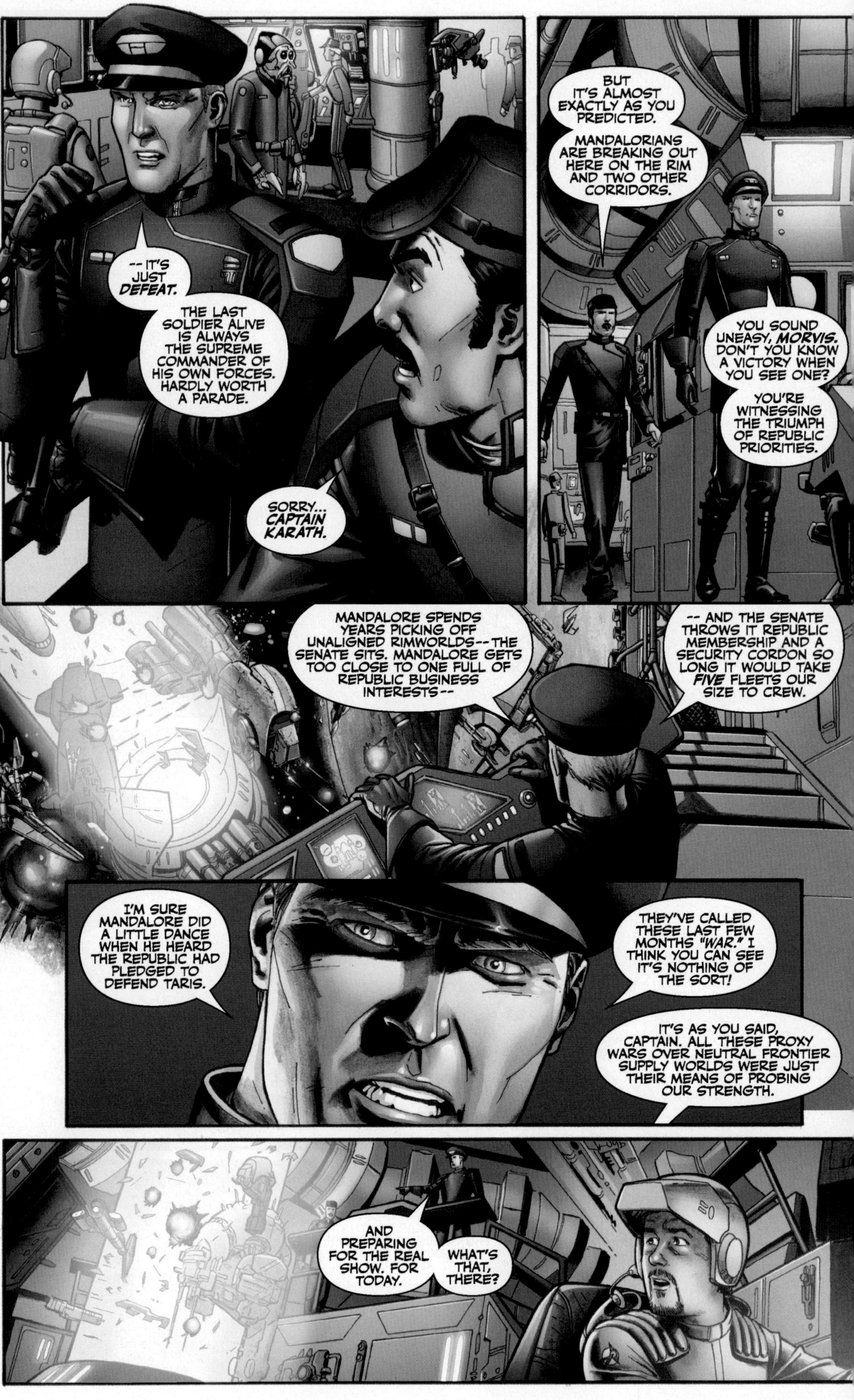
-- IT'S JUST *DEFEAT.*
THE LAST SOLDIER ALIVE IS ALWAYS THE SUPREME COMMANDER OF HIS OWN FORCES. HARDLY WORTH A PARADE.
SORRY... *CAPTAIN KARATH.*
BUT IT'S ALMOST EXACTLY AS YOU PREDICTED.
MANDALORIANS ARE BREAKING OUT HERE ON THE RIM AND TWO OTHER CORRIDORS.
YOU SOUND UNEASY, *MORVIS.* DON'T YOU KNOW A VICTORY WHEN YOU SEE ONE?
YOU'RE WITNESSING THE TRIUMPH OF REPUBLIC PRIORITIES.
MANDALORE SPENDS YEARS PICKING OFF UNALIGNED RIMWORLDS--THE SENATE SITS. MANDALORE GETS TOO CLOSE TO ONE FULL OF REPUBLIC BUSINESS INTERESTS--
-- AND THE SENATE THROWS IT REPUBLIC MEMBERSHIP AND A SECURITY CORDON SO LONG IT WOULD TAKE *FIVE* FLEETS OUR SIZE TO CREW.
I'M SURE MANDALORE DID A LITTLE DANCE WHEN HE HEARD THE REPUBLIC HAD PLEDGED TO DEFEND TARIS.
THEY'VE CALLED THESE LAST FEW MONTHS "*WAR.*" I THINK YOU CAN SEE IT'S NOTHING OF THE SORT!
IT'S AS YOU SAID, CAPTAIN. ALL THESE PROXY WARS OVER NEUTRAL FRONTIER SUPPLY WORLDS WERE JUST THEIR MEANS OF PROBING OUR STRENGTH.
AND PREPARING FOR THE REAL SHOW. FOR TODAY.
WHAT'S THAT, THERE?

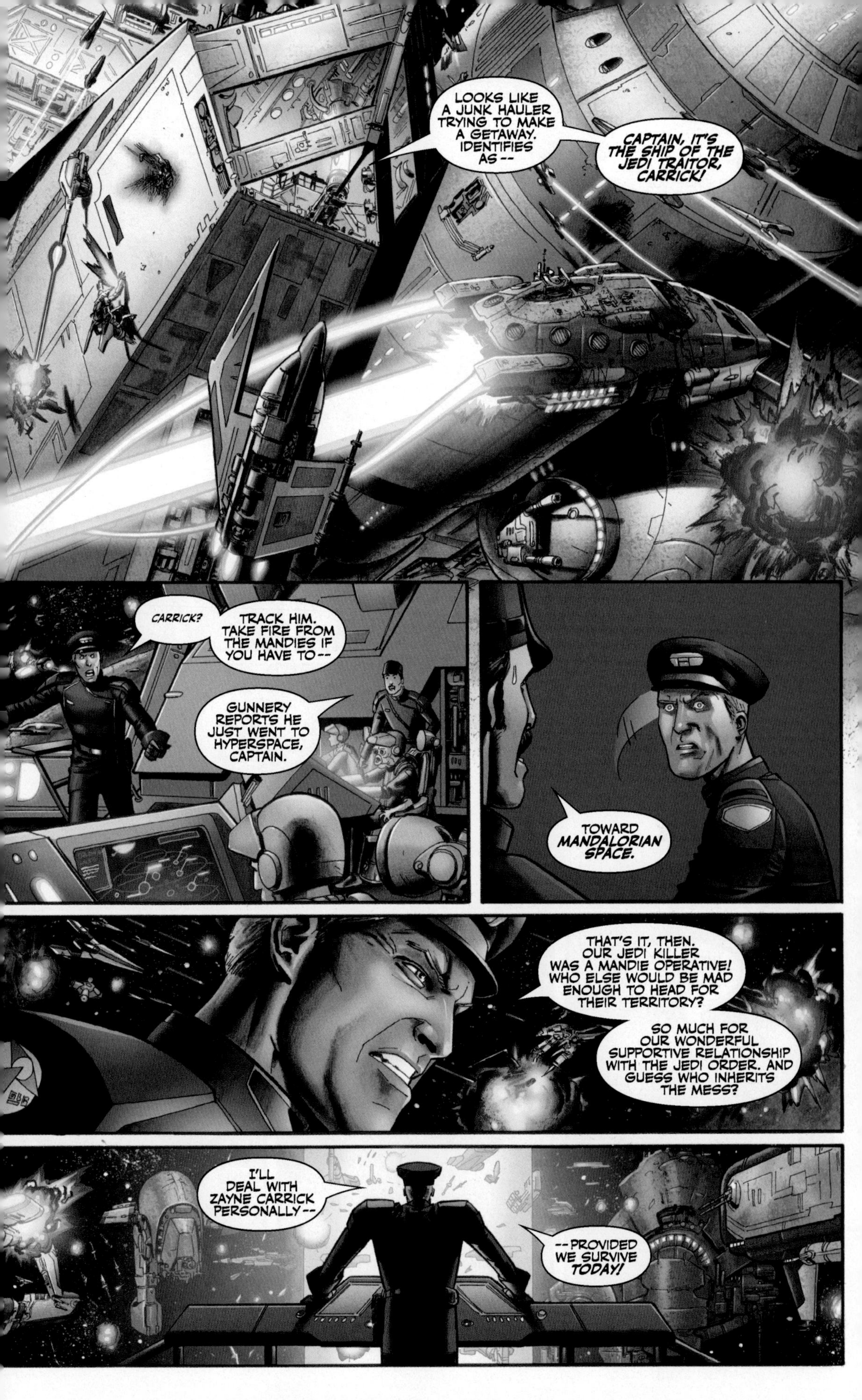
LOOKS LIKE A JUNK HAULER TRYING TO MAKE A GETAWAY. IDENTIFIES AS --
CAPTAIN, IT'S THE SHIP OF THE JEDI TRAITOR, CARRICK!
CARRICK?
TRACK HIM. TAKE FIRE FROM THE MANDIES IF YOU HAVE TO --
GUNNERY REPORTS HE JUST WENT TO HYPERSPACE, CAPTAIN.
TOWARD MANDALORIAN SPACE.
THAT'S IT, THEN. OUR JEDI KILLER WAS A MANDIE OPERATIVE! WHO ELSE WOULD BE MAD ENOUGH TO HEAD FOR THEIR TERRITORY?
SO MUCH FOR OUR WONDERFUL SUPPORTIVE RELATIONSHIP WITH THE JEDI ORDER. AND GUESS WHO INHERITS THE MESS?
I'LL DEAL WITH ZAYNE CARRICK PERSONALLY --
-- PROVIDED WE SURVIVE TODAY!

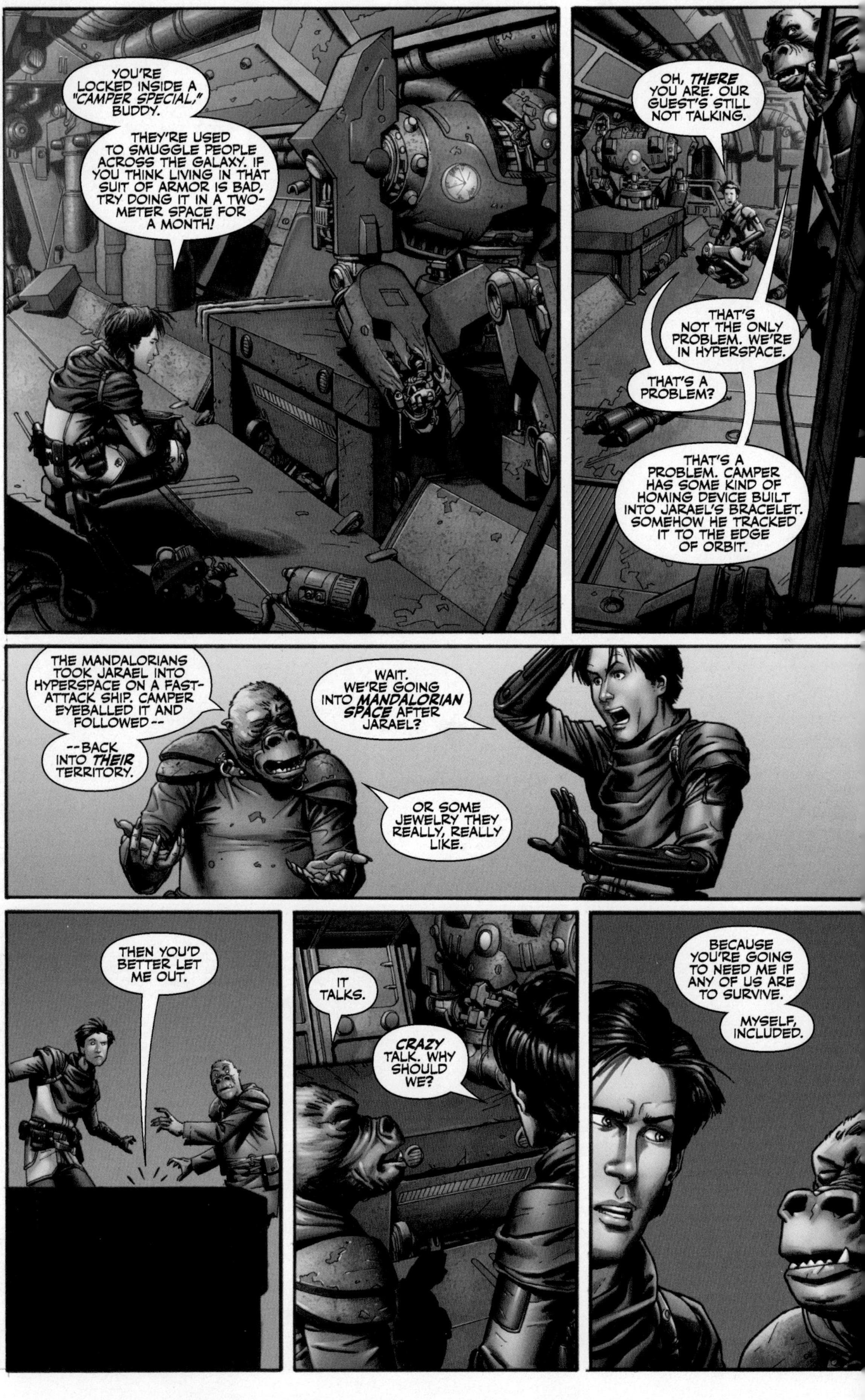
YOU'RE LOCKED INSIDE A "CAMPER SPECIAL," BUDDY.
THEY'RE USED TO SMUGGLE PEOPLE ACROSS THE GALAXY. IF YOU THINK LIVING IN THAT SUIT OF ARMOR IS BAD, TRY DOING IT IN A TWO-METER SPACE FOR A MONTH!
OH, THERE YOU ARE. OUR GUEST'S STILL NOT TALKING.
THAT'S NOT THE ONLY PROBLEM. WE'RE IN HYPERSPACE.
THAT'S A PROBLEM?
THAT'S A PROBLEM. CAMPER HAS SOME KIND OF HOMING DEVICE BUILT INTO JARAEL'S BRACELET. SOMEHOW HE TRACKED IT TO THE EDGE OF ORBIT.
THE MANDALORIANS TOOK JARAEL INTO HYPERSPACE ON A FAST-ATTACK SHIP. CAMPER EYEBALLED IT AND FOLLOWED--
--BACK INTO THEIR TERRITORY.
WAIT. WE'RE GOING INTO MANDALORIAN SPACE AFTER JARAEL?
OR SOME JEWELRY THEY REALLY, REALLY LIKE.
THEN YOU'D BETTER LET ME OUT.
IT TALKS.
CRAZY TALK. WHY SHOULD WE?
BECAUSE YOU'RE GOING TO NEED ME IF ANY OF US ARE TO SURVIVE.
MYSELF, INCLUDED.

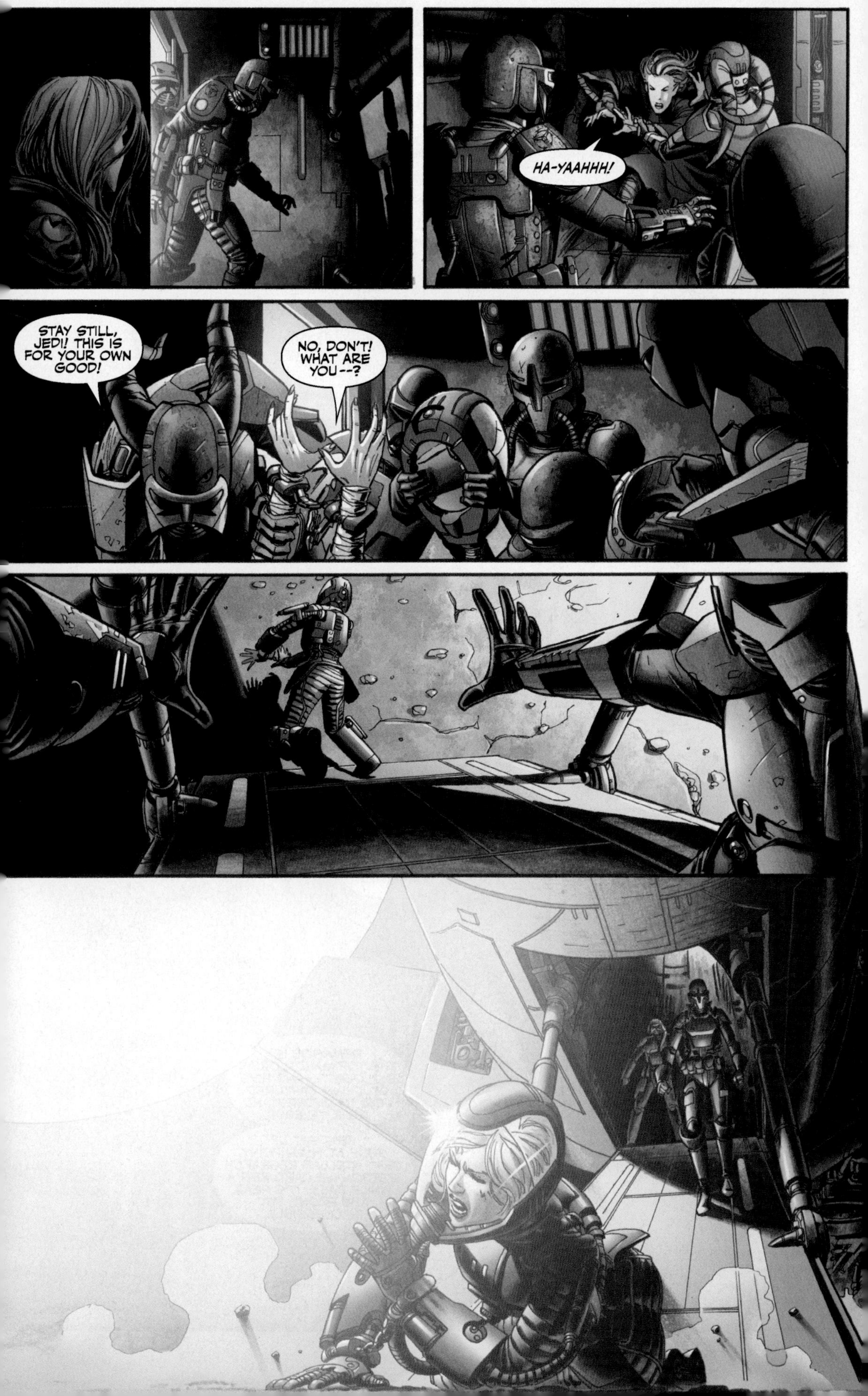
HA-YAAHHH!
STAY STILL, JEDI! THIS IS FOR YOUR OWN GOOD!
NO, DON'T! WHAT ARE YOU --?

KEEP AN EYE ON HIM, KID.

DON'T BOTHER. YOU'RE AS TRAPPED AS I AM. THEY'RE GOING TO *FLASHPOINT.*

WAS YOUR FRIEND A JEDI?

NO. I AM.

...MORE OR LESS.

WELL, THE TROOPS MUST THINK YOUR FRIEND'S A JEDI, BECAUSE *FLASHPOINT* IS WHERE WE'VE BEEN TAKING THE CATCH.

THE CATCH? *THE CATCH?*

SHE HAD MY LIGHTSABER. MAYBE THEY THOUGHT--

THEY WOULDN'T HAVE TAKEN TIME TO THINK. SINCE YOUR JEDI SCOUTS STARTED NOSING AROUND THE FRONTIER, WE'VE GOT A STANDING ORDER--

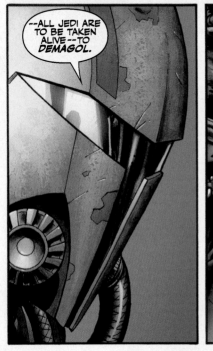

--ALL JEDI ARE TO BE TAKEN ALIVE--TO *DEMAGOL.*

WHAT'S A DEMAGOL?

DEMAGOL IS THE TOP MANDALORIAN BIOLOGIST--AND HE'S STUDYING CAPTURED JEDI TO UNDERSTAND THEIR TALENTS.

HE'S SET UP SHOP AT FLASHPOINT, THAT STELLAR RESEARCH STATION WE CAPTURED A WHILE BACK. IT'S NEAR THE FRONT, YET INACCESSIBLE.

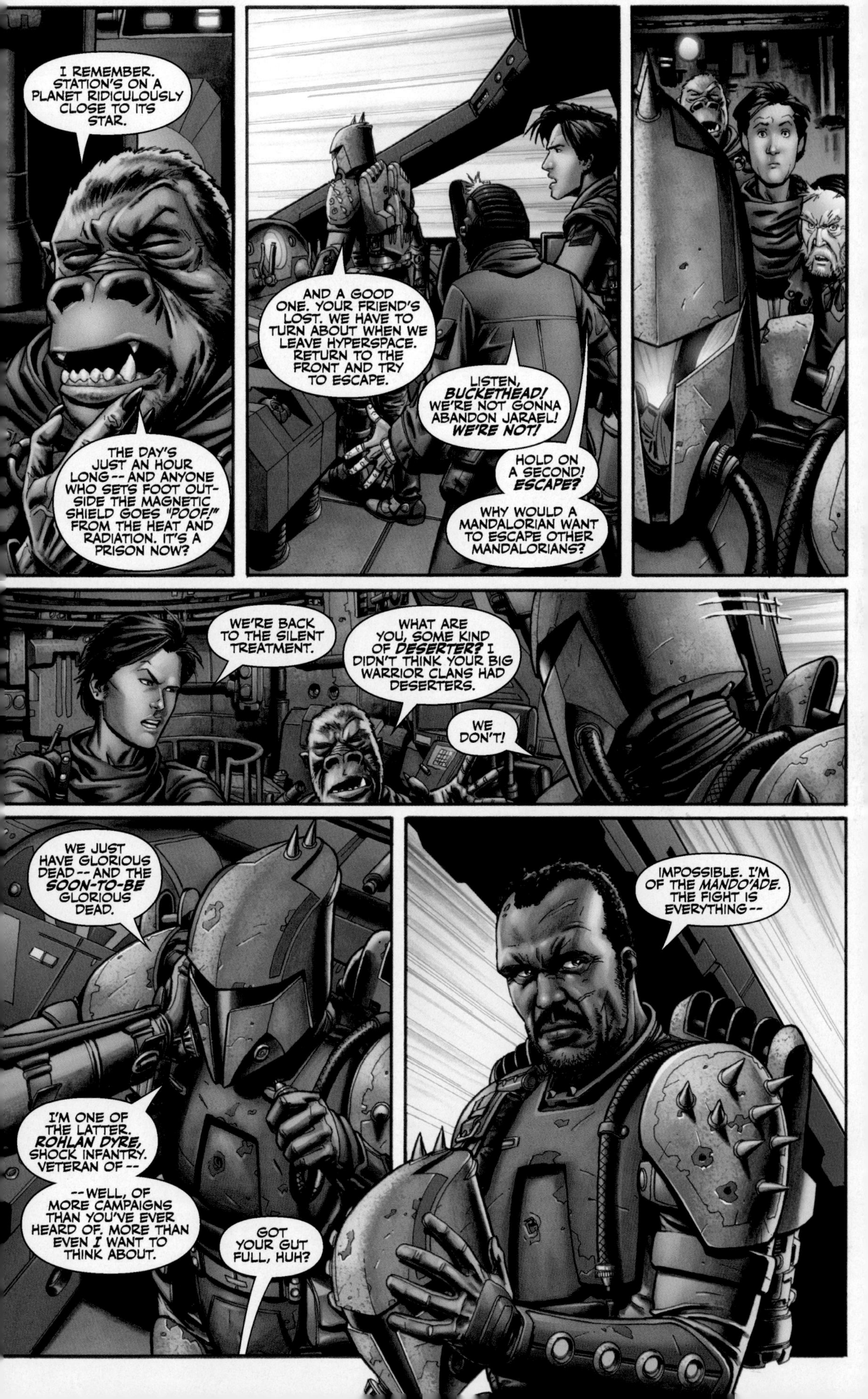
I REMEMBER. STATION'S ON A PLANET RIDICULOUSLY CLOSE TO ITS STAR.
THE DAY'S JUST AN HOUR LONG--AND ANYONE WHO SETS FOOT OUTSIDE THE MAGNETIC SHIELD GOES "POOF!" FROM THE HEAT AND RADIATION. IT'S A PRISON NOW?
AND A GOOD ONE. YOUR FRIEND'S LOST. WE HAVE TO TURN ABOUT WHEN WE LEAVE HYPERSPACE. RETURN TO THE FRONT AND TRY TO ESCAPE.
LISTEN, BUCKETHEAD! WE'RE NOT GONNA ABANDON JARAEL! WE'RE NOT!
HOLD ON A SECOND! ESCAPE?
WHY WOULD A MANDALORIAN WANT TO ESCAPE OTHER MANDALORIANS?
WE'RE BACK TO THE SILENT TREATMENT.
WHAT ARE YOU, SOME KIND OF DESERTER? I DIDN'T THINK YOUR BIG WARRIOR CLANS HAD DESERTERS.
WE DON'T!
WE JUST HAVE GLORIOUS DEAD--AND THE SOON-TO-BE GLORIOUS DEAD.
I'M ONE OF THE LATTER. ROHLAN DYRE, SHOCK INFANTRY. VETERAN OF--
--WELL, OF MORE CAMPAIGNS THAN YOU'VE EVER HEARD OF. MORE THAN EVEN I WANT TO THINK ABOUT.
GOT YOUR GUT FULL, HUH?
IMPOSSIBLE. I'M OF THE MANDO'ADE. THE FIGHT IS EVERYTHING--

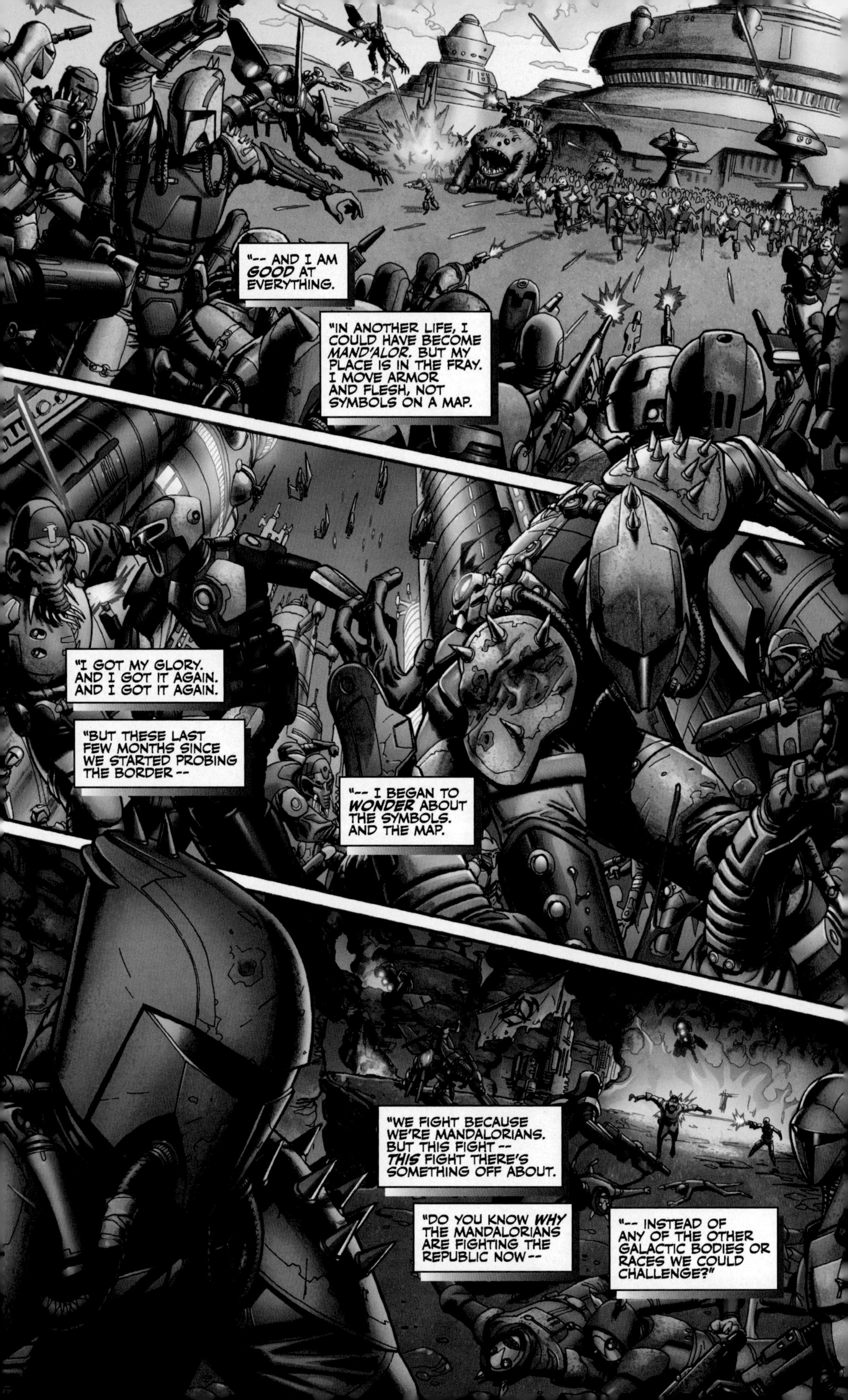
"-- AND I AM GOOD AT EVERYTHING.
"IN ANOTHER LIFE, I COULD HAVE BECOME MAND'ALOR. BUT MY PLACE IS IN THE FRAY. I MOVE ARMOR AND FLESH, NOT SYMBOLS ON A MAP.
"I GOT MY GLORY. AND I GOT IT AGAIN. AND I GOT IT AGAIN.
"BUT THESE LAST FEW MONTHS SINCE WE STARTED PROBING THE BORDER --
"-- I BEGAN TO WONDER ABOUT THE SYMBOLS. AND THE MAP.
"WE FIGHT BECAUSE WE'RE MANDALORIANS. BUT THIS FIGHT -- THIS FIGHT THERE'S SOMETHING OFF ABOUT.
"DO YOU KNOW WHY THE MANDALORIANS ARE FIGHTING THE REPUBLIC NOW --
"-- INSTEAD OF ANY OF THE OTHER GALACTIC BODIES OR RACES WE COULD CHALLENGE?"

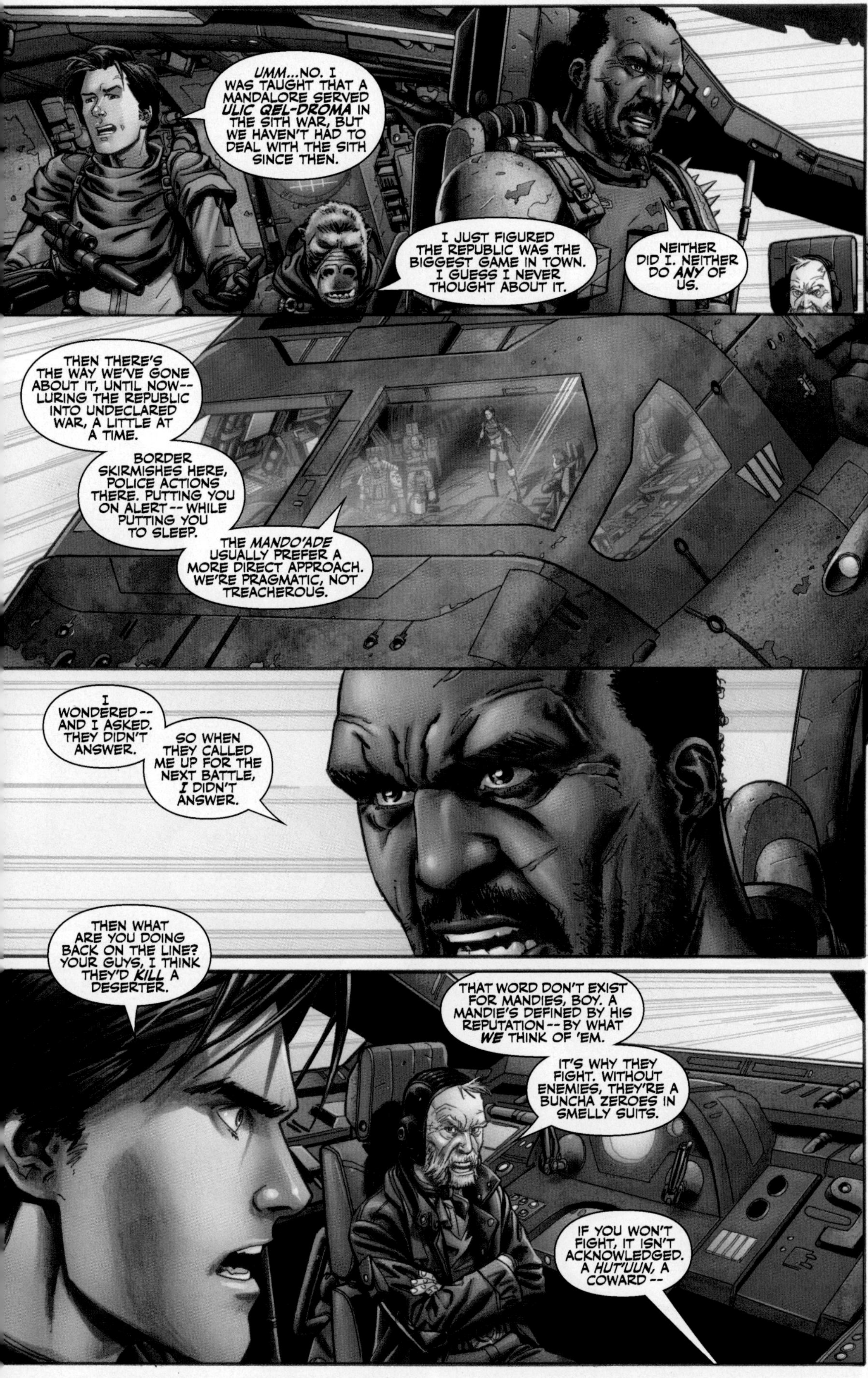
UMM...NO. I WAS TAUGHT THAT A MANDALORE SERVED ULIC QEL-DROMA IN THE SITH WAR, BUT WE HAVEN'T HAD TO DEAL WITH THE SITH SINCE THEN.
I JUST FIGURED THE REPUBLIC WAS THE BIGGEST GAME IN TOWN. I GUESS I NEVER THOUGHT ABOUT IT.
NEITHER DID I. NEITHER DO ANY OF US.
THEN THERE'S THE WAY WE'VE GONE ABOUT IT, UNTIL NOW-- LURING THE REPUBLIC INTO UNDECLARED WAR, A LITTLE AT A TIME.
BORDER SKIRMISHES HERE, POLICE ACTIONS THERE. PUTTING YOU ON ALERT-- WHILE PUTTING YOU TO SLEEP.
THE MANDO'ADE USUALLY PREFER A MORE DIRECT APPROACH. WE'RE PRAGMATIC, NOT TREACHEROUS.
I WONDERED-- AND I ASKED. THEY DIDN'T ANSWER.
SO WHEN THEY CALLED ME UP FOR THE NEXT BATTLE, I DIDN'T ANSWER.
THEN WHAT ARE YOU DOING BACK ON THE LINE? YOUR GUYS, I THINK THEY'D KILL A DESERTER.
THAT WORD DON'T EXIST FOR MANDIES, BOY. A MANDIE'S DEFINED BY HIS REPUTATION-- BY WHAT WE THINK OF 'EM.
IT'S WHY THEY FIGHT. WITHOUT ENEMIES, THEY'RE A BUNCHA ZEROES IN SMELLY SUITS.
IF YOU WON'T FIGHT, IT ISN'T ACKNOWLEDGED. A HUT'UUN, A COWARD--

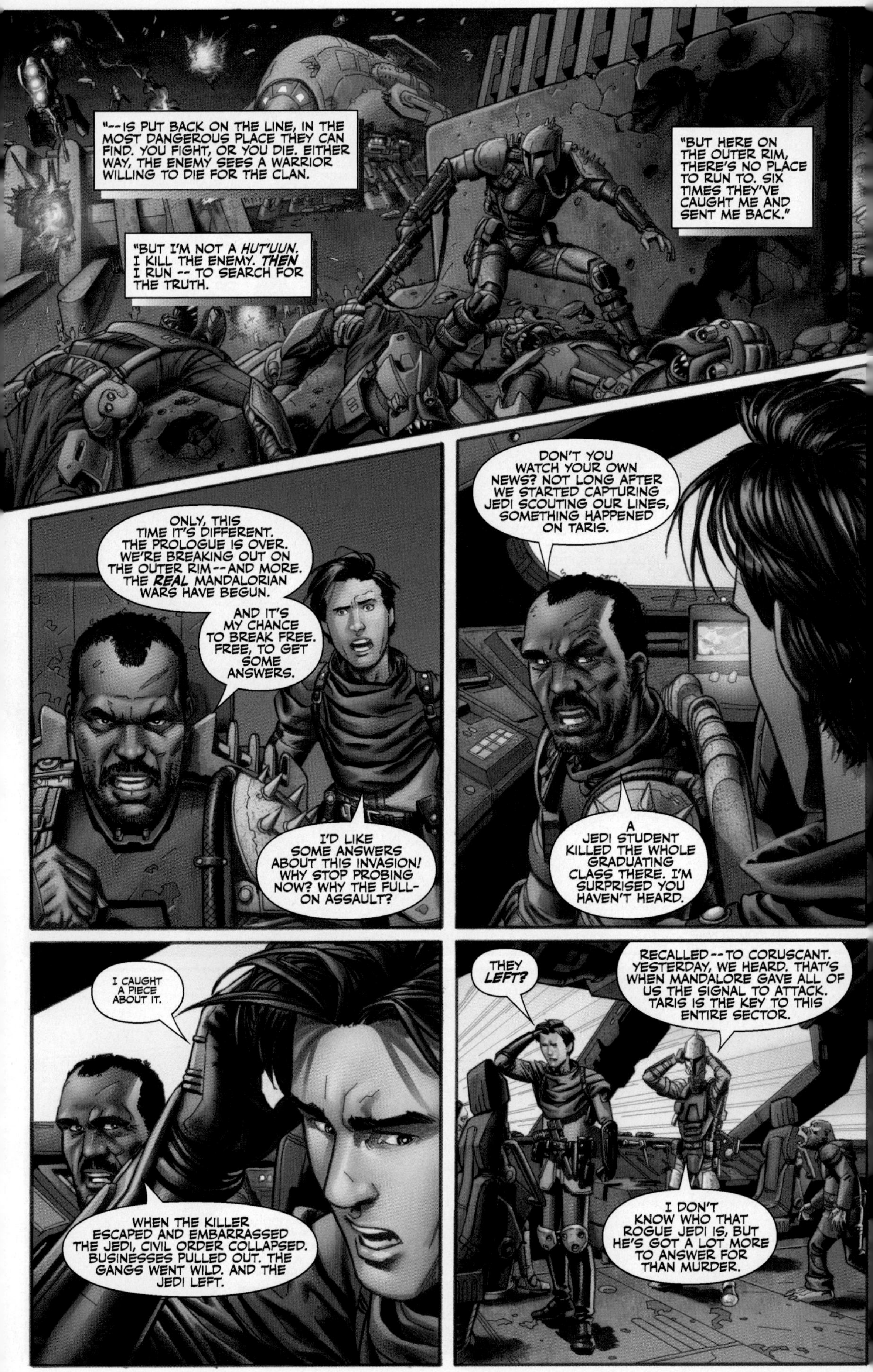
"--IS PUT BACK ON THE LINE, IN THE MOST DANGEROUS PLACE THEY CAN FIND. YOU FIGHT, OR YOU DIE. EITHER WAY, THE ENEMY SEES A WARRIOR WILLING TO DIE FOR THE CLAN.
"BUT I'M NOT A *HUT'UUN*. I KILL THE ENEMY. *THEN* I RUN -- TO SEARCH FOR THE TRUTH.
"BUT HERE ON THE OUTER RIM, THERE'S NO PLACE TO RUN TO. SIX TIMES THEY'VE CAUGHT ME AND SENT ME BACK."
ONLY, THIS TIME IT'S DIFFERENT. THE PROLOGUE IS OVER. WE'RE BREAKING OUT ON THE OUTER RIM--AND MORE. THE *REAL* MANDALORIAN WARS HAVE BEGUN.
AND IT'S MY CHANCE TO BREAK FREE. FREE, TO GET SOME ANSWERS.
I'D LIKE SOME ANSWERS ABOUT THIS INVASION! WHY STOP PROBING NOW? WHY THE FULL-ON ASSAULT?
DON'T YOU WATCH YOUR OWN NEWS? NOT LONG AFTER WE STARTED CAPTURING JEDI SCOUTING OUR LINES, SOMETHING HAPPENED ON TARIS.
A JEDI STUDENT KILLED THE WHOLE GRADUATING CLASS THERE. I'M SURPRISED YOU HAVEN'T HEARD.
I CAUGHT A PIECE ABOUT IT.
WHEN THE KILLER ESCAPED AND EMBARRASSED THE JEDI, CIVIL ORDER COLLAPSED. BUSINESSES PULLED OUT. THE GANGS WENT WILD. AND THE JEDI LEFT.
THEY *LEFT?*
RECALLED--TO CORUSCANT. YESTERDAY, WE HEARD. THAT'S WHEN MANDALORE GAVE ALL OF US THE SIGNAL TO ATTACK. TARIS IS THE KEY TO THIS ENTIRE SECTOR.
I DON'T KNOW WHO THAT ROGUE JEDI IS, BUT HE'S GOT A LOT MORE TO ANSWER FOR THAN MURDER.

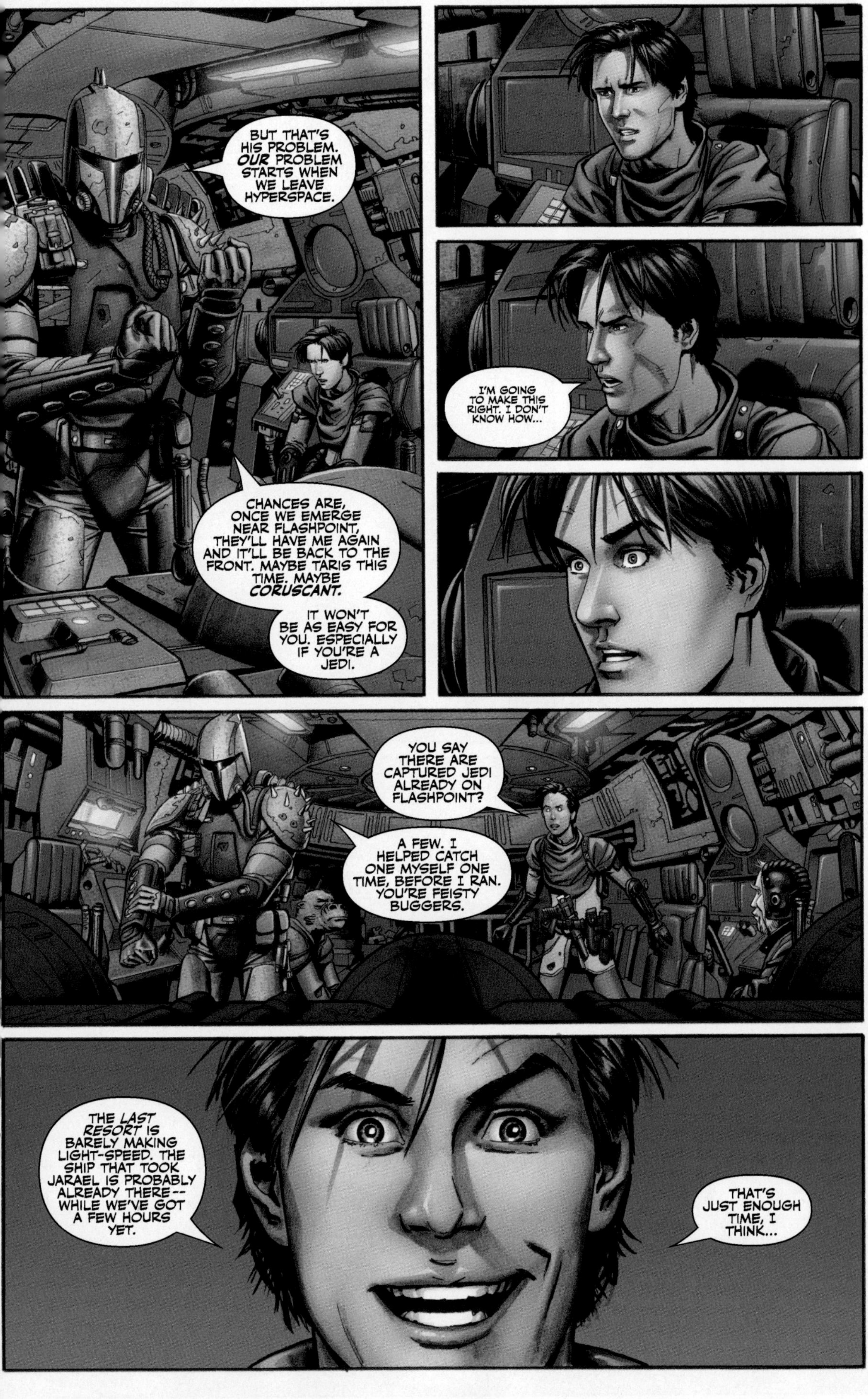

BUT THAT'S HIS PROBLEM. *OUR* PROBLEM STARTS WHEN WE LEAVE HYPERSPACE.
I'M GOING TO MAKE THIS RIGHT. I DON'T KNOW HOW...
CHANCES ARE, ONCE WE EMERGE NEAR FLASHPOINT, THEY'LL HAVE ME AGAIN AND IT'LL BE BACK TO THE FRONT. MAYBE TARIS THIS TIME. MAYBE ***CORUSCANT.***
IT WON'T BE AS EASY FOR YOU. ESPECIALLY IF YOU'RE A JEDI.
YOU SAY THERE ARE CAPTURED JEDI ALREADY ON FLASHPOINT?
A FEW. I HELPED CATCH ONE MYSELF ONE TIME, BEFORE I RAN. YOU'RE FEISTY BUGGERS.
THE *LAST RESORT* IS BARELY MAKING LIGHT-SPEED. THE SHIP THAT TOOK JARAEL IS PROBABLY ALREADY THERE-- WHILE WE'VE GOT A FEW HOURS YET.
THAT'S JUST ENOUGH TIME, I THINK...

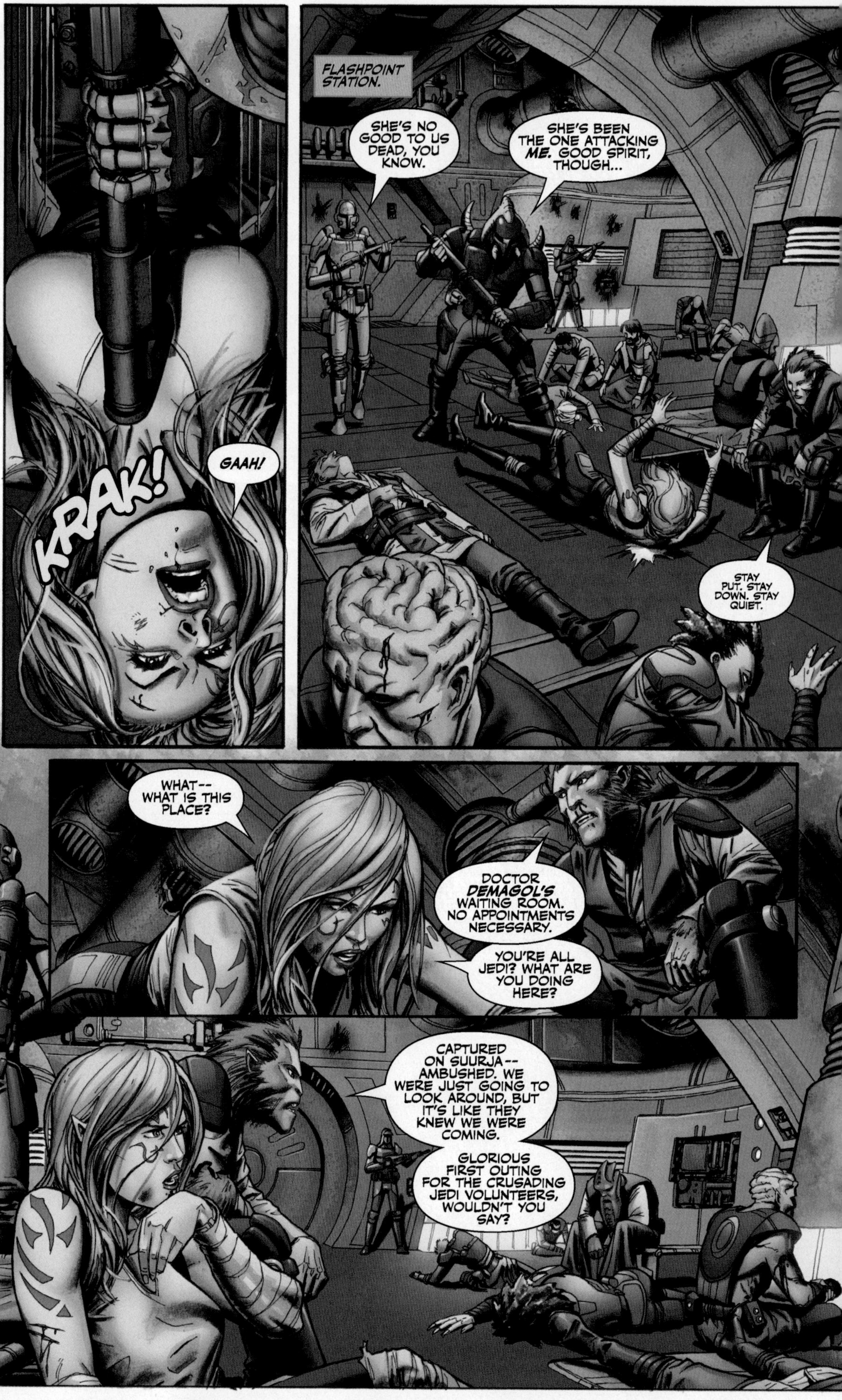
KRAK!
GAAH!
FLASHPOINT STATION.
SHE'S NO GOOD TO US DEAD, YOU KNOW.
SHE'S BEEN THE ONE ATTACKING ME. GOOD SPIRIT, THOUGH...
STAY PUT. STAY DOWN. STAY QUIET.
WHAT-- WHAT IS THIS PLACE?
DOCTOR DEMAGOL'S WAITING ROOM. NO APPOINTMENTS NECESSARY.
YOU'RE ALL JEDI? WHAT ARE YOU DOING HERE?
CAPTURED ON SUURJA-- AMBUSHED. WE WERE JUST GOING TO LOOK AROUND, BUT IT'S LIKE THEY KNEW WE WERE COMING.
GLORIOUS FIRST OUTING FOR THE CRUSADING JEDI VOLUNTEERS, WOULDN'T YOU SAY?

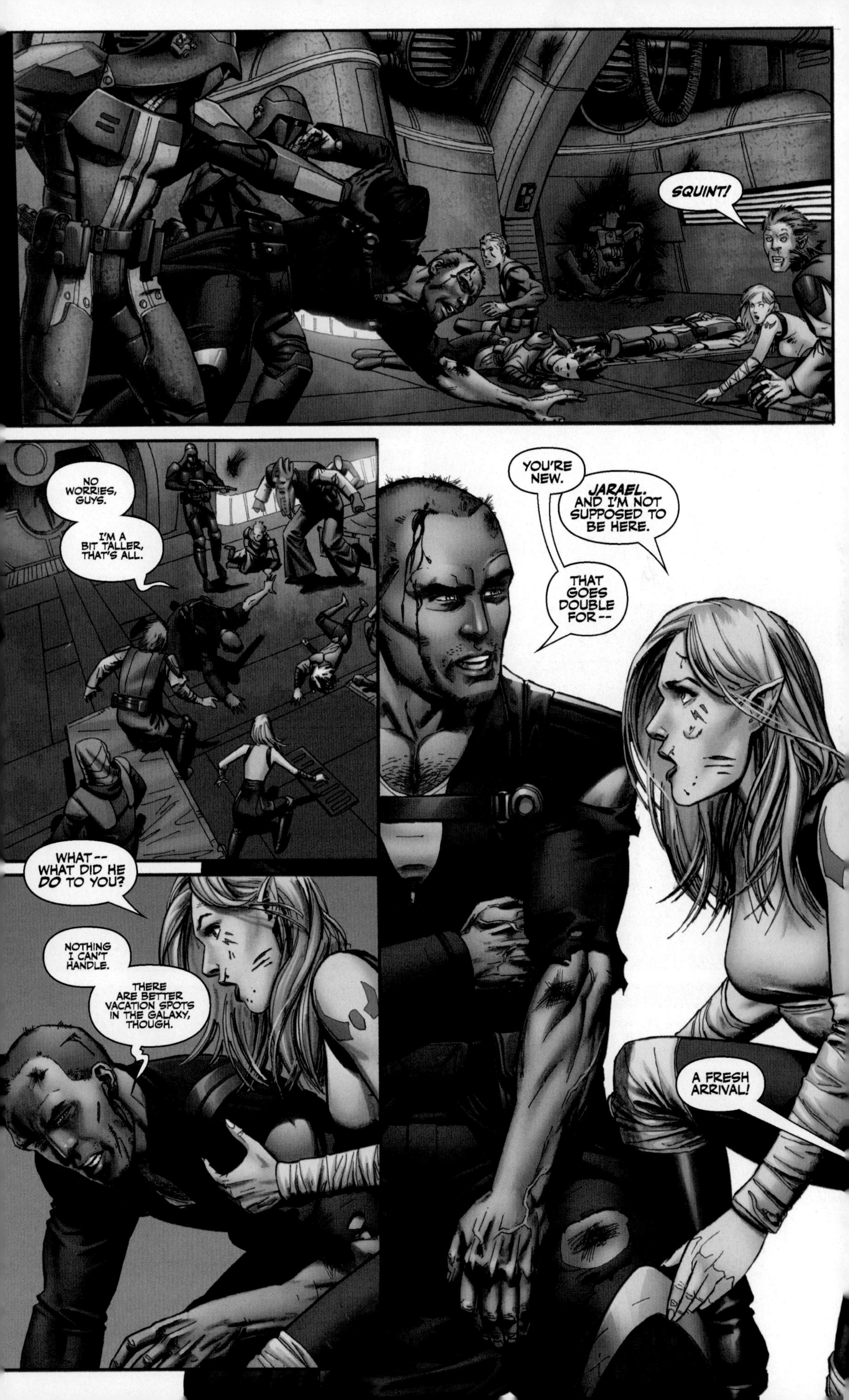
SQUINT!
NO WORRIES, GUYS.
I'M A BIT TALLER, THAT'S ALL.
WHAT-- WHAT DID HE DO TO YOU?
NOTHING I CAN'T HANDLE.
THERE ARE BETTER VACATION SPOTS IN THE GALAXY, THOUGH.
YOU'RE NEW.
JARAEL. AND I'M NOT SUPPOSED TO BE HERE.
THAT GOES DOUBLE FOR--
A FRESH ARRIVAL!

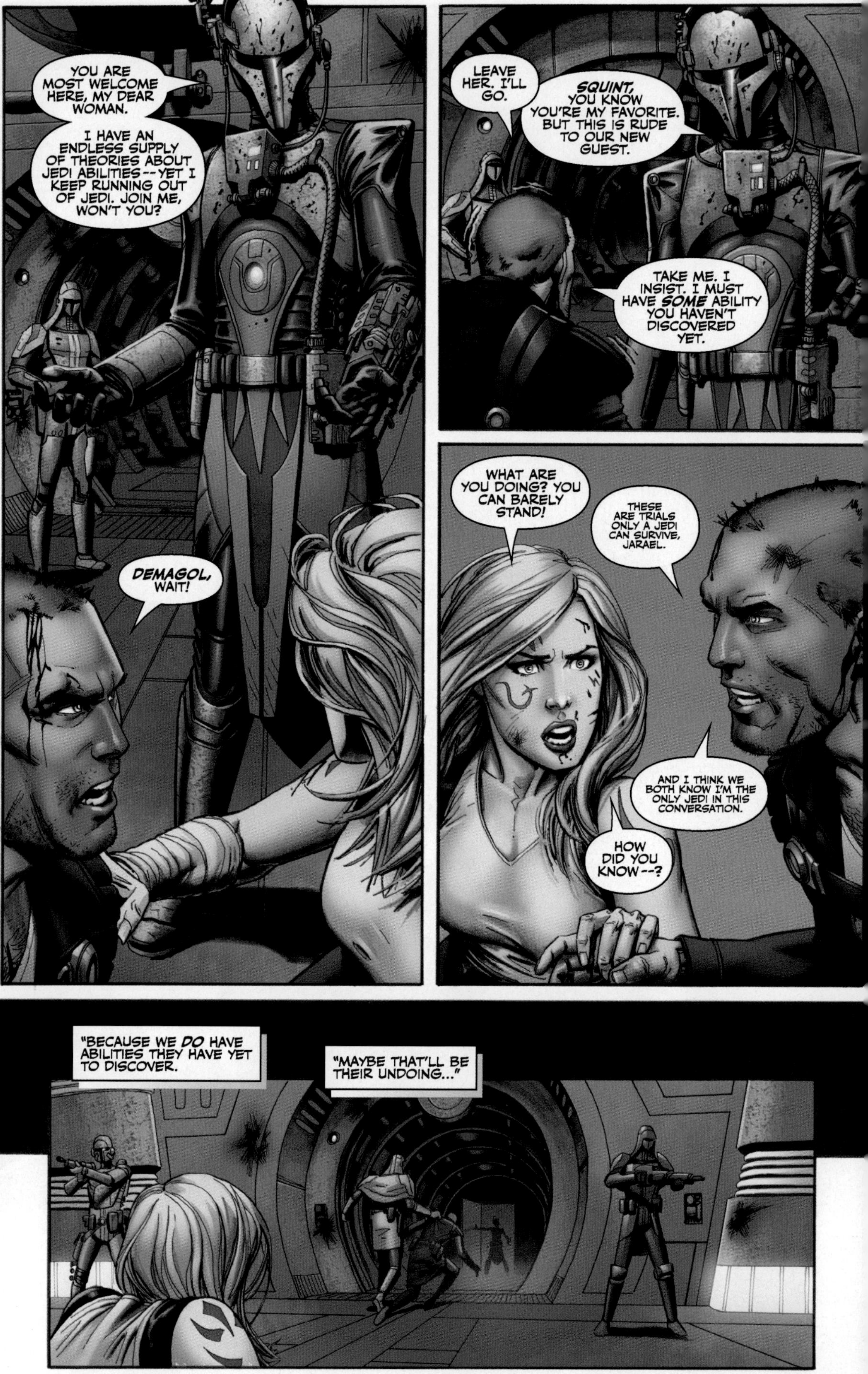
YOU ARE MOST WELCOME HERE, MY DEAR WOMAN.
I HAVE AN ENDLESS SUPPLY OF THEORIES ABOUT JEDI ABILITIES--YET I KEEP RUNNING OUT OF JEDI. JOIN ME, WON'T YOU?
DEMAGOL, WAIT!
LEAVE HER. I'LL GO.
SQUINT, YOU KNOW YOU'RE MY FAVORITE. BUT THIS IS RUDE TO OUR NEW GUEST.
TAKE ME. I INSIST. I MUST HAVE SOME ABILITY YOU HAVEN'T DISCOVERED YET.
WHAT ARE YOU DOING? YOU CAN BARELY STAND!
THESE ARE TRIALS ONLY A JEDI CAN SURVIVE, JARAEL.
AND I THINK WE BOTH KNOW I'M THE ONLY JEDI IN THIS CONVERSATION.
HOW DID YOU KNOW--?
"BECAUSE WE DO HAVE ABILITIES THEY HAVE YET TO DISCOVER.
"MAYBE THAT'LL BE THEIR UNDOING..."

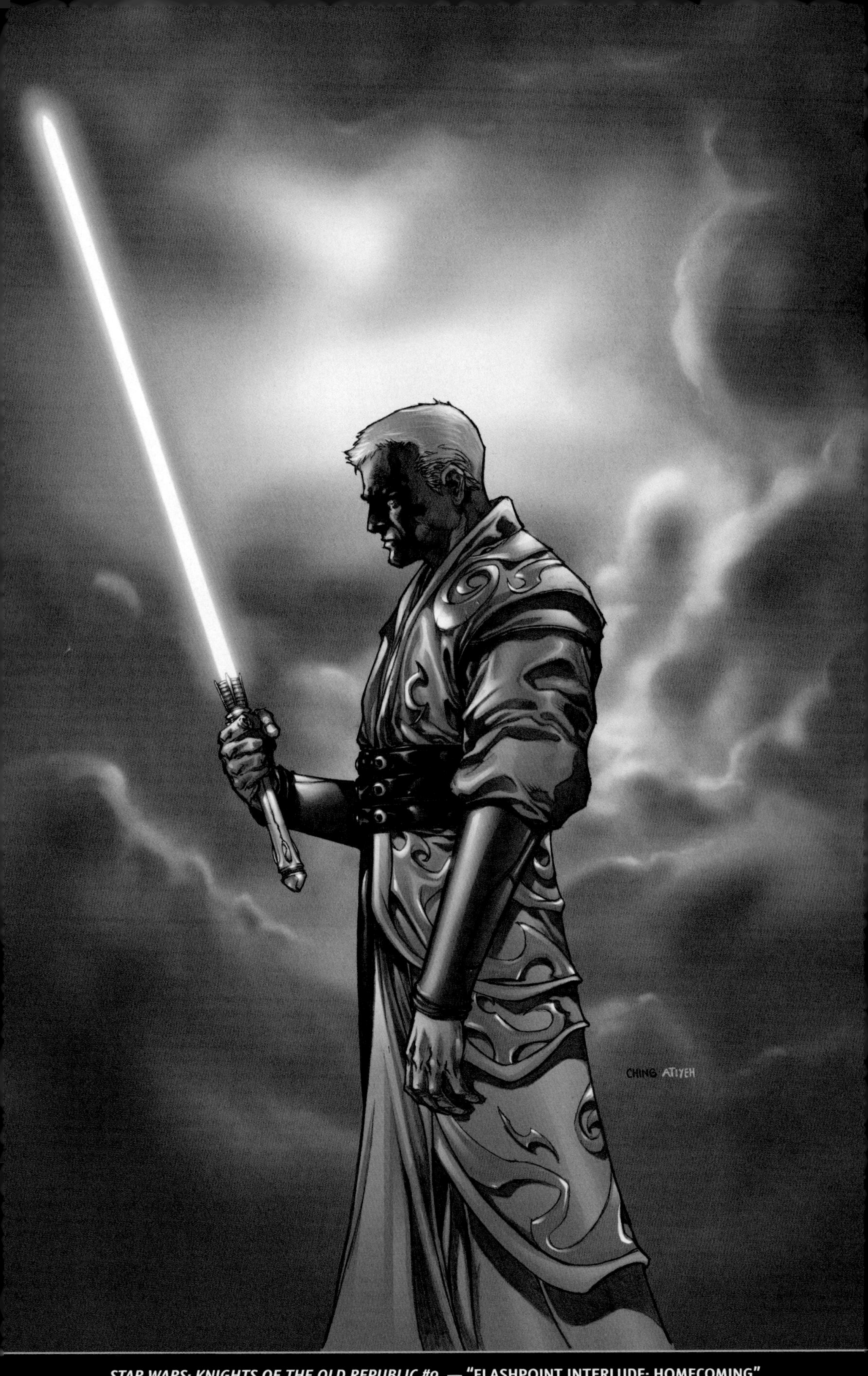
CHING ATIYEH

STAR WARS: KNIGHTS OF THE OLD REPUBLIC #9 — "FLASHPOINT INTERLUDE: HOMECOMING"

WRITER: JOHN JACKSON MILLER • ARTIST: BRIAN CHING • COLORIST: MICHAEL ATIYEH • LETTERER: MICHAEL HEISLER
ASSISTANT EDITOR: DAVE MARSHALL • EDITOR: JEREMY BARLOW • COVER ARTISTS: BRIAN CHING & MICHAEL ATIYEH

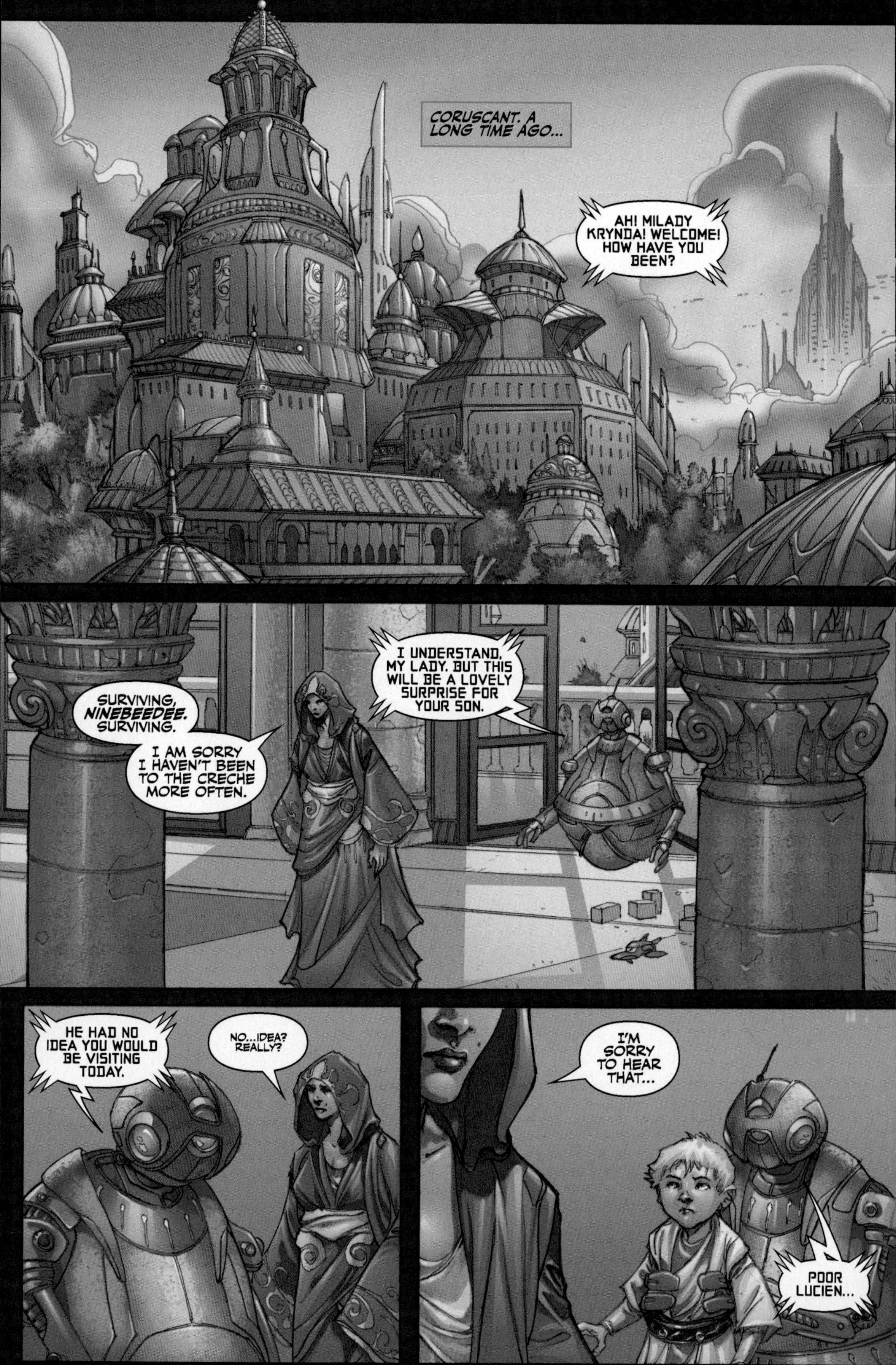
CORUSCANT. A LONG TIME AGO...
AH! MILADY KRYNDA! WELCOME! HOW HAVE YOU BEEN?
SURVIVING, NINEBEEDEE. SURVIVING.
I AM SORRY I HAVEN'T BEEN TO THE CRECHE MORE OFTEN.
I UNDERSTAND, MY LADY. BUT THIS WILL BE A LOVELY SURPRISE FOR YOUR SON.
HE HAD NO IDEA YOU WOULD BE VISITING TODAY.
NO...IDEA? REALLY?
I'M SORRY TO HEAR THAT...
POOR LUCIEN...

CORUSCANT. TODAY.

WHERE ARE YOU?

I'M SORRY, BUT THE DRAAY ESTATE IS CLOSED TO --

OH! *MASTER LUCIEN!* I DIDN'T KNOW YOU HAD RETURNED TO CORUSCANT!

IT WAS A SUDDEN DECISION. I NEED TO SEE MY MOTHER.

I'M SORRY, BUT HER LADYSHIP IS NOT SEEING GUESTS AT THIS TIME.

I'M NOT A GUEST, NINEBEEDEE! THIS IS MY HOUSE!

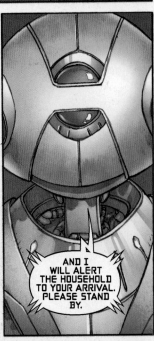

AND I WILL ALERT THE HOUSEHOLD TO YOUR ARRIVAL. PLEASE STAND BY.

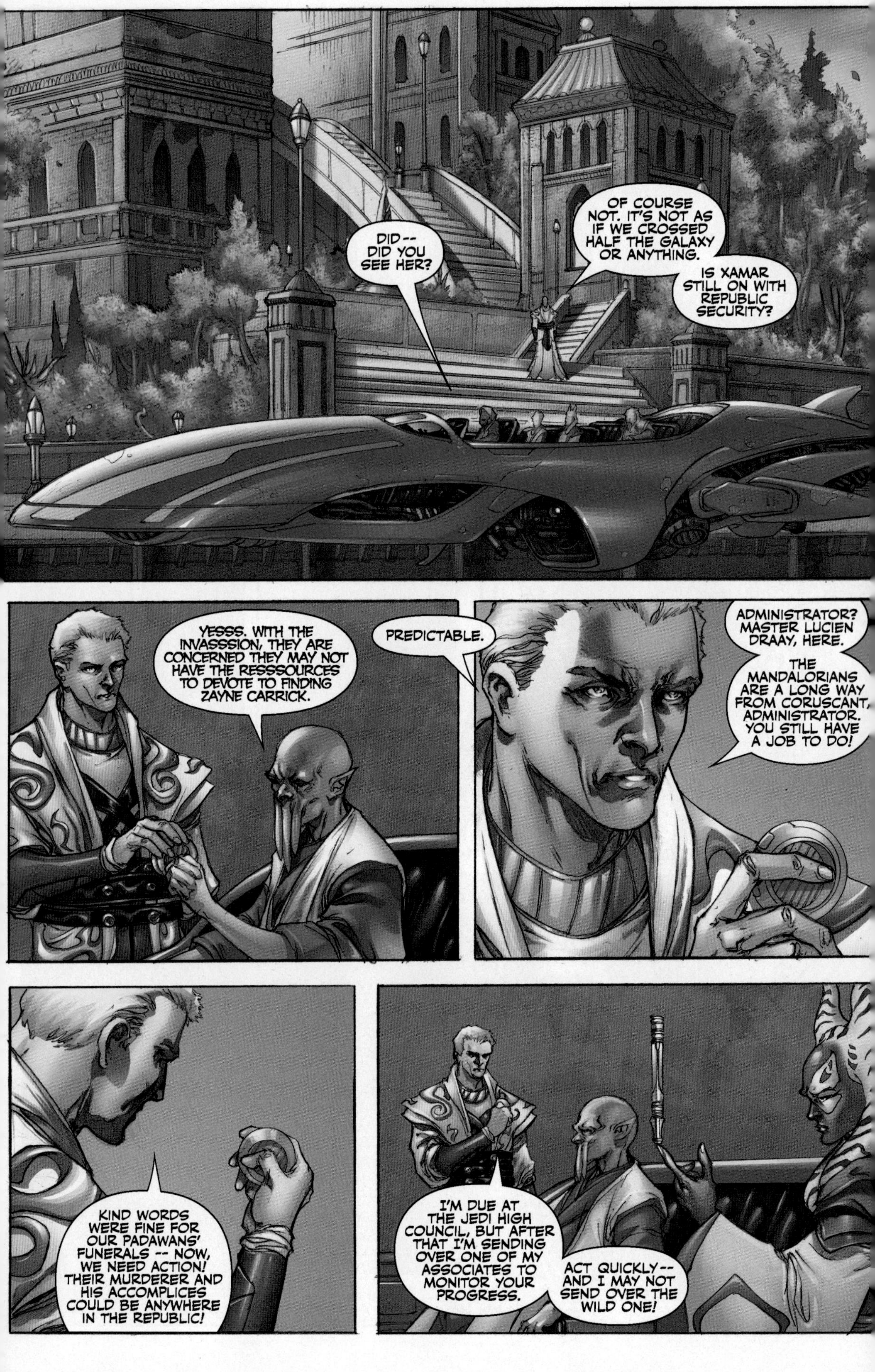
DID-- DID YOU SEE HER?
OF COURSE NOT. IT'S NOT AS IF WE CROSSED HALF THE GALAXY OR ANYTHING.
IS XAMAR STILL ON WITH REPUBLIC SECURITY?
YESSS. WITH THE INVASSSION, THEY ARE CONCERNED THEY MAY NOT HAVE THE RESSSOURCES TO DEVOTE TO FINDING ZAYNE CARRICK.
PREDICTABLE.
ADMINISTRATOR? MASTER LUCIEN DRAAY, HERE.
THE MANDALORIANS ARE A LONG WAY FROM CORUSCANT, ADMINISTRATOR. YOU STILL HAVE A JOB TO DO!
KIND WORDS WERE FINE FOR OUR PADAWANS' FUNERALS -- NOW, WE NEED ACTION! THEIR MURDERER AND HIS ACCOMPLICES COULD BE ANYWHERE IN THE REPUBLIC!
I'M DUE AT THE JEDI HIGH COUNCIL, BUT AFTER THAT I'M SENDING OVER ONE OF MY ASSOCIATES TO MONITOR YOUR PROGRESS.
ACT QUICKLY-- AND I MAY NOT SEND OVER THE WILD ONE!

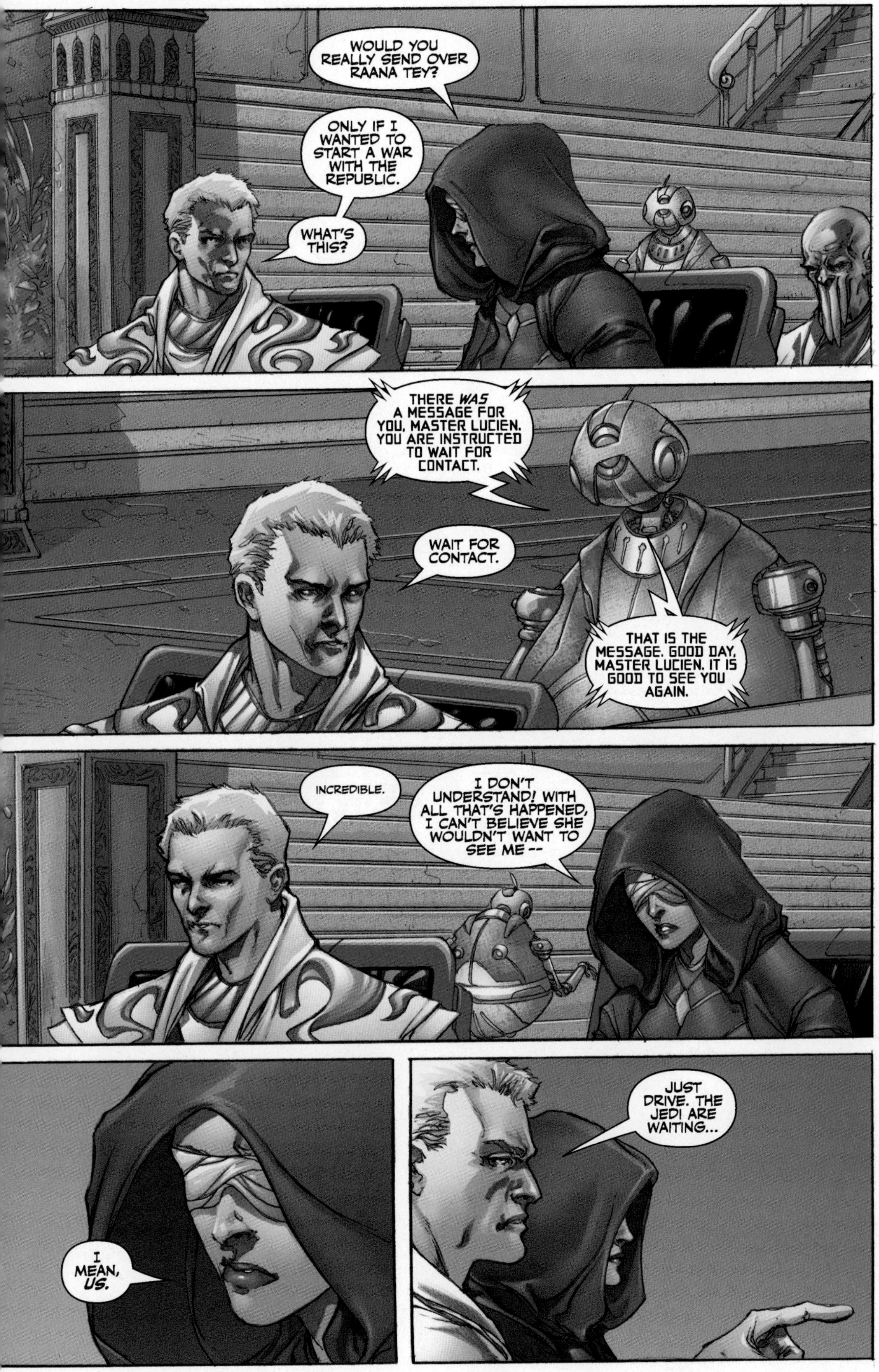
WOULD YOU REALLY SEND OVER RAANA TEY?
ONLY IF I WANTED TO START A WAR WITH THE REPUBLIC.
WHAT'S THIS?
THERE *WAS* A MESSAGE FOR YOU, MASTER LUCIEN. YOU ARE INSTRUCTED TO WAIT FOR CONTACT.
WAIT FOR CONTACT.
THAT IS THE MESSAGE. GOOD DAY, MASTER LUCIEN. IT IS GOOD TO SEE YOU AGAIN.
INCREDIBLE.
I DON'T UNDERSTAND! WITH ALL THAT'S HAPPENED, I CAN'T BELIEVE SHE WOULDN'T WANT TO SEE ME --
I MEAN, *US*.
JUST DRIVE. THE JEDI ARE WAITING...

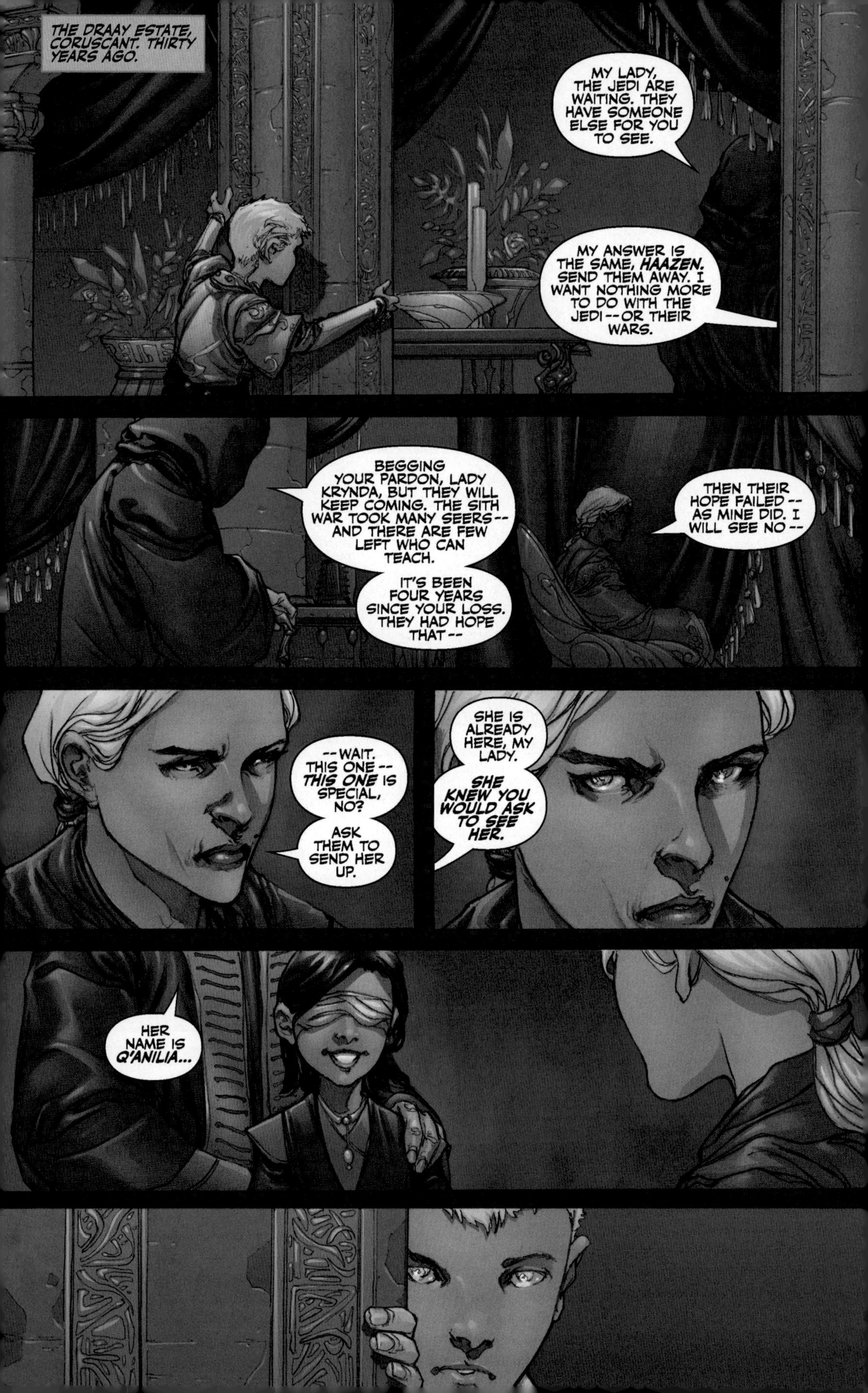
THE DRAAY ESTATE, CORUSCANT. THIRTY YEARS AGO.
MY LADY, THE JEDI ARE WAITING. THEY HAVE SOMEONE ELSE FOR YOU TO SEE.
MY ANSWER IS THE SAME, HAAZEN. SEND THEM AWAY. I WANT NOTHING MORE TO DO WITH THE JEDI--OR THEIR WARS.
BEGGING YOUR PARDON, LADY KRYNDA, BUT THEY WILL KEEP COMING. THE SITH WAR TOOK MANY SEERS--AND THERE ARE FEW LEFT WHO CAN TEACH.
IT'S BEEN FOUR YEARS SINCE YOUR LOSS. THEY HAD HOPE THAT--
THEN THEIR HOPE FAILED--AS MINE DID. I WILL SEE NO--
--WAIT. THIS ONE--THIS ONE IS SPECIAL, NO?
ASK THEM TO SEND HER UP.
SHE IS ALREADY HERE, MY LADY.
SHE KNEW YOU WOULD ASK TO SEE HER.
HER NAME IS Q'ANILIA...

THE JEDI HIGH COUNCIL, CORUSCANT. TODAY.

...AND WHILE YOUR REPORT ON WHAT YOU SAW AT *ONDERON* AND *DXUN* IS, OF COURSE, DISTURBING--

-- NONETHELESS, YOU HAD NO BUSINESS INVESTIGATING ON YOUR OWN!

WE'RE STILL REBUILDING OUR RANKS FROM THE LAST WAR. WE CAN'T AFFORD THIS KIND OF ADVENTURISM, EVEN IF WE *WERE* SUPPORTING IT!

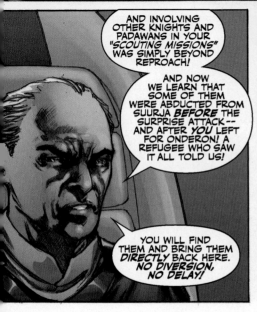

AND INVOLVING OTHER KNIGHTS AND PADAWANS IN YOUR "SCOUTING MISSIONS" WAS SIMPLY BEYOND REPROACH!

AND NOW WE LEARN THAT SOME OF THEM WERE ABDUCTED FROM SUURJA *BEFORE* THE SURPRISE ATTACK -- AND AFTER *YOU* LEFT FOR ONDERON! A REFUGEE WHO SAW IT ALL TOLD US!

YOU WILL FIND THEM AND BRING THEM *DIRECTLY* BACK HERE. NO DIVERSION, NO DELAY!

THERE WAS NO PLACE FOR THE ORDER IN THE WRANGLING OVER THE OUTER RIM, AND THERE IS CERTAINLY NO PLACE FOR IT IN A WIDER MANDALORIAN WAR!

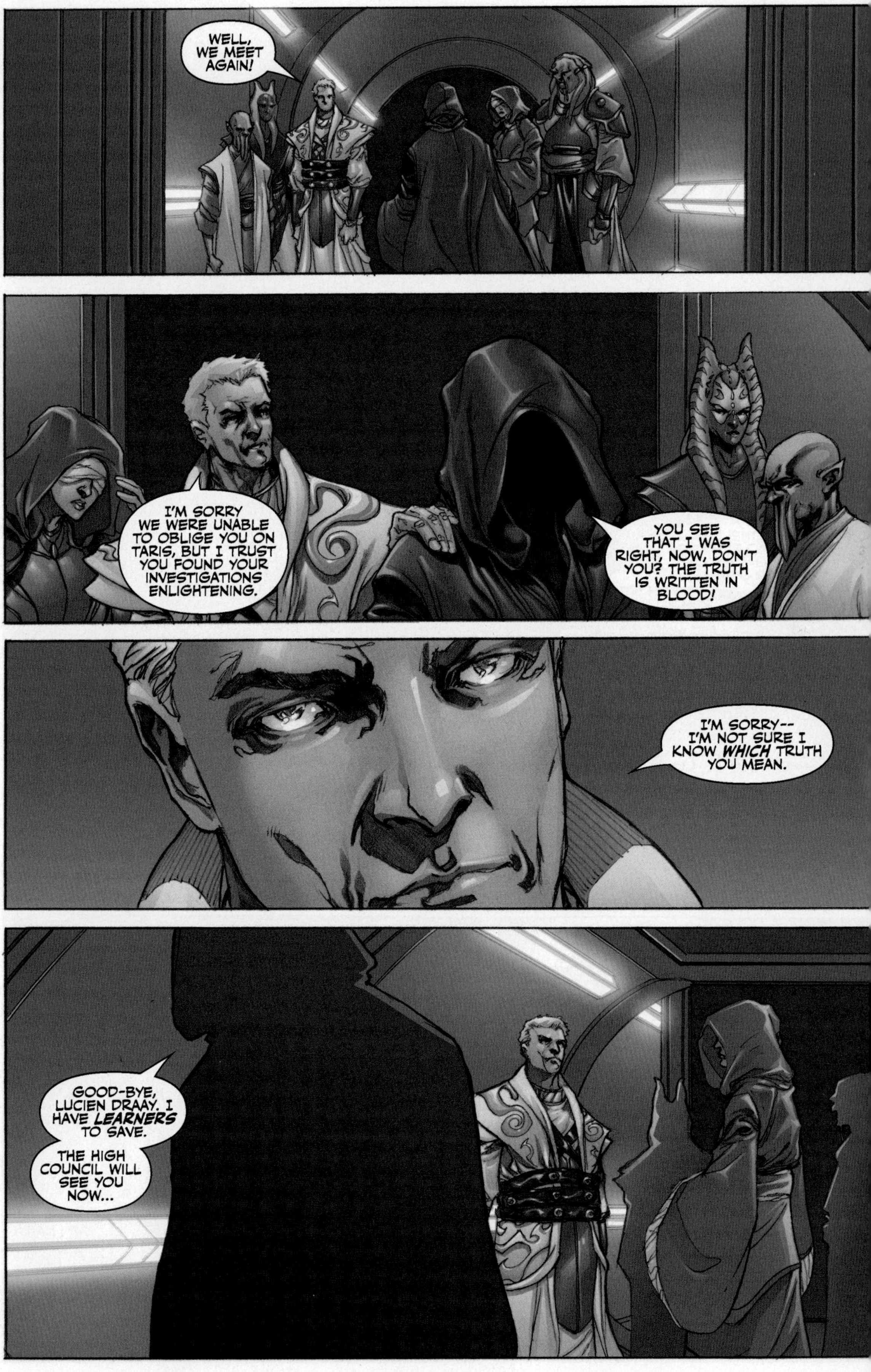
WELL, WE MEET AGAIN!
I'M SORRY WE WERE UNABLE TO OBLIGE YOU ON TARIS, BUT I TRUST YOU FOUND YOUR INVESTIGATIONS ENLIGHTENING.
YOU SEE THAT I WAS RIGHT, NOW, DON'T YOU? THE TRUTH IS WRITTEN IN BLOOD!
I'M SORRY-- I'M NOT SURE I KNOW WHICH TRUTH YOU MEAN.
GOOD-BYE, LUCIEN DRAAY. I HAVE LEARNERS TO SAVE.
THE HIGH COUNCIL WILL SEE YOU NOW...

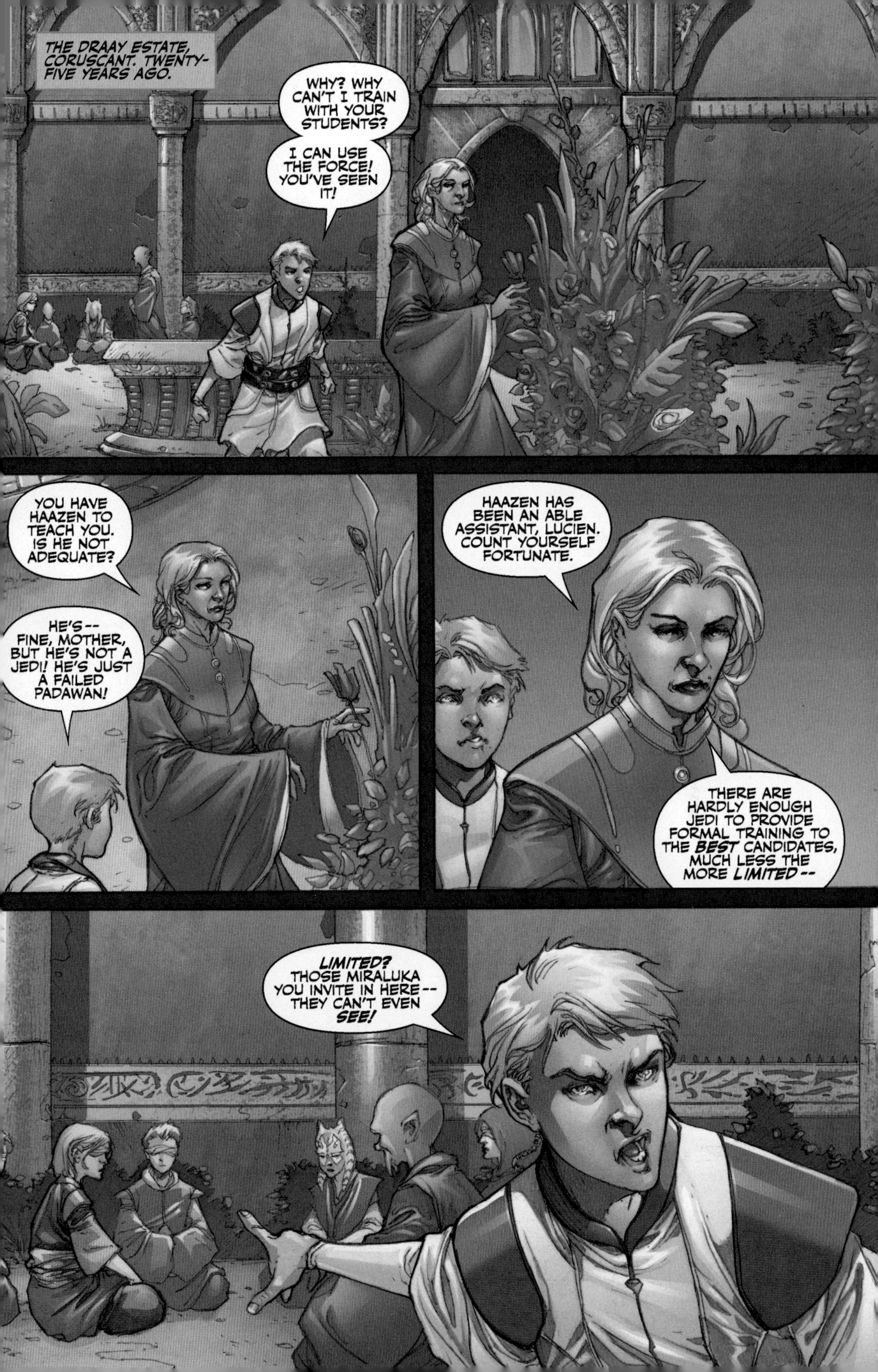
THE DRAAY ESTATE, CORUSCANT. TWENTY-FIVE YEARS AGO.
WHY? WHY CAN'T I TRAIN WITH YOUR STUDENTS?
I CAN USE THE FORCE! YOU'VE SEEN IT!
YOU HAVE HAAZEN TO TEACH YOU. IS HE NOT ADEQUATE?
HE'S-- FINE, MOTHER, BUT HE'S NOT A JEDI! HE'S JUST A FAILED PADAWAN!
HAAZEN HAS BEEN AN ABLE ASSISTANT, LUCIEN. COUNT YOURSELF FORTUNATE.
THERE ARE HARDLY ENOUGH JEDI TO PROVIDE FORMAL TRAINING TO THE BEST CANDIDATES, MUCH LESS THE MORE LIMITED--
LIMITED? THOSE MIRALUKA YOU INVITE IN HERE-- THEY CAN'T EVEN SEE!

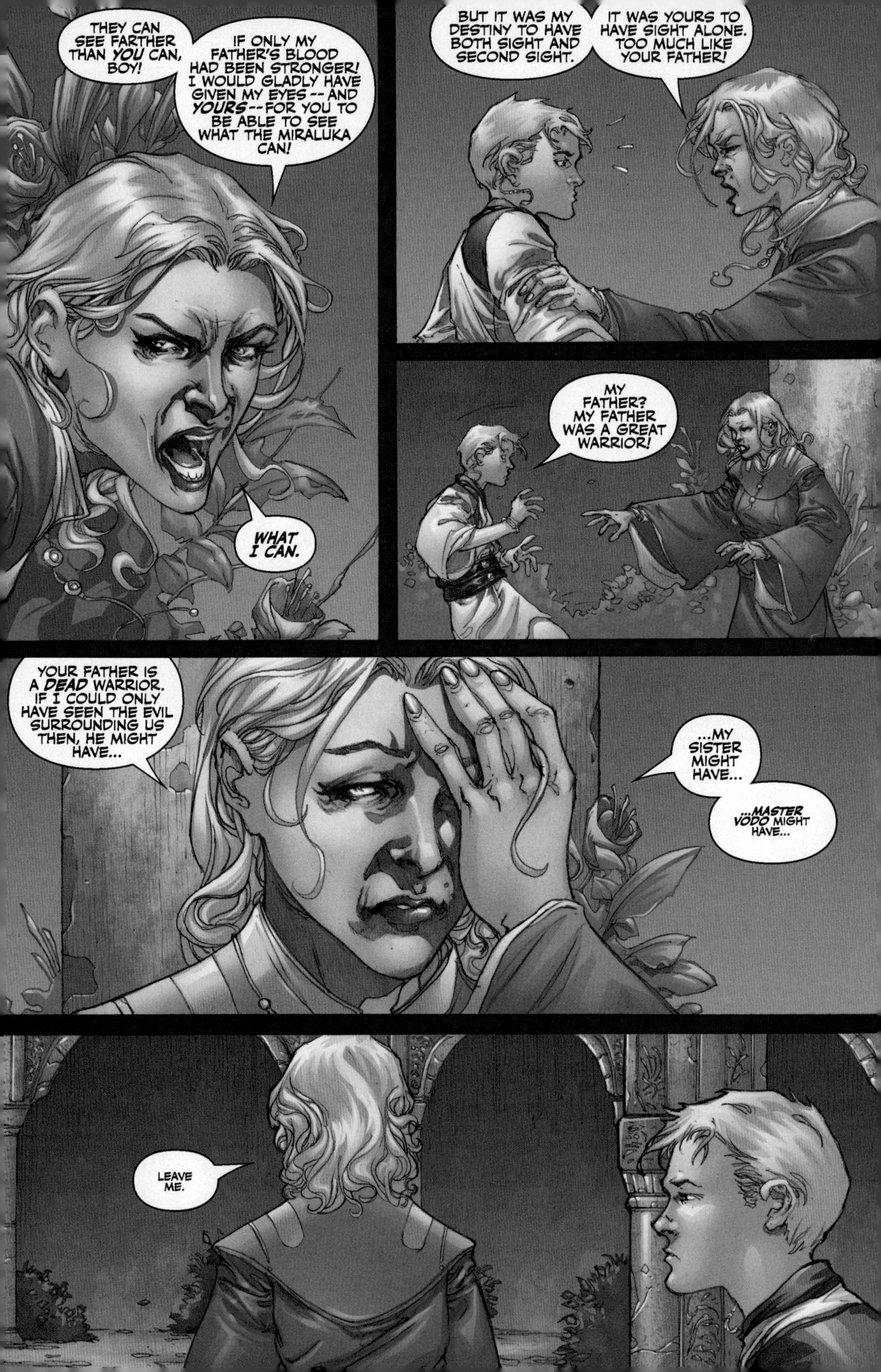
THEY CAN SEE FARTHER THAN *YOU* CAN, BOY!
IF ONLY MY FATHER'S BLOOD HAD BEEN STRONGER! I WOULD GLADLY HAVE GIVEN MY EYES -- AND *YOURS* -- FOR YOU TO BE ABLE TO SEE WHAT THE MIRALUKA CAN!
WHAT I CAN.
BUT IT WAS MY DESTINY TO HAVE BOTH SIGHT AND SECOND SIGHT.
IT WAS YOURS TO HAVE SIGHT ALONE. TOO MUCH LIKE YOUR FATHER!
MY FATHER? MY FATHER WAS A GREAT WARRIOR!
YOUR FATHER IS A *DEAD* WARRIOR. IF I COULD ONLY HAVE SEEN THE EVIL SURROUNDING US THEN, HE MIGHT HAVE...
...MY SISTER MIGHT HAVE...
...*MASTER VODO* MIGHT HAVE...
LEAVE ME.

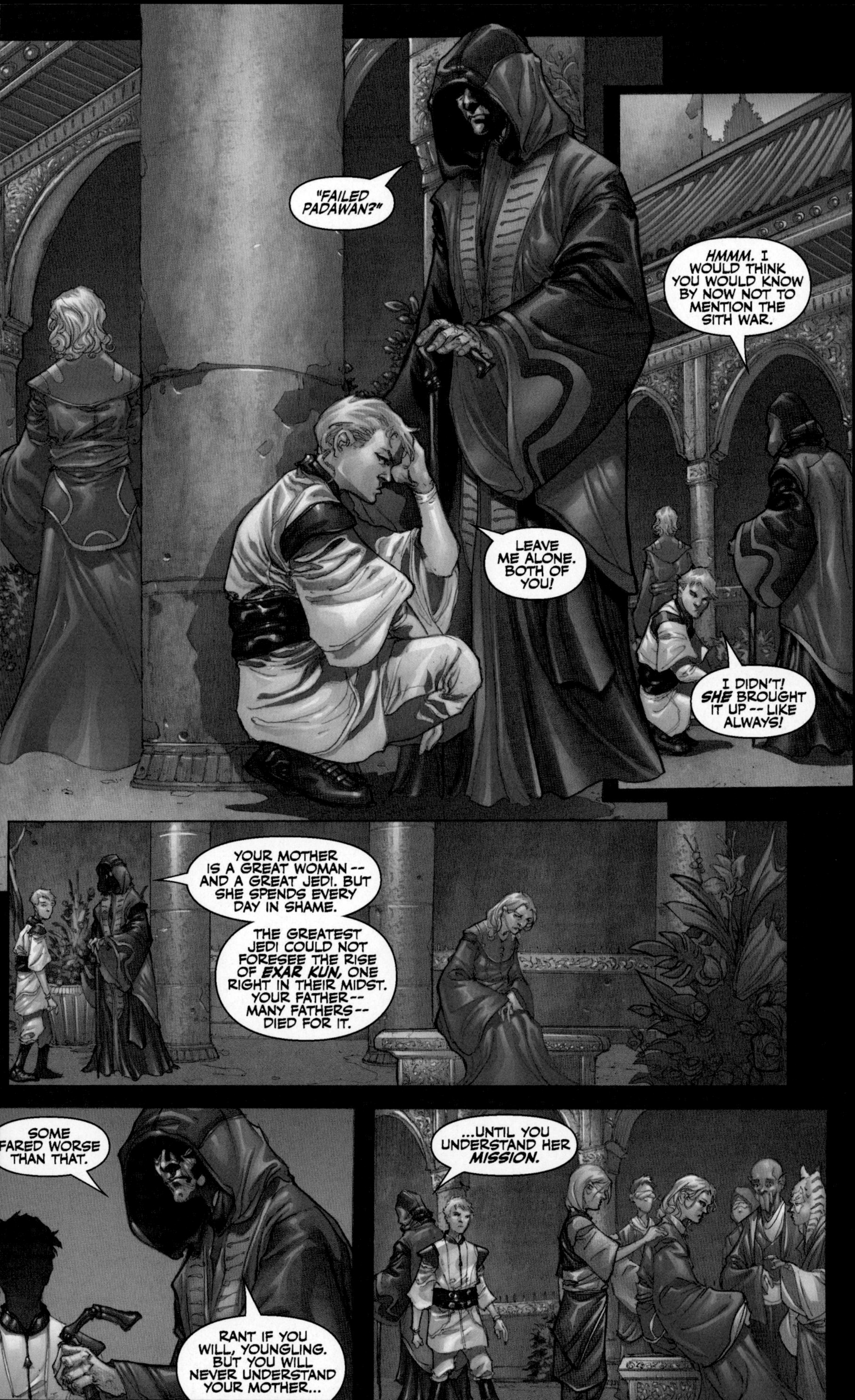
"FAILED PADAWAN?"
HMMM. I WOULD THINK YOU WOULD KNOW BY NOW NOT TO MENTION THE SITH WAR.
LEAVE ME ALONE. BOTH OF YOU!
I DIDN'T! SHE BROUGHT IT UP -- LIKE ALWAYS!
YOUR MOTHER IS A GREAT WOMAN -- AND A GREAT JEDI. BUT SHE SPENDS EVERY DAY IN SHAME.
THE GREATEST JEDI COULD NOT FORESEE THE RISE OF EXAR KUN, ONE RIGHT IN THEIR MIDST. YOUR FATHER -- MANY FATHERS -- DIED FOR IT.
SOME FARED WORSE THAN THAT.
RANT IF YOU WILL, YOUNGLING. BUT YOU WILL NEVER UNDERSTAND YOUR MOTHER...
...UNTIL YOU UNDERSTAND HER MISSION.

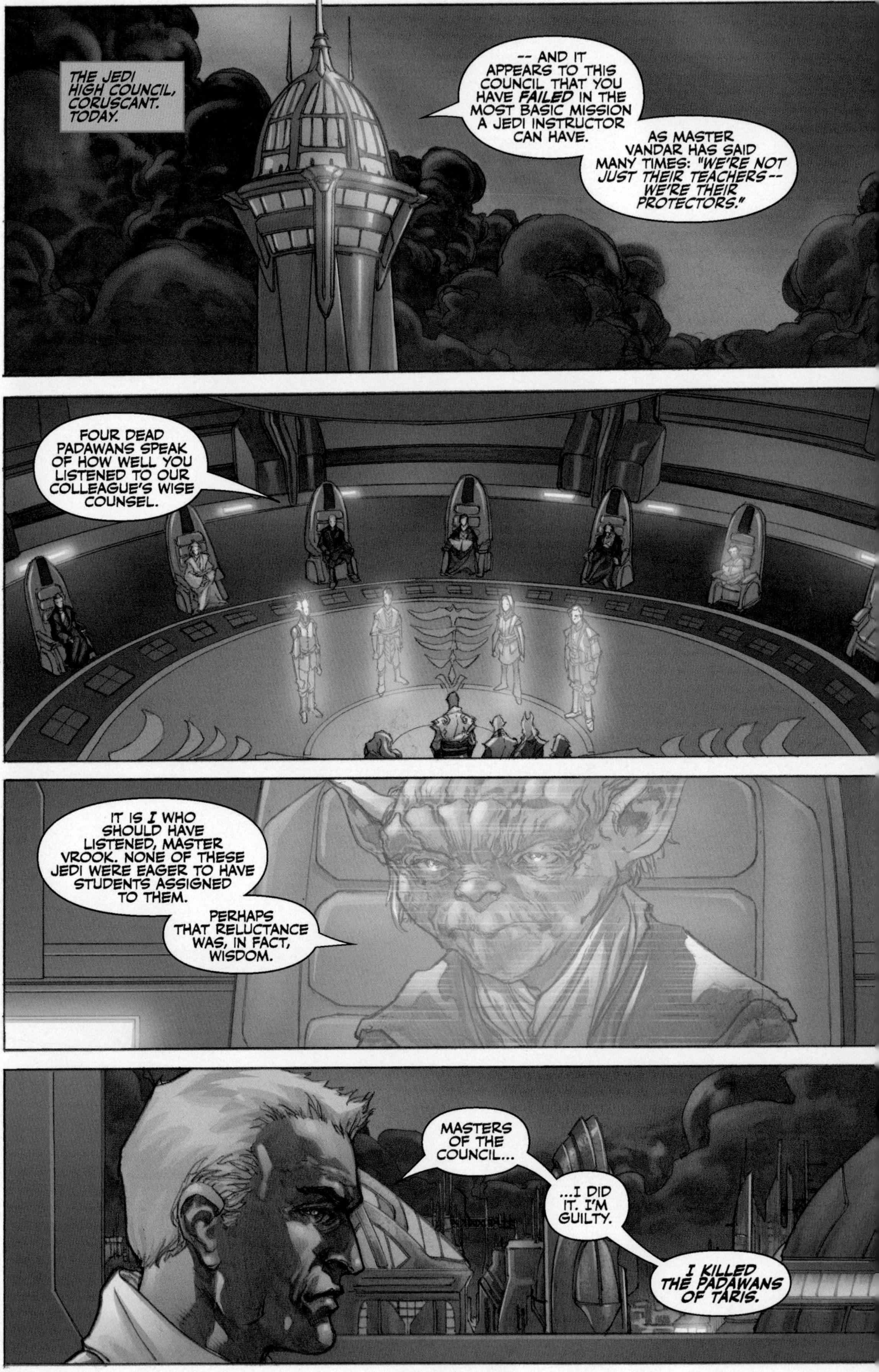
THE JEDI HIGH COUNCIL, CORUSCANT. TODAY.
-- AND IT APPEARS TO THIS COUNCIL THAT YOU HAVE FAILED IN THE MOST BASIC MISSION A JEDI INSTRUCTOR CAN HAVE.
AS MASTER VANDAR HAS SAID MANY TIMES: "WE'RE NOT JUST THEIR TEACHERS -- WE'RE THEIR PROTECTORS."
FOUR DEAD PADAWANS SPEAK OF HOW WELL YOU LISTENED TO OUR COLLEAGUE'S WISE COUNSEL.
IT IS I WHO SHOULD HAVE LISTENED, MASTER VROOK. NONE OF THESE JEDI WERE EAGER TO HAVE STUDENTS ASSIGNED TO THEM.
PERHAPS THAT RELUCTANCE WAS, IN FACT, WISDOM.
MASTERS OF THE COUNCIL...
...I DID IT. I'M GUILTY.
I KILLED THE PADAWANS OF TARIS.

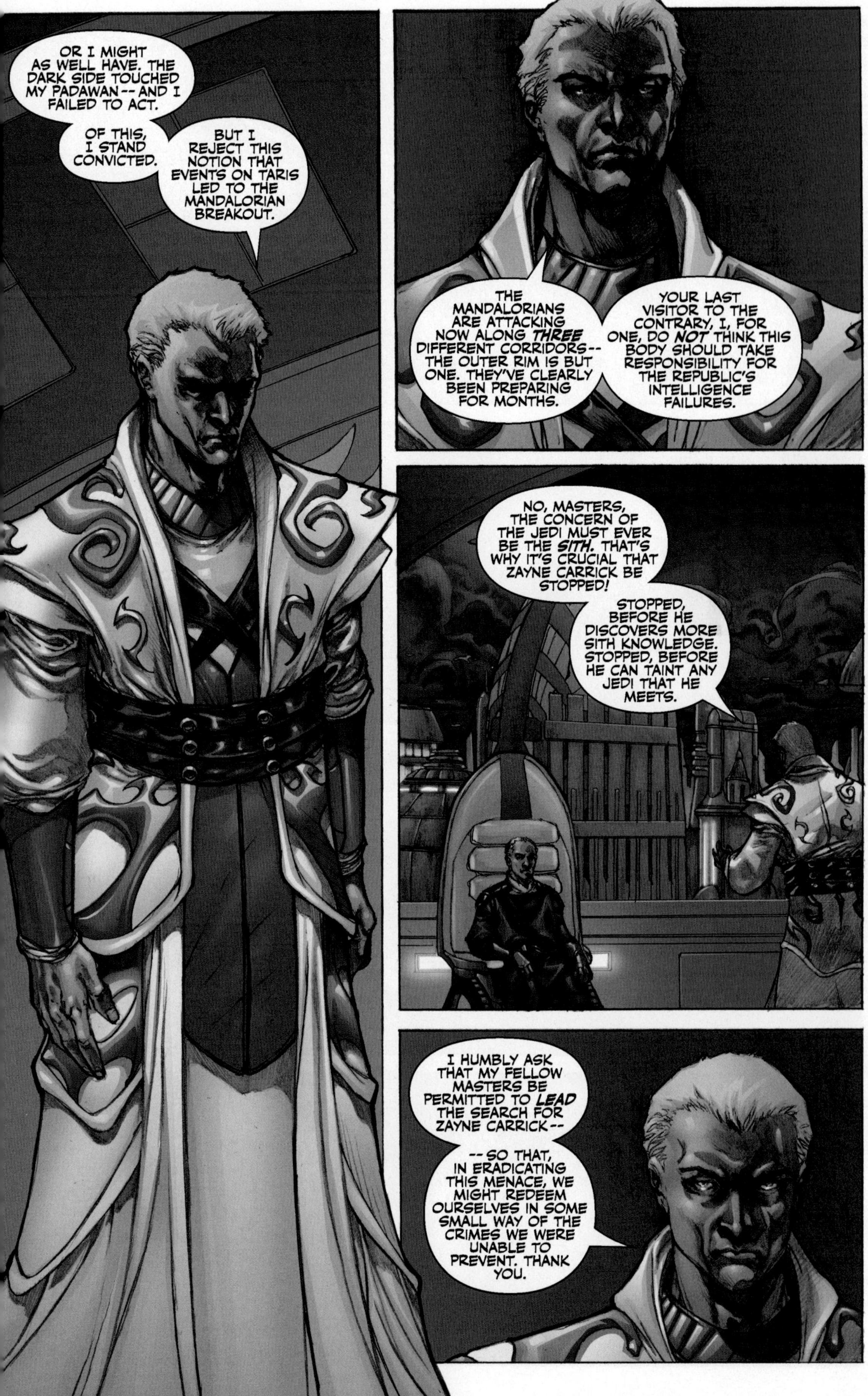
OR I MIGHT AS WELL HAVE. THE DARK SIDE TOUCHED MY PADAWAN--AND I FAILED TO ACT.
OF THIS, I STAND CONVICTED.
BUT I REJECT THIS NOTION THAT EVENTS ON TARIS LED TO THE MANDALORIAN BREAKOUT.
THE MANDALORIANS ARE ATTACKING NOW ALONG THREE DIFFERENT CORRIDORS--THE OUTER RIM IS BUT ONE. THEY'VE CLEARLY BEEN PREPARING FOR MONTHS.
YOUR LAST VISITOR TO THE CONTRARY, I, FOR ONE, DO NOT THINK THIS BODY SHOULD TAKE RESPONSIBILITY FOR THE REPUBLIC'S INTELLIGENCE FAILURES.
NO, MASTERS, THE CONCERN OF THE JEDI MUST EVER BE THE SITH. THAT'S WHY IT'S CRUCIAL THAT ZAYNE CARRICK BE STOPPED!
STOPPED, BEFORE HE DISCOVERS MORE SITH KNOWLEDGE. STOPPED, BEFORE HE CAN TAINT ANY JEDI THAT HE MEETS.
I HUMBLY ASK THAT MY FELLOW MASTERS BE PERMITTED TO LEAD THE SEARCH FOR ZAYNE CARRICK--
--SO THAT, IN ERADICATING THIS MENACE, WE MIGHT REDEEM OURSELVES IN SOME SMALL WAY OF THE CRIMES WE WERE UNABLE TO PREVENT. THANK YOU.

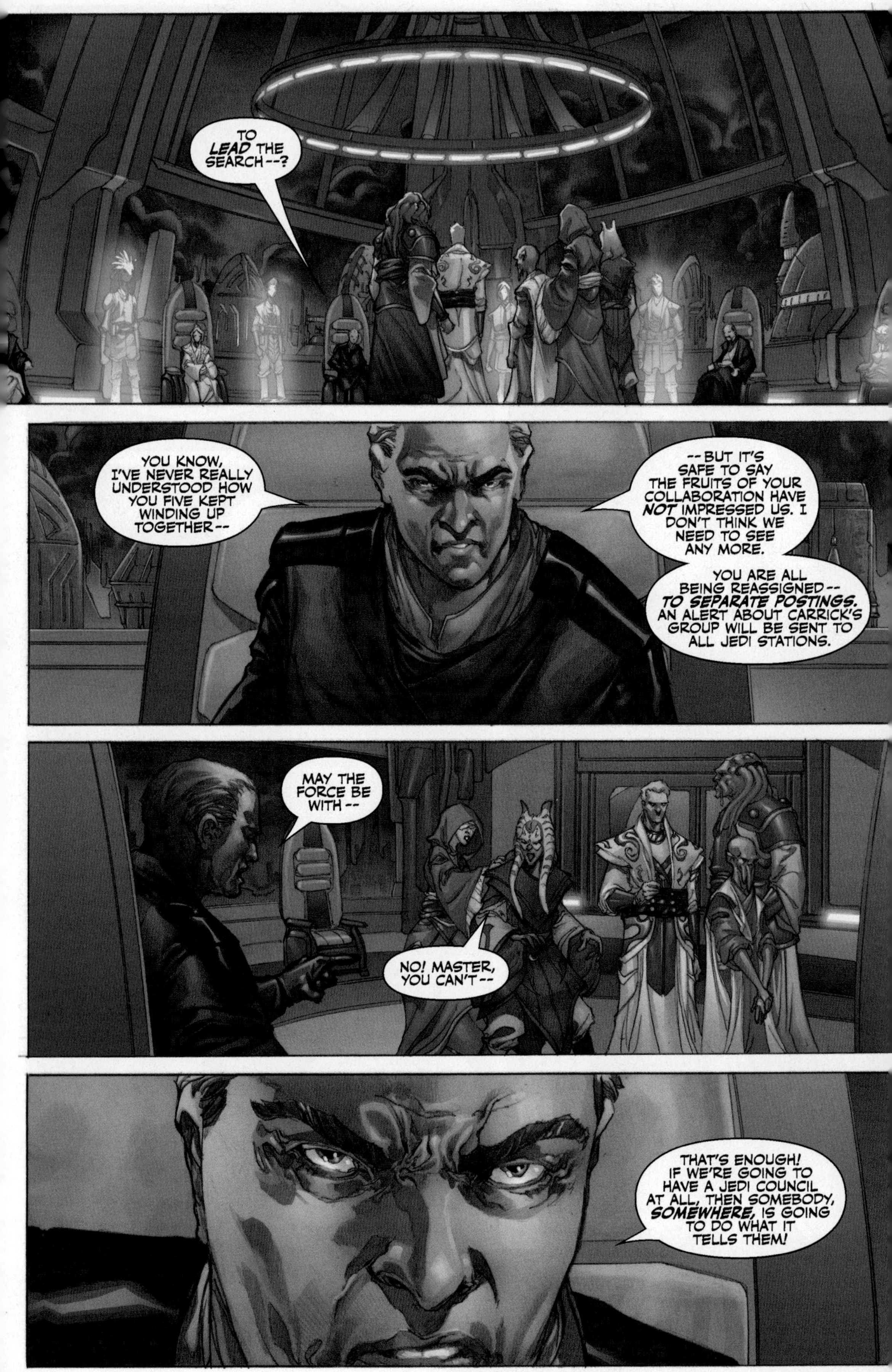
TO LEAD THE SEARCH--?
YOU KNOW, I'VE NEVER REALLY UNDERSTOOD HOW YOU FIVE KEPT WINDING UP TOGETHER--
--BUT IT'S SAFE TO SAY THE FRUITS OF YOUR COLLABORATION HAVE NOT IMPRESSED US. I DON'T THINK WE NEED TO SEE ANY MORE.
YOU ARE ALL BEING REASSIGNED-- TO SEPARATE POSTINGS. AN ALERT ABOUT CARRICK'S GROUP WILL BE SENT TO ALL JEDI STATIONS.
MAY THE FORCE BE WITH--
NO! MASTER, YOU CAN'T--
THAT'S ENOUGH! IF WE'RE GOING TO HAVE A JEDI COUNCIL AT ALL, THEN SOMEBODY, SOMEWHERE, IS GOING TO DO WHAT IT TELLS THEM!

I DO NOT UNDERSSSSTAND WHY WE DO NOT TELL THEM ALL WE HAVE FORESSSSEEN FOR ZAYNE.

AN ALERT! THAT'S A BANDAGE ON A GUSHING WOUND.

IF THEY KNEW WHAT ISSS AT SSSTAKE --

DID YOU *MISS* THE LAST HOUR? THE MANDALORIANS ARE *INVADING* AND THEY'RE STILL NOT LISTENING TO PROPHECIES ABOUT *THEM!*

A SITH LORD COULD WALK RIGHT IN FRONT OF THE COUNCIL AND THEY'D LECTURE HIM ABOUT NEUTRALITY!

LESS PASSION, RAANA. WE HAVE TO SEE CLEARLY --

-- ALTHOUGH RIGHT NOW, I SEE ONLY MORE OBSTACLES AHEAD.

THE FURTHER THE MANDALORIANS STAB, THE MORE TRACTION OUR COLLEAGUE BACK THERE WILL GET. THE JEDI COULD LOSE WHAT LITTLE FOCUS THEY HAVE.

YEAH. BACK HOME, RECLAIMING GROUND LOST IN WAR WAS THE NOBLEST CAUSE YOU COULD HAVE.

JURMAARZ, WE CALLED IT -- WHAT'S THE BASIC WORD?

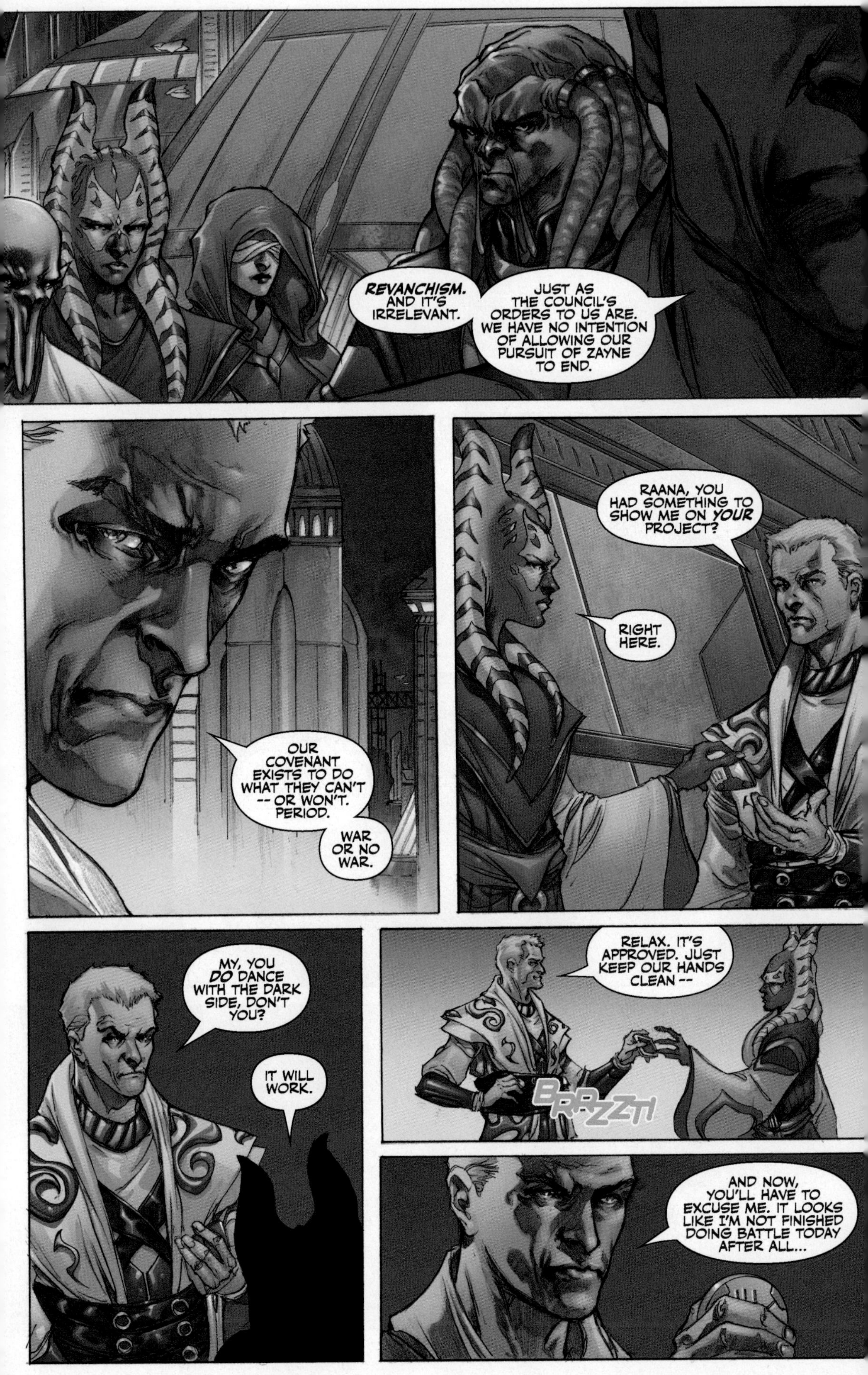
REVANCHISM. AND IT'S IRRELEVANT.
JUST AS THE COUNCIL'S ORDERS TO US ARE. WE HAVE NO INTENTION OF ALLOWING OUR PURSUIT OF ZAYNE TO END.
OUR COVENANT EXISTS TO DO WHAT THEY CAN'T -- OR WON'T. PERIOD.
WAR OR NO WAR.
RAANA, YOU HAD SOMETHING TO SHOW ME ON YOUR PROJECT?
RIGHT HERE.
MY, YOU DO DANCE WITH THE DARK SIDE, DON'T YOU?
IT WILL WORK.
RELAX. IT'S APPROVED. JUST KEEP OUR HANDS CLEAN --
BRRZZT!
AND NOW, YOU'LL HAVE TO EXCUSE ME. IT LOOKS LIKE I'M NOT FINISHED DOING BATTLE TODAY AFTER ALL...

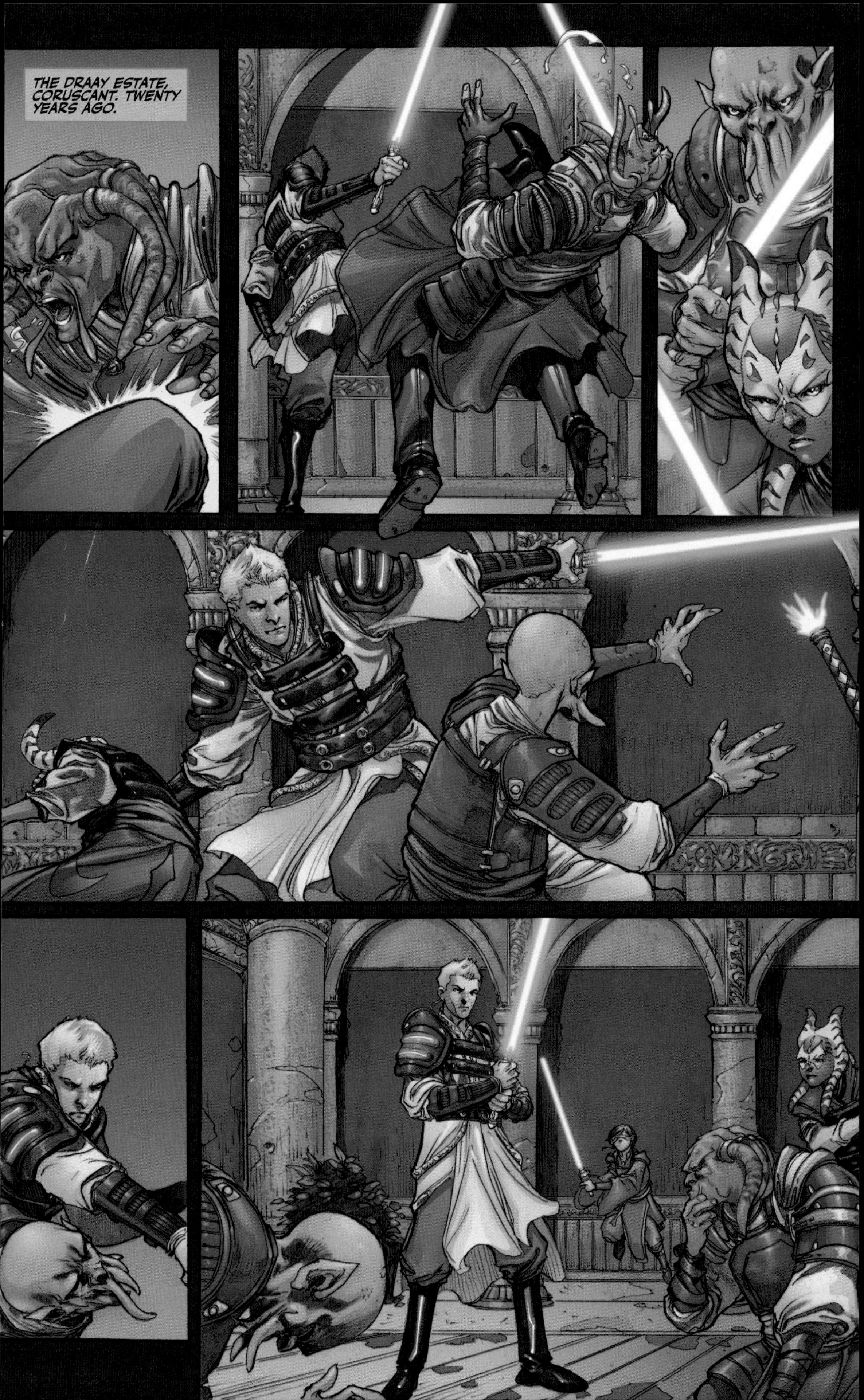
THE DRAAY ESTATE, CORUSCANT. TWENTY YEARS AGO.

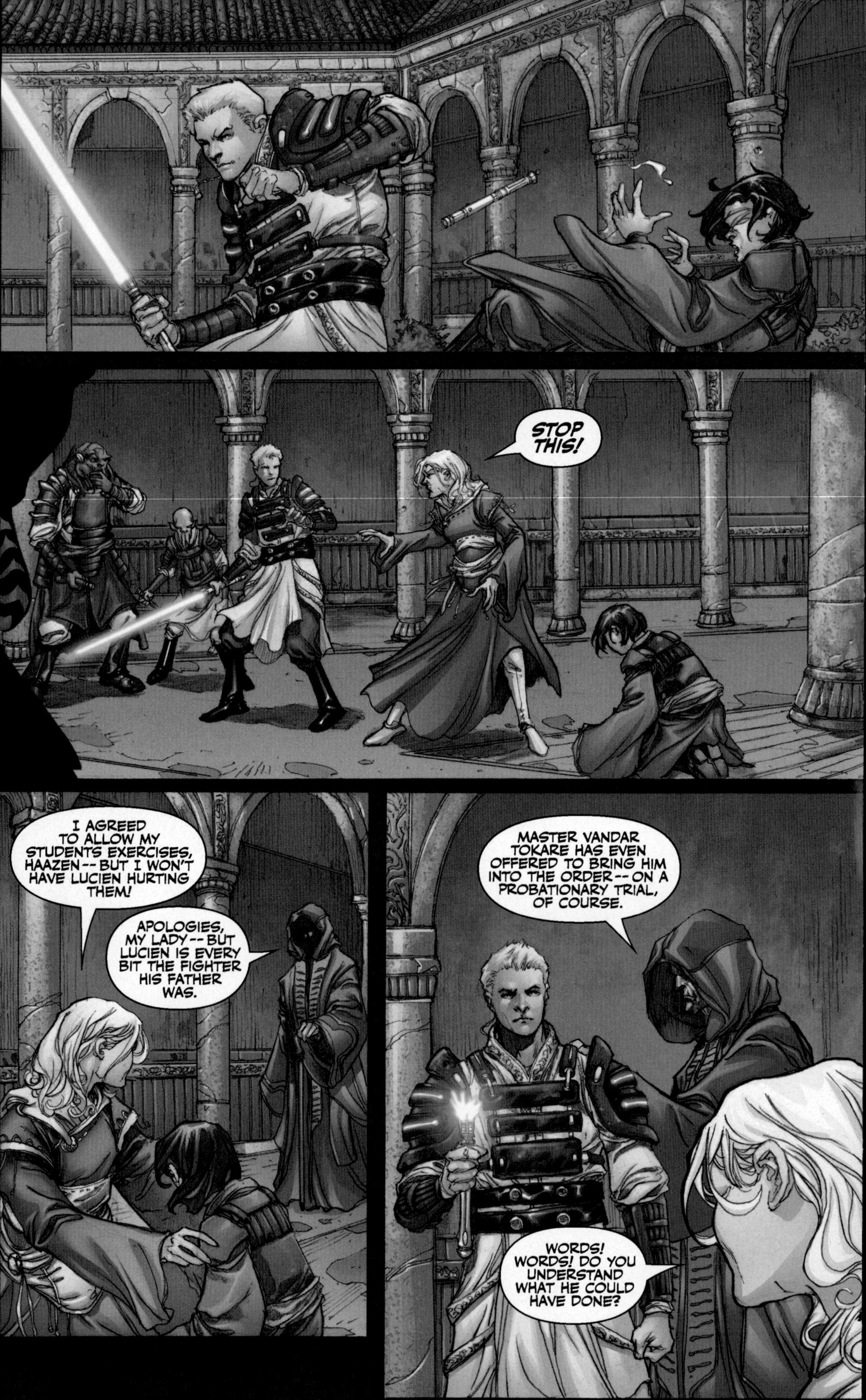
STOP THIS!
I AGREED TO ALLOW MY STUDENTS EXERCISES, HAAZEN-- BUT I WON'T HAVE LUCIEN HURTING THEM!
APOLOGIES, MY LADY-- BUT LUCIEN IS EVERY BIT THE FIGHTER HIS FATHER WAS.
MASTER VANDAR TOKARE HAS EVEN OFFERED TO BRING HIM INTO THE ORDER-- ON A PROBATIONARY TRIAL, OF COURSE.
WORDS! WORDS! DO YOU UNDERSTAND WHAT HE COULD HAVE DONE?

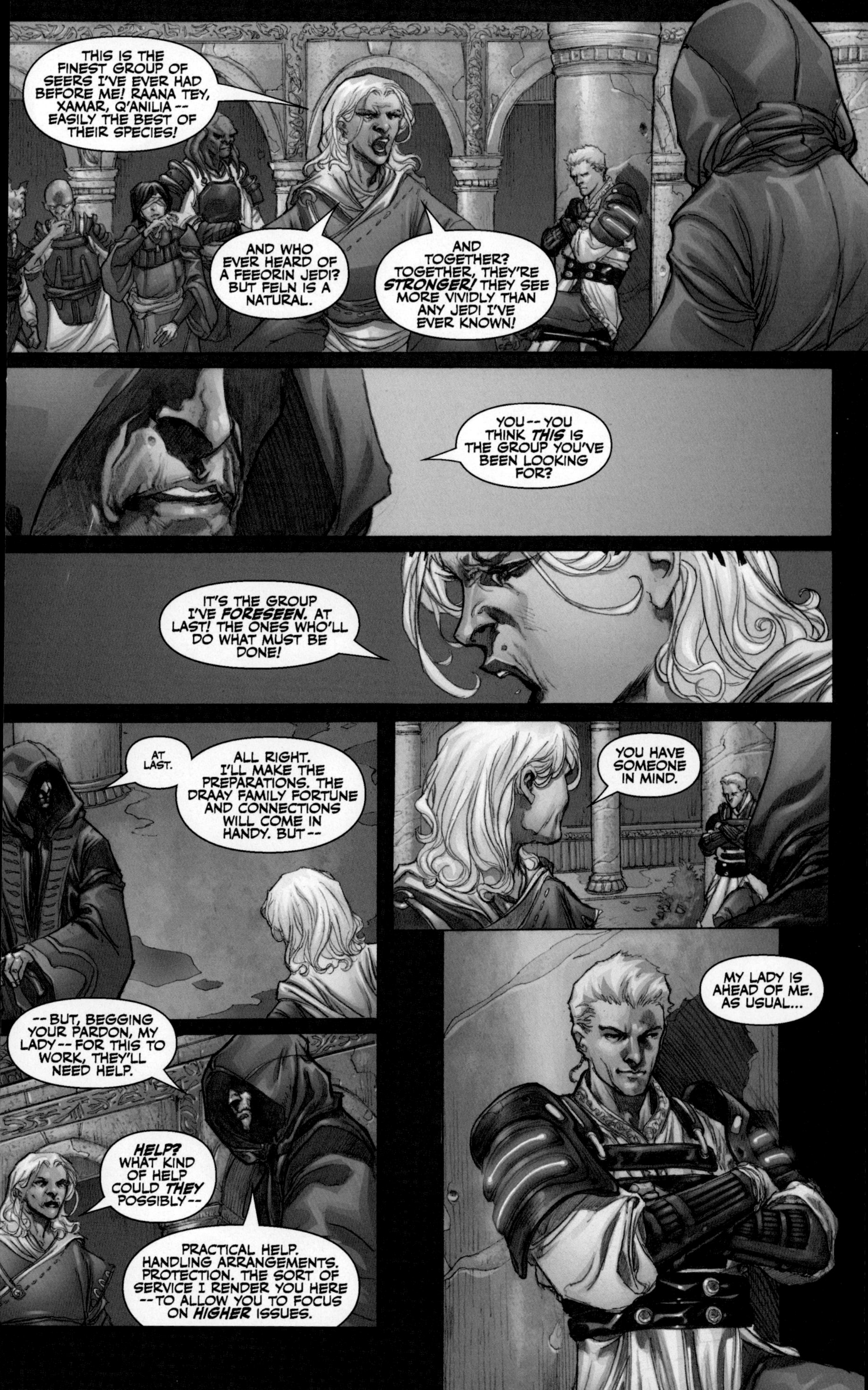
THIS IS THE FINEST GROUP OF SEERS I'VE EVER HAD BEFORE ME! RAANA TEY, XAMAR, Q'ANILIA -- EASILY THE BEST OF THEIR SPECIES!
AND WHO EVER HEARD OF A FEEORIN JEDI? BUT FELN IS A NATURAL.
AND TOGETHER? TOGETHER, THEY'RE STRONGER! THEY SEE MORE VIVIDLY THAN ANY JEDI I'VE EVER KNOWN!
YOU -- YOU THINK THIS IS THE GROUP YOU'VE BEEN LOOKING FOR?
IT'S THE GROUP I'VE FORESEEN. AT LAST! THE ONES WHO'LL DO WHAT MUST BE DONE!
AT LAST.
ALL RIGHT. I'LL MAKE THE PREPARATIONS. THE DRAAY FAMILY FORTUNE AND CONNECTIONS WILL COME IN HANDY. BUT --
YOU HAVE SOMEONE IN MIND.
-- BUT, BEGGING YOUR PARDON, MY LADY -- FOR THIS TO WORK, THEY'LL NEED HELP.
HELP? WHAT KIND OF HELP COULD THEY POSSIBLY --
PRACTICAL HELP. HANDLING ARRANGEMENTS. PROTECTION. THE SORT OF SERVICE I RENDER YOU HERE -- TO ALLOW YOU TO FOCUS ON HIGHER ISSUES.
MY LADY IS AHEAD OF ME. AS USUAL...

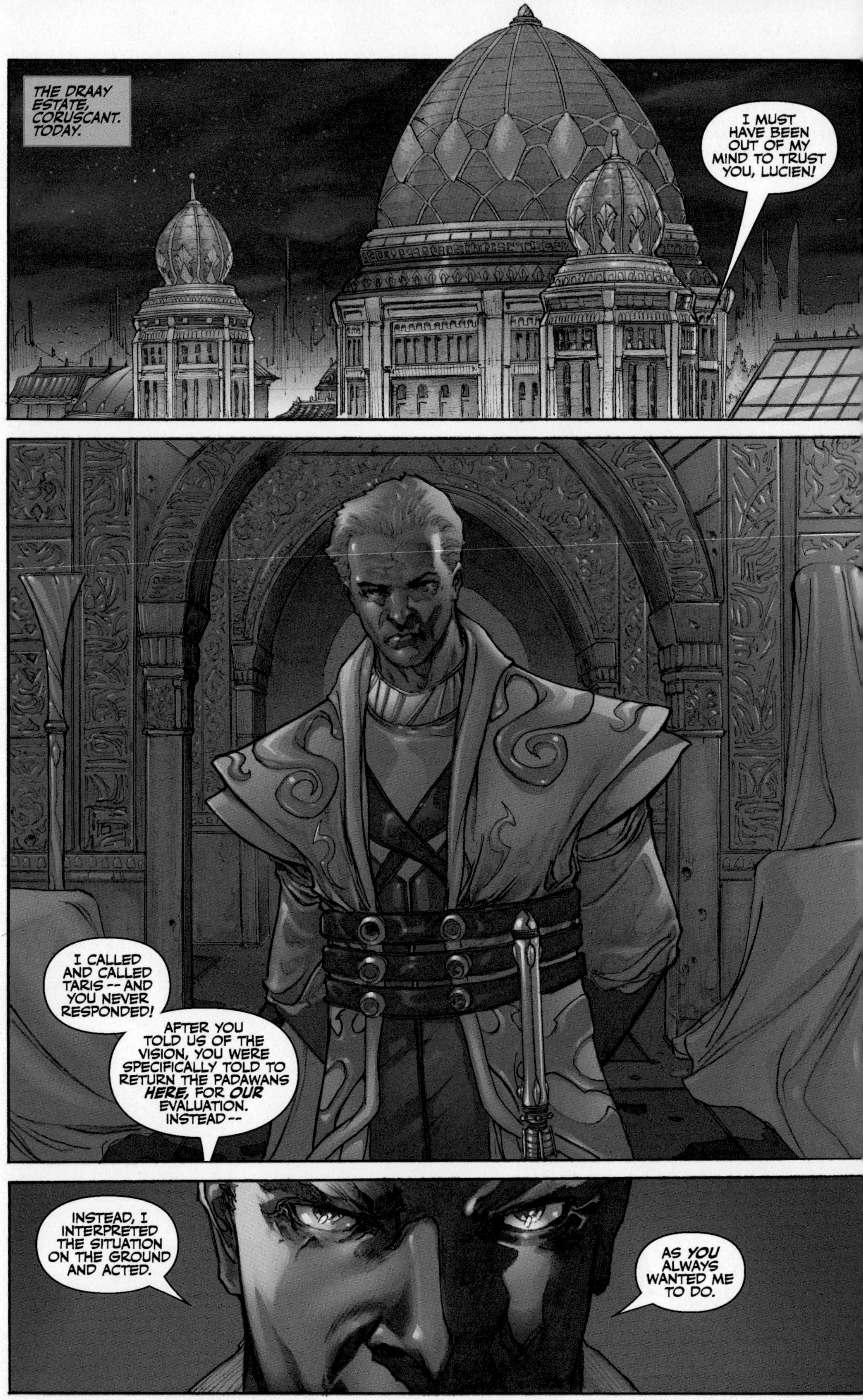
THE DRAAY ESTATE, CORUSCANT. TODAY.
I MUST HAVE BEEN OUT OF MY MIND TO TRUST YOU, LUCIEN!
I CALLED AND CALLED TARIS -- AND YOU NEVER RESPONDED!
AFTER YOU TOLD US OF THE VISION, YOU WERE SPECIFICALLY TOLD TO RETURN THE PADAWANS HERE, FOR OUR EVALUATION. INSTEAD --
INSTEAD, I INTERPRETED THE SITUATION ON THE GROUND AND ACTED.
AS YOU ALWAYS WANTED ME TO DO.

I NEVER WANTED YOU TO DO *THAT*.

NOW, THE COVENANT'S ONLY BARELY ESCAPED EXPOSURE, AND YOUR EFFECTIVENESS IS GREATLY REDUCED.

WHERE'S MY MOTHER, HAAZEN?

SHE'S HERE. CAN'T YOU FEEL HER PRESENCE?

NO. I MEAN, *YES*. I MEAN --

YOU'RE GETTING AS FEEBLE WITH THE PRESENT AS YOU ARE WITH THE FUTURE. YOUR HANDLING OF THE TARIS AFFAIR IS PROOF OF THAT!

AND I'VE BEEN EXAMINING SOME OF THE REPORTS IN VANDAR'S FILES. WHY DIDN'T YOU TELL US ABOUT ZAYNE CARRICK'S *"SPECIAL RELATIONSHIP"* WITH THE FORCE?

THERE WAS NO REASON TO. IT'S OF NO USE TO ANYONE.

YOU MEAN, THE JEDI DIDN'T KNOW WHAT TO DO WITH IT. MAYBE IT WAS HIS TEACHERS WHO WERE OF NO USE TO HIM! I WAS A SO-CALLED *"FAILED PADAWAN,"* MYSELF.

NO NEED TO GET NOSTALGIC, HAAZEN. YOU STILL ARE.

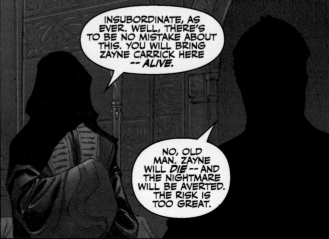

INSUBORDINATE, AS EVER. WELL, THERE'S TO BE NO MISTAKE ABOUT THIS. YOU WILL BRING ZAYNE CARRICK HERE -- *ALIVE*.

NO, OLD MAN. ZAYNE WILL *DIE* -- AND THE NIGHTMARE WILL BE AVERTED. THE RISK IS TOO GREAT.

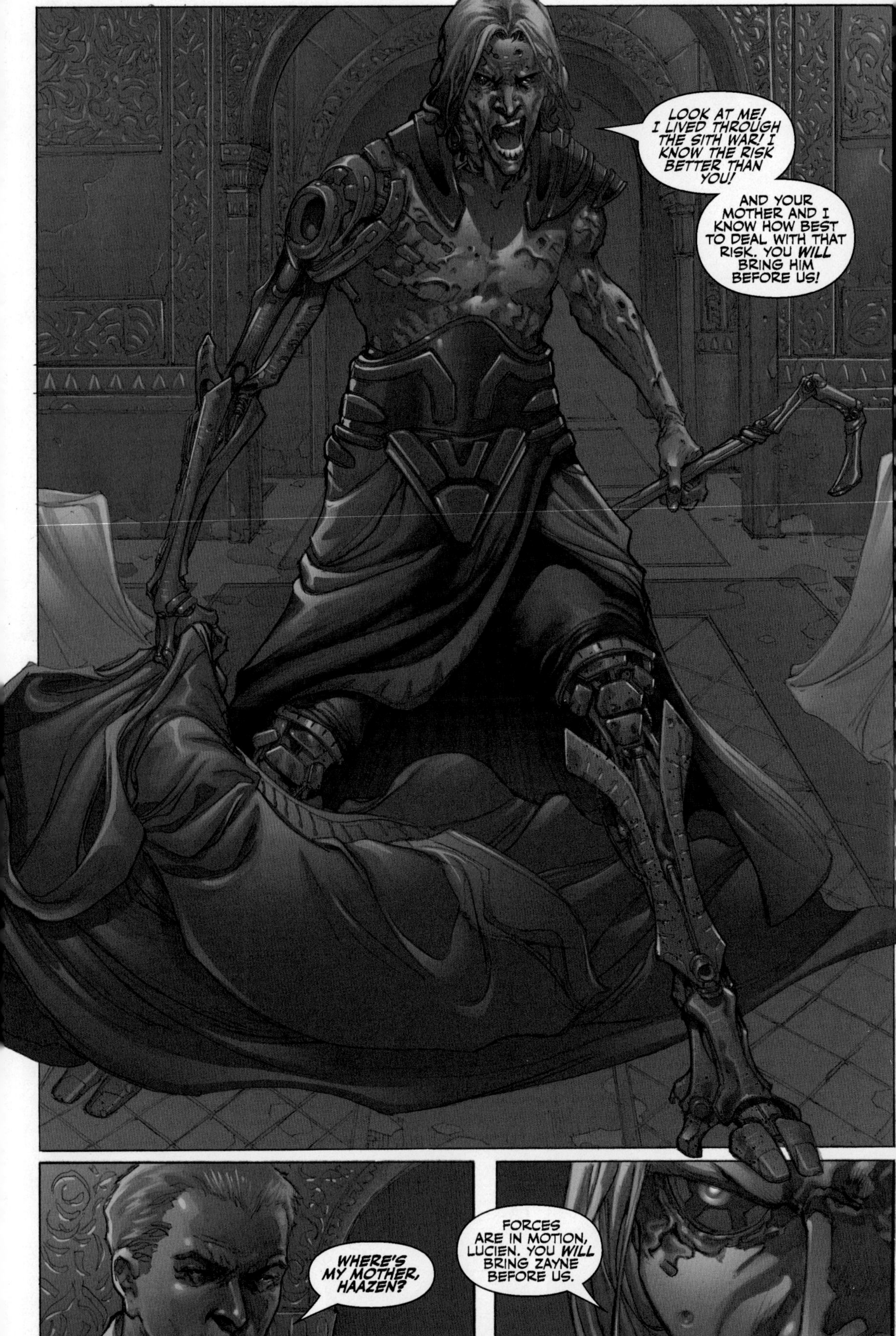
LOOK AT ME! I LIVED THROUGH THE SITH WAR! I KNOW THE RISK BETTER THAN YOU!
AND YOUR MOTHER AND I KNOW HOW BEST TO DEAL WITH THAT RISK. YOU WILL BRING HIM BEFORE US!

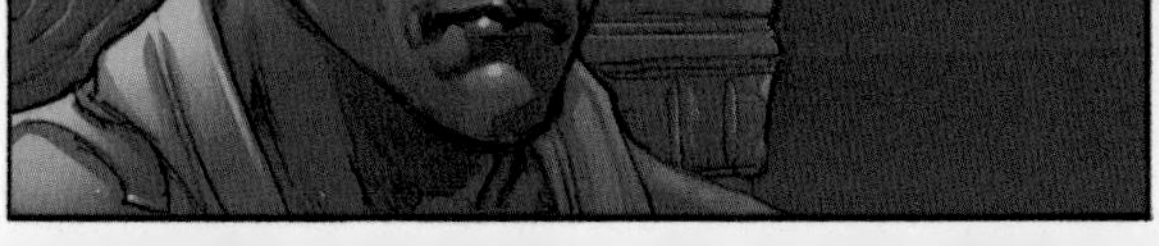
WHERE'S MY MOTHER, HAAZEN?

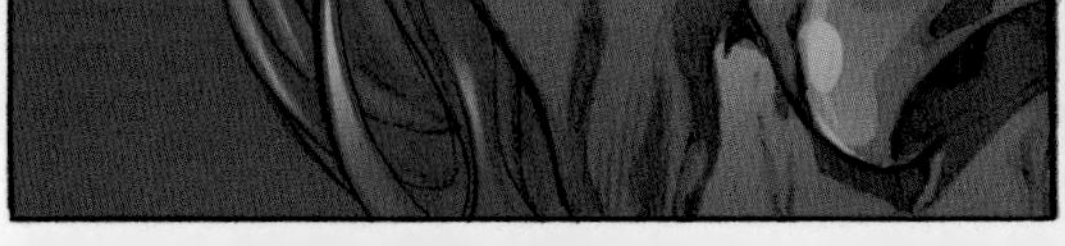
FORCES ARE IN MOTION, LUCIEN. YOU WILL BRING ZAYNE BEFORE US.

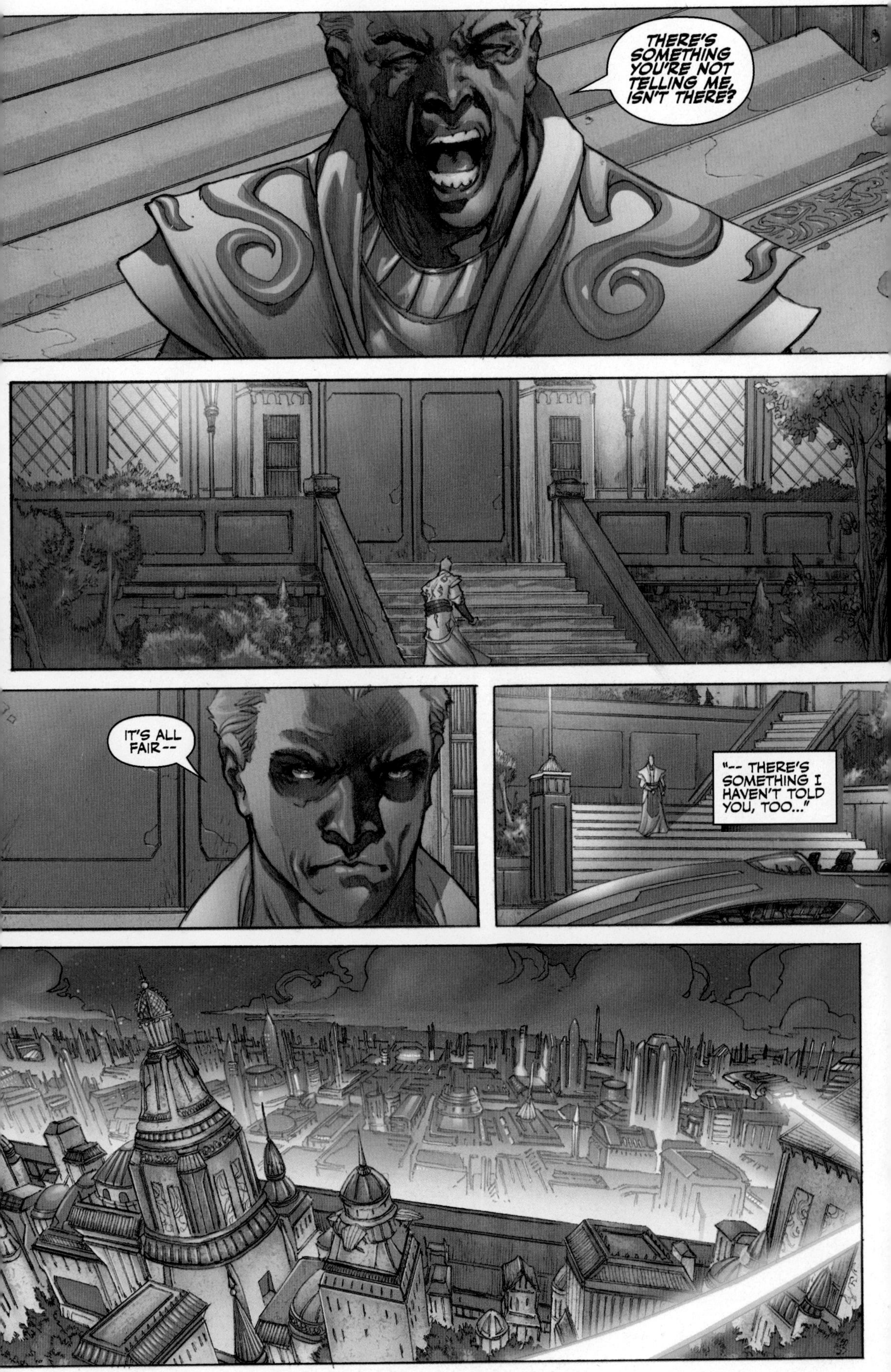
THERE'S SOMETHING YOU'RE NOT TELLING ME, ISN'T THERE?
IT'S ALL FAIR--
"-- THERE'S SOMETHING I HAVEN'T TOLD YOU, TOO..."

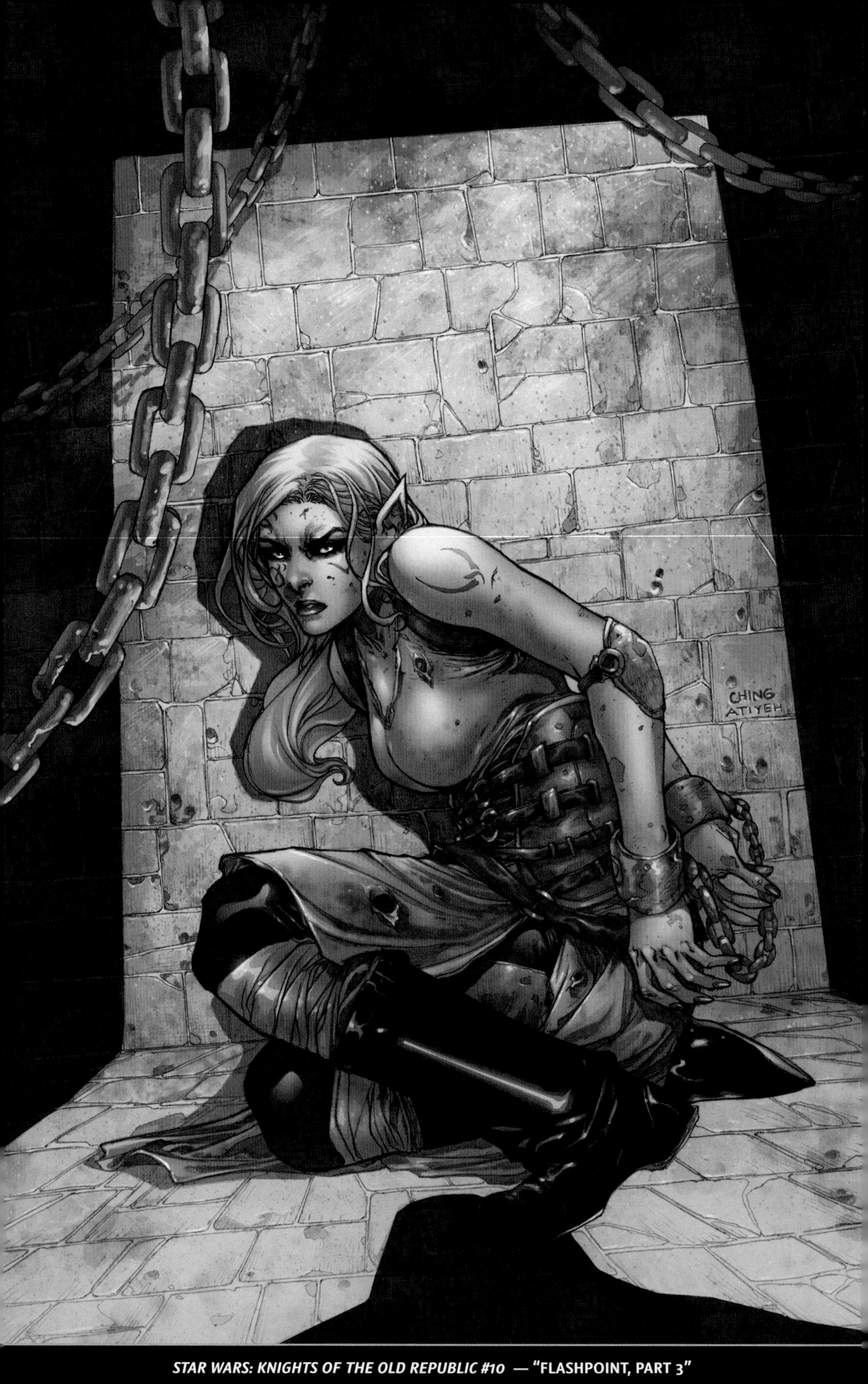
CHING
ATIYEH

STAR WARS: KNIGHTS OF THE OLD REPUBLIC #10 — "FLASHPOINT, PART 3"

WRITER: JOHN JACKSON MILLER • ARTIST: DUSTIN WEAVER • COLORIST: MICHAEL ATIYEH • LETTERER: MICHAEL HEISLER
ASSISTANT EDITOR: DAVE MARSHALL • EDITOR: JEREMY BARLOW • COVER ARTISTS: BRIAN CHING & MICHAEL ATIYEH

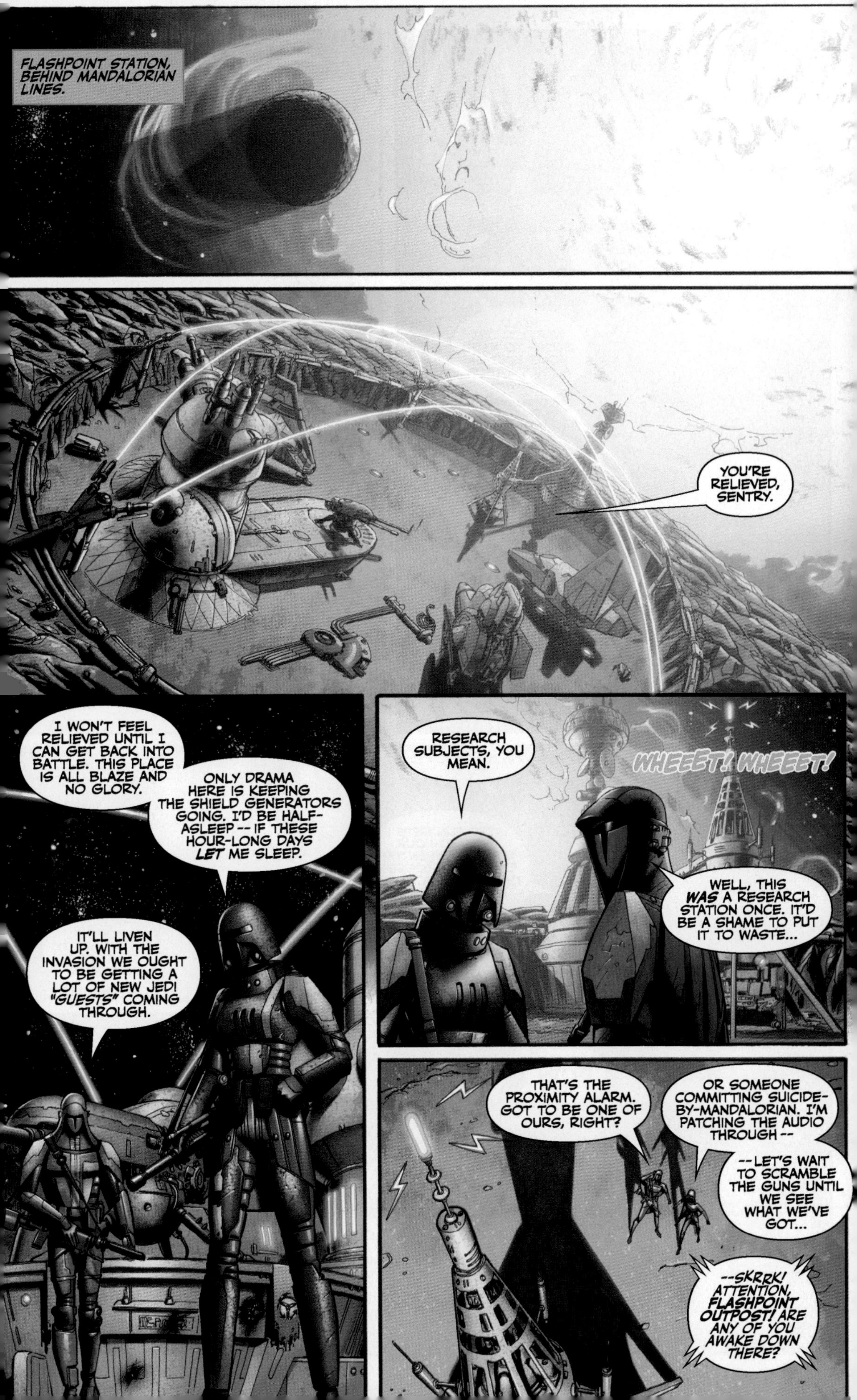
FLASHPOINT STATION, BEHIND MANDALORIAN LINES.
YOU'RE RELIEVED, SENTRY.
I WON'T FEEL RELIEVED UNTIL I CAN GET BACK INTO BATTLE. THIS PLACE IS ALL BLAZE AND NO GLORY.
ONLY DRAMA HERE IS KEEPING THE SHIELD GENERATORS GOING. I'D BE HALF-ASLEEP -- IF THESE HOUR-LONG DAYS LET ME SLEEP.
IT'LL LIVEN UP. WITH THE INVASION WE OUGHT TO BE GETTING A LOT OF NEW JEDI "GUESTS" COMING THROUGH.
RESEARCH SUBJECTS, YOU MEAN.
WHEEET! WHEEET!
WELL, THIS WAS A RESEARCH STATION ONCE. IT'D BE A SHAME TO PUT IT TO WASTE...
THAT'S THE PROXIMITY ALARM. GOT TO BE ONE OF OURS, RIGHT?
OR SOMEONE COMMITTING SUICIDE-BY-MANDALORIAN. I'M PATCHING THE AUDIO THROUGH --
--LET'S WAIT TO SCRAMBLE THE GUNS UNTIL WE SEE WHAT WE'VE GOT...
--SKRRK! ATTENTION, FLASHPOINT OUTPOST! ARE ANY OF YOU AWAKE DOWN THERE?

REPEAT, I NEED CLEARANCE TO LAND! I HAVE A PRISONER FROM VANQUO. OPEN THE MAGNETIC FIELD!

HOLD, WARRIOR. I'M GOING TO NEED SOME KIND OF AUTHORIZATION FROM--

DON'T GIVE ME THAT REARGUARD GARBAGE! I DON'T KNOW HOW IT IS DOWN THERE--

-- BUT ON THE FRONT WHEN A REAL MANDALORIAN CAPTURES A JEDI IN HIS OWN SHIP, THEY PAY HIM HEED! NOW OPEN THE FIELD!

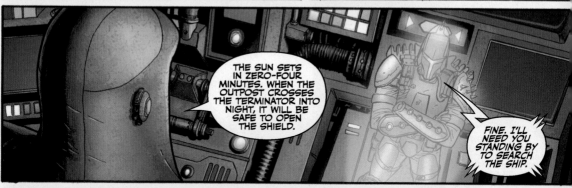

THE SUN SETS IN ZERO-FOUR MINUTES. WHEN THE OUTPOST CROSSES THE TERMINATOR INTO NIGHT, IT WILL BE SAFE TO OPEN THE SHIELD.

FINE. I'LL NEED YOU STANDING BY TO SEARCH THE SHIP.

WHAT DO YOU THINK?

LET'S SCRAMBLE THE GUNS ANYWAY. HE AS MUCH AS WAGGLES FUNNY, WE'LL BE PICKING HIM OUT OF THE WRECKAGE...

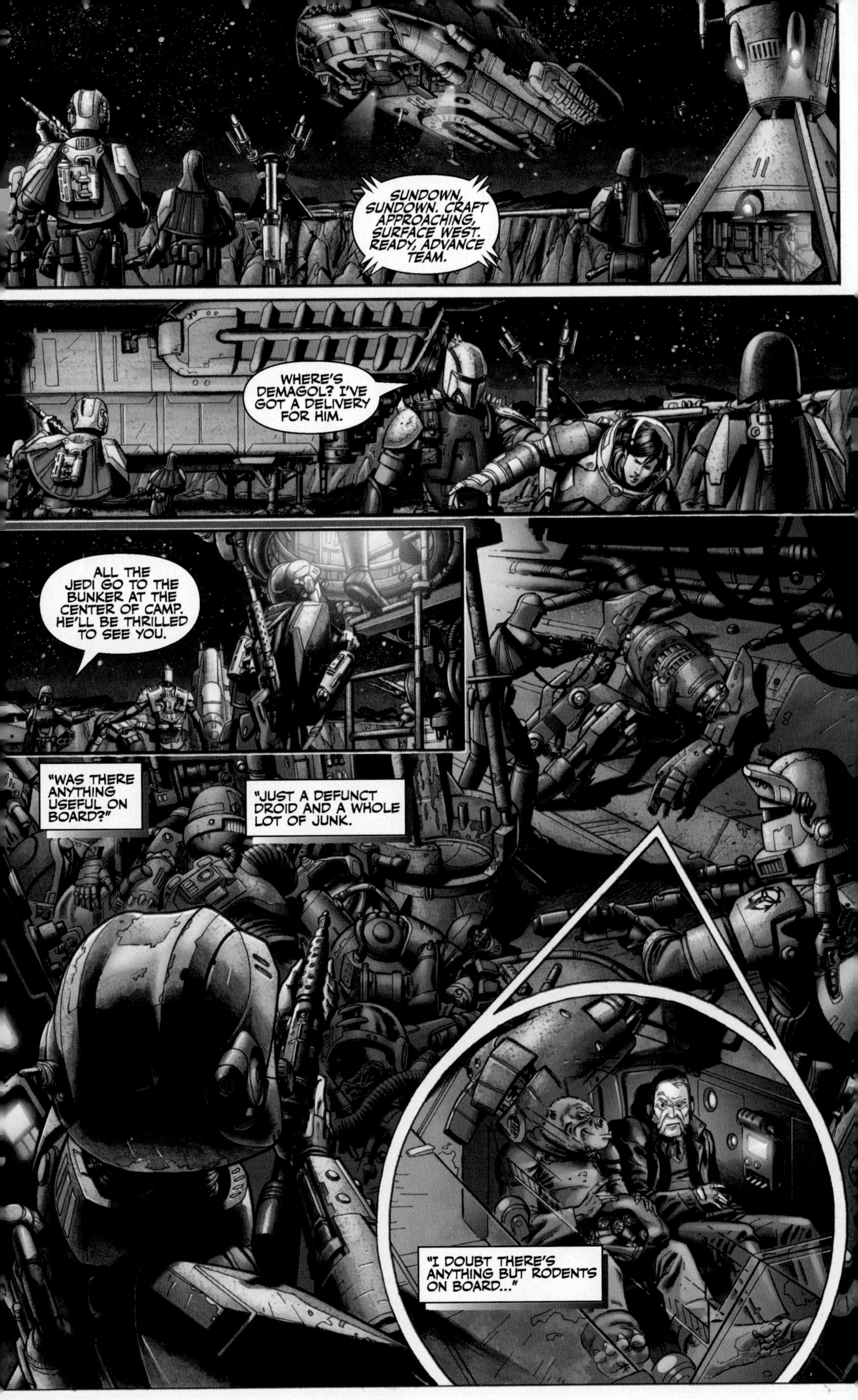
SUNDOWN, SUNDOWN. CRAFT APPROACHING, SURFACE WEST. READY, ADVANCE TEAM.
WHERE'S DEMAGOL? I'VE GOT A DELIVERY FOR HIM.
ALL THE JEDI GO TO THE BUNKER AT THE CENTER OF CAMP. HE'LL BE THRILLED TO SEE YOU.
"WAS THERE ANYTHING USEFUL ON BOARD?"
"JUST A DEFUNCT DROID AND A WHOLE LOT OF JUNK.
"I DOUBT THERE'S ANYTHING BUT RODENTS ON BOARD..."

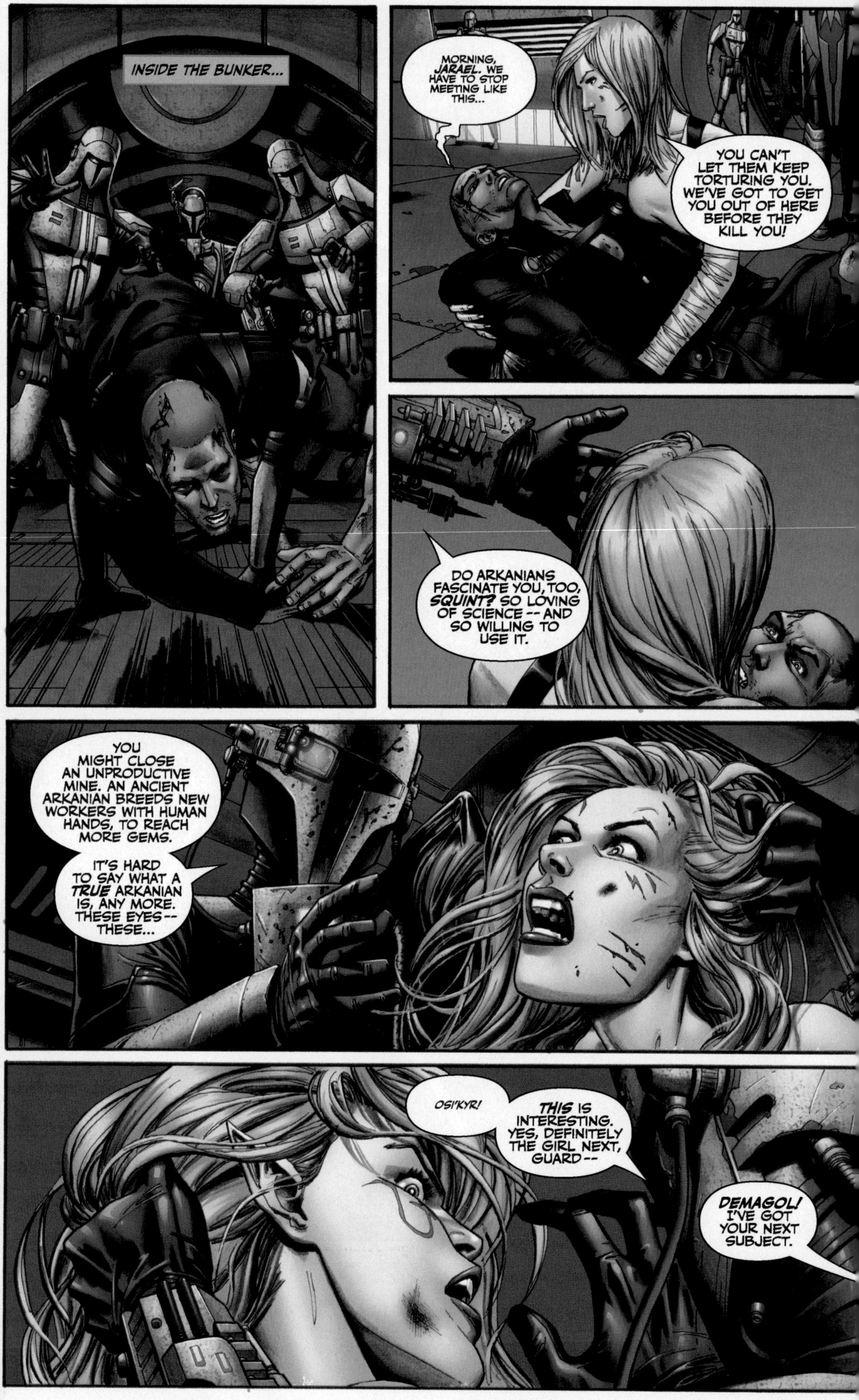
INSIDE THE BUNKER...
MORNING, JARAEL. WE HAVE TO STOP MEETING LIKE THIS...
YOU CAN'T LET THEM KEEP TORTURING YOU. WE'VE GOT TO GET YOU OUT OF HERE BEFORE THEY KILL YOU!
DO ARKANIANS FASCINATE YOU, TOO, SQUINT? SO LOVING OF SCIENCE -- AND SO WILLING TO USE IT.
YOU MIGHT CLOSE AN UNPRODUCTIVE MINE. AN ANCIENT ARKANIAN BREEDS NEW WORKERS WITH HUMAN HANDS, TO REACH MORE GEMS.
IT'S HARD TO SAY WHAT A TRUE ARKANIAN IS, ANY MORE. THESE EYES -- THESE...
OSI'KYR!
THIS IS INTERESTING. YES, DEFINITELY THE GIRL NEXT, GUARD --
DEMAGOL! I'VE GOT YOUR NEXT SUBJECT.

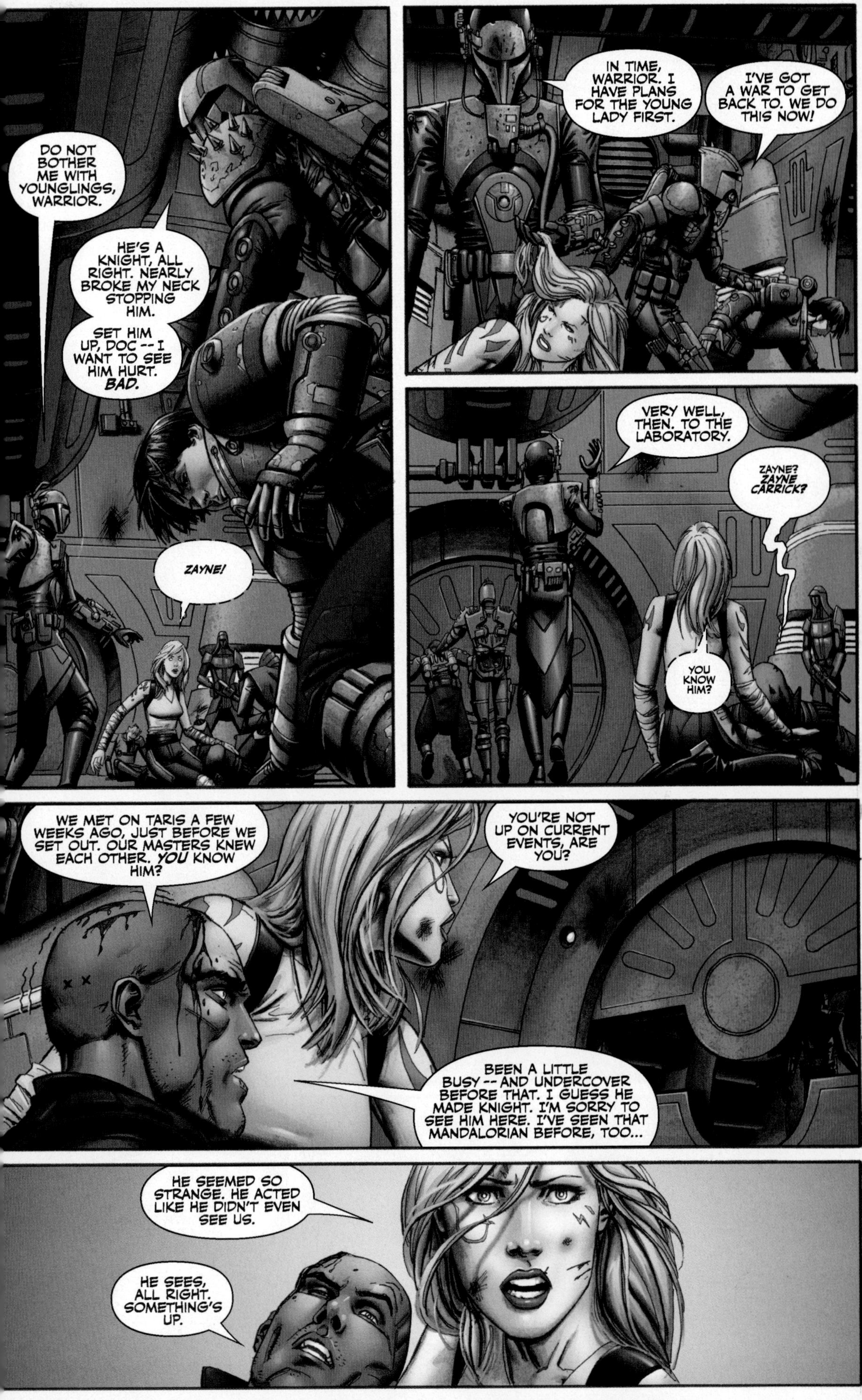
DO NOT BOTHER ME WITH YOUNGLINGS, WARRIOR.
HE'S A KNIGHT, ALL RIGHT. NEARLY BROKE MY NECK STOPPING HIM.
SET HIM UP, DOC -- I WANT TO SEE HIM HURT. BAD.
ZAYNE!
IN TIME, WARRIOR. I HAVE PLANS FOR THE YOUNG LADY FIRST.
I'VE GOT A WAR TO GET BACK TO. WE DO THIS NOW!
VERY WELL, THEN. TO THE LABORATORY.
ZAYNE? ZAYNE CARRICK?
YOU KNOW HIM?
WE MET ON TARIS A FEW WEEKS AGO, JUST BEFORE WE SET OUT. OUR MASTERS KNEW EACH OTHER. YOU KNOW HIM?
YOU'RE NOT UP ON CURRENT EVENTS, ARE YOU?
BEEN A LITTLE BUSY -- AND UNDERCOVER BEFORE THAT. I GUESS HE MADE KNIGHT. I'M SORRY TO SEE HIM HERE. I'VE SEEN THAT MANDALORIAN BEFORE, TOO...
HE SEEMED SO STRANGE. HE ACTED LIKE HE DIDN'T EVEN SEE US.
HE SEES, ALL RIGHT. SOMETHING'S UP.

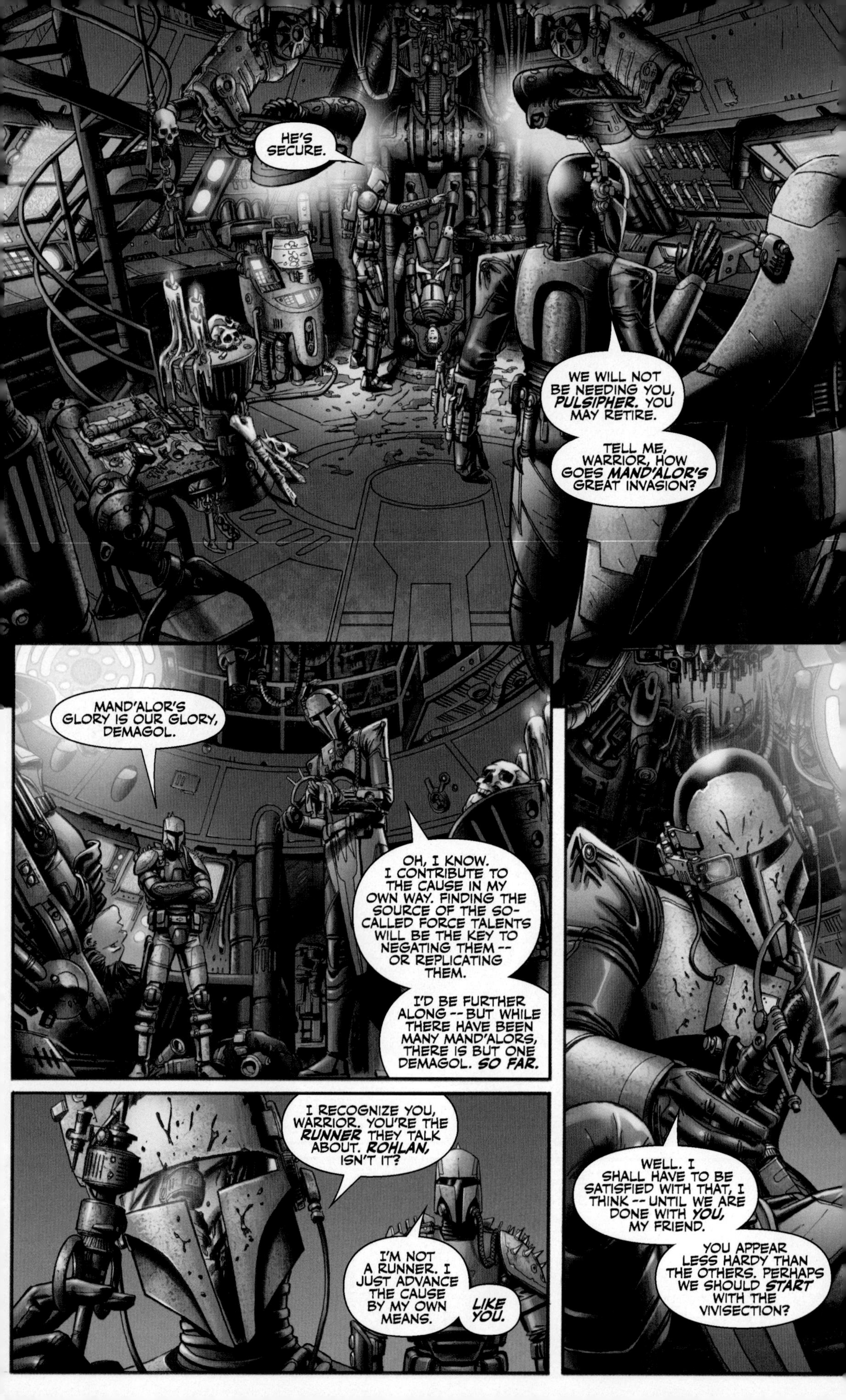
HE'S SECURE.
WE WILL NOT BE NEEDING YOU, *PULSIPHER.* YOU MAY RETIRE.
TELL ME, WARRIOR, HOW GOES *MAND'ALOR'S* GREAT INVASION?
MAND'ALOR'S GLORY IS OUR GLORY, DEMAGOL.
OH, I KNOW. I CONTRIBUTE TO THE CAUSE IN MY OWN WAY. FINDING THE SOURCE OF THE SO-CALLED FORCE TALENTS WILL BE THE KEY TO NEGATING THEM -- OR REPLICATING THEM.
I'D BE FURTHER ALONG -- BUT WHILE THERE HAVE BEEN MANY MAND'ALORS, THERE IS BUT ONE DEMAGOL. *SO FAR.*
I RECOGNIZE YOU, WARRIOR. YOU'RE THE *RUNNER* THEY TALK ABOUT. *ROHLAN,* ISN'T IT?
I'M NOT A RUNNER. I JUST ADVANCE THE CAUSE BY MY OWN MEANS.
LIKE YOU.
WELL. I SHALL HAVE TO BE SATISFIED WITH THAT, I THINK -- UNTIL WE ARE DONE WITH *YOU,* MY FRIEND.
YOU APPEAR LESS HARDY THAN THE OTHERS. PERHAPS WE SHOULD *START* WITH THE VIVISECTION?

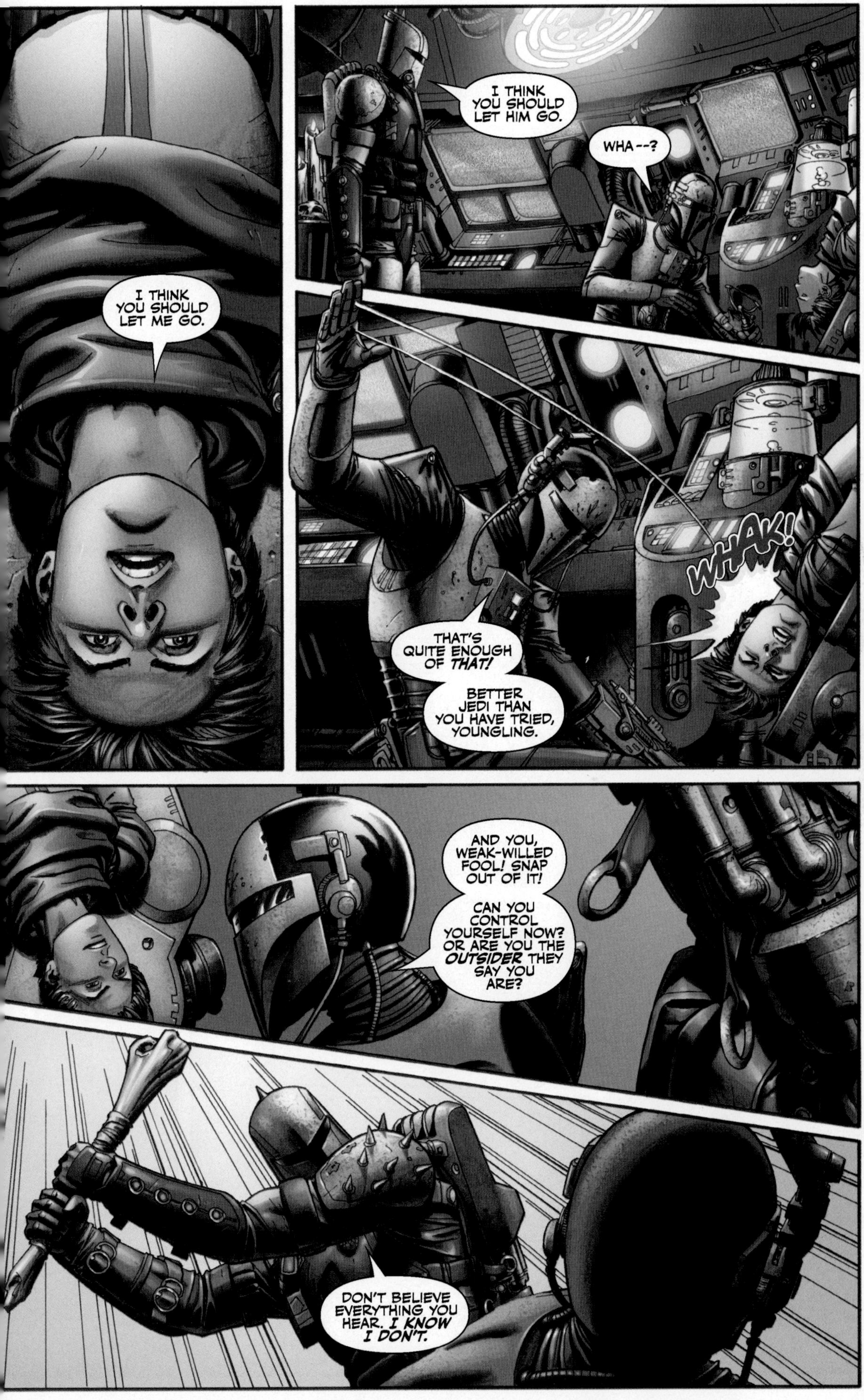
I THINK YOU SHOULD LET ME GO.
I THINK YOU SHOULD LET HIM GO.
WHA--?
WHAK!
THAT'S QUITE ENOUGH OF *THAT!*
BETTER JEDI THAN YOU HAVE TRIED, YOUNGLING.
AND YOU, WEAK-WILLED FOOL! SNAP OUT OF IT!
CAN YOU CONTROL YOURSELF NOW? OR ARE YOU THE *OUTSIDER* THEY SAY YOU ARE?
DON'T BELIEVE EVERYTHING YOU HEAR. *I KNOW I DON'T.*

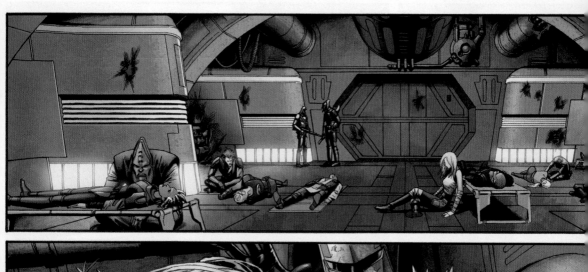

ANIMAL!

OOOF!

OOOF!

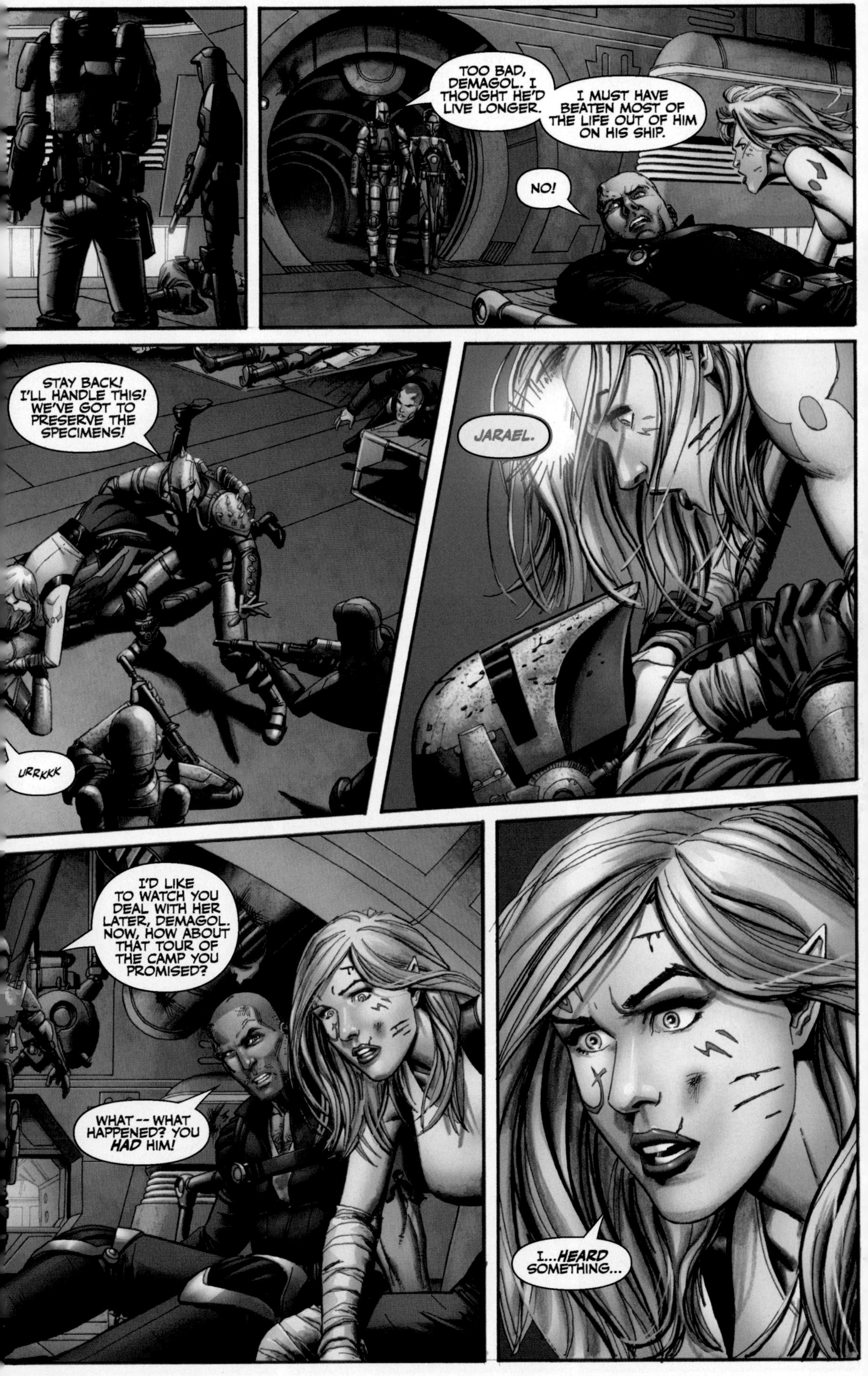

TOO BAD, DEMAGOL. I THOUGHT HE'D LIVE LONGER.
I MUST HAVE BEATEN MOST OF THE LIFE OUT OF HIM ON HIS SHIP.
NO!
STAY BACK! I'LL HANDLE THIS! WE'VE GOT TO PRESERVE THE SPECIMENS!
URRKKK
JARAEL.
I'D LIKE TO WATCH YOU DEAL WITH HER LATER, DEMAGOL. NOW, HOW ABOUT THAT TOUR OF THE CAMP YOU PROMISED?
WHAT -- WHAT HAPPENED? YOU HAD HIM!
I...HEARD SOMETHING...

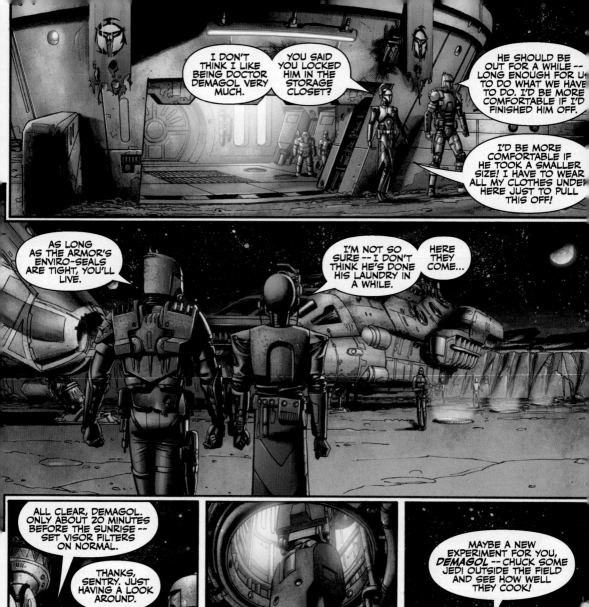

I DON'T THINK I LIKE BEING DOCTOR DEMAGOL VERY MUCH.

YOU SAID YOU LOCKED HIM IN THE STORAGE CLOSET?

HE SHOULD BE OUT FOR A WHILE -- LONG ENOUGH FOR U— TO DO WHAT WE HAVE TO DO. I'D BE MORE COMFORTABLE IF I'D FINISHED HIM OFF.

I'D BE MORE COMFORTABLE IF HE TOOK A SMALLER SIZE! I HAVE TO WEAR ALL MY CLOTHES UNDER HERE JUST TO PULL THIS OFF!

AS LONG AS THE ARMOR'S ENVIRO-SEALS ARE TIGHT, YOU'LL LIVE.

I'M NOT SO SURE -- I DON'T THINK HE'S DONE HIS LAUNDRY IN A WHILE.

HERE THEY COME...

ALL CLEAR, DEMAGOL. ONLY ABOUT 20 MINUTES BEFORE THE SUNRISE -- SET VISOR FILTERS ON NORMAL.

THANKS, SENTRY. JUST HAVING A LOOK AROUND.

HOW'S THE DUTY HERE?

NOT MUCH ACTION, OF COURSE. AND IF YOUR VISOR GOES OUT, YOU'RE IN BIG TROUBLE.

THE FORCE FIELD CUTS THE HEAT AND THE RADIATION, BUT IT STILL HURTS TO LOOK UP.

MAYBE A NEW EXPERIMENT FOR YOU, DEMAGOL -- CHUCK SOME JEDI OUTSIDE THE FIELD AND SEE HOW WELL THEY COOK!

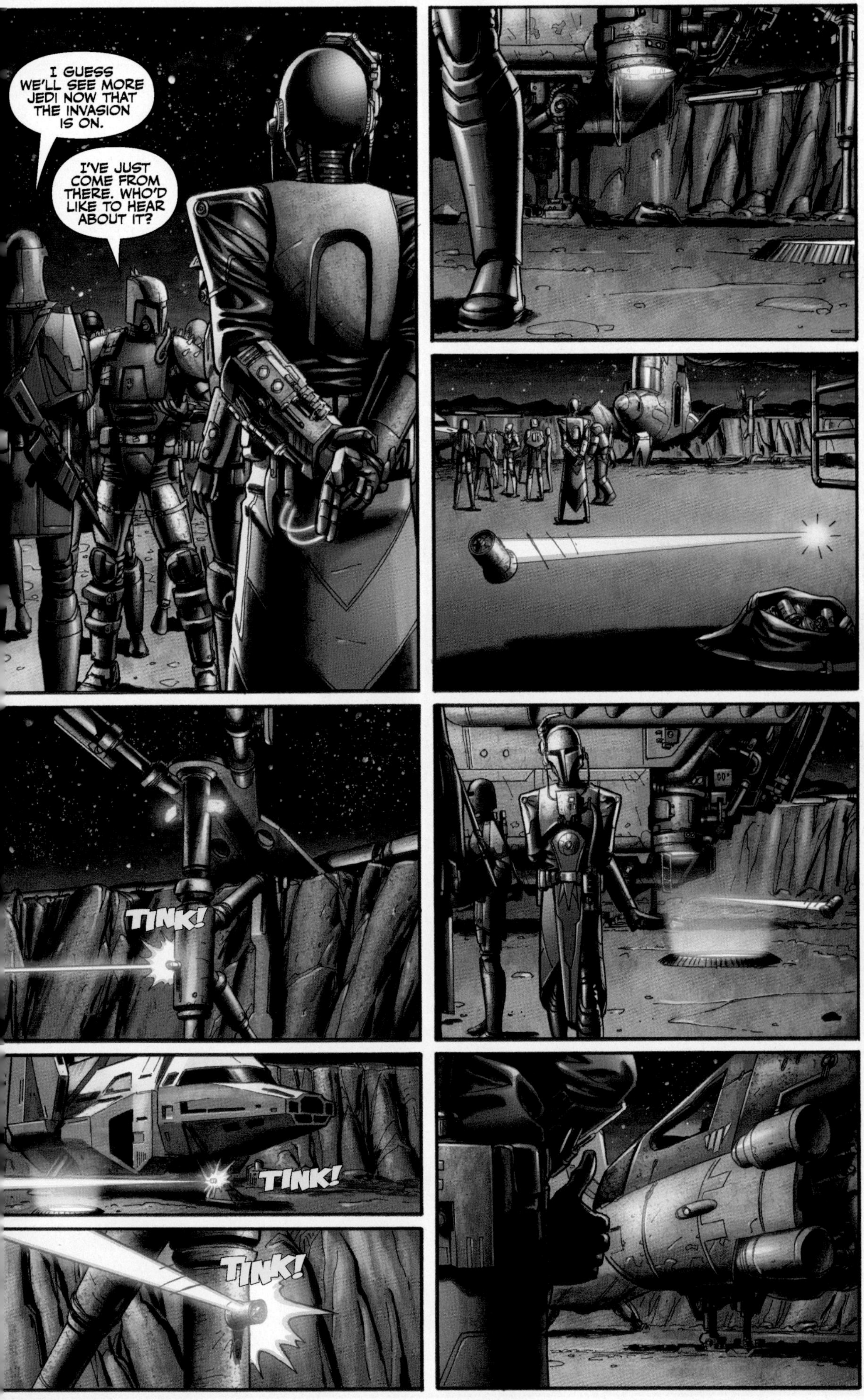
I GUESS WE'LL SEE MORE JEDI NOW THAT THE INVASION IS ON.
I'VE JUST COME FROM THERE. WHO'D LIKE TO HEAR ABOUT IT?
TINK!
TINK!
TINK!

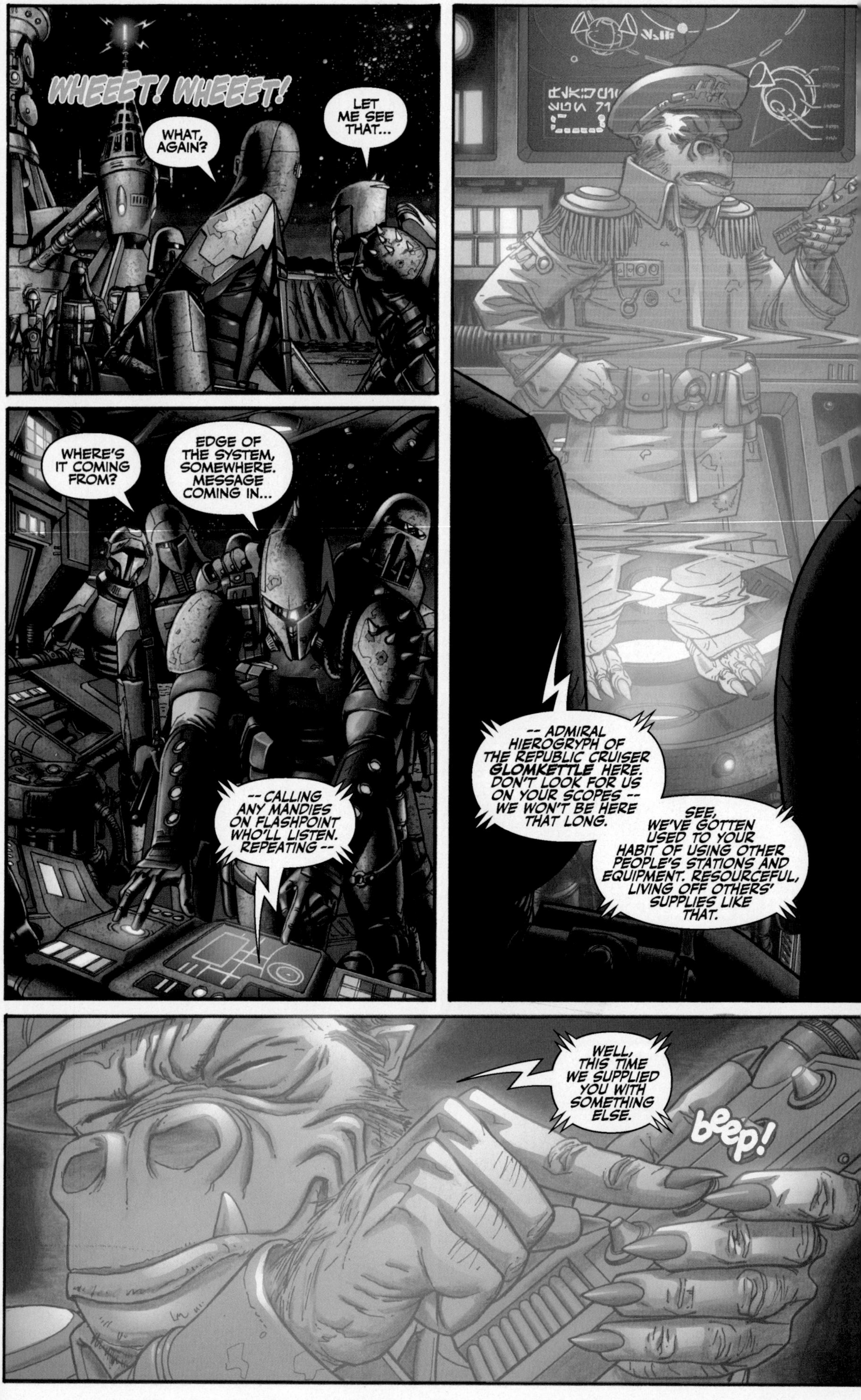
WHEEET! WHEEET!
WHAT, AGAIN?
LET ME SEE THAT...
WHERE'S IT COMING FROM?
EDGE OF THE SYSTEM, SOMEWHERE. MESSAGE COMING IN...
--CALLING ANY MANDIES ON FLASHPOINT WHO'LL LISTEN. REPEATING --
-- ADMIRAL HIEROGRYPH OF THE REPUBLIC CRUISER GLOMKETTLE HERE. DON'T LOOK FOR US ON YOUR SCOPES -- WE WON'T BE HERE THAT LONG.
SEE, WE'VE GOTTEN USED TO YOUR HABIT OF USING OTHER PEOPLE'S STATIONS AND EQUIPMENT. RESOURCEFUL, LIVING OFF OTHERS' SUPPLIES LIKE THAT.
WELL, THIS TIME WE SUPPLIED YOU WITH SOMETHING ELSE.
beep!

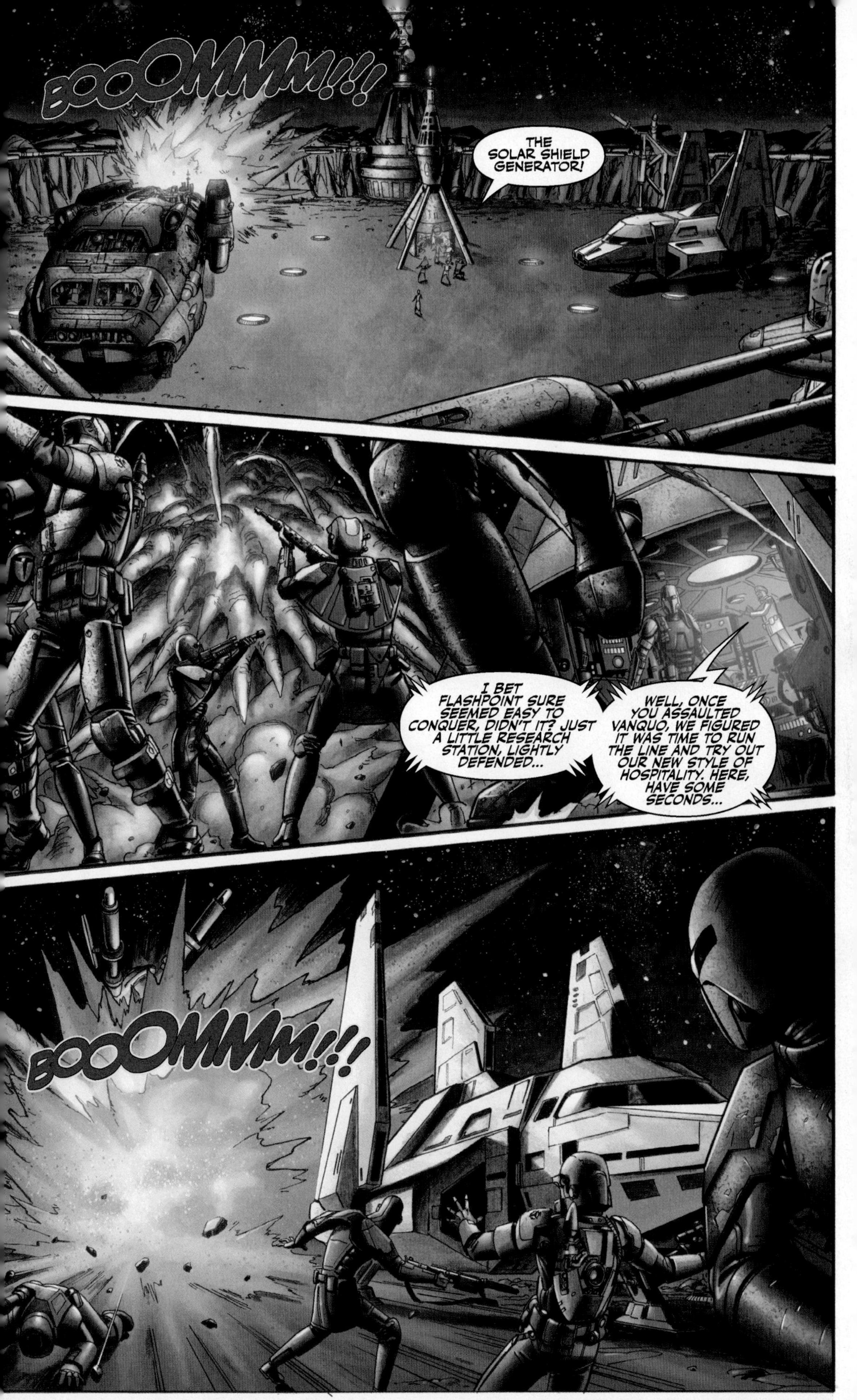
BOOOMMM!!!
THE SOLAR SHIELD GENERATOR!
I BET FLASHPOINT SURE SEEMED EASY TO CONQUER, DIDN'T IT? JUST A LITTLE RESEARCH STATION, LIGHTLY DEFENDED...
WELL, ONCE YOU ASSAULTED VANQUO, WE FIGURED IT WAS TIME TO RUN THE LINE AND TRY OUT OUR NEW STYLE OF HOSPITALITY. HERE, HAVE SOME SECONDS...
BOOOMMM!!!

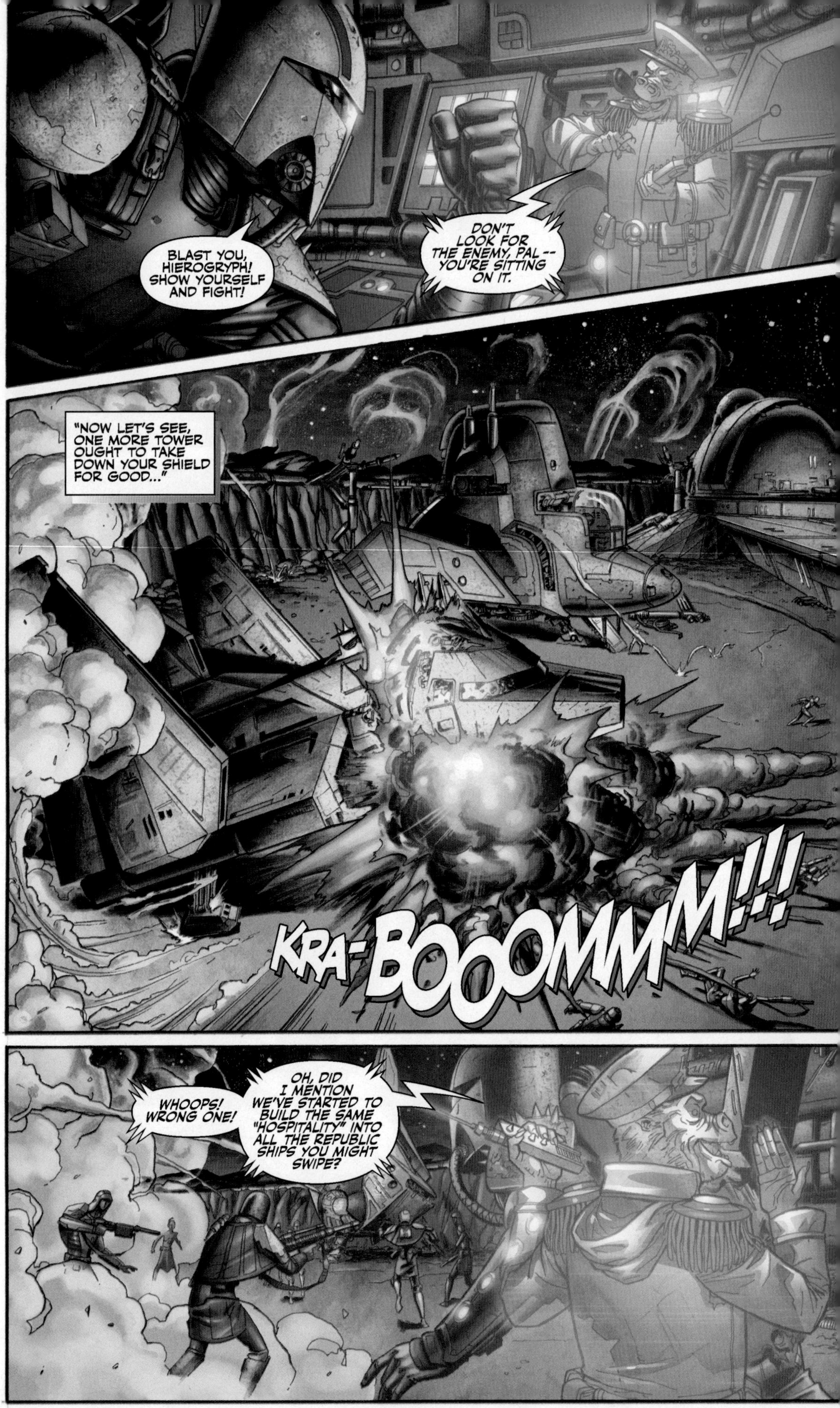
BLAST YOU, HIEROGRYPH! SHOW YOURSELF AND FIGHT!
DON'T LOOK FOR THE ENEMY, PAL-- YOU'RE SITTING ON IT.
"NOW LET'S SEE, ONE MORE TOWER OUGHT TO TAKE DOWN YOUR SHIELD FOR GOOD..."
KRA-BOOOMMM!!!
WHOOPS! WRONG ONE!
OH, DID I MENTION WE'VE STARTED TO BUILD THE SAME "HOSPITALITY" INTO ALL THE REPUBLIC SHIPS YOU MIGHT SWIPE?

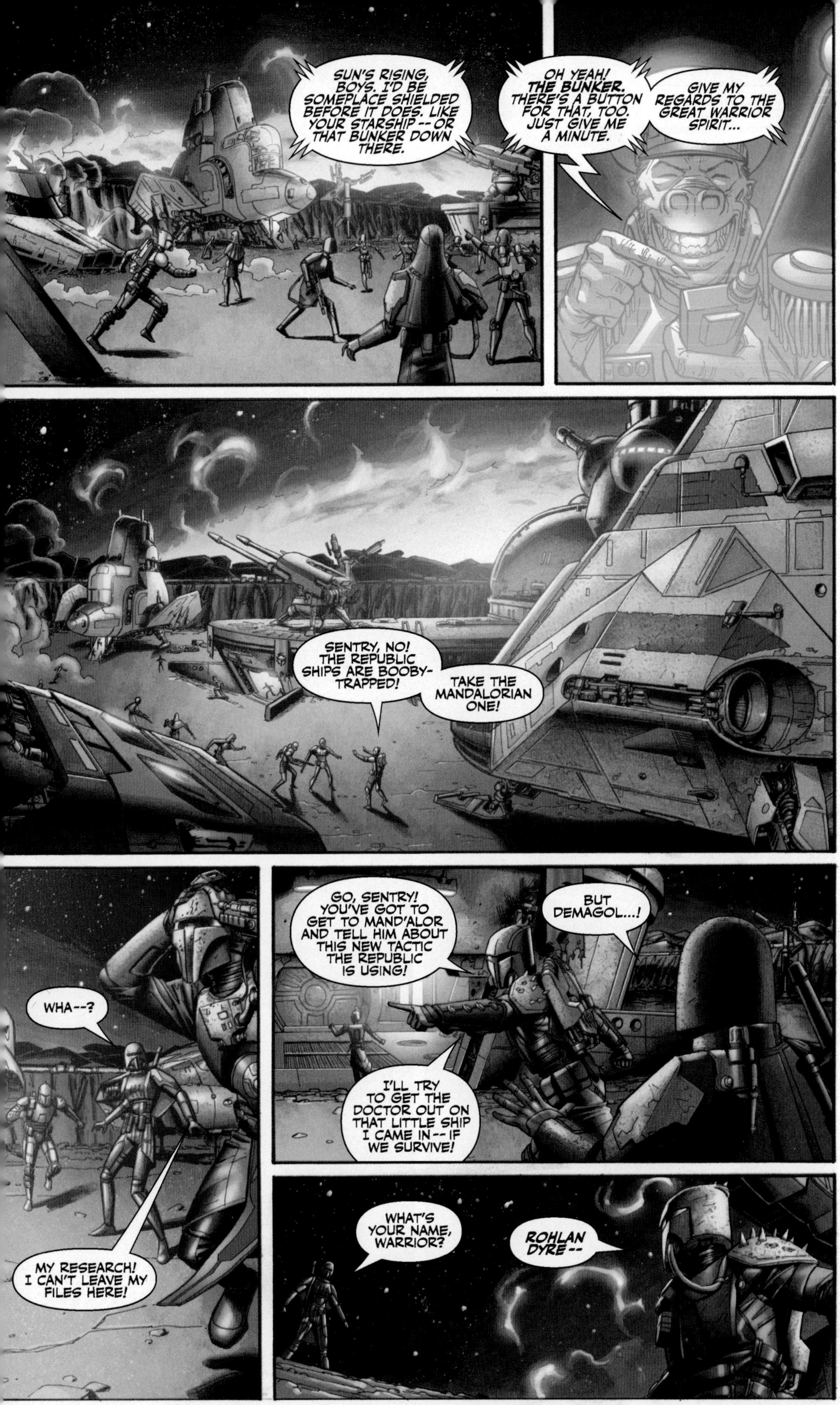
SUN'S RISING, BOYS. I'D BE SOMEPLACE SHIELDED BEFORE IT DOES. LIKE YOUR STARSHIP -- OR THAT BUNKER DOWN THERE.
OH YEAH! THE BUNKER. THERE'S A BUTTON FOR THAT, TOO. JUST GIVE ME A MINUTE.
GIVE MY REGARDS TO THE GREAT WARRIOR SPIRIT...
SENTRY, NO! THE REPUBLIC SHIPS ARE BOOBY-TRAPPED!
TAKE THE MANDALORIAN ONE!
WHA--?
MY RESEARCH! I CAN'T LEAVE MY FILES HERE!
GO, SENTRY! YOU'VE GOT TO GET TO MAND'ALOR AND TELL HIM ABOUT THIS NEW TACTIC THE REPUBLIC IS USING!
BUT DEMAGOL...!
I'LL TRY TO GET THE DOCTOR OUT ON THAT LITTLE SHIP I CAME IN -- IF WE SURVIVE!
WHAT'S YOUR NAME, WARRIOR?
ROHLAN DYRE --

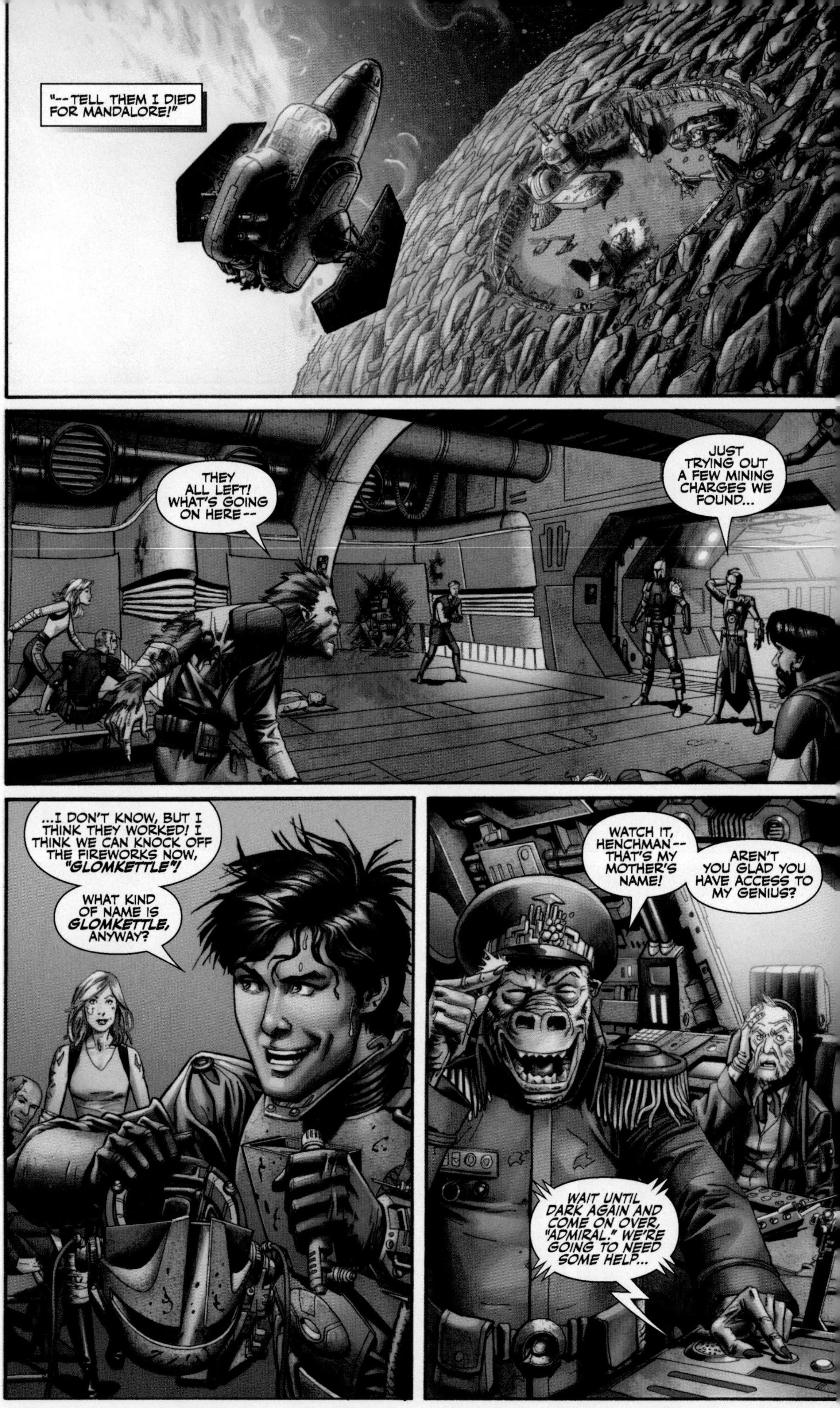
"--TELL THEM I DIED FOR MANDALORE!"
THEY ALL LEFT! WHAT'S GOING ON HERE--
JUST TRYING OUT A FEW MINING CHARGES WE FOUND...
...I DON'T KNOW, BUT I THINK THEY WORKED! I THINK WE CAN KNOCK OFF THE FIREWORKS NOW, "GLOMKETTLE"!
WHAT KIND OF NAME IS GLOMKETTLE, ANYWAY?
WATCH IT, HENCHMAN-- THAT'S MY MOTHER'S NAME!
AREN'T YOU GLAD YOU HAVE ACCESS TO MY GENIUS?
WAIT UNTIL DARK AGAIN AND COME ON OVER, "ADMIRAL." WE'RE GOING TO NEED SOME HELP...

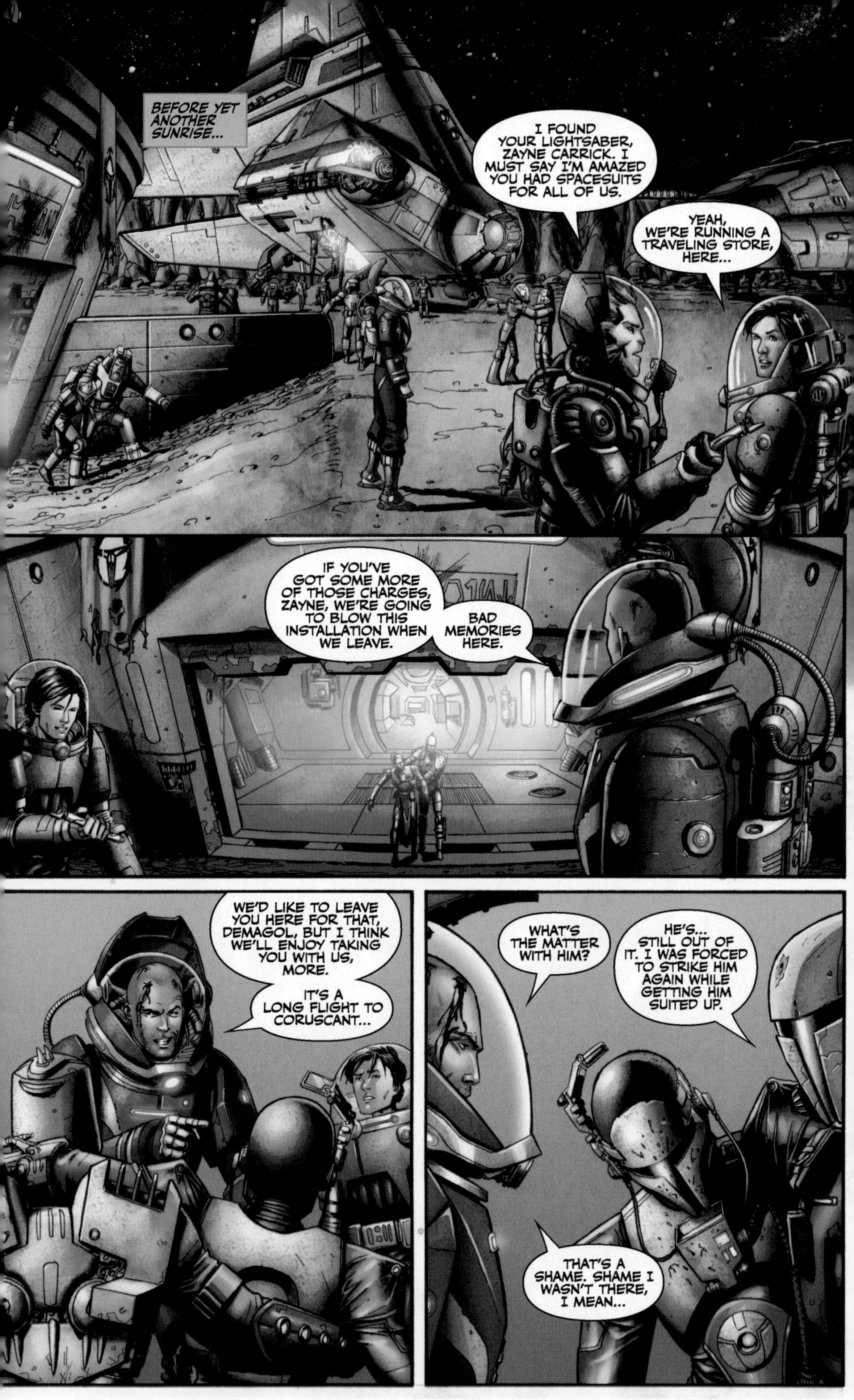
BEFORE YET ANOTHER SUNRISE...
I FOUND YOUR LIGHTSABER, ZAYNE CARRICK. I MUST SAY I'M AMAZED YOU HAD SPACESUITS FOR ALL OF US.
YEAH, WE'RE RUNNING A TRAVELING STORE, HERE...
IF YOU'VE GOT SOME MORE OF THOSE CHARGES, ZAYNE, WE'RE GOING TO BLOW THIS INSTALLATION WHEN WE LEAVE.
BAD MEMORIES HERE.
WE'D LIKE TO LEAVE YOU HERE FOR THAT, DEMAGOL, BUT I THINK WE'LL ENJOY TAKING YOU WITH US, MORE.
IT'S A LONG FLIGHT TO CORUSCANT...
WHAT'S THE MATTER WITH HIM?
HE'S... STILL OUT OF IT. I WAS FORCED TO STRIKE HIM AGAIN WHILE GETTING HIM SUITED UP.
THAT'S A SHAME. SHAME I WASN'T THERE, I MEAN...

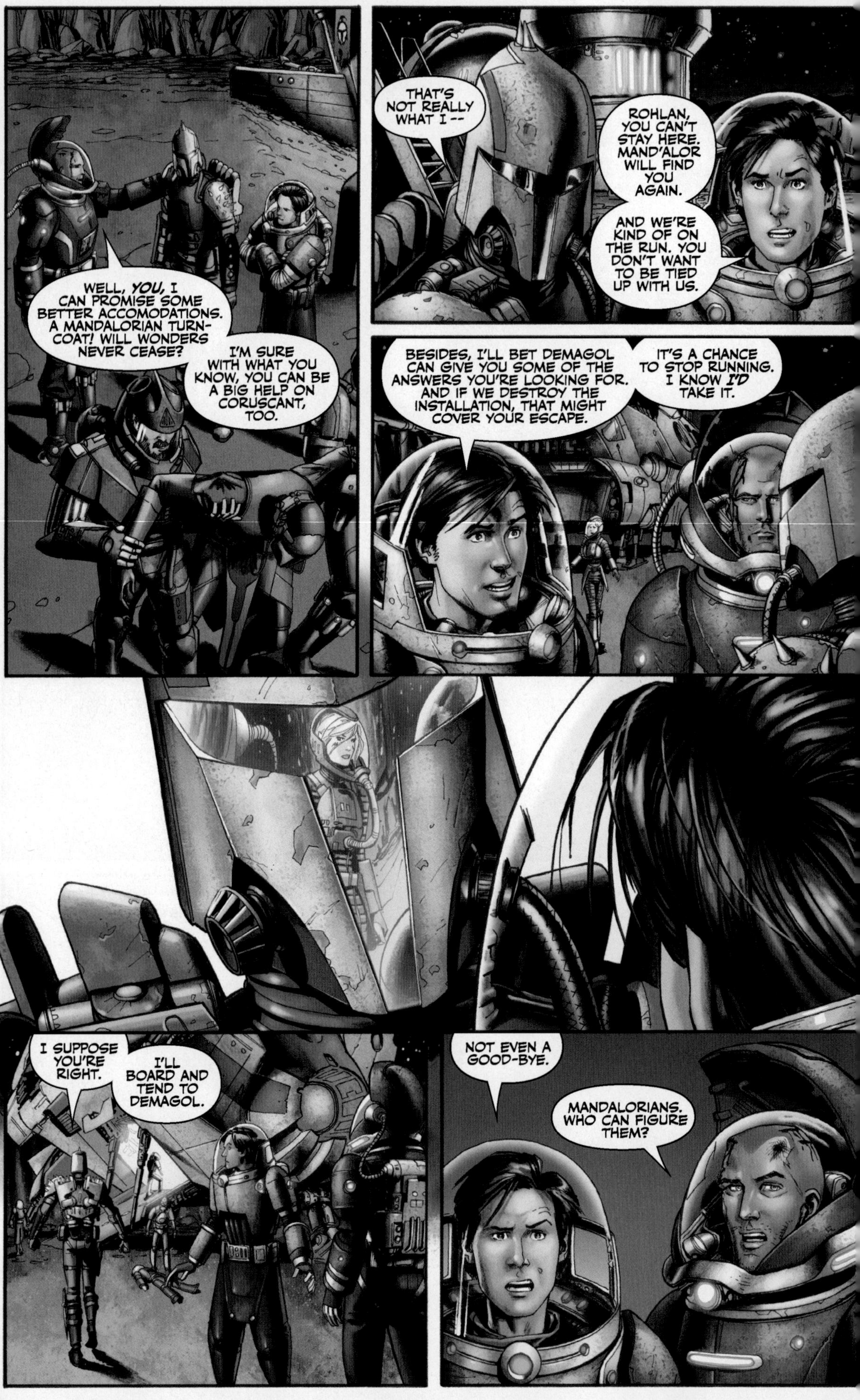
WELL, *YOU,* I CAN PROMISE SOME BETTER ACCOMODATIONS. A MANDALORIAN TURN-COAT! WILL WONDERS NEVER CEASE?
I'M SURE WITH WHAT YOU KNOW, YOU CAN BE A BIG HELP ON CORUSCANT, TOO.
THAT'S NOT REALLY WHAT I --
ROHLAN, YOU CAN'T STAY HERE. MAND'ALOR WILL FIND YOU AGAIN.
AND WE'RE KIND OF ON THE RUN. YOU DON'T WANT TO BE TIED UP WITH US.
BESIDES, I'LL BET DEMAGOL CAN GIVE YOU SOME OF THE ANSWERS YOU'RE LOOKING FOR. AND IF WE DESTROY THE INSTALLATION, THAT MIGHT COVER YOUR ESCAPE.
IT'S A CHANCE TO STOP RUNNING. I KNOW *I'D* TAKE IT.
I SUPPOSE YOU'RE RIGHT.
I'LL BOARD AND TEND TO DEMAGOL.
NOT EVEN A GOOD-BYE.
MANDALORIANS. WHO CAN FIGURE THEM?

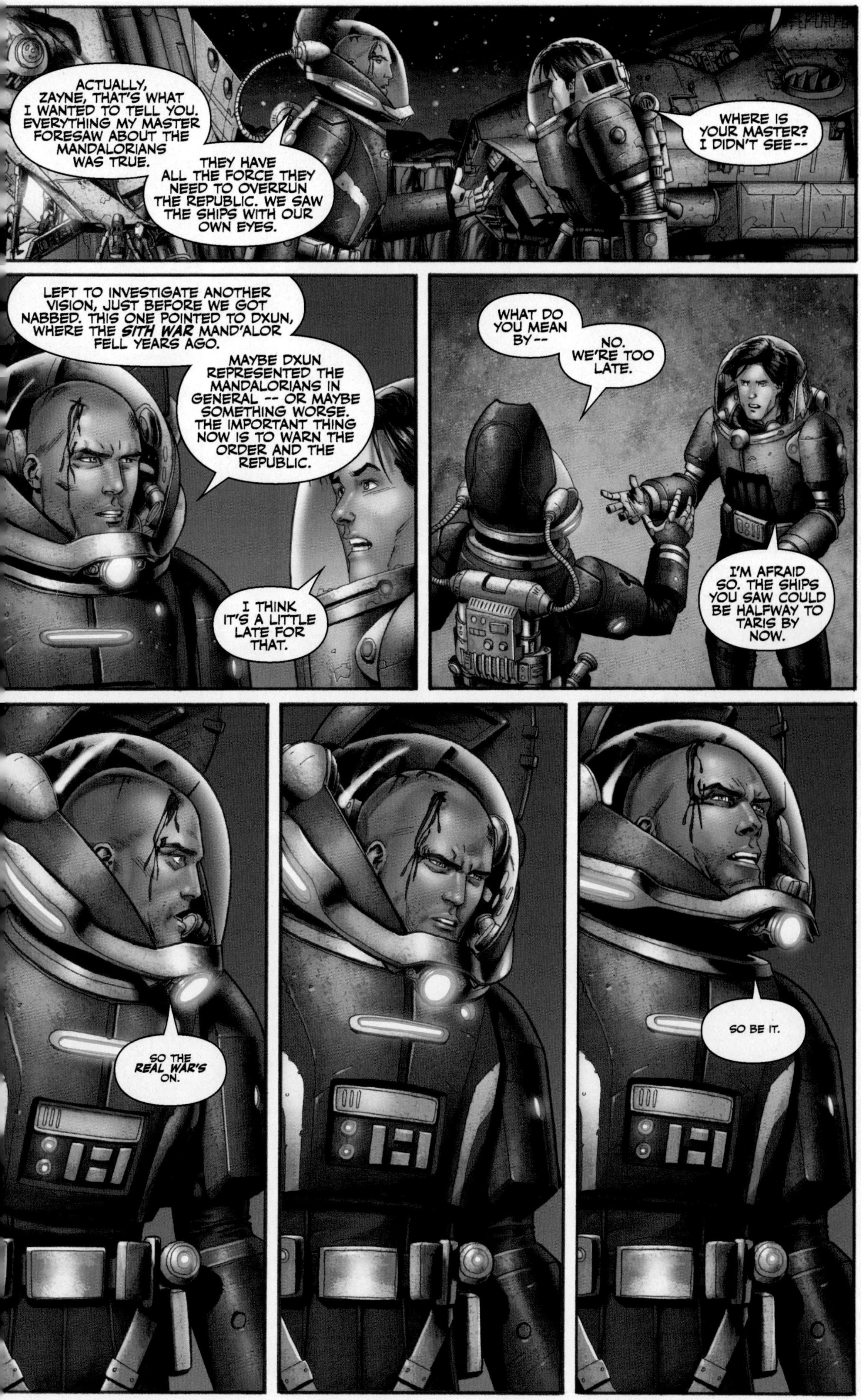
ACTUALLY, ZAYNE, THAT'S WHAT I WANTED TO TELL YOU. EVERYTHING MY MASTER FORESAW ABOUT THE MANDALORIANS WAS TRUE.
THEY HAVE ALL THE FORCE THEY NEED TO OVERRUN THE REPUBLIC. WE SAW THE SHIPS WITH OUR OWN EYES.
WHERE IS YOUR MASTER? I DIDN'T SEE--
LEFT TO INVESTIGATE ANOTHER VISION, JUST BEFORE WE GOT NABBED. THIS ONE POINTED TO DXUN, WHERE THE SITH WAR MAND'ALOR FELL YEARS AGO.
MAYBE DXUN REPRESENTED THE MANDALORIANS IN GENERAL -- OR MAYBE SOMETHING WORSE. THE IMPORTANT THING NOW IS TO WARN THE ORDER AND THE REPUBLIC.
I THINK IT'S A LITTLE LATE FOR THAT.
WHAT DO YOU MEAN BY--
NO. WE'RE TOO LATE.
I'M AFRAID SO. THE SHIPS YOU SAW COULD BE HALFWAY TO TARIS BY NOW.
SO THE REAL WAR'S ON.
SO BE IT.

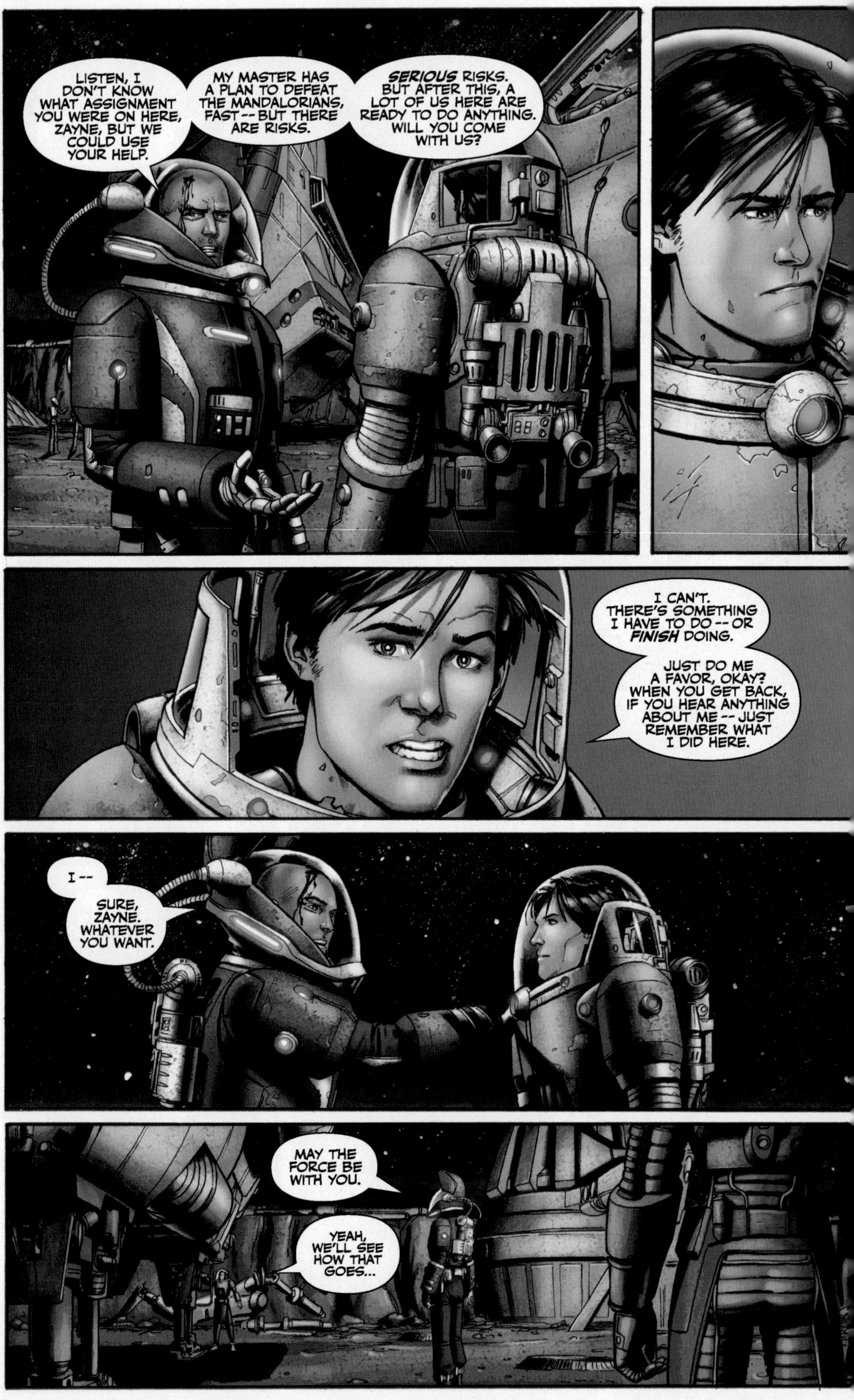
LISTEN, I DON'T KNOW WHAT ASSIGNMENT YOU WERE ON HERE, ZAYNE, BUT WE COULD USE YOUR HELP.
MY MASTER HAS A PLAN TO DEFEAT THE MANDALORIANS, FAST -- BUT THERE ARE RISKS.
SERIOUS RISKS. BUT AFTER THIS, A LOT OF US HERE ARE READY TO DO ANYTHING. WILL YOU COME WITH US?
I CAN'T. THERE'S SOMETHING I HAVE TO DO -- OR FINISH DOING.
JUST DO ME A FAVOR, OKAY? WHEN YOU GET BACK, IF YOU HEAR ANYTHING ABOUT ME -- JUST REMEMBER WHAT I DID HERE.
I --
SURE, ZAYNE. WHATEVER YOU WANT.
MAY THE FORCE BE WITH YOU.
YEAH, WE'LL SEE HOW THAT GOES...

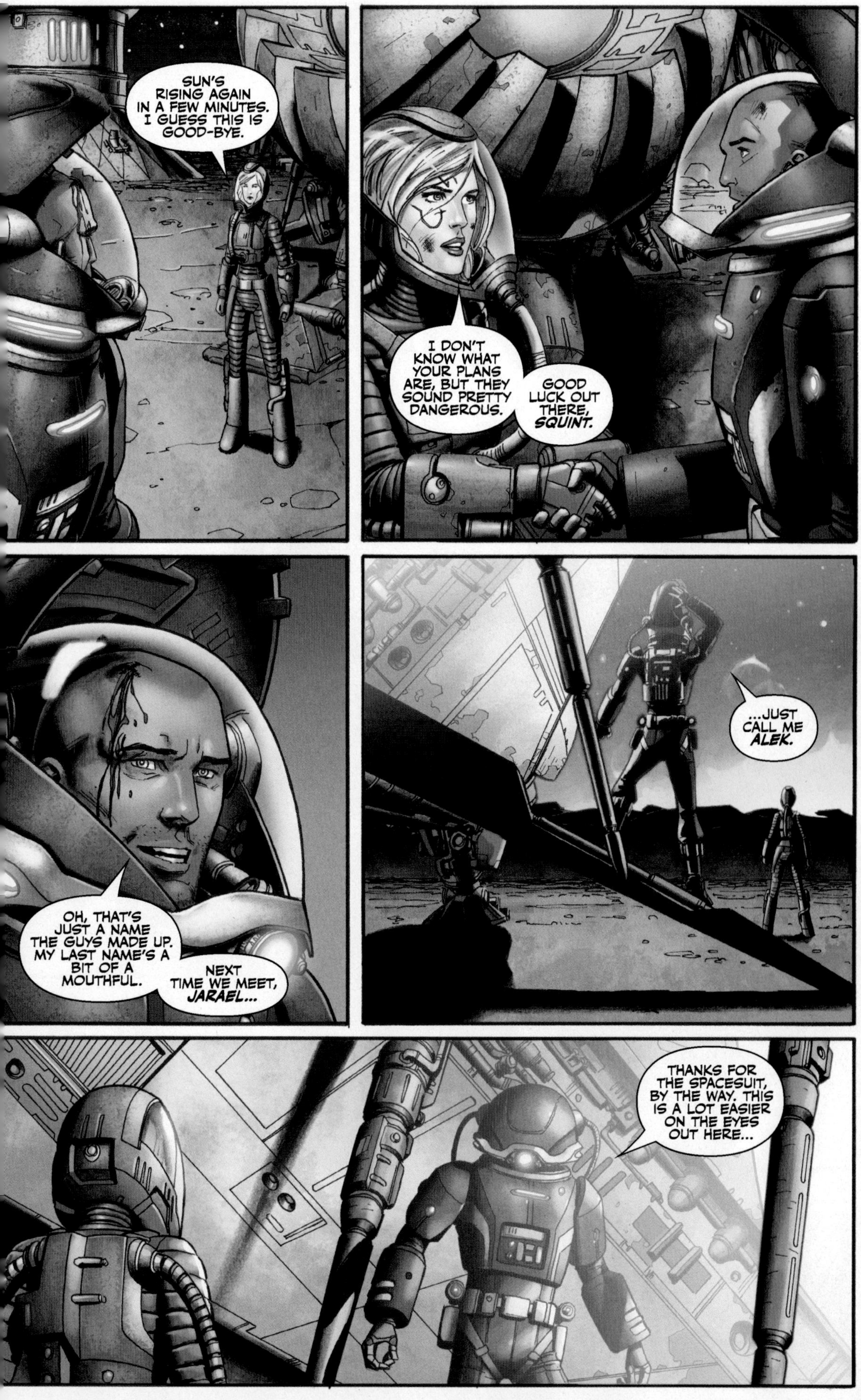
SUN'S RISING AGAIN IN A FEW MINUTES. I GUESS THIS IS GOOD-BYE.
I DON'T KNOW WHAT YOUR PLANS ARE, BUT THEY SOUND PRETTY DANGEROUS.
GOOD LUCK OUT THERE, SQUINT.
OH, THAT'S JUST A NAME THE GUYS MADE UP. MY LAST NAME'S A BIT OF A MOUTHFUL.
NEXT TIME WE MEET, JARAEL...
...JUST CALL ME ALEK.
THANKS FOR THE SPACESUIT, BY THE WAY. THIS IS A LOT EASIER ON THE EYES OUT HERE...

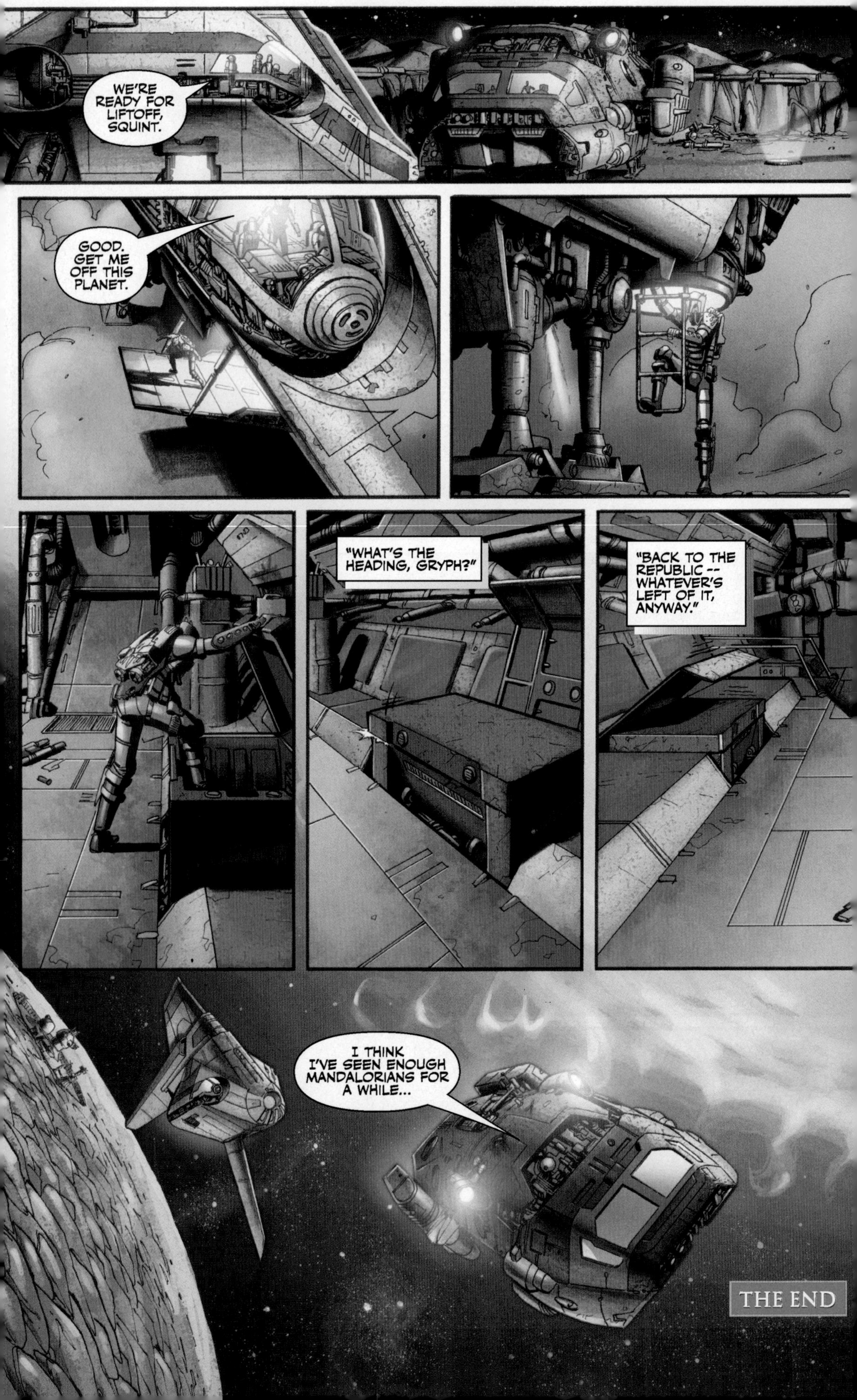

WE'RE READY FOR LIFTOFF, SQUINT.
GOOD. GET ME OFF THIS PLANET.
"WHAT'S THE HEADING, GRYPH?"
"BACK TO THE REPUBLIC -- WHATEVER'S LEFT OF IT, ANYWAY."
I THINK I'VE SEEN ENOUGH MANDALORIANS FOR A WHILE...
THE END

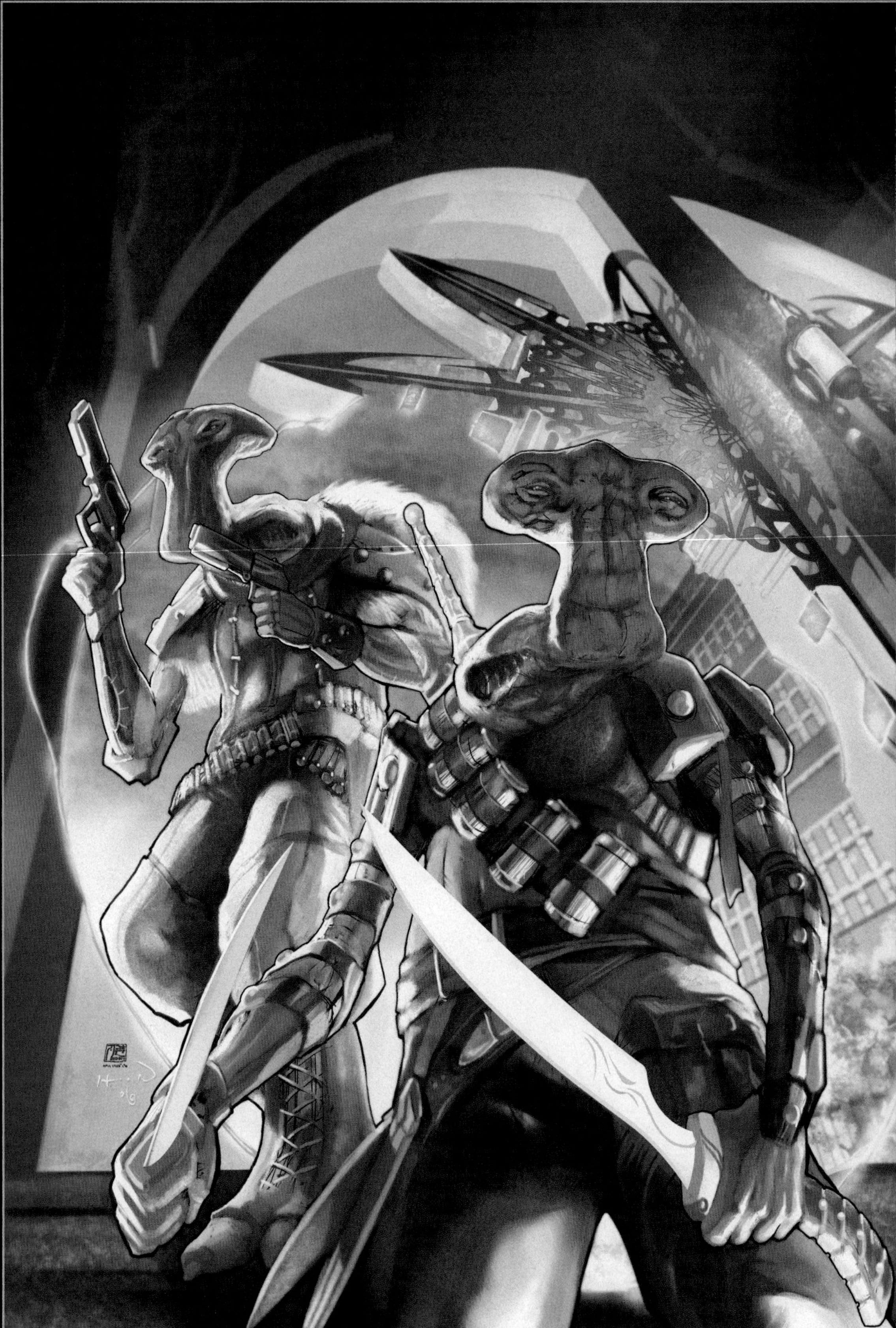

STAR WARS: KNIGHTS OF THE OLD REPUBLIC #11 **— "REUNION, PART 1"**

WRITER: JOHN JACKSON MILLER • ARTIST: BRIAN CHING • COLORIST: MICHAEL ATIYEH • LETTERER: MICHAEL HEISLER
ASSISTANT EDITOR: DAVE MARSHALL • EDITOR: JEREMY BARLOW • COVER ARTIST: HOON

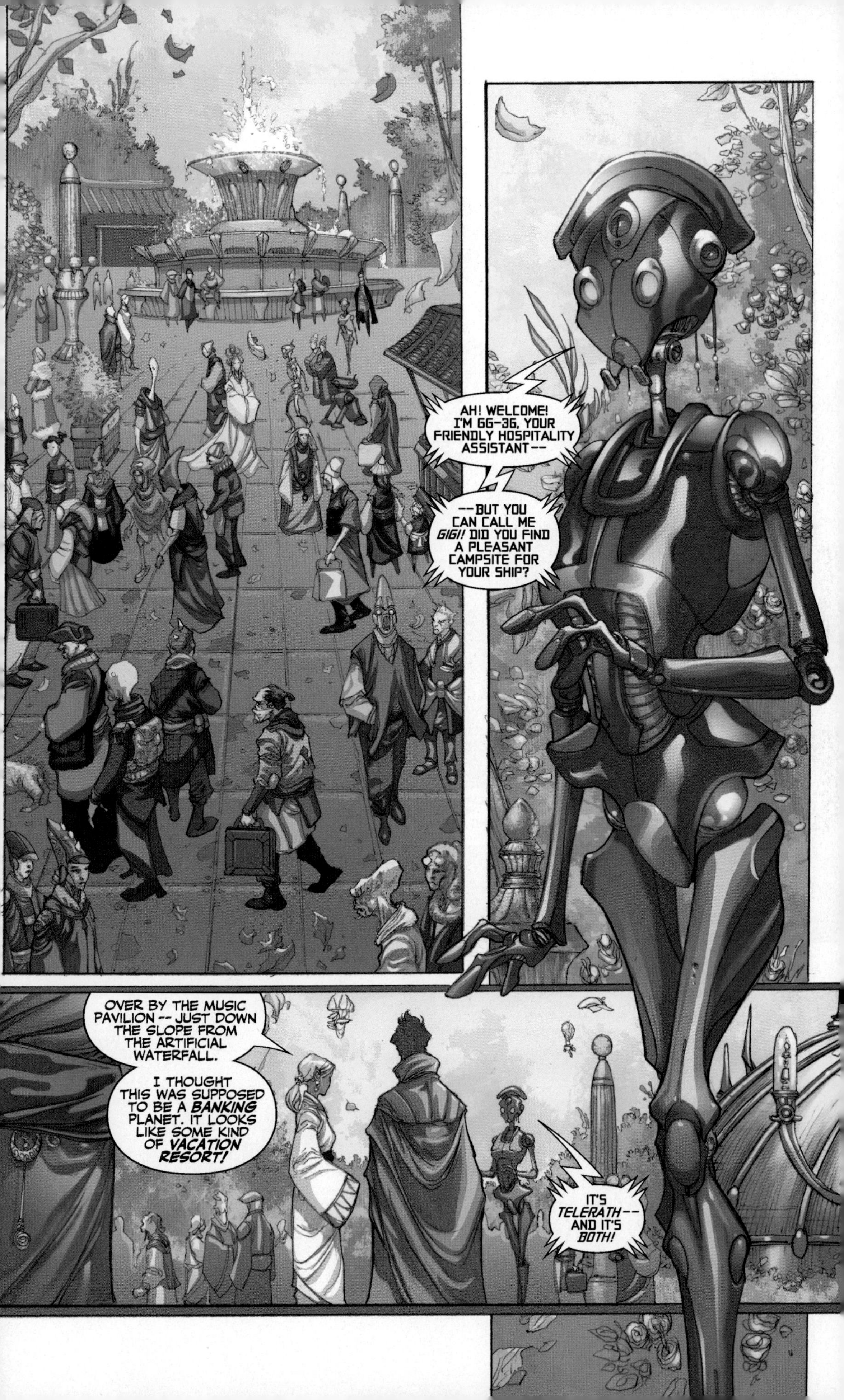
AH! WELCOME! I'M GG-36, YOUR FRIENDLY HOSPITALITY ASSISTANT--
--BUT YOU CAN CALL ME *GIGI!* DID YOU FIND A PLEASANT CAMPSITE FOR YOUR SHIP?
OVER BY THE MUSIC PAVILION -- JUST DOWN THE SLOPE FROM THE ARTIFICIAL WATERFALL.
I THOUGHT THIS WAS SUPPOSED TO BE A *BANKING* PLANET. IT LOOKS LIKE SOME KIND OF ***VACATION RESORT!***
IT'S *TELERATH*-- AND IT'S *BOTH!*

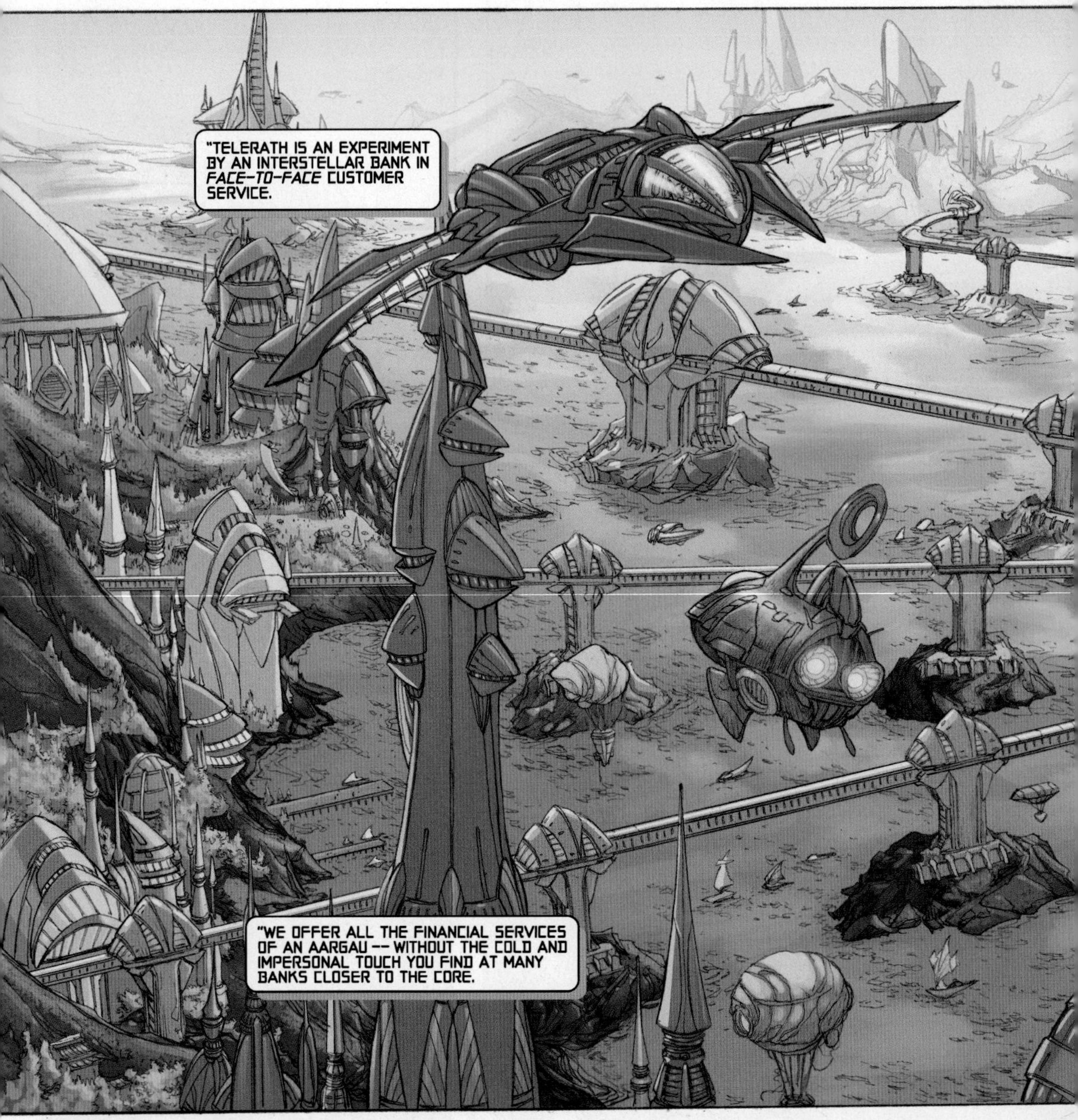
"TELERATH IS AN EXPERIMENT BY AN INTERSTELLAR BANK IN *FACE-TO-FACE* CUSTOMER SERVICE.
"WE OFFER ALL THE FINANCIAL SERVICES OF AN AARGAU -- WITHOUT THE COLD AND IMPERSONAL TOUCH YOU FIND AT MANY BANKS CLOSER TO THE CORE.

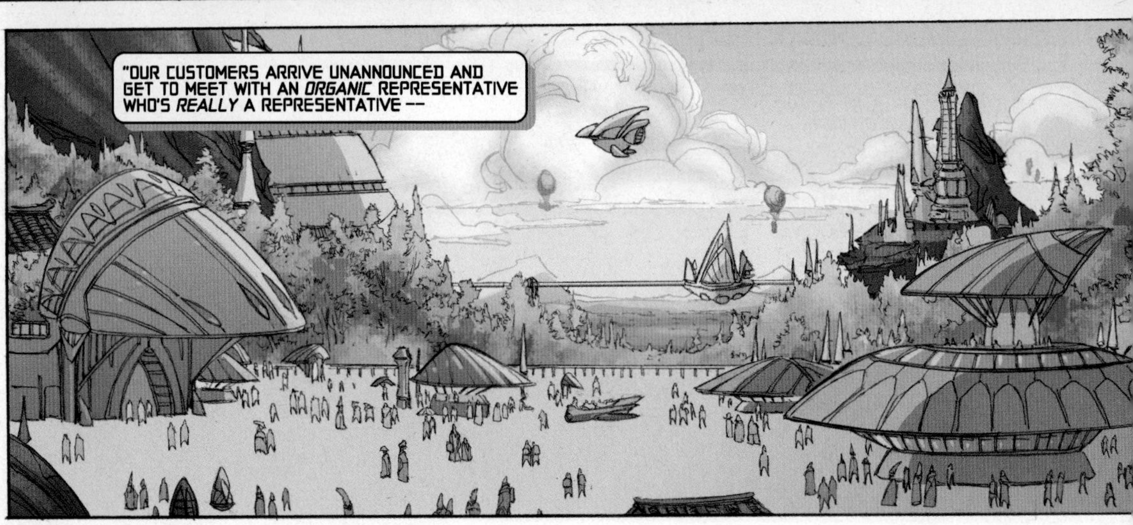
"OUR CUSTOMERS ARRIVE UNANNOUNCED AND GET TO MEET WITH AN *ORGANIC* REPRESENTATIVE WHO'S *REALLY* A REPRESENTATIVE --

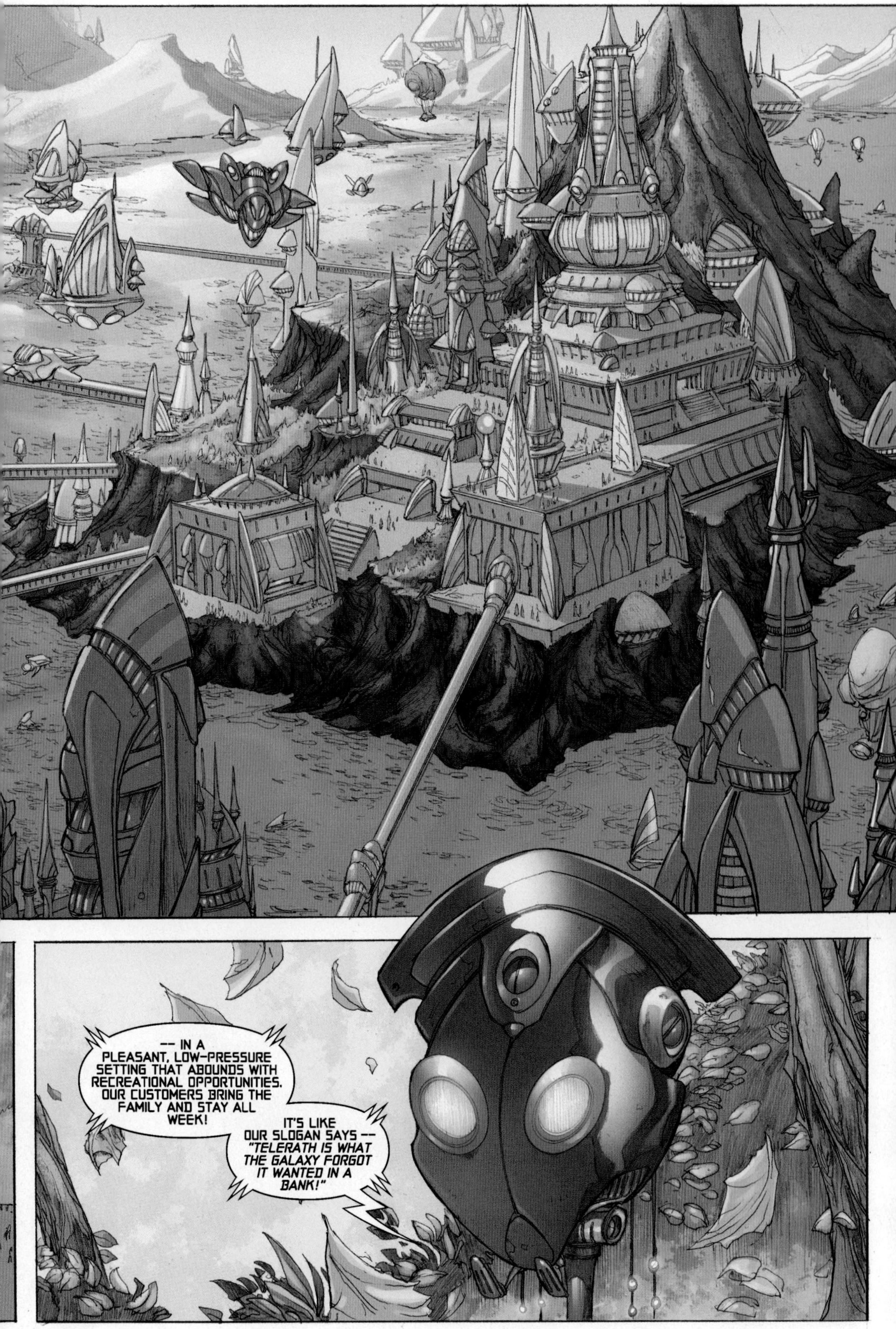
-- IN A PLEASANT, LOW-PRESSURE SETTING THAT ABOUNDS WITH RECREATIONAL OPPORTUNITIES. OUR CUSTOMERS BRING THE FAMILY AND STAY ALL WEEK!
IT'S LIKE OUR SLOGAN SAYS -- *"TELERATH IS WHAT THE GALAXY FORGOT IT WANTED IN A BANK!"*

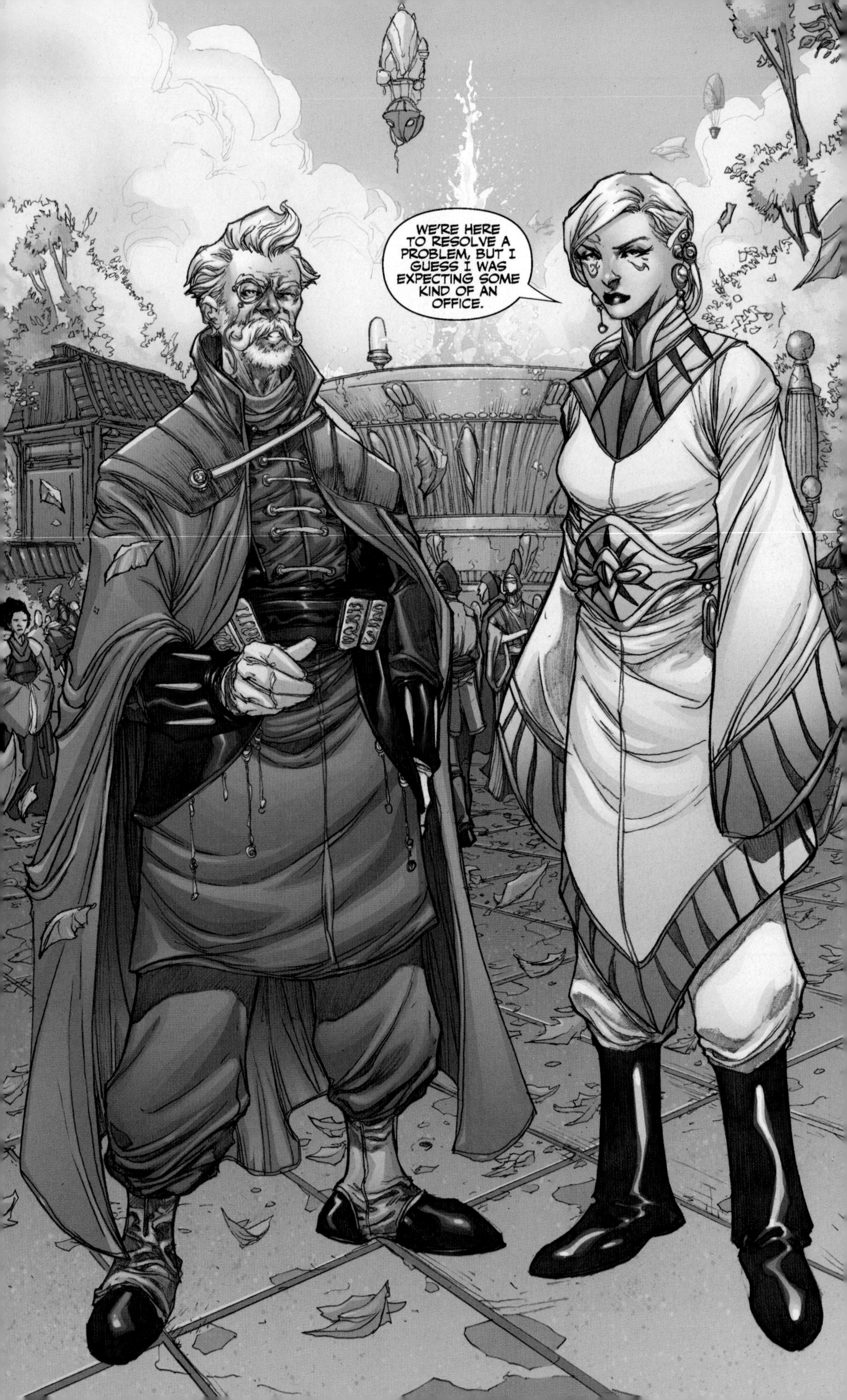
WE'RE HERE TO RESOLVE A PROBLEM, BUT I GUESS I WAS EXPECTING SOME KIND OF AN OFFICE.

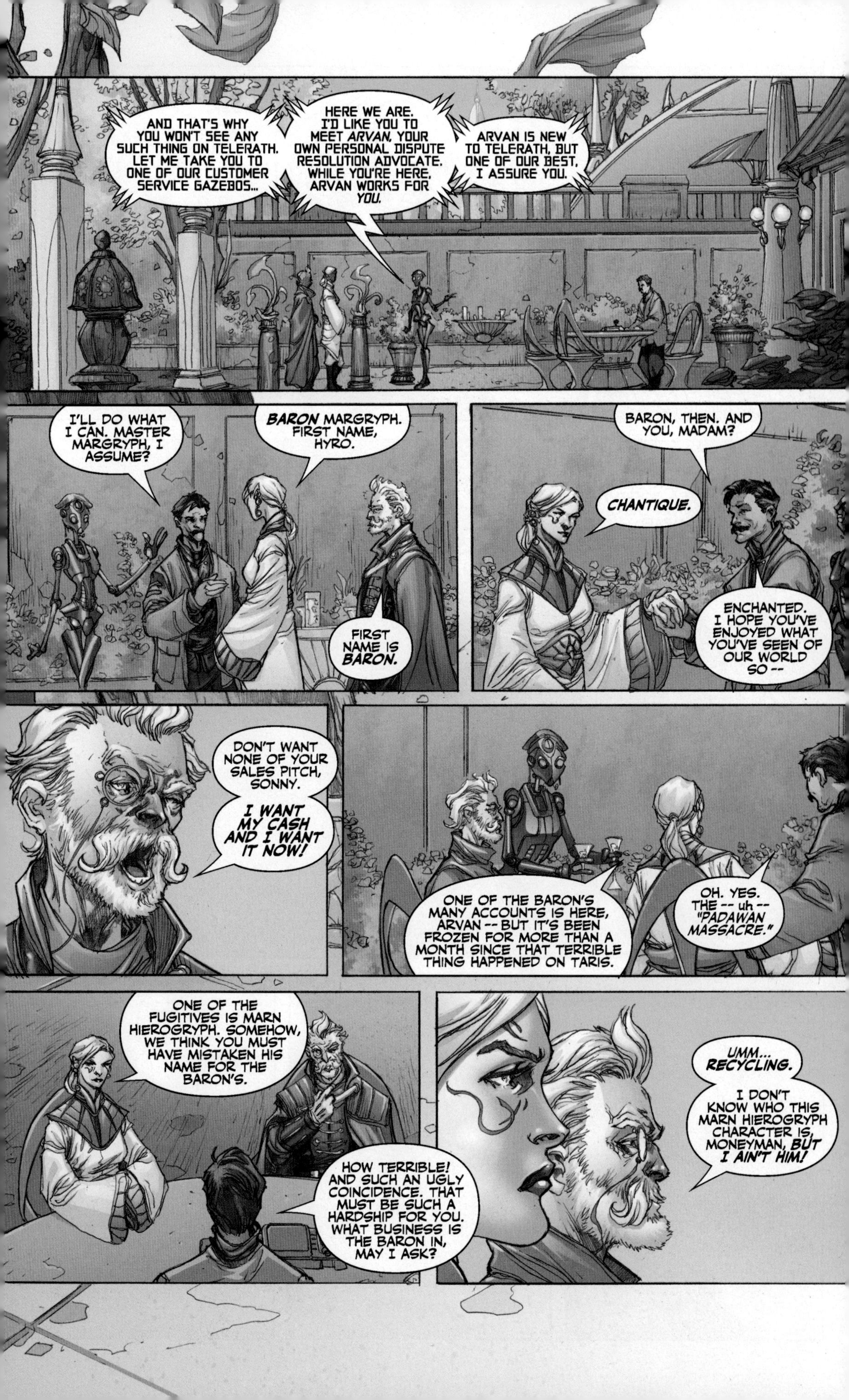
AND THAT'S WHY YOU WON'T SEE ANY SUCH THING ON TELERATH. LET ME TAKE YOU TO ONE OF OUR CUSTOMER SERVICE GAZEBOS...
HERE WE ARE. I'D LIKE YOU TO MEET *ARVAN*, YOUR OWN PERSONAL DISPUTE RESOLUTION ADVOCATE. WHILE YOU'RE HERE, ARVAN WORKS FOR *YOU*.
ARVAN IS NEW TO TELERATH, BUT ONE OF OUR BEST, I ASSURE YOU.
I'LL DO WHAT I CAN. MASTER MARGRYPH, I ASSUME?
BARON MARGRYPH. FIRST NAME, HYRO.
FIRST NAME IS *BARON.*
BARON, THEN. AND YOU, MADAM?
CHANTIQUE.
ENCHANTED. I HOPE YOU'VE ENJOYED WHAT YOU'VE SEEN OF OUR WORLD SO --
DON'T WANT NONE OF YOUR SALES PITCH, SONNY.
I WANT MY CASH AND I WANT IT NOW!
ONE OF THE BARON'S MANY ACCOUNTS IS HERE, ARVAN -- BUT IT'S BEEN FROZEN FOR MORE THAN A MONTH SINCE THAT TERRIBLE THING HAPPENED ON TARIS.
OH. YES. THE -- uh -- *"PADAWAN MASSACRE."*
ONE OF THE FUGITIVES IS MARN HIEROGRYPH. SOMEHOW, WE THINK YOU MUST HAVE MISTAKEN HIS NAME FOR THE BARON'S.
HOW TERRIBLE! AND SUCH AN UGLY COINCIDENCE. THAT MUST BE SUCH A HARDSHIP FOR YOU. WHAT BUSINESS IS THE BARON IN, MAY I ASK?
UMM... RECYCLING.
I DON'T KNOW WHO THIS MARN HIEROGRYPH CHARACTER IS, MONEYMAN, *BUT I AIN'T HIM!*

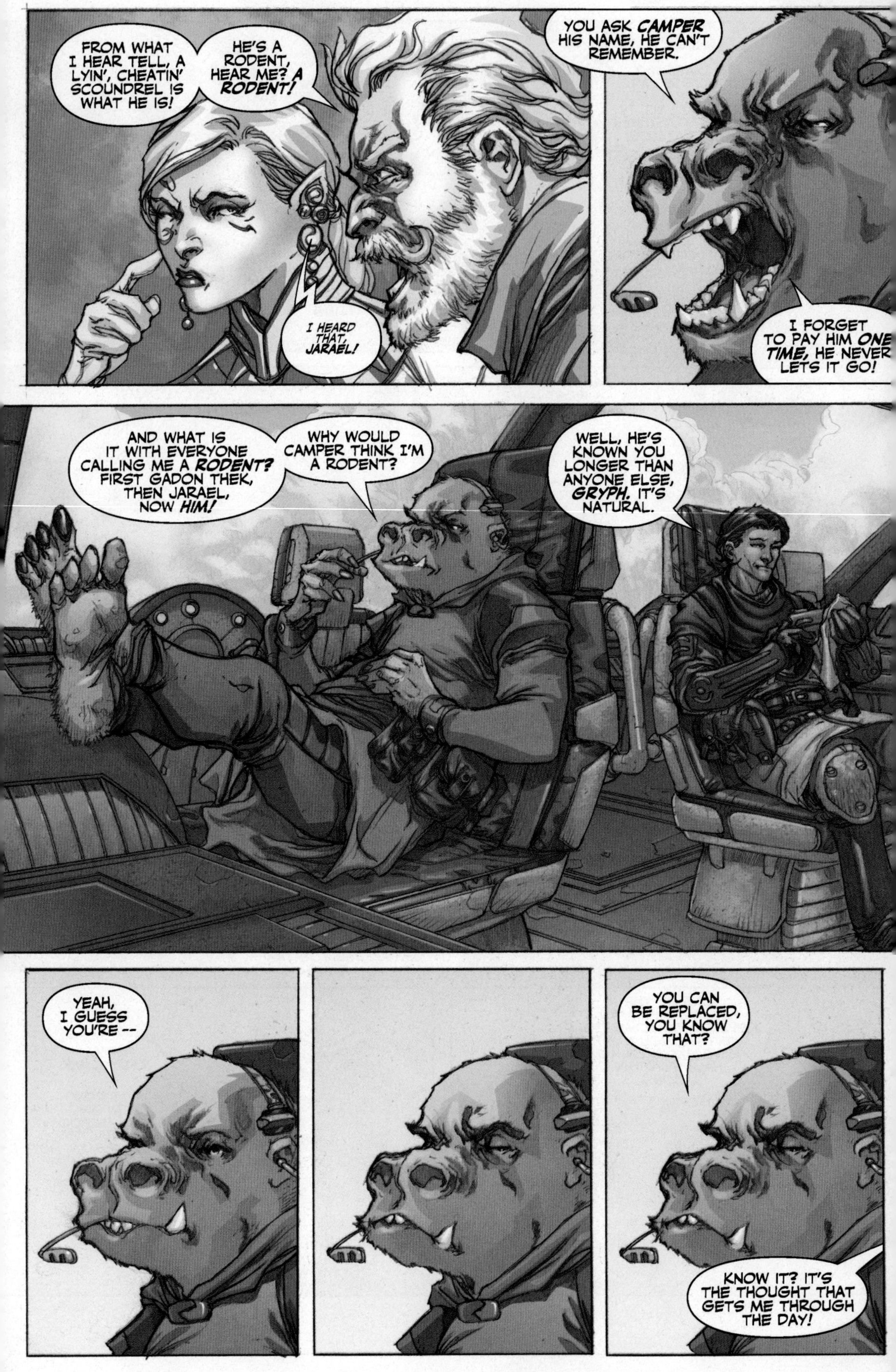
FROM WHAT I HEAR TELL, A LYIN', CHEATIN' SCOUNDREL IS WHAT HE IS!
HE'S A RODENT, HEAR ME? A RODENT!
I HEARD THAT, JARAEL!
YOU ASK CAMPER HIS NAME, HE CAN'T REMEMBER.
I FORGET TO PAY HIM ONE TIME, HE NEVER LETS IT GO!
AND WHAT IS IT WITH EVERYONE CALLING ME A RODENT? FIRST GADON THEK, THEN JARAEL, NOW HIM!
WHY WOULD CAMPER THINK I'M A RODENT?
WELL, HE'S KNOWN YOU LONGER THAN ANYONE ELSE, GRYPH. IT'S NATURAL.
YEAH, I GUESS YOU'RE --
YOU CAN BE REPLACED, YOU KNOW THAT?
KNOW IT? IT'S THE THOUGHT THAT GETS ME THROUGH THE DAY!

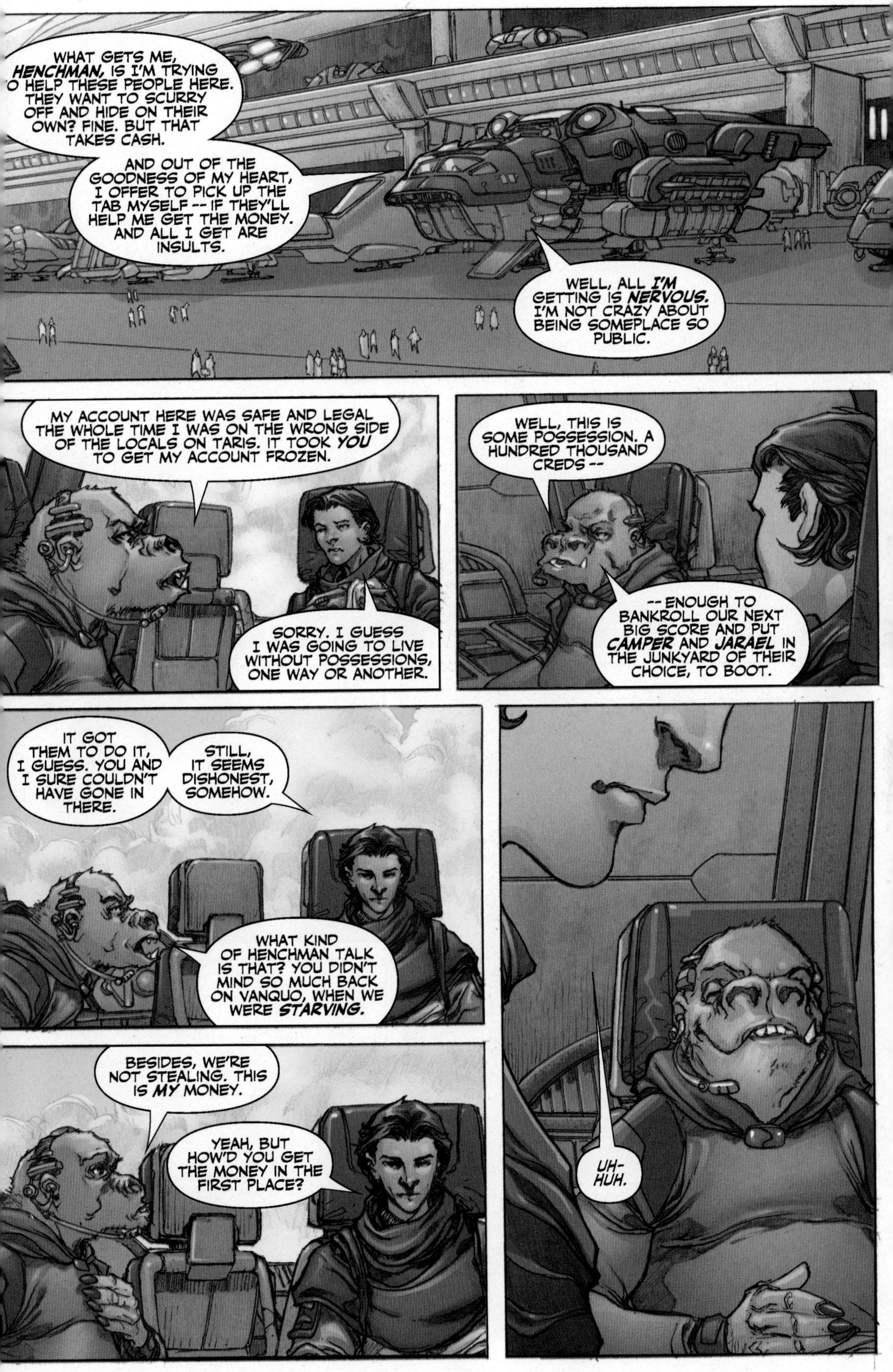
WHAT GETS ME, HENCHMAN, IS I'M TRYING TO HELP THESE PEOPLE HERE. THEY WANT TO SCURRY OFF AND HIDE ON THEIR OWN? FINE. BUT THAT TAKES CASH.
AND OUT OF THE GOODNESS OF MY HEART, I OFFER TO PICK UP THE TAB MYSELF -- IF THEY'LL HELP ME GET THE MONEY. AND ALL I GET ARE INSULTS.
WELL, ALL I'M GETTING IS NERVOUS. I'M NOT CRAZY ABOUT BEING SOMEPLACE SO PUBLIC.
MY ACCOUNT HERE WAS SAFE AND LEGAL THE WHOLE TIME I WAS ON THE WRONG SIDE OF THE LOCALS ON TARIS. IT TOOK YOU TO GET MY ACCOUNT FROZEN.
SORRY. I GUESS I WAS GOING TO LIVE WITHOUT POSSESSIONS, ONE WAY OR ANOTHER.
WELL, THIS IS SOME POSSESSION. A HUNDRED THOUSAND CREDS --
-- ENOUGH TO BANKROLL OUR NEXT BIG SCORE AND PUT CAMPER AND JARAEL IN THE JUNKYARD OF THEIR CHOICE, TO BOOT.
IT GOT THEM TO DO IT, I GUESS. YOU AND I SURE COULDN'T HAVE GONE IN THERE.
STILL, IT SEEMS DISHONEST, SOMEHOW.
WHAT KIND OF HENCHMAN TALK IS THAT? YOU DIDN'T MIND SO MUCH BACK ON VANQUO, WHEN WE WERE STARVING.
BESIDES, WE'RE NOT STEALING. THIS IS MY MONEY.
YEAH, BUT HOW'D YOU GET THE MONEY IN THE FIRST PLACE?
UH-HUH.

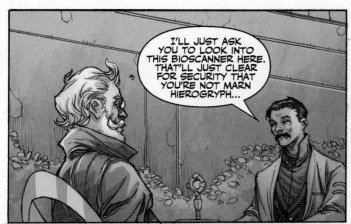

I'LL JUST ASK YOU TO LOOK INTO THIS BIOSCANNER HERE. THAT'LL JUST CLEAR FOR SECURITY THAT YOU'RE NOT MARN HIEROGRYPH...

...AND, OBVIOUSLY, YOU'RE NOT. THANK YOU, BARON.

DING!

ALL WE SHOULD NEED NOW IS YOUR 30-DIGIT ACCOUNT ACCESS CODE. I'M SURE YOU BROUGHT THAT WITH YOU?

NO PROBLEM, JARAEL...CAMPER'S GOT THE NUMBER RIGHT THERE WITH HIM ON HIS MANIFEST.

YOU MEAN THIS MANIFEST?

YEAH, THAT'S THE ONE.

TERRIFIC.

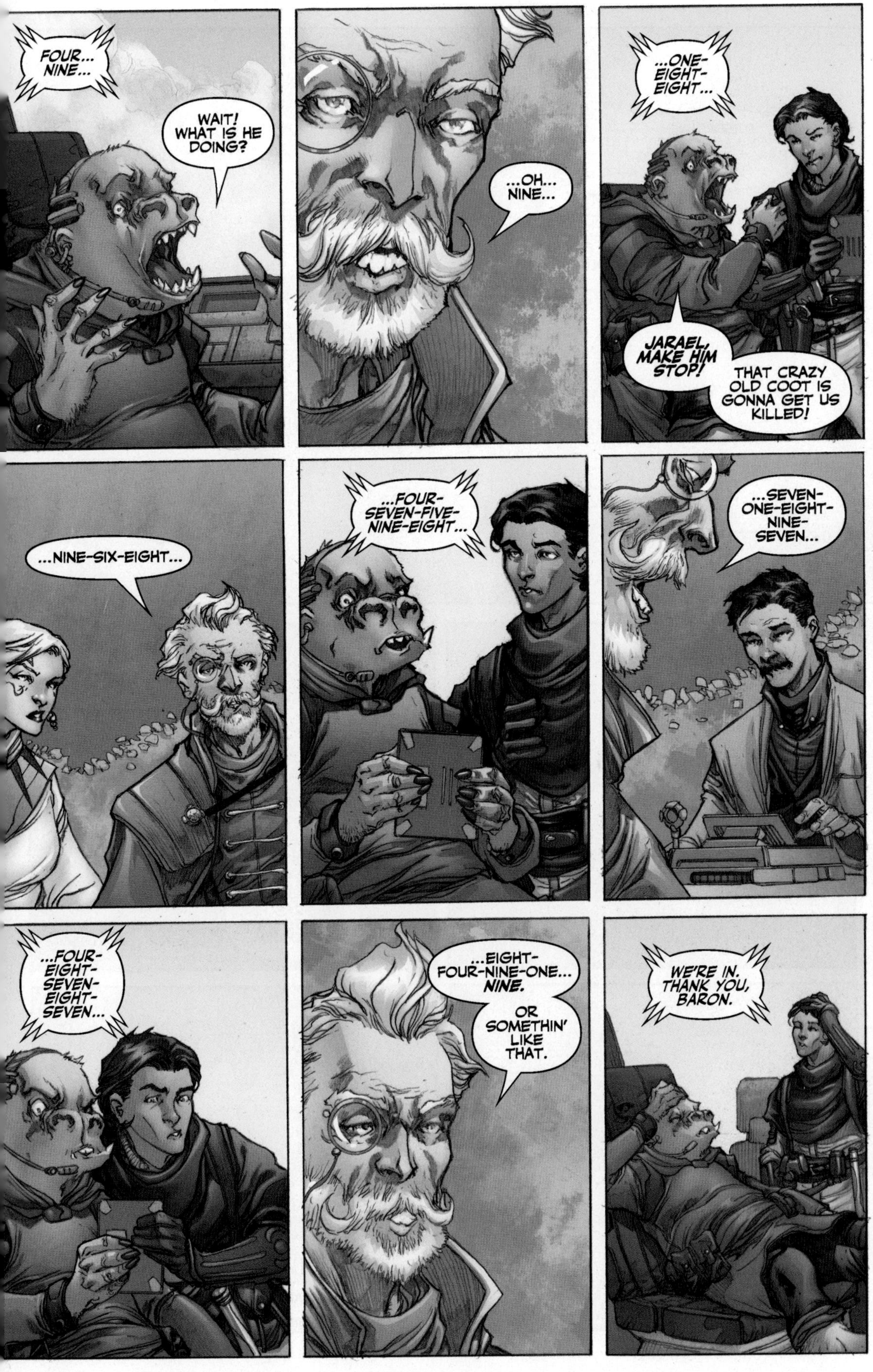
FOUR... NINE...
WAIT! WHAT IS HE DOING?
...OH... NINE...
...ONE-EIGHT-EIGHT...
JARAEL, MAKE HIM STOP!
THAT CRAZY OLD COOT IS GONNA GET US KILLED!
...NINE-SIX-EIGHT...
...FOUR-SEVEN-FIVE-NINE-EIGHT...
...SEVEN-ONE-EIGHT-NINE-SEVEN...
...FOUR-EIGHT-SEVEN-EIGHT-SEVEN...
...EIGHT-FOUR-NINE-ONE... NINE.
OR SOMETHIN' LIKE THAT.
WE'RE IN. THANK YOU, BARON.

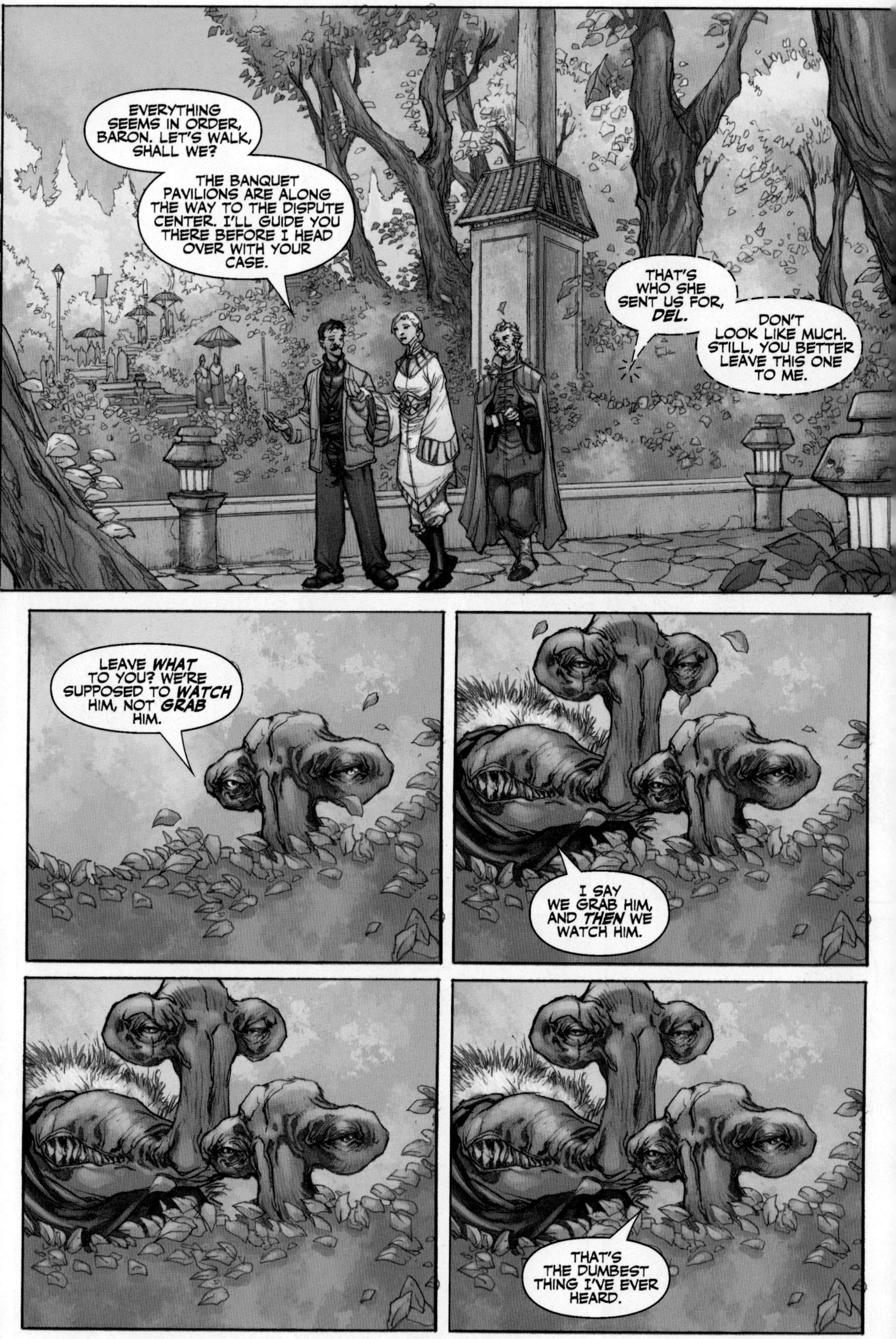
EVERYTHING SEEMS IN ORDER, BARON. LET'S WALK, SHALL WE?
THE BANQUET PAVILIONS ARE ALONG THE WAY TO THE DISPUTE CENTER. I'LL GUIDE YOU THERE BEFORE I HEAD OVER WITH YOUR CASE.
THAT'S WHO SHE SENT US FOR, DEL.
DON'T LOOK LIKE MUCH. STILL, YOU BETTER LEAVE THIS ONE TO ME.
LEAVE WHAT TO YOU? WE'RE SUPPOSED TO WATCH HIM, NOT GRAB HIM.
I SAY WE GRAB HIM, AND THEN WE WATCH HIM.
THAT'S THE DUMBEST THING I'VE EVER HEARD.

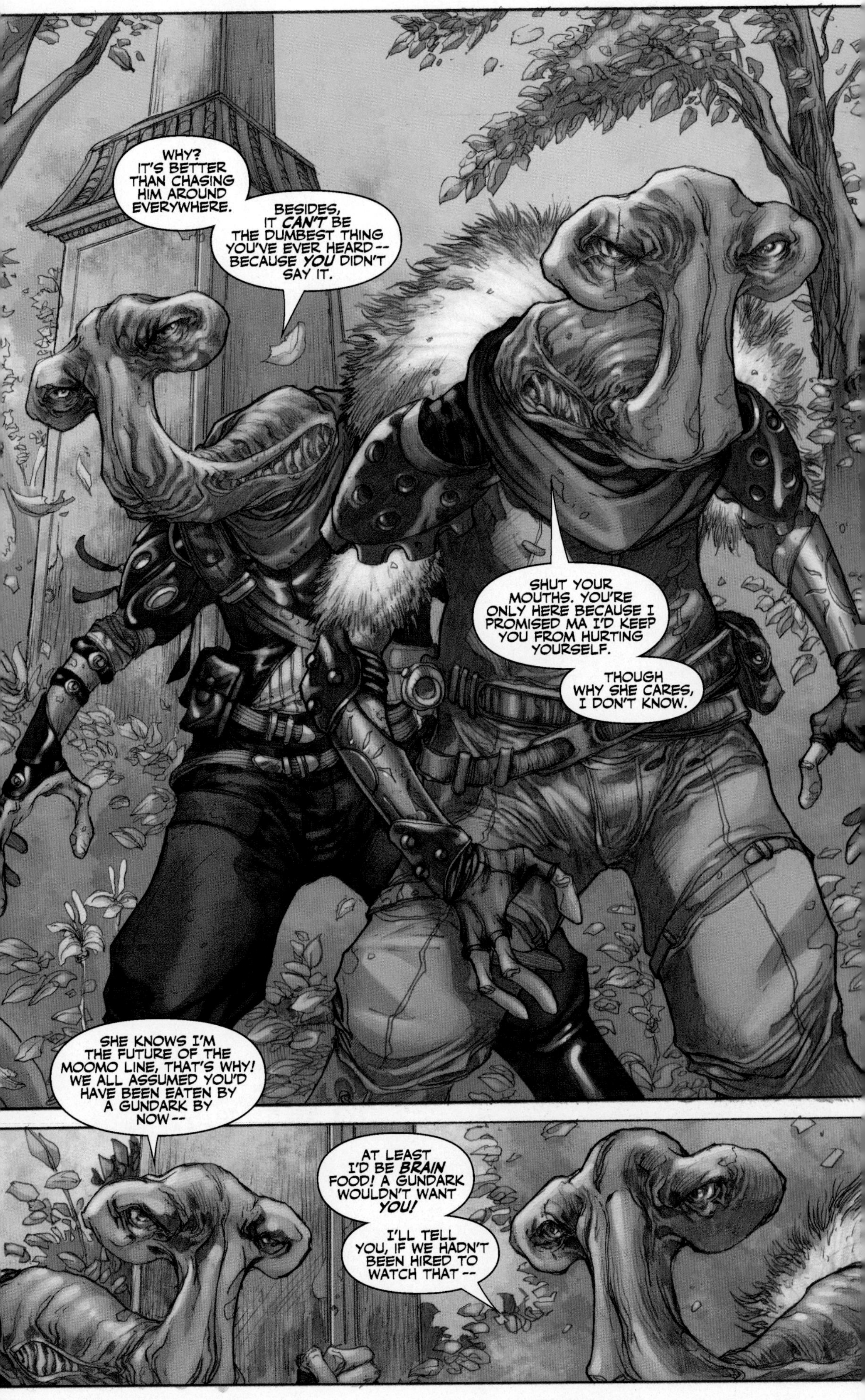
WHY? IT'S BETTER THAN CHASING HIM AROUND EVERYWHERE.
BESIDES, IT CAN'T BE THE DUMBEST THING YOU'VE EVER HEARD-- BECAUSE YOU DIDN'T SAY IT.
SHUT YOUR MOUTHS. YOU'RE ONLY HERE BECAUSE I PROMISED MA I'D KEEP YOU FROM HURTING YOURSELF.
THOUGH WHY SHE CARES, I DON'T KNOW.
SHE KNOWS I'M THE FUTURE OF THE MOOMO LINE, THAT'S WHY! WE ALL ASSUMED YOU'D HAVE BEEN EATEN BY A GUNDARK BY NOW--
AT LEAST I'D BE BRAIN FOOD! A GUNDARK WOULDN'T WANT YOU!
I'LL TELL YOU, IF WE HADN'T BEEN HIRED TO WATCH THAT--

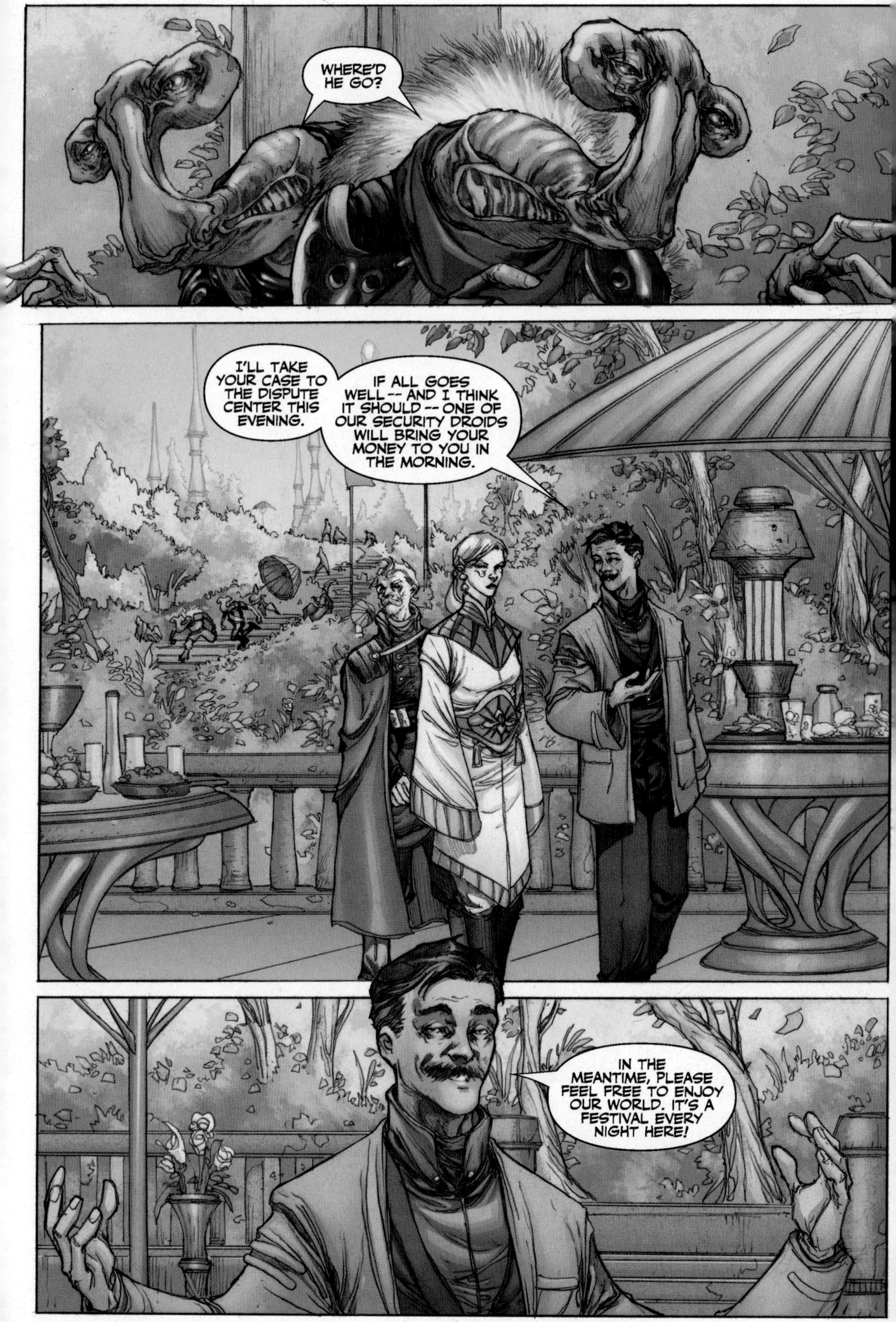
WHERE'D HE GO?
I'LL TAKE YOUR CASE TO THE DISPUTE CENTER THIS EVENING.
IF ALL GOES WELL-- AND I THINK IT SHOULD-- ONE OF OUR SECURITY DROIDS WILL BRING YOUR MONEY TO YOU IN THE MORNING.
IN THE MEANTIME, PLEASE FEEL FREE TO ENJOY OUR WORLD. IT'S A FESTIVAL EVERY NIGHT HERE!

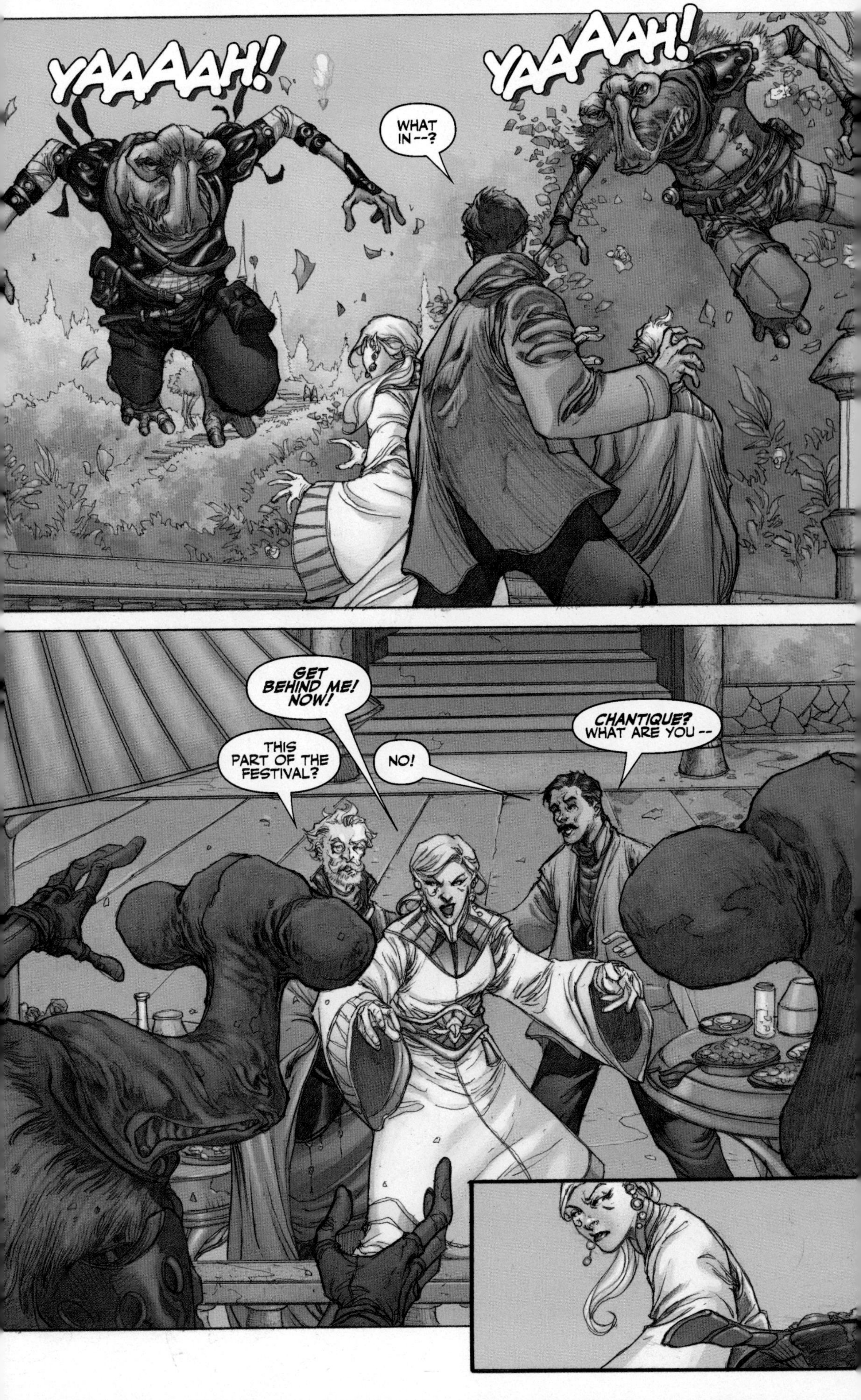
YAAAAH!
WHAT IN--?
YAAAAH!
GET BEHIND ME! NOW!
THIS PART OF THE FESTIVAL?
NO!
CHANTIQUE? WHAT ARE YOU --

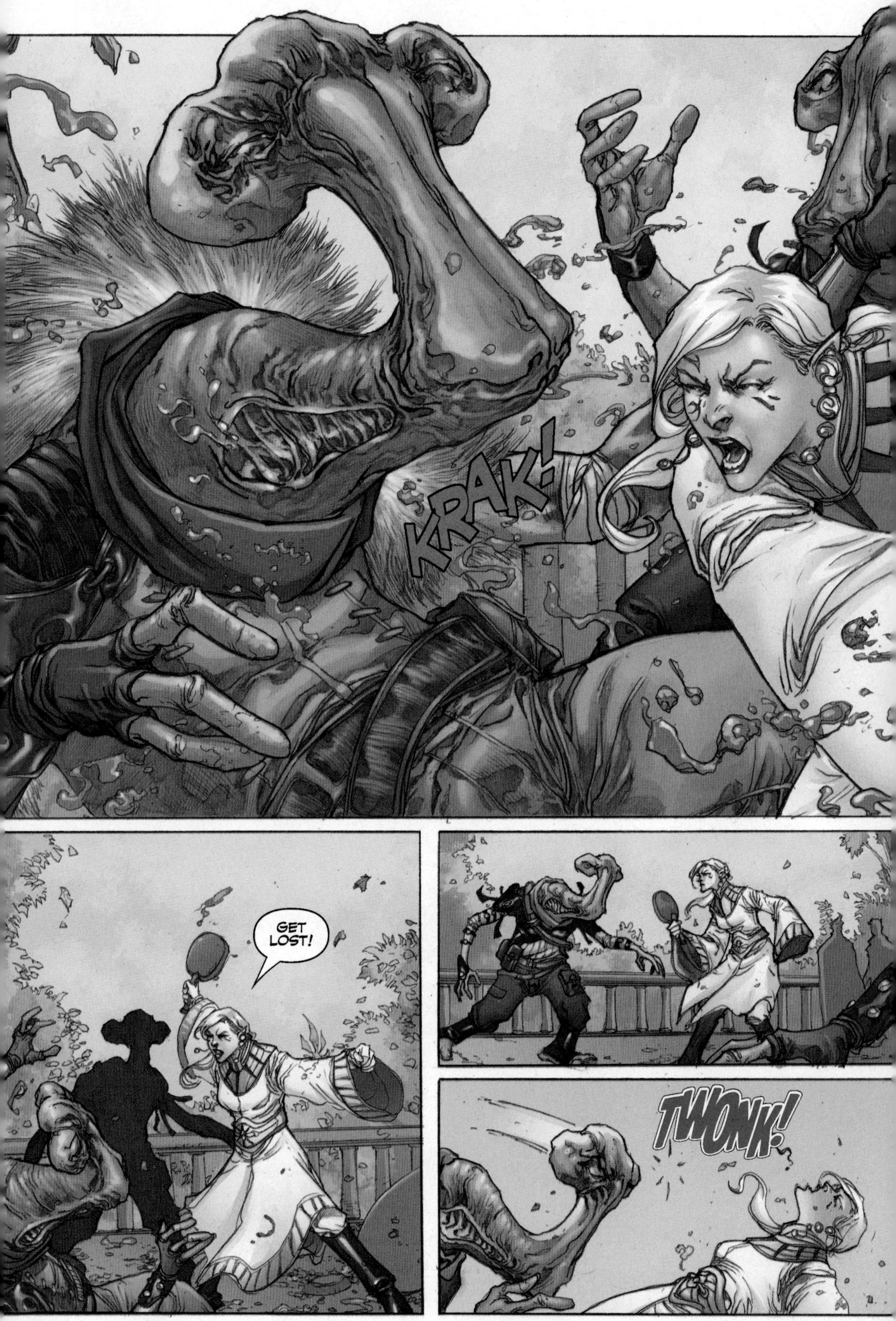
KRAK!
GET LOST!
TWONK!

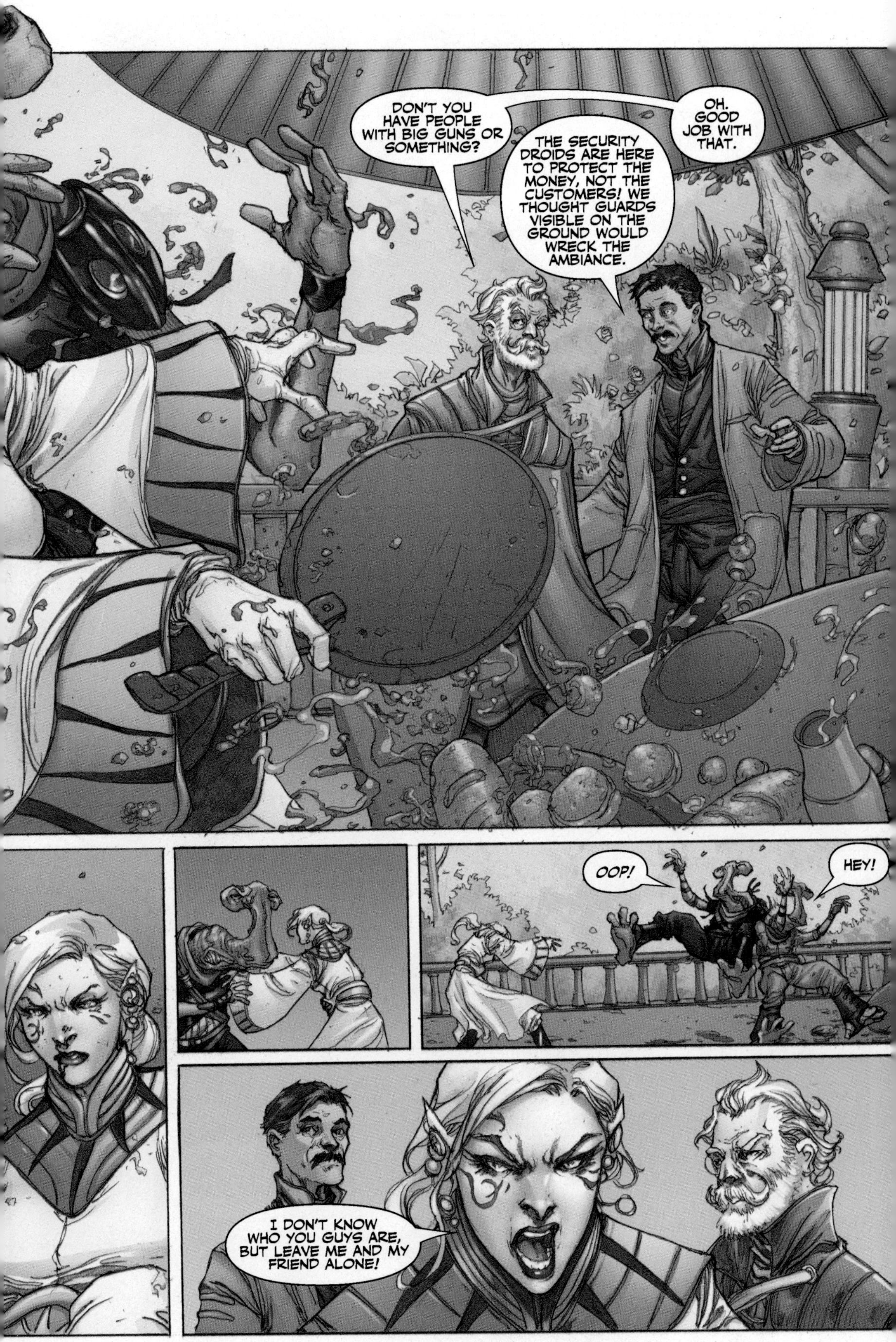
DON'T YOU HAVE PEOPLE WITH BIG GUNS OR SOMETHING?
THE SECURITY DROIDS ARE HERE TO PROTECT THE MONEY, NOT THE CUSTOMERS! WE THOUGHT GUARDS VISIBLE ON THE GROUND WOULD WRECK THE AMBIANCE.
OH. GOOD JOB WITH THAT.
OOP!
HEY!
I DON'T KNOW WHO YOU GUYS ARE, BUT LEAVE ME AND MY FRIEND ALONE!

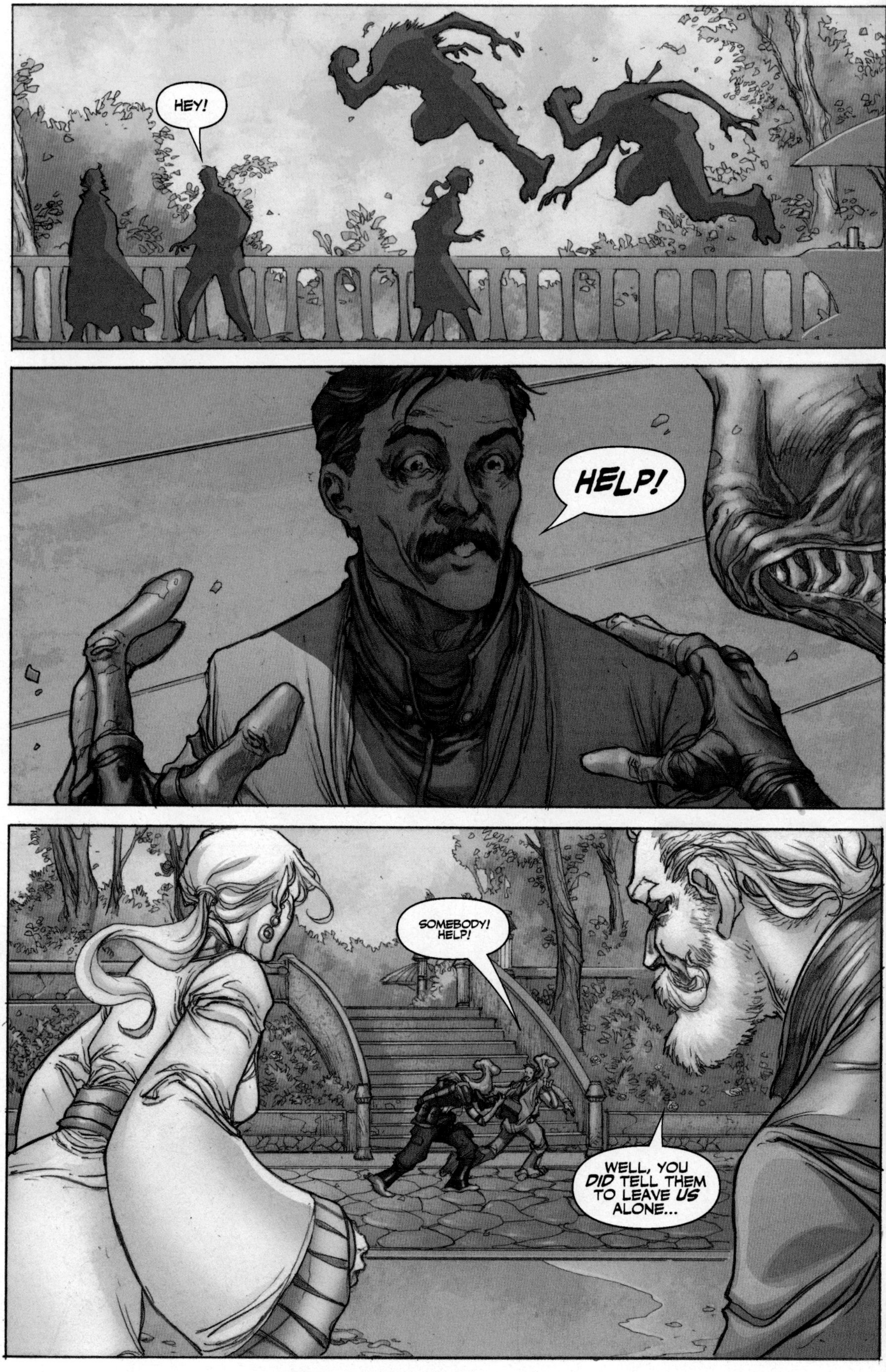
HEY!
HELP!
SOMEBODY! HELP!
WELL, YOU DID TELL THEM TO LEAVE US ALONE...

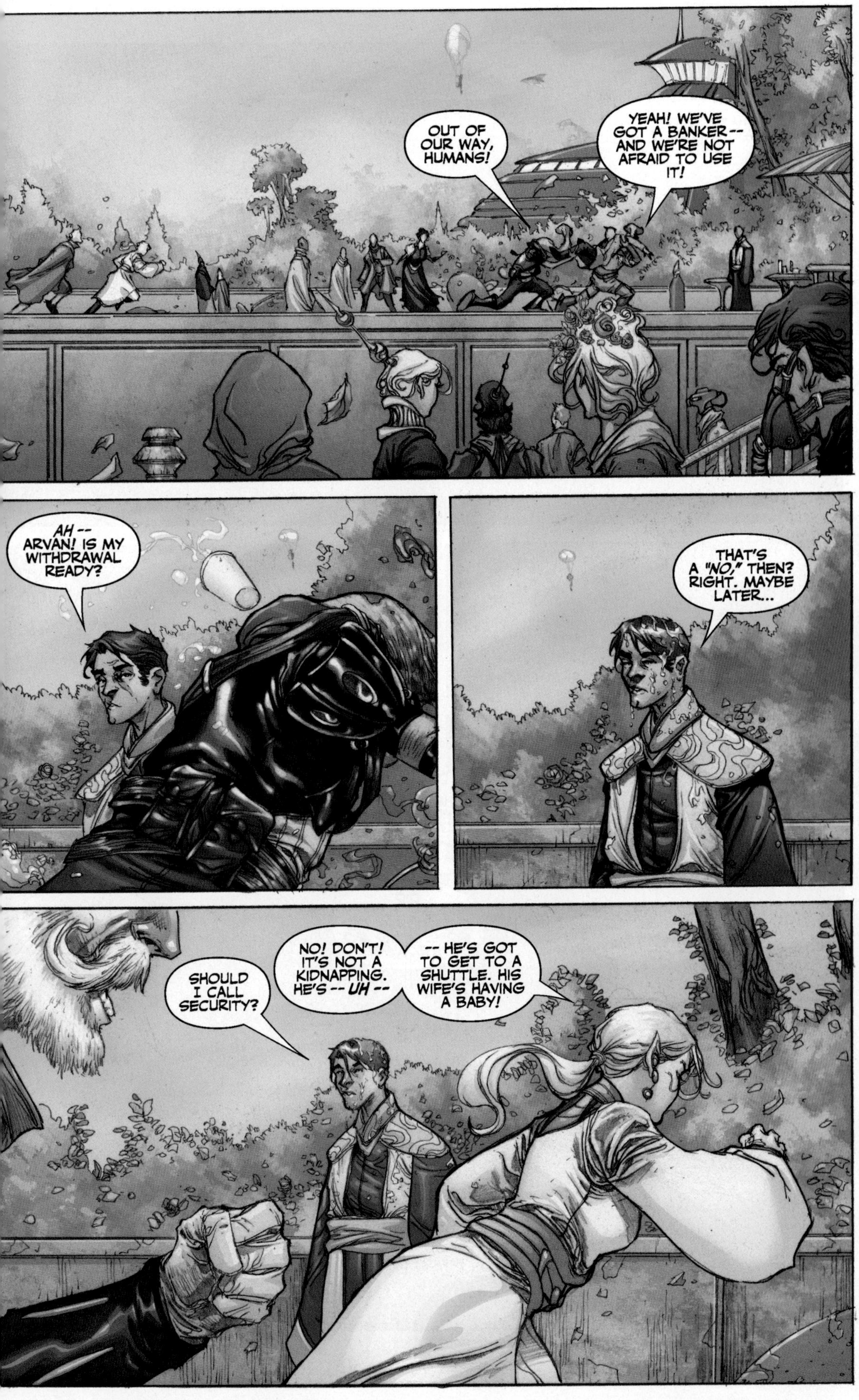
OUT OF OUR WAY, HUMANS!
YEAH! WE'VE GOT A BANKER-- AND WE'RE NOT AFRAID TO USE IT!
AH -- ARVAN! IS MY WITHDRAWAL READY?
THAT'S A "NO," THEN? RIGHT. MAYBE LATER...
SHOULD I CALL SECURITY?
NO! DON'T! IT'S NOT A KIDNAPPING. HE'S -- UH --
-- HE'S GOT TO GET TO A SHUTTLE. HIS WIFE'S HAVING A BABY!

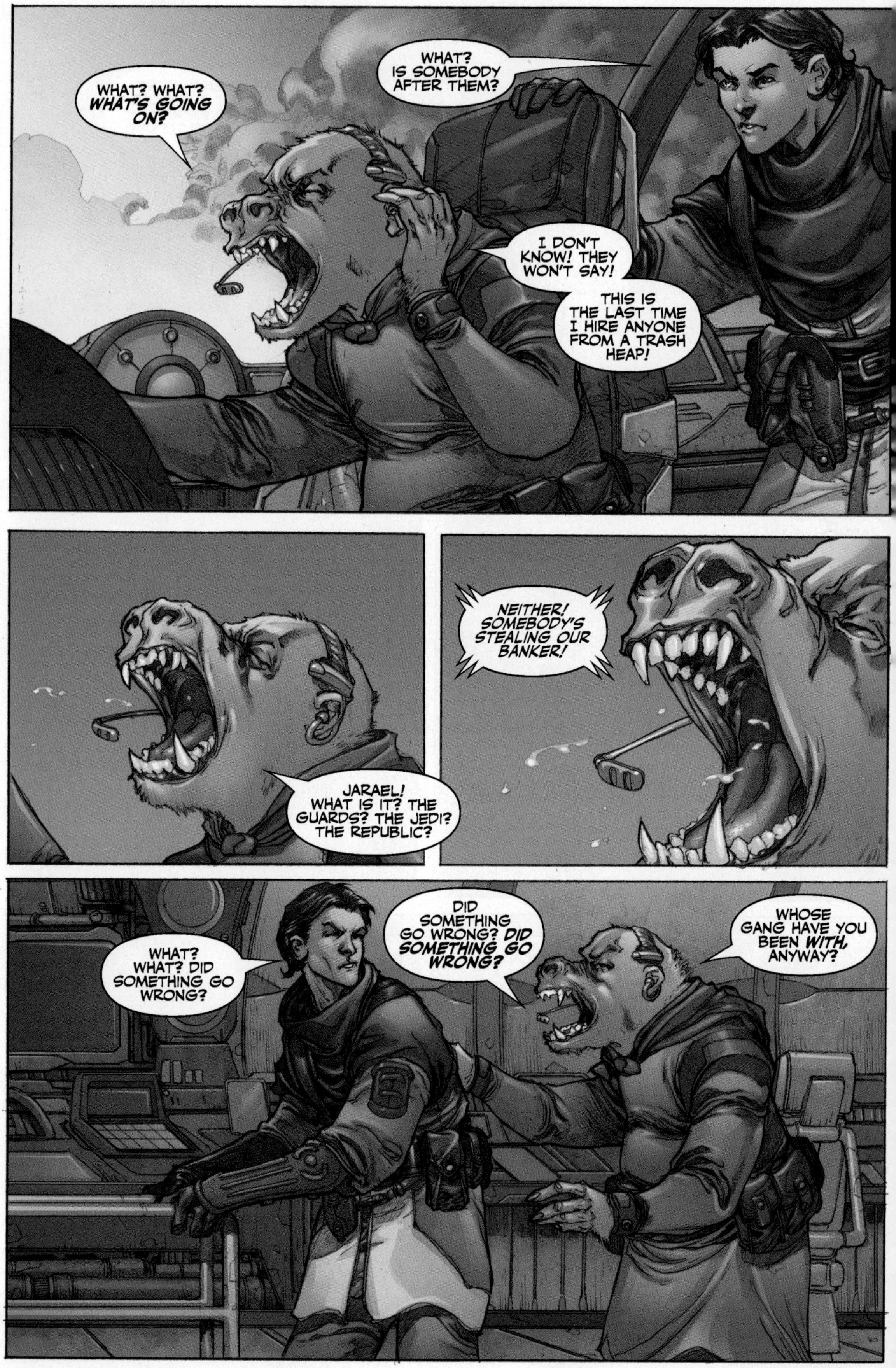
WHAT? WHAT? WHAT'S GOING ON?
WHAT? IS SOMEBODY AFTER THEM?
I DON'T KNOW! THEY WON'T SAY!
THIS IS THE LAST TIME I HIRE ANYONE FROM A TRASH HEAP!
JARAEL! WHAT IS IT? THE GUARDS? THE JEDI? THE REPUBLIC?
NEITHER! SOMEBODY'S STEALING OUR BANKER!
WHAT? WHAT? DID SOMETHING GO WRONG?
DID SOMETHING GO WRONG? DID SOMETHING GO WRONG?
WHOSE GANG HAVE YOU BEEN WITH, ANYWAY?

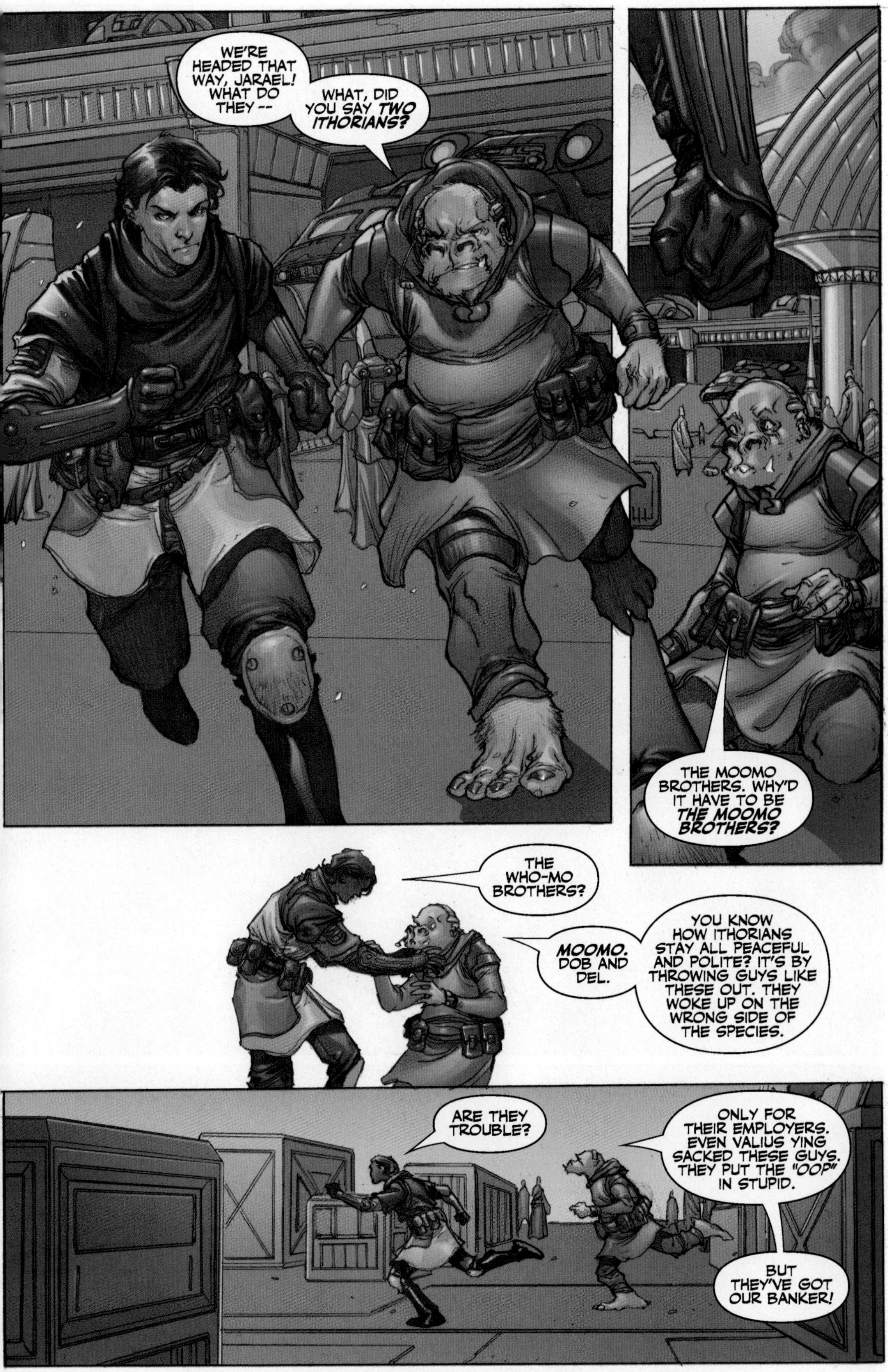
WE'RE HEADED THAT WAY, JARAEL! WHAT DO THEY --
WHAT, DID YOU SAY *TWO ITHORIANS?*
THE MOOMO BROTHERS. WHY'D IT HAVE TO BE *THE MOOMO BROTHERS?*
THE WHO-MO BROTHERS?
MOOMO. DOB AND DEL.
YOU KNOW HOW ITHORIANS STAY ALL PEACEFUL AND POLITE? IT'S BY THROWING GUYS LIKE THESE OUT. THEY WOKE UP ON THE WRONG SIDE OF THE SPECIES.
ARE THEY TROUBLE?
ONLY FOR THEIR EMPLOYERS. EVEN VALIUS YING SACKED THESE GUYS. THEY PUT THE *"OOP"* IN STUPID.
BUT THEY'VE GOT OUR BANKER!

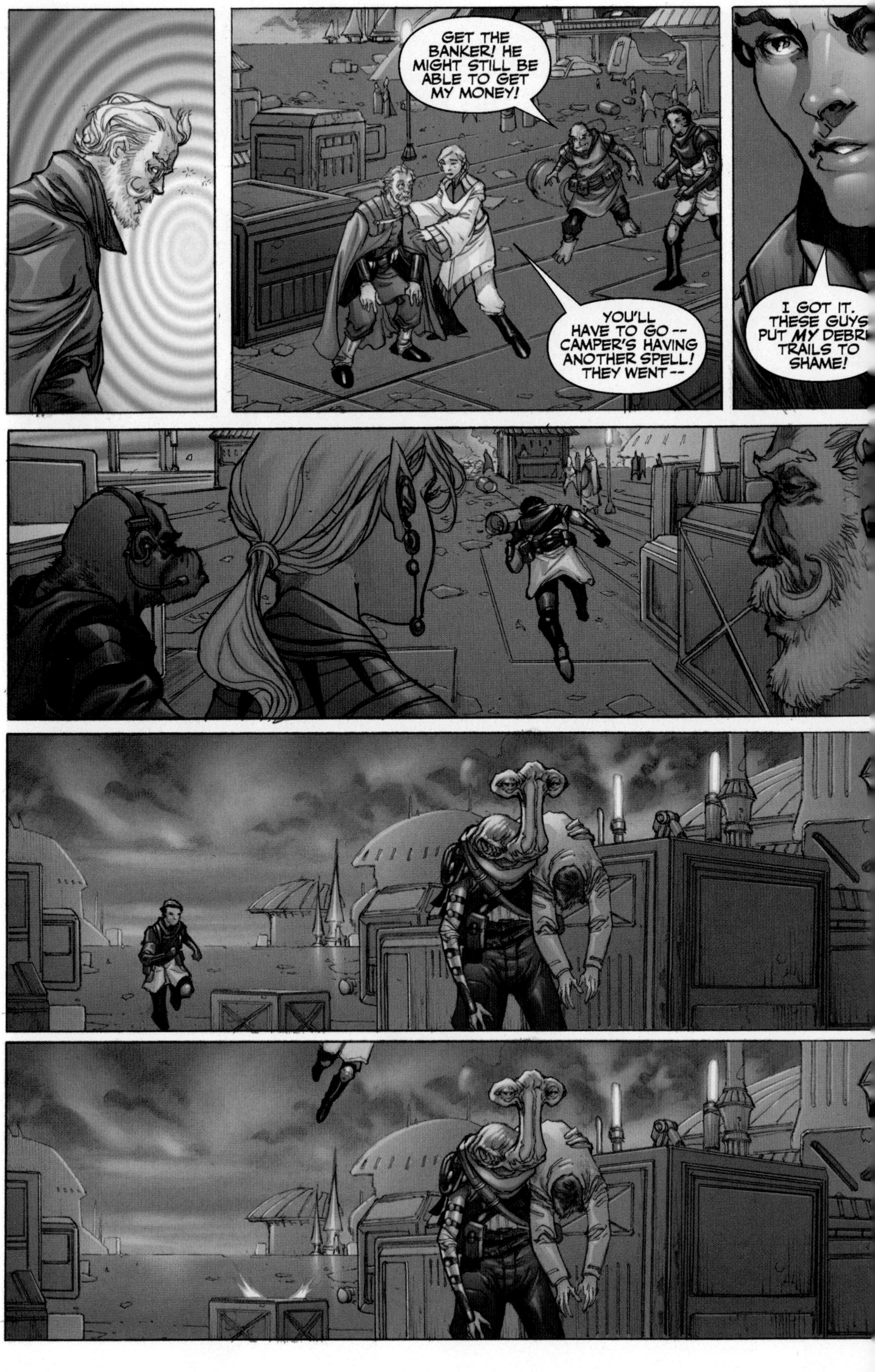
GET THE BANKER! HE MIGHT STILL BE ABLE TO GET MY MONEY!
YOU'LL HAVE TO GO -- CAMPER'S HAVING ANOTHER SPELL! THEY WENT --
I GOT IT. THESE GUYS PUT MY DEBR TRAILS TO SHAME!

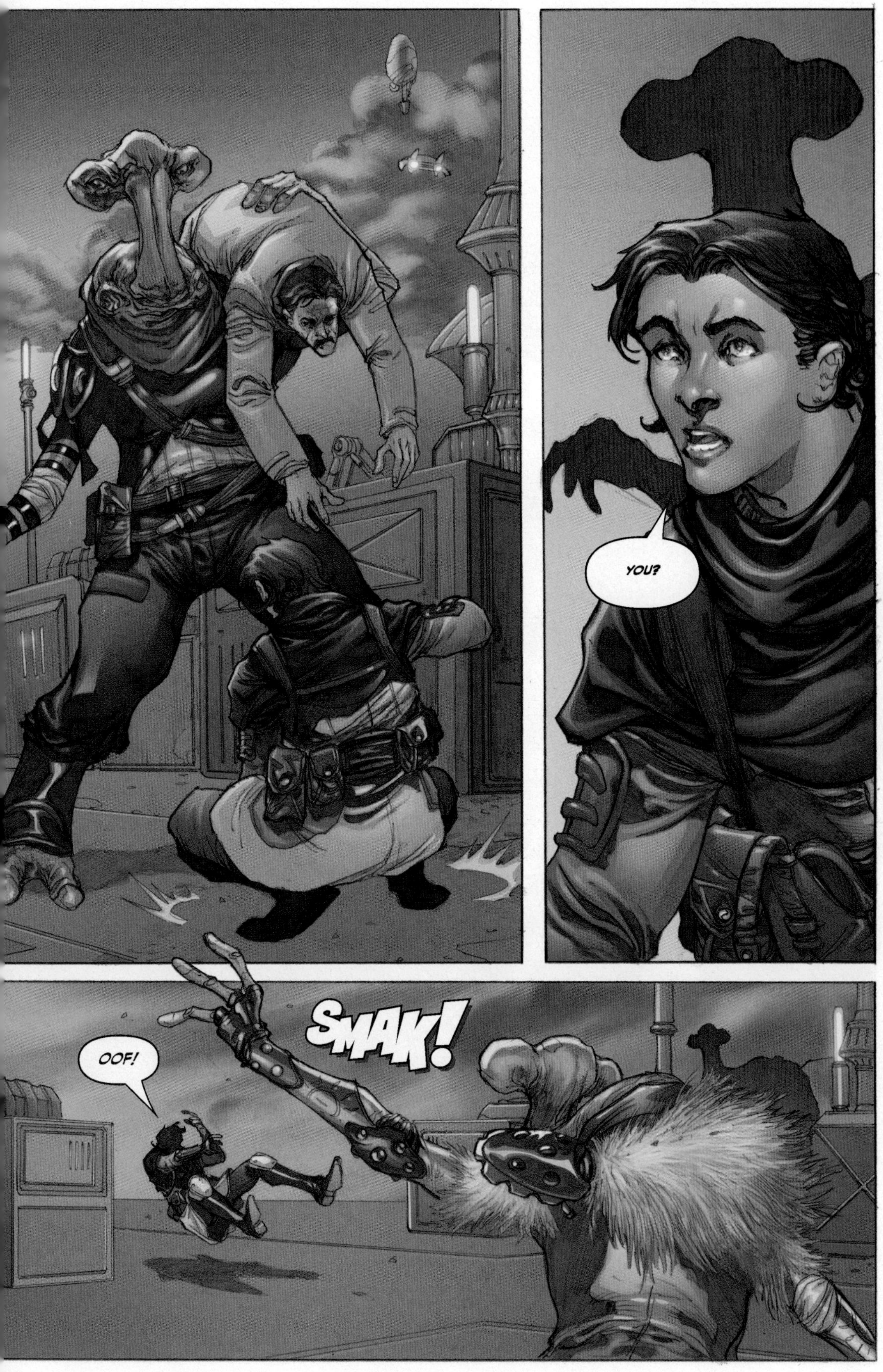
YOU?
SMAK!
OOF!

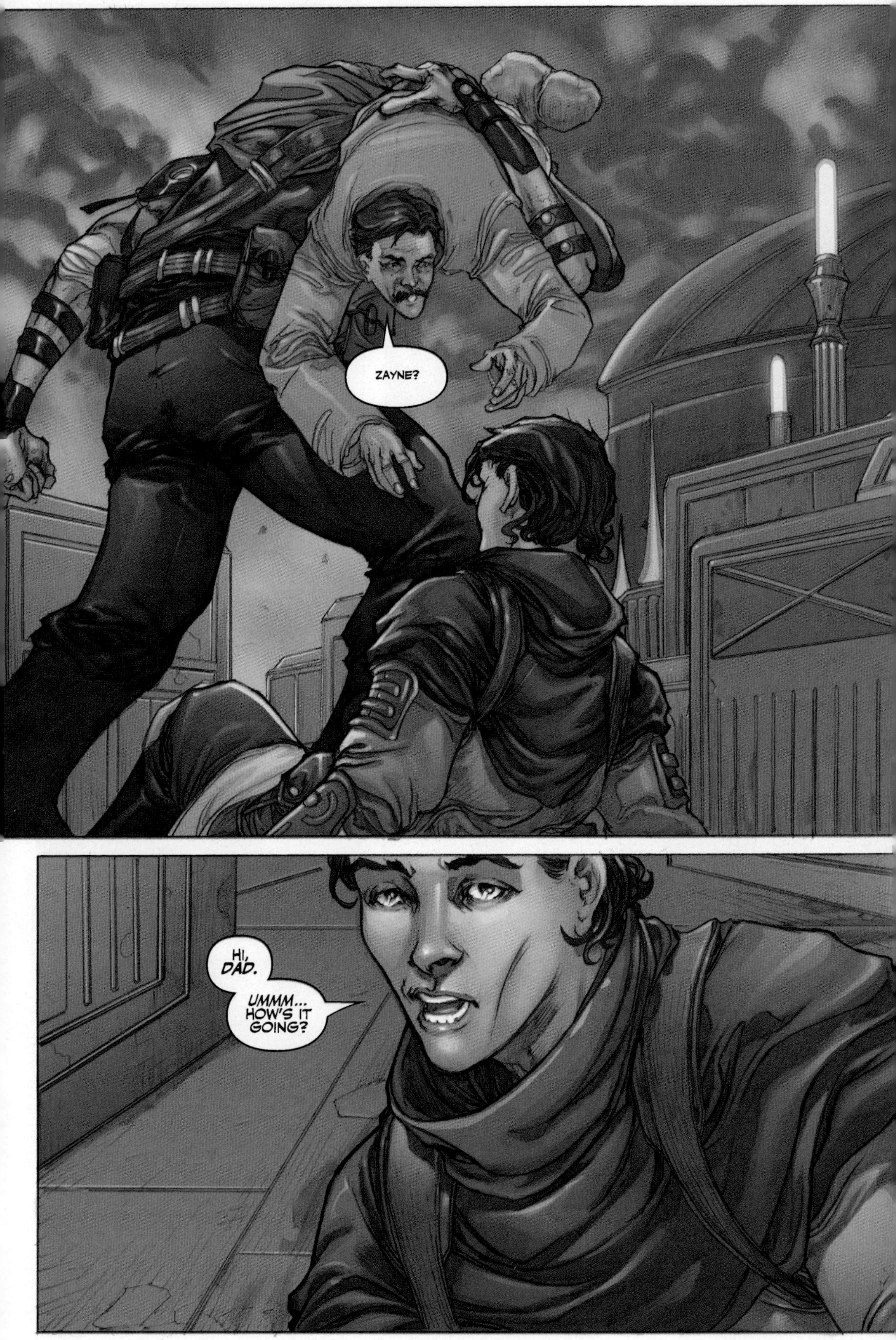
ZAYNE?
HI, DAD.
UMMM... HOW'S IT GOING?

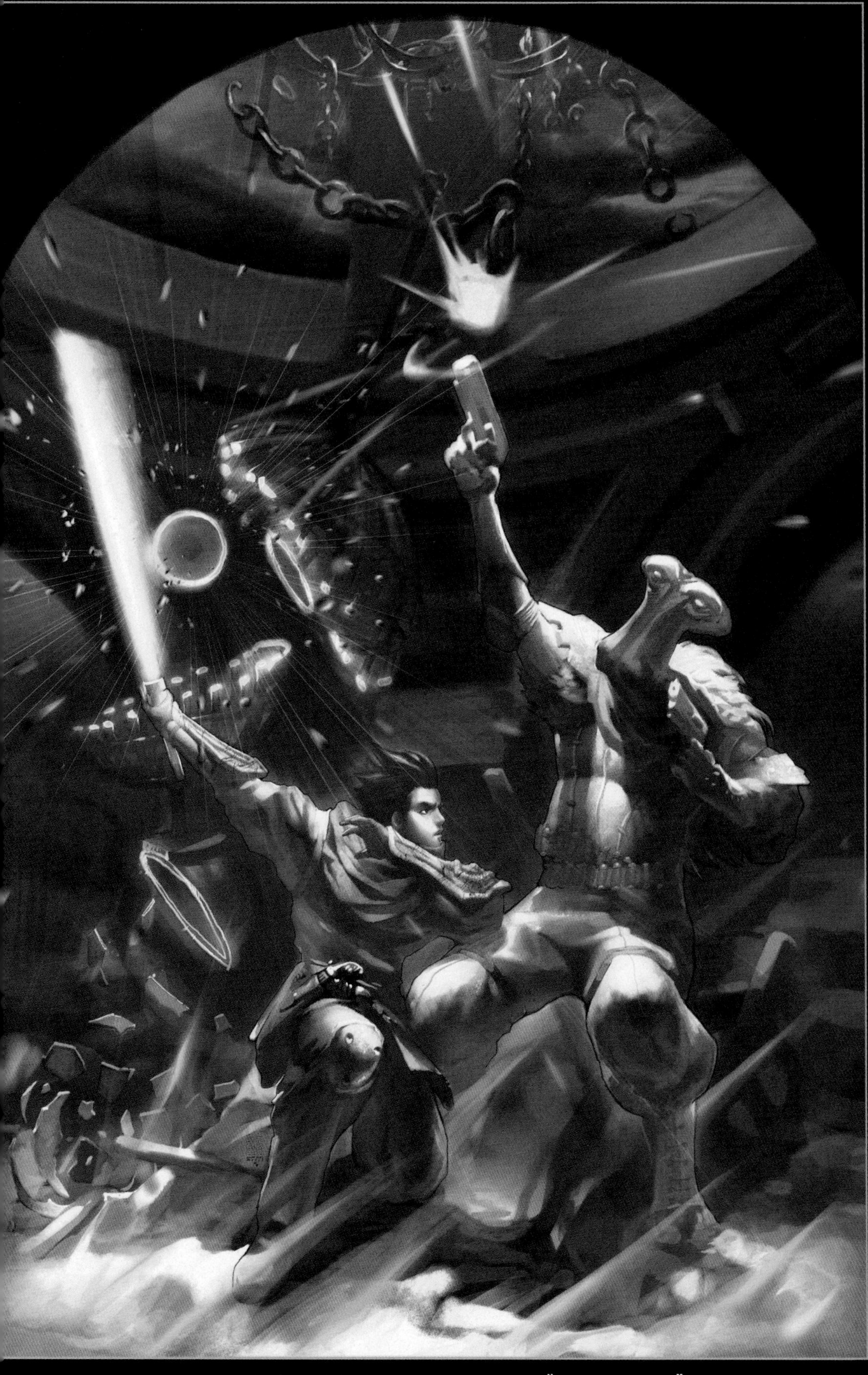

STAR WARS: KNIGHTS OF THE OLD REPUBLIC #12 — "REUNION, PART 2"

WRITER: JOHN JACKSON MILLER • ARTIST: HARVEY TOLIBAO WITH SPECIAL THANKS TO CRYSTAL FAITH CELESTIAL • COLORIST: JAY DAVID RAMOS
LETTERER: MICHAEL HEISLER • ASSISTANT EDITOR: DAVE MARSHALL • EDITOR: JEREMY BARLOW • COVER ARTIST: HOON

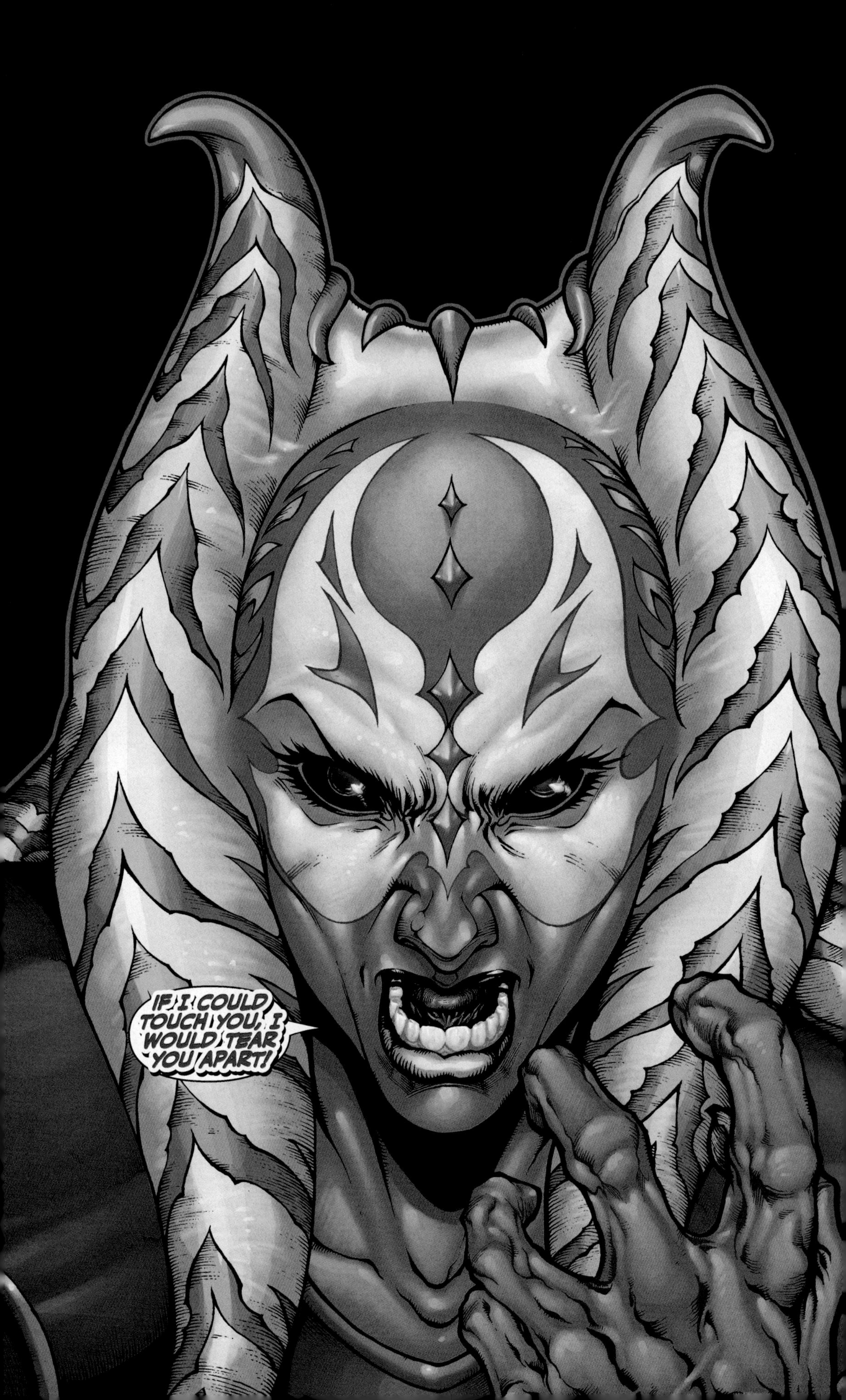
IF I COULD TOUCH YOU, I WOULD TEAR YOU APART!

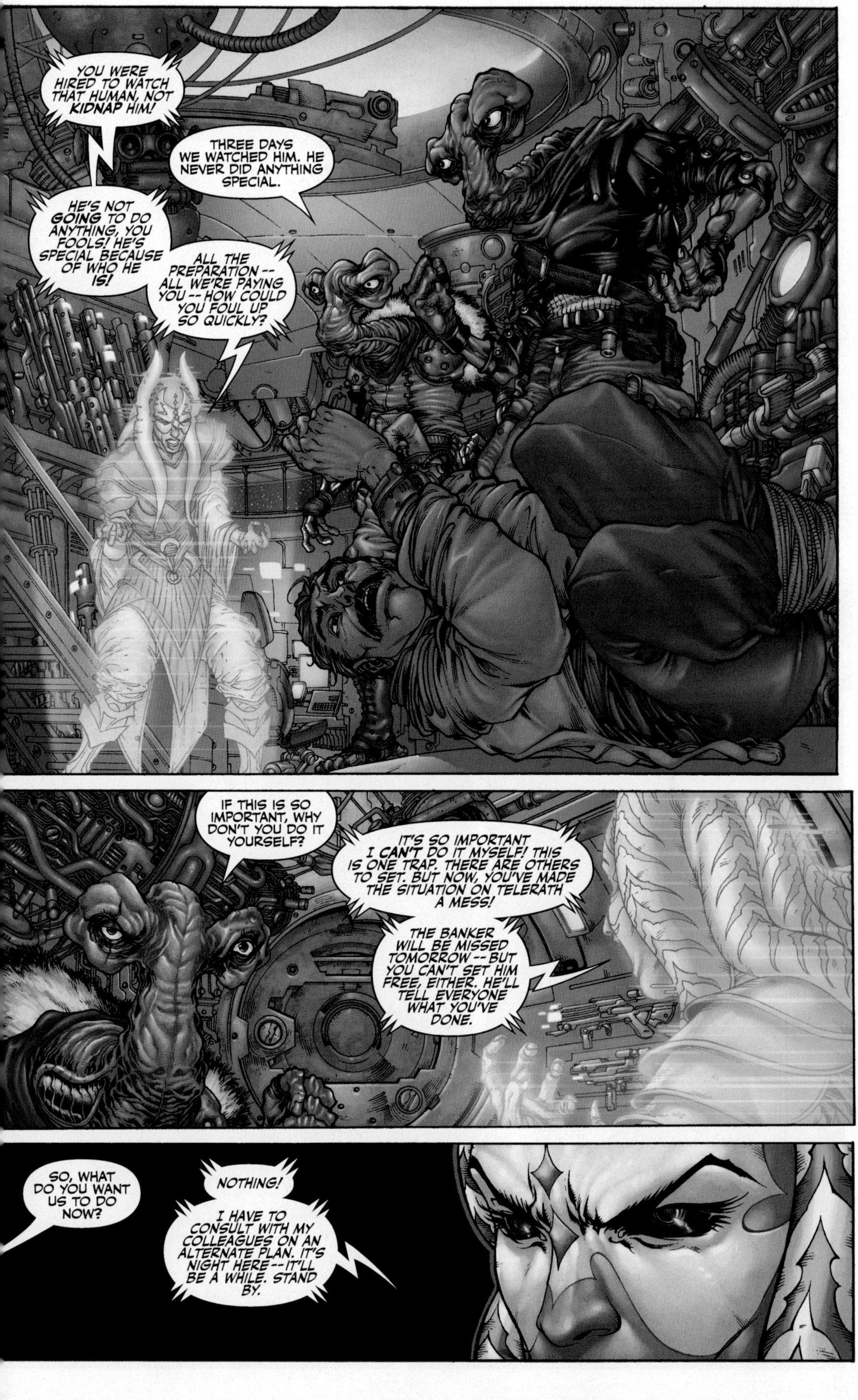

YOU WERE HIRED TO WATCH THAT HUMAN, NOT KIDNAP HIM!
THREE DAYS WE WATCHED HIM. HE NEVER DID ANYTHING SPECIAL.
HE'S NOT GOING TO DO ANYTHING, YOU FOOLS! HE'S SPECIAL BECAUSE OF WHO HE IS!
ALL THE PREPARATION -- ALL WE'RE PAYING YOU -- HOW COULD YOU FOUL UP SO QUICKLY?
IF THIS IS SO IMPORTANT, WHY DON'T YOU DO IT YOURSELF?
IT'S SO IMPORTANT I CAN'T DO IT MYSELF! THIS IS ONE TRAP. THERE ARE OTHERS TO SET. BUT NOW, YOU'VE MADE THE SITUATION ON TELERATH A MESS!
THE BANKER WILL BE MISSED TOMORROW -- BUT YOU CAN'T SET HIM FREE, EITHER. HE'LL TELL EVERYONE WHAT YOU'VE DONE.
SO, WHAT DO YOU WANT US TO DO NOW?
NOTHING!
I HAVE TO CONSULT WITH MY COLLEAGUES ON AN ALTERNATE PLAN. IT'S NIGHT HERE--IT'LL BE A WHILE. STAND BY.

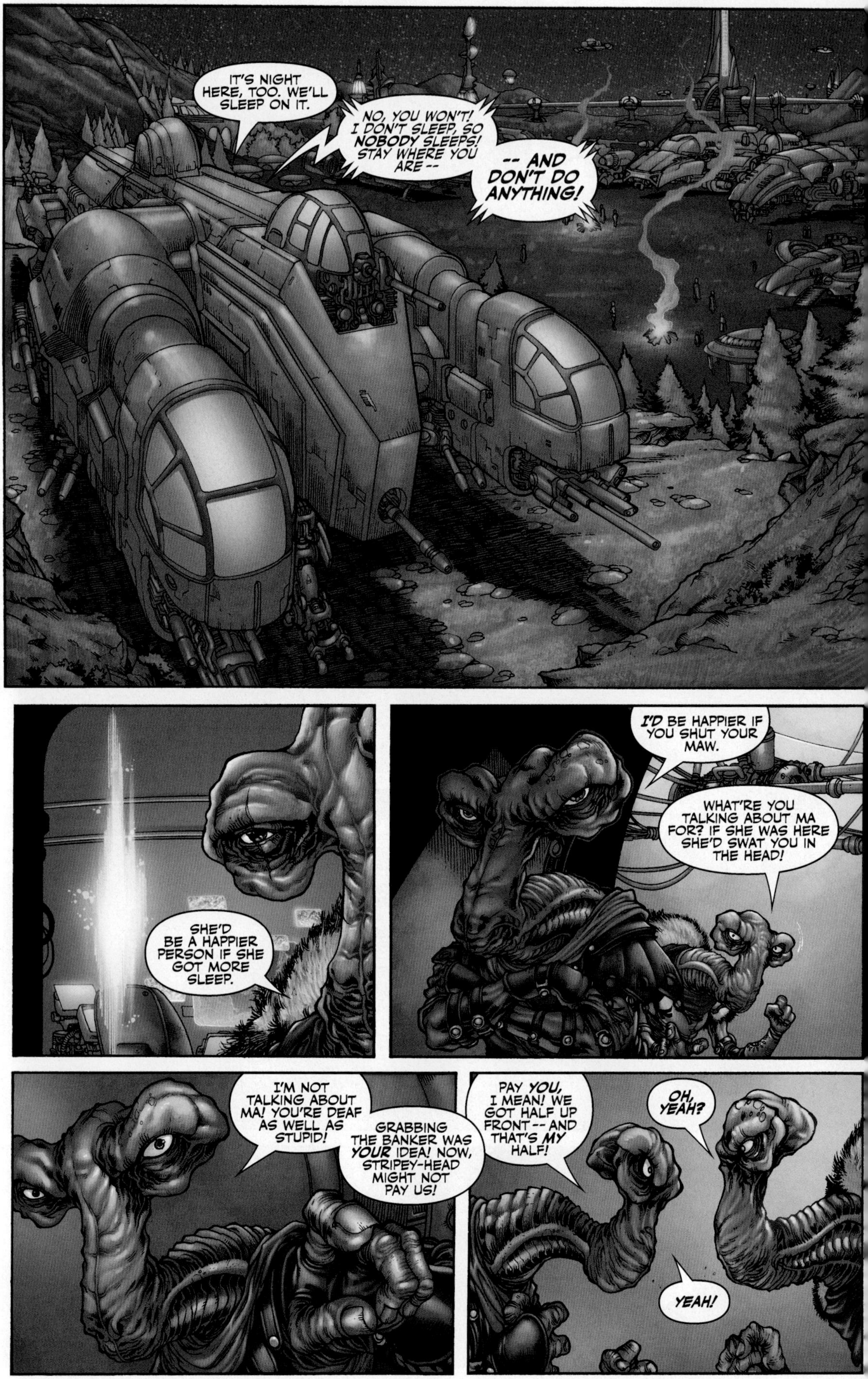
IT'S NIGHT HERE, TOO. WE'LL SLEEP ON IT.
NO, YOU WON'T! I DON'T SLEEP, SO NOBODY SLEEPS! STAY WHERE YOU ARE --
-- AND DON'T DO ANYTHING!
SHE'D BE A HAPPIER PERSON IF SHE GOT MORE SLEEP.
I'D BE HAPPIER IF YOU SHUT YOUR MAW.
WHAT'RE YOU TALKING ABOUT MA FOR? IF SHE WAS HERE SHE'D SWAT YOU IN THE HEAD!
I'M NOT TALKING ABOUT MA! YOU'RE DEAF AS WELL AS STUPID!
GRABBING THE BANKER WAS YOUR IDEA! NOW, STRIPEY-HEAD MIGHT NOT PAY US!
PAY YOU, I MEAN! WE GOT HALF UP FRONT -- AND THAT'S MY HALF!
OH, YEAH?
YEAH!

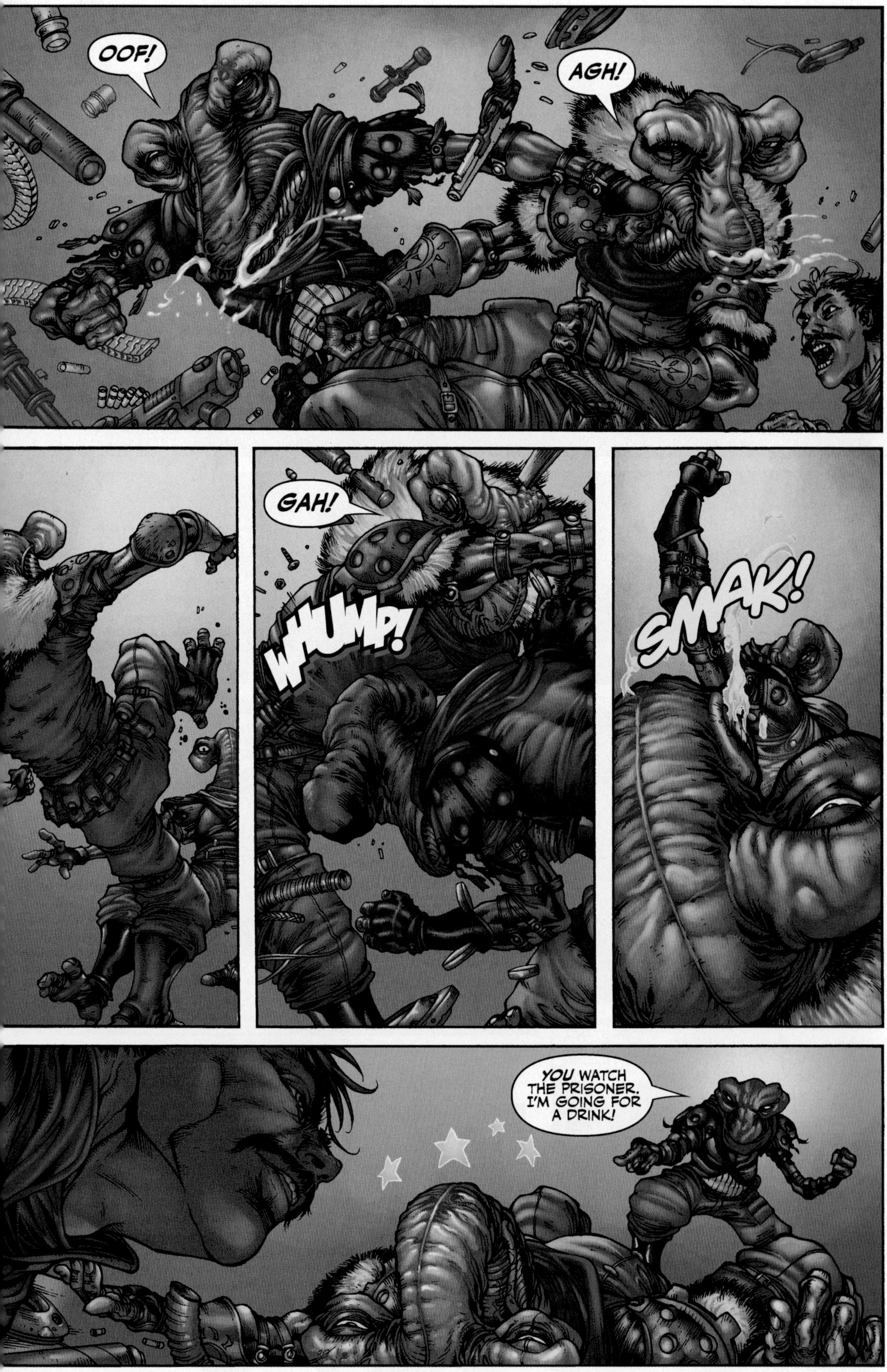
OOF!
AGH!
GAH!
WHUMP!
SMAK!
YOU WATCH THE PRISONER. I'M GOING FOR A DRINK!

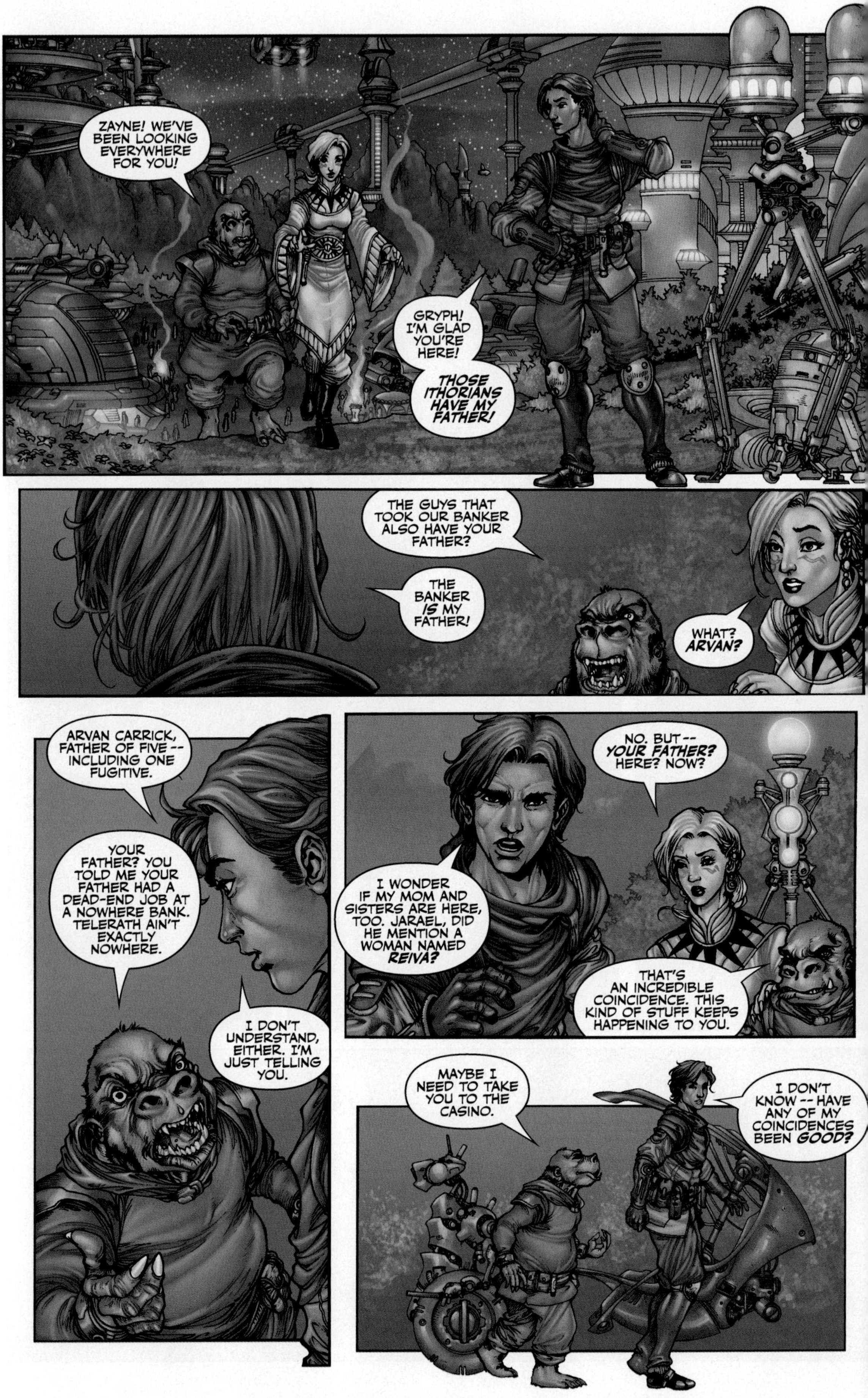
ZAYNE! WE'VE BEEN LOOKING EVERYWHERE FOR YOU!
GRYPH! I'M GLAD YOU'RE HERE!
THOSE ITHORIANS HAVE MY FATHER!
THE GUYS THAT TOOK OUR BANKER ALSO HAVE YOUR FATHER?
THE BANKER IS MY FATHER!
WHAT? ARVAN?
ARVAN CARRICK, FATHER OF FIVE -- INCLUDING ONE FUGITIVE.
YOUR FATHER? YOU TOLD ME YOUR FATHER HAD A DEAD-END JOB AT A NOWHERE BANK. TELERATH AIN'T EXACTLY NOWHERE.
I DON'T UNDERSTAND, EITHER. I'M JUST TELLING YOU.
NO. BUT -- YOUR FATHER? HERE? NOW?
I WONDER IF MY MOM AND SISTERS ARE HERE, TOO. JARAEL, DID HE MENTION A WOMAN NAMED REIVA?
THAT'S AN INCREDIBLE COINCIDENCE. THIS KIND OF STUFF KEEPS HAPPENING TO YOU.
MAYBE I NEED TO TAKE YOU TO THE CASINO.
I DON'T KNOW -- HAVE ANY OF MY COINCIDENCES BEEN GOOD?

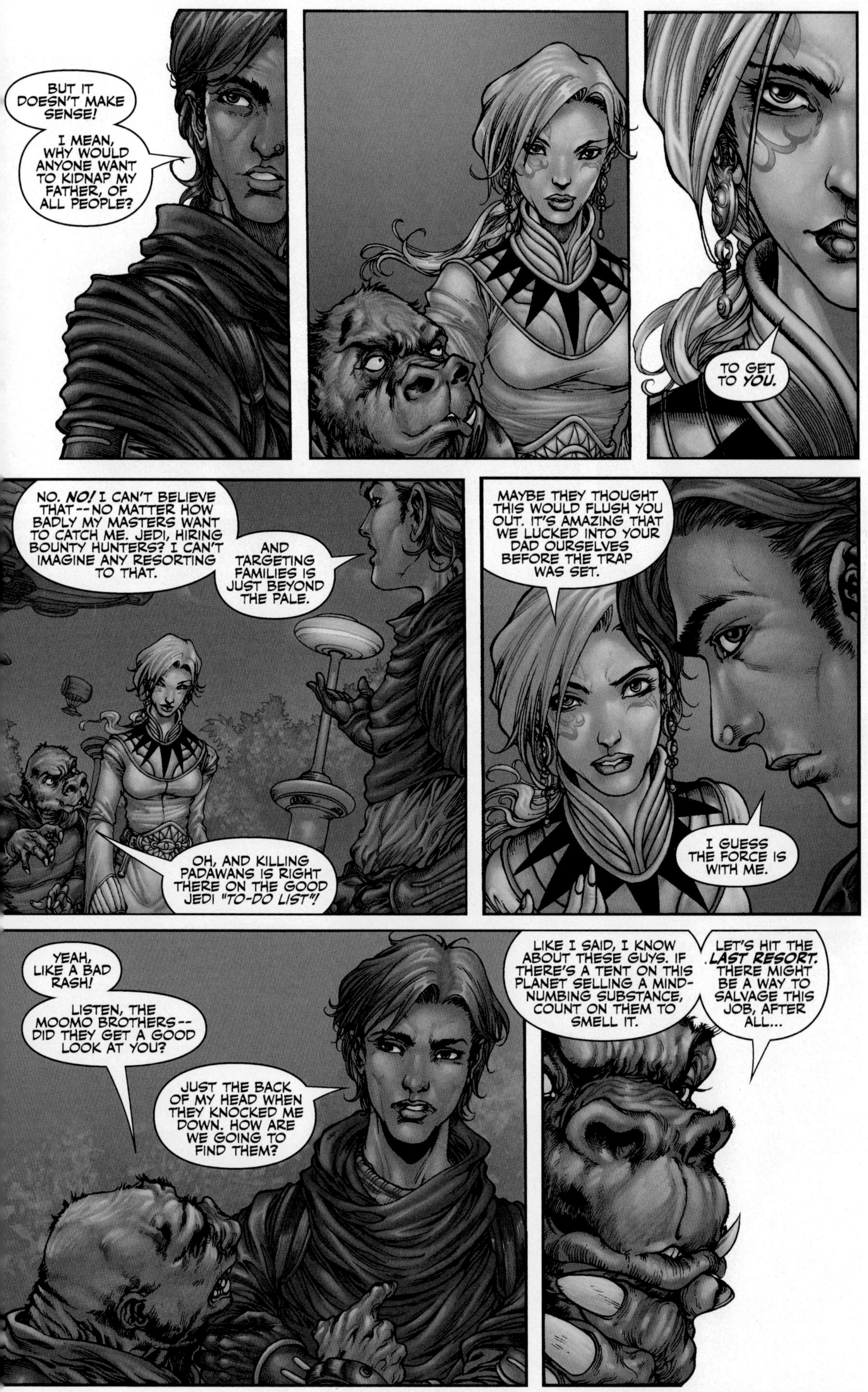
BUT IT DOESN'T MAKE SENSE!
I MEAN, WHY WOULD ANYONE WANT TO KIDNAP MY FATHER, OF ALL PEOPLE?
TO GET TO *YOU.*
NO. *NO!* I CAN'T BELIEVE THAT--NO MATTER HOW BADLY MY MASTERS WANT TO CATCH ME. JEDI, HIRING BOUNTY HUNTERS? I CAN'T IMAGINE ANY RESORTING TO THAT.
AND TARGETING FAMILIES IS JUST BEYOND THE PALE.
OH, AND KILLING PADAWANS IS RIGHT THERE ON THE GOOD JEDI *"TO-DO LIST"!*
MAYBE THEY THOUGHT THIS WOULD FLUSH YOU OUT. IT'S AMAZING THAT WE LUCKED INTO YOUR DAD OURSELVES BEFORE THE TRAP WAS SET.
I GUESS THE FORCE IS WITH ME.
YEAH, LIKE A BAD RASH!
LISTEN, THE MOOMO BROTHERS--DID THEY GET A GOOD LOOK AT YOU?
JUST THE BACK OF MY HEAD WHEN THEY KNOCKED ME DOWN. HOW ARE WE GOING TO FIND THEM?
LIKE I SAID, I KNOW ABOUT THESE GUYS. IF THERE'S A TENT ON THIS PLANET SELLING A MIND-NUMBING SUBSTANCE, COUNT ON THEM TO SMELL IT.
LET'S HIT THE *LAST RESORT.* THERE MIGHT BE A WAY TO SALVAGE THIS JOB, AFTER ALL...

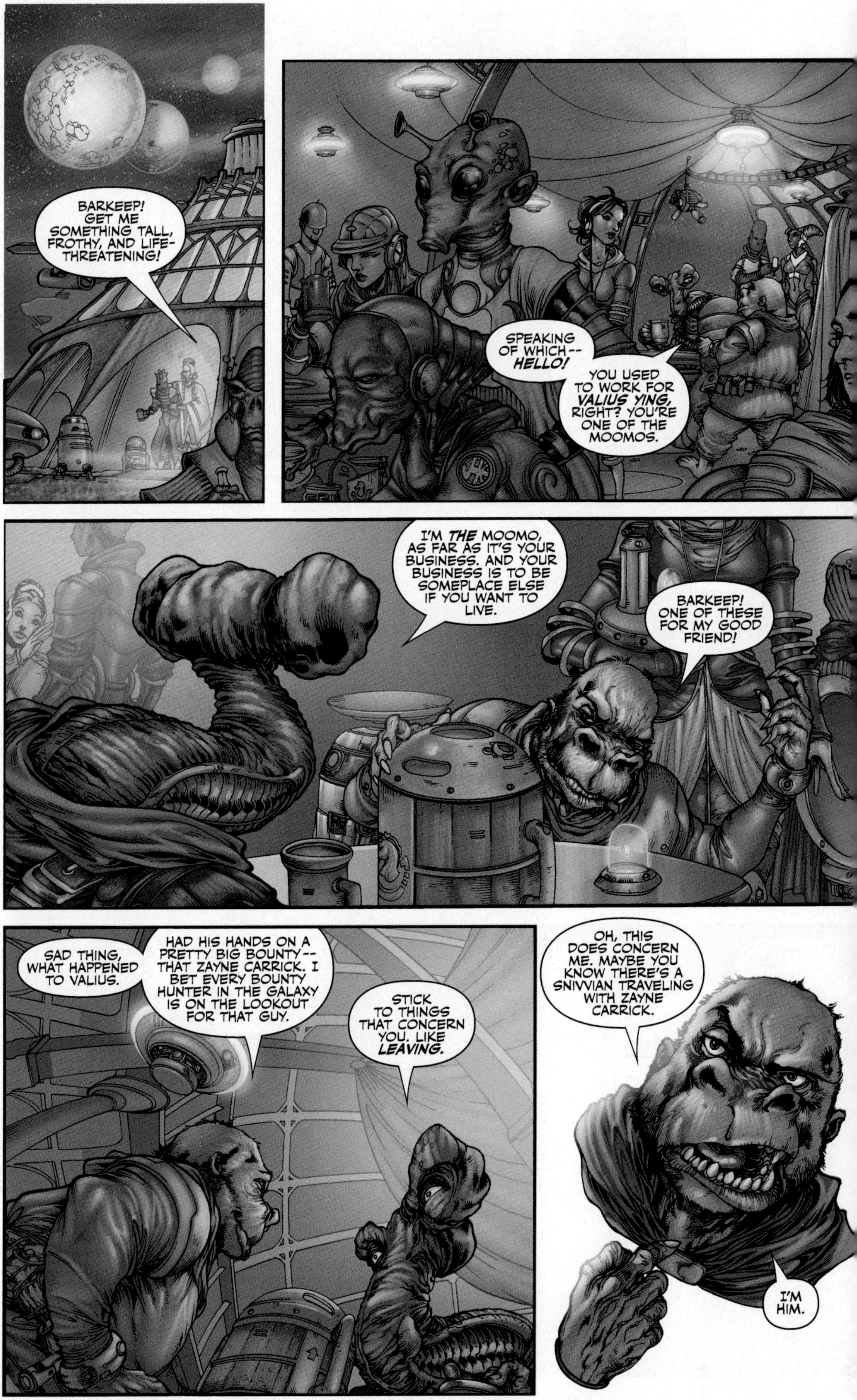
BARKEEP! GET ME SOMETHING TALL, FROTHY, AND LIFE-THREATENING!
SPEAKING OF WHICH-- HELLO!
YOU USED TO WORK FOR VALIUS YING, RIGHT? YOU'RE ONE OF THE MOOMOS.
I'M THE MOOMO, AS FAR AS IT'S YOUR BUSINESS. AND YOUR BUSINESS IS TO BE SOMEPLACE ELSE IF YOU WANT TO LIVE.
BARKEEP! ONE OF THESE FOR MY GOOD FRIEND!
SAD THING, WHAT HAPPENED TO VALIUS.
HAD HIS HANDS ON A PRETTY BIG BOUNTY-- THAT ZAYNE CARRICK. I BET EVERY BOUNTY HUNTER IN THE GALAXY IS ON THE LOOKOUT FOR THAT GUY.
STICK TO THINGS THAT CONCERN YOU. LIKE LEAVING.
OH, THIS DOES CONCERN ME. MAYBE YOU KNOW THERE'S A SNIVVIAN TRAVELING WITH ZAYNE CARRICK.
I'M HIM.

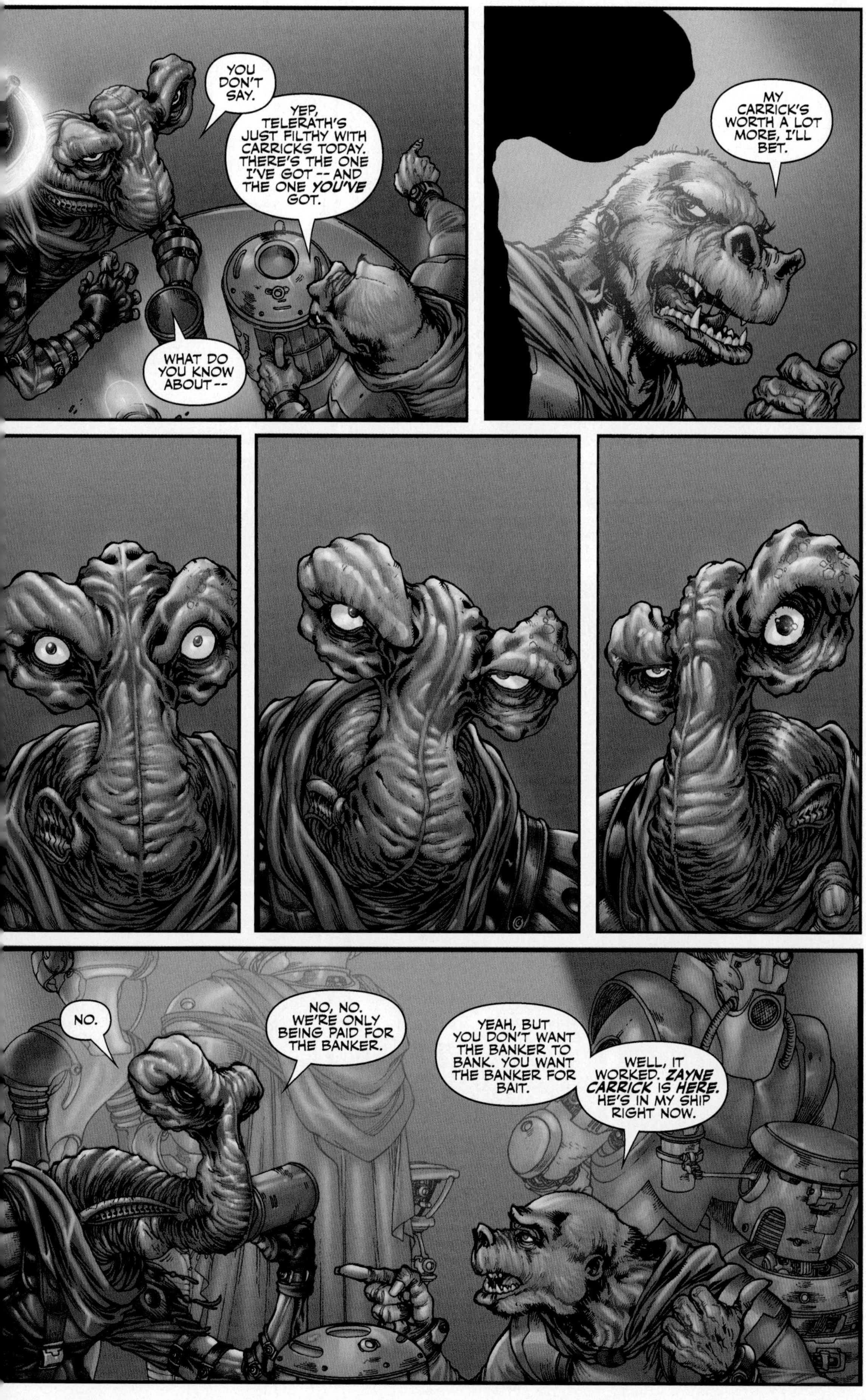
YOU DON'T SAY.
YEP, TELERATH'S JUST FILTHY WITH CARRICKS TODAY. THERE'S THE ONE I'VE GOT -- AND THE ONE *YOU'VE* GOT.
WHAT DO YOU KNOW ABOUT --
MY CARRICK'S WORTH A LOT MORE, I'LL BET.
NO.
NO, NO. WE'RE ONLY BEING PAID FOR THE BANKER.
YEAH, BUT YOU DON'T WANT THE BANKER TO BANK. YOU WANT THE BANKER FOR BAIT.
WELL, IT WORKED. *ZAYNE CARRICK* IS *HERE.* HE'S IN MY SHIP RIGHT NOW.

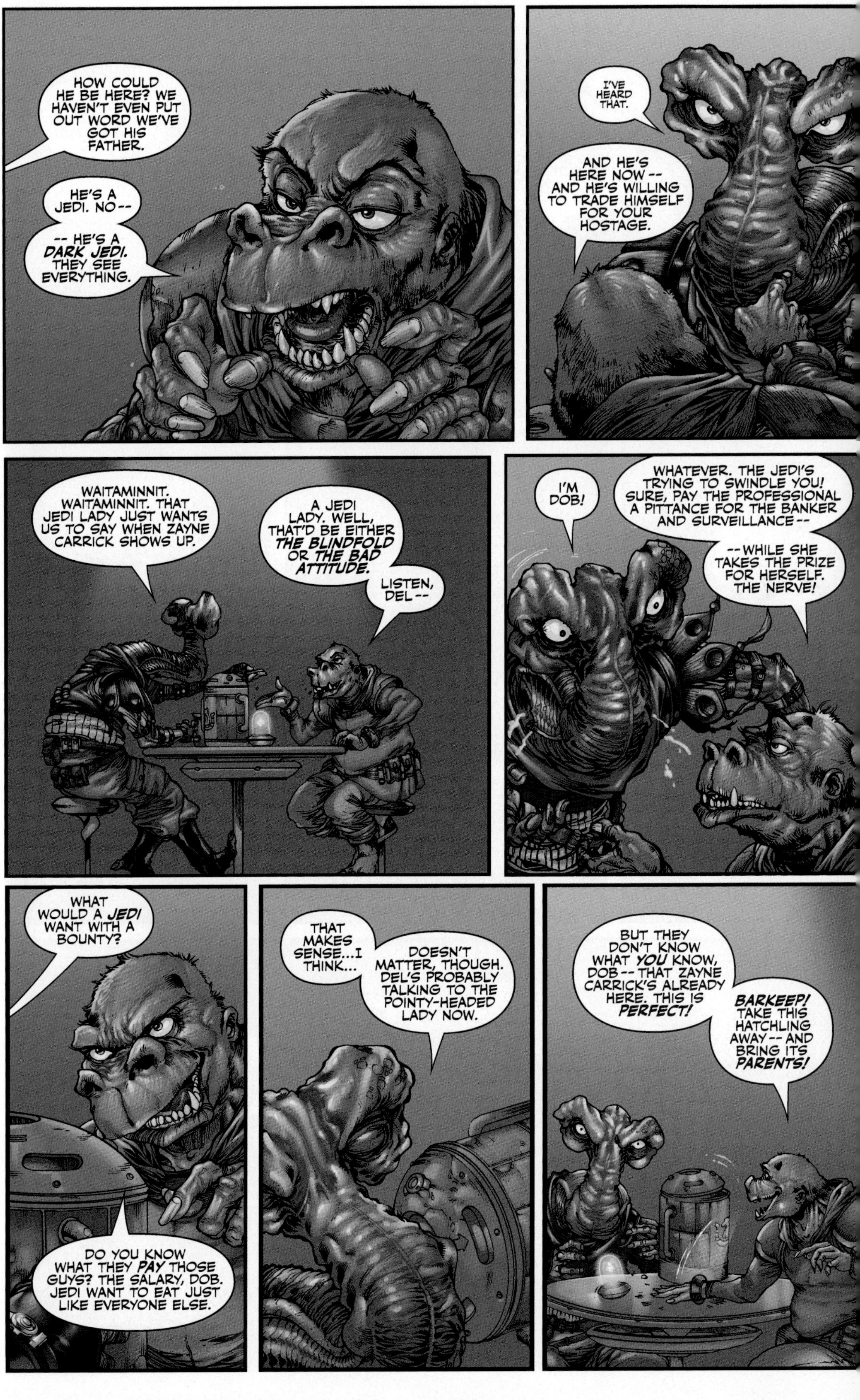
HOW COULD HE BE HERE? WE HAVEN'T EVEN PUT OUT WORD WE'VE GOT HIS FATHER.
HE'S A JEDI. NO--
-- HE'S A DARK JEDI. THEY SEE EVERYTHING.
I'VE HEARD THAT.
AND HE'S HERE NOW -- AND HE'S WILLING TO TRADE HIMSELF FOR YOUR HOSTAGE.
WAITAMINNIT. WAITAMINNIT. THAT JEDI LADY JUST WANTS US TO SAY WHEN ZAYNE CARRICK SHOWS UP.
A JEDI LADY. WELL, THAT'D BE EITHER THE BLINDFOLD OR THE BAD ATTITUDE.
LISTEN, DEL--
I'M DOB!
WHATEVER. THE JEDI'S TRYING TO SWINDLE YOU! SURE, PAY THE PROFESSIONAL A PITTANCE FOR THE BANKER AND SURVEILLANCE--
--WHILE SHE TAKES THE PRIZE FOR HERSELF. THE NERVE!
WHAT WOULD A JEDI WANT WITH A BOUNTY?
DO YOU KNOW WHAT THEY PAY THOSE GUYS? THE SALARY, DOB. JEDI WANT TO EAT JUST LIKE EVERYONE ELSE.
THAT MAKES SENSE...I THINK...
DOESN'T MATTER, THOUGH. DEL'S PROBABLY TALKING TO THE POINTY-HEADED LADY NOW.
BUT THEY DON'T KNOW WHAT YOU KNOW, DOB -- THAT ZAYNE CARRICK'S ALREADY HERE. THIS IS PERFECT!
BARKEEP! TAKE THIS HATCHLING AWAY -- AND BRING ITS PARENTS!

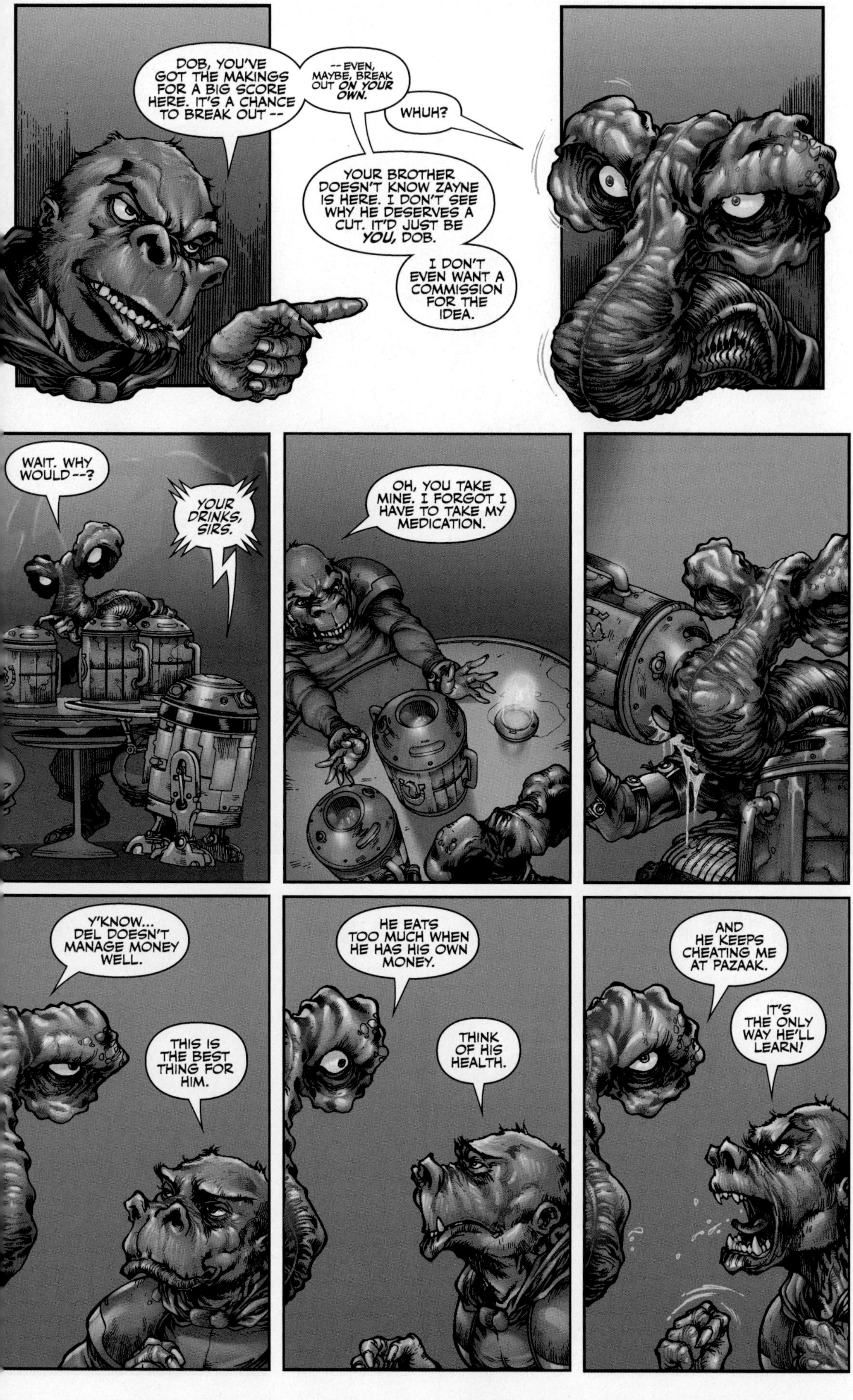
DOB, YOU'VE GOT THE MAKINGS FOR A BIG SCORE HERE. IT'S A CHANCE TO BREAK OUT --
-- EVEN, MAYBE, BREAK OUT *ON YOUR OWN.*
WHUH?
YOUR BROTHER DOESN'T KNOW ZAYNE IS HERE. I DON'T SEE WHY HE DESERVES A CUT. IT'D JUST BE *YOU,* DOB.
I DON'T EVEN WANT A COMMISSION FOR THE IDEA.
WAIT. WHY WOULD--?
YOUR DRINKS, SIRS.
OH, YOU TAKE MINE. I FORGOT I HAVE TO TAKE MY MEDICATION.
Y'KNOW... DEL DOESN'T MANAGE MONEY WELL.
THIS IS THE BEST THING FOR HIM.
HE EATS TOO MUCH WHEN HE HAS HIS OWN MONEY.
THINK OF HIS HEALTH.
AND HE KEEPS CHEATING ME AT PAZAAK.
IT'S THE ONLY WAY HE'LL LEARN!

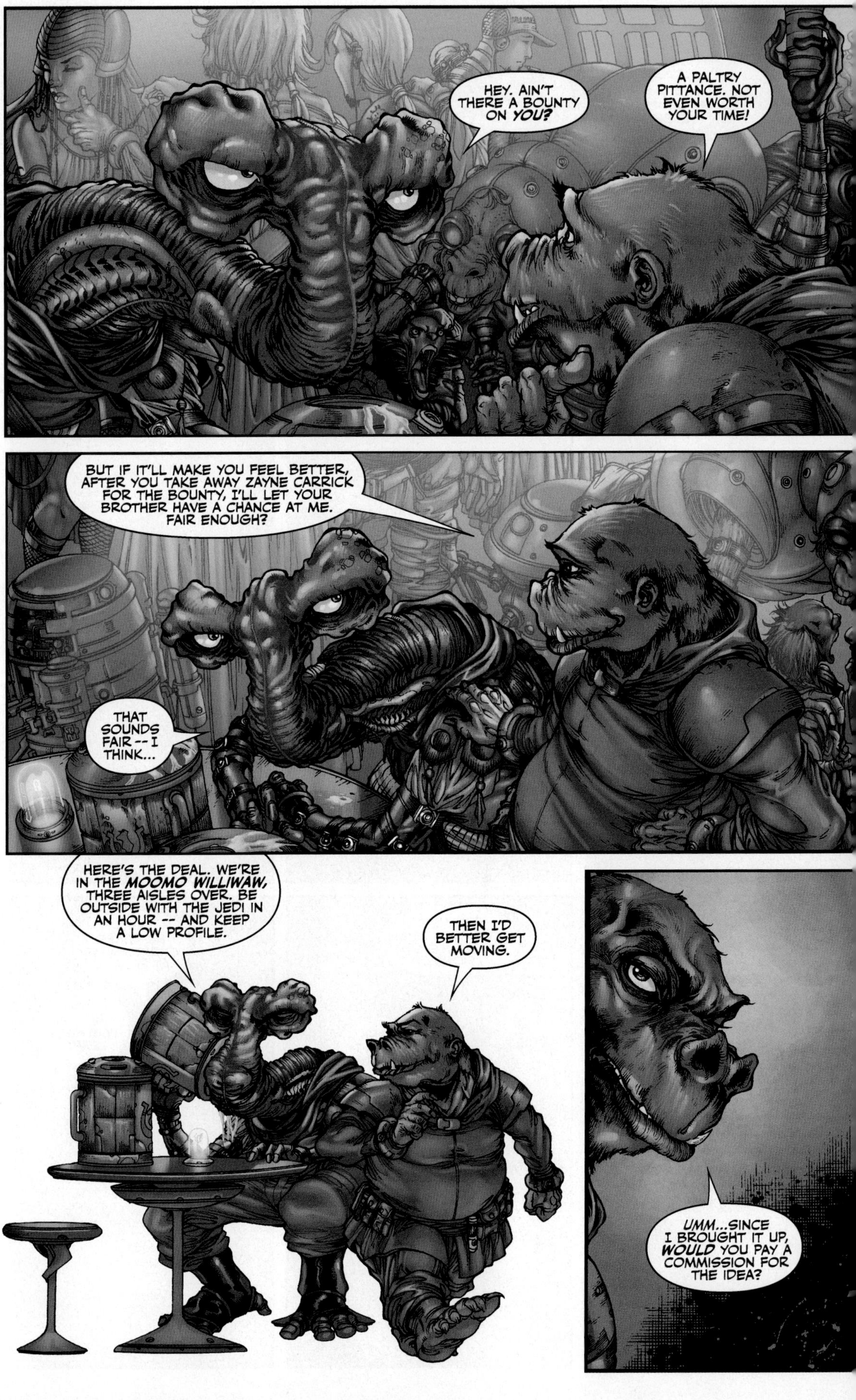
HEY. AIN'T THERE A BOUNTY ON *YOU?*
A PALTRY PITTANCE. NOT EVEN WORTH YOUR TIME!
BUT IF IT'LL MAKE YOU FEEL BETTER, AFTER YOU TAKE AWAY ZAYNE CARRICK FOR THE BOUNTY, I'LL LET YOUR BROTHER HAVE A CHANCE AT ME. FAIR ENOUGH?
THAT SOUNDS FAIR -- I THINK...
HERE'S THE DEAL. WE'RE IN THE *MOOMO WILLIWAW,* THREE AISLES OVER. BE OUTSIDE WITH THE JEDI IN AN HOUR -- AND KEEP A LOW PROFILE.
THEN I'D BETTER GET MOVING.
UMM...SINCE I BROUGHT IT UP, *WOULD* YOU PAY A COMMISSION FOR THE IDEA?

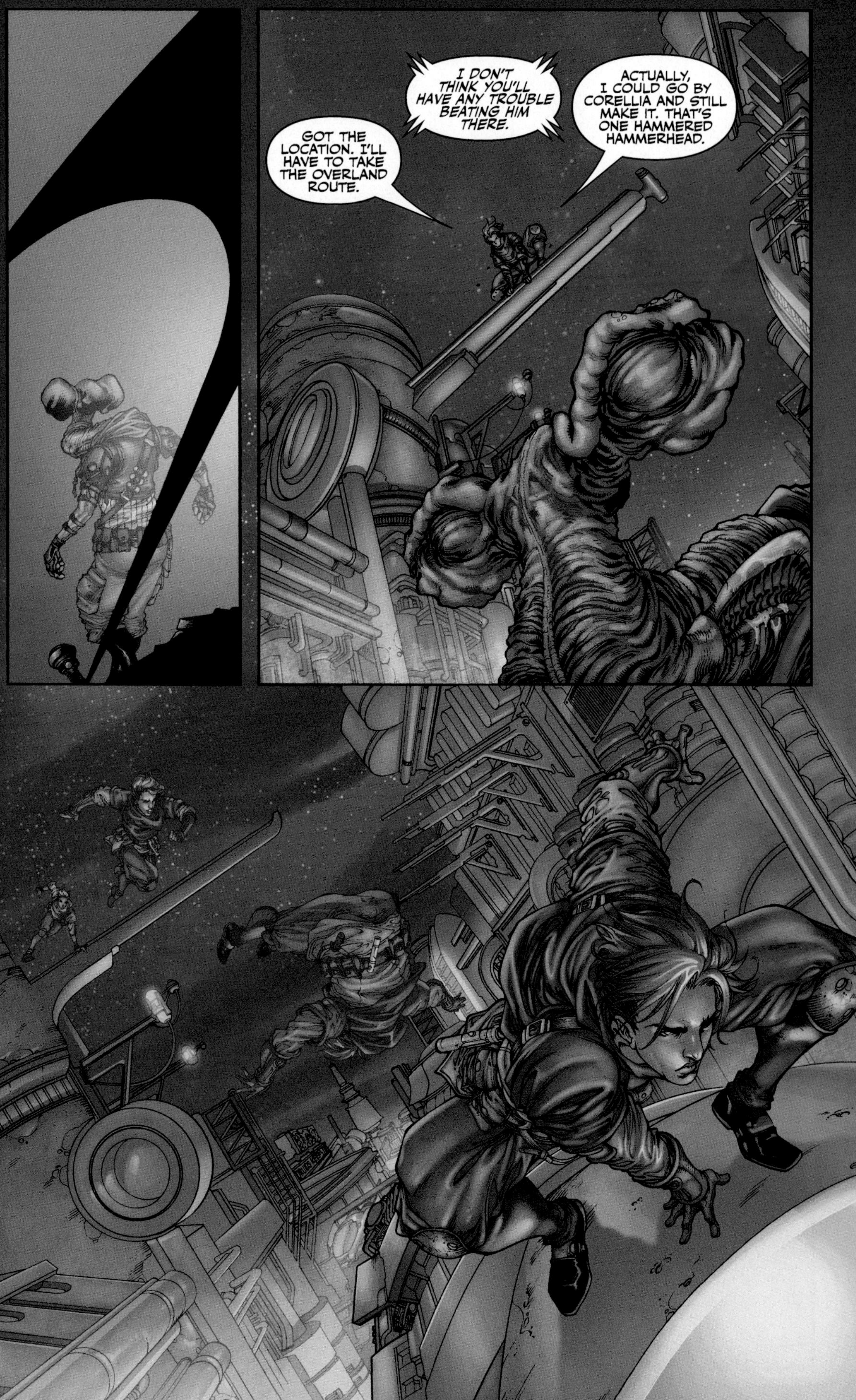
GOT THE LOCATION. I'LL HAVE TO TAKE THE OVERLAND ROUTE.
I DON'T THINK YOU'LL HAVE ANY TROUBLE BEATING HIM THERE.
ACTUALLY, I COULD GO BY CORELLIA AND STILL MAKE IT. THAT'S ONE HAMMERED HAMMERHEAD.

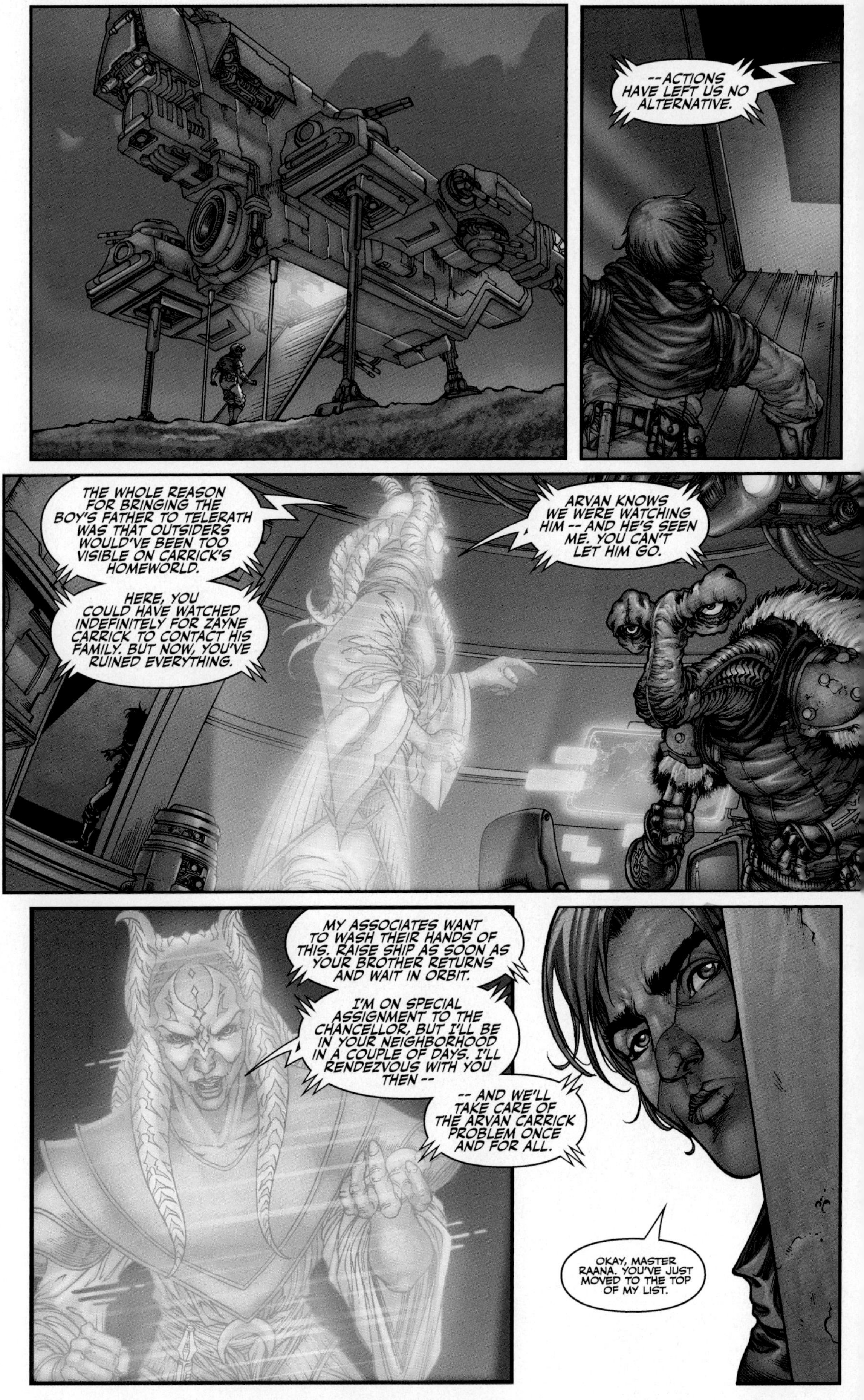
--ACTIONS HAVE LEFT US NO ALTERNATIVE.
THE WHOLE REASON FOR BRINGING THE BOY'S FATHER TO TELERATH WAS THAT OUTSIDERS WOULD'VE BEEN TOO VISIBLE ON CARRICK'S HOMEWORLD.
HERE, YOU COULD HAVE WATCHED INDEFINITELY FOR ZAYNE CARRICK TO CONTACT HIS FAMILY. BUT NOW, YOU'VE RUINED EVERYTHING.
ARVAN KNOWS WE WERE WATCHING HIM -- AND HE'S SEEN ME. YOU CAN'T LET HIM GO.
MY ASSOCIATES WANT TO WASH THEIR HANDS OF THIS. RAISE SHIP AS SOON AS YOUR BROTHER RETURNS AND WAIT IN ORBIT.
I'M ON SPECIAL ASSIGNMENT TO THE CHANCELLOR, BUT I'LL BE IN YOUR NEIGHBORHOOD IN A COUPLE OF DAYS. I'LL RENDEZVOUS WITH YOU THEN --
-- AND WE'LL TAKE CARE OF THE ARVAN CARRICK PROBLEM ONCE AND FOR ALL.
OKAY, MASTER RAANA. YOU'VE JUST MOVED TO THE TOP OF MY LIST.

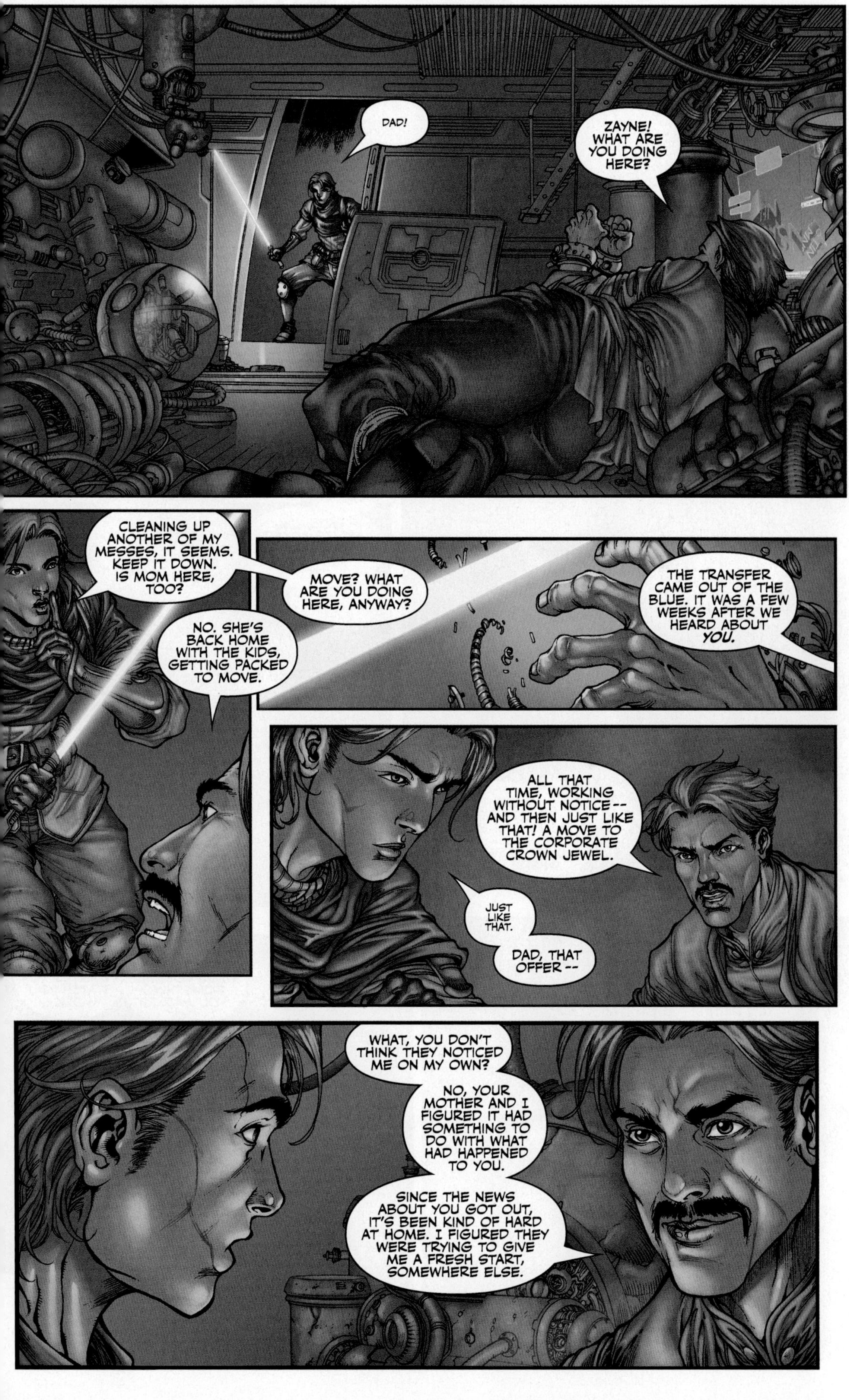
DAD!
ZAYNE! WHAT ARE YOU DOING HERE?
CLEANING UP ANOTHER OF MY MESSES, IT SEEMS. KEEP IT DOWN. IS MOM HERE, TOO?
NO. SHE'S BACK HOME WITH THE KIDS, GETTING PACKED TO MOVE.
MOVE? WHAT ARE YOU DOING HERE, ANYWAY?
THE TRANSFER CAME OUT OF THE BLUE. IT WAS A FEW WEEKS AFTER WE HEARD ABOUT *YOU.*
ALL THAT TIME, WORKING WITHOUT NOTICE-- AND THEN JUST LIKE THAT! A MOVE TO THE CORPORATE CROWN JEWEL.
JUST LIKE THAT.
DAD, THAT OFFER--
WHAT, YOU DON'T THINK THEY NOTICED ME ON MY OWN?
NO, YOUR MOTHER AND I FIGURED IT HAD SOMETHING TO DO WITH WHAT HAD HAPPENED TO YOU.
SINCE THE NEWS ABOUT YOU GOT OUT, IT'S BEEN KIND OF HARD AT HOME. I FIGURED THEY WERE TRYING TO GIVE ME A FRESH START, SOMEWHERE ELSE.

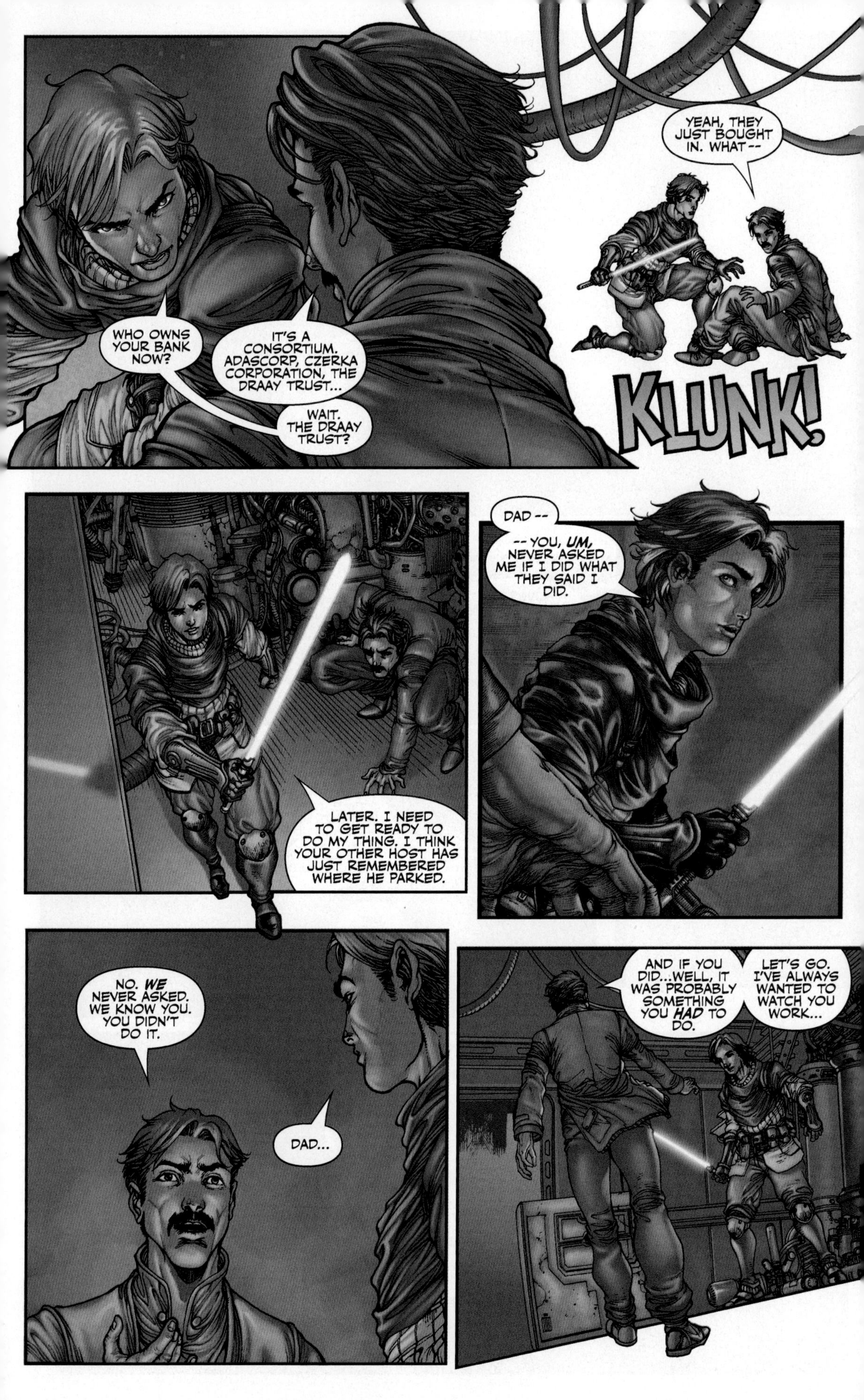
WHO OWNS YOUR BANK NOW?
IT'S A CONSORTIUM. ADASCORP, CZERKA CORPORATION, THE DRAAY TRUST...
WAIT. THE DRAAY TRUST?
YEAH, THEY JUST BOUGHT IN. WHAT --
KLUNK!
LATER. I NEED TO GET READY TO DO MY THING. I THINK YOUR OTHER HOST HAS JUST REMEMBERED WHERE HE PARKED.
DAD --
-- YOU, UM, NEVER ASKED ME IF I DID WHAT THEY SAID I DID.
NO. WE NEVER ASKED. WE KNOW YOU. YOU DIDN'T DO IT.
DAD...
AND IF YOU DID...WELL, IT WAS PROBABLY SOMETHING YOU HAD TO DO.
LET'S GO. I'VE ALWAYS WANTED TO WATCH YOU WORK...

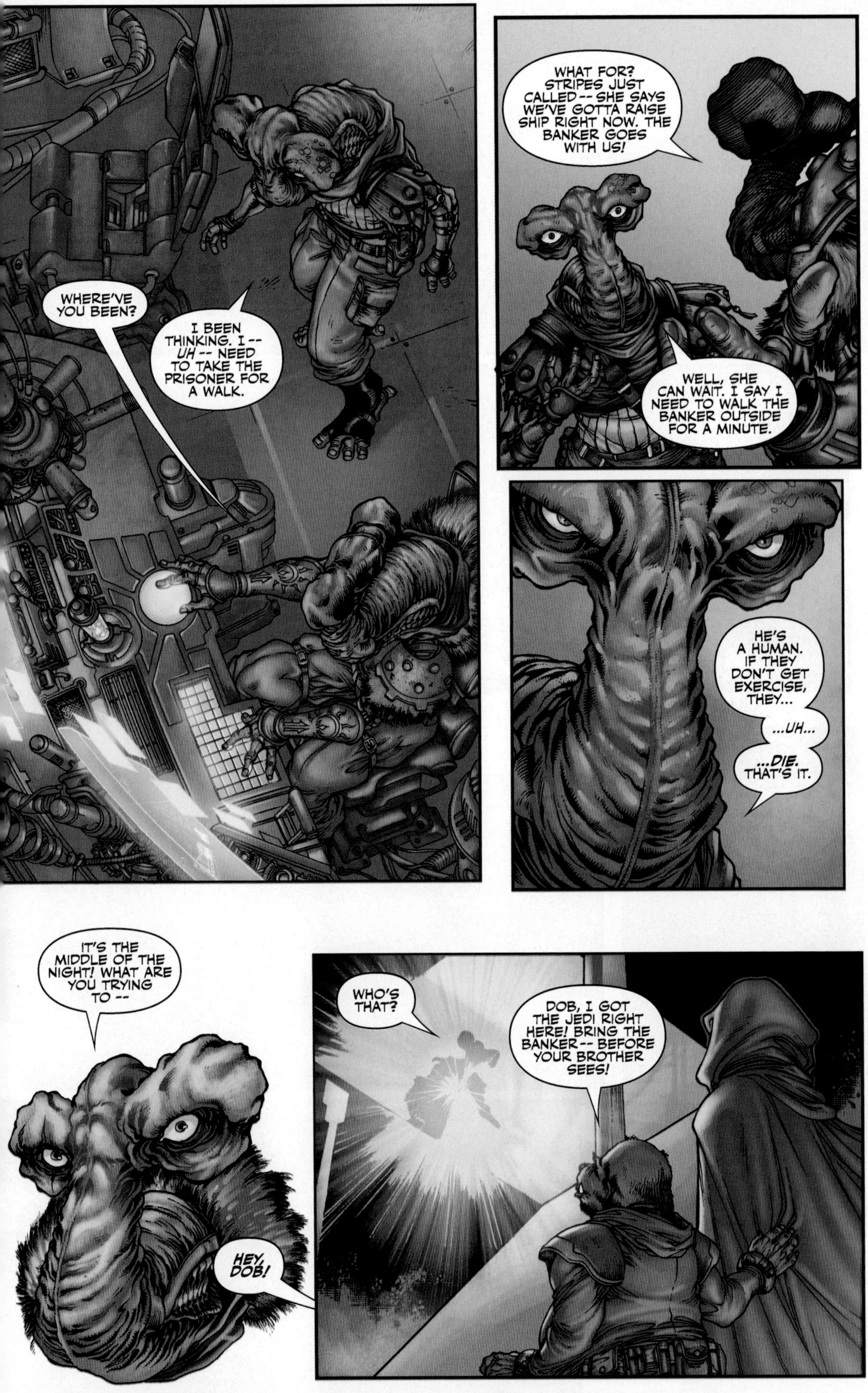
WHERE'VE YOU BEEN?
I BEEN THINKING. I -- *UH* -- NEED TO TAKE THE PRISONER FOR A WALK.
WHAT FOR? STRIPES JUST CALLED -- SHE SAYS WE'VE GOTTA RAISE SHIP RIGHT NOW. THE BANKER GOES WITH US!
WELL, SHE CAN WAIT. I SAY I NEED TO WALK THE BANKER OUTSIDE FOR A MINUTE.
HE'S A HUMAN. IF THEY DON'T GET EXERCISE, THEY...
...*UH*...
...***DIE***. THAT'S IT.
IT'S THE MIDDLE OF THE NIGHT! WHAT ARE YOU TRYING TO --
HEY, DOB!
WHO'S THAT?
DOB, I GOT THE JEDI RIGHT HERE! BRING THE BANKER -- BEFORE YOUR BROTHER SEES!

TOUCH ME AGAIN, *SNOUT,* AND I'M GONNA CHOP THAT PAW OFF AND ATTACH IT TO ELBEE.

YOU OWE ME *MUMBLECHOPS.* BESIDES, JARAEL SAID SHE'D NEVER PRETEND TO BE A JEDI AGAIN!

WHAT'S GOING ON? WHAT ARE YOU TRYING TO PULL?

NOTHIN'! IT'S JUST A COUPLE OF SPICEHEADS ACTING CRAZY. GO BACK TO SLEEP!

TELL YOU WHAT. LET ME WALK THE BANKER, AND I'LL GET RID OF THEM!

NO, YOU DON'T! WE'RE LEAVING, NOW!

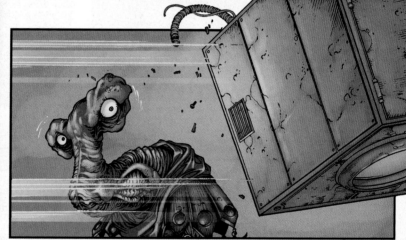

KRAK!

GAHH!

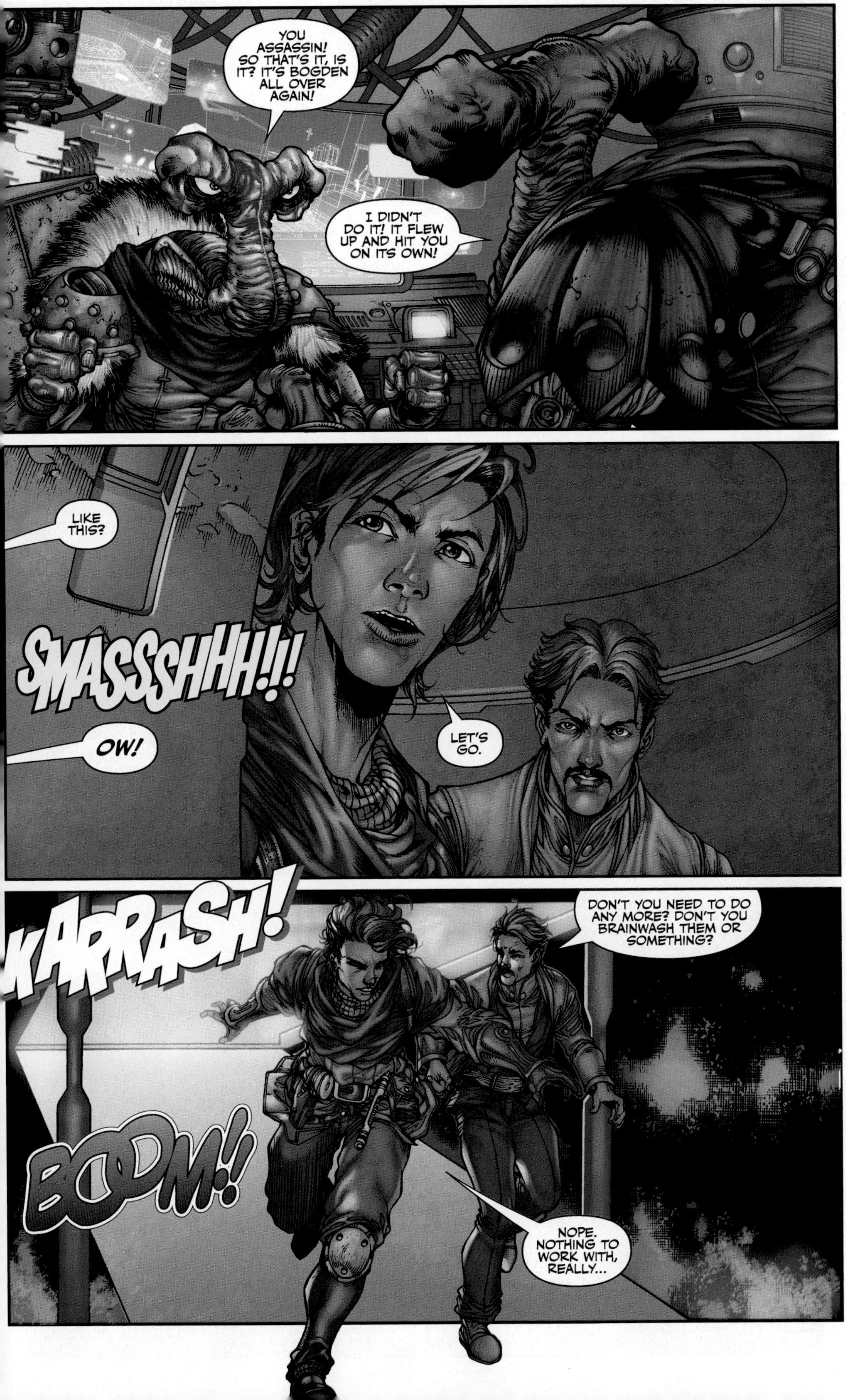
YOU ASSASSIN! SO THAT'S IT, IS IT? IT'S BOGDEN ALL OVER AGAIN!
I DIDN'T DO IT! IT FLEW UP AND HIT YOU ON ITS OWN!
LIKE THIS?
SMASSSHHH!!!
OW!
LET'S GO.
KARRASH!
BOOM!
DON'T YOU NEED TO DO ANY MORE? DON'T YOU BRAINWASH THEM OR SOMETHING?
NOPE. NOTHING TO WORK WITH, REALLY...

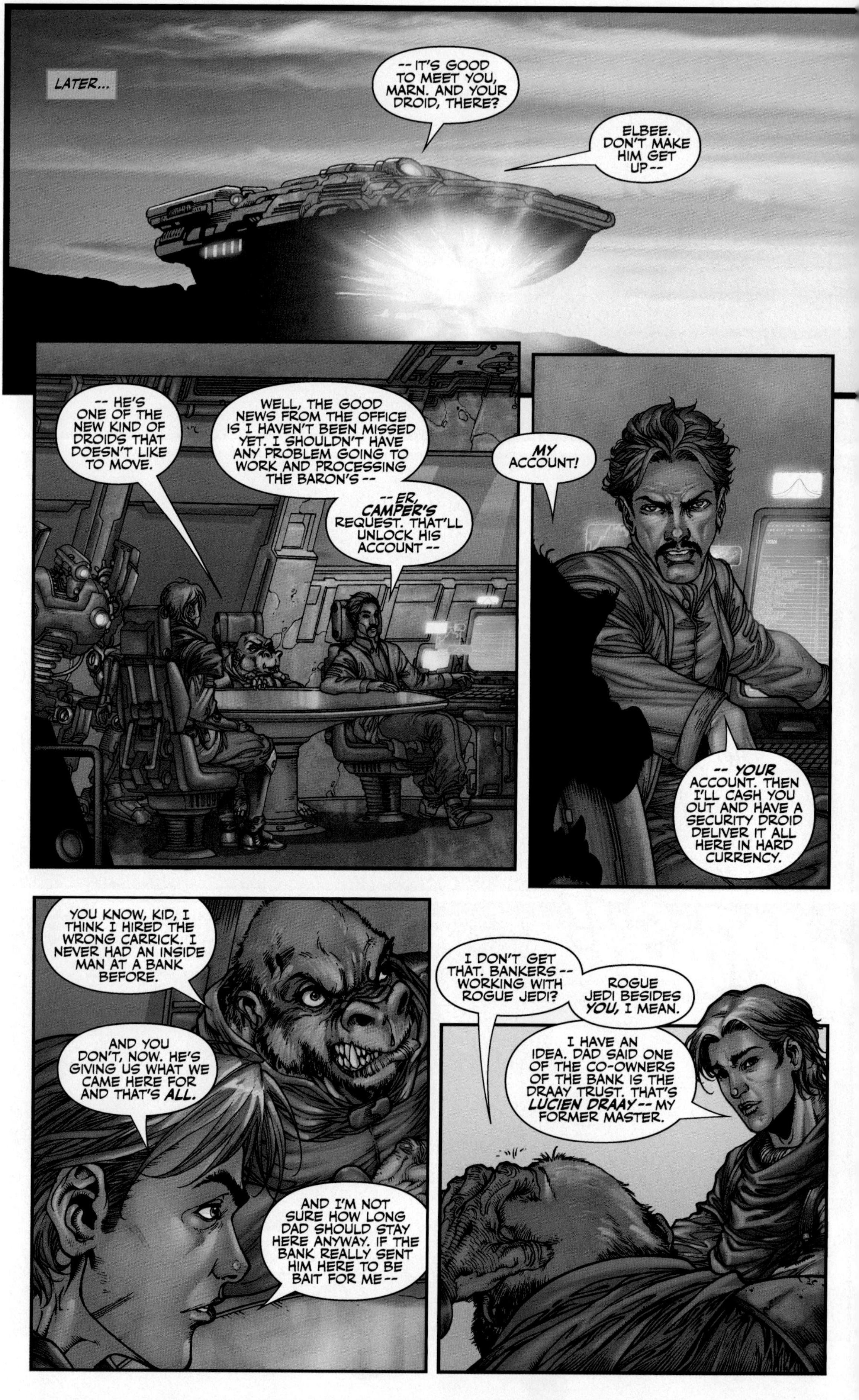
LATER...
-- IT'S GOOD TO MEET YOU, MARN. AND YOUR DROID, THERE?
ELBEE. DON'T MAKE HIM GET UP --
-- HE'S ONE OF THE NEW KIND OF DROIDS THAT DOESN'T LIKE TO MOVE.
WELL, THE GOOD NEWS FROM THE OFFICE IS I HAVEN'T BEEN MISSED YET. I SHOULDN'T HAVE ANY PROBLEM GOING TO WORK AND PROCESSING THE BARON'S --
-- ER, CAMPER'S REQUEST. THAT'LL UNLOCK HIS ACCOUNT --
MY ACCOUNT!
-- YOUR ACCOUNT. THEN I'LL CASH YOU OUT AND HAVE A SECURITY DROID DELIVER IT ALL HERE IN HARD CURRENCY.
YOU KNOW, KID, I THINK I HIRED THE WRONG CARRICK. I NEVER HAD AN INSIDE MAN AT A BANK BEFORE.
AND YOU DON'T, NOW. HE'S GIVING US WHAT WE CAME HERE FOR AND THAT'S ALL.
AND I'M NOT SURE HOW LONG DAD SHOULD STAY HERE ANYWAY. IF THE BANK REALLY SENT HIM HERE TO BE BAIT FOR ME --
I DON'T GET THAT. BANKERS -- WORKING WITH ROGUE JEDI?
ROGUE JEDI BESIDES YOU, I MEAN.
I HAVE AN IDEA. DAD SAID ONE OF THE CO-OWNERS OF THE BANK IS THE DRAAY TRUST. THAT'S LUCIEN DRAAY -- MY FORMER MASTER.

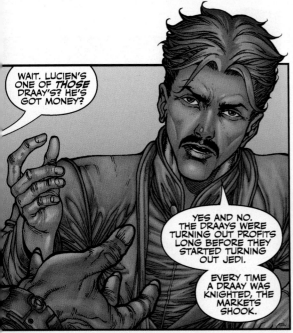

WAIT. LUCIEN'S ONE OF *THOSE* DRAAY'S? HE'S GOT MONEY?

YES AND NO. THE DRAAYS WERE TURNING OUT PROFITS LONG BEFORE THEY STARTED TURNING OUT JEDI.

EVERY TIME A DRAAY WAS KNIGHTED, THE MARKETS SHOOK.

BUT THE ORDER NEEDS RECRUITS -- AND HAVING SOME FROM THE ELITES SENDS THE MESSAGE THAT JEDI CAN COME FROM ANY WALK OF LIFE.

LUCIEN'S FATHER, *BARRISON,* HIT ON THE COMPROMISE. THE DRAAY TRUST KEEPS THE FORTUNE TOGETHER, MAKING MONEY FOR CHARITABLE CAUSES --

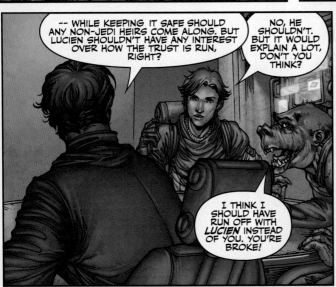

-- WHILE KEEPING IT SAFE SHOULD ANY NON-JEDI HEIRS COME ALONG. BUT LUCIEN SHOULDN'T HAVE ANY INTEREST OVER HOW THE TRUST IS RUN, RIGHT?

NO, HE SHOULDN'T. BUT IT WOULD EXPLAIN A LOT, DON'T YOU THINK?

I THINK I SHOULD HAVE RUN OFF WITH *LUCIEN* INSTEAD OF YOU. YOU'RE BROKE!

THAT REMINDS ME. NOW THAT YOU'RE GETTING ALL THIS MONEY, GRYPH --

-- PAY ME.

AHEM. YOU JUST SAID THE JEDI WEREN'T INTO THE WHOLE MATERIAL THING.

I'M A HENCHMAN, NOT A JEDI. I HENCH, YOU PAY. NOW PAY ME.

THERE'S NOTHING LEFT TO BELIEVE IN ANYMORE.

HERE, THIS AMOUNT SEEMS FAIR.

MY HAND SLIPPED! MY HAND SLIPPED!

THIS HAS ALL BEEN VERY HARD ON MY NERVES...

GRYPH!

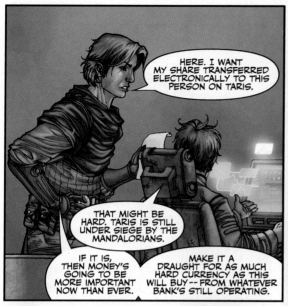

HERE. I WANT MY SHARE TRANSFERRED ELECTRONICALLY TO THIS PERSON ON TARIS.

THAT MIGHT BE HARD. TARIS IS STILL UNDER SIEGE BY THE MANDALORIANS.

IF IT IS, THEN MONEY'S GOING TO BE MORE IMPORTANT NOW THAN EVER.

MAKE IT A DRAUGHT FOR AS MUCH HARD CURRENCY AS THIS WILL BUY -- FROM WHATEVER BANK'S STILL OPERATING.

I SHOULD BE ABLE TO DO THAT. WHAT THEN?

THEN YOU NEED TO CALL YOUR MANAGEMENT AND TELL THEM YOU'VE HAD A CHANGE OF HEART -- THAT YOU WANT TO GO SOMEWHERE ELSE.

TAKE A LOOK.

THERE?!

IT'S THE ONLY WAY. I'M NOT SURE HOW FAR THIS CONSPIRACY GOES -- BUT THIS IS NEAR SOMEONE I STILL THINK I CAN TRUST.

THEY'LL HAVE A HARDER TIME MOVING AGAINST YOU THERE.

I HAVE A LOT TO DO BEFORE THIS IS OVER -- AND I NEED TO KNOW YOU'RE ALL SAFE.

I'M SORRY THIS HAS AFFECTED YOU. I KNOW IT'S NOT WHAT YOU HAD IN MIND FOR YOURSELF.

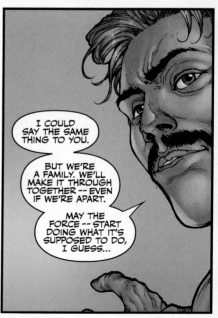

I COULD SAY THE SAME THING TO YOU.

BUT WE'RE A FAMILY. WE'LL MAKE IT THROUGH TOGETHER -- EVEN IF WE'RE APART.

MAY THE FORCE -- START DOING WHAT IT'S SUPPOSED TO DO, I GUESS...

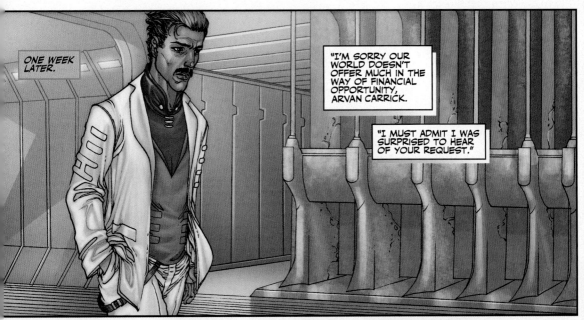

ONE WEEK LATER.

"I'M SORRY OUR WORLD DOESN'T OFFER MUCH IN THE WAY OF FINANCIAL OPPORTUNITY, ARVAN CARRICK.

"I MUST ADMIT I WAS SURPRISED TO HEAR OF YOUR REQUEST."

"TRUST MEANS A LOT IN BANKING. ZAYNE ALWAYS SPOKE OF YOU AS SOMEONE HE FELT HE COULD TRUST.

"AND WHILE HIS MOTHER AND I CAN'T EXPLAIN WHAT HE'S ACCUSED OF -- OR WHY --

" -- WE'RE AS INTERESTED IN THE SEARCH FOR HIM AS YOU ARE. AND WE'RE SURE YOU'D LIKE TO KEEP US CLOSE."

IN CASE SOMETHING HAPPENS, OF COURSE.

OF COURSE.

EVEN THE JEDI ACADEMY OF DANTOOINE HAS FINANCES TO MANAGE.

VANDAR TOKARE IS HONORED BY YOUR PRESENCE. YOU AND YOUR FAMILY ARE WELCOME HERE -- FOR AS LONG AS YOU LIKE.

THE END

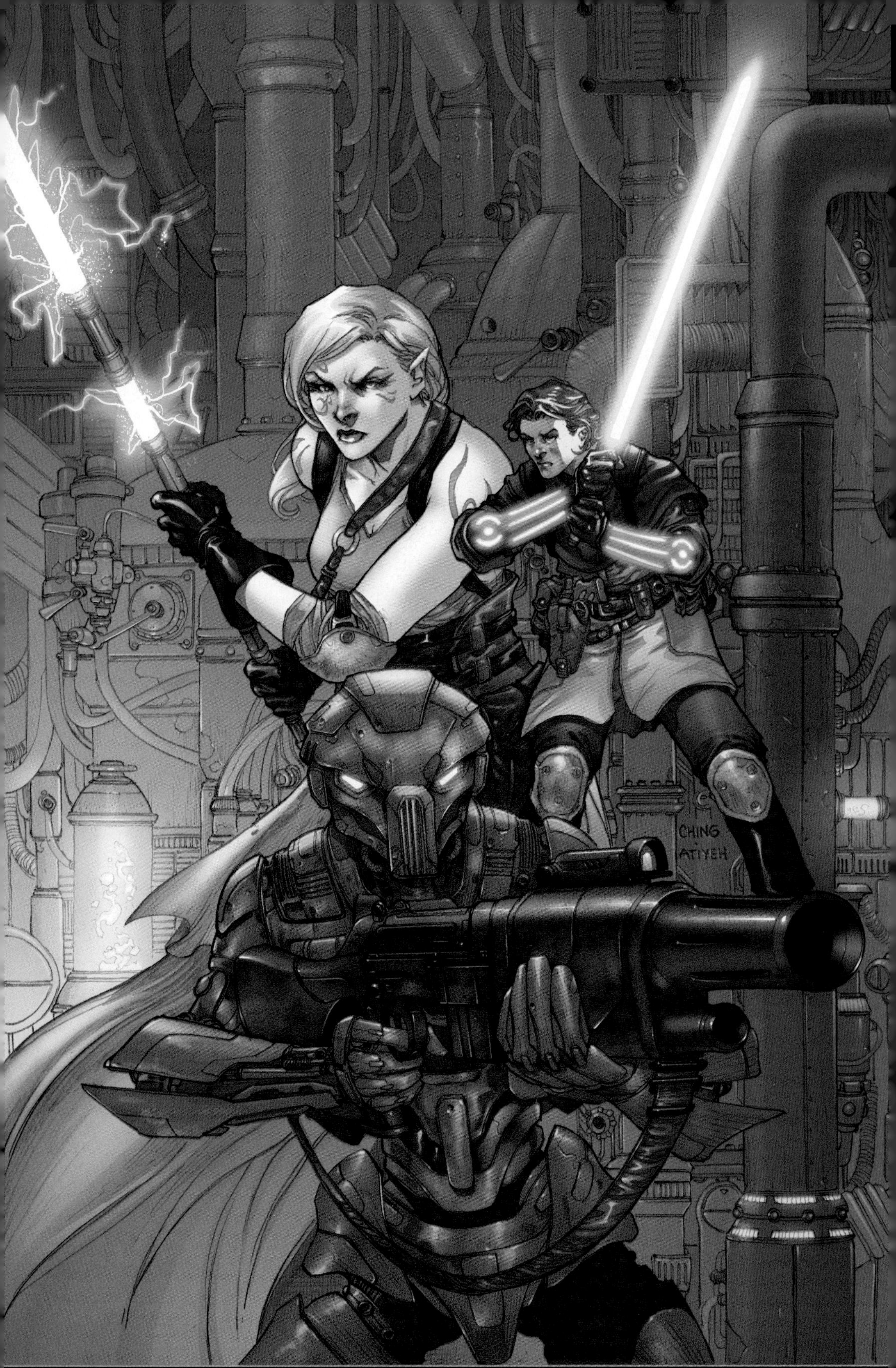
CHING
ATIYEH

STAR WARS: KNIGHTS OF THE OLD REPUBLIC #13 — "DAYS OF FEAR, PART 1"

WRITER: JOHN JACKSON MILLER • ARTIST: DUSTIN WEAVER • COLORIST: MICHAEL ATIYEH • LETTERER: MICHAEL HEISLER
ASSISTANT EDITOR: DAVE MARSHALL • EDITOR: JEREMY BARLOW • COVER ARTISTS: BRIAN CHING & MICHAEL ATIYEH

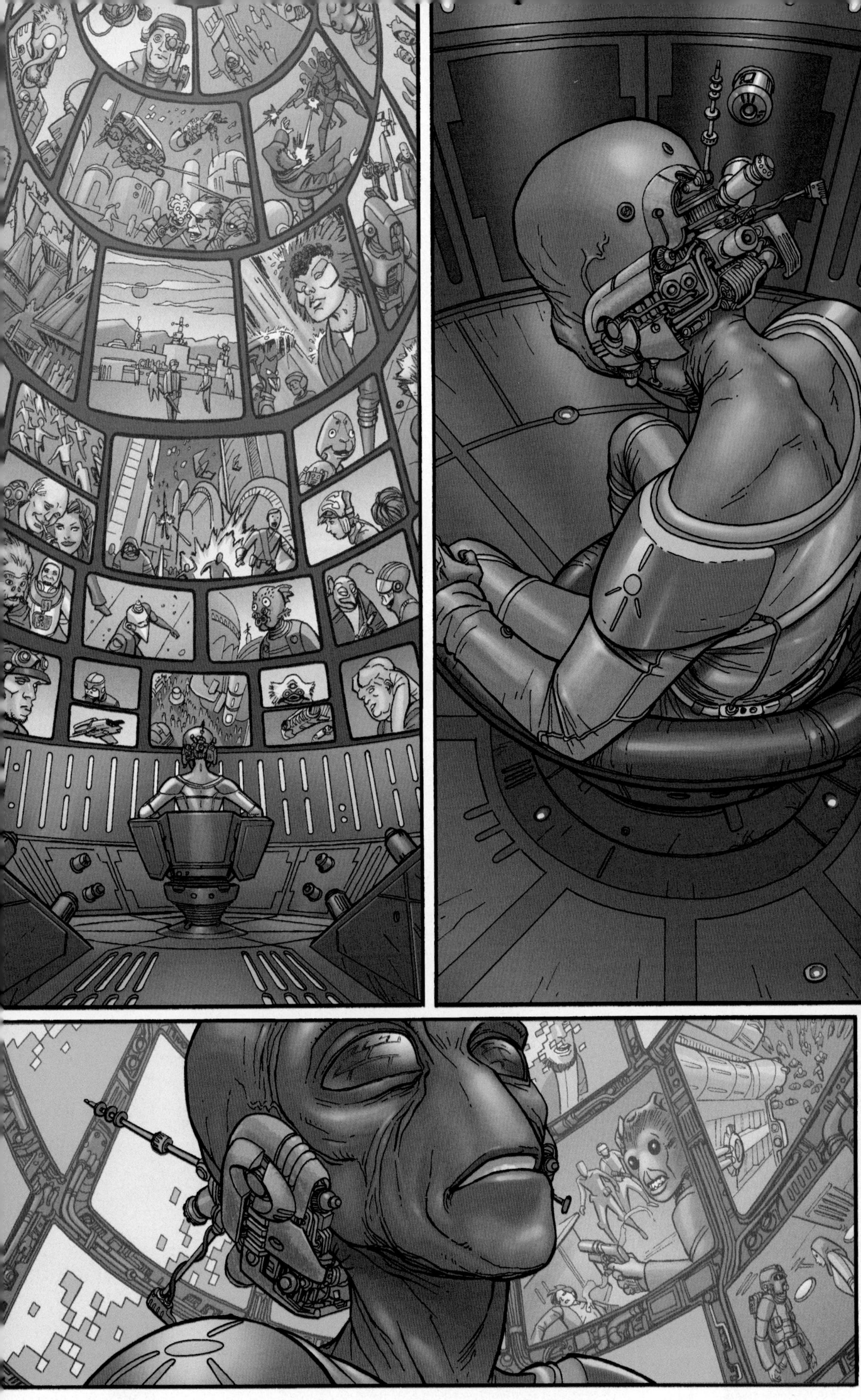

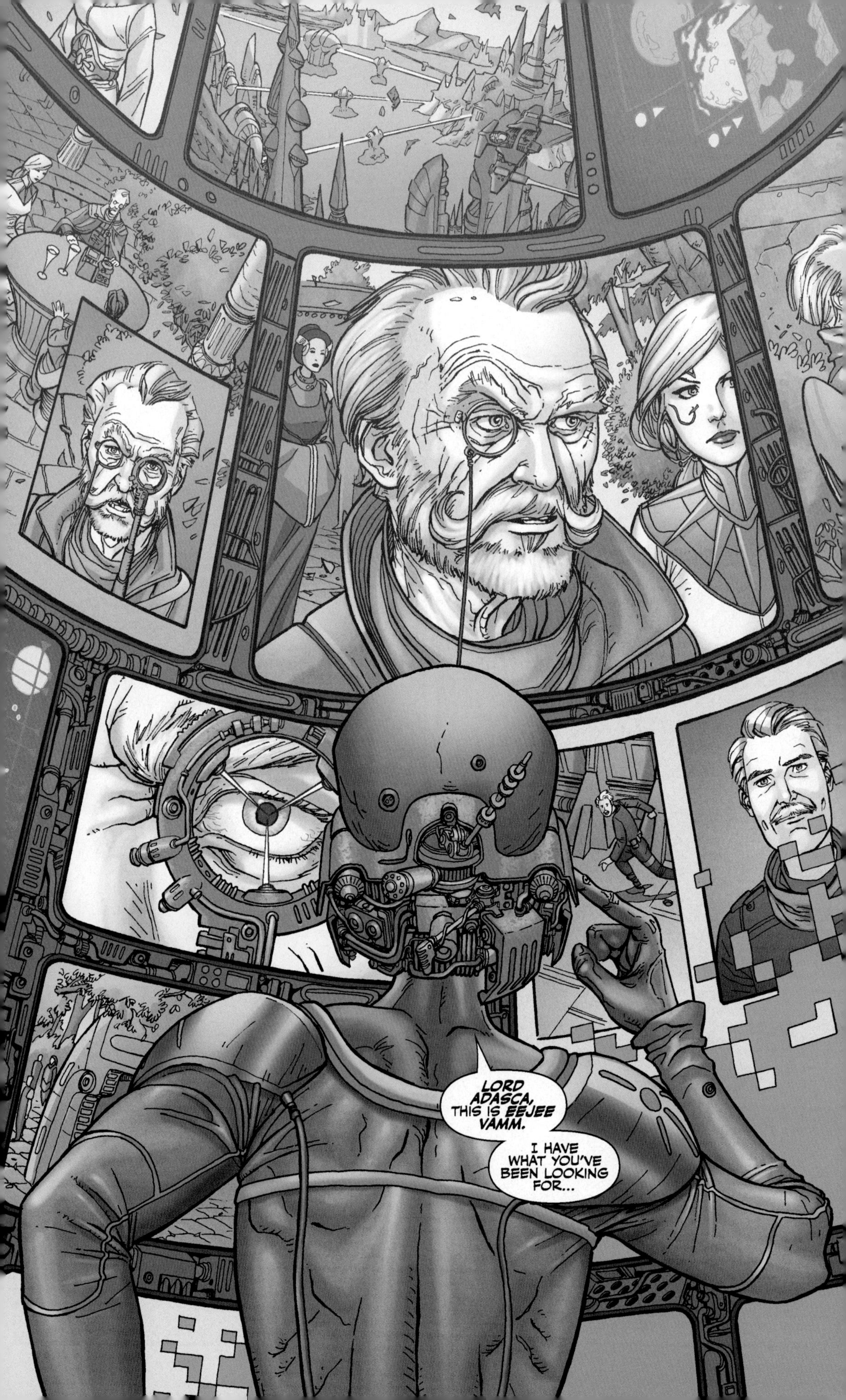
LORD ADASCA, THIS IS EEJEE VAMM.
I HAVE WHAT YOU'VE BEEN LOOKING FOR...

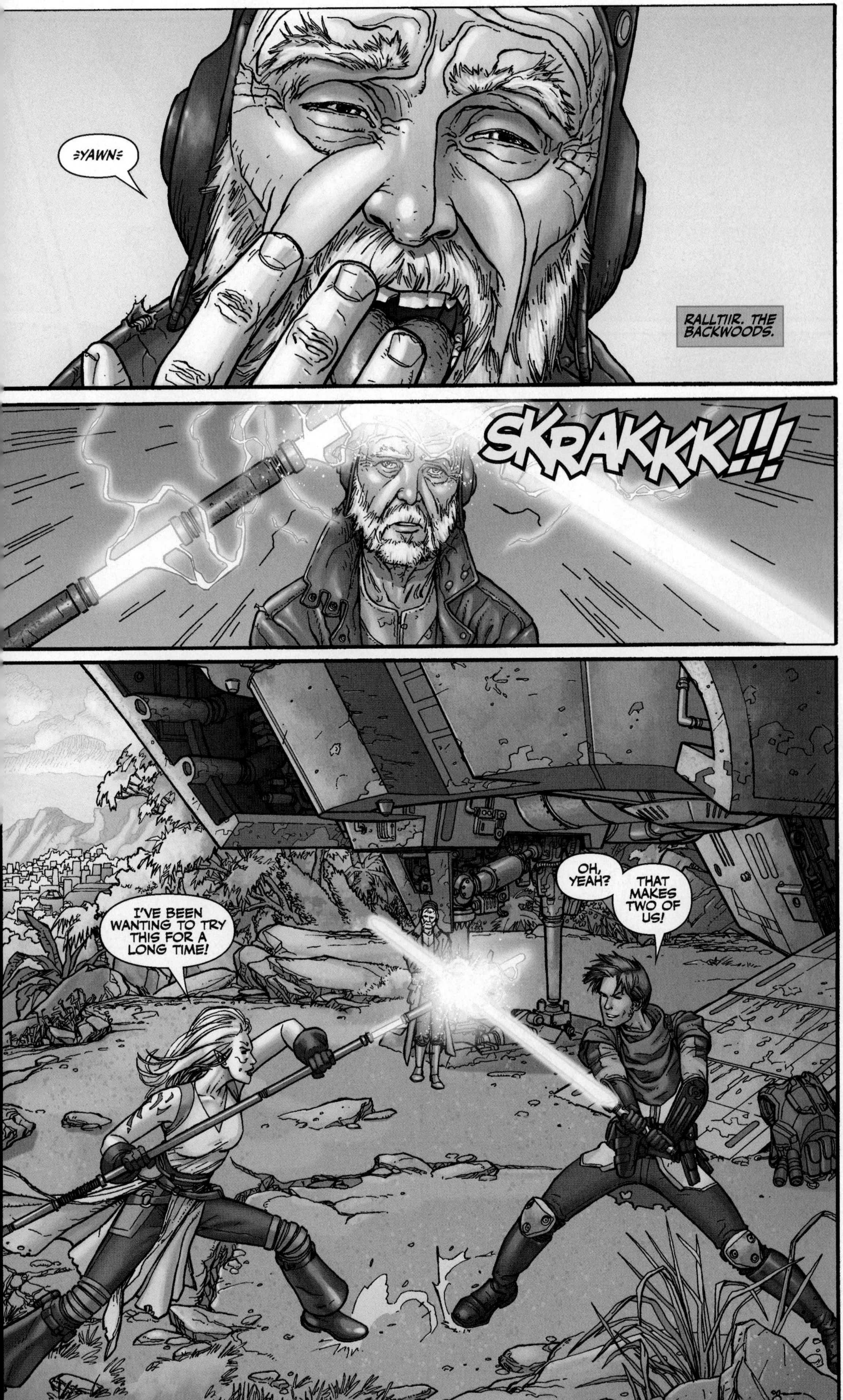

=YAWN=
RALLTIIR. THE BACKWOODS.
SKRAKKK!!!
I'VE BEEN WANTING TO TRY THIS FOR A LONG TIME!
OH, YEAH?
THAT MAKES TWO OF US!

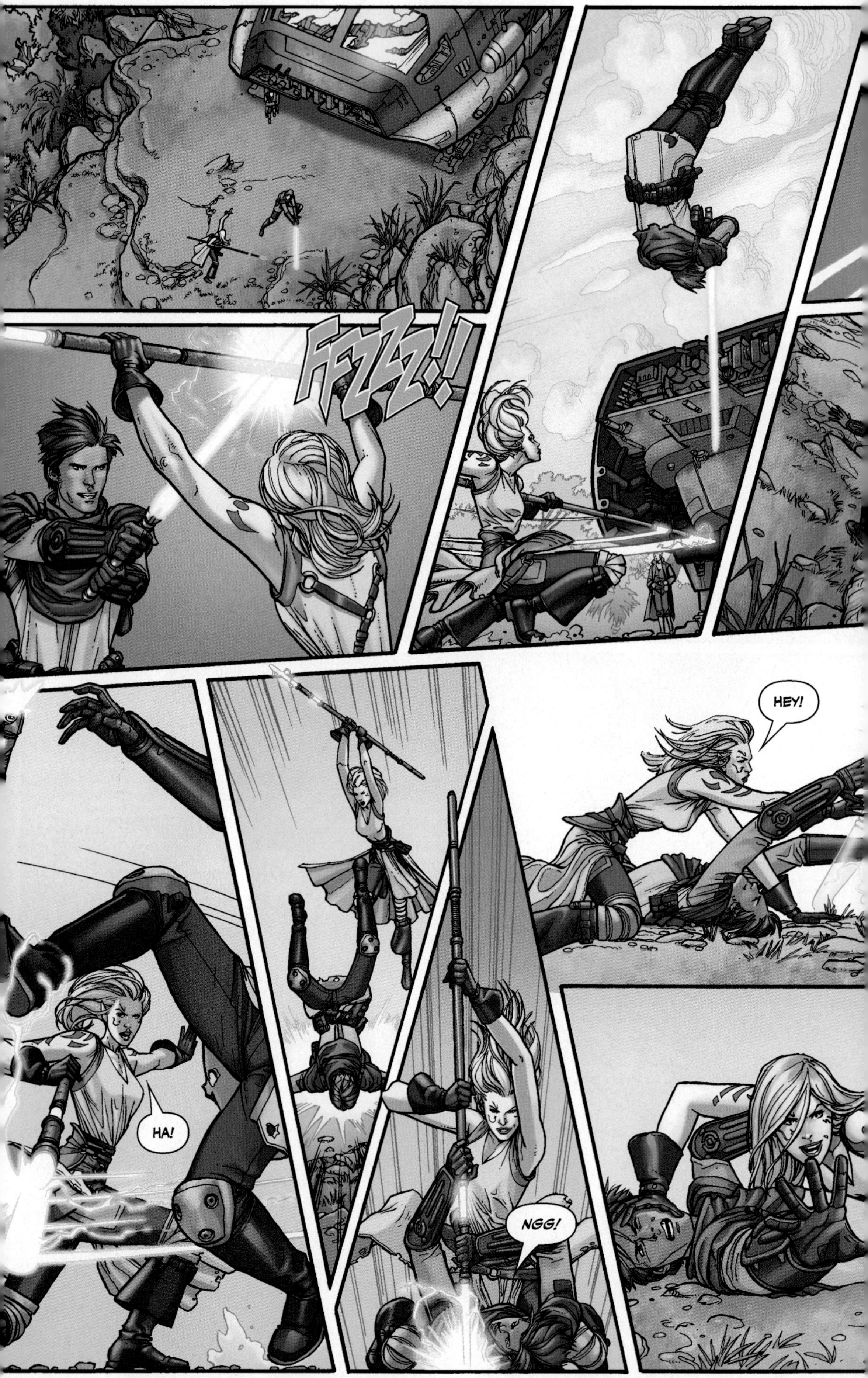
FFZZZ!!
HEY!
HA!
NGG!

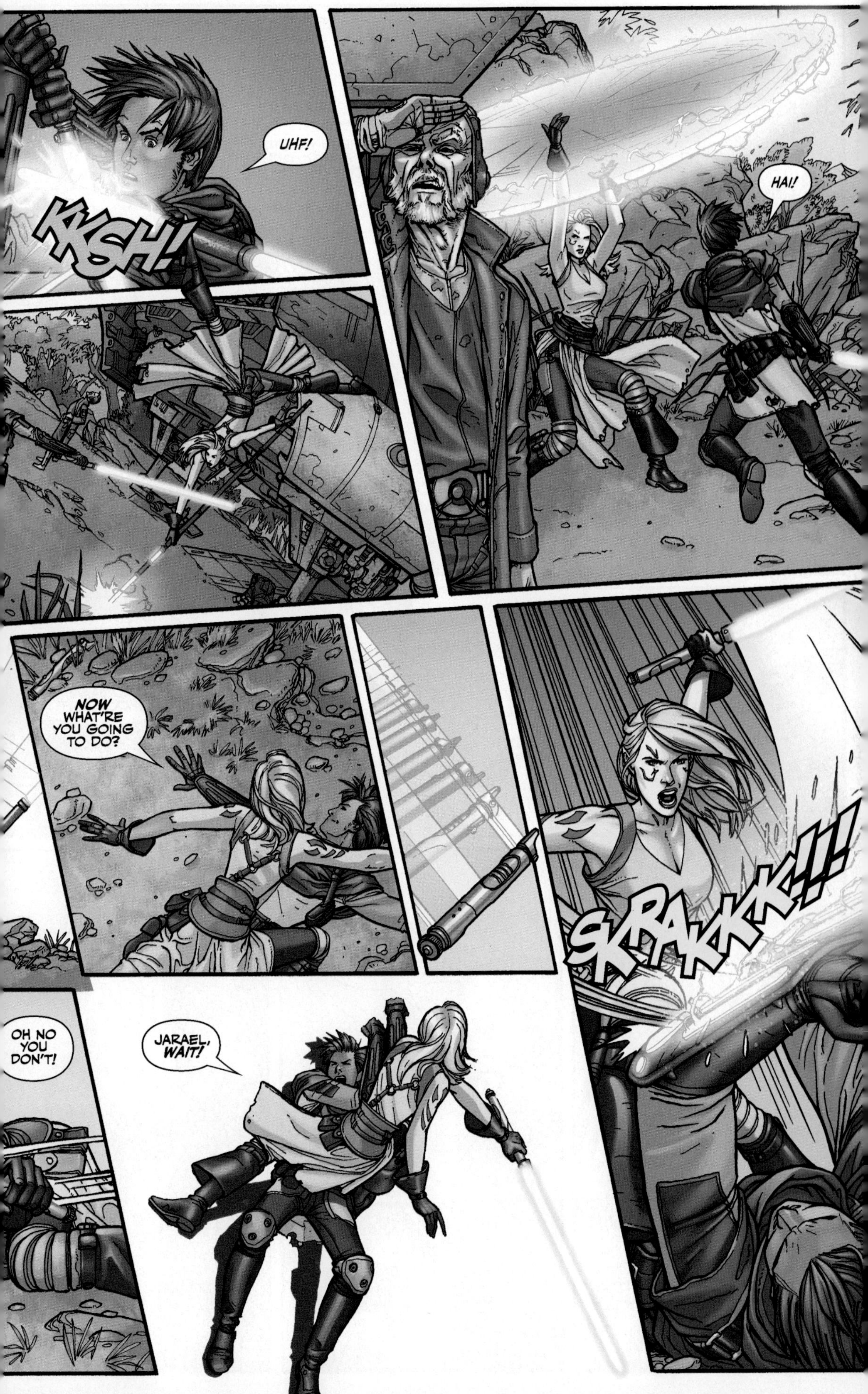
UHF!
KKSH!
HAI!
NOW WHAT'RE YOU GOING TO DO?
SKRAKKK!!!
OH NO YOU DON'T!
JARAEL, WAIT!

I STILL HAVE A HAND!

WHAT ARE THESE AGAIN?

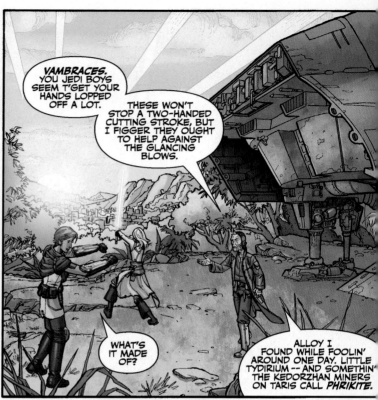

VAMBRACES. YOU JEDI BOYS SEEM T'GET YOUR HANDS LOPPED OFF A LOT.

THESE WON'T STOP A TWO-HANDED CUTTING STROKE, BUT I FIGGER THEY OUGHT TO HELP AGAINST THE GLANCING BLOWS.

WHAT'S IT MADE OF?

ALLOY I FOUND WHILE FOOLIN' AROUND ONE DAY. LITTLE TYDIRIUM -- AND SOMETHIN' THE KEDORZHAN MINERS ON TARIS CALL PHRIKITE.

USED T'TRADE WITH 'EM WHEN THEY'D FIND SOME. WASN'T OFTEN. TOOK YEARS TO GET ENOUGH FOR WHAT'S IN THOSE -- AND JARAEL'S SHOCKSTAFF.

BUT IT STOPS LIGHTSABERS. DO YOU KNOW WHAT THIS COULD BE WORTH?

YUP. AND THAT'S WHY IT STAYS RIGHT UP HERE. ONLY I KNOW HOW--

-- HOW --

-- WHAT WERE WE TALKIN' ABOUT?

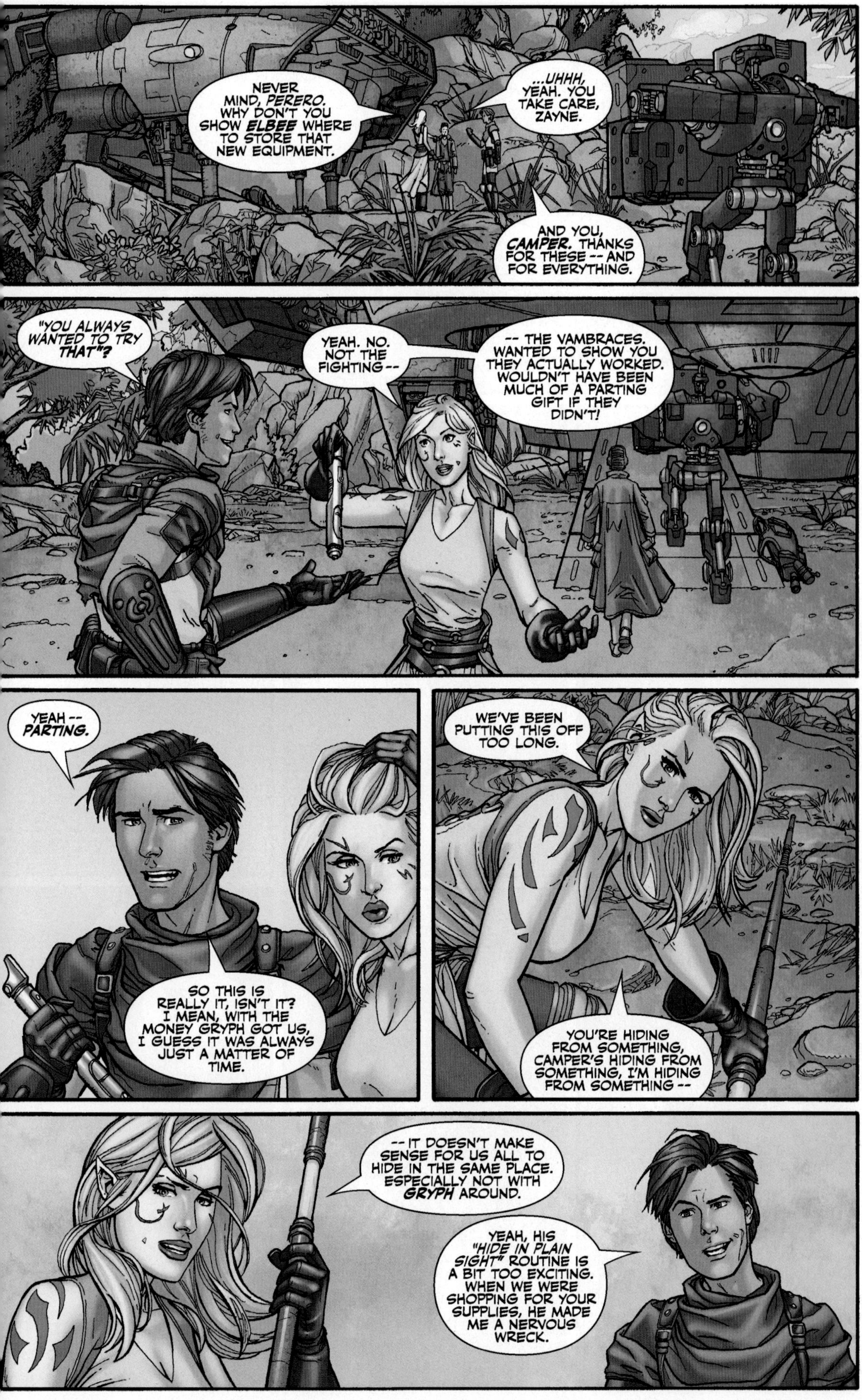
NEVER MIND, PERERO. WHY DON'T YOU SHOW ELBEE WHERE TO STORE THAT NEW EQUIPMENT.
...UHHH, YEAH. YOU TAKE CARE, ZAYNE.
AND YOU, CAMPER. THANKS FOR THESE -- AND FOR EVERYTHING.
"YOU ALWAYS WANTED TO TRY THAT"?
YEAH. NO. NOT THE FIGHTING --
-- THE VAMBRACES. WANTED TO SHOW YOU THEY ACTUALLY WORKED. WOULDN'T HAVE BEEN MUCH OF A PARTING GIFT IF THEY DIDN'T!
YEAH -- PARTING.
SO THIS IS REALLY IT, ISN'T IT? I MEAN, WITH THE MONEY GRYPH GOT US, I GUESS IT WAS ALWAYS JUST A MATTER OF TIME.
WE'VE BEEN PUTTING THIS OFF TOO LONG.
YOU'RE HIDING FROM SOMETHING, CAMPER'S HIDING FROM SOMETHING, I'M HIDING FROM SOMETHING --
-- IT DOESN'T MAKE SENSE FOR US ALL TO HIDE IN THE SAME PLACE. ESPECIALLY NOT WITH GRYPH AROUND.
YEAH, HIS "HIDE IN PLAIN SIGHT" ROUTINE IS A BIT TOO EXCITING. WHEN WE WERE SHOPPING FOR YOUR SUPPLIES, HE MADE ME A NERVOUS WRECK.

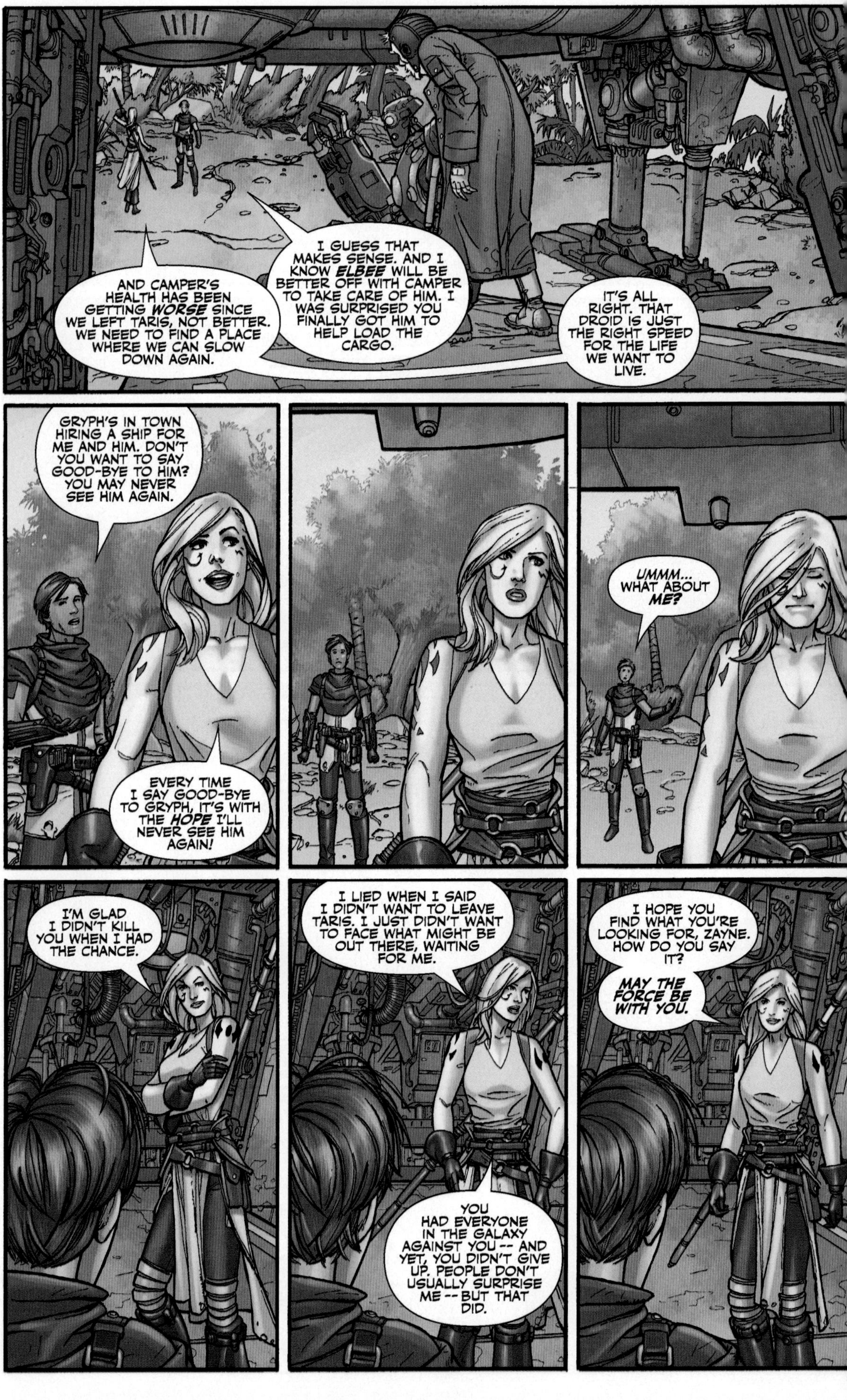
AND CAMPER'S HEALTH HAS BEEN GETTING *WORSE* SINCE WE LEFT TARIS, NOT BETTER. WE NEED TO FIND A PLACE WHERE WE CAN SLOW DOWN AGAIN.
I GUESS THAT MAKES SENSE. AND I KNOW *ELBEE* WILL BE BETTER OFF WITH CAMPER TO TAKE CARE OF HIM. I WAS SURPRISED YOU FINALLY GOT HIM TO HELP LOAD THE CARGO.
IT'S ALL RIGHT. THAT DROID IS JUST THE RIGHT SPEED FOR THE LIFE WE WANT TO LIVE.
GRYPH'S IN TOWN HIRING A SHIP FOR ME AND HIM. DON'T YOU WANT TO SAY GOOD-BYE TO HIM? YOU MAY NEVER SEE HIM AGAIN.
EVERY TIME I SAY GOOD-BYE TO GRYPH, IT'S WITH THE *HOPE* I'LL NEVER SEE HIM AGAIN!
UMMM... WHAT ABOUT ***ME?***
I'M GLAD I DIDN'T KILL YOU WHEN I HAD THE CHANCE.
I LIED WHEN I SAID I DIDN'T WANT TO LEAVE TARIS. I JUST DIDN'T WANT TO FACE WHAT MIGHT BE OUT THERE, WAITING FOR ME.
YOU HAD EVERYONE IN THE GALAXY AGAINST YOU -- AND YET, YOU DIDN'T GIVE UP. PEOPLE DON'T USUALLY SURPRISE ME -- BUT THAT DID.
I HOPE YOU FIND WHAT YOU'RE LOOKING FOR, ZAYNE. HOW DO YOU SAY IT?
MAY THE FORCE BE WITH YOU.

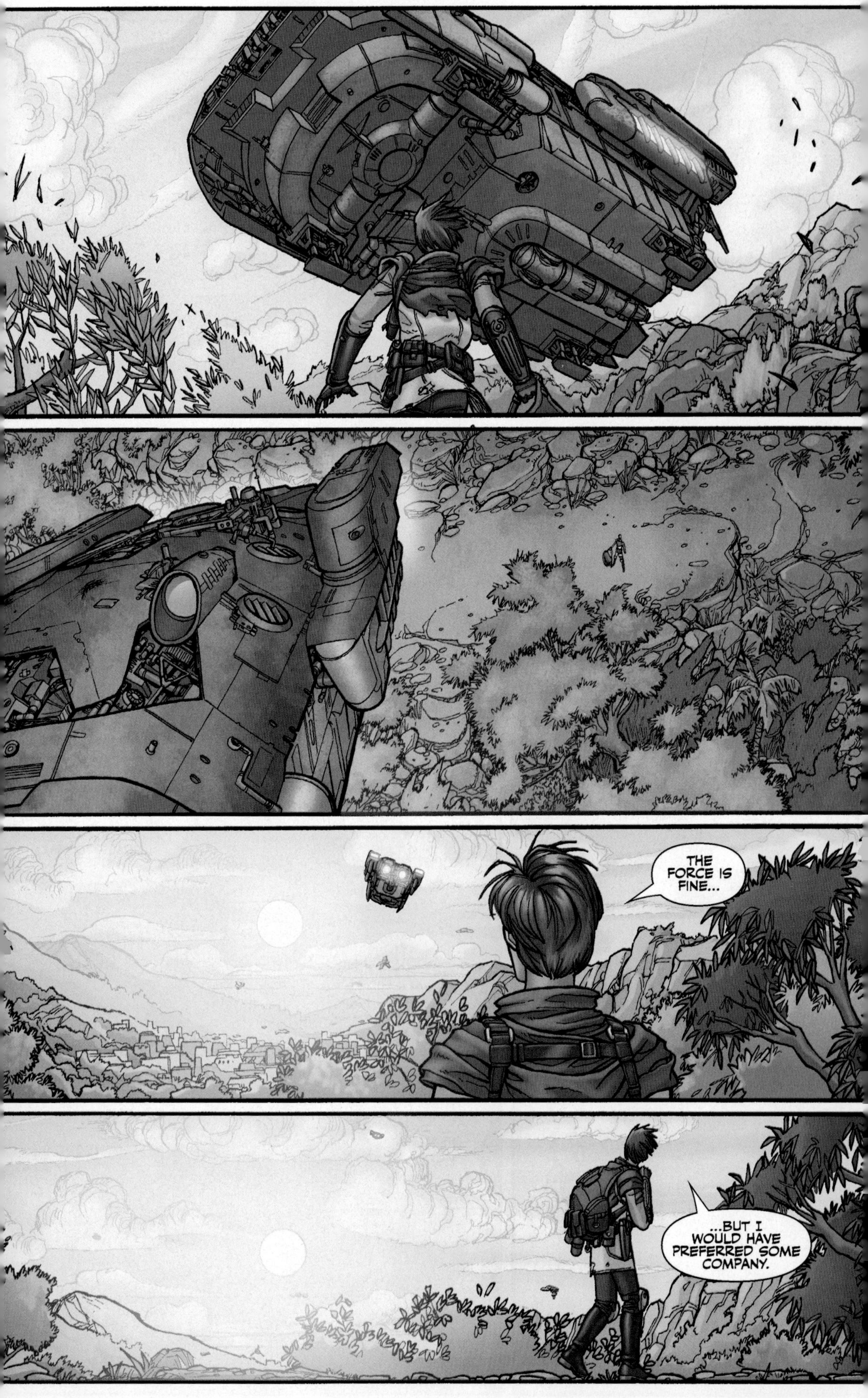
THE FORCE IS FINE...
...BUT I WOULD HAVE PREFERRED SOME COMPANY.

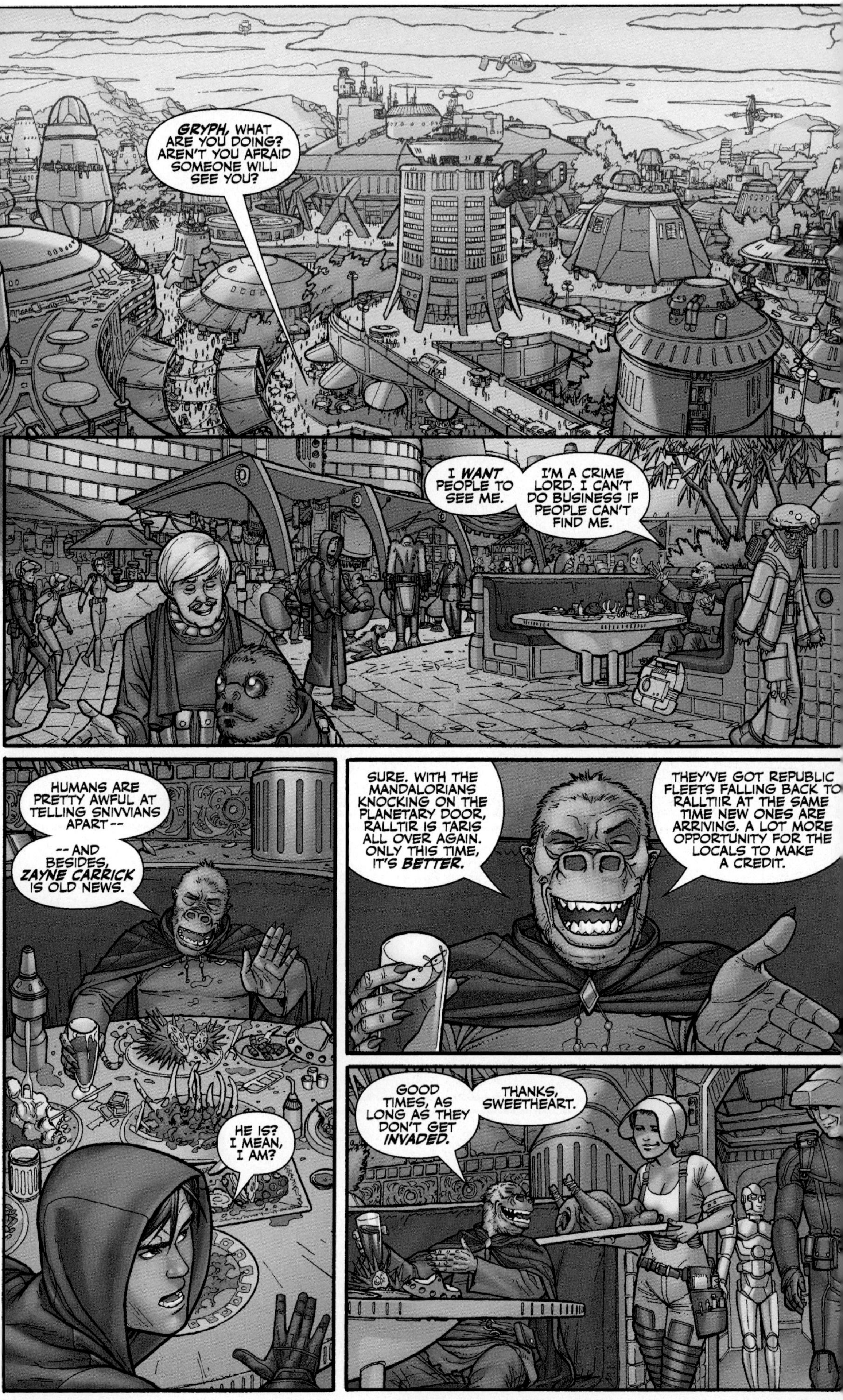
GRYPH, WHAT ARE YOU DOING? AREN'T YOU AFRAID SOMEONE WILL SEE YOU?
I WANT PEOPLE TO SEE ME.
I'M A CRIME LORD. I CAN'T DO BUSINESS IF PEOPLE CAN'T FIND ME.
HUMANS ARE PRETTY AWFUL AT TELLING SNIVVIANS APART --
-- AND BESIDES, ZAYNE CARRICK IS OLD NEWS.
HE IS? I MEAN, I AM?
SURE. WITH THE MANDALORIANS KNOCKING ON THE PLANETARY DOOR, RALLTIR IS TARIS ALL OVER AGAIN. ONLY THIS TIME, IT'S BETTER.
THEY'VE GOT REPUBLIC FLEETS FALLING BACK TO RALLTIIR AT THE SAME TIME NEW ONES ARE ARRIVING. A LOT MORE OPPORTUNITY FOR THE LOCALS TO MAKE A CREDIT.
GOOD TIMES, AS LONG AS THEY DON'T GET INVADED.
THANKS, SWEETHEART.

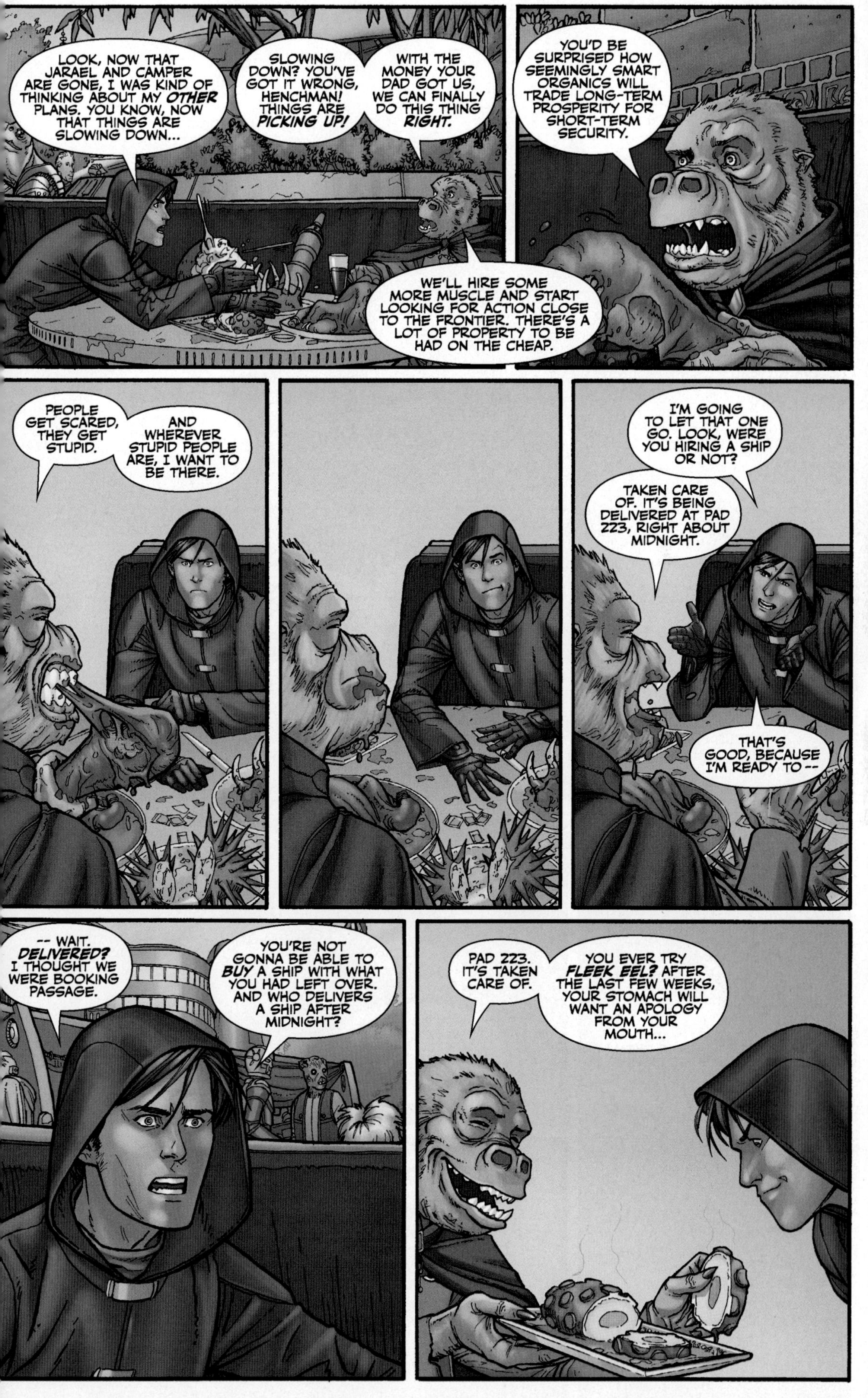
LOOK, NOW THAT JARAEL AND CAMPER ARE GONE, I WAS KIND OF THINKING ABOUT MY OTHER PLANS. YOU KNOW, NOW THAT THINGS ARE SLOWING DOWN...
SLOWING DOWN? YOU'VE GOT IT WRONG, HENCHMAN! THINGS ARE PICKING UP!
WITH THE MONEY YOUR DAD GOT US, WE CAN FINALLY DO THIS THING RIGHT.
WE'LL HIRE SOME MORE MUSCLE AND START LOOKING FOR ACTION CLOSE TO THE FRONTIER. THERE'S A LOT OF PROPERTY TO BE HAD ON THE CHEAP.
YOU'D BE SURPRISED HOW SEEMINGLY SMART ORGANICS WILL TRADE LONG-TERM PROSPERITY FOR SHORT-TERM SECURITY.
PEOPLE GET SCARED, THEY GET STUPID.
AND WHEREVER STUPID PEOPLE ARE, I WANT TO BE THERE.
I'M GOING TO LET THAT ONE GO. LOOK, WERE YOU HIRING A SHIP OR NOT?
TAKEN CARE OF. IT'S BEING DELIVERED AT PAD 223, RIGHT ABOUT MIDNIGHT.
THAT'S GOOD, BECAUSE I'M READY TO --
-- WAIT. DELIVERED? I THOUGHT WE WERE BOOKING PASSAGE.
YOU'RE NOT GONNA BE ABLE TO BUY A SHIP WITH WHAT YOU HAD LEFT OVER. AND WHO DELIVERS A SHIP AFTER MIDNIGHT?
PAD 223. IT'S TAKEN CARE OF.
YOU EVER TRY FLEEK EEL? AFTER THE LAST FEW WEEKS, YOUR STOMACH WILL WANT AN APOLOGY FROM YOUR MOUTH...

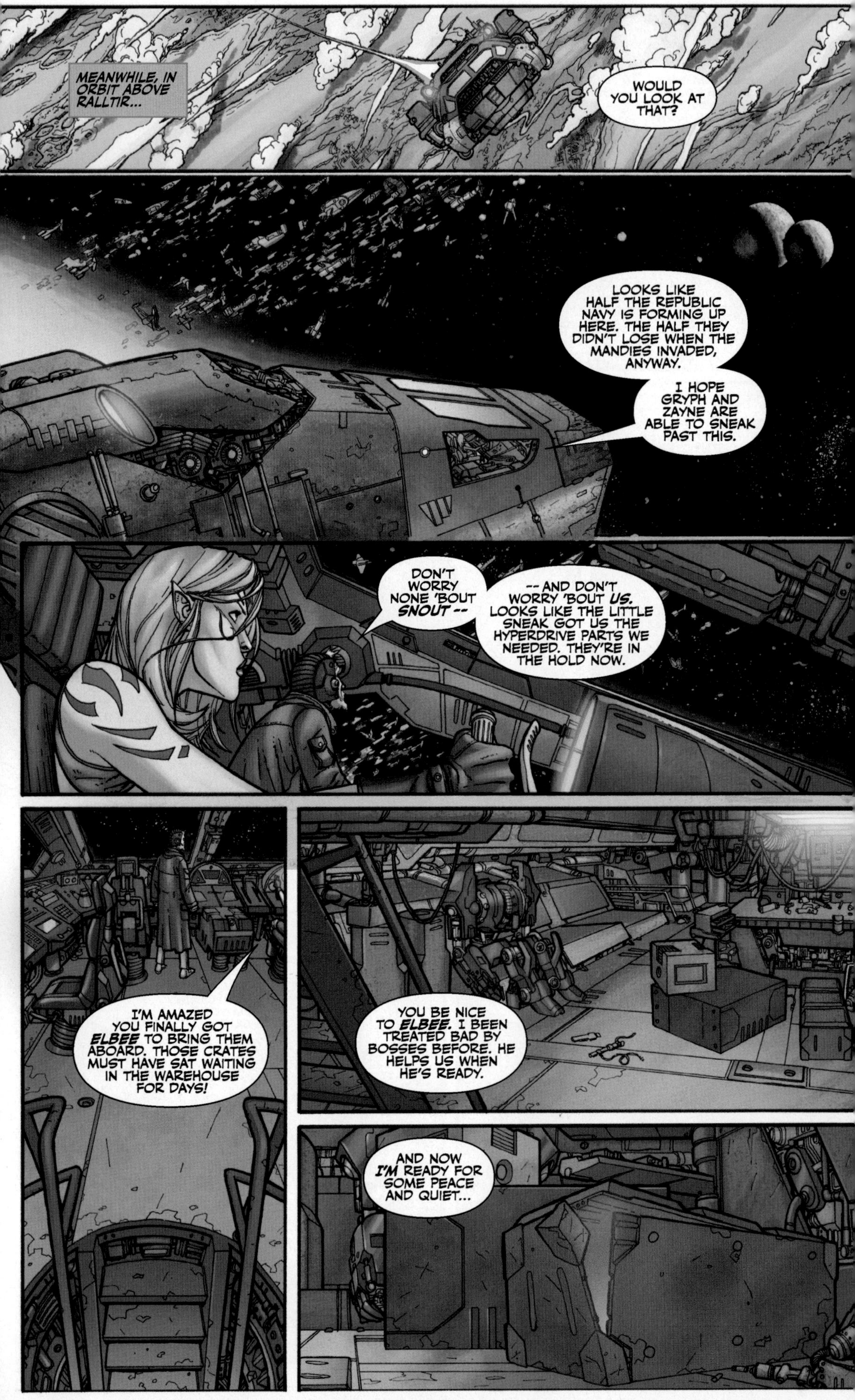
MEANWHILE, IN ORBIT ABOVE RALLTIR...
WOULD YOU LOOK AT THAT?
LOOKS LIKE HALF THE REPUBLIC NAVY IS FORMING UP HERE. THE HALF THEY DIDN'T LOSE WHEN THE MANDIES INVADED, ANYWAY.
I HOPE GRYPH AND ZAYNE ARE ABLE TO SNEAK PAST THIS.
DON'T WORRY NONE 'BOUT SNOUT --
-- AND DON'T WORRY 'BOUT US. LOOKS LIKE THE LITTLE SNEAK GOT US THE HYPERDRIVE PARTS WE NEEDED. THEY'RE IN THE HOLD NOW.
I'M AMAZED YOU FINALLY GOT ELBEE TO BRING THEM ABOARD. THOSE CRATES MUST HAVE SAT WAITING IN THE WAREHOUSE FOR DAYS!
YOU BE NICE TO ELBEE. I BEEN TREATED BAD BY BOSSES BEFORE. HE HELPS US WHEN HE'S READY.
AND NOW I'M READY FOR SOME PEACE AND QUIET...

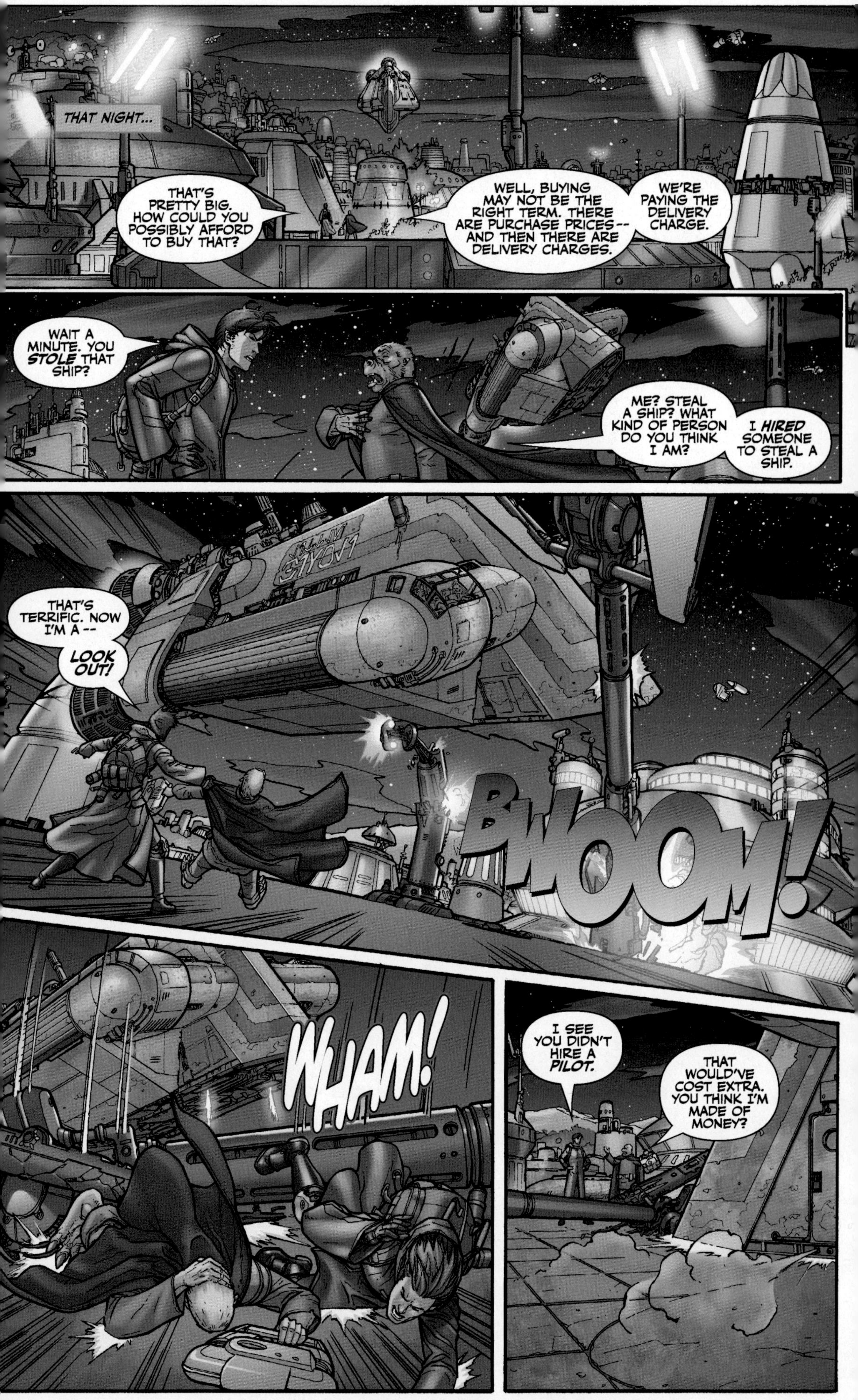
THAT NIGHT...
THAT'S PRETTY BIG. HOW COULD YOU POSSIBLY AFFORD TO BUY THAT?
WELL, BUYING MAY NOT BE THE RIGHT TERM. THERE ARE PURCHASE PRICES-- AND THEN THERE ARE DELIVERY CHARGES.
WE'RE PAYING THE DELIVERY CHARGE.
WAIT A MINUTE. YOU STOLE THAT SHIP?
ME? STEAL A SHIP? WHAT KIND OF PERSON DO YOU THINK I AM?
I HIRED SOMEONE TO STEAL A SHIP.
THAT'S TERRIFIC. NOW I'M A --
LOOK OUT!
BWOOM!
WHAM!
I SEE YOU DIDN'T HIRE A PILOT.
THAT WOULD'VE COST EXTRA. YOU THINK I'M MADE OF MONEY?

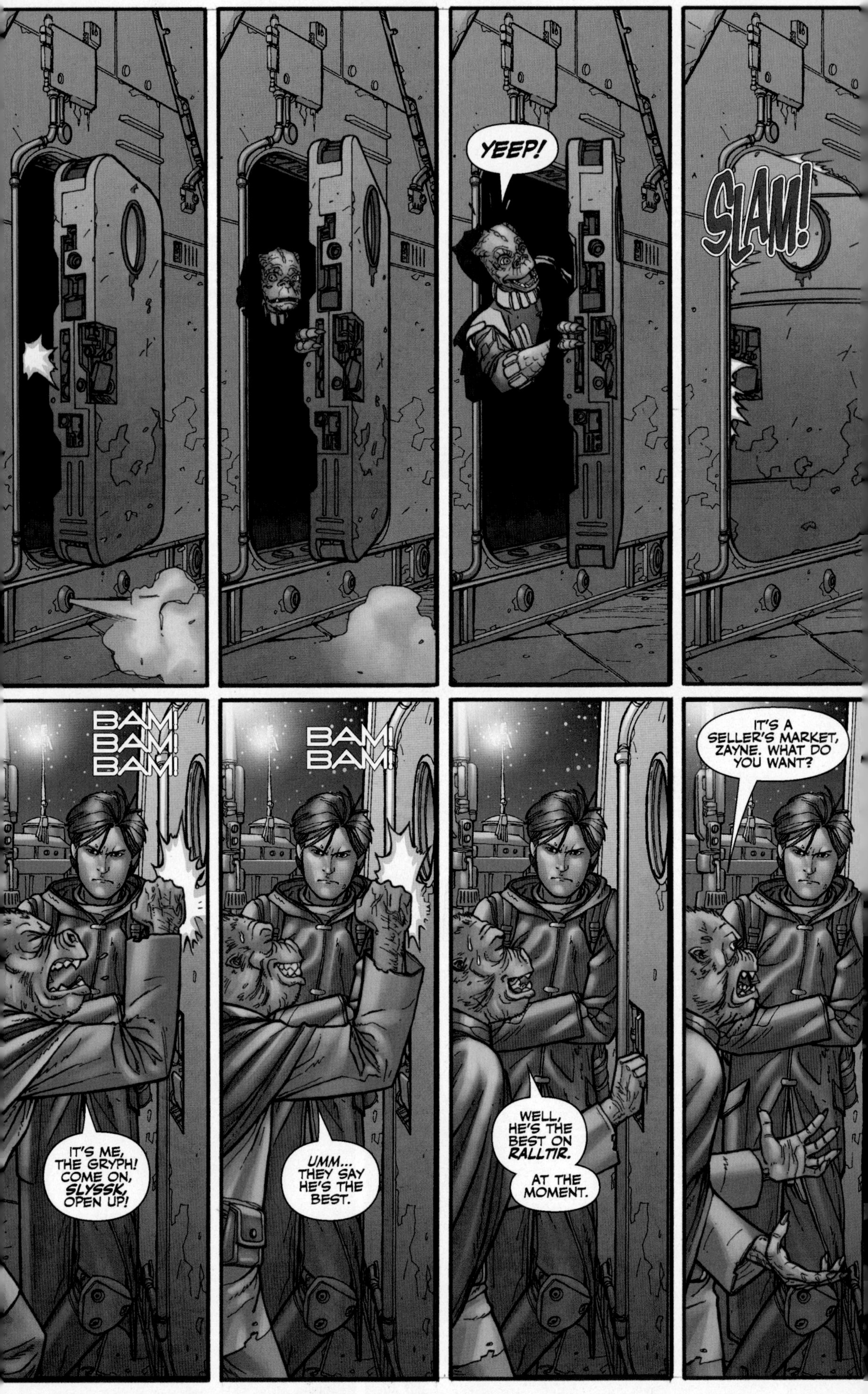
YEEP!
SLAM!
BAM! BAM! BAM!
IT'S ME, THE GRYPH! COME ON, SLYSSK, OPEN UP!
BAM! BAM!
UMM... THEY SAY HE'S THE BEST.
WELL, HE'S THE BEST ON RALLTIR.
AT THE MOMENT.
IT'S A SELLER'S MARKET, ZAYNE. WHAT DO YOU WANT?

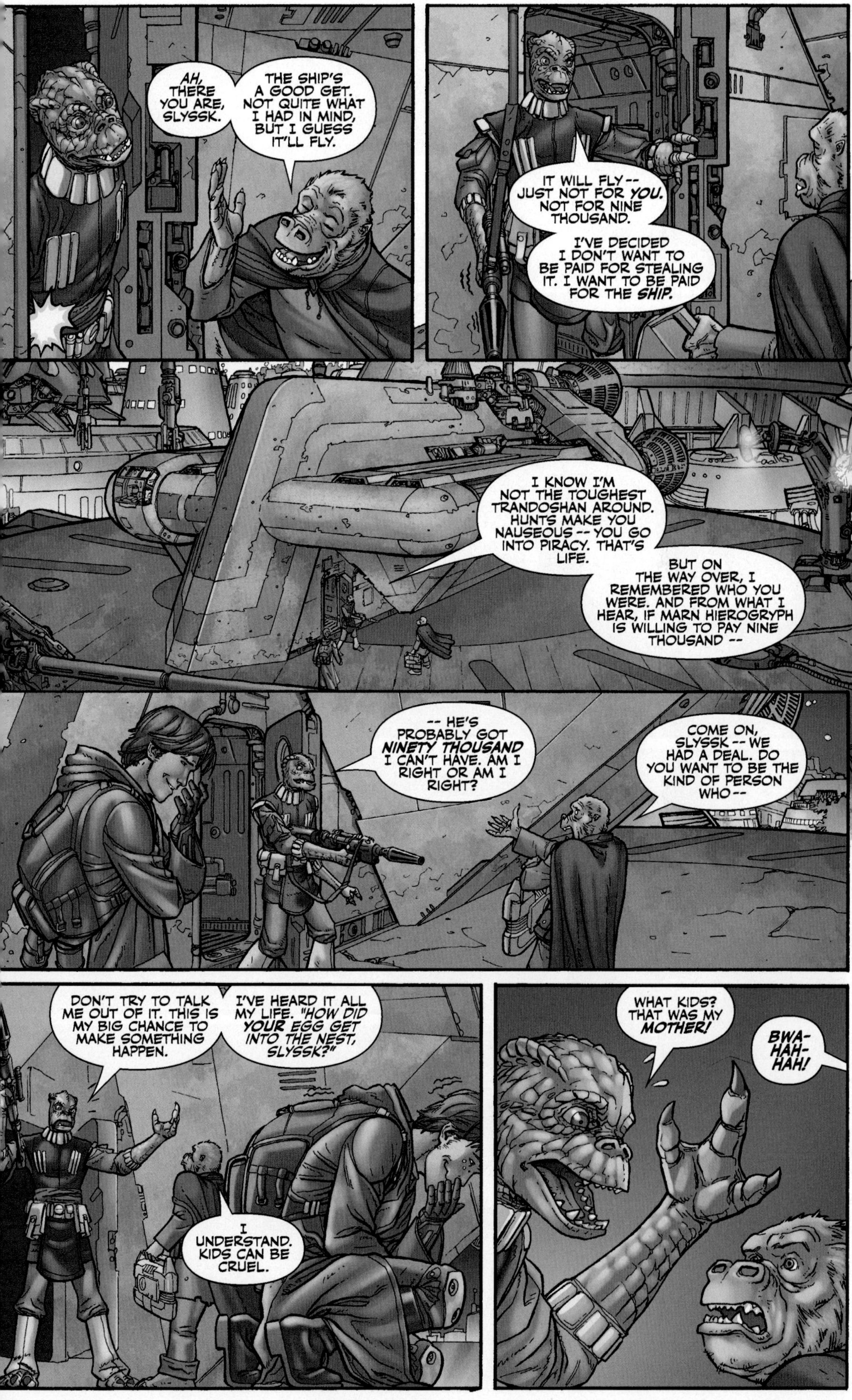
AH, THERE YOU ARE, SLYSSK.
THE SHIP'S A GOOD GET. NOT QUITE WHAT I HAD IN MIND, BUT I GUESS IT'LL FLY.
IT WILL FLY -- JUST NOT FOR YOU. NOT FOR NINE THOUSAND.
I'VE DECIDED I DON'T WANT TO BE PAID FOR STEALING IT. I WANT TO BE PAID FOR THE SHIP.
I KNOW I'M NOT THE TOUGHEST TRANDOSHAN AROUND. HUNTS MAKE YOU NAUSEOUS -- YOU GO INTO PIRACY. THAT'S LIFE.
BUT ON THE WAY OVER, I REMEMBERED WHO YOU WERE. AND FROM WHAT I HEAR, IF MARN HIEROGRYPH IS WILLING TO PAY NINE THOUSAND --
-- HE'S PROBABLY GOT NINETY THOUSAND I CAN'T HAVE. AM I RIGHT OR AM I RIGHT?
COME ON, SLYSSK -- WE HAD A DEAL. DO YOU WANT TO BE THE KIND OF PERSON WHO --
DON'T TRY TO TALK ME OUT OF IT. THIS IS MY BIG CHANCE TO MAKE SOMETHING HAPPEN.
I'VE HEARD IT ALL MY LIFE. "HOW DID YOUR EGG GET INTO THE NEST, SLYSSK?"
I UNDERSTAND. KIDS CAN BE CRUEL.
WHAT KIDS? THAT WAS MY MOTHER!
BWA-HAH-HAH!

HA-HA-HA-HA!

EXCUSE ME FOR A MOMENT, WON'T YOU? I HAVE TO CONFER WITH MY ASSOCIATE.

OR KILL HIM.

IT'S THE -- IT'S THE -- CURSE OF THE MOOMO BROTHERS!

MAYBE WITH ALL THAT MUSCLE YOU NEED TO HIRE A BRAIN, TOO!

THAT'S RIGHT, THAT'S RIGHT.

MASTER JEDI NEVER SCREWS ANYTHING UP. HO, HO, HO.

YOU WANT ME TO DO MY THING?

NO, YOUR OTHER THING. LISTEN CLOSELY...

STEP OVER BY THE LIGHT, SLYSSK...

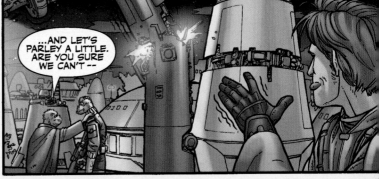

...AND LET'S PARLEY A LITTLE. ARE YOU SURE WE CAN'T --

SNAP!

HUH?

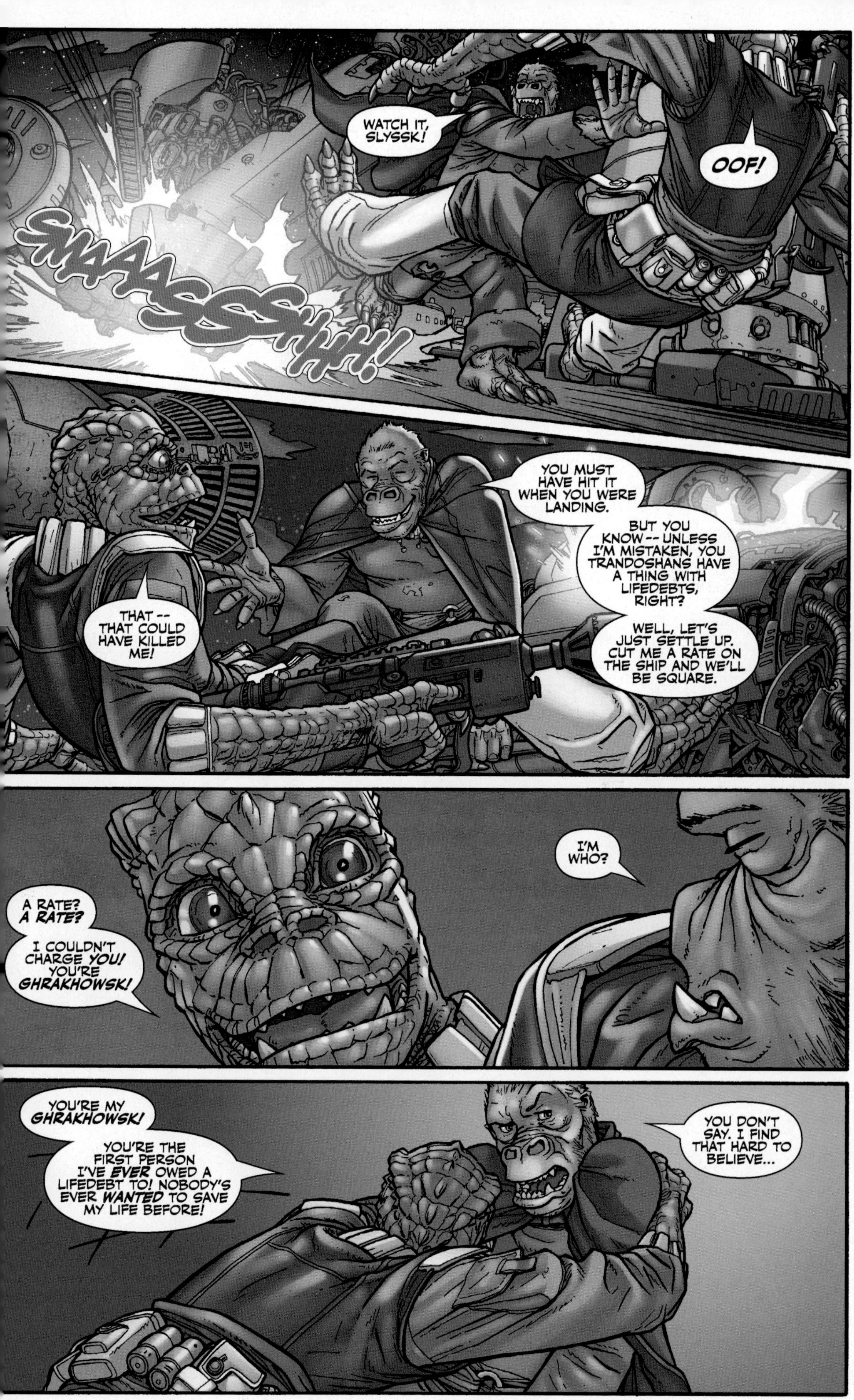

WATCH IT, SLYSSK!
OOF!
SMAAASSHHH!
YOU MUST HAVE HIT IT WHEN YOU WERE LANDING.
BUT YOU KNOW-- UNLESS I'M MISTAKEN, YOU TRANDOSHANS HAVE A THING WITH LIFEDEBTS, RIGHT?
WELL, LET'S JUST SETTLE UP. CUT ME A RATE ON THE SHIP AND WE'LL BE SQUARE.
THAT -- THAT COULD HAVE KILLED ME!
A RATE? A RATE?
I COULDN'T CHARGE YOU! YOU'RE GHRAKHOWSK!
I'M WHO?
YOU'RE MY GHRAKHOWSK!
YOU'RE THE FIRST PERSON I'VE EVER OWED A LIFEDEBT TO! NOBODY'S EVER WANTED TO SAVE MY LIFE BEFORE!
YOU DON'T SAY. I FIND THAT HARD TO BELIEVE...

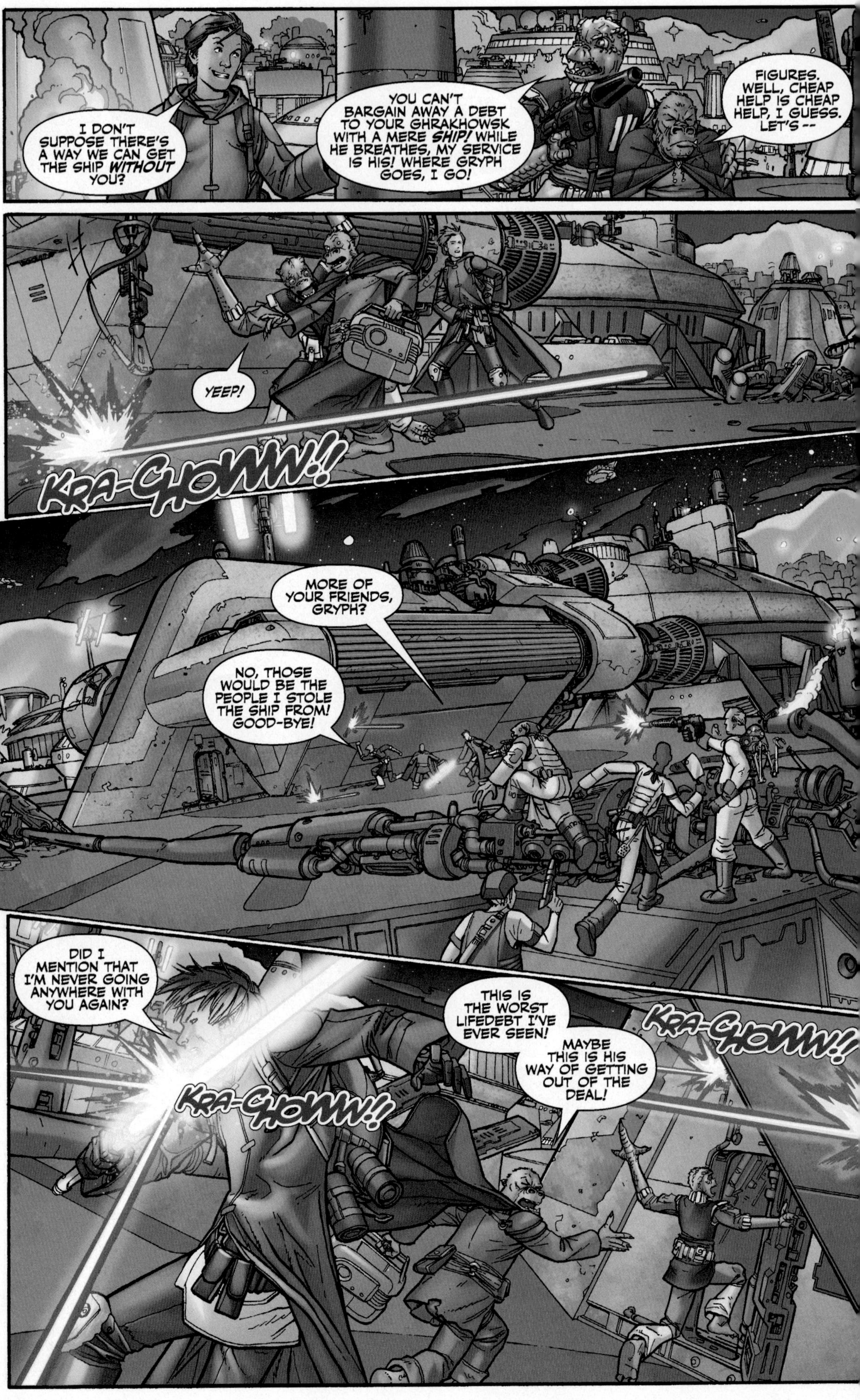
I DON'T SUPPOSE THERE'S A WAY WE CAN GET THE SHIP *WITHOUT* YOU?
YOU CAN'T BARGAIN AWAY A DEBT TO YOUR GHRAKHOWSK WITH A MERE *SHIP!* WHILE HE BREATHES, MY SERVICE IS HIS! WHERE GRYPH GOES, I GO!
FIGURES. WELL, CHEAP HELP IS CHEAP HELP, I GUESS. LET'S --
YEEP!
KRA-CHOWW!!
MORE OF YOUR FRIENDS, GRYPH?
NO, THOSE WOULD BE THE PEOPLE I STOLE THE SHIP FROM! GOOD-BYE!
DID I MENTION THAT I'M NEVER GOING ANYWHERE WITH YOU AGAIN?
THIS IS THE WORST LIFEDEBT I'VE EVER SEEN!
KRA-CHOWW!!
MAYBE THIS IS HIS WAY OF GETTING OUT OF THE DEAL!
KRA-CHOWW!!

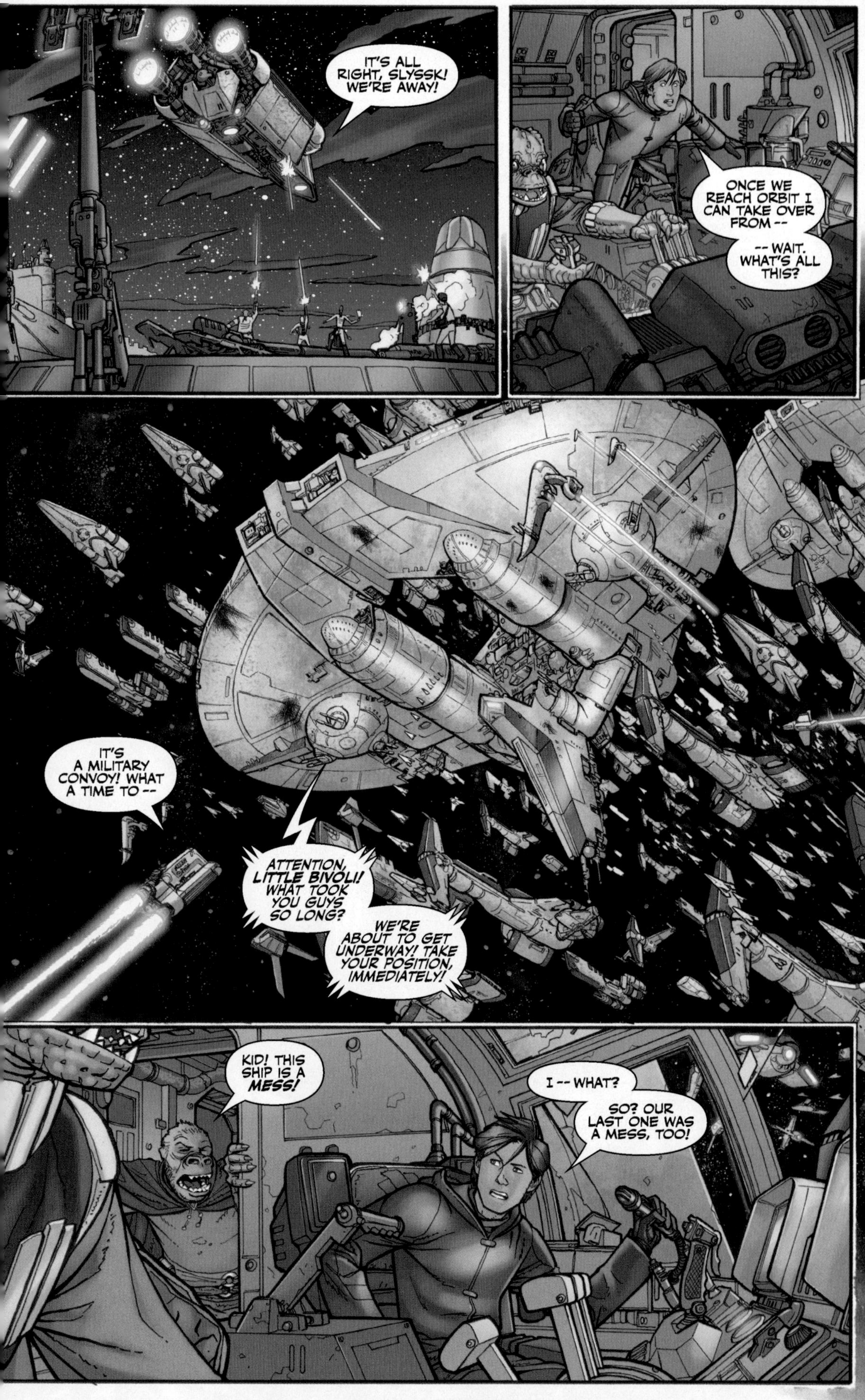
IT'S ALL RIGHT, SLYSSK! WE'RE AWAY!
ONCE WE REACH ORBIT I CAN TAKE OVER FROM --
-- WAIT. WHAT'S ALL THIS?
IT'S A MILITARY CONVOY! WHAT A TIME TO --
ATTENTION, LITTLE BIVOLI! WHAT TOOK YOU GUYS SO LONG?
WE'RE ABOUT TO GET UNDERWAY! TAKE YOUR POSITION, IMMEDIATELY!
KID! THIS SHIP IS A MESS!
I -- WHAT?
SO? OUR LAST ONE WAS A MESS, TOO!

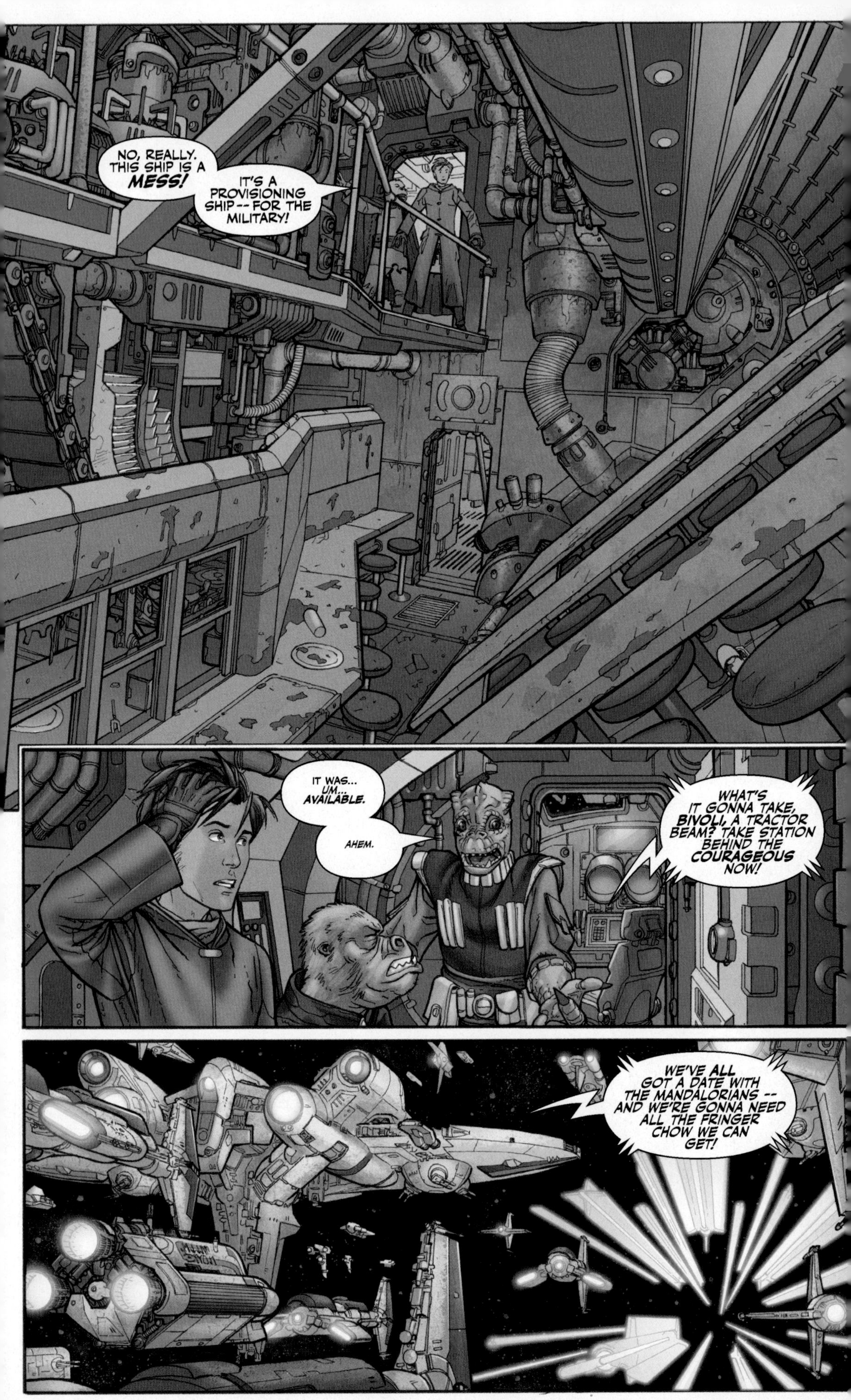
NO, REALLY. THIS SHIP IS A MESS!
IT'S A PROVISIONING SHIP -- FOR THE MILITARY!
IT WAS... UM... AVAILABLE.
AHEM.
WHAT'S IT GONNA TAKE, BIVOLI, A TRACTOR BEAM? TAKE STATION BEHIND THE COURAGEOUS NOW!
WE'VE ALL GOT A DATE WITH THE MANDALORIANS -- AND WE'RE GONNA NEED ALL THE FRINGER CHOW WE CAN GET!

IN HYPERSPACE, ABOARD THE *LAST RESORT*...

...COURSE THE JUMP IS ROUGH, HAVEN'T *FLOWN* IN YEARS...LUCKY WE'VE GOTTEN THIS FAR, SHE SAYS...AIN'T LUCK, IT'S *SKILL*, BUT THEY NEVER PAID ME LIKE I ~

-- WAIT. DIDN'T OPEN THAT, DID I?

STARTIN' TO *GO* AGAIN. BEEN WORSE SINCE WE LEFT TARIS.

CLANK!

WHAT WAS --

STATEMENT: ARKANIAN OFFSHOOT, MALE, ELDERLY. OBJECTIVE CONFIRMED.

OH, NO!

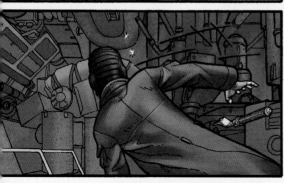

CAMPER? WHAT WAS THAT NOISE? CAMPER?

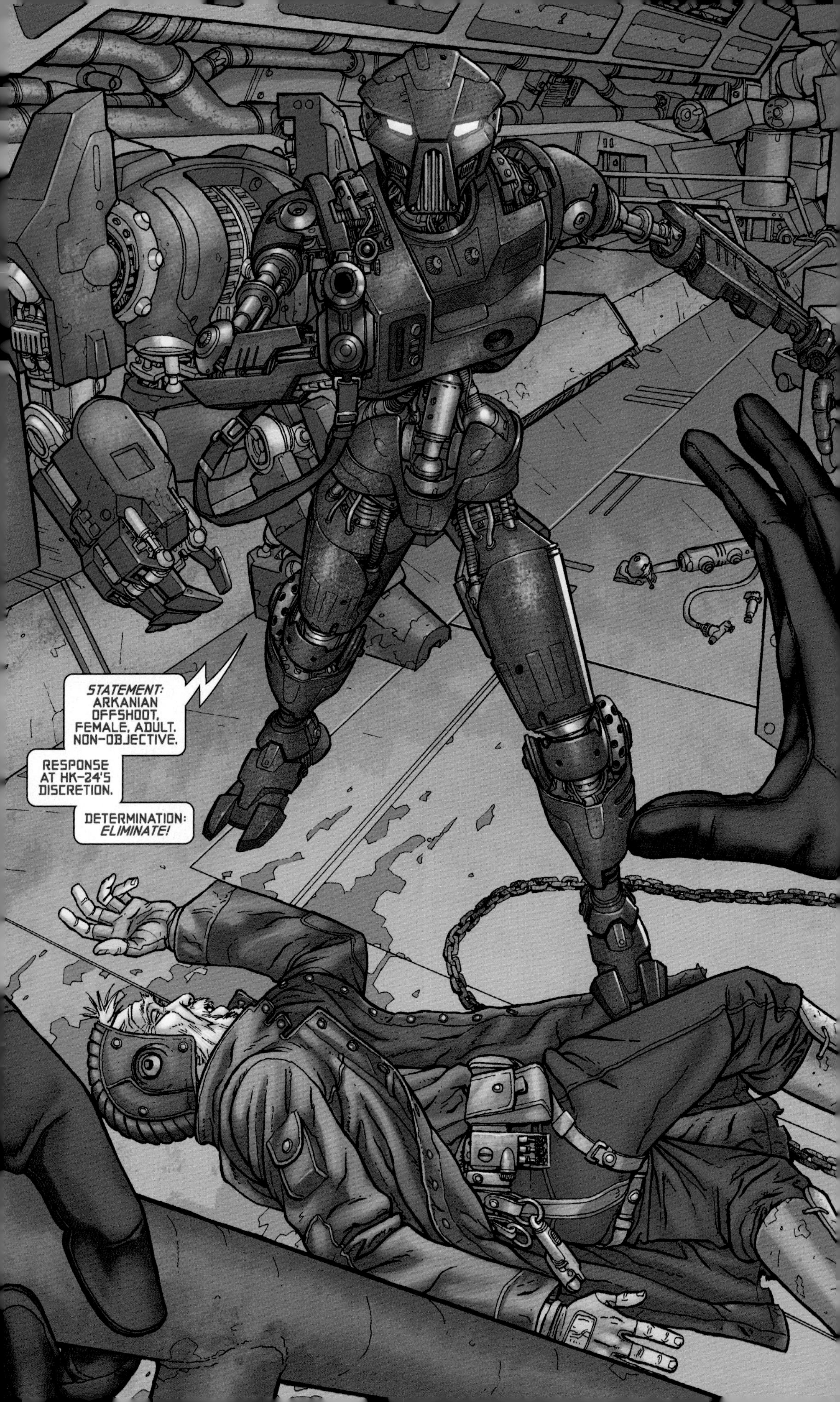
STATEMENT: ARKANIAN OFFSHOOT, FEMALE, ADULT. NON-OBJECTIVE.
RESPONSE AT HK-24'S DISCRETION.
DETERMINATION: ELIMINATE!

THE ADMIRAL'S LIST

THE OFFICIAL COMMUNIQUÉ FROM THE REPUBLIC NAVY

JIMAS VELTRAA MEMORIAL EDITION

ADMIRAL VELTRAA REMEMBERED

Hero of Taris feted in Coruscant ceremony

Admiral Jimas Veltraa, who perished in the defense of Taris against the surprise advance of Mandalorian forces along three fronts (now known by the popular media as "The Onslaught"), was memorialized in a service at Admiralty Plaza on Coruscant.

When the Jebble-Vanquo-Tarnith line became indefensible, Veltraa heroically reformed remnants of the Outer Rim fleets into a line protecting Taris. Veltraa died when his flagship, *Reliance*, was destroyed with all hands lost. Speaking at the memorial service, the Chancellor credited Veltraa's sacrifice with delaying the Mandalorians' siege of Taris, which is still ongoing.

Discussion had been given to rechristening the new class of warship, recently approved for construction in the spaceyards at Corellia, in honor of the late admiral. However, the Chancellor spoke in favor of the original name, *Interdictor*-class, which Veltraa himself had proposed.

Admiral Saul Karath, whose strong defense of and escape from Vanquo resulted in his recent promotion, was not able to attend but sent a message honoring the late Admiral and dedicating his upcoming campaign to Veltraa's memory.

SELECT to learn more...

STATUS OF FRINGERS DISPUTED

Admiral Noma Sommos, inactive since her injuries following the collapse of the line on the Outer Rim, filed an official complaint from her field hospital at Wayland over the growing presence of fringers, or freelance tradespeople, in naval groups.

"The combat and spacelift duties of the navy are inconsistent with providing protection for irregular and unaffiliated units," the complaint read.

Provisioning problems for ground units had begun to attract more fringers even before the Mandalorian onslaught. Sommos cited the logistical complications of running a modern navy in her request to the Republic for relief.

"Fringers will always be with us as long as there are armies to feed," said Catronus Steffans, defense official for the Republic. "The greater question is whether we wish to abandon the commercial opportunities this Republic is known for in the name of military expedience. We must remember what we're fighting for, after all."

SELECT to learn more...

PROMOTIONS LIST

In addition to the already-reported promotion of Saul Karath of the *Courageous* to Rear Admiral, the latest promotions were handed down from the Republic Navy, including many official confirmations of field promotions assigned during the Onslaught.

To Captain:
Teelo Vang, of Coruscant
Bask Modl, of Bestine

To Commander:
Dias Athacorr, of Arkania
Owen Delstar, of Coruscant

To Lieutenant:
Jerrit, of Mon Calamari
Carth Onasi, of Telos
Rutu, of Moltok

SELECT to see more...

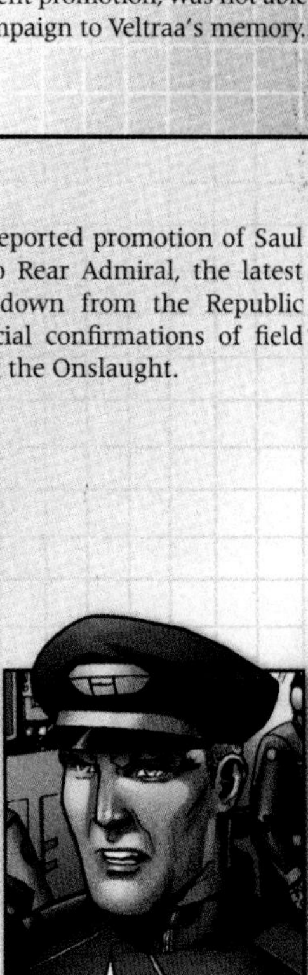

SAUL KARATH
Rear Admiral

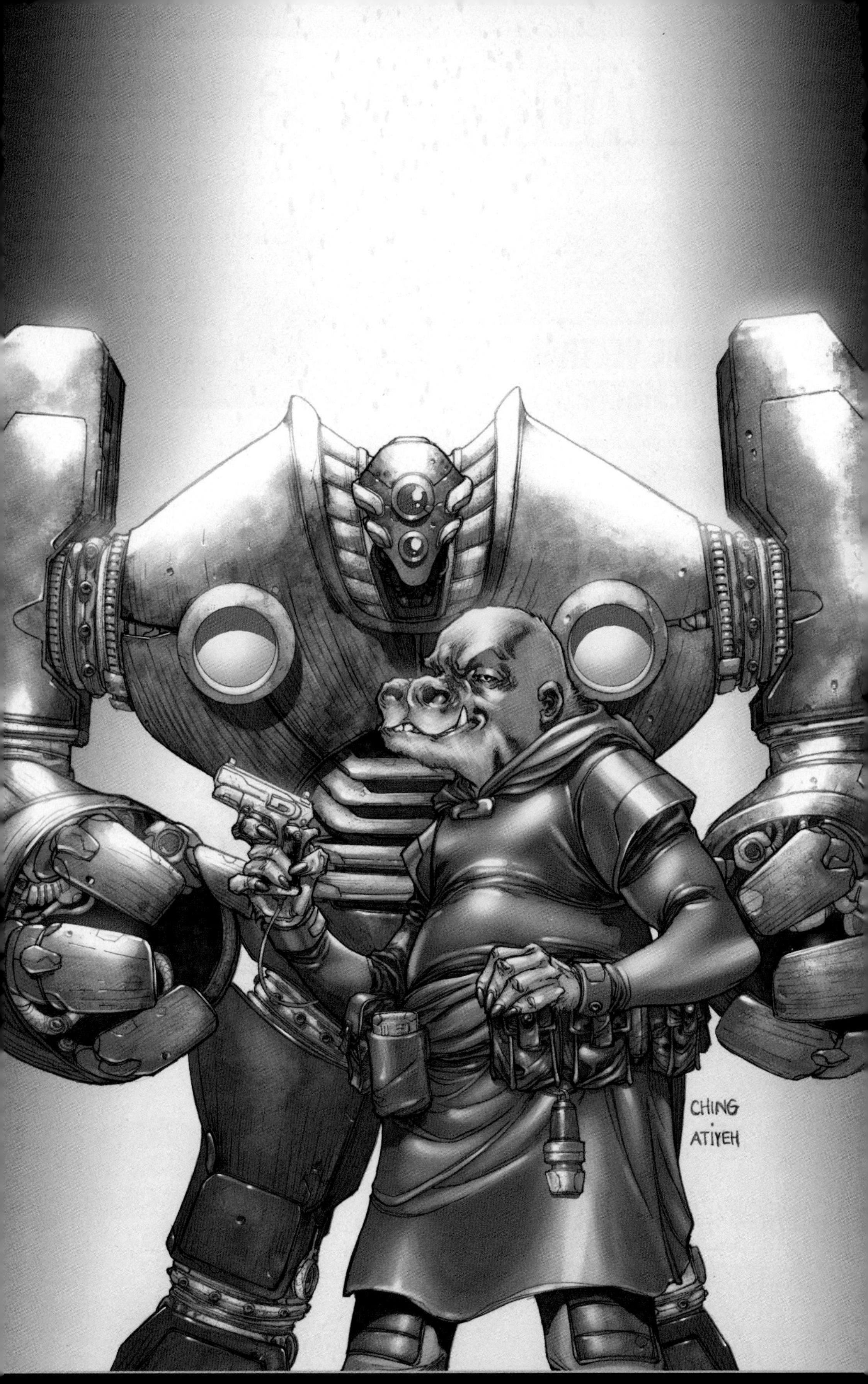
CHING
ATIYEH

STAR WARS: KNIGHTS OF THE OLD REPUBLIC #14 — "DAYS OF FEAR, PART 2"

WRITER: JOHN JACKSON MILLER • ARTIST: BRIAN CHING • COLORIST: MICHAEL ATIYEH • LETTERER: MICHAEL HEISLER
ASSISTANT EDITOR: DAVE MARSHALL • EDITOR: JEREMY BARLOW • COVER ARTISTS: BRIAN CHING & MICHAEL ATIYEH

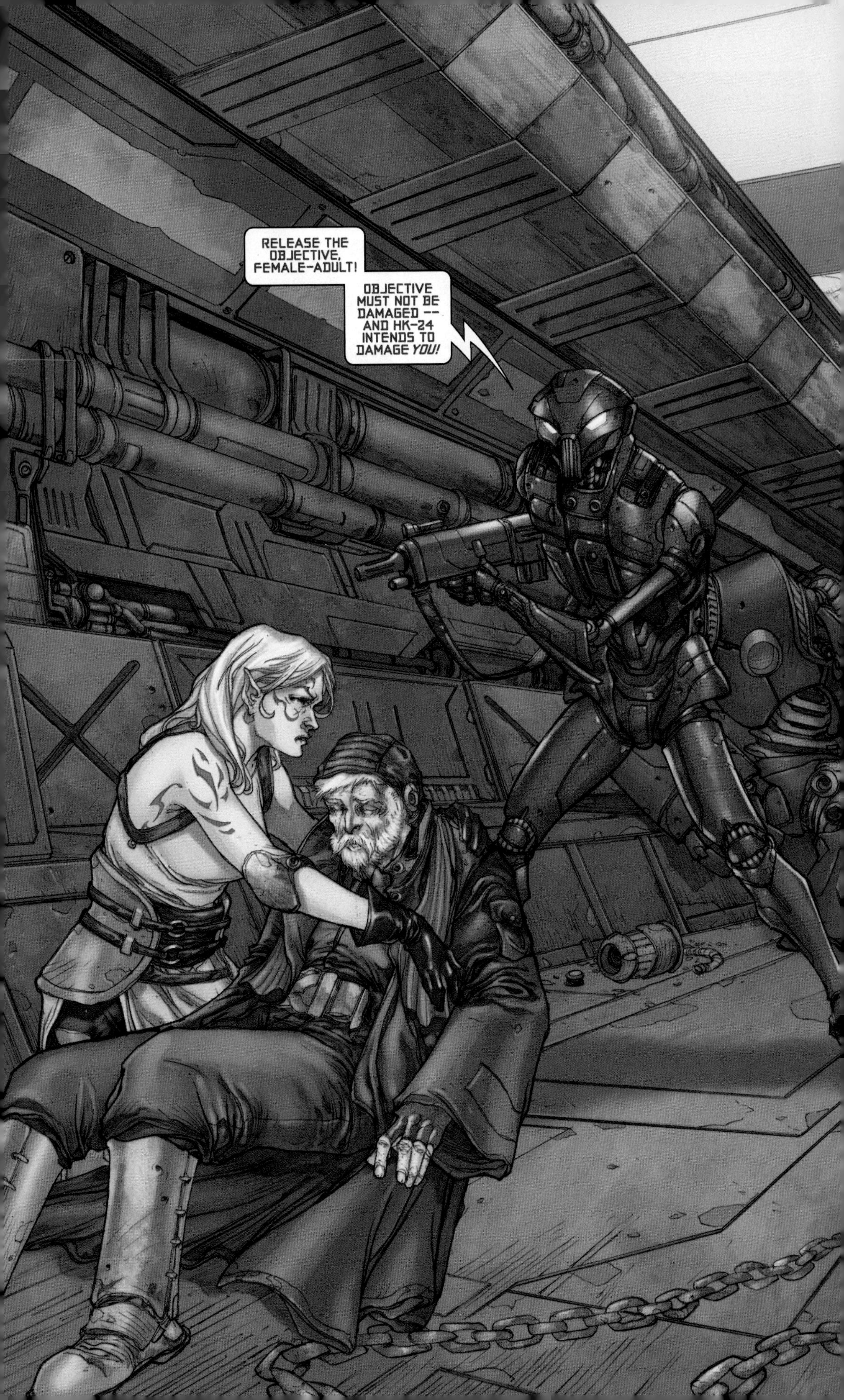
RELEASE THE OBJECTIVE, FEMALE-ADULT!
OBJECTIVE MUST NOT BE DAMAGED -- AND HK-24 INTENDS TO DAMAGE *YOU!*

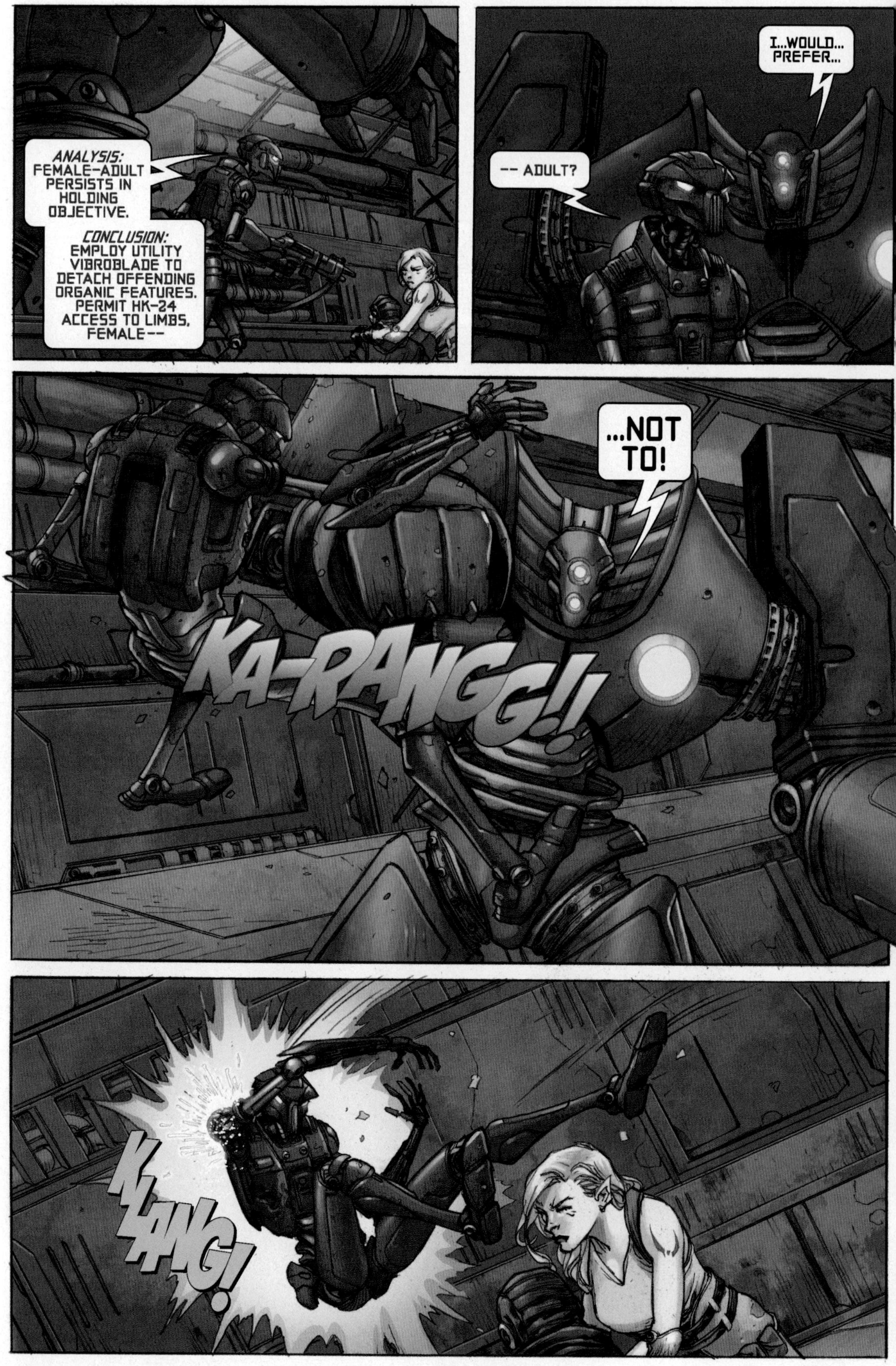
ANALYSIS: FEMALE-ADULT PERSISTS IN HOLDING OBJECTIVE.
CONCLUSION: EMPLOY UTILITY VIBROBLADE TO DETACH OFFENDING ORGANIC FEATURES. PERMIT HK-24 ACCESS TO LIMBS, FEMALE--
I...WOULD... PREFER...
-- ADULT?
...NOT TO!
KA-RANGG!!
KLANG!

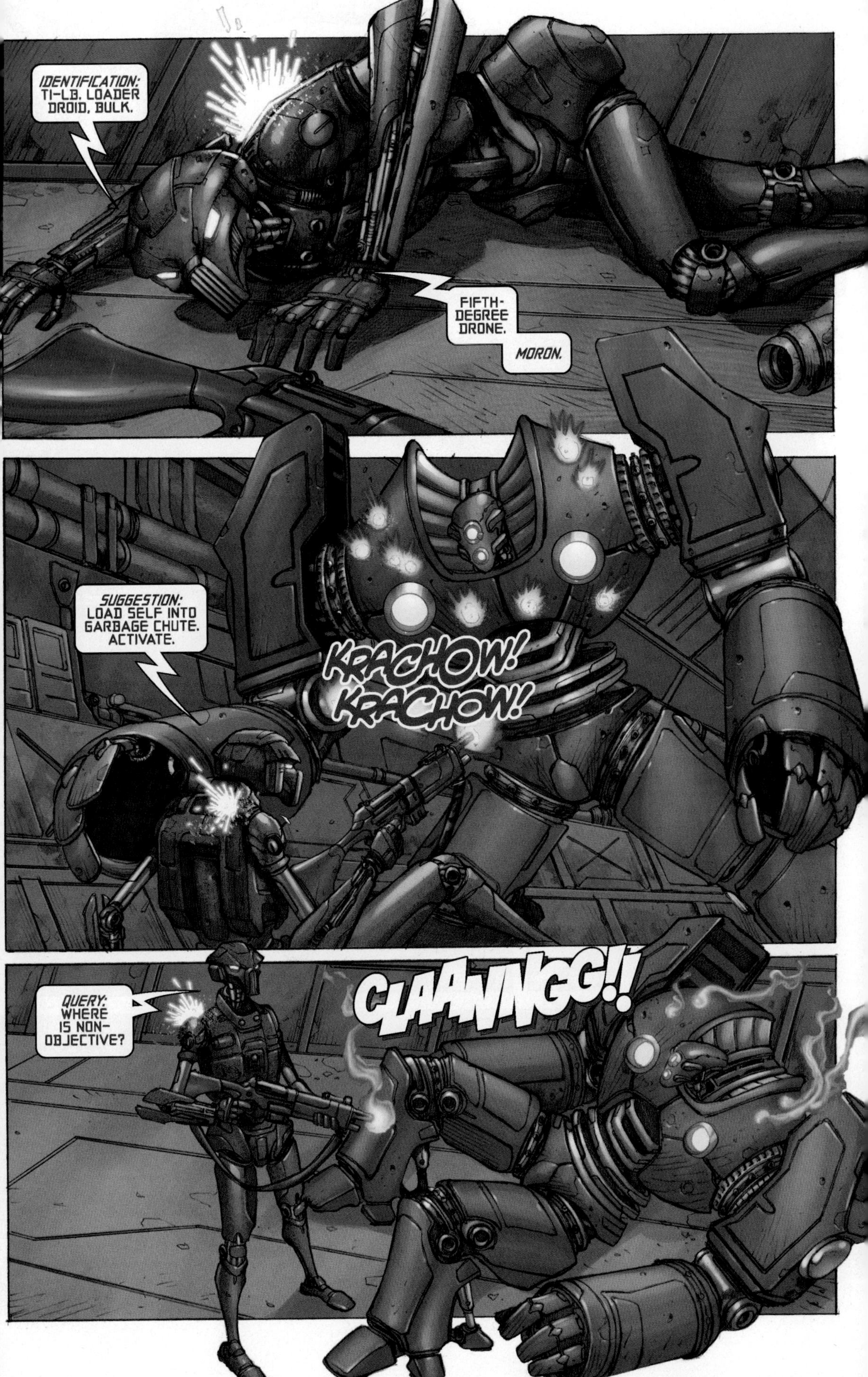
IDENTIFICATION: TI-LB. LOADER DROID. BULK.
FIFTH-DEGREE DRONE.
MORON.
SUGGESTION: LOAD SELF INTO GARBAGE CHUTE. ACTIVATE.
KRACHOW! KRACHOW!
QUERY: WHERE IS NON-OBJECTIVE?
CLAANNGG!!

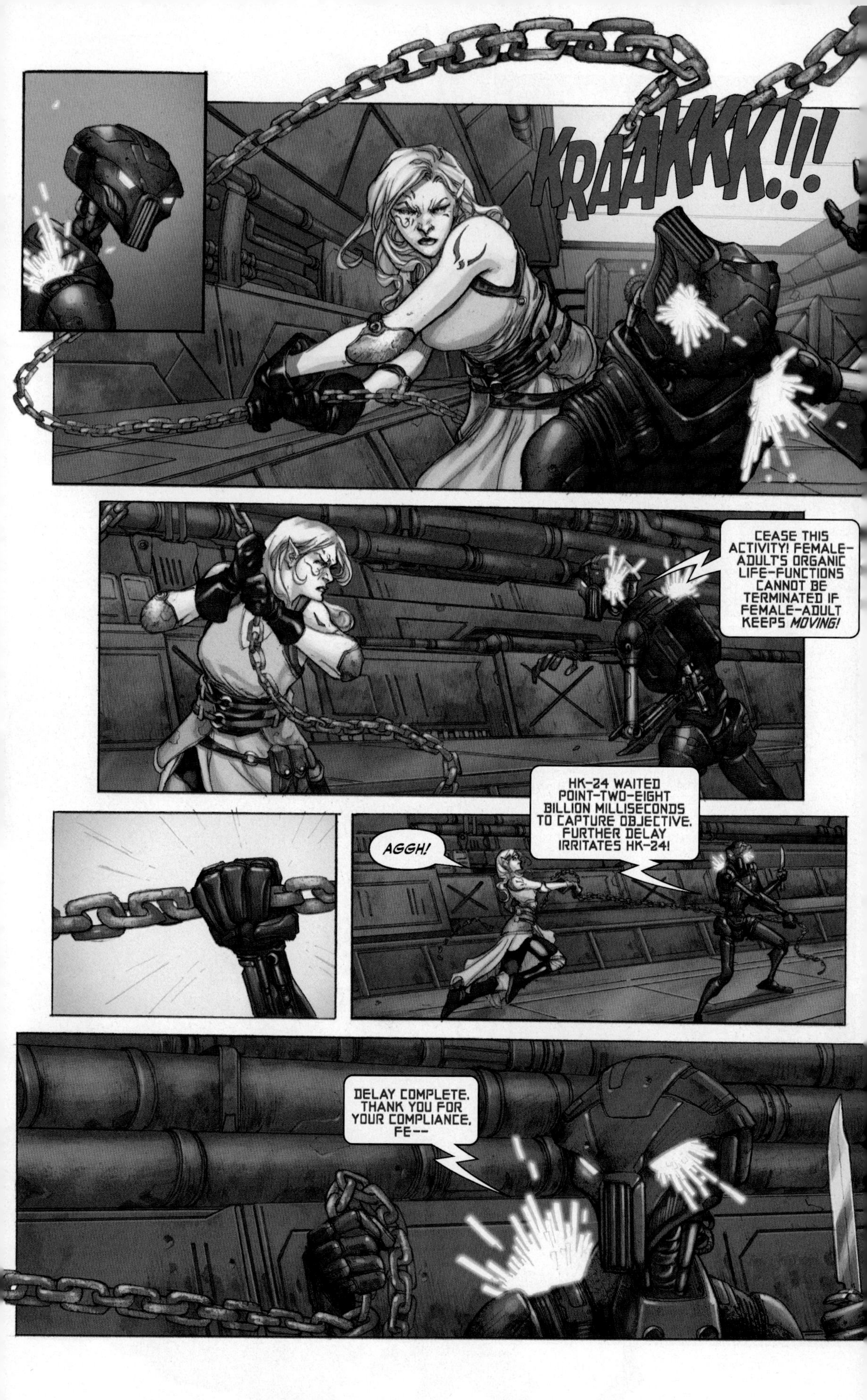
KRAAKKK!!!
CEASE THIS ACTIVITY! FEMALE-ADULT'S ORGANIC LIFE-FUNCTIONS CANNOT BE TERMINATED IF FEMALE-ADULT KEEPS *MOVING!*
HK-24 WAITED POINT-TWO-EIGHT BILLION MILLISECONDS TO CAPTURE OBJECTIVE. FURTHER DELAY IRRITATES HK-24!
AGGH!
DELAY COMPLETE. THANK YOU FOR YOUR COMPLIANCE, FE--

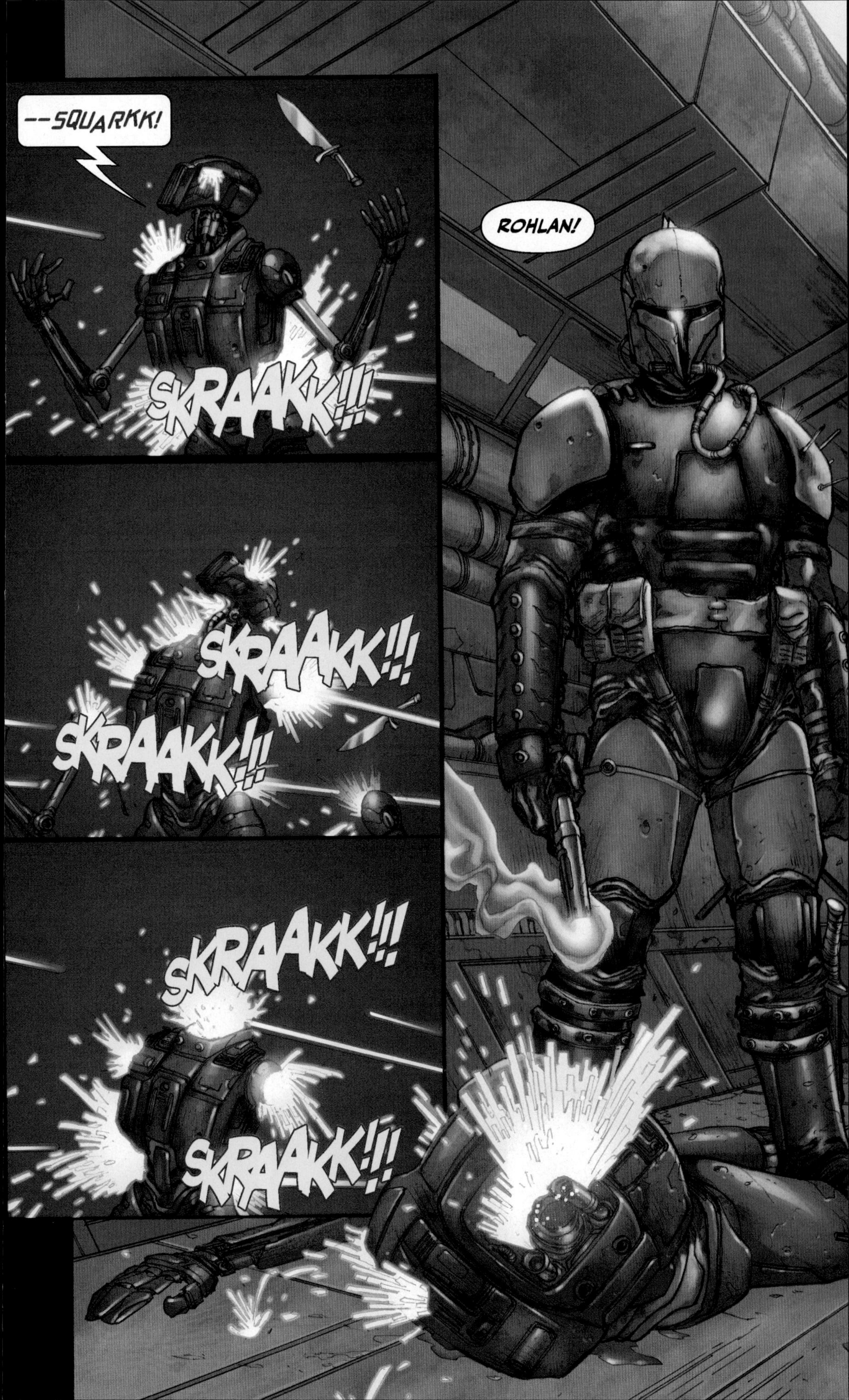
--SQUARKK!
SKRAAKK!!!
SKRAAKK!!!
SKRAAKK!!!
SKRAAKK!!!
SKRAAKK!!!
ROHLAN!

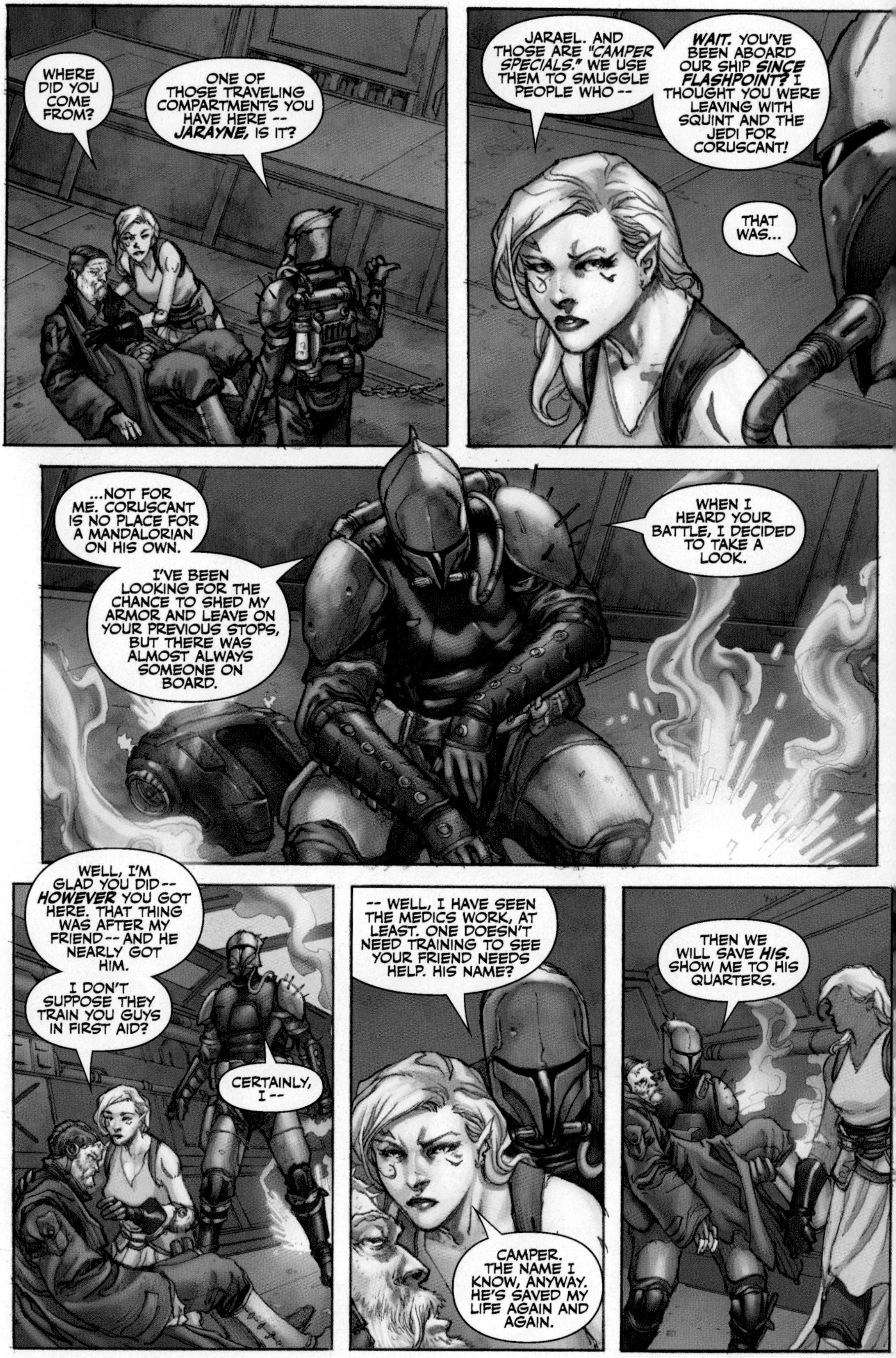
WHERE DID YOU COME FROM?
ONE OF THOSE TRAVELING COMPARTMENTS YOU HAVE HERE -- JARAYNE, IS IT?
JARAEL. AND THOSE ARE "CAMPER SPECIALS." WE USE THEM TO SMUGGLE PEOPLE WHO --
WAIT. YOU'VE BEEN ABOARD OUR SHIP SINCE FLASHPOINT? I THOUGHT YOU WERE LEAVING WITH SQUINT AND THE JEDI FOR CORUSCANT!
THAT WAS...
...NOT FOR ME. CORUSCANT IS NO PLACE FOR A MANDALORIAN ON HIS OWN.
I'VE BEEN LOOKING FOR THE CHANCE TO SHED MY ARMOR AND LEAVE ON YOUR PREVIOUS STOPS, BUT THERE WAS ALMOST ALWAYS SOMEONE ON BOARD.
WHEN I HEARD YOUR BATTLE, I DECIDED TO TAKE A LOOK.
WELL, I'M GLAD YOU DID-- HOWEVER YOU GOT HERE. THAT THING WAS AFTER MY FRIEND-- AND HE NEARLY GOT HIM.
I DON'T SUPPOSE THEY TRAIN YOU GUYS IN FIRST AID?
CERTAINLY, I --
-- WELL, I HAVE SEEN THE MEDICS WORK, AT LEAST. ONE DOESN'T NEED TRAINING TO SEE YOUR FRIEND NEEDS HELP. HIS NAME?
CAMPER. THE NAME I KNOW, ANYWAY. HE'S SAVED MY LIFE AGAIN AND AGAIN.
THEN WE WILL SAVE HIS. SHOW ME TO HIS QUARTERS.

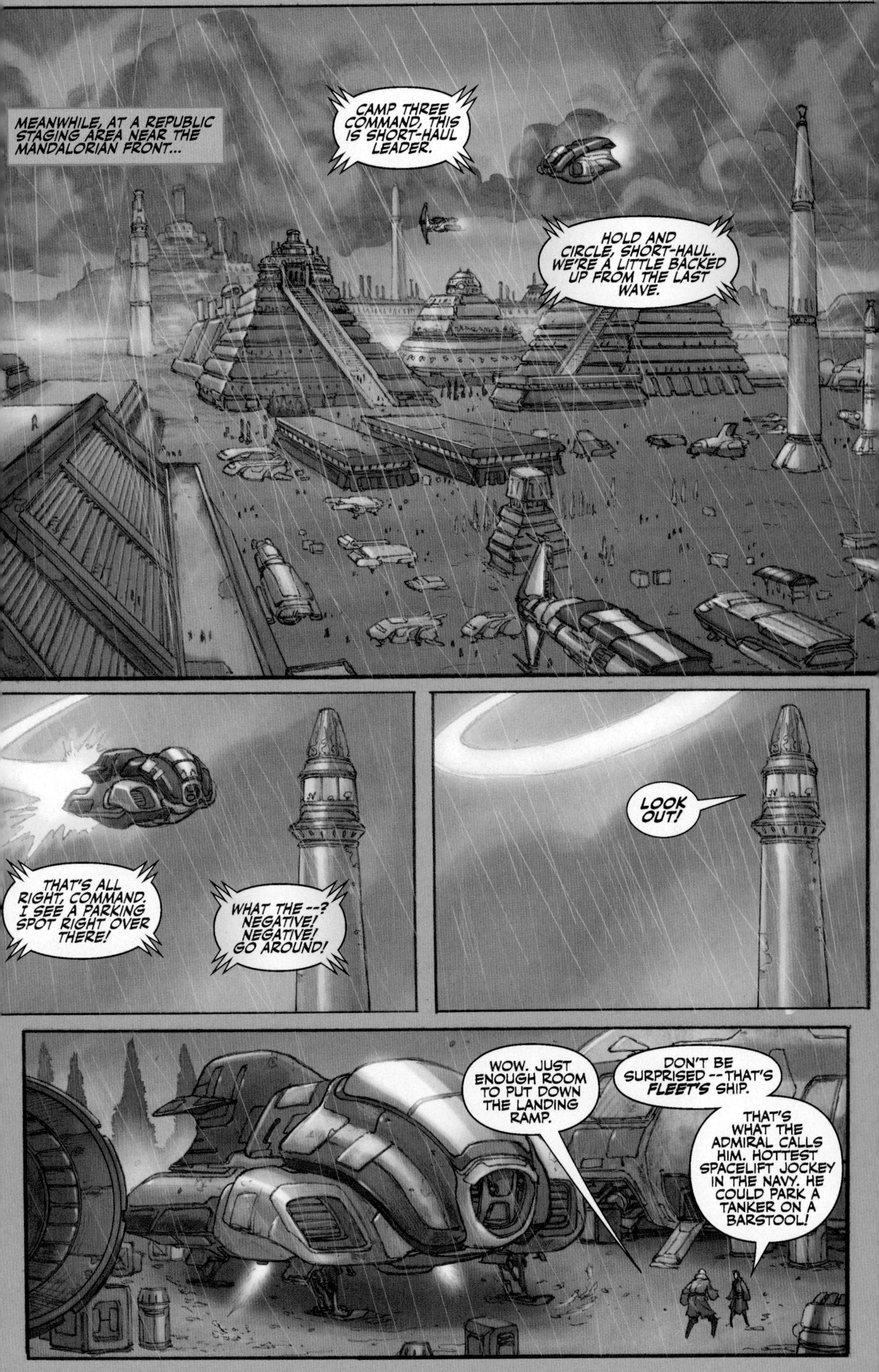
MEANWHILE, AT A REPUBLIC STAGING AREA NEAR THE MANDALORIAN FRONT...
CAMP THREE COMMAND, THIS IS SHORT-HAUL LEADER.
HOLD AND CIRCLE, SHORT-HAUL. WE'RE A LITTLE BACKED UP FROM THE LAST WAVE.
THAT'S ALL RIGHT, COMMAND. I SEE A PARKING SPOT RIGHT OVER THERE!
WHAT THE --? NEGATIVE! NEGATIVE! GO AROUND!
LOOK OUT!
WOW. JUST ENOUGH ROOM TO PUT DOWN THE LANDING RAMP.
DON'T BE SURPRISED -- THAT'S FLEET'S SHIP.
THAT'S WHAT THE ADMIRAL CALLS HIM. HOTTEST SPACELIFT JOCKEY IN THE NAVY. HE COULD PARK A TANKER ON A BARSTOOL!

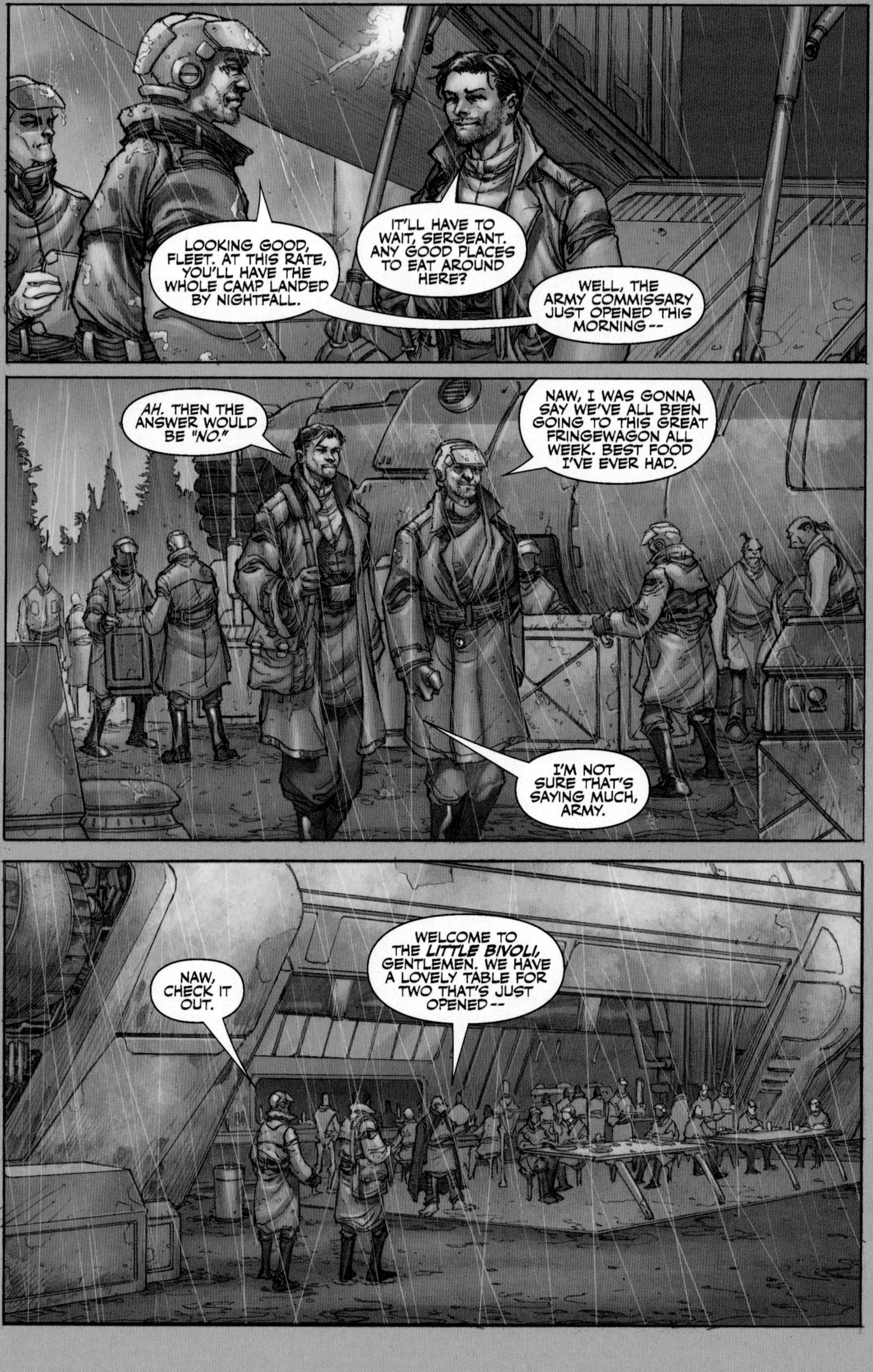
LOOKING GOOD, FLEET. AT THIS RATE, YOU'LL HAVE THE WHOLE CAMP LANDED BY NIGHTFALL.
IT'LL HAVE TO WAIT, SERGEANT. ANY GOOD PLACES TO EAT AROUND HERE?
WELL, THE ARMY COMMISSARY JUST OPENED THIS MORNING--
AH. THEN THE ANSWER WOULD BE *"NO."*
NAW, I WAS GONNA SAY WE'VE ALL BEEN GOING TO THIS GREAT FRINGEWAGON ALL WEEK. BEST FOOD I'VE EVER HAD.
I'M NOT SURE THAT'S SAYING MUCH, ARMY.
NAW, CHECK IT OUT.
WELCOME TO THE *LITTLE BIVOLI,* GENTLEMEN. WE HAVE A LOVELY TABLE FOR TWO THAT'S JUST OPENED--

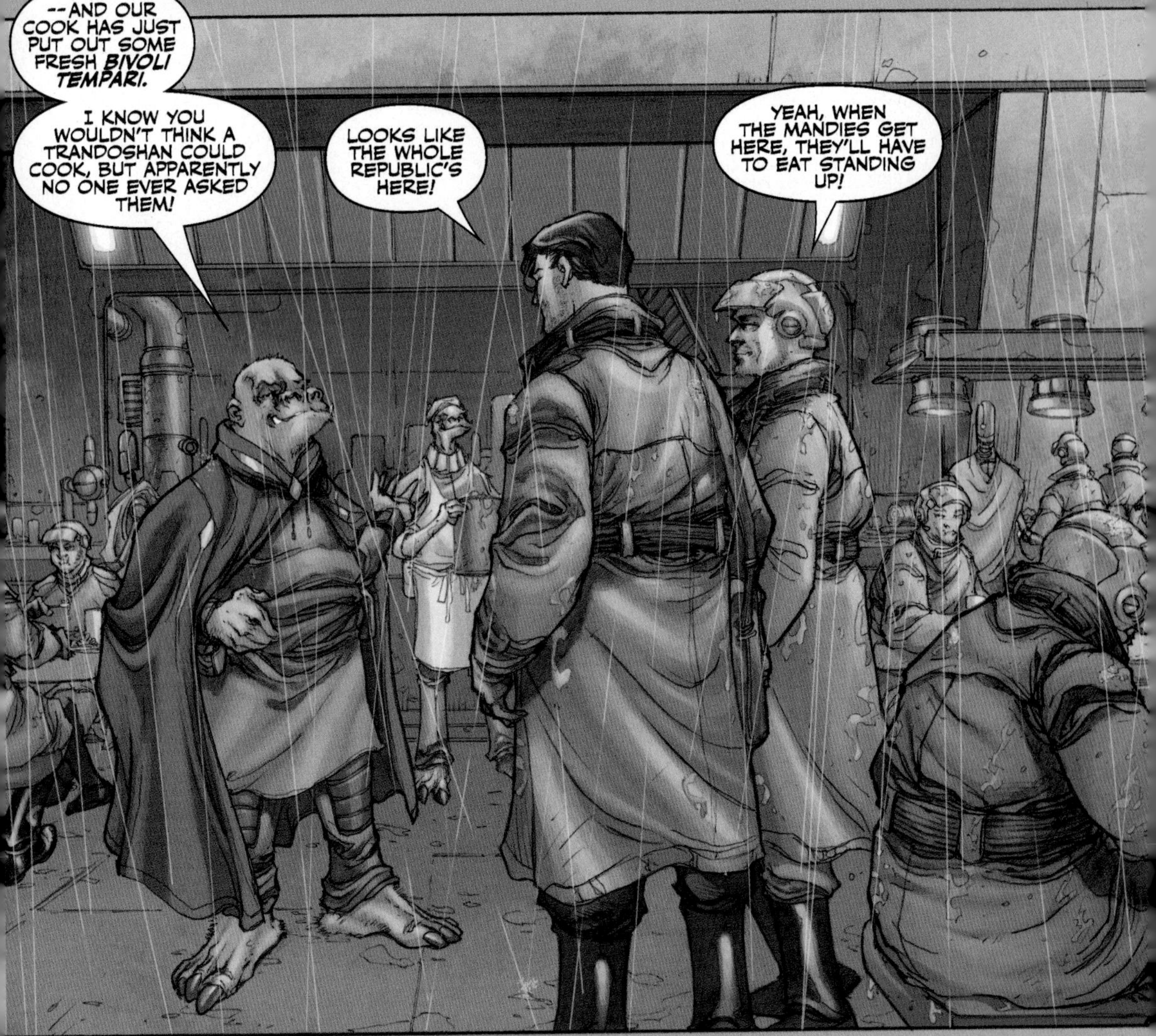
--AND OUR COOK HAS JUST PUT OUT SOME FRESH BIVOLI TEMPARI.
I KNOW YOU WOULDN'T THINK A TRANDOSHAN COULD COOK, BUT APPARENTLY NO ONE EVER ASKED THEM!
LOOKS LIKE THE WHOLE REPUBLIC'S HERE!
YEAH, WHEN THE MANDIES GET HERE, THEY'LL HAVE TO EAT STANDING UP!

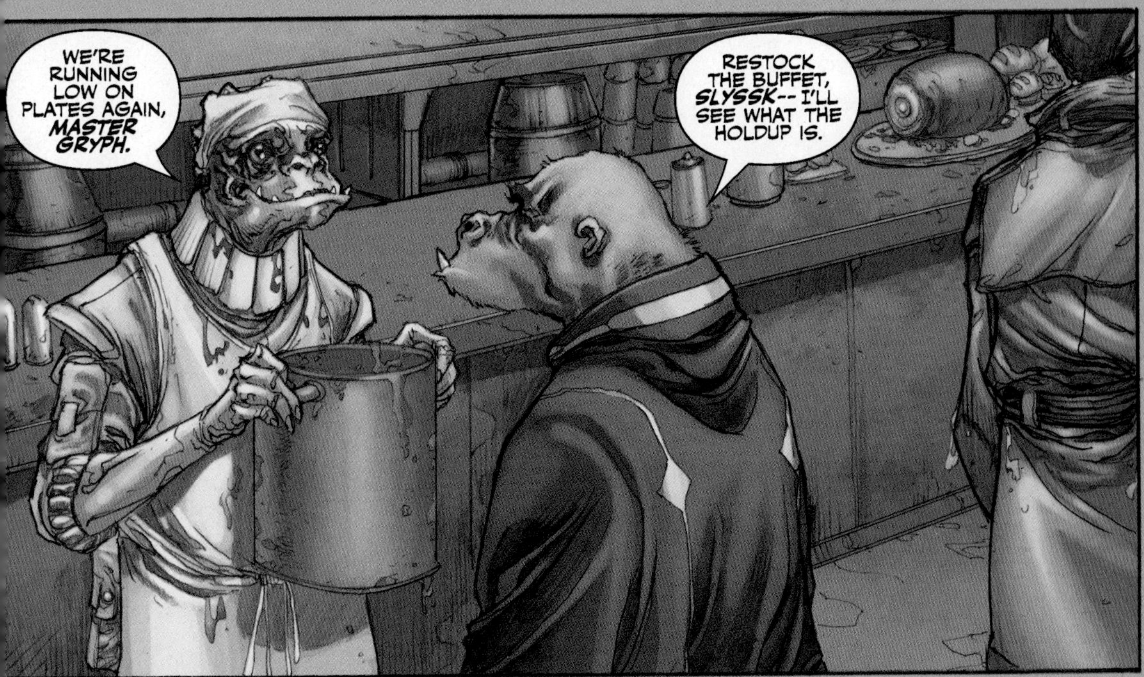
WE'RE RUNNING LOW ON PLATES AGAIN, MASTER GRYPH.
RESTOCK THE BUFFET, SLYSSK-- I'LL SEE WHAT THE HOLDUP IS.

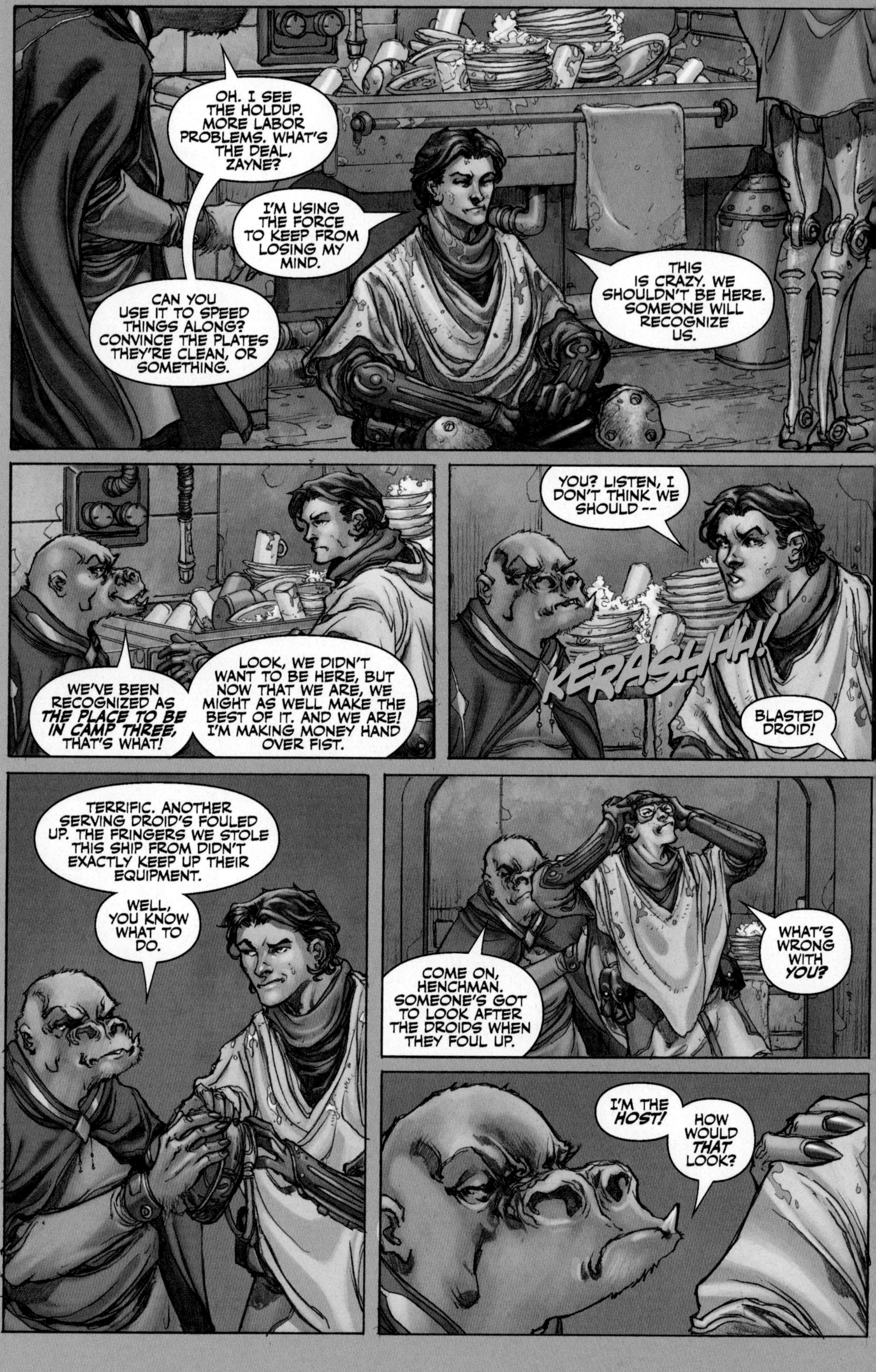

OH. I SEE THE HOLDUP. MORE LABOR PROBLEMS. WHAT'S THE DEAL, ZAYNE?
I'M USING THE FORCE TO KEEP FROM LOSING MY MIND.
CAN YOU USE IT TO SPEED THINGS ALONG? CONVINCE THE PLATES THEY'RE CLEAN, OR SOMETHING.
THIS IS CRAZY. WE SHOULDN'T BE HERE. SOMEONE WILL RECOGNIZE US.
WE'VE BEEN RECOGNIZED AS *THE PLACE TO BE IN CAMP THREE,* THAT'S WHAT!
LOOK, WE DIDN'T WANT TO BE HERE, BUT NOW THAT WE ARE, WE MIGHT AS WELL MAKE THE BEST OF IT. AND WE ARE! I'M MAKING MONEY HAND OVER FIST.
YOU? LISTEN, I DON'T THINK WE SHOULD --
KERASHHH!
BLASTED DROID!
TERRIFIC. ANOTHER SERVING DROID'S FOULED UP. THE FRINGERS WE STOLE THIS SHIP FROM DIDN'T EXACTLY KEEP UP THEIR EQUIPMENT.
WELL, YOU KNOW WHAT TO DO.
COME ON, HENCHMAN. SOMEONE'S GOT TO LOOK AFTER THE DROIDS WHEN THEY FOUL UP.
WHAT'S WRONG WITH *YOU?*
I'M THE *HOST!*
HOW WOULD *THAT* LOOK?

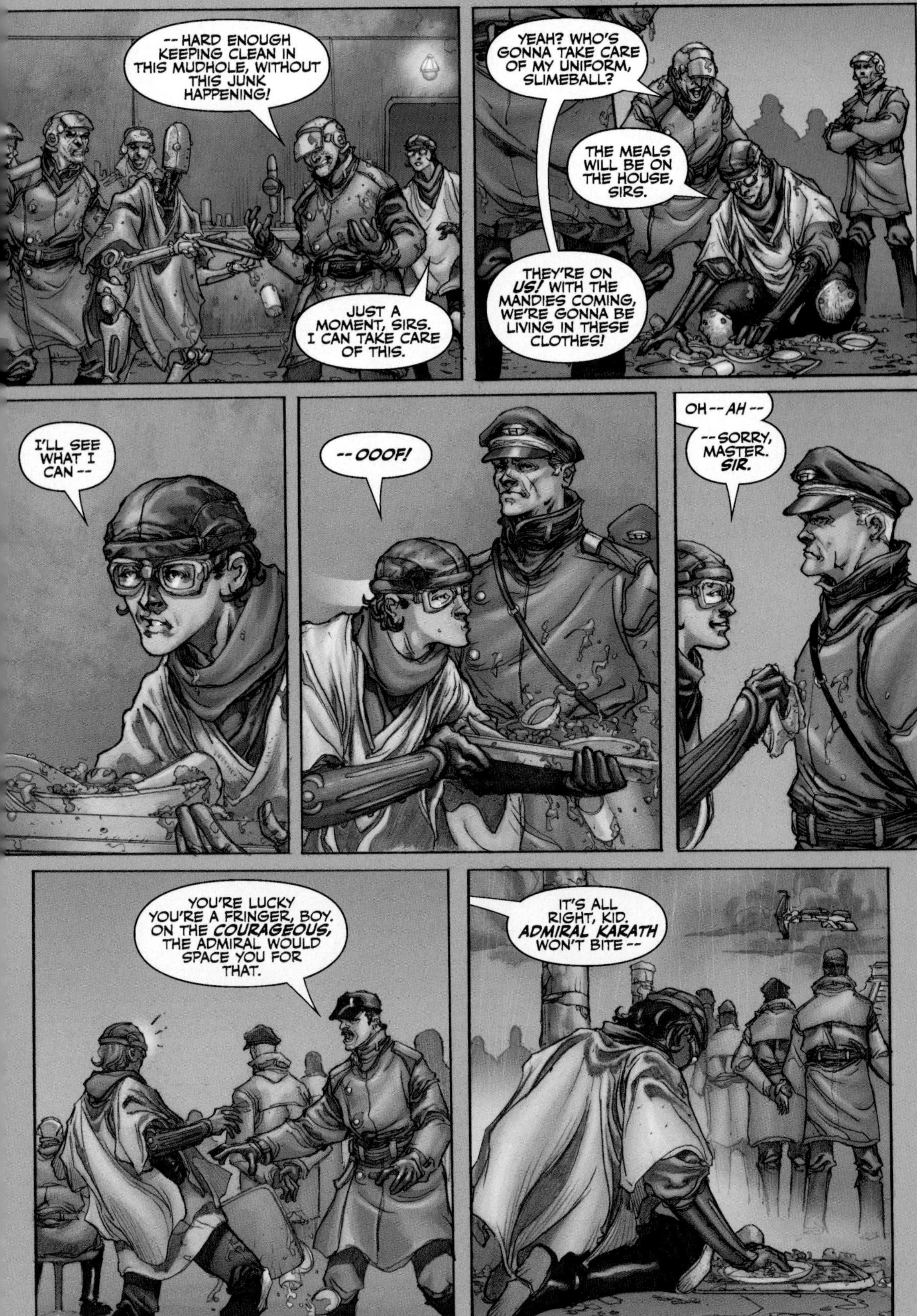
--HARD ENOUGH KEEPING CLEAN IN THIS MUDHOLE, WITHOUT THIS JUNK HAPPENING!
JUST A MOMENT, SIRS. I CAN TAKE CARE OF THIS.
YEAH? WHO'S GONNA TAKE CARE OF MY UNIFORM, SLIMEBALL?
THE MEALS WILL BE ON THE HOUSE, SIRS.
THEY'RE ON US! WITH THE MANDIES COMING, WE'RE GONNA BE LIVING IN THESE CLOTHES!
I'LL SEE WHAT I CAN--
--OOOF!
OH--AH--
--SORRY, MASTER. SIR.
YOU'RE LUCKY YOU'RE A FRINGER, BOY. ON THE COURAGEOUS, THE ADMIRAL WOULD SPACE YOU FOR THAT.
IT'S ALL RIGHT, KID. ADMIRAL KARATH WON'T BITE--

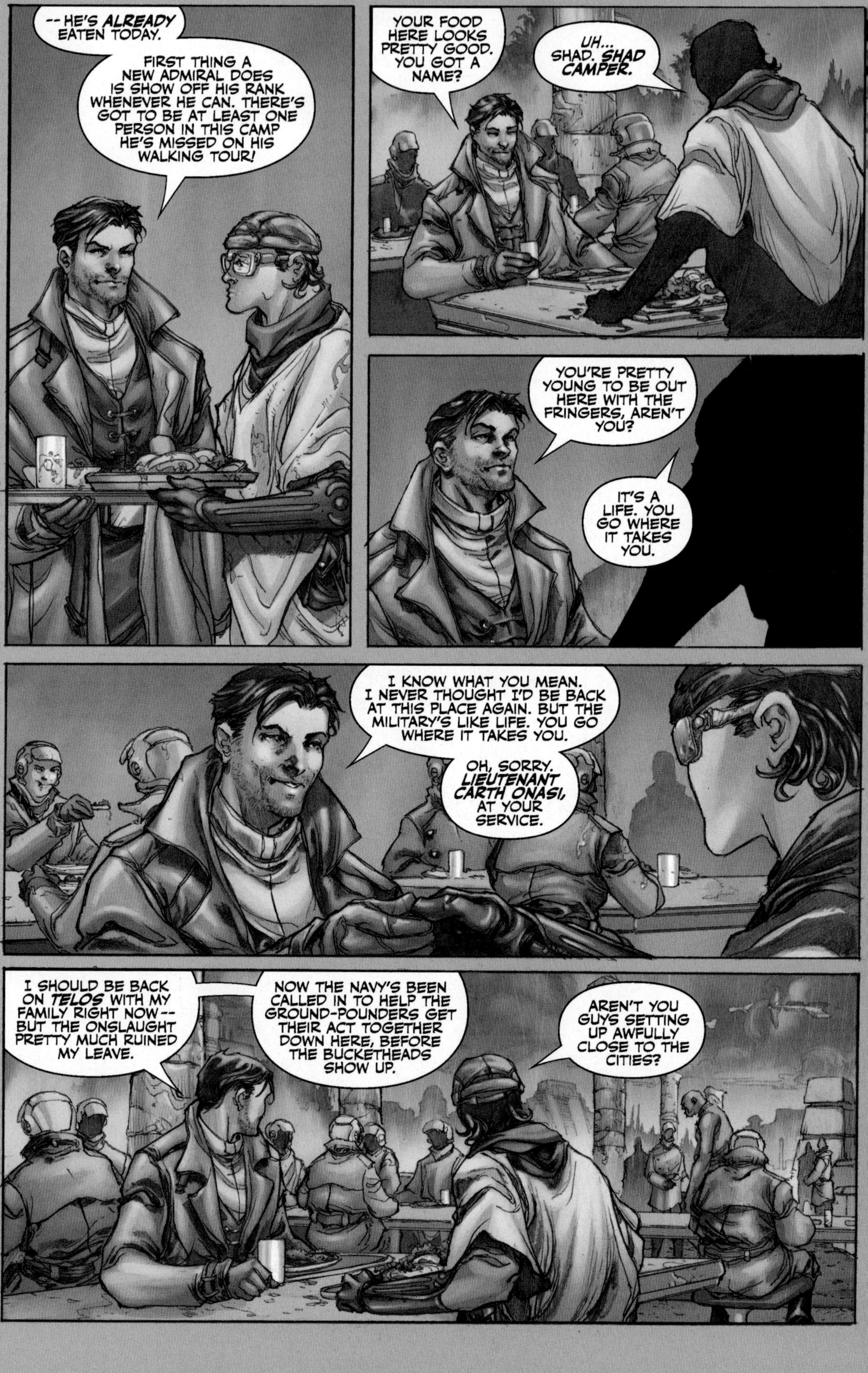

--HE'S ALREADY EATEN TODAY.
FIRST THING A NEW ADMIRAL DOES IS SHOW OFF HIS RANK WHENEVER HE CAN. THERE'S GOT TO BE AT LEAST ONE PERSON IN THIS CAMP HE'S MISSED ON HIS WALKING TOUR!
YOUR FOOD HERE LOOKS PRETTY GOOD. YOU GOT A NAME?
UH... SHAD. SHAD CAMPER.
YOU'RE PRETTY YOUNG TO BE OUT HERE WITH THE FRINGERS, AREN'T YOU?
IT'S A LIFE. YOU GO WHERE IT TAKES YOU.
I KNOW WHAT YOU MEAN. I NEVER THOUGHT I'D BE BACK AT THIS PLACE AGAIN. BUT THE MILITARY'S LIKE LIFE. YOU GO WHERE IT TAKES YOU.
OH, SORRY. LIEUTENANT CARTH ONASI, AT YOUR SERVICE.
I SHOULD BE BACK ON TELOS WITH MY FAMILY RIGHT NOW--BUT THE ONSLAUGHT PRETTY MUCH RUINED MY LEAVE.
NOW THE NAVY'S BEEN CALLED IN TO HELP THE GROUND-POUNDERS GET THEIR ACT TOGETHER DOWN HERE, BEFORE THE BUCKETHEADS SHOW UP.
AREN'T YOU GUYS SETTING UP AWFULLY CLOSE TO THE CITIES?

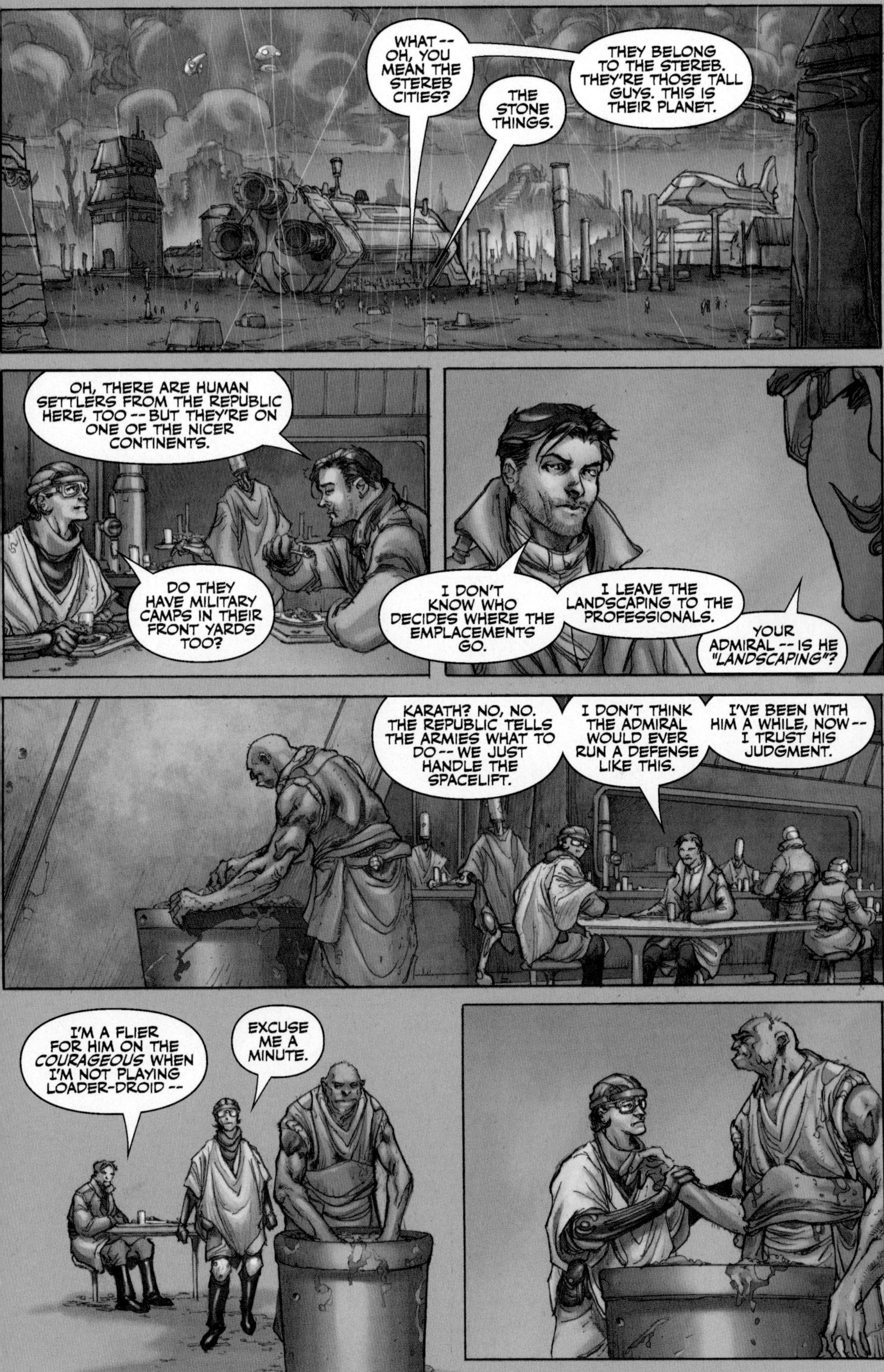
WHAT -- OH, YOU MEAN THE STEREB CITIES?
THE STONE THINGS.
THEY BELONG TO THE STEREB. THEY'RE THOSE TALL GUYS. THIS IS THEIR PLANET.
OH, THERE ARE HUMAN SETTLERS FROM THE REPUBLIC HERE, TOO -- BUT THEY'RE ON ONE OF THE NICER CONTINENTS.
DO THEY HAVE MILITARY CAMPS IN THEIR FRONT YARDS TOO?
I DON'T KNOW WHO DECIDES WHERE THE EMPLACEMENTS GO.
I LEAVE THE LANDSCAPING TO THE PROFESSIONALS.
YOUR ADMIRAL -- IS HE "LANDSCAPING"?
KARATH? NO, NO. THE REPUBLIC TELLS THE ARMIES WHAT TO DO -- WE JUST HANDLE THE SPACELIFT.
I DON'T THINK THE ADMIRAL WOULD EVER RUN A DEFENSE LIKE THIS.
I'VE BEEN WITH HIM A WHILE, NOW -- I TRUST HIS JUDGMENT.
I'M A FLIER FOR HIM ON THE COURAGEOUS WHEN I'M NOT PLAYING LOADER-DROID --
EXCUSE ME A MINUTE.

THAT'S COMING OUT OF YOUR CUT, YOU KNOW.

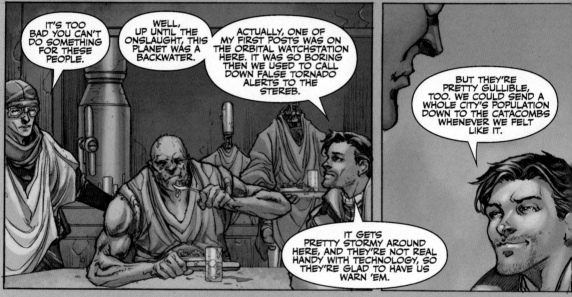

IT'S TOO BAD YOU CAN'T DO SOMETHING FOR THESE PEOPLE.

WELL, UP UNTIL THE ONSLAUGHT, THIS PLANET WAS A BACKWATER.

ACTUALLY, ONE OF MY FIRST POSTS WAS ON THE ORBITAL WATCHSTATION HERE. IT WAS SO BORING THEN WE USED TO CALL DOWN FALSE TORNADO ALERTS TO THE STEREB.

BUT THEY'RE PRETTY GULLIBLE, TOO. WE COULD SEND A WHOLE CITY'S POPULATION DOWN TO THE CATACOMBS WHENEVER WE FELT LIKE IT.

IT GETS PRETTY STORMY AROUND HERE, AND THEY'RE NOT REAL HANDY WITH TECHNOLOGY, SO THEY'RE GLAD TO HAVE US WARN 'EM.

DURING SPORTING EVENTS, FESTIVALS -- YOU NAME IT. KIND OF FUN TO WATCH FROM ABOVE -- FOR A WHILE, ANYWAY.

IT STOPPED BEING FUN?

SENATOR COMPLAINED.

ALSO, I GOT DOWN HERE AND MET A FEW -- DIDN'T SEEM SO FUN AFTER THAT...

WELL, I'VE A LOT OF METAL TO MOVE, SHAD CAMPER. *THE MANDALORIANS* WILL BE DROPPING IN TOMORROW.

TOMORROW?

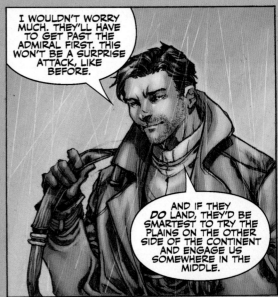

I WOULDN'T WORRY MUCH. THEY'LL HAVE TO GET PAST THE ADMIRAL FIRST. THIS WON'T BE A SURPRISE ATTACK, LIKE BEFORE.

AND IF THEY *DO* LAND, THEY'D BE SMARTEST TO TRY THE PLAINS ON THE OTHER SIDE OF THE CONTINENT AND ENGAGE US SOMEWHERE IN THE MIDDLE.

BESIDES, IT'S LIKE YOU SAY. THEY COME HERE, THEY'VE GOT A GOOD CHANCE OF WRECKING THE CITIES. MANDIES DON'T LIKE TO SPOIL THE SPOILS OF WAR.

HERE.

THAT'S FOR ME -- AND FOR THE *STEREB*. TAKE IT EASY, KID.

AND MY COMPLIMENTS TO THE CHEF.

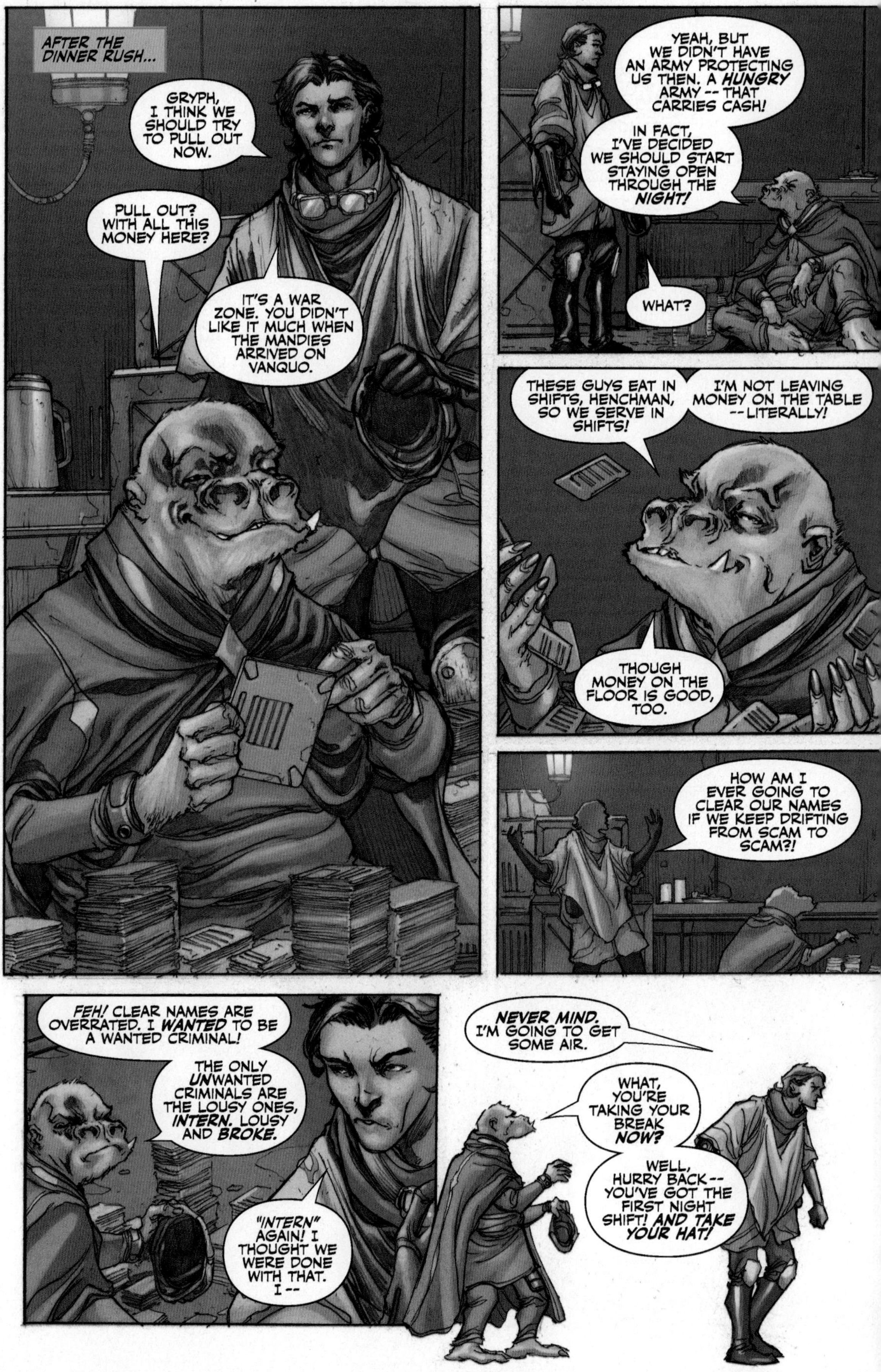
AFTER THE DINNER RUSH...
GRYPH, I THINK WE SHOULD TRY TO PULL OUT NOW.
PULL OUT? WITH ALL THIS MONEY HERE?
IT'S A WAR ZONE. YOU DIDN'T LIKE IT MUCH WHEN THE MANDIES ARRIVED ON VANQUO.
YEAH, BUT WE DIDN'T HAVE AN ARMY PROTECTING US THEN. A HUNGRY ARMY -- THAT CARRIES CASH!
IN FACT, I'VE DECIDED WE SHOULD START STAYING OPEN THROUGH THE NIGHT!
WHAT?
THESE GUYS EAT IN SHIFTS, HENCHMAN, SO WE SERVE IN SHIFTS!
I'M NOT LEAVING MONEY ON THE TABLE --LITERALLY!
THOUGH MONEY ON THE FLOOR IS GOOD, TOO.
HOW AM I EVER GOING TO CLEAR OUR NAMES IF WE KEEP DRIFTING FROM SCAM TO SCAM?!
FEH! CLEAR NAMES ARE OVERRATED. I WANTED TO BE A WANTED CRIMINAL!
THE ONLY UNWANTED CRIMINALS ARE THE LOUSY ONES, INTERN. LOUSY AND BROKE.
"INTERN" AGAIN! I THOUGHT WE WERE DONE WITH THAT. I --
NEVER MIND. I'M GOING TO GET SOME AIR.
WHAT, YOU'RE TAKING YOUR BREAK NOW?
WELL, HURRY BACK-- YOU'VE GOT THE FIRST NIGHT SHIFT! AND TAKE YOUR HAT!

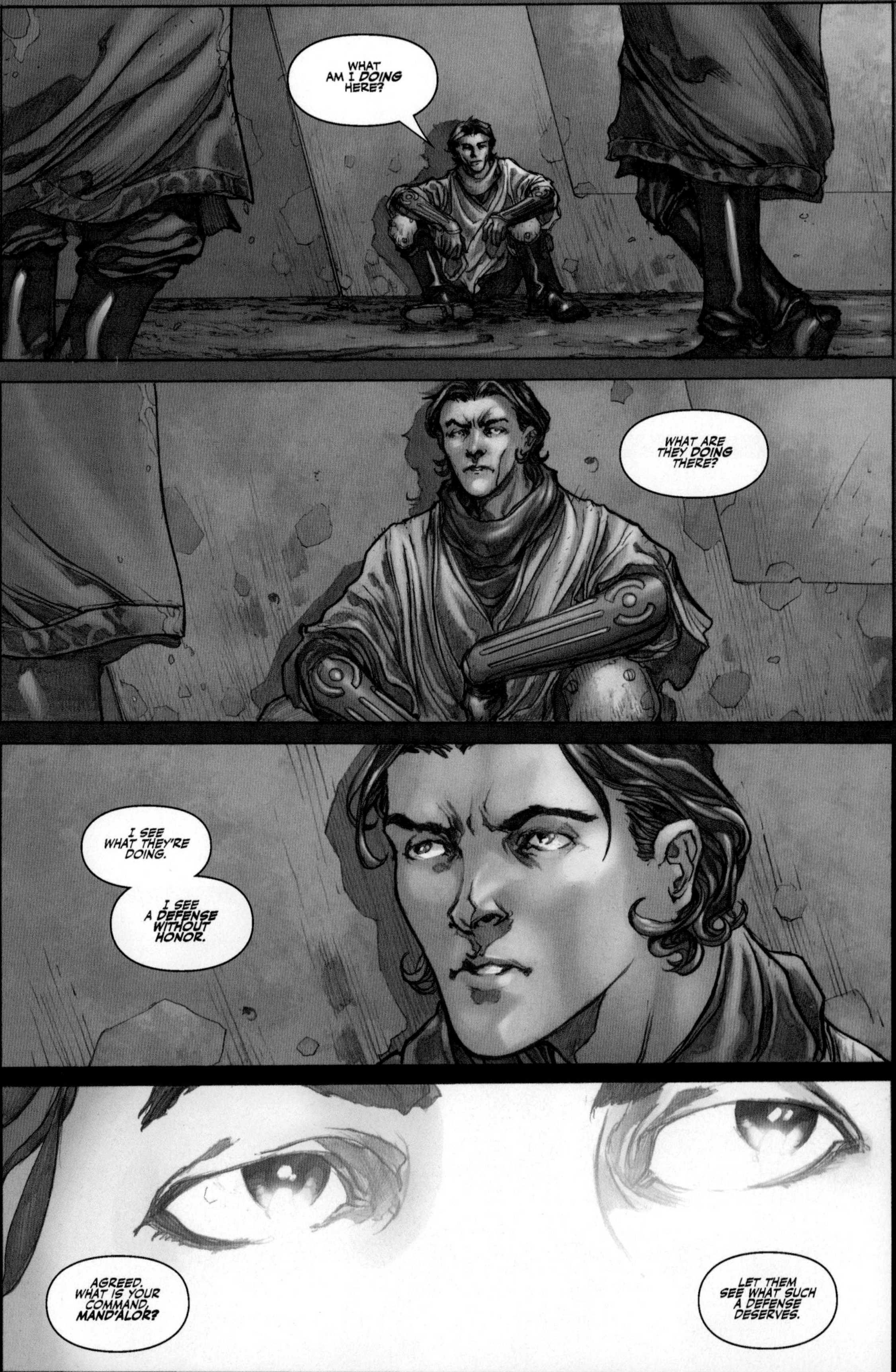
WHAT AM I DOING HERE?
WHAT ARE THEY DOING THERE?
I SEE WHAT THEY'RE DOING.
I SEE A DEFENSE WITHOUT HONOR.
AGREED. WHAT IS YOUR COMMAND, MAND'ALOR?
LET THEM SEE WHAT SUCH A DEFENSE DESERVES.

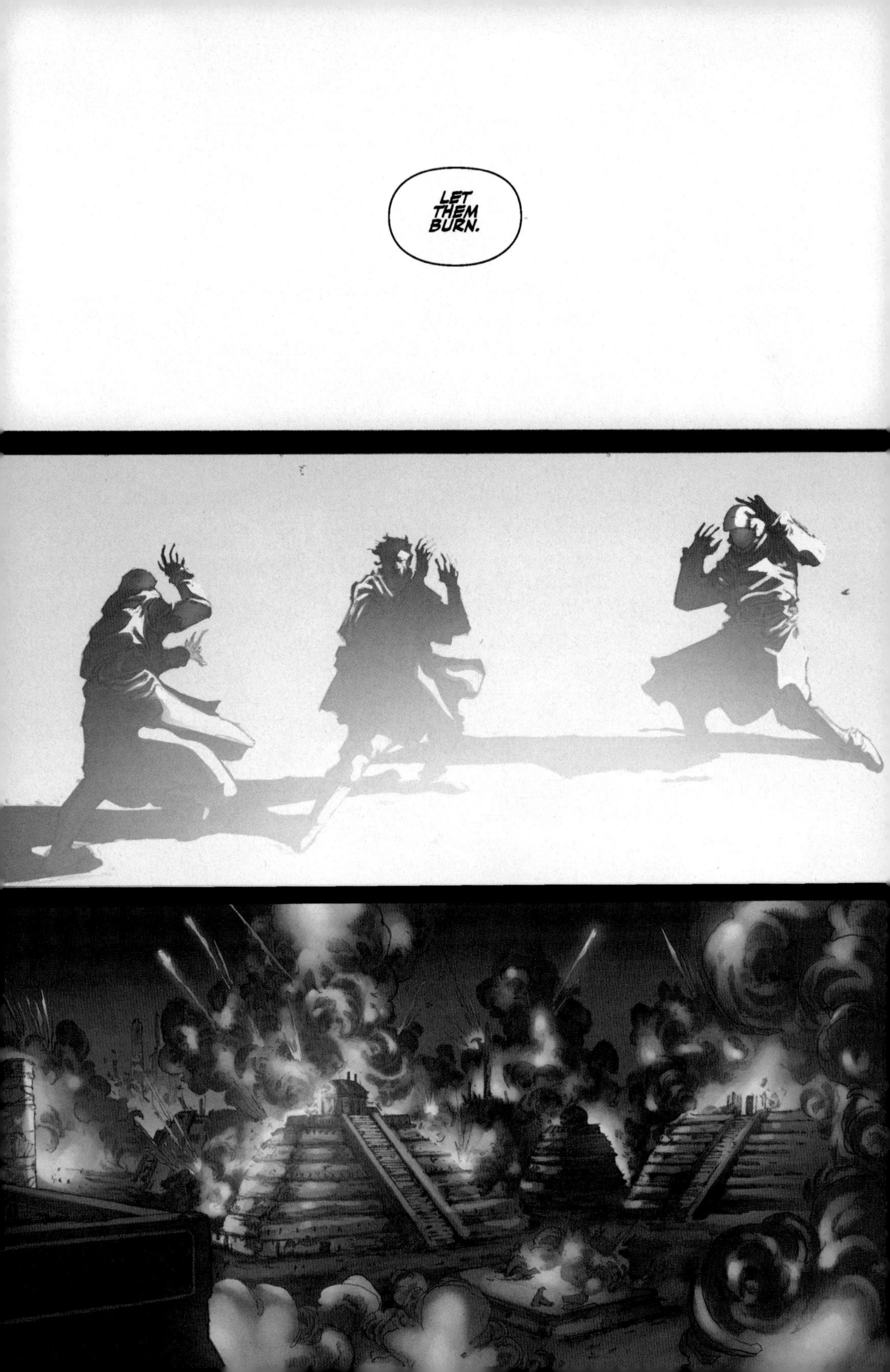
LET THEM BURN.

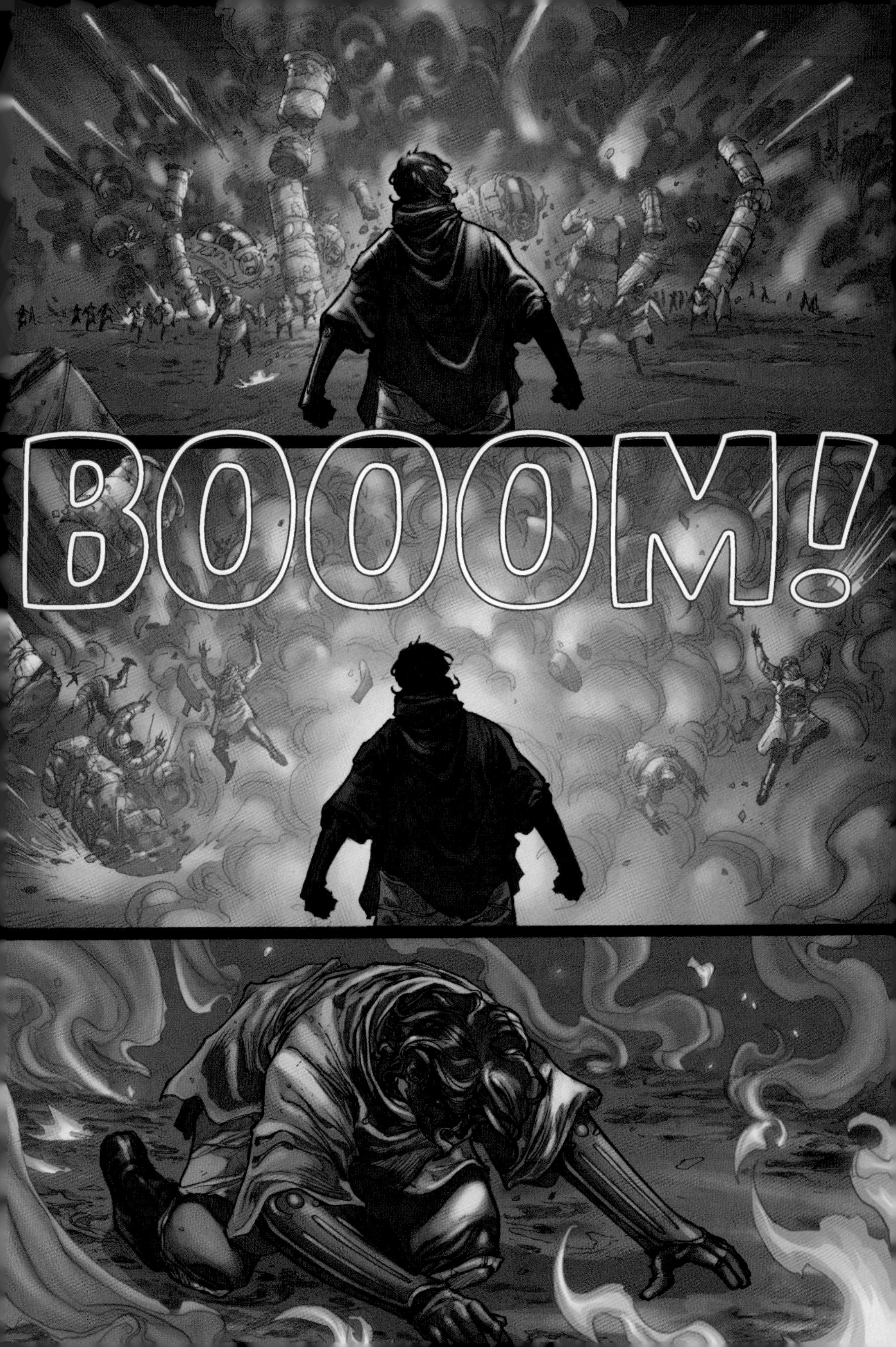
BOOOM!

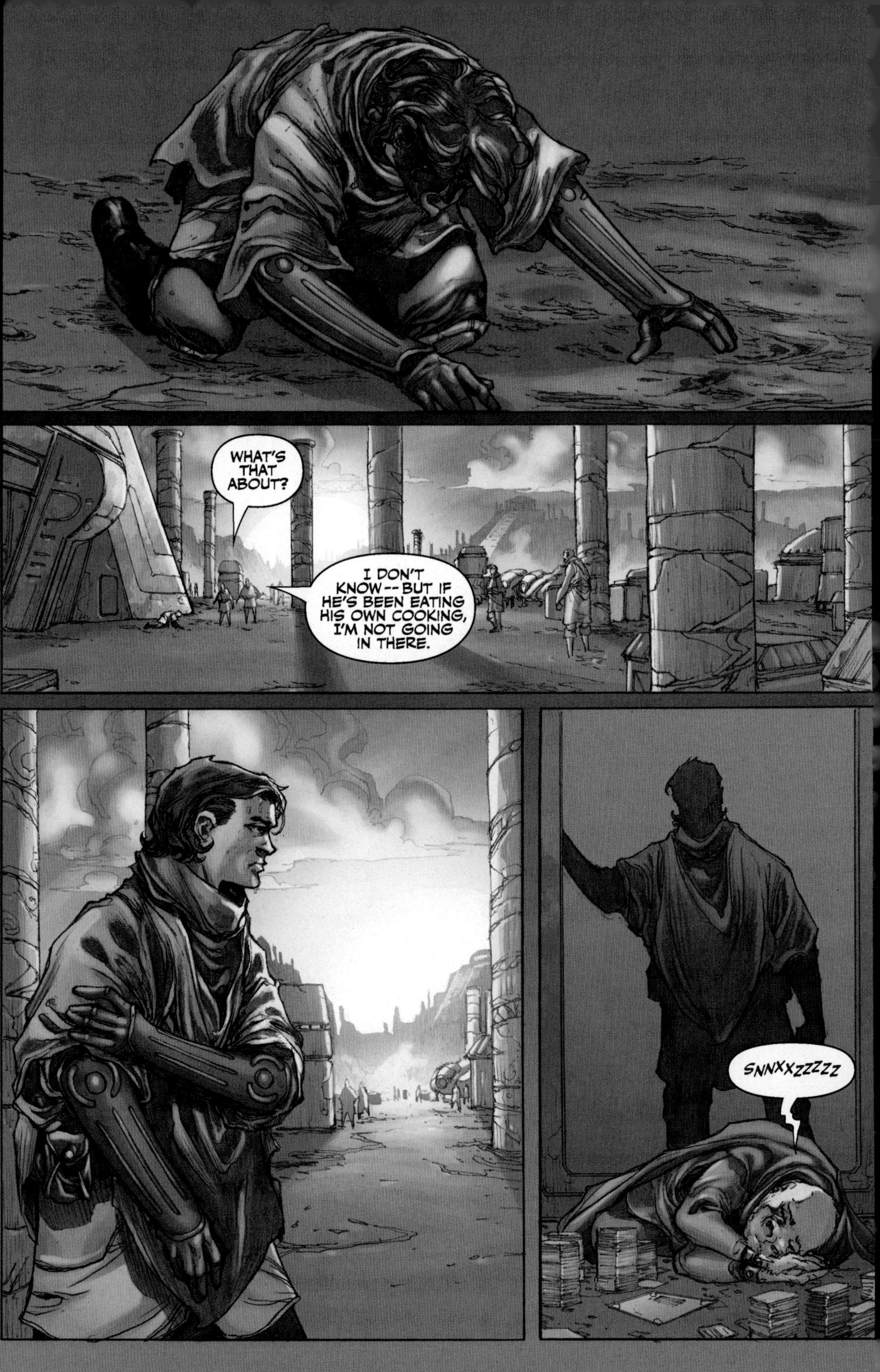
WHAT'S THAT ABOUT?
I DON'T KNOW--BUT IF HE'S BEEN EATING HIS OWN COOKING, I'M NOT GOING IN THERE.
SNNXXZZZZZ

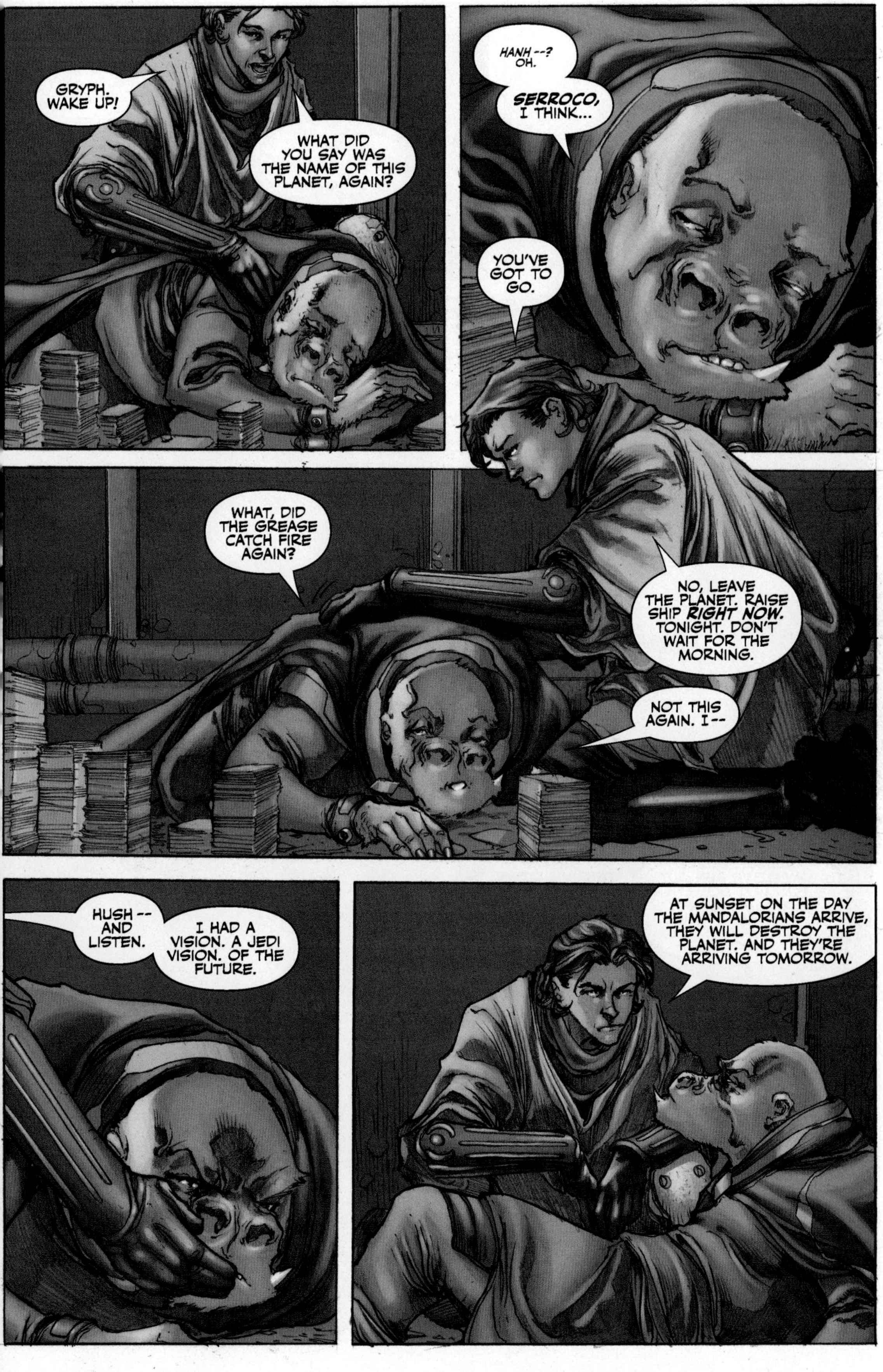

GRYPH. WAKE UP!
WHAT DID YOU SAY WAS THE NAME OF THIS PLANET, AGAIN?
HANH --? OH.
SERROCO, I THINK...
YOU'VE GOT TO GO.
WHAT, DID THE GREASE CATCH FIRE AGAIN?
NO, LEAVE THE PLANET. RAISE SHIP RIGHT NOW. TONIGHT. DON'T WAIT FOR THE MORNING.
NOT THIS AGAIN. I --
HUSH -- AND LISTEN.
I HAD A VISION. A JEDI VISION. OF THE FUTURE.
AT SUNSET ON THE DAY THE MANDALORIANS ARRIVE, THEY WILL DESTROY THE PLANET. AND THEY'RE ARRIVING TOMORROW.

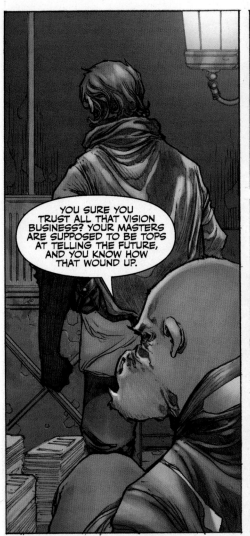

YOU SURE YOU TRUST ALL THAT VISION BUSINESS? YOUR MASTERS ARE SUPPOSED TO BE TOPS AT TELLING THE FUTURE, AND YOU KNOW HOW THAT WOUND UP.

THEY WERE *TRYING* TO SEE THE FUTURE. I WASN'T.

ALMOST NEVER *WORKS* WHEN I TRY. WHEN I SEE SOMETHING I *WASN'T* LOOKING FOR... WELL, I THINK THE FORCE REALLY MEANS IT.

I DON'T LIKE IT ONE BIT. THERE'S MONEY TO BE MADE HERE -- AND I DON'T MEAN BY ME. THIS PLANET'S *WORTH* SOMETHING.

WHO TRASHES SOMETHING VALUABLE?

SOMEONE WHO WANTS TO MAKE A POINT.

ALL RIGHT. I'LL SAY WE'VE RUN OUT OF FOOD OR SOMETHING. THEY WON'T WANT US HERE WHEN THE SHOOTING STARTS, ANYWAY.

START TEARING DOWN THE TABLES AND WE'LL GET OUT OF HERE.

YOU'LL HAVE TO DO THAT. I CAN'T --

--BECAUSE I'M NOT GOING WITH YOU.

I HAVE TO TALK TO ADMIRAL KARATH.

THE ADJUDICATOR

The Freelance Security Professional's Holofeed

Special Report: The Outer Rim

KRAV'S HOT LIST

They're hot—and they're worth a lot!

Got some decent picks this week to add to the list, plus the same-old-same-old.

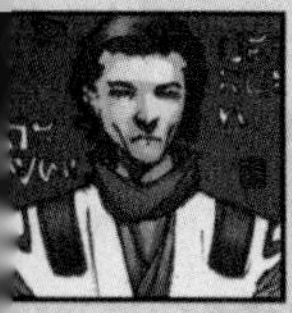

Zayne Carrick
Bounties: Nine, totaling 61,000 credits
Wanted for: Murder, treason, destruction of property, traffic infractions

Status on some of those bounties is iffy (see column this issue) but we hear a Coruscant player may step in and guarantee the ones in doubt. Not how I'd spend it, but hey, it's your money…

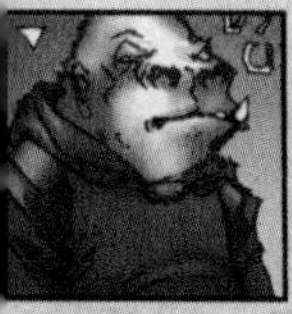

Marn Hierogryph
Bounties: Seven, totaling 24,000 credits
Wanted for: Accomplice to murder, treason, destruction of property, racketeering, fraud

Sightings of "The Gryph" are so common, it's almost not worth talking about. Seems like all the Snivvians in the galaxy comb their hair the same way.

picture not available

Kelven Garnatrope
Bounties: Three, totaling 38,000 credits
Wanted for: Murder

They say he's the "Corellian Strangler," but I'll believe it when they can get a decent picture for us to go on. How are we supposed to catch this guy, start checking I.D.s?

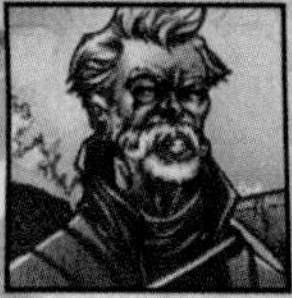

Baron Hyro Margryph
Bounties: One, totaling 100,000 credits
Wanted for: Who cares?

New to the list is this guy: only got the name and image. An Arkanian offshoot—no idea what he did. Doesn't look too dangerous, but the money's amazing and the issuer looks solid. This fossil's buried treasure!

SELECT to continue list...

OUTER RIM BOUNTIES: STILL ANY GOOD?

Mandie assault ruins it for the rest of us
By KRAV NOBLIS, *Adjudicator* Editor

And we thought the Jedi were spoilsports.

With the Mandalorians gobbling up Republic worlds on the Outer Rim, it's not just hurting the freelancers who work there. Many of the perps on the run in Republic territory (or, at least, what's Republic territory for the moment) are only valuable to parties that now have other things to worry about.

The most glaring example is Zayne Carrick, the Padawan who, with his accomplice Marn Hierogryph, whacked the rest of his class on Taris. The biggest of the bounties was guaranteed by the Taris Chamber of Commerce, which, last this reporter heard, was in danger of some serious Mandalorian redecoration. You can't very well cough up the credits with a bomb dropped in your lobby!

Don't get me wrong—I still wouldn't turn down a chance to nab either one of 'em, though. There's more than enough cash put up on Coruscant alone. But on a Zovius Mendu, forget it. I'm not in this for my health!

It's worse than you may think. I was trying to turn in a sniveling executive-type perp on Wayland the other day, when who should I see in the hallway of the constabulary but the Constable—carrying boxes to the exit, and leading what looked like his whole family. Seeing the guy was busy, I just asked for a voucher to take to the Lhosan Industries building. No joy! It's full of Basilisks, he says. Industrial espionage just ain't the big problem it once was for them!

Until lately, our trade's had a good run. When guys like the Moomo Brothers can get work, anybody can. But if the Mandies keep knocking off the customers, those times may be over. The bucketheads seem to like to chase their own baddies well enough. Almost makes you think a Mandalorian would make a decent bounty hunter, if circumstances were different!

SELECT to learn more...

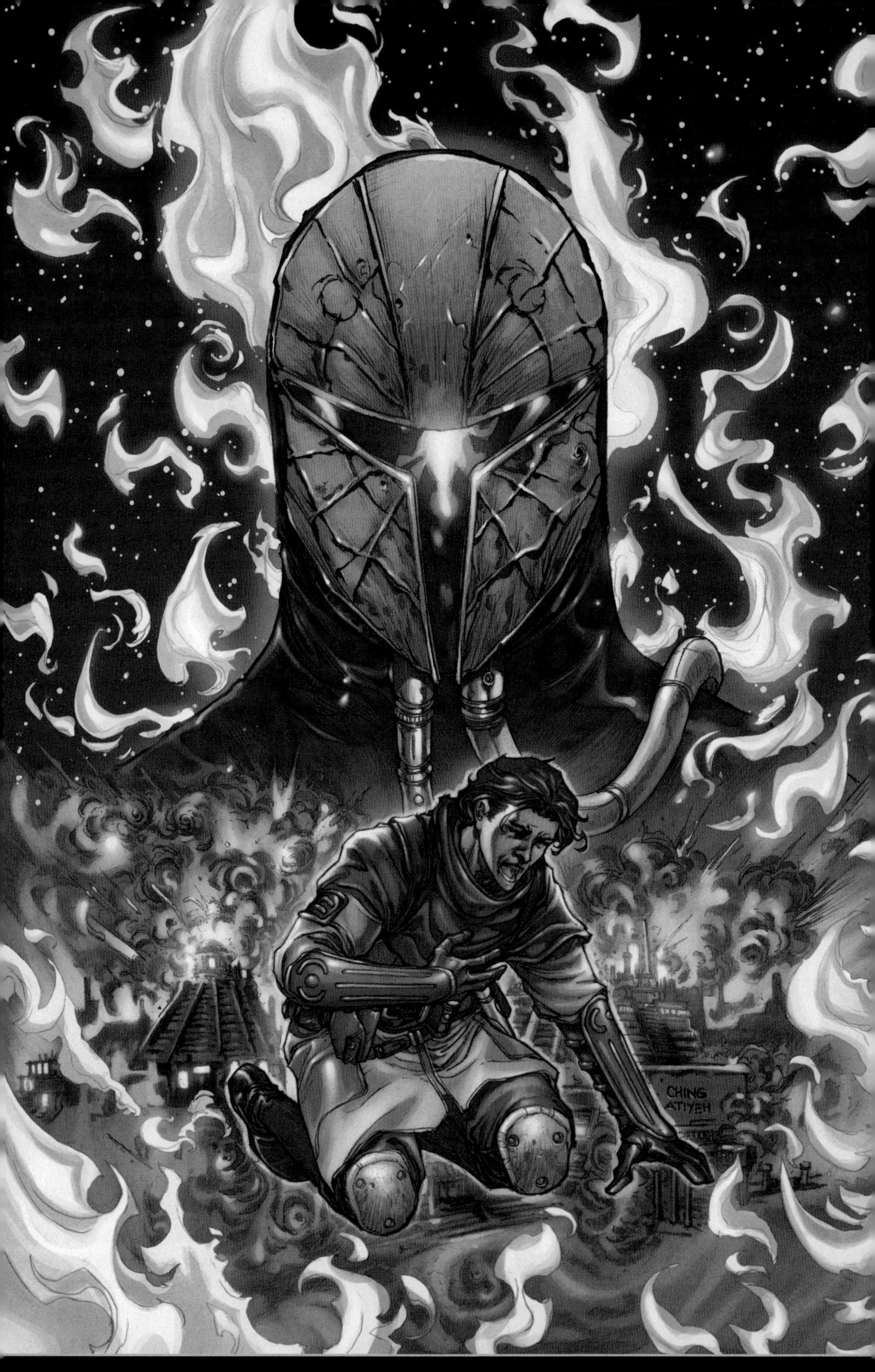
CHING
ATIYEH

STAR WARS: KNIGHTS OF THE OLD REPUBLIC #15 — "DAYS OF FEAR, PART 3"

WRITER: JOHN JACKSON MILLER • ARTIST: DUSTIN WEAVER • COLORIST: MICHAEL ATIYEH • LETTERER: MICHAEL HEISLER
ASSISTANT EDITOR: DAVE MARSHALL • EDITOR: JEREMY BARLOW • COVER ARTISTS: BRIAN CHING & MICHAEL ATIYEH

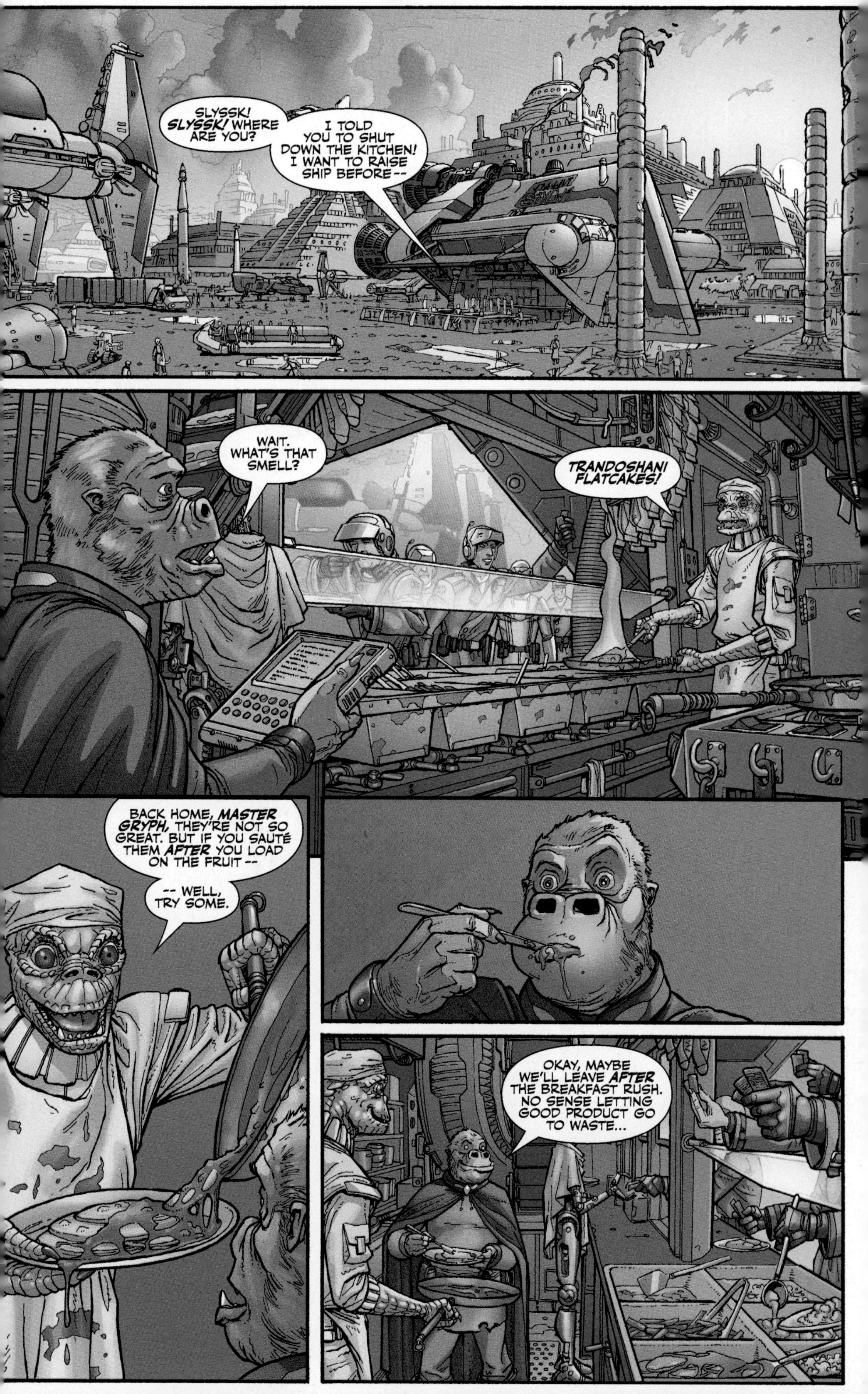

SLYSSK! SLYSSK! WHERE ARE YOU?
I TOLD YOU TO SHUT DOWN THE KITCHEN! I WANT TO RAISE SHIP BEFORE--
WAIT. WHAT'S THAT SMELL?
TRANDOSHANI FLATCAKES!
BACK HOME, MASTER GRYPH, THEY'RE NOT SO GREAT. BUT IF YOU SAUTÉ THEM AFTER YOU LOAD ON THE FRUIT --
-- WELL, TRY SOME.
OKAY, MAYBE WE'LL LEAVE AFTER THE BREAKFAST RUSH. NO SENSE LETTING GOOD PRODUCT GO TO WASTE...

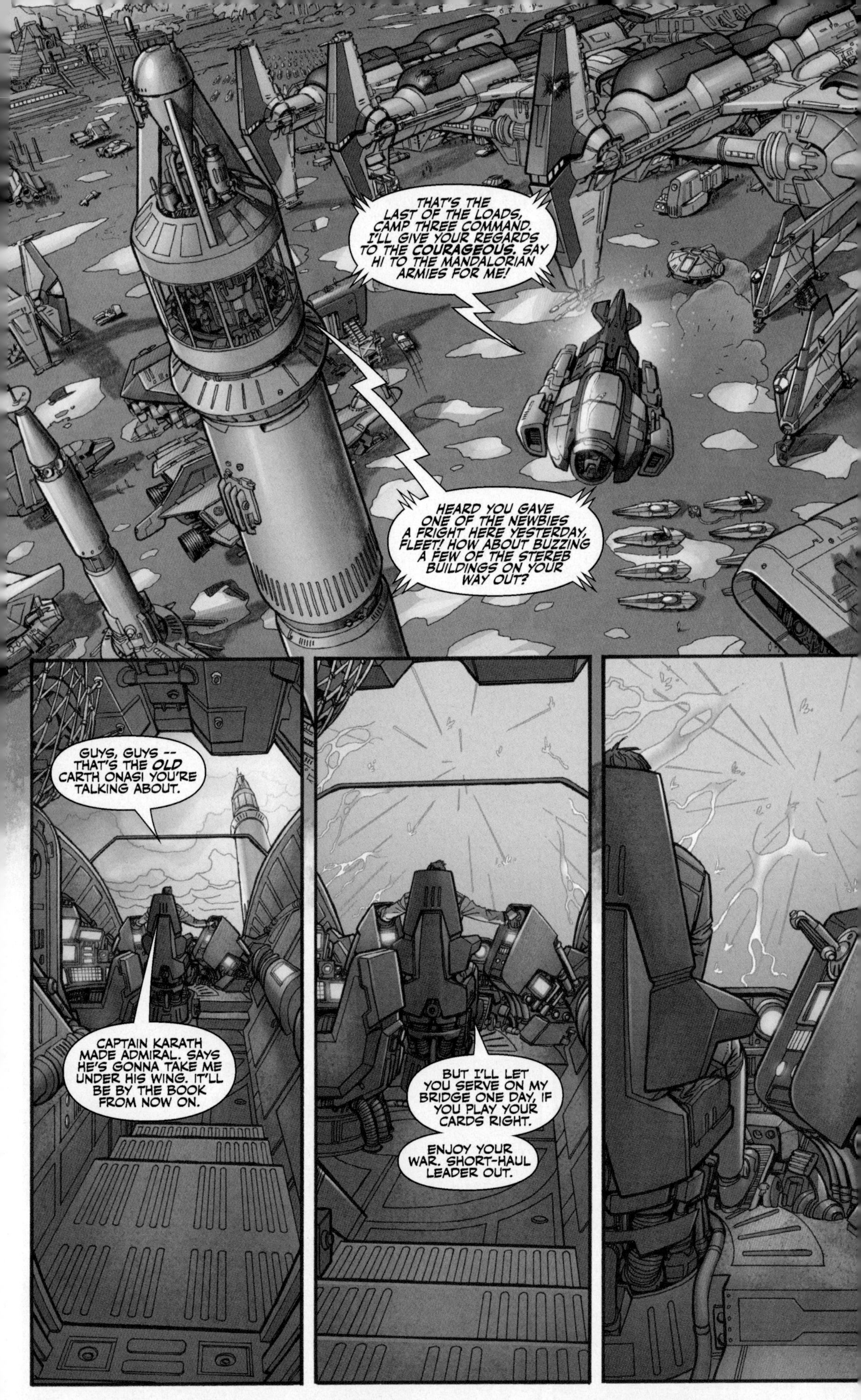
THAT'S THE LAST OF THE LOADS, CAMP THREE COMMAND. I'LL GIVE YOUR REGARDS TO THE COURAGEOUS. SAY HI TO THE MANDALORIAN ARMIES FOR ME!
HEARD YOU GAVE ONE OF THE NEWBIES A FRIGHT HERE YESTERDAY, FLEET! HOW ABOUT BUZZING A FEW OF THE STEREB BUILDINGS ON YOUR WAY OUT?
GUYS, GUYS -- THAT'S THE OLD CARTH ONASI YOU'RE TALKING ABOUT.
CAPTAIN KARATH MADE ADMIRAL. SAYS HE'S GONNA TAKE ME UNDER HIS WING. IT'LL BE BY THE BOOK FROM NOW ON.
BUT I'LL LET YOU SERVE ON MY BRIDGE ONE DAY, IF YOU PLAY YOUR CARDS RIGHT.
ENJOY YOUR WAR. SHORT-HAUL LEADER OUT.

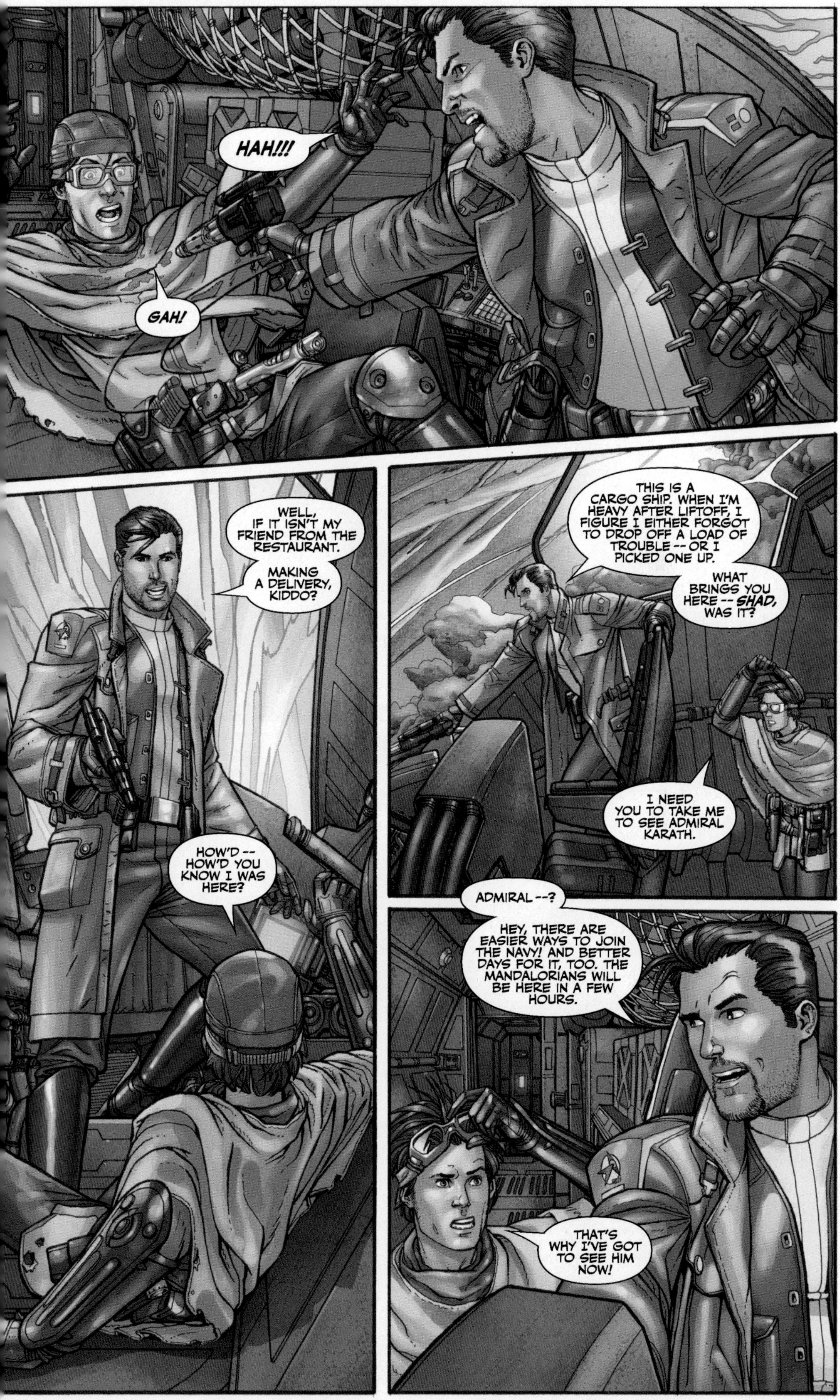
HAH!!!
GAH!
WELL, IF IT ISN'T MY FRIEND FROM THE RESTAURANT.
MAKING A DELIVERY, KIDDO?
HOW'D -- HOW'D YOU KNOW I WAS HERE?
THIS IS A CARGO SHIP. WHEN I'M HEAVY AFTER LIFTOFF, I FIGURE I EITHER FORGOT TO DROP OFF A LOAD OF TROUBLE -- OR I PICKED ONE UP.
WHAT BRINGS YOU HERE -- SHAD, WAS IT?
I NEED YOU TO TAKE ME TO SEE ADMIRAL KARATH.
ADMIRAL --?
HEY, THERE ARE EASIER WAYS TO JOIN THE NAVY! AND BETTER DAYS FOR IT, TOO. THE MANDALORIANS WILL BE HERE IN A FEW HOURS.
THAT'S WHY I'VE GOT TO SEE HIM NOW!

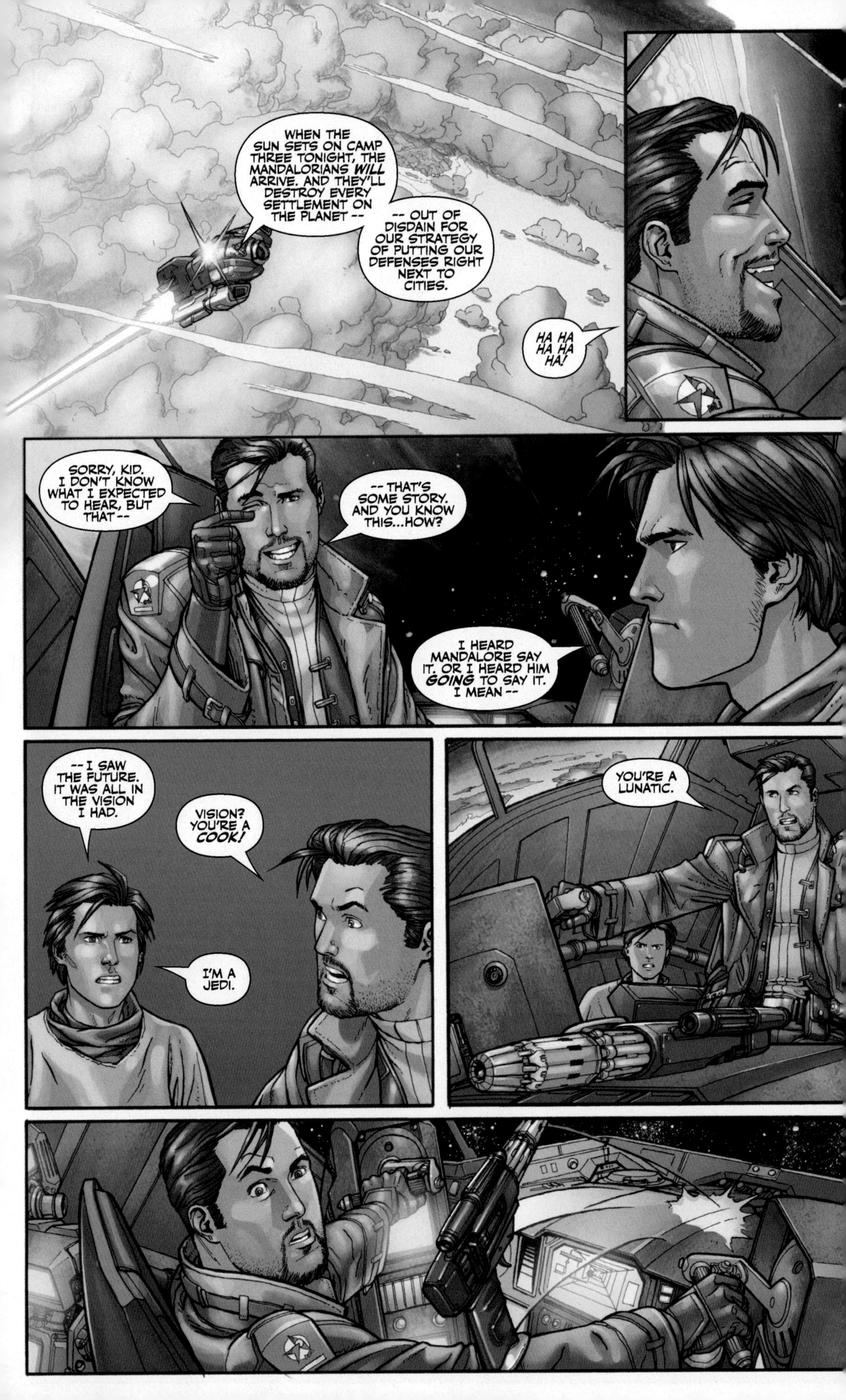
WHEN THE SUN SETS ON CAMP THREE TONIGHT, THE MANDALORIANS *WILL* ARRIVE. AND THEY'LL DESTROY EVERY SETTLEMENT ON THE PLANET --
-- OUT OF DISDAIN FOR OUR STRATEGY OF PUTTING OUR DEFENSES RIGHT NEXT TO CITIES.
HA HA HA HA HA!
SORRY, KID. I DON'T KNOW WHAT I EXPECTED TO HEAR, BUT THAT --
-- THAT'S SOME STORY. AND YOU KNOW THIS...HOW?
I HEARD MANDALORE SAY IT. OR I HEARD HIM *GOING* TO SAY IT. I MEAN --
-- I SAW THE FUTURE. IT WAS ALL IN THE VISION I HAD.
VISION? YOU'RE A *COOK!*
I'M A JEDI.
YOU'RE A LUNATIC.

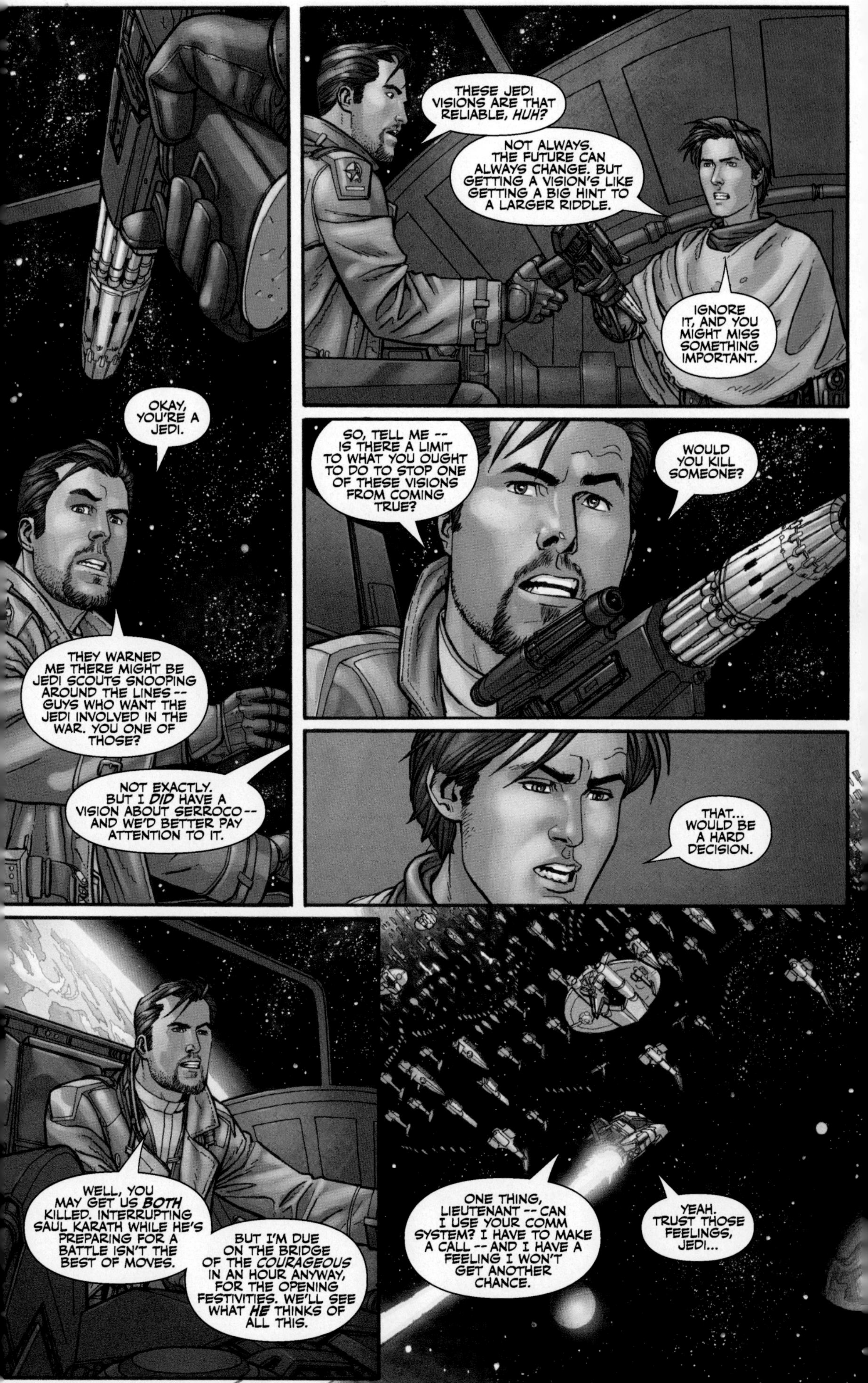
THESE JEDI VISIONS ARE THAT RELIABLE, *HUH*?
NOT ALWAYS. THE FUTURE CAN ALWAYS CHANGE. BUT GETTING A VISION'S LIKE GETTING A BIG HINT TO A LARGER RIDDLE.
IGNORE IT, AND YOU MIGHT MISS SOMETHING IMPORTANT.
OKAY, YOU'RE A JEDI.
THEY WARNED ME THERE MIGHT BE JEDI SCOUTS SNOOPING AROUND THE LINES -- GUYS WHO WANT THE JEDI INVOLVED IN THE WAR. YOU ONE OF THOSE?
NOT EXACTLY. BUT I *DID* HAVE A VISION ABOUT SERROCO -- AND WE'D BETTER PAY ATTENTION TO IT.
SO, TELL ME -- IS THERE A LIMIT TO WHAT YOU OUGHT TO DO TO STOP ONE OF THESE VISIONS FROM COMING TRUE?
WOULD YOU KILL SOMEONE?
THAT... WOULD BE A HARD DECISION.
WELL, YOU MAY GET US *BOTH* KILLED. INTERRUPTING SAUL KARATH WHILE HE'S PREPARING FOR A BATTLE ISN'T THE BEST OF MOVES.
BUT I'M DUE ON THE BRIDGE OF THE *COURAGEOUS* IN AN HOUR ANYWAY, FOR THE OPENING FESTIVITIES. WE'LL SEE WHAT *HE* THINKS OF ALL THIS.
ONE THING, LIEUTENANT -- CAN I USE YOUR COMM SYSTEM? I HAVE TO MAKE A CALL -- AND I HAVE A FEELING I WON'T GET ANOTHER CHANCE.
YEAH. TRUST THOSE FEELINGS, JEDI...

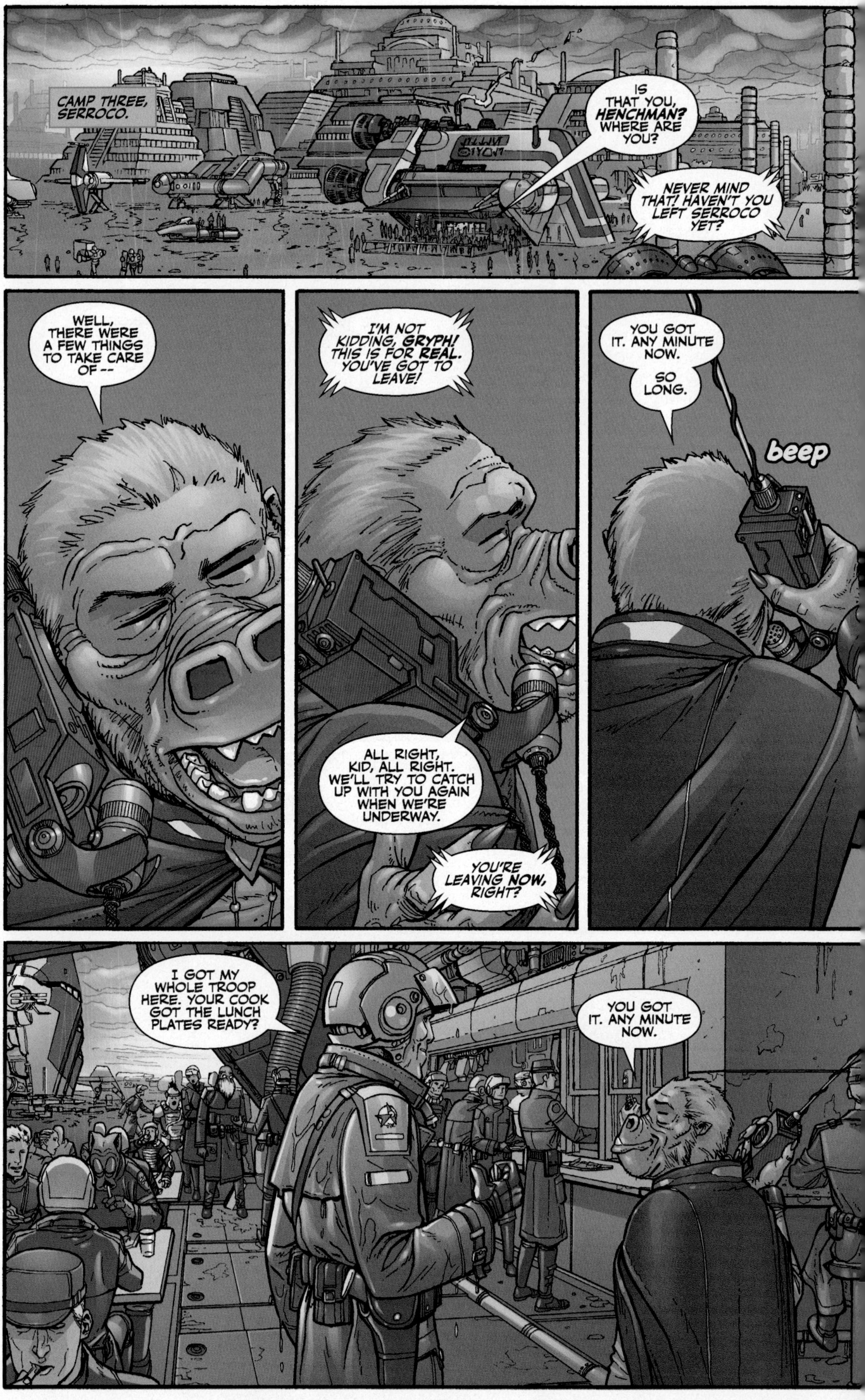
CAMP THREE, SERROCO.
IS THAT YOU, HENCHMAN? WHERE ARE YOU?
NEVER MIND THAT! HAVEN'T YOU LEFT SERROCO YET?
WELL, THERE WERE A FEW THINGS TO TAKE CARE OF --
I'M NOT KIDDING, GRYPH! THIS IS FOR REAL. YOU'VE GOT TO LEAVE!
ALL RIGHT, KID, ALL RIGHT. WE'LL TRY TO CATCH UP WITH YOU AGAIN WHEN WE'RE UNDERWAY.
YOU'RE LEAVING NOW, RIGHT?
YOU GOT IT. ANY MINUTE NOW.
SO LONG.
beep
I GOT MY WHOLE TROOP HERE. YOUR COOK GOT THE LUNCH PLATES READY?
YOU GOT IT. ANY MINUTE NOW.

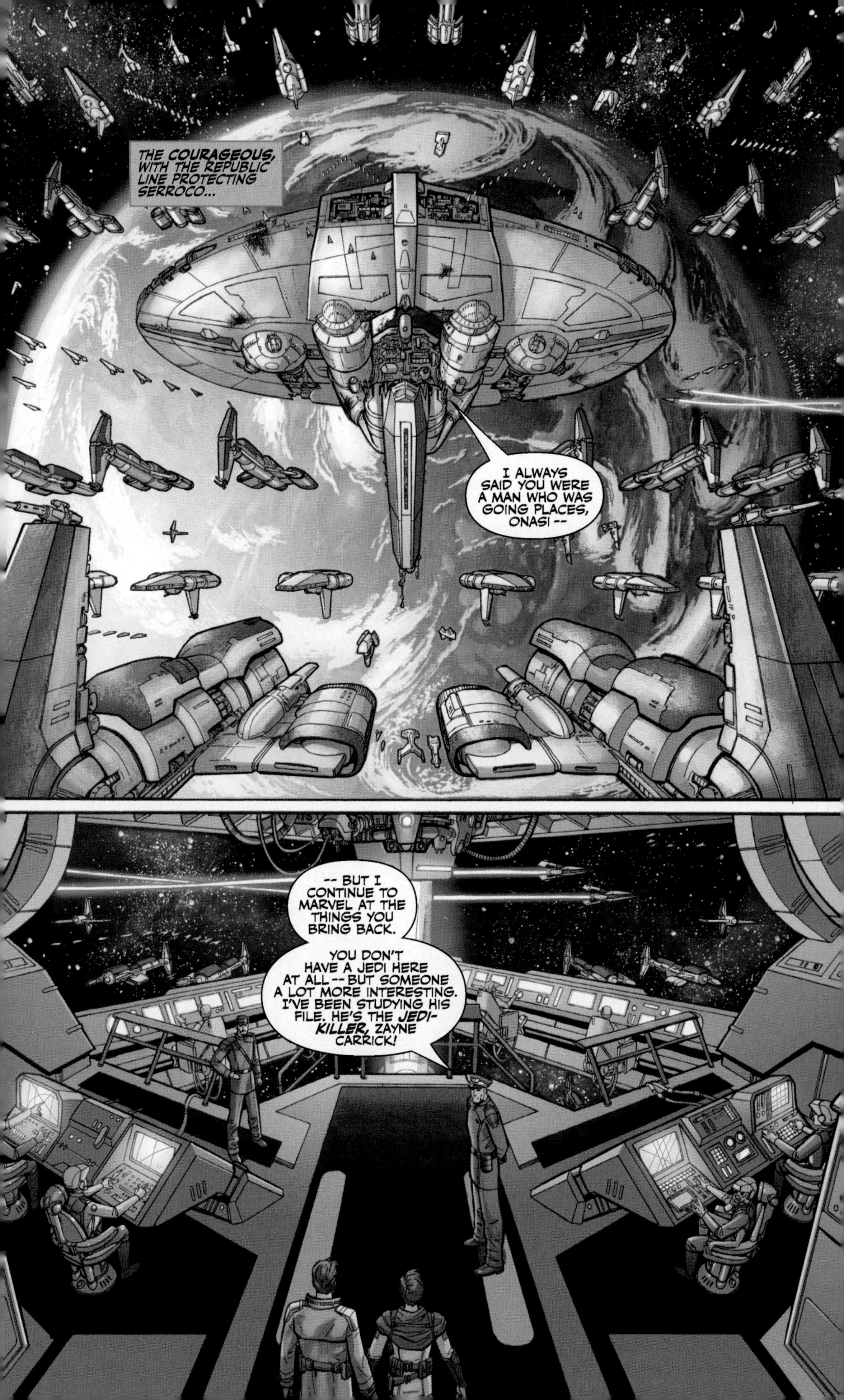
THE COURAGEOUS, WITH THE REPUBLIC LINE PROTECTING SERROCO...
I ALWAYS SAID YOU WERE A MAN WHO WAS GOING PLACES, ONASI --
-- BUT I CONTINUE TO MARVEL AT THE THINGS YOU BRING BACK.
YOU DON'T HAVE A JEDI HERE AT ALL -- BUT SOMEONE A LOT MORE INTERESTING. I'VE BEEN STUDYING HIS FILE. HE'S THE JEDI-KILLER, ZAYNE CARRICK!

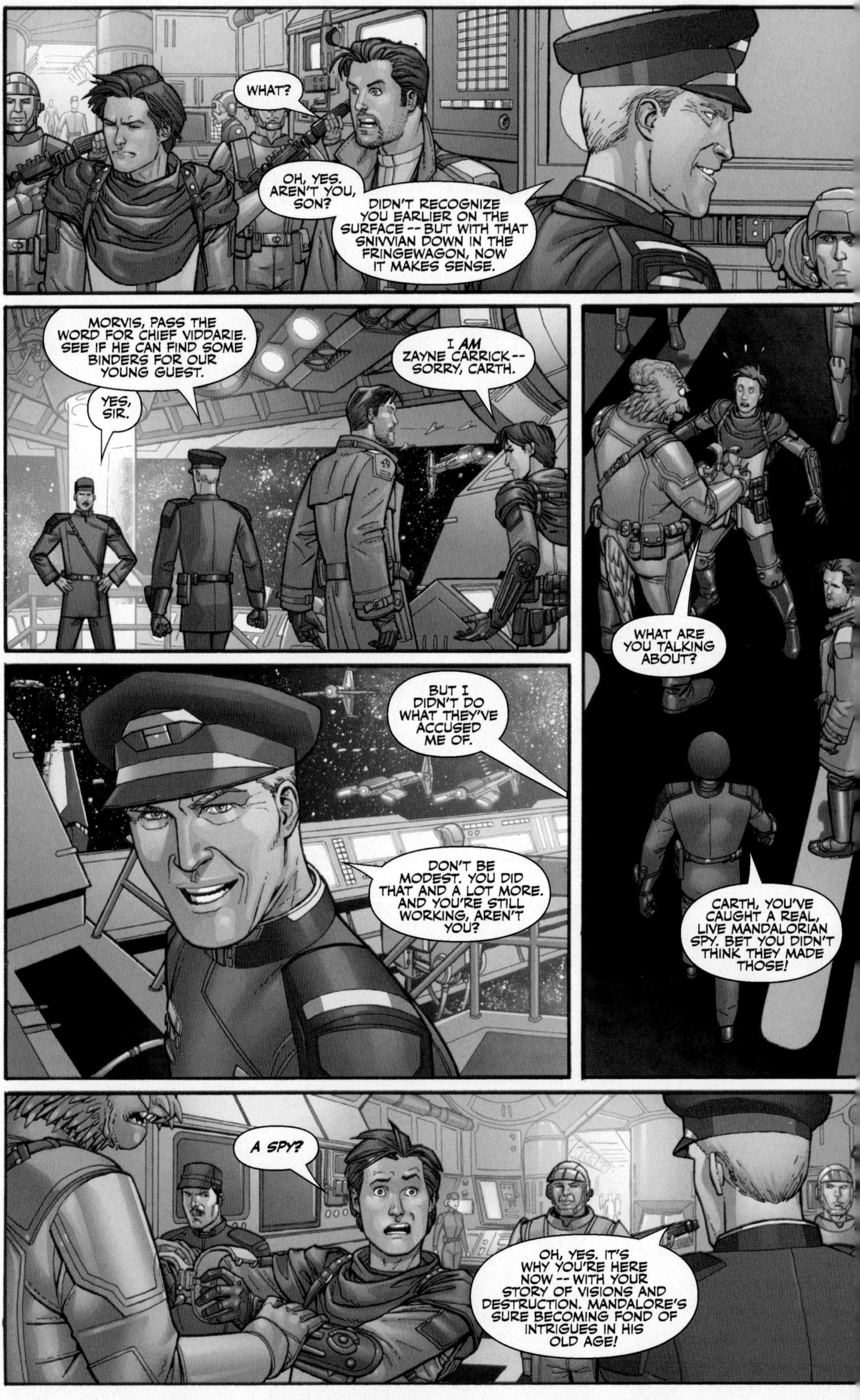

WHAT?
OH, YES. AREN'T YOU, SON?
DIDN'T RECOGNIZE YOU EARLIER ON THE SURFACE -- BUT WITH THAT SNIVVIAN DOWN IN THE FRINGEWAGON, NOW IT MAKES SENSE.
MORVIS, PASS THE WORD FOR CHIEF VIDDARIE. SEE IF HE CAN FIND SOME BINDERS FOR OUR YOUNG GUEST.
YES, SIR.
I *AM* ZAYNE CARRICK -- SORRY, CARTH.
WHAT ARE YOU TALKING ABOUT?
BUT I DIDN'T DO WHAT THEY'VE ACCUSED ME OF.
DON'T BE MODEST. YOU DID THAT AND A LOT MORE. AND YOU'RE STILL WORKING, AREN'T YOU?
CARTH, YOU'VE CAUGHT A REAL, LIVE MANDALORIAN SPY. BET YOU DIDN'T THINK THEY MADE THOSE!
A SPY?
OH, YES. IT'S WHY YOU'RE HERE NOW -- WITH YOUR STORY OF VISIONS AND DESTRUCTION. MANDALORE'S SURE BECOMING FOND OF INTRIGUES IN HIS OLD AGE!

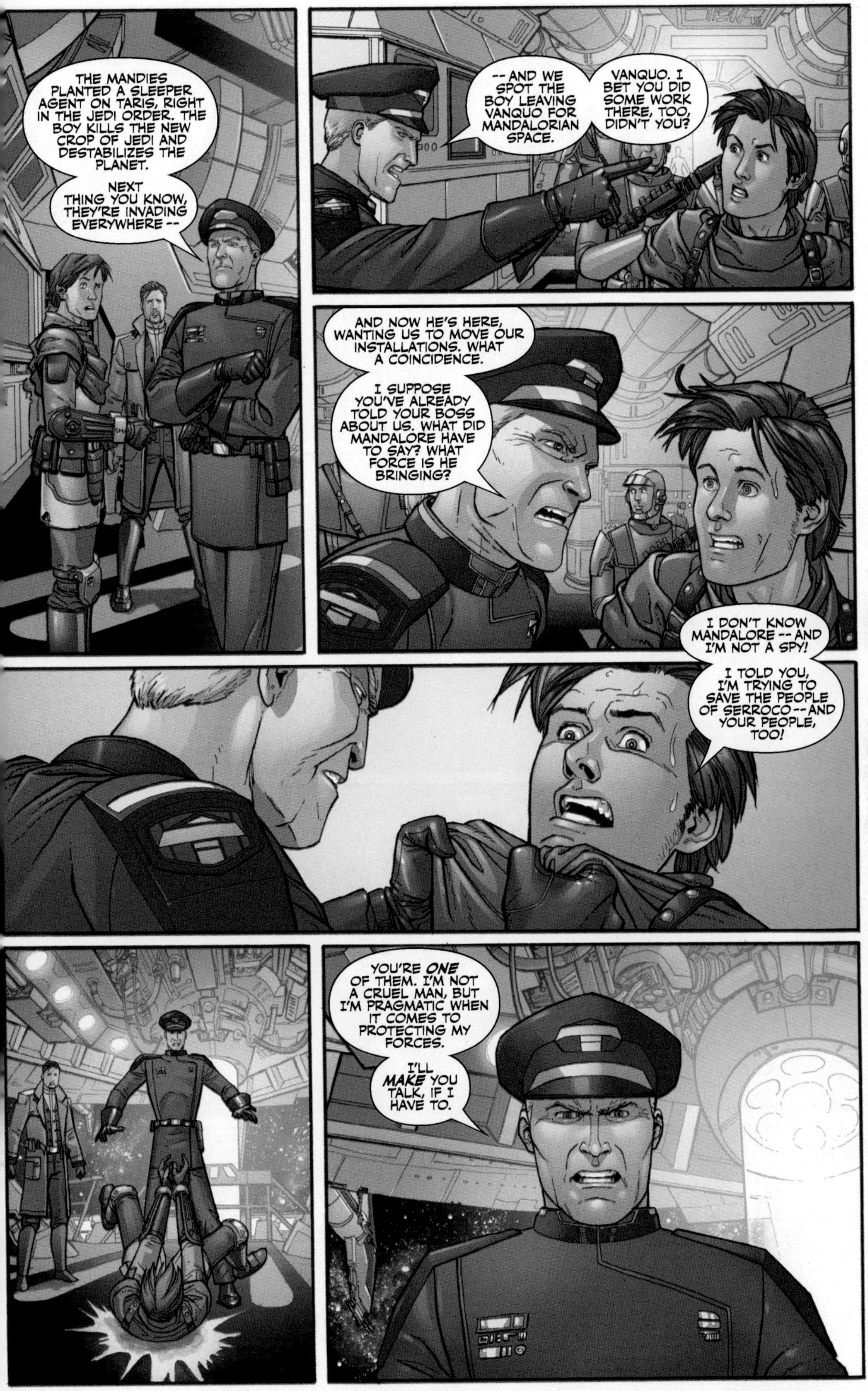
THE MANDIES PLANTED A SLEEPER AGENT ON TARIS, RIGHT IN THE JEDI ORDER. THE BOY KILLS THE NEW CROP OF JEDI AND DESTABILIZES THE PLANET.
NEXT THING YOU KNOW, THEY'RE INVADING EVERYWHERE --
-- AND WE SPOT THE BOY LEAVING VANQUO FOR MANDALORIAN SPACE.
VANQUO. I BET YOU DID SOME WORK THERE, TOO, DIDN'T YOU?
AND NOW HE'S HERE, WANTING US TO MOVE OUR INSTALLATIONS. WHAT A COINCIDENCE.
I SUPPOSE YOU'VE ALREADY TOLD YOUR BOSS ABOUT US. WHAT DID MANDALORE HAVE TO SAY? WHAT FORCE IS HE BRINGING?
I DON'T KNOW MANDALORE -- AND I'M NOT A SPY!
I TOLD YOU, I'M TRYING TO SAVE THE PEOPLE OF SERROCO -- AND YOUR PEOPLE, TOO!
YOU'RE ONE OF THEM. I'M NOT A CRUEL MAN, BUT I'M PRAGMATIC WHEN IT COMES TO PROTECTING MY FORCES.
I'LL MAKE YOU TALK, IF I HAVE TO.

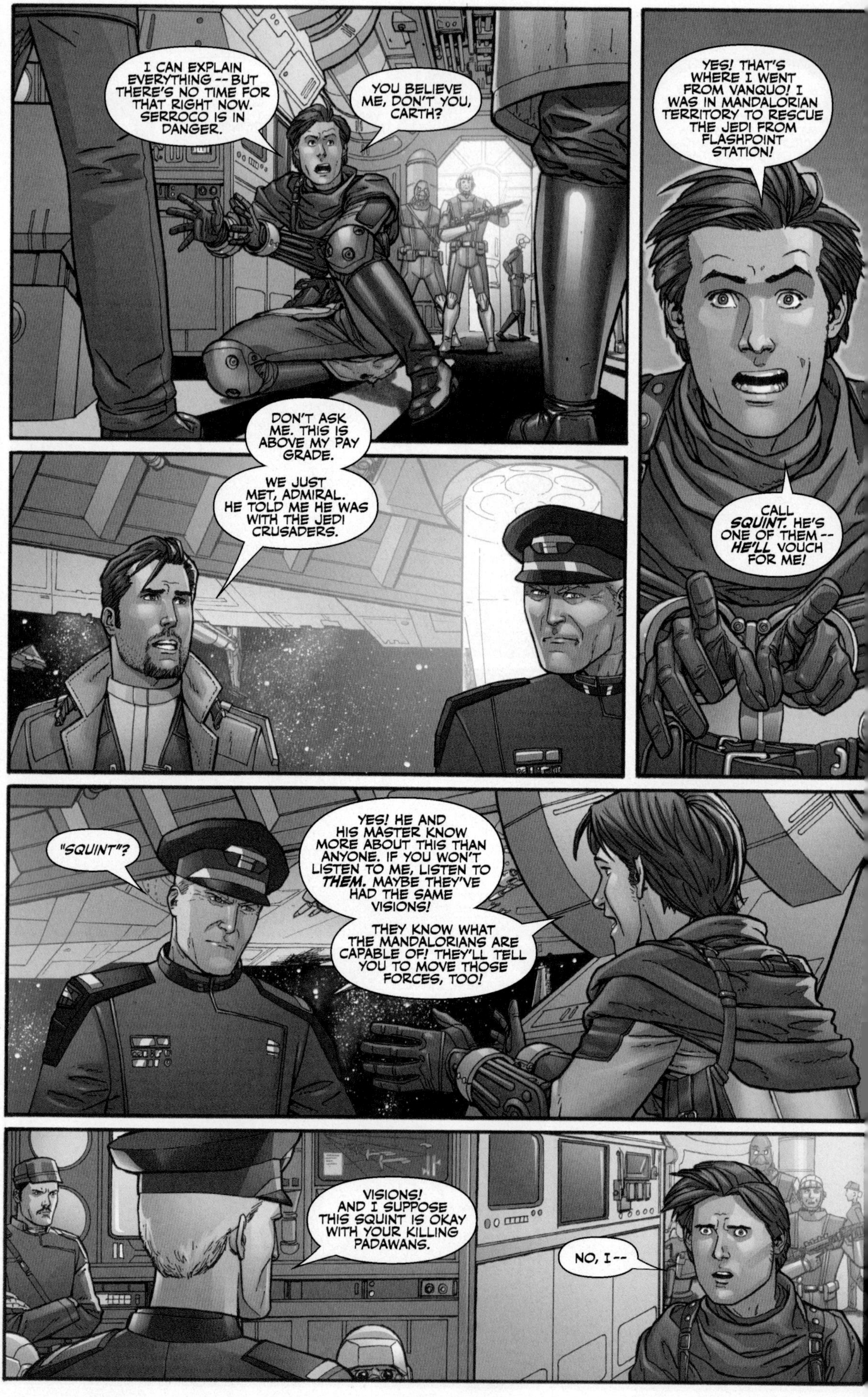
I CAN EXPLAIN EVERYTHING -- BUT THERE'S NO TIME FOR THAT RIGHT NOW. SERROCO IS IN DANGER.
YOU BELIEVE ME, DON'T YOU, CARTH?
DON'T ASK ME. THIS IS ABOVE MY PAY GRADE.
WE JUST MET, ADMIRAL. HE TOLD ME HE WAS WITH THE JEDI CRUSADERS.
YES! THAT'S WHERE I WENT FROM VANQUO! I WAS IN MANDALORIAN TERRITORY TO RESCUE THE JEDI FROM FLASHPOINT STATION!
CALL *SQUINT.* HE'S ONE OF THEM -- *HE'LL* VOUCH FOR ME!
"SQUINT"?
YES! HE AND HIS MASTER KNOW MORE ABOUT THIS THAN ANYONE. IF YOU WON'T LISTEN TO ME, LISTEN TO *THEM.* MAYBE THEY'VE HAD THE SAME VISIONS!
THEY KNOW WHAT THE MANDALORIANS ARE CAPABLE OF! THEY'LL TELL YOU TO MOVE THOSE FORCES, TOO!
VISIONS! AND I SUPPOSE THIS SQUINT IS OKAY WITH YOUR KILLING PADAWANS.
NO, I --

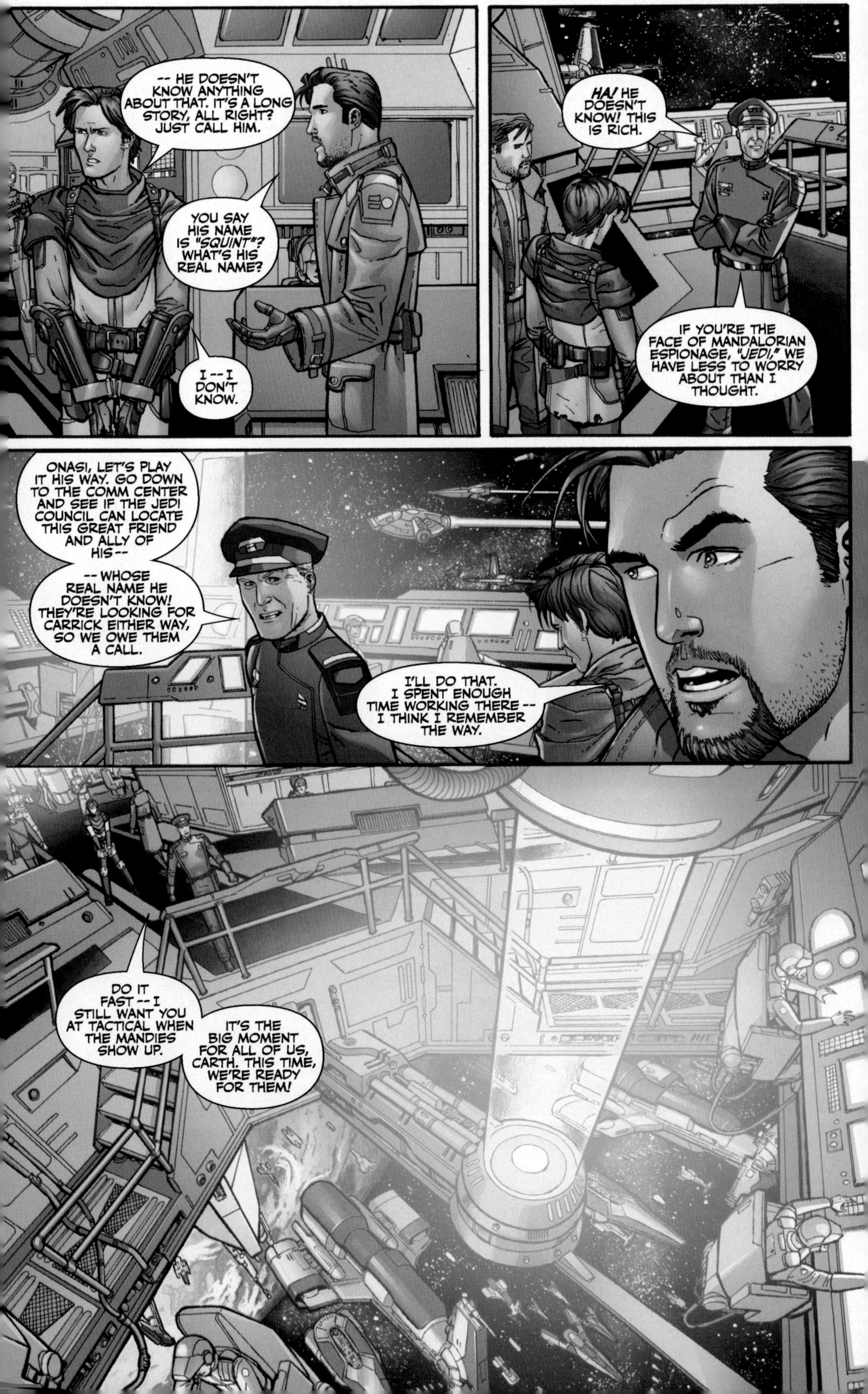
-- HE DOESN'T KNOW ANYTHING ABOUT THAT. IT'S A LONG STORY, ALL RIGHT? JUST CALL HIM.
YOU SAY HIS NAME IS "SQUINT"? WHAT'S HIS REAL NAME?
I -- I DON'T KNOW.
HA! HE DOESN'T KNOW! THIS IS RICH.
IF YOU'RE THE FACE OF MANDALORIAN ESPIONAGE, "JEDI," WE HAVE LESS TO WORRY ABOUT THAN I THOUGHT.
ONASI, LET'S PLAY IT HIS WAY. GO DOWN TO THE COMM CENTER AND SEE IF THE JEDI COUNCIL CAN LOCATE THIS GREAT FRIEND AND ALLY OF HIS--
-- WHOSE REAL NAME HE DOESN'T KNOW! THEY'RE LOOKING FOR CARRICK EITHER WAY, SO WE OWE THEM A CALL.
I'LL DO THAT. I SPENT ENOUGH TIME WORKING THERE -- I THINK I REMEMBER THE WAY.
DO IT FAST -- I STILL WANT YOU AT TACTICAL WHEN THE MANDIES SHOW UP.
IT'S THE BIG MOMENT FOR ALL OF US, CARTH. THIS TIME, WE'RE READY FOR THEM!

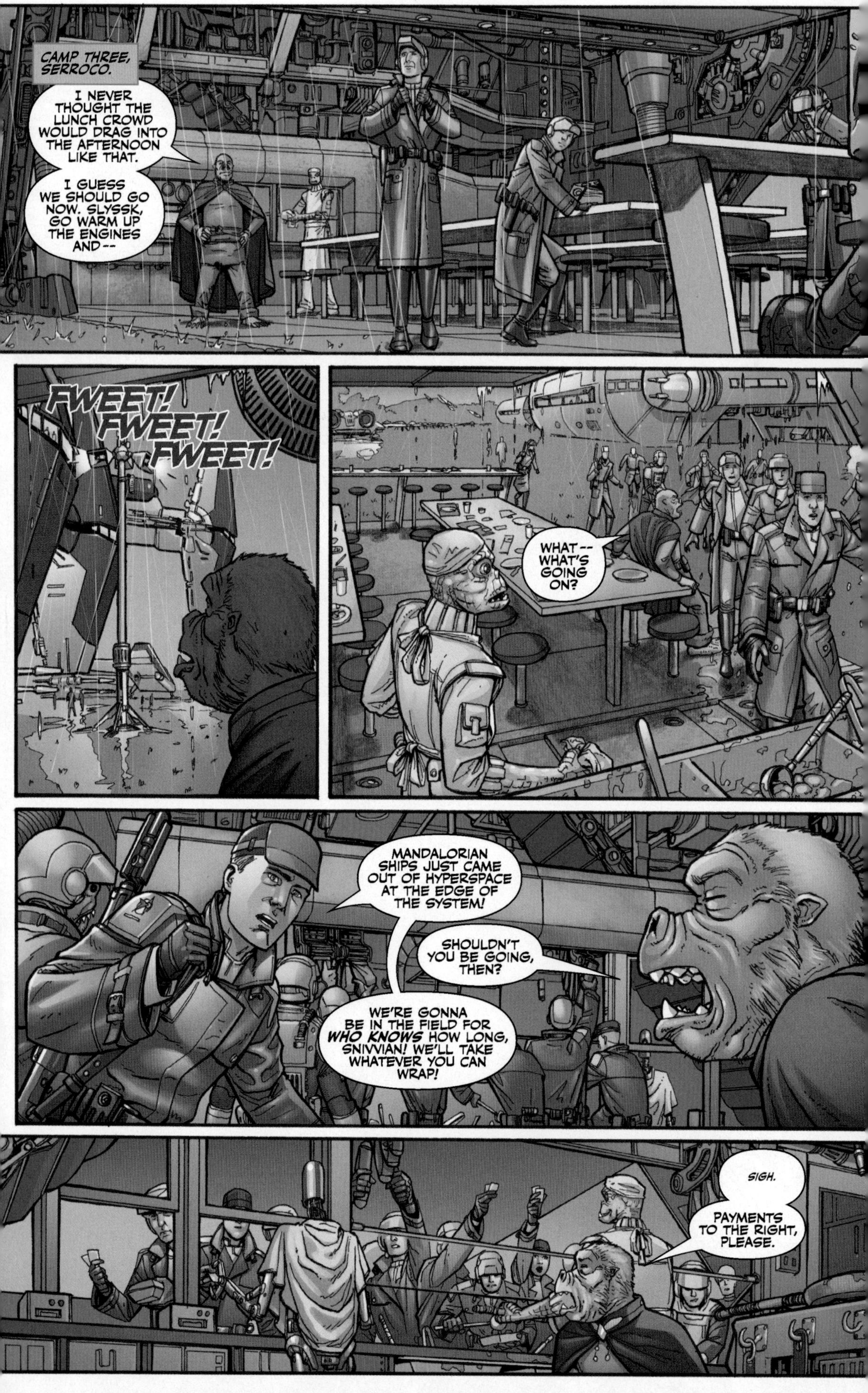
CAMP THREE, SERROCO.
I NEVER THOUGHT THE LUNCH CROWD WOULD DRAG INTO THE AFTERNOON LIKE THAT.
I GUESS WE SHOULD GO NOW. SLYSSK, GO WARM UP THE ENGINES AND--
FWEET! FWEET! FWEET!
WHAT-- WHAT'S GOING ON?
MANDALORIAN SHIPS JUST CAME OUT OF HYPERSPACE AT THE EDGE OF THE SYSTEM!
SHOULDN'T YOU BE GOING, THEN?
WE'RE GONNA BE IN THE FIELD FOR WHO KNOWS HOW LONG, SNIVVIAN! WE'LL TAKE WHATEVER YOU CAN WRAP!
SIGH.
PAYMENTS TO THE RIGHT, PLEASE.

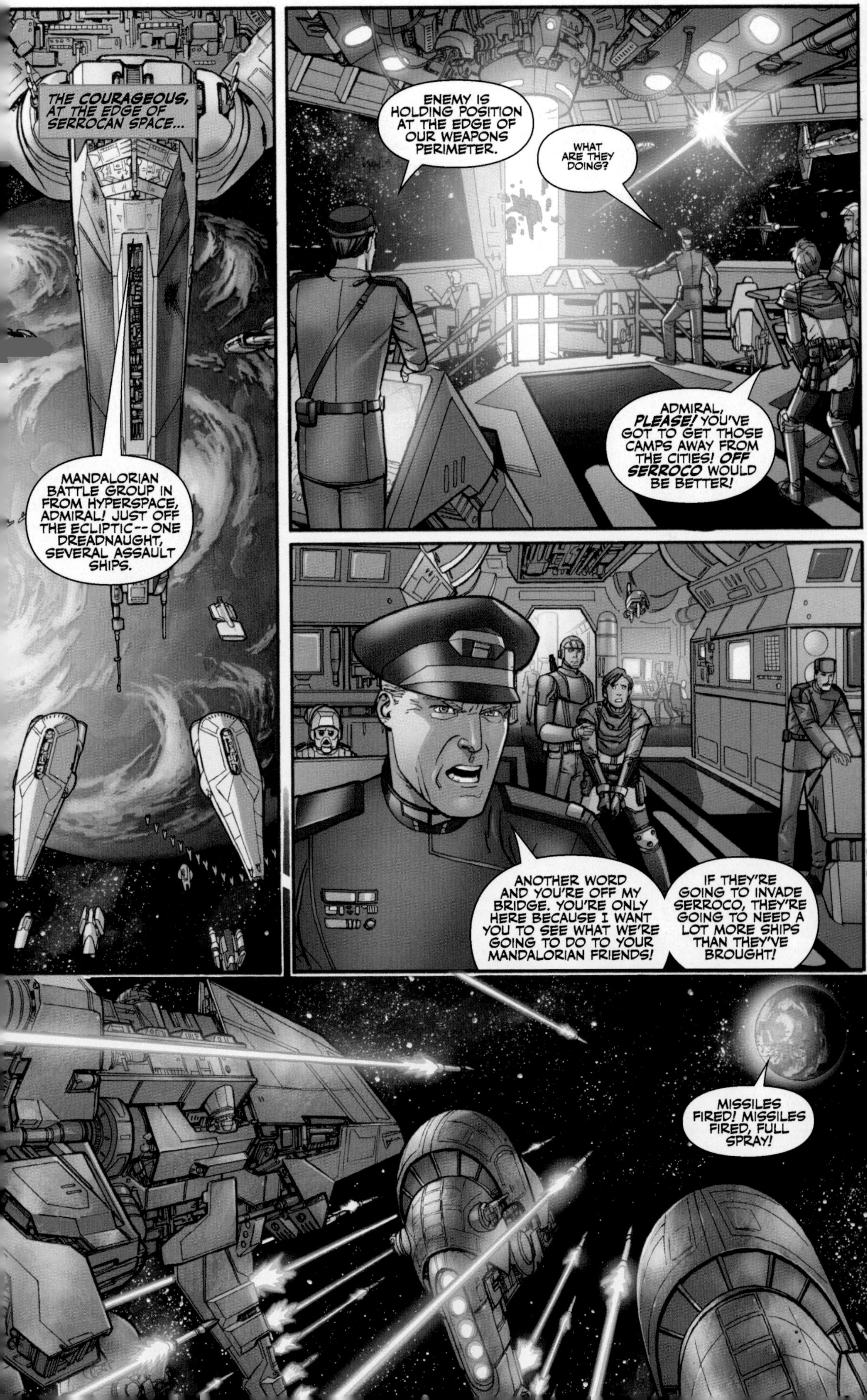
THE COURAGEOUS, AT THE EDGE OF SERROCAN SPACE...
MANDALORIAN BATTLE GROUP IN FROM HYPERSPACE, ADMIRAL! JUST OFF THE ECLIPTIC--ONE DREADNAUGHT, SEVERAL ASSAULT SHIPS.
ENEMY IS HOLDING POSITION AT THE EDGE OF OUR WEAPONS PERIMETER.
WHAT ARE THEY DOING?
ADMIRAL, PLEASE! YOU'VE GOT TO GET THOSE CAMPS AWAY FROM THE CITIES! OFF SERROCO WOULD BE BETTER!
ANOTHER WORD AND YOU'RE OFF MY BRIDGE. YOU'RE ONLY HERE BECAUSE I WANT YOU TO SEE WHAT WE'RE GOING TO DO TO YOUR MANDALORIAN FRIENDS!
IF THEY'RE GOING TO INVADE SERROCO, THEY'RE GOING TO NEED A LOT MORE SHIPS THAN THEY'VE BROUGHT!
MISSILES FIRED! MISSILES FIRED, FULL SPRAY!

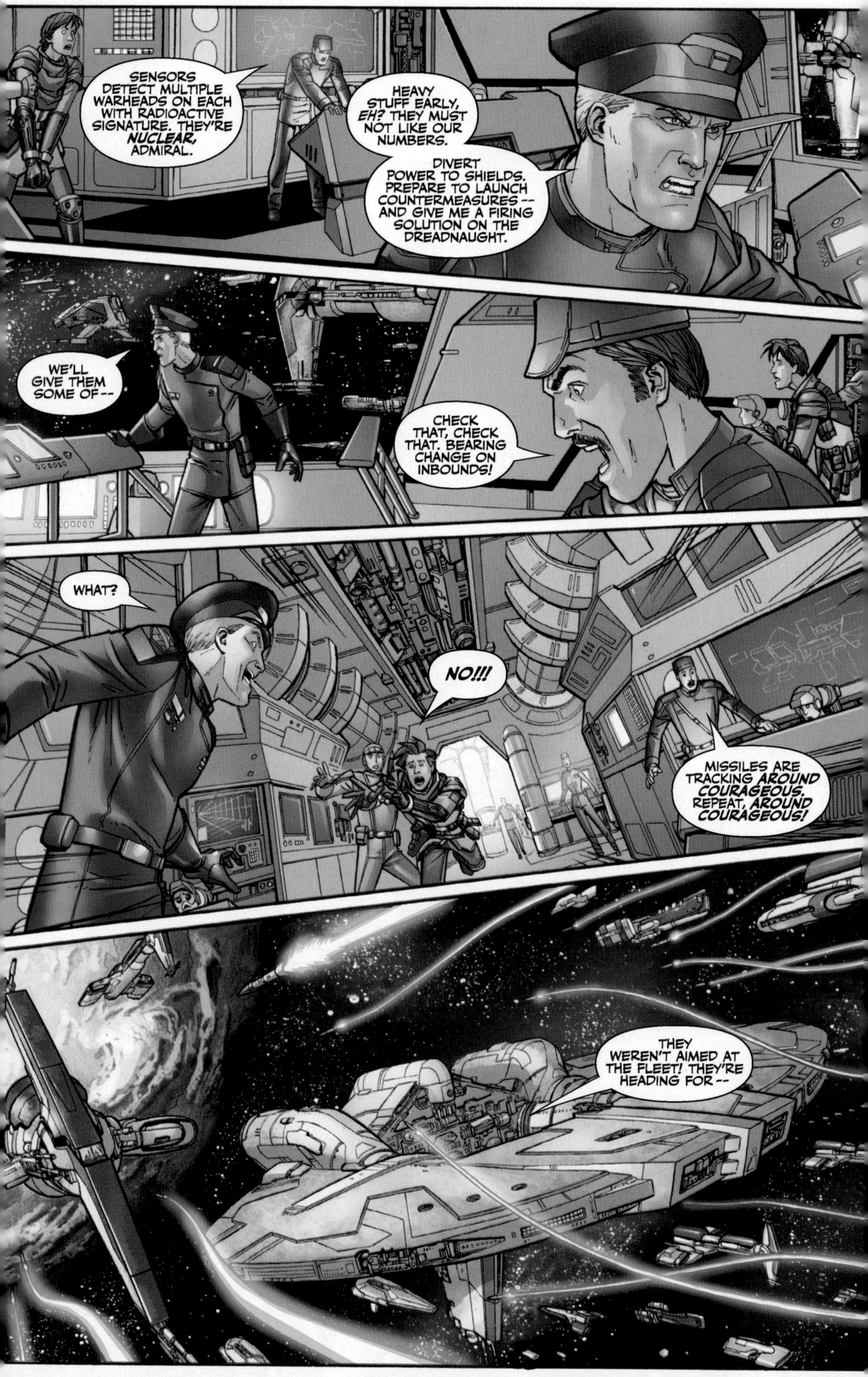
SENSORS DETECT MULTIPLE WARHEADS ON EACH WITH RADIOACTIVE SIGNATURE. THEY'RE *NUCLEAR,* ADMIRAL.
HEAVY STUFF EARLY, *EH?* THEY MUST NOT LIKE OUR NUMBERS.
DIVERT POWER TO SHIELDS. PREPARE TO LAUNCH COUNTERMEASURES -- AND GIVE ME A FIRING SOLUTION ON THE DREADNAUGHT.
WE'LL GIVE THEM SOME OF --
CHECK THAT, CHECK THAT. BEARING CHANGE ON INBOUNDS!
WHAT?
NO!!!
MISSILES ARE TRACKING *AROUND COURAGEOUS.* REPEAT, *AROUND COURAGEOUS!*
THEY WEREN'T AIMED AT THE FLEET! THEY'RE HEADING FOR --

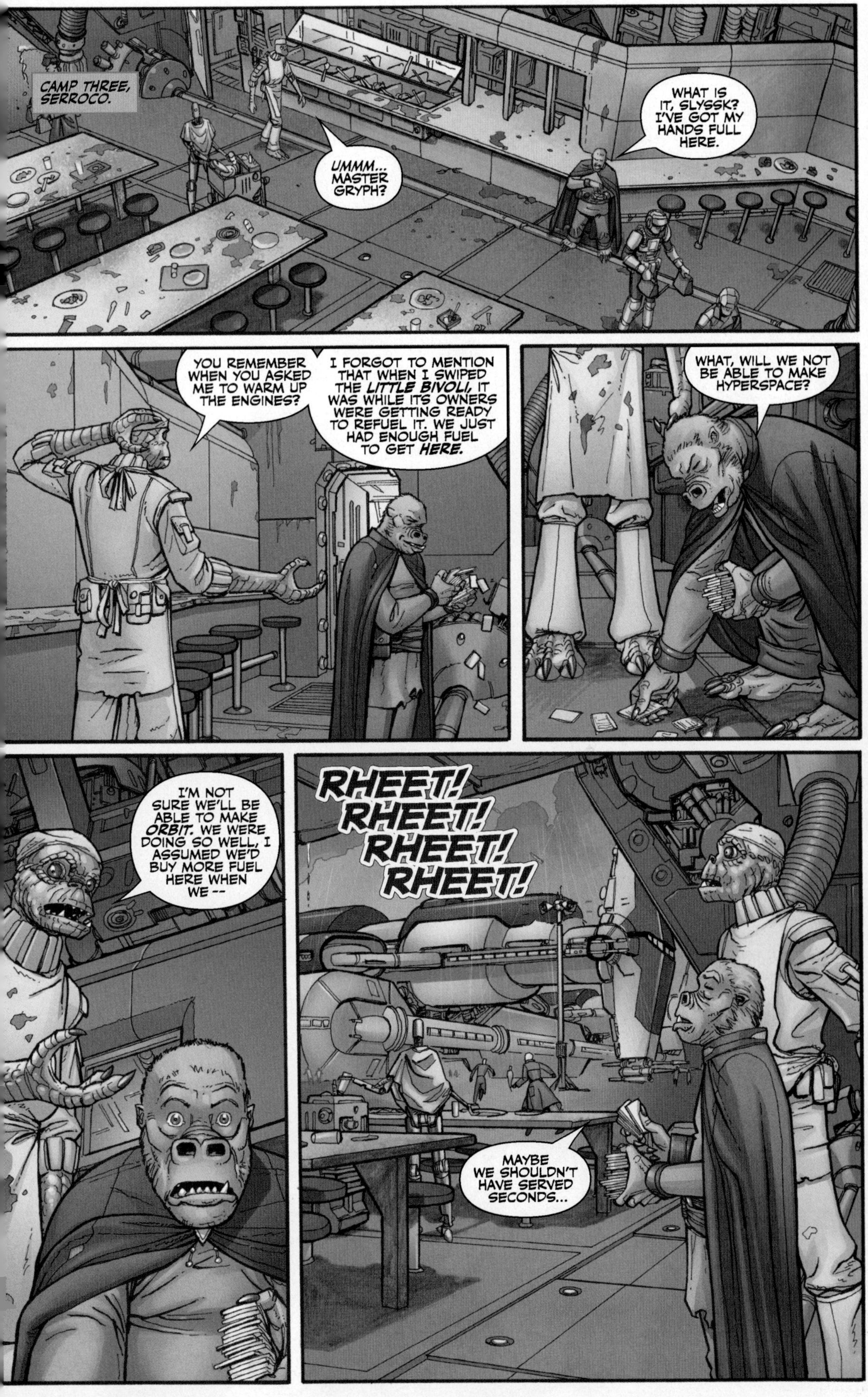
CAMP THREE, SERROCO.
UMMM... MASTER GRYPH?
WHAT IS IT, SLYSSK? I'VE GOT MY HANDS FULL HERE.
YOU REMEMBER WHEN YOU ASKED ME TO WARM UP THE ENGINES?
I FORGOT TO MENTION THAT WHEN I SWIPED THE *LITTLE BIVOLI,* IT WAS WHILE ITS OWNERS WERE GETTING READY TO REFUEL IT. WE JUST HAD ENOUGH FUEL TO GET *HERE.*
WHAT, WILL WE NOT BE ABLE TO MAKE HYPERSPACE?
I'M NOT SURE WE'LL BE ABLE TO MAKE *ORBIT.* WE WERE DOING SO WELL, I ASSUMED WE'D BUY MORE FUEL HERE WHEN WE --
RHEET! RHEET! RHEET! RHEET!
MAYBE WE SHOULDN'T HAVE SERVED SECONDS...

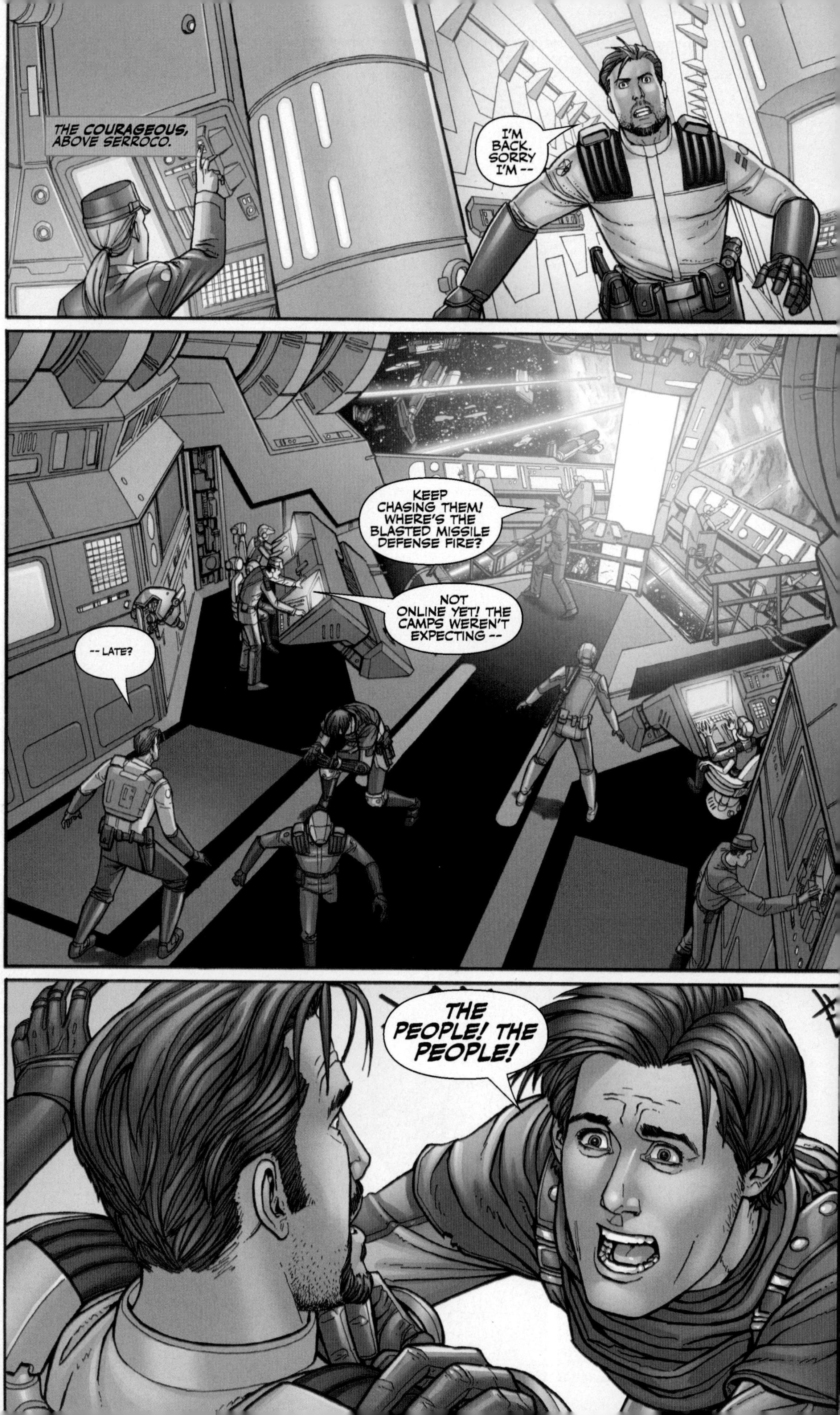
THE COURAGEOUS, ABOVE SERROCO.
I'M BACK. SORRY I'M --
KEEP CHASING THEM! WHERE'S THE BLASTED MISSILE DEFENSE FIRE?
NOT ONLINE YET! THE CAMPS WEREN'T EXPECTING --
-- LATE?
THE PEOPLE! THE PEOPLE!

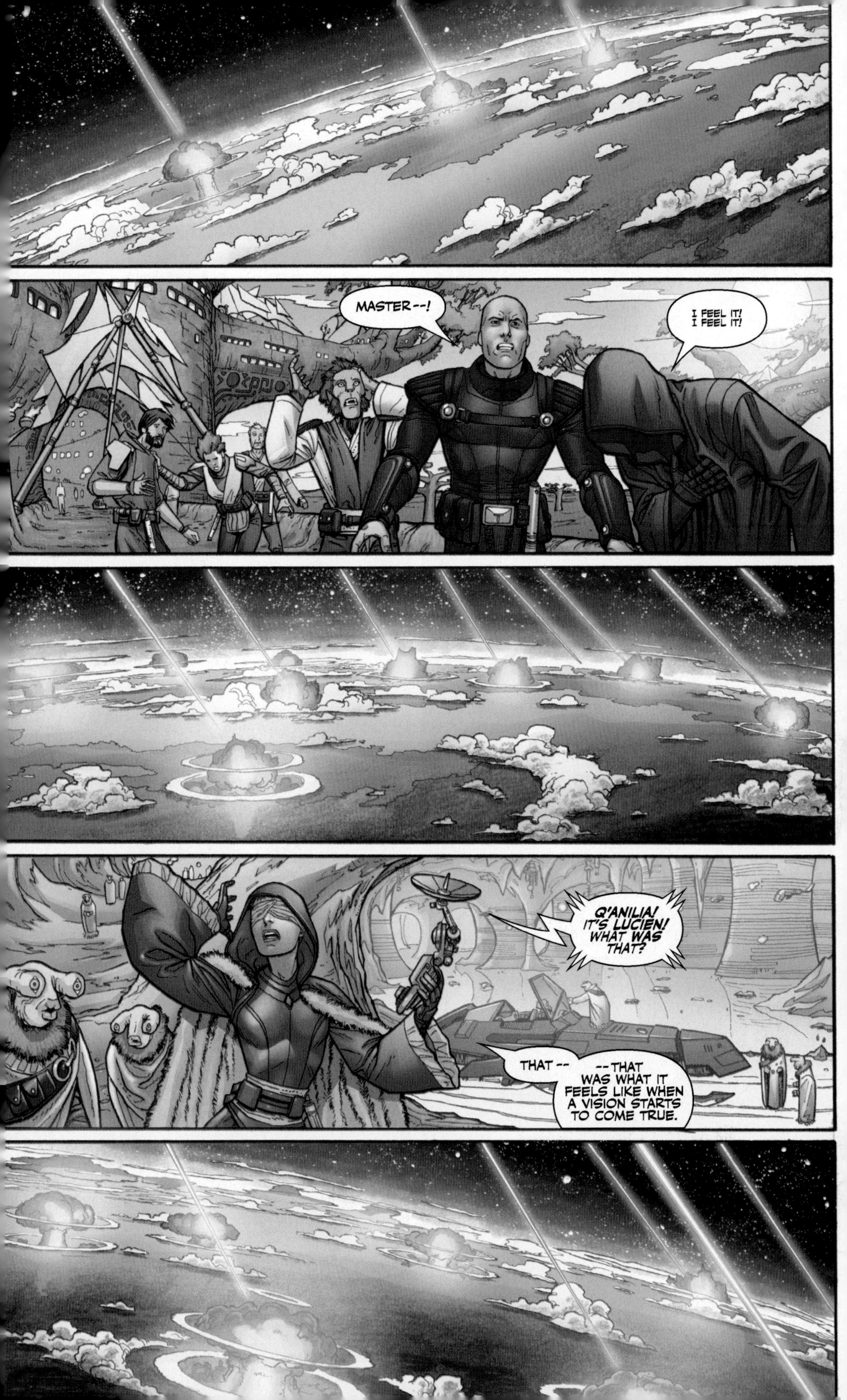
MASTER--!
I FEEL IT! I FEEL IT!
Q'ANILIA! IT'S LUCIEN! WHAT WAS THAT?
THAT--
--THAT WAS WHAT IT FEELS LIKE WHEN A VISION STARTS TO COME TRUE.

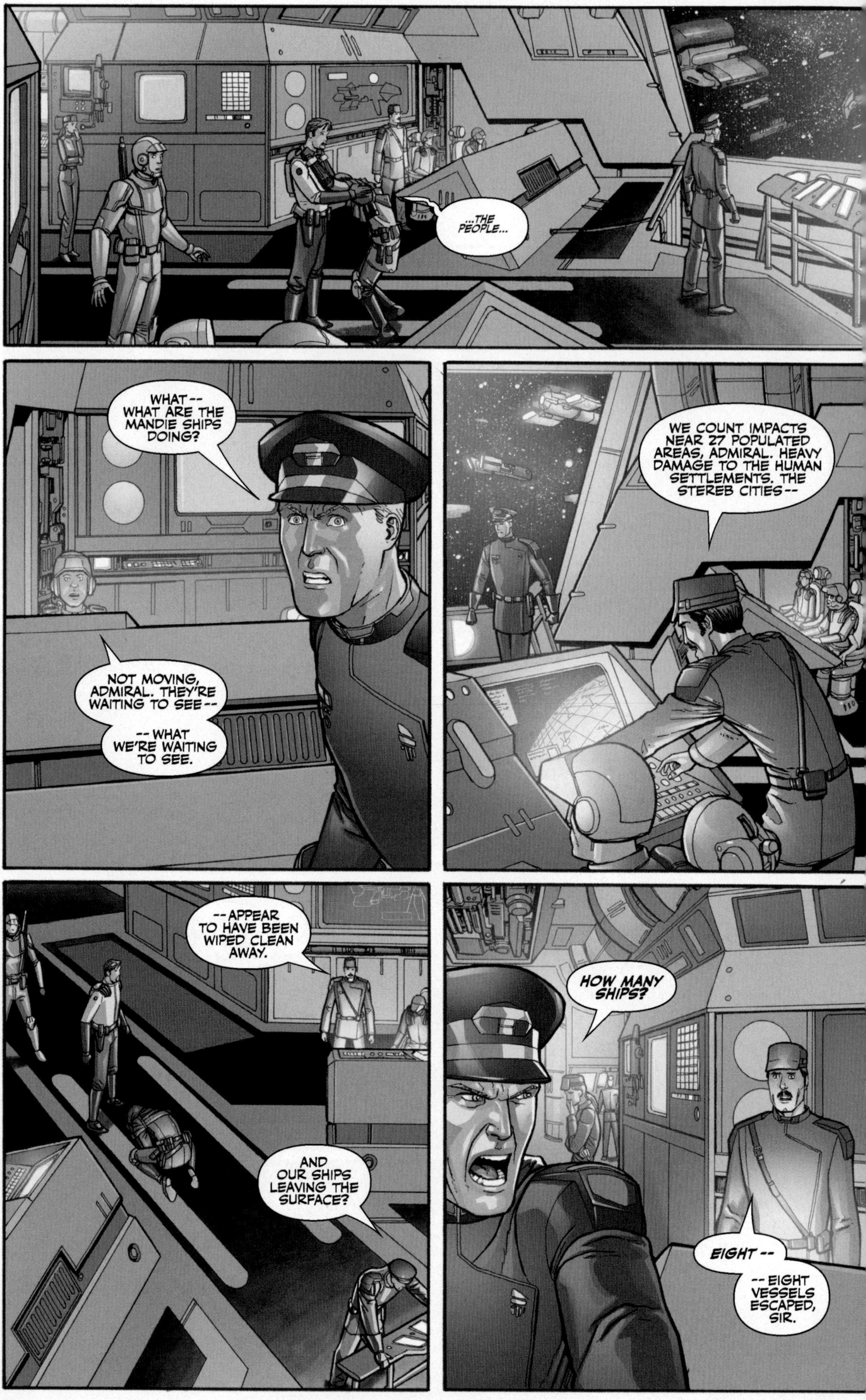
...THE PEOPLE...
WHAT-- WHAT ARE THE MANDIE SHIPS DOING?
NOT MOVING, ADMIRAL. THEY'RE WAITING TO SEE--
--WHAT WE'RE WAITING TO SEE.
WE COUNT IMPACTS NEAR 27 POPULATED AREAS, ADMIRAL. HEAVY DAMAGE TO THE HUMAN SETTLEMENTS. THE STEREB CITIES--
--APPEAR TO HAVE BEEN WIPED CLEAN AWAY.
AND OUR SHIPS LEAVING THE SURFACE?
HOW MANY SHIPS?
EIGHT--
--EIGHT VESSELS ESCAPED, SIR.

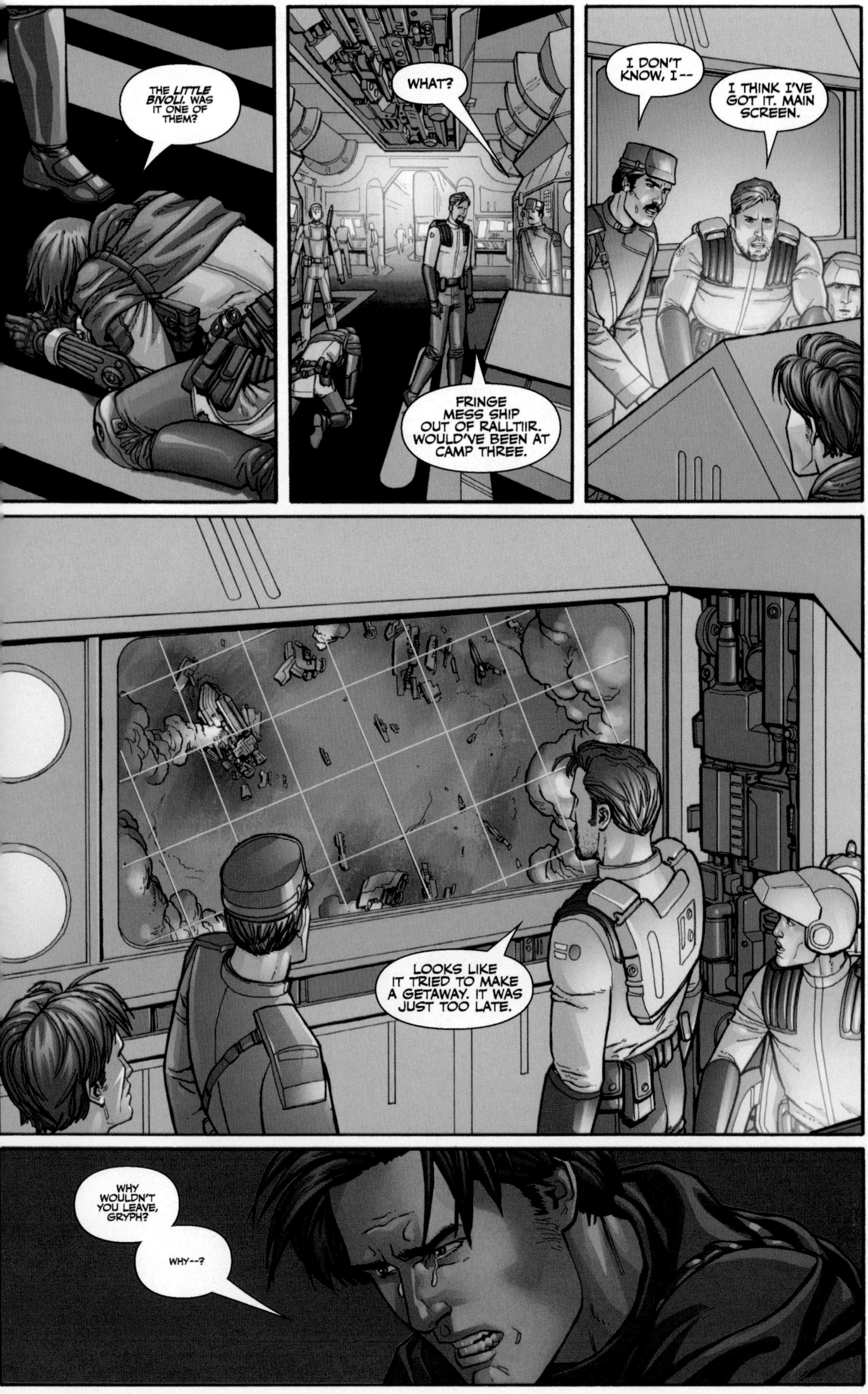
THE *LITTLE BIVOLI*. WAS IT ONE OF THEM?
WHAT?
FRINGE MESS SHIP OUT OF RALLTIIR. WOULD'VE BEEN AT CAMP THREE.
I DON'T KNOW, I--
I THINK I'VE GOT IT. MAIN SCREEN.
LOOKS LIKE IT TRIED TO MAKE A GETAWAY. IT WAS JUST TOO LATE.
WHY WOULDN'T YOU LEAVE, GRYPH?
WHY--?

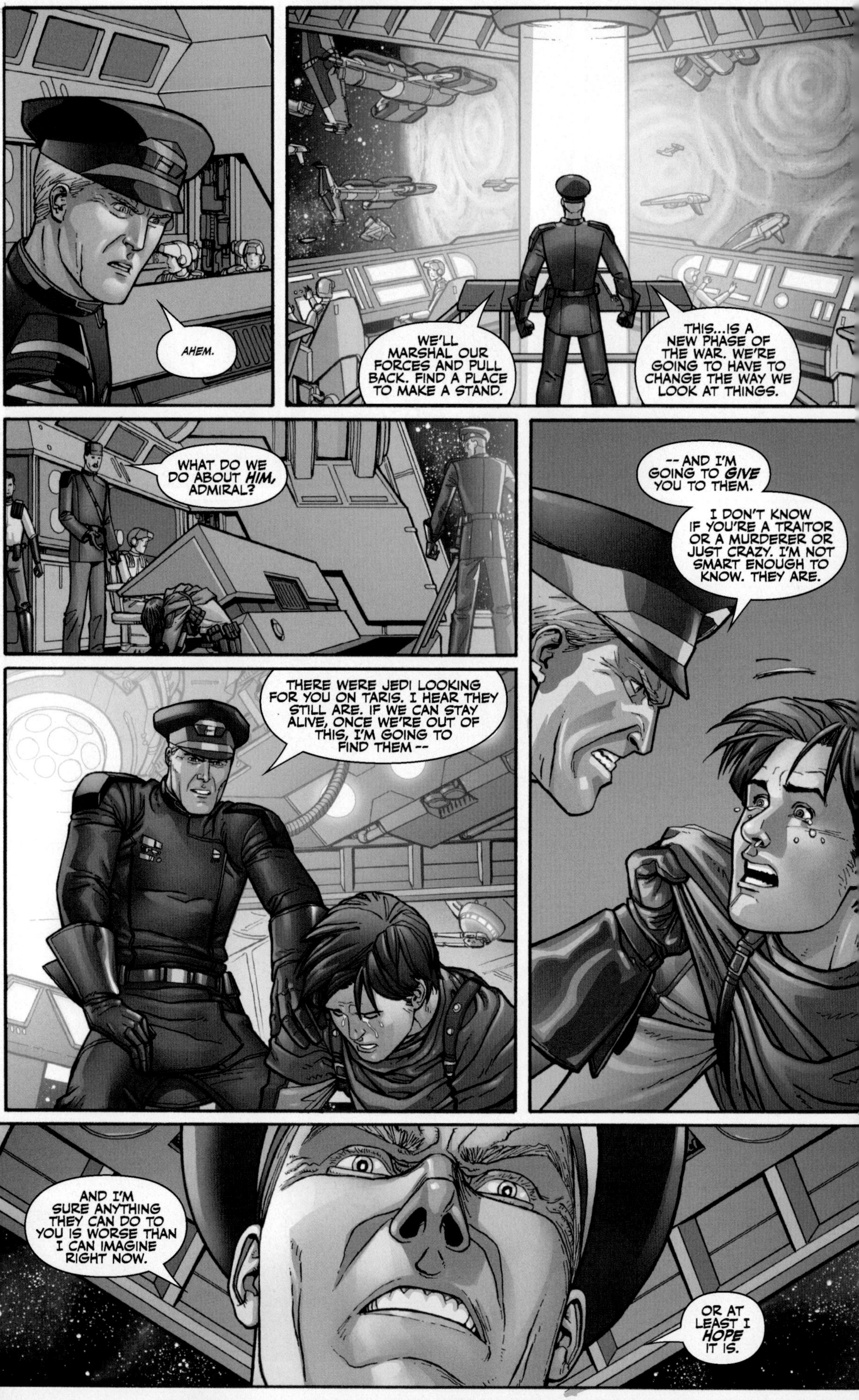
AHEM.
WE'LL MARSHAL OUR FORCES AND PULL BACK. FIND A PLACE TO MAKE A STAND.
THIS...IS A NEW PHASE OF THE WAR. WE'RE GOING TO HAVE TO CHANGE THE WAY WE LOOK AT THINGS.
WHAT DO WE DO ABOUT *HIM,* ADMIRAL?
THERE WERE JEDI LOOKING FOR YOU ON TARIS. I HEAR THEY STILL ARE. IF WE CAN STAY ALIVE, ONCE WE'RE OUT OF THIS, I'M GOING TO FIND THEM --
-- AND I'M GOING TO *GIVE* YOU TO THEM.
I DON'T KNOW IF YOU'RE A TRAITOR OR A MURDERER OR JUST CRAZY. I'M NOT SMART ENOUGH TO KNOW. THEY ARE.
AND I'M SURE ANYTHING THEY CAN DO TO YOU IS WORSE THAN I CAN IMAGINE RIGHT NOW.
OR AT LEAST I *HOPE* IT IS.

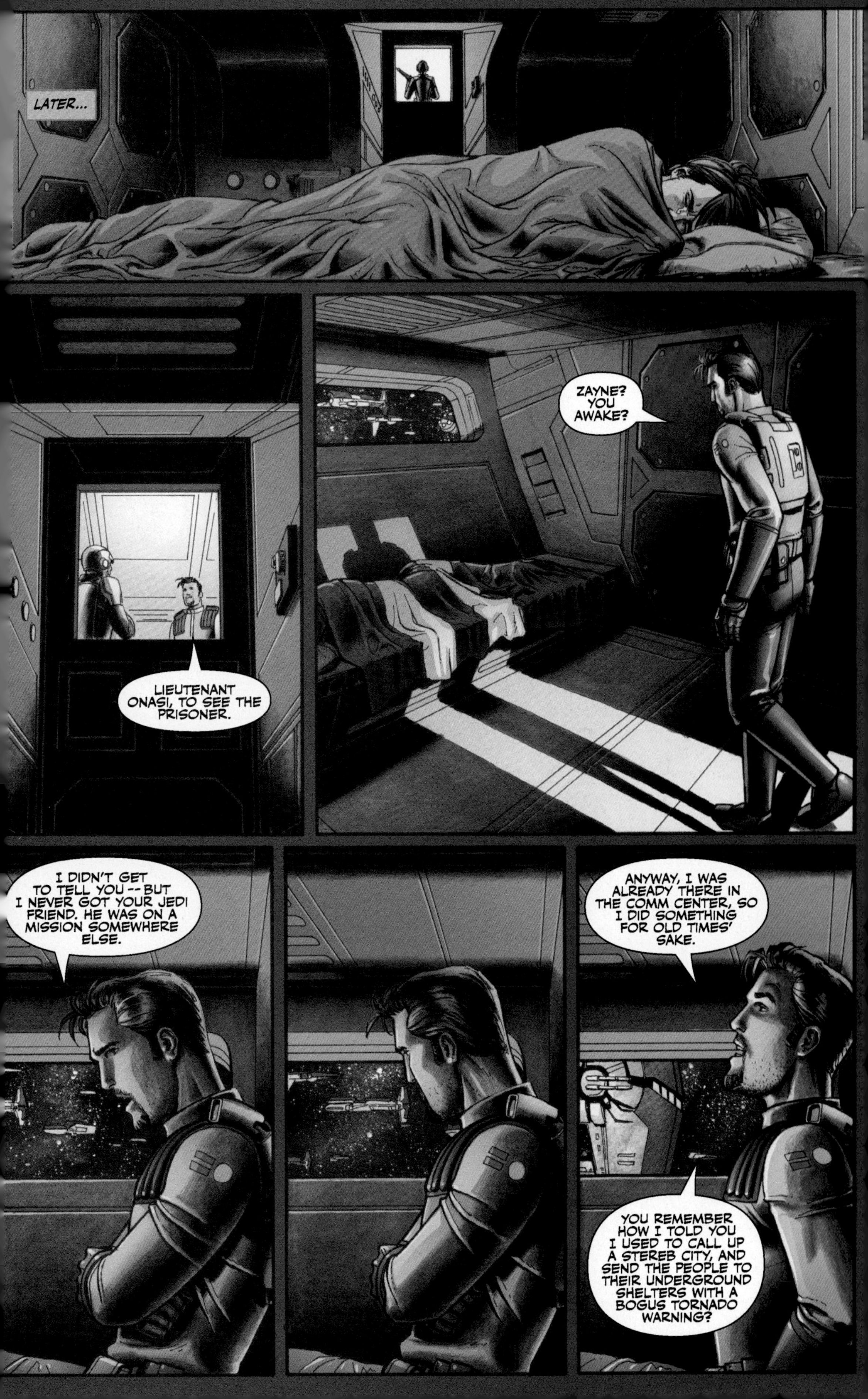
LATER...
LIEUTENANT ONASI, TO SEE THE PRISONER.
ZAYNE? YOU AWAKE?
I DIDN'T GET TO TELL YOU -- BUT I NEVER GOT YOUR JEDI FRIEND. HE WAS ON A MISSION SOMEWHERE ELSE.
ANYWAY, I WAS ALREADY THERE IN THE COMM CENTER, SO I DID SOMETHING FOR OLD TIMES' SAKE.
YOU REMEMBER HOW I TOLD YOU I USED TO CALL UP A STEREB CITY, AND SEND THE PEOPLE TO THEIR UNDERGROUND SHELTERS WITH A BOGUS TORNADO WARNING?

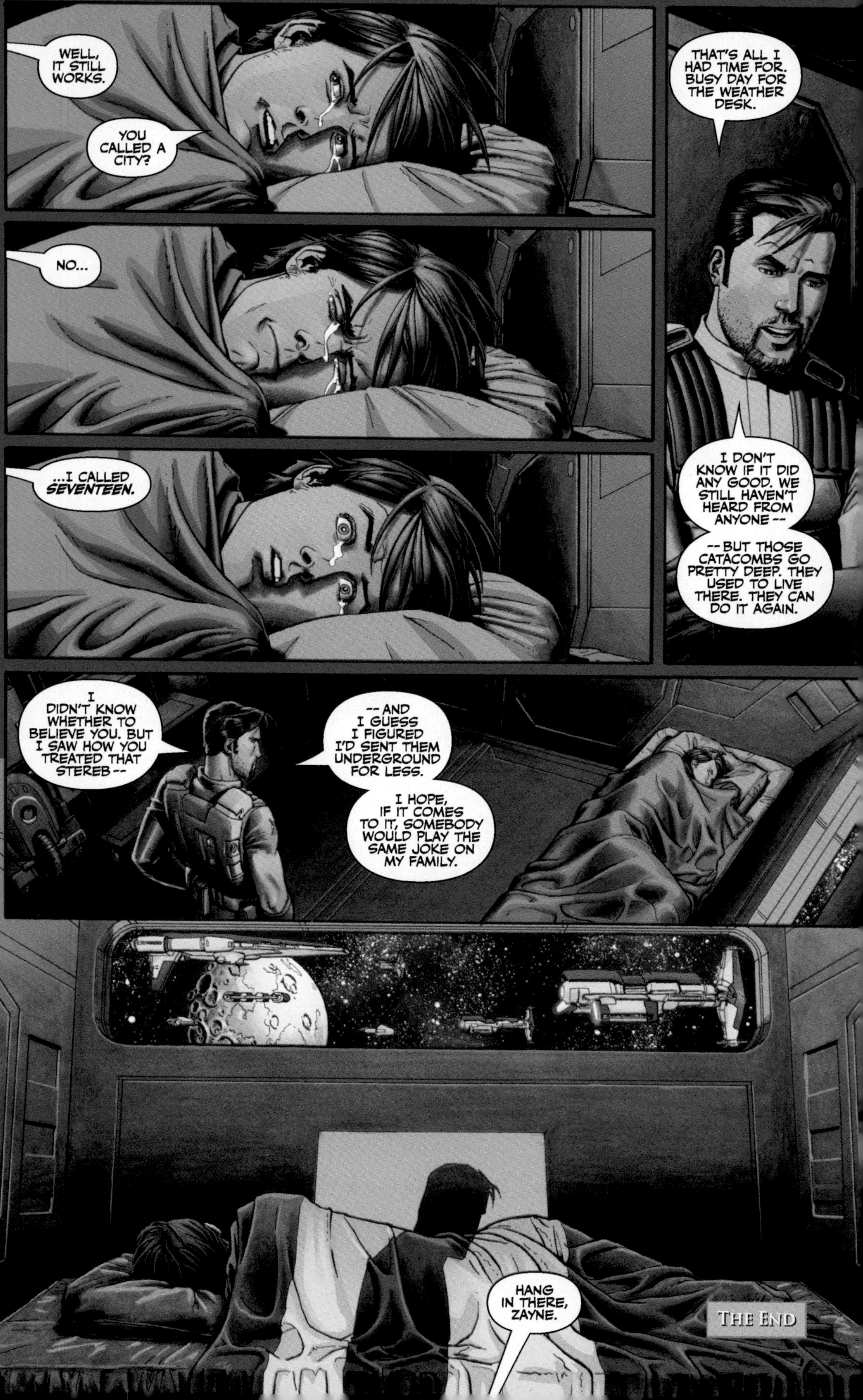
WELL, IT STILL WORKS.
YOU CALLED A CITY?
NO...
...I CALLED SEVENTEEN.
THAT'S ALL I HAD TIME FOR. BUSY DAY FOR THE WEATHER DESK.
I DON'T KNOW IF IT DID ANY GOOD. WE STILL HAVEN'T HEARD FROM ANYONE --
-- BUT THOSE CATACOMBS GO PRETTY DEEP. THEY USED TO LIVE THERE. THEY CAN DO IT AGAIN.
I DIDN'T KNOW WHETHER TO BELIEVE YOU. BUT I SAW HOW YOU TREATED THAT STEREB --
-- AND I GUESS I FIGURED I'D SENT THEM UNDERGROUND FOR LESS.
I HOPE, IF IT COMES TO IT, SOMEBODY WOULD PLAY THE SAME JOKE ON MY FAMILY.
HANG IN THERE, ZAYNE.
THE END

THE TARIS HOLOFEED

SIEGE EDITION

NO END IN SIGHT FOR MANDALORIAN SIEGE

More kilotons of destructive force rained down on Taris today, as yet another Mandalorian Dreadnaught joined the offensive in orbit. The most intense bombardment in weeks left several heretofore-untouched sectors of the Middle City in ruins.

Losses included the historic Lhosan Industries plant near Machineville, known throughout the riding community as the "birthplace of the swoop-bike." Abandoned by the manufacturer in the run-up to the siege, many beings had taken refuge inside its cavernous walls. Loss of life is estimated to be high.

Sorties of planetary defense fighters continued to scream skyward throughout the night, again meeting with defeat as they reached the Mandalorian perimeter. Sources with the Home Guard reported that the planet may soon have to turn to law enforcement vehicles for defense, although military sources with the Republic denied the story.

Speaking remotely, Republic defense official Catronus Steffans took time in his news conference about the Serroco tragedy to spare a few words for Taris. "It is when the Republic faces its greatest tests that the true spirit of our people shines through—whether in responding to the horrific crime of Serroco, or in defending our homes on Taris."

SELECT to learn more . . .

WHO LOST TARIS?

AN EDITORIAL BY THE PUBLISHER

The story, by now, is an old and familiar one to anyone who's lived through it: Three years ago, with the Mandalorians beginning to threaten Taris's resource worlds of Vanquo, Tarnith, Suurja, and Jebble, the Republic suddenly changed its policy and offered protection to a world on the Outer Rim.

No matter that the number of vessels needed to extend such protection far outstripped what the Republic had to offer. Money talks—and it did. Lhosan Industries convinced the Republic to give membership to our tiny island on a remote stellar sea—and its go-between with the Senate, Gorravus, became our first Senator himself as payment for his efforts. "Payment" may once have seemed a strong term—but it hardly matters now, with Mandalorian bombs falling.

Bombs, which could not be stopped by a Republic Navy, spread too thin. Nor by well-meaning Jedi such as the Revanchist leader, who only too late proved that the threat we faced was real. Nor by Lhosan chairman Jervo, who had once seemed to care so much about protecting his interests here—only to pull his company offworld before the Mandies even showed up. Nor by Senator Gorravus—who had begun to evolve into a true champion for Taris's cause, only to disappear before the shooting started . . .

SELECT to learn more . . .

HYSTERICS AMID THE HYSTERIA

A lighter moment in the darkness came yesterday when observers reported a comical sight in the Middle City.

A city surveillance droid, its logic center unable to integrate the recent events with its customary duties, attempted to issue a parking citation to an unexploded Mandalorian bomb.

No one was injured in the ensuing blast, which was said to have lightened the hearts of overworked rescuers nearby. "Wished I'd seen that sight a thousand times before," said one, who asked not to be named.

SELECT to learn more . . .

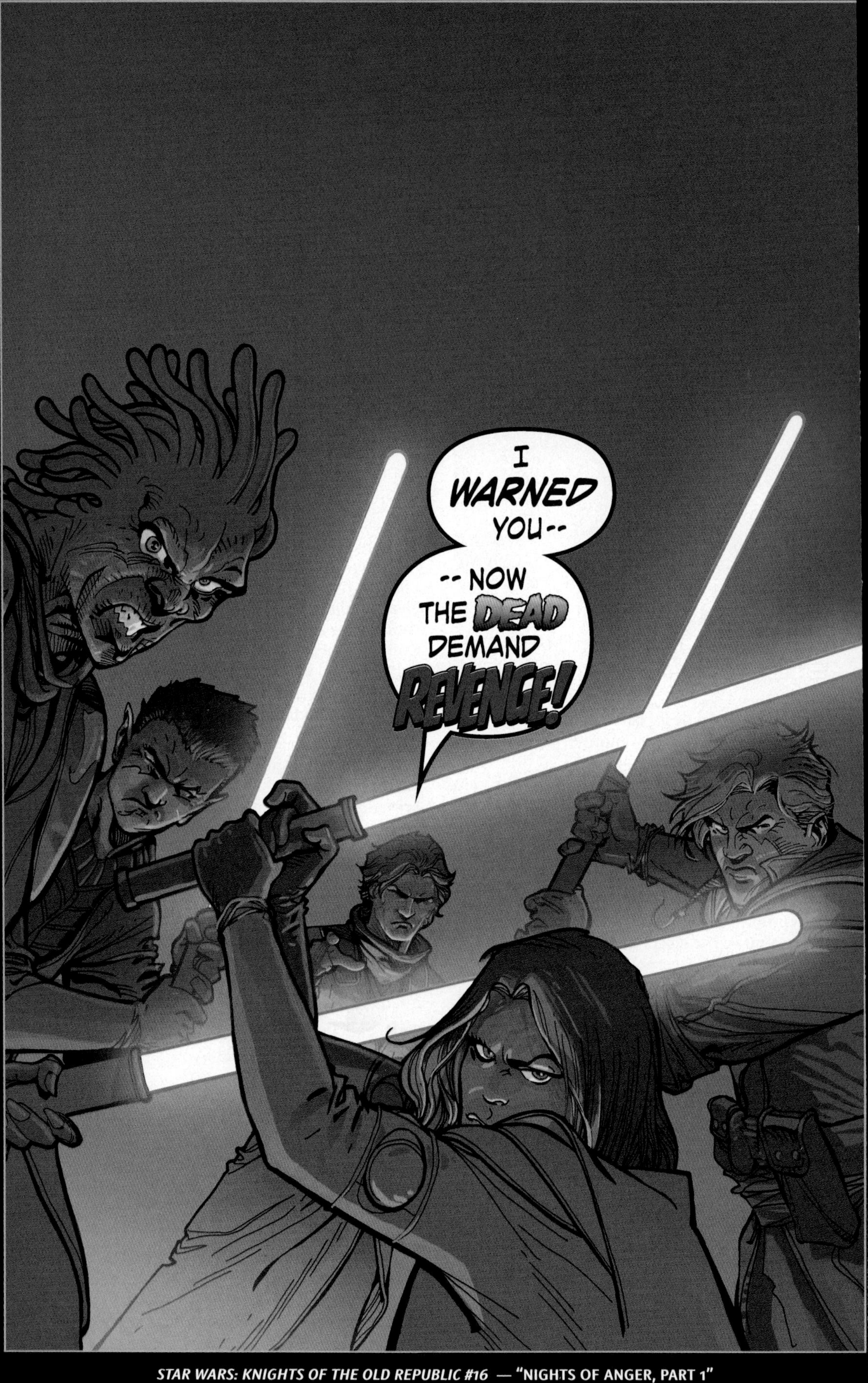
I WARNED YOU--
-- NOW THE DEAD DEMAND REVENGE!

STAR WARS: KNIGHTS OF THE OLD REPUBLIC #16 — "NIGHTS OF ANGER, PART 1"

WRITER: JOHN JACKSON MILLER • ARTIST: BRIAN CHING • COLORIST: MICHAEL ATIYEH • LETTERER: MICHAEL HEISLER
ASSISTANT EDITOR: DAVE MARSHALL • EDITOR: JEREMY BARLOW • COVER ARTIST: COLIN WILSON

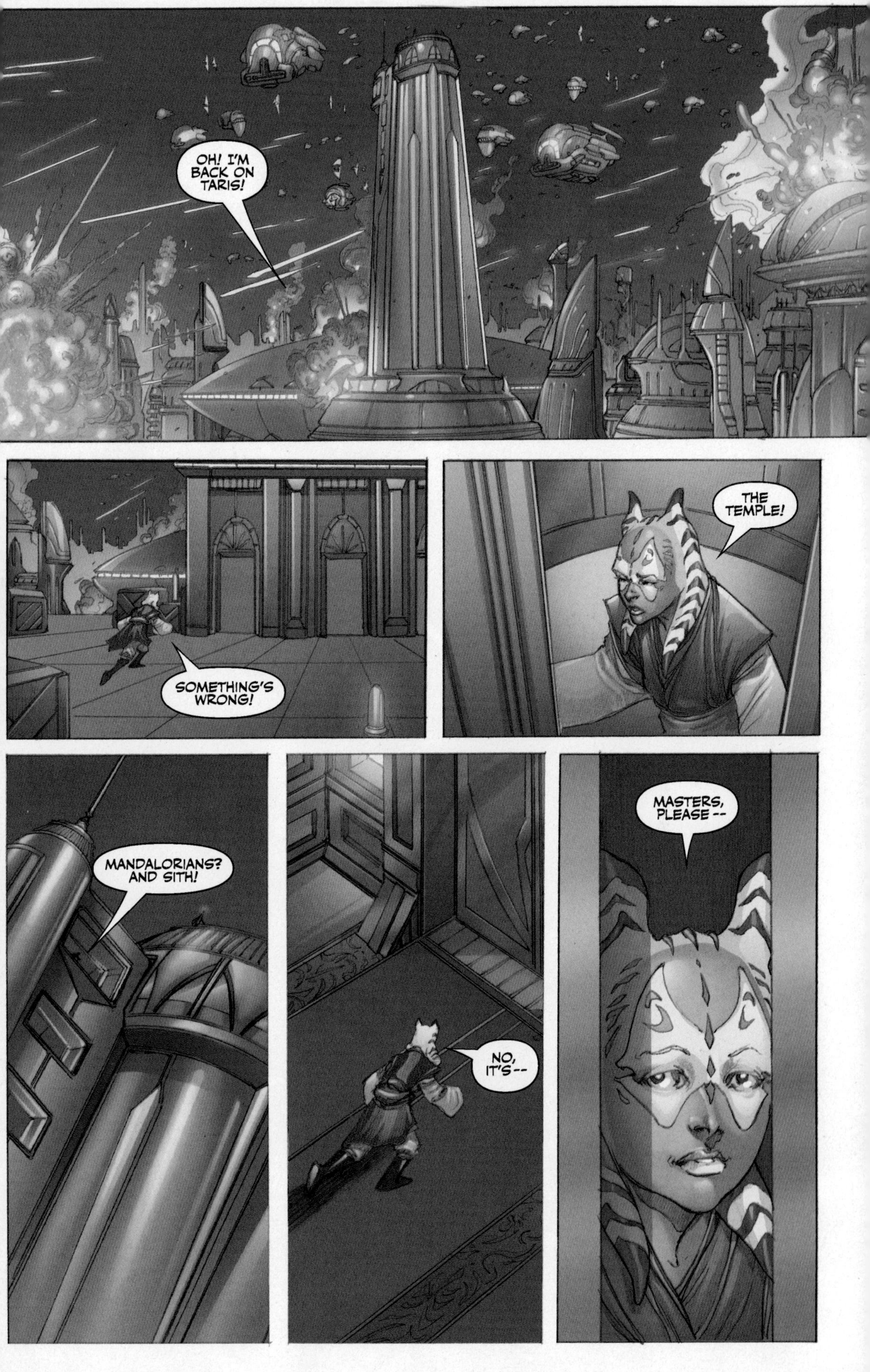
OH! I'M BACK ON TARIS!
SOMETHING'S WRONG!
THE TEMPLE!
MANDALORIANS? AND SITH!
NO, IT'S--
MASTERS, PLEASE --

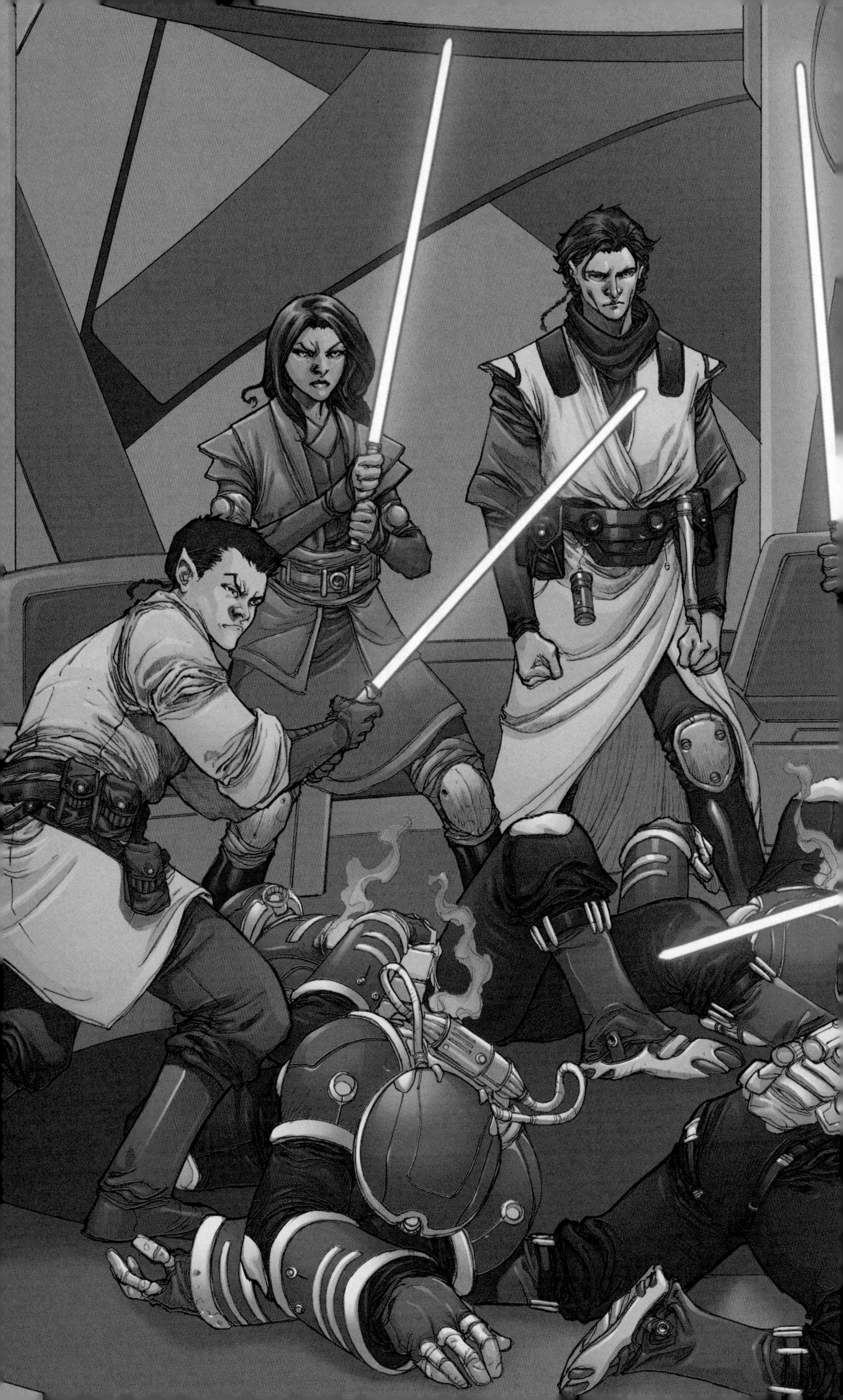

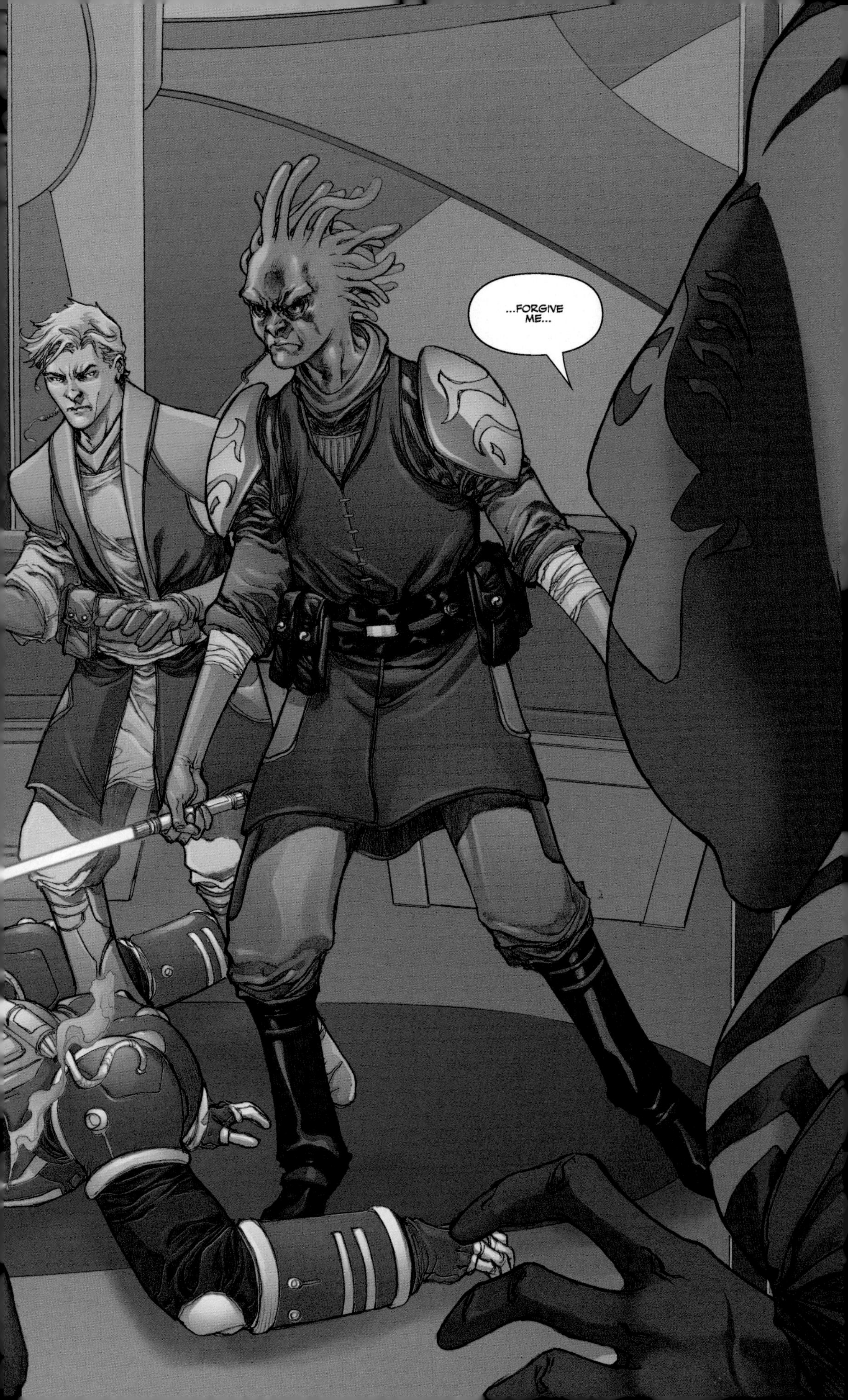
...FORGIVE ME...

YOU'RE LATE, YOUNG ONE.

THIS -- THIS IS THE TEMPLE ON TARIS.

W--W--WE ABANDONED IT.

WE NEVER LEFT IT.

AND NOW YOU'RE BACK WITH US, MASTER RAANA TEY.

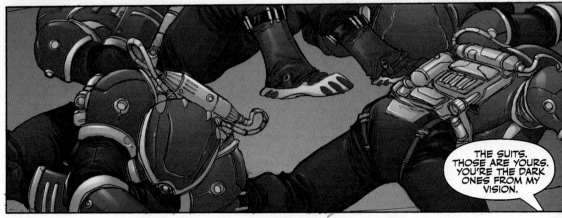

THE SUITS. THOSE ARE YOURS. YOU'RE THE DARK ONES FROM MY VISION.

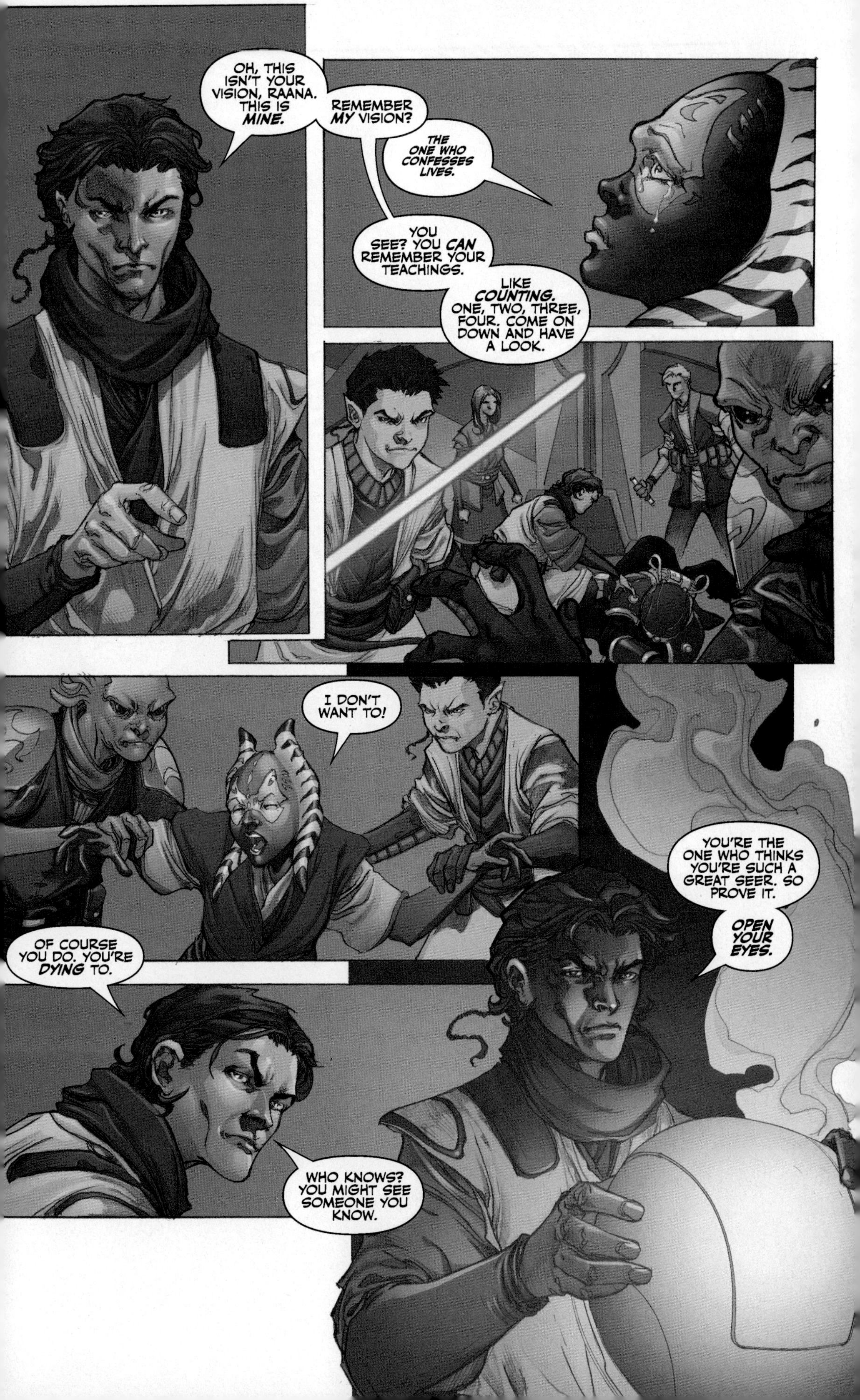
OH, THIS ISN'T YOUR VISION, RAANA. THIS IS MINE.
REMEMBER MY VISION?
THE ONE WHO CONFESSES LIVES.
YOU SEE? YOU CAN REMEMBER YOUR TEACHINGS.
LIKE COUNTING. ONE, TWO, THREE, FOUR. COME ON DOWN AND HAVE A LOOK.
I DON'T WANT TO!
OF COURSE YOU DO. YOU'RE DYING TO.
WHO KNOWS? YOU MIGHT SEE SOMEONE YOU KNOW.
YOU'RE THE ONE WHO THINKS YOU'RE SUCH A GREAT SEER. SO PROVE IT.
OPEN YOUR EYES.

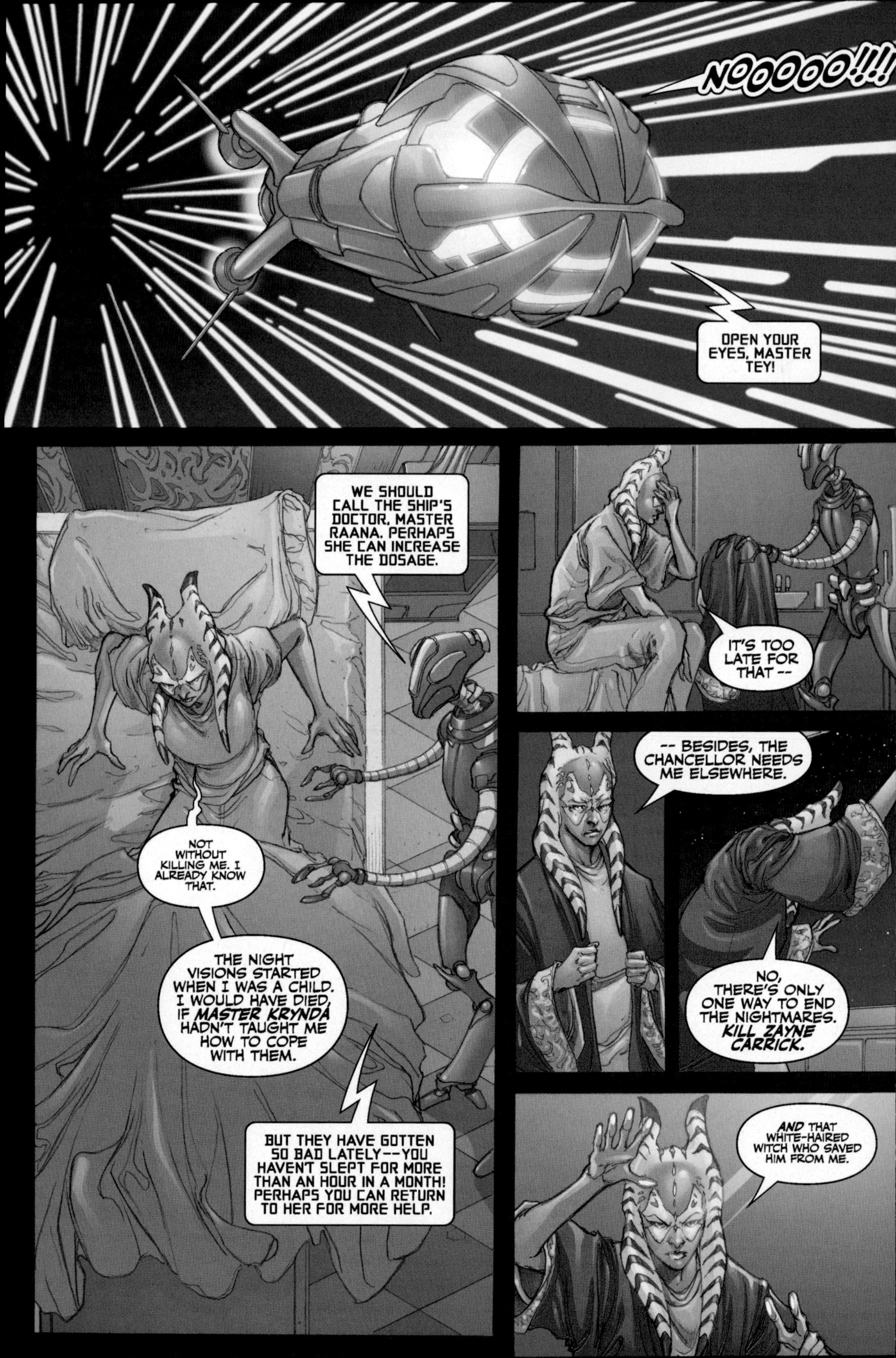
NOOOOO!!!!
OPEN YOUR EYES, MASTER TEY!
WE SHOULD CALL THE SHIP'S DOCTOR, MASTER RAANA. PERHAPS SHE CAN INCREASE THE DOSAGE.
NOT WITHOUT KILLING ME. I ALREADY KNOW THAT.
THE NIGHT VISIONS STARTED WHEN I WAS A CHILD. I WOULD HAVE DIED, IF MASTER KRYNDA HADN'T TAUGHT ME HOW TO COPE WITH THEM.
BUT THEY HAVE GOTTEN SO BAD LATELY--YOU HAVEN'T SLEPT FOR MORE THAN AN HOUR IN A MONTH! PERHAPS YOU CAN RETURN TO HER FOR MORE HELP.
IT'S TOO LATE FOR THAT --
-- BESIDES, THE CHANCELLOR NEEDS ME ELSEWHERE.
NO, THERE'S ONLY ONE WAY TO END THE NIGHTMARES. KILL ZAYNE CARRICK.
AND THAT WHITE-HAIRED WITCH WHO SAVED HIM FROM ME.

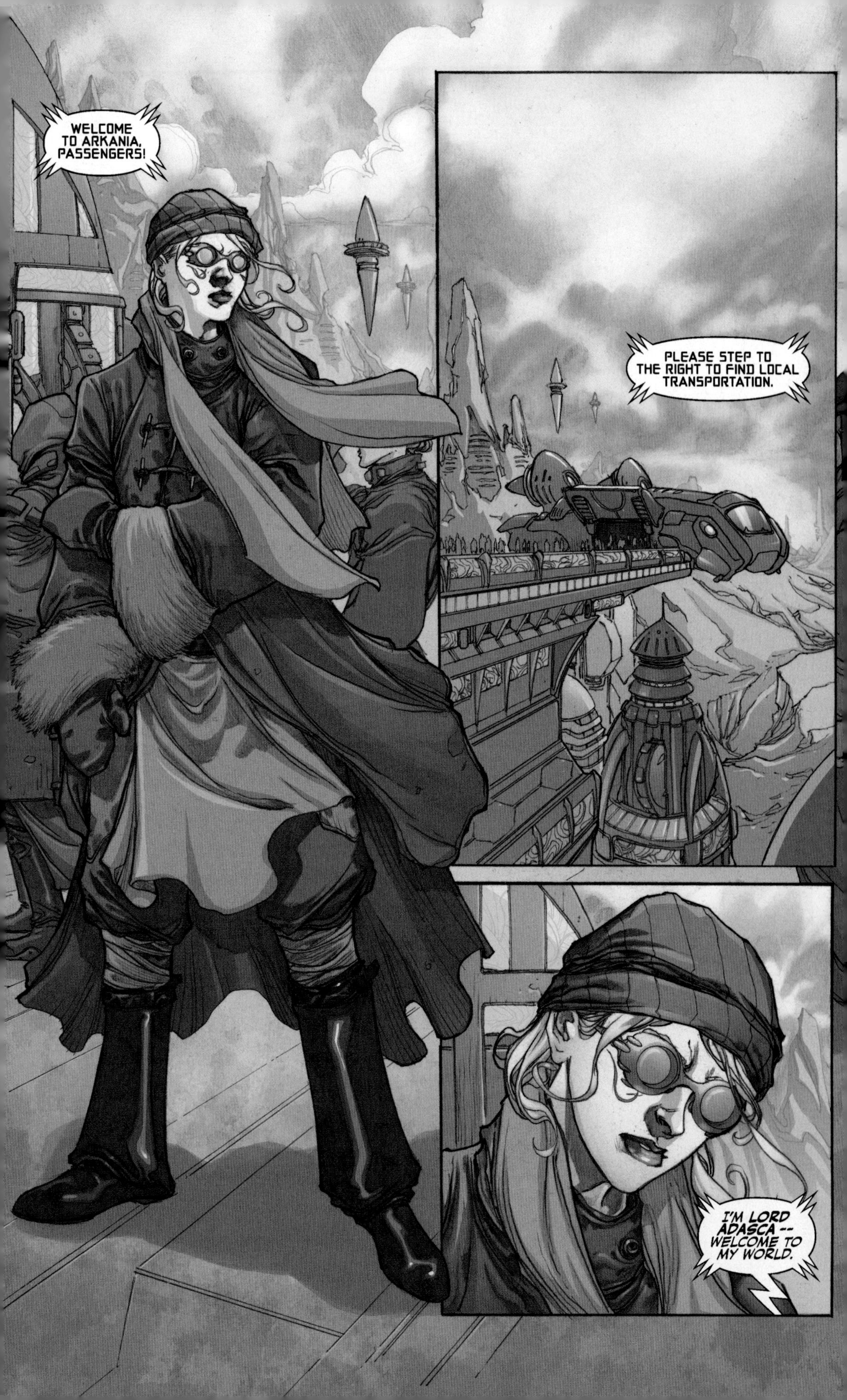

WELCOME TO ARKANIA, PASSENGERS!
PLEASE STEP TO THE RIGHT TO FIND LOCAL TRANSPORTATION.
I'M LORD ADASCA -- WELCOME TO MY WORLD.

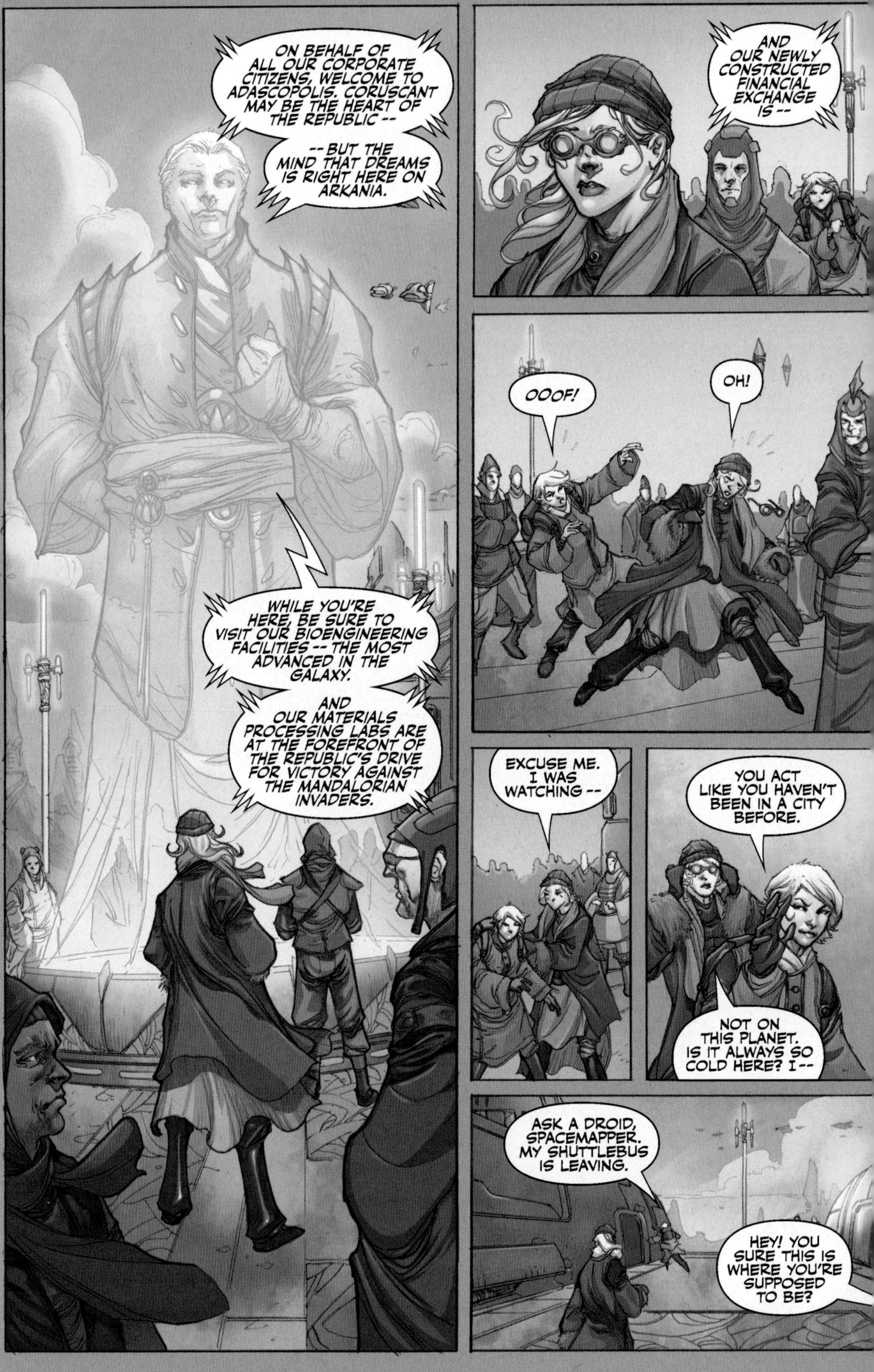
ON BEHALF OF ALL OUR CORPORATE CITIZENS, WELCOME TO ADASCOPOLIS. CORUSCANT MAY BE THE HEART OF THE REPUBLIC --
-- BUT THE MIND THAT DREAMS IS RIGHT HERE ON ARKANIA.
WHILE YOU'RE HERE, BE SURE TO VISIT OUR BIOENGINEERING FACILITIES -- THE MOST ADVANCED IN THE GALAXY.
AND OUR MATERIALS PROCESSING LABS ARE AT THE FOREFRONT OF THE REPUBLIC'S DRIVE FOR VICTORY AGAINST THE MANDALORIAN INVADERS.
AND OUR NEWLY CONSTRUCTED FINANCIAL EXCHANGE IS --
OOOF!
OH!
EXCUSE ME. I WAS WATCHING --
YOU ACT LIKE YOU HAVEN'T BEEN IN A CITY BEFORE.
NOT ON THIS PLANET. IS IT ALWAYS SO COLD HERE? I --
ASK A DROID, SPACEMAPPER. MY SHUTTLEBUS IS LEAVING.
HEY! YOU SURE THIS IS WHERE YOU'RE SUPPOSED TO BE?

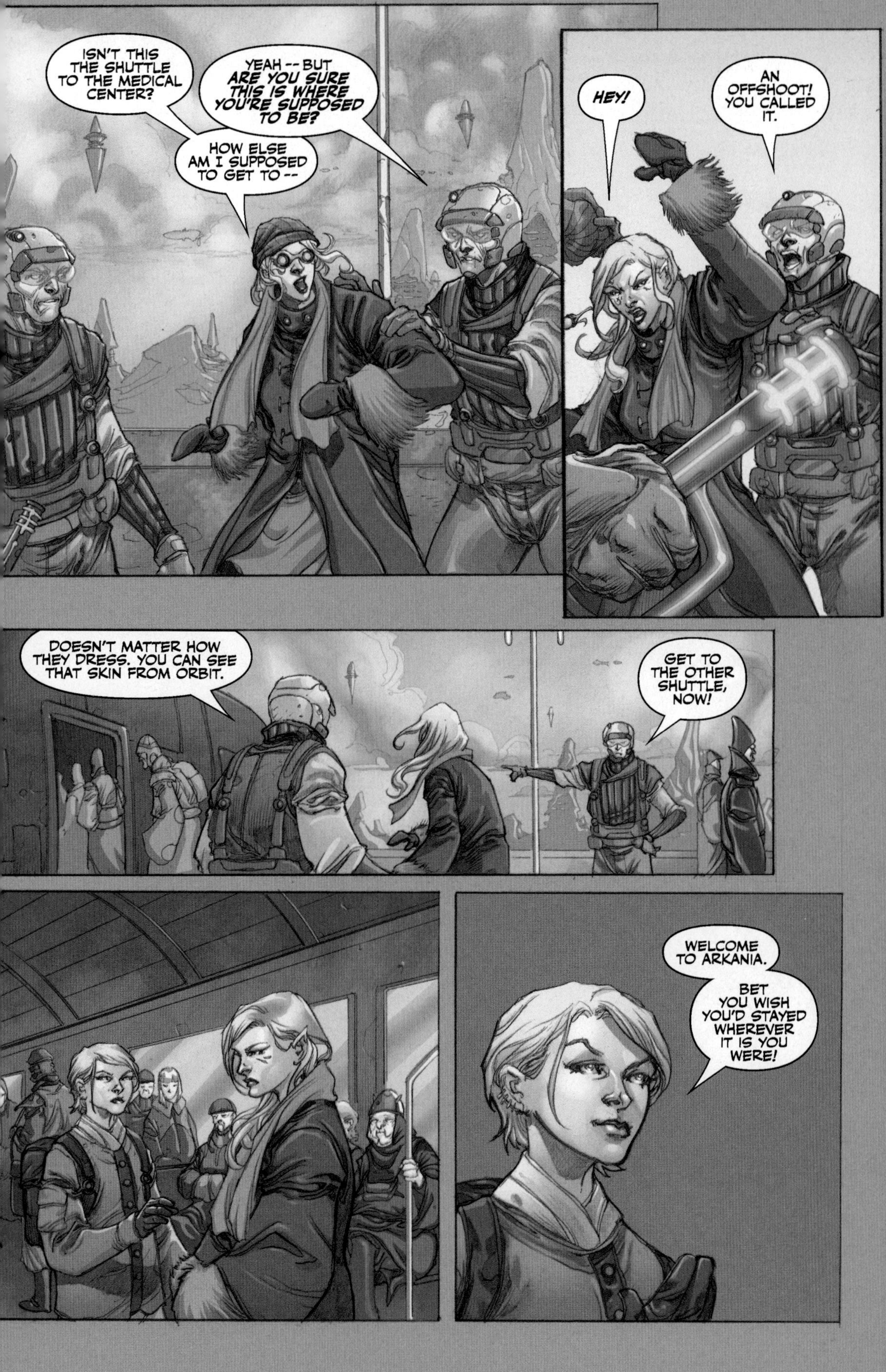
ISN'T THIS THE SHUTTLE TO THE MEDICAL CENTER?
YEAH -- BUT ARE YOU SURE THIS IS WHERE YOU'RE SUPPOSED TO BE?
HOW ELSE AM I SUPPOSED TO GET TO --
HEY!
AN OFFSHOOT! YOU CALLED IT.
DOESN'T MATTER HOW THEY DRESS. YOU CAN SEE THAT SKIN FROM ORBIT.
GET TO THE OTHER SHUTTLE, NOW!
WELCOME TO ARKANIA.
BET YOU WISH YOU'D STAYED WHEREVER IT IS YOU WERE!

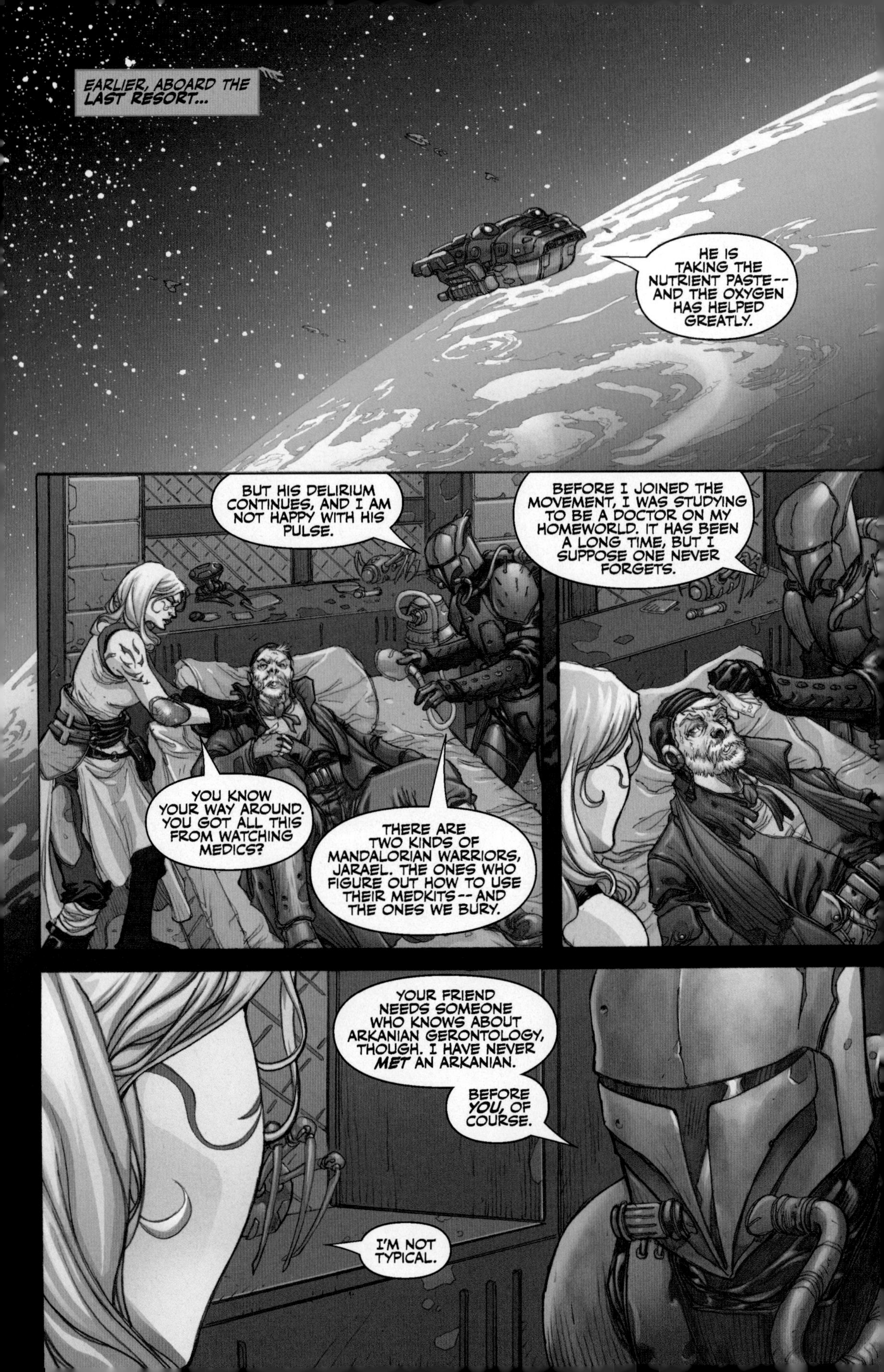
EARLIER, ABOARD THE LAST RESORT...
HE IS TAKING THE NUTRIENT PASTE-- AND THE OXYGEN HAS HELPED GREATLY.
BUT HIS DELIRIUM CONTINUES, AND I AM NOT HAPPY WITH HIS PULSE.
YOU KNOW YOUR WAY AROUND. YOU GOT ALL THIS FROM WATCHING MEDICS?
THERE ARE TWO KINDS OF MANDALORIAN WARRIORS, JARAEL. THE ONES WHO FIGURE OUT HOW TO USE THEIR MEDKITS-- AND THE ONES WE BURY.
BEFORE I JOINED THE MOVEMENT, I WAS STUDYING TO BE A DOCTOR ON MY HOMEWORLD. IT HAS BEEN A LONG TIME, BUT I SUPPOSE ONE NEVER FORGETS.
YOUR FRIEND NEEDS SOMEONE WHO KNOWS ABOUT ARKANIAN GERONTOLOGY, THOUGH. I HAVE NEVER MET AN ARKANIAN.
BEFORE YOU, OF COURSE.
I'M NOT TYPICAL.

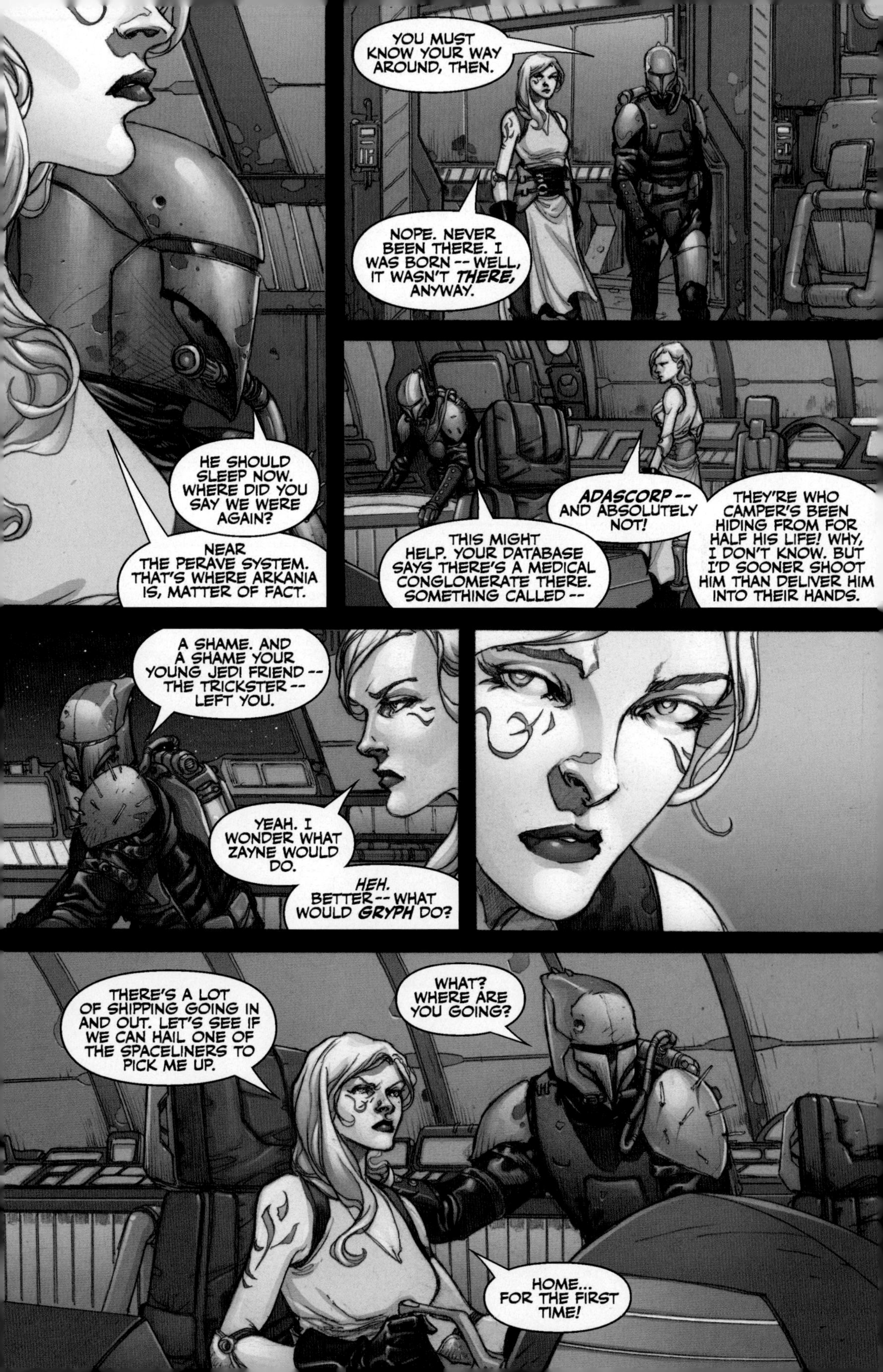
YOU MUST KNOW YOUR WAY AROUND, THEN.
NOPE. NEVER BEEN THERE. I WAS BORN -- WELL, IT WASN'T THERE, ANYWAY.
HE SHOULD SLEEP NOW. WHERE DID YOU SAY WE WERE AGAIN?
NEAR THE PERAVE SYSTEM. THAT'S WHERE ARKANIA IS, MATTER OF FACT.
THIS MIGHT HELP. YOUR DATABASE SAYS THERE'S A MEDICAL CONGLOMERATE THERE. SOMETHING CALLED --
ADASCORP -- AND ABSOLUTELY NOT!
THEY'RE WHO CAMPER'S BEEN HIDING FROM FOR HALF HIS LIFE! WHY, I DON'T KNOW. BUT I'D SOONER SHOOT HIM THAN DELIVER HIM INTO THEIR HANDS.
A SHAME. AND A SHAME YOUR YOUNG JEDI FRIEND -- THE TRICKSTER -- LEFT YOU.
YEAH. I WONDER WHAT ZAYNE WOULD DO.
HEH. BETTER -- WHAT WOULD GRYPH DO?
THERE'S A LOT OF SHIPPING GOING IN AND OUT. LET'S SEE IF WE CAN HAIL ONE OF THE SPACELINERS TO PICK ME UP.
WHAT? WHERE ARE YOU GOING?
HOME... FOR THE FIRST TIME!

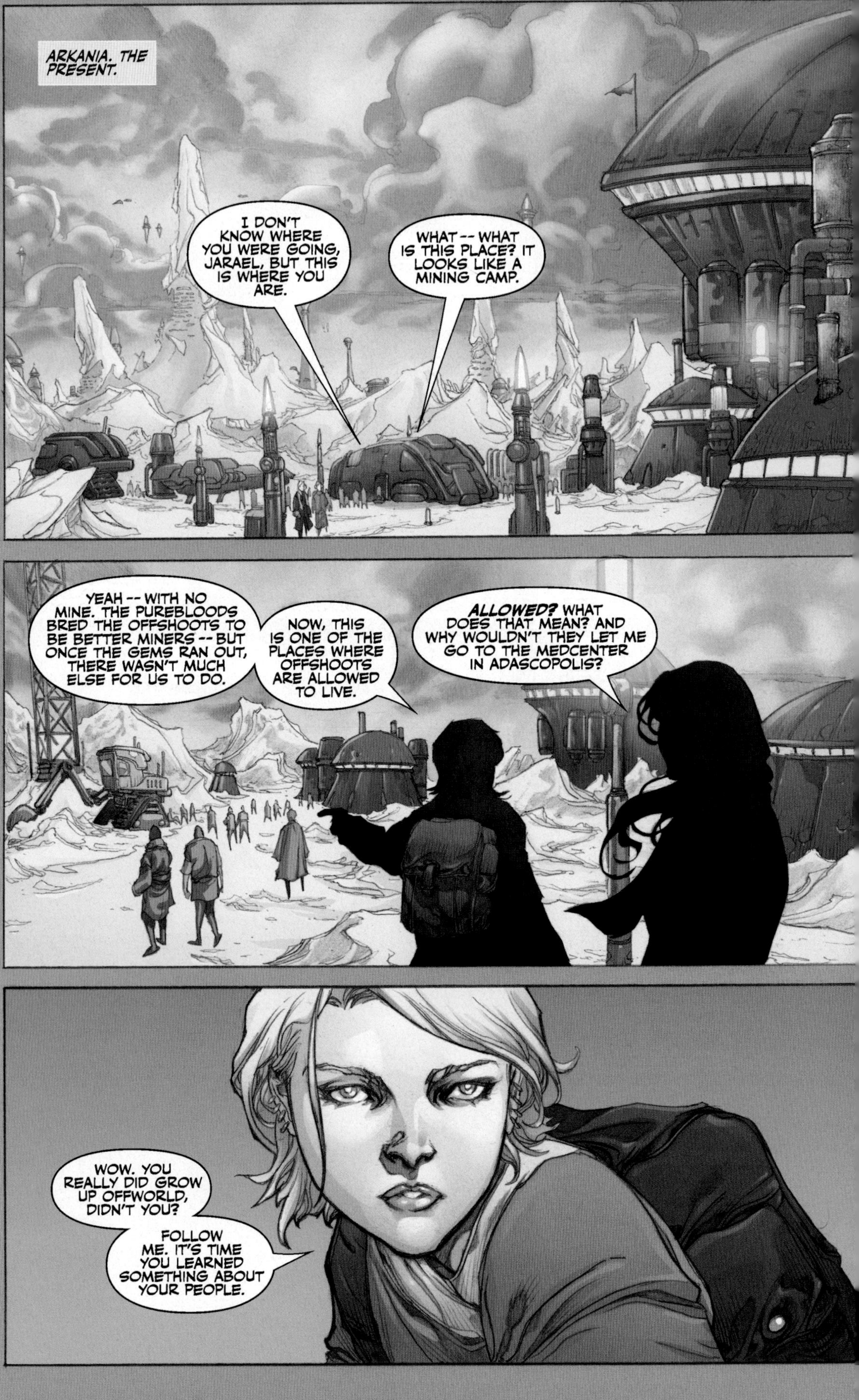
ARKANIA. THE PRESENT.
I DON'T KNOW WHERE YOU WERE GOING, JARAEL, BUT THIS IS WHERE YOU ARE.
WHAT -- WHAT IS THIS PLACE? IT LOOKS LIKE A MINING CAMP.
YEAH -- WITH NO MINE. THE PUREBLOODS BRED THE OFFSHOOTS TO BE BETTER MINERS -- BUT ONCE THE GEMS RAN OUT, THERE WASN'T MUCH ELSE FOR US TO DO.
NOW, THIS IS ONE OF THE PLACES WHERE OFFSHOOTS ARE ALLOWED TO LIVE.
ALLOWED? WHAT DOES THAT MEAN? AND WHY WOULDN'T THEY LET ME GO TO THE MEDCENTER IN ADASCOPOLIS?
WOW. YOU REALLY DID GROW UP OFFWORLD, DIDN'T YOU?
FOLLOW ME. IT'S TIME YOU LEARNED SOMETHING ABOUT YOUR PEOPLE.

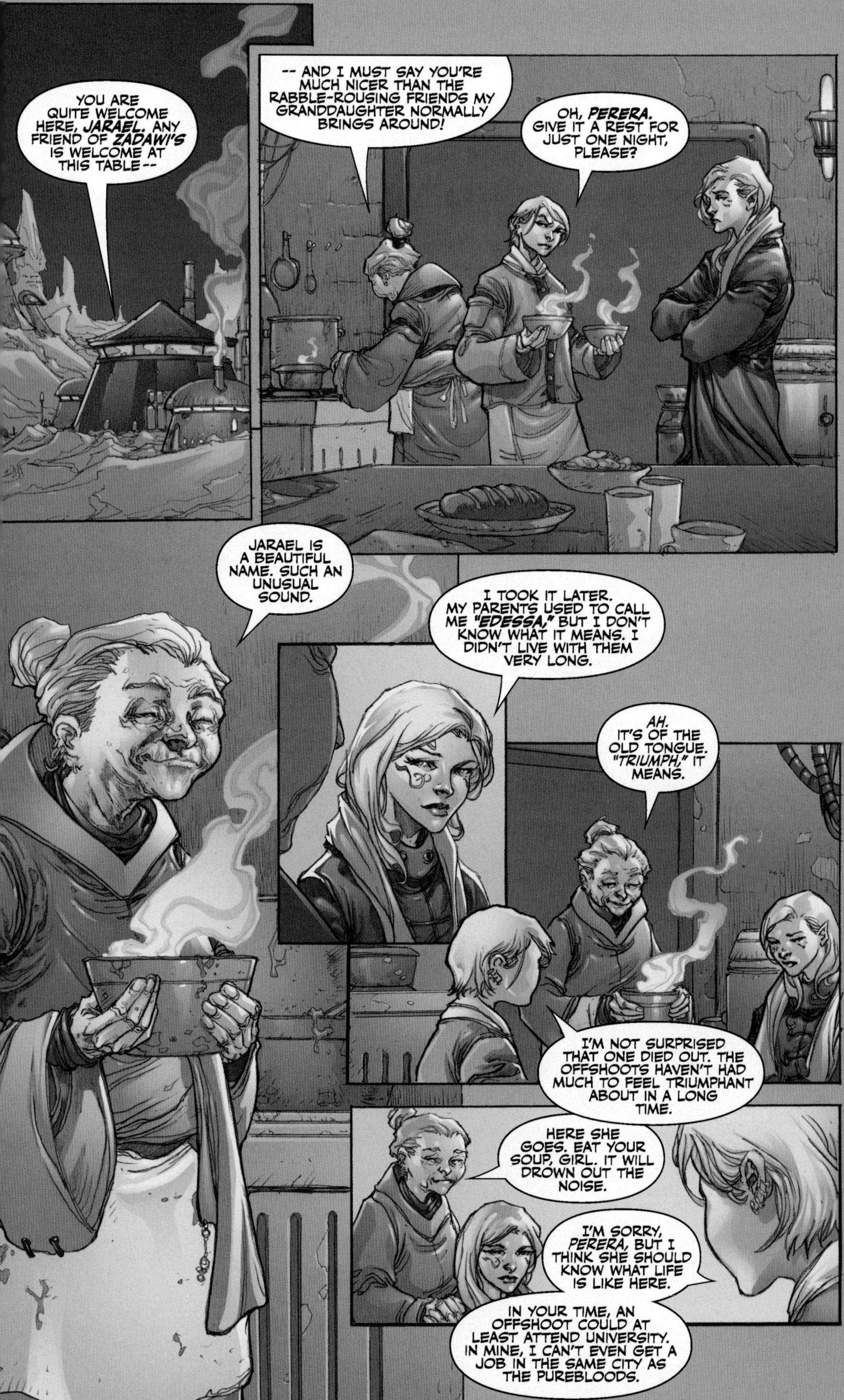
YOU ARE QUITE WELCOME HERE, JARAEL. ANY FRIEND OF ZADAWI'S IS WELCOME AT THIS TABLE--
-- AND I MUST SAY YOU'RE MUCH NICER THAN THE RABBLE-ROUSING FRIENDS MY GRANDDAUGHTER NORMALLY BRINGS AROUND!
OH, PERERA. GIVE IT A REST FOR JUST ONE NIGHT, PLEASE?
JARAEL IS A BEAUTIFUL NAME. SUCH AN UNUSUAL SOUND.
I TOOK IT LATER. MY PARENTS USED TO CALL ME "EDESSA," BUT I DON'T KNOW WHAT IT MEANS. I DIDN'T LIVE WITH THEM VERY LONG.
AH. IT'S OF THE OLD TONGUE. "TRIUMPH," IT MEANS.
I'M NOT SURPRISED THAT ONE DIED OUT. THE OFFSHOOTS HAVEN'T HAD MUCH TO FEEL TRIUMPHANT ABOUT IN A LONG TIME.
HERE SHE GOES. EAT YOUR SOUP, GIRL. IT WILL DROWN OUT THE NOISE.
I'M SORRY, PERERA, BUT I THINK SHE SHOULD KNOW WHAT LIFE IS LIKE HERE.
IN YOUR TIME, AN OFFSHOOT COULD AT LEAST ATTEND UNIVERSITY. IN MINE, I CAN'T EVEN GET A JOB IN THE SAME CITY AS THE PUREBLOODS.

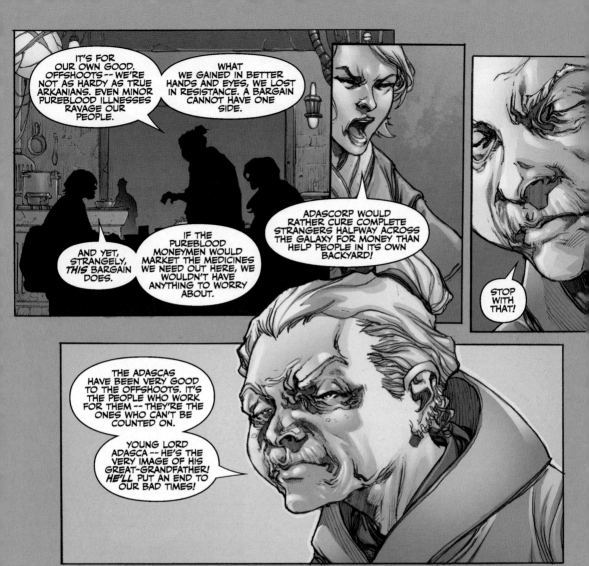

IT'S FOR OUR OWN GOOD, OFFSHOOTS -- WE'RE NOT AS HARDY AS TRUE ARKANIANS. EVEN MINOR PUREBLOOD ILLNESSES RAVAGE OUR PEOPLE.

WHAT WE GAINED IN BETTER HANDS AND EYES, WE LOST IN RESISTANCE. A BARGAIN CANNOT HAVE ONE SIDE.

AND YET, STRANGELY, *THIS* BARGAIN DOES.

IF THE PUREBLOOD MONEYMEN WOULD MARKET THE MEDICINES WE NEED OUT HERE, WE WOULDN'T HAVE ANYTHING TO WORRY ABOUT.

ADASCORP WOULD RATHER CURE COMPLETE STRANGERS HALFWAY ACROSS THE GALAXY FOR MONEY THAN HELP PEOPLE IN ITS OWN BACKYARD!

STOP WITH THAT!

THE ADASCAS HAVE BEEN VERY GOOD TO THE OFFSHOOTS. IT'S THE PEOPLE WHO WORK FOR THEM -- THEY'RE THE ONES WHO CAN'T BE COUNTED ON.

YOUNG LORD ADASCA -- HE'S THE VERY IMAGE OF HIS GREAT-GRANDFATHER! *HE'LL* PUT AN END TO OUR BAD TIMES!

GIVE HIM TIME -- I KNOW HE WILL. HE'LL --

MOTHER, RELAX. YOU'LL TAKE ILL AGAIN.

DO YOU SEE WHAT YOU STARTED?

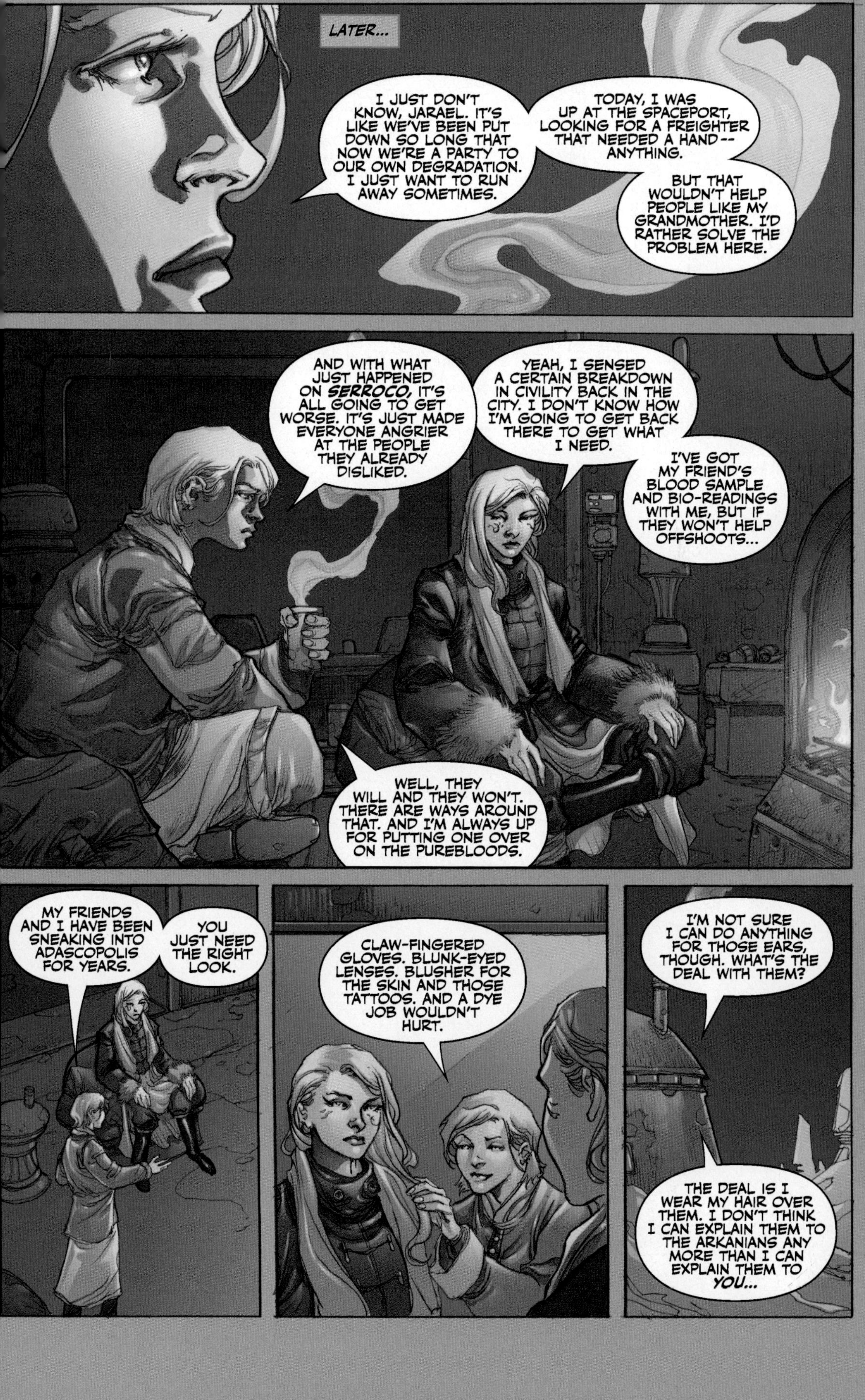
LATER...
I JUST DON'T KNOW, JARAEL. IT'S LIKE WE'VE BEEN PUT DOWN SO LONG THAT NOW WE'RE A PARTY TO OUR OWN DEGRADATION. I JUST WANT TO RUN AWAY SOMETIMES.
TODAY, I WAS UP AT THE SPACEPORT, LOOKING FOR A FREIGHTER THAT NEEDED A HAND-- ANYTHING.
BUT THAT WOULDN'T HELP PEOPLE LIKE MY GRANDMOTHER. I'D RATHER SOLVE THE PROBLEM HERE.
AND WITH WHAT JUST HAPPENED ON SERROCO, IT'S ALL GOING TO GET WORSE. IT'S JUST MADE EVERYONE ANGRIER AT THE PEOPLE THEY ALREADY DISLIKED.
YEAH, I SENSED A CERTAIN BREAKDOWN IN CIVILITY BACK IN THE CITY. I DON'T KNOW HOW I'M GOING TO GET BACK THERE TO GET WHAT I NEED.
I'VE GOT MY FRIEND'S BLOOD SAMPLE AND BIO-READINGS WITH ME, BUT IF THEY WON'T HELP OFFSHOOTS...
WELL, THEY WILL AND THEY WON'T. THERE ARE WAYS AROUND THAT. AND I'M ALWAYS UP FOR PUTTING ONE OVER ON THE PUREBLOODS.
MY FRIENDS AND I HAVE BEEN SNEAKING INTO ADASCOPOLIS FOR YEARS.
YOU JUST NEED THE RIGHT LOOK.
CLAW-FINGERED GLOVES. BLUNK-EYED LENSES. BLUSHER FOR THE SKIN AND THOSE TATTOOS. AND A DYE JOB WOULDN'T HURT.
I'M NOT SURE I CAN DO ANYTHING FOR THOSE EARS, THOUGH. WHAT'S THE DEAL WITH THEM?
THE DEAL IS I WEAR MY HAIR OVER THEM. I DON'T THINK I CAN EXPLAIN THEM TO THE ARKANIANS ANY MORE THAN I CAN EXPLAIN THEM TO YOU...

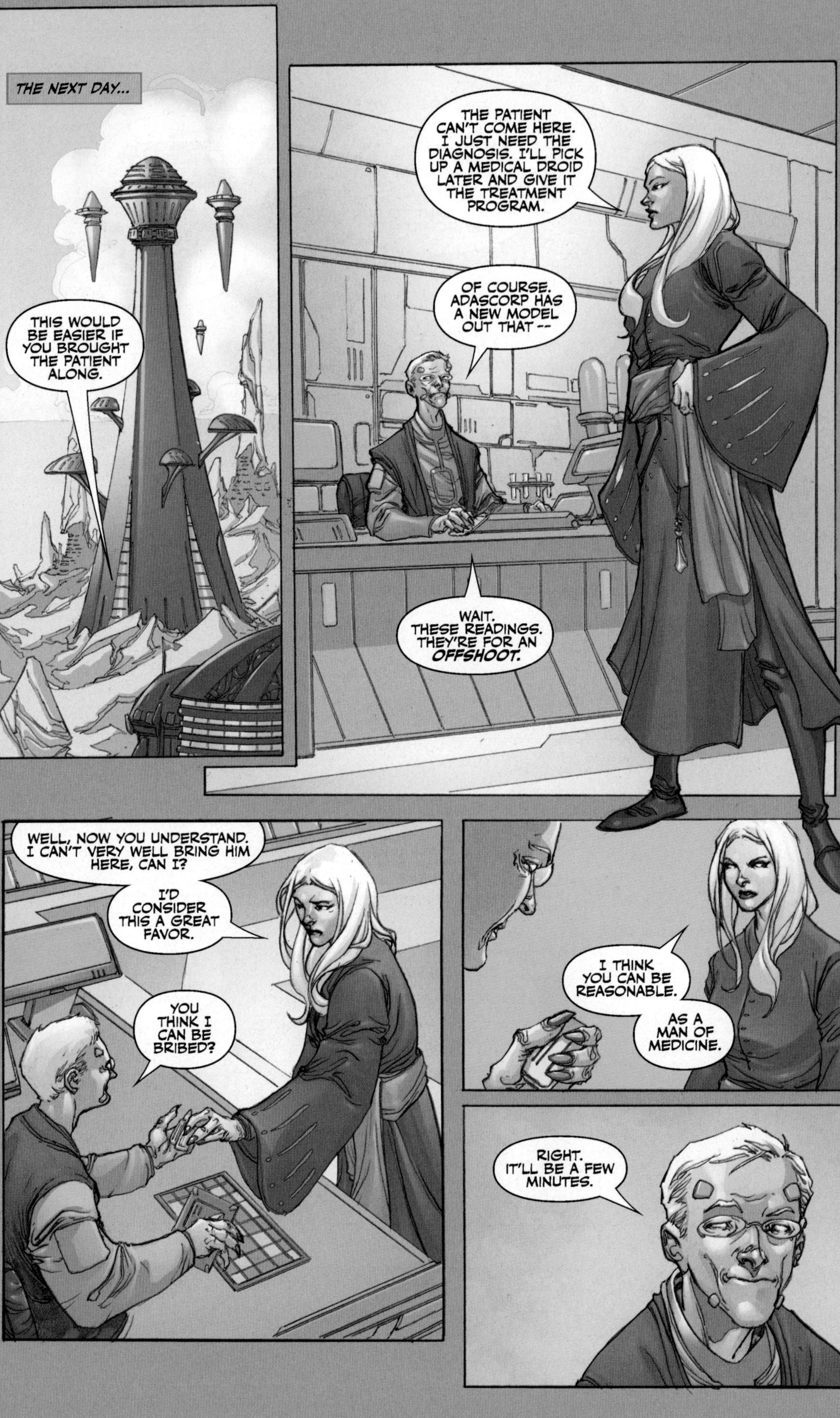
THE NEXT DAY...
THIS WOULD BE EASIER IF YOU BROUGHT THE PATIENT ALONG.
THE PATIENT CAN'T COME HERE. I JUST NEED THE DIAGNOSIS. I'LL PICK UP A MEDICAL DROID LATER AND GIVE IT THE TREATMENT PROGRAM.
OF COURSE. ADASCORP HAS A NEW MODEL OUT THAT --
WAIT. THESE READINGS. THEY'RE FOR AN OFFSHOOT.
WELL, NOW YOU UNDERSTAND. I CAN'T VERY WELL BRING HIM HERE, CAN I?
I'D CONSIDER THIS A GREAT FAVOR.
YOU THINK I CAN BE BRIBED?
I THINK YOU CAN BE REASONABLE.
AS A MAN OF MEDICINE.
RIGHT. IT'LL BE A FEW MINUTES.

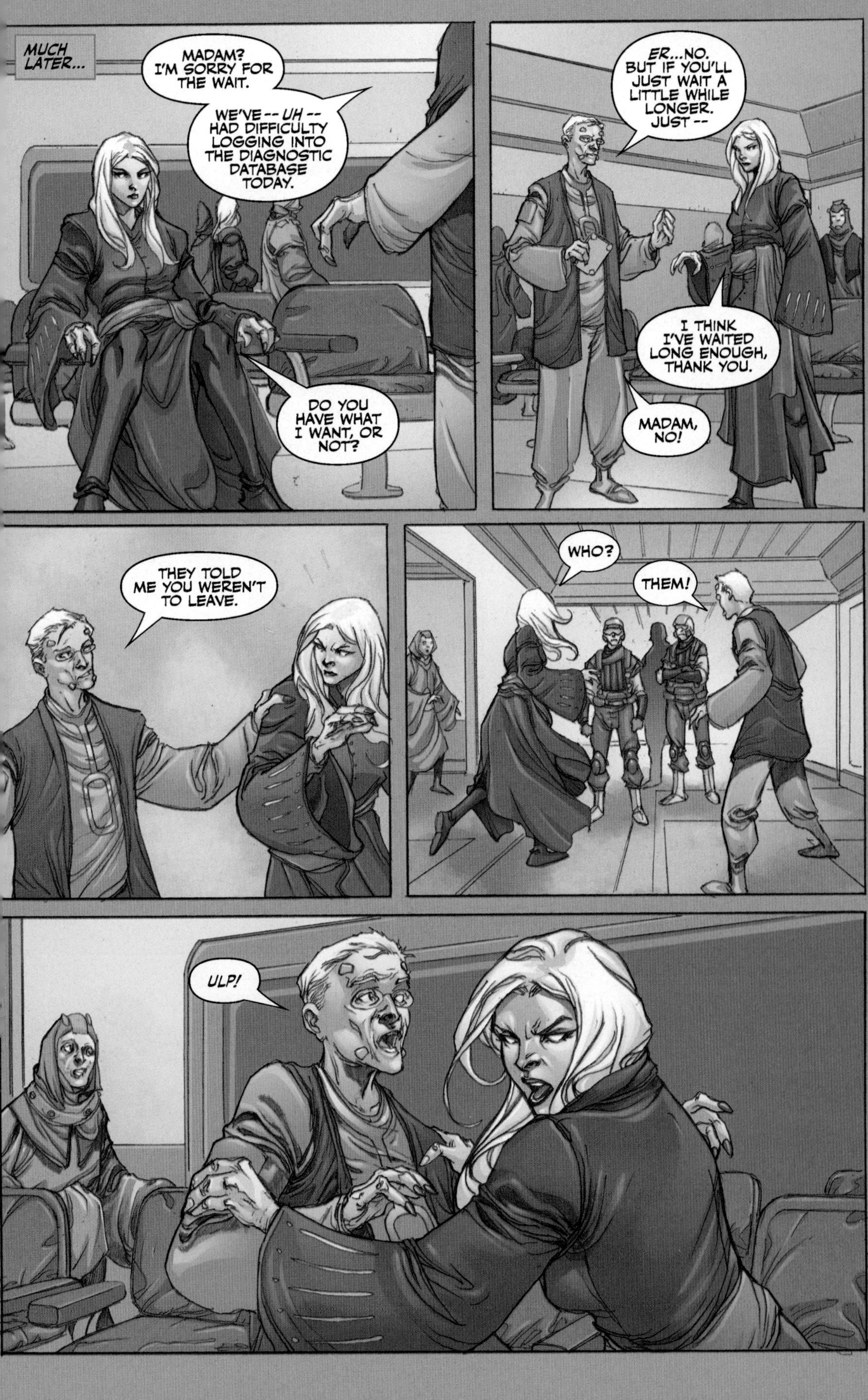
MUCH LATER...
MADAM? I'M SORRY FOR THE WAIT.
WE'VE -- UH -- HAD DIFFICULTY LOGGING INTO THE DIAGNOSTIC DATABASE TODAY.
DO YOU HAVE WHAT I WANT, OR NOT?
ER...NO. BUT IF YOU'LL JUST WAIT A LITTLE WHILE LONGER. JUST --
I THINK I'VE WAITED LONG ENOUGH, THANK YOU.
MADAM, NO!
THEY TOLD ME YOU WEREN'T TO LEAVE.
WHO?
THEM!
ULP!

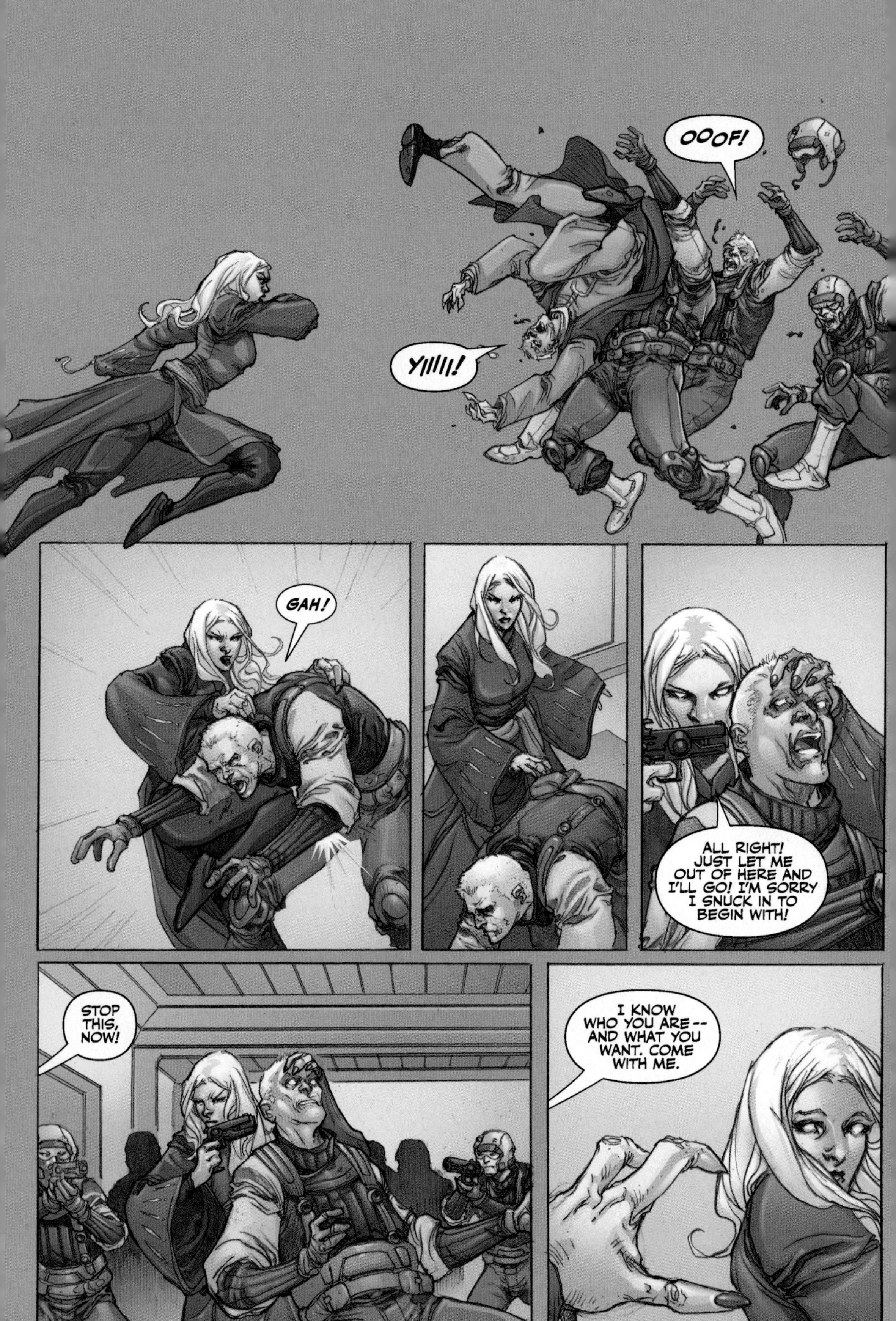
OOOF!
YIIIII!
GAH!
ALL RIGHT! JUST LET ME OUT OF HERE AND I'LL GO! I'M SORRY I SNUCK IN TO BEGIN WITH!
STOP THIS, NOW!
I KNOW WHO YOU ARE -- AND WHAT YOU WANT. COME WITH ME.

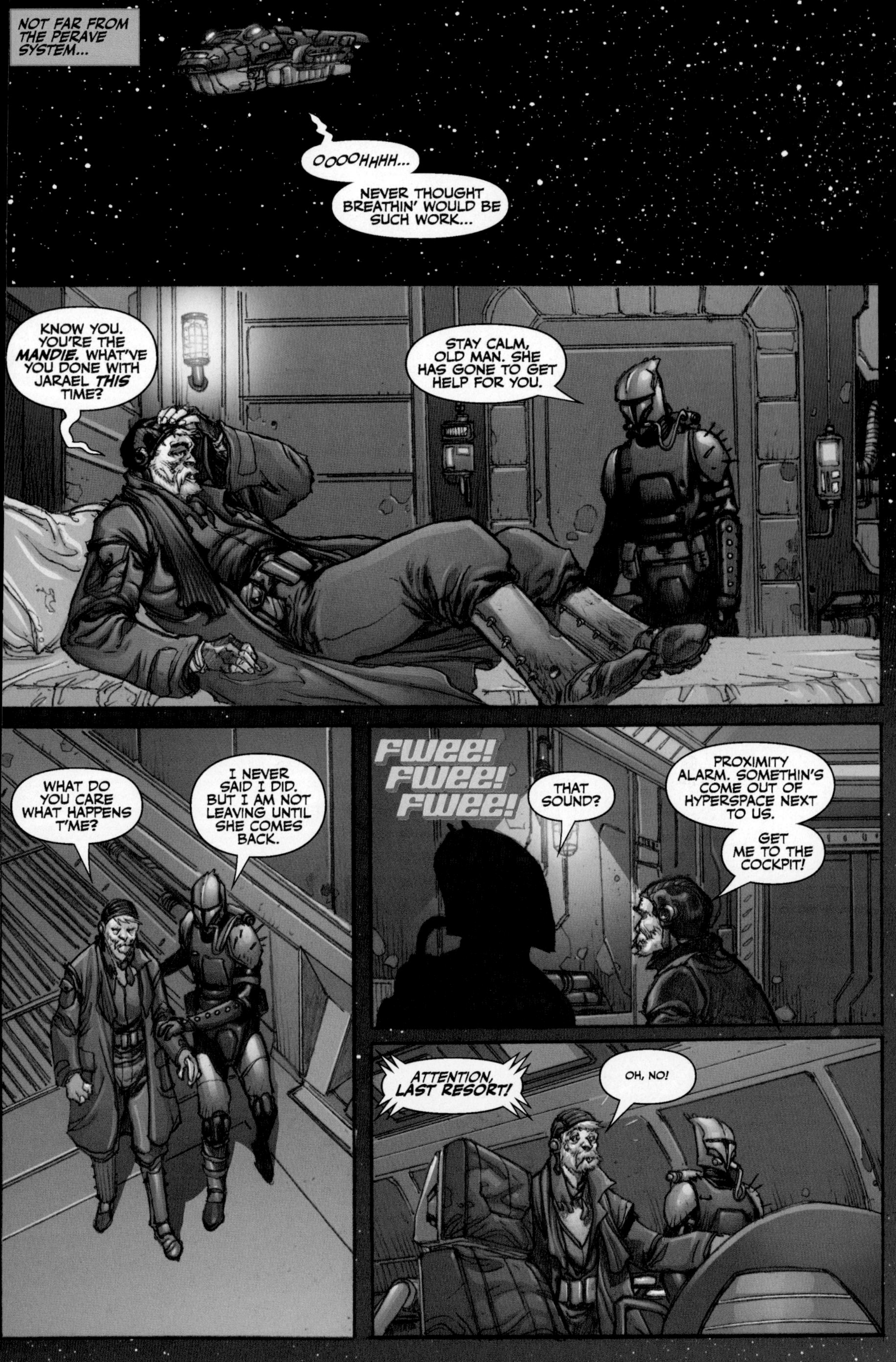
NOT FAR FROM THE PERAVE SYSTEM...
OOOOHHHH...
NEVER THOUGHT BREATHIN' WOULD BE SUCH WORK...
KNOW YOU. YOU'RE THE MANDIE. WHAT'VE YOU DONE WITH JARAEL THIS TIME?
STAY CALM, OLD MAN. SHE HAS GONE TO GET HELP FOR YOU.
WHAT DO YOU CARE WHAT HAPPENS T'ME?
I NEVER SAID I DID. BUT I AM NOT LEAVING UNTIL SHE COMES BACK.
FWEE! FWEE! FWEE!
THAT SOUND?
PROXIMITY ALARM. SOMETHIN'S COME OUT OF HYPERSPACE NEXT TO US.
GET ME TO THE COCKPIT!
ATTENTION, LAST RESORT!
OH, NO!

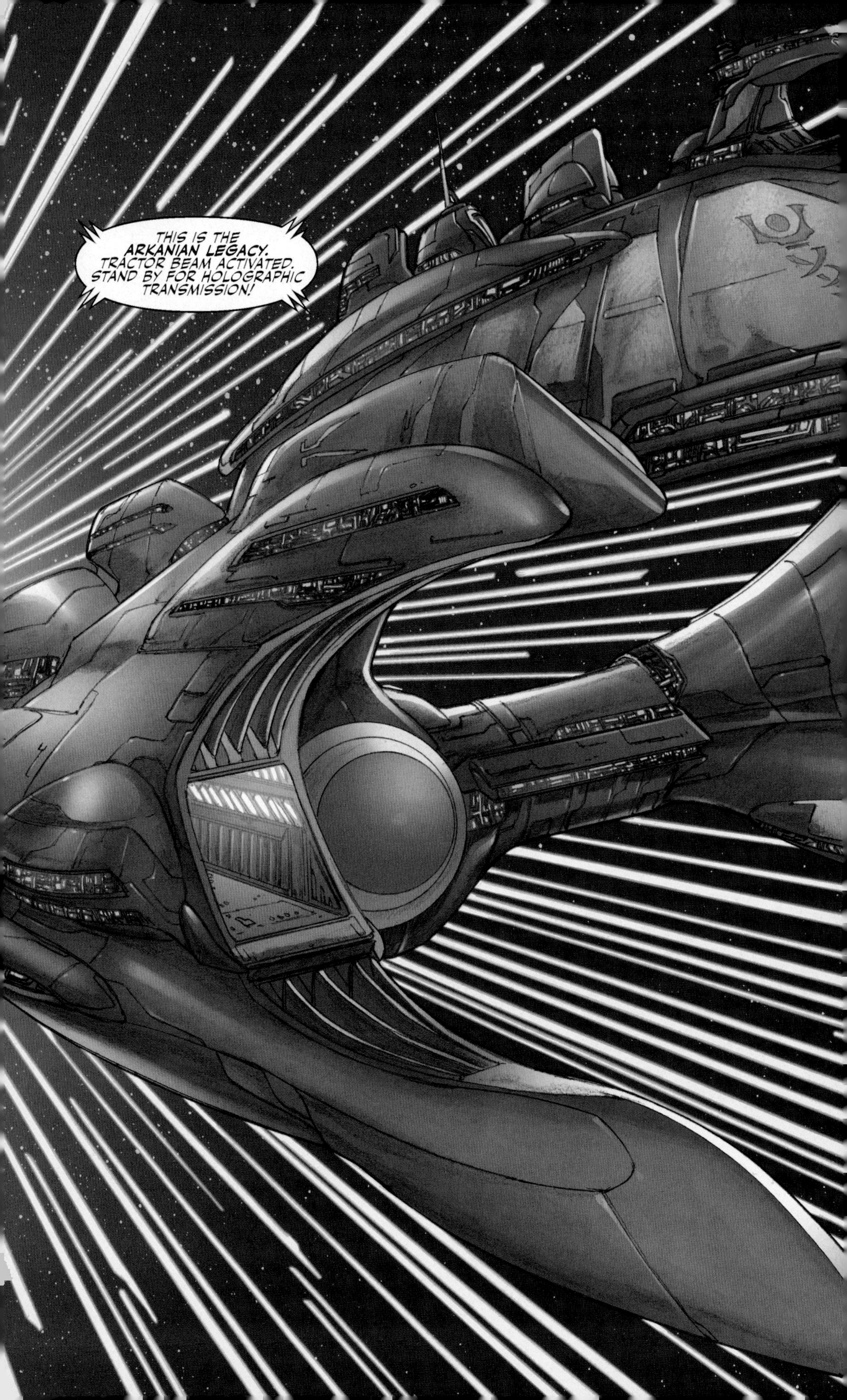
THIS IS THE ARKANIAN LEGACY. TRACTOR BEAM ACTIVATED. STAND BY FOR HOLOGRAPHIC TRANSMISSION!

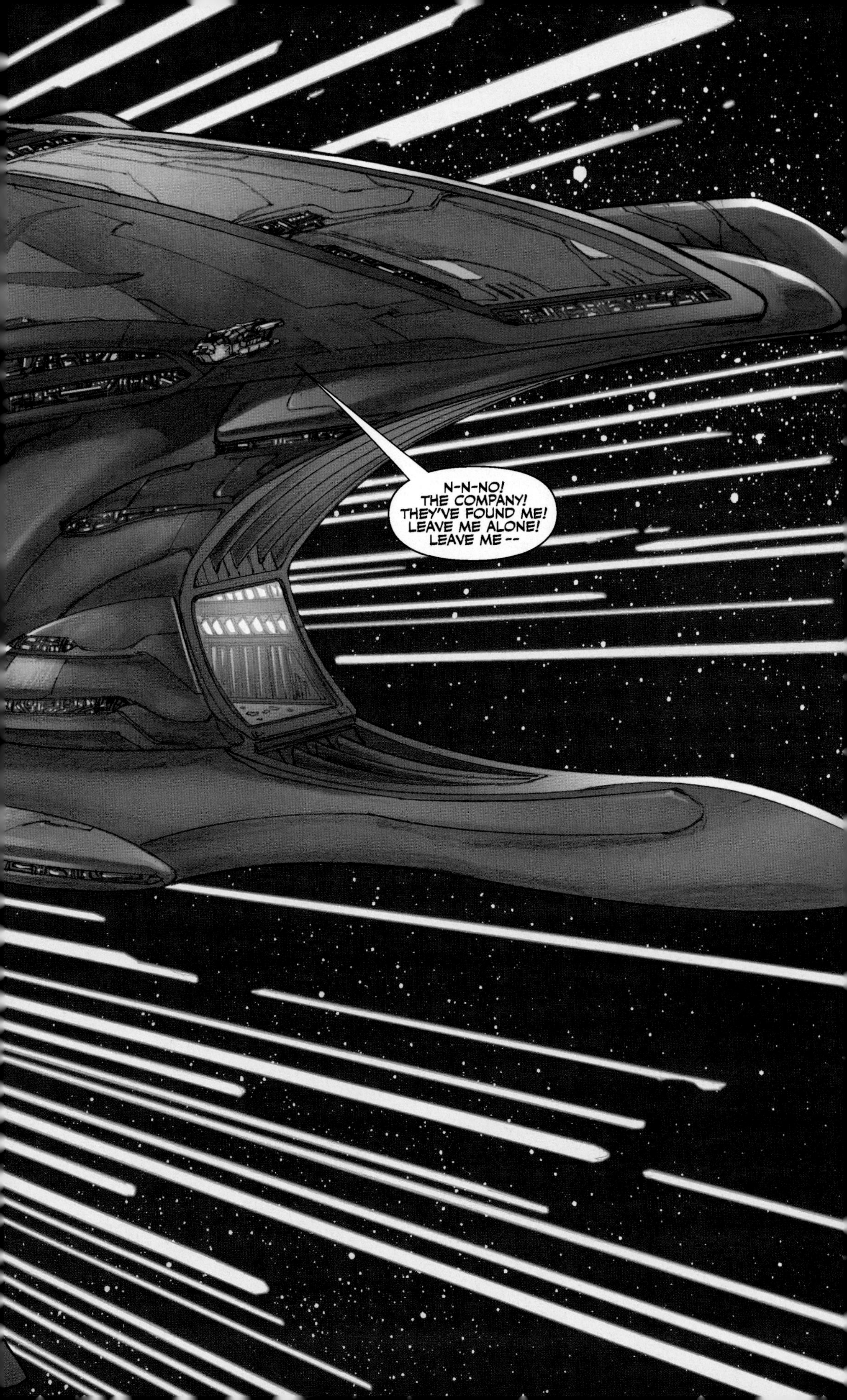
N-N-NO! THE COMPANY! THEY'VE FOUND ME! LEAVE ME ALONE! LEAVE ME --

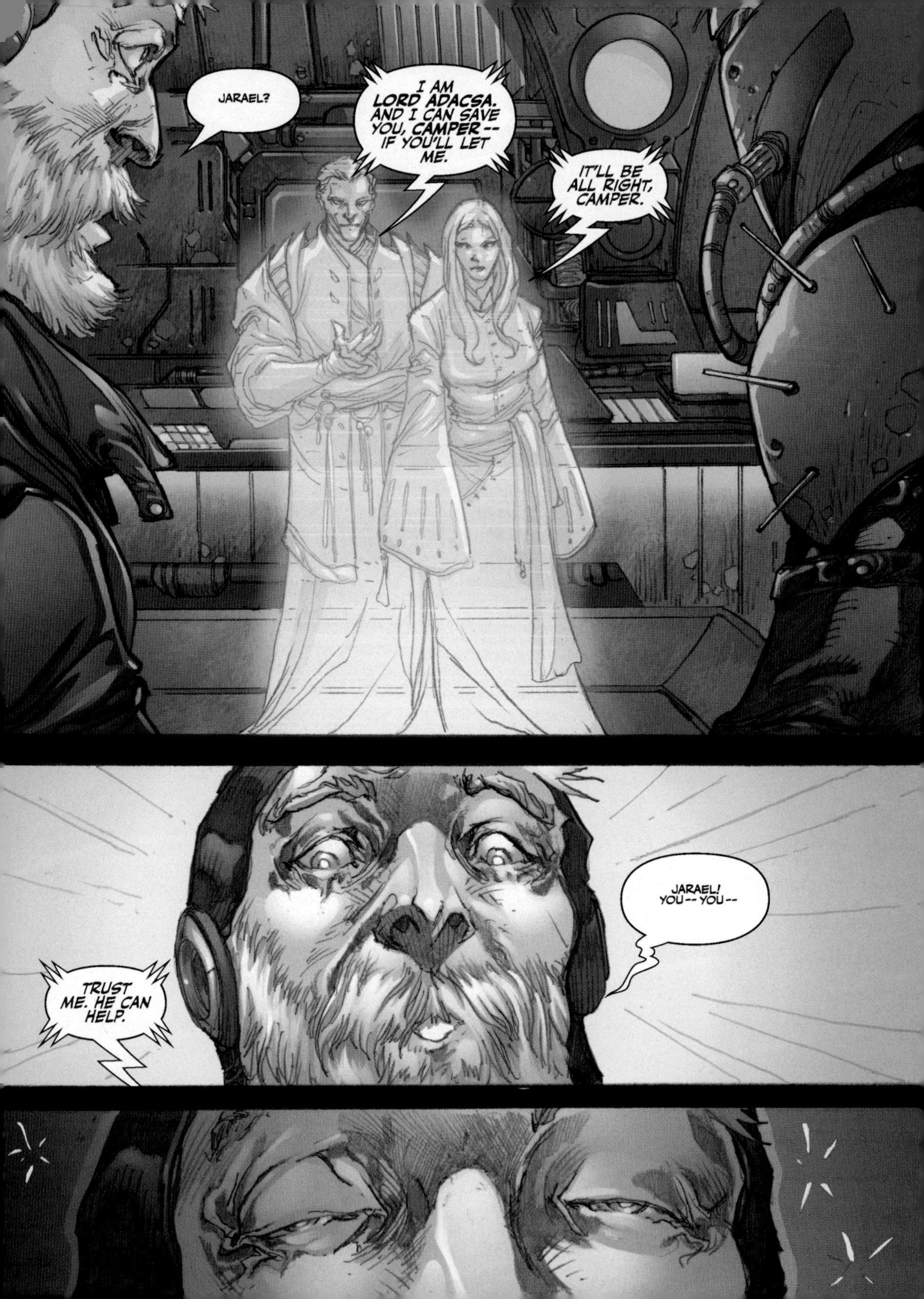
JARAEL?
I AM LORD ADACSA. AND I CAN SAVE YOU, CAMPER -- IF YOU'LL LET ME.
IT'LL BE ALL RIGHT, CAMPER.
JARAEL! YOU -- YOU --
TRUST ME. HE CAN HELP.

THE ADMIRAL'S LIST

THE OFFICIAL COMMUNIQUÉ FROM THE REPUBLIC NAVY

REMEMBER SERROCO! EDITION

HOPE FADES FOR SERROCO SURVIVORS

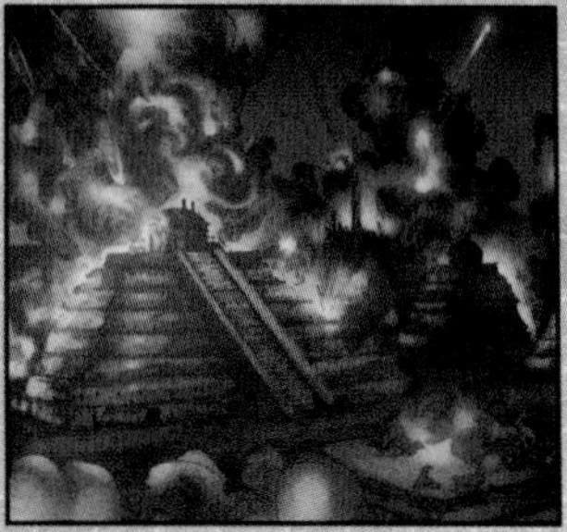

Number rescued unchanged; escapees under fire

Recent days have yielded little hope for additional survivors from the cowardly Mandalore's incineration of the Republic forces building on Serroco. No new vessels have arrived in Republic space, and the group returning with Admiral Saul Karath continues under fire (see dispatch).

Meanwhile, the Admiral of the Fleet signaled his intention to lodge an official protest with the Republic over the army's positioning of forces near Serrocan population centers.

"No one acquainted with the rules of war could have expected the shocking and abhorrent acts of the abomination called Mandalore," said Catronus Steffans, Republic defense official. However, with such populated worlds as Telerath, Ralltiir, and Arkania potentially under threat next, Steffans indicated that future policy was under review.

SELECT to learn more...

CASUALTY LIST

Here are the latest confirmed additions to the record of ships lost at Serroco:

SERVICE:
Perspicacity, Cruiser
CX-03, Cargolift Vessel
CX-09, Cargolift Vessel
CX-14, Cargolift Vessel

CIVILIAN:
Queen of Taris, spaceliner
Little Bivoli, fringe supply vessel
Grubstake, fringe supply vessel

SELECT to continue list...

DISPATCHES FROM THE FRONT

Admiral Karath fights to elude his pursuers

The following dispatch arrived from the *Courageous* battle group two days ago to the Admiral of the Fleet on Coruscant:

Sir,

I have the duty and the grave responsibility to report to you the disposition of my forces, still under pursuit on the lanes from Serroco to Telerath.

Since departing Serroco, our ranks have been reduced to [force disposition classified]. I am hopeful that we will be able to make Myrkr or the Ryyk Nebula, where we might reform with the Tremendous group arriving from [point of origin classified].

I should like to commend Lieutenant Carth Onasi, whose swift thinking has been a service to the fleet. The conduct of Commander Dallan Morvis has also been exemplary. I also appreciate your forwarding my message, submitted in my last dispatch, to the Jedi order.

I regret that I cannot make a more detailed report, but we have repeatedly been called upon to defend the flotilla. I have pledged not to allow any of the ships escaping the cauldron of Serroco to fall prey to the Mandalorians without a fight.

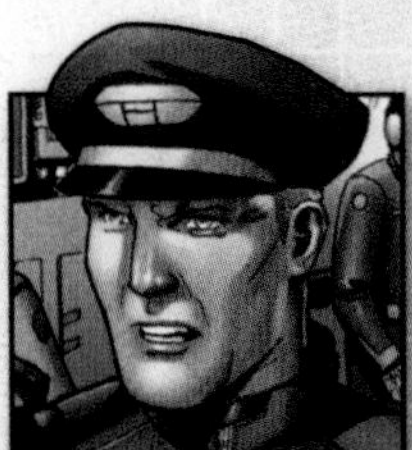

Yours in duty,
SAUL KARATH
Republic Ship *Courageous*

SELECT to learn more...

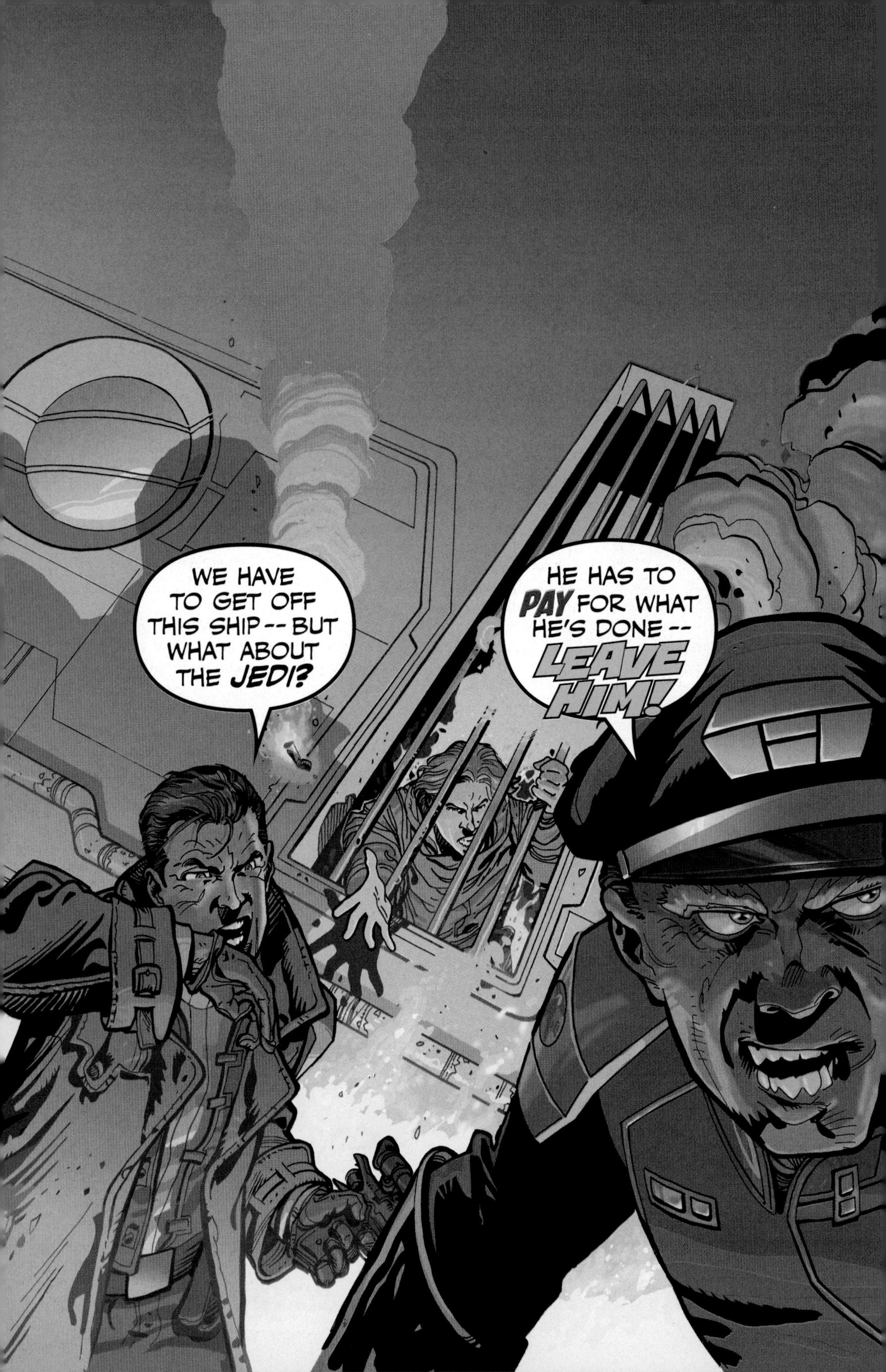
WE HAVE TO GET OFF THIS SHIP -- BUT WHAT ABOUT THE JEDI?
HE HAS TO PAY FOR WHAT HE'S DONE -- LEAVE HIM!

STAR WARS: KNIGHTS OF THE OLD REPUBLIC #17 — "NIGHTS OF ANGER, PART 2"

WRITER: JOHN JACKSON MILLER • ARTIST: HARVEY TOLIBAO • COLORIST: MICHAEL ATIYEH • LETTERER: MICHAEL HEISLER

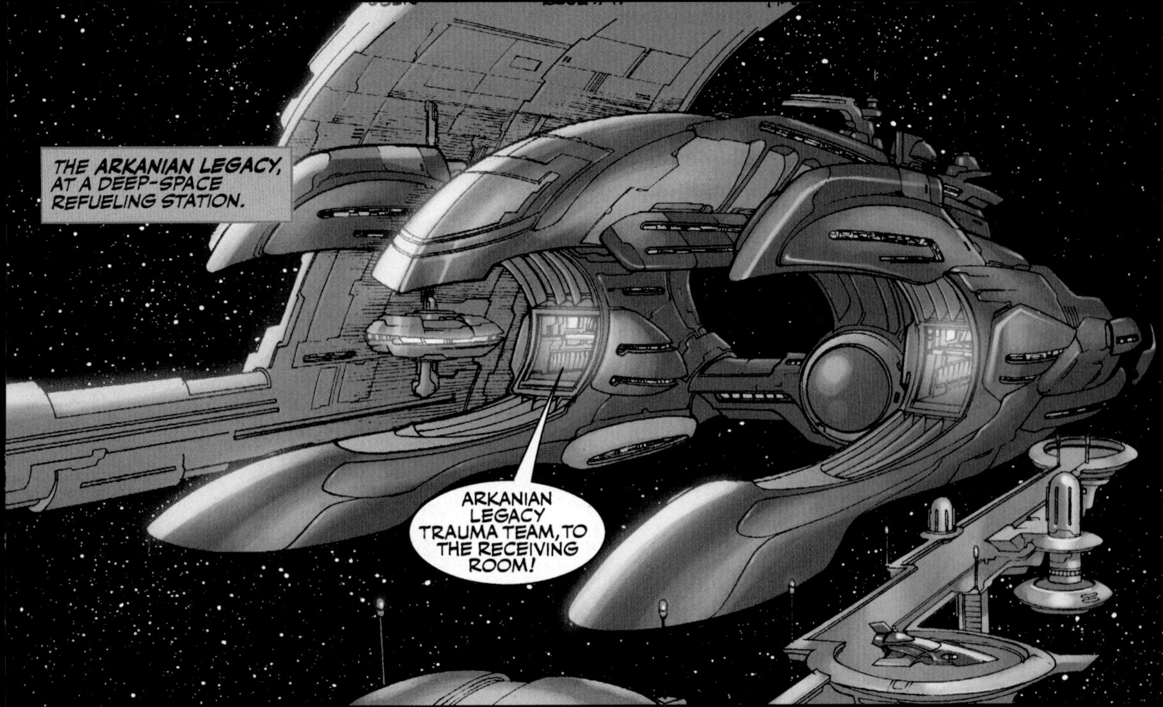
THE ARKANIAN LEGACY, AT A DEEP-SPACE REFUELING STATION.
ARKANIAN LEGACY TRAUMA TEAM, TO THE RECEIVING ROOM!

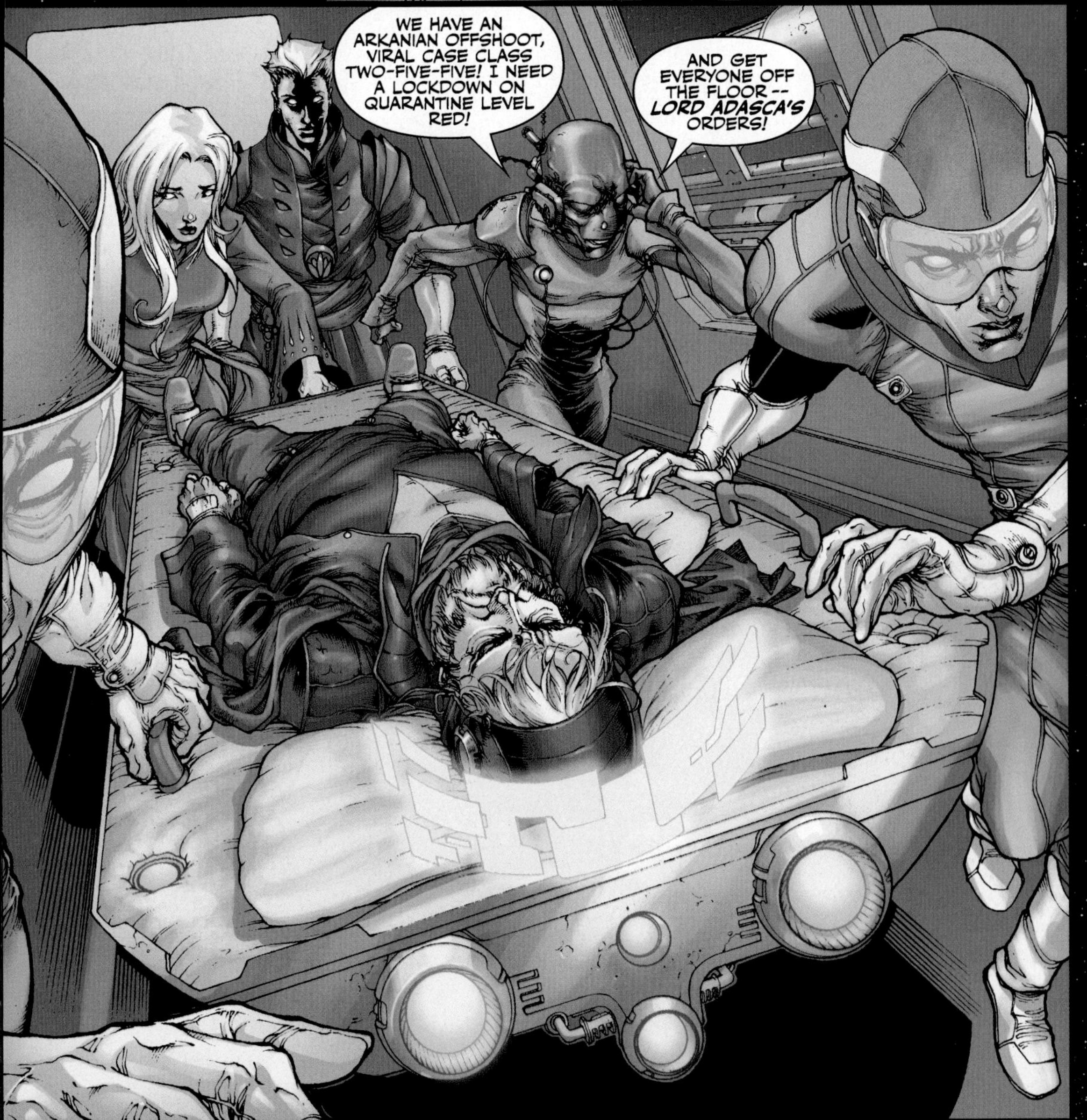
WE HAVE AN ARKANIAN OFFSHOOT, VIRAL CASE CLASS TWO-FIVE-FIVE! I NEED A LOCKDOWN ON QUARANTINE LEVEL RED!
AND GET EVERYONE OFF THE FLOOR -- LORD ADASCA'S ORDERS!

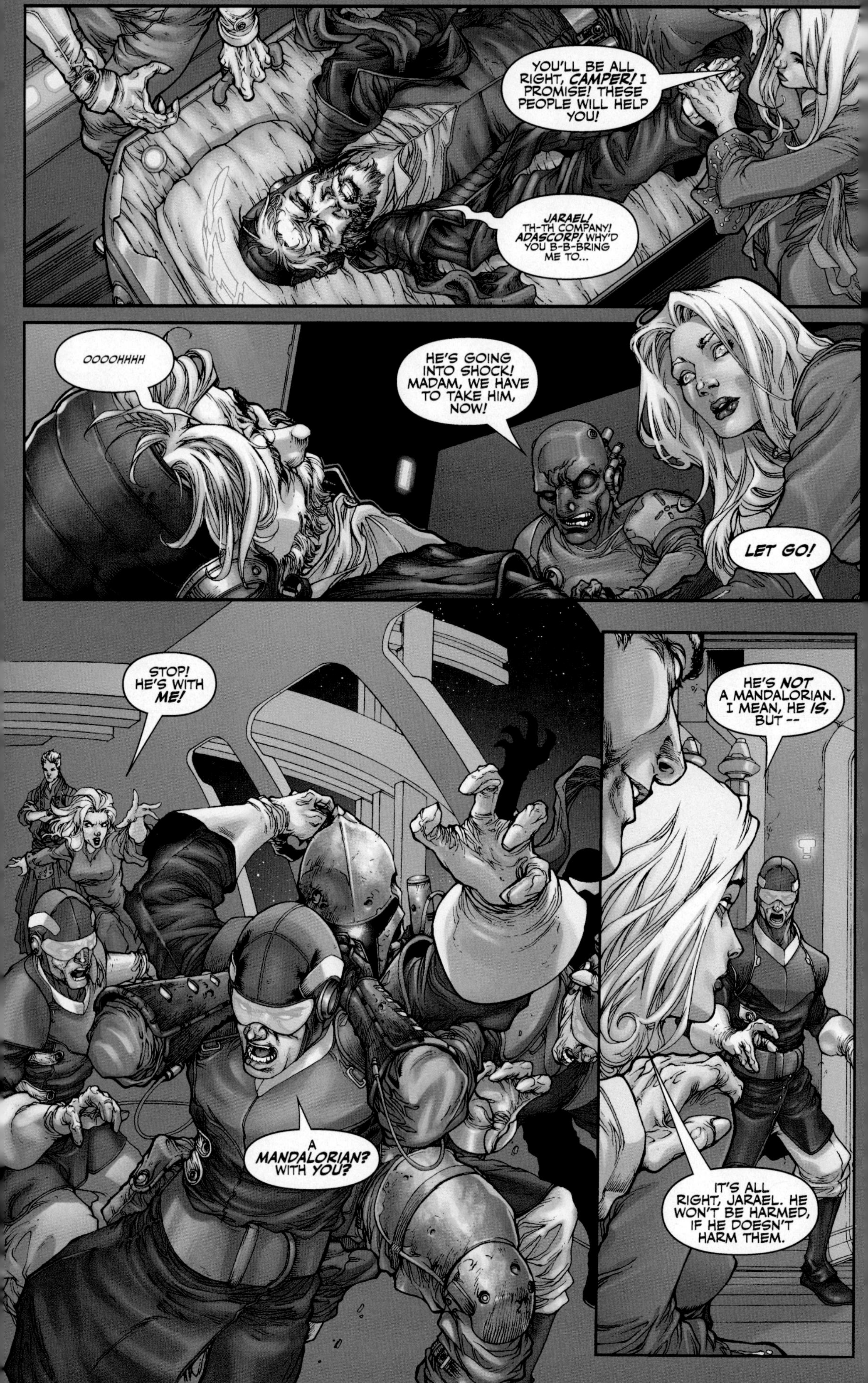
YOU'LL BE ALL RIGHT, CAMPER! I PROMISE! THESE PEOPLE WILL HELP YOU!
JARAEL! TH-TH COMPANY! ADASCORP! WHY'D YOU B-B-BRING ME TO...
OOOOHHHH
HE'S GOING INTO SHOCK! MADAM, WE HAVE TO TAKE HIM, NOW!
LET GO!
STOP! HE'S WITH ME!
A MANDALORIAN? WITH YOU?
HE'S NOT A MANDALORIAN. I MEAN, HE IS, BUT --
IT'S ALL RIGHT, JARAEL. HE WON'T BE HARMED, IF HE DOESN'T HARM THEM.

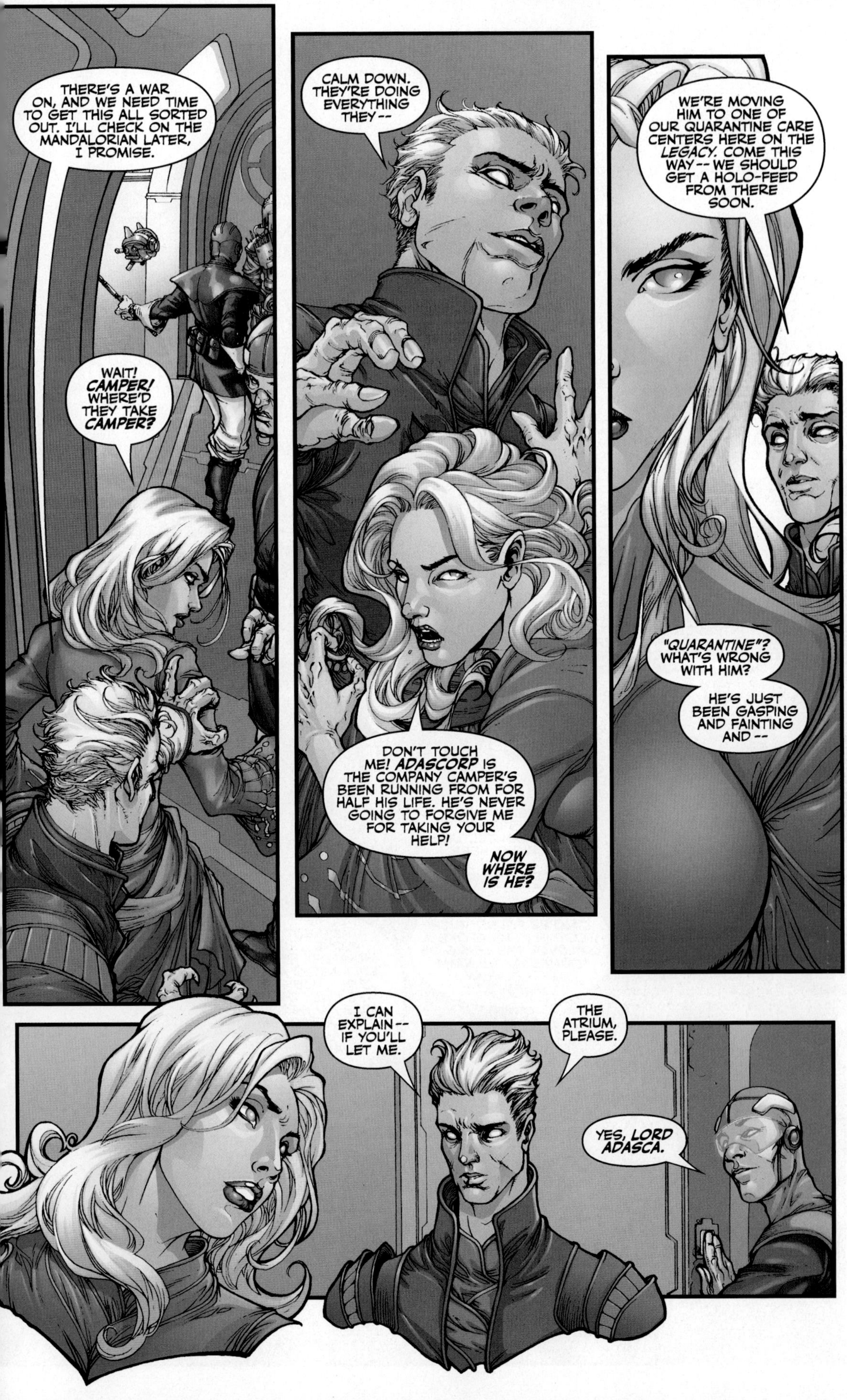
THERE'S A WAR ON, AND WE NEED TIME TO GET THIS ALL SORTED OUT. I'LL CHECK ON THE MANDALORIAN LATER, I PROMISE.
WAIT! CAMPER! WHERE'D THEY TAKE CAMPER?
CALM DOWN. THEY'RE DOING EVERYTHING THEY --
DON'T TOUCH ME! ADASCORP IS THE COMPANY CAMPER'S BEEN RUNNING FROM FOR HALF HIS LIFE. HE'S NEVER GOING TO FORGIVE ME FOR TAKING YOUR HELP!
NOW WHERE IS HE?
WE'RE MOVING HIM TO ONE OF OUR QUARANTINE CARE CENTERS HERE ON THE LEGACY. COME THIS WAY -- WE SHOULD GET A HOLO-FEED FROM THERE SOON.
"QUARANTINE"? WHAT'S WRONG WITH HIM?
HE'S JUST BEEN GASPING AND FAINTING AND --
I CAN EXPLAIN -- IF YOU'LL LET ME.
THE ATRIUM, PLEASE.
YES, LORD ADASCA.

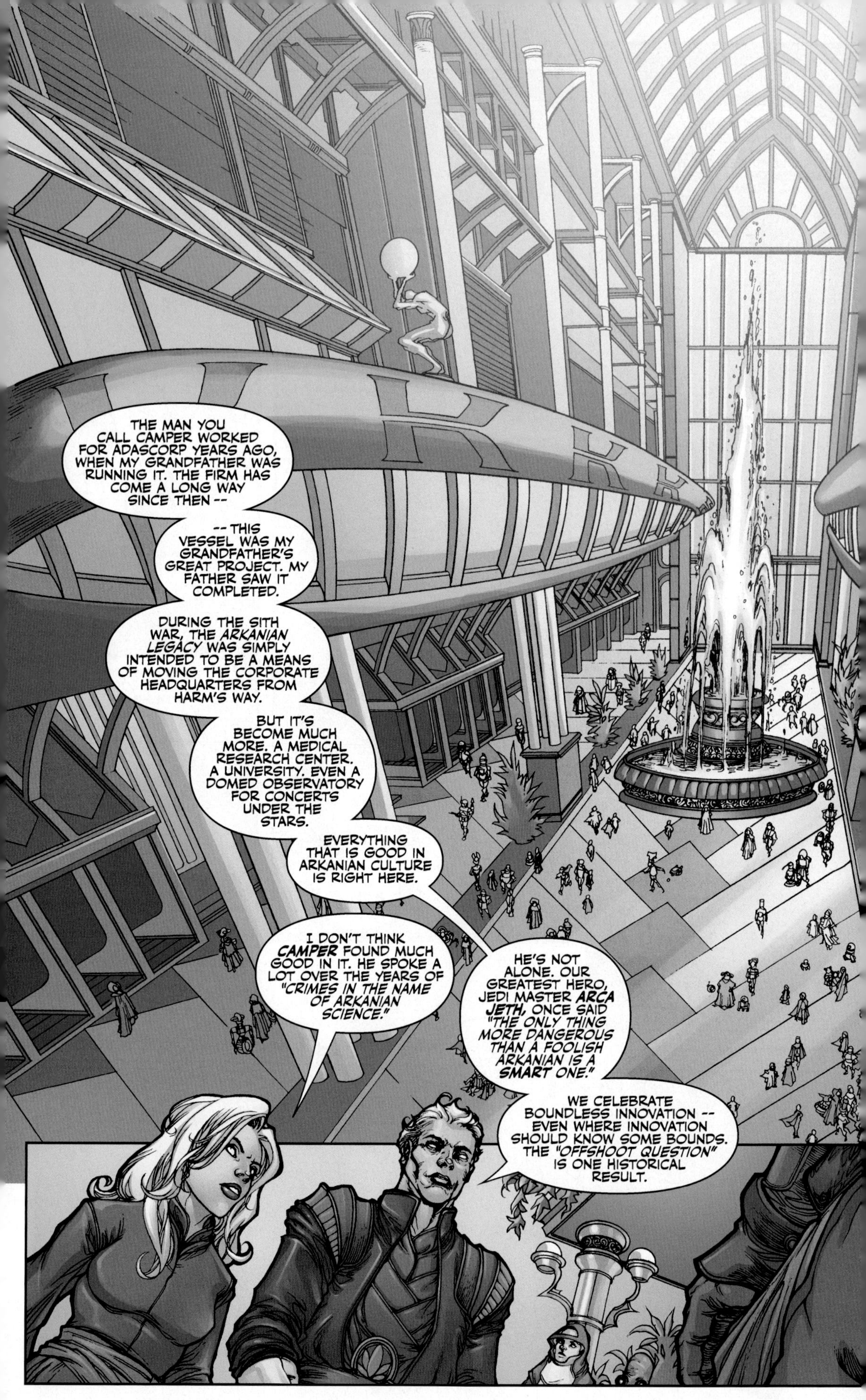
THE MAN YOU CALL CAMPER WORKED FOR ADASCORP YEARS AGO, WHEN MY GRANDFATHER WAS RUNNING IT. THE FIRM HAS COME A LONG WAY SINCE THEN --
-- THIS VESSEL WAS MY GRANDFATHER'S GREAT PROJECT. MY FATHER SAW IT COMPLETED.
DURING THE SITH WAR, THE *ARKANIAN LEGACY* WAS SIMPLY INTENDED TO BE A MEANS OF MOVING THE CORPORATE HEADQUARTERS FROM HARM'S WAY.
BUT IT'S BECOME MUCH MORE. A MEDICAL RESEARCH CENTER. A UNIVERSITY. EVEN A DOMED OBSERVATORY FOR CONCERTS UNDER THE STARS.
EVERYTHING THAT IS GOOD IN ARKANIAN CULTURE IS RIGHT HERE.
I DON'T THINK ***CAMPER*** FOUND MUCH GOOD IN IT. HE SPOKE A LOT OVER THE YEARS OF *"CRIMES IN THE NAME OF ARKANIAN SCIENCE."*
HE'S NOT ALONE. OUR GREATEST HERO, JEDI MASTER ***ARCA JETH,*** ONCE SAID *"THE ONLY THING MORE DANGEROUS THAN A FOOLISH ARKANIAN IS A **SMART** ONE."*
WE CELEBRATE BOUNDLESS INNOVATION -- EVEN WHERE INNOVATION SHOULD KNOW SOME BOUNDS. THE *"OFFSHOOT QUESTION"* IS ONE HISTORICAL RESULT.

HE WAS ONE OF THE LAST TRULY BRILLIANT OFFSHOOT STUDENTS TO COME OUT OF THE ARKANIAN UNIVERSITIES -- BEFORE DISEASE CLOSED OFF ADMISSIONS.

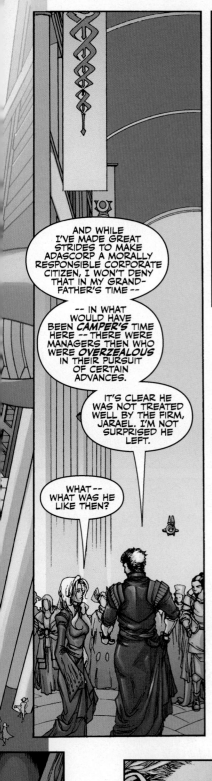

AND WHILE I'VE MADE GREAT STRIDES TO MAKE ADASCORP A MORALLY RESPONSIBLE CORPORATE CITIZEN, I WON'T DENY THAT IN MY GRAND-FATHER'S TIME --

-- IN WHAT WOULD HAVE BEEN *CAMPER'S* TIME HERE -- THERE WERE MANAGERS THEN WHO WERE *OVERZEALOUS* IN THEIR PURSUIT OF CERTAIN ADVANCES.

IT'S CLEAR HE WAS NOT TREATED WELL BY THE FIRM, JARAEL. I'M NOT SURPRISED HE LEFT.

WHAT -- WHAT WAS HE LIKE THEN?

HE WAS A WONDER WITH THINGS BOTH ORGANIC AND INORGANIC -- AS KNOWLEDGEABLE ABOUT BIOLOGY AS HE WAS ABOUT TECHNOLOGY. WE HIRED HIM IMMEDIATELY.

BUT IN HIS YEARS OF WORKING IN THE CORPORATE LABS, HE WAS EXPOSED TO *BALINQUAR'S VIRUS*, A PATHOGEN THAT SEEMED HARMLESS AT THE TIME.

WE NOW KNOW THAT IN OFFSHOOTS, IT LIES DORMANT UNTIL OLD AGE, WHEN IT TRIGGERS A SERIES OF WORSENING SYMPTOMS --

-- WELL, YOU SAW THE RESULT. THAT'S HOW WE FOUND YOU, ACTUALLY.

WHEN MY STAFF ANALYZED HIS SAMPLE, THEY SAW THE VIRUS -- AND RECOGNIZED HIS GENETIC PROFILE FROM OUR RECORDS. WE KNEW WE HAD TO HELP RIGHT AWAY.

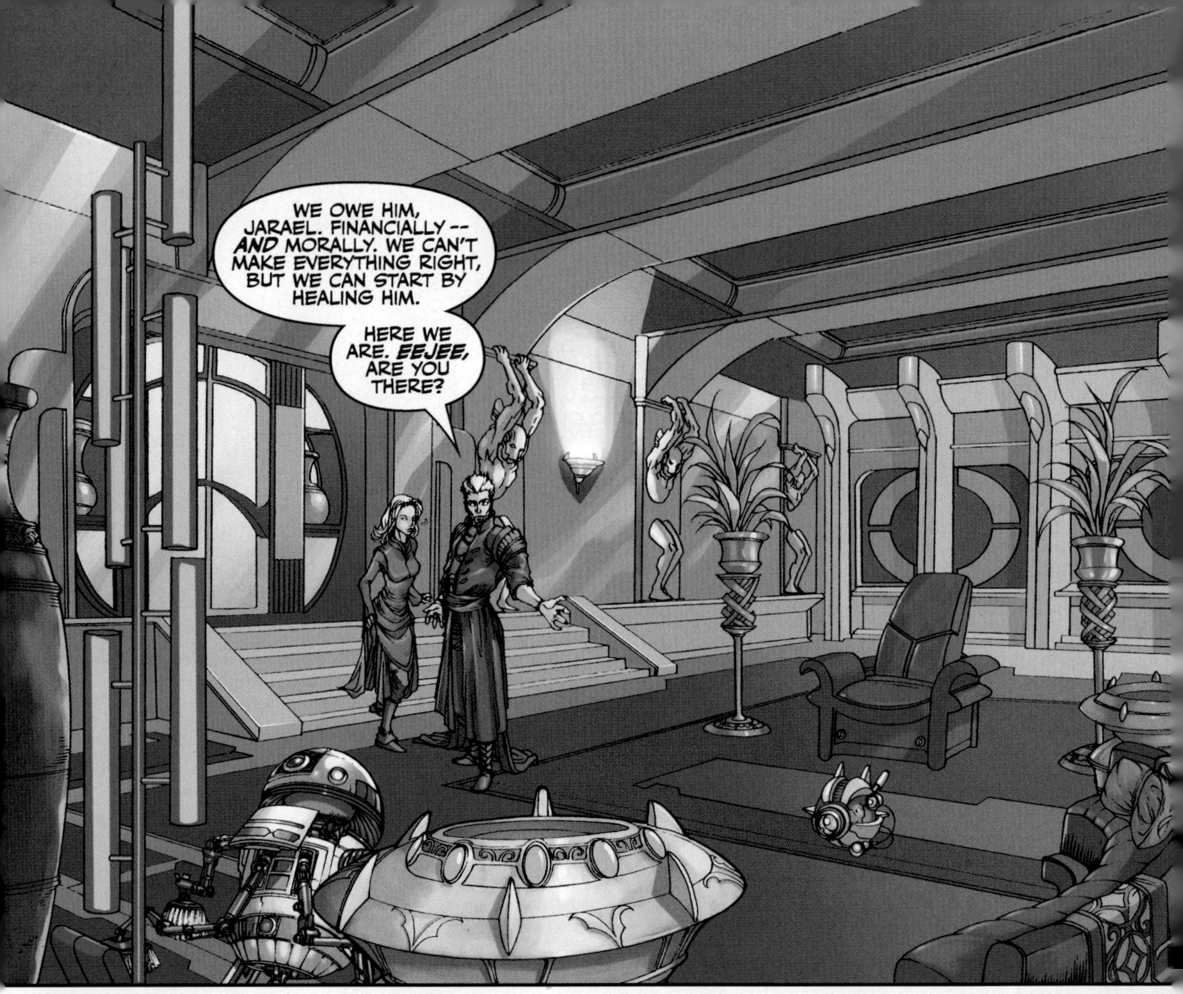
WE OWE HIM, JARAEL. FINANCIALLY -- AND MORALLY. WE CAN'T MAKE EVERYTHING RIGHT, BUT WE CAN START BY HEALING HIM.
HERE WE ARE. EEJEE, ARE YOU THERE?

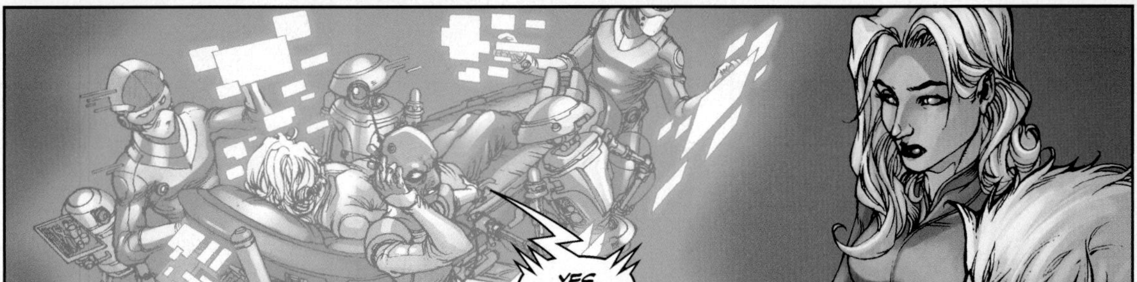
YES, MILORD.
THE PATIENT IS COMATOSE. IT'S WHAT WE THOUGHT.

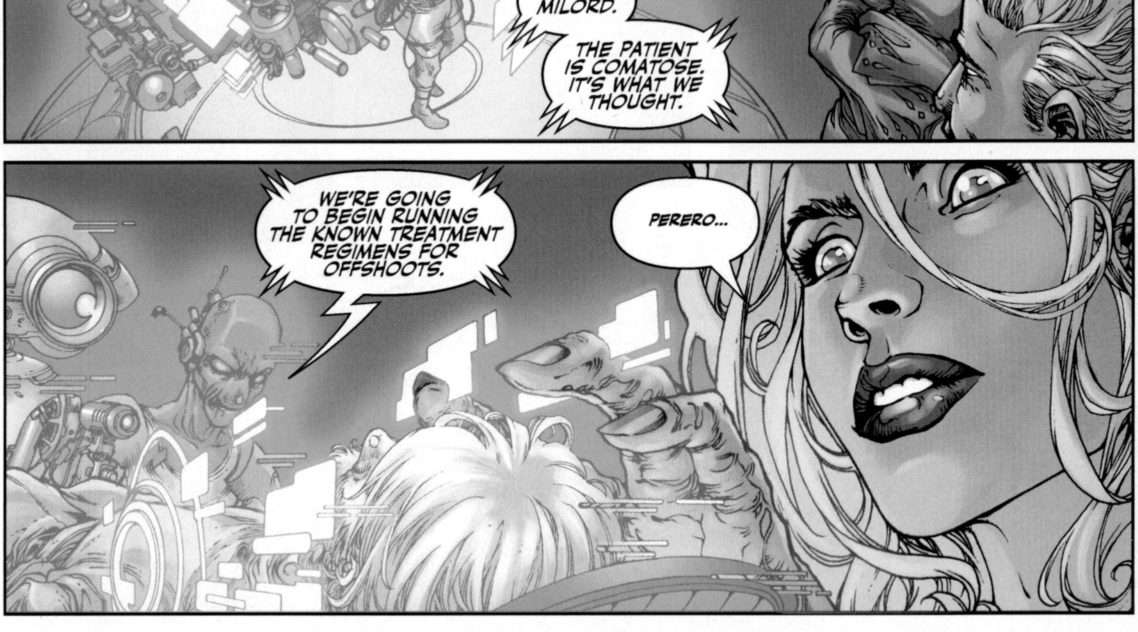
WE'RE GOING TO BEGIN RUNNING THE KNOWN TREATMENT REGIMENS FOR OFFSHOOTS.
PERERO...

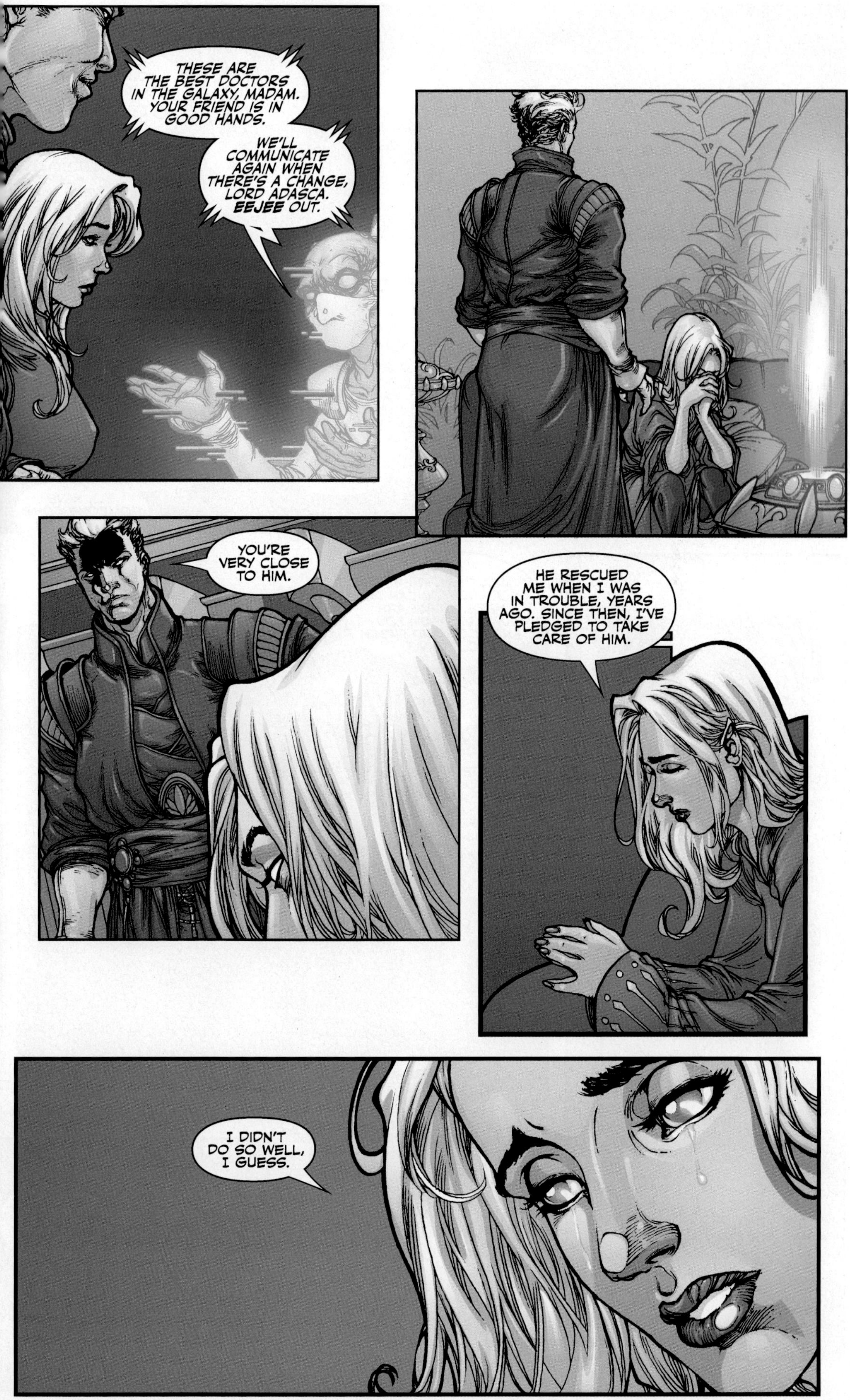
THESE ARE THE BEST DOCTORS IN THE GALAXY, MADAM. YOUR FRIEND IS IN GOOD HANDS.
WE'LL COMMUNICATE AGAIN WHEN THERE'S A CHANGE, LORD ADASCA. EEJEE OUT.
YOU'RE VERY CLOSE TO HIM.
HE RESCUED ME WHEN I WAS IN TROUBLE, YEARS AGO. SINCE THEN, I'VE PLEDGED TO TAKE CARE OF HIM.
I DIDN'T DO SO WELL, I GUESS.

NONSENSE. YOU BROUGHT HIM TO THE RIGHT PLACE. HE IS LUCKY TO HAVE HAD SUCH A GUARDIAN.

I WISH THE CARETAKERS AT MY HOSPITALS WERE SO COMMITTED.

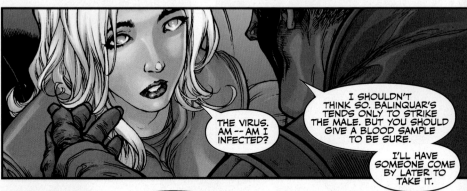

THE VIRUS. AM -- AM I INFECTED?

I SHOULDN'T THINK SO. BALINQUAR'S TENDS ONLY TO STRIKE THE MALE. BUT YOU SHOULD GIVE A BLOOD SAMPLE TO BE SURE.

I'LL HAVE SOMEONE COME BY LATER TO TAKE IT.

IN THE MEANTIME, THERE'S NOTHING YOU CAN DO HERE. THERE ARE QUARTERS FOR YOU -- AND FOOD AND FRESH CLOTHING.

I DON'T WANT --

PLEASE. I WANT YOU TO FEEL -- *AND* LOOK -- LIKE YOURSELF AGAIN.

FROM WHAT I'M TOLD, LIFE ON THE *LAST RESORT* MUST HAVE BEEN VERY SPARE. I THINK YOU'LL FIND THE *ARKANIAN LEGACY* TO BE A GREAT COMFORT -- WHILE YOU WAIT.

WHILE WE *ALL* WAIT.

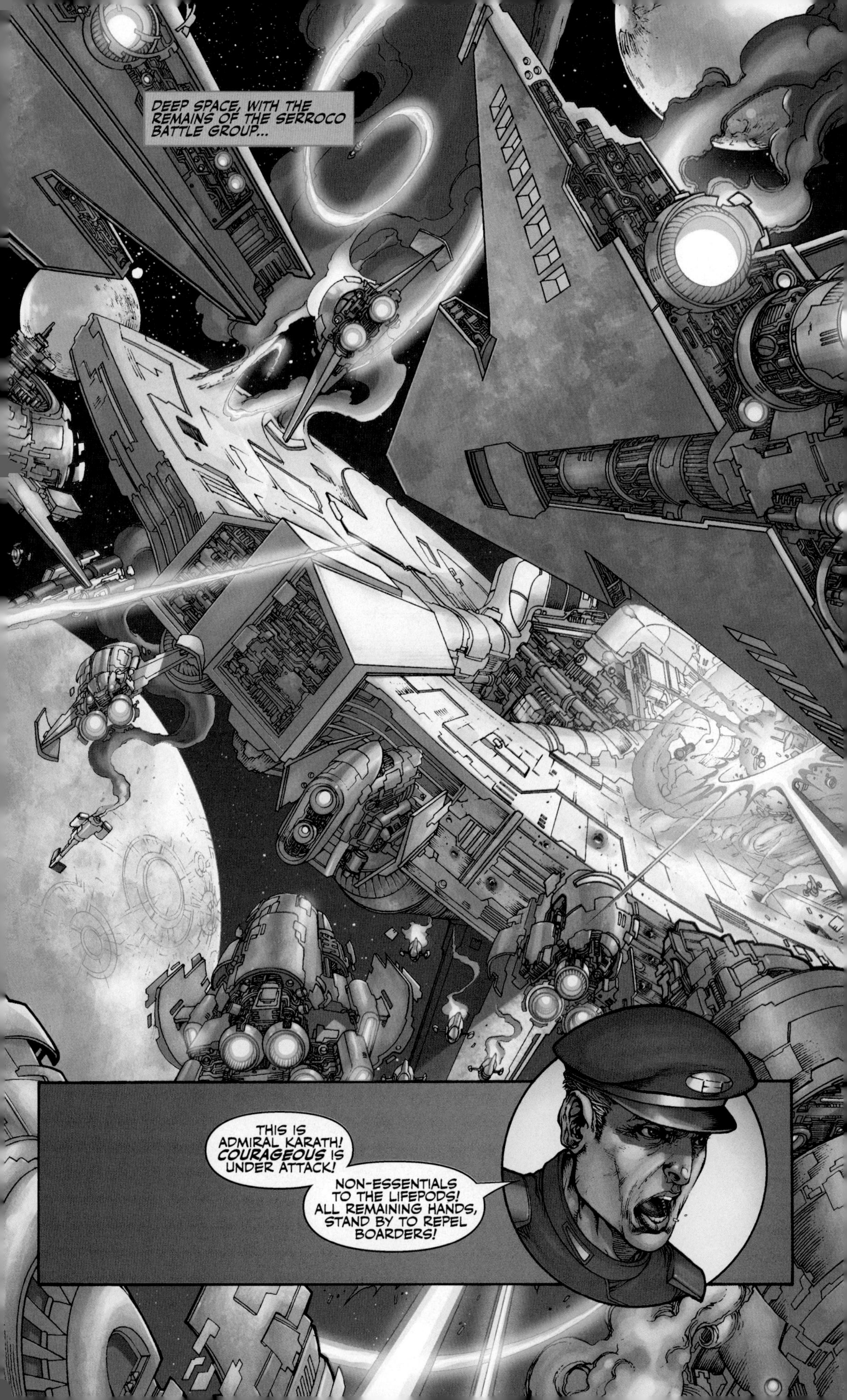
DEEP SPACE, WITH THE REMAINS OF THE SERROCO BATTLE GROUP...
THIS IS ADMIRAL KARATH! COURAGEOUS IS UNDER ATTACK!
NON-ESSENTIALS TO THE LIFEPODS! ALL REMAINING HANDS, STAND BY TO REPEL BOARDERS!

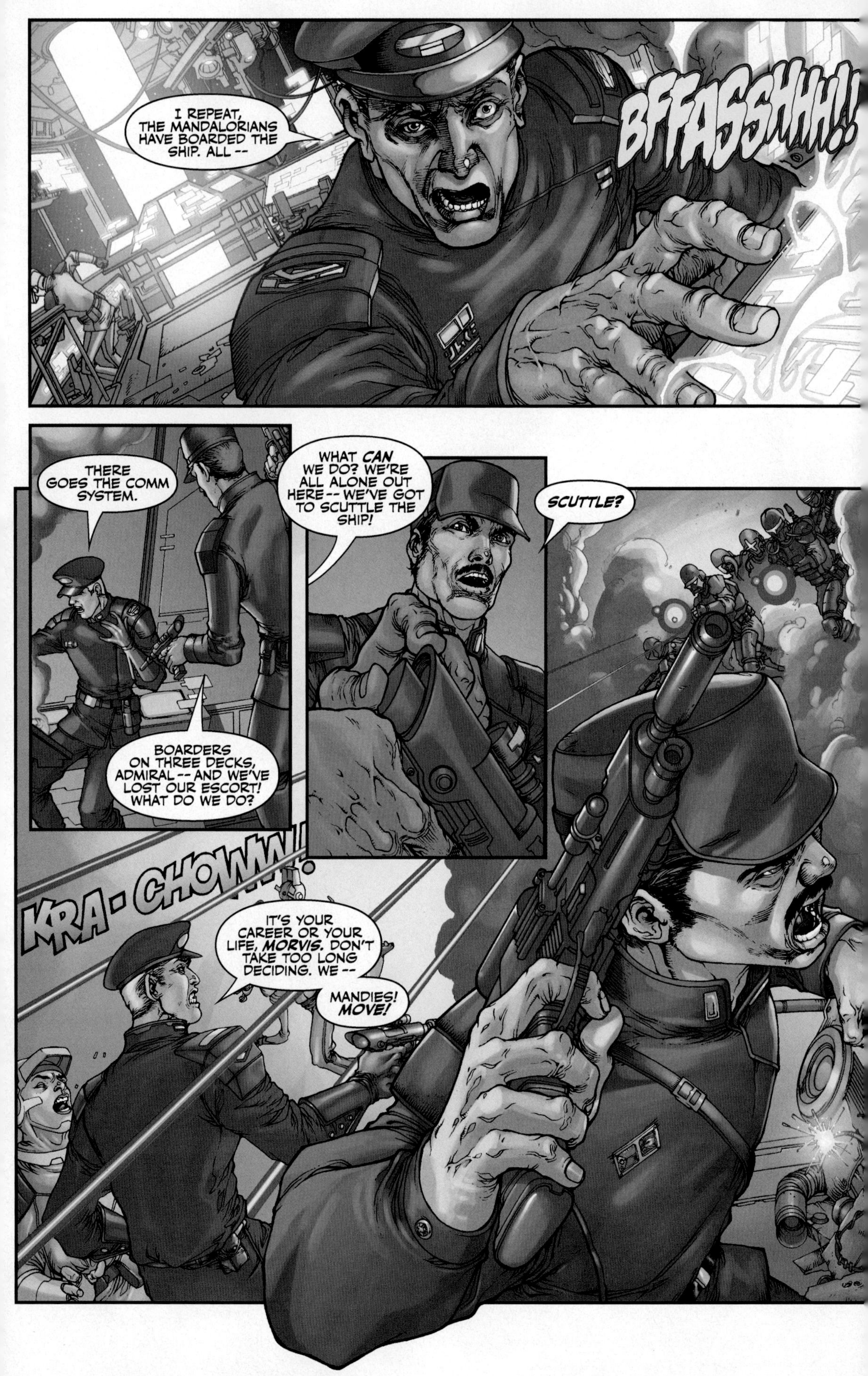
I REPEAT, THE MANDALORIANS HAVE BOARDED THE SHIP. ALL --
BFFASSHHH!!
THERE GOES THE COMM SYSTEM.
BOARDERS ON THREE DECKS, ADMIRAL -- AND WE'VE LOST OUR ESCORT! WHAT DO WE DO?
WHAT *CAN* WE DO? WE'RE ALL ALONE OUT HERE -- WE'VE GOT TO SCUTTLE THE SHIP!
SCUTTLE?
KRA-CHOWW!!
IT'S YOUR CAREER OR YOUR LIFE, *MORVIS*. DON'T TAKE TOO LONG DECIDING. WE --
MANDIES! *MOVE!*

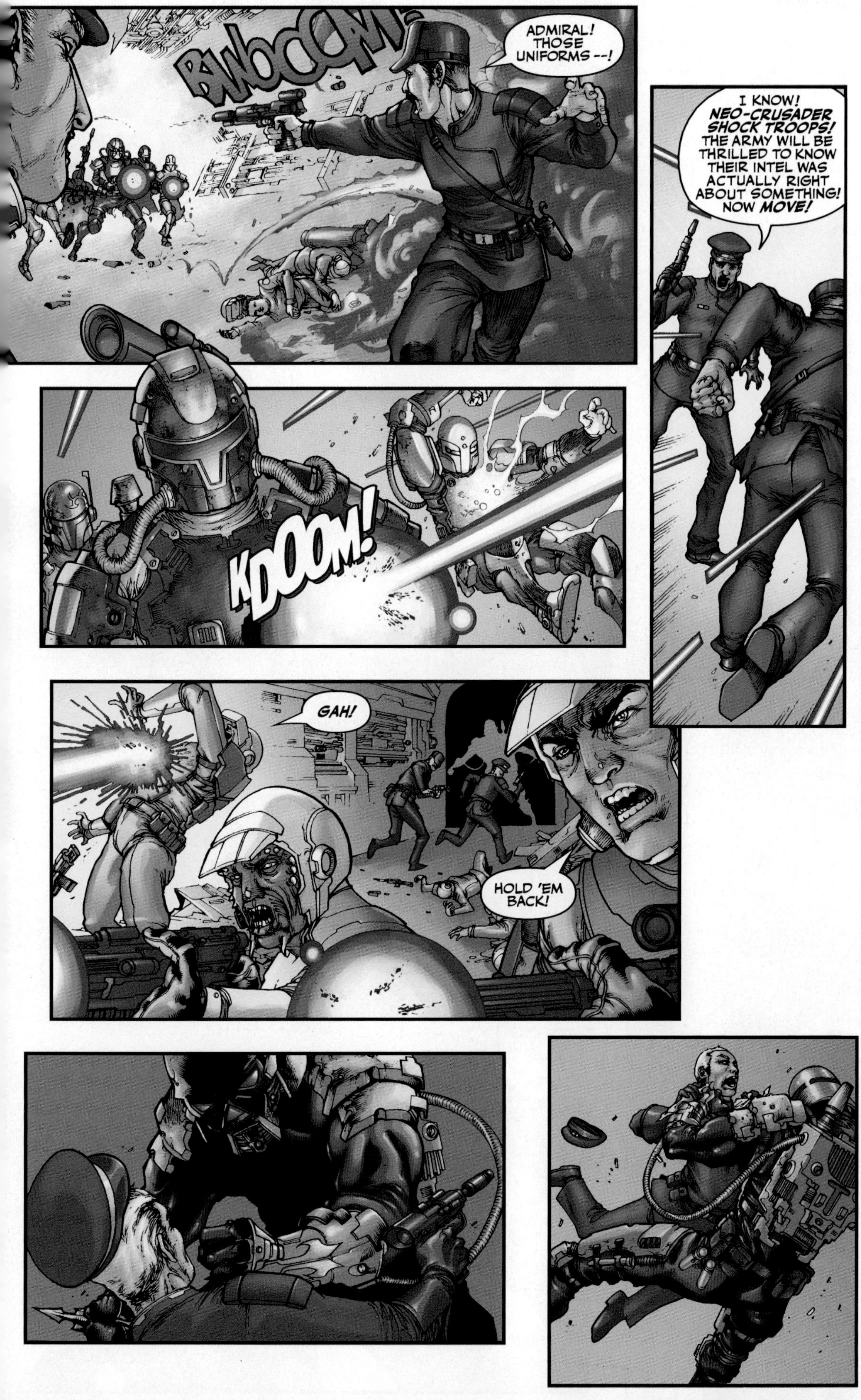
BWOOOM!
ADMIRAL! THOSE UNIFORMS --!
I KNOW! NEO-CRUSADER SHOCK TROOPS! THE ARMY WILL BE THRILLED TO KNOW THEIR INTEL WAS ACTUALLY RIGHT ABOUT SOMETHING! NOW MOVE!
KDOOM!
GAH!
HOLD 'EM BACK!

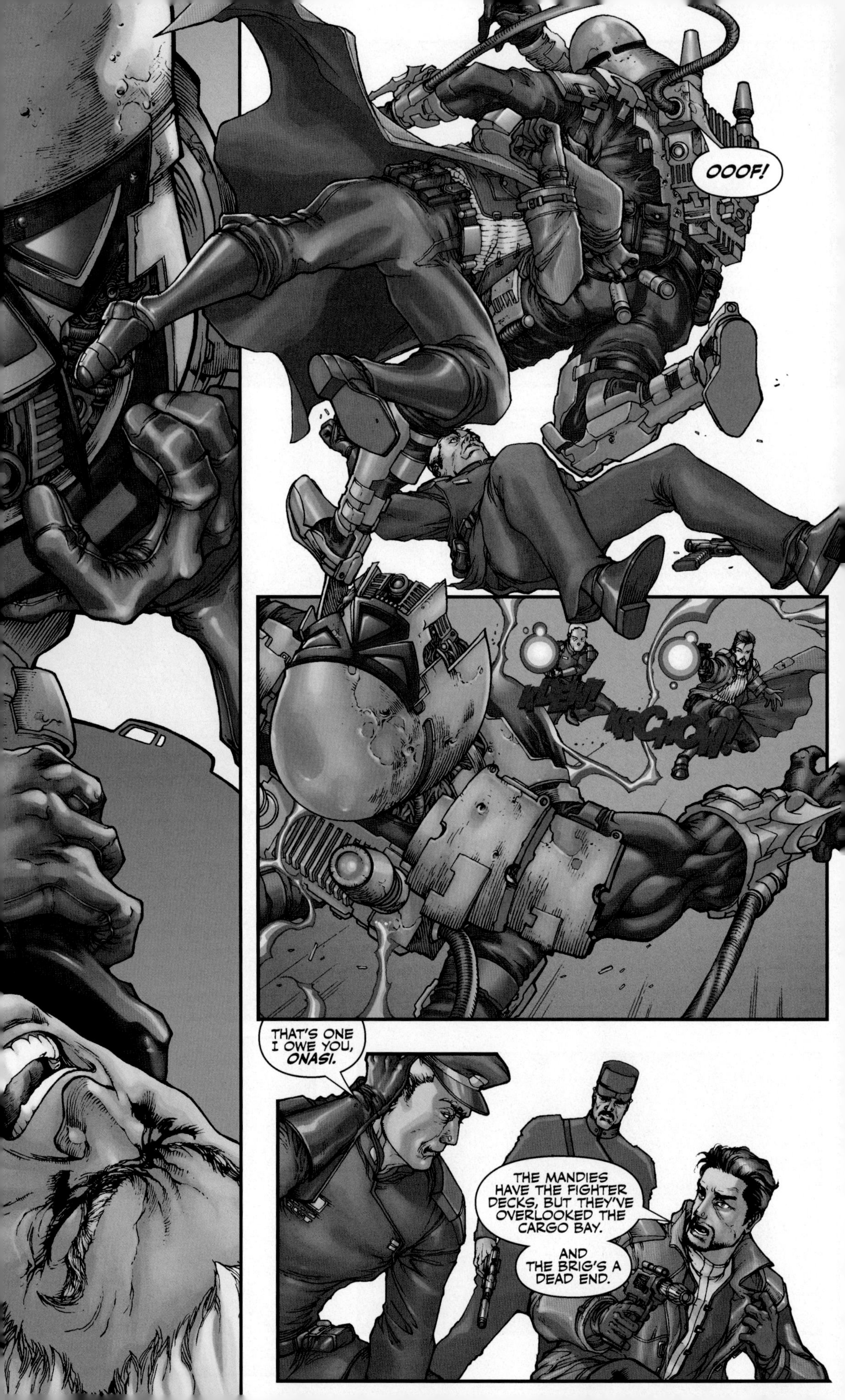
OOOF!
THAT'S ONE I OWE YOU, ONASI.
THE MANDIES HAVE THE FIGHTER DECKS, BUT THEY'VE OVERLOOKED THE CARGO BAY.
AND THE BRIG'S A DEAD END.

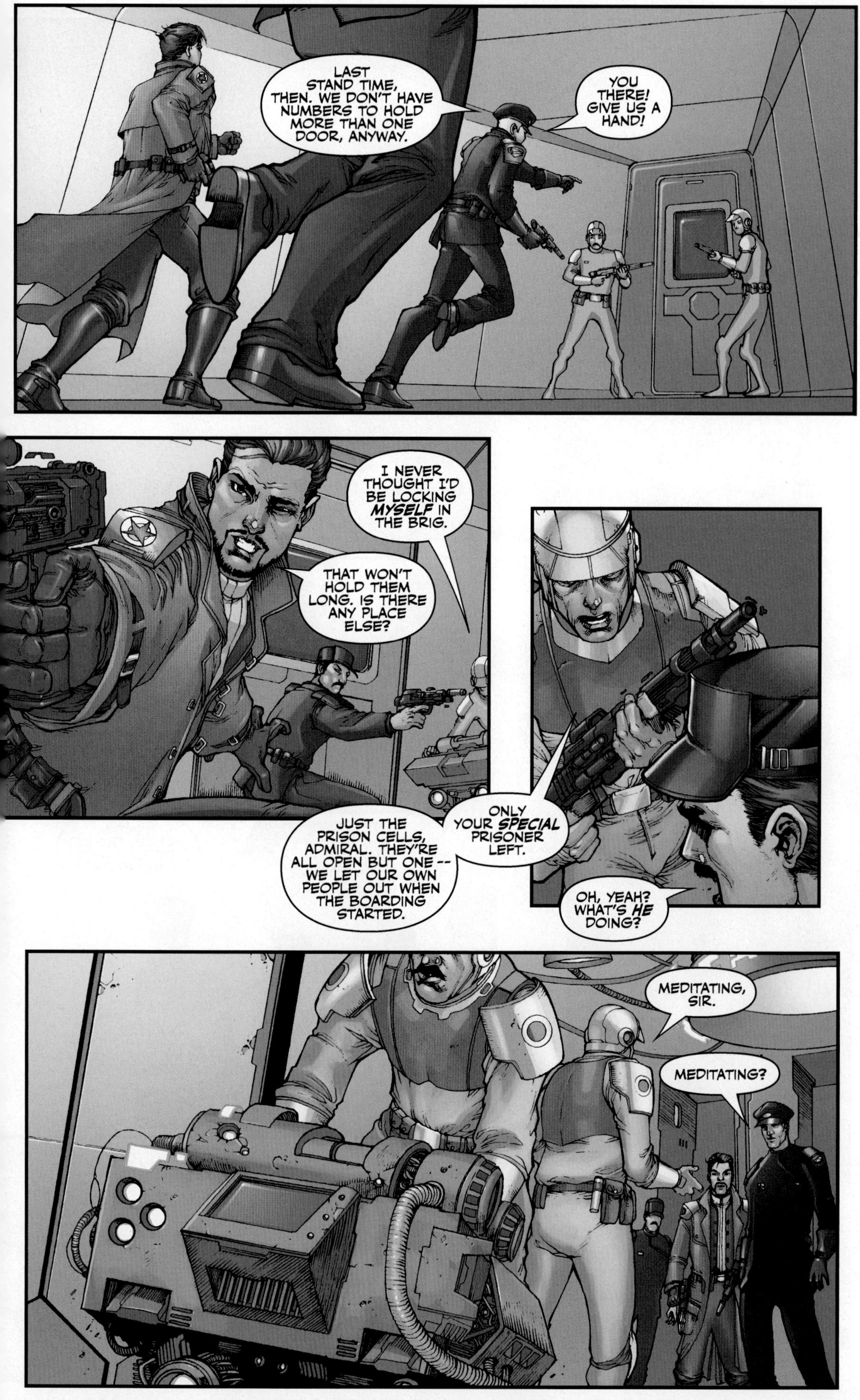
LAST STAND TIME, THEN. WE DON'T HAVE NUMBERS TO HOLD MORE THAN ONE DOOR, ANYWAY.
YOU THERE! GIVE US A HAND!
I NEVER THOUGHT I'D BE LOCKING *MYSELF* IN THE BRIG.
THAT WON'T HOLD THEM LONG. IS THERE ANY PLACE ELSE?
JUST THE PRISON CELLS, ADMIRAL. THEY'RE ALL OPEN BUT ONE -- WE LET OUR OWN PEOPLE OUT WHEN THE BOARDING STARTED.
ONLY YOUR *SPECIAL* PRISONER LEFT.
OH, YEAH? WHAT'S *HE* DOING?
MEDITATING, SIR.
MEDITATING?

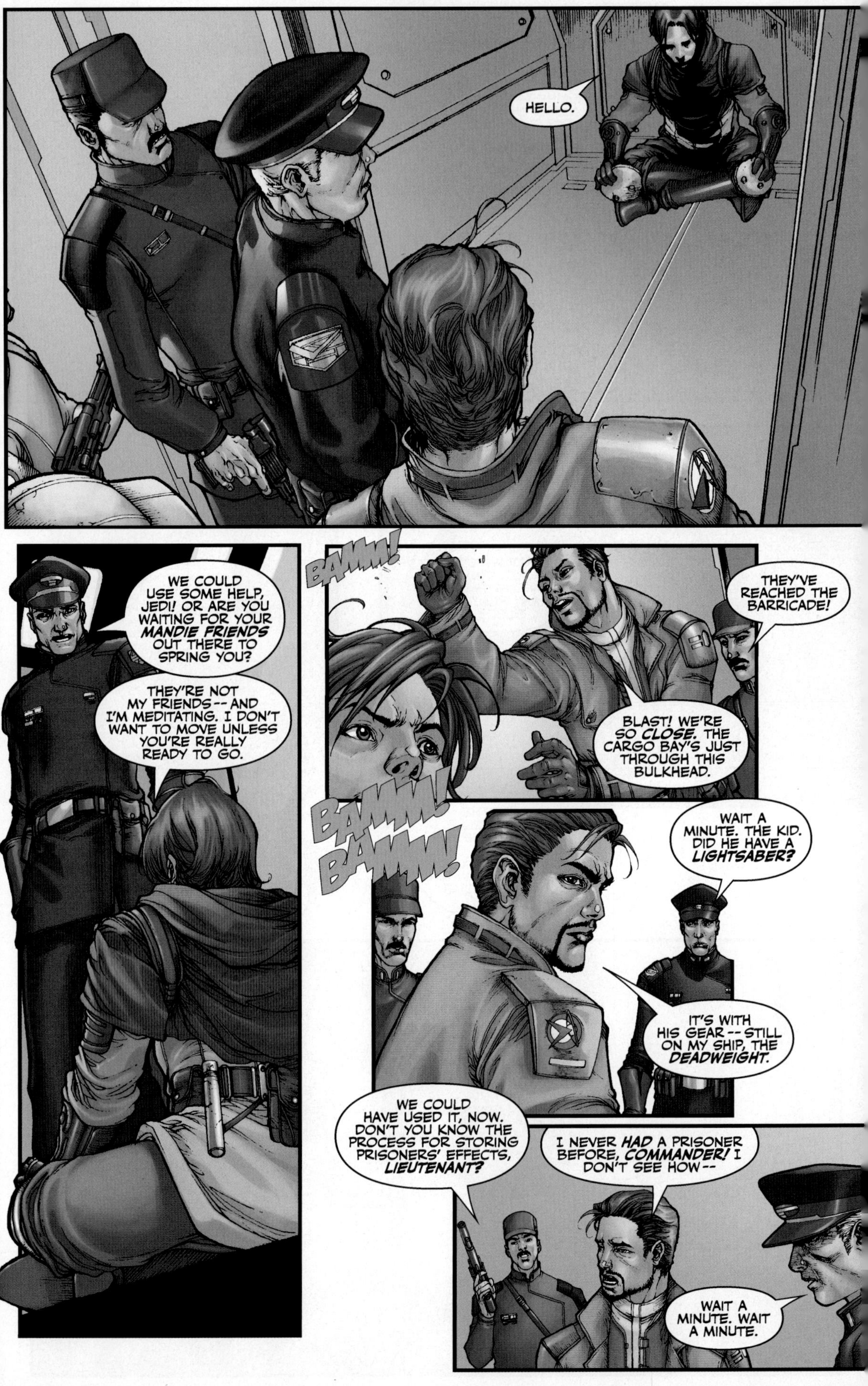
HELLO.
WE COULD USE SOME HELP, JEDI! OR ARE YOU WAITING FOR YOUR *MANDIE FRIENDS* OUT THERE TO SPRING YOU?
THEY'RE NOT MY FRIENDS--AND I'M MEDITATING. I DON'T WANT TO MOVE UNLESS YOU'RE REALLY READY TO GO.
BAMM!
THEY'VE REACHED THE BARRICADE!
BLAST! WE'RE SO *CLOSE.* THE CARGO BAY'S JUST THROUGH THIS BULKHEAD.
BAMMM! BAMMM!
WAIT A MINUTE. THE KID. DID HE HAVE A *LIGHTSABER?*
IT'S WITH HIS GEAR--STILL ON MY SHIP, THE *DEADWEIGHT.*
WE COULD HAVE USED IT, NOW. DON'T YOU KNOW THE PROCESS FOR STORING PRISONERS' EFFECTS, *LIEUTENANT?*
I NEVER *HAD* A PRISONER BEFORE, *COMMANDER!* I DON'T SEE HOW--
WAIT A MINUTE. WAIT A MINUTE.

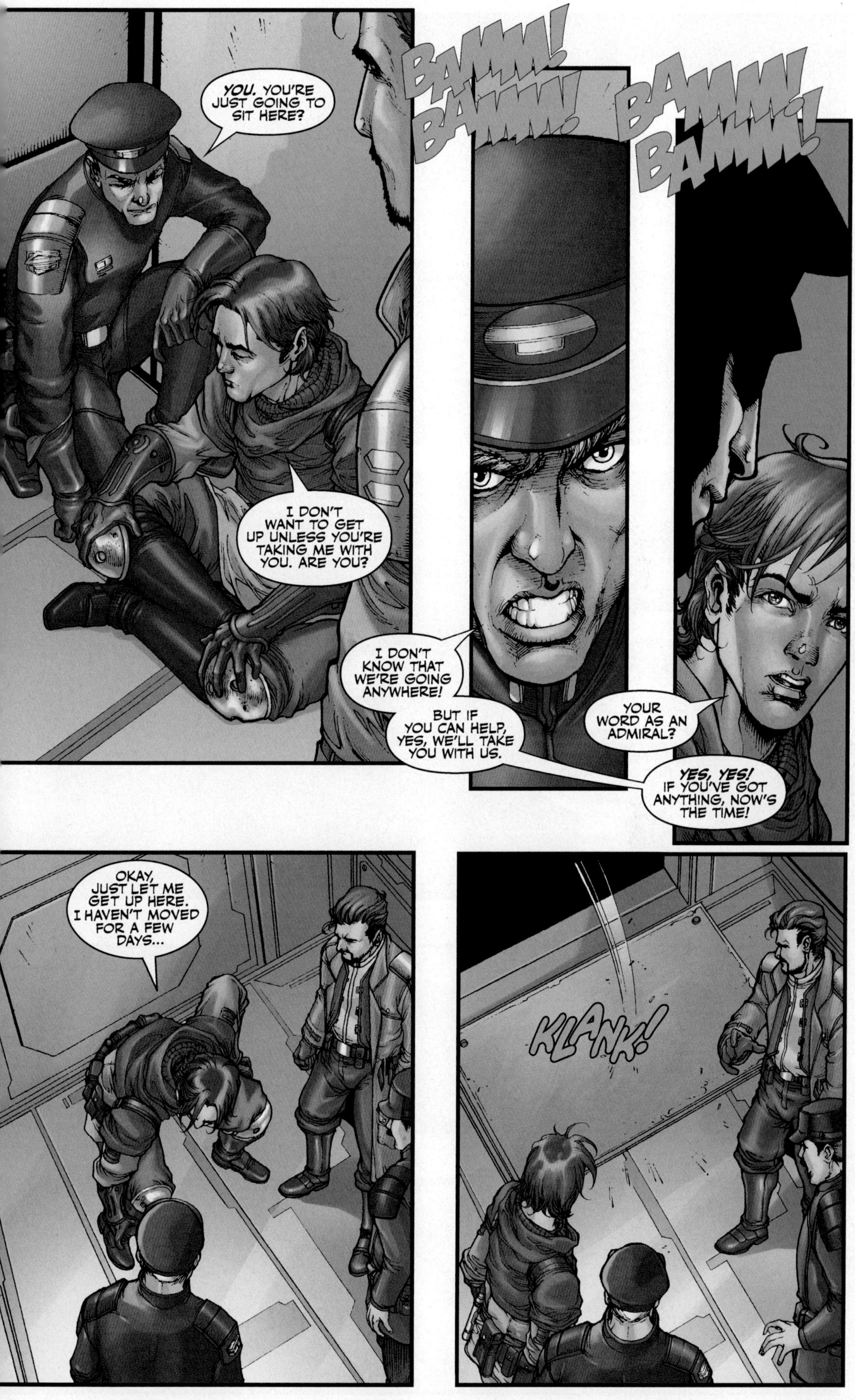

YOU. YOU'RE JUST GOING TO SIT HERE?
I DON'T WANT TO GET UP UNLESS YOU'RE TAKING ME WITH YOU. ARE YOU?
BAMM! BAMM! BAMM! BAMM!
I DON'T KNOW THAT WE'RE GOING ANYWHERE!
BUT IF YOU CAN HELP, YES, WE'LL TAKE YOU WITH US.
YOUR WORD AS AN ADMIRAL?
YES, YES! IF YOU'VE GOT ANYTHING, NOW'S THE TIME!
OKAY, JUST LET ME GET UP HERE. I HAVEN'T MOVED FOR A FEW DAYS...
KLANK!

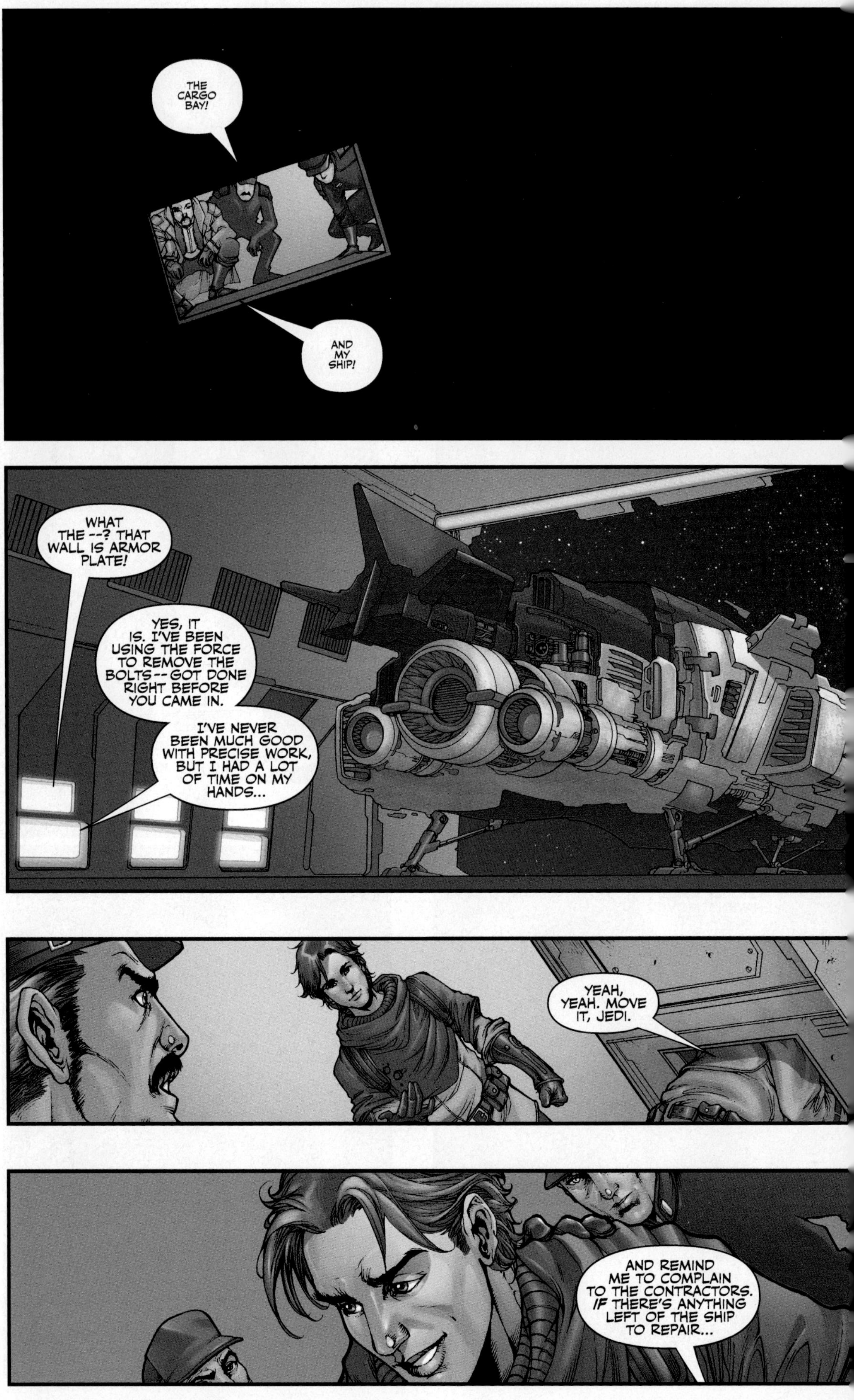
THE CARGO BAY!
AND MY SHIP!
WHAT THE --? THAT WALL IS ARMOR PLATE!
YES, IT IS. I'VE BEEN USING THE FORCE TO REMOVE THE BOLTS--GOT DONE RIGHT BEFORE YOU CAME IN.
I'VE NEVER BEEN MUCH GOOD WITH PRECISE WORK, BUT I HAD A LOT OF TIME ON MY HANDS...
YEAH, YEAH. MOVE IT, JEDI.
AND REMIND ME TO COMPLAIN TO THE CONTRACTORS. *IF* THERE'S ANYTHING LEFT OF THE SHIP TO REPAIR...

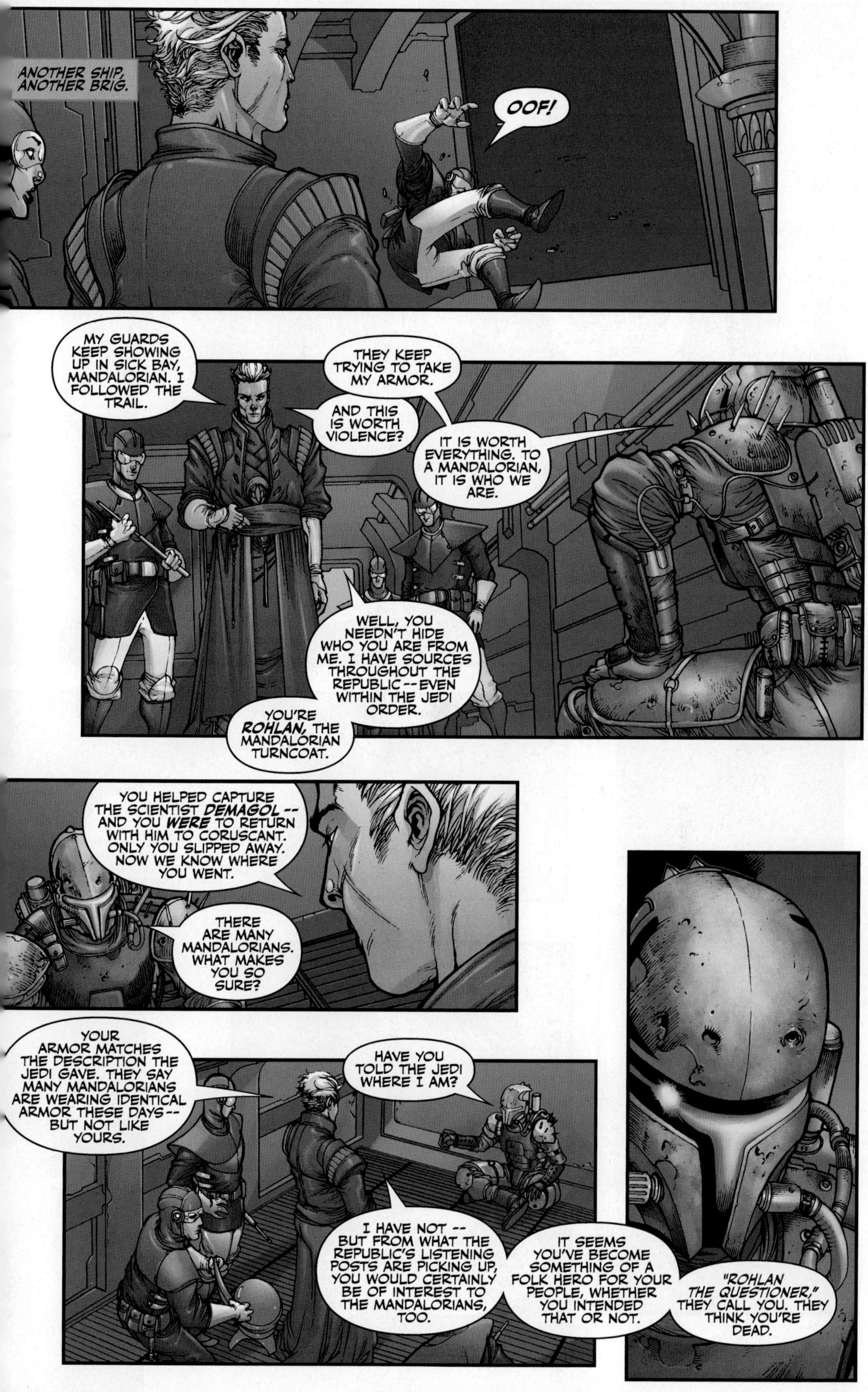
ANOTHER SHIP, ANOTHER BRIG.
OOF!
MY GUARDS KEEP SHOWING UP IN SICK BAY, MANDALORIAN. I FOLLOWED THE TRAIL.
THEY KEEP TRYING TO TAKE MY ARMOR.
AND THIS IS WORTH VIOLENCE?
IT IS WORTH EVERYTHING. TO A MANDALORIAN, IT IS WHO WE ARE.
WELL, YOU NEEDN'T HIDE WHO YOU ARE FROM ME. I HAVE SOURCES THROUGHOUT THE REPUBLIC--EVEN WITHIN THE JEDI ORDER.
YOU'RE *ROHLAN,* THE MANDALORIAN TURNCOAT.
YOU HELPED CAPTURE THE SCIENTIST *DEMAGOL* -- AND YOU *WERE* TO RETURN WITH HIM TO CORUSCANT. ONLY YOU SLIPPED AWAY. NOW WE KNOW WHERE YOU WENT.
THERE ARE MANY MANDALORIANS. WHAT MAKES YOU SO SURE?
YOUR ARMOR MATCHES THE DESCRIPTION THE JEDI GAVE. THEY SAY MANY MANDALORIANS ARE WEARING IDENTICAL ARMOR THESE DAYS-- BUT NOT LIKE YOURS.
HAVE YOU TOLD THE JEDI WHERE I AM?
I HAVE NOT -- BUT FROM WHAT THE REPUBLIC'S LISTENING POSTS ARE PICKING UP, YOU WOULD CERTAINLY BE OF INTEREST TO THE MANDALORIANS, TOO.
IT SEEMS YOU'VE BECOME SOMETHING OF A FOLK HERO FOR YOUR PEOPLE, WHETHER YOU INTENDED THAT OR NOT.
"ROHLAN THE QUESTIONER," THEY CALL YOU. THEY THINK YOU'RE DEAD.

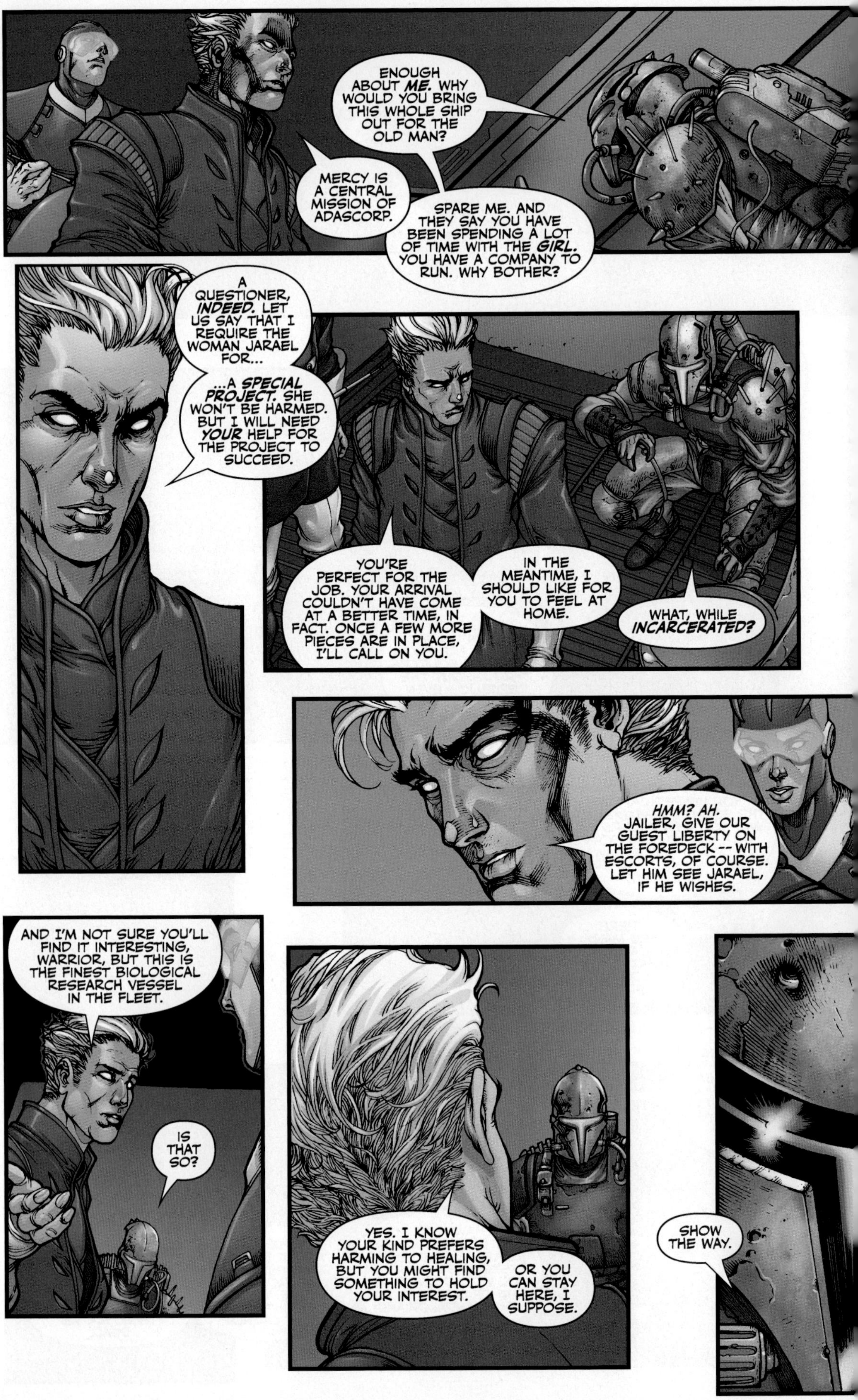
ENOUGH ABOUT *ME.* WHY WOULD YOU BRING THIS WHOLE SHIP OUT FOR THE OLD MAN?
MERCY IS A CENTRAL MISSION OF ADASCORP.
SPARE ME. AND THEY SAY YOU HAVE BEEN SPENDING A LOT OF TIME WITH THE *GIRL.* YOU HAVE A COMPANY TO RUN. WHY BOTHER?
A QUESTIONER, *INDEED.* LET US SAY THAT I REQUIRE THE WOMAN JARAEL FOR...
...A *SPECIAL PROJECT.* SHE WON'T BE HARMED. BUT I WILL NEED *YOUR* HELP FOR THE PROJECT TO SUCCEED.
YOU'RE PERFECT FOR THE JOB. YOUR ARRIVAL COULDN'T HAVE COME AT A BETTER TIME, IN FACT. ONCE A FEW MORE PIECES ARE IN PLACE, I'LL CALL ON YOU.
IN THE MEANTIME, I SHOULD LIKE FOR YOU TO FEEL AT HOME.
WHAT, WHILE *INCARCERATED?*
HMM? AH. JAILER, GIVE OUR GUEST LIBERTY ON THE FOREDECK -- WITH ESCORTS, OF COURSE. LET HIM SEE JARAEL, IF HE WISHES.
AND I'M NOT SURE YOU'LL FIND IT INTERESTING, WARRIOR, BUT THIS IS THE FINEST BIOLOGICAL RESEARCH VESSEL IN THE FLEET.
IS THAT SO?
YES. I KNOW YOUR KIND PREFERS HARMING TO HEALING, BUT YOU MIGHT FIND SOMETHING TO HOLD YOUR INTEREST.
OR YOU CAN STAY HERE, I SUPPOSE.
SHOW THE WAY.

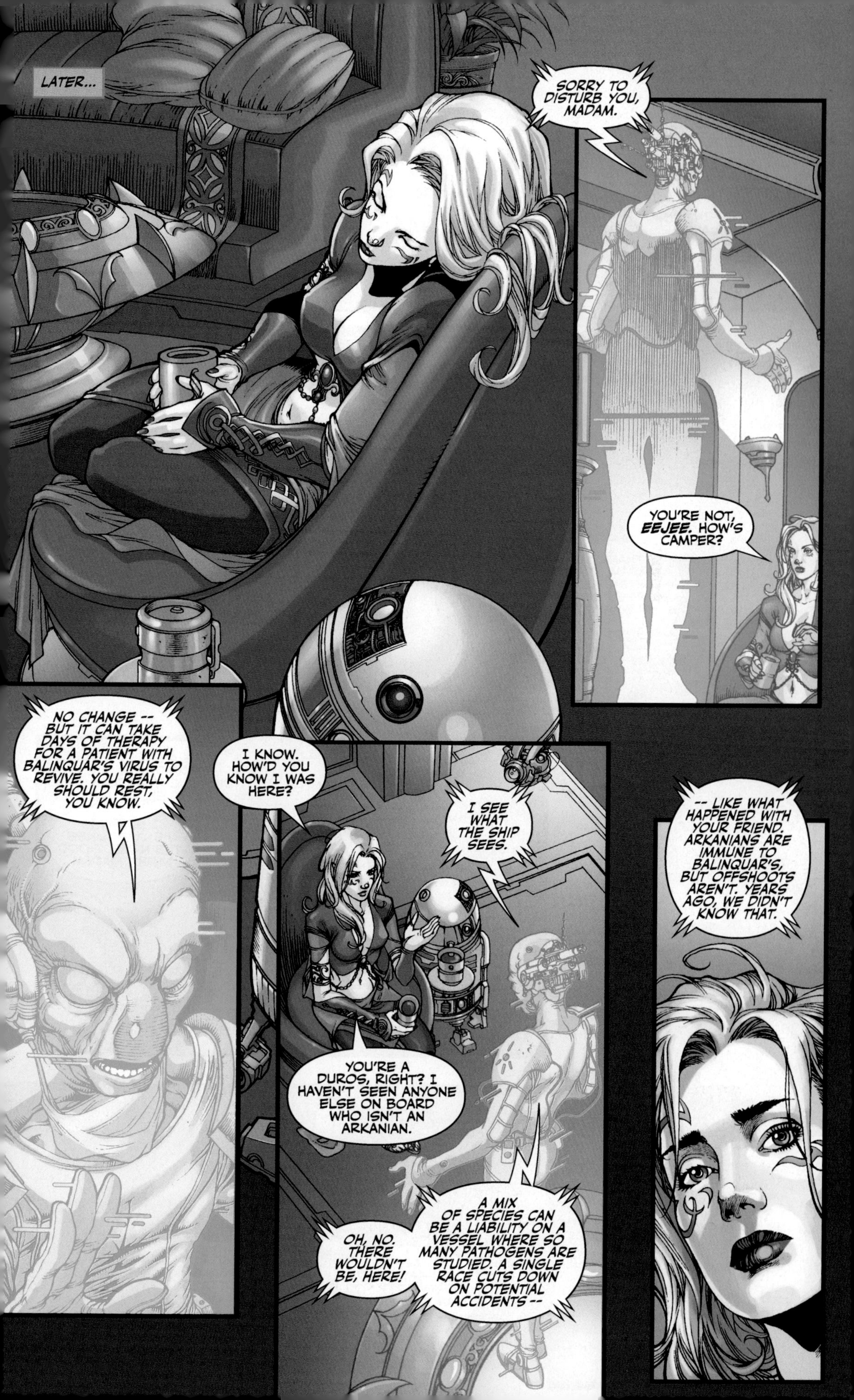
LATER...
SORRY TO DISTURB YOU, MADAM.
YOU'RE NOT, EEJEE. HOW'S CAMPER?
NO CHANGE -- BUT IT CAN TAKE DAYS OF THERAPY FOR A PATIENT WITH BALINQUAR'S VIRUS TO REVIVE. YOU REALLY SHOULD REST, YOU KNOW.
I KNOW. HOW'D YOU KNOW I WAS HERE?
I SEE WHAT THE SHIP SEES.
YOU'RE A DUROS, RIGHT? I HAVEN'T SEEN ANYONE ELSE ON BOARD WHO ISN'T AN ARKANIAN.
OH, NO. THERE WOULDN'T BE, HERE!
A MIX OF SPECIES CAN BE A LIABILITY ON A VESSEL WHERE SO MANY PATHOGENS ARE STUDIED. A SINGLE RACE CUTS DOWN ON POTENTIAL ACCIDENTS --
-- LIKE WHAT HAPPENED WITH YOUR FRIEND. ARKANIANS ARE IMMUNE TO BALINQUAR'S, BUT OFFSHOOTS AREN'T. YEARS AGO, WE DIDN'T KNOW THAT.

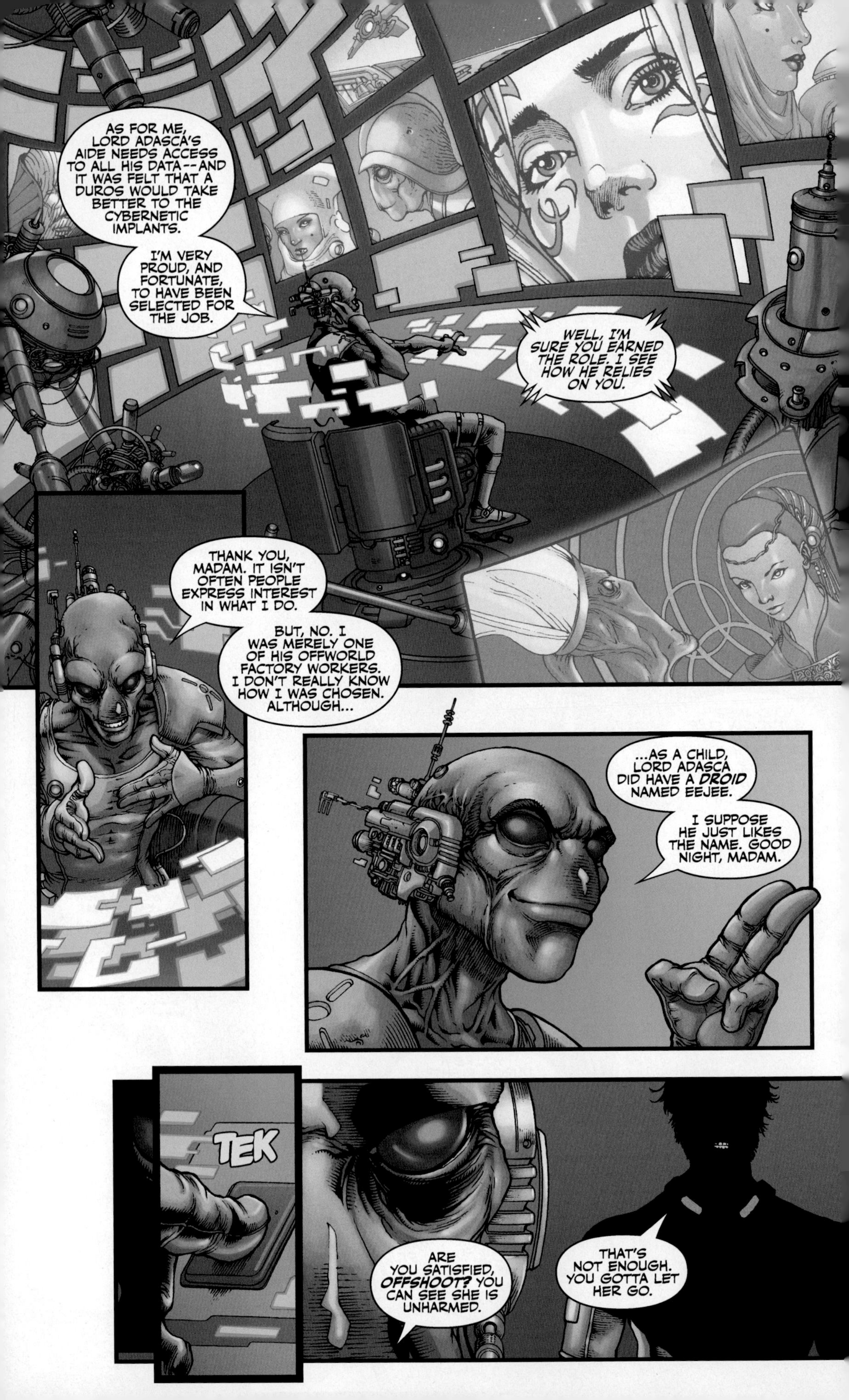
AS FOR ME, LORD ADASCA'S AIDE NEEDS ACCESS TO ALL HIS DATA--AND IT WAS FELT THAT A DUROS WOULD TAKE BETTER TO THE CYBERNETIC IMPLANTS.
I'M VERY PROUD, AND FORTUNATE, TO HAVE BEEN SELECTED FOR THE JOB.
WELL, I'M SURE YOU EARNED THE ROLE. I SEE HOW HE RELIES ON YOU.
THANK YOU, MADAM. IT ISN'T OFTEN PEOPLE EXPRESS INTEREST IN WHAT I DO.
BUT, NO. I WAS MERELY ONE OF HIS OFFWORLD FACTORY WORKERS. I DON'T REALLY KNOW HOW I WAS CHOSEN. ALTHOUGH...
...AS A CHILD, LORD ADASCA DID HAVE A *DROID* NAMED EEJEE.
I SUPPOSE HE JUST LIKES THE NAME. GOOD NIGHT, MADAM.
TEK
ARE YOU SATISFIED, *OFFSHOOT?* YOU CAN SEE SHE IS UNHARMED.
THAT'S NOT ENOUGH. YOU GOTTA LET HER GO.

YOU SHOULD BE THANKFUL TO US, OLD MAN. WE'VE CURED YOU.

FEH! WHAT WAS ALL THAT JUNK ABOUT *BALINQUAR'S VIRUS?* THAT'S GARBAGE, AND YOU KNOW IT!

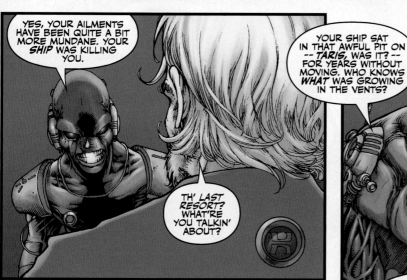

YES, YOUR AILMENTS HAVE BEEN QUITE A BIT MORE MUNDANE. YOUR *SHIP* WAS KILLING YOU.

YOUR SHIP SAT IN THAT AWFUL PIT ON -- *TARIS*, WAS IT? -- FOR YEARS WITHOUT MOVING. WHO KNOWS *WHAT* WAS GROWING IN THE VENTS?

TH' *LAST RESORT?* WHAT'RE YOU TALKIN' ABOUT?

WHATEVER IT WAS, IT DIDN'T LIKE YOU. AS SOON AS YOU LEFT THE PLANET AND ACTUALLY STARTED USING THE CIRCULATION SYSTEM, YOU BECAME MORE AND MORE ILL.

YOU WERE GOING INTO SHOCK WHEN YOU CAME ABOARD. ONCE WE IDENTIFIED THE ALLERGEN, IT WAS AN EASY MATTER TO WIPE YOU CLEAN.

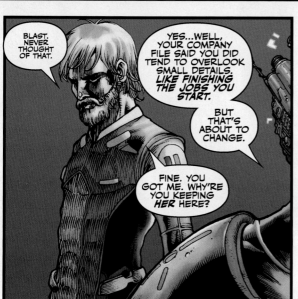

BLAST. NEVER THOUGHT OF THAT.

YES...WELL, YOUR COMPANY FILE SAID YOU DID TEND TO OVERLOOK SMALL DETAILS. *LIKE FINISHING THE JOBS YOU START.*

BUT THAT'S ABOUT TO CHANGE.

FINE. YOU GOT ME. WHY'RE YOU KEEPING *HER* HERE?

FOR THE SAME REASON WE CURED YOU, OFFSHOOT-- WE NEED YOU *BOTH.*

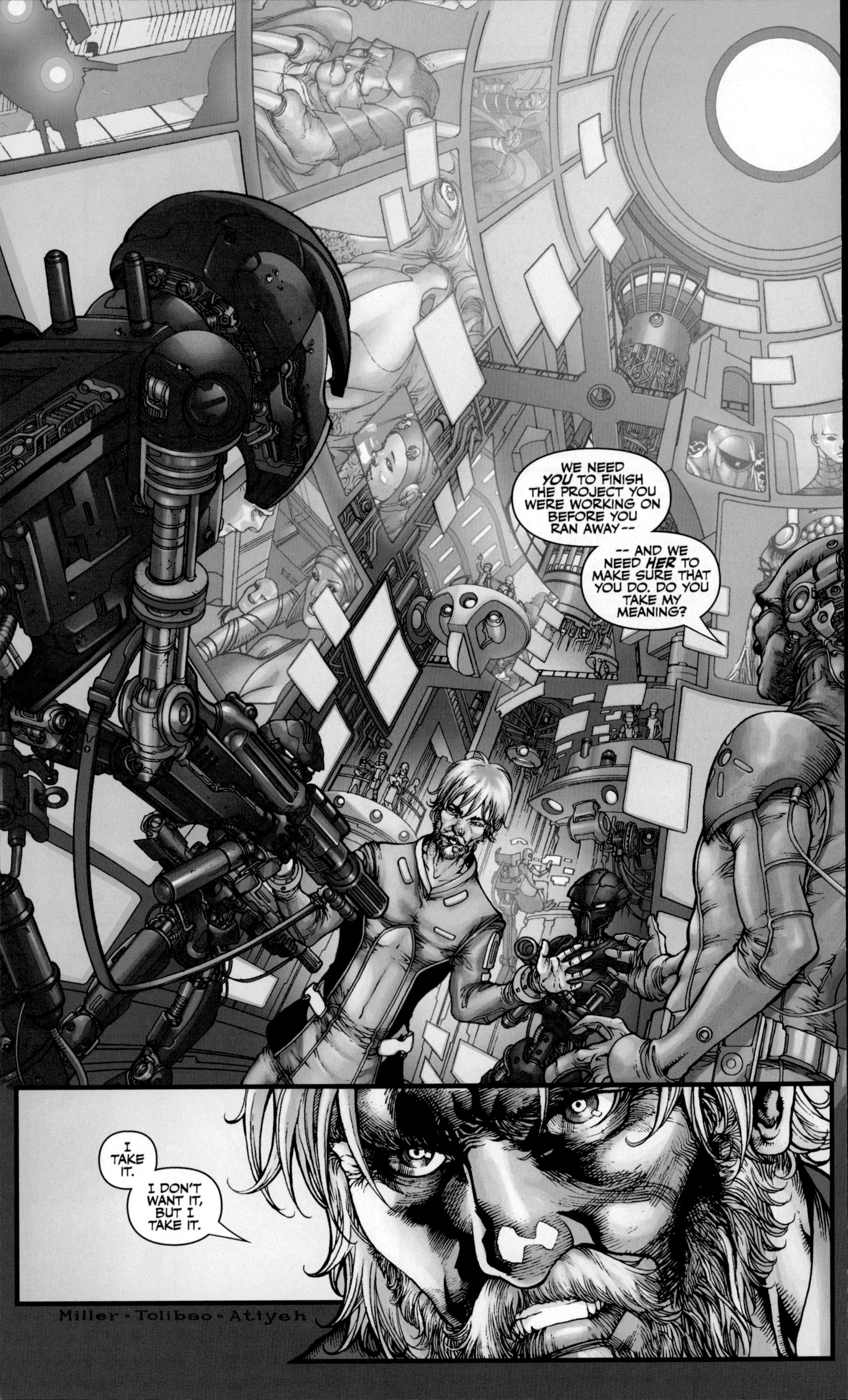
WE NEED YOU TO FINISH THE PROJECT YOU WERE WORKING ON BEFORE YOU RAN AWAY--
-- AND WE NEED HER TO MAKE SURE THAT YOU DO. DO YOU TAKE MY MEANING?
I TAKE IT.
I DON'T WANT IT, BUT I TAKE IT.
Miller • Tolibao • Atiyeh

ADASCORP

FISCAL PERIOD FINANCIAL REPORT AND OUTLOOK

Message from the Chief Executive
Arkoh, the Eighth Lord Adasca

On behalf of the employees and managers of **The Adasca BioMechanical Corporation of Arkania**, it is my great pleasure to welcome all readers to the Adascorp financial report.

The devastating surprise attack by the Mandalorians on the Republic contributed to much instability during this financial period, affecting not simply our own business operations, but the lives of many of the customers for our products. Nevertheless, through the diligence of management and our devoted employees, Adascorp managed to **meet or exceed all financial targets** for the period in every sector in which it operates.

The **medical services** division of Adascorp continued its market leadership, expanding its research into battlefield prosthetics and genetic manipulation. New viral therapy products continued to show promise. And sales of automated field hospitals and medical droids to the Republic reached an all-time high.

As there are healers, so are there warriors—and Adascorp's new **Military Research and Development Division** released a number of new products to market. More than half of our Adascorp-branded armament revenue came from the sale of battle-droid artificial musculature components to the Republic. Adascorp researchers first recognized the synergies between medical prosthetics and droid manufacture, and the frontiers of this promising field continue to be explored.

Our **financial services** continued to expand in the period just ended. The opening of the **Adascopolis Financial Exchange** promises to move the center of commercial gravity closer to the Colonies.

And our pending purchase of much of the Draay Trust's share of the **Telerath Interstellar Banking Iniative** at market price gives the Corporation controlling interest in an enterprise which is clearly the wave of the future for personal banking in the galaxy.

The **mining sector** continued to face a challenging environment, owing to declining Arkanian gem production, the siege of Taris, and the loss of operations on Vanquo. But our ongoing dispatch of droid-operated mining stations to systems inhospitable for organics continues to show promise. The uptick in military ship-building also promises to fuel growth in our materials processing operations.

Even in these uncertain times, my confidence in the Corporation's future is high. So high that I have personally authorized **the purchase of 17 billion shares** to add to the Adasca family's controlling interest, thus protecting, for all investors, the share price against the current instability. We all look forward to happier—and more profitable—days ahead.

Very best to yours,
ARKOH, Lord ADASCA
Chief Executive Officer

SELECT to see Financial Summary Statement
SELECT to see Business Environment and Risk Assessment
SELECT to see Individual Sector Drilldowns

The Corporation ["The Adasca BioMechanical Corporation of Arkania," herein known as "Adascorp"] affirms that all information appearing in the summary and attached report is true to the best of the knowledge of all Officers of the Corporation, and does not omit any facts material to the information presented. Disclosures made herein are in full accordance with the Coruscant Financial Exchange Establishment Act and all its codicils. However, the Corporation cautions that affirmations in this report relating to future results and conditions are forward-looking statements based on The Corporation's educated expectations. Actual results in future timeframes could differ materially from projections in those forward-looking statements due to changes in the business environment's risk quotient. For a discussion of factors affecting the Corporation's risk quotient, see Attachment 6A.

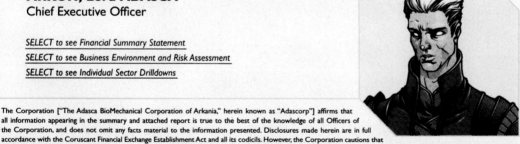

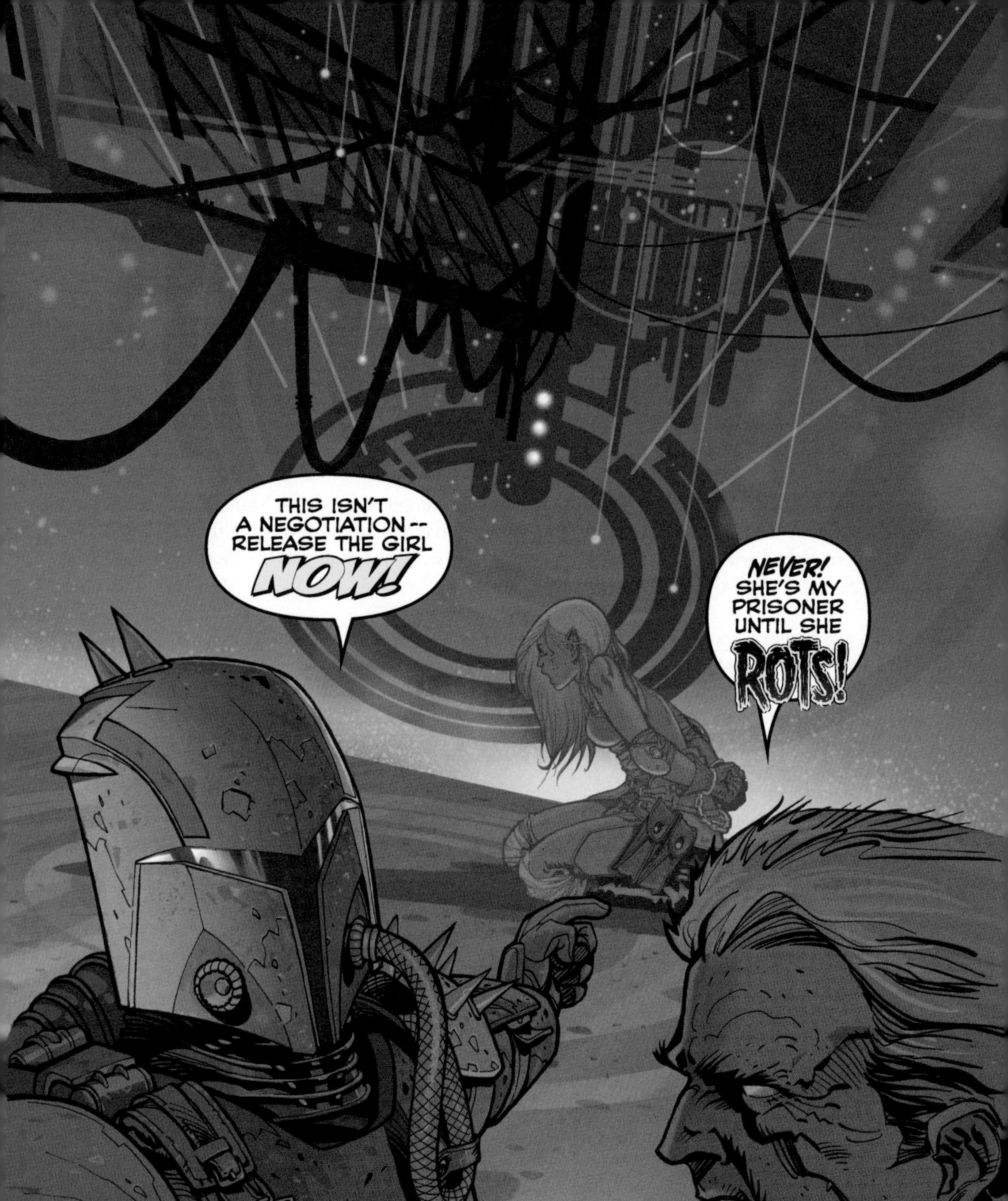
THIS ISN'T A NEGOTIATION -- RELEASE THE GIRL NOW!
NEVER! SHE'S MY PRISONER UNTIL SHE ROTS!

STAR WARS: KNIGHTS OF THE OLD REPUBLIC #18 — "NIGHTS OF ANGER, PART 3"

WRITER: JOHN JACKSON MILLER • ARTIST: HARVEY TOLIBAO • COLORIST: MICHAEL ATIYEH • LETTERER: MICHAEL HEISLER
ASSISTANT EDITOR: DAVE MARSHALL • EDITOR: JEREMY BARLOW • COVER ARTIST: COLIN WILSON

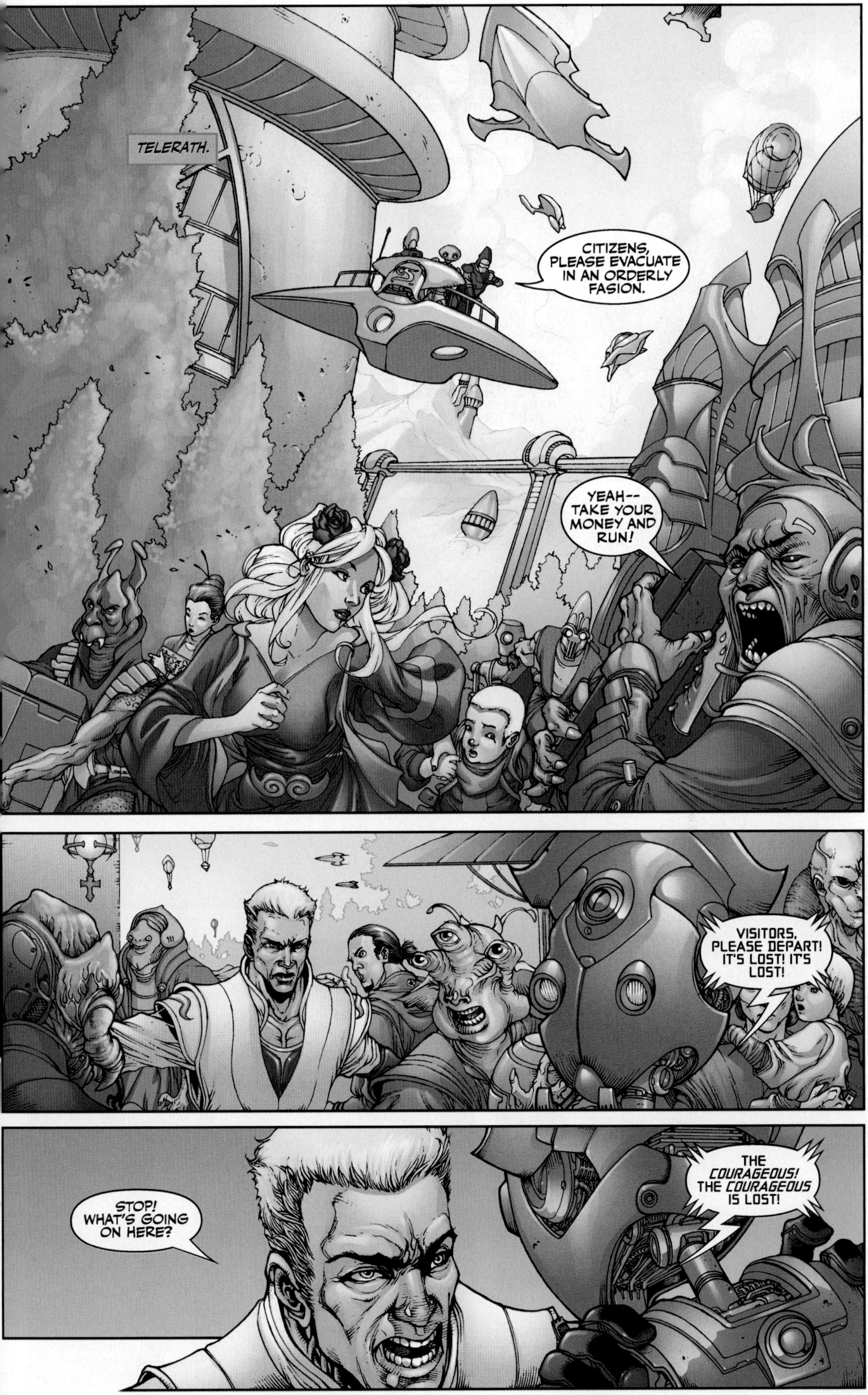
TELERATH.
CITIZENS, PLEASE EVACUATE IN AN ORDERLY FASION.
YEAH-- TAKE YOUR MONEY AND RUN!
VISITORS, PLEASE DEPART! IT'S LOST! IT'S LOST!
STOP! WHAT'S GOING ON HERE?
THE *COURAGEOUS!* THE *COURAGEOUS* IS LOST!

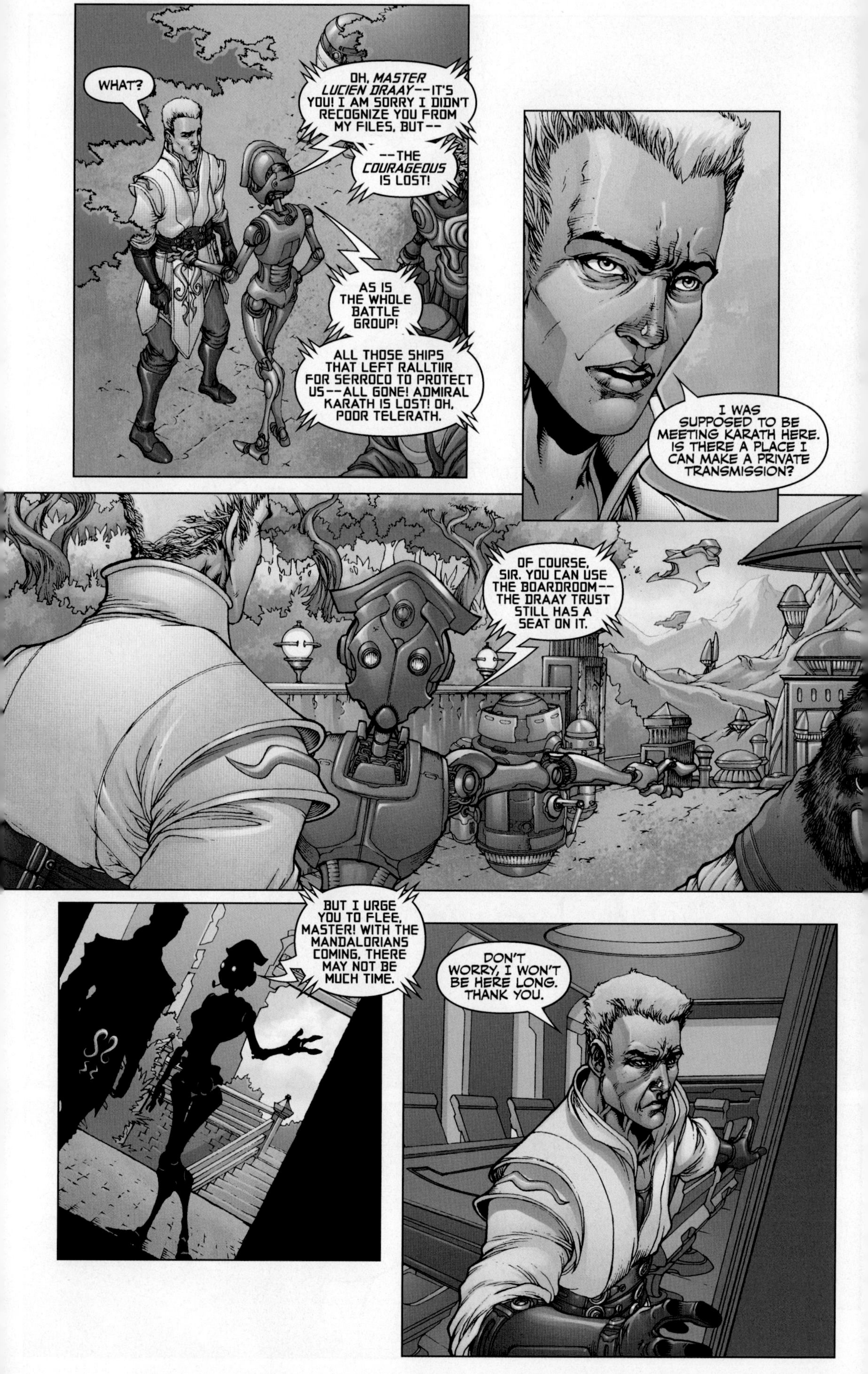
WHAT?
OH, MASTER LUCIEN DRAAY--IT'S YOU! I AM SORRY I DIDN'T RECOGNIZE YOU FROM MY FILES, BUT--
--THE COURAGEOUS IS LOST!
AS IS THE WHOLE BATTLE GROUP!
ALL THOSE SHIPS THAT LEFT RALLTIIR FOR SERROCO TO PROTECT US--ALL GONE! ADMIRAL KARATH IS LOST! OH, POOR TELERATH.
I WAS SUPPOSED TO BE MEETING KARATH HERE. IS THERE A PLACE I CAN MAKE A PRIVATE TRANSMISSION?
OF COURSE, SIR. YOU CAN USE THE BOARDROOM--THE DRAAY TRUST STILL HAS A SEAT ON IT.
BUT I URGE YOU TO FLEE, MASTER! WITH THE MANDALORIANS COMING, THERE MAY NOT BE MUCH TIME.
DON'T WORRY, I WON'T BE HERE LONG. THANK YOU.

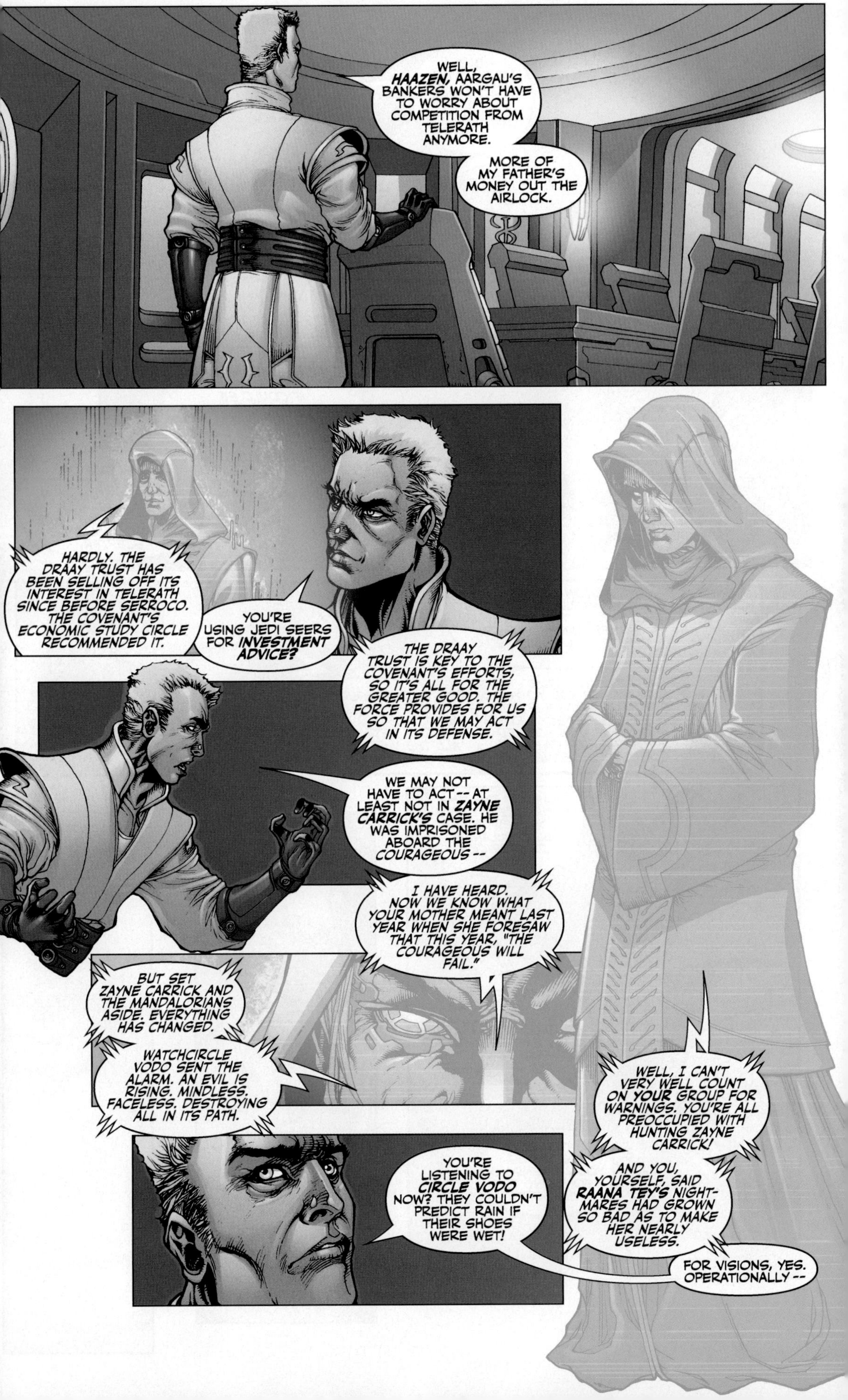
WELL, HAAZEN, AARGAU'S BANKERS WON'T HAVE TO WORRY ABOUT COMPETITION FROM TELERATH ANYMORE.
MORE OF MY FATHER'S MONEY OUT THE AIRLOCK.
HARDLY. THE DRAAY TRUST HAS BEEN SELLING OFF ITS INTEREST IN TELERATH SINCE BEFORE SERROCO. THE COVENANT'S ECONOMIC STUDY CIRCLE RECOMMENDED IT.
YOU'RE USING JEDI SEERS FOR INVESTMENT ADVICE?
THE DRAAY TRUST IS KEY TO THE COVENANT'S EFFORTS, SO IT'S ALL FOR THE GREATER GOOD. THE FORCE PROVIDES FOR US SO THAT WE MAY ACT IN ITS DEFENSE.
WE MAY NOT HAVE TO ACT -- AT LEAST NOT IN ZAYNE CARRICK'S CASE. HE WAS IMPRISONED ABOARD THE COURAGEOUS --
I HAVE HEARD. NOW WE KNOW WHAT YOUR MOTHER MEANT LAST YEAR WHEN SHE FORESAW THAT THIS YEAR, "THE COURAGEOUS WILL FAIL."
BUT SET ZAYNE CARRICK AND THE MANDALORIANS ASIDE. EVERYTHING HAS CHANGED.
WATCHCIRCLE VODO SENT THE ALARM. AN EVIL IS RISING. MINDLESS. FACELESS. DESTROYING ALL IN ITS PATH.
YOU'RE LISTENING TO CIRCLE VODO NOW? THEY COULDN'T PREDICT RAIN IF THEIR SHOES WERE WET!
WELL, I CAN'T VERY WELL COUNT ON YOUR GROUP FOR WARNINGS. YOU'RE ALL PREOCCUPIED WITH HUNTING ZAYNE CARRICK!
AND YOU, YOURSELF, SAID RAANA TEY'S NIGHT-MARES HAD GROWN SO BAD AS TO MAKE HER NEARLY USELESS.
FOR VISIONS, YES. OPERATIONALLY --

-- BUT NEVER MIND. WHAT DOES MY *MOTHER* SAY ABOUT THE CIRCLE'S VISION?

THE *LADY KRYNDA* CONCURS. SHE'S UPSTAIRS NOW WORKING WITH ANOTHER GROUP OF PADAWANS TO FIND OUT WHAT MORE SHE CAN.

THIS MUCH WE KNOW: THIS NEW THREAT -- IT DOESN'T SEEM TO BE A SITH FORCE. IT'S LESS SEDUCTIVE, MORE RAW AND BRAZEN. ALMOST...A *HUNGER.*

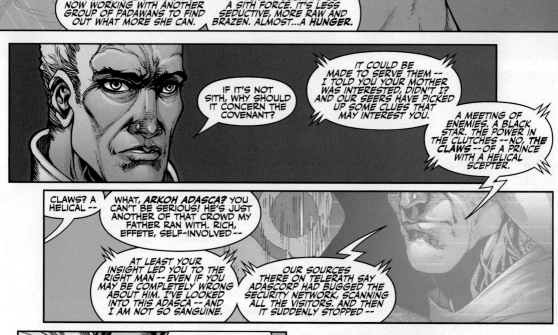

IF IT'S NOT SITH, WHY SHOULD IT CONCERN THE COVENANT?

IT COULD BE MADE TO SERVE THEM -- I TOLD YOU YOUR MOTHER WAS INTERESTED, DIDN'T I? AND OUR SEERS HAVE PICKED UP SOME CLUES THAT MAY INTEREST YOU.

A MEETING OF ENEMIES. A BLACK STAR. THE POWER IN THE CLUTCHES -- NO, *THE CLAWS* -- OF A PRINCE WITH A HELICAL SCEPTER.

CLAWS? A HELICAL --

WHAT, *ARKOH ADASCA?* YOU CAN'T BE SERIOUS! HE'S JUST ANOTHER OF THAT CROWD MY FATHER RAN WITH. RICH, EFFETE, SELF-INVOLVED --

AT LEAST YOUR INSIGHT LED YOU TO THE RIGHT MAN -- EVEN IF YOU MAY BE COMPLETELY WRONG ABOUT HIM. I'VE LOOKED INTO THIS ADASCA -- AND I AM NOT SO SANGUINE.

OUR SOURCES THERE ON TELERATH SAY ADASCORP HAD BUGGED THE SECURITY NETWORK, SCANNING ALL THE VISITORS. AND THEN IT SUDDENLY STOPPED --

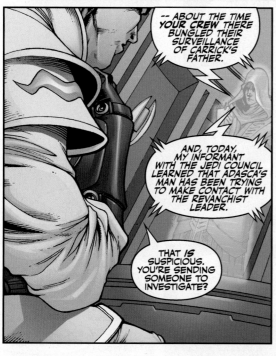

-- ABOUT THE TIME *YOUR CREW* THERE BUNGLED THEIR SURVEILLANCE OF CARRICK'S FATHER.

AND, TODAY, MY INFORMANT WITH THE JEDI COUNCIL LEARNED THAT ADASCA'S MAN HAS BEEN TRYING TO MAKE CONTACT WITH THE REVANCHIST LEADER.

THAT *IS* SUSPICIOUS. YOU'RE SENDING SOMEONE TO INVESTIGATE?

NOT JUST ANYONE. YOU ARE IN THE NEIGHBORHOOD -- AND YOU KNOW HIM. AND WITH CARRICK DEAD OR IN A MANDALORIAN PRISON, YOU ARE VERY MUCH AT YOUR LEISURE.

DISCOVER WHAT THIS DARK POWER IS -- AND REPORT TO ME!

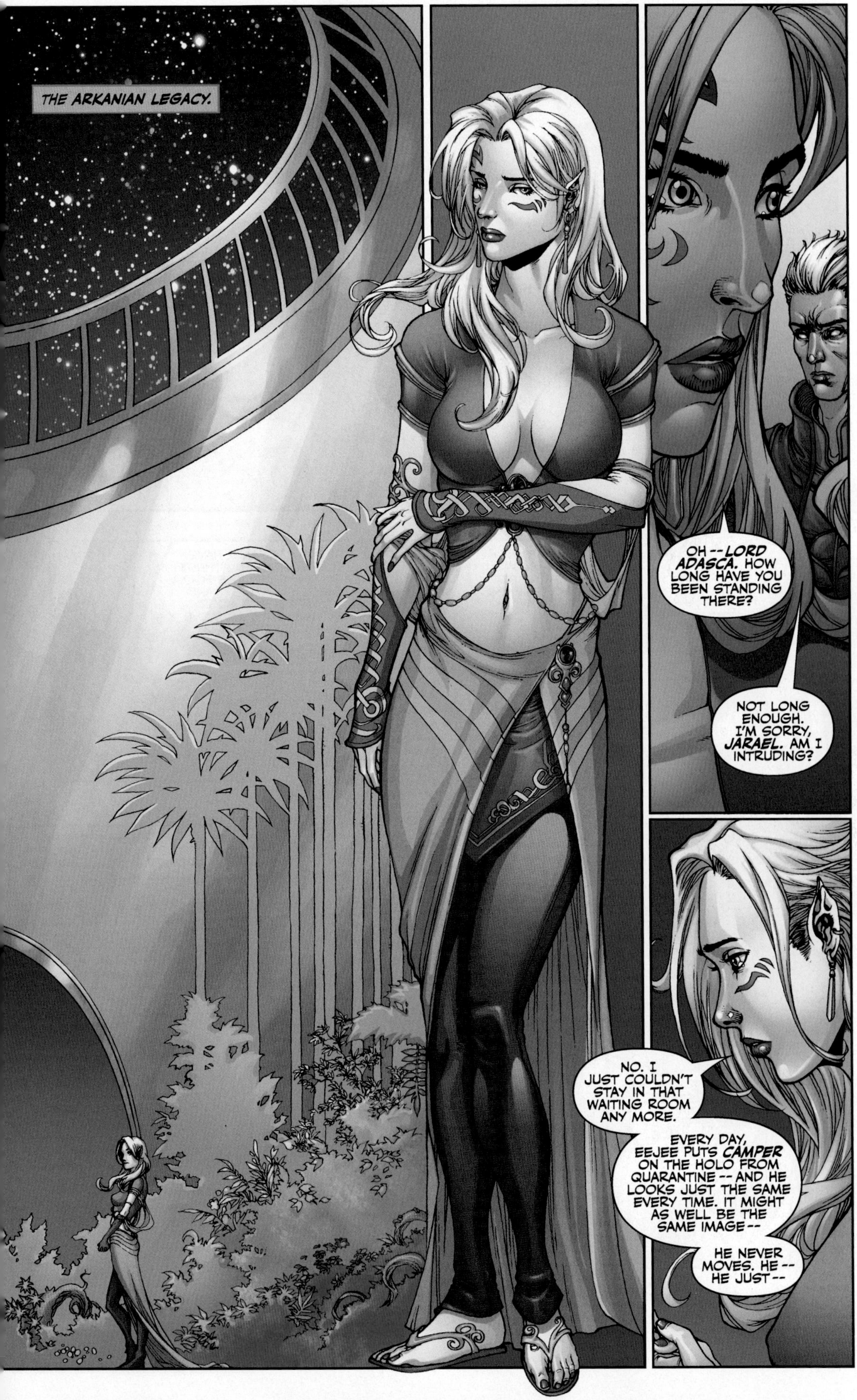
THE ARKANIAN LEGACY.
OH -- LORD ADASCA. HOW LONG HAVE YOU BEEN STANDING THERE?
NOT LONG ENOUGH. I'M SORRY, JARAEL. AM I INTRUDING?
NO. I JUST COULDN'T STAY IN THAT WAITING ROOM ANY MORE.
EVERY DAY, EEJEE PUTS CAMPER ON THE HOLO FROM QUARANTINE -- AND HE LOOKS JUST THE SAME EVERY TIME. IT MIGHT AS WELL BE THE SAME IMAGE--
HE NEVER MOVES. HE -- HE JUST --

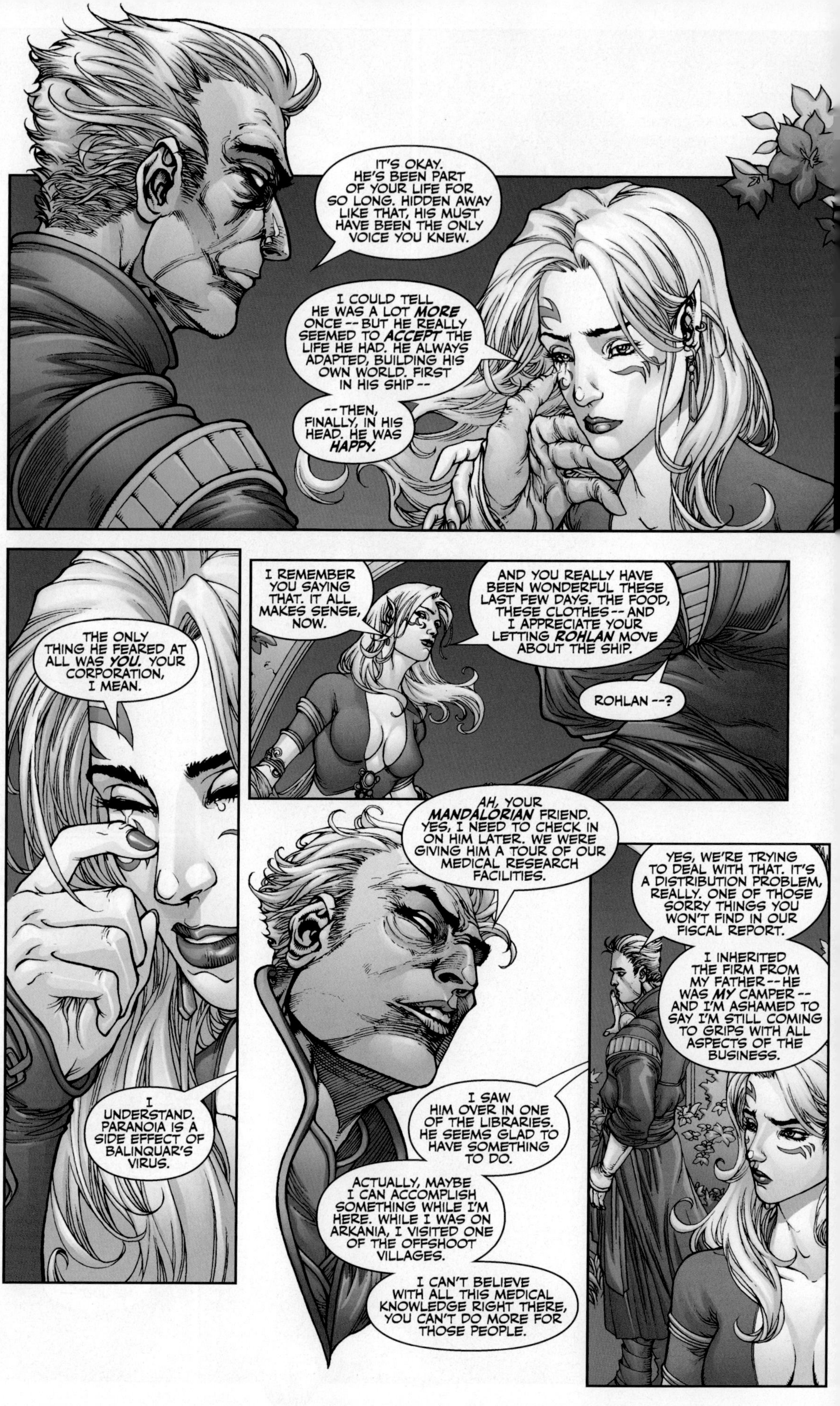
IT'S OKAY. HE'S BEEN PART OF YOUR LIFE FOR SO LONG. HIDDEN AWAY LIKE THAT, HIS MUST HAVE BEEN THE ONLY VOICE YOU KNEW.
I COULD TELL HE WAS A LOT MORE ONCE -- BUT HE REALLY SEEMED TO ACCEPT THE LIFE HE HAD. HE ALWAYS ADAPTED, BUILDING HIS OWN WORLD. FIRST IN HIS SHIP --
-- THEN, FINALLY, IN HIS HEAD. HE WAS HAPPY.
THE ONLY THING HE FEARED AT ALL WAS YOU. YOUR CORPORATION, I MEAN.
I UNDERSTAND. PARANOIA IS A SIDE EFFECT OF BALINQUAR'S VIRUS.
I REMEMBER YOU SAYING THAT. IT ALL MAKES SENSE, NOW.
AND YOU REALLY HAVE BEEN WONDERFUL THESE LAST FEW DAYS. THE FOOD, THESE CLOTHES -- AND I APPRECIATE YOUR LETTING ROHLAN MOVE ABOUT THE SHIP.
ROHLAN --?
AH, YOUR MANDALORIAN FRIEND. YES, I NEED TO CHECK IN ON HIM LATER. WE WERE GIVING HIM A TOUR OF OUR MEDICAL RESEARCH FACILITIES.
I SAW HIM OVER IN ONE OF THE LIBRARIES. HE SEEMS GLAD TO HAVE SOMETHING TO DO.
ACTUALLY, MAYBE I CAN ACCOMPLISH SOMETHING WHILE I'M HERE. WHILE I WAS ON ARKANIA, I VISITED ONE OF THE OFFSHOOT VILLAGES.
I CAN'T BELIEVE WITH ALL THIS MEDICAL KNOWLEDGE RIGHT THERE, YOU CAN'T DO MORE FOR THOSE PEOPLE.
YES, WE'RE TRYING TO DEAL WITH THAT. IT'S A DISTRIBUTION PROBLEM, REALLY. ONE OF THOSE SORRY THINGS YOU WON'T FIND IN OUR FISCAL REPORT.
I INHERITED THE FIRM FROM MY FATHER -- HE WAS MY CAMPER -- AND I'M ASHAMED TO SAY I'M STILL COMING TO GRIPS WITH ALL ASPECTS OF THE BUSINESS.

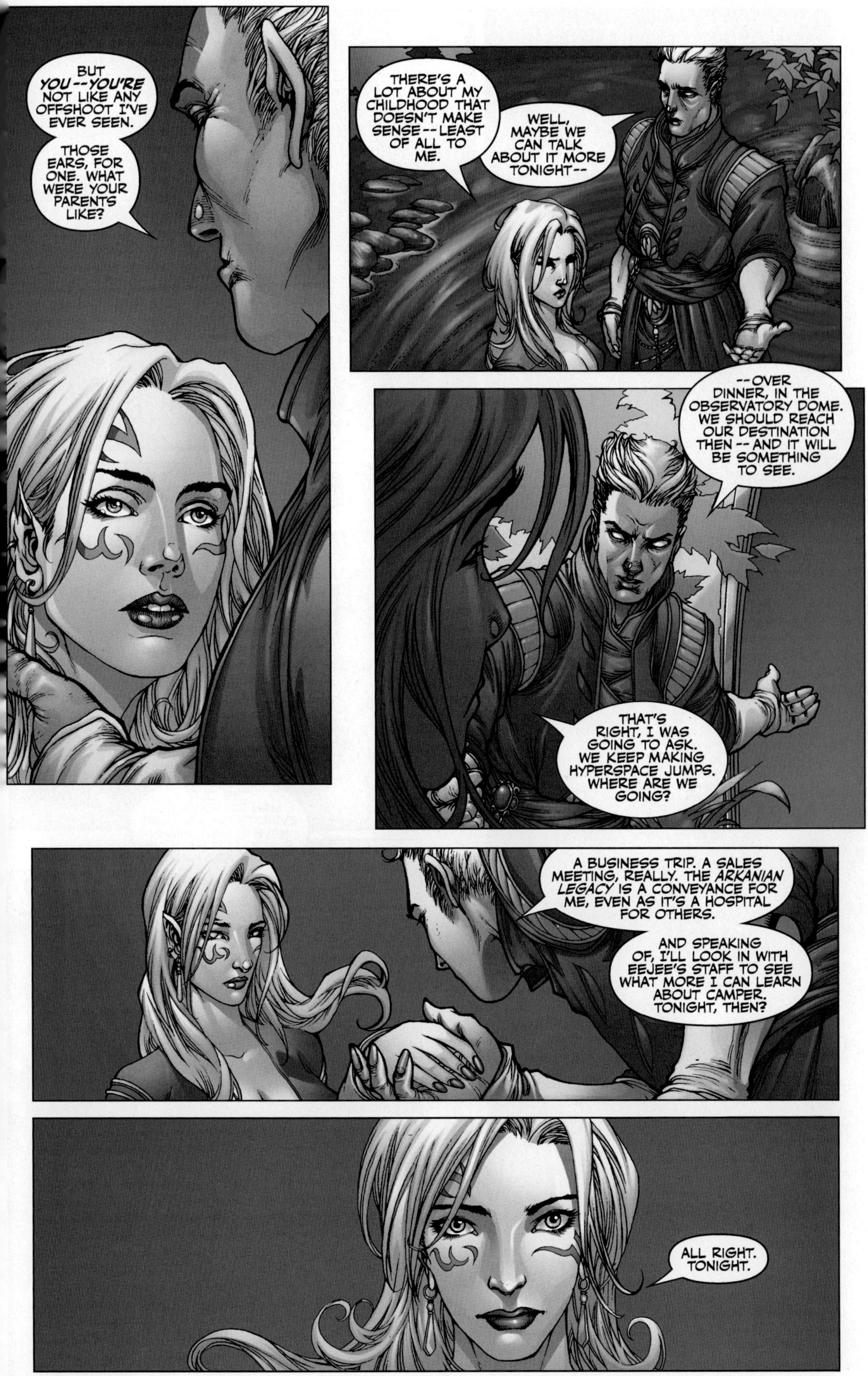
BUT YOU--YOU'RE NOT LIKE ANY OFFSHOOT I'VE EVER SEEN.
THOSE EARS, FOR ONE. WHAT WERE YOUR PARENTS LIKE?
THERE'S A LOT ABOUT MY CHILDHOOD THAT DOESN'T MAKE SENSE--LEAST OF ALL TO ME.
WELL, MAYBE WE CAN TALK ABOUT IT MORE TONIGHT--
--OVER DINNER, IN THE OBSERVATORY DOME. WE SHOULD REACH OUR DESTINATION THEN--AND IT WILL BE SOMETHING TO SEE.
THAT'S RIGHT, I WAS GOING TO ASK. WE KEEP MAKING HYPERSPACE JUMPS. WHERE ARE WE GOING?
A BUSINESS TRIP. A SALES MEETING, REALLY. THE ARKANIAN LEGACY IS A CONVEYANCE FOR ME, EVEN AS IT'S A HOSPITAL FOR OTHERS.
AND SPEAKING OF, I'LL LOOK IN WITH EEJEE'S STAFF TO SEE WHAT MORE I CAN LEARN ABOUT CAMPER. TONIGHT, THEN?
ALL RIGHT. TONIGHT.

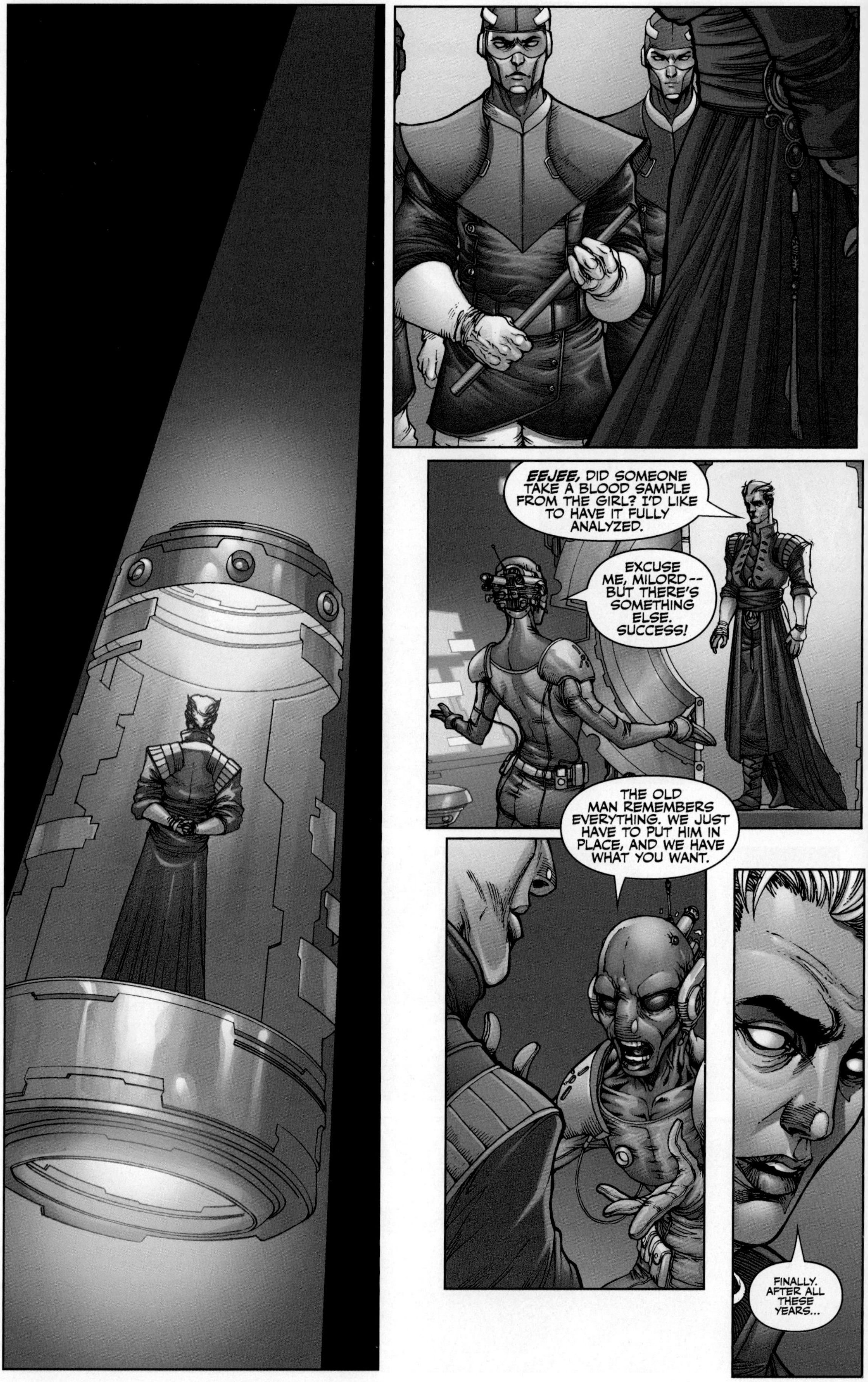
EEJEE, DID SOMEONE TAKE A BLOOD SAMPLE FROM THE GIRL? I'D LIKE TO HAVE IT FULLY ANALYZED.
EXCUSE ME, MILORD-- BUT THERE'S SOMETHING ELSE. SUCCESS!
THE OLD MAN REMEMBERS EVERYTHING. WE JUST HAVE TO PUT HIM IN PLACE, AND WE HAVE WHAT YOU WANT.
FINALLY. AFTER ALL THESE YEARS...

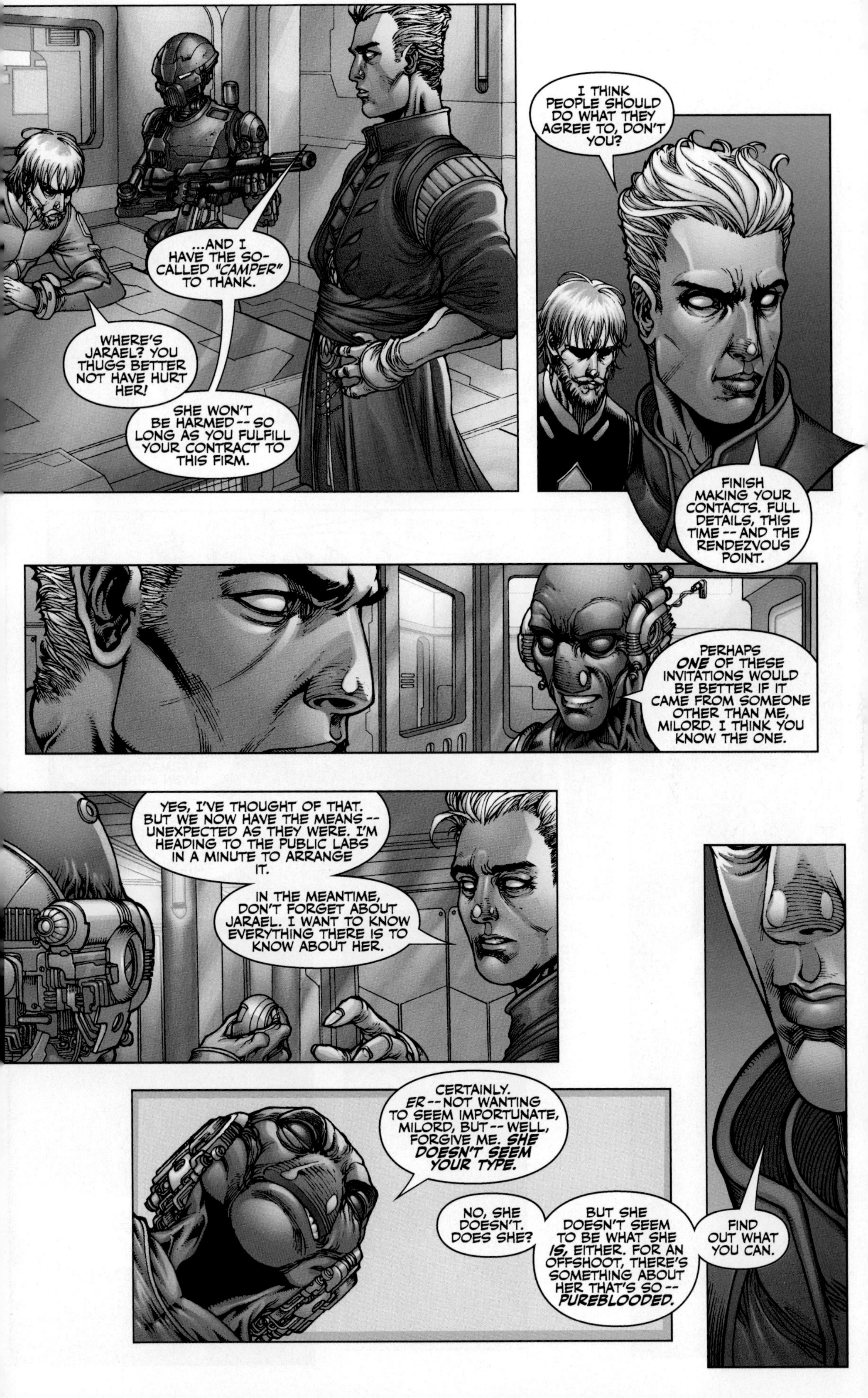
...AND I HAVE THE SO-CALLED "CAMPER" TO THANK.
WHERE'S JARAEL? YOU THUGS BETTER NOT HAVE HURT HER!
SHE WON'T BE HARMED -- SO LONG AS YOU FULFILL YOUR CONTRACT TO THIS FIRM.
I THINK PEOPLE SHOULD DO WHAT THEY AGREE TO, DON'T YOU?
FINISH MAKING YOUR CONTACTS. FULL DETAILS, THIS TIME -- AND THE RENDEZVOUS POINT.
PERHAPS ONE OF THESE INVITATIONS WOULD BE BETTER IF IT CAME FROM SOMEONE OTHER THAN ME, MILORD. I THINK YOU KNOW THE ONE.
YES, I'VE THOUGHT OF THAT. BUT WE NOW HAVE THE MEANS -- UNEXPECTED AS THEY WERE. I'M HEADING TO THE PUBLIC LABS IN A MINUTE TO ARRANGE IT.
IN THE MEANTIME, DON'T FORGET ABOUT JARAEL. I WANT TO KNOW EVERYTHING THERE IS TO KNOW ABOUT HER.
CERTAINLY. ER -- NOT WANTING TO SEEM IMPORTUNATE, MILORD, BUT -- WELL, FORGIVE ME. SHE DOESN'T SEEM YOUR TYPE.
NO, SHE DOESN'T. DOES SHE?
BUT SHE DOESN'T SEEM TO BE WHAT SHE IS, EITHER. FOR AN OFFSHOOT, THERE'S SOMETHING ABOUT HER THAT'S SO -- PUREBLOODED.
FIND OUT WHAT YOU CAN.

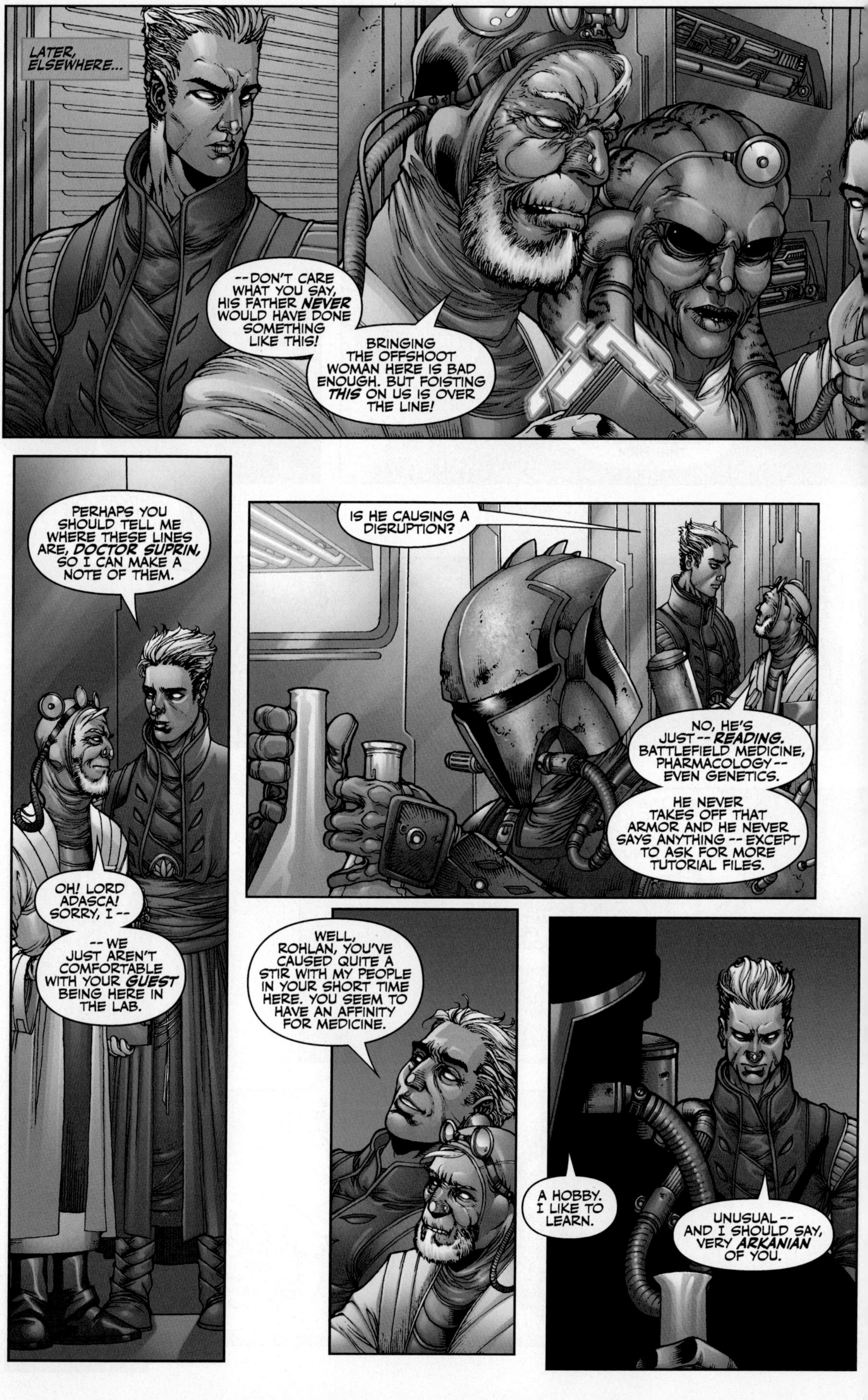
LATER, ELSEWHERE...
--DON'T CARE WHAT YOU SAY, HIS FATHER NEVER WOULD HAVE DONE SOMETHING LIKE THIS!
BRINGING THE OFFSHOOT WOMAN HERE IS BAD ENOUGH. BUT FOISTING THIS ON US IS OVER THE LINE!
PERHAPS YOU SHOULD TELL ME WHERE THESE LINES ARE, DOCTOR SUPRIN, SO I CAN MAKE A NOTE OF THEM.
OH! LORD ADASCA! SORRY, I --
-- WE JUST AREN'T COMFORTABLE WITH YOUR GUEST BEING HERE IN THE LAB.
IS HE CAUSING A DISRUPTION?
NO, HE'S JUST -- READING. BATTLEFIELD MEDICINE, PHARMACOLOGY -- EVEN GENETICS.
HE NEVER TAKES OFF THAT ARMOR AND HE NEVER SAYS ANYTHING -- EXCEPT TO ASK FOR MORE TUTORIAL FILES.
WELL, ROHLAN, YOU'VE CAUSED QUITE A STIR WITH MY PEOPLE IN YOUR SHORT TIME HERE. YOU SEEM TO HAVE AN AFFINITY FOR MEDICINE.
A HOBBY. I LIKE TO LEARN.
UNUSUAL -- AND I SHOULD SAY, VERY ARKANIAN OF YOU.

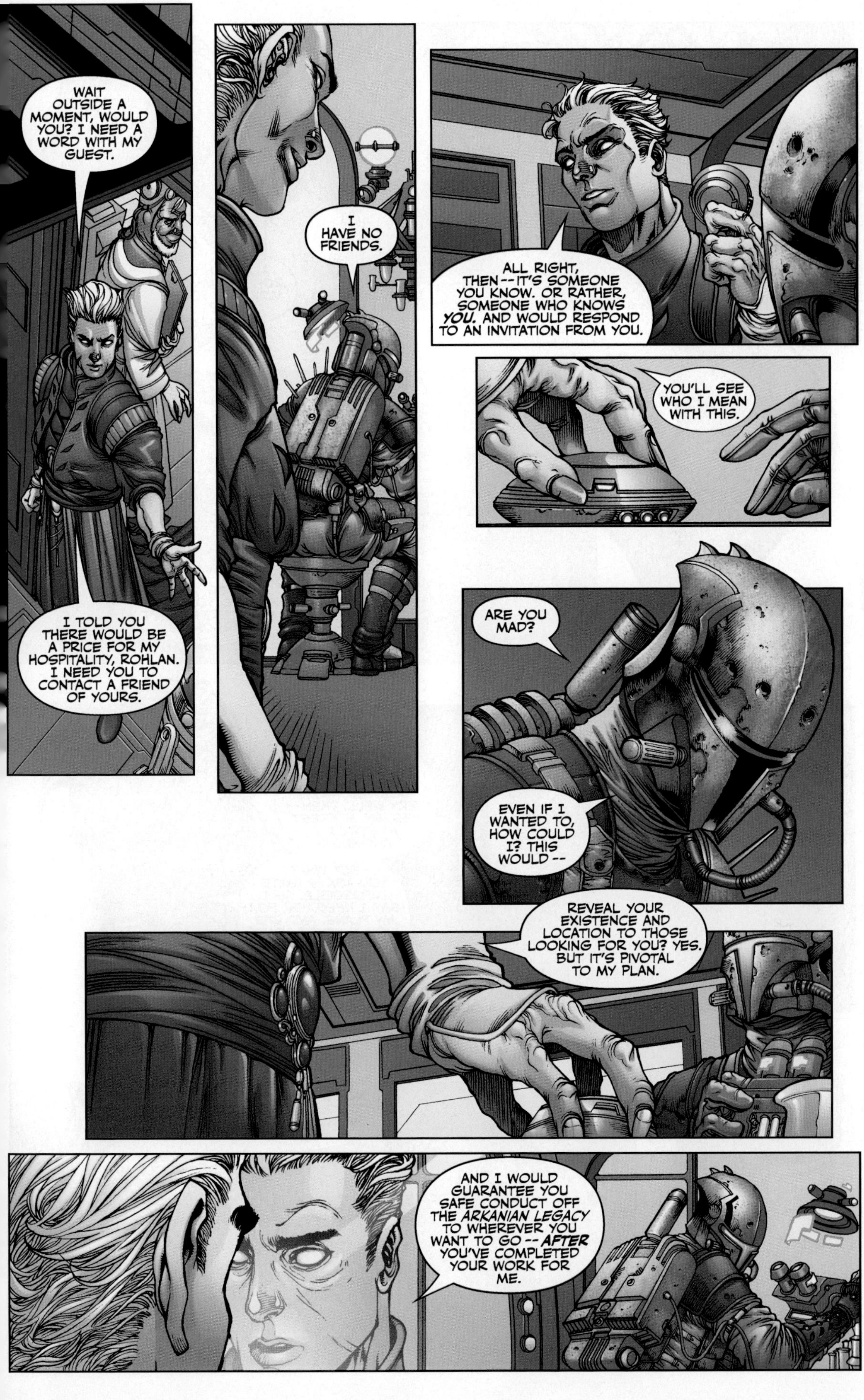
WAIT OUTSIDE A MOMENT, WOULD YOU? I NEED A WORD WITH MY GUEST.
I TOLD YOU THERE WOULD BE A PRICE FOR MY HOSPITALITY, ROHLAN. I NEED YOU TO CONTACT A FRIEND OF YOURS.
I HAVE NO FRIENDS.
ALL RIGHT, THEN--IT'S SOMEONE YOU KNOW. OR RATHER, SOMEONE WHO KNOWS *YOU.* AND WOULD RESPOND TO AN INVITATION FROM YOU.
YOU'LL SEE WHO I MEAN WITH THIS.
ARE YOU MAD?
EVEN IF I WANTED TO, HOW COULD I? THIS WOULD --
REVEAL YOUR EXISTENCE AND LOCATION TO THOSE LOOKING FOR YOU? YES. BUT IT'S PIVOTAL TO MY PLAN.
AND I WOULD GUARANTEE YOU SAFE CONDUCT OFF THE *ARKANIAN LEGACY* TO WHEREVER YOU WANT TO GO -- *AFTER* YOU'VE COMPLETED YOUR WORK FOR ME.

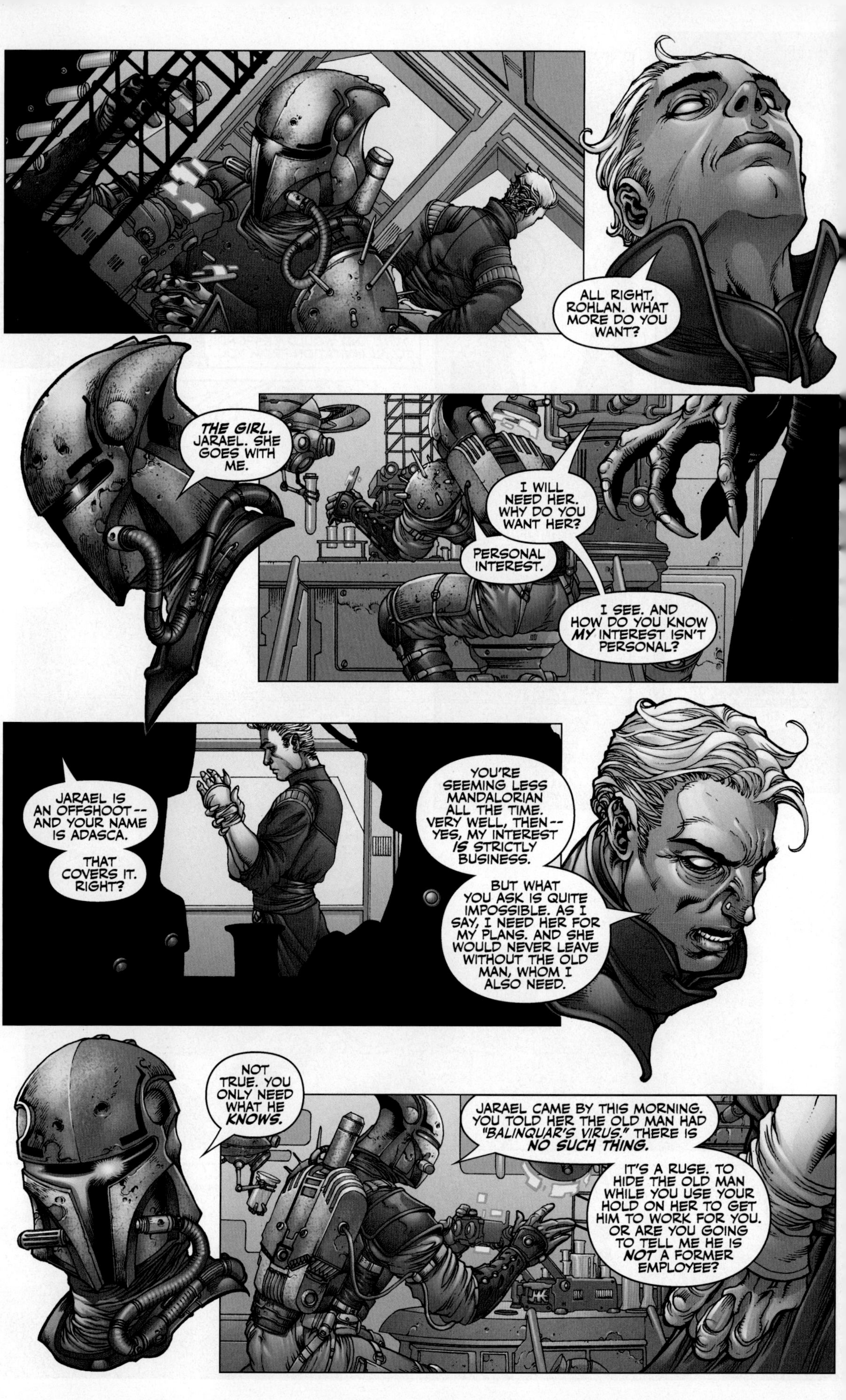
ALL RIGHT, ROHLAN. WHAT MORE DO YOU WANT?
THE GIRL. JARAEL. SHE GOES WITH ME.
I WILL NEED HER. WHY DO YOU WANT HER?
PERSONAL INTEREST.
I SEE. AND HOW DO YOU KNOW MY INTEREST ISN'T PERSONAL?
JARAEL IS AN OFFSHOOT-- AND YOUR NAME IS ADASCA.
THAT COVERS IT. RIGHT?
YOU'RE SEEMING LESS MANDALORIAN ALL THE TIME. VERY WELL, THEN-- YES, MY INTEREST IS STRICTLY BUSINESS.
BUT WHAT YOU ASK IS QUITE IMPOSSIBLE. AS I SAY, I NEED HER FOR MY PLANS. AND SHE WOULD NEVER LEAVE WITHOUT THE OLD MAN, WHOM I ALSO NEED.
NOT TRUE. YOU ONLY NEED WHAT HE KNOWS.
JARAEL CAME BY THIS MORNING. YOU TOLD HER THE OLD MAN HAD "BALINQUAR'S VIRUS." THERE IS NO SUCH THING.
IT'S A RUSE. TO HIDE THE OLD MAN WHILE YOU USE YOUR HOLD ON HER TO GET HIM TO WORK FOR YOU. OR ARE YOU GOING TO TELL ME HE IS NOT A FORMER EMPLOYEE?

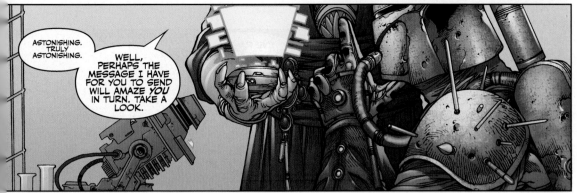

ASTONISHING. TRULY ASTONISHING.

WELL, PERHAPS THE MESSAGE I HAVE FOR YOU TO SEND WILL AMAZE *YOU* IN TURN. TAKE A LOOK.

THIS -- THIS IS AMAZING! *THIS* WAS LOCKED IN THE OLD MAN'S HEAD?

INDEED. YOU SHOULD *SEE* WHAT'S GOING ON ELSEWHERE ON THE SHIP -- THIS LEVEL ONLY DEALS WITH MEDICAL MATTERS.

THIS *WILL* PROVOKE A RESPONSE, DON'T YOU THINK?

DEFINITELY.

SEND IT. SEND IT, AND I WILL GIVE YOU YOUR FREEDOM.

AND IF THE OLD MAN PROVES NO LONGER NECESSARY, YES, I WILL GIVE YOU THE GIRL.

ALL RIGHT. JUST SHOW ME WHERE TO GO.

EXCELLENT. I'LL HAVE EEJEE SET YOU UP A SECURE CHANNEL.

I *AM* IMPRESSED. SUPRIN, TEACH HIM WHATEVER HE WANTS TO KNOW.

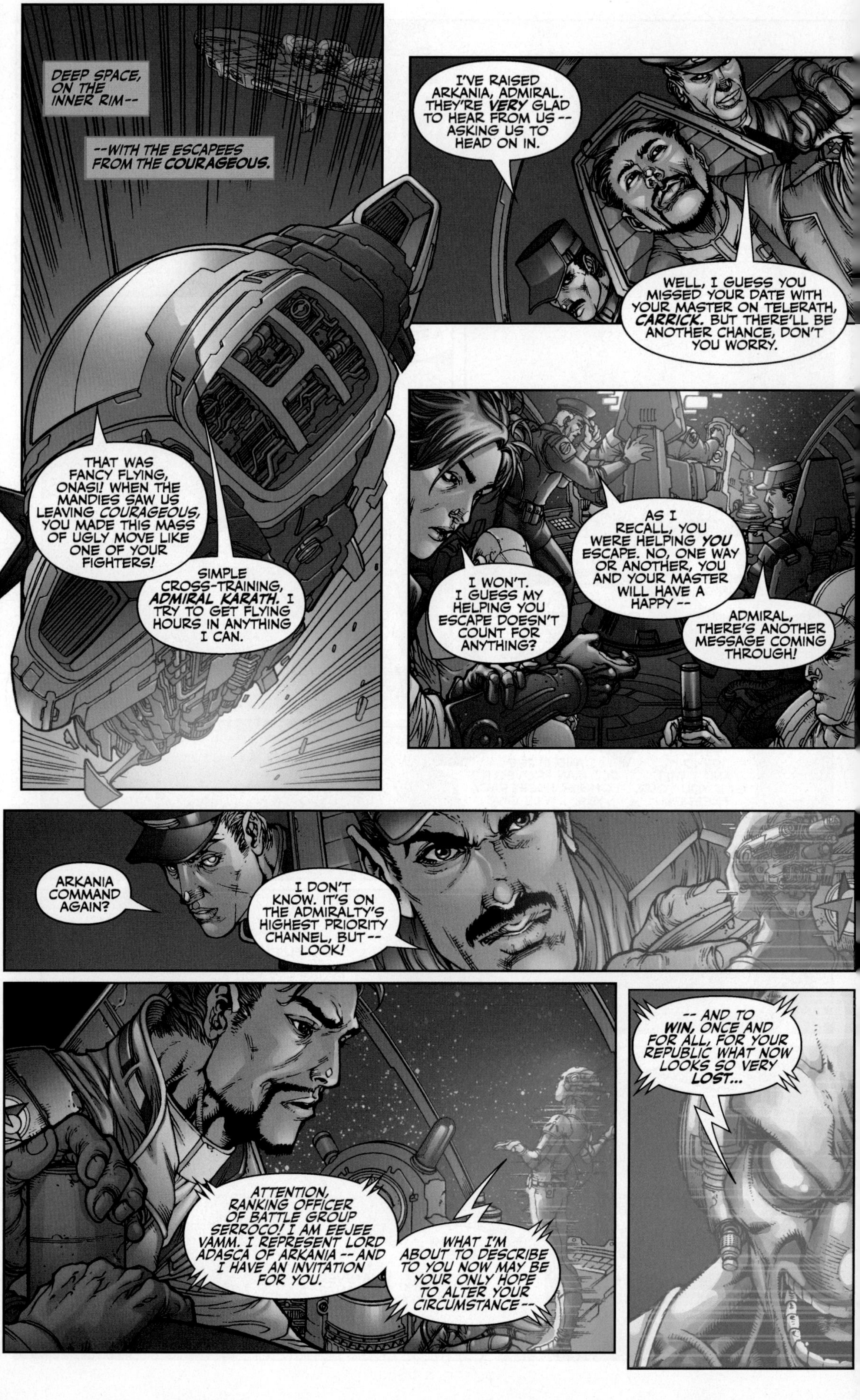
DEEP SPACE, ON THE INNER RIM--
--WITH THE ESCAPEES FROM THE COURAGEOUS.
THAT WAS FANCY FLYING, ONASI! WHEN THE MANDIES SAW US LEAVING COURAGEOUS, YOU MADE THIS MASS OF UGLY MOVE LIKE ONE OF YOUR FIGHTERS!
SIMPLE CROSS-TRAINING, ADMIRAL KARATH. I TRY TO GET FLYING HOURS IN ANYTHING I CAN.
I'VE RAISED ARKANIA, ADMIRAL. THEY'RE VERY GLAD TO HEAR FROM US -- ASKING US TO HEAD ON IN.
WELL, I GUESS YOU MISSED YOUR DATE WITH YOUR MASTER ON TELERATH, CARRICK. BUT THERE'LL BE ANOTHER CHANCE, DON'T YOU WORRY.
I WON'T. I GUESS MY HELPING YOU ESCAPE DOESN'T COUNT FOR ANYTHING?
AS I RECALL, YOU WERE HELPING YOU ESCAPE. NO, ONE WAY OR ANOTHER, YOU AND YOUR MASTER WILL HAVE A HAPPY --
ADMIRAL, THERE'S ANOTHER MESSAGE COMING THROUGH!
ARKANIA COMMAND AGAIN?
I DON'T KNOW. IT'S ON THE ADMIRALTY'S HIGHEST PRIORITY CHANNEL, BUT -- LOOK!
ATTENTION, RANKING OFFICER OF BATTLE GROUP SERROCO! I AM EEJEE VAMM. I REPRESENT LORD ADASCA OF ARKANIA -- AND I HAVE AN INVITATION FOR YOU.
WHAT I'M ABOUT TO DESCRIBE TO YOU NOW MAY BE YOUR ONLY HOPE TO ALTER YOUR CIRCUMSTANCE --
-- AND TO WIN, ONCE AND FOR ALL, FOR YOUR REPUBLIC WHAT NOW LOOKS SO VERY LOST...

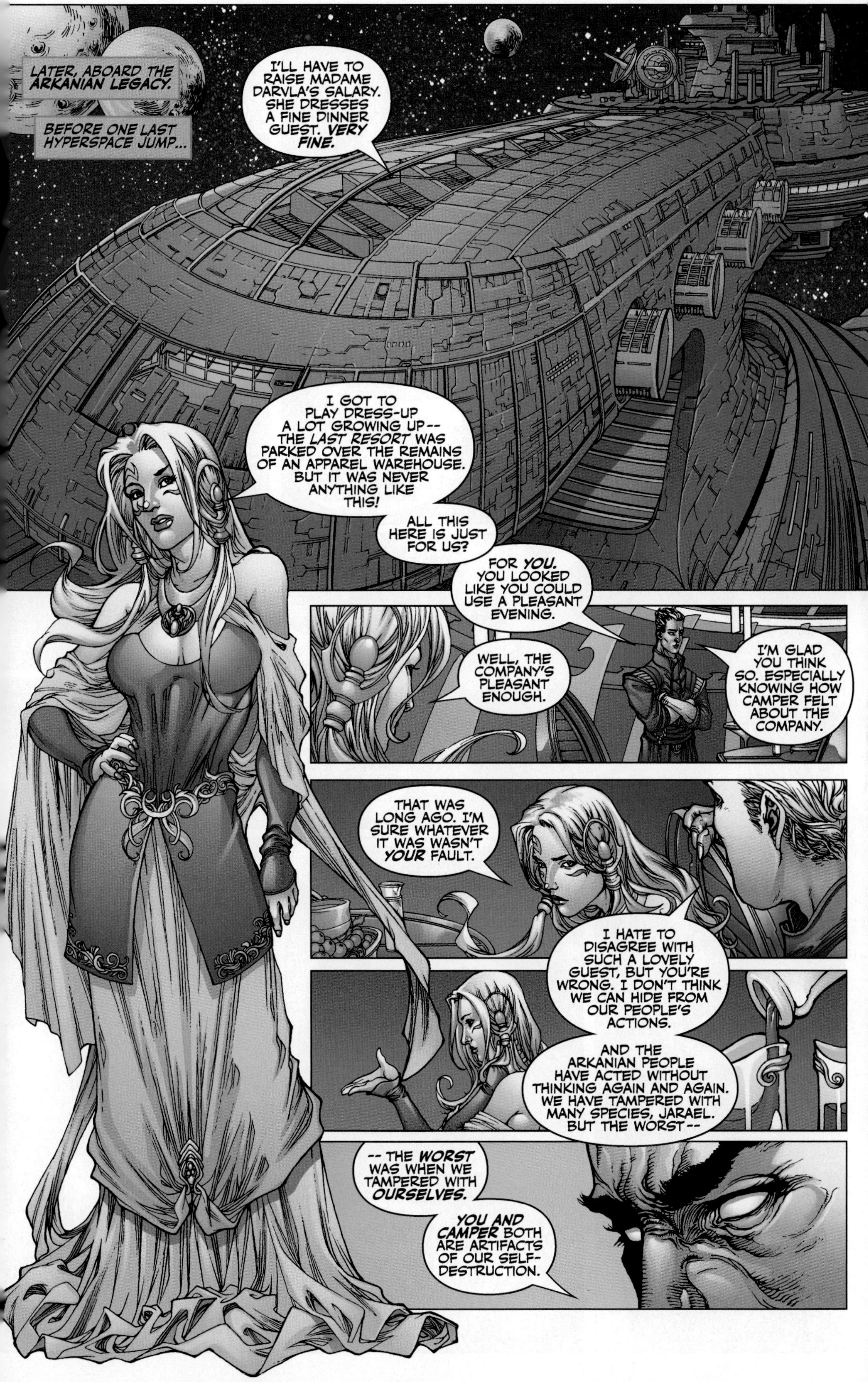
LATER, ABOARD THE ARKANIAN LEGACY.
BEFORE ONE LAST HYPERSPACE JUMP...
I'LL HAVE TO RAISE MADAME DARVLA'S SALARY. SHE DRESSES A FINE DINNER GUEST. VERY FINE.
I GOT TO PLAY DRESS-UP A LOT GROWING UP-- THE LAST RESORT WAS PARKED OVER THE REMAINS OF AN APPAREL WAREHOUSE. BUT IT WAS NEVER ANYTHING LIKE THIS!
ALL THIS HERE IS JUST FOR US?
FOR YOU. YOU LOOKED LIKE YOU COULD USE A PLEASANT EVENING.
WELL, THE COMPANY'S PLEASANT ENOUGH.
I'M GLAD YOU THINK SO. ESPECIALLY KNOWING HOW CAMPER FELT ABOUT THE COMPANY.
THAT WAS LONG AGO. I'M SURE WHATEVER IT WAS WASN'T YOUR FAULT.
I HATE TO DISAGREE WITH SUCH A LOVELY GUEST, BUT YOU'RE WRONG. I DON'T THINK WE CAN HIDE FROM OUR PEOPLE'S ACTIONS.
AND THE ARKANIAN PEOPLE HAVE ACTED WITHOUT THINKING AGAIN AND AGAIN. WE HAVE TAMPERED WITH MANY SPECIES, JARAEL. BUT THE WORST--
-- THE WORST WAS WHEN WE TAMPERED WITH OURSELVES.
YOU AND CAMPER BOTH ARE ARTIFACTS OF OUR SELF-DESTRUCTION.

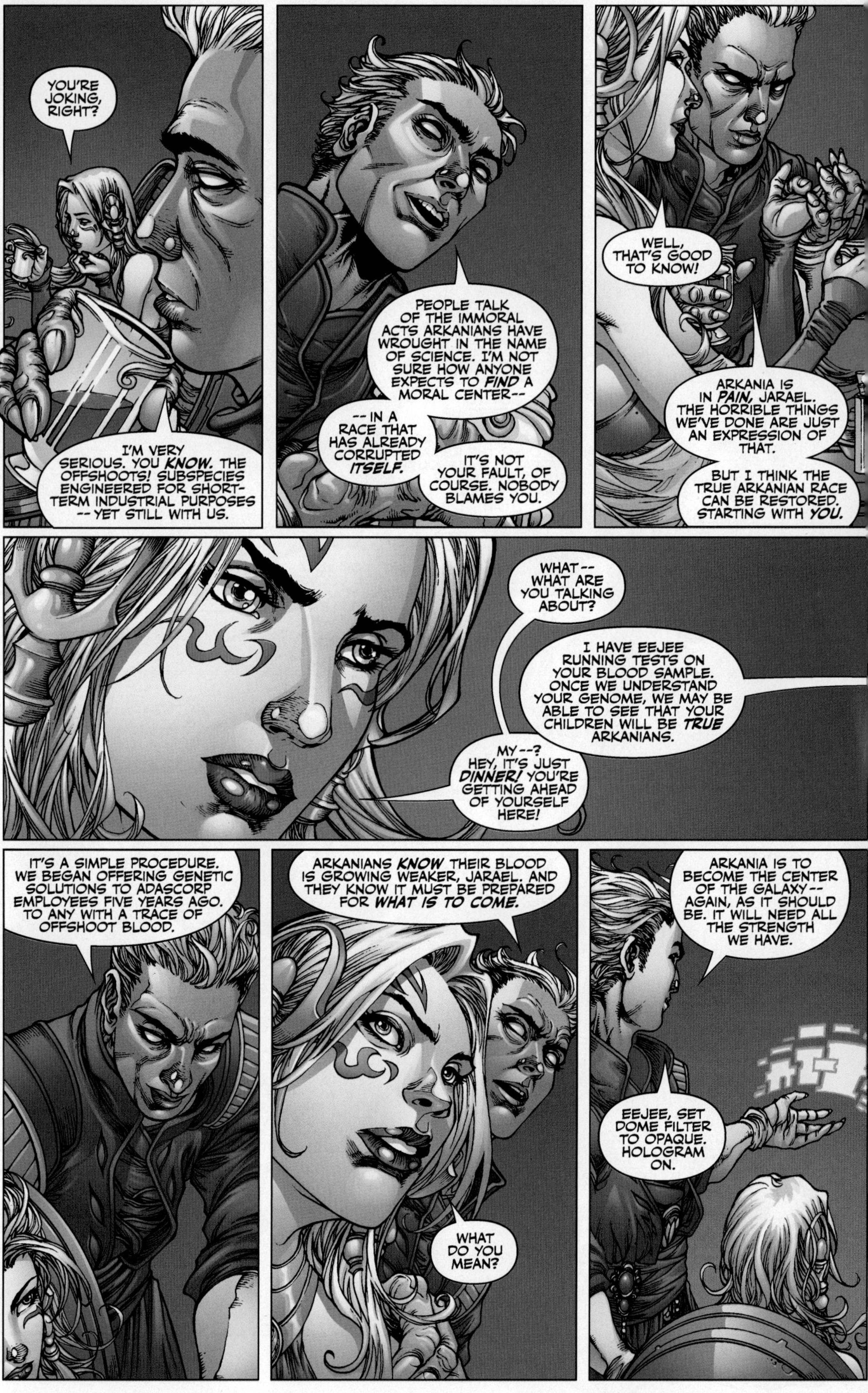
YOU'RE JOKING, RIGHT?
I'M VERY SERIOUS. YOU KNOW. THE OFFSHOOTS! SUBSPECIES ENGINEERED FOR SHORT-TERM INDUSTRIAL PURPOSES --YET STILL WITH US.
PEOPLE TALK OF THE IMMORAL ACTS ARKANIANS HAVE WROUGHT IN THE NAME OF SCIENCE. I'M NOT SURE HOW ANYONE EXPECTS TO FIND A MORAL CENTER--
--IN A RACE THAT HAS ALREADY CORRUPTED ITSELF.
IT'S NOT YOUR FAULT, OF COURSE. NOBODY BLAMES YOU.
WELL, THAT'S GOOD TO KNOW!
ARKANIA IS IN PAIN, JARAEL. THE HORRIBLE THINGS WE'VE DONE ARE JUST AN EXPRESSION OF THAT.
BUT I THINK THE TRUE ARKANIAN RACE CAN BE RESTORED. STARTING WITH YOU.
WHAT-- WHAT ARE YOU TALKING ABOUT?
I HAVE EEJEE RUNNING TESTS ON YOUR BLOOD SAMPLE. ONCE WE UNDERSTAND YOUR GENOME, WE MAY BE ABLE TO SEE THAT YOUR CHILDREN WILL BE TRUE ARKANIANS.
MY--? HEY, IT'S JUST DINNER! YOU'RE GETTING AHEAD OF YOURSELF HERE!
IT'S A SIMPLE PROCEDURE. WE BEGAN OFFERING GENETIC SOLUTIONS TO ADASCORP EMPLOYEES FIVE YEARS AGO. TO ANY WITH A TRACE OF OFFSHOOT BLOOD.
ARKANIANS KNOW THEIR BLOOD IS GROWING WEAKER, JARAEL. AND THEY KNOW IT MUST BE PREPARED FOR WHAT IS TO COME.
WHAT DO YOU MEAN?
ARKANIA IS TO BECOME THE CENTER OF THE GALAXY-- AGAIN, AS IT SHOULD BE. IT WILL NEED ALL THE STRENGTH WE HAVE.
EEJEE, SET DOME FILTER TO OPAQUE. HOLOGRAM ON.

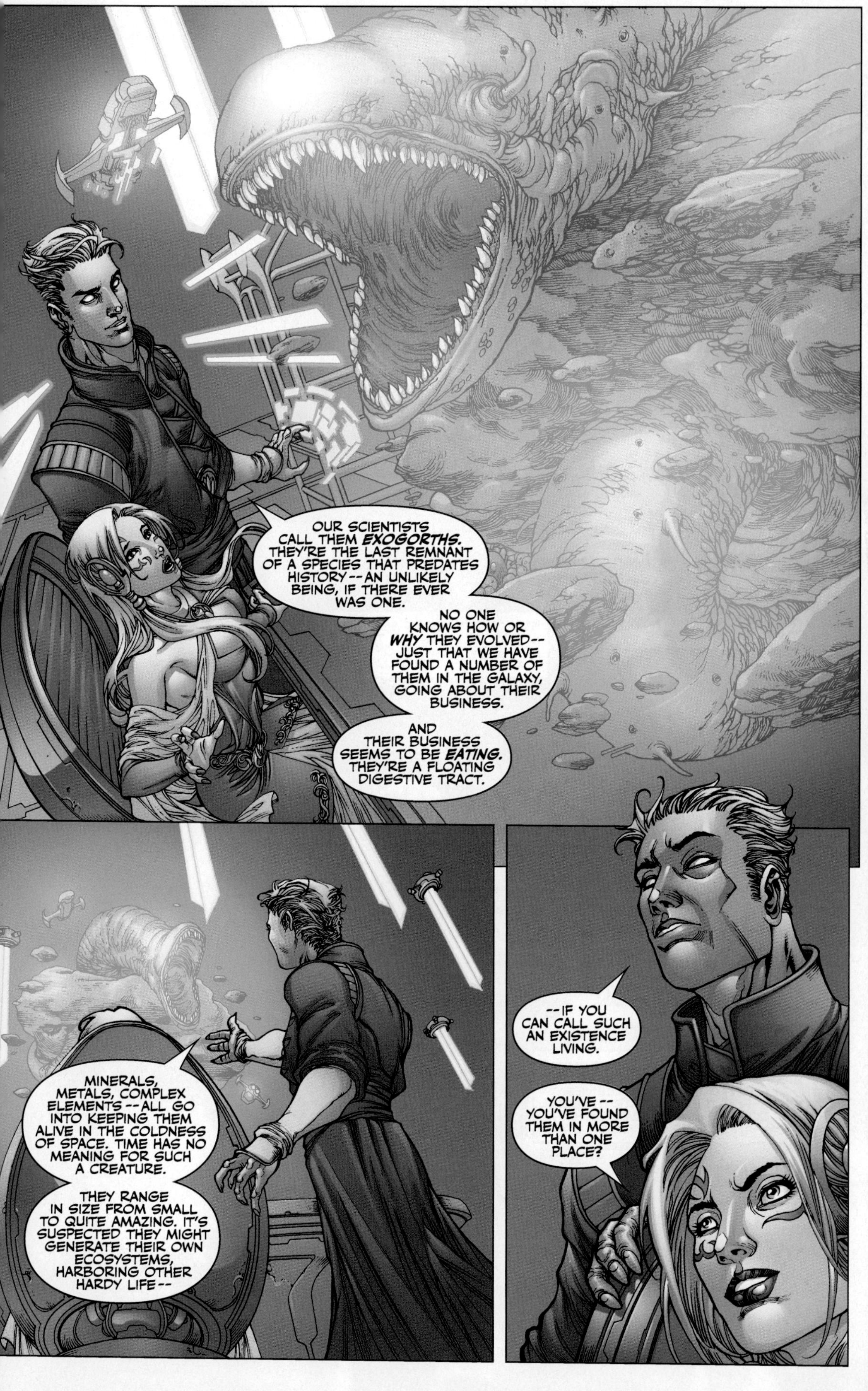
OUR SCIENTISTS CALL THEM EXOGORTHS. THEY'RE THE LAST REMNANT OF A SPECIES THAT PREDATES HISTORY--AN UNLIKELY BEING, IF THERE EVER WAS ONE.
NO ONE KNOWS HOW OR WHY THEY EVOLVED--JUST THAT WE HAVE FOUND A NUMBER OF THEM IN THE GALAXY, GOING ABOUT THEIR BUSINESS.
AND THEIR BUSINESS SEEMS TO BE EATING. THEY'RE A FLOATING DIGESTIVE TRACT.
MINERALS, METALS, COMPLEX ELEMENTS--ALL GO INTO KEEPING THEM ALIVE IN THE COLDNESS OF SPACE. TIME HAS NO MEANING FOR SUCH A CREATURE.
THEY RANGE IN SIZE FROM SMALL TO QUITE AMAZING. IT'S SUSPECTED THEY MIGHT GENERATE THEIR OWN ECOSYSTEMS, HARBORING OTHER HARDY LIFE--
--IF YOU CAN CALL SUCH AN EXISTENCE LIVING.
YOU'VE--YOU'VE FOUND THEM IN MORE THAN ONE PLACE?

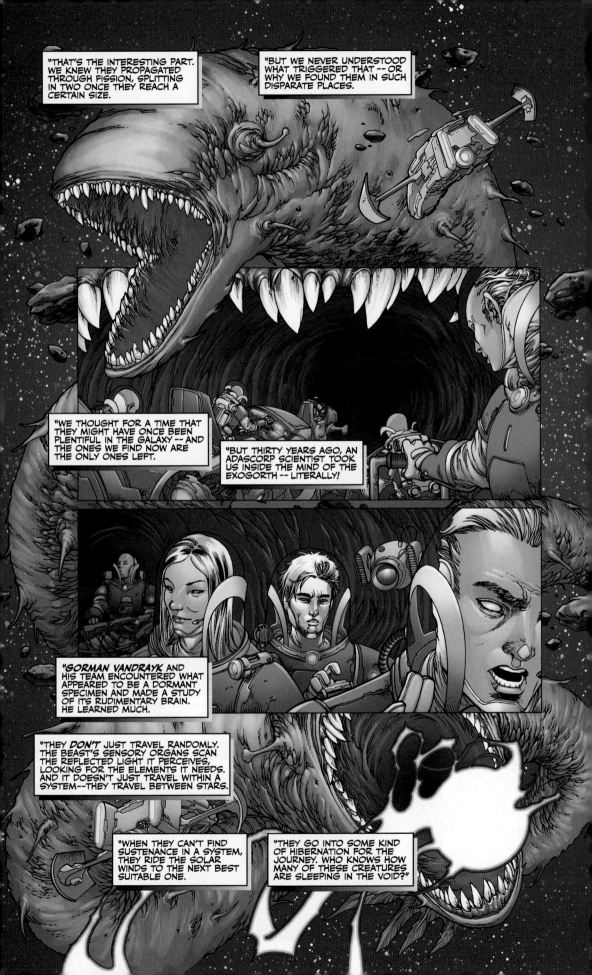

"THAT'S THE INTERESTING PART. WE KNEW THEY PROPAGATED THROUGH FISSION, SPLITTING IN TWO ONCE THEY REACH A CERTAIN SIZE.

"BUT WE NEVER UNDERSTOOD WHAT TRIGGERED THAT -- OR WHY WE FOUND THEM IN SUCH DISPARATE PLACES.

"WE THOUGHT FOR A TIME THAT THEY MIGHT HAVE ONCE BEEN PLENTIFUL IN THE GALAXY -- AND THE ONES WE FIND NOW ARE THE ONLY ONES LEFT.

"BUT THIRTY YEARS AGO, AN ADASCORP SCIENTIST TOOK US INSIDE THE MIND OF THE EXOGORTH -- LITERALLY!

"*GORMAN VANDRAYK* AND HIS TEAM ENCOUNTERED WHAT APPEARED TO BE A DORMANT SPECIMEN AND MADE A STUDY OF ITS RUDIMENTARY BRAIN. HE LEARNED MUCH.

"THEY *DON'T* JUST TRAVEL RANDOMLY. THE BEAST'S SENSORY ORGANS SCAN THE REFLECTED LIGHT IT PERCEIVES, LOOKING FOR THE ELEMENTS IT NEEDS. AND IT DOESN'T JUST TRAVEL WITHIN A SYSTEM--THEY TRAVEL BETWEEN STARS.

"WHEN THEY CAN'T FIND SUSTENANCE IN A SYSTEM, THEY RIDE THE SOLAR WINDS TO THE NEXT BEST SUITABLE ONE.

"THEY GO INTO SOME KIND OF HIBERNATION FOR THE JOURNEY. WHO KNOWS HOW MANY OF THESE CREATURES ARE SLEEPING IN THE VOID?"

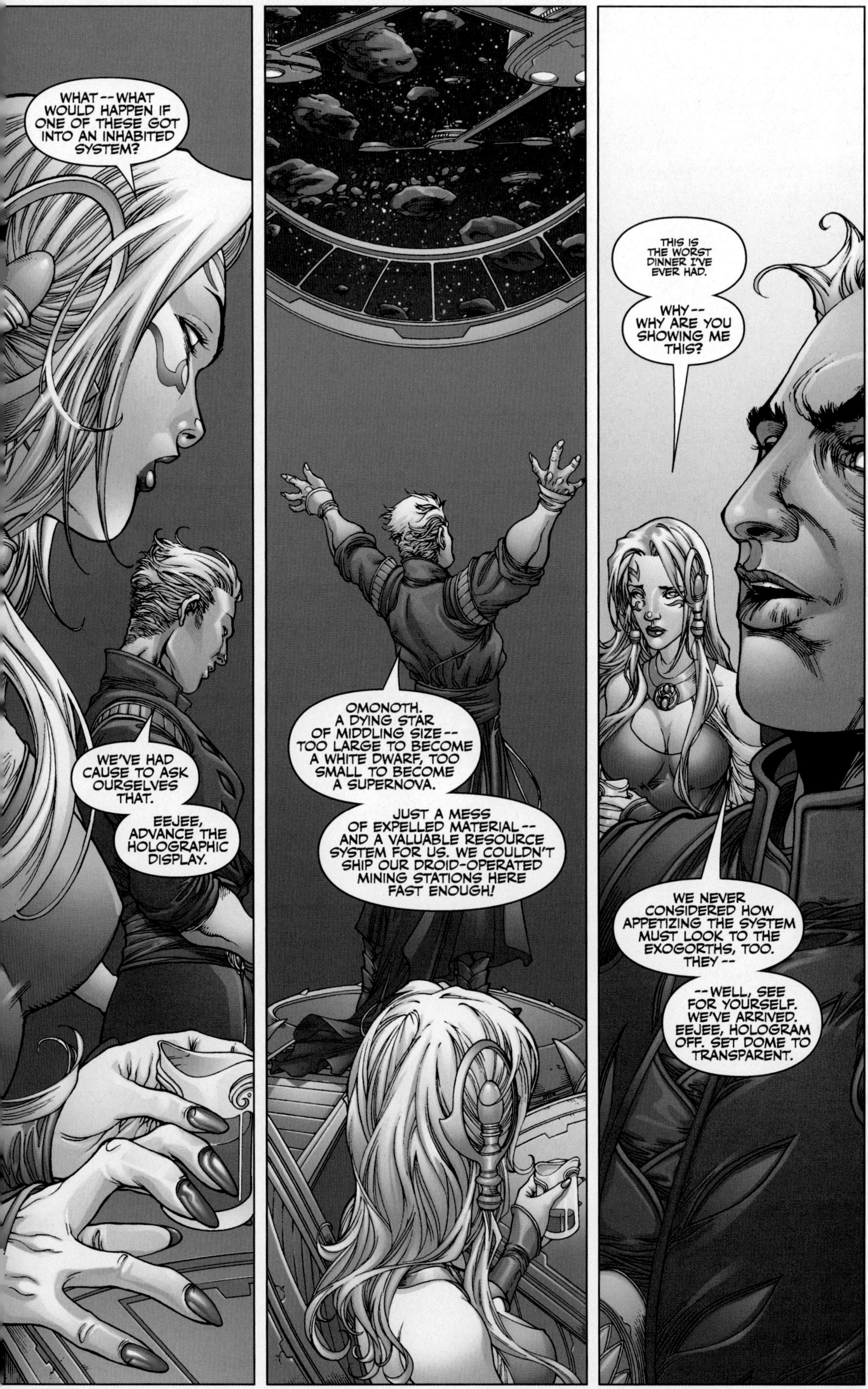
WHAT--WHAT WOULD HAPPEN IF ONE OF THESE GOT INTO AN INHABITED SYSTEM?
WE'VE HAD CAUSE TO ASK OURSELVES THAT.
EEJEE, ADVANCE THE HOLOGRAPHIC DISPLAY.
OMONOTH. A DYING STAR OF MIDDLING SIZE--TOO LARGE TO BECOME A WHITE DWARF, TOO SMALL TO BECOME A SUPERNOVA.
JUST A MESS OF EXPELLED MATERIAL--AND A VALUABLE RESOURCE SYSTEM FOR US. WE COULDN'T SHIP OUR DROID-OPERATED MINING STATIONS HERE FAST ENOUGH!
THIS IS THE WORST DINNER I'VE EVER HAD.
WHY--WHY ARE YOU SHOWING ME THIS?
WE NEVER CONSIDERED HOW APPETIZING THE SYSTEM MUST LOOK TO THE EXOGORTHS, TOO. THEY--
--WELL, SEE FOR YOURSELF. WE'VE ARRIVED. EEJEE, HOLOGRAM OFF. SET DOME TO TRANSPARENT.

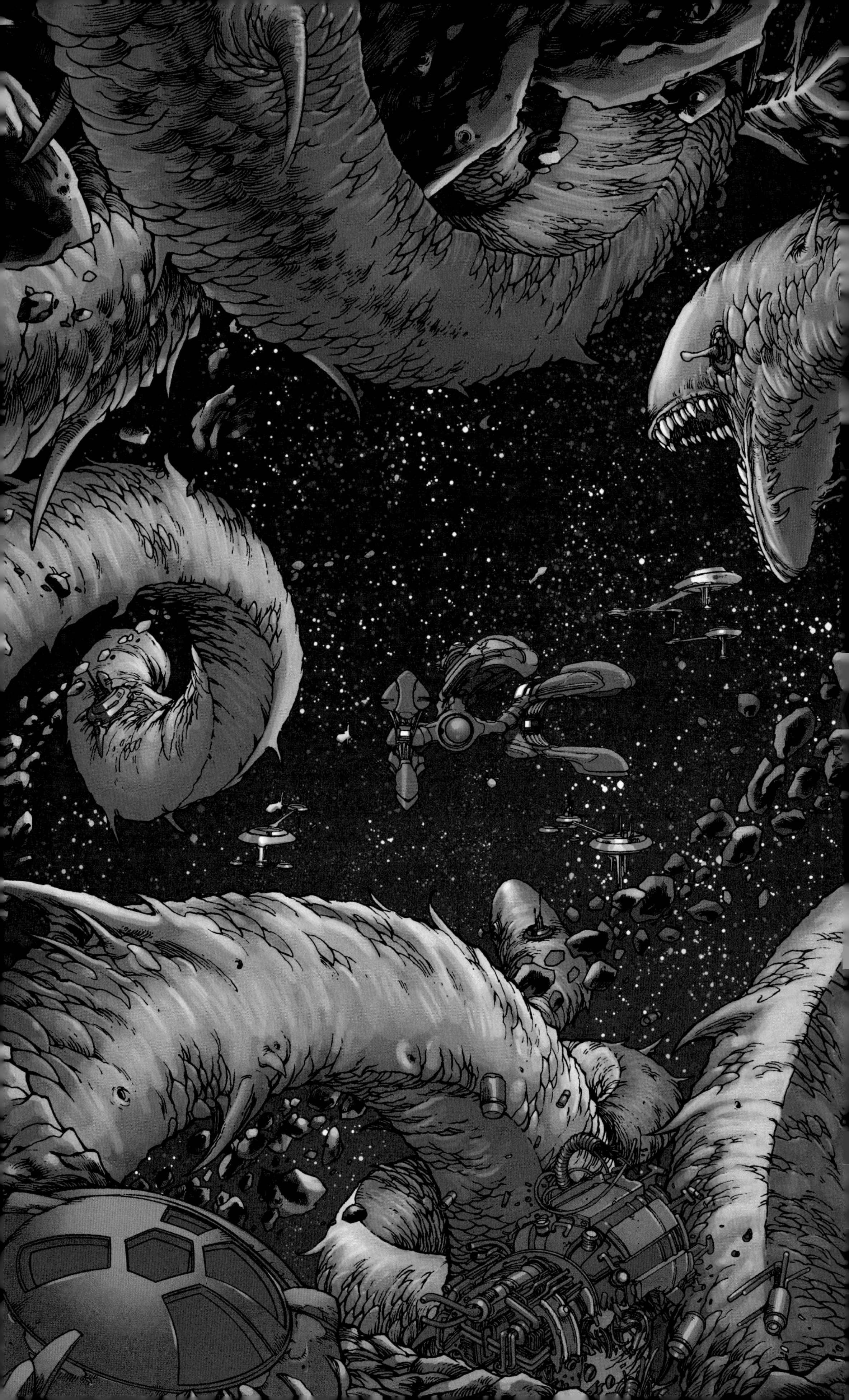

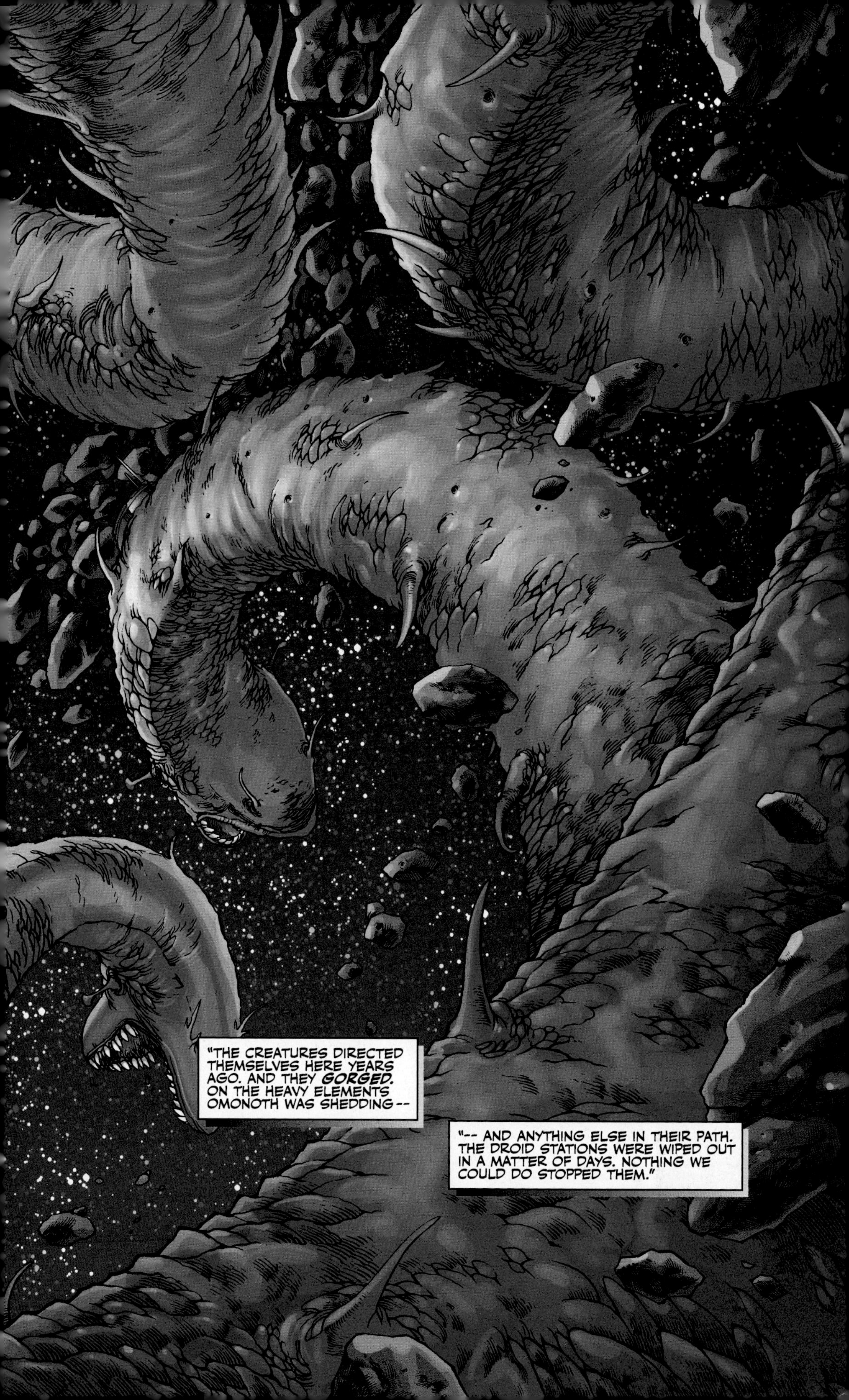
"THE CREATURES DIRECTED THEMSELVES HERE YEARS AGO. AND THEY *GORGED*. ON THE HEAVY ELEMENTS OMONOTH WAS SHEDDING--
"-- AND ANYTHING ELSE IN THEIR PATH. THE DROID STATIONS WERE WIPED OUT IN A MATTER OF DAYS. NOTHING WE COULD DO STOPPED THEM."

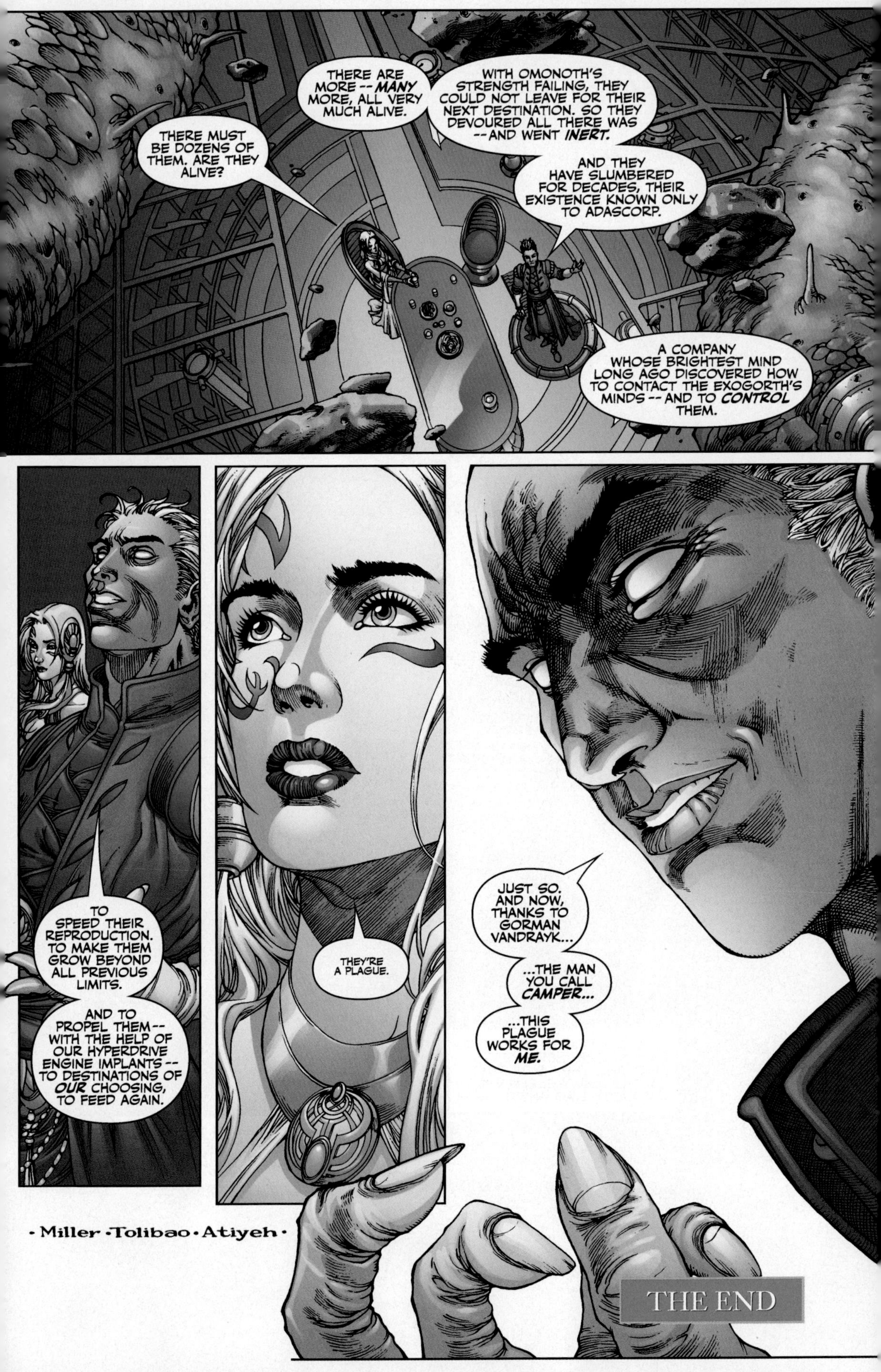
THERE MUST BE DOZENS OF THEM. ARE THEY ALIVE?
THERE ARE MORE -- MANY MORE, ALL VERY MUCH ALIVE.
WITH OMONOTH'S STRENGTH FAILING, THEY COULD NOT LEAVE FOR THEIR NEXT DESTINATION. SO THEY DEVOURED ALL THERE WAS -- AND WENT INERT.
AND THEY HAVE SLUMBERED FOR DECADES, THEIR EXISTENCE KNOWN ONLY TO ADASCORP.
A COMPANY WHOSE BRIGHTEST MIND LONG AGO DISCOVERED HOW TO CONTACT THE EXOGORTH'S MINDS -- AND TO CONTROL THEM.
TO SPEED THEIR REPRODUCTION. TO MAKE THEM GROW BEYOND ALL PREVIOUS LIMITS.
AND TO PROPEL THEM -- WITH THE HELP OF OUR HYPERDRIVE ENGINE IMPLANTS -- TO DESTINATIONS OF OUR CHOOSING, TO FEED AGAIN.
THEY'RE A PLAGUE.
JUST SO. AND NOW, THANKS TO GORMAN VANDRAYK...
...THE MAN YOU CALL CAMPER...
...THIS PLAGUE WORKS FOR ME.
•Miller •Tolibao•Atiyeh•
THE END

THE TARIS HOLOFEED
INVASION EDITION

THE MANDLORIANS HAVE LANDED!

Taris is being invaded.
Repeat, Taris is being invaded!

This is the report from the scene here in the Upper City. After seemingly endless days under the siege of orbiting forces above, the Mandalorians began landing in the polar areas of the planet late last night! Other incursions in the equatorial regions followed, and at this hour they very nearly appear all over the map. It's difficult to say—the last report from the civil defense holofeed came hours ago, and we've been relying on everything from weather sensors to word of mouth.

The reader will forgive any lapses in journalistic standards. The Mandalorians have just landed at Highpoint, and the offices which source this Holofeed there were struck two days ago by some kind of explosive. Since that time—not counting a nervous night hiding in the back room of Kebla Yurt's Equipment Emporium—this reporter and staff have been stationed at the Senatorial Suite of the Junavex Hotel.

The choice wasn't made from avarice—it provides a good view of the city and its construction is sound—though your correspondent will admit to some intentional irony. Many exclusive haunts previously off-limits to normal folk sit completely abandoned today—and, of course, our own senator has been missing since the weeks following the Padawan Massacre. Wherever you are, Gorravus, we're keeping an eye on the place for you!

Mandalorian shock troopers can now be seen on the streets of the Upper City, and armored figures astride metal horrors called basilisks can be seen darting through the city canyons toward the regions below. Reports say Cassus Fett is running the show, and if so, he's doing it with macabre efficiency. The taking of Market Street this morning barely gave a moment's respite between the looters leaving and the invaders arriving!

At least the swoop gangs had the decency to fire a few parting shots at the Mandies before streaking back to their holes. It's more than the Republic has done. Even before the Republic announced Taris "indefensible," they weren't able to do much. For weeks, people on Taris have asked why the Republic would invite the planet to join if it didn't intend to protect them. It's plain now. They didn't want you, Master and Mistress Taris—they wanted your business!

They say the Chancellor has launched an investigation into how Taris got fast-tracked into the Republic in the first place. This reporter has a few choice words for any investigator who decides to drop in. But it's already a busy day for visitors!

Where will the Mandalorians stop? What do they want? Taris has asked for weeks! Report is that they're asking it tonight on Telerath. Serroco asked and never found out! They could be asking soon on—where? Arkania? Ralltiir? Alderaan? And where else? Who can understand the—

Flash! There are reports of Mandalorians in the building! Middle floors, roof. We're sealing the door, will try to hold out! Does anyone know if Mandies take prisoners? They're close now. Voices in a strange language. Blasters going off! There's nowhere to move, so this broadcast will continue until th—

TRANSMISSION INTERRUPTION

NO SIGNAL

NO SIGNAL

NO SIGNAL

*****

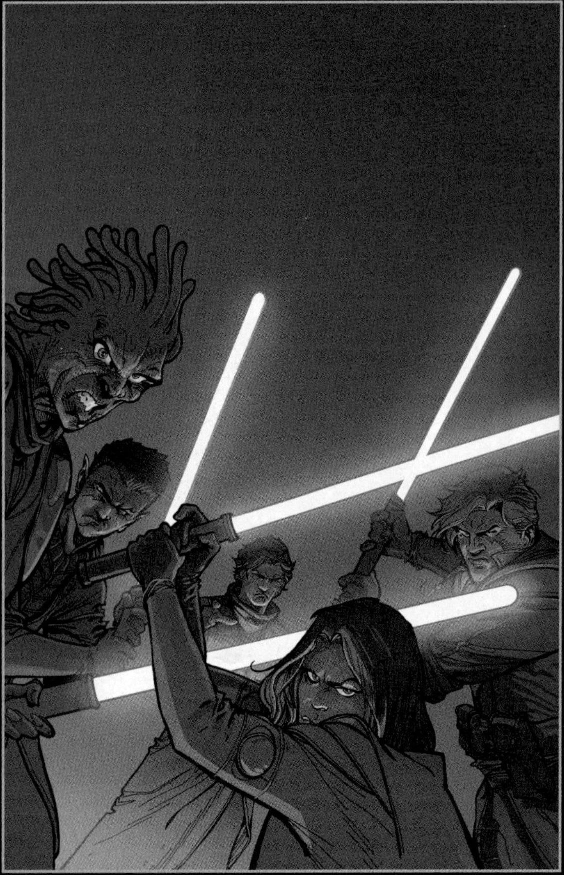
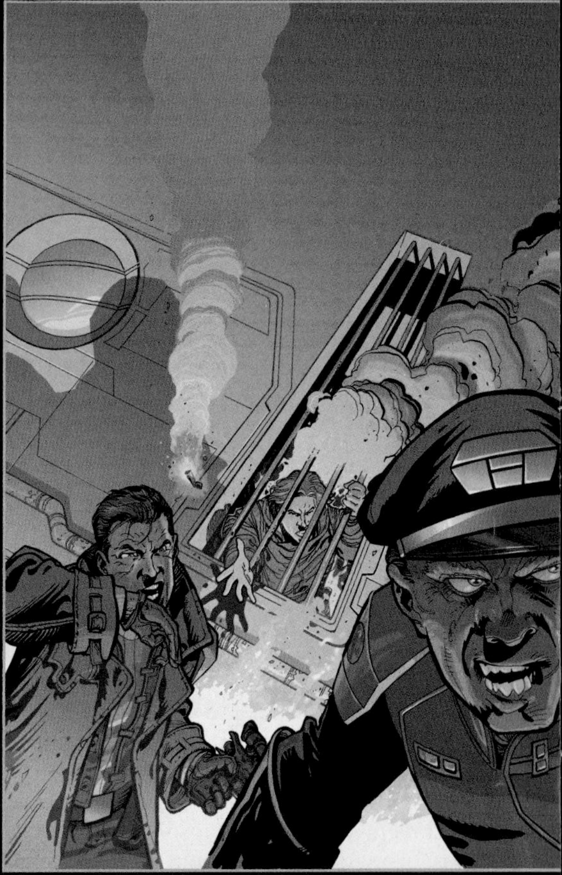
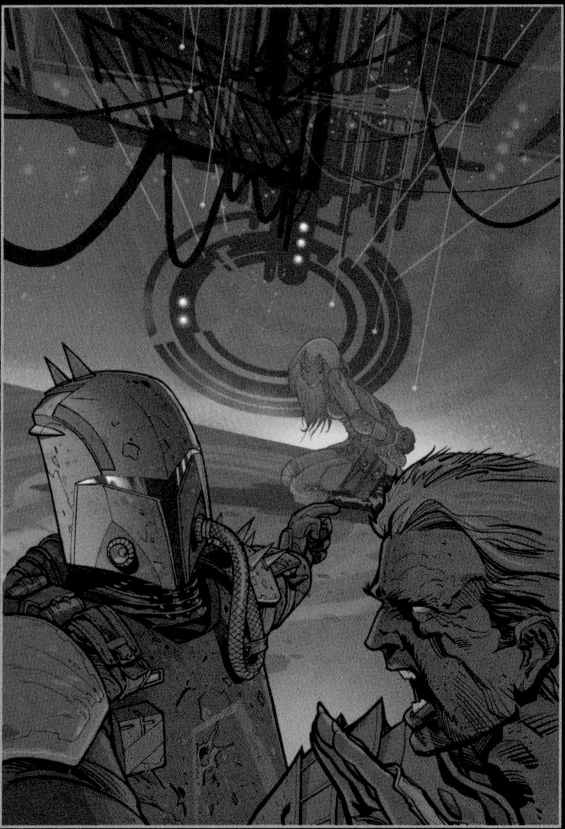